1985 Which? Wir

CW01667555

W.W.G.85.—I

1985 Which? Wine Guide

Edited by Kathryn McWhirter

Published by
Consumers' Association and
Hodder & Stoughton

Which? Wine Guide 1985 is published by
Consumers' Association, 14 Buckingham Street,
London WC2N 6DS and
Hodder & Stoughton Ltd, 47 Bedford Square,
London WC1B 3DP

British Library Cataloguing in Publication Data

Which? wine guide.–1985
1. Wine and wine making–Great Britain–
Directories
641.2'2'0294 HD9381.3

ISBN 0-340-36088-7

Cover design Paul Bowden
Cover photograph Trevor Melton

Cartography by David L Fryer & Co, Henley-on-Thames, Oxon
The maps are based on Ordnance Survey maps with the permission of the Controller of Her Majesty's Stationery Office. Crown copyright reserved

Typesetting by Rowland Phototypesetting Limited
Bury St Edmunds, Suffolk

Printed and bound in Great Britain by
Hazell, Watson & Viney Limited
Member of the BPCC Group
Aylesbury, Bucks

The editor

KATHRYN MCWHIRTER became interested in wine while working during school and university vacations in bars and restaurants in France, Germany and Italy. She worked briefly in the wine trade in London before joining the wine trade magazine *Wine & Spirit*, which she edited for four years until her appointment in 1984 as the editor of *Which? Wine Guide* and its associated newsletter, *Which? Wine Monthly*. She has also contributed articles to *Good Housekeeping* and *The Tatler*.

Acknowledgements

Consultant
Edmund Penning-Rowsell

Contributors

Jim Ainsworth
Christopher Ann
Nicholas Belfrage MW
Jeremy Bell
Marilyn Bright
Gordon Brown
Anthony Byrne
Oz Clarke
Clive Coates MW
Peter Collins
Fiona Cook
John Davies
Nicholas Faith
Christopher Fielden
Neville Filar
Richard Freeman
Michael Garner
Mark Greengrass
Bill Gunn MW
Ted Hale MW
Aileen Hall
Roger Harris
Richard Hayden
Ian Jamieson MW
Robert Joseph
Anthony and Novella Lacey
John Livingstone-Learmonth
Simon Loftus MW
Charles Metcalfe
Angela Muir MW
Nigel Munton
Stephen Nixon
Sebastian Payne
David Pipon
Helen Priday
Mary Redgate
Adam Richardson
Geoffrey Roberts
James Rogers
Declan Ryan
Mark Savage MW
Mark Sherston
Caroline Stacey
Paul Tholen MW
Nancy Thompson
Roger Voss
Bill Warre MW
John Weedy
John Wyndham-Lewis

NOTE Masters of Wine (MWS) are those who have passed the British wine trade's stiffest test of proficiency in practical as well as theoretical examinations. There are now just over 100 of them.

Contents

The wine regions (continued)

Part II WHERE TO BUY

Part III DRINKING OUT

Introduction

This new edition of *Which? Wine Guide* is an even more practical guide than its predecessors. We hope you will find yourself consulting all its sections throughout the year, rather than perusing the book once and for all as you down your first bottle of Beaujolais Nouveau or digest your Christmas pudding.

You probably have a specific problem in mind when you reach for a wine guide: whatever shall we drink with the turkey, or with that new fish recipe? This *Guide* will help you to make the choice. It leads you first through a WINE WITH FOOD section, suggesting the types and categories of wine that match different foods and dishes. You may be signposted to a grape variety whose flavour blends well with your chosen dish, in which case a flick through GRAPES ON THE LABEL will tell you which country or region uses that variety to make wines of the style you are seeking; or you may be directed straight to a choice of specific countries or regions.

This year we look in more detail at what each wine-producing region has to offer and suggest which vintages and styles to buy to drink now, in late 1984, and throughout 1985, and what to buy to lay down and when it might be ready to drink; we also list information – and point out any pitfalls – that might be vital to your decision when faced with a bewildering array of bottles on the shelf (who would guess, for example, that Bourgogne Grand Ordinaire is more *'ordinaire'* than Bourgogne Ordinaire?). And we highlight for each wine-producing area the 'names to look out for' – a selection of some of the best producers and merchants whose wines are available in this country, with brief run-downs on their style, reputation and any special forte.

Europe in general has been slow to make proper use of modern wine-making methods and equipment. But as winemakers' sons and daughters pour out of agricultural college and oenology school and back into the family cellars, and as governments and a generous EEC pour millions into vineyards and cellar improvements in the way of subsidies (particularly to the benefit of the wine co-operatives), the wines of all European wine regions have been changing very much for the better. For this reason, Spain and Italy get more coverage in this year's *Guide*, since both countries still suffer from poor reputations as producers of plonk only and deserve a new and more extensive assessment.

The wines of Burgundy also get a close inspection this year, in a section contributed by wine writer Robert Joseph. Burgundies have had to swallow some rough words from journalists and authors in recent years: deservedly so in the case of perhaps the majority of wines leaving the region's cellars, if quality is judged in ratio to price. Yet some of the world's very best wines, value for money even when expensive, also come from those Burgundian cellars, and we hope this *Guide* will help you to pick your way through the bewildering variety.

In terms of volume, over half the wine bought in this country is now selected from supermarket shelves. Many wine drinkers, indeed, never use a 'real' wine merchant. So this year's WHERE TO BUY section, as well as covering specialised merchants, also includes a brief assessment of Britain's licensed supermarkets and of the specialised chains of wine shops, some of which – like Oddbins, Cullen's, Sainsbury's or The Market – can rival Britain's top merchants for range and value, though few would pretend to offer any of the extras that make up a good wine merchant's service. The other way to buy wine is through auction, and once again we provide an up-to-date guide to wine-buying in Britain's auction houses.

Most wine shoppers go out to buy with a specific price range in view, so this year we have introduced symbols throughout THE WINE REGIONS and the WHERE TO BUY sections to give an indication of the price bracket into which various wines or categories of wines fit: [£] for wines under £3 a bottle, [££] for wines from £3 to £5, and [£££] for wines over £5. Because of the wide variation in mark-up, this cannot, of course, apply in the sections on restaurants and wine bars.

The scope of these last two sections has also been extended in the *1985 Guide*. By appointing 'scouts' in each area of the country we have been able to widen our coverage considerably; this year 148 restaurants and 300 wine bars have been selected (and many more were inspected but failed to gain a place in the *Guide*).

A final useful addition this year are the London maps, to guide you more quickly to wine bars, restaurants and merchants in different parts of the city. Outside London, there are the usual country maps and gazetteer.

We hope you will enjoy finding your way around wine

drinkers' Britain with the *1985 Which? Wine Guide*; also that you will continue to help us to improve it. Some of the *Guide*'s most valuable input comes from those who use it; we have appreciated each comment, criticism and suggestion received from our readers. So please don't hesitate to write to us (on the special forms at the back of the book, or by letter if you prefer) with your comments on any merchant, restaurant or wine bar you have visited, whether included or not in this year's *Guide*. We look forward to hearing your views, and wish you, meanwhile, happy wine drinking throughout 1985.

KATHRYN MCWHIRTER

The Which? Wine Guide awards

Key to symbols

Ⓥ This is an award for good value which goes to establishments *whose prices are lower than average*, though it is awarded only to those whose wines we also judge to be particularly good. You may well find good value elsewhere, even when prices are higher, if the higher prices are a justifiable result of the costs of providing exceptional service or maintaining enormous stock holdings.

This is an award to merchants, bars or restaurants with a particularly extensive range of good wines. This often means a good spread from throughout the wine-growing world, but may also be awarded for a particularly fine and thorough coverage of just one country.

☞ This award goes to merchants, restaurants and bars which give an especially personal, helpful, friendly service, and provide a range of extras such as newsletters, tastings, clubs, advice, rapid delivery as well as good wines.

Wine price categories

[£] Under £3 a bottle
[££] £3 to £5 a bottle
[£££] Over £5 a bottle

Part I

What to buy

Wine with food

Drinking and eating should be fun, not a cause for anxiety as you wonder about the 'right' combination of the two elements. After all, a tannic red wine with your fish and chips is just as palatable as the tannic cup of tea many Englishmen would choose, and sweet wine with meat is no more horrifying than a sweet glass of orange juice.

But if you want to be a perfectionist, for your own private pleasure or when entertaining, it's just as important to match the wine to the dish you'll eat with it as it is to match the sauce to the food over which you will pour it. Used to complement food, wine is indeed a sort of supplementary sauce.

Any serious cook will think about the tastes of the meat or the fish he/she is about to prepare, and may choose a sauce to match the meat's heaviness, lightness or richness; alternatively, the sauce can counterbalance a feature – even a defect – of the main ingredient: acidic lemon juice in a sauce for fried fish, for example. And wine provides yet another set of complex flavours that can also either blend with or usefully counterbalance those of the food. So conjure up the flavour of the dish you'll be eating before choosing the wine. You may remember a wine that has a similar flavour or opt for one that has a little sharpness or toughness to correct the oiliness or richness of the food.

Weight and richness are the first qualities in wine and food that need to be matched – a big bouncer of a California Chardonnay would instantly overpower a feeble prawn; a casseroled hare would swamp a lily-livered Liebfraumilch. Tartness in the food is also better matched by a wine of similar acidity, such as a wine from Northern Europe, or a fresh white wine from elsewhere made from grapes picked early, still tart and not too ripe. Lemon juice or acidity in a sauce will only make a flat and flabby wine seem flatter. Similarly, sauces containing fruit will make an ageing, fruitless wine seem even duller, so a young, zippy, fruity wine, white or red, will blend in best.

Smoked food is an interesting flavour to match. Its aromatic tang has a certain similarity to the spiciness of certain grape varieties – like the Gewürztraminer, the Grüner Veltliner of Austria, the Sauvignon Blanc, or the young, aromatic fruit of a good Gamay, like a Beaujolais. *(See the section on* GRAPES ON THE LABEL *for guidelines on the taste of wines from different grapes in different parts of the world.)*

But if the food is oily, fried or rich, a contrast may be better than a match: a light, sharply acid wine will cut through the fat and make life easier for your digestive system, too. Tannin in a tough red wine can work the same alchemy on richness or oiliness in food.

A cookery book recently published by top chefs Albert and Michel Roux suggests 'muted wines to complement exquisite food, and low-key food for exquisite wines'. If you're serving really fine wines, you may, as they say, prefer to avoid the risk of all the compliments going to the cook, whose triumphs may inadvertently distract your guests' taste buds. But if you choose your wine as sensibly as you choose your sauce, neither wine nor food need step on the other's toes.

There are one or two foods that consistently seem to clash with wine, or at least make its appreciation difficult: chocolate, particularly the more bitter types, can linger distractingly in the mouth so that you taste little else; so can dill, and citrus fruits or vinegar in excess can take a bit of washing down. Chillies or curry or any mouth-searing concoctions may be a good way of getting rid of bad wine buys, though lagers are far better fire-quenchers – or try lassee, made from plain yoghourt, the Indians' own solution. Don't waste your best wines on any of these.

Because tastes that have gone before can dull the palate or alter the taste of things that follow, it's best, if you are serving a succession of wines at a formal dinner, to ensure that wines and foods that begin a meal don't swamp more delicate flavours to come. (If they must, then generally a neutralising chomp at a piece of bread or a swig or two of water will help to clear the way.) But it's preferable to drink light wines before heavy ones, young and fruity before old, dry before sweet.

Having the right wine in your glass to drink with the cheese can be a problem, if you want to drink sweet wines with the pud. If you and your guests prefer cheese *after* the pudding, even a tough red wine with the cheese will taste odd. Port is the traditional answer, but its spirity sweetness tastes peculiar with pungent cheeses like ripe Camembert or Brie, and overpowers delicate flavours like Leicester. So it makes some sense to follow the Continental example, and drink up the red wine with the cheese *before* moving on to sweeter liquid and solid flavours.

And if you are drinking a sweet wine with the pudding, do try some of it before you start eating. Otherwise, if the food is sweeter than the wine, the wine may seem dry and acid in contrast, and you may never taste it at its best.

Taste categories of wine

The first of the following lists divides the wines of the world into broad taste categories, and identifies each group by a letter. The second list groups a wide range of dishes under type/main ingredient (eg Starters, Fish, Cheese), and then cross-refers each dish to the relevant category/categories of wine by the appropriate letter(s); anything in these categories should then be suitable. If one or more specific wines are particularly suitable, then these are mentioned by name in the food list. To give you some idea of price, £ stands for wines £3 and under, ££ for wines £5 and under, and £££ for wines over £5. Starred wines in the 'categories' list are likely to have fairly high acidity. Wines or areas marked with a star and question mark *may* produce wines with good acidity, but not always. Turn to the sections on 'GRAPES ON THE LABEL' and 'THE WINE REGIONS' for more specific advice on what to buy within each category.

A Aromatic dry whites

All Alsace wines, particularly Gewürztraminer * ££
Austrian wines, especially Grüner Veltliner *? £–££
Sancerre, Pouilly Fumé etc (Eastern Loire) * ££–£££
Sauvignon de Touraine (Loire) * £
Sauvignon du Haut Poitou (Loire) * £

Grapes on the label: Gewürztraminer, Traminer, Sauvignon, Grüner Veltliner, dry Muscat (though you may find the latter too grapy to accompany food)

B Light dry whites

Alsace * ££
England * £–£££
Most New Zealand wines * £–£££
Champagne * and other sparklers *? £–£££
Muscadet (Loire) * £–££
Anjou or Saumur Blanc (Loire) * £–£££
White Bordeaux £–££
Chablis * ££–£££
Northern Italian whites *? £–££
New-style Spanish whites (Rioja, Catalonia) *? £–££
Vinho verde * (Portugal) £
German trocken and halbtrocken wines, and some Kabinetts * £–££
Most freshly made vins de pays *? £

Grapes on the label: Light Chardonnay and Riesling, Kerner, Sauvignon, Müller-Thurgau, Viura, Chenin Blanc, Pinot Blanc, Pinot Gris

C Medium-bodied dry whites

Lighter Burgundies * £–££
Wines of North-West USA (not California) * £££
Fuller New Zealand wines *? ££
Richer Alsace wines * ££–£££
Some vins de pays *? £
Mid to Southern Italian whites £–££

Grapes on the label: Chardonnay, Aligoté, Riesling, Chenin Blanc, Sauvignon (in California and Australia)

D Full-bodied dry whites

Most Australian and California whites £££
Good, full Burgundies * ££–£££
Northern Rhônes, Condrieu, Hermitage, St Joseph ££–£££
Old style Riojas £–££

Grapes on the label: Chardonnay, Semillon

E Medium-dry, fruity whites

German wines, Tafelwein–Kabinett * £–££
Austrian wines (usually sold sweeter here than in Austria) *? £–££

Grapes on the label: Riesling, Kerner, Weissburgunder

F Medium-sweet whites

German Kabinett and Spätlese * ££–£££
Austrian Kabinett, Spätlese and Ausbruch *? ££–£££
Some Vouvray (Loire) * ££–£££

Grapes on the label: Riesling

G Very sweet whites

Muscat de Beaumes de Venise (Rhône–fortified) £££
Moscatel de Setúbal (Portugal–fortified) ££–£££
Tokay ££–£££
Sweet Champagne * £££
Sweet Loire, Coteaux du Layon *, Quarts de Chaume *, Bonnezeaux * and some Vouvray * ££–£££
Sauternes, Barsac ££–£££
Other sweet Bordeaux £–££
Monbazillac ££
Sweet Germans * and Austrians *? (Auslese–Trockenbeerenauslese) ££–£££

Grapes on the label: Muscat, Riesling

H Fresh, lively, light reds

Beaujolais (except the fuller crus) * £–££
Anjou and Touraine Gamay (Loire) * £–££

Cabernet Rouge from Anjou or Saumur (Loire) * £–££
Chinon, Bourgueil, St-Nicolas-de-Bourgueil (Loire) * ££–£££
New style Côtes-du-Rhône £–££
Young Chianti (after 1981) *? £–££
All nouveau, nuevo, novello or primeur reds * £
North-Eastern and Central North Italian reds, Friuli, Trentino, the best of the lighter Valpolicellas and Bardolinos *? £

Grapes on the label: Gamay

I Medium-bodied reds

Most Riojas £–££, many Catalonian reds *? £–££
Older Chianti (before 1981) *? ££
Valpolicella £ and other fuller Northern Italian reds *? £
Fuller and old style Côtes-du-Rhône £–£££
Loire Cabernets of better years * £–££
Bergerac * £–££
Young, light clarets * £–££
Light Burgundies *? £–£££
Beaujolais crus * ££–£££
Many vins de pays *? £
Wines of the Midi £–££

Grapes on the label: Cabernet, Pinot Noir, Merlot, Barbera, Dolcetto

J Full reds

Châteauneuf-du-Pape £££
Northern Rhône reds, Hermitage, Côte-Rôtie, Crozes-Hermitage £££
Some Côtes-du-Rhône ££
Fuller Burgundy and Bordeaux reds *? ££–£££
Fuller Riojas ££ and the bigger wines of Catalonia ££
Bulgarian and Chilean Cabernet Sauvignon £–££
Reds from North-West USA *? £££

K Powerful reds

Australian reds £££
Most California reds £££
Portuguese reds £–££
Rich Burgundies and clarets ££–£££
Barolo, Barbaresco, Valtellina £–£££

Grapes on the label: Syrah, Shiraz, Cabernet Sauvignon, Zinfandel, Nebbiolo

L Dry rosés

Rosé de Loire * £
Tavel rosé (Rhône) ££
Lirac rosé ££
Provence rosé £–££
Pinot Noir from Alsace * (theoretically red) ££
German, Austrian and Swiss reds (nearly rosé) £–£££

M Medium-dry rosé

Rosé d'Anjou * £
Cabernet d'Anjou * ££

Mixing and matching wines with food

Aperitifs or drinks parties

A B H, or slightly sweeter E if there are less regular wine drinkers in the party. It may be best anyway to provide something from category E, as well as whatever else you choose.

Starters

Artichokes Rather metallic, so choose cheaper wine, and match the wine to the sauce. A–E, I–L.

Asparagus Flavour might overpower subtle, fine wine; match wine to sauce. B C. You may enjoy fino sherry with asparagus.

Avocado B C.

Caviar B C. Champagne. With saltier versions, try schnapps or aquavit.

Champignons à la grecque Acidic dish, so choose a wine with good, fresh acidity. B C H.

Eggs Undiluted, yolks tend to coat the mouth and dull a fine wine, so drink cheaper H I J, or whatever's on hand. Used diluted to thicken or enrich a sauce, eggs are not really a problem, nor when cooked and lightened in a soufflé.

Foie gras Fatty by definition, so cut through the fat with acidity, and/or match it with richness, even sweet richness. Champagne, Alsace (especially vendange tardive) or rich, mature Burgundy with good acidity. Try it with Sauternes and see if you like the sweet-rich blend. A C D E F, unfortified G.

Gravad lax *(see FISH)*

Guacamole Cheap aromatic wine to match the spiciness. A.

Hummus A – D.

Mushrooms *(see champignons)*

Mussels *(see FISH)*

Onion dishes A H.

Parma ham A H, or E if it's served with melon.

Pasta + fish A B C.

Pasta + meat H – J.

Pasta + oil, garlic, cream C D H I.

Pâté, fish A B C, match to the type of fish.

Pâté, meat H I J.

Quiches H, or A – C for fish.

Rillettes Fatty, so choose an acidic white or red. A B C H.

Salads as starters Acid wine to cope with the dressing, not too expensive. B C H. But your wine can safely go up-market if you make the dressing with lots of oil and a little lemon juice, which is kinder to wine than vinegar.

Salmon *(see FISH)*

Soups Match the ingredients. But do you want to drink *more* liquid? It can make a pleasant hot–cold contrast.

Snails (bourguignonne) Wine needs acidity and body to cope with the butter and garlic. C D H J.

Taramosalata Needs wine with good acidity to cope with the lemon and garlic. A B C.

Terrine of fish A B C.

Terrine of meat H I J.

Terrine of vegetables B C H.

Sauces

Butter sauces (eg beurre blanc, hollandaise) Cut through the fat with a sharp, dry white, maybe also with richness to match. A B C D. The richness of the sauce can cope with sweeter wines with balancing acidity. E F. But bear in mind the main meat or fish ingredient, too.

Cream sauces Rich whites. D. But match other ingredients.

Curry and chilli sauces If it's a strong, mouth-stinging concoction, bring out your bad buys and drink them up. Better still, drink beer. If the curry is lightly flavoured, try a well-flavoured, aromatic H or a cheap D.

Dill sauces Dill is a difficult flavour for a wine to cope with. Try solid, rustic whites. Old-style Rioja, white Northern Rhônes. C D.

Egg-yolk sauces Cut through the slightly tongue-coating yolks with a wine of good acidity, especially if there's lemon juice or vinegar in the sauce. A B C D.

Fruit sauces (apricots, cherries, prunes, apples etc) Fruity white wine with sweetness to match the dish, but balancing acidity. E F. Or a plain young fruity H.

Mayonnaise An acidic wine to match the lemon or vinegar and cut through the oil. B.

Mint sauce Both the mint and the vinegar are difficult to match for taste intensity. A strong Cabernet from North or South America or Australia, or a Shiraz or Zinfandel can usually cope. K.

Mustard sauce A strong-flavoured A, D or H. Alsace Riesling, cheaper white Burgundy, Cabernet Rouge d'Anjou. But if there's lots of mustard in the sauce, go for a cheaper wine.

Tartare sauce Match acidity with B. Don't waste expensive wines.

Tomato sauces Match acidity and lightness of a *nouvelle cuisine* coulis de tomates with A B H. Italian-style tomato sauces may be quite acid, too, but not always. C D I J will go with a richer, less sharp sauce.

Fish

Bass (see white fish)

Caviar *(see STARTERS)*

Cod *(see white fish)*

Coquilles St Jacques *(see scallops)*

Crab Rich meat, so D with good acidity. California or Australian Chardonnay. Burgundy. Expensive white Bordeaux.

Crayfish C D.

Eel C D.

Eel, smoked A, or Dutch gin.

Gravad lax You'll need to match the slight sweetness, though the vinegar and dill would spoil a good wine. E with good acidity. Or resort to aquavit.

Haddock C D.

Haddock, smoked Go for a rich A, D.

Halibut *(see white fish)*

Herrings Need acidity in the wine to cut the richness. B C D. Unless they're pickled, in which case try aquavit or schnapps.

Kedgeree A D.

Kippers B C D with good acidity.

Lobster, plain B C D. Champagne, rich Alsace.

Lobster, rich sauce C D or a very good E or F. California or Australian Chardonnay, good white Burgundy, German or Austrian Spätlese, if you like sweet-rich combinations.

Mackerel, plain A B C D with acidity to cut the richness.

Mackerel, smoked A D.

Monkfish *(see white fish)*

Mussels B.

Oysters Light, very dry A B with very good acidity. Drink very cheap wine if you like to douse your oysters with vinegar.

Oysters, cooked Match the sauce.

Paella (fish) C D to match the richness, flavour and garlic.

Plaice *(see white fish)*

Prawn Delicate white A B.

Salmon, fresh A B C.

Salmon, smoked Alsace, Gewürztraminer, Chardonnay from Australia or California. A D. Try fino sherry.

Sardines (fresh) B with acidity to cut richness.

Scallops A D.

Scampi *(see prawn)* But go for something more acidic if it's fried, and richer if it's garlicky.

Shrimps *(see prawn)*

Sole *(see white fish)*

Taramosalata *(see STARTERS)*

Trout Light, flowery A B.

Trout, smoked Aromatic A.

Turbot *(see white fish)*

Whitebait B with good acidity.

White fish, plain, grilled A B C D, useful to show off fine whites.

White fish, rich sauce or fried Acid B to cut the richness, C D to balance it. Or match the flavours to the sauce.

Meat

Barbecued meat Straight, gutsy reds, not too expensive. Rioja, Catalonia, good fruity Italians, Zinfandel. J K.

Beef, roast, cold H I J for more delicate beef flavour.

Beef, roast, hot J K.

Beef stew J K.

Chicken, fried As roast, but choose a wine with good acidity to cut the fat. C D H I J

Chicken, plain, roast C D H I J. Use it as a bland background to show off good wines.

Chili con carne A useful way of using up bad red buys, while your palate is overcome by the heat. Or cheaper J K.

Cold meats The flavour becomes more delicate when cold. So move down a notch or two in category – especially to H.

Confit d'oie, de canard *(see duck)*

Coq au vin J K.

Curry *(see SAUCES)*

Duck Acid and rich A or D, or young tannic J to cut the richness. Young red Cabernet d'Anjou, young claret, or a sturdy F to match richness with sweetness.

Duck in sweet sauce A sturdy F, or fruity H.

Game J K. Well-hung game matches well the gaminess of Rhônes. Plain roasted game often blends well with mature fine wines.

Goose Fattier, heavier in texture than duck, sweeter in taste. A good Mosel goes well, a cru Beaujolais, a Chinon or Bourgeuil, or another aromatic H.

Goose in sweet sauce A sturdy F or a fruity H.

Goulash H J K.

Grouse *(see game)*

Ham H I L. E if the ham is sugar-glazed or served with fruit.

Hare J K, especially Rhônes.

Kidneys H J. But match also to sauce.

Lamb, cold, roast H I *(see cold meats)*

Lamb, hot, roast I J.

Liver H J for strongly flavoured liver. Try E or F with liver and onions. C with lighter-flavoured liver eg chicken.

Moussaka H J K.

Oxtail H to cut the fat or J K to match the richness.

Paella (meat only) C D H I.

Partridge *(see game)*

Pigeon C D H I.

Pork, cold C H *(see cold meats)*

Pork, hot H to cut the fat and cope with apple sauce and sage stuffing. Plain pork is a good, neutral background to fine reds. I J.

Pork, smoked Aromatic C or H.

Pork with sweet sauce F or a fruity H.

Poultry B C D H I L.

Quail Delicate-flavoured wines. B H I.

Rabbit C D H I. Match also to the sauce.

Steaks J K.

Steak tartare I J.

Sweetbreads Very rich, and often served in rich sauce, so D, a mature I J, or a sweetish F.

Tongue H I.

Tripe D H I J.

Turkey Most wines 'go' with turkey, but a fullish wine is best. D J K. But nice also with a fruity H.

Veal C D L.

Venison K.

Wiener Schnitzel B C D E H with good acidity.

Wild boar K.

Wild duck K.

Cheese

Bleu de Bresse *(see Stilton)*

Blue *(see Stilton)*

Brie Tastes odd with port because of the ammoniac overtone, especially when ripe. Rich reds can cope, Rhônes ££ – £££, Zinfandels ££ and other California and Australian reds £££, or cheaper Ds.

Camembert *(see Brie)*

Cheddar *(see English cheeses)*

Cheshire *(see English cheeses)*

Dolcelatte *(see Stilton)* But less powerful, softer Dolcelatte goes well with J K.

Emmenthal *(see Gruyère)*

English cheeses (except Stilton) I J, richer wines for more mature cheese. English cheeses are a good background for fine wines.

Gloucester *(see English cheeses)*

Goat cheese Mature goat's cheese tastes better with a clean, dry white than with a red. Try the aromatic wines of the Upper Loire. A D. But an H or I will taste good with a fresher goat's cheese.

Gorgonzola *(see Stilton)*

Gruyère Overpowered by reds. Try fullish whites.

Lymeswold *(see Brie)* But Lymeswold is less ammoniac. I J.

Munster Like the aptly named German 'Stinkkäse' (stink cheese) this is extremely powerful and few wines can cope. Try a tough, fairly acidic, coarse-flavoured Gewürztraminer – Munster would spoil a good one.

Parmesan Try a full, dry white C D. Goes with port, but don't sacrifice a fine port to a salty Parmesan.

Roquefort *(see Stilton)*

Soft, mild French cheeses (eg Brillat-Savarin) I J.

Stilton It's traditional to drink port, and the spirity sweetness does cope with the salty tang of the cheese. Try Sauternes and Barsac for similar sweet-salt contrast-blend. The acidity of sweet Loires or sweet Germans doesn't quite work, nor does the grapy flavour of sweet Muscat. But all blue cheeses will kill fine table wines – so don't choose anything expensive.

Wensleydale *(see English cheeses)*

Puddings and desserts

Almond puddings and desserts Muscat de Beaumes de Venise, Moscatel de Setúbal go particularly well with almonds. G.

Apple pies and puddings Sweet wine with good acidity, like Coteaux du Layon, Bonnezeaux, Quarts de Chaume. G.

Apricots (cooked) Muscat de Beaumes de Venise. G.

Cheesecakes Match the tartness and the sweetness with an Austrian or German G, or a sweet Loire.

Chocolate cake, mousse, soufflé Unless the chocolate content is very low, most unfortified sweet wines won't taste of much through a mouthful of chocolate. Muscat de Beaumes de Venise, Muscat de Rivesaltes, or Moscatel de Setúbal can usually cope.

Christmas pudding Try a mature, sweet German or Austrian G to match the spiciness. Or one of the more mature, wood-aged sweet fortified wines, Portuguese Moscatel de

Setúbal (6 or 25-year-old), or a sweet Tokay from Hungary. G.

Creams and custards The less acidic of the sweet unfortified wines are best: Sauternes and Tokay, rather than the Loires and Germans.

Crème brûlée The flavour goes particularly well with Sauternes or Barsac, especially if it's mature.

Crêpes *(see pancakes)*

Fruit flans and pies Loires and German Gs for more acidic fruits, Sauternes, Barsac, Tokay for fruit that's less tart.

Fruit, fresh Loire and German Gs. Other Gs.

Fruit salad Asti Spumante or sweet Muscat, particularly if you pour some into the fruit bowl, too.

Ice-cream Drink the sweet wine first, before the ice-cream numbs your mouth.

Meringue Very sweet, so have a good few minutes just drinking the sweet wine first – the meringue's sugar will probably overpower it. Don't waste your best sweet wines.

Nuts Tawny port, Madeira, oloroso sherry, dry or sweet.

Oranges Too acid to drink wine.

Pancakes Sweet German Gs or Loires with good acidity.

Pears Sauternes and Barsac go well with very ripe pears.

Raspberries German and Loire Gs to match the acidity.

Sorbets *(see ice-cream)*

Strawberries Sweet Loire and German Gs, Asti Spumante, sweet Muscats, sweet Champagne and sweet Bordeaux all go well.

Zabaglione Sauternes, Barsac, Sweet Austrians, or more of the Marsala you used to make it.

Serving and storing wine

Serving wine

Temperature Port, and medium-bodied and heavier reds need to be served warm enough for their aromas to evaporate; chilling white, rosé, light red, sweet or sparkling wines in the fridge for a couple of hours adds to their freshness; while chilling any poor wine will help disguise its defects. A good, full-bodied white such as a California or Australian Chardonnay, a fine white Burgundy or a fino sherry needs less chilling – just half an hour to an hour in the fridge is enough, or the aromas will not be released.

If you're caught short of cold wine, ten minutes in the freezer will certainly do the wine no harm – but beware of lollipops in broken bottles. In desperation, for a not particularly fine wine, ice cubes are the other obvious solution – though it's a shame to water down a *good* wine. Once your bottle is cool, a good alternative to the ice bucket is a plastic insulating sleeve sold under the brand name 'Vinicool', and insulated portable bottle-bags useful for picnics are also available.

It's more difficult instantly to warm up a bottle of red without overheating parts of the bottle and risking spoiling the wine's aromas. Be gentle. Pour it into a warm, not hot, decanter. Or better still, just wait for it to warm up in the glass – cupping in your hands will help.

Glasses To taste a wine at its best and catch all the aromas, use a glass that curves in at the upper edges, and is big enough to hold a reasonable amount. The thinner and finer the glass, the finer the wine will taste: experiment and see. Any engraving, and particularly smokiness or colour in the glass, will of course make it impossible to inspect the wine's colour properly. Filling the glass just half to two-thirds full (like the one on the *Guide*'s cover) leaves an air-space into which the aromas can evaporate and remain trapped, until sniffed out. It also leaves wine experts scope to swirl the wine around their glass without putting table cloth or carpet at risk. Nowadays the flat coupe-shaped Champagne glasses (bizarrely reputed to have been modelled on Marie-Antoinette's breasts) are fortunately less common: they are hopeless, allowing expensive bubbles to escape in a flash from their enormous surface. Best are the tall, thin Champagne flutes, with only a tiny surface area, but there's nothing wrong with using an ordinary large wine glass for Champagne and other sparkling wines.

Opening Remove the foil or plastic capsule completely, or cut it well underneath the bottle lip, so that it cannot possibly come into contact with the wine: this would be just messy with modern aluminium foil or plastic, potentially poisonous in the long term if it's the old-fashioned lead variety! If the cork won't budge, hold the neck for a minute or so under fairly hot running water and try again. For corks that drop into the bottle, there's a long spindly-legged plastic gadget called a 'Decorker'; you may have to resort to a coffee filter if you make unacceptable quantities of cork crumbs.

Champagne corks Hold the top firmly and be careful where you point the bottle: people have lost eyes through flying corks. If the mushroom top breaks off as you twist the cork or the bottle, carefully use a corkscrew. Always disturb the bottle as little as possible, and keep a glass on hand to catch accidental fountains.

Checking the quality If it has a deposit, decant it *(see below)*. If not, pour some for *yourself* first to check that it is sound before serving your guests; and don't forget to check subsequent bottles. There may be a difference between two bottles of a quite simple wine, so make sure any wine connoisseurs amongst your guests have finished up the dregs of one bottle in their glass before serving them from the next; they may be deeply shocked if you mix bottles, especially of different wines! Non-winos will think this nonsense – so just top them up.

Unfinished bottles Still wines can just be recorked, or poured into a smaller bottle for better keeping. To stopper half-drunk Champagnes or sparkling wines, there are special clamp tops available.

Storing wine

Few people are fortunate enough today to own a cellar. It is possible to buy air-conditioned/chilled cabinets storing a considerable number of bottles. Those with neither cellar nor cabinet should choose a spot in the house where there is least risk of vibration (away from scampering feet) and where the temperature is fairly constant (away from central heating and water pipes, and away from outer walls). Wine will mature more quickly in a warm place, and may spoil or re-ferment if suddenly exposed to heat-wave conditions. Very cold conditions may cause it to deposit more solids in the bottle, though most medium- to low-priced wines are now chilled before bottling to forestall this risk. Avoid these extremes and temperature fluctuations, and you should have no problems. The bottles should lie on their side, to keep the cork moist. Dried-up corks let air into the bottle and are also difficult to remove. It takes some time, however, for a properly capsuled bottle to come to any harm.

For the cellared few, the main problem can be dampness, which can obscure and rot the labels. The best answer is plastic bottle sleeves, or clingfilm, or spraying the labels with hair spray! And beware of introducing rare, cellar-blackened bottles. Our consultant Edmund Penning-Rowsell has cellar walls, bottles and labels sprouting slowly with healthy (and harmless) black cellar mould, all the results of one aged bottle of Champagne from a French cellar.

Decanting – finishing school or euthanasia?

Many fine, expensive old wines are never tasted at their best because they are opened and decanted too early. Wine books and articles often recommend opening clarets and Burgundies or vintage ports hours before the meal. For tough wines like Barolo and Dão, writers have been known to maintain that the wines improve if opened as long as a day before drinking. Unfortunately, these generalisations – like the maxim 'red wine with meat, white wine with fish' – can be misleading and even disastrous in certain instances.

All wines that have developed for most of their life in bottle – like claret and vintage port – will begin to lose their fruit towards the end of their life. The process may take decades, or it may take just a year or two, depending on the raw materials and the initial winemaking methods. Many of the rich, ripe 1976 clarets and Burgundies, for example, already have the slightly spicy, slightly decaying flavour of mature wine, and a fading fruit. Opened and decanted too early, mature wines will lose all the fruit that remains, as the fruitiness combines with oxygen. And the aromas may float away on the dining room air if you wait too long.

Younger, or less delicate wines, or wines that have been left to age a long time in wood (like Barolo, old-fashioned Burgundy, Rhônes, or Chiantis, where much of the combination with oxygen will have taken place earlier, before bottling) may not change much with an airing. However, long cellaring in old wooden barrels tends to encourage 'volatile acidity', a slight vinegariness sometimes detectable in Burgundies, Barolos or Chiantis, and this can increase to a much more noticeable level if the wine is left open for more than a few hours.

Blind tests run recently by the catering press comparing decanted and non-decanted youngish, fairly sturdy wines failed to establish any tastable difference. So if a wine sometimes tastes better at the latter stages of a meal it may be the influence of the food's flavours – and also, perhaps, alcohol's happy tendency to make the whole world look, taste, smell and feel rather better.

It's unlikely, in fact, with younger, tougher wines, that you can do much harm by opening them for an hour or two. Indeed, any off-smells from the sulphur compounds derived from the necessary preservatives will have time to disperse, particularly if the wine is sloshed into a decanter: little is likely to escape through the bottle neck.

That's one *good* reason for decanting a little while in advance. You may also feel the wine looks better in decanter than in bottle. You may just feel inclined to play mean tricks in public on wine-buff friends, or give them, for that matter, an educational blind tasting test. So go ahead and decant. Of course, if the bottle has thrown a sludgy deposit – as a vintage port or an old claret or Burgundy will certainly have done – you will need to decant it before drinking. (Either stand the bottle upright two or three days ahead to allow the deposit to collect in the base, or keep it well-settled on its side, carefully draw the cork, and pour, shining a torch or, more romantically, a candle through the bottle neck and watching carefully for the deposit to reach the bottle shoulder. If delirium tremens foils your attempts, resort to a coffee filter!)

Once decanted, the volatile substances in the wine will begin to evaporate, creating the bouquet. This also happens fairly rapidly in the glass; the warmer the wine is, the more rapidly it happens. If the wine is mature and fragile, the aroma can be off and away in no time.

Many restaurants, in our view, are guilty of 'euthanasia' on elderly wine. How often are customers consulted when they order an expensive old bottle of red to follow their white as to whether they really *want* the bottle opened when they begin their meal?

Few wines suffer from late decanting. If you are unsure, try experimenting with different opening times next time you're serving two or more bottles of the same wine to unproblematic guests.

The bag-in-box trap

Bags-in-boxes, used sensibly, are a good solution for any household that drinks no more than one or two glasses in total a day. But beware! This form of packaging has not yet been perfected, and there is *no doubt* that wine deteriorates much more rapidly in box than in bottle. One major problem is metal fatigue (known in the trade as 'flexing') in the protective aluminium inner layer between the inner and outer plastic layers of the bags. Bags that have flopped gently from bagging line to the laboratory shelf for testing will not suffer from this; a bag that has jolted along on a fork lift truck, and then by lorry to reach the depot, then out again to the shop shelf will have about half the protective properties it had at the outset. Bag manufacturers are working on this (double metal layers help, as do new sorts of plastic that don't need metal) but the baggers have so far been reluctant to pay the extra that these improvements cost. Anyway, almost every bagging machine in use in this country puts more air into the three-litre bag than you would find in three equivalent litre glass bottles. Air can also get trapped *between* the layers of the bag when it is made and so has a shorter distance to penetrate into the wine (though most bags are now 'ironed' to solve this problem); and air also gets in through the tap, both before and, to a greater extent, after the box has been used for the first time. (It helps considerably if you store the box with the tap *downwards*, and keep the bag cool.) So although manufacturers might claim that the wine is of an acceptable condition after four months, it *will* have deteriorated – and their idea of 'acceptable' might not be yours!

It's not only on opening that the problem starts. Oxygen will begin getting into the wine through the bag, and a bit through the tap from the moment it is bagged; and that bagged-in air from the filling-hall will get to work immediately, acting first on the sulphur and other preservatives, then moving on to the wine itself. So it is vital to buy a freshly filled box. Only Waitrose print a packing date on the outside of the box – others use codes, or a coded, sometimes decipherable, date under the flap or inside the box. Most producers will admit in private that it would be fairer to print a sell-by or bottled-on date for all eyes to see, but have not had the commercial guts to do so – because they know that turn-over is not always as rapid as it should be, and that their trade customers will not want to take the risk of being left with ageing stocks on their hands. All *you* can do is go to a shop with a fast turnover in boxes – shops with smaller box ranges are likely to turn over individual brands more quickly – and pick one that hasn't gathered dust! Beware at Christmas especially. All bagging firms will have anticipated big sales, and many will have been building up a stock of filled boxes well before you started counting the shopping days.

And wine boxes aren't like washing powder – you aren't getting a bargain because you are buying a bumper pack. The bag-in-box is an expensive form of packaging, more expensive than glass, except for the firms bagging in really huge quantities.

The quality of many of the wines inside leaves much to be desired, too. There's such competition in this growing market that producers' margins are tiny – and their solution has often been simply to cut corners on the quality of the wine.

So, think carefully about your requirements before you plump for a box. Most wines will keep well in the fridge for two days, many for three. So if you can manage a bottle between you within two or three days, you will be assured of better quality, given wines in bag and bottle of a similar quality at the outset. There's all the more reason to go for bottles if you are a crowd, at a party or dinner party. Why risk poor quality when you are certain to drink several bottles at one session? Anyway, its much more fun to hear the pop.

Grapes on the label

Different grape varieties, just like different varieties of apples or any other fruit, have their own distinct flavours, but each will change subtly or dramatically depending on the climate, and how the wine is made. The following grape varieties are sometimes used alone to make solo grape-variety wines and their names may appear on the label, rather than the regional name, as the chief means of identification of what's in the bottle. For this reason it is useful to know how wines from these varieties are likely to taste from different parts of the world. If you want to know more, turn to the 'WHAT TO DRINK NOW' and 'UNDERSTANDING THE LABEL' sections of the wine regions mentioned here. You may find a few rarer grapes explained in the UNDERSTANDING THE LABEL sections of THE WINE REGIONS.

Solo white grapes

Aligoté Light, tart wines from Burgundy, slightly cheaper than the cheapest Chardonnays. Sometimes a hint of buttermilk soap, sometimes a gentle hint of glue. In ripe years in Burgundy (like 1983), the Aligoté makes good, well-flavoured wines, and manages to balance its tartness [££].

Chardonnay Makes a great variety of wine styles, from light, appley and delicate in Bulgaria [££], Northern Italy [££] and central France [£]–[££] to rich, vegetably or honey-flavoured, sometimes heavy, in Australia [£££], California [£££] and South Africa [£££]. In Burgundy, it makes a whole range from simple [££] to rich, complex wines with a spread of flavours [£££], and it is making light, well-flavoured wines in the North-West USA [£££] and New Zealand [££], too. Ages well to a spicy, meaty, complex wine. Dry, alcoholic wines, generally with balanced acidity. Often aged in oak barrels, its flavour marries well with the wood. The grape of most white Burgundy. Makes blanc de blancs Champagne, and forms part of most other Champagne blends. Grown in almost every wine-making country of the world.

Chenin Blanc Made into dry wine, the Chenin is fairly neutral, sometimes faintly appley or flowery, sometimes a bit honeyed, generally high in acidity. It sometimes has a positively unpleasant, 'vomity' smell. Often dull in the Loire [£], but *some* steely, dry, honeyed wines are made in Anjou [££]–[£££]. Some good dry wines in South Africa where the grape is sometimes called **Steen** [££] and New Zealand [££].

Sometimes quite good in Australia ££ and the USA £££. But it can make delicious sweet wines in the Loire (Coteaux du Layon, Bonnezeaux, Quarts de Chaume and Vouvray – expensive when ready for drinking £££), which, in good years, keep and grow more complex for decades.

Colombard A straightforward grape which can be pleasant, flowery and gulpable if well made – look for pale, light colour. Some from the South of France £, some from the USA ££, where it's known as **French Colombard**.

Gewürztraminer Richly spiced, pungent grape, sometimes like the Chinese fruit lychee. Delicate and rich Gewürztraminers come from Alsace ££–£££, Northern Italy ££, Austria ££, New Zealand ££. Sometimes short of acidity in a warm climate, sometimes oily in texture. Always blatantly flavoursome.

Grüner Veltliner Crisp, fruity, lightly spicy wines of light to medium body, often with a light, refreshing prickle. Best very young. An Austrian speciality £–££.

Kerner One of the best of the new German crossings (half Riesling) with the good, crisp acidity and a lot of the elegance of Riesling. Its smell is close to that of Riesling, sometimes with a whiff of Muscat-like grapiness. It usually makes poor wines in bad years. Found commercially in Germany £–££.

Müller-Thurgau Smells like elderberry or blackcurrant bushes or, put less delicately, cats' pee, but a less pure, less steely flavour than the Sauvignon *(see below)*. It's softer, grapier, still with fairly good acidity. Used for most of the cheaper German wines, including Liebfraumilch £. Also grown in Eastern Europe £. There are some good ones from New Zealand ££.

Muscat Headily grapy, perfumed, fruity wines, often made sweet (in Asti for the Spumante ££, sweet and fortified with alcohol in Muscat de Beaumes-de-Venise £££, the sweet, fortified Portuguese Moscatel de Setúbal £££ or the delicious heavy dessert Muscats of Australia £££). Alsace makes a good, aromatic, well-flavoured dry version ££. Morio Muscat from Germany has a very similar flavour, but it's in fact a crossing of Silvaner and Weisser Burgunder (Pinot Blanc) that somehow tastes Muscaty by mistake. Like the real Muscat, its wines are for drinking young.

Pinot Blanc Genetically a poor cousin of the Chardonnay, with some of its flavour but much less character. Makes clean, dry, quite alcoholic wines in Alsace ££, Northern Italy £–££ (also good sparkling wines ££). In Germany and Austria, it is called the **Weisser Burgunder** or **Weissburgunder**, and is made medium-dry (dry in Austria for home consumption, though it is generally sweetened up for us in Britain) £–££.

Pinot Gris Crisp, dry wines, often quite high in alcohol, lowish in acidity, sometimes with a slight nuttiness, but generally rather neutral. In Alsace they like to call it **Tokay**, whatever the EEC may say to the contrary ££. It's called the **Ruländer** in Germany and Austria £–££, and the **Pinot Grigio** (formerly sometimes **Tocai**) in Italy £.

Riesling (pronounced *Reesling*, and also called Rheinriesling, Weisser Riesling, Johannisberg Riesling, Riesling Renano in Italy and Rajnski Rizling in Yugoslavia.) When young, these are crisp, fruity, flowery wines with good acidity, sometimes honeyed, and the good ones age with several years in bottle to give an increasingly petrolly bouquet and flavour – sounds awful, tastes delicious. Australian Rieslings develop this character quicker than most, sometimes in two or three years £££. Delicious, flowery steely-crisp wines in Alsace £–£££. Sometimes dry, sometimes sweeter in California and North-West USA £££. The top quality grape of Germany, where it makes some dry, mostly medium to sweet wines £–£££. Some excellent dry and sweet wines also in Austria, where the wines mature quicker £–£££. (Not to be confused with Welschriesling, Riesling Italico, Riesling Italianski, or Laski or Lutomer Riesling which are not the same thing at all, but make decent, drinkable, but dull wines in Italy, Austria and Eastern Europe £.) Riesling alone on the label anywhere in the world *should* mean Rheinriesling, the real stuff, but you can't always rely on it.

Sauvignon (Sauvignon Blanc) Crisp, steely, gooseberry, elderflower, or cats' pee flavour and smell, very aromatic wines, with good acidity. Best when young. Fresh, light and delicate in Sancerre and Pouilly Fumé ££–£££, light, fresh, less delicate in Touraine £–££ and Haut Poitou £–££. Heavier, fatter as a rule in Bordeaux £–£££, where the whites are sometimes pure Sauvignon and will generally say so on the label, sometimes a mix of Sauvignon and Sémillon *(see below)*. They are heavier and fuller still, often very rich and ripe, in California £££ and Australia £££. Sometimes called Fumé Blanc (after Pouilly Blanc Fumé) in the USA. Some firm, fresh Sauvignons are being made in Chile £–££. Grown all over the world.

Scheurebe Along with Kerner and Müller-Thurgau, the best of the new German vine crossings (Silvaner × Riesling). A steely, Riesling-like acidity, but can be coarse-flavoured if unripe. Ripe, it has an agreeable, fresh bouquet, often a bit reminiscent of grapefruit skins. Found only in Germany £–££ and well worth trying. (Pronounced 'shoy-rayber'.)

Sémillon Rich, subdued, heavy wine, with low acidity, and a sweetish aroma even when it's bone dry. Yellow to deep golden colour, and best a year or two old. Grown and bottled as a separate variety in the Hunter Valley of Australia £££. It's the main constituent (usually with a little Sauvignon) of the great sweet wines of Sauternes and Barsac ££–£££, also flavoured in most years by a fungus – noble rot or botrytis – which shrivels and concentrates the grapes.

Silvaner/Sylvaner (The first spelling in Germany, the second in Alsace.) Fairly neutral, sometimes acid grape without much distinguishing flavour, grown in Alsace [££]. Sometimes seen on German labels, particularly the flask-bottles of Franconia (Franken) [££].

Traminer Banned now as a name in the EEC except in the South Tyrol (Alto Adige) in Italy, where it originated. The same grape as Gewürztraminer *(see above).*

Viura (Called the **Macabeo** or **Macabeu** in Catalonia.) A Spanish grape. Most of the Viura wines imported into Britain are now made fresh, sold young, and their taste is lightly flowery, often rather neutral, often with a 'cardboard' aftertaste. *Very* well made (and Marqués de Cáceres in the only such one we've tasted), it can taste almost like Sauvignon.

Solo black grapes

Barbera Ruby-red, dry, acid wines, medium-bodied, tannic when young, from North-West Italy [£]–[££]. Nice lightly chilled.

Cabernet Franc A bit like Cabernet Sauvignon *(see below)*, but even more grassy and fragrant, lighter coloured and lighter bodied, less tannic wines. One of the three main constituents of claret. The grape of the fragrant Chinon and Bourgueil wines of the Loire [££]–[£££], and usually half of the blend of Cabernet Rouge d'Anjou [£]–[££]. Also made into single variety wines in North-East Italy [£].

Cabernet Sauvignon Inky purple-black when young, ageing to tawny-amber, intensely flavoured wines, tasting sometimes of blackcurrant fruit or blackcurrant leaves, sometimes of mint, rather herbaceous in cooler climates. In Northern France, it makes simple, gutsy, herbaceous wines, often mixed in with Cabernet Franc [£]–[££], and in Bulgaria it makes simple, gutsy, jammy, cheap and good-value wines [£]–[££]. Chilean [££] and South African Cabernets are dark, fat and smoky, and it makes particularly powerful, richly fruity alcoholic reds in California and Australia [£££], a bit lighter in North-West USA [£££]. It's one of the major grapes of Bordeaux. In Anjou, mixed with the Cabernet Franc, it makes a sweetish, aromatic rosé, also with that characteristic blackcurrant flavour [££].

Dolcetto Not sweet, despite the name: dry, grapy, very fruity wines with a refreshingly bitter almond after-taste. Often an inky-rich red. From North-West Italy [£]–[££]. Best young and cool.

Gamay Purplish-crimson, light to medium light coloured reds with an appealing boiled-fruit-sweet aroma. Generally not very tannic except for the best wines of the Beaujolais, which need two or three years to soften [££]. Otherwise good, easy-gulping wines from Beaujolais [£]–[££], Burgundy [£]–[££], the Loire (Anjou and Touraine) [£]–[££] and Austria, where it is known as the Blaufränkisch [£]–[££].

Merlot Round, fat, plummy, alcoholic wines, with a sweetish taste, even when there's in fact no sugar there. Sometimes a gamy aroma.

Easy drinking: lots of tannin, but not as hard as in Cabernet Sauvignon. (Merlot is an important softening part of the claret blend in St-Emilion and Pomerol and to a lesser extent elsewhere in Bordeaux.) Made as a single variety, rich and velvety, in California and North-West USA [£££]. Rather lighter and thinner versions come from Northern Italy [£].

Nebbiolo Often intensely scented (liquorice, prunes, though those of higher gastronomic habits have been known to say truffles), full-bodied and slightly bitter grape from North-West Italy. It's the grape of the tough Barolo, Barbaresco, Spanna, Gattinara etc [££]–[£££] but wines from this area labelled simply 'Nebbiolo' [££] are likely to be softer (relatively, that is), more approachable and drinkable earlier, within five or six years of the vintage – and a bit cheaper.

Pinot Noir A fussy grape, which many winemakers can't handle to appetising effect. When it's good, it's rich, with pure, raspberry-like fruit. It smells sweet, even if it's quite, quite dry. Made badly, or grown in a poor year or in the wrong place, Pinot Noir is thin and light, often with a cabbagy, beetrooty aroma, maybe from elsewhere in the vegetable plot or even the compost heap. Good ones age well for many years (though not as long as Cabernet) and age tends to accentuate the 'sweet' and vegetably characteristics. Exquisite to good to appalling in Burgundy [££]–[£££]. Lighter, but generally good, clear-flavoured, sometimes a bit acid, in Sancerre [£££]. Usually disappointing in California, New Zealand and Australia [£££]. It's called the Blauburgunder in Austria and Germany, where it makes thin and weedy, near-rosé wines, best avoided if something else can be had instead [£]–[££], and light, almost rosé red wines in Alsace [££]. (White juice from the Pinot Noir goes into practically all Champagnes.)

Pinotage A cross between the Pinot Noir and the Cinsault of Southern France. Widely grown in South Africa [££]–[£££], and increasingly in New Zealand (not yet imported here). Big, jammy, sometimes rather coarse.

Syrah (**Shiraz** in Australia) Inky-black, rich, intensely fruity, tannic wines, full of flavour, almost tarry, and very perfumed, with a raspberry-and-tar aroma. They improve with age. The grape of the powerful Northern Rhône reds [££]–[£££] and also blended into Southern Rhônes such as Côtes-du-Rhône [££] and Châteauneuf-du-Pape [£££] to give extra beef, perfume, fruit and colour, and also into lesser wines of the South of France (Midi) [£]. Called the Shiraz in Australia, it can have a flavour some describe as 'sweaty saddle'! Australian Shiraz is fat, very full, pleasantly sweetish [£££]. The Australians often blend it effectively with Cabernet Sauvignon, which adds a more lingering flavour. California Syrah can be good, Northern Rhône-like wine [£££]. (The Californians also grow a tough, not-so-appealing and quite unrelated grape they call the Petite Sirah.)

Zinfandel Makes rich, fat wines, sometimes jammy, sometimes tough, but always fruity. It often smells like bramble jelly, occasionally like tinned loganberries. Exclusive to California [££].

The wine regions

This section on the wine regions of the world aims to give you all the *practical* information you need to make your choice when faced with a daunting array of bottles or names on the shop shelf or wine list. It won't tell you anything about the wines' history, nor about which grapes grow on the south-facing slope. What matters to you is how the wine tastes, how much it costs, and what is best value for money. In each section, where appropriate, you will find advice on which vintages to buy now to drink now, which to buy now to lay down for the future, and when they should be ready to drink; an explanation of any terms to be found on the wine label that might be confusing or unfamiliar; the names of our choice of the most reliably good to excellent producers and wines, compiled by our team of experts in conjunction with the editor; where to go in Britain to find a wide selection of the wines, and our top choice of wines that represent particularly good value.

Wines and categories of wines are marked throughout with a symbol denoting the price range into which they generally fall. [£] means a wine under £3, [££] a wine between £3 and £5, and [£££] a wine over £5. For further information, or if you have trouble tracking down specific wines, the organisations mentioned at the end of each section should be able to help.

Australia

A group of Australian wine importers sent a questionnaire out earlier this year. Amongst the members of the wine trade canvassed, only 31 per cent could name more than four areas of Australian wine production, and 42 per cent could name fewer than three. Members of the public were also canvassed, and 82 per cent were unable to name a single area. This wouldn't be particularly distressing, were it not for the fact that, of those questioned, 100 per cent of the trade sample were satisfied with their purchase of Australian wine – and 100 per cent of the general public who had tried Australian wines thought them enjoyable and good value. As to availability, 92 per cent of the trade, and 96 per cent of the public, thought these wines were not easily available to the consumer.

Value for money

Any Australian wine in good condition is almost certain to be value for money. The Australians are making too much wine, and there's only so much you can expect an Anglo-Saxon to knock back and still do a 40 hour week. So they *must* export. Prices start at less than £10 per dozen (ex-cellars). The shipping is no more expensive than from Marseilles, the duty's a bit more, but the eventual retail price could easily be less than £2.50 a bottle for full-flavoured, cleanly made, ripe, fruity wine. £5–£6 will buy you some of the best wines on the British market.

Most of what the Australians themselves drink is cheap and comes out of a wine box. **Australian wine boxes** are the best on the British market: clean fruity reds and whites. The reds are often particularly good value because, unlike the European wines generally found in boxes, they have enough alcohol and body to resist the ravages of oxidation. **North East Victoria Muscats** [£££] are superb, strong, sweet wines and cheap at the price, getting more out of the Muscat grape than any other region can. They are like a concentrated essence of the grape, though they are difficult to find *(see below)*. **Chardonnays** [££]–[£££], except for the most expensive, are particularly good value, and start at around £3.30. The wines are soft and creamy with oak, and the quality is as good as any except fine Côte d'Or Burgundies. Also excellent value are the widely available **Coonawarra reds** [££]–[£££]. Both the Shiraz and the Cabernet grown in Coonawarra make lovely wines, drawing out lovely fruit and mint flavours, backed up by oak, but almost always surprisingly light for the amount of flavour.

The 1984 vintage

By the summer of 1984, we already had some 1984s in the form of Hill-Smith Old Triangle Riesling [£] *(see below)*. Good though 1983 was, 1984 looks better, because for once, the Australians had a long, cool summer. Australia has an eternal battle to keep alcohol levels down and acid levels up. Whereas 1983 was frequently harvested in drought conditions, except where flash floods swept six feet of water through the exhausted vineyards, the 1984 ripening and picking season, for over four months, was cloudy from the warmest to the coolest parts. It is a vintage which will once more reinforce Australia's growing reputation for high-class whites and the more elegant, fragrant reds.

What to drink now, what to keep

Except for a very few massive reds, Australian wines are not made to cellar endlessly. Few Australians will lay wine down, and so the wines are ready on release. Even so, they will mostly age extremely well for a few years, and Cabernet, Semillon and Rhine Riesling will completely change character. Choose laying-down wine by winemaker rather than by vintage. Producers like Taltarni, Bailey's of Bundarra, Brokenwood, Hardy's, Marienberg, Chateau Tahbilk, Rothbury, and Hill-Smith all make red wines that can age for up to ten years. But remember that the producers see any such ageing as merely an added bonus: the wines will be delicious without.

Understanding the Australian label

There are only three small 'appellation' areas in Australia, and the general feeling is that a French-style AC system would be unhelpful, to say the least, since there's a long tradition of innovative blending to make the desired style of wine, as well as of hauling grapes hundreds of miles from vineyard to winery. In 1983, Mitchelton in Victoria bought grapes in Western Australia and drove them across the Nullarbor Desert. Anakie Vineyards flew grapes in from Tasmania.

The only legal limits which must be respected are:

Grape type

If labelled as a varietal, 80 per cent must be of that type. One of the best Shiraz wines available in Britain is blended with five per cent Trebbiano – simply to improve the taste. If it is more than an 80–20 blend, the larger percentage grape is stated first. There have been a couple of labelling scandals in Australia in the last 12 months, but with the high standard of wine we're getting, don't let that worry you.

Region

If more than one region's wine is substantially included, the chief contributing area must be listed first, but a widely available high quality wine like Wynns Ovens Valley Shiraz is blended with a little Coonawarra fruit – presumably to improve the taste – and because the proportion is small, they have no need to mention this on the label.

New South Wales The most famous area, but not much seen in Britain, except for Rosemount Estates. Others include Tyrrell, Rothbury, Lake's Folly, Brokenwood, Allandale, Wyndham, De Bortoli.

South Australia They truck grapes all over the place here, and the best wines with any label definition will be from the Coonawarra or the cooler fringes of the Barossa. From the Coonawarra come Wynns, Rosemount, Penfolds, Mildara; from elsewhere: Gawler River, Hill-Smith, Orlando, Jim Barry, Berri Estates/Renmano.

Tasmania Lovely cool climate, wines with good acidity and clear character. Moorilla, Piper's Brook, Heemskerk.

Victoria A wealth of good wines, covering all styles. Bailey's of Bundarra, Stanton & Killeen, Taltarni, Chateau Tahbilk, Bests Great Western, Cathcart Ridge, Tisdall, Brown Brothers, Chateau Remy, Yellowglen, Wynns Ovens Valley, Warrenmang. There are many others, but samples of these should be available in the UK *(see below)*.

Western Australia Houghtons is the only producer providing real value for money here – big, old style, but worth it. Otherwise, more modern and expensive wineries include Moss Wood, Wiyabrup, Vasse Felix and Leeuwin Estate.

Australian names to look out for

New South Wales

Tyrrell Full, intense and famous whites especially VAT 47 Chardonnay. *(Averys)*

Rothbury Estate The Semillon and Shiraz experts, individual and high quality. *(Geoffrey Roberts)*

Brokenwood High quality, very concentrated reds. *(Australvin UK)*

Rosemount Widely available fair priced reds and whites. *(Rosemount [UK] Ltd)*

McWilliams Good stocky reds and attractive well-priced whites. *(Averys)*

South Australia

Orlando Good William Jacob blends and excellent value varietals, especially Chardonnay and Cabernet. *(Colman's of Norwich)*

Gawler River Very good, fair priced reds and whites, particularly Hermitage and dry Muscat. *(Blackshaw & Jowers International)*

Hill-Smith Excellent blended red, very good Cabernet and Shiraz and 'immediate release' *('nouveau')* Riesling. *(A Huesgen [UK] Ltd)*

Wynns Wonderful, light, fragrant Cabernet and Shiraz and some good whites. *(Australian Forwarding Agency)*

Hardy Heavy but enjoyable old-style reds, and some attractive fresh whites. *(Australian Forwarding Agency)*

Berri/Renmano Excellent low-price reds and whites, especially Cabernet and 'fruity Gordo'. Good red Cabernet–Shiraz wine box. *(Shaftesbury Marketing)*

Tasmania

Moorilla High quality and expensive Cabernet and Riesling. *(Geoffrey Roberts)*

Victoria

Yellowglen Primarily high quality Champagne method fizz, but strong reds too. *(Hicks & Hayes, Emmons Wholesale)*

Chateau Tahbilk Best for big intense reds though chunky whites are also good. *(Spedding Nicholson, Christopher & Co)*

Taltarni First-class modern reds and whites. *(Caxton Wines)*

Tisdall Marvellous Chardonnay and Cabernet based reds. *(Hicks & Hayes)*

Brown Bros Remarkable array of excellent whites and good reds. *(Walter Siegel)*

Baileys Stunning old style reds and brilliant Muscats. *(W H Cullen)*

Western Australia

Houghton Old-style Cabernet and 'non-Chardonnay' white Burgundy style. *(Australian Forwarding Agency)*

Where to buy Australian wines

Geoffrey Roberts, The Wine Studio, Les Amis du Vin, W H Cullen, Averys of Bristol.

BEST AUSTRALIAN BUYS [££] Killawarra Chardonnay *(Victoria Wine; importer: Australian Forwarding Agency)* [££] Orlando Chardonnay *(Carrefour, Peter Dominic, Bottoms Up [selected stores], Roys of Wroxham, Chard Brothers [Weston-super-Mare]; McKerchar & MacNaughton; importer: Colmans)* [££] Rosemount Estates Show Chardonnay *(Peter Dominic [Orange Street], Victoria Wine; importer: Rosemount UK)* [££] Wynn's Ovens Valley or Coonawarra Shiraz *(Oddbins; importer: Australian Forwarding Agency)* [££] Hill-Smith Estate Red *(Cullens, Dolamore, Ashe & Nephew; importer: A Heusgen UK)* [££] Wynn's Coonawarra Estate Cabernet Sauvignon *(Oddbins, Case Wines [Bristol], A W Turpins [Notts]; importer: Australian Forwarding Agency)* [£££] Renmano Chairman's Selection Cabernet Sauvignon *(Davy & Co; importer: Shaftesbury Marketing)* [£££] Stanton & Killeen Muscat à Petits Grains (fortified) *(Peter Dominic [Orange Street only], The Wine Studio, David Alexander of Maidenhead; importer: Hicks & Hays)* [£££] Bailey's Liqueur Muscat *(Cullens)*

For further information contact: The Australian Trade Commission, Australia House, The Strand, London WC2B 4LA; tel: 01-438 8205.

Austria

The 1983 Vintage

The year 1983 was a great one in Austria, though not among the greatest. Early predictions that it would prove to be 'the vintage of the century' have proved, as usual, to be unfounded, though 1983 will certainly take its place in the first league. The one flaw, it seems, was a lack of vital humidity in Lower Austria and the Burgenland for the making in any quantity of the great sweet Prädikat wines, which crowned such truly classic years as 1917, 1947 or 1949. (Botrytis needs a humid atmosphere.)

The 1983 harvest was above average in size, but well down on the record yield of the previous year; 1983 wines reflect this in their better construction. Natural sugar levels in the grapes at the vintage were high, though the average acidity of most wines is a little on the low side to guarantee a long shelf-life. (Acidity, like the vinegar in pickles, helps wine to keep.

The key words to look for on the label in connection with the Austrians of 1983 are **Kabinett** ££ (a high proportion of the wines fall into this category: light, elegant wines for early drinking) and **Grüner Veltliner** (the mouthwatering freshness and lively acidity of this predominant Austrian variety are well matched this year, with a necessary counterbalance of natural grape sugars). If you can find both names in conjunction, then you will find probably the most typical expression of an excellent year, though there will be other prizes in store for the discerning. Lenz Moser, for example, have announced with pride that they have made two *Eisweine* £££ in Lower Austria, the first since 1978; there will also be some excellent Voslau red wines from the 1983 vintage.

Value for money

Basic Grüner Veltliner own-labels on the market are excellent value at around £2. The Prädikat wines are also good value ££–£££, maturing more quickly than their German counterparts. And there are some bargains to be found in the ££ price range.

What to drink now, what to keep

The ruling principle in drinking Austrian wines is 'the fresher the better': arguably, one can never improve on the green, prickling 'Heurigen' which never feel the confines of bottle and cork, and are drunk in Austria fresh from the cask through the winter following the vintage. Few wines, apart from the sweetest and greatest, either keep for long or are made to do so; it follows, therefore, that wines bearing a vintage earlier than 1980 should be viewed with circumspection, especially those without Prädikat. Austrian Prädikat wines have less acidity than most German wines, and mature more quickly. The following can be only a general guide:

1983 *(See above)*

1982 Light wines, agreeable, fresh but unlikely to keep. Drink now.

1981 A good year. Drinking well now. Keep Prädikat wines for a maximum of two to three years.

1980 A difficult year. Choose reliable shippers only *(see below under* NAMES TO LOOK OUT FOR).

1979 A good year. Prädikat wines drinking well. Others probably on the downward slope.

1978 A poor year. Exceptional bottles only.

1977, 1976 Good vintages, but all but Prädikat wines will be showing their age.

Looking further back, 1971 and 1969 were excellent vintages, the former (as in Germany) characterised by an excellent acid/sugar balance, which has given the wines unusual longevity. The best of them are still superb.

Understanding the Austrian label

Austrian wines, though very different from their German neighbours, use broadly the same geographical and descriptive codes and quality grading system. This glossary, therefore, is limited to those terms which are uniquely Austrian (the ending -er denotes a wine from the village whose name precedes it):

Apetlon(er) Village on the eastern shore of the Neusiedlersee, near the Hungarian border. Famous for sweet wines.

Ausbruch Quality level between Spätlese and Auslese, rarely found in Britain.

Ausstich Selected top-quality wines, set aside after the vintage.

Bouviertraube Aromatic, fast-maturing grape variety.

Burgenland Austria's easternmost wine district, embracing the shallow Neusiedlersee. Its sandy soils and warm, humid climate produce rich dessert wines from botrytis-affected grapes.

Dürnstein Best-known (and spectacular) village of the Wachau (*see below*), home of the Wachau WZG (co-operative).

Falkenstein(er) Village of Lower Austria, north-west of Vienna, producing plentiful wines mainly from Grüner Veltliner. Increasingly available in the UK.

Grüner Veltliner Austria's leading grape variety, producing green, slightly austere, dry wines; delicious young, but only Prädikat grades (Kabinett and above) are for keeping. *(See also* GRAPES ON THE LABEL.)

Gumpoldskirchen(er) District south of Vienna producing rich, heady white wines.

Heurigen 'Jug wines' drawn from the barrel: a speciality of the Viennese suburbs, where the wine bar–pubs are also called 'Heurigen'.

Klosterneuburg Government testing-station, viticultural school, and quality-wine producer all rub shoulders in this imposing, green-domed Abbey complex on the Danube west of Vienna. *(See* NAMES TO LOOK OUT FOR.)

Krems(er)/Langenlois(er) Quality districts adjoining the Wachau.

Muskat Ottonel An aromatic grape-variety not uniquely Austrian, but worthy of mention nevertheless. The best are difficult to surpass. The name is said to derive from an Irish emigrant named O'Connell.

Neuburger Lesser grape-variety of the Wachau.

Niederösterreich Lower Austria, the largest wine region, divided into several sub-districts (eg Wachau).

Riede Single vineyard (equivalent to German 'Lage').

Rust Lake-shore village of Burgenland, famous for Ruster Ausbruch (dessert wine likened to Tokay).

St Laurent Red grape-variety, producing deep, plum-coloured wines with distinctive flavour.

Schilcher Dry rosé, a Styrian speciality.

Spätrot-Rotgipfler Blend of two grape varieties, from which Gumpoldskirchener is made.

Voslau Austria's best-known red-wine district.

Wachau Terraced vineyards lining the Danube gorge that produce classic wines from Rheinriesling and lesser varieties, often with keeping qualities rare for the country as a whole. The leading district for dry and semi-dry wines, as Burgenland is for the sweet dessert types.

Zweigeltrebe A Gamay × St Laurent cross, producing light, agreeable red wines.

Austrian names to look out for

H Augustin Good quality, clean wines, increasingly available in Britain. [£]–[££] *(H Augustin Ltd)*

Bründlmayer Traditional producer based in Langenlois. Fine quality. [££]→[£££] *(Lawlers/Charles Heidsieck)*

Döblinger Herrenhaus The national co-operative, a major producer of generic wines. [£]–[££] *(Tower Wine Shippers)*

Sepp Hold Burgenland producer of classic sweet wines. [££]–[£££] *(City Vintagers)*

Johann Kattus One of the few Viennese houses represented in UK, producer of both still and sparkling wines (eg Hochriegl Sekt). [££]–[£££] *(Tower Wine Shippers)*

Klosterneuburg A major producer, both as estate owner and négociant. A benchmark of quality. [££]–[£££] *(Klosterneuburg Ltd)*

Klosterkeller Siegendorf Good Burgenland producer. [££]–[£££] *(Amann-Seethaler Ltd)*

Lenz Moser The doyen of the Austrian trade, based at Röhrendorf near Krems. Source of 'Schluck', 'Blue Danube' brands and an ascending scale of estate wines. £–£££ *(Lawlers/Charles Heidsieck)*

Fritz Saloman Small company making good characterful wines. ££ *(Tower Wine Shippers)*

Schlosskellerei Uhlheim Good small producer and merchant based in Styria. Source of an excellent St Laurent 'Ausstich' from Voslau. ££ *(Tower Wine Shippers)*

Alexander Unger Producer of classic Burgenland wines for the sweet-toothed. ££–£££ *(Tower Wine Shippers)*

Winzergenossenschaft This impressive word (WZG for short) simply means wine co-operative, of which Austria has a great number. Among the most respected are those at **Gumpoldskirchen** *(Tower Wine Shippers)*, **Krems** *(House of Austria)*, **Loiben**, **Retz** and **Dürnstein (WZG Wachau)** *(Tower)*. The latter has just started to sell in Britain four excellent dry white wines in a Burgundy-shaped bottle, including Grüner Veltliner Kabinett 1982 and Riesling Kabinett 1982. ££

Where to buy Austrian wines

Austrian wines, good as they are, are not always easy to find in Britain. The wine trade is unwilling to stock them because the public, who know little about them, are slow to buy. Try, for a start, the slightly bigger than average Austrian ranges of the following retailers: Victoria Wine, Cullens, Selfridges, Arthur Rackham, West End Wine Centre, House of Austria, Alston Wines, McKerchar & MacNaughton, Philip Morgan.

BEST AUSTRIAN BUYS £ Own-label Grüner Veltliner from Sainsbury's, Littlewoods, Victoria Wine, Grants of St James's, and from Tesco (these are all around £2); ££ St Leopold Red and White Litres (Klosterneuburg) *(Oddbins, Wm Morrison)*, ££ St Laurent Ausstich 1979/1981 Schlosskellerei Uhlheim *(West End Wine Centre)*, ££ Kremser Wachtberg Traminer Kabinett 1982, Fritz Salomon *(by the case from Tower Wine Shippers)*, ££–£££ Sweet Austrians from Selfridges, Victoria Wine, Sainsbury's Vintage Selection, and stockists listed in the previous paragraph.

For further information, including addresses of importers, contact: The Austrian Trade Commission, 1 Hyde Park Gate, London SW7 5ER; tel: 01-584 4411.

The 'Names to look out for' sections point out our selection of the most reliable growers, producers or merchants. Some good producers may have been omitted because they are hard to find in British shops.

China

The 'Great Wall', China's premier wine, has crumbled, owing, we are told, to the inconsistency of quality and difficulty in getting supplies. However, a new dragon has appeared – 'Dynasty' – imported by Reid, Pye and Campbell and sold at the moment by Harrods [££]. Made from the Muscat grape, it has the Muscat's usual floweriness, but whether it is worth the asking price is doubtful.

Cyprus

Though nothing remotely exciting is coming out of Cyprus at the moment, we can expect some sound, gulpable wines in a year or two. The government is putting a lot of money and effort into wine research at the Cypriot Department of Agriculture's Model Winery in Limassol, and the knowledge gained is being passed on to the island's winemakers. Of the Cypriot wines currently available in the UK, however, the reds are without exception dull; best amongst the readily available whites is Bellapais (lightly sparkling and medium dry).

For further information contact: Cyprus Trade Centre, 213 Regent Street, London W1; tel: 01-734 4791.

Eastern Europe

BULGARIA

Value for money

The bustling Bulgarians continue to set the pace for Eastern European wines on the British market, and in terms of value for money their offerings are hard to beat. Relatively limited in range, but of uniformly good quality, the wines are now found on most supermarket and off-licence shelves and are even penetrating the hotel and restaurant trade as consistent and reliable 'house wines'.

What to drink now

All the Bulgarian wines are imported ready for drinking. The better, fatter reds *(see below)* may benefit from being aged a year or so after you buy them, but are also very good new.

Understanding the Bulgarian label

An important part of the success the Bulgarians have achieved here is due to the efforts they have made to tailor their labels, as well as the wines themselves, to the British market: the days of contorted cyrillics are long past, and the wines are sold simply under branded or varietal names. The latter are often qualified by their **region of origin**, such as **Suhindol** or **Schumen**, which are best identified with a map of Bulgaria in hand. **Asenovgrad** is a sort of super-appellation, commanding a substantial premium on the home market [££]. Perhaps the only other name requiring explanation is **'Gamza'** (or **'Gumza'**), the name of a lesser Bulgarian varietal which produces a rather tough red.

The basic Bulgarian range, red, medium white and a new sweet white (with nice acidity to match the sweetness) is found either under the **Mehana** brand [£] or under the retailer's own generic label, eg Asda Bulgarian Red [£]. The red, made from a local variety called the Pamid, is garnet-coloured, light in body, soft and highly quaffable, the whites faintly aromatic (a whiff of Muscat is apparent), soft, grapy, fresh and nicely balanced. At well under £2 per bottle, excellent value.

A few rungs up the quality scale, one finds the range of varietal wines which first put Bulgaria on our map. The **Riesling** [£] is of immediate appeal: scented, off-dry, with pleasant green acidity, now widely available in both bottles and litres. Two other whites have been added to the range: a **Pinot Chardonnay** [£], which is pleasant if a little short on varietal character (though the Bulgarians are bringing in a new, crisper style, which augurs well: look for it in a 'Burgundy' bottle, as opposed to the green 'Bordeaux' of its predecessor) and a **Sauvignon** [£], which is delicious: full and soft on the palate (with some 12 per cent of alcohol), but with all the fresh aroma and green 'bite' that one looks for in this variety.

The reds are equally impressive: the **Cabernet Sauvignon** [£] (currently 1979 vintage) is the closest of the Eastern European examples to the Bordeaux model, with a rich, plummy quality overlaying a firm, cedary core. The **Merlot** [£], also 1979, is similarly attractive, with the ripe, mellow qualities of the varietal.

At the top end of the range are two wines of some individuality, with distinctive white labels. The first of these is a 1977 **Mavrud** from **Asenovgrad** [££]: Mavrud being a dark, tannic indigenous variety much prized in Bulgaria. With this degree of maturity, the wine softens agreeably, and is well worth a try. The **Sakar Mountain Cabernet Sauvignon** (the 1976 vintage is on sale as we go to press) [££] is also recommended: fully mature, with an agreeable touch of oakiness.

Names to look out for

All Bulgarian wines are marketed here under the auspices of the state monopoly, which trades as the Bulgarian Vintners Company Ltd (BVC). Many shippers and retailers have, however, negotiated a direct supply from Bulgaria, though the blends vary only slightly from the standard range described above. BVC will be able to help you trace stockists; their address is: 156 Caledonian Road, London N1; tel: 01-278 8047.

BEST BULGARIAN BUYS [£] Bulgarian Riesling (supermarket or BVC labels), [£] Bulgarian Cabernet Sauvignon (supermarket or BVC labels), both available from many sources; and [££] Asenovgrad Mavrud 1977 *(Victoria Wine, Peter Dominic, Harveys of Bristol)*

For further information contact: Bulgarian Vintners Co Ltd, 156 Caledonian Road, London N1; tel: 01-278 8047.

CZECHOSLOVAKIA

Wine importers Stowells have conceded defeat with their Zigani brand, which is no longer available, reasonable value though it was. To drink the excellent Czech whites, one will now have to visit the country: a good excuse for a dirty weekend in Prague.

HUNGARY

Value for money

There are early signs of change on the Hungarian wine scene, which can only be for the better. As one of the poorer Eastern bloc countries, Hungary has been late in adopting modern wine-making techniques, and her wines (with the exception of timeless Tokay) have suffered by comparison with those of the westernised Yugoslavs and the ambitious Bulgarians. Now it seems that competition is increasing on the British market, partly as a spin-off from the increase in reciprocal trading symbolised by Mrs Thatcher's visit to Budapest. Improvements in quality should result.

What to drink now

All the Hungarian wines are imported ready for drinking. Tokay can keep a long time. Vintages back to 1957 and up to nearly £42 a half-litre bottle are available from Adnams. La Vigneronne usually also has old vintages. But the younger vintages on the market now in Britain are quite ready for drinking, though they will keep.

Understanding the Hungarian label

Badacsony(i) Quality wine-district (mainly white wines) on the northern shore of Lake Balaton.

Balaton(i) Wines from Lake Balaton, the Hungarian 'inland sea', which enjoys a favourable micro-climate.

Egri Wines from the Eger district in north-eastern Hungary. 'Egri Bikaver' translates as 'Bull's Blood of Eger'.

Puttonyos Measures of grape-paste from nobly rotted grapes added to fermenting Tokay, which determine the level of sweetness. Tokay is sold with three, four or five puttonyos, the last being the sweetest.

Tokay Aszu The classic Tokay, containing the 'puttonyos' of sweetening-paste. Not all Tokay is 'Aszu': look for the word on the label if you want the traditional dessert wine.

Tokay Aszu Eszencia The most concentrated, and expensive, Tokay Aszu, made entirely of nobly rotted grapes. Worth the premium £££.

Tokay Furmint A heavy, and rather dull, dry table wine.

Tokay Szamorodni Tokay made without the addition of 'puttonyos' of 'aszu' paste. It may be sweet or dry, according to vintage, and is rather dull.

Hungarian names to look out for

Colman's of Norwich continue to dominate the market as a result of their trading agreements with Monimpex, the Hungarian monopoly. Wisely, though, they have recently decided to bow to the inevitable, concentrate on their established sellers, and withdraw from the market some of the more obscure speciality wines, which were really more interesting for their polysyllables than for their content.

The new, pruned selection is headed by the ever popular, chewy red **Bull's Blood** £, which is available in both bottle and box and also in a Hungarian-bottled version (**'Egri Bikaver'**); cognoscenti will recognise a touch more body and bottle age in the latter. **Olasz (Welsch/Laski) Riesling** £ comes in three styles: dry, from **Kecskemet** on the Great Plain, medium from **Pecs** (pronounced Paish) in Southern Hungary, and sweet from **Balatonfured** on the shores of Lake Balaton. All three are commercial, well-made wines with a touch more spice and body than the Yugoslav equivalents.

Relatively new arrivals on the Hungarian scene are **Cabernet Sauvignon** and **Chardonnay** varietals £, which one finds in a number of supermarkets. Both are sound wines if lacking any pronounced varietal characteristics.

Soproni Kekfrankos and **Kadarka** £ are two of the Hungarian specialities that may outlive their departed stablemates (such as Egri Leanyka, Mori Ezerjo, and Debroi Harslevelu); the former is a dark, sweetened red from the Austrian border, Kadarka a gutsy, positive red from the Plain, the traditional match for goulash.

Crowning the Hungarian assortment is **Tokay** ££ in its distinctive ninepin half-litre bottles.

BEST HUNGARIAN BUY ££ Tokay 5 Puttonyos *(Selfridges, Peter Dominic and quite widely elsewhere; importer: Colman's of Norwich)*

RUMANIA

Rumanian wines are still available only in a limited way on our market. Such wines as one does find are generally sound and attractive, if usually on the sweet side (including reds), but there is little progress to report.

What to drink now

Anything on the market here will be at its peak.

Understanding the Rumanian label

Rumanian labels tend if anything to err on the wordy side in their descriptive copy but often forget to provide the one vital piece of information: whether the wine is sweet or dry! So if in doubt, ask the retailer. Generally speaking, the wines are marketed under varietal names, qualified by region.

The most widely distributed range of wines consists of a sweetened red **Merlot** [£] from the **Dealul Mare**, a quality production zone in the Carpathians, and a medium-dry white from **Tarnave** in **Transylvania** [£], made from the indigenous **Feteasca** variety (also known as Mädchentraube). For a sweetened wine, the red is well made and harmonious, and by no means objectionable; the white is aromatic and luscious, with a pleasant, grapy flavour. Both are usually priced competitively and are consequently good value.

A slightly more serious contender is the **Minis** brand [£] of **Cabernet Sauvignon**, which is a good, workmanlike varietal, though lacking the class of the Bulgarian equivalent.

Rumania also produces a range of **Rieslings** (predominantly **Laski**), the sandy **Banat** area in the west of the country being the main source. They compare well with Yugoslav equivalents, and one marketed under the **Vinoroman** label [£] is particularly good. White wines from **Murfatlar**, on the Black Sea, tend to be made for the local market, which favours a golden, slightly oxidised style. *These labels are best avoided.*

BEST RUMANIAN BUYS [£] Merlot *(Victoria Wine Co and supermarkets)*

USSR

Sweet Russian sparkling wines have a cult following in several European countries, but perhaps we are more discerning. The best-known brand, **Krim**, is regularly available only from *The Russian Shop* in High Holborn, London WC1 (who offer a mail-order service to any part of the UK). **Ruby of Crimea**, a sweetened red, is also available from here and from those specialists who want another exotic heading for their price list. They are worth tasting to slake your curiosity, but you probably won't go back for a second bottle.

YUGOSLAVIA

The Yugoslav contenders on our shelves consist almost exclusively of the 'superbrand' Lutomer, its only competitor worthy of the title, Cloberg, a rash of retailers' own label Laski Rieslings, a smattering of other varietals . . . and that is that. It is a pity the list is so short, because Yugoslavia has probably a greater wealth of interesting and individual wines to offer than any of her Eastern European neighbours. Somehow these other wines don't seem to reach us, notwithstanding the honest endeavours of the specialist Yugoslav importers such as

Teltscher Bros and Vitkovitch Bros to offer a selection wider than the commonplace.

What to drink now

Yugoslav wines are imported generally ready for drinking. But try ageing the tannic Vranac brand for a couple of years.

Understanding the Yugoslav label

Beli Burgundec Pinot Blanc.

Dingac Sweetish red wine from the Dalmatian coast.

Fruska Gora Quality white wine-producing area of Serbia.

Gamé Gamay.

Jeruzalem Vineyard area of Slovenia, where crusaders stopped for a rest and stayed to grow wine.

Kombinat Co-operative winery.

Modri Burgundec Pinot Noir.

Neoplanta A crossing of Traminer and Smederevka varieties, making pleasant, scented white wines.

Prosek Rich dessert wine from Dalmatia.

Srem (or Sremski Karlovci) The former 'Carlowitz', a reputed vineyard area on the Danube north of Belgrade.

Zilavka Reputed white wine from Bosnia–Herzegovina. Deep, straw-coloured and tangy: an acquired taste.

There can be very few retailers in this country who fail to carry at least one **Laski Riesling** from Yugoslavia. The great virtue of these wines is their consistency; it will be a rare bottle that disappoints and *that* will probably be from an old bottling. They come in the main from Slovenia, Kontinentalna Hrvatska (Croatia), Velika Morava or Vojvodina (the northern part of Serbia) and are generally sold without a vintage, and in the medium dry style prescribed for the British market.

The same areas, all in the northern half of the country and leading up towards the Austrian border, produce a wide range of white varietal wines, including **Sauvignon**, **Traminer** and **Renski** (Rhine) **Riesling**. In Slovenia especially, these wines are characterised in their natural state by a lively, fresh acidity and pure varietal flavour matched only in certain regions of Austria and South Tyrol (Alto Adige). Milder versions of Sauvignon and Traminer can be found on the UK market in the Grants of St James's carafe range of varietal wines.

Yugoslav red wines come from the warmer and drier central and southern republics, including Serbia (embracing the region of **Kosmet**), **Montenegro** and **Macedonia**. The **Cabernet Sauvignon** and **Merlot** varietals can be excellent; **Pinot Noir** and **Gamay** are sound but less recognisable by true varietal standards. Two local specialities occasionally seen here are **Prokupac**, a soft agreeable red, and **Vranac** (literally 'Black Stallion'), a powerful, tannic red from Montenegro which, though intimidating when young, softens appealingly with age. Both are well worth a try.

Yugoslav names to look out for

The three most significant producers for the British market are the two major Slovene combines of **Slovin** in Ljubljana (source of Lutomer), **Vinag** in Maribor, and **Navip** in Belgrade-Zemun. Their names do occasionally appear on labels, and can be relied upon. Other good sources are the **Kombinat** at **Ptuj** in Slovenia, and the **22 Iuli Kombinat** at Titograd, who make good Vranac.

BEST YUGOSLAV BUYS [£] Own-label Laski Riesling *(supermarkets)*, [£] Renski Riesling *(widely stocked; importers: Teltscher Bros)*, [£] Vranac *(widely stocked; importers: Vitkovitch)*

For further information contact: The Yugoslav Wine Information Centre, 6 Vigo Street, London W1X 1AH; tel: 437 5927

England

The 1983 vintage

In terms of quantity, 1983 was the best year for English wines ever since vineyards began to be planted again 20 years ago. Yields were very high – ten tons or more per acre, compared with the paltry two to four the English grower can usually hope for, if he's lucky, in our climate, which is really far from ideal for grape-growing. More than two million bottles were produced in 1983, double the quantity made in 1982. And, most important, quality is good, with greater concentration of flavour than in recent years, and higher natural alcohol, owing to sunny weather at the end of October after a reasonable summer. The wines have gradually been improving also because the vines themselves are now mature, the majority having been planted 10 or 11 years ago – young vines produce thin wines. And, of course, the English winemakers are maturing, too; the standard of winemaking has risen greatly, even in the past couple of years.

Send us **your** views on the report forms at the back of the book.

What to drink now

1983 is the vintage to drink now. There is in any case precious little of previous vintages around. Any bottles you have stashed away of 1976 could be very good, mature wines as this was an exceptionally hot summer, and many wines were very rich, but often still with good acidity to help them to keep.

Value for money

English wines are for patriots, tourists and the curious: pleasant in a good year like 1983, rather like German wines in style, but *expensive* compared to similar wines on the market. This is natural enough, since the grower's costs must be extraordinarily high to cover years when our dreadful English weather ruins or vastly reduces his crop. Many prices did drop by 50p or so, however, after the big harvest in 1984 [£]–[££]. You will certainly find better value for money elsewhere. But it's nevertheless fun to drink the local produce.

Understanding the English label

English or British?

It is important to establish first of all that you are buying a *real* wine. **British** wines officially and legally speaking are wines made in industrial proportions from imported grape juice concentrate (like Carrow Prior and Moussec). They may, like these two, bear brand names which might lead you to believe that they came straight from an English or French vineyard. They are likely to be fairly sound, cheap and bland. **English**, **Welsh or Irish** wines are made from fresh grapes grown in the 1,000 acres of vineyard in the southern parts of those countries, where there were 205 commercial growers in 1984. It is illegal for a British (ex-concentrate) wine producer to label his wines as 'English'.

Certification trade mark

This is Britain's 'Appellation Contrôlée' system, set up a couple of years ago. Growers can submit their wines for stringent testing in the early part of the summer following the vintage, and wines successful in laboratory tests and tasting tests conducted by a panel of experts and Masters of Wine are granted a small gold seal, which will always appear on the bottles of these certified wines. It is wrong to believe, however, that a wine without a seal is necessarily poor. Some small growers are loath to pay the entry fees and laboratory costs, so do not submit their wines; and often the quantities produced are so small that they can easily sell their whole crop over the farm gate. The seal in any case means only that the wines are acceptable – pass level is fairly low.

Prices are correct to the best of our knowledge in summer 1984.

Grapes on the label

Gutenborner A rather neutral-tasting grape, a crossing of the Müller-Thurgau and the Chasselas Napoléon, grown in England because it ripens very early.

Huxelrebe Rather rough and acid in poor years but, when properly ripe, rather Muscat-like, quite full, with good, firm acidity. Good in 1983. A crossing of two rather obscure grapes, the Weisser Gutedel and the Courtillier Musqué.

Müller-Thurgau The grape most planted in this country. Medium-bodied wines of good acidity with a smell reminiscent of blackcurrant or elderflower leaves. Ripe and fruity in 1983. It is a crossing, done over 100 years ago, thought for years to have been of Riesling with Sylvaner, but now believed to be possibly a crossing of two strains of Riesling.

Ortega Suited to poor English summers because it ripens very early, this is a crossing between the Müller-Thurgau and the Siegerebe, the latter itself a Madeleine Angevine x Gewürztraminer crossing. At their best, when properly ripe, Ortega wines have a peachy nose and full fruit, and age well in bottle. But the wines can be a little bitter if the grapes are not properly ripe.

Reichensteiner One of the most popular grapes amongst English growers. A rather neutral wine, however, without much bouquet or flavour. It is a crossing, again containing rather obscure varieties: the familiar Müller-Thurgau, and a previous crossing of the Madeleine Angevine and Calabreser-Fröhlich.

Schönburger Well suited to this country, because it doesn't rot as easily as most other varieties. Its wines are spicy, fruity, and in England, in contrast to Schönburgers grown elsewhere, have plenty of balancing acidity. It's a crossing of the Pinot Noir and an Italian table grape variety, developed from a crossing of the Chasselas and the Muscat Hamburg – the spiciness comes from the Muscat, but it actually smells rather more like Gewürztraminer.

Names to look out for

See the BEST ENGLISH BUYS on page 57.

The Wine Development Board is a small organisation with the responsibility of encouraging more people to drink wine. They may be able to supply literature and general promotional material. Contact them at: Five Kings House, Kennet Wharf Lane, Upper Thames Street, London EC4V 3BH; TEL 01–248 5835.

Where to buy English wines

At the vineyard gate

Many English vineyards accept visitors and offer guided tours, the opportunity to buy from a vineyard shop, and sometimes even wine bar type food with home-grown wine. The vineyards listed below accepted visitors in 1984, and a similar list will be published by the English Vineyards Association early in the summer of 1985, obtainable from the Association at The Ridge, Lamberhurst Down, Kent, TN3 8ER; tel: (0892) 890734. It is always advisable to telephone the vineyard beforehand. The vintage generally takes place from mid to late October and growers are obviously terribly busy at this time. The English Vineyards Association also sells by post large and very attractive maps and provides information about English wines.

Key to the vineyard list

V Visitors welcome (particularly, the EVA leaflet points out, those who wish to buy wine).

CP Coach parties accepted with prior booking.

OD Open days – growers welcome visitors on certain days acceptable to them. *Always* telephone or write first.

VA Visitors by appointment only.

Counties containing vineyards that accept visitors

Berkshire Ascot, Cane End, Hillfoot, The Holt, Westbury

Buckinghamshire Wickenden

Cornwall Polmassick

Devon Loddiswell, Whitmoor House, Whitstone, Yearlstone

Dorset Kings Green

Essex Felstar, Nevards

Glamorgan Croffta

Gloucestershire Tapestry Wines, Three Choirs

Hampshire Aldermoor, Beaulieu, Hambledon, Hill Grove, Lymington

Hereford and Worcester Broadfield, Croft Castle, Kinver

Hertfordshire Frithsden, Rowney

Isle of Wight Barton Manor

Kent Bardingley, Biddenden, Conghurst, Elham Valley, Harbourne, Ightham, Lamberhurst, Leeds Castle, Penshurst, St Nicholas, Staple, Syndale Valley, Tenterden, Three Corners

Norfolk Elmham Park, Lexham Hall, Pulham

Oxfordshire Flints

Somerset Brympton d'Evercy, Pilton Manor, Spring Farm, Staplegrove, Whatley, Wootton, Wraxall

Suffolk Boyton, Brandeston, Bruisyard, Cavendish Manor, Chickering, Snape

Sussex Berwick Glebe, Breaky Bottom, Carr Taylor, Chilsdown, Ditchling, The English Wine Centre, Five Chimneys, Hooksway, Pine Ridge, Rock Lodge, St George's, Swiftsden

Wiltshire Elms Cross, Sherston Earl, Stitchcombe, Tytherley

British vineyards open to the public

Aldermoor (6 acres) **OD VA**
M F and W A Baerselman, Picket Hill, Ringwood, Hants. *Tel*: Ringwood (042 54) 2911

Ascot (2.5 acres) **V CP VA**
Col A R Robertson, Ascot Farm, Winkfield Road, Ascot, Berks. *Tel*: Ascot (0990) 23563

Bardingley (2.5 acres) **VA**
H S and B Turner, Babylon Lane, Hawkenbury, Staplehurst, Kent. *Tel*: Staplehurst (0580) 892264

Barton Manor (5.7 acres) **V CP OD VA** – Mr and Mrs A H Goddard, Whippingham, East Cowes, Isle of Wight. *Tel*: Cowes (0983) 292835

Beaulieu (6 acres) **V CP VA**
Lord Montagu of Beaulieu, Bealieu, Nr Brockenhurst, Hants. *Tel*: Beaulieu (0590) 612345

Berwick Glebe (2 acres) **VA**
Jane Broster and Doreen Birks, Frensham Cottage, Berwick, Nr Polegate, Sussex. *Tel*: Alfriston (0323) 870361

Biddenden (18 acres) **V CP VA**
R A Barnes, Little Whatmans, Biddenden, Ashford, Kent. *Tel*: Biddenden (0580) 291726

Boyton (4 acres) **V CP**
Michael W Crisp, Boyton End, Stoke by Clare, Suffolk. *Tel*: Haverhill (0440) 61893

Brandeston Priory (7 acres) **V CP**
Mr and Mrs P Dow, The Priory, Brandeston, Woodbridge, Suffolk. *Tel*: Earl Soham (072 882) 462

Breaky Bottom (4 acres) **CP VA**
Peter Hall, Rodwell, Lewes, Sussex. *Tel*: Lewes (079 16) 6427

Broadfield (10 acres) **OD VA**
K R H James, Broadfield Court Estate, Bodenham, Hereford and Worcester. *Tel*: Bodenham (056 884) 274 and 438

Brympton d'Evercy (1 acre) **V CP OD**
Charles E B Clive-Ponsonby-Fane, Brympton d'Evercy, Yeovil, Somerset. *Tel*: Yeovil (039 586) 2528

Bruisyard (10 acres) **V CP**
Mr and Mrs I H Berwick, Church Road, Bruisyard, Saxmundham, Suffolk. *Tel*: Badingham (072 875) 281

Cane End (6 acres) **VA**
Mr L E Hordern and Mr M A Hordern, Cane End Farm, Cane End, Reading, Berks. *Tel*: Reading (0734) 722217

Carr Taylor (21 acres) **V CP OD VA**
David Carr Taylor, Westfield, Hastings, East Sussex. *Tel*: Hastings (0424) 752501

Cavendish Manor (8.5 acres) **V CP**
B T Ambrose, Nether Hall Manor, Cavendish, Sudbury, Suffolk. *Tel*: Glemsford (0787) 280221

Chickering (2.5 acres) **VA**
P H Day, Chickering Hall, Hoxne, Eye, Suffolk. *Tel*: Hoxne (037 975) 227

Chilsdown (10.5 acres) **V CP OD**
Ian and Andrew Paget, The Old Station House, Singleton, Chichester, West Sussex. *Tel*: Singleton (0243 63) 398

Conghurst (0.5 acre) **VA**
Mrs B Bridgewater, Conghurst Oast, Conghurst Lane, Hawkhurst, Kent. *Tel*: Hawkhurst (058 05) 2634

Croft Castle (0.5 acre) **V CP**
Hon Mrs F Uhlman, Croft Castle, Nr Leominster, Hereford and Worcester. *Tel*: Yarpold (056 885) 246

Croffta (3 acres) **V CP OD VA**
J L M Bevan, Groes-Faen, Pontyclun. *Tel*: Glamorgan (0443) 223876

Ditchling (5 acres) **VA**
David and Ann Mills, Claycroft, Beacon Road, Ditchling, Hassocks, Sussex. *Tel*: Hassocks (079 18) 2634

Elham Valley (1.6 acres) **VA**
Mrs J V Allen and Mr P W Warden, Breach, Barham, Kent. *Tel*: Barham (022 782) 266

Elmham Park (7.5 acres) **CP VA**
R S Don, Elmham House, North Elmham, Dereham, Norfolk. *Tel*: Dereham (036 281) 571 and 363

Elms Cross (2.75 acres) **V**
Alan R Shaw, Elms Cross, Bradford-on-Avon, Wiltshire. *Tel*: Bradford-on-Avon (022 16) 6917

The English Wine Centre (1 acre) **V CP OD**
Christopher and Lucy Ann, Valley Wine Cellars, Drusillas Corner, Alfriston, East Sussex. *Tel*: Alfriston (0323) 870532

Felstar (10.5 acres) **V CP OD VA**
J G and I M Barrett, The Vineyards, Cricks Green, Felsted, Essex. *Tel*: Chelmsford (0245) 361504

Five Chimneys (4.5 acres) **VA**
Mr William Russell, Five Chimneys Farm, Hadlow Down, Uckfield, East Sussex. *Tel*: Buxted (082 581) 2541

Flints (0.25 acre) **V VA**
J Elliott, Flints, Hambleden, Henley-on-Thames, Oxon. *Tel*: Hambleden (049 166) 514

Frithsden (2.5 acres) **VA**
Peter and Ann Latchford, 38 Crouchfield, Boxmoor, Hemel Hempstead, Herts. *Tel*: Hemel Hempstead (0442) 57902

Hambledon (7.5 acres) **V CP OD VA**
Sir Guy and Lady Salisbury-Jones, Mill Down, Hambledon, Portsmouth, Hants. *Tel*: Hambledon (070 132) 475

Harbourne (3 acres) **VA**
L S Williams, High Halden, Ashford, Kent. *Tel*: Ashford (0233) 37916

Hillfoot (5 acres) **V CP**
Roger Jones, Beenham Road, Beenham, Berkshire. *Tel*: Woolhampton (0734) 712701

Hillgrove (8 acres) **V CP VA**
C J Hartley, Swanmore, Hants. *Tel*: Droxford (0489) 877435

The Holt (1.5 acres) **VA**
Col and Mrs W G R Turner, The Holt, Woolton Hill, Newbury, Berkshire. *Tel*: Highclere (0635) 253680

Hooksway (3 acres) **VA**
S R Moore, Hooksway, North Mardon, West Sussex. *Tel*: Midhurst (073 081) 3317

Ightham (3 acres) **VA**
Mr and Mrs J M B Corfe, Mote Road, Ivy Hatch, Nr Sevenoaks, Kent. *Tel*: Sevenoaks (0732) 810348

Kings Green (4 acres) **VA**
Mr and Mrs J H Doran, Bourton, Gillingham, Dorset. *Tel*: Shaftesbury (0747) 840218

Kinver (2.25 acres) **V VA**
E I Garrett and J M Duncan, Dunsley House, Kinver, Hereford and Worcester. *Tel*: Kinver (0384) 872206

Lamberhurst (32 acres) **V CP VA**
K McAlpine, Ridge Farm, Lamberhurst, Nr Tunbridge Wells, Kent. *Tel*: Lamberhurst (0892) 890844

Leeds Castle (2.75 acres) **V CP OD VA** Leeds Castle Foundation, Leeds Castle, Maidstone, Kent. *Tel*: Maidstone (0622) 65400

Lexham Hall (8 acres) **CP VA**
W R B Foster and Partners, Lexham Hall, Nr Litcham, King's Lynn, Norfolk. *Tel*: Litcham (032 876) 288

Loddiswell (4 acres) **V CP OD VA**
R H, B E and E J Sampson, Lilwell, Loddiswell, Kingsbridge, Devon. *Tel*: Loddiswell (054 855) 221

Lymington (6 acres) **V OD VA**
C W and M M Sentance, Wainsford Road, Pennington, Lymington, Hants. *Tel*: Lymington (0590) 72112

Nevards (1 acre) **V VA** R E Barrett, Nevards, Boxted, Colchester, Essex. *Tel*: Boxted (0206) 36325

Penshurst (12 acres) **V CP OD VA** W H Westphal, Grove Road, Penshurst, Kent. *Tel*: Penshurst (0892) 870255

Pilton Manor (6.5 acres) **V CP OD VA** N de M Godden, Pilton, Shepton Mallet, Somerset. *Tel*: Pilton (074 989) 325

Pine Ridge (1 acre) **V** W R Cook, Staplecross, Robertsbridge, East Sussex. *Tel*: Staplecross (058 083) 715

Polmassick (1.5 acres) **CP OD** Mr and Mrs P Crowe, Polmassick, St Ewe, St Austell, Cornwall. *Tel*: Mevagissey (0726) 842239

Pulham (6 acres) **CP VA** Peter W Cook, Mill Lane, Pulham Market, Diss, Norfolk. *Tel*: Pulham Market (037 976) 342

Rock Lodge (3.5 acres) **V CP OD VA** Norman D Cowderoy, Scaynes Hill, Sussex. *Tel*: Scaynes Hill (044 486) 224

Rowney (2 acres) **VA** D G Hall, D N Hall and M Lilley, Rowney Farm, Chaseways, Herts. *Tel*: Harlow (0279) 410275

St George's (5 acres) **V CP OD** Peter and Gay Biddlecombe, Waldron Village, Nr Heathfield, East Sussex. *Tel*: Heathfield (043 53) 2156

St Nicholas (2 acres) **V VA** J Wilkinson, Moat Farm House, Moat Lane, Ash, Canterbury, Kent. *Tel*: Ash (0304) 812670

Sherston Earl (3.5 acres) **V CP** Norman Sellers, Sherston, Nr Malmesbury, Wilts. *Tel*: Malmesbury (0666) 840716

Snape (1.5 acres) **VA** R P and J I Basham, Snape Farm Road, Clopton, Woodbridge, Suffolk. *Tel*: Charsfield (047 337) 270

Spring Farm (12 acres) **V** T B Rees, Moorlynch, Bridgwater, Somerset. *Tel*: Ashcott (0458) 210393

Staple (7 acres) **V** W T Ash, Church Farm, Staple, Canterbury, Kent. *Tel*: Ash (0304) 812571

Staplegrove (3.5 acres) **VA** M M Cursham, Burlands Farm, Staplegrove, Taunton, Somerset. *Tel*: Kingston St Mary (082 345) 217

Stitchcombe (5 acres) **V CP OD VA** Kennet Valley Wine Co, Stitchcombe, Marlborough, Wiltshire. *Tel*: Marlborough (0672) 52297

Swiftsden (3 acres) **VA** Mr and Mrs W D Gammell, Swiftsden House, Hurst Green, Sussex. *Tel*: Hurst Green (058 086) 287

Syndale Valley (9 acres) **VA** J H Abbs & Partners, 'Lady's Wood', Newnham, Sittingbourne, Kent. *Tel*: Eastling (079 589) 693

Tapestry Wines (3 acres) **V CP VA** David M Jones, Wells Farm, Apperley, Glos. *Tel*: Tirley (045 278) 435

Tenterden (10 acres) **V CP VA** S P Skelton, Spots Farm, Small Hythe, Tenterden, Kent. *Tel*: Tenterden (058 06) 3033

Three Choirs (17.5 acres) **V CP OD VA** T W Day, Fairfields Fruit Farm Ltd, Rhyle House, Welsh House Lane, Newent, Glos. *Tel*: Dymock (053 185) 223

Three Corners (1.5 acres) **VA** Lt Col C S Galbraith, Beacon Lane, Woodnesborough, Sandwich, Kent. *Tel*: Ash (0304) 812025

Tytherley (1.25 acres) **VA** J R M Donald, The Garden House, West Tytherley, Salisbury, Wilts. *Tel*: Lockerley (0794) 40644

Westbury (12 acres) **V CP VA** B H Theobald, Westbury Farm, Purley, Reading, Berks. *Tel*: Pangbourne (073 57) 3123

Whatley (4 acres) **VA** M J E Witt, Old Rectory, Whatley, Frome, Somerset. *Tel*: Nunney (037 384) 467

Whitmoor House (1 acre) **VA**
Dr Richard R Trussell, Whitmoor House, Ashill, Cullompton, Devon. *Tel*: Craddock (0884) 40145

Whitstone (1.5 acres) **OD VA**
George and Laura Barclay, Bovey Tracey, Bovey, South Devon. *Tel*: Tracey (0626) 832280

Wickenden (3.5 acres) **CP OD VA**
Raymond Lock, Wickenden, Cliveden Road, Taplow, Bucks. *Tel*: Maidenhead (0628) 29455

Wootton (6 acres) **V CP**
Major C L B Gillespie, North Wootton, Shepton Mallet, Somerset. *Tel*: Pilton (074 989) 359

Wraxall (6 acres) **V CP OD VA**
A S Holmes & Partners, Wraxall, Shepton Mallet, Somerset. *Tel*: Ditcheat (074 986) 331 and 486

Yearlstone (1.5 acres) **OD VA**
Miss Gillian Pearkes, Chilton, Bickleigh, Tiverton, Devon. *Tel*: Bickleigh (088 45) 450

Where to buy in the high street

Many wine merchants stock the wines of one or two vineyards. The following retail shops and chains have an especially good selection of English wines: Vintners Wain, Arthur Rackham, Valley Wine Cellars, Harrods, Fortnum and Mason.

BEST ENGLISH BUYS

Gold Biddenden Ortega 1983 *(English Wine Centre [Alfriston]; Lurcocks [Blenheim]; The Grapevine [Folkestone]; Mermaid Inn [Rye]; Bottles Off Licence [Ashford]; Bournes Stores [Brenchley]).*

Silver Three Choirs Huxelrebe 1983 *(Peter Green, Edinburgh; Soho Wine Supplies; Yorkshire Fine Wines)*, Queen Court 1983 *(Shepherd Neame, Faversham Brewery)*

Bronze Barton Manor Medium Dry 1983 (*Vintners Wain [14 Buckingham Palace Road, SW1]; several small off-licences in the Isle of Wight)*, Axbridge Müller-Thurgau Dry 1983 *(mail order by the case from: Axbridge Vineyard, 7 Sunnyside, Frome, Somerset [0373] 71079; or retail from Axbridge Wine Vaults, The Square, Axbridge, Somerset)*, Biddenden Vineyards Huxelrebe 1983 *(English Wine Centre [Alfriston]; Lurcocks [Blenheim]; The Grapevine [Folkestone]; Mermaid Inn [Rye]; Bottles Off Licence [Ashford]; Bournes Stores [Brenchley]*, Penshurst Müller-Thurgau Dry 1983 *(The Pantiles Vintry [Tunbridge Wells]; Vintners Wain [London SW1])*

For further information contact: The English Vineyards Association, The Ridge, Lamberhurst Down, Kent, TN3 8ER; tel: Lamberhurst (0892) 890734.

France

ALSACE

The 1983 vintage

Whether the 1983 vintage has made the finest wines since 1976 or since 1921 in Alsace depends on either your memory or your tasting experience. However, one thing is certain – the long, fine autumn proved ideal for making the *vendange tardive* and *sélection de grains nobles* wines *(see below)* in quantities hitherto unknown. Until recently, these late-picked specialities have been made by a small number of growers; indeed, Hugel is probably the only house to have attempted the *sélection de grains nobles* previously. This year, they were by no means alone. The vintage was generous also in quantity. This poses certain problems, as the 1982 crop was enormous and stocks are still in abundance; the wines are good, but not great, and might be difficult to sell now that the 1983s are on the market.

Value for money

Alsace wines tend to be on the expensive side ££–£££, but quality is reliably good to excellent. Wine merchants are reluctant to stock a big range, since they are slow to sell. They are still excellent value for money.

What to drink now, what to keep

Generally, the wines of Alsace should be drunk young, so that their main charm, their fresh fruitiness, can be appreciated. Therefore an Edelzwicker, Sylvaner, Pinot Blanc and, to a lesser extent, Pinot Gris should be drunk up to two years old, or up to four years old in the best vintages. The more fully flavoured Riesling and Gewürztraminer will last longer – up to eight or ten years in the best vintages. Here are the recent vintages:

1983 Really excellent vintage of full-bodied wines. Good for current drinking. Buy the better ones to keep, too.

1982 Soft and early maturing. Good at present, but not to be kept.

1981 Above average in quality, but not a truly long distance runner. Many are now too old.

1980 Almost no Gewürztraminer produced, and what is left of the rest should be treated with caution.

1979 Fair quality but, apart from the better wines from the better houses, now probably over the hill.

1978 A great vintage – buy those Rieslings you can still find. Good to drink now.

1977 To be avoided.

1976 Excellent. Try the *vendange tardive* wines, which are beautiful now, but can mostly still be kept.

Understanding the Alsace label

Solo grapes

Generally speaking, the three important facts on an Alsace wine label are the grape variety, the vintage and the producer.

Of the grape varieties, there are two groups in the local hierarchy: what might be called the 'humble' and the 'noble'. Alsace wines are usually made from only one grape variety and this will appear by name on the label. If the wine is made from a blend of grapes, or from the Chasselas (which for some perverse reason may not be mentioned by name), it will appear under a brand name or be described as **Edelzwicker**. The following varieties do appear on the label. *(See* GRAPES ON THE LABEL *in the* WINE WITH FOOD *section for further details on how these varieties taste.)*

The 'humble' varieties are:
The **Sylvaner**, grown more towards the northern end of the Alsace vineyards. It generally produces sound, easy-drinking wines, but rather neutral-flavoured. On occasions, especially in the village of Mittelbergheim, it can make something really outstanding.

The **Pinot Noir** has, until recently, produced pale but fruity imitations of Burgundy. Now some houses are making fuller wines, aged in oak. These can be excellent. Try the Rouge d'Alsace of the Eguisheim Co-operative.

Pinot Blanc or **Clevner** is a soft, simple wine without great pretensions. It is now often used for making sparkling wine.

The four 'noble' varieties are:
The **Riesling**, in the top rank of Alsace wines. The best are firm and full-flavoured and will keep well. The finest come from such villages as Riquewihr, Ribeauvillé and Eguisheim.

The **Tokay d'Alsace** is sometimes – and if the civil servants of Brussels have their way, will always be – called the **Pinot Gris**. In Alsace, it gives rich, rather succulent wines, often high in alcohol.

The **Muscat** is a difficult wine to match with food for it has a pronounced grapy, Muscatel taste, whilst remaining totally dry. The production is small, but it is worth seeking out, even if it is drunk on its own.

The **Gewürztraminer** is the distinctive wine of the region, for it, too, has a concentrated, spicy flavour. For the wine-beginner it is very appealing because of its distinctiveness. It gives some superb late-picked wines.

Other terms on the labels

Crémant d'Alsace [££] Fine sparkling wines are now being made by the Champagne method by a number of companies. Crémant is the term for sparkling in Alsace, and doesn't imply a slightly less fizzy sparkle, as it does in Champagne. The base grape is normally the Pinot Blanc – but often with some Riesling added. **Dopff au Moulin** have had the longest experience – and it shows.

Grand cru [££]–[£££] Certain of the better vineyards are being granted the right to name their wines thus, if made from one of the four noble varieties and of a sufficient degree of alcohol. As a result of much local in-fighting, some of the finest vineyards, such as the Sporen at Riquewihr, and the Kaefferkopf at Ammerschwihr, will not have this classification, so its total validity must be in doubt.

Réserve Personnelle, Sélection Spéciale, Cuvée Spéciale [££]–[£££] Such terms have no legal backing, but generally are used for the better quality wines of the individual producer.

Sélection de Grains Nobles [£££] For some growers, the perfection in Alsace wine; for others total anathema. These wines are rich and opulent, rare and expensive, and are made from individually picked over-ripe grapes. Until the 1983 vintage, they were the sole preserve of Hugel.

Vendange tardive [£££] This is the equivalent of the German Spätlese – late-picked – wines. Some Alsatian growers still make it as a dry wine – Léon Beyer, for example; others, such as Hugel, give it a sweeter style. Unfortunately, there is rarely any indication of sweetness on the label.

Medals and things

Because it is often difficult for the consumer to differentiate between qualities of wine under the same name from different suppliers, much store in Alsace is set by medals. These, too, vary in worth, but perhaps the best would be one from the **Concours Agricole**, in Paris, or the **National Wine Fair** in Mâcon. Even more valuable is the seal of the **Confrérie Saint Etienne** on a bottle.

Names to look out for

Producers' names

There are three types of producer whose wines you might see in this country: the growers, the merchants and the co-operatives. The growers will sell only wine from their own vineyards, home-bottled. The merchants will buy in wine and grapes from outside to supplement those from their own vineyards and those that they have under exclusive contract. The co-operatives take grapes from their numerous members, and sell the resultant wine either in bulk to merchants or in bottle under their own label.

The growers

There are over 9,000 growers in Alsace, many of whom bottle no wine, preferring to sell it to the trade. Here is just a handful of the best:

Théo Faller, Kaysersberg Superb wines from the single vineyard, the Weinbach, Clos des Capucins. Now under the direction of Mme Faller. Especially good are the Rieslings and Gewürztraminers. They also make some *vendange tardive* wines. *(O W Loeb)*

Eugène Klipfel, Barr One of the best domains of the Bas-Rhin. Outstanding is the Clos Zisser Gewürztraminer. Well respected for *vendange tardive* wines. Associated with the merchants André Lorentz. *(Walter S Siegel)*

A & O Muré, Rouffach Their vineyard, the Clos Saint Landelin, is one of the steepest in Alsace. Good Rieslings. They are also merchants, under a different label. *(James Bell & Co, Bishopsmead Wine Co)*

Schlumberger, Guebwiller The largest domain in the Alsace vineyards, with more than three hundred acres. Single vineyard wines from the Kitterlé, Saering and Kessler. Full-bodied and succulent wines of which the best may be their Gewürztraminers, especially the late-picked ones. *(Lawlers of London)*

Sick-Dreyer, Ammerschwihr Unfortunately named growers who make very clean, frank wines. Rieslings and Gewürztraminers from the Kaefferkopf vineyard. *(Caxtòn Wines)*

Henri Wiederhirn, Riquewihr Fine wines across the range. *(High Breck Vintners)*

Zind-Humbrecht, Wintzenheim A fascinating range of wines from the villages of Turckheim, Wintzenheim and Thann. All their single vineyard wines are excellent: perhaps of most interest is the Riesling from the Clos Saint Urbain at Thann, the only vineyard on volcanic soil in Alsace. *(Laytons)*

The merchants

Léon Beyer, Eguisheim Superb, steely wines. Even his **vendange tardive** wines are dry. *(Michael Druitt Wines)*

E Boeckel, Mittelbergheim Amongst the best are the Sylvaner from the Zotzenberg and Riesling from the Brandluft vineyards. *(Churton Cousins Ltd)*

Dopff au Moulin, Riquewihr One of the great innovators in Alsace. The first to sell wine in bottle and the first sparkling wine maker. Single wines of note: Riesling Schoenenberg and Gewürztraminer Eichberg. Try their Crémant d'Alsace. *(Mentzendorff & Co)*

Dopff et Irion, Riquewihr Introverted wines that need to age to appear at their best. A large vineyard holding. *(J B Reynier)*

Hugel et Fils, Riquewihr Deservedly the market leaders in Britain for all that they have done to introduce us to the wines of Alsace. Soft, florid wines of real quality. Look particularly for their Réserve Personnelle range and their late-picked specialities. *(In England Dreyfus Ashby; in Scotland Peter Thomson of Perth; in Ireland Grants of Ireland)*

Kuehn, Ammerschwihr A traditional house that has recently been absorbed by a co-operative cellar. The co-operative has had the good sense to leave well alone. Try their Charme d'Alsace if you want to know what a Chasselas wine tastes like. *(Tanners, Lay & Wheeler)*

Kuentz-Bas, Husseren les Châteaux This is a small family house making excellent wines. Their first *vendange tardive* wines have just appeared and are very good. *(Dolamore/Rawlings Voigt)*

J Preiss-Zimmer, Riquewihr The Rieslings are perhaps the best wines from here, though all are first-class in a rather firm, crisp style. *(Hatch, Mansfield)*

Pierre Sparr A small family firm who also own their own vineyards making firm, well-flavoured wines. Try particularly their Gewürztraminer from the Mambourg vineyard. *(Barwell & Jones)*

F E Trimbach, Ribeauvillé A smallish company, but with a very high reputation for very clean wines of a rather austere nature. Their Clos Sainte-Hune Riesling is the highest rated in the region. *(H Parrot & Co)*

Co-operatives

There are some eighteen of these in Alsace and their importance is growing fast. The largest is that of **Eguisheim** (Gewürztraminers and sparkling wines are good) and the smallest is that of **Cleebourg** in an enclave of vines in the north of Alsace on the German border (Pinot Auxerrois). Amongst the other good ones are those of **Beblenheim** and **Bennwihr** (both make good Pinot Blanc), **Westhalten** and **Ribeauvillé**.

Where to buy Alsace wines

Specialists No-one stocks a large range of different Alsace houses, but most retailers have at least one Alsace wine, if not a small selection from one grower. Try *La Vigneronne* for older vintages.

BEST ALSACE BUYS [£] Grants of St James's Alsace *(Victoria Wine)*, [£]–[£££] Wines of the 1983 vintage, [££]–[£££] Vendange Tardive and Sélection de Grains Nobles

BEAUJOLAIS

The 1983 vintage

The wine grower is a farmer and like most farmers he never seems happy. Though on the face of it he might appear to have a comfortable life, in actual fact, he is never making any money. However, as far as the 1983 vintage is concerned, the Beaujolais grower can have had little ground for complaint. Its quality was outstanding, probably the best since 1976, and the quantity was some 20 per cent above average. It was good for his bank balance, too. The prices rose and a third of the total crop was sold as Beaujolais Nouveau.

In many ways, the 1983 wines from the Beaujolais are not typical, for they are bigger, and many will take longer to mature than normal. Even so, one leading producer in the area suggests that even the finest wines will be at their best before their third birthday.

Value for money

Whilst Beaujolais still represents good value, it has moved out of the cheap wine bracket and more care has to be taken now in purchasing to guarantee value for money. Sadly, on some wine-store shelves, and in very many restaurants and wine bars, bottles of Beaujolais are on sale which do little credit to the appellation. The best value is to be found in the single domaine or château wines from the crus.

What to drink now, what to keep

1984 Still on the vines as we went to press.

1983 Big atypical wines, often rather introverted and with some tannin. The better cru wines can be bought for laying down.

1982 Many of the wines of this vintage lack depth of Gamay flavour. Sound but not exciting for Beaujolais-Villages and above. Ordinary Beaujolais now probably past its best. Avoid 1982 and buy 1983 whenever you can.

1981 A good vintage with a lot of fruit. The cru wines should still give much pleasure.

1980 The best wines from the best producers might be worth a gamble, but a gamble it would be.

Older wines should be avoided, but well-kept crus from the 1978 and 1976 vintages might give some pleasant surprises. As it ages, a good, firm Beaujolais takes on an extraordinary Pinot Noir-like character.

Understanding the Beaujolais label

In the Beaujolais region, there is a hierarchy in the quality of the wines, dependent on geographical source, that has been built up over the centuries. At the bottom of the scale comes plain **Beaujolais** [£]–[££]. Whilst this can come from anywhere within the region, in effect it comes from the southern half of the area, between Villefranche and the northern outskirts of Lyons. Beaujolais should be soft and fruity – but it is often very mediocre wine. The majority of it nowadays is sold as Beaujolais Nouveau *(see below)*.

From the northern half of the vineyards comes **Beaujolais-Villages** [££]. This should have rather more depth of fruit and body and should take rather longer to reach its peak. Some of the better 'new' Beaujolais will also come from here. It was the Beaujolais region that started the demand for early supply of wines of the new vintage. **Beaujolais Nouveau** and **Beaujolais Primeur** [£]–[££] have traditionally been released on 15 November, though this date may now be changed, depending on the characteristics of the vintage. But whenever possible, the wines are rushed through to meet the famous date.

Whilst many other regions have tried to cash in on the habit, none has succeeded to the same extent. Beaujolais, however, is now having to pay the price of this success. Because more than half of ordinary Beaujolais is now being sold as Nouveau, there is little left for the rest of the year, and since the best vats of wine are often chosen for the Nouveau, the straight Beaujolais that come out later are often poor wines. Efforts are now being made by the merchants in the Beaujolais region to play down Beaujolais Nouveau. They would rather make more money selling the wines more expensively later in the year, and pay less overtime at bottling time for Beaujolais Nouveau, but naturally the growers are resisting this, as for them it is very profitable.

What is the difference between Beaujolais Nouveau and Beaujolais Primeur? The former is simply the wine of the last vintage, whilst the latter is a wine that has been released before the 15 December following the vintage, when most *appellation contrôlée* wines are first permitted to appear on the market.

The crus [££]–[£££]

From within the Beaujolais Villages area come the nine **crus**. These are single villages that have the right to their own appellation. Their styles vary considerably. Generally speaking, **Brouilly** makes the cru wines which mature the earliest, though this may not be true in 1983. It also has the largest production. The wine should be rather soft and fruity, with a long aftertaste. **Château de la Chaize** is a good single vineyard.

Côte de Brouilly has a much smaller production of bigger, slightly more alcoholic wines, with a great deal of elegance. (Try **Château Thivin**.)

Certainly of the 1983 wines, those of **Chiroubles** seem to have matured the quickest, and are light and supple. The most pleasant to drink at the present. (**Château Javernand** is good.)

Saint Amour lies at the very north of the region, where the vineyards overlap those of the Mâconnais. The wines are soft and round and have the most important virtue in the Beaujolais – they slip down very easily! (**Domaine des Billards** is good.)

Fleurie tastes flowery. It may seem trite, but it is true. It should have a good purple colour and after a couple of years be very silky. (Try **Clos des Quatre Vents**.)

Juliénas produces one of the bigger wines of the region, which should be given two or three years' ageing before drinking. It has a spicy taste and lasts well in the mouth. (Try **Château des Capitans, Domaine de la Dîme, Domaine de la Vieille Eglise**.)

Morgon wines have a certain style with a big, deep perfume and a full body. (Try **Les Versauds, Charmes, Princesse Lieven**)

Chénas has the smallest production of all, and most of this disappears to Switzerland. At its best, the wines can be the biggest in the Beaujolais – the 1983 vintage has been very successful here. Opulent and long lasting.

The aristocrat of the Beaujolais is **Moulin-à-Vent**. Its wines are deep and often tannic. In a great year, they are capable of lasting for a very long time. **(Château des Jacques, Château Portier, Domaine de la Tour du Bief.)**

Names to look out for

As Beaujolais is considered part of Burgundy as far as wines are concerned, much of it appears under the labels of merchants from Beaune and elsewhere *(see* BURGUNDY *section)*. Here are the names of some specialists actually in the Beaujolais region, whose wines we would recommend:

Chanut Frères, Romanèche-Thorins: Excellent Nouveaux. *(Eldridge Pope)*

Desvignes Aîné, Pontaneveaux *(Charles Dakin)*

Chevalier Fils, Charnay-lès-Mâcon *(G Bravo & Sons)*

David et Foillard, Saint-Georges-de-Reneins *(John Harvey & Sons et al)*

Jacques Dépagneux, Villefranche

Georges Duboeuf, Romanèche-Thorins The specialist of single vineyard wines made by carbonic maceration. Very fruity wines. Often described as 'jammy' by some of his competitors. A sound choice, if you like the new style. *(Berkmann Wine Cellars. Their Nez Rouge Club stocks a good range.)*

Pierre Ferraud, Belleville *(K F Butler)*

Loron et Fils, Pontanevaux Sound, full, fruity wines. *(Ernst Gorge)*

Pasquier-Desvignes, Saint Lager Good, solid wines in a rather austere style. *(Dolamore/Rawlings Voigt)*

Sarrau, Saint-Jean d'Ardières Firm, lasting wines. *(Sarrau Wines)*

Louis Tête, Saint-Didier-sur-Beaujeu *(F & E May)*

Thorin, Pontanevaux Château des Jacques, Moulin-à-Vent and Château de Loyse, white Beaujolais. *(Findlater Matta)*

Where to buy Beaujolais

Roger Harris Wines, Weston Longville, Norfolk (mail order) specialise exclusively in Beaujolais, stock over 60 wines; Le Nez Rouge Wine Club and Anthony Byrne Fine Wines have a full Duboeuf range.

BEST BEAUJOLAIS BUYS [££] 1983 Beaujolais from Duboeuf *(Lay & Wheeler, Christopher Piper, Berkmann Wine Cellars/Le Nez Rouge)*, [££] 1983 Beaujolais from Sarrau *(Yorkshire Fine Wines, Morans of Bristol)*, [££] Morgon, Félix Longepierre 1983 *(Haynes, Hanson & Clark)*

BORDEAUX

The 1983 vintage

For the third year in succession, thus making seven out of the last nine, 1983 was a very good vintage in Bordeaux. For the second year in a row, the crop was very large.

Dry whites [£]–[££] The wines are light, crisp and fruity, with more zip of acidity than in 1982. For the most part, they will develop soon. More and more, the Bordelais are switching over from white grapes to red, and today less than a third of the crop is white, the reverse of a generation ago. Why the Bordeaux growers should have failed to cash in on the current fashion for dry white wine remains a mystery. Also, too much cheap Bordeaux white remains dull and over-sulphured. At best, good, dry, simple 1983 Bordeaux Blanc Sec and Sauvignon at little over £2.20 a bottle is a bargain. Too much is still rather dreadful. Cheaper white Bordeaux is always best young, so, failing a disastrous harvest, drink the 1984 whites (apart from the more expensive [£££], of course) as soon as they become available, early in 1985.

Reds In general, the quality gets proportionately better as one climbs up the hierarchy from Bordeaux Rouge to classed growth. It is also better in the Graves and the Médoc than in St-Emilion and Pomerol, because the later-ripening Cabernet did better in 1983 than the early Merlot, of which there is more in St-Emilion and Pomerol.

Petits-châteaux and petits bourgeois growths [£]–[££] (Under the appellations of Bordeaux, Bordeaux Supérieur, Côtes de Bourg, Premières Côtes de Bordeaux and Premières Côtes de Blaye.) Here, the quality is certainly inferior to the 1982 vintage, and also less consistent. The wines are healthy, ripe and fruity, but lack the character and charm of the 1982s. They will develop reasonably soon. Expect to see some on the market and *ready for drinking from the middle of 1985 onwards*. The better wines will be ready from 1986.

The lesser wines of the Libournais [£]–[££] (Fronsac, Lalande de Pomerol, the satellites of St-Emilion and the unclassified wines of St-Emilion itself.) In general, the same remarks can be applied as above. The wines, being more expensive, can be expected to have more personality. *They will be ready from 1986 onwards.*

St-Emilion and Pomerol – the best wines [£££] A good vintage, but not, in general, as good as 1982 or 1981, and with some disappointments. The wines are quite full and sturdy, ripe and generous, though they lack the fatness of 1982, but some also lack both concentration and depth. There are many delicious wines, however, and this is certainly a vintage to buy. *Ready from 1987 onwards. The very best wines will not be ready until the early 1990s.*

Médoc and Graves – the 'bourgeois' wines [££]–[£££] A better vintage than across the river in St-Emilion and Pomerol. Good, full, rich, tannic wines, which have plenty of ripe fruit and will last well. Proportionately better value than the petits-châteaux. Not as good as the 1982s, though some are close, but apart from that, the best since at least 1978, perhaps 1970. There is so much excellent wine at relatively inexpensive prices, from hardworking and consistent properties, that this area is a must for those who buy now for future drinking. *The wines will be ready from 1988 onwards. Some will need ten years before they mature.*

Médoc and Graves – the crus classés [£££] This is where the 1983 vintage was at its most successful. There are more than a few wines which are better than the same 1982s. Others are very close in quality to that celebrated vintage. The wines have a splendid colour, are high in alcohol and extract, rich, full and concentrated, and have heaps of fruit. These wines are classic claret, and *need keeping until the early 1990s, if not later*. A must for those who lay down.

Sauternes and the other sweet wines [££]–[£££] Thanks to the glorious Indian summer, this is the best Sauternes vintage since at least 1976 and 1975, and perhaps will be better than either. Not only are the wines splendidly rich and concentrated, with good acidity and delicious, complex fruit, but there are plenty of them. The 1983 Sauternes are exceptional. While Sauternes is unexpectedly delicious when young, and indeed can be enjoyed almost as soon as it has had time to settle down in bottle, *leave the best 1983s for ten years, and even the lesser wines until 1986.*

Value for money

Apart from the first-growths and the most fashionable among the rest – the so-called 'super seconds' – Bordeaux wines are not expensive, particularly by comparison with the equivalent in quality in Burgundy – or California. Opening prices of petits-châteaux have hardly moved since 1979, and even the better wines, despite the demand, and what seemed extravagant prices for the 1982s, have not risen by more than inflation over the last five years.

Many of the 1983s, helped by the size of the harvest, opened at more or less the same price as last year's did. There are still bargains to be had, particularly if one buys *'en primeur'*, that is, taking advantage of the many opening offers mailed by the specialist British firms in the summer after the vintage.

What to drink now, what to keep

	Petits Châteaux	Bourgeois growths	Top wines
1983	now–1990	1987–94	1990–2000+
1982	now–1988	1986–92	1990–2000+
1981	now–1988	1986–91	1989–2000
1980	drink up	now–1987	1985–1992
1979	drink up	now–1990	1986–1996
1978	now–1986	1986–1992	1988–2000+
1977	showing age	drink up	now–1990
1976	showing age	now–1987	now–1990
1975	drink up	now–1990	1986–2000
1974			now–1990
1973			now–1990
1972	showing age	drink up	drink up
1971			now–1990
1970		now–1990	1986–2000

We have tried to make the *1985 Which? Wine Guide* as comprehensive as possible, but we should love to hear from you about any other establishments you feel deserve an entry, or your comments on existing entries. Write to us either by letter or using the report forms supplied at the back of the book.

Understanding the Bordeaux label

Classifications Red Bordeaux ranges from regional or generic 'Bordeaux Rouge', to the produce of famous estates like Ch Lafite. However, the region is the home of several thousand wine estates, a substantial proportion of which are large enough to be self-sufficient in wine terms, and who sell their wine under their property or 'château' name – even if the 'château' is little more than a farmhouse! At various times, particularly in 1855 and for the various separate districts since the 1950s, most of the top properties have been officially classified. These wines are the **'classed growths'** or **'cru classés'**, and most classifications sub-divide into various categories from **premier (grand) cru classé** or **first growth** downwards. Beneath this classification, lesser proportions have been designated **cru exceptionnel** or **cru bourgeois** (in the Médoc) or **grand cru** (in St-Emilion). (The St-Emilion classification is being revised for the 1984 vintage onwards.) There are also the **'second wines'** of the top properties, made from their young vines or less successful vats, and many of these are at least as good as good 'bourgeois' wines, or even a lesser classed growth.

There is, however, no single up-to-date official classification of all the top Bordeaux wines together, and so a cru classé in one region may not necessarily be at the same level of quality as an apparently similar wine in another district. The most up-to-date classification is that of St-Emilion, revised in 1984, and one is due for the leading Graves châteaux in 1985. But since it is the property and not the wine that is being classified, and vintages can vary and reputations rise and fall, one should never treat any classification as an invariable guarantee of quality. It is always better to taste for oneself or put one's faith in the advice of a reputable source of supply than simply to buy names.

Lesser areas to look out for on the label

Above 'Bordeaux' and 'Bordeaux Supérieur', but beneath 'Cru Bourgeois' and 'Cru Classé', you will find a host of good red wines and a large number of relatively small and often overlooked appellations. This is the £3 to £6 bottle, wines that are normally at their best from two to five years after bottling. This is a field full of riches, with some marvellous value.

Premières Côtes de Blaye, Côtes de Bourg ££ – £££ From the east of the Gironde estuary. Sturdy, sometimes robust wines with a strong *goût de terroir* (an earthy taste which in bad hands becomes farmyardy.) Choose with care. **Look for:** [Blaye] Haut Sociando, Segonzac, Cantemerle; [Bourg] Moulin de Roussellet, Rousselle, de Barbe, La Croix Millorit, Guionne, Haut Guiraud.

Premières Côtes de Bordeaux ££ – £££ A narrow strip of vineyards on slopes facing west towards the Garonne on the edge of the Entre-Deux-Mers. Soft, elegant wines, less 'rustic' in general than the above. Good value. **Look for:** Jean Bernard, Lezongars, Fardet.

Côtes Canon Fronsac/Fronsac ££–£££ These adjoining districts lie north-west of Pomerol, and are much underrated. More expensive than the areas above, but better than the satellites of St-Emilion, which are the same price. Excellent, abundantly fruity wines, round and attractive. **Look for:** Richotey, Canon de Brem, La Dauphine, Mayne Vieil, Vrai-Canon-Boyer, Jumayne, Lariveau, Moulin Pey Labrie, du Tasta, Zauzet.

Other possibly confusing terms on the label

Château . . . A specific property. Often, nowadays, not inhabited because upkeep is too expensive. It may be no more, however, than a modest farmhouse.

Domaine . . . Looser: can be a blend from several properties owned by the same proprietor.

Cuvée de . . ., Sélection de . . ., Réserve de . . . Even looser: does not denote any specific origin – or any particular quality – though it would be misleading if a producer's 'réserve' were inferior to his 'ordinaire'.

Mise en bouteilles au château/à la propriété par . . . The 'propriété' may well be a co-operative. 'Château' might mean a warehouse five miles away registered as a château annexe. But it most often really means what it says – not necessarily a guarantee of *good* bottling.

Grand Vin de Bordeaux Aren't they all?

Grand Cru (without the word classé) Anyone can describe his/her own wine as 'Grand'.

Names to look out for

Red wines

Médoc and Graves

The Haut-Médoc is undoubtedly the greatest stretch of quality wine-making land in the world. The sixty or so classed growths, mainly situated in the communes of St-Estèphe, Pauillac, St-Julien and Margaux, are merely the cream, and even with today's high prices, one does not necessarily have to be a millionaire in order to enjoy superb wines, though it certainly helps to take advantage of 'opening offers' and buy the wines as young as possible when they are at their cheapest.

Of the many hundreds of fine properties – and it is idle to mention the premier crus – the following are particular favourites £££ and also normally consistently good, year in, year out.

> *Which? Wine Guide* does not accept payment for inclusion, and there is no sponsorship or advertising.

At the very top level £££ **Ducru-Beaucaillou, Léoville-Las-Cases, Pichon-Longueville, Lalande** and **Palmer** in the Haut-Médoc; **Domaine de Chevalier** and **La Mission-Haut-Brion** in the Graves. These wines are often of indisputable first-growth quality.

Among the rest of the classed growths £££ **Cos d'Estournel, Grand-Puy-Lacoste, Mouton-Baronne-Philippe, Lynch-Bages, Léoville-Barton**, the little-known **St-Pierre-Sevaistre, Malescot, Prieuré-Lichine** (Alexis Lichine's own property), **Issan, La Lagune** and **du Tertre**, all in the Haut-Médoc; **Haut-Bailly** in the Graves. All these produce wines which, as *Cocks et Ferret*, the 'Bible of Bordeaux', puts it, are *'actuellement très supérieur à leur classement'*.

The best bourgeois £££ **Angludet, Gloria, Lalande-Borie, Terry-Gros-Caillou** (also sold as **Hortevie**), **Du Glana, Chasse-Spleen, Phélan-Ségur, de Pez, Poujeaux** (also known as **Poujeaux-Theil**), **Labegorce-Zédé**: these all come from the Haut-Médoc and would be classed growths in any reclassification; **Larrivet-Haut-Brion** in the Graves.

Other good bourgeois £££ (cheaper than the above) **Caronne-St-Gemme, Citran, Fourcas-Hosten, Fourcas-Dupré, Les Ormes de Pez, La Tour de By, Patache d'Aux, Potensac, Coufran, Verdignan** and **Loudenne**. Some of these can be really remarkable value if bought early.

Good 'second' wines £££ **Clos du Marquis (Léoville-Las-Cases), La Croix (Ducru-Beaucaillou), Réserve de la Comtesse (Pichon-Longueville, Lalande), Haut-Bages-Averous (Lynch-Bages).** These are normally the same price as the wines in the 'best bourgeois' category, and equally good, if not better.

St-Emilion and Pomerol

Pomerols are particular favourites. They can be incredibly rich, full yet with a soft concentration of ripe fruit in a good year. Unfortunately, many of the properties are very small, and so some of the wines are difficult to find, and they are often expensive.

At the top level £££ **Trotanoy, La Fleur** (both exceptional), **La Fleur-Pétrus, Vieux-Château-Certan, Latour (à Pomerol), Certan-de-May, Evangile, La Conseillante**, all in Pomerol; **Figeac, Belair, Canon** and **Magdelaine** in St-Emilion.

Good to best bourgeois level £££ **La Dominique, La Grave Trigant de Boisset, Lagrange, L'Eglise-Clinet, Feytit-Clinet, La Pointe** in Pomerol; **Cadet-Piola, Trois-Moulins, Fonroque, Larcis-Ducasse, La Cluserie, Dassault Larmande, La Tour-Figeac, La Tour-du-Pin-Figeac** (Moueix) and **Canon-La-Gaffelière** in St-Emilion.

Dry White Wines

There is little dry white Bordeaux of really superlative quality, and when you find it, from **Haut-Brion, Laville-Haut-Brion**, or **Domaine de Chevalier**, it is very expensive. Lower down in the hierarchy, good white is made at **Bouscaut, Fieuzal** and **Carbonnieux** £££, but again, not often seen.

The best value in dry white Bordeaux is at the petits-châteaux or petits bourgeois level £–££. Look for a merchant who specialises in these wines, and buys from a reputable source such as **Pierre Coste** in Langon. Look also for the dry white wines, such as **Guiraud Sec**, or **Doisy-Daëne Sec** ££, made on the famous Sauternes estates.

Sweet wines

The best sweet wines come from the Sauternes region, from five communes including Barsac. Apart from **Yquem**, the best of the premiers crus are **Suduiraut, Climens, Coutet, Guiraud** (since 1979), **Rieussec, Lafaurie-Peyraguey, Clos Haut-Peyraguey** and **Sigalas-Rabaud** £££. Even these, however, are inconsistent. It pays to take advice from a reputable merchant.

Among the deuxième crus £££, **Doisy-Daëne** and **Nairac** stand out. Other good estates are **Broustet** and **Suau** (both second growths), **Liot, Bastor-Lamontagne** and **Ch La Chartreuse**.

The merchants of Bordeaux

Because the vast majority of Bordeaux wine is château-bottled, or, at the cheaper end of the scale, bottled by UK merchants in Bordeaux with a British firm's name on the label as their house claret or whatever, the names of merchants *(négociants)* in Bordeaux do not impinge much on the British public – unlike, for example, their equivalents in Burgundy, Beaujolais or Alsace. Some names, however, may be familiar. Here is a guide to the best of them:

Cordier Soft, fruity, well-made wines. *(Cordier UK)*

E Coste et Fils, Langon Pierre Coste is one of the best-respected tasters in Bordeaux, and his small but thriving firm has many followers in the UK. He is one of the few reliable merchants for dry white wine, and for early drinking soft, fruity reds.

Gallaire et Fils Owned by Peter Sichel, who also owns Ch d'Angludet and part of Ch Palmer. Excellent, well-chosen and consistent lesser red wines.

J P Moueix Easily the most important merchant for the wines of St-Emilion and Pomerol, and owners, farmers or exclusive agents for a host of the best properties in the area, including Ch Pétrus.
An excellent source for minor St-Emilions and Pomerols and Fronsacs under their own bottling, as well as lesser red wines.
(Walter S Siegel Ltd, Corney & Barrow)

Nathaniel Johnston et Fils Long established Chartronnais firm and exclusive agents for many minor red wine properties, whose wines they bottle in their premises in Bordeaux.

Many Bordeaux merchants have tried, and are continuing to try, with greater or lesser success, to market their own generic wines, or to create Bordeaux Rouge brand names. The most famous of these, if not the most exciting, is Mouton Cadet, which also comes in a white version, from La Baronnie in Pauillac. Others prominent in this field are Cordier (owners of a number of properties, including Ch Gruaud-Larose and Talbot), Dourthe (with Beau-Mayne), Borie Manoux and Barton & Guestier. For the most part, however, you will find as good a wine, at a cheaper price, either from an individual petit-château, or under a Bordeaux Rouge or house claret label of a British wine merchant.

Where to buy Bordeaux

The following **specialist** wine merchants, all of whom sell by mail order, have a significant list of clarets and white Bordeaux, but also sell wine *'en primeur'*. All also offer, or can arrange, storage at nominal prices:
Adnams; Les Amis du Vin; Averys of Bristol Ltd; Ballantynes of Cowbridge; Balls Bros; Bibendum Wines Ltd; Christopher & Co Ltd; Corney & Barrow Ltd; Findlater; Mackie Todd & Co Ltd; Greens; Haynes, Hanson & Clark; Hatch Mansfield & Co Ltd; Michael Harris Wines; The Hungerford Wine Company; S H Jones Ltd; Justerini & Brooks Ltd; Lay & Wheeler Ltd; Laytons; Mackie & Co; Malmaison Wine Club; Russell & McIver; Tanners Wines Ltd; Henry Townsend & Co; The Wine Society.
Those of the above who are especially noted for the depth and range of older, mature red wines include: Adnams, Averys, Bibendum, Corney & Barrow, Hatch Mansfield, Lay & Wheeler, Tanners and The Wine Society.

Chains

Victoria Wine, Peter Dominic, Oddbins.

Supermarkets

Few, if any, have any great selection of the wines of Bordeaux (as their policy is to stock only what sells in volume, and to buy from hand to mouth). This does not, however, stop what they do have from being well-chosen and good value. Marks & Spencer and the Sainsbury's Vintage Selection have been noteworthy in this field.

BEST BORDEAUX BUYS

Dry white Bordeaux [£] Ch Rolland, 1983 *(Les Amis du Vin)*, [£] Ch Reynon, 1983 *(Adnams, Caves de la Madeleine, Balls Bros)*, [££] Ch Montalivet, Graves, 1983 *(Les Amis du Vin, Caves de la Madeleine, Balls Bros)*, [££] Ch Thieuley, 1983 *(Adnams, Lay & Wheeler, Tanners)*

Cheap red Bordeaux Ch Bellevue, 1983 Bordeaux AC mise J P Moueix *(Les Amis du Vin)*, ££ Pierre Coste Graves, 1982/3 *(Adnams, Caves de la Madeleine)*

Better Wines Clos du Marquis 1978 *(Peatling and Cawdron)*, £££ Ch Chasse-Spleen 1979 *(Adnams, Lay & Wheeler)*

BURGUNDY AND CHABLIS

The 1983 vintage

In 1983, Burgundy, so they said, had the vintage of the century. Again. But, as is so often the case, the region's vines produced a crop that tested the skill of both growers and merchants to their limits.

It was a big harvest, not as enormous as the record-beating 1982, but still a third up on the average for the previous decade, and amounting to around 45 million bottles in the supposedly top-class vineyards of the Côte d'Or. The best wines will be stupendously good, but there will also be a big crop of really bad wine. Buy wisely, and you will find some of the best, most long-lived red Burgundies in years; buy carelessly, and you will have poorly made, overpriced vinegar.

After the over-plentiful and often anaemically thin wines of 1982 (another 'vintage of the century') the 1983s often proved *too* rich. Ripening all at once, packed with sugar and often short of acidity, grapes of both colours often weighed in with an almost unheard of alcoholic potential. A few white Burgundies, from genuinely nobly rotten grapes, were sweet enough to be dubbed 'Meursaulternes' by those who tasted them; even some of the most lily-livered and humble wines had alcohol to spare. At their best, the whites are often rather like the 1976s: rich, heavy and ripe, delicious perhaps, but often short of acidity and not really typical white Burgundy. Acidification, which is perfectly legal within limits, and which proved necessary for white wines throughout the Côte d'Or, brought its own problems. Tartaric acid added early enough should have blended in with the rest of the wine; added after fermentation, as was often the case, it may have thrown the wine out of balance completely.

Rot, if unwelcome in the whites, proved an even greater problem in the reds – particularly those of the Côte de Nuits from in and around Chambolle-Musigny. Even in the hallowed cellars of the Hospices de Beaune, the musty, dank flavour of rotten grapes was clearly to be found in several barrels of wine. There *were* good wines made in every village, even those hit by rot and hail, but they need careful seeking out.

With the surfeit of sugar and the shortage of natural acidity, fermentation had to be managed with great dexterity. Many vats simply stopped in mid-process – no longer grape juice, and not yet wine – allowing volatile acidity (vinegar to the layman) to take over.

But good growers made good wine. If they chose the right moment to pick their grapes, checked for rot, watched the vats and barrels zealously and acidified slightly if necessary, their reds will be fruity, solid and tannic. They will not be wines for drinking in a year or so, like many of the 1979s and 1982s, but real, old-fashioned 'lay-it-down-till-it's-ready' Burgundy. *Plain Bourgogne Rouge and wines from the humbler villages should be ready for drinking in 1987*, whilst *grands crus*, if they are worth their salt, *should be forgotten until 1994*. Whites, given their low acidity, may well be ready sooner, and indeed may not last long.

If it was difficult for growers to make good wine, it was doubly difficult for the merchants to buy it. Safest buys will be from the soundest producers, from merchants' own vineyards *(see the list of merchants below)* and from the handful of merchants whose wines are generally reliable. The 1983 vintage is certainly not one to buy 'blind'.

Value for money

Burgundy prices are in a state of complete turmoil. On the one hand, there are growers used to asking and getting 50 francs a bottle for their Pommard or Gevrey-Chambertin, and who see no point in reducing their prices as they try to survive in an inflation-racked France. On the other, there are producers whose cellars are full of 1982 and 1983 wines, and whose bank managers and tax inspectors are getting restive. So there will be bargains to be found. Unfortunately, many of these bargains will be far from the producers' best – in some cases they will be very poor indeed. At their worst, prices of red Burgundies should remain stable, although some wines at the bottom end of the scale may be attractively inexpensive.

As for the whites, demand in the United States remains so strong that no one making anything worth drinking should have any difficulty selling it for the price he wants. Pouilly-Fuissé, for instance, is now going for astronomical prices, and 1983 Chablis is selling for at least 25 per cent more than the 1982 vintage. Saint-Véran and Bourgogne Aligoté should be the best bargains around.

What to drink now, what to keep

1982 A very big vintage with many easy-to-drink, soft wines, often short of the acidity and tannin they need to keep them going. Côte de Beaune reds are mostly better than Côte de Nuits. Chablis are very attractive, but lack bite.

1981 A generally disappointing but very varied vintage which was half the size of an average harvest. There are good wines from all over the Côte d'Or, but they are few and far between – most are thin and unappealing. Stick to known and trusted producers. Whites were better, and there are some really first-class Chablis.

1980 Whites of the Côte d'Or often suffered from rot, seeming prematurely aged when they were first made. Good wines are coming round now. Côte de Nuits reds from good growers are also repaying anyone who had confidence in them during their acid youth. Côte de

Beaune reds are often less good. Chablis were highly acid, but are softening now.

1979 Absolutely ready to drink now – only the best examples should be kept for very much longer. Many reds have too much alcohol for their fruit (because of heavy sugaring of thin juice at the vintage). Whites also suffered from low acidity and should be drunk up.

1978 A truly 'great' Burgundy vintage. Some whites – and indeed some reds – are beginning to tire, but good examples should still improve with keeping.

1977 Some of the Côte d'Or reds of this unattractive vintage are beginning to soften up. They still tend to have a slightly metallic aftertaste. A dodgy vintage unless you are very confident in the grower or merchant.

1976 Hailed as the vintage of the century, 1976 sorted Burgundian sheep from goats. Those who got it wrong with their reds – arguably a majority – made wine that seemed fruitless and over-tannic when young and, now that the tannin is fading, seems simply fruitless. Some wines are dying without ever passing through an attractive stage at all; others may become truly great. Even fine winemakers failed, so buy warily. Some of the whites, however, too big and rich ever to be thought typical Burgundy, make an appealing alternative to fat California wines.

1975 Rain – and rot – stopped play, except in Chablis and the Mâconnais, where there are some glorious, if rarely encountered, whites.

1974 Drink up any remaining bottles.

1973 Far better for whites than reds. A gambler's wine these days.

1972 Original unattractive acidity has begun to soften off recently, leaving some truly excellent wine. Fine Côte de Nuits may have developed superbly.

1971 The other 'great' vintage of the decade. Some wines made for keeping are very good now. But the trend to lighter winemaking had already set in, and many good wines are now tiring. Gutsy Côte de Nuits are probably the best bets among the reds. Well-made whites are still certainly worth having.

Understanding the Burgundian label

Who would guess that **Bourgogne Grand Ordinaire**, is more 'ordinaire' than **Bourgogne Ordinaire**? That Bourgogne Rouge *has* to be made exclusively from the Pinot Noir grape – unless it comes from a few of the southernmost vineyards of the region? Or that the presence on the label of a vineyard name – or what looks like a vineyard name – may mean nothing whatsoever? A cynic might well suppose that Burgundian labelling laws were deliberately designed to confuse the unwary. The following list may help you find your way around.

Aligoté White and generally, but not always, rather acidic wine made from the Aligoté grape. The traditional partner for Cassis in Kir.

Bourgogne If white, it must be 100 per cent Chardonnay, or the rare Pinot Blanc, and produced from vines which are at least four years old, and planted on authorised land somewhere between Chablis in the north and the Mâconnais in the south. If red, and from the Côte d'Or, Côte Chalonnaise or the Mâconnais, it has to be 100 per cent Pinot Noir. From further south from the nine Beaujolais Crus vineyards, however, it can be Gamay, and to the north, in Chablis, it can be made from the César and Tressot. In other words, a Bourgogne Rouge can legally contain no Pinot Noir, and thus no true Burgundian Pinot flavour at all.

Bourgogne Côte de Beaune (or Côte de Nuits) Villages Can be very good value, coming from vines which do not quite fit into the village appellations of the two Côtes, but are a cut above simple Bourgogne. Well made, they should show the characteristics of their 'Côte'.

Bourgogne (Saint-Romain) (or one of a number of other Côtes de Beaune villages) -Côte de Beaune Simply indicates that the wine in the bottle is red, and comes from the village in question. So a bottle of Chassagne-Montrachet rouge will be identical to one labelled Chassagne-Montrachet-Côte de Beaune. The use of the suffix is supposed to attract customers' attention towards wines they might not otherwise know. Without it, how many people would recognise Saint-Aubin as a Burgundy at all?

Bourgogne Hautes Côtes de Beaune (or Côte de Nuits) Wines grown in the highest vineyards just above those producing wine that could call itself Côte de Beaune (or Côte de Nuits) Villages, and championed by a single co-operative, a couple of merchants and several eager growers. These wines can be first-class in good years and certainly have their fans, but they are often disappointing, and frequently overpriced. Even so, Hautes-Côtes supporters continue to hail the wines' virtues. There were some good examples in 1983, however.

Bourgogne Passe-tout-grains By law, a blend of two-thirds Gamay and one-third Pinot Noir, but in practice often biased more in the other direction. This is a pity: the attraction of this wine lies in the fruity character of the Gamay.

Bourgogne Ordinaire and Bourgogne Grand Ordinaire Very difficult to find nowadays, and officially the lowest form of wine life in Burgundy. Made from a variety of grapes, including the Gamay and Pinot Noir for the red, and the Chardonnay, Pinot Blanc, Aligoté and even the almost extinct Melon de Bourgogne (which, in the Loire, produces Muscadet) for the white.

Château Means nothing at all in Burgundy where most growers work from tiny, and very unimposing, village houses. There *are* a few châteaux in Burgundy, and some can produce good wine, but afford them no undue respect.

Côte de Beaune A very rare appellation, covering a smallish area around the town of Beaune itself. It should not be confused with Côtes de Beaune Villages which stretches over a far greater terrain.

Grand Cru Traditionally the very finest vineyards in the Côte d'Or and Chablis. The reds are all – except the Corton – on the Côte de Nuits, whilst the Côte de Beaune has all the (non-Chablis) whites. As in Bordeaux, there is some controversy over why certain vineyards were never considered worthy of grand cru status; it is certain that a well-made Meursault-Perrières or Volnay-Caillerets (both premiers crus) will more than match a mediocre Bâtard-Montrachet or Clos de la Roche. In theory at least, grand cru vineyards are allowed to produce a smaller quantity of grapes per acre than premier cru and simple village wines. Sticklers for detail can go back to the pre-1936 maps, which show how the vineyards are designated as first, second and third class. Grand Cru Chablis is – with few exceptions – always a cut above its neighbouring vineyards.

Hospices de Beaune All wine bought at the annual Hospices de Beaune charity auction is sold with the recognisable Hospices label, which also shows, in rather small print, the name of the wine's purchaser. This name is always more important than the Hospices label itself; the wines originally come from good vineyards and are well made, but mischief can and does occur between auction and bottling line, since much will depend on how the wine is looked after and topped up by the merchant who bought it, or his agent.

Hospices de Nuits Relatively little known in Britain, and overshadowed by the glamour of the Beaune auction every November, the sale of the Hospices de Nuits wines takes place several months later in March, when at least the wines are much easier to taste.

Négociant-Éleveur A merchant who has bought and *'élevé'* – matured – the wine. In practice, this describes virtually all of Burgundy's merchants, almost none of whom buys wine which is already in bottle and which has thus already been *'élevé'* by its grower.

Premier Cru The second rank of greatness. All but the most humble Côte d'Or villages have at least a few premier cru vineyards, and several – Beaune, for example – have nothing greater. Growers and merchants are not obliged to put the words 'premier cru' on their labels and can content themselves simply by printing the name of the village, followed by that of the vineyard – Meursault-Charmes for example. Confusingly, the names of other, non-premier cru, vineyards (*'lieux-dits'*) can appear in just the same way *but in smaller print*. So if the letters of the vineyard name are in type that is more than half the size of that used for the village name, the wine must be a premier cru. As if matters weren't already sufficiently confusing, some producers print the premier cru names in very small type too. One clear (?) indication that you are dealing with a *lieu-dit* rather than a premier cru lies in the insertion of the village name between the words Appellation Contrôlée – eg Appellation Meursault Contrôlée. Producers with batches of wine from different premier cru vineyards in the same village which are too small to sell under individual names can mix them and sell the blend under the village appellation adding the words 'Premier Cru' eg Beaune Premier Cru. Also beware of the fact that in the Côte Chalonnaise and Montagny, the words 'premier cru' can refer to the minimum alcohol level of a wine, rather than its provenance.

Propriétaire-Récoltant (or Viticulteur) Literally, the owner and harvester. In other words, certainly not a merchant.

Tastevinage The generally underrated, and too little known, annual tasting by local growers, brokers, merchants and *'amateurs'* of wines produced anywhere in Burgundy. Those which pass the rigorous test bear the recognisable – to some, gaudy – tastevinage label. Do not confuse the serious tastevinage tasting with the *'folklorique'* mock-mediaeval dinners of the Chevaliers de Tastevin which are fun for those who enjoy them, but have little to do with great wine. A *'tasteviné'* Bourgogne Rouge or Blanc is well worth looking out for.

Burgundian names to look out for

Choosing a good bottle of Burgundy is far more difficult than choosing a claret. Even the most rudimentary knowledge and experience of Bordeaux will enable you to recognise certain châteaux as reliable favourites; all you have to do is consider the merits or demerits of particular vintages. In Burgundy, everything depends on who made the wine. Just compare France's two greatest white wines. Ch d'Yquem produces some 65,000 bottles of wine a year, all made by one winemaker. Burgundy's Le Montrachet, with just four hectares and less than 20,000 bottles, derives its produce from 14 individual owners, most of whom sell part of what they make to several different merchants. Allowing for the use of merchants' pseudonyms, there could, in any given year, be as many as 100 producers' or merchants' names appearing at the bottom of the labels of wines being sold as Le Montrachet. And there will be at least 14 different wines behind those labels. One grower may have vines which are older and thus better, another may be using more new oak barrels, a third may have forgotten to spray his plants against rot. . . . So the name of the producer is as important – often more important – than that of the wine.

But even this essential knowledge is not enough to get you past the hurdles. Each of Burgundy's several thousand growers will produce wines of several separate appellations – a Bourgogne Rouge, a Beaune Premier Cru, a Meursault and a Pommard, for example. It is rare for each of these wines to be of an equally high standard: some vineyards will inevitably be better situated than others or the grower may be better at making white than red. There *are* a few growers all of whose wines do seem to be well made from year to year, but they are the exceptions to the general rule.

The merchants have an even more difficult job trying to offer consistent quality. Their customers expect them to list wines from every village and vineyard in the region. They own only a smallish proportion of the vines, so are largely at the mercy of the growers, whose wines they will buy and blend. Some own better vineyards than others; some are better blenders. Virtually none now offers a complete range of truly first-class wine. The best buys generally come from the merchants' own vineyards, where the merchant has as much control over the final product as if he were an individual grower.

The following list of merchants and growers should give some indication of which names to look out for. The list is not comprehensive, but merchants' names which appear on labels but not in these pages could well be secondary brands, for pseudonyms are used by all of the region's merchants when selling to several different importers.

The merchants

Bacheroy-Josselin Successful, and expanding, Chablis merchant with over 40 hectares of vines divided between the Domaine Laroche and the Domaine de la Jouchère. The best wines sold under the former label benefit from ageing in oak.

Albert Bichot An enormous company whose wines you are almost sure to have tasted – though possibly under one of the over three dozen brand names the firm uses including, rather cheekily, **Jean Bouchard** and **Paul Bouchard** – which must further confuse those Burgundy lovers who have enough trouble remembering which of Beaune's two old firms is Bouchard Aîné, and which Bouchard Père et Fils. The **Chablis, La Moutonne** is worth looking out for, as may be wines from the Bichot-owned **Clos Frantin** vines in Gevrey-Chambertin, Vosne-Romanée, Clos de Vougeot, Echézeaux, Corton and Nuits-St-Georges. Other labels include: Caves Syndicales de Bourgogne; Charles Drapier; Labaume Aîné et Fils; Fortier Picard; Rémy-Gauthier; Bouchot-Ludot; Léon Rigault; Maurice Dard; Lupé Cholet (a wholly owned subsidiary). *(Unwins)*

Jean-Claude Boisset Extremely dynamic, if often uninspired twenty-year old firm with over twenty acres of vines. Best wines are from the domaine **Boisset Deschamps** in Nuits-lès-Damodes, **Gevrey-Chambertin, Côte de Nuits-Villages** and **Bourgogne Rouge**. Other labels include Honoré Lavigne, Blanchard de Cordambles; Georges Meurgey; Louis Deschamps.

Bouchard Aîné Not one of Burgundy's brightest burning stars, nor one of its dimmest. A large chunk of the firm's 62 acres of vines are in **Mercurey** on the Côte Chalonnaise and the Bouchard Aîné white from this village is arguably one of their best value wines. In the Côte d'Or, vineyards owned include several in Beaune, Fixin and Chambertin, Clos de Bèze. Other labels include H Audiffred. *(Bouchard Aîné Ltd)*

Bouchard Père et Fils Burgundy's largest merchant, founded in 1731 and now with around 80 hectares of vines. The wines are by no means uniformly fine, but some are excellent, particularly those from Bouchard's own vines, of which nearly 70 hectares are premiers and grands crus. Red wines from the estate all go into new oak barrels and are bottled fairly early, in order to maintain their freshness. The firm is especially well known for its **Beaunes**, including its exclusive **Grèves 'Vigne de l'Enfant Jésus'**, **Clos St-Landry** and **Clos de la Mousse**, as well as large slices of **Les Avaux**, **Les Aigrots**, **Cent Vignes** and **Marconnets**. Amongst Bouchard's other most notable holdings are **Le Montrachet**; **Chevalier-Montrachet**; **Corton**; **Corton-Charlemagne**; **Volnay 'Ancienne Cuvée Carnot'** (part of Volnay Caillerets, made from particularly old vines); **Chambertin**, and **Savigny Les Lavières**. The firm also distribute the Aux Regnots Premier Cru from the Château de Vosne-Romanée on the Côte de Nuits, wines from the Château de Mandelot in the Hautes Côtes de Beaune, and the Clos-St-Marc, a Nuits-St-Georges Premier Cru. Particularly good value are the **Aligotés** from the village of **Bouzeron** on the Côte Chalonnaise, where Bouchard own around two-thirds of the vines. *(Morgan Furze)*

Lionel J Bruck Relatively little known firm in the UK, though occasionally seen under their second name of Hasenklever, this firm's wines often do well at the Tastevinage *(see above)*. Director Henri-François Cruse is a Bordelais who seems to favour tough, tannic wines. Wines come from growers with whom the firm have contracts throughout the Côte d'Or. Look out for **Corton**, **Clos-du-Roi**, **Nuits-St-Georges**, **Les St-Georges**, and **Savigny**, **Clos-des-Guettes**. The original Mr Bruck came from the Liverpool cotton trade.

Champy Père & Cie Another firm that do well at the Tastevinage, this is one of the oldest merchants in Burgundy, still owned by the family that founded it in 1720. The firm's vineyards include parts of **Clos de Vougeot**; **Beaune**, **Clos des Mouches** and **Les Avaux**, and **Savigny**, **La Dominode**.

Chanson Père & Fils Voltaire used to buy from Chanson. Would he do so if he were alive today? The wines are generally good rather than great, and the whites more interesting than the reds. The firm's own 40 hectares include an impressive range of **Beaunes**. Of these, the **Clos des Fèves** can be interestingly meaty, and the **Marconnets**, **Clos du Roi**, **Les Bressandes**, **Champs Pimont**, **Marconnets, Blanches Fleurs**, **Grèves**, **Clos des Mouches** and **Teurons** all reasonably reliable. Amongst the whites, most noteworthy are probably Chanson's own Pernand-Vergelesses, a Bourgogne Blanc 'Cuvée Alexis Chanson' and Chablis, Mont de Milieu. *(Morans of Bristol)*

F Chauvenet (also Louis Max) Better known on the other side of the Atlantic, where the firm own vines – in California – and sell sparkling red Burgundy under the name 'Red Cap'. Well thought of in France are a Bourgogne Blanc called 'Château Marguerite de Bourgogne', a 'Domaine de Pérignon' Passe-tout-grains from vines grown near Chablis, and a Pouilly-Fuissé. Visitors to Beaune may have encountered, though perhaps not memorably, Chauvenet wines at the Hôtel de la Poste, under the Marc Chevillot label.

Raoûl Clerget The Clergets were making wine in Volnay in 1270, and the family still owns the firm, which remains small. The **Saint-Aubins** – both red and white – are generally excellent, as are their other **white Burgundies**.

Coron A century old, this firm's three hectares of vines include **Beaune, Les Cent Vignes, Clos Du Roi**; **Clos des Mouches**; **Les Grèves** and **Champs Pimont**. Also use the name Amsler-Lecouvreur.

M Doudet-Naudin The epitome of 'old style' Burgundy the way our grandfathers used to like it; but then they weren't given the chance to compare it with the lighter, fresher, more characterful wines preferred by today's Burgundy lovers. Still, there *are* those who still like their Burgundies dark, jammy and thick-tasting with an almost cooked flavour – Auberon Waugh, for example, remains a fan – so these wines are not to be dismissed. The firm's cellars are in Savigny, and they own vineyards there, in Beaune and Aloxe-Corton. The wines tend to taste rather similar, but have the merit (thanks to their generous alcohol content) of lasting almost indefinitely. Berry Bros and Rudd and Buckingham's should have some. Elsewhere they may be sold under the Albert Brenot or Georges Germain labels.

Joseph Drouhin Now perhaps one of the two most reliable Burgundy merchants, and one which have found their form once again after a poorish patch in the early 1970s following a major fire. Robert Drouhin prides himself on selling no basic branded table wines, concentrating instead on Burgundies and Beaujolais. Drouhin are noteworthy for their careful use of new oak – experimenting with different woods and various ratios of old barrels to new. Best of the wines from the firm's own vines is probably the **Beaune, Clos des Mouches**, of which some is **white** – a rare beast. Other holdings extend over 51 hectares, an area the firm is sensibly continuing to expand, and include 27 hectares of **Chablis**; **Puligny, Clos du Cailleret**; **Corton-Charlemagne**; **Corton-Bressandes, Bâtard-Montrachet**; **Volnay, Clos des Chênes**; **Griotte-Chambertin**; **Chambertin**; **Chambolle-Musigny, Les Amoureuses**; **Musigny**; **Echézeaux**; **Clos de Vougeot**; and **Bonnes-Mares**. Drouhin also make and sell the excellent **Marquis de Laguiche Le Montrachet**. *(Dreyfus Ashby)*

Georges Duboeuf King of the Beaujolais, where he makes excellent fruity, gulpable wines, and champion of **Saint-Véran**. Many people consider St-Véran 'the poor man's Pouilly-Fuissé'. Duboeuf's St-Véran wines are better than most, and his **Mâcon Blancs** are good too. Other names include Marc Dudet and Jacques Gonard. *(Berkmann Wine Cellars)*

Dufuleur Frères A small Nuits-St-Georges-based firm with vines at **Mercurey, Clos-Vougeot**, **Musigny** and **Nuits-St-Georges** itself. *(Barwell & Jones)*

Joseph Faiveley Another family firm which went through a thin patch, Faiveley have recently begun to re-establish themselves under the direction of 34-year-old president François Faiveley. They have more vines than any other firm in the region – over 100 hectares – including large holdings in **Mercurey** (close to those of Bouchard Aîné), **Rully**; **Clos-Vougeot**; **Corton, Clos de Cortons, Nuits, Clos de la Maréchale** (rented); **Mazis** and **Latricières-Chambertin**; **Clos de Bèze and Echézeaux**. Faiveley's **reds** tend to be better than their whites. *(Laurence Hayward)*

Geisweiler Although their Côte d'Or wines seldom impinge on the memory for their character and quality, Geisweiler are to be praised for championing the cause of the Hautes-Côtes de Nuits, where they have two domains. The Domaine des Dames Hautes covers some 17 hectares, and the Domaine de Bévy around 70 hectares, including over 20 of Chardonnay, an unusual plant for this corner of the Côte d'Or, where Pinot Noir and a little Gamay are almost in control. Amongst other labels are Colcombet Frères, Duret, Larbalestier, A Roussigneux and J Goubard. *(Geisweiler & Fils UK)*

Jaboulet-Vercherre Originally related to – but now unconnected with – the great winemaking Jaboulets of the Rhône, Jaboulet-Vercherre produce a range of Burgundies of which few would serve as characteristic examples to place in a blind tasting. People who like their wines full and velvety may not mind this, however. The flagship of the Jaboulet fleet remains their **Château de Pommard**, and the four-hectare **Clos de la Commaraine** that surrounds it. Until recently, the firm regularly bought the Hospices de Beaune Corton-Charlemagne, paying in 1982 the equivalent of £50 per bottle for the wine in its raw state on the day of the auction. In 1983, Jaboulet-Vercherre took a tighter hold on their purse strings – and declined to bid. Their vineyards include **Pommard**, **Clos Blanc**; **Chambertin**; **Clos de Vougeot**; **Corton, Les Bressandes**; **Beaune-Clos de l'Ecu Monopole** and **Volnay-Caillerets**. *(Grierson-Blumenthal)*

Louis Jadot One of Burgundy's best merchants, their finest wines are without question their **whites** (Corton-Charlemagne, Chevalier-Montrachet, Les Demoiselles, Puligny-Montrachet, Les Referts and Les Folatières) and their Beaunes (most notably the 2.5 hectare Clos des Ursules which forms part of the Vignes Franches). There are some excellent 1980s but unfortunately a number of wines from recent vintages show some all-too-frequent Burgundian merchant characteristics and are thinnish and over-alcoholic. Even these wines are still a cut above many of those offered by most of the region's other merchants, but only a small cut. Wines to look out for are the **Bourgogne Rouge** and **Blanc**, and the **Rully Rouge**; other vineyards forming part of the domaine include **Corton**; **Pougets Corton**

Charlemagne; **Beaune Clos du Roi**; **Les Teurons**; **Les Bressandes**; **Les Vignes Franches**, and **Les Boucherottes**, and **Pernand-Vergelesses en Caradeux, Clos de la Croix de Pierre Monopole**. *(Hatch Mansfield)*

Jaffelin Owned by Joseph Drouhin since 1969, but maintaining a wholly separate identity, this is a firm the French would call *'sérieux'*. They have only 3.5 hectares of vines (in Clos de Vougeot; Beaune, Les Bressandes and Les Avaux) so rely on what they can purchase from growers.

Labouré-Roi This firm is not widely known in Britain, but often produce remarkably good wine, particularly from the six-hectare **René Manuel** domaine, whose wines they sell. The domaine comprises **Meursault, Poruzots**, and **Bouches Chères**, and the red **Meursault, Clos de la Baronne**.

Lamblin & Fils Small but very serious Chablis firm with seven hectares of good vineyards and an attitude which is at once go-ahead and traditionalist. Look for the **Chablis, Mont-de-Milieu**.

Louis Latour For many years, almost the 'Château Latour' of Burgundy, the unassailable peak against which other merchants were to be compared. Recent years have, however, seen a certain erosion of that pre-eminence. The brouhaha which surrounded Anthony Hanson's revelation in his excellent book *Burgundy* that Louis Latour's red Burgundies are all pasteurised has somewhat distracted people's attention from the fact that some of the firm's red wines from the last few vintages have, in any case, less than dazzled their tasters. In Burgundy, Louis Latour himself has become quite unpopular following his strong criticism of the 1980 vintage by calling it the worst in his memory, and by refusing to purchase any of its wine (a disaster for growers who had come to rely on his custom). All the stranger, since many prefer the 1980 Côte de Nuits wines to the 1981s that followed.

Most of Latour's vines are in Corton: the Château de Corton-Grancey; Corton, Clos de la Vigne au Saint-Monopole, Corton-Charlemagne, and Aloxe-Corton, Les Chaillots. Others include Romanée-Saint-Vivant, Quatre Journeaux; Chambertin, Clos des Héritiers; Chevalier-Montrachet, Les Demoiselles; Pommard, Les Epenots; Beaune, Clos du Roi, Les Vignes Franches, Les Grèves and Les Perriès. Louis Latour **white** Burgundies are almost always of a good standard, the **Corton-Charlemagne** and the **Chevalier-Montrachet, Les Demoiselles** outstanding, and the **Montagny** – a village Latour has done much to promote – particularly good value. *(H Parrot & Co)*

Leroy A quirky firm, outside the mainstream of the Burgundian trade and not just in terms of their Auxey-Duresses address. Madame Bize-Leroy, who is also known as an accomplished mountain climber and co-owner of the Domaine de la Romanée-Conti, has a simple and unswerving attitude towards her wines and her business. She sells almost no wine which does not come from the Côte d'Or – and emphatically nothing from outside Burgundy. She certainly would not dream of being associated with such nonsense as Beaujolais Nouveau. Her wines are almost always tough and unyielding when young, developing with age into fine, absolutely typical Burgundies. Since customers rarely have the patience to wait for this to happen, Leroy do a great deal of storage themselves, selling off fully mature wines at horrendously high prices. But where else can you be certain to find fine 1959 Musigny? Owning vineyards in **Pommard, Meursault, Auxey-Duresses, Chambertin, Clos de Vougeot** and **Musigny**, Madame Leroy is just as idiosyncratic about the way she buys wine. Sometimes she will support an unpopular vintage in which she believes, like 1972, and on occasion she will decide not to buy a popular vintage. The most basic, **Leroy d'Auvenay red and white** ££ are possibly the best Burgundy bargains on the market. *(Gonzalez Byass)*

Loron & Fils A variably reliable Beaujolais merchant with good quality **Mâcon Blancs** and **Saint-Vérans**. *(Ernst Gorge)*

P de Marcilly Frères Although owning vineyards in **Chassagne-Montrachet (Clos Saint-Jean, Morgeot, La Conière, Bâtard-Montrachet, and Criots-Bâtard-Montrachet), Beaune (Premier Cru and Les Grèves)**, and **Chambertin**, de Marcilly specialise in good **Bourgogne Rouge** and **Blanc**, sold as **Marcilly Première** or **Marcilly Réserve** ££, and including wines made in the above-listed plots. These basic wines are consequently amongst the best plain Burgundies available. De Marcilly's more up-market Burgundies seem disappointing in comparison.

Prosper Maufoux Santenay-based, this modern firm does produce good wines – red and white – from their vines in that village. Their other wines, particularly the reds from recent vintages, can, however, be very dull indeed, and it sometimes seems that although most of Maufoux's wines are exported, the best do not always reach these shores. Amongst the best of the firm's non-**Santenay** wines are their **Meursault-Charmes** and **Puligny-Montrachet Les Folatières**. Reds from older vintages may still be showing well, though; Maufoux wines have a reputation for longevity. Marcel Amance *(Laytons)* is an alternative name. *(Deinhard & Co)*

Moillard Known as Burgundy's bankers – not in the financial sense, but in the way in which this firm can normally supply their neighbouring merchants with almost any wine they require. The wines are variable and, as a whole, unexciting, though the whites can be fair. Moillard's own vineyards include **Chambertin, Clos de Bèze, Romanée-St-Vivant, Vosne-Romanée, Aux Malconsorts** and **Les Beaumonts, Nuits-St-Georges, Clos de Thorey Monopole, La Richemone, Les Grandes Vignes Monopole; Beaune, Grèves; Corton, Clos de Vergennes** and **Clos de Vougeot**. They also distribute Volnay, Clos de la Barre and Corton, Clos de Vergennes. The wines may also be sold under such names as Pierre Olivier, Toursier, Javelier-Laurin, Henri de Bahèzre, and Thomas Frères. *(Lawlers-Charles Heidsieck Ltd)*

Mommessin A big merchant in the Mâconnais, where their wines are generally of a fair quality. Mommessin also own the entire 7.5-hectare **Clos de Tart Grand Cru** vineyard in Morey-St-Denis. Another label is J Curtil.

Moreau Rivalling only the Cave Co-opérative, Moreau is the big name in Chablis, owning more land, and selling more wine, than anyone else. The wines they sell are good and reliable, if not sublime, and for those who like to drink their **Chablis** young, Moreau is a good name to look for.

Pasquier-Desvignes A five-hundred-year-old company in the Beaujolais with some good quality wines from the **Mâconnais**. *(Dolamore/Rawlings Voigt)*

Patriarche Père & Fils Arousing enormous jealousy amongst other, older-established Burgundy merchants, this Johnny-Come-Lately now takes in more francs, dollars and pounds every year than any of their competitors. Of course, much of this turnover is raised by brands such as Père Patriarche and Kriter, which have nothing whatsoever to do with Burgundy's vines and wines, but Patriarche do sell a large amount of wine from the region itself. Much of this does little credit to the labels, but there *are* some creditable wines, particularly from the **Château de Meursault** estate, taken over and refurbished by Patriarche several years ago. Vineyards include **Beaune**, **Les Fèves**, **Les Grèves**, **Les Avaux**, **Les Bressandes**, **Les Cent Vignes**, **Les Toussaints**, **Les Blanches Fleurs**, and **Clos du Roi**; **Volnay Clos des Chênes**; **Meursault**, **Charmes** and **Les Perrières**. The **Clos du Château Bourgogne Blanc** £££ is a nice wine with a Meursault-like character, but it is not cheap, and you may well wonder whether you are not being asked to pay for the prettily shaped bottle and the impressive label. *(Matthew Clark)*

Piat Père & Fils Another Beaujolais house, and one that puts its wines into attractive pot-shaped bottles. Few are worth a detour, though the **Mâcon-Viré** can be of a reasonable quality. *(IDV)*

Pierre Ponnelle This firm was once a good source of old wine, but stocks of such treasures are now very depleted. Their own vineyards include Vougeot, Domaine du Prieuré; Clos de Vougeot; Beaune, Clos du Roi and Les Grèves; Corton, Clos-du-Roi, Chambolle-Musigny; Charmes-Chambertin; Musigny and Bonnes-Mares. *(Hayward Bros)*

A Régnard & Fils (also sold as **Albert Pic**) Another family firm in Chablis, which owns no vines, but buys carefully from a regular set of growers. Their **Chablis Fourchaumes** is always particularly good.

La Reine Pédauque Over five million visitors troop through this firm's cellars in Beaune, and many leave bearing bottles. Other people order wines from La Reine Pédauque (or P A André, Gauthey Cadet, Abel Laporte, Société d'Elevage des Grands Vins or any of a number of other sub-names used by the company) in restaurants. The firm market wines from the Domaine de la Juvinière (Clos de Vougeot; Corton, Clos du Roi, Combes and Pougets, Clos des Langres; Savigny; Pommard; Aloxe-Corton); the Domaine Les Terres Vineuses (Corton, Clos du Roi, Charlemagne and Renardes; Aloxe-Corton Premier Cru and Ladoix, Clos les Chagnots Monopole), and Mâcon from the Domaine Viticole des Carmes. *(City Vintagers)*

Remoissenet Père et Fils Côte d'Or, broker to the Paris firm of Nicolas and supplier to Averys of Bristol and The Wine Society for many years, Remoissenet have always been well thought of for their white wines in particular (including the **Domaine Thénard Le Montrachet**) and their own **Beaunes** (**Marconnets, Toussaints, Grèves** and **Bressandes**). *(Averys and The Wine Society)*

Antonin Rodet Very popular amongst France's starred restaurants, Rodet specialise in wines of the **Côte Chalonnaise** where their own cellars are situated. Look out for the **Château de Chamiray Mercurey**. Also use the name Pierre Desruelles. *(French Wine Farmers Ltd)*

Ropiteau Frères Traditionally best known for their **Meursault**, the village where most of the Ropiteau estate vines are situated, Ropiteau Frères are gradually raising their standards, concentrating on a smaller range of better wines. Domaine vineyards include plots in **Chambolle Musigny, Clos Vougeot, Volnay, Pommard, Beaune Grèves, Echézeaux, Monthélie** and **Premier Cru Puligny-Montrachet**, as well as **Meursault** and **Meursault-Genevrières, Perrières, Goutte d'Or, Poruzots, Clous and Chevalières.** *(Christopher & Co)*

Simmonet-Febvre A fairly small, but bustling, Chablis firm, always a source for red **Irancy** wines from the area, as well as **Chablis, Les Preuses** and **Mont-de-Milieu** from their own vines. Other wines are generally reliable too. *(Christopher & Co)*

Thorin Also known as Faye, Héritiers Forest, Union des Producteurs and, of course, Henri Bouchard, Thorin is a Mâconnais merchant with some **fair white wines**. *(Findlater Matta)*

Charles Viénot This firm's vineyards include a Nuits-St-Georges Monopole (Clos Saint Marc), three hectares of Corton, one of Richebourg, some Vosne-Romanée and some Aloxe-Corton.

Henri de Villamont Swiss-owned and relatively recently established, de Villamont sprang into the limelight when the firm bought the treasure trove of Dr Arthur Barolet's ancient Burgundies in 1968. Nowadays, using the Barolet name and several others (including François Marthenot, Caves de Valclair, Etienne Vergey, Louis Serrignon, Paul Rolland, Mesnard and Brocard et Fils), de Villamont sell largely unexceptionable wines. They are involved in the promotion of the wines of the Hautes-Côtes, and have their own vines in Grands-Echézeaux, Chambolle-Musigny and Savigny, Clos des Guettes. *(Buckingham Vintners)*

Burgundian growers

The following growers may generally be relied upon for wine from the appellations under which they are listed:

Chablis

René Dauvissat
Paul Droin
Marcel Duplessis
Jean Durup
William Fèvre
Cave La Chablisienne
Henri Laroche
Louis Michel
Louis Pinson
François Raveneau
Gérard Rottiers
Marcel Servin
Jacques Tremblay
Gérard Tremblay
Robert Vocoret

Côte de Nuits

André Bart
Etablissements Bertagna
Domaine Georges Bryzceck
Domaine Camus
Yves Chaley
Domaine Chevalier
Robert Chevillon
Domaine Clair-Daü
Georges Clerget
Domaine Jean Confuron & Fils
Domaine Cornu
Domaine Damoy
Robert Dubois & Fils
Domaine Dujac
Domaine René Engel
Domaine Pierre Gelin
Domaine Elmerich Gouachon
Domaine Henri Gouges
Jean Grivot
Domaine Jean Gros
Domaine Antonin Guyon
Domaine Henri Lamarché
Domaine Lignier
Domaine Machard de Gramont
Henri Magnien
Domaine Manière-Noirot
Alain Michelot
Mugneret-Gibourg
Domaine Mugneret-Gouachon
Domaine Naigeon-Chauveau
Domaine Ponsot
Domaine de la Poulette
Domaine Jacques Prieur
Charles Quillardet
Henri Remoriquet & Fils
Domaine Rion
Domaine de la Romanée-Conti
Philippe Rossignol
Joseph Roty
Domaine G Roumier
Domaine Armand Rousseau
Thévenot-Le-Brun & Fils
Domaine Tollot-Beaut & Fils
Domaine Tollot-Voarick
Domaine F Tortochot
Domaine Louis Trapet
Domaine des Varoilles
Domaine Michel Voarick
Domaine Comte Georges de Vogüé

Côte de Beaune

Robert Ampeau
Domaine Marquis d'Angerville
Domaine Bachelet-Ramonet Père & Fils
Domaine Besancenot
Simon Bize
Domaine Henri Boillot
Domaine Bonneau de Martray
Denis Boussey
Alain Burguet
Domaine Capron-Manieux
Louis Carillon
Domaine Chandon de Briailles
Louis Chapuis
Domaine Clerget
Domaine de Madame Bernard de Courcel
Domaine Darnat
Domaine Delagrange-Bachelet
Domaine Dubreuil-Fontaine
Domaine Duchet
Domaine du Clos des Epenaux
Jacques Gagnard-Delagrange
Domaine F Gaunoux
Domaine Michel Gaunoux
Domaine Germain au Château de Chorey
Jean Germain
Henri Germain
Domaine Alain Gras
Bernard & Louis Glantenay
Domaine Jean Joliot
Domaine Michel Lafarge
Domaine des Comtes Lafon
Domaine Laleure-Piot
Jean Lamy & Fils
Domaine Leflaive
Domaine Lequin-Roussot

£ means that a wine costs, from most producers and in most British shops, under £3 a bottle, ££ that it costs between £3 and £5, and £££ that it costs over £5.

Domaine Lucien Jacob
Leroy
Domaine Machard de Gramont
Domaine du Duc de Magenta
Château de la Maltroye
Domaine Joseph & Pierre Matrot
Mazilly Père & Fils
Domaine Prince Florent de Merode
Mestre Père & Fils
Domaine Michelot-Buisson
Domaine Jean Monnier & Fils
Domaine René Monnier
Domaine de Montille
Albert Morey & Fils
Domaine Mussy
Domaine Parent
Pavelot Père & Fils
Henri Potinet-Ampeau
Domaine de la Pousse d'Or
Domaine Jacques Prieur
Ramonet Prudhon
Domaine Quenot-Meuneveaux
Rapet Père & Fils
Domaine P Rossignol
Domaine Roux Père & Fils
Domaine Etienne Sauzet
Domaine Daniel Sénard
Robert de Suremain
Domaine Tollot-Beaut & Fils
Domaine Tollot-Voarick
Domaine Michel Voarick
Joseph Voillot

Côte Chalonnaise
Chanzy Frères
Jean-François Delorme
Michel Derain
Du Gardin Michel Goubard
Henri & Paul Jacquesson
Domaine Michel Juillot
Paul & Yves de Launay
Jean Maréchal
Domaine Michel
Armand Monassier
Domaine Noël-Bouton (Domaine de la Folie)
François Protheau & Fils
Domaine Ragot
Domaine Roy-Thévenin
Domaine Saier
Domaine Steinmaier
Hugues de Suremain
Soc. Civile du Domaine Thénard
A and P de Villaine
Cave des Vignerons de Buxy

Mâconnais
Cave de Buxy
Cave de Viré
Cave de Prissé
Château de Beauregard
Georges Chagny
André Chavet
Joseph Corsin
Jacques Dépagneux
Hubert Desbois
R Duperron
Roger Duboeuf
Domaine Ferret
Claude Guérin
Maurice Luquet
Lycée Agricole de Davaye
Jean Mathias
Gilles Noblet
Jean Thévenet
Marcel Vincent (Château de Fuissé)

Where to buy Burgundy

O W Loeb, Domaines Direct, Adnams, Corney & Barrow, Lay & Wheeler, Edward Sheldon, Tanners, Les Amis du Vin, Russell & McIver, Christopher Piper Wines, Wine Society.

BEST BURGUNDY BUYS [££] Leroy d'Auvenay red and white *(Barretts, Cavendish House [Cheltenham], Haslemere Wine Company, T & W Wines [Thetford], Morleys Off Licence [Croydon], white only, Selfridges; importer: Gonzalez Byass [UK] Ltd)*; [££] Marcilly Première and Marcilly Réserve, red and white *(Bow Wine Vaults, Richard Harvey Wines [Wimborne], Rose Tree Fine Wines [Cheltenham], Luckin [Great Dunmow]; importer: France Vin Ltd)*; [£££] Daniel Rion Wines *(André Simon, H Allen Smith, Alex Findlater; importer: Morris & Verdin)*

In general: Rully, Mercurey, Montagny, Hautes Côtes de Nuits/Beaune 1983, Auxey-Duresses, St-Aubin 1979, St-Véran 1982/3, St-Romain 1979, Ladoix 1979.

CHAMPAGNE

The 1983 Vintage

This was the largest vintage in the history of Champagne when over 300 million bottles were produced. The previous record was in 1982 (295 million bottles) which compensated for the lean years of 1978, 1980 and 1981. The 1983 quality is high. It will certainly be a vintage year, for the wine is perhaps slightly better than in 1982, which had less acidity. The 1983 Chardonnay wines will be superior to the 1982s, but only time will tell which Pinot year will be the better.

Value for money

Champagne producers now have plentiful stocks. This is likely to have a favourable influence on current price levels, although dramatic reductions should not be expected in the well-known brands. But a lot of companies are selling younger Champagnes cheaply under a secondary label, or for own-label to supermarkets. In Champagne terms, the quality of these cheapest Champagnes is low. But tasted against other sparklers, they are often good value for money.

What to drink now, what to keep

The best recent vintages were 1971, 1975 and 1976, followed by the reasonably good 1978 and a very good 1979, neither of which have had sufficient time to mature to show their best; buyers should snap up the delicious Champagnes of 1975. The less long-lasting 1976 Champagnes are perfect for current drinking, though some are already a little flabby, and losing fruit. Don't hurry to drink the 1979s. These Champagnes will be lovely in a couple of years' time.

Understanding the Champagne label

In this minefield, look first for the word **'Champagne'**, which is the guarantee of origin. Then look for the name of the maker, which you may already know. **Vintage** champagnes, wines blended from one particular year, are dated on both the label and the cork. Vintages are declared only when the quality of the wines is sufficiently good, but do not expect all vintages to be of equal standard. Champagne makers try to maintain a consistent style with their non-vintage blends. A good non-vintage Champagne may therefore be better value than a vintage from a less than exceptional year.

There are two significant dates for a bottle of vintage Champagne – the date of the harvest, and the date the Champagne was disgorged (the last stage of the Champagne method, when the sediment is removed and the bottle topped up). Only very rarely do the Champagne makers disclose the date of disgorging, even though this would be of great use to the consumer. It is all-important, because it shows how long the vintage Champagne has been maturing in the maker's cellar. Bollinger have a lovely vintage champagne – Bollinger **RD** – which stands for

'Récemment Dégorgé' (recently disgorged). A special label on the back of the bottle tells you that date – a most creditable practice. (Otherwise you might be able to make some sense out of the code on the cork.)

Most Champagnes are blends of Chardonnay and the two Pinot varieties, Pinot Noir and Pinot Meunier. Very few champagnes are made only from black grapes **(Blanc de Noirs)**, although there are many excellent Champagnes made only from Chardonnay grapes. These are the **Blanc de Blancs** Champagnes.

Chardonnay grapes are sometimes used from only one village to produce quite remarkable wines. Look for the names of the very best villages, such as **Avize**, **Cramant** or **Le Mesnil**. But make sure you are buying pure Avize or pure Cramant, because the village names are occasionally to be found on the label signifying little more than the fact that the wine was made at the local co-operative. The place where the wine was made does not guarantee the provenance of the grapes, which may come from anywhere outside that well-known and respected village. Perhaps the most famous of all the single village Champagnes is Salon le Mesnil, a superb and long-lasting wine of immense character, now regrettably overpriced in this country. But some Champagnes do not even boast of their origin on the label so that cannot be counted on as a clear indicator. There are in any case some superb blended Blanc de Blancs too; look out for Dom Ruinart and Taittinger Comtes de Champagne.

Revealing codes The critical information on the label is the tiny numbering system. The maker can be traced through the number, but the letters will give most of the clues you need.

NM means the Champagne was made by a merchant (*négoçiant*) who has the right to buy grapes and wine from elsewhere to make his blend. All the major houses have this status, so if you rely on the letters **NM** you will not go far wrong. The name and reputation of the maker is on the line, although even some of the most reputable houses sometimes suffer from inconsistencies of quality.

RM signifies that the maker is a grower, who must make wine from his own produce with only five per cent or less from other grapes. If his vines are in a good village (villages are officially rated on a quality scale from 80 to 100 per cent) and the vintage is good, the results should be superb, but a wine from a poorly rated village in a bad year could be awful. Look for **'grand cru'** which signifies a 100 per cent rating, or **'premier cru'** which means a rating above 90 per cent. But, again, you cannot rely on this system because these descriptions are often omitted.

MA shows that the Champagne has been made for a merchant who has put his own label on the bottle – it's a 'buyer's own brand'. Some such Champagnes are excellent wines, but some are not. Although you need to be careful here, at the current low prices, even these least good Champagnes compare favourably with most other sparkling wines for value for money.

CM shows that the wine has been made by a co-operative. Again, this is little guarantee of quality. Co-operative wines range from the exquisite to the awful.

How dry? You will want to know how sweet or dry the Champagne is. **'Brut'** means very dry, although some wines are made bone dry without the addition of any sugar in the dosage (final topping-up mix of wine and sugar to replace the wine lost with the sediment). These are called names such as **Ultra Brut**, **Brut Zéro** or **Brut Sauvage**. Laurent-Perrier Ultra Brut and Piper-Heidsieck Brut Sauvage are very appealing examples, but the same is not true of all these extra-dry wines. **'Extra dry'** is slightly less dry, and **'sec'** is even less so. **'Demi-sec'**, **'doux'** or **'rich'** are sweet Champagnes for drinking at the end of a meal. Try Veuve Clicquot Demi-Sec.

Rosé Champagne is a blend, normally with red still Champagne wine added to give colour.

Crémant is fermented to a lower pressure and has slightly less sparkle.

Names to look out for

A huge number of Champagnes are imported into this country. The choice is made easier if you decide you like the style of a predominantly Pinot blend or one which is primarily Chardonnay in character. The weighty wines, with a higher proportion of Pinot, often come from Ay or Reims; examples are **Bollinger**, **Deutz**, **Ayala**, **Gosset**, **Alfred Gratien**, **Goulet** or **Veuve Clicquot**. Delicate and balanced blends, containing more Chardonnay, are made by **Pol Roger**, **Perrier-Jouët**, **Moët & Chandon** and many of the **Epernay houses**. **Krug** is a complex blend in a class of its own, whereas **Laurent-Perrier** has its own specially smooth style. **Roederer** makes a full but well-balanced blend, but **Taittinger** has a lighter character. **Mumm** and **Pommery**, like **Moët & Chandon**, **Lanson** and **Mercier** are all in the mass production class, but nevertheless good; Canard-Duchêne, Charles Heidsieck, Besserat and Veuve Clicquot are also big producers. Many houses vary their blends between their vintage and non-vintage wines. There are many other good brands and a number of reputable growers such as **Bonnaire-Bouquemont** from Cramant and **George Vesselle** from Bouzy.

Many of the great houses produce wonderful de luxe Champagnes, some of which are well worth the money; others are dreadfully overpriced. Be sure you know what you are buying at £20 or more. Amongst the luxury brands, you will not be disappointed by **Bollinger RD**, **Cuvée William Deutz**, **vintage Krug**, **Pol Roger PR**, **Dom Pérignon**, **Dom Ruinart**, **Taittinger Comtes de Champagne** or **Roederer Cristal**, but shop around, as prices vary enormously.

Where to buy Champagne

Fortnum & Mason have a serious list with a first-class selection of many of the major producers' wines. **Oddbins** offer an excellent range at competitive prices. **The Champagne House** offer a superb and rigorously selected list of some of the best Champagnes available. **Camden Wine & Food** have an excellent selection at good prices.

Freddie Barratt's Liquor Stores are a good place to look for reasonable quality cheaper Champagnes – often the cheapest on the market. **La Vigneronne** have some good older vintages.

BEST CHAMPAGNE BUYS

Non-vintage Albert Le Brun Cuvée Réservée *(The Champagne House)*; Perrier-Jouët Grand Brut *(Sainsbury's, Stones of Belgravia, Woodcox of Cirencester, Selfridges, Harrods; importer: M Druitt)*; Pol Roger White Foil *(La Réserve, Oddbins, Vintage Wines of Nottingham, Davy & Co, The Champagne House; importer: Dent & Reuss)*; Roederer Extra Quality *(Oddbins, Bottoms Up [selected stores]; importer: Rutherford, Osborne & Perkin)*

Blanc de Blancs Albert Le Brun *(The Champagne House)*; Dom Ruinart *(Victoria Wine [selected shops]; importer: Moët & Chandon)*

Vintage Bruno Paillard 1973 *(French Wine Centre, Wineheads; importer: Ehrmanns)*; Pol Roger 1976 *(Davy's, Oddbins, Stones of Belgravia; importer: Dent & Reuss)*; Cuvée William Deutz 1975 *(Malmaisonl importer: Laytons)*; Perrier-Jouët 1978 *(Sainsburys)*

Crémant Mumm Crémant de Cramant *(Fields, Kershaws Wine Warehouse, Army & Navy, Champagne House; importer: Seagram)*

For further information contact: The Champagne Bureau, 34 Dean Street, London W1; tel 01-437 3526.

JURA

There can be no vineyard area in France which owes so much to one company as the Jura does to Henri Maire. For it is this company alone which has built up the reputation of the wines of the region from almost nothing to their present sound position in the hierarchy of appellation contrôlée wines. This has brought with it certain problems, however. Although in recent years Maire has sold more than 70 per cent of the total production of Jura wines, he also sold vast quantities of wine from elsewhere in France, which the consumer might have mistaken for Jura wine since his name is so tightly linked with the Jura area in the public's mind. In addition, the recent financial problems of Henri Maire have been reflected throughout the wine trade of the whole region. His wines are sound, but highly overpriced, owing to an enormous advertising and promotion budget.

Of the ordinary table wines, the best are probably the rosés, made from the Poulsard grape, which have the reputation of being the finest

> Importers (in brackets) will supply names of retail outlets stocking any wines you have difficulty in finding. Food & Wine from France, 41–46 Piccadilly, London W1; TEL 01–439 8371 will put you in contact with the importers.

in France after those of Tavel. Full-bodied red wines come from the Trousseau and sound whites from the Chardonnay. The best come under the appellation Arbois, lesser wines under Côtes du Jura. Good white wines come also from Pupillin and l'Étoile.

There are three regional specialities: least important is **macvin**, rather similar to white port; secondly, **vin de paille**, a fiendishly expensive dessert wine, made from grapes hung in bunches from house rafters to ripen over the winter; finally – and most importantly – there is **vin jaune**. This can be likened to an old fino sherry and is made in a similar way, by leaving the wine to age in cask for a long time. A **flor** fungus grows on the surface and the wine is reputed to gain in strength. It may not be sold less than six years old, but can age indefinitely. It appears in the peculiar 64cl bottle, the *clavelin*, though this can last only as long as it remains unnoticed by the civil servants of Brussels. Vin Jaune is made from the Savagnin grape. The best comes from the village of Château Châlon, with Arbois, l'Étoile, Poligny and Pupillin close seconds.

Names to look out for

After Maire, the most important supplier must be the co-operative, the Fruitière Viticole. Outstanding single vineyards are **Château d'Arlay** *(France Vin Ltd)* and **Domaine de la Pinte**.

THE LOIRE: Anjou/Touraine/Muscadet

The 1983 Vintage

The 1983 vintage was successful for the Touraine red wines, notably the Gamays, but since they are intended for early drinking while they still contain a lively acidity, the 1984 vintage (unpicked as we go to press) is likely to be the one to buy as soon as possible. The 1983 Chinons, Bourgueils and Saumur Champignys are all better than the 1982s, which was also a good, rich and tannic vintage, and will evolve well over the next five years. They have good colour and fruit. The whites are fruity with appealing freshness and will not fade quickly like the 1982s. There are some very good Anjou dry whites, and in Muscadet, the high-quality 1983s will develop well for those interested in this wine when it has aged a little.

Value for money

Muscadet prices rose last year despite a big harvest. There is a lot of poor, dull Muscadet around, so you need to choose well to get value for money. The whites of Anjou and Touraine are cheap [£] and good value, especially the well-made Touraine Sauvignons and the better new Anjou whites which have had a boost of Chardonnay or Sauvignon added to the rather dull base of dry Chenin Blanc. Single variety wines (Sauvignon and Chardonnay) labelled 'Vin de Pays du Jardin de la France' can be especially good value [£] and, from a good grower, better than the AC Anjou Blanc. Reds from Anjou have improved enormously in the past few years, and are now generally more richly coloured, fruity and aromatic, good value at [£]+.

What to drink now, what to keep

The 1982 whites from Touraine – Sauvignons and Chardonnays notably – need drinking up as they have become flabby and flat-tasting. The same applies to many Muscadets. The year was better for some of the Chenin wines like Jasnières. Otherwise, great care should be taken when buying 1982 whites or rosés from the middle and lower Loire. The 1983s, on the other hand, can be bought with confidence.

The 1982 reds from Anjou, Saumur Champigny and Touraine have, in some instances, started to lose their already low acidity and do not look worth hanging on to, though the better ones (eg Richou – *see below*) will still repay keeping. Go for the **1983** of the lighter reds and start drinking the Champignys in a couple of years, the Bourgueils in maybe four or five. Anjou rouge Cabernet from 1981 is also a good wine now – look for domaines like Richou, Lebreton, Dhomme, Chauvin and Banchereau.

The two vintages before 1981 to look out for in **Chinon** and **Bourgueil** are the **1978** and **1976**. They are reaching their peak very nicely, showing the soft flavours of early age.

Understanding the label

Anjou blanc sec A dry white made principally from the austere and rather dull Chenin grape, often successfully softened with some Sauvignon or Chardonnay. These wines are steadily improving in standard.

Anjou demi-sec or doux A semi-sweet or sweet version of this wine.

Rosé d'Anjou This indicates a sweet rosé wine, the workhorse of the region, made mainly from the Grolleau grape.

Cabernet d'Anjou (rosé) A generally semi-sweet rosé made from the Cabernet Franc more often than the Cabernet Sauvignon. It can age for many years.

Anjou cépage Cabernet A red wine made from the Cabernet (usually a mix of Franc and Sauvignon). These, too, have recently improved enormously.

Rosé de la Loire A dry rosé made from Cabernet, Grolleau and Gamay. It is a clear, fresh wine.

Vouvray sec When young a rasping, dry wine, one that benefits from several years' ageing. When there is no indication, the wine is often slightly sweet, not cloying, and agreeable as an aperitif if well chilled.

Vouvray mousseux The slightly less fizzy version of **Vouvray pétillant**, the latter being the full sparkler. **Montlouis** wines are similarly described.

Names to look out for

Touraine

Confrérie des Vignerons de Oisly et Thésée, particularly their **Baronnie d'Aignan** £ brand of white Touraine sec, a crisp and impressive wine. *(Hawkins & Nuirick)*

Jasnières ££, a Chenin white that needs ageing for a minimum of four or five years, from J-B Pinon. *(Yapp, La Vigneronne)*

Domaine de la Charmoise, Henri Marionnet, Touraine Gamay

Prince Poniatowski, Vouvray ££ *(Caves de la Madeleine, La Vigneronne)*

J-P Leblois, Montlouis

Marc Brédif, Vouvray ££, *(Bow Wine Vaults and others)*

Gaston Huet, Vouvray ££ *(The Wine Society)*

Raymond Desbourdes, Chinon £££ *(Yapp)*

Olga Raffault, Chinon £££ *(Wine Society)*

A Donabella Domaine de Ronce, Chinon £££

Charles Joguet, Chinon £££ *(O W Loeb)*

G Audebert, Domaine de Grand Clos, Bourgueil ££ *(Berry Bros)*

J-P Mabileau, St Nicolas-de-Bourgueil ££

Lame-Delille-Boucard, Bourgueil £££ *(La Vigneronne)*

Anjou

Domaine Richou, Anjou Rouge Cabernet ££ *(Haynes, Hanson & Clark, Angevin Wines [UK] Ltd)*

Domaine des Rochettes, Gérard Chauvin £ *(Waitrose)*

Send us your views on the report forms at the back of the book.

Muscadet

Louis Métaireau, Muscadet [£]

Château de la Galissonnière, Muscadet [££]

Château de Chasseloir, Chereau-Carré, Muscadet [££]

Château de la Ragotière, Muscadet [££]

Saumur Cave Co-opérative des Vignerons de Saumur [£]

Saumur Champigny Paul Filliatreau [££]

Saumur Champigny Denis Duveau [££]

Where to buy Muscadet/Anjou/Touraine wines

Yapp Bros and *Lorne House Vintners* have an excellent range, La Vigneronne has older vintages. Also Mackie, The Wine Society.

BEST LOIRE BUYS [££] Sauvignon, Vignerons de Oisly et Thésée Baronnie d'Aignan *(André Simon, Gerard Harris, Jacques Matthieu, Hurlingham; agents: Hawkins & Nuirick)*, [££] Domaine Richou Gamay and Cabernet *(Haynes, Hanson & Clark, Angevin [UK] Ltd)*, [£££] Chinon Charles Joguet *(G H Gare & Co, Thos Baty, Caves de la Madeleine, Henry Townsend; importer: O W Loeb)*, [£££] Savennières, Domaine de la Bizolière 1983 *(Sainsbury's)*, [£] Saumur blanc 1983 Cave Co-op St Cyr *(Robert James & others)*, [£££] Chinon L'Arpenty 1983 R Desbourdes *(Yapp)* [££] Muscadet, Château de Chasseloir, Comte Leloup *(Lorne House)*

THE LOIRE: sweet wines

The 1983 vintage

Sweet wines made from the Chenin Blanc grape are very slow to develop and lose their early sharpness. Growers are pleased with their 1983 sweet wines, which at present have a firm, pale lemon colour, and an acid, rather raw fruit on the palate. The bouquet will take six years to open up in the better Layons. The 1983s should keep well – easily 15 to 30 years.

Value for money

Prices of sweet Loires have crept up over the past three years, particularly for well-aged wines. By far the best value buys at present are wines from the late 1960s and early 1970s – £7 to £9 on most lists – which are very good to drink now, but which can live and mature for another five to ten years without problem. Young vintages may well be good value for laying down at just over £3.

What to drink now, what to keep

The **1982** sweet Loires are a little unformed, rather bitter and do not match the 1983s' potential. It is a middle-weight vintage and better value can be obtained from the **1981** and **1978**, both still full of young fruit but developing the honey-and-apricot flavours that come with age. **1976** is a major keeping vintage, as are **1969**, **1964**, **1961** and the legendary **1959**, the last named remarkable for its complex, honeyed flavours and clean, tangy finish.

Before 1959, Layons, their underrated neighbour Coteaux de l'Aubance and Vouvray moelleux should all be delicious if well cellared, but they are expensive at starting prices of £16+. The old Anjou whites – eg 1928 – that have sprung on to the market following the Prunier cellar sale are good but not startling, and are hardly snips at £18–£25 a bottle.

The two best lightweight vintages giving **good drinking now** are **1975** and **1967**.

Understanding the sweet Loire label

The principal sweet Loire region is **Coteaux du Layon**, south of Angers. Rather as in Beaujolais, there is a basic category of wine called simply Coteaux du Layon. Then there is a step up to the **Coteaux du Layon Villages**, seven communities (**Beaulieu, Faye, Rablay, Rochefort, Saint-Aubin, Saint-Lambert and Chaume**) who put their village name on the label as an indication of a higher natural alcohol degree. Their wine is more concentrated than the ordinary Coteaux du Layon, with greater selection of noble rot grapes in the vineyards, and represents good value for money. The driest style of wine comes from Rochefort and Saint-Aubin. Chaume is the king of this group, with a lower yield per hectare allowed, and two summit wines, **Quarts de Chaume** and **Bonnezeaux** have their own appellation. Only about 50,000 bottles of Quarts de Chaume are made in any one year.

Coteaux de l'Aubance Borders Layon. Its wines are also made from the Chenin blanc grape, age just about as well, and are good buys. A key word to look out for is **moelleux**. This denotes a grower's sweet wine, often made only in better years: eg 'Vouvray moelleux'.

Names to look out for

Château de la Guimonière, Coteaux du Layon Chaume *(La Vigneronne)*
Domaine de la Croix de Mission, René Renou, Bonnezeaux *(Yapp, Hurlingham, Lay & Wheeler, and Harrods have young vintages)*
Domaine d'Ambinos, J-P Chêne, Coteaux du Layon Beaulieu *(Robert James)*
Domaine de la Soucherie, Coteaux du Layon *(Sainsbury's)*
Domaine des Rochettes, G Chauvin, Coteaux de l'Aubance *(Waitrose)*

Specialists in the UK

Yapp Brothers (broad selection from four growers, high quality), La Vigneronne (good selection of older, rarer wines), High Breck Vintners (several vintages of Chaume), Adnams (vintages of sweet Anjou Moulin Touchais 1929–75), Mackie & Co.

BEST BUYS ££ Coteaux de l'Aubance, provided it is cheaper than Layon, is a sound buy *(Waitrose)*, £££ Coteaux du Layon from the Villages in vintages 1967, 1969, 1975, 1976 *(La Vigneronne, Sainsbury's)*

UPPER LOIRE (Sancerre, Pouilly Fumé etc)

The 1983 vintage

Rot and mildew affected the crop, so that some wines are not as fresh as they might be. But the wines have better acidity than the 1982s, and are generally marked by a crisp fruitiness. The large crop has meant that quality was good, but perhaps not as outstanding as had been hoped.

Value for money

Sancerre prices continue to creep up to a level where they are strained to offer such good value as high-priced wines like Chablis. Pouilly Fumé is beginning to represent possibly better value.

What to drink now, what to keep

The 1982 Sancerres and Pouilly Fumés should be drunk soon. But better, turn to *the remaining 1981s and the 1983s*. 1983 will also be better for the red Sancerres than 1982, while the *1983 Quincys are a good buy*.

Understanding the Upper Loire label

Quincy, Reuilly and **Ménétou-Salon** are vineyards that lie south-west of Sancerre, their white wines all made from the Sauvignon grape. **Sancerre red** is made with the Pinot Noir, while the unusual **Reuilly rosé** comes from the Pinot Gris grape. **Pouilly Fumé** is sometimes labelled **Blanc Fumé de Pouilly** – two ways of saying the same thing. But Pouilly-sur-Loire is an inferior wine, made from the neutral Chasselas grape. You will rarely see it in England.

Names to look out for

Sancerre, Vacheron *(Wine Society and others)*
Sancerre, H Bourgeois *(Yeo, Ratcliffe & Dawe Ltd)*
Sancerre, Jean Vatan *(Yapp)*
Sancerre, Clos du Chêne Marchand T Merlin *(La Vigneronne and others)*
Pouilly Fumé, Bailly *(Wine Society)*

Pouilly Fumé, Ladoucette *(Sainsbury's and others)*
Ch de Tracy, Pouilly Fumé
Pouilly Fumé, Robert Pesson
Quincy, Raymond Pipet *(Yapp)*
Quincy, Pierre Mardon *(Bow Wine Vaults)*
Menetou-Salon, H Pellé *(Wine Society)*
Reuilly, Cordier *(Yapp)*

BEST BUYS [££]–[£££] Quincy 1983, R Pipet *(Yapp)*, Pouilly Fumé, Ch de Tracy 1982 *(G E Bromley, Leicester)*, Pouilly Fumé, Bailly 1983 *(Wine Society)*, Sancerre, H Bourgeois 1983 *(Yeo, Ratcliffe & Dawe)*

THE MIDI

Don't write off the South of France as a land of plonk – things have been changing – and still are.

The great common denominator in red and rosé wine-making in France's Mediterranean regions of Languedoc–Roussillon and Provence is the Carignan grape, which produces a firm, tannic wine. But it is now being partially replaced by new plantings of the so-called *cépages améliorateurs* (improver varieties) such as Grenache, Cinsault, Syrah, Cabernet Sauvignon, Merlot and Mourvèdre. This last variety is a native of the area and is capable of producing full, aromatic, long-lived wines like those of Bandol. The Grenache gives a good degree of alcohol, fruit and body and the Syrah, Cabernet Sauvignon and Merlot especially are used in Coteaux d'Aix-en-Provence, the Gard, the Hérault and the Aude either to give a wine a particular style (only ten to 15 per cent of one or other is needed) or to make single grape variety wines, which can be quite delicious in their own right. The traditional white varieties are Clairette, Ugni Blanc, Bourboulenc and (Roussillon only) Maccabeo. But now the Sauvignon is planted quite widely and is bringing a degree of acidity and fresh fruit to white wines from the Midi, virtually unknown ten years ago.

New methods of vinification have also been very important in improving quality: both co-operatives and individual growers have invested heavily in stainless steel equipment, better presses and filtration equipment and, perhaps most important of all, temperature-controlled fermentation vats, in which white wines can ferment slowly at a maximum of 22°C, thus retaining more of their fragrance and eliminating the former 'cooked' character of so many southern wines. Carbonic maceration (fermenting whole grapes in the absence of oxygen) is also used and is just one of the methods of extracting more colour, immediate fruit and bouquet. It is particularly used in Corbières but usually only for a proportion of wines going into the final blend.

The 1983 vintage

There need be no worries about the vintage as the Mediterranean climate nearly always assures a mature harvest picked in good conditions. That of 1983 is no exception, although particularly the Grenache fruit failed in bad weather early in the season so the average yield in red wines was significantly lower than usual.

Value for money

In many ways the Midi represents the most exciting part of France from a wine lover's point of view. If you cannot afford always to drink the wine of your choice from more northerly and expensive climes, the Midi offers an increasingly attractive range of wines in all three colours at comparatively low prices. This huge wine-growing area, running from Nice round to Perpignan, produces over half the total French output in terms of volume and is still devoted predominantly to red and rosé, but the low quality image of its wine is deservedly changing for the better. Of course there remains a proportion of low degree and characterless (or worse) red wine but in the British market we would see it only, if at all, in very cheap French or EEC vin de table blends. Much of it will be distilled. Good wines from the Midi need cost only a few tens of centimes more per bottle ex-cellars and wine trade buyers do not find much difficulty in spotting the difference!

Prices in the Midi have risen only very slightly, much to the growers' chagrin, but the favourable exchange rate and our drop in duty have saved British consumers from increases.

What to drink now, what to keep

Since the wine harvest in the Midi starts in September, a good three weeks earlier than in the more northerly vineyards, and in late August in the case of some white grapes, it is quite normal to be offered white wines from the new vintage before Christmas, and for red wines, which are usually sold without vintage, to be freshened (depending on stocks) with increasing amounts of the new wine into the new year. Even with the latest vinification techniques, *it is preferable to drink the white wines within a year of the harvest. Most 1983 reds, whether vintaged or not, will be drinking well now and any wines showing any earlier vintage will be ready for drinking.* The exceptions to this are the bigger domaine or château bottled wines from Bandol, Fitou and Côtes-du-Roussillon-Villages and a few others like the extraordinary Mas de Daumas Gassac from the Hérault (*see below*).

Understanding the South-of-France label

The principal appellation areas going from East to West are **Côtes de Provence AC** [££], **Coteaux d'Aix-en-Provence VDQS** [£]–[££], **Costières du Gard VDQS** [£], **Coteaux du Languedoc VDQS** [£], **Minervois VDQS** [£]–[££], and **Côtes du Roussillon AC** [£]. This last is subdivided into two parts, as in Beaujolais, with the higher quality **Côtes-du-Roussillon-Villages** wines coming from the more mountainous communes. In fact, the Midi is going through another transitional period in terms of AOC and it is almost certain that 1985 will see the disappearance of the VDQS classification, the better parts of the areas achieving full AC status and the rest classified as vin de pays de zone (*see below*).

This is by far the most confusing part of the four-tier classification system at present. Readers should try to discover whether a given vin de pays is a **vin de pays départmental**: **Vin de Pays du Var, des Bouches-du-Rhône** or **du Gard** for instance, or a **vin de pays de zone**. Here there is a plethora of names from more distinct districts within the nine departments such as **Vin de Pays des Sables du Golfe du Lion, des Collines de la Moure** and **de la Haute Vallée de l'Aude**. While it might be difficult to detect exactly where these wines come from even with the help of a yellow Michelin map, the wines coming from a more closely defined region should be more characterful. It does not help that the words 'vin de table' also have to be shown on vin de pays labels.

Clearly vin de table itself is the least specific classification since it may be labelled only as French, from the EEC or whatever, even if its provenance is the Gard, for instance.

Names to look out for

Bellet AC ££+ The very small appellation just behind Nice, most of whose wine is drunk 'sur place' but some of which escapes to be offered by *Yapp Bros.* **Château de Crémet** in red, white and rosé and generic Bellet in white and rosé made at the château from the neighbours' grapes. These are wines of real character made from some very ancient grape varieties like Folle Noir for the red and Rolle for the white, with only a little Cinsault and Grenache in the blends.

Côtes de Provence AC ££ A huge area, 18,000 hectares of vines, which was granted full AC status in 1977. The rosés are still the most popular and should be drunk as young as possible – beware of wines of a brown-pink colour, which will be getting a bit past it. Great progress has been made in red and white wines. Whites now account for a tenth of the production and tend to be made from a proportion of Sauvignon picked before full maturity to avoid excessive tannin from sun-thickened skins and to preserve acidity. Look for **l'Estandon** among branded wines, for the expensive but delicious wines of **Domaines Ott** (available from *Bibendum* and *Lay & Wheeler, Tanners* and *Yorkshire Fine Wines*), and for the **Domaine des Hauts de St Jean** and **Domaine des Féraud** (from *Yapp* and *Caves de la Madeleine* respectively). In vin de pays, try *Adnams'* **Domaine des Chaberts Vin de Pays des Coteaux Varois** red.

Bandol AC ££–£££ A very small appellation, which preceded Côtes de Provence in AC status along with Bellet, Cassis and Palette and whose terraced vineyards above Toulon produce perhaps the finest wines in Provence. The reds must include a minimum of 50 per cent Mourvèdre, giving considerable depth of colour, fruit and ageing potential. The rosés must be kept in wood for a minimum of eight months and thus have a slightly orange hue; the total production of whites is not much more than 10,000 cases a year. Clairette, Bourboulenc and Ugni Blanc make a rich and fragrant white wine. We would recommend **Domaine Tempier** (from *Berkmann, Milroy's* and *O W Loeb*), **Mas de la Rouvière** *(Yapp)*, and **Château des Vannières** *(Yorkshire Fine Wines)*.

Cassis AC ££–£££ A small area of 150 hectares next door to Bandol known best for its white wines made principally from the Clairette, Ugni Blanc, Marsanne and Sauvignon grapes but with touches of one or two lesser-known varieties, giving a very crisp dry wine with little acidity which should be drunk young. An outstanding wine is **Domaine du Paternel**. **Clos Sainte-Magdeleine** is also excellent *(Yapp)*.

Palette AC £££ The last of the tiny appellations whose red, white and rosé wines, while being vinified from mixes of the same grapes as above, need some time in bottle before reaching their best. **Château Simone** is virtually the only source *(Yapp, Malmaison)*.

Coteaux d'Aix-en-Provence £ About one sixth the size of Côtes de Provence, Coteaux d'Aix lies mostly to the south and east of Aix itself and produces predominantly red and rosé wines with a very distinctive taste. The most attractive wines are those from the estates of the **Marquis de Saporta**, which are the exception to the rule in making one of the best white wines in the Midi: early picking, cold fermentation, the addition of 20 per cent Sauvignon, and great attention to detail, combine to create a fresh and fragrant wine with a touch of acidity, suggesting the Loire or Alsace on blind tasting. *Harrods, Justerini & Brooks* and the *Merchant Vintners (Adnams, Tanners, Lay & Wheeler, and others)* sell the wines in all three colours from **Château de Fonscolombe** itself, *Bibendum* and *Luc Lacerre* sell the wines under the name of the Marquis, *Peter Dominic* sell the red from the **Domaine de la Crémade** and *Berry Bros* the white **Domaine de Paradis**. **Château Vignelaure** is a very good, if expensive, example of the art of making a Cabernet Sauvignon wine outside Bordeaux, and Château de la Gaude is a more typical red wine of the old style, made from the oldest vines in the area – *Yapp Bros* sell the 1981 Cuvée Spéciale and the rosé.

In Vin de Pays, the *Wine Growers' Association*'s red and white **Domaine de Boulléry, Vin de Pays des Bouches du Rhône** represent outstanding value.

Coteaux des Baux VDQS £–££ A tiny appellation, which has become known for its wines in large measure as a result of the promotional efforts of the three *Michelin*-starred restaurants at Les Baux. The best wines are exceptions, but can be very good. We recommend *Yapp*'s **Domaine de Trévallon** ££ (60 per cent Cabernet Sauvignon and 40 per cent Syrah), also available at the *La Réserve* shops.

Côtes du Lubéron VDQS £–££ From the Montagne du Lubéron, the range of hills extending along the north bank of the Durance river.

Being relatively high, the vineyards are suited to growing **white** wines as well as red and rosé. Nearly all the wine is produced by the extremely modern and efficient co-operative. It is widely available in supermarkets and off-licences, usually under the **Cellier du Marrenon** label, and both red and white are light and fruity in style. But beware older vintages of the white. These wines are made to drink in the year after the vintage, but there are a lot of older vintages around, which have now become dull. More interesting is the **La Vieille Ferme** ££ white made totally from Chardonnay, albeit made to produce very high yields *(Laytons, André Simon, Crawfords* and *La Réserve)*. Try also the red **Côtes du Lubéron, Château de Canorgue** ££ from *Yapp*.

Costières du Gard VDQS £ An area of about 4,000 hectares round Nîmes producing almost entirely red and rosé wines of a more spicy character than in neighbouring appellations. For a generic Costières du Gard, try that of *Bow Wine Vaults* from **La Méridionale**, a group of some thirty co-operatives now making some very good wines – one sixtieth, in fact, of the total French production. Otherwise, Gallaire et Fils bottle the excellent **Domaine La Perdrix** in red and white *(Tanners)* and **Château de Belle Coste** is a château-bottled red from *Luc Lacerre*.

Vin de Pays du Gard £ now tends to be flavoured up with five per cent or so of either Syrah or of Cabernet Sauvignon. Whichever is the case, the wine will have less depth than the VDQS but it nonetheless represents good value, also in the **Peter Dominic** and **Stowells bag-in-boxes** always provided that they are *very* freshly 'bagged'.

Vin de Pays des Sables du Golfe du Lion £ Vines growing in the sandy soil, derived from marine deposits and drift from the lower Rhône, running west from the Camargues round the wonderful walled town of Aigues-Mortes and down to the sea at the lighthouse of l'Espiguette. **Listel**, a name corrupted from 'Ile de Stel' or sand island, is the very successful branded range of wines produced by the Domaines Viticoles des Salins du Midi, which own over 1,000 hectares in the immediate area and many more outside it. The **Listel Dry** is a delicate, dry white which nonetheless achieves 12° *(Victoria Wine, Arthur Cooper, Lennons)*. The company's ultra-modern methods of vinification have been developed in order to extract the maximum flavour from the Ugni Blanc, Clairette and touch of Sauvignon and they are now producing **Brut de Listel**, a superior non-appellation vin mousseux from the same grape varieties, as well as some newly-introduced varietal wines – try the **Cabernet Sauvignon**, Chardonnay and Sauvignon.

Coteaux du Languedoc VDQS £ If the reds are generally less aromatic than the Costières du Gard, they can still be full-bodied and quite classy, especially domaine wines from the hills round the Pic St-Loup. The only white wines of the area to achieve VDQS status – **Picpoul de Pinet** – are those grown nearer the coast near Sète. Made almost entirely from the Picpoul grape, these wines are best drunk very young and very chilled at one of the many fish restaurants overlooking the canals in the old town of Sète, still the largest wine port in the world.

Vins de Pays de l'Hérault [£], also from this area, range from the very ordinary to the most exotic wines in the South of France. At the top of the first category must come the excellent and very well-priced **Domaine du Chapître** red and white, made at the institute of oenology at Montpellier *(Asda, Morris & Verdin)*. The second is the **Mas de Daumas Gassac** [££]–[£££], which has been queryingly hailed as the 'Lafite Languedocien?' by *Gault Millau*, and which consists of 20 hectares of the only glacial soil known to remain in the Midi of the type found in some of the best parts of the Médoc and Burgundy. A cool micro-climate, a classic Bordeaux fermentation inspired by Emile Peynaud (including the use of a proportion of new barrels each year and otherwise second-year barrels from Châteaux Margaux and Palmer), and 70 per cent of Cabernet Sauvignon, combine to make a very dark, tannic and complex wine which will improve for many years. A classic wine available in the 1982 vintage from several specialist wine merchants across the country including *La Vigneronne, Rose Tree Fine Wines, Eaton Elliot Wine Brokers, Moray Quality Wines* and *Bow Wine Vaults.*

Minervois VDQS [£] Usually sound red wines made to the north-west of Narbonne from a higher proportion of Carignan (50 per cent and more) together with Grenache and Cinsault. The wines may not be very weighty in character but they are cheap, so it is worth seeking out single property wines such as the **Domaine St-Eulalie** from *Adnams*, the **Cuvée Jean d'Alibert** from *Lay & Wheeler* and the **Château de Gourgazaud** from *Tanners*, which most represent the velvety depth and length that the best wines from this region achieve.

In vins de pays from the area, we would recommend the **Vins de Pays de la Haute Vallée de l'Aude**, an impressive district towards Limoux, where a lot of Cabernet Sauvignon and Merlot have been planted. A good example made from 100 per cent Cabernet is shipped by *Eldridge Pope.*

Corbières VDQS [£]–[££] A large area straddling the Languedoc and the Roussillon, whose red wines are strong in colour, meaty in flavour and usually generous in alcohol. At the cheapest end, one can meet tired wines, which have been blended in large part from wines made by the carbonic maceration method of fermentation (made rather like Beaujolais Nouveau for early drinking) and which have been kept too long in stock by importers. The tendency in the region, however, seems to be to return to more traditional methods of vinification, giving full-bodied wines that will last. The **Château de Montrabech** produces dependable wine of this type and has the merit of being quite widely available.

Fitou AC [££] A small commune sandwiched between the hills of the Corbières and the plain running south to Perpignan. The wines of Fitou are distinguished by having to include a minimum of 70 per cent of Carignan and to be aged in wood for 18 months before bottling. Wonderful ruby red wines of great depth are produced and they should be drunk three to five years after the vintage.

Côtes de Roussillon £ and **Côtes-de-Roussillon-Villages AC** £–££
Long recognised as one of the best wine-producing areas in the Midi. (AOC status was granted in 1973.) By contrast with Fitou, the red wines must have a maximum of 70 per cent of Carignan, and most are now based on Grenache, which gives the wines great depth of colour, softness, good fruit and a long finish. These are warming wines being a minimum of 11.5° in the straight AC and 12° in the Villages, the best areas in the foothills of the Pyrenees. **Vignerons Catalans** produce consistent wines in great volume. **Coteaux Catalans** are also very good – try their 13° Côtes-du-Roussillon-Villages, available from *Arthur Cooper* and *Roberts* shops. Amongst single properties, *Peter Dominic, Sainsbury Bros* in Bath and *Luc Lacerre* sell the **Château de Corneilla**, and *Ashe & Nephew* sell the **Château de Villeclare**. White wines from the area are made from the Maccabeo grape and are usually vinified after early picking and sold as *'vin vert'*. These wines have very little acidity, tire easily and are best drunk in the Roussillon. The **Vin de Pays Catalans** and **Vin de Pays des Pyrénées-Orientales** £ come in considerable volume in both red and white. The reds are very good value but can be earthy, and indeed rough at times. (Know your wine merchant or supermarket!) The whites, made from Ugni Blanc and Clairette as well as the Maccabeo of the region, tend to be pleasant enough but should be drunk young.

Vins Doux Naturels (VDN) These are naturally sweet wines made mainly from Muscat and Grenache grapes in the area around Sète and in the Roussillon. The technique is to stop the fermentation at about 7° by adding a dash of very powerful but neutral grape brandy, leaving a very rich dessert wine with a total of between 15° and 22° in alcohol and plenty of unfermented sugar. The best-known names in the Grenache-based wines are **Banyuls** £££ and **Maury** ££ from the Roussillon; the **Muscats** are perhaps more to the British palate. Look for **Muscats de Frontignan** ££ and **de Mireval** ££. *Luc Lacerre, Vannick Wines* and *Crawfords* stock the **Muscat de Rivesaltes** ££ from **Château Corneilla**, and *Cullens* have a very good Muscat de Rivesaltes called **Aphrodis**.

Where to buy wines of the Midi

Adnams, Yapps, La Réserve, Tanners, Luc Lacerre, Crawfords.

BEST BUYS £ Listel wines *(many stockists including a number of supermarkets)*, ££ Domaine de Trévallon *(Yapps, La Réserve)*, ££ La Vieille Ferme *(Laytons, André Simon, Crawfords, La Réserve)*; other wines mentioned above.

RHÔNE: the North

All Northern Rhône **reds** are made from the Syrah grape, though Côte-Rôtie may be lightened with a little of the white Viognier. Smelling of vanilla and black cherries when young, these wines mature to a warm, spicy opulence. The best are very long-lived (up to twenty years). All the **whites** use the Marsanne and Roussanne grapes, except Condrieu, which is made from the Viognier. The Marsanne and Roussanne mix produces full-flavoured wines, smelling of blackthorn and lime blossom. Viognier makes wines reminiscent of greengages and red gooseberries.

The 1983 vintage

'We had five months of summer; it was a great year.' Louis Jaboulet's opinion is echoed by all the top growers. Marcel Guigal even talks of a vintage that may have produced wines better than the fabled 1978s.

The size of the 1983 crop was normal and the wines were slightly less alcoholic than in 1982 (when exceptional heat in the autumn hastened the grapes to a slightly unbalanced maturity).

Both 1982 and 1983 were excellent vintages in the Northern Rhône. But the 1983s will almost certainly be the better vintage. Max Chapoutier compares them with 1953 and 1952. '1982 is like 1953, producing wines very high in alcohol but supple and ripe. 1983 is like 1952. The wines have more character, more tannin and are more severe and more difficult to taste at this stage than the 1982s were. Now, after thirty years, if we compare 1952 and 1953 we find both are good. This is very surprising because we thought the 1953s would fade before the 1952s.'

Our own tastings confirm the quite exceptional concentration in the 1983s. A deep purple, almost black, they have the character of black cherries and vanilla that we often associate with young Syrah. They are clearly made to last.

The white wines are probably better balanced than the 1982s with slightly higher acidity and lower alcohol.

Value for money

Production is small and quality high, with prices to match ££–£££, often well worth it. Try Crozes-Hermitage ££ for cheaper Northern Rhônes, ready in two to five years after a good vintage, whereas the others are more expensive and generally need longer maturation.

What to drink now, what to keep

Northern Rhône reds

St Joseph, Crozes-Hermitage ££ Fairly straightforward wines, normally best drunk relatively young. 1983 and 1982 should be kept but anything earlier can be enjoyed now (some single-vineyard wines need five to ten years' maturity). St-Joseph reds are generally good buys.

Cornas ££–£££ Sturdy, forceful wine that needs keeping. Lay down 1983 and 1982. Avoid 1981. Drink older vintages but keep 1978 (if you can find it) for at least another five years.

Côte-Rôtie, Hermitage £££ The grandest red wines of the Rhône. Côte-Rôtie tends to be more elegant (and quicker maturing) while

Hermitage is a big wine that needs time. Don't miss the classic 1983s (and some fine 1982s) for laying down. Avoid 1981. Keep 1980, 1979 and 1978 (this last is the great vintage of recent times). *Drink 1972 and 1975.*

Northern Rhône Whites

St Joseph, St Péray, Crozes-Hermitage (blanc) [£££] *Drink young,* 1983 for preference.

Hermitage (blanc) [£££] There are two styles of winemaking. Jaboulet's white Hermitage should be drunk young (1982 or 1983) but Chave, Chapoutier and Grippat make their wines to keep. From these producers, lay down 1983 and 1982 and keep most older vintages as long as you can. The best years last indefinitely.

Condrieu, Château Grillet [£££] Delicious wines that should be drunk young, so *choose 1983 or 1982.* Anything older than that is likely to be a curiosity.

Names to look out for

St Joseph [££] **Jean-Louis Grippat** *(Yapp)* and **Bernard Gripa** are the two best growers.

Crozes-Hermitage [££]–[£££] **Jaboulet's Crozes-Hermitage, Thalabert** *(Loeb)* and **Chapoutier's Les Meysonniers** *(H Parrot)* are probably the best. Other wines of this appellation can be dull.

Cornas [££]–[£££] **Auguste Clape** *(Yapp)* make intense, long-lived wines. **Guy de Barjac's Cornas** is slightly softer, more open.

Côte-Rôtie [£££] **Guigal** *(Tanners, Adnams)* make the best (and the most expensive), followed by **Jasmin** *(Yapp)* who make very elegant wines, and the very reliable **Vidal-Fleury** *(K F Butler).*

Hermitage [£££] **Gérard Chave** *(Yapp, Adnams)* produce the finest Hermitage (red and white) from vineyards owned by the family for 500 years. **Jaboulet**'s La Chapelle *(Loeb)* is a classic, long-lived red, but their white is for early drinking. **Chapoutier** *(H Parrot)* make a fine, middle-weight red and a classic old-fashioned white that is wonderful with a decade or more of bottle-age. **Jean-Louis Grippat** *(Yapp)* make classic white Hermitage and **Sorrel** produces a reliable red.

Condrieu and Château Grillet [£££] **Guigal** *(Majestic, Corney & Barrow)* make the best Condrieux, followed closely by **Georges Vernay** *(Yapp)* and Paul Multier's **Ch de Rozay** *(Yapp).* **Ch Grillet** *(Yapp)* is not as good as it was.

[£] indicates wines under £3, [££] wines £3–£5 and [£££] wines over £5.

RHÔNE: the South

The principal red grape is Grenache, which is normally blended with one or more of the following varieties: Syrah, Cinsault, Mourvèdre. The wines are rich red, often herby, and should have plenty of fruit. They are uncomplicated, for relatively early drinking, except Châteauneuf-du-Pape.

The 1983 vintage

As in several recent vintages, the quality in the Southern Rhône was good but not outstanding, and less satisfactory than in the north. Very little Grenache was picked in 1983 as a result of crop failure in the spring. The worst-affected areas seem to have been around the villages of Gigondas and Beaumes-de-Venise. But it was an excellent year for Syrah and Mourvèdre, neither of which was affected by the spring weather. Most red wines have more colour than the 1982s and a perfectly respectable constitution for medium-term drinking. The whites are adequate, but sometimes lack acidity, the usual problem in the Southern Rhône.

Value for money

Because of the small size of the crop, prices are firm, but should remain fairly steady in the UK until the spring of 1985. Southern Rhônes still offer excellent value for money. Domain-bottled Châteauneuf-du-Pape – whoever the producer, is especially good value. Look for the Châteauneuf papal keys symbol moulded into the glass.

What to drink now, what to keep

Côtes du Ventous, Côtes-du-Rhône, Côtes-du-Rhône-Villages (including **Cairanne**, and **Vacqueyras**) [£]–[££] Straightforward, flavoursome. The best can be strong and mouthfilling. *Drink the 1983 vintage* (better than the 1982) over the next year or two. Earlier vintages should be finished quickly, except for best estates.

Lirac (rouge) [££], **Gigondas** [£££] Lirac is often soft and plummy while Gigondas is more firmly structured. The same comments apply to Lirac and Côtes-du-Rhône-Villages except that Gigondas often lasts a year or two longer.

Châteauneuf-du-Pape [££]–[£££] Inexpensive Châteauneuf costs about the same as Gigondas and is rarely as good. Stick to domaine-bottled wines from the top estates (*see below for list of recommended producers*). Good Châteauneuf is strong-flavoured and long-lived. Buy 1983 and 1981 for laying down. *Pre-1981 vintages can be drunk now* but the best (eg 1978) will continue to improve if kept for up to twelve years from the harvest.

Southern Rhône rosé and white

Tavel, Lirac (rosé) ££ Strong-coloured, full-flavoured dry rosé which must be drunk young and fresh. *Drink 1983 or 1982.*

Côtes-du-Rhône (blanc) ££, **Châteauneuf-du-Pape (blanc)** £££ Most white Côtes-du-Rhône is dull stuff for immediate consumption but the best whites from the top Châteauneuf estates such as Beaucastel or Rayas can be intense, characterful wines that deserve a few years' bottle-age. *Buy 1983 for laying down, 1979 and earlier for drinking.*

Understanding the Southern Rhône label

Watch out for **Châteauneuf-du-Pape** ££–£££. The best domaine wines come in bottles embossed with the papal keys but this bottle is also used by some co-operatives. A number of fine producers are recommended below.

Don't confuse the name of Jaboulet-Vercherre (a Burgundy-based merchant of no great prestige) with **Jaboulet-Aîné** (one of the best producers in the Rhône).

Côtes-du-Rhône-Villages ££ is normally better than Côtes-du-Rhône (same principle as Beaujolais-Villages) but some single-vineyard Côtes-du-Rhône wines can be outstanding.

Names to look out for

Côtes du Ventoux £–££ **Domaine des Anges** *(Ehrmanns, Adnams)* has striking concentration; **La Vieille Ferme** *(Laytons, Yorkshire Fine Wines, Bibendum)* is a consistently decent brand.

Côtes-du-Rhône £–££ **Château du Grand Moulas** *(Adnams)* is a peppery, characterful wine from a high, stony vineyard; **'Parallèle 45'** brand-name of Jaboulet Aîné *(O W Loeb)* consistently good; **Chusclan Co-operative** *(Bordeaux Direct)*·round, aromatic; **Cellier du Troubadour** *Tanners, Adnams)* **Vacqueyras Co-operative** *(Berkmann Wines)* Well structured, elegant.

Côtes-du-Rhône Villages ££ The **co-operatives of Vacqueyras** *(Berkmann)* and **Chusclan** *(Bordeaux Direct)* produce excellent wines. **Arnoux et Fils** make good Côtes-du-Rhône Villages and Vacqueyras from bought-in grapes, while **Roger Combe** *(Adnams)* produces particularly rich, concentrated Vacqueyras from his own domaine.

Gigondas ££–£££ The **Gigondas village co-operative** makes good, middle-weight wines as does **Pascal** *(Laytons, La Vigneronne)*. For greater concentration, try **Roger Combe's L'Ousteau Fauquet** *(Tanners)*, **Domaine St Gayon** *(Yapp)* or **Domaine de Verquière.**

Châteauneuf-du-Pape ££–£££ **Château Rayas** *(Loeb)* is excellent, especially if you can find pre-1976 vintages; **Château de Beaucastel** *(agent: Mistral Wines)* is an elegant, complex wine made from all thirteen permitted grape varieties – excellent, if expensive; **Domaine du Vieux Télégraphe** *(Adnams, Tanners)* (dark, concentrated, long-lived classic); **Domaine de Mont-Redon** *(J B Reynier)* large, very traditional estate; **Clos des Papes** big, tannic, long-lived; **Domaine de Beaurenard** softer style, made for earlier drinking; **Chante Cigale** *(Yapp)* another big, concentrated wine, not to be confused with a similarly-named brand of pleasant plonk. **Jaboulet** *(Loeb)* and **Chapoutier** *(H Parrot)* both make good Châteauneuf.

Tavel and Lirac [££] **Domaine de la Genestière**; **Domaine Maby** *(Yapp)*; **Domaine de Castel Oualou** (including red Lirac); **Château de Trinquevedel.**

Where to buy Rhônes, North and South

Adnams, Yapp, Lay & Wheeler, Tanners, O W Loeb.

BEST RHÔNE BUYS

[£] Côtes-du-Rhône, Domaine du Vieux Chêne *(Justerini & Brooks)* [££] Côtes-du-Rhône, Cru du Coudoulet *(Bibendum, Bart's Cellars, Luc Lacerre, Crawfords; agent: Mistral Wines)* [££] Châteauneuf, Domaine du Vieux Télégraphe *(Lay & Wheeler, Adnams, Tanners)* [£££] Châteauneuf, Ch de Beaucastel *(Bibendum, Les Amis du Vin, Waters of Coventry, Luc Lacerre, Bart's Cellars, Seckford Wines)* [£££] Gigondas, Domaine St-Gayon *(Yapp)* [££] St-Joseph, Co-opérative de St-Désirat-Champagne *(Yapp)* [££] Crozes Hermitage, Thalalbert, P Jaboulet Aîné *(Adnams, Bow Wine Vaults, Loeb)* [£££] Condrieux white, Georges Vernay *(Yapp)* [£££] Hermitage, J L Chave *(Yapp)* [£££] Côte-Rôtie, Guigal *(Adnams, Tanners, Majestic)* [£££] Côte-Rôtie, Jeantaz Dervieux *(Richards & Walford)* [£££] Muscat de Beaumes-de-Venise, Domaine de Coyeux *(Laytons, Chaplin & Sons, Ebury Wine Co, La Vigneronne, Windrush Wines)* [£££] Muscat de Beaumes-de-Venise, Domaine de Durban *(Yapp, Victoria Wine)*

SAVOIE

The wines of Savoie are little seen in Britain, for they are largely consumed in the Alpine resorts. Of the few that are imported, the most common are the sparkling wines of **Seyssel**, from vineyards on both sides of the Rhône, where the river turns eastwards towards Lake Geneva. The outstanding producer is **Varichon et Clerc**.

The still wines of Savoie are named after either the village or the grape from which they come, and, occasionally, from a combination of the two. The best-known villages are Crépy (white wines with a slight prickle) Abymes, Apremont, Chignin and Montmélian.

The white wines, which account for a large majority of the production, are made from the Jacquère, for the most part, though the best are from the Roussette, Altesse and Chardonnay. The red wines come from the Gamay and the Pinot Noir, though a local speciality is the curiously flavoured Mondeuse.

Names to look out for

Over half the wine comes from the five co-operative cellars, and most of the rest appear under the labels of small growers. Three suppliers to look out for are **Magnin** of Belley, **Le Vigneron Savoyard** of Apremont, and **Mercier** of Crépy. *(No regular importer.)*

SOUTH-WEST FRANCE

The major thing to remember about the scattered vineyard pockets of South-West France is that the closer they are to Bordeaux, the more they become pale imitations of Bordeaux styles. They have similar grapes, soils and climatic conditions. Where they are cheaper than their Bordelais equivalents, they are normally worth an experimental buy because no importer is going to risk bringing in something with an obscure name unless he is impressed with its value for money.

Béarn (red, rosé and dry white) [£]–[££], **Jurançon (AC Jurançon, dry and sweet whites)** [££] Interesting, more for curiosity than any other purpose. The 1983s are quite good. In Béarn, a good red is Pot au Poule, a hard, astringent but fruity and long-tasting red. The whites are heavy and often neutral in style. Most Bordeaux ACs are better value. Age improves the best of the sweet whites. There is one co-operative, which produces the cheapest wines, at Gan. Other than this, most production is sold under its estate name. The Ch Jolys Jurançon is amongst the most reliable.

Bergerac Region [£]–[££] **(ACs Bergerac, dry red, dry white; Montravel, dry white; Côtes de Bergerac, medium white; Pécharmant, very rare, red; Monbazillac sweet)** The 1983 vintage was good and plentiful, just as in Bordeaux. Prices are cheap but the majority of dry and medium whites do not keep well. *Reds should nearly always be drunk within months of buying.* A very few do keep. There are some very good value 1982 and 1983 reds here and there. Monbazillacs for export are normally carefully chosen to avoid the more acetic, sulphury offerings and can be excellent value. These will almost invariably keep well. Great Sauternes vintages (1983 is one) are normally good here, too. **Unidor**, the big co-operative producer, is very reliable but not great. **Ch la Jaubertie** *(High Breck Vintners)*, owned by Nick Ryman of Ryman Conran fame, is getting better and better. But this is mainly a region of small properties that have not yet discovered modern technology in a big way. When they are lucky, they make good wine. Don't look for continuity yet, with the exception of the above.

Buzet [££] **(AC Côtes de Buzet)** The vintage quality here is very important. 1982 and 1983 are both good, but a poor Bordeaux vintage is to be avoided like the plague as the wines (all red, from Bordelais grapes) become thin, attenuated imitations of poor Bordeaux with little or no price advantage. Production is almost totally in the hands of the co-operative whose winemaker has a fixation with wood ageing. This suits his top wine, brand-named Napoléon, in a good year. It keeps three to five years and is well worth a try, if not cheap [££].

Cahors (AC Cahors [££]; Vin de Pays Coteaux de Quercy [£]) 1983 produced tough, concentrated dry red wines. Bad Cahors is dull and very tough and the vin de pays is often very harsh; good Cahors is also tough, and needs to be kept for longer than the growers, the merchants or the importers will consider financing. It is therefore strictly for laying down, for six or seven years at least. The wines have only just generally started to come into their own because there has been a lot of re-planting since the early 1970s. (Young vines do not produce enough body to make for good keeping.) Good 1982s and 1983s will keep for eight to ten years or more. Expect to pay £3 to £5 because they are fashionable in France. The co-operative (**Côtes d'Olt**) makes cheap, reasonable value wines, but the **individual châteaux** are better and more interesting. Try **Château St Didier** *(Ehrmanns)*, **Château Chambert** *(Richard Kihl, Dakin & Co)* especially, and **Domaine Mas d'El Perrié**. These are all fruitier, and less harshly tannic than one might expect.

Duras/Marmandais [£] (ACs Côtes de Duras, dry white, red; VDQS Côtes du Marmandais) Another little Bordeaux: therefore good 1983s. Duras prices are inclined to be a bit high because of the passing tourist trade. Marmandais, which is largely produced by the co-operative, has fallen on much harder times and therefore is good value for 1982 and 1983s. Both drinking now. 'Tête de Cuvée' on the white Duras labels is normally the pick of the crop and worth trying and varietal labelling is also common. The Merlot reds are very attractive when young. The crisp, sharp Sauvignons need to be young. The Union de Producteurs makes a good one.

Fronton [£] (AC Côtes Frontonnais, red) Down the motorway from Bordeaux to Toulouse, Fronton produces warmer and softer wines than the Bordeaux reds. Both 1982 and the slightly tougher 1983s are good. If you can find them, they are excellent value for money. There are really only three major producers: two **co-operatives** and **Château Bellevue la Forêt** *(Hatch Mansfield)*. These wines have not got the recognition they deserve.

Gaillac [£] (ACs Gaillac red, white, rosé and perlé; Vin de Pays des Côtes du Tarn) There was a big crop here, too, in 1983. The vin de pays whites are best as non-vintage and are some of the most reliable cheap whites from the South, with, at best, a pleasant lemon-soapy style. AC Gaillac tends to be on the expensive side for fairly undistinguished wine. The whites certainly do not keep and the reds only for two to three years. Gaillac **Perlé** semi-sparkling [£], produced by the co-operative at **Labastide de Lévis**, makes an interesting aperitif *(Findlater, Mackie & Todd, Richard Harvey Wines, K F Butler)*. This co-operative is really the only good one of the area. Most Domaines are expensive and, apart from Stowells' white wine box, most other wines from here are anonymous and characterless.

Gers (AC Madiran [££], heavy red; VDQS Côtes de St-Mont [£]; Vin de Pays Côtes de Gascogne [£], Comté Tolosan [£], reds and whites) Very good, easy year in 1982, fair but more concentrated in 1983. Madiran is famous in France and therefore a little expensive. It is a lively, dry, tough wine which repays laying down for five to eight years. Both 1982 and 1983 are good. The major improvement is in the white wines. Vin de pays and VDQS are both now being properly made by a group of co-operatives who dominate production in this region, the Producteurs de Plaimont. Watch in particular for the **French Colombard** [£] grape type *(Waitrose, Eldridge Pope, Waters of Coventry, Les Amis du Vin)*. These wines are not expensive and are excellent value. Go for the latest possible vintage, as they soon tire. **Sainsbury's Dry White Vin de Pays Carafe** and **Nicolas Dry White** are two widely available examples.

Blanquette de Limoux [££] Excellent Champagne method sparkler. Almost all of it is produced by the co-operative. A good one is stocked by *Oddbins, Waitrose* and *Gough Bros* and others, and *Christopher's* sell the vintage, rather better, and just a bit more expensive.

There are other names in the South-West such as **Montravel** next to Bergerac (very similar, normally not so good), **Irouleguy** in Béarn, **Tursan** in the Gers, but these are so rarely available in this country because of their irregular nature or scarce production that we have not included them.

Where to buy wines of the South-West

High Breck Vintners, Adnams, Sélection Gault-Millau, Lay & Wheeler, Ehrmanns

BEST BUYS [££] Sparkling Blanquette de Limoux *(Oddbins, Christopher's, Waitrose, Gough Bros, Stones of Belgravia)*, [£] Château la Jaubertie, Bergerac *(High Breck Vintners)*, [£] Colombard, Producteurs de Plaimont *(Eldridge Pope, Waters of Coventry, Les Amis du Vin, Adnams)*.

For further information on all French wines, contact:
Food & Wine from France, Nuffield House, 41–46 Piccadilly, London W1 (they expect to move during 1985); tel: 01-439 8371, or The French Embassy, 12 Stanhope Gardens, London W1; tel: 01-493 5021.

Germany

The 1983 vintage

In 1983, Germany produced a large, good quality vintage. The Riesling, which withstands the idiosyncrasies of the German climate better than most vines, produced some marvellously elegant wines. In the Mosel–Saar–Ruwer, their fruit and acidity and tremendous ripeness make them about the best that the region has known since the 'classic' 1975 vintage; some are even being likened to the great 1971s. In the small, quality-conscious part of the Nahe region between Bad Kreuznach and Schlossböckelheim, where the wines are often thought to resemble Moselles, the Riesling again performed at its best. In the Rheingau, nobody complains about the stylish Kabinett and Spätlese wines, but the lack of Auslesen, for which a fair amount of sugar-enhancing noble rot is almost a prerequisite, was disappointing. The richest Rheingau wines in 1983 were the amazing Eisweine (ice wines). Franken (Franconia), a region that can suffer enormous crop losses through its climate, reported an even bigger yield in 1983 than in the mammoth 1982 vintage, and the wines are firm and concentrated.

In good years, the late-ripening vines come into their own, but in 1983, the very dry summer was too much for the early Müller-Thurgau, from which much of the cheapest wine is usually made. The sugar content of its grapes was less than had been hoped, but the yield remained high, so these wines are thin.

Value for money

The problem of excess stocks after two large vintages has created Germany's own cheap wine lake for the first time since she joined the EEC. Distillation to industrial alcohol has provided an outlet, but it is one to which growers have turned only in desperation. Production costs are increasing in a market that cannot absorb the wine on offer, and if the problem is not solved soon, many will abandon their vines.

A short-term benefit to the German consumer from the troubles of the wine producers has been the drop in prices at all quality levels. But at the cheapest end of the market for German wine in the UK, prices can have less to do with quality than with marketing policy and individual companies' methods of costing. (At a UK retail price per bottle below £1.90, the cost of the wine is quite insignificant compared to that of the duty, shipping and distribution costs.)

For fine estate-bottled Kabinett or Spätlese wines, prices charged by the producer in Germany have dropped during the last 12 months by anything up to ten per cent for the 1982 vintage. And because there is so much wine about, the excellent 1983s were being offered by growers last spring at only two to five per cent up on prices charged in 1983 for the 1982s.

Relatively small and volatile price movements are not usually reflected in UK retail prices. They are averaged out by the importers to provide the continuity expected by the wine trade and hotel and catering industry. This steadiness of price has sometimes produced interesting situations in which long-maturing Auslesen in top-quality vintages have been cheaper in the UK than in their homeland. However, in spite of the character and quality of its fine wines, statistics show that much that is exported from Germany is very cheap, with possibly 25 to 30 per cent being blended wine of non-German origin.

What to drink now, what to keep

1983 Started to arrive in the UK in the summer of 1984. Cleaner than 1982. Some excellent Riesling. Some merchants, such as *Henry Townsend of Amersham* and *O W Loeb* have specialised in the vintage. Drink up the cheaper wines of the QbA category. Riesling Kabinetts and Spätlesen will be good now and throughout 1985. Auslesen, of which there are few, will age well *(see Riesling below)*.

1982 Well-chosen wines are sound, and like the 1983s are at their most successful in the Mosel–Saar–Ruwer region. Some of the 1982s have a bitter flavour as a result of wet weather immediately before and during the harvest. Many are flabby and low in acidity, and many have an off-flavour owing to hot fermentations and panic in cramped cellars in this huge vintage. Even the best wines are rather low in acidity and dull. Drink up.

1981 Relatively small vintage, still listed by many merchants, offers Kabinett and Spätlese wine with an attractive fresh but mature style. Drink now.

1980 Very ordinary wines; not many are still around. Avoid any you find!

1979 Stocks are low. Again, a very successful vintage on good estates. Drink now.

1976 The last vintage to produce large quantities of rich Riesling Auslese wines. They can be drunk now or kept longer.

Maturing Riesling It is not obligatory to state on a bottle label the type or types of grape from which the wine is made, but it is useful information. Because of the high reputation of the Riesling, the grape name is usually included in the title. Rieslings are pleasant enough when they are young but need varying amounts of time in bottle to show their best, subtle qualities. As a rule of thumb, Rieslings, in their different quality categories, reach their peak when kept for the following minimum number of years after the vintage.

Send us **your** views on the report forms at the back of the book.

Category		Years
QbA	(simple quality wine)	1½
QmP	(quality wine with distinction)	
	Kabinett	1½
	Spätlese	2
	Auslese	5
	Beerenauslese, Eiswein, Trockenbeerenauslese	7 or more

Understanding the German label

The detail on a German wine label includes all the information you are likely to need other than an up-to-date tasting comment. Behind each word lie paragraphs of German and EEC law. A typical German quality wine label will include most of the following information:

Country of origin
Produce of Germany

Region
Ahr, Mosel–Saar–Ruwer, Mittelrhein, Rheingau, Nahe, Rheinhessen, Rheinpfalz, Hessische Bergstraße, Franken, Württemberg, Baden

Quality category
Tafelwein, Landwein, Qualitätswein bestimmter Anbaugebiete (QbA) Qualitätswein mit Prädikat (QmP)

Vintage
1983

Distinction
Kabinett, Spätlese, Auslese, Beerenauslese, Eiswein, Trockenbeerenauslese

Vine variety
Riesling, Müller-Thurgau, Kerner etc

Commune and vineyard site
eg Niersteiner Ölberg

Quality control number
Amtliche Prüfungs Nr eg 4 123 456 78 84

Estate bottled
Erzeugerabfüllung

Name of bottler
eg Weingut H F Schmitt

Address
eg Nierstein-am-Rhein

e 750 ml
Bottled in accordance with EEC regulations. Liquid content

The following are the most common terms, descriptions, and regional names that appear on German wine labels:

Abfülling Bottled by.

Ahr Small region, just south of Bonn known mainly for light red wine.

Amtliche Prüfungsnummer Official quality control number, often shortened to A P Nr, and followed by the appropriate number.

Auslese Describes quality wine made from selected bunches of grapes. Rare and rich.

Bacchus New grape variety with a rather coarse flavour grown mainly in the Rheinhessen.

Baden Region producing soft but fresh wines in south Germany. Brown bottles.

Beerenauslese Describes quality wine made from individually selected grapes, possible only in very good vintages. Tremendously rich.

Deutscher Tafelwein German table wine, below the quality wine category. Not all dry wines bear this description.

Diabetikerwein Diabetic wine, containing less than four g/l sugar. Very dry.

Eiswein Describes wine made from frozen grapes. Concentrated and sweet.

Erzeugerabfüllung Bottled by the producer, estate bottled.

Franken (Franconia) Region producing quality wines sold in a flagon-shaped bottle.

Halbtrocken Medium dry wines, which often taste thin owing to lack of sugar to round them out.

Hessische Bergstrasse Small region on the Rhine south of Mainz. Firm, steely wines. Brown bottles.

Kerner New vine variety, producing stylish wine. Good acidity. Related to the Riesling, and shares some of its quality.

Landwein Top of the table wine category, equivalent to vin de pays. Good value in good vintages (like 1983) since Germany produces little table wine, and QbA wines are often declassified to Landwein.

Liebfraumilch Most popular German quality wine, mainly from the Rheinhessen and Rheinpfalz. Medium sweet.

Mittelrhein Region close to the Rhine between Bonn and the Rheingau. Much Riesling planted. Brown bottles.

Mosel–Saar–Ruwer Best-known German wine-producing region. Light, stylish wine in slim green bottles.

Müller-Thurgau Most widely planted vine in Germany, covering over a quarter of the vineyards. Wine is soft, with a nettly flavour, agreeable but usually lacks distinction.

Nahe Region of sound quality wines. Some very stylish.

Rheingau Best Rhineland region. Many fine estates.

Rheinhessen Largest vine-growing region. Much ordinary wine and some made from the Riesling that is top-quality. The source of much of the Liebfraumilch.

Rheinpfalz Large region producing full-bodied, distinguished Riesling wines as well as others that are cheap and cheerful.

Riesling A great vine, can produce superbly elegant wines in good sites.

Ruländer Grey Pinot vine. More flavour, but less style than Riesling.

Scheurebe Vine crossing. Wine known for a grapefruit skins smell and good acidity. Along with Kerner (*see above*) one of the best new vine crossings for quality wine production.

Silvaner Vine making neutral-flavoured wine.

Trocken Dry, as opposed to sweet.

Trockenbeerenauslese Richest of all quality wines made from grapes dried on the vine. Very rare.

Wein aus verschiedenen Ländern der EG Wine from different countries of the EEC. To ensure that the wine you buy is German, and not simply a blend of wines from different countries put together in Germany, it is necessary to read the label closely. Many of these EEC blends seem to be deliberately dressed to deceive, presenting a totally Germanic appearance.

Weingut Wine-making estate.

Weinkellerei Wine merchant's cellar.

Winzergenossenschaft Co-operative cellar.

Winzerverein Co-operative cellar.

Württemberg Region making white and red wine drunk mainly within its borders.

Names to look out for

German wines in the UK can be loosely divided into three overlapping categories:

Under £2.20 The wines are light, usually medium sweet (ie, contain between 18 and 45 grammes per litre of residual sugar), probably with much Müller-Thurgau (*see above*) in their blend. They are exported by many large, commercial cellars *(Weinkellereien)*, and sometimes also by well-known wine shippers under their own or, coyly, subsidiary company names. Such wines should be agreeable, without any claims to distinction. Many are sold under the familiar names Liebfraumilch, Niersteiner Gutes Domtal, and Piesporter Michelsberg, probably followed in frequency by Oppenheimer Krötenbrunnen, Bernkasteler Kurfürstlay, and Rüdesheimer Rosengarten.

£2.20 to £3.50 These wines should show their quality by their acidity and positive flavour. It is an area occupied by most of the widely advertised branded wines.

£3.50 and upwards Into this category fall estate-bottled wines, and it is here that true individuality of style and variety of flavour will be found.

Co-operative cellars are also allowed by law to sell their wines as **'estate-bottled'** *('Erzeugerabfüllung')* – even the very cheapest.

Estates The popular impression of an estate as being a private or state-owned property where the vine-growing and wine-making are all under one control seems more comprehensible than the use of the term for a co-operative bottling. There are many estates in Germany, with over 15,000 selling wine in bottle. Amongst the best-known are the following, with the name of a UK source of supply in brackets:

Anheuser, Weingut Ökonomierat August E Fine Nahe grower, making particularly racy Kreuznacher Rieslings. *(Berry Bros & Rudd, Justerini & Brooks)*

Anheuser, Weingut Paul Another branch of the Anheuser family, best-known in the USA for beer-making. Top quality Nahe wines at Kreuznach, Schlossböckelheim etc. *(Corney & Barrow, Lay & Wheeler, Anthony Byrne)*

Badischer Winzergenossenschaften eG, Zentralkellerei Largest co-operative cellar in Germany dealing in well-made wines of quality from all over Baden. *(Victoria Wine and many others)*

Balbach Erben, Weingut Bürgermeister Anton Important Rheinhessen estate, planted 80 per cent in Riesling. Fresh, modern wine-making. *(Justerini & Brooks, Harveys)*

Bassermann-Jordan, Weingut Geheimer Rat Dr von A 13th-century estate, aiming by 1987 to grow Riesling only, with holdings in the Rheinpfalz at Deidesheim and Forst. Fine wine production. *(Harveys, Lay & Wheeler)*

Bischöfliche Weingüter, Verwaltung der Four fine, formerly church-owned estates based on Trier with top-quality holdings in the Mosel–Saar–Ruwer. Beautiful cask-matured wines. *(Adnams, Townsend)*

Buhl, Weingut Reichsrat von Great Rheinpfalz estate, making fine wine at Forst, Deidesheim and Ruppertsberg from very extensive vineyards (97 hectares). *(Ehrmanns, Gerard Harris)*

Bürklin-Wolf, Weingut Dr 100-hectare estate, based on Wachenheim. Possibly the best-known in the Rheinpfalz. Careful, dedicated wine-making. *(Berry Bros & Rudd, La Vigneronne)*

Deidesheim, eG, Winzerverein Good quality co-operative cellar. The members own 220 hectares in Deidesheim, Forst, and Wachenheim in the Rheinpfalz.

Diefenhardt'sches Weingut Rheingau estate of 12.2 hectares based on Martinsthal, selling fine Eltviller and Rauenthaler Riesling wines with the pronounced acidity typical of the Rheingau. *(Ehrmanns)*

Deinhard, Gutsverwaltung Large 100-hectare estate with holdings uniquely in the Rheingau, Mosel–Saar–Ruwer and Rheinpfalz, capitalising on the Riesling qualities of freshness and long-life. *(Harrods, Sanderson of Morpeth)*

Eltville, Verwaltung der Staatsweingüter Largest estate in Germany owned by Hessen covering 160 hectares in the Rheingau and the Hessische Bergstrasse, directed by the leading writer on German wine Dr Hans Ambrosi. Wines with body and style are the aim. *(Harveys, Tanners of Shrewsbury)*

Forschungsanstalt, Geisenheim The viticulture and oenology school of the Rheingau sells some of its wines; exemplary wine-making, of course! *(Ehrmanns)*

Forster Winzerverein eG Fine co-operative cellar producing stylish wine from the best sites at Forst in the Rheinpfalz, planted 66 per cent in Riesling.

Friedrich-Wilhelm-Gymnasium, Stiftung Staatliches A 16th-century, Jesuit-founded estate with holdings in 45 hectares of the Mosel–Saar–Ruwer, based on Trier. Fine wines with just enough sweetness to balance. *(Gerard Harris, Townsend)*

Kesselstatt, Weingut Reichsgraf von Large combination of four estates at Graach, Piesport, Kasel and Oberemmel. Close ties with a number of other Mosel–Saar–Ruwer estates. Now owned by Herr Günther Reh. Fine, classic wines. *(Justerini & Brooks, Townsend, Anthony Byrne)*

Müller-Scharzhof, Weingut Egon Great and ancient Saar estate planted 96 per cent in Riesling, lying at the foot of its most famous site, the Scharzhofberg. Intensity of flavour and finesse are characteristic of the wines in good years. Naturally sweet Auslesen represent Saar wine at its very considerable best, and only QmP (wines) are sold under the Scharzhofberg name.

Niederhausen-Schlossböckelheim, Verwaltung der Staatlichen Weinbaudomänen Important Nahe estate of 45 hectares based on Niederhausen, producing outstandingly fresh and stylish Riesling wines. *(Les Amis du Vin, Lay & Wheeler)*

Ferdinand Pieroth Weingut Weinkellerei GmbH Direct selling operation dealing mainly in QmP wines at prices that reflect the high cost of distribution in six-bottle cartons to private addresses. Better value for money may well be supplied by your local off-licence. *(Sold in the UK by an assiduous band of door-to-door salesmen.)*

Plettenburg'sche Verwaltung, Reichsgräflich von An 18th century estate of 48 hectares spread over Schlossböckelheim, Bad Kreuznach, Norheim and other less wellknown Nahe villages. Skilled and efficient winemaking produces fresh, attractively grapy wines.

Prüm, Weingut JJ Moselle Riesling estate of some 14 hectares based on Wehlen, whose reputation could not be improved. The wines are matured in wood and built to last. All J J Prüm bottlings are worth tasting, but at Auslese level in a fine vintage like 1983 the Wehlener Sonnenuhr will be simply superb.

Schloss Reinhartshausen, Administration Prinz Friedrich von Preussen Owned by the great-grandchildren of Kaiser Wilhelm II, a 67-hectare estate based on Erbach in the Rheingau. Fine holdings in fine sites, producing the expected Rieslings, as well as Chardonnay and Weissburgunder (Pinot Blanc). *(Justerini & Brooks, La Vigneronne)*

Schloss Schönborn, Domänenweingut Fine, old Rheingau estate. Big wines, 91 per cent Riesling. *(La Vigneronne, Tanners of Shrewsbury)*

C von Schubert'sche Gutsverwaltung Distinguished estate, first mentioned in 966, lying at the foot of its 32-hectare vineyards at Maximin Grünhaus on the Ruwer near Trier. Top-quality wines reach ambrosial heights in the best years. *(Ehrmanns)*

Vereinigte Hospitien, Güterverwaltung Ancient Trier-based estate, with some of the oldest cellars in Germany. Top-quality cask-matured wines. *(Berry Bros & Rudd, La Vigneronne)*

Thanisch, Weingut Wwe Dr H A 13-hectare estate at Bernkastel, with further holdings at Brauneberg and Graach. Fine Moselle wine-making. *(Adnams, Corney & Barrow)*

Weil, Weingut Dr R Estate with holdings entirely at Kiedrich in the Rheingau, producing wines with pronounced acidity and Riesling freshness. *(Ehrmanns, Lay & Wheeler, Saintsbury)*

Where to buy German wines

Adnams, Les Amis du Vin, Berry Bros & Rudd, Anthony Byrne, D Byrne & Co, Corney & Barrow, Ehrmanns, German Food Centre, German Wine Club, Gerard Harris, Harveys of Bristol, Justerini & Brooks, Lay & Wheeler, O W Loeb, Otto's Winetasters' Warehouse, Saintsbury, Sanderson of Morpeth, Tanners of Shrewsbury, Henry Townsend, La Vigneronne, The Wine Society, Kabinett Wines.

BEST GERMAN BUYS [£££] Amongst the wealth of different bottlings of German wine available in the UK, the following from the two great vintages of the 1970s recommend themselves strongly. Except in 1983 in the Mosel–Saar–Ruwer, there has not been a vintage since to challenge their superiority: [£££] **1976Wiltinger Hölle Riesling Auslese QmP, estate-bottled Vereinigte Hospitien.** *(Berry Bros Rudd & Co)* [£££] **1976 Brauneberger Juffer-Sonnenuhr Riesling Auslese QmP, estate-bottled Dr Thanisch.** *(Corney & Barrow)* [£££] **1976 Deidesheimer Herrgottsacker Riesling Auslese QmP, estate-bottled von Buhl.** *(Henry Townsend)* [£££] **1976 Forster Ungeheuer Riesling Auslese QmP, estate-bottled Bassermann-Jordan.** *(Harveys)* [£££] **1971 Hattenheimer Wisselbrunnen Riesling Spätlese QmP estate-bottled Schloss Reinhartshausen.** *(Harris)* [£££] **1976 Johannisberger Hölle Riesling Auslese QmP estate-bottled Deinhard.** *(Morris's Wine Stores, Solihull)*

Greece

Sadly, an officious bureaucracy is currently hampering the efforts of the more go-ahead companies, and providing an unwelcome disincentive to further investment in what could be a bright future. In its efforts to bolster the co-operatives, the current Greek administration has firmly opted for the road marked 'quantity' rather than 'quality', and, barring any U-turn, the few pioneers of the Greek (as opposed to Cypriot) wines on our highly selective market will have to work even harder at their very laudable task. *Almost* without exception, Greek wines are heavy, and tend to be oxidised. Occasionally, Retsinas can be good, and a pleasure or a penance according to your preference.

The only wine, apart from Retsina, that we would positively recommend is Ch Carras Red, deep, rich, with a positive, curranty flavour. It is made of the Bordeaux grapes, aged in oak, by a shipping magnate turned wine-maker who studied winemaking in Bordeaux. It is expensive at nearly £5, and interesting to try out of curiosity, but not really good value for money. The Carras white is less interesting, though made from the Sauvignon grape. *(See below for stockists.)* Acceptable red brands are Apollo [£] *(Waitrose)*, Castel Danielis [£] *(Peter Dominic)*, and Demestica [£] *(Peter Dominic)*. Amongst the heavy whites, Apollo Dry White [£] is drinkable *(Waitrose)*. Best of the Retsinas are Kourtakis and Metaxas [£].

BEST GREEK BUYS [£] Kourtakis Retsina *(Arthur Rackham, Cullens, Victoria Wine)*, [£] Metaxas Retsina *(Soho Wine Supply)*, [££] Château Carras Red *(Bibendum, Victoria Wine, La Vigneronne, Westover Wines, Hicks & Don, The Wine Society)*.

For further information, contact: Greek Embassy Commercial Section, 1A Holland Park, London W11 tel: 01-727 8040.

Israel

Outside the Jewish community, Israeli wines are seldom seen. Many people believe that they are all sweet, but this no longer true. The Cabernet Sauvignon for red and Sauvignon for white are beginning to produce some nice wines; a good example is the 1979 from Société Grandes Caves sold by *La Vigneronne* [££]. At just under £5, the competition comes from Chile, Lebanon and Australia and, although the wine is interesting, its quality does not reach the standard of the others. For the more basic wines, the Carmel Wine Company still holds the whip hand. The wines vary from dry to sweet, still and sparkling [££]. Without so much patriotic support, these wines would not be able to stand on their own feet. There are far better wines for the price in all categories. Selfridges stock a big range.

Italy

Value for money

The nation usually producing the greatest quantity of wine on earth continues to make tremendous headway in terms of quality. Every conceivable style of wine is available from Italy, and there is great value for money to be had at every level. However, a tendency remains on the parts of trade and consumer alike to buy on price, and there are quantities of duff wines on the market under well-known denominations. Look out for the producers' names given below and you will both avoid disappointment and be pleasantly surprised.

(**Stockists** *British stockists mentioned are generally wholesalers. Their addresses may be obtained from the Italian Trade Centre, 37 Sackville Street, London W1; tel: 01-734 2412. Wholesalers can supply names of retailers, restaurants, etc*)

Understanding the Italian label

Italian labels provide some or all of the following information:
The **denomination** – eg *Valpolicella* (name of place where the grapes were grown), or *Barbera d'Asti* (name of grape and place) or *Tignanello* (name of vineyard), or *Est! Est!! Est!!!* (fantasy name).

Classico As in Chianti, Valpolicella, Soave et al; denotes wine from the heart of the delimited area.

Superiore In general merely signifies extra alcohol. Not necessarily indicative of superior quality.

Riserva (Speciale) Supposed to indicate extra ageing, usually in barrel; more significant in Chianti than Barolo/Barbaresco. Not necessarily an advantage – wines are often kept *too* long in barrel. But the best, richest wines are likely to have been selected in the first place to become Riservas.

Quality description

DOC Like France's AOC, a guarantee of origin, not necessarily of quality.

DOCG Supposedly a greater guarantee of quality than DOC, but this is debatable. Now appearing on Vino Nobile, to be followed by Barbaresco, Barolo, Brunello and Chianti.

Vino da tavola Not necessarily modest quality. Some of Italy's best are 'table wines', just because they do not conform to the DOC of their zone.

Vino Tipico is an up-market version of vino da tavola now appearing and has more to do with red tape than anything else.

VQPRD EEC's equivalent of DOC.

VSQPRD EEC's equivalent of DOC for sparkling wine.

Qualitätswein South Tyrolean (Alto Adige) equivalent of DOC.

Imbottigliato dal viticoltore (bottled by the grower), **all'origine** (at the place of origin), **dai produttori** (by the producers – usually the co-op), **nella zona di produzione** (in the zone of production).

Name of producer eg Masi. This is the ultimate guarantee of quality.

Type of establishment

Azienda Agricola (vine-grower), **Azienda Vinicola** (bottler, not grower; probably large, but can be excellent), **Cantina Sociale** (growers' co-operative), **Fattoria** (winery, not factory), **Villa, Castello, Tenuta, Podere** (single estates).

Other indications

Consortium seal (below capsule) Means wine has passed analytical and tasting tests organised by producers' consortium. Generally not terribly significant, Chianti Classico (Black Cockerel) and Chianti Putto (Cherub) excepted.

VIDE (as collar label): means that the winery belongs to an association of quality producers and that this particular wine has passed genuinely stringent tests.

NORTH-WEST ITALY

The North-West is Italy's most traditional wine zone, with the exception of the southern mainland. The Piemontesi in particular are notoriously conservative, and since they produce the best red wines in the land, it is not surprising that they are slow to move. But things *are* changing, with a growing tendency away from barrel-ageing of reds towards maturation in bottle or stainless steel. New grape varieties are being planted – notably Cabernet, Pinot Bianco and Chardonnay. White wines and sparklers are on the increase, at the expense of reds.

Barolo and Barbaresco ££–£££

Meanwhile, Italy's greatest wine remains **Barolo**, which for the sake of convenience may be considered alongside **Barbaresco** (they are both 100 per cent Nebbiolo and come from the vicinity of the town of Alba in Piedmont).

> Importers (in brackets) will supply names of retail outlets. You can contact the importers through: The Italian Trade Centre, 37 Sackville Street, London W1; TEL 01–734 2412.

What to drink, what to keep

Note that Barolo cannot be sold before it has been aged for three years (two years for Barbaresco), so the youngest wines on the market will be of the **1981** vintage (fair), though **1980s** are more likely (good). **1979** should still be about (very good), as should **1978s** (excellent; for keeping). Other top vintages include **1982** (great; for keeping), **1974**, **1971**, **1970**.

Names to look out for

Abbazia dell'Annunziata The great Renato Ratti produces outstanding Barolo, also excellent Barbaresco, Barbera and Dolcetto. *(Cynthia Bacon)*

Borgogno Old vintages back to 1947 are stocked by *Italian Wine Agencies*.

Cavallotto Small producer, Barolo specialist. Remarkable 1971 Riserva Speciale may still be available. *(Cynthia Bacon)*

Ceretto Top quality Barolo from the vineyards **Bricco Rocche** and **Zonchetta**; **Barbaresco Asili**. *(Alivini-Trestini)*

Fontanafredda Sound, reliable Barolo, Barbaresco, also Pinot Bianco, Dolcetto, Barbera. *(Enotria)*

Franco-Fiorina Archetypal Barolo and Barbaresco. *(Alivini-Trestini)*

Gaja A Barbaresco specialist, super-expensive, super wines. *(Adnams; Peppercorn & Sutcliffe)*

Giacosa, Bruno A great name, especially in Barbaresco. *(Barwell & Jones)*

Marcarini Tight, rich, quintessential Barolo – especially 1979 La Serra. *(Recount Wines)*

Marchesi di Barolo Long established, good house. *(Giordano)*

Oddero Sound, typical wines at extremely reasonable prices. *(Alivini-Trestini)*

I Paglieri Another top quality Barbaresco specialist.

Pio Cesare Essence of traditional Barolo and Barbaresco, now modernising somewhat. Their 1978 Barolo is superb. Also produce excellent Barbera d'Alba, Nebbiolo d'Alba and a barrique-aged Gavi. *(Findlaters)*

Produttori di Barbaresco Reliable and inexpensive, as are **Terre del Barolo** – both co-operatives. *(European Vintners)*

Vietti Big Barolos, rather short on fruit. Good 1982 Nebbiolo and Barbera. *(Cynthia Bacon)*

Vigna in Rabaya Single-vineyard Barbaresco; 1979 is outstanding. *(Italian Wine Agencies)*

Other good producers of Barolo/Barbaresco/Nebbiolo: Accademia Torregiorgi *(Adnams)*; **Bersano** *(Bacchus Caves)*; **Prunotto** *(Peppercorn & Sutcliffe)*; **Sandrone** *(Ehrmanns)*; **Gigi Rosso** *(Maison* DOC; **Gemma** *('Sunday Times' Wine Club)*.

An excellent oak-matured Nebbiolo-Barbera blend is made by **Rocche dei Manzoni**. *('Sunday Times' Wine Club)*

Other Nebbiolos [£]–[£££]

The Nebbiolo grape is also responsible for other high quality wines from the North-West. Prominent among these:

Carema [£££] **Ferrando** virtually monopolises the market for this very fine red which must be aged for a minimum of four years; seek out their **Black Label**, expensive but excellent. *(Alivini-Trestini)*

Gattinara [££] **Dessilani**; **Antoniolo** *(Enotria)* – Antoniolo also do an excellent Spanna, which is a synonym for Nebbiolo; **Nervi** *(Belloni)*.

Lessona [££] **Sella** are *the* producers – another very classy wine.

Valtellina [££] (with sub-denominations **Inferno, Sassella, Grumello**) **Nera** *(Alivini-Trestini)* is excellent. (Try his Sforzato, a rich and powerful winter warmer); **Enologica Valtellinese** *(Barwell & Jones)*; **Rainoldi** *(Cynthia Bacon)*.

Other North-Western reds

Dolcetto [£]–[££] is a wine (named after the grape) which cries out for greater recognition. It is the Piemontese luncheon wine *par excellence*. Most Barolo/Barbaresco shippers do one – that of **Fontanafredda** *(Enotria)* is good value; that of **Ceretto** good but dear. **Poggio Giuseppe** *(Adnams)*, a grower who is a Dolcetto specialist, produces the very best; another excellent one is made by **Sandrone** *(Ehrmanns)*.

Barbera [£]–[££] is Piemonte's most produced red grape. The wine tends to be acidic, zingy, sometimes slightly frothing; ideal with pasta or garlicky, oily dishes. The best are called **Barbera d'Alba (Pio Cesare, Vietti**); most common in every sense is Barbera del Monferrato. Try the **Ronco** 1982. *(Millevini)*

Other north-western reds worth trying: **Frecciarossa Rosso '79, Oltrepò Pavese, Oddero** [££] *(Millevini)*; **Franciacorta Rosso**, **Cá del Bosco** *(Alivini-Trestini)*.

North-Western Sparklers [£]–[£££]

Sparkling wines are a North-Western speciality. They come in various styles:

Asti Spumante and Moscato d'Asti [££] Light, sweet and grapy, good as aperitif, or with puddings or dessert. **Fontanafredda** *(Enotria* and *Gilbey Vintners)* is consistently the best. **Gancia** *(Hedges & Butler)*, **Martini** *(Martini & Rossi)*, and **Riccadonna** *(Saccone & Speed)* are all good. European Vintners do a charming, cheap, Moscato-based sweet slightly sparkling (*frizzante*) wine called **Piemontello**. The Vietti's **Moscato del Piemonte** *(Cynthia Bacon)* is excellent, too, if rather more expensive.

Champagne-method sparklers [£££], mainly Pinot are also made in the area. Good ones are: Cá del Bosco *(Trestini)*, especially interesting being the Cá del Bosco extra brut **Dosage Zero**; **Contessa Rosa** *(Enotria)*; **Cinzano** *(Cinzano)*.

Dry (non-Champenoise) sparklers [££] Two good examples are **President Brut** *(Saccone & Speed)*, and **Bersano Brut** *(Bacchus Caves)*.

Still dry North-Western whites

Still dry white wines are not strong here. Perhaps the best known, but little seen, is **Gavi** [£££] – **La Giustiniana** *(Trestini)*, **Tenuta San Pietro** *(Italian Wine Agencies)*, **La Chiara** *('Sunday Times' Wine Club)*, **Pavese** *(Stonehaven)* are respectable. The best are called Gavi dei Gavi. Another good one from the Cortese grape is Cortese **Ronco** [££] *(Millevini)*. Arneis [££] is an obscure Piemonte grape producing delicious wine for **La Cornarea** *(Trestini)* and **Vietti** *(Cynthia Bacon)*. Of interest is the white Nebbiolo blanc de noirs of **Fontanafredda** called **Vino Fiore** [££] *(Enotria)*.

NORTH-EAST ITALY

The North-East is Italian wine's experimental hotbed as well as her main producer of quality wines. French and German grapes thrive here alongside Italian varieties of more or less ancient lineage.

What to drink now, what to keep

White wines should in general be drunk as young as possible and this applies also to light reds, which in the UK are often too old.

Big reds such as **Amarone, Cabernet (Riserva), Refosco** and **Teroldego**, as well as **some Pinot Nero** and **Merlot**, can age well, and only for these are vintages really significant. **1983** was very good for reds, **1982** good but variable (low acidity), **1981** modest, **1980** somewhat weak, **1979** very good, **1978** good but variable. There has not really been a 'vintage of the century' for at least a decade.

Soave, Valpolicella and Bardolino [£]–[££]

The major traditional area as far as the UK is concerned, is Verona, centre for Soave, Valpolicella and Bardolino – not just the industrial stuff, but some increasingly fine wines as well.

> We have tried to make the *1985 Which? Wine Guide* as comprehensive as possible, but we should love to hear from you about any other establishments you feel deserve an entry, or your comments on existing entries. Write to us either by letter or using the report forms supplied at the back of the book.

Names to look out for

Allegrini Strong in Valpolicella and Amarone. *('Sunday Times' Wine Club)*

Anselmi Wines are excellent, especially Capitel Foscarino. *(Dolamore)*

Bertani Especially good is their Valpolicella Valpantena. *(Belloni)*

Bolla Fair quality. Their Valpolicella cru Jago is excellent, and is considered by some pundits as supreme. It's not yet available in the UK – try it in Italy. *(Hedges & Butler)*

Boscaini Look especially for Le Cane. *(Italian Wine Agencies)*

Campagnola Reliable. *(Eurowines)*

Cantina Sociale di Valpolicella and the **Cantina Sociale di Soave** are both dependable producers capable of unexpected heights. Try Valpolicella's Amarone and Soave's Costalta.

Fabiano Reliable. *(Enotria)*

Guerrieri-Rizzardi Boast a first-class selection and are especially adept in Bardolino. *(Barwell & Jones)*

Lenotti Reliable. *(Bacchus Caves)*

Masi Good, basic Valpolicella, two first-class vini da tavola – Masianco white and Campo Fiorin red, outstanding Amarone, especially Cru Campolongo and Mazzano. *(Alivini-Trestini)*

Pieropan Are tops in Soave. *(Alivini-Trestini)*

Quintarelli A superlative producer (if you can find him).

Le Ragose Probably unequalled in normal Valpolicella. *(Stonehaven)*

Santa Sofia A good range of whites and reds (especially good Bianco di Custoza).

Serego-Alighieri Almost unequalled in normal Valpolicella. *(Alivini-Trestini)*

Speri Have good Valpolicella and Amarone. *(Peppercorn & Sutcliffe)*

Tedeschi Their Soave, Bianco di Custoza, Valpolicella and Amarone are all very good; Capital San Rocco Rosso vino da tavola ££ is excellent; the sweet Recioto Capitel Monte Fontana ££ is superb – Italy's answer to vintage port. *(Italian Wine Agencies)*

Other Veneto wines

Outside Verona, the treasures of the Veneto are somewhat scattered.

Carpene-Malvolti are particularly well considered for their sparkling Prosecco di Conegliano [££]. *(Giordano)*

Castello di Belvedere of the Colli Berici have an interesting range of wines of French grapes (Cabernet, Merlot, Sauvignon) in the Italian style. [£] *(Cynthia Bacon)* **Lazzarini** are better in the same style but are at present unavailable in the UK.

La Fattoria do a delicious Tocai di Lison and a classic, coppery Pinot Grigio di Summaga [£]. *(Recount Wines)*

La Fornarina are strong in Raboso di Annone [£]. *(Harvey Prince)*

Maculan of Breganze do an outstanding sweet white based on the Vespaiolo grape called Torcolato [£££] a full, fragrant, fresh, dry Breganze Bianco [£££], and a very classy Cabernet Sauvignon [£££], aged in barrique. *(Alivini-Trestini)*

Santa Margherita are high volume producers of goodish wines, notably Pinot Grigio (this is Italy's most widely distributed Pinot Grigio) and Chardonnay [£]–[££]. *(Findlater Matta)*

Venegazzù have been much praised for their **Riserva della Casa** [££], an elegant Bordeaux-style blend from the Montello hills, but the wine has an unfortunate tendency to petillance. Their Prosecco [£]–[££] and Metodo Champenois [££] are more convincing as sparkling wines. *(Enotria Wines)*

Friuli-Venezia Giulia [£]–[££]

Friuli-Venezia Giulia has until recently been viewed as the producer of Italy's finest (and most expensive) whites, especially those from the Collio and the Colli Orientali del Friuli. Some of the best producers' wines are not available in the UK (notably **Schiopetto**), but of those that are, the following are noteworthy:

Jermann Outstanding Pinot Grigio, Chardonnay; their blend, **Vintage Tunina** [£££], is considered by some to be Italy's greatest white, but it is expensive and almost unobtainable, though it has been imported. *(Peppercorn & Sutcliffe)*

Marco Felluga and **Livio Felluga** (Ciborio) Both produce excellent Tocai del Collio (no relation to Tokay d'Alsace, which is in fact Pinot Gris or Grigio), as well as Pinot Bianco, Pinot Grigio and Sauvignon. *(Belloni)*

Borgo Conventi A tasty Pinot Bianco.

Eno Friulia Sauvignon *(Recount Wines; Joseph Berkmann)*, **Abbazia di Rosazzo** Tocai *('Sunday Times' Wine Club)*, **Formentini** Pinot Bianco and **Attems** Pinot Grigio (both *Stonehaven*) can also be recommended. An example of Italy's most expensive sweet white, Picolit [£££], is available through *Stonehaven* from **Butussi**.

The Grave del Friuli [£]–[££]

In the Grave del Friuli, **Collavini** *(Italian Wine Agencies)* otherwise known as **Catemario** *(Trestini)* are certainly among the leaders; their reds, notably Cabernet, and their elegant sparkler **Il Grigio** [££] are perhaps more interesting than their whites. Other good red wine producers of the Friuli include **Valle** *(Maison DOC)* – their Cabernet is good; **Vinicola Udinese** *(Recount Wines)* – try their Malbeck; **Pradio** *(Continental Wine & Food)* the Cabernet Franc is worth a go; and **La Delizia** *(Buyers' Own Brand)* – a good Merlot.

Perhaps Friuli's best red grape is the indigenous Refosco [££]. If you have not tasted this consistently good, deep-coloured wine, full of personality, try a bottle from **Butussi**, **La Delizia**, **Plozner** *(Peppercorn & Sutcliffe)* or best of all from **Ronchi di Fornaz** *('Sunday Times' Wine Club)*.

The South Tyrol [££] (Alto Adige)

The South Tyrol (Alto Adige) is making rapid headway, especially in whites. Here you find wineries with California-like ranges of 20 wines or more.

Names to look out for

Alois Lageder is a top producer of this region, his Cabernet Riserva being one of Italy's best examples of this variety. **Chardonnay Cru Buchholz**, and Sauvignon are perhaps his best whites. *(Alivini-Trestini)*

Herbert Tiefenbrunner of **Schloss Turmhof** is probably the greatest magician of the lot, producing outstanding Rheinriesling, Müller-Thurgau, Gewürztraminer, Pinot Bianco, Pinot Grigio, Chardonnay and a fine Goldmuskateller among the whites, plus delicious Lagrein Kretzer (rosé), Lagrein Dunkel, Cabernet, Pinot Noir, Kalterersee Auslese (from the Schiava grape) and Rosenmuskateller, a rosé which smells just like fresh roses. All Tiefenbrunner wines are dry. *(Mitchells of Lancaster, Ehrmanns)*

The Union of South Tyrolean Co-operatives is by far the largest bottler of these parts, but their quality is outstanding. Their **Gewürztraminer Tenuta Trattmannhof** is perhaps South Tyrol's best, and **Chardonnay di Appiano** and Cabernet are very good value. *(Italian Wine Agencies)*

Importers (in brackets) will supply names of retail outlets. You can contact the importers through: The Italian Trade Centre, 37 Sackville Street, London W1; TEL 01–734 2412.

Other good Tyrolean producers are Schloss Schwanburg *(Tower Wine Shippers)* – especially their Pinot Bianco; **Wilhelm Walch** *(Continental Wine & Food)* – especially their Gewürztraminer; **Josef Niedermayr** – try their Lagrein Dunkel; **Hofstätter** *(Wine Society)* – for their Cabernet and Sankt Magdalener. The most outstanding of all Sankt Magdaleners (probably South Tyrol's most famous wine, made from Schiava or Vernatsch grapes grown on steep terraces overlooking Bolzano) is that of **Heinrich Rottensteiner** *(Bordeaux Direct)*.

Trentino [££]

The Trentino, another up-and-coming area and, like the South Tyrol, of outstanding natural beauty, boasts a number of excellent wineries, from the valley floor on up the mountains to 700 metres and more.

The Cantina Sociale Mezzacorona makes good Cabernet and Chardonnay.

CAVIT This vast but quality-conscious co-operative makes excellent low-cost house wines *(Adnams; Café St Pierre; The Market)* under the DOC names **Valdadige Bianco** and **Casteller** (light red). *(Ehrmanns)*

Conte Fedrigotti (*Ciborio*) make a good Cabernet-Merlot blend called **Foianeghe**.

Conti Martini make wines of consistent excellence. Their Pinot Trentino is perhaps Italy's finest Pinot Bianco. Their Goldmuskateller, dry and delicately perfumed, is stunning. Their Teroldego Rotaliano *(Adnams)* is of a beautiful chocolaty richness, and few can rival their deep, elegant Lagrein Scuro. *(Maison DOC)*

The Istituto San Michele make one of Italy's finest Chardonnays *('Sunday Times' Wine Club)* plus an excellent Cabernet-Merlot blend called **Castel San Michele**. *(Trestini)*

Letrari have an excellent Cabernet-Merlot blend under the name **Maso Lodron** *(Bacchus Caves)* and sell to *The Wine Society* a good Cabernet Riserva del Trentino.

Pojer & Sandri do an amazing, dry but scented Müller-Thurgau, to run rings around anything from Germany. *(Peppercorn & Sutcliffe)*

Zeni are leading producers of Pinot Bianco and Chardonnay. *(Italian Wine Agencies)*

Sparkling Trentino wines [££]–[£££]

CAVIT This big co-operative makes a good Champagne method wine made from Pinot grapes called **Equipe 5** [£££], and also a fairly good tank method sparkler called Gran Cavit [££]. *(Ehrmanns)*

Ferrari Brut £££ is perhaps the best Champagne method sparkler from hereabouts, made from 95 per cent Chardonnay and five per cent Pinot Noir. *(Italian Wine Agencies)*

Teroldego and Marzemino ££ Trentino's two most individual grape varieties, both red, are Teroldego, all of which comes from North of Trento, and Marzemino, which is found only South of Trento. Top producers of the former are **Barone de Cles** *(Peppercorn & Sutcliffe)*; and **Conti Martini, de Tarczal** *(Italian Wine Agencies)* is usually considered the tops in Marzemino, along with **Donati** *(Stonehaven)* and **Conti Fedrigotti**. In good years, Teroldego can age marvellously well, though *'l'eccellente Marzemino'* (as Don Giovanni refers to it in Mozart's opera) is a lightish wine to be drunk relatively young.

CENTRAL ITALY

Covering everything from the Po Valley to the Deep South, this is a vast land of vast production. The dominant grapes here are Sangiovese on the red side, Trebbiano on the white, though there are plenty of others. The Sangiovese *can* make rich, long-lasting wines, and do sometimes in this area. But many of the Sangiovese vines are degenerate, and produce thin, astringent wines. The Trebbiano is a rather neutral-tasting grape, the Ugni Blanc of France.

What to drink now, what to keep (Central Italy)

It all depends on the style of the wine-making. Drink all non-riserva wines as young as possible – they should be ready when they appear on the shelves. Riservas must in any case be aged by the producer for three years before release, but again the idea is that they should be ready at the time of release. Some vintages are tougher, however, and will repay keeping. (The comments below apply also to Brunello, Vino Nobile and Carmignano, which can be treated as Chianti Riserva equivalents.)

1983 Generally a good to very good vintage, though the midsummer drought damaged some wines, so some care will be needed in selection. Some good riservas were made, but they will not be on the market until 1986.

1982 A must to lay down when they come out in 1985. Production was not huge, and the wines have a lot of concentration, very good colour, and quite a lot of tannin. These wines should be good stayers, the really concentrated ones for 10–15 years. Those who like wines young and tannic will be able to drink these Chiantis next year; others should leave them until at least 1988.

1981 Good, not outstanding. Drinking well in 1985.

1980 Mediocre, light; drink up.

1978 Patchy, some good quality.

1977 Good riserva year. Drink now. Strongly recommended.

1976 Very poor. Avoid.

1975 Excellent, superb top quality vintage. Drink riservas now, or keep still longer. Strongly recommended.

1974 Little left. Not bad.

1973 Finished.

1972 Finished.

1971 Still a bit to be found. A long-living vintage. If you can find it, it could be very good.

Chianti £–££

Tuscany's Chianti is easily the most important wine here, at least from the point of view of volume production (three times more than the next largest DOC, which is Soave). It is important to distinguish between Chianti Classico (with the black cockerel necklet, theoretically better wines from the central area), Chianti Putto (a league of producers from outside the central Classico area, including lesser regions like Rufina, Colli Senesi) and ordinary Chianti, cheap supermarket or Italian restaurant stuff either in bottle or flask, usually to be avoided. But many good (yet very few great) Chiantis are available in the UK. Some producers make small quantities of exceptional wine, basically from Chianti grapes, very largely Sangiovese, possibly with the addition of Cabernet Sauvignon (up to 15 per cent is allowed), and often enough aged in barrique. These include:

Exceptional wines from the Chianti area £££

Tignanello from Antinori 15 per cent Cabernet Sauvignon. *(Belloni)*

Prima Vigna from Castello Vicchio Maggio Old vines. *John Matta)*

Coltassala from Castello di Volpaia 95 per cent Sangioveto, barrique-aged. *(Christopher Tatham)*

Sodi San Niccolo Riserva from Castellare *(Alivini-Trestini)*

Montesodi from Frescobaldi Single vineyard Chianti Rufina DOC.(Rufina is the smallest of the Chianti zones, making some of the best wines, not to be confused with the company Ruffino.) *(Bacchus Caves)*

Pergole Torte from Monte Vertine *(Peppercorn & Sutcliffe)*

La Corte from Querceto *(Peppercorn & Sutcliffe)*

Concerto from Castello di Fonterutoli 30 per cent Cabernet Sauvignon *(Geoffrey Roberts)*

> Wine in bag-in-box ages and spoils quicker than in bottle. If you buy boxes, buy and drink up one box before you buy the next. Boxes in the store-cupboard will lose their freshness. Used or unopened, a wine box will keep better if you store it tap downwards, keeping wine, not air, in the valve.

The above are all producers of very good Chianti indeed. The following are also excellent, more traditionally composed Chiantis:

Highly recommended Chiantis ££–£££

Capezzana, Montalbano *(Market Finders)*

Castello di Rampolla, Classico *(Stapylton Fletcher)*

Castello di San Polo in Rosso, Classico *(Peppercorn & Sutcliffe)*

Riecine, Classico *(Cockburn & Campbell)*

Villa di Vetrice, Rufina *(Ehrmanns, Adnams)*

Other good Chiantis £–££

Casavecchia di Nittardi, Classico *(Grapevine)*

Castell' in Villa, Classico *(Recount)*

Castillo di Uzzano, Classico *(Stonehaven)*

Coiano, Colli Fiorentini *(Harvey Prince)*

Fontodi, Classico *(Millevini)*

Fossi, Classico *(Hamilton Hubbard)*

Montegufoni, Colli Fiorentini *(Ellis Son & Vidler)*

Montellori, Colli Fiorentini*(Alivini-Trestini)*

Pagliarese, Classico *(Italian Wine Agencies)*

Le Pici, Classico *(Millevini)*

Rocca Delle Macie, Classico UK's biggest selling Chianti Classico *(Enotria)*

Ruffino Riserva Ducale, Classico (*Hedges & Butler*)

Spalletti Poggio Reale, Rufina *(Fiandaca)*

Vistarenni, Classico *(Vendemmia Italiana)*

£ means that a wine costs, from most producers and in most British shops, under £3 a bottle, ££ that it costs between £3 and £5, and £££ that it costs over £5.

Companies in brackets after the name of a wine in this section are either the agent or importer of that wine, or in some cases a major stockist. Some of these are retailers, from whom you can buy direct, some wholesalers, who will be able to put you in contact with retail stockists if you have trouble tracing a particular wine. At the end of each section on a country or region you will find the address of an organisation that can put you in contact with these firms.

Other Sangioveses

Other good to excellent wines based on the Sangiovese grape are:

Brunello di Montalcino £££ Italy's most expensive wine, reputed to have great longevity in good vintages.

Biondi-Santi is number one here, in price and in quality. **Altesino** *(Fiandaca)* is an excellent youngish property, as is **Caparzo** *(Cynthia Bacon)*. **Argiano** *(Italian Wine Agencies)* can be good, certainly historic. **Fattoria dei Barbi** is very consistent. Some of these make a Rosso dai Vigneti di Brunello which can be amazing value.

Vino Nobile di Montepulciano ££–£££ This was the first of the DOCGs to appear (all Vino Nobile di Montepulciano must be DOCG from the 1980 vintage, or be relegated to vino da tavola). Let's hope this will make a psychological difference, if nothing else, for Vino Nobile can be disappointing. Exceptions to this rule are:

Avignonesi *('Sunday Times' Wine Club)*, **Boscarelli** *(Ciborio)*, **Fassati** *(Belloni)*, **Carletti della Giovanpaola** *(Alivini-Trestini)*, **Fognano** *(Barwell & Jones)*.

Carmignano £££ A DOC which allows ten per cent Cabernet in the blend. Ugo Contini-Bonacossi's Villa di Capezzana *(Market Finders)* is indisputably on top here. Gilbey Vintners sell in the UK a delicious youngish **Tenuta di Capezzana**. The excellent **Villa di Trefiano** *(Market Finders)* is from the same stable. Only rivals: **Artimino** *(Giordano)* and **Bachereto**.

Torgiano ££ (Sometimes known as Rubesco – a brand name.) A Chianti-type wine from Umbria. **Lungarotti** *(Belloni)* has a virtual monopoly. The Riserva 1975 is one of Italy's great reds. They also do a Sangiovese–Cabernet blend called **San Giorgio**, which is *very* expensive.

Sangiovese di Romagna £–££ There's not a lot of good Sangiovese di Romagna about. **Pasolini** *(Dreyfus Ashby)* do a good version. The one from **Fattoria Paradiso** is probably best if you can find it. The 1983 **Vallunga** *(Maison DOC)* is also very tasty.

From the Marche and Abruzzi There's a variety of wines from these regions based on Sangiovese and/or the Montepulciano grape (not to be confused with the Tuscan town of that name).

Santa Christiana *(Continental Wine & Food)* produce both Rosso Conero (more Montepulciano than Sangiovese) and Rosso Piceno (the reverse) to a fairly high standard. Other good makers of Rosso Piceno are **Villa Pigna** *(Lega)*, who also do an excellent, Vellutato (which means velvety red).

Morellino di Scansano £ Little-known but good light wine from Tuscany. The one from the **Cantina Sociale** *(Maison DOC)* is well worth trying.

Montepulciano d'Abruzzo ££ Can be really delicious, gutsy but balanced. **Colle Secco Tollo** *(Alivini-Trestini)* is a very good one, as is **Illuminati** *(Giordano)*, especially the 'Invecchiato'. **Casal Thaulero** *(Lega)* can also be recommended, especially the 'Numerata' (numbered bottle) series. **Nicodemi** *('Sunday Times' Wine Club)* is well worth obtaining, as is **Barone Cornacchia** *(Stonehaven)*.

The Cabernet Invasion ££–£££

Cabernet Sauvignon has caught on in Central Italy in no small way. The Tuscan **Sassicaia** £££ *(Hunt & Braithwaite)* is the front runner by a mile, but others are catching up. The **Lungarotti** version £££ from Umbria is excellent, as is **Bonacossi's** Cabernet–Merlot blend **Ghiaie della Furba**. All these wines receive oak ageing, either in barrique or large barrel. But **Vallania** ££ *(Maison DOC)*, whose Cabernet is very highly considered, completely rejects oak-ageing for red wine as well as for white; definitely worth trying.

Other Central Reds £–££

Other reds from these parts include **Gutturnio** ££; **Romagnoli** *(Belloni)* and **Fugazza** *(Italian Wine Agencies)* are worth seeking out; and of course **Lambrusco** £, which is difficult to recommend, although **Giacobazzi** *(Belloni)* and **Cavicchioli** *(Enotria)* may be said to produce potable versions.

Central Italian Whites £–££

White wines are making progress in Central Italy, but have a long way to go before they catch up with reds in importance. The main problem is that the ubiquitous Trebbiano vine variety is of somewhat insipid character.

Tuscan and Umbrian whites Most Chianti producers make a white, but it is rarely worth mentioning. **Antinori** *(Belloni)* do a couple of good ones £–££; Galestro (a brand name – light and vinous) and Orvieto (fuller flavour). Their Orvieto Castello della Sala is a wine whose abboccato version (sweet) is raved about in some quarters for some reason – we wouldn't recommend it. **Le Vellette** *(Ciborio)* is another acceptable Orvieto.

Trebbiano d'Abruzzo £ (a finer clone of the Trebbiano vine) can work better than the Tuscan version, so look out for **Illuminati**, **Casal Thaulero**, **Barone Cornacchia** and especially **Nicodemi**.

Montecarlo ££ is basically Trebbiano with other varieties thrown in. **Fattoria di Buonamico** *(Adnams)* do the best, **Mazzini** *(Stonehaven)* being a good alternative.

Verdicchio £ is a white from the Marches which has captured a certain audience, perhaps just because it is neutral. **Fazi-Battaglia** *(Belloni)*, **Umani Ronchi** *(Hedges & Butler)* alias **Bianchi** *(Enotria)* are adequate. **Santa Chiara** *(Bishopsmead)* is the only one which might inspire mild enthusiasm.

Frascati £, from near Rome, is of somewhat more interest, being made from the potentially tasty Malvasia Bianco. **Colli di Catone** £–££ frosted bottle *(Alivini-Trestini)* is undoubtedly the best, **Gotto d'Oro** *(Belloni)* and **Ambra** *(Enotria)* from the Cantina Sociale di Marino are best inexpensive options. **Fontana Candida** has become very boring in the hands of producer-owners Winefood. Actually, Trestini's humble **Velletri** £ (from near Frascati) is possibly the best of the lot, at a knock-down price: nobody has heard of it, so no one will stock it (except *The Market*).

Vernaccia di San Gimignano ££ is easily the most interesting of Central Italy's native whites. In this field, **Teruzzi & Puthod** *(Enotria)* are unrivalled, though they do tend to have re-fermentation problems. **Falchini** *(Bishopsmead)* claims to be the best, but is a bit too 'cold fermentation', ie fresh and boring, for some. **Strozzi** is the most famous.

The Chardonnay invasion £–£££

The Chardonnay grape is beginning now to make inroads in Central Italy. **Pomino 'Il Benefizio'** £££ by **Frescobaldi** *(Bacchus Caves)*, in which Chardonnay is mixed with certain other grapes and aged in Bordeaux-type small oak barrels, is the most interesting version – like a very old Burgundy. **Vallania's Terre Rosse** ££ *(Maison DOC)* is outstanding of the un-oaked style. The **Lungarotti Miralduolo** £££ *(Belloni)* version, more expensive, is less interesting, and less good value for money.

THE ITALIAN SOUTH AND THE ISLANDS

The 'Mezzogiorno', that large tract of land stretching from south of Rome to Sicily, is very like France's 'Midi' of 15 years ago: an historic not to say ancient wine-country of enormous potential but, at present, producing little enough of high quality. This is wine-lake country, and UK importers are as wary of it as they were in the early 1970s of Southern France. However, there *are* a few decent bottles drifting our way, and some amazing value. The same may be said of Sardinia, which is now witnessing a stirring of interest from the British trade. The following are the best of the selection so far:

From Campania come the wines of **Mastroberardino** *(Italian Wine Agencies)*, the rich, refined **Taurasi** £££ (which is sometimes compared with great Barolo; Italian Wine Agencies have old vintages back to 1968), the highly regarded, fine but rather expensive dry whites Fiano di Avellino and Greco di Tufo and Lacryma Christi (red and white) from the vineyards of Vesuvius. An interesting range of Lacryma Christi (dry, medium, sweet and lightly sparkling (*frizzante*) white, red and sparkling rosé) [££] is on offer from **Saviano** *(Giordano)*.

From Basilicata hail the more easily affordable Aglianico del Vulture reds [££] from **Fratelli d'Angelo** (another *Italian Wine Agencies* agency). (Aglianico is made from the same grape as Taurasi.) The 1981 is excellent and the 1977 Riserva is outstanding value – unusual full, rich, fruity wines.

Puglia is represented in the UK notably by wines which have found their way anonymously into other Italian wines, not to mention certain 'French' wines which have needed doctoring. A few pioneers are, however, producing fine wine, notably **Rivera** of Castel del Monte (excellent rosé and a brilliant red called **Il Falcone**). **Simonini (Favonio)** who has had the courage to plant Pinot Bianco, Chardonnay and Cabernet Franc in a favourable if improbable micro-climate near Foggia; and **Leone de Castris** *(Lega)* whose **Five Roses** rosé [££] is world famous and whose **Salice Salentino** Red [££] (especially the 1977 Riserva) is capable of great longevity. (The 1962 is also still available at an elevated price [£££]. The **Cantina Sociale Locorotondo** *('Sunday Times' Wine Club)* do a fine white which is 'crisp and lively on the palate', according to Burton Anderson (who made all the 'Sunday Times' selections).

Sardinia has always produced wines of big alcohol and body, and there are some excellent examples on offer. Sherry-lovers looking for something similar-but-different might try the 1974 Vernaccia di Oristano Riserva from **Fratelli Contini** *('Sunday Times' Wine Club)*, not unlike a dry amontillado. Port-lovers, on the other hand, might appreciate a drop of Anghelu Ruju by **Sella & Mosca** *(Belloni)*, a rich, sweet dessert wine made from the Cannonau grape. Sella & Mosca, Sardinia's biggest private and most go-ahead concern, also produce a good red table wine from Cannonau and two delicious, light, summery dry whites called Torbato and Vermentino. All three carry the geographic indication 'di Alghero'. An excellent Sardinian co-operative is **Dolianova** [£] *(Eurowines)*, whose characterful Cannonau DOC is really tasty for an inexpensive wine and whose magnum-size non-DOC Cannonau and Vermentino represent probably the best value in jug wine around.

Sicily is the region of Italy that has advanced most dramatically over the past ten years. One of Italy's best red wines is made here, the Rosso del Conte [££] of **Regaleali** *(Italian Wine Agencies)*; Regaleali's normal red and dry white [££] are also outstanding. **Corvo** red and white [£]–[££] *(Hedges & Butler)* are very reliable wines, while **Corvo Colomba Platino** [££] is an up-market white deserving special attention. The whites of the Alcamo zone have perhaps made the greatest strides: **Rapitalà** [£] *(Alivini-Trestini)* is a meaty but rather neutral-flavoured wine with 'Northern' freshness. Perhaps the best cheap table wines of Sicily come from the co-operative **Settesoli** [£] *(Ciborio)*.

Marsala £££ Fortified wines are a traditional speciality here, Marsala being the best known. There is some talk now of declassifying the 'special' Marsalas made with egg, banana-flavouring, almond-essence etc. If this results in a revaluation of genuine Marsala, it will be a good thing, since Marsala Vergine, a dry, nutty wine, often of considerable age and tasting something like a cross between sherry and Madeira, is potentially one of the world's great fortified wines. The **Vecchia Riserva** of **Pellegrino** *(European Vintners)* is an excellent example. The dry SOM (Superior old Marsala) and sweet **Garibaldi** wines of **Alagna** *(Giordano)* are other versions of authentic Marsala worth a taste. The finest Marsala of them all, however, is not so called. It is a dry, relatively light aperitif named Vecchio Samperi from **De Bartoli** *(Alivini-Trestini)* a vino da tavola, since it has only 16.5° of alcohol instead of the statutory 18°. This wine is particularly distinguished since it is unfortified.

Moscato Passito di Pantelleria £££ Finally, from a small island south of Sicily near Africa comes another excellent fortified wine called Moscato Passito di Pantelleria. **Tanit** *(Italian Wine Agencies)* have a virtual monopoly on production of this creamy, luscious dessert wine.

Where to buy Italian wines

Adnams, Cynthia Bacon, Barwell & Jones, Millevini, Stonehaven Wines, Wine Society.

BEST ITALIAN BUYS

North West 1978 Barolo, Pio Cesare *(Adnams, The Market; importers: Findlater Matta Agency – for laying down)*, 1978 Barolo Abbazia Dell'Annunziato, Ratti *(Cynthia Bacon – for laying down)*, 1982 Dolcetto, Sandrone *(Ehrmanns; importers: Ehrmanns)*, Asti Spumante, Fontanafredda *(Peter Dominic; importers: Enotria Wines Ltd)*, Piemontello, Moscato Frissante *(Threshers, Safeways, Tesco, Cullen's; importers: European Vintners)*

North East 1978 Campo Fiorin, Masi *(Oddbins, Luigi Delicatessens, Harrods, Fratelli Camisa; importer: Alivini-Trestini)*, 1983 Soave Costalta *(Ehrmanns; importer: Ehrmanns)*, 1983 Chardonnay di Appiano Viticoltori Alto Adige *(Wine Growers' Association; importers: Italian Wine Agency)*, 1983 Valdadige Bianco, Cavit *(Adnams, The Market; importer: Ehrmanns)*, 1983 Pinot Blanc Tiefenbrunner *(Ehrmanns, Adnams, The Market, The Wine Bin, G Hush, Bellavini; importers: Mitchells of Lancaster)*, 1981 Cabernet Lageder *(Luigi Delicatessens, Fratelli Camisa; importers: Alivini-Trestini)*

Central Italy 1979 Tignanello, Antinori *(André Simon, Victoria Wines; importers: Belloni)*, 1982 Chianti Rufina, Villa di Vetrice *(The Market, Ehrmanns; importer: Ehrmanns)*, 1983 Velletri Villa Ginetti *(The Market, Luigi Delicatessens; importers: Alivini-Trestini)*, 1981 Carmignano, Tenuta di Capezzana *(Peter Dominic; importer: Peter Dominic)*

South and Islands 1981 Aglianico del Vulture, D'Angelo *(Wine Growers' Association; importers: Italian Wine Agency)*, 1982/83 Torbato di Alghero, Sella & Mosca *(some branches of Galleon Wines and Augustus Barnett; importers: Hedges & Butler)*, 1982 Bianco, Regaleali *(Wine Growers' Association; importers: Italian Wine Agency)*, 1.5 litre Cannonau (red) and Vermentino (white), Dolianova *(The Market; importers: Euro Wines)*, Marsala Vergine Vecchia Riserva, Pellegrino *(no retailers)*

For further information, contact: The Italian Trade Centre, 37 Sackville Street, London W1; tel: 01-734 2412

Japan

Nothing successful apart from Sake (rice wine) and Akadana (plum wine) has been seen in this country, and even these are sold only in Japanese restaurants, and Chinese supermarkets and grocery shops.

Lebanon

Ironically, the Lebanon has benefited in some small way from the troubles of war: in the publicity its wines have received. Serge Hochar of Ch Musar (the only Lebanese wine on sale in Britain) was declared 'Wine Man of the Year' by *Decanter* magazine, and the press, television and radio reacted enthusiastically – here was a story! Mr Hochar's vineyards are only ten miles east of Beirut, his winery the same distance to the north. The 1983 vintage had to be picked at night and, remarkably, 90 per cent of the harvest was saved.

Mr Hochar has three grape varieties. The Château wines virtually always have a predominance of Cabernet Sauvignon, the remaining portion of the wine being a blend of Cinsault and Syrah. The skill of each vintage is to recognise each variety's assets and deficiencies and blend accordingly. The 1975 was 70 per cent Cabernet, 20 per cent Cinsault and 10 per cent Syrah £££, whereas the 1977 was 74 per cent Cabernet and equal proportions of Syrah and Cinsault ££. Cuvée Musar, on the other hand, is the reverse proportion of Syrah and Cinsault to Cabernet £.

What to drink now

The two vintage wines currently available are the 1975 and 1977. The 1975 is more akin to the softer Margaux style of Bordeaux, whereas the 1977 is at its more natural 'gamy' best. Cuvée Musar, the house wine, is currently from the 1980 vintage, and has a richness verging on the sweet – something that the devotee of the 'Château' wine does not appreciate. The 1975 is now quite scarce, the 1977 should still be around at the beginning of the year, and the 1978 has just been released. Stockists include Peter Dominic, Victoria Wine, Cullens,

Christophers, Adnams, Peter Green (Scotland), Grants (Ireland) and many others.

Luxembourg

The wines of Luxembourg have a certain similarity to those from our own shores: mainly Germanic grape varieties, Rhine Riesling, Müller-Thurgau, Gewürztraminer, etc. Very little is stocked here, but Heritage Wines import a range of which the Gewürztraminer ££ is the best example. The others tend to be rather weak.

For further information, contact: The Luxembourg Embassy, 27 Wilton Crescent, London SW1; tel: 01-235 6961

New Zealand

Comparing Australia with New Zealand just because they are both in the Pacific is like comparing Germany with France just because they're both in the Common Market. New Zealand has vineyards closer to the South Pole than any other country and this daunting generalisation alone could be used to mark out her wines. They have acidity, and superbly pointed varietal tastes. They are usually light – rarely reaching 12 degrees of alcohol – and some of the most skilful and most technologically advanced winemaking in the world is done in New Zealand.

Reds Until recently, these *have* been less impressive than the whites, quite understandably so when you think that there's little but penguins between them and Antarctica. But things are looking up. 1982, with the red grape vineyards now reasonably mature and with a perfect summer, produced tremendous deep, dry, blackcurrant-and-green-pepper Cabernets from Vidal and Neudorf, as well as a wonderful Burgundian style Pinot Noir from Saint Helena. First sightings of 1983 show even greater promise: the spicy, ripe Cabernet from Cooks is the best they've yet made. However, the UK market is still dominated by the earlier vintages, and we suggest you try the light oak and grassy fruity **Nobilo 1978 Cabernet** £££, and the **Nobilo Pinotage 1978** £££ *(both Averys)*; the **Montana Cabernet** £££, light, grassy, but straight *(Oddbins, Gough; importer: Seagrams)* and either the very dry **Cooks Pinot Noir 1981** £££ *(Unwins, some Victoria Wine and Peter Dominic; importer: Cooks New Zealand Wines [UK])*, or the excellent **Cooks New Zealand Dry Red** £ *(Gough, Waitrose, Bottoms Up, Peter Dominic; importer Cooks New Zealand Wines [UK])*.

Whites These are still the forte. They should be as young as possible. **Montana**'s best wine is the **Sauvignon**, ££ (*Oddbins, Gough; importer:Seagram)* stingingly fresh with the typical flavour of the Sauvignon grape. Their **Chardonnay** ££ is also good in a rather dry, oaked, 'Chablis' style. **Cooks' 1983 Chardonnay** £££ is an exciting example of high acidity, good honeyed fruit, and rich, buttery oak *(Laytons, Parker & Walton, Peter Dominic Orange Street; importer: Cooks New Zealand Wines UK)*. The **1982 Chenin** *(Peter Dominic, Cullens, Lay & Wheeler, Sandersons, etc)* is prickly, fruit-juice fresh, while the **Late Pick Riesling Sylvaner** *(Peter Dominic Orange Street)* is incredibly rich for a wine that hasn't been affected by noble rot. The **Delegats Chardonnay** £££ matches richness with a savoury dryness in a way that Burgundy rarely manages, and **Matawhero Gewürztraminer** £££ *(Averys)* stands out as one of the great Gewürzes of the world.

BEST BUYS £ Cooks New Zealand Dry Red *(Gough, Waitrose, Bottoms Up, Peter Dominic; importer: Cooks New Zealand Wines [UK])*, ££ Montana Sauvignon *(Gough, Oddbins, Victoria Wines; importer: Seagrams)*, £££ Matawhero Gewürztraminer *(Averys)*

Further information from: New Zealand High Commission, New Zealand House, 80 Haymarket, London SW1; tel: 01-930 8422.

North Africa

Of the three North African countries, **Morocco** is the only one that seriously exports its wine to this country. Although wines of great blending qualities, they tend on their own to be rather one-dimensional. Grown on sandy soil and subjected to intensive heat, the wines are very big, but lack the necessary acidity to make a 'complete' wine. The main grape variety is Cinsault, although Grenache and Carignan are quite prevalent. This blend is the structure of **Tarik** sold by Oddbins at around £2. The 1981 vintage is curiously bottled in Belgium but is worth the money to further your experience of world wines. Even better is a straight Cinsault from the Appellation Guerrouane, **Sidi Brahim**, a 12° wine also from the 1981 vintage. This wine will no doubt improve with bottle age. Imported by *Jeffrey Benson Wines*, it is also sold at around the £2 mark at *Buckingham Vintners* and *Del Monicos*.

Portugal

The 1983 vintage

The crop was about a fifth smaller than normal. But the quality of the wine was generally very good throughout the country, particularly in Madeira, where 1983 was considered outstanding.

Value for money

With the exception of vinhos verdes, we are unlikely to see many of these wines in the UK for some time. Most Portuguese wine is matured for a number of years (some would say for too many) before bottling, and because of this, a range of vintages that extends back into the late 1960s and early 1970s is readily available in Britain.

All these older wines are traditional in style – full, dry whites which are often rather oxidised, and tough, robust reds with a quite aromatic character but an inevitable astringency. This is all very well for the Portuguese or for the intrepid traveller, but the world market demands different styles: fresh, fruity whites and younger, softer reds which can be enjoyed without food. Portuguese wines are nevertheless cheap, with all but the oldest selling at £3 or below. The stars of the export markets have always been the slightly sweet, slightly sparkling, slightly dull rosés, and in the past few years a new style of white *vinho verde*, sweetened up and with extra, added prickle, has increased sales dramatically in the UK. It is encouraging that one can now find a few younger Dão and Bairrada wines with a fruitier, more generous character, demonstrating that, despite their natural resistance to change, the Portuguese are gradually accepting that to thrive they must produce wines acceptable to a wider public. One estate that has done this with great results is Quinta da Bacalhôa, near Lisbon, whose excellent red is made by an Australian with Cabernet grapes.

What to drink now, what to keep

Provided one appreciates the rather uncompromising style of Portuguese wines, the shelves of Britain's wine merchants offer a wide selection of older vintages and remarkable value for money. It is unusual to pay more than £3.50 a bottle, and 16-year-old wines of considerable quality are still less than £5.

Vinho verde, of course, is made to be enjoyed as young and fresh as possible and is almost always sold without a vintage.

Vintages of other wines currently seen in the UK:
Bucelas (white): 1979, 1981
Dão (white): 1978, 1979, 1980, 1981
Dão (red): 1970, 1974, 1978, 1979
Bairrada: 1970, 1979, 1980
Douro (red): 1979
Colares (red): 1971
Other regions (usually *reservas* or *garrafeira* wines from reputable shippers); 1963, 1968, 1970, 1974, 1978, 1980

Most of these wines are ready for drinking, and quality depends rather more on the way the wine has been handled (or manhandled) than on the vintage. But the younger Bairradas and Dãos will benefit from further bottle ageing.

Understanding the Portuguese label

Portuguese labels hold few mysteries, but beware one unique aspect of their wine marketing: some of the best bottles are to be found *without* the name of any recognised region but merely a vintage, the producer's name and a word or two to indicate that the wine is a reserva or garrafeira.

Look out for the following terms:

Colheita Vintage or harvest (eg Colheita 1970).

Engarrafado Bottled (by).

Garrafeira A wine merchant's best selected wine matured for a number of years in cask and bottle.

Maduro Mature wine (as opposed to *vinho verde*, young green wine).

Região Demarcada Demarcated region. A system, not unlike France's AOC laws, which governs grape varieties, yield, production methods, etc.

Reserva A wine specially chosen and set aside by a shipper for more careful handling and longer ageing.

Velho (or Velhas) Old, aged.

The regions

Bairrada [£] A new quality region producing mainly red and Champagne method sparkling wines.

Bucelas [£] A small region near Lisbon that produces dry, quite austere white wines.

Carcavelhos [£] Almost extinct. Now only one vineyard swamped by the resort of Estoril, where a slightly sweet fortified wine is made.

Colares [£] Unique in that its vineyards are in deep sand and therefore on ungrafted vines. Huge red wines that need much ageing.

Dão [£] The best-known region for quality (but mostly tough and astringent) red wines and many whites. The best of these dry, austere wines can achieve excellence.

Douro [£] The most recently demarcated area (for table wine, that is, since the region was first identified for the production of port wine as early as 1756). Large quantities of average to very good wines. The base wine for Mateus Rosé comes from here and Bairrada.

Madeira [££]–[£££] Unique fortified wines of considerable style from this Atlantic island. Four main types from the nearly dry (Sercial, Verdelho) to the rich and sweet (Bual, Malmsey).

Moscatel de Setúbal [££]–[£££] Excellent fortified dessert wines from a peninsula south of Lisbon. Quite outstanding when aged for many years in cask, but some prefer the younger, fruitier, and less expensive six-year-old.

Vinho verde [£] Largest of the demarcated regions, in the cool North, producing a quarter of Portugal's wine. Although nearly three-quarters of it is red, we see only the white version in Britain.

Names to look out for

Caves Aliança Based in Bairrada and making some of its best table and sparkling wines, as well as a full range of Dãos, Vinhos Verdes and Douros. *(Portuguese Wine Distributors)*

Quinta da Aveleda Not only does this company produce the popular and commercial Aveleda vinho verde, but also an excellent estate bottled wine, labelled **Quinta da Aveleda**. *(Hedges & Butler)*

Borges & Irmão An Oporto company whose good **Gatão** brand is Britain's leading vinho verde and who also produce a full portfolio of wines from other regions. *(Grants of St James's)*

Carvalho, Ribeiro & Ferreira Shippers, rather than producers of an excellent range of wines mainly from undemarcated regions. Best known is **Serradayres** from the Ribatejo area, but their finest wines are mainly old **reservas** and **garrafeiras**. *(D & F Wine Shippers)*

J M da Fonseca The second largest producer of wine in Portugal, famous for **Moscatel de Setúbal** and the consistently good **Periquita** and **Pasmados** wines from the undemarcated regions around their headquarters in Azeitão (and the unremarkable Lancers rosé). *(Viniberia)*

SOGRAPE Portugal's largest producer. Notable mainly for Mateus Rosé, although its brand of Dão, Grão Vasco, is one of the best known from the region *(Hedges & Butler)*. They have recently launched a good commercial **vinho verde, Gazela**. *(Stevens Garnier)*

Caves Velhas The sole producer of Bucelas and also well-known for the Romeira range of table wines. *(D & F Wine Shippers)*

Where to buy Portuguese wines

Bottoms Up (a wide range of wines, covering most regions and styles), Peter Dominic (basic branded table wine as well as some better wines at sensible prices), A O L Grilli, Cranbrook, Kent (a one-man band who has made it a personal crusade to list good Portuguese wines), Oddbins (certainly the most comprehensive range and keenest prices available in the UK today; some exciting bargains to be found), Sainsbury's (to be praised for helping increase sales of vinho verde and Dão by their own-label campaign, and making a success of Quinta da Bacalhôa), Waitrose (a good supermarket chain with a small range including the excellent Tinta da Anfora).

BEST PORTUGUESE BUYS:

Vinho verde: £ Gazela *(Davisons, Barretts, Buckinghams, Cullens)* £ Quinta da Aveleda *(wine in the drier, traditional style just being introduced: Hedges & Butler)*

Dão £ Dom Ferraz Reserva 1974 *(big, fruity: Bottoms Up, Threshers, Waitrose)*, £ Conde de Santar 1978 *(estate wine: Oddbins, Victoria Wine [selected stores])*

Bairrada £ Montanha Reserva 1970 *(Bottoms Up)*

Undemarcated £ Pasmados *(Oddbins, Cockburns of Leith, A O L Grilli)*, Periquita *(Cockburns of Leith, A O L Grilli, Les Amis du Vin)*, Camarate *(Oddbins, Cockburns of Leith, A O L Grilli)* all from J M da Fonseca, ££ Quinta de Bacalhôa *(Sainsbury's Vintage Selection)* and Tinta da Anfora *(Waitrose)*, £££ **Madeira** Henriques & Henriques Verdelho *(Harrods, Cockburns of Leith, S H Jones, McKechnie Wines)*, £££ Blandy's Ten-Year-Old Malmsey *(superb classic wine of remarkable concentration) (Hedges & Butler, Peter Dominic (selected stores), Selfridges, Harrods, Fortnum & Mason, Buckinghams, G C Harvey)*

For further information contact: Portuguese Government Trade Office, 4th Floor, New Bond Street House, 1–5 New Bond Street, London W1; tel: 01-493 0212.

PORT

The 1983 vintage

Port is a fortified wine, 20 per cent alcohol by volume. So it is not possible to assess fully the quality of top grade ports, particularly wines which may become vintage ports, until 12 to 15 months after the wines are made, since the spirit predominates. When this *Guide* is published, it may be that 1983 will have been declared suitable for vintage port. At the time of writing, we can only be glad that decent wine was made at all in 1983 after the bad weather in the early months of the year. But the autumn weather was excellent, and the quality was saved. Since several port firms decided not to declare the 1982 vintage, the likelihood of a 1983 vintage declaration is the greater. But vintage port is a tiny two to three per cent of the whole. The quality of the whole area is what matters.

Value for money

Prices continue upwards in Portugal. Inflation is around five to six times greater than in the UK. Only the gradual devaluation of the Portuguese currency protects us from horrific increases, but it can be confidently stated that good port will never be cheap again, as in the 25 to 30 years after 1945. Generally, the prices of vintage ports in Britain are influenced by economic factors here rather than rising production costs in Portugal. Any wine over about 12 years of age tends to be in short supply, hence expensive.

What to drink now, what to lay down

Generally, it is worth paying for the medium to upper price brackets within each category of port, but particularly for cask-matured ports, non-vintage or LBV (Late Bottled means four to six years after the vintage).

Leading supermarkets often sell their own-label ports alongside advertised brands. These wines are well worth trying. Never poor, and often very good, they represent very keen value. Most, but not all, have been Oporto-bottled. All such wines have a black-printed, numbered white seal on the neck, issued by the Portuguese government. Ports bottled in Britain have no seal, but all are tasted and issued with a certificate of origin before shipment.

Remember, only a few ports need laying down for ageing. Most are ready to drink at once. If in doubt, ask a merchant.

Vintages Under this heading we include all ports which are made for laying down for maturing in bottle. (This excludes many dated LBVs, which are intended for immediate drinking.)

1955, 1958, 1960 Mature, fully ready, but stocks are low.

1963 Full potential not yet realised. A classic year. Some wines ready, the greatest will repay keeping.

1966 An under-rated vintage. Not many wines available, but most are excellent and a few need another five to eight years.

1967 A useful, but not great year. Quite ready in 1985. Only four or five shippers declared.

★1968 Graham's Malvedos and Fonseca-Guimaraens, bottled 1970, are excellent un-declared wines. Ready now.

1970 A near-classic year, generally declared by all shippers of vintage to the UK. Although these will be delicious wines in 1985, the best will keep ten years longer at least.

1972 Dow, Offley and Taylor's Vargellas may still be found. All quite ready.

★1974 Warre and Smith Woodhouse bottled in 1978 wines for crusting. Good value and ready.

1975 A generally declared year that has matured faster than expected. Drink now and before the 1970, 1966 and 1963s, if possible.

• *Single Quinta ports are rightly becoming more widely distributed. The quality is always next highest to vintage and the prices lower. Normally bottled at two years (vintage ports have to be bottled before they are two-and-a-half years old), they are either the produce of one vineyard of high quality or a blend using top-area ports only.*

1977 A classic port. Some experts believe it is the best for 50 years. Hold on to it, or lay it down for young children.

1980 A small quantity of excellent wine which should be ready before the 1977s, say by 1995.

1982 Declared a vintage by a minority of leading shippers, this year produced good wines. However, a certain lack of evenness in top vineyards' production means less than half of the known names will be bottling this vintage in autumn 1984.

Understanding the port label

On a port label, you will find:

The brand or description of the wine and the unqualified word 'Port'; the shipper or responsible bottler's name and an address; the content of the bottle at time of filling, expressed in centilitres; the country of origin – Portugal.

Only wine certified by the Portuguese authorities may legally be called Port in the United Kingdom. Any port indicating its age will have been bottled at source.

You will find amongst the qualities on sale the following:

Crusted port This term refers nowadays to a blend of very good wines averaging some three to four years in wood, bottled as for vintage port. Being somewhat older when bottled than vintage, crusted will mature more quickly in bottle. It generally needs five to ten years from the year of bottling, which should be mentioned on the label. A very good alternative to vintage port. It will need to have 'crust' or sediment decanted off.

Dry White Aperitif A very few shippers import this attractive pre-prandial drink.

Fine Ruby or Fine Old Ruby (similar for Tawny and White) This indicates a basic quality either with full colour (ruby) or lighter (tawny). The wines will average two-and-a-half to three years' age.

Finest Old Tawny, 10 years or 20 years or 30 years of age The price of these will indicate their qualities. Usually from £7 a bottle upwards. Blended very fine wines with little colour but great flavour and softness. 'The Wine Trade's favourite drink.'

1979 Late Bottled Vintage or vintage character, bottled 1985 (see below under NAMES TO LOOK OUT FOR) A few of these are crusting ports which need decanting; most are good quality cask-matured wines of single years, with no deposit, ready for drinking.

1968 Quinta de . . . If the year does not appear on wine charts, this will mean that the port was not declared a full vintage, but that the firm owning the quinta (farm, estate) wanted to sell some vintage-style wine. It is sure to be good value and good wine.

Ruby *see 'Fine Ruby'.*

1980 (eg) Vintage Bottled two years after picking and declared by individual firms only when outstanding quality is available from the top-grade vineyards. Must be kept on its side, label upwards, for anything from ten to 30-plus years (*see under* WHAT IS AVAILABLE NOW). The capsule or seal will probably be marked with shipper and year. Some bottles are embossed on the shoulder with this information. The cork will be branded and extra long, of finest quality.

Vintage Character, LB or Late Bottled Vintage (with a date) These indicate superior qualities of cask-matured ports, either of blended years or of single years. Ready for immediate drinking. Likely to be five to seven years of age. Pro-rata, better value than the cheapest ports.

White Port *see 'Dry White Aperitif'.*

There are a few dated wood ports (matured in cask), which must have been kept for a minimum of eight years in cask and so will have got rid of their deposit before bottling. Not to be confused with Vintage Port, which throws its deposit in the bottle, and so needs decanting.

Names to look out for

Middle range ££ As duty is the same for an inexpensive port as for a very old one, it is best to search the middle range of prices. Here, Vintage Character and Late Bottled Vintage are the two descriptions to remember. Leaders in this group we recommend are: **Dow 1979 LBV**, soft and slightly dry, with excellent balance; **Fonseca Bin 27**, sweeter than some, with good, firm fruit; **Graham 1978 LBV**, oak-matured, soft but rich; **Taylor 1978 LBV**, powerful but long and balanced; **Gould Campbell Vintage Character**, velvety with very long flavour.

For Old Tawny £££ wines in the £7 plus bracket, look for: **Delaforce His Eminence's Choice**, fruity but showing cask age; **Graham 10-year-old**, nutty and rich; **Ferreira Duke of Bragança 20-year-old** shows the quality of this leading Portuguese shipper; **Smith Woodhouse Old Lodge**, undated but of excellent softness and style; **Warre 10-year-old**, smart bottle matches the quality; **Dow Boardroom**, dry finish on a lovely, nutty style.

Single Quinta Ports £££, shippers' second string vintage ports. Bottled after two years, they develop like vintage but tend to mature more quickly and sell for less. The best now are: **Graham Quinta dos Malvedos 1968, Fonseca Guimaraens 1968, Taylor Quinta de Vargellas 1972**. All of these are rich and from top quality vineyards, ready for drinking from 1984. (Unlike the majority of LBV ports, they need decanting.) In a similar category to single quintas, look for **Warre 1974, bottled 1978** and **Smith Woodhouse 1974** both good, rich wines. Six or seven years in bottle works wonders when the wine starts out with sufficient body.

Shippers and brands

Cockburn, Smithes Part of Allied-Lyons group. Has the largest share of the home market. They promote heavily 'Special Reserve', a 'vintage character' bottled here, but one of the less exciting. Distribute a single Quinta (estate), **Eire Velha**, since the 1978. Vintage reputation less good than formerly. *(Harveys)*

Croft Now part of Grand Metropolitan's IDV. Their leading quality wood port is now **1978 LBV**, which is reasonable but not outstanding. Also ship cheaper Gilbey range. They own a fine **Quinta, Roeda**, which maintains the high standard of their **vintages**. *(IDV)*

Delaforce Same group as Croft. Managed by the original family. **Vintage character and old tawny** both Oporto-bottled and sound. Quinta da Corte is too recent (1980) to judge fully. *(Dent & Reuss)*

Dow Brand belonging to Silva & Cosens in privately owned group with Graham and Warre. One of the leading **vintage** houses. Dry, elegant but long-lasting wines. *(Christophers)*

Fonseca Brand of Guimaraens. British control within the Taylor group. Big sweet long-lasting ports of consistent character. *(Menzendorff)*

Ferreira Largest Portuguese firm. The brewers Whitbread (Stowells) have the UK agency. A fine range of well-presented qualities. *(Stowells of Chelsea)*

Grahams One of the leading shippers. Quality is always very good across the range.

Noval Name of a very fine quinta which now names the firm. They plan to bottle the wines at the estate. Good reputation in Britain, based on excellent **vintages**, particularly 1931 to 1960s. *(Rutherford, Osborne & Perkin)*

Sandeman Very large world-wide sales. Owned by Seagram and working to re-establish the market leadership they have lost to Cockburn. Qualities in the lower and middle range not thrilling. *(Sandeman UK)*

Taylor British-run private firm with high, well-deserved reputation for **vintages**. Rich, fruity wines seem to be always youthful. Old tawnies, 10- and 20-year-olds are good but costly. **Quinta de Vargellas** is frequently first-class. *(Deinhard)*

Warre Reputed to be the oldest British shipper. Part of larger independent group in Oporto. **Vintage** reputation now high, particularly since 1945. Sound, elegant ports distributed in the UK by brewers Bass. *(J E Fells)*

Where to buy port

Berry Bros & Rudd, Corney & Barrow, Davy's of London, The Halesworth Vintner, John Harvey & Sons, Harrods, Justerini & Brooks, Richard Kihl, Andrew Mead.

BEST BUYS £££ Vargellas 1972, Smith Woodhouse Old Priory, Smith Woodhouse Crusted, Dow 1979 LBV, Fonseca Bin 27, Gould Campbell Crusted, Warre 10-year-old

For further information, contact: Portuguese Government Trade Office, 4th Floor, New Bond Street House, 1–5 New Bond Street, London W1; tel: 01-493 0212.

Spain

The 1983 vintage

The 1983 vintage in Spain was in general a good, but not very good, one. The best wines produced are without doubt the whites of the Mediterranean region, especially Penedès and Valencia, whereas some of the reds will show a certain harshness. There will, of course, be exceptions. So far, there are very good reports coming out of Jumilla and Yecla (inland from Alicante) for their red wines, which have plenty of fruit and colour.

One region to look out for, so far as the 1983 vintage is concerned, is Navarra. The production is down slightly on 1982, but the quality is up, both in whites and reds. We should begin to see the whites on the market during the first part of 1985, and they will certainly be worth looking out for. The reds will not appear for some while yet, but again, well worth hunting for once they do. They have lots of fruit, good tannin balance and will be good stayers.

The centre of Spain, La Mancha especially, has produced a great deal of wine on top of a previous glut. Most of the wine produced here goes, via the co-operatives, into branded wines and the surplus should help to keep the price of Spanish brands stable in the foreseeable future.

CATALONIA

Following Rioja, this autonomous region in the North-West of Spain produces some of the country's best light wines, both still and sparkling. The region comprises five separate Denominación de Origen areas; these are: Ampurdan Costa Brava, Tarragona, Alella, Priorato and Penedès.

Importers (in brackets) will supply names of retail outlets. You can contact the importers through:
Vinos de España, 22 Manchester Square, London W1; TEL 01–935 6140.

Value for money

The best value wines from these regions are without doubt the whites, both still and sparkling, and the rosados (rosés). In Catalonia as a whole, the use of controlled temperature fermentation techniques, which retain fruit and acidity in the wine, have gone a long way to changing the image of Spanish white wine. The wines are now much fresher and more appealing, without having lost the individual characteristics of the grape varieties, though some are a bit neutral.

The reds are good in general, perhaps not as long-lived as the best Riojas, but normally more drinkable when young. Fair value is to be found in Catalonia in the sparkling wines made by the Champagne method, known as 'cava' in Spain – if you like the rather odd, earthy taste. Although the Spanish regulations do not restrict production of cava to Catalonia, 90 per cent of it is made there; mostly in the Penedès region, around the town of San Sadurní de Noya. Cava can be either non-vintage (nine months' maturation) or vintage (three years' maturation) and it is often the cheaper, fresher (because younger) cavas that are the best buy.

What to drink now, what to keep

The whites to look for are the young wines – 1983 and, as soon as they appear in the spring, the 1984s. Whilst lovely when young they do tend to lose their fruit rather early. There are exceptions, of course, but unfortunately it is difficult to show how to determine which of the whites have gone through any wood maturation, unless the producer prints the information on a back label. Good wood-matured whites to look out for are **Jean León's Chardonnay** [£££], which is fermented in oak and has good, round flavour. Look for the 1982 for keeping two or three more years. Also in this category is the **Torres Gran Viña Sol Green Label** [££], a blend of Parellada and Sauvignon Blanc, which receives some six months' wood maturation. Current vintages available are 1981 and 1982, both of which will keep a while.

For **reds**, look for wines from the **1978 and 1980 vintages** – those from 1981, 1982 and 1983 are not ready yet but will be good in three or four years' time. The one vintage to avoid is 1979, which produced some lightweight, acid wines. Older wines to avoid are 1972 and 1974. The 1972s were a disaster and most of the 1974s tasted recently have lost their fruit. There are some 1970s and 1971s still available at high prices (£10 minimum). But, as in Rioja, **1975** and **1976** are lovely, mature and very good value, and at £5–£6 a bottle are tasting good now and will hold a little longer. *Sainsburys* stock a **Vallformosa 1975** [£], which is great value.

Understanding the Catalan label

Many producers use grape varieties to indicate the style of the wine. The principal ones in Catalonia are **Xarel-lo** – white, produces mainly dry wines with good acid; **Parellada** – softer, fruitier wines, also white;

Macabeo – this is the Viura of Rioja, firm, full, sturdy white wines when young, with an odd, cardboardy after-taste; **Ull de Llebre** – the firm, fruity elegant red, the Tempranillo of Rioja; and **Garnacha** – red, fruity, full-bodied. There are, however, in Penedès especially, some very interesting wines made from classic grape varieties such as Cabernet Sauvignon not indigenous to Spain.

The **vintage** of the wine is normally expressed in English now, but the Spanish is **cosecha** or **vendimia**. There is often an expression of the dryness of the wine on the label, most often in Spanish on cava labels. The driest is **Brut Natur**, followed by **Brut**, **Semi Seco**, **Semi Dulce** and **Dulce** in ascending order of sweetness.

Quality status is legally defined only by the Denominación de Origen seal on the label. Some producers use the words **Reserva** and **Gran Reserva**; whereas in Rioja these terms are legally defined, in Penedès they are not, and simply mean that in the producer's opinion these are the best of his wines.

Whilst **Penedès** (Denominación de Origen, South-West of Barcelona) undoubtedly produces some of the best whites, the growers of **Alella** (a Denominación de Origen area up the coast from Barcelona) are making great strides in producing better, fresher wines.

Catalan names to look out for

René Barbier Denominación de Origen Penedès. On the same estate as the fair value **Conde de Caralt**, this ex-Rumasa firm makes a fresh white wine under the brand name Kraliner [£], as well as sound red wines. *(Harrison Wells)*

Jean León, SA Denominación de Origen Penedès. A small property which grows all its own grapes. The owner is a restaurant patron from Beverly Hills, California. Consequently, the majority of the production goes to the United States. Two wines are produced: an oak-fermented and aged Chardonnay [£££], and a powerful Cabernet Sauvignon [£££], both of which are of very high quality. The Chardonnay loses some of its freshness by being too oaky but ages well, and the latest vintage of Cabernet (1981) is rather over-powerful, almost rummy, and disappointing after previous vintages. *(Laymont & Shaw)*

Marqués de Alella Brand from Alta Alella SA, the only large company producing Alella wines, superbly equipped, in a very modern winery. Try this pleasant, fresh, off-dry white [£]. *(Espavino)*

Masía Bach Sweet dessert wines are making a spirited comeback, and the Catalonia region specialises in luscious wines from the Moscatel and Malvasía grapes. The best known, and probably the best, is **Extremisimo Bach** [£££], made by Masía Bach, a company owned by the giant sparkling wine producer Codorníu. Extremisimo is oak matured, deep, full-flavoured and lusciously sweet. There is also a fairly good red. *(Codorníu UK)*

Raïmat Large estate in Lerida in the West of Catalonia, also owned by Codorníu. Reds contain Cabernet (the most expensive, 100 per cent) [££], the whites Chardonnay (an oaked 100 per cent Chardonnay may be imported to Britain for the first time in 1985) [££]. Some of the finest winemaking equipment in Spain. Whites much improved since the 1983 vintage. *(Victoria Wine, Hatch Mansfield)*

Bodegas Torres Denominación de Origen Penedès. Far and away the best known Catalan wine producer. Long established family firm, constantly innovative in vinification techniques. Along with Jean León, one of the first to adapt French, German and Alsace grape varieties to the Penedès. Dry, fresh and fruity Viña Sol [£], Gran Viña Sol [££] (with a proportion of Chardonnay) and Gran Viña Sol Green Label [£££] (with a proportion of oak-aged Sauvignon Blanc); semi-dry Viña Esmeralda [££], a spicy blend of Muscat d'Alsace and Gewürztraminer. Reds are aged for a maximum of two years in oak and are consequently very fruity: full-bodied Tres Torres [£] (Garnacha and Cariñena), and Coronas [£]–[££] from local varieties with its Reserva Gran Coronas [££], incorporating 50 per cent Cabernet Sauvignon. Recently released is the Gran Magdala [£££], which blends together Pinot Noir and Pinot Meunier, big brother to the Pinot Noir and Cariñena blend, Viña Magdala [££]. The 'Gran Coronas' Black Label [£££] is very good, rich wine, and is now a blend of 90 per cent Cabernet Sauvignon and ten per cent Cabernet Franc. *(Sichel – very widely stocked)*

Vallformosa Large estate in Penedès, producing excellent reds [£] *(Sainsburys)*

BEST BUYS

Whites

All the Torres whites *(Very widely stocked)*, Raïmat Chardonnay Blanco *(Victoria Wine)*, Cavas del Castillo Perelada NV *(Hay Wine Co, House of Townend)*

Reds

All the Torres reds *(Very widely stocked)*, Valformosa *(Ehrmanns, and Sainsbury's)*, Raïmat Abadia *(Victoria Wine)*

NAVARRA

The vineyards of Navarra adjoin the north-east edge of those of Rioja. The more far-sighted producers are abandoning the traditional heavyweight red and rosé wines made from the Garnacha, in favour of lighter, fruitier wines from the Tempranillo grape for red wines, and the Viura for whites. Look out for some big improvements in the next couple of years. Navarra wines are generally less expensive all round than Riojas, and for under £3 there are already some very good, well-made, basic wines to be found, especially those that have not been aged in oak, and more particularly the following:

Names to look out for

Agronavarra Under the brand names **Agramont** [££] (the top quality) and **Campo Nuevo** [£] (very good, basic quality), excellent, fresh, young reds, whites and rosés, new to the British market *(importer about to be appointed).*

Julian Chivite Quite fresh, clean, well-made wines, especially the **Gran Fuedo** [£] range. *(Laymont & Shaw)*

Monte Ory Brand name of Bodegas Villafranca. Interesting red 'nuevo' (nouveau style) [£], good reds [£]–[££] and quite good whites. *(Ehrmanns)*

BEST BUYS [£]–[££] Reds, whites and rosés of Agramont and Campo Nuevo

RIOJA

The 1983 vintage

The 1983 vintage should be a very satisfactory year in Rioja. Coming after the two splendid harvests of 1981 and 1982, 1983 had a lot to live up to, and was certainly a disappointment in terms of quantity, owing to a long drought. Quality is good for whites and reds.

Value for money

Although only about seven per cent down in quantity on the previous harvest, the price of grapes shot up in Rioja to twice that of last year. This will inevitably mean a small increase in the price that has to be paid per bottle in the UK. But red Riojas particularly still remain excellent value for money.

What to drink, what to keep

White Rioja
Gone are the days when white Rioja was either oaky, rich and a worthy rival to the great white Burgundies or, quite frankly, not a pleasant drink. Nowadays, apart from the bodegas which still produce those splendidly traditional wines, every Rioja exporter can turn out fresh, fruity white wines, fermented cool and bottled young. They are often recognisable by a pineapply-fruit style, often a little neutral. They are made to be drunk young, too, and are generally beginning to tire by the time the next vintage is out of the vats. So don't be fobbed off with 1981s or 1982s. *Insist on 1983 young style whites and, as soon as they become available, buy the 1984s.*

The traditionalist bodegas, the exceptions to this rule, are the Marqués de Murrieta, CVNE, López de Heredia, La Rioja Alta and Paternina. In every case, the best wines are the Crianzas and Reservas. They will have spent enough time in wood to gain the deep vanilla flavour that balances the sharp fruit of the Viura grape from which these wines are made.

Recommended vintages for 'old-style' whites: 1981, 1980, 1978, 1973, 1970.

Red Rioja

It is difficult to generalise about which vintages are available now, or what style to expect. The climate in Rioja does vary more from year to year than in other areas of Spain, but differences are to be put down rather more to the winemaking policy of the different firms than to the vagaries of the weather.

Traditionally in Rioja, red wine is barrel-aged, often in old oak barrels, though the best bodegas will renew their barrels, on a rotation basis, every five years or so, to give new oak flavour to their wines. (Flavour merchants claim to do big business in Rioja with oak-type flavourings and extracts, too!) Different bodegas have different policies as far as wood ageing is concerned, some ageing their wines for the minimum legal time, some preferring to have them longer in wood. A lighter vintage will also generally spend less time in wood than a fuller wine. Time in wood varies also with the different qualities of red Rioja – Crianza, Reserva and Gran Reserva. The best, richest wines of the vintage will generally be selected for the Gran Reservas, for longer wood ageing, the next best for Reserva wines, and the rest will be sold younger, as Crianza wines (*see below for definitions*). And styles of winemaking vary enormously from bodega to bodega.

Until the last few years, there was much jiggery-pokery with vintages, blending years together and claiming that the wine was from a single vintage, and/or that wines were older than in reality. The authorities in Rioja have considerably tightened up on this. But it's worth bearing in mind, particularly if you're buying Rioja vintages of the mid-'70s or earlier. In general, however, the following vintages are now on sale in Britain:

Wines without barrel-ageing 1983, 1982, 1981.
Crianza wines 1981, 1980, 1979, 1978.
Reserva wines 1979, 1978, 1976, 1975, 1973.
Gran reserva wines 1975, 1973, 1970.

There may also be isolated occurrences of wines from older vintages, such as 1964 and 1955, on restaurant lists and from some specialist merchants. *The best recent vintages for red wine are 1982, 1981, 1978, 1976, 1975, 1973 and 1970.*

Understanding the Rioja label

Rioja labels, indeed, Spanish labels in general, are not very informative. But matters have progressed from the old days when the date on a label bore as much relationship to the year in which the wine was made as to the winemaker's telephone number. Now, at least 85 per cent of the wine in a bottle on which the vintage is marked *must* be from the vintage stated. Well, 85 per cent is better than none! But the following terms do contribute to one's knowledge of what is inside the Rioja bottle:

Clarete Red wine of a lighter style than most. The term is not much used nowadays.

Cosechero *(See Nuevo).*

Crianza 'Nursing' literally – aged wine – but not very. The legal minimum is 12 months in oak cask and 12 in bottle, for both white and red.

Gran reserva The tops. Minimum periods are two years in barrel, followed by three in bottle, for reds, and four years for whites and rosés, of which six months must be in barrel. In addition, red wines must have lain at the same bodega for a minimum of seven years. Not every bodega uses 'gran reserva' as a description when entitled to do so. In a good vintage, about a third of a bodega's production will be made into reservas and gran reservas.

Nuevo Rioja's answer to Beaujolais Nouveau. Made in the same way, with no ageing in barrel.

Reserva Good quality wine, aged for a minimum of three years, of which one must be in barrel for red wines. Whites and rosés have a shorter minimum period, two years, of which six months must be in barrel.

Tinto Full-bodied red wine. Some bodegas, Muga, for example, make a very pale, delicate red, and still call it tinto.

Viña Vineyard.

Names to look out for

Bodegas Alavesas Soft, light but concentrated red wines, made, unusually, almost entirely from grapes from one area only, the Rioja Alavesa. The Crianza and Reservas are sold as Solar de Samaniego, and there is also a young, partially carbonic maceration red (very fruity because the grapes are fermented whole, all air excluded), with a delicious, fragrantly plummy character. *(Arriba Kettle)*

Bodegas Berberana Modernists who believe in starting the maturation of red wines in new barrels (to take up more oak flavour), and then bottling sooner. In the young wines, this gives an immediate, fruity character, and those that have spent two years in barrel (Grants of St James's Rioja, for instance) have more of Rioja's typical oaky-vanilla flavour and aroma. *(Michael Druitt Wines Ltd)*

Bodegas Beronia Owned by Gonzales Byass, the famous sherry house, and producers of good, soft, oaky reds, and good fresh whites.

Bodegas Campo Viejo A real 'factory', but capable of making excellent red wine. Huge installations on the edge of Logroño turn out enormous quantities. The reds are all made in a plummy, fruity style, except the prestige brand, Marqués de Villamagna, which is concentrated, oaky and soft. *(Gonzales Byass UK Ltd)*

CVNE (Compania Vinicola del Norte de España) One of the oldest bodegas, and producer of an excellent range of traditional-style wines. Monopole is one of the few well-made old-style white Riojas, a blend of fresh fruit with oak. The reds are impressive throughout, from the Clarete to the Imperial Gran Reserva, plummily fragrant in the younger wines, and deepening and filling out in the reservas. *(Direct Wine Suppliers)*

Bodegas Faustino Good, well-made reds, in expensive-looking bottles, the Gran Reserva, Faustino I, coming complete with fake, sprayed-on dust. But inside the bottles, the wine is an attractive blend of oak and intense fruit, which repays keeping till fully mature. *(Findlater Matta)*

Bodegas Lagunilla Owned by Grand Metropolitan Hotels, a modern bodega producing reliable red wines. Soft, and very much the popular idea of what red Riojas should be *(Croft & Co)*

Bodegas Lan Modern producers of good young wines. Lan Blanco is one of the best new-style whites around, without the 'cardboardy' finish of many others. The red crianza wines are fragrantly reminiscent of the Côte de Beaune, with attractive, uncomplicated strawberry fruit well married to the oaky vanilla. *(Phipps Johnson)*

Bodegas López de Heredia A gloriously old-fashioned bodega, with its own cooperage, and cellars tunnelled into sandstone. A limited range of wines, called Tondonia, the white traditionally honeyed and nutty, the reds intensely strawberry-flavoured, with overtones of oak, delicate but concentrated. *(Roy Gunn Wines)*

Bodegas Marqués de Cáceres One of the most go-ahead properties in Rioja. Enrique Forner, the owner, studied in Bordeaux and still has a part share in two successful châteaux there. He was the first Rioja winemaker to install cooling equipment for white and rosé fermentation, and is still amongst the producers who make best use of it. He believes in making wine with grapes from a very small and specific area: in his case, the village of Cenicero, in the Rioja Alta. The maximum time his red wines spend in oak barrels is two years – the rest of their ageing is done in bottle. *(Caxton Wines)*

Bodegas Marqués de Murrieta When he first started at Ygay, outside Logrono, in 1877, the then Marqués won prizes for honey, olive oil, hops *and* wine. Now it's just wine, and wonderful wine at that. This is the most traditional bodega – everything is done by hand. They don't *sell* wine; people come to *buy*. Probably the best white Riojas, the Marqués de Murrieta whites typify the way in which Riojas can approach the character of great white Burgundy when carefully made and matured. The reds are made to last, with extra tartaric acid added (quite legally), and are positively unattractive when young. But it's worth buying the reserva early, and keeping it as one would a fine claret. *(Percy Fox & Co)*

Bodegas Montecillo Ultra-modern bodega owned by the giant Osborne sherry/brandy house. Highly mechanised, with a bulk wine storage area that would be a public lavatory attendant's fantasy – rows of dazzling white-tiled tanks. Good reds: Viña Cumbrero, light strawberry flavour with nice oakiness, and Viña Monty, a rich, complex reserva that ages very well. *(Teltscher Bros)*

Bodegas Muga Although founded only in 1932, this is one of the most traditionally minded bodegas. Isaac Muga still uses beaten egg whites to fine his wines. The reds are amongst the most delicate in Rioja, very light in colour and body, but full of unexpected aromas, with staying power. Muga is one of the best winemakers in the whole area. *(Sherston)*

Bodegas Federico Paternina One of the oldest, and newest, bodegas in Rioja. The frontage of the modern buildings in Haro comes straight out of *'Dallas'*, but the old cellars in Ollauri are encrusted with ancient fungus and filled with old bottles dating from 1872. Banda Azul *can* be very good. The 1981 is honeyed and reminiscent of good Cru Beaujolais. *(Wooley, Duval & Beaufoys Ltd)*

Bodegas La Rioja Alta Another Haro traditionalist producing one of the most successful ranges of wines in all Rioja. Metropole is another rare old-style white which works, and develops into rich, buttery harmony as it ages. The red Viña Alberdi sets the style for the rest in a curranty, minty way. Viña Arana, Viña Ardanza and finally Reserva 904 increase in complexity and character as the price mounts. *(Laymont & Shaw)*

Where to buy Riojas

Specialists

Laymont & Shaw, Truro, Cornwall agents for the excellent La Rioja Alta wines, with many other top bodegas on their list; **Sherston Wine Company, Malmesbury** UK agent for the ultra-traditional wines of Bodegas Muga, with comprehensive list of other fine Riojas; **Arriba Kettle, Birmingham** agent for the soft, attractive wines of Bodegas Alavesas, with three bodegas from the Rioja Alta region, La Rioja Alta, Marqués de Cáceres and Berberana, also featured. **Wines of Spain,**

Liverpool Bodegas Campo Viejo agents, offering a tinto at under £3 up and back to the 1970 Marqués de Villamagna Gran Reserva at £7, with wines from La Rioja Alta, Murrieta, CVNE, Riscal and Faustino along the way; **Corney & Barrow** city merchants offering a good selection from CVNE, old-style bodega in Haro. **Adnams of Southwold** carefully chosen list, with both old and new style whites (La Rioja Alta and Marqués de Cáceres), and good reds; **Dolamore** agents for Bodegas Bilbainas.

BEST RIOJA BUYS

[£] **white** 1983 Marqués de Cáceres Blanco *(very widely stocked)*, 1983 Lan Blanco *(Harveys, Sherston; importer: Phipps Johnson)*

[£] **red** 1980 Viña Alberdi *(Sainsbury)*

[££] **white** 1981 Monopole (Crianza), CVNE *(very widely stocked)*

[££] **red** 1975 Solar di Samaniego Reserva, Bodegas Alavesas *(Laymont & Shaw, D Byrne, Camden Wine & Cheese, Moreno Wines; importer: Arriba Kettle)*, 1975 Monty Reserva, Montecillo *(Howgate Wines, Vineyard Wine Stores, SE1; importers: Teltscher Bros)*, 1975 Viña Lanciano Reserva, Lancorta *(Waitrose, Malmaison; importer: Phipps Johnson)*, 1976 Viña Ardanza, La Rioja Alta *(J Moreno Wines, James Aitken, La Vigneronne; importer: Laymont & Shaw)*

OTHER SPANISH TABLE WINES

The Eastern Seaboard

The Eastern Seaboard, between Valencia and Alicante and stretching inland to Murcia and Albacete, houses six Denominations of Origin – Valencia, Alicante, Almansa, Utiel-Requena, which produce mainly red wines for local consumption and blending, and which are seldom seen on the UK market – plus **Jumilla** and **Yecla** to the south of the region, which make mainly full-bodied red wines, mainly in co-operatives. Those imported into the UK are of the best, the most suited to Northern European palates. Historically, the wines have been very high in alcohol – sometimes as high as 18° – but the more enlightened producers have now started to make much lighter wines.

Vintages this far south are fairly unimportant, as the weather is so consistently good, so if a vintage is indicated, look for the younger ones.

The areas are dominated by two massive co-operatives – **San Isidro** in Yecla and **La Purisima** in Jumilla. Apart from these, look for **Bodegas Bleda** in Jumilla and their **Castillo de Jumilla** at around £2. Also from Jumilla is an own-label wine from *Sainsbury's* at about the same price. However, the star of the region must be Viña Montana from Yecla, a wine with sufficient elegance to suggest it may have been produced further north.

BEST BUY [£] *Sainsbury's* Jumilla 1978 from Castillo de Los Molinos at under £2, [£] Viña Montana from Yecla, also under £2. *(City Wines, Norwich)*

The Central Plateau

The Central Plateau comprises three separate Denominations of Origin – Mentrida, La Mancha and Valdepeñas – the last lying within La Mancha. Mentrida and La Mancha produce a great deal of Spain's basic blending wines, and for years they have been very ordinary, and the subject of great abuse, most of it deserved. However, things are changing. A new range of **Don Cortez** wines [£] has been produced, ranging in style from a dry white to a full red, and for the price, well under £2 per bottle, they are good.

Valdepeñas has always been rated as the best of the region and although the production is mainly of whites, the reds are by far the best. They are made from the classic red grape of Spain – the Tempranillo, although here it is known as the Cencibel. Most of the reds are aged for two years in wood and take a little time in bottle to settle down, so *the 1978s, if still available, and the 1980s are the years to look for.* Again, avoid anything from 1979. The best producers are **Visan**, who make a red Castillo de Mudela at around £2 *(Moreno)* and **Bodegas Felix Solis**, who produce a red Viña Albalí, at around £2. *(Sainsbury's and Ehrmanns)*

To the north of Madrid, there are two more areas worthy of note. Firstly, **Rueda**, making mainly white wines from the Viura and Verdejo grapes. These are wines for drinking young and are normally produced without a vintage date. The most notable is the *Marqués de Riscal* white (the red is a Rioja). The wine is produced in two styles, a young fresh, fruity white [£], and a Reserva Limousin [££] which has been aged in wood and is a much firmer, mature wine which could be kept for a couple of years. *(Hatch Mansfield/Victoria Wine)*

The upper valley of the Douro, in Spain called the Duero, is the recently created appellation of **Ribera del Duero**. Here are produced some very good, firm red wines, the most famous being *Vega Sicilia* [£££], from a vineyard planted in the last century in Bordeaux grape varieties. The wine will age for a very long time and is probably at its peak at about thirty years. From the same source come more quickly maturing red wines under the Valbuena [£££] label. Even this latter must be considered an expensive wine *(Laymont & Shaw)*. The co-operative at Peñafiel also makes fine red wines from the local Tinto del País. The finest quality appears under the *Protos* [£££] brand, younger wines under the name Ribera Duero [£]–[£££] *(Laymont & Shaw)*. Another excellent producer of red wines is **Antonio Fernández**, whose **Tinto Pesquera** appears without a vintage, but in a range of qualities. Some excellent red wines have also just been imported from Bodegas Peñalba Lopez under the brand name Torremilanos.

Where to buy Spanish wines

Specialists Arriba Kettle, Ehrmanns, Laymont & Shaw, Martinez Fine Wine, Mi Casa, J Moreno, Sherston Wine Co, Wines of Spain of Liverpool.
Supermarkets Sainsbury's Waitrose, Tesco.

The following also stock a good range: Cullens, Bottoms Up, Oddbins, Tanners of Shrewsbury, Lay & Wheeler, Hynard Hughes of Leicester, Waters of Coventry, David Byrne of Clitheroe.

BEST BUYS [£] Don Cortes *(Victoria Wine)*, Castillo de Mudela *(Moreno)*, Viña Albalí *(Sainsbury's; importer: Ehrmanns)*

SHERRY AND MONTILLA

Sherry is a fortified wine from the south-west of Spain, strengthened with grape alcohol to about 17.5°, though some sherries can attain this strength without aid. Montilla is another Andalusian wine, grown on similar calcareous slopes in the hills near Córdoba, in the south of Spain, east of Jerez. Similar to sherry in many ways, it can be drunk whenever sherry is appropriate, but has different nuances of flavour, even the best being far less fine and complex than the better sherries. It is also cheaper.

Value for money

Compared with most quality wines, sherry is very cheap and Montilla even cheaper, so the value on offer is excellent. The very cheapest of either is never a good buy, though. The quality you get by paying a little more is disproportionately higher and the most expensive wines are often the best value of all.

Understanding the label

The following are the various styles, beginning with the lightest and going on to the heaviest and sweetest. But remember that all sherry is by nature dry. It is sweetened by blending with specially prepared wines.

Manzanilla The lightest style of sherry (a bit like a fino, though more delicate), matured in cool bodegas by the estuary of the Guadalquivir. Generally very dry and best served chilled. Manzanilla deteriorates very quickly, even unopened, so try to make sure you buy it from a shop with a quick turnover, and treat it as a light wine – drink it up in a few days.

Fino Light in style and colour with a fine aroma and pronounced flavour. Best when very dry. Fino also deteriorates rapidly, so the same advice goes as for manzanilla. Serve chilled.

Amontillado Darker than fino in colour with a 'nutty' aroma and great depth of flavour. As these come about through age, amontillado must be relatively expensive if genuine. Alas, many of the wines shipped as amontillados are not – they are simply young wines sweetened to the medium sweetness the British have been led to expect of 'amontillado'. Although sometimes shipped bone dry, it does taste good blended with sweetening wine. But dry amontillados are delicious.

Medium A sherry or Montilla of any style blended with sweetening wine to be of medium sweetness.

Palo Cortado A sherry that can be produced only in small quantities, in style somewhere between an amontillado and an oloroso but with a subtle distinction of its own – great fragrance and depth. Usually shipped bone dry, but occasionally sweetened. Genuine Palo Cortado is very expensive [£££].

Oloroso Darker in colour than an amontillado, with a different and less penetrating aroma and a blander flavour. Rarely shipped bone dry, it is well adapted to be sweetened as a dessert wine. Dry, old ones are delicious.

Cream A sweetened dessert sherry or Montilla oloroso blended to be light in colour. Pale Cream is now very popular, usually made from sweetened fino sherry, but particularly light oloroso can be used.

Amoroso A relatively light but sweet oloroso sherry blend.

Brown Sherry A very dark, very sweet oloroso blend, usually of mediocre quality.

These are the principal kinds. There are a vast number of subtle variants, though, some of which have special, but rarely encountered, names. Many sherries and Montillas are sold under fancy names or distinguished by their degree of sweetness rather than style.

Names to look out for

Some of the small and little-known houses ship good wine. It is impossible to list all of them. The largest group, controlling about half the sherry trade, is Rumasa, part of a conglomerate recently taken over by the state. Even though the future is uncertain, at present the individual houses are left to go their own way. Here are some of the reliable sherry names:

Barbadillo Spanish house in which Harveys have an interest. Notable for their excellent **manzanillas**, also very good **fino** [£]–[££]. *(Hicks & Don)*

Croft An English company. Ships a small range of good wines. *(IDV)*

Domecq A very large, Spanish house shipping excellent wines such as fino **La Ina** [££], an amontillado, **Botaina**, and a dry oloroso, **Rio Viejo** [££]. *(Dent & Reuss)*

Duff Gordon Independent Spanish. **El Cid** [££] is one of the better medium sherries. *(City Vintagers)*

Garvey Part of Rumasa. **Fino San Patricio** [££], amontillado **Tio Guillermo** [££], oloroso **Flor de Jerez** [££] and other high quality wines. *(Garvey (UK) Ltd)*

Gonzalez Byass A very large, independent, Anglo-Spanish firm with a fine range of wines. The best known is their excellent **Tio Pepe** [££]. **Elegante** [£] is a cheaper, good fino. Their **Apostoles** [£££] range of very special wines is expensive and worth every penny. *(Gonzalez Byass UK)*

Harvey English. They ship a very extensive range. Luncheon Dry is a fair fino at a very competitive price, **Fine Old Amontillado** [£££] and **Palo Cortado** [£££] are both excellent. *(Harveys of Bristol)*

La Riva Connected with Domecq. **Tres Palmas** is a pungent, dry, austere fino [££].

Emilio Lustau Independent Spanish house. The Dry Lustau range of excellent dry sherries [£] and also **almacenista sherries** [££]–[£££] *(see below)*.

Osborne The same company as Duff Gordon but shipping a different range of not very exciting wines. *(Teltscher Bros)*

Ruiz Mateos, Zoilo A Rumasa company – indeed its abbreviated name is the origin of the 'Rumasa' name. **Don Zoilo Fino** [££] is an intense, aromatic, spicily complex wine, rather fuller than most finos.

Sancho Romate Excellent **Fino Marismeno** [££], one of the best. *(Ehrmanns)*

Sandeman Now owned by Seagrams. They ship a wide range of sherries including one of the better **pale creams**. *(Sandeman UK)*

Valdespino An independent Spanish house whose excellent wines include the fino **Inocente** [££] and amontillado **Tio Diego** [££].

Williams & Humbert Part of Rumasa, shipping a wide range of good wines including a fino, **Pando** [££], a well-known medium sherry, **Dry Sack** [££], and an excellent palo cortado, **Dos Cortados**. *(European Vintners Ltd)*

Wisdom & Warter Connected with Gonzalez Byass. Good wines include dry **Royal Palace** amontillado [££]. *(House of Townend)*

Almacenista sherries

Almacenistas are private wholesalers, often doctors or lawyers or other professionals who dabble in sherry in their spare time, selling it in 'parcels' of one or more barrels. These are very individual sherries, some of the most interesting and delicious on the market, and a range

> You can get help in contacting stockists, through the importers, from The Sherry Institute of Spain, 22 Manchester Square, London W1; TEL 01–935 6140.

is offered here by *Emilio Lustau UK Ltd (Arch 12, Leake Street, London SE1 7BE; tel: 01-928 4390)*, who will provide a list of stockists in your area. **Deinhard** have their own label almacenista range – an excellent manzanilla passada [££], dry amontillado and very old oloroso [£££]. Stockists of these can also be obtained from the offices of Emilio Lustau UK Ltd.

Where to buy sherry

Most merchants have at least some sherries under their own labels. Those with particularly extensive and interesting lists include:

Adnams of Southwold (long list including good old olorosos); Arriba Kettle, Birmingham (lists a range of recommended shippers' sherries); Averys of Bristol (extensive range of excellent wines, Elizabetha fino, Oloroso 4th Criadera, dry); Berry Bros & Rudd, London (includes old bottled sherries); Findlater, Mackie, Todd, London (Tia Lola, fino and Cecilia amontillado); Laymont & Shaw, Truro (long list of good shippers' wines); Tanners, Shrewsbury (excellent, wide range; Mariscal Manzanilla and Jerez Cortado are good examples).

BEST BUYS: [£] Manzanilla and Fino de Balbaina from Barbadillo *(Laymont & Shaw, Windrush Wines, Laurence Smith; agents: Hicks & Don)*, [££] Tio Guillermo, Amontillado, Garvey *(Laymont & Shaw)*, [£££] Jerez Cortado *(Tanners)*, [£££] Oloroso 4th Criadera *(Averys)*, [££]–[£££] Deinhard almacenista sherries *(G C Harvey of Norwich, Alex Findlater, La Vigneronne, Evingtons of Leicester, Les Amis du Vin)*.

Málaga

An old favourite in this country, now making something of a comeback, is **Málaga**, also from the deep South. Most commonly, this is a very grapy dessert wine, but can appear in drier styles. The British market is dominated by **Scholtz Hermanos** *(Laymont & Shaw)* but look also for the wines of **Larios** (better known for their gins), **Lopez Hermanos** and **Bacarles**.

For further information on Spanish wines contact: Vinos de España, 22 Manchester Square, London W1; tel: 01-935 6140.

South Africa

White wines from South Africa are invariably made from the Chenin Blanc grape (also called Steen) and range from bone dry through off dry, flowery (owing to a little residual sugar) to late harvested sweet styles. Red wines will either be straight Cabernet Sauvignon, Pinotage (the only native South African grape) or blends, usually with some Cabernet Sauvignon content. They will vary from the dry, slightly hard type to the supple, lightish, softly fruity versions.

The 1984 vintage

On average, the quality in South Africa in 1984 is good, better than 1983, with the red wines from the better areas showing plenty of promise.

But for many producers, heat waves pushed sugar levels up and kept acidity levels down, always a problem in the Cape. Unusually, rot was a big problem, and equally unusually in some areas, the different grape varieties reached maturity almost simultaneously, giving the wine-makers difficulties. The hot spells took their greatest toll in the non-irrigated quality growing areas of Stellenbosch and Paarl. Stellenbosch's crop was 13.5 per cent down on 1983, and Paarl nine per cent, but the higher sugar levels have favoured the red wines, which showed good colour and varietal character. Despite problems with acidity levels, some fine white wines were made from the Steen grape, and in the Breede River Valley, a key area for quality white wines, similar results were obtained.

Value for money

South African wines are fair value at all price levels if your politics permit.

What to drink now

It has only really been in the last decade that the concept of cellaring wines to allow them to mature further in bottle has become part of the drinking pattern of the South African wine lover. So it is only recently that the wineries, large and small, have started to respond to the market for such wines.

White wines generally are made fresh, crisp and ready for immediate drinking, red wines light bodied, quick maturing and drinkable in the warm to hot South African climate.

A handful of estate wines have always had the potential for bottle maturation, particularly the full, deep, old-style reds. Now the big wineries and many more estates are producing such wines, and with the introduction of Chardonnay and Sauvignon Blanc vines, some white wines are also being produced that will age in bottle.

In Britain, almost all the South African wines available are ready for immediate drinking. The white wines will improve no further, and should be drunk for their youthful charm. The red wines are generally ready, though a year or two in the cellar will do them no harm.

Understanding the South African label

South Africa has its own appellation laws, called the **Wine of Origin System** [WOS]. Not all wines come under this system, as a winemaker may be using grapes grown outside a defined growing area or new grape varieties not yet officially approved. The wine may be just as good as wines within the WOS rules. In Britain, it is unlikely that any wines will be found that are not Wines of Origin.

The WOS is essentially a guarantee of the claims made by the producer on his label, in regard to the area of origin, the grape variety used, and the vintage. To get this authentication, the producer must provide certain information to the issuing authority, and the wine must pass tasting tests carried out by an independent panel.

The WOS is indicated by a small certificate glued to the neck of a bottle of South African wine, covering part of the capsule. The certificate, usually referred to as the 'bus ticket' by the producers, is white. On it are three colour bands: blue, indicating the wine has been certified as coming from the region, district or ward where the grapes were grown; green, indicating that the wine is made from the grape variety specified on the label (though this may not necessarily mean it is a 100 per cent varietal wine) and has the characteristics of that variety; and red, certifying the vintage date, though under the current rules, the wine need be only 75 per cent of the year indicated.

Because a large amount of blending goes on in South Africa, some wines may be certified for, say, only vintage, and not area of origin or grape variety. Some may be certified for two of the three, some for all three, and it is largely up to the producer to decide which of the criteria he asks his wine to be certified for.

The WOS certificate is not a guarantee of quality, only of authenticity. However, if the 'bus ticket' is gold in colour, it indicates that the wine is **Superior**, a new category introduced in 1982 involving further tests to determine whether the wine is 'superior of its type'.

The 'bus ticket' may also have a strip on it with the word **'Estate'** which means that the wine comes from grapes grown and vinified on one of the sixty-odd Cape wine estates, roughly equivalent to a château or domaine in concept, though certainly not in appearance, and all privately owned.

Names to look out for

The South African wine industry is dominated by three companies: the Oude Meester group (**Fleur du Cap, Grunberger, Stellenryck** and **Cellar Cask** labels), the Ko-operative Wijnbouwers Vereniging (**KWV** labels) and Stellenbosch Farmers' Winery (the **Nederburg** range). Most of the South African wines available in Britain come from these three wineries, all of which produce sound wines [££].

Two other big producers also represented here are Gilbeys South Africa (Bertrams labels) and Union Wine (the Bellingham and Culemborg labels). A very limited amount of estate wine from a handful of producers is also available [££]–[£££]: **Meerlust, De Wetshof, Meerendal, Fairview, Backsburg, Spier, Le Bonheur, Twee Jongegezellen and Koopmaskloof.** This is of excellent quality.

Where to buy South African wine

The importer specialising in Cape wines is Cape Province Wine Importers. Another specialist is Jeffrey Phillips. Henry C Collison (owned by the Oude Meester Group) has a wide selection of wines from the parent company, plus wines from several estates. David Baillie Vintners stock a fair range. The Cape Wine Centre in Soho was due to close down as we went to press.

BEST SOUTH AFRICAN BUYS [£] KWV Chenin Blanc, KWV Roodeberg *(Victoria Wine, Arthur Cooper, Threshers, Gough Bros, Roberts, Cullens)*, [£] KWV Cape Foret 1982 [wood matured Chenin Blanc] *(W H Cullen)*, [££] Fleur du Cap Chenin Blanc *(Community Wines, Bristol, Cape Province Wines, Jeffrey Phillips, J W Lees, Le Riche Stores)*, [££] Grunburger Steen *(Victoria Wine, Cape Province Wines)*, [££] Fleur du Cap Cabernet Sauvignon *(Collisons, Cape Province Wines)*, [££] Nederburg Paarl Riesling *(Dolamore)*, [££] Nederburg Fonternel (semi-dry white) *(Dolamore)*, [££] Nederburg Cabernet Sauvignon *(Dolamore)*, [£££] Nederburg Edelkeur (botrytised dessert wine) *(Cape Province Wines – also older vintages)*, [£££] Meerlust Estate 1980 Cabernet Sauvignon *(Henry Collison, Cape Province Wines)*, [£££] Meerlust Estate 1980 Rubicon *(Henry Collison, Cape Province Wines)*.

South America

The wines of South America that are pertinent to the British market come from the neighbouring slopes and plains of the Andes mountains in Chile and Argentina.

ARGENTINA

Obviously this country has taken a back seat over the last two years. Wines like Franchette and other own-labelled wines had gained a fine reputation at the bottom end of the market. The leading varietal wines were Andean Cabernet Sauvignon (1975) and Andean Chardonnay (1980) which are still available at Cullens for around £3. The Cabernet is drinking superbly, whereas the Chardonnay is now rather blowsy.

Owing to a surfeit of wine and the Argentinians' need for currency, the Russians bought 25 million litres of wine at 1 US cent per litre for sale in the USSR! But the wine lake remains, so if the merchants in Britain, and of course the public, can be enticed back in due course, there will be some good bargain wine from Argentina.

CHILE

When one of the great winemakers of the world decides to cross both an ocean and a continent to grow grapes, there must be a good reason.

Miguel Torres, from Penedès, Spain, has done just this. Chilean reds have always had a fine reputation, but the whites appealed only to the local community. Miguel Torres immediately adopted the method of cold fermentation for the vinification of his white wines. The Chileans objected to this new crisp taste, but we are already benefiting. The 1984 vintage is very good.

Understanding the Chilean label

Chilean wines are all of a varietal nature whether single (Cabernet Sauvignon) or blended (Sauvignon/Sémillon) with the predominant grape named first. Single grape variety wines almost without exception are 100 per cent as stated, although the law does not require it.

What to drink now, what to keep

Concha y Toro have a wide range. Their **box wines** which are 75 per cent Cabernet/25 per cent Merlot for red and 90 per cent Sauvignon/ten per cent Sémillon for white, are two of the few quality wines that are packaged this way; their alcohol content (12°) makes them relatively sound. They work out at between £14–£15 per 5 litres. Concha y Toro's **Cabernet Sauvignon** (1980) [£] is sold to drink now, but a few more years in bottle would greatly enhance its quality. The **Oro del Rhin** [£] (blend of Sauvignon, Muscat and Sémillon) will be enormously improved by refrigeration techniques in the vinification. Watch for the 1984 vintage. The two newcomers are a **sparkling rosé** which, although rather orange in colour, is quite pleasant, and the **1983 Chardonnay** [££], fully flavoured and an infinite improvement on the 1981 Cousiño Macul Chardonnay, which is most disappointing. However, the current **Cousiño Macul Antiguas Reservas Cabernet Sauvignon 1977** [££] is the best vintage since 1973. Beautifully balanced, with good fruit and tannin, this wine should be laid down for five years to reach perfection. One of the great wines of the New World.

The secret of the Torres white wines will be to balance the inherent character of Chilean wine with the freshness and acidity produced by cold fermentation. The 1984 Viña Santa Digna is the best produced so far, recognisably Sauvignon and a good, fresh, fruity and enjoyable wine.

Where to buy Chilean wines

The main importers are *Valdeca* from Rottingdean (Concha y Toro and Cousiño Macul), *Christophers* (Cousiño Macul), *Stevens Garnier* (Viña Linderos), and *Sichel* (Torres). Retailers include *Cullens, Victoria Wine, Waitrose, Oddbins, and The Wine Society*.

BEST BUYS [£] Concha y Toro Cabernet Sauvignon *(Cullens, and quite widely elsewhere)*, [££] Cousiño Macul Antiguas Reservas Cabernet Sauvignon 1977 *(Christophers, Cullens, La Vigneronne, Balls Bros, Henry Townsend)*, [£] Viña Santa Digna 1984, Torres *(Bottoms Up, Tanners)*

Switzerland

When your cheapest wine starts at £5, high quality must be instantly recognisable. This is unfortunately not so in the case of Switzerland. A strong currency, limited supplies and a buoyant home market have prevented a serious look at an export market. For experimentation, the *Swiss Centre*, Leicester Square, London, is the main source of supply for our market. The whites from the Vaud and the Valais are best.

USA

CALIFORNIA

The 1983 vintage

The 1983 vintage was not a great one and goes to prove that the weather is not always perfect in California. The wines will be on the light side and quite high in acid. Quantity was below that of 1982 by an average of 20 per cent. Fine wines were made, but it is a vintage where the name and reputation of the producer will be all-important when choosing which wines to buy.

Napa Valley 1983 was a mixed vintage where only the best makers produced fine wine. More than twice the average rainfall, both before and during the harvest, caused severe problems of rot in the vineyards. But by careful grape selection, some fine wine has been made. The whites look a better bet than the reds, which may be on the light side. Generally, wine made from grapes harvested after late September will not be as good as that made from early-picked grapes.

Sonoma County Heavy rains in September caused real problems for this area. Very selective picking was necessary and production was down between 20 and 50 per cent on 1982. Again, white wines seemed to have fared better than reds and as one would imagine, some superb botrytised Rieslings, Gewürztraminers and Sauvignon Blancs have been made.

Mendocino County Problems caused by heavy rains were compounded by a 100° heatwave in July, which damaged grape skins, making them even more vulnerable to rot. Almost 40 per cent of the crop was lost to rot and much of the wine made from this area will be no better than average.

Monterey County and Santa Barbara County Although above average rainfall was suffered in the southern area, it was not quite as great as on the North Coast. However, loss from rot was around 30 per cent and selective picking was essential. Cabernet was markedly better here than in most North Coast areas and generally the reds seem good. Whites on the other hand, look unbalanced and seem no better than average.

Value for money

Prices do not seem to be going up in California and we can hope for stabilisation and even some price reductions. Thanks to large crops in 1981 and 1982, there is no shortage of wine, and competition from Europe is encouraging keen prices and making California wines a better buy than for many years, despite the strong dollar.

What to drink, what to keep

In white varietals, the **1982 Chardonnays** are now available and are mostly of good quality, ready for drinking. Try also the **1981 Chardonnays** as these are drinking well now. The **1980s** were a mixed bunch, mostly rather high in alcohol and tending to be out of balance, so best avoided unless you know the wine.

For red varietals, go for the **1978 Cabernets**, if you can find them. This was an excellent vintage for all red wines. The **1979 reds** are well balanced, quite elegant and good for drinking now. Buy the **1980s** for big, rich wines with time ahead of them. Of the earlier vintages, *drink up the 1977s* as these are mostly at the top now, as are the *1975s*, though some of them will still benefit from further cellaring.

Understanding the California label

For the energetic enthusiast, the UK offers a rewarding range of California wines. But they do have to be sought out. Most of the famous names are represented over here and several of them are readily available. Indeed, it is difficult to find a supermarket which does not stock the Paul Masson Carafes.

California labels are often extremely informative and if read and understood can tell the drinker a great deal about the wine in the bottle. Many wines carry a back label, which may give extra information on the origins of the wine, the style of winemaking, and even a history of the winery.

On the front label, certain essential pieces of information appear: **The name of the vendor of the wine,** eg 'Joseph Phelps Vineyards'. This will be in large letters prominently displayed. Go then to the bottom of the label to find out more information about the vendor. Did he actually make the wine, and if so, did he make it from his own grapes or did he buy in grapes? Or did he simply buy the wine ready made and only bottle and label it?

If the phrase '**Estate grown**' or '**Grown, produced and bottled by**' features, then the wine has been made by the vendor from his own grapes. If '**Produced and bottled by**' appears, he will have bought in the grapes. (This is not a bad sign, as many winemakers prefer to leave grape growing to grape growers.) If simply '**Bottled by**' or even '**Cellared and bottled by**' appear, the wine will have been bought in bulk and finished off (filtered etc) by the vendor.

All this is useful information, but does not necessarily reveal the quality of the wine.

Grape variety If 75 per cent of the wine has been made from one grape, its name will normally be featured. It cannot by law be featured alone if its proportion is less than that percentage. The two most successful varietals are **Cabernet Sauvignon** and **Chardonnay**. As in Bordeaux, Cabernet will often be blended with another grape, usually Merlot, to add complexity, or otherwise to enhance the wine. A good producer will blend only to increase the quality of the wine, not to lower the cost. White grape varietals are not usually blended. In red wines, blending has become more accepted at home in America in the last few years and few labels now boast 100 per cent Cabernet as if this made their wine better than one with ten or 20 per cent Merlot.

Other varietals to look out for are (in red) **Zinfandel, Pinot Noir, Merlot, Syrah, Petite Sirah**, and, in white – **Sauvignon Blanc** (also called **Fumé Blanc**), **Chenin Blanc, Pinot Blanc, Johannisberg Riesling** and **Gewürztraminer**.

Brand names If the wine is a blend with no predominant grape, then it will have a brand name, eg Premium White. Usually this will denote a simple, everyday drinking wine with a price to match. Some notable exceptions are the **Joseph Phelps Insignia**, a blend of Cabernet Sauvignon, Merlot and Cabernet Franc and consistently one of California's greatest red wines, and the **Trefethen Eshcol** red and white wines which are better than many varietals.

Alcohol content Normally, the alcohol content will be printed. Under Californian law, this need only be accurate to within 1.5 per cent, so the figure may be only a rough guide. If the content is stated as 13 per cent or more, assume the wine will be rich and full-bodied. If less, the wine will be lighter and more suitable for lunchtime drinking. Most California Cabernets and Chardonnays are between 12.5 per cent and 14 per cent. Zinfandels and Pinot Noirs can go higher, while Rieslings and Gewürztraminers will be lower.

Sweet or dry? Indications of how dry or sweet the wine is will not always be apparent. The words **'Late Harvest'** or **'Selected Late Harvest'** indicate that the wine was made from grapes left on the vine, which will probably have been affected by botrytis (noble rot). These phrases will be found on Rieslings, Gewürztraminers, or Sauvignon Blancs, which will be dessert wines. A few Zinfandels are made from late-picked grapes, resulting in a port-style wine. Mayacamas is famous for 'Late Picked' Zinfandels.

Vintages Most varietals are vintage wines. The significance of each vintage in California is not so great as in France. However, each year produces wines of differing styles and, of course, knowing the age of the wine is important.

Production region The region most prominently marked will be where the grapes were grown. The actual winery could well be in another region. An example of this would be the fine Cabernet Sauvignon called York Creek (a Napa Valley vineyard) made by Ridge Vineyards (a

Santa Cruz Mountains winery). **The Napa Valley** is particularly well known for Cabernet and Chardonnay. Other good areas to look out for are the **Alexander Valley, Dry Creek Valley** and **Russian River Valley,** all in **Sonoma County,** and the **Edna Valley** and **Santa Ynez Valley** south of San Francisco. **Monterey County** and **Mendocino County** also make good wines.

California names to look out for

Beringer Vineyards (Napa Valley) Medium-sized producer of sound varietals. **Chardonnay** and **Cabernet** especially good. *(Victoria Wine)*

Buena Vista (Sonoma) Under new German owners, the wines have improved dramatically. Try their unique **'Spiceling'**, a blend of Riesling and Gewürztraminer. *(Wine Studio)*

Chalone Vineyards (Monterey) Very fine, small producer. **Chardonnay, Pinot Blanc** and especially **Pinot Noir**. *(Les Amis, Adnams)*

Chateau Montelena (Napa Valley) Tiny producer of superb **Cabernet** and **Chardonnay** at an appropriate price. *(Wine Studio)*

Chateau St Jean (Sonoma) White wine producer of great quality. **Chardonnay** and **botrytised Rieslings** particularly. Expensive. *(Majestic, Oddbins)*

Christian Brothers (Napa Valley) Large, historic winery. Quality is improving. Good value. *(Peter Dominic)*

Clos du Bois (Sonoma County) Medium-sized winery making sound **Cabernet, Chardonnay** and particularly **Merlot**. *(Majestic, Les Amis)*

Clos du Val (Napa Valley) Small producer with a French winemaker. Wines are elegant and well balanced. Particularly good **Merlot**. Also **Chardonnay** and **Cabernet**. *(Reid Wines, Averys)*

Dry Creek (Sonoma) Better whites than reds. **Fumé Blanc** and **Chenin Blanc** especially good. *(Wine Studio)*

Edna Valley Vineyards (Edna Valley) New producer of soft, fresh **Chardonnay**. Excellent value. *(The Market, Laytons, La Réserve, La Vigneronne)*

Firestone Vineyards (Santa Ynez) Drop-out members of the tyre-making family producing big, sturdy wines full of flavour. Well-made and good value. Try the **Merlot** particularly. *(Caves de la Madeleine, Sainsbury's, Bottoms Up, Justerini & Brooks)*

Freemark Abbey (Napa Valley) Old established small producer. Good **Chardonnay** and **Cabernet**. Expensive. *(Wine Studio)*

Gallo (Modesto) California's largest producer, making over 50 million cases a year. Much of it excellent plonk. The varietals are on the dull side. *(Wine Studio)*

Grgich Hills Cella (Napa Valley) Big, rich **Chardonnays at a high** price. *(Averys)*

Heitz Wine Cellars (Napa Valley) Famous small producer of top quality Cabernets from different vineyards, **Martha's Vineyard** and **Bella Oaks** being the best. Also good **Chardonnay** and **Zinfandel** wines. High prices. *(Les Amis, H Allen Smith, La Réserve, Wine Studio)*

Iron Horse (Sonoma County) Small producer making excellent **Cabernet** and **Chardonnay**. Now also making very good sparkling wine. *(Caves de la Madeleine, Wine Studio)*

Jordan Winery (Alexander Valley) A no-expense spared producer of excellent **Cabernet** and **Chardonnay**. Wines are elegant and mostly ready for drinking when released. *(Curzon Wine Co)*

Paul Masson (Sarratoga) Huge producer of the ubiquitous **Carafe**. Also makes decent varietals at modest prices. A reliable name in the medium-price range. Try their '**Pinnacle**' selection for a little extra quality. *(Wine Studio and many others)*

Mayacamas Vineyards (Napa Valley) Tiny producer of long-lasting **Cabernet** and **Chardonnay** of superb quality. Occasionally also port-style **late-harvest Zinfandel**. *(Wine Studio)*

Robert Mondavi Winery (Napa Valley) The bench-mark producer of all Napa Valley wines. Always reliable and lately excellent value, since prices in Britain dropped in late 1983, for marketing reasons. The **Fumé Blanc** never fails to impress and **Cabernet**, **Chardonnay** and even **Pinot Noir** are all high quality. Try the very good *'Reserve'* varietals. *(Lay & Wheeler, André Simon, Tanners, Bow Wine Vaults, Alex Findlater)*

Monticello Cellars (Napa Valley) New small producer making very good **Chardonnay**. *(Wine Studio)*

Opus One (Napa Valley) The new wine from the joint venture between Robert Mondavi Winery and Ch Mouton-Rothschild in Bordeaux. Both quality and price are very high. *(Wine Studio)*

Parducci Cellars (Mendocino County) A large, family-owned producer making straightforward no-nonsense wines. Always well made and good value. *(Adnams)*

Joseph Phelps Vineyards (Napa Valley) Excellent all-round producer of both red and white varietals. Particularly noted for **sweet Rieslings** and **Gewürztraminers**. *(Caves de la Madeleine)*

Ridge Vineyards (Santa Cruz Mountains) Small, old-established maker of fine **Zinfandel** and **Cabernet**. All wines are vineyard designated. The **Montebello Cabernet** is one of California's finest with a price to match. *(Adnams, La Vigneronne)*

Rutherford Hill (Napa Valley) Medium-sized producer offering good all-round quality varietals. *(Bibendum)*

Schramsberg Vineyards (Napa Valley) Historic producer of California's finest sparkling wines. Made in the same way as Champagne and of comparable quality. *(Buckingham Vintners, Bibendum, Les Amis)*

Stag's Leap Wine Cellars (Napa Valley) Small producer of superb **Cabernet**, **Merlot** and **Chardonnay**. Top quality. *(Corney & Barrow)*

Sterling Vineyards (Napa Valley) Small high quality producer of **Cabernet** and **Chardonnay**. Interesting **Sauvignon Blanc** in 'Graves style'. *(Caves de la Madeleine)*

Trefethen Vineyards (Napa Valley) Small producer of **excellent Chardonnay**. Good **Cabernet** and **Pinot Noir**. Also noted for their second wines under the *'Eshcol'* label. *(Wine Society, Bottoms Up, Lay & Wheeler, Tanners)*

Wente Bros (Alameda County) Medium-sized family producers. Good quality varietals at a reasonable price. *(Wine Studio)*

Mark West Vineyards (Russian River Valley) Elegant, high-acid **Chardonnays**. Also **late harvest Riesling**. *(Staypleton Fletcher, La Vigneronne)*

Where to buy California wines

Wine Studio Widest range of California wines in UK and older vintages.

Wine Society Society's red and white [££].

La Vigneronne Good range of older Cabernets and half-bottles.

Les Amis du Vin Own-label red and white [£]. Trefethen Eshcol [££] wines and Chalone Chardonnay [£££].

Adnams Ridge wines and Chalone [£££].

Sainsbury's Firestone Pinot Noir 1979 [£££], Robert Mondavi Fumé Blanc 1981 [£££].

Oddbins Geoffrey Roberts California Reserve Red [£] and Firestone Merlot 1979 [££].

Cullens *Geoffrey Roberts Reserve Red and White* £.

Justerini & Brooks *Parducci Cabernet Sauvignon* £££.

Bibendum *Good range. Schramsberg* sparkling wines £££.

Littlewoods *Own label red and white* £.

BEST CALIFORNIA BUYS *See above in* 'WHERE TO BUY CALIFORNIA WINES'

NEW YORK STATE

Until very recently almost unknown in Britain, the second largest wine-producing state in the USA is now turning out some really excellent and individual wines. These most emphatically do not include wines made from the native 'Labrusca' grapes which have been called 'foxy' by the charitable and some rather ruder names by the more forthright. Better are the wines made from such unfamiliar hybrid varieties as the Vidal, Ravat, Seyval Blanc (also now being grown with some success in this country), the Baco Noir, de Chaunac and the Maréchal Foch. All are characterful, combining flavour with a crisper acidity than is usually found in wines from California.

More to the European palate however are the better examples made from 'vinifera' (European type) grapes, such as the Cabernet Sauvignon and the Riesling. So far, whites are decidedly better than reds, with **Chardonnays** from **Gold Seal** in the Finger Lakes, and the **Hargrave Winery** on Long Island; **Rieslings** from **Great Western, Gold Seal** and **Glenora**; and **Cabernet** from **Hargrave**. Particularly interesting is the prospect of late-picked Rieslings and Eiswein from the cool winter Finger Lake Region to the north of the state. But New York State sparkling wines almost all seem to have a slightly bitter tang, which comes from the grape varieties used, and are not recommended. Gold Seal, however, is now making a Pinot Noir blanc de noirs of some class.

The commitment of Canadian giant (and Paul Masson owner) Seagram to three wineries in the Finger Lake Region would indicate that a larger selection of these wines is likely to reach Britain during 1985. Prices are often lower than their Californian counterparts, transport costs less savage, and styles more suited to European wine drinkers.

W H Cullen and *Harrods* stock **Gold Seal Chardonnay 1981** £££ and **Hargrave**. The *Great American Food & Wine Company* have **Gold Seal Riesling, Chardonnay** £££ and transfer method sparkling wine.

BEST BUYS £££ Gold Seal Chardonnay *(Cullens)*

> We should very much appreciate further comments and suggestions of establishments of particular interest to the wine lover. There are report forms at the back of this book.

NORTH-WEST USA

The 1983 vintage

This is likely to be one of the most successful vintages in the modern era of winemaking in the region.

Value for money

Prices should remain stable, since production has been going ahead even faster than demand. Like Californian prices, they are nevertheless high in the UK, owing to the exchange rate. Compared with fine Côte d'Or prices, however, they are not high, indeed often cheaper for wines which are more delicate in flavour, more European in style than California equivalents.

What to drink, what to keep

The following is a rough generalisation, based on the wines available now in Britain.

Pinot Noir (Oregon)

1982 Drink late 1985 to end of decade.

1980 Drink now, or lay down for up to three years.

Cabernet Sauvignon (Washington)

1981 Leave until 1986/7. Some will keep ten years.

1980 Drinkable now, and until 1988.

Riesling Best young and fresh.

Chenin Blanc Best young.

Chardonnay Unlike most California Chardonnays, these wines are likely to improve with age for two, three or more years, since their acidity is high. But the plantings are new, and there is as yet no track record.

Understanding the label

Most wines are identified quite simply by the name of the producer and the principal grape variety involved. North-West labelling laws are stricter than those in California. No European generic names such as 'Chablis' or 'Burgundy' are permitted.

In **Oregon**, the varieties to look for are **Pinot Noir** (lighter, more 'Burgundian' flavour than one would expect to find in California), **Riesling**, and **Chardonnay**, while in **Washington State**, **Cabernet Sauvignon** and **Merlot** are increasingly successful, in addition to the more popular and widespread **Riesling**.

Names to look out for

(All the following are available by mail order from Windrush Wines of Cirencester, who are importers of all the wines and will be able to supply names of other retailers for some of them)

Oregon

The Eyrie Vineyards David Lett's pioneer **Pinot Noir** vines, planted as early as 1966, produce stylish wines [£££] that have done most so far to establish the potential of the area. Low yields and intense care are reflected in high, but not inflated prices.

Knudsen Erath Oregon's largest and most versatile producer is right at the good end of the quality spectrum with its **Pinot Noir** [£££], **Chardonnay** [£££] and **Riesling** [£££]. Champagne method sparkling wines are now being released.

Tualatin Professional winemaking from Bill Fuller has produced fine **Riesling** [£££] and **Gewürztraminer** [££] and, more recently, fast improving **Pinot Noir** [£££] and **Chardonnay** [£££], with a style and balance very reminiscent of Burgundy.

Elk Cove Remarkable **Pinot Noir** [£££] now emerging, and some promising **Riesling** [£££], too. Small (Burgundian-style) grower/producer who has made great strides in the past four years. Grapes from different vineyard sites vinified separately, following traditional Burgundian techniques.

Washington State and Idaho

Ste Michelle The largest producer, with two enormous wineries, one near Seattle and a new, even larger one near the Columbia River in Eastern Washington. High quality and large volume production here prove that the two can go together.

Associated Vintners Well-established (1962) producer with David Lake MW as winemaker. Famous for their **Gewürztraminer** [££], but look out for an exciting though still very hard and young **1981 Cabernet** [££] from the Willow Creek Vineyard (Yakima Valley). The blended 'Valley White' can be a good buy too.

Preston Wine Cellars Washington's largest family-owned winery, run by genial, all-American Bill Preston. Second largest in the state, founded in 1976, produces a wide range of reliable and good value for money wines. Based at Pasco in Eastern Washington, surrounded by their own vineyards.

Ste Chapelle Vineyards high up (2,500 ft) in the Snake River valley. Best known for its **Chardonnay** [£££], rather Californian in style, but with higher acid to match the alcohol. Very promising late harvest **Riesling** and **Gewürztraminer**.

Quail Run Important new Yakima Valley winery making good medium-dry and late harvest **Riesling** [£££], also a Germanic style Aligoté.

Latah Creek Small producer near Spokane. Good **Riesling** and very interesting **Chenin Blanc** [££]+.

Where to buy North-West American wines

Distribution at present is limited, because the strength of the dollar in the past couple of years has discouraged potential importers from taking the risk. If your local merchant cannot help, try *Windrush Wines* in Cirencester. In London, the *Wine Studio* have one or two, and both *Adnams* and *Lay & Wheeler* in East Anglia may oblige.

BEST NORTH-WEST USA BUYS [££] Associated Vintners' Bordeaux-look-alike Cabernet *(Windrush Wines)*, [£££] Tualatin Chardonnay and Riesling *(Windrush Wines)*, [£££] Knudsen Erath Pinot Noir *(Windrush Wines)*, [£££] Ste Chapelle Chardonnay *(Windrush Wines)*.

For further information on all American wines, contact: American Chamber of Commerce, 75 Brook Street, London W1; tel: 01-493 0381.

Non-Champagne dry sparkling wines

Further details on the following dry sparkling wines, some cheap, some very expensive, will be found in the individual regions.

France

Blanquette de Limoux [££] A good fresh, appley sparkler from Languedoc-Roussillon, most being made in the very modern co-operative. There are two qualities of these co-operative wines on the British market, with about 40p between them. The better is brand-named 'Fleur de Lys', but both are very good. *(Oddbins, Christophers; importer: Christophers)*

Clairette de Die Brut [££] Good Champagne method sparkler from the Northern Rhône.

Sparkling Saumur [££] Clean, fruity, pleasant but rather neutral-tasting sparkling wines from Saumur, between Tours and Angers on the Loire. Most producers now add some Cabernet or Chardonnay to beef up the dull Chenin Blanc. Saumur Crémant is the finer, slightly more expensive version. In Champagne, 'crémant' means lower pressure, less fizz; in Saumur, a crémant will have just as much fizz as a Saumur mousseux but will have been made under much more stringent rules of production (lighter pressing of the grapes, longer maturation). Names to look out for especially are Gratien & Meyer *(Peter Dominic, Wine Society, Arthur Rackham)*, Veuve Amiot *(Threshers; importers: Stowells)* and Langlois-Château *(Bibendum; importers:Mentzendorff)*.

Vouvray [££] Firm, earthy-spicy, honey-fruit wines at their best, always with high acidity and varying in sweetness, but mostly dry to medium. Vouvray mousseux is the slightly less fizzy version of Vouvray pétillant. Names to look out for: Marc Brédif *(Bow Wine Vaults, Oddbins)*, Prince Poniatowski *(Caves de la Madeleine, La Vigneronne)*, Gaston Huet *(Wine Society)*, Foreau *(Loeb)*.

Other French sparklers A good, straight, fresh sparkling wine is made by Listel in the middle of the South coast – Listel Brut, excellent value at just over £3 *(importer: Grande Île Wines)*. Sparkling wines from Alsace and Burgundy may sometimes be rather acid, and dear [££]–[£££].

Germany

The best are made from the Riesling grape, grown in Germany. Look for 'Riesling' on the label; Deutscher Sekt may just mean that the bubbles were German-made, not the base wine, which is generally imported from Italy or Southern France. 'Sekt' simply means 'sparkling wine' in German. Names to look out for: Deinhard Lila [££]–[£££] *(Vintners Wain; importers: Deinhard)*, Deinhard Moselle Riesling [££] *(Vintners Wain; importers: Deinhard)*, Fürst von Metternich [££] *(Oddbins, German Food Centre; importers: Atkinson Baldwin)*.

Italy

Some good dry sparkling wines are now being made in the North of Italy. Unusually good is Ferrari Brut, Champagne method sparkling wine made with Chardonnay and a bit of Pinot Noir. It is very mature, indeed too mature for some [£££] *(Wine Growers' Association)*. Other, simpler wines to look out for are Pinot di Pinot from Gancia [££] *(Galleon Wines; importer: Hedges & Butler)*, and President Brut [££] *(Peter Dominic)*.

Spain

Earthy-peppery Champagne method ('cava' in Spanish) sparklers that easily lose their fruit. The cheaper ones are often the best buys within a company's range, since they are younger and generally fresher and fruitier. Names to look out for: Castellblanch *(Augustus Barnett, Bottoms Up, Buckinghams, Army & Navy; importer: Garvey UK)*; Freixenet Cordon Negro *(Ashe & Nephew, Europa Foods; importer: Direct Wine Suppliers)*; Codorníu Brut *(Victoria Wine; importer: Grants of St James's)* and Segura Viudas *(Waitrose, Cullens, Bottoms Up; importer: The Wine Gallery)*.

USA

Of the many California sparkling wines, only a few are available here. The Paul Masson sparkler is fresh and of decent quality [££] *(importer: Seagram)*. Best are the Schramsberg wines [£££], made by the Champagne method and very difficult to tell from the real thing – and very expensive *(Les Amis du Vin; importer: Geoffrey Roberts)*. A newcomer is Gold Seal from New York State, a soft, well-made bottle-fermented wine *(Great American Food and Wine Co)*.

Part II

Where to buy

Where to buy

The range of wines on sale on British merchants' shelves and lists in the mid-1980s is so enormous that the bewildered customer can be forgiven for reaching out for the nearest bottle in his price range or that reassuring brand. Wine merchants could give so much more help. Often highly privileged wine drinkers, with years of experience, travelling and prolific tasting behind them, many of them have an immense amount of knowledge to impart. A large number do, but many more would give a far better service to their customers if they took the time to slip even an occasional tasting note on to their shelves, and to annotate their lists with useful comments. Most, for example, lump clarets all together, leaving the customer at a loss as to whether to spend the £5 for the evening's dinner party on the Ch Paviel de Luze, Margaux 1978, the Ch Loudenne 1979 or the Ch La Cardonne, Blaignan Médoc 1981. Are they ready? How do they taste? Hugh Johnson is not always to pocket. Merchants may be ready and willing to offer advice, but not everyone has the time or the courage to ask, not every shop assistant knows, and there are simply those times when the shop is full and there isn't the time to help.

The Victoria Wine chain has been a pioneer in several informative ways. The first to introduce a sweetness shelf-rating for whites and a body-weight rating for reds, they began in 1984 to shelve their wines according to taste category rather than, as traditionally, by country of origin, realising that taste was the uppermost question in the minds of most customers who entered their shops. Cullens have very recently introduced their own shelf symbols directing customers to good wine and food matches, as a supplement to their taste-rating symbols. Some specialist merchants are getting left behind. The public is eager to learn, and will discover more interesting out-of-the-way wines more quickly given a gentle, informative nudge in the right direction.

Notes on information

Discounts Often do not apply on credit card sales.
Glass hire Generally available only with a wine order, which may have to be of a minimum sum.
Cellarage Generally only for wines bought from the company.

See page 12 for an explanation of our special awards Ⓥ and

Prices and price categories were correct to the best of our knowledge as we went to press. They, and ranges of wines stocked, are likely to change during the course of 1985, and are intended as a rough indication of an establishment's range and prices.

Most wine merchants will hire out glasses free of charge, provided they are collected and returned clean, and that you are buying enough wine to fill them! In most cases, it's first come, first served, so get your order in early to ensure supply.

Specialist Merchants

William Addison (Newport) Ltd

67 High Street, Newport, Shropshire TEL (0952) 810627
35 Mill Street, Stafford, Staffordshire TEL (0785) 52735

OPEN Mon–Sat 9 am–5 pm CLOSED Sun, public holidays CREDIT CARD Visa
DISCOUNTS Not for private customers DELIVERY Free within 30 miles of Newport, min 1 case; thereafter at cost GLASS HIRE Free
TASTINGS AND TALKS On request; wines charged at cost CELLARAGE Free

Around the world in a host of brands – anyone in search of the likes of Black Tower or Veuve du Vernay will be sure to find it here. But there is more to Addisons of Newport than brands: plenty of sound if rarely exciting choice at the cheap end, and a large range of clarets, ports and Burgundies. Prices are fair, too, sometimes very good, though Champagne prices are extraordinarily high. Business in the old High Street premises of this family business has been rather superseded in importance in recent years by their cash-and-carry trade wholesale business at the Village Farm, Lilleshall: which explains how the retail shops can carry such an extensive range – and also, no doubt, the vast array of brands. Addisons stock a very good range of vintage ports, back to 1934 (Martinez) and 1935 (Taylor) with three 1955s and plenty of '60s, '63s and '66s: all at fairly standard prices, sometimes 20p or so a bottle up on the average. There are some good basic clarets (Nathaniel Johnston, Pierre Coste [£]–[££]) and a good selection of classed growths from the 1970s and early '80s, many of them from Cordier, at fair prices; an extensive list of red and white Burgundies concentrates mostly in the lower Burgundian price brackets, with a few (mostly Louis Latour) overstepping £10. Moreau wines, sound but not exciting, are much in evidence. If they are not sold out by the time the *Guide* is published, beware the rather aged English wines – 1983 is the vintage to go for, not 1978 and 1979. Why, like so many merchants, do Addisons take fright when they come to list their German and Italian wines and leave us guessing who the producer is? It matters no less here than anywhere else in the world. Try Lungarotti's Rubesco Torgiano in the Italian section. CVNE Riojas, Marqués de Cáceres and the Torres range are always a safe bet, just a bit pricier than average.

BEST BUYS [£]–[£££] Clarets

Adega Wines Ⓥ

132 Stoke Lane, Westbury-on-Trym, Bristol TEL (0272) 620584

OPEN Mon–Fri 10 am–1 pm, 2 pm–6 pm (Fri till 8 pm) Sat 9.30 am–6 pm Sun 11 am–1 pm CLOSED Public holidays CREDIT CARDS Access/Euro, Visa DISCOUNTS Not available DELIVERY Free within Bristol City boundary, min 1 case; Avon County 60p per case on 2+ cases; elsewhere mainland UK £3.50 per case for 1–2 cases, £1.79 per case third case + GLASS HIRE Free TASTINGS AND TALKS Occasionally by invitation CELLARAGE In bond and duty paid £1.20 per case per year

Roy Maggs, managing director of Adega Wines, re-emerged from retirement in Madeira a few years ago with a burning mission to sell good Portuguese wines to the British public, and for those who like the rather tough and woodily dry style of (almost all) Portuguese wines, this is a good source. Best amongst the reds are probably the Pasmados wines, liked by some, though this *Guide*'s editor can find no pleasure in them. Both the Moscatels de Setúbal (1978 and 25-year-old) are pleasant dessert wines (£5.45 and £7.69) especially the fruitier, younger and cheaper wine. There is also now a big range of wines from elsewhere, and these, like the Portuguese wines, are at very reasonable prices, mostly in the £1.50–£2.50 range, comparing well with prices of the same wines elsewhere. Best value are the Bulgarian wines at under £2; the Riojas, especially the Muga, Marqués de Cáceres, Rivarey and Olarra wines at well under £3 and Viña Tondonia 1975 at £4.35; the Chilean wines, mostly around £3; Australians from Rosemount [££]; a small range of good California wines; and the Lustau sherries [£]. The French range has been greatly extended in the October 1984 list, mostly unexcitingly, with very many wines from the cellars of Desvignes Aîné, which we have found very disappointing; similarly the wines from Rémy Pannier.

BEST BUYS [£] Riojas, [£]–[££] Chilean wines

Adnams and Company

Sole Bay Brewery, Southwold, Suffolk TEL (0502) 722424
Adnams Wine Shop, South Green, Southwold, Suffolk TEL (0502) 722138
Market Place Off-Licence, Halesworth, Suffolk TEL (096 87) 2563
Olde Wine Shop, Aldeburgh, Suffolk TEL (072 885) 2298

OPEN MAIN OFICES Mon–Fri 9 am–1 pm, 2 pm–5 pm SHOPS Mon–Sat 10 am–7.30 pm CLOSED Sun, public holidays, Wed pm CREDIT CARDS Not accepted; only personal and business accounts DISCOUNTS 69p per case on 5–10 cases, greater discounts thereafter; £2.30 per case cash & carry DELIVERY Free throughout mainland UK for 2 or more cases; rates elsewhere on demand; £2.30 on single case deliveries, except certain special offers GLASS HIRE Free; 50p per glass deposit TASTINGS AND TALKS For groups at wine cost CELLARAGE £2.76 per case per annum

The wines on the Adnams list are consistently outstanding, from the cheapest to the top of the range, thanks to the fine palate of Simon Loftus, director of the Sole Bay Brewery's wine arm. Like Tanners of Shrewsbury and Lay & Wheeler of Colchester, Adnams are a member of the Merchant Vintners' buying group, set up by a number of small, regional merchants to pool buying experience and benefit from quantity discounts – though prices at Adnams are nevertheless high. Simon Loftus has been largely responsible for the group's purchases from the Rhône and Bordeaux, and his experience in these areas shines through these two extensive sections of his list: (Guigal, Chave, Chapoutier [££]–[£££] and many more from the Rhône; Pierre Coste's light fruity Bordeaux are well worth trying amongst the 'house wines' [£]–[££]. Adnams offer a fine – if rather expensive – list *'en primeur'* and a good selection, red and white, of fine Bordeaux back in one case to 1945. The Burgundy section has been bolstered this year by a long selection of well-chosen red and particularly white 1982s, many of them from small growers. There is also a good selection from elsewhere in France. A well-bought clutch of Italian wines at all price levels is featured for the first time (Pio Cesare, Tedeschi, Tiefenbrunner, and many more, are good). California and North West USA wines tend to fall into the up-market, upper price ranges of these expensive areas. There is a short but carefully selected German list. Spain, tucked away at the back, now deserves a spell of Simon Loftus's attention – but the current seven bottles are good ones (CVNE, La Rioja Alta, Marqués de Cáceres [££]). But beware old white vintages. The Adnams selection is by no means cheap, but always good value, and well worth the effort and small extra cost of exploring by mail order. Simon Loftus's expensively produced and well-illustrated list is a mine of self-opinionated but nevertheless fascinating information. 'When to drink' symbols are extremely useful. But the new, much heralded 'food for wine' snippets by 'friend, customer and remarkably good cook' Victor Gordon, scattered throughout the list, are often preciously written, sometimes misleading or insensitive in their suggestions of wine–food combinations, and full of culinary information in no way directly relevant to wine. One small maggot in an exceptional whole! Adnams hope, incidentally, to open a restaurant in Southwold in spring 1985 with a 'huge wine list'.

BEST BUYS Most things on the list, special sample case offers, [£]–[££] Bordeaux – Pierre Coste, [££] Ch Thieuley, Sauvignon, [££] Dolcetto Poggio Giuseppe, [££]–[£££] Rhône – Chave, and Jaboulet, Hermitage, Vieux Télégraphe, [£££] Burgundy – Tollot-Beaut, Leflaive, Comte Lafon

Roger Aldridge (Wines) Ltd

29 Selcroft Road, Purley, Surrey TEL 01-668 0666

OPEN Mon–Fri 9 am–7.30 pm Sat 9 am–1 pm CLOSED Sun, public holidays
CREDIT CARDS Not accepted DISCOUNTS On application; better rates for

4 cases + DELIVERY Free on UK mainland, min 1 case GLASS HIRE Free TASTINGS AND TALKS On request CELLARAGE Not provided

Prices are fair and concentrated at the lower end, mostly under £5, on Roger Aldridge's list, except on the fine wine supplement, for which most of the stock is sensibly kept in Customs bond, requiring a little time for clearance. The regular list provides a scattering from across France: some reasonable basics at around £3, including the good wines from Ch la Jaubertie, a few clarets up to £4.40, a few reasonable Burgundies, Alsace wines from Haag and Gisselbrecht, George Goulet Champagnes, and some lesser-known Californias: Cassayre-Forni, Cuvaison, Stonegate [£££]. Interesting to taste would be the Swiss Vin des Chanoines, Fendant, Provins, Valais 1978, though expensive at £4.59. The company occasionally offers mixed cases, such as a selection of half-bottles, or 'Nick Ryman's case' from Ch la Jaubertie. They hold a telephone 'wine surgery' every evening between 6 and 7 pm, offering advice to customers, and, interestingly, will arrange the fitting of made-to-measure steel and wooden wine racks.

BEST BUYS [£]–[££] Ch la Jaubertie

Alison's Wine Shop

299 Canongate, Edinburgh TEL (031-557) 3484

OPEN Mon–Thurs 10 am–6 pm Fri, Sat 10 am–7 pm CLOSED Sun, Chr Day, Boxing Day, 1 and 2 Jan CREDIT CARDS Access/Euro, Diners, Visa; business and personal accounts DISCOUNTS 5% on case orders DELIVERY Free on UK mainland, min 2 cases; 1 case free in Edinburgh, elsewhere £3.50 GLASS HIRE Free TASTINGS AND TALKS Wine dinners and tutored tastings on request CELLARAGE Free duty paid; in bond, £1.50 per case per year

Sparkling wines and Champagnes are a speciality at Alison's. The numerous NV, vintage and special Champagnes are unpriced on the list, apart from the good-value Paillard range. Blanquette de Limoux and the Deinhard sparklers are the ones to go for amongst the sparkling wines. For best value in still wines, look to the Riojas – the delicious Muga red (the white is rather heavy), Marqués de Cáceres, a little expensive here, and the fruity Olarras and Domecq Domaine; Garvey sherries are good, too. To the Loire wines have been added this year the bargain Bonnezeaux of René Renou: the 1982 vintage is only £3, and will repay keeping for many years, while his Bonnezeaux Tête de Cuvée of the same vintage, a finer wine, is £4.48. There is a good selection of Alsace wines, including four special wines of the 1976 vintage from Hugel. You will find vintage ports back to 1955, and a large range of clarets, confusingly arranged by price, with vintages, drinkables and not-yet-drinkables, the fine and the modest all in a jumble. Burgundies, Beaujolais and Rhônes are less interesting, Italians less so still, and the German estate wines are not of very exciting vintages. Beware if you are ordering from home – the prices in the list do not include VAT.

BEST BUYS ££ Riojas, ££ Bonnezeaux René Renou, ££ Blanquette de Limoux

H Allen Smith Ltd

7–11 Justice Walk (off Lawrence Street), London, SW3 TEL 01-352 4114
29 Heath Street, London, NW3 TEL 01-435 6845

OPEN (Justice Walk) Mon–Fri 9 am–7 pm Sat 10 am–1 pm CLOSED Sun, public holidays OPEN (Heath Street) Mon–Sat 9 am–9 pm Sun 12 noon–2 pm CLOSED Public holidays CREDIT CARDS Access/Euro, Visa; personal and business accounts DISCOUNTS 5% on case orders, 10% on 10 cases + DELIVERY Free within greater London (within 24 hours), min 1 case; elsewhere on UK mainland £6 per case GLASS HIRE Free TASTINGS AND TALKS Possibly in 1985 CELLARAGE £2 per case per year (plus VAT)

This old-established London firm was bought out of receivership at the end of 1983, and the new owners and management have worked a transformation. Their aims were 'to take a traditional approach to customer service and return the company to its former position as one of the leading London wine merchants, offering an extensive range of wines'. And an extensive list they already have, mostly French, though with some good Spanish (Jean León Cabernet 1978 at £5.95), Italian Sassicaia of different vintages £££, numerous vintages of Lebanese Ch Musar back to 1961 (at prices rather over the going rate for the earlier ones); and from the New World a few good Australians (try especially Tyrells Vat 47 Chardonnay 1982 for £8.95) and some rarely encountered California wines: Zinfandel 1981 from Heitz is delicious and at £6.95 a good way of tasting the expensive wines of this cellar (Martha's Vineyard at prices over £20 a bottle is also on the reasonably long list). Mark West Pinot Noir Blanc (actually a rosé) at £4.95 is also very good; then there's the lovely Edna Valley Chardonnay 1982, and lots of Mondavi. But France takes up the greater part of the list. There are some interesting vins de pays £, excellent Rhônes (Salavert, Paul Jaboulet Aîné, Chave, La Vielle Ferme Côtes du Ventoux), and an occasional rarity such as Ch Grillet white 1976 for £36 a bottle, which will no doubt all have gone by the time this *Guide* reaches the bookshelves. Look for older vintages, too: Châteauneuf-du-Pape, Les Cèdres 1967, P Jaboulet was £7.95 for a half-bottle on the summer 1984 list. Burgundies include Faiveley wines, the excellent Rion wines and some unusual single vineyard Beaujolais. There's plenty of claret, too, from basics upwards and backwards to Ch Lafite 1945 for £350 a bottle. There are also older vintages of Sauternes and Barsac: Ch Doisy-Daëne 1949 at £48.95 or Rieussec 1961 for £24.95. Praise is due to H Allen Smith for the helpful tasting notes on their spacious list (though one or two vintages are missing from the simpler wines). It is helpful, too, to group the sweet wines together at the back as well as within their respective regions. Their Chelsea cellars, full of historic wine trade bits and antique pieces, are well worth a visit.

BEST BUYS Most things on the list

Alston Wines

Front Street, Alston, Cumbria TEL (0498) 81800

OPEN Mon–Thur 9.30 am–5.30 pm Fri and public holidays 9.30 am–7 pm Sat 9 am–7 pm CLOSED Sun, Chr Day, Boxing Day, New Year's Day, Good Friday CREDIT CARDS Access/Euro; business accounts DISCOUNTS 5% on unmixed cases, 3% on mixed cases DELIVERY Free within 5 miles, min half a case; free within Northern England and Southern Scotland, min 1 case; elsewhere, details on application GLASS HIRE Free TASTINGS AND TALKS; CELLARAGE Not provided

Alston Wines have a beautifully balanced list. Spoilt for choice, you might plump for something from the unusual and extensive collection of Austrian wines [£]–[£££], rising from the simple up to Trockenbeerenauslesen: or for one of the excellent Tieffenbrunner wines at £3 or just over from the Italian South Tyrol amongst the very respectable Italian section. Prices of the Marqués de Cáceres Riojas are very good; try also the CVNE Riojas. Germans are well chosen, mostly simple QbA wines [£]–[££], and there are Bulgarians for discerning penny-pinchers, as well as some good Chilean wines [££]. The New World is worth a look, too: Australians from Ch Tahbilk and Taltarni [££], Nederburg wines from South Africa and some good Californias from Jekel, Fetzer, Zaca Mesa and Burgess [££]–[£££]. If your tastes are more traditional, you will dabble happily in Mac Brown's French selection, too. Try the excellent Jacquesson Champagnes, the Hermitage from Chave [£££], some good Loires, Alsace wines from Sick-Dreyer and Schleret, and a fair range of clarets and Burgundies (Chanson, Picard). Sherries from Valdespino are excellent, too, as are the lovely liqueurs of Gabriel Boudier: with white wine try his Liqueur de Myrtilles (bilberries or wimberries as folks in these parts might say) in place of Cassis as a variation on Kir.

BEST BUYS [£]–[££] Marqués de Cáceres Rioja, [£]–[££] Austrian wines, [££]–[£££] California and Australian wines

Les Amis du Vin

7 Ariel Way, Wood Lane, London, W12 TEL 01-740 0053 (warehouse) 01-743 2066 (orders)

OPEN Tue–Fri 11 am–7 pm Sat and Sun 11 am–4 pm (prepared orders may be collected during office hours 9 am–5.30 pm; orders may be left on answering machine) CLOSED Mon

51 Chiltern Street, London, W1 TEL 01-487 3419

OPEN Tue–Fri 10.30 am–7 pm Sat 9.30 am–7 pm CLOSED Sun, Mon

30 James Street, London, WC2 TEL 01-836 4666

OPEN Mon–Sat 11 am–7 pm CLOSED Sun

CREDIT CARDS All accepted, plus banker's orders of 50% for orders over £250, payable over 6 months (members only) DISCOUNTS (Non-members) 5% for unmixed cases, 2.5% extra for 6+ cases and 5% extra for 10+ cases. (Members) 5% for bottles, 10% for unmixed cases, extra quantity discounts as above DELIVERY Free on UK mainland, min 2 cases (non-members), on orders over £35 (members); £3 for under 2 cases (non-members), £2 for orders less than £35 (members) GLASS HIRE Free TASTINGS AND TALKS Excellent regular club tastings, open also to non-members at higher fee CELLARAGE £2.30 per case per year ('to be increased marginally when temperature-controlled storage is offered')

Les Amis sensibly decided in 1984 to prune their wonderful but commercially unwieldy list and to concentrate on a still extensive selection of 250 wines from Bordeaux, Burgundy, the Rhône, Loire, the lesser regions of France and California; they still aim, though, over the long term, to provide a full range to members, if not to casual shoppers, by making regular offers of special purchases. In 1984 these turned out to be 'Beaujolais 1983 and Mâconnais 1983', 'Opening offer on German wines', 'Older vintages of German wines', 'Opening offer on Burgundies' and 'Pomerol', as well as a Christmas offer. These 'specials' are available only by the case, but at very reasonable prices. Membership of Les Amis (£10 for life) brings a 5 per cent discount off single bottles, 10 per cent off unmixed cases, cheaper delivery (free for smaller quantities, *see above*), offers of the 'special purchases', a businesslike but friendly monthly newsletter, and favourable rates for the Les Amis tastings and 'L'Ecole des Amis' which began last year. The Wine Workshops are an excellent way for anyone living within reach of London to learn more about wine. There might be a 'vertical' tasting of Ch d'Issan 1983 to 1970, given by the proprietor himself (£14.95 to members/£17.50 to non-members), or a tutored blind tasting (£7.50/£10). The 'Ecole', five evenings per session, is rather expensive at £75/£67.50 and includes a very small supper, four tasting wines and schooling on such things as decanting, storage, 'the food and wine connection' and how to run a wine tasting, though course content will vary. Members have reported efficient delivery over the past year – in fact a smaller and better Grand Frère has arrived right on cue to record your wine preferences as well as your orders, enabling Les Amis to make only offers relevant to *you*. Much of the autumn 1984 list remains the same – good-value Les Amis own-label wines, an initial selection under £3 (though many just top £3 in the 'VAT inc' column), mostly from the lesser regions of France. The fine California section [£££], presided over by in-house California expert Geoffrey Roberts, remains as good as ever, and Bordeaux and Burgundy have been slightly fattened out, in response to members' requests in the survey carried out in 1984. Clarets are sensibly divided into two sections: wines ready for drinking now or likely to reach maturity within the next few months, beginning with Les Amis Claret at around £3 up to mature classed growths (there's a note on each, as there is on every wine in this useful list); then wines for laying down, with an indication of when they are likely to be ready. Les Amis made a big opening offer of 1983 clarets across the price range, from quite cheap and simple wines to Ch Latour at £314 per case, and prices, at members' rates, were quite competitive. The Burgundy list contains some good names, and there is good value to be had in the Loire, too: try the excellent Quarts de Chaume 1980 at £9.11 from this little Layon cru's best producer Jean Baumard – but not too soon, as it will improve for years. Rhônes are also tempting, with a lot of Paul Jaboulet Aîné and others. Watch out for interesting mixed case offers.

BEST BUYS [£] Own-label wines; most things on the list

J Arkell & Sons Ltd

Kingsdown Brewery, Upper Stratton TEL (0793) 823026
Swindon, Wiltshire

OPEN Mon–Fri 9 am–1 pm, 2 pm–5 pm CLOSED Sat, Sun, public holidays CREDIT CARDS Not accepted DISCOUNTS; DELIVERY Not available GLASS HIRE Free TASTINGS AND TALKS On request CELLARAGE Free

The wine department of this small family brewery carries a wide range of wines, which get rather expensive once you fish out your calculator and sort out the real prices *with* VAT. Ports go back to 1960 but are expensive. There's a fair range of Champagnes, and a page of clarets, starting cheaply [£] and remaining good value – Ch Gruaud Larose 1978 is £7.45 and Ch Beychevelle 1952 (an enormous time leap from the nearest vintage, 1976) is £12.65. Burgundy, Beaujolais and Rhône, all stirred up (list-wise), are less interesting, but there are some good Germans, including some estate wines, from Deinhard, and the excellent Deinhard Lila Riesling Sekt at just over £5, and a fair but unexciting sprinkling of lower-priced wines [£]–[££] from elsewhere.

BEST BUYS [££]–[£££] German wines, [£££] Deinhard Lila Riesling Sekt

The John Arlott Wine Club

17 Lettice Street, London, SW6 TEL 01-736 7878 (24 hours)

OPEN Mon–Fri 9.15 am–7 pm Sat 9.15 am–1 pm CLOSED Sun, public holidays CREDIT CARDS Access/Euro and Visa for mixed cases only DISCOUNTS None: list already discounted DELIVERY Free in Central London, min one case, may be mixed; elsewhere on UK mainland, £2.80 on single case deliveries, £2 per case for 2 cases, thereafter free GLASS HIRE Free TASTINGS AND TALKS For members in London CELLARAGE At cost in public warehouses, on request MAIL ORDER SPECIALISTS

The club is run in partnership by Guardian Publications and wine merchants Haynes Hanson & Clark, with the Great Man of Cricket tasting and approving from afar in his Channel Island retreat. The wines, always by the case, sometimes mixed, are selected from the excellent Haynes Hanson & Clark list *(see below)*; and charged, if unmixed, at wholesale rate (ten per cent down on retail price). A well-annotated offer goes out to 'members' (ie anyone who has previously ordered) every two months, and there are occasional offers in *The Guardian*.

BEST BUYS £–££ Marqués de Cáceres

Army and Navy

101 Victoria Street, London, SW1 TEL 01-834 1234
High Street, Guildford, Surrey TEL (0483) 68171
West Street, Chichester, West Sussex TEL (0234) 786551
Terminus Road, Eastbourne, East Sussex TEL (0323) 27663

OPEN Mon–Sat 9 am (Tue 9.30 am)–5.30 pm CLOSED Sun, public holidays
CREDIT CARDS All accepted; monthly accounts (inc House of Fraser)
DISCOUNTS 5% on unmixed cases if not on special offer; large order discount on application DELIVERY Free in van area; elsewhere from £2 (for 1 bottle) to £6.50 (1 case) or £12.50 (2 cases); 3 cases, quotation supplied GLASS HIRE £1 per doz
TASTINGS AND TALKS In-store wine of the month and promotions
CELLARAGE £2.75 per case per year

Defence cuts seem to have hit this House of Fraser operation and they have retreated from a couple of stores, including Barkers of Kensington. But the manual still lists the big guns from Bordeaux: château bottlings from most of the best claret years since 1970, like Ch Gruaud-Larose 1979 (£8.95) for the officers' mess and, for other ranks, a fresh, youthful, well-made NV Army & Navy Claret (£2.95) or a classy Malésan Bordeaux Rouge 1979 (£3.29), both bottled in Bordeaux (but give a wide berth to the Malésan Entre-Deux-Mers 1982). Red Burgundies are more extensive than whites, going back to 1971, with wines from respectable houses like Loron at between £5 and £10 (eg Savigny-lès-Beaune Les Lavières 1978 from Remoissenet, £8.75). They are happily still listing heavily to port, with own bottlings of vintages from 1954 (Offley £30) up to 1970 (of which there are half a dozen at £14 each); 1977s to lay down include a Taylor at £12 – far from the best prices you can find. Champagne and Germany seem sound, but vintages and producers are not specified in the catalogue so mail-orderers, if there are any at these carriage prices, should check first. Otherwise, there is not a lot else to go overboard about: Italy, Spain and the rest of France hold the odd treat (eg Marqués de Riscal, £4.15). Undoubtedly the best value for money are the wine sales advertised in the national press, when you might save £20 or £30 a case on list prices, and when delivery is free!

BEST BUYS Special wine sales

Arnold Wine Stock

Priory Lodge, Follifoot, Harrogate, N Yorks TEL (0423) 872130

OPEN Evenings, weekends (for mail and telephone orders) CREDIT CARDS Not accepted DISCOUNTS Not available DELIVERY Free for case orders in Harrogate, Leeds, Westbury GLASS HIRE Free with £30 order TASTINGS AND TALKS On request at cost CELLARAGE Not available MAIL ORDER SPECIALISTS

Once you carve through the lengthy but very useful 'verbal encouragement', the list of this helpful one-couple band is short. Though shippers' and producers' names are sparse, prices are good when you consider that delivery is included, making this a useful source of some good wines for anyone living in the delivery area. Pat and John Arnold sell only by the case, but are happy to mix it any way you please. Mehana Bulgarian red and Bulgarian Cabernet Sauvignon are good value at around £2 a bottle (though we are sure the Cabernet is not *really* a 1969!); also worth trying, no doubt, is the anonymous Gamay de l'Ardèche at just over £3. Just four clarets range from Domaine de Roussert 1981, Bourg, also at just over £3, to half-bottles of Ch Lafite 1969 at £5.70. Pierre Sparr Alsace wines are good value at around £3, and the prolific sweet Moulin Touchais wines have reached Follifoot, too: the 1959 is £6.10 and the venerable 1949, £11.50.

BEST BUYS [££] Pierre Sparr Alsace, [££] Gamay de l'Ardèche

Arriba Kettle & Co

Ⓥ ☞

5 St Philips Place, Birmingham, W Midlands TEL 021-236 8186

CREDIT CARDS Not accepted DISCOUNTS £1 per case on 4–6 cases, £1.75 per case on 7–10 cases, £2.50 per case on 12 cases + DELIVERY Min 1 case, may be mixed; £1.75 per case on single case orders GLASS HIRE Free TASTINGS AND TALKS For groups at wine cost CELLARAGE Not available MAIL ORDER ONLY

This specialist Spanish mail order business is the time-consuming hobby of Birmingham architect Barry Kettle, who goes to such extraordinary lengths of customer service as printing his home telephone number in his list in case of evening or weekend queries. Prices are good. Prominent on the 100-strong list is a good range of older vintages of red Riojas, with the best of the old-style oaked white Riojas, plus a few of the new, lighter wines. Particularly worth buying are the Torres range [££], Marqués de Cáceres (and second label Rivarey) white and red [£]–[££], Chardonnay Jean León 1980 (£7.53) and Protos 1974 (£6), cheaper neighbour of the expensive Vega Sicilia. The Lustau Fino (£3.38) is good on the short sherry list. Vital information is occasionally omitted from the list, such as vintages or producer – the Torres wines, for example, appear anonymously under just their brand names.

BEST BUYS [£]–[££] Bodegas Alavasas wines (Solar de Samaniego)

ASDA

See CHAINS AND SUPERMARKETS

Ashe & Nephew

See CHAINS AND SUPERMARKETS

Ashley Scott ☞

PO Box 28, The Highway, Hawarden TEL (0244) 531655
Deeside, Clwyd, Wales

OPEN Mon–Sat 8.30 am–6 pm (but customers may telephone 'at any reasonable time') CLOSED Sun CREDIT CARDS Not accepted; personal and business accounts DISCOUNTS 5% on 6+ cases DELIVERY Free in Wales, Cheshire, Lancashire, Merseyside and Shropshire; min 1 case, may be mixed; elsewhere delivered at cost GLASS HIRE Free TASTINGS AND TALKS For local groups. Selective wine tastings for customers CELLARAGE Not available
MAIL ORDER ONLY

Wales is a vinous desert, and this particular watering-hole, only nine miles from Chester, was fairly recently dug – Ashley Scott was set up in May 1981 by wine company manager of 18 years' standing Michael Scott and his accountant wife Jean. The company deliver free throughout Wales and adjoining counties; they offer a friendly and helpful service by telephone (there is no shop) and will visit and advise customers on request. They have only a wholesale licence, so sell by the case, which may be mixed at no extra cost. The selection is generally sound, with some very good buys, and prices are very fair. Bin-end sales are especially good value. Their Italians are not exciting, but the Germans are reliable from Guntrum, as are Loires from Gratien, Meyer & Seydoux. Try the excellent and reasonably priced Sancerre and Pouilly Fumé from Gitton [££], and Châteauneuf-du-Pape Chante-Cigale 1980 (£5.13) (not to be confused with the similarly named vin de pays). There's a reasonable range of fairly cheap ready-to-drink petits-châteaux. Burgundies are not all recommendable. Montagny 1981 from the excellent co-operative Vignerons de Buxy is fairly cheap (£4.41). Sauzet's Puligny-Montrachet 1982 is good (£9.23), and the Chablis are from the very reliable Michel Rémon [££] – [£££]. Advice and tasting notes would be useful additions to the list.

BEST BUYS [££] Montagny, Vignerons de Buxy, [££] Sancerre and Pouilly Fumé from Gitton

Prices are only a rough indication, and were current in summer 1984.

Jacques Aubrée Wines Ltd

Farleigh House, Frome Road, Bradford-on-Avon, Wiltshire TEL (02216) 5891

OPEN Mon–Fri 9 am–6 pm Sat 10 am–4 pm CLOSED Sun, public holidays, 60 days a year CREDIT CARDS Not accepted; accounts, with bank reference DISCOUNTS 10% on orders £150+ COD, £1 per case cash & carry DELIVERY Free within 15 miles, min 1 case; free on UK mainland, min 5 cases or £150, otherwise £3 per case GLASS HIRE Free TASTINGS AND TALKS On request, in cellars for up to 120 people, buffet or barbecue optional, min £8 per head CELLARAGE £1 per case per year + insurance

Frenchman and now West-Countryman Jacques Aubrée conducts his business with panache – not least during the two July weeks of the Bristol Wine Fair. Indeed, were it not for M Aubrée, the organisers of the Fair would no doubt find themselves with a good deal of empty space on their hands. The Aubrée list is entirely French, from the main AC areas, though it is an original selection from growers otherwise not seen on the UK market, plus a few co-operatives. Prices are fair and almost everything on the list is under £5. Watch out for good-value bin-end sales. Jacques Aubrée's wines can also be bought from Casewines Ltd of Bristol, Classic Wines of Halifax, and France-Ecosse Vintner in Scotland. Since the company has only a wholesale licence, you must buy by the case, which may be mixed.

Averys of Bristol

11 Park Street, Bristol, Avon TEL (0272) 214141

OPEN Mon–Fri 9 am–6 pm Sat 9 am–5 pm CLOSED Sun, public holidays CREDIT CARDS Not accepted DISCOUNTS £1.68 per case, 2.5% off case rate for cash and carry orders DELIVERY Free on mainland UK, min 2 cases; in Northern Ireland, £5 per case up to 10 cases, thereafter free GLASS HIRE 40p per doz (max 360) TASTINGS AND TALKS June tasting for customers, free tasting Thur & Fri in shop CELLARAGE £2.50 per case per year

Stories still occasionally drop into our letter-box about slow delivery from Averys, but service appears to have improved since the arrival on the Board of shareholders from two other Bristol firms, who now hold a significant share in this traditional family business. A lot of old stock was sold off last yar, some of it in a treasure trove of a bin-end sale at the Bristol Wine Fair, some at Christie's, and chaos has been alleviated by the installation of a sophisticated computer system. Let's hope your stories this year will be more encouraging. So the Averys list no longer stretches back to such venerable vintages. There are nevertheless a few old white Burgundies back to 1959 at prices that compare favourably with equivalent wines from the 1981 vintage! And the Burgundy list is still very good, if not exactly cheap. Clarets and red Burgundies now go back to 1970. There are some sound German estate wines, some nice Italians (Ratti, Sassicaia) and good but expensive Californias from

Beaulieu and Clos du Val. Wines of which there is insufficient stock to last the year are now left out of the annual list, so it's still worth enquiring if you're after an old, extra-gutsy favourite. John Avery, still the major shareholder, was the first wine merchant to bring a significant range of New World wines to the UK. His predilection for buying and hoarding large quantities of Antipodean wines has been unfortunate, no doubt, for the company's cash flow, because Averys have been slow to persuade the wine-drinking West Countrymen to take the plunge and sample these delights from Down Under. The list has been reduced, further again this year, but there are still some red vintages back to 1975 of the pair of wineries (Tyrrells and McWilliams) that hog the Australian list. Tyrrell's Vat 47 Chardonnay 1982 is delicious at £7.42, as are other wines from this excellent winery. Three new wineries have been added in the latest list. The New Zealand whites from Matawhero ££–£££ are some of the country's best. The Inniskillin Canadian wines are not brilliant, but worth trying as an oddity ££. You won't find many bargains but Averys range is still good. Get to know the man behind the counter and you may come up with some extraordinarily interesting off-the-list buys.

BEST BUYS ££–£££ German estate wines, ££–£££ Burgundies, ££–£££ New Zealand and Australian wines

Avon Fine Wines/Sparling

35 New King Street, Bath, Avon TEL (0225) 333486

OPEN Mon–Thur 10 am–9 pm Fri, Sat 10 am–9.30 pm Sun and public holidays 12 noon–2 pm, 7 pm–9 pm CLOSED Chr Day, Boxing Day, Good Friday, Easter CREDIT CARDS Access/Euro, Visa DISCOUNTS 75p per case on 5+ cases DELIVERY Free within 40 miles of Bath, min 1 case; elsewhere £2 per case for under 5 cases GLASS HIRE Free TASTINGS AND TALKS Wines always open for tasting (at a small cost) in shop; wine tasting lunches every Thur with country theme; £1 per head includes sandwiches and 2 wines, subsequent wines (up to 8) 25p a glass CELLARAGE £1 per case per year

'Once tasted, always bought,' Avon Fine Wines boast. And tastings are frequent, because the company's new off-licence, Sparling, also has an on-licence and serves wine by the glass, so that you can taste before you buy – four 'tasters' for £1. There is always a wine of the week, too, with 20p off per bottle – an incentive to try something new. The focus is mostly European, but with California, Australia and New Zealand quite well represented, too. The German range is particularly good, with a vast selection from the reliable Müller £–£££, a number from Dr Kern's estate of Schloss Deidesheim, plus some more from Sichel and Deinhard. Champagnes are good value, beginning with a cheapie, Marquis de Conflans Brut NV, at £6.30 a bottle, then De Lahaye Brut NV at £7.10, or the pink Jacqueline De Lahaye (NV at £8.15, 1973 at £9.57), and good prices for vintage and NV Bollinger. The Italian wines and the few Spanish are well chosen. There's a good range of 30 clarets, including a few 1966s, and a few Burgundies, some of them from small growers. The Beaujolais range includes the good Sarrau wines. There's Heim from Alsace, some interesting-looking Rhônes and the vins de pays and VDQSs look worth a try, too. And you might enjoy comparing some of the different grape varieties grown in England amongst the ranges of Westbury, Spots Farm and Wraxall. A few very old ports are listed such as Sandeman 1934 and 1935 and Taylor 1927 – prices on request.

BEST BUYS [£] Vins de pays, [£]–[£££] German wines

Cynthia Bacon, Fine Italian Wines

ffowlers' Bucke, South Harting, Petersfield, Hants TEL (073 085) 471

OPEN Mon–Fri 9 am–1 pm, 2.30 pm–5.30 pm Sat 9 am–1 pm CLOSED Sun, public holidays DISCOUNTS 2.5% on unmixed cases DELIVERY Min one case, may be mixed; 5+ cases free within 20 miles of Harting, 1–4 cases in that area £1.75 per case; England and Wales £3.25 per case, Scotland £3.50 TASTINGS AND TALKS On request CELLARAGE Not available

Cynthia Bacon's 100-strong list specialises in the wines of Northern Italy, especially Piedmont, with an occasional foray down south as far as Tuscany. It's a good, in places outstanding, selection, at all price ranges. There's useful information at the back about the style of the wines, with sound ideas for accompanying food. Regular tastings are held at ffowlers' Bucke, the Bacons' 500-year-old former inn.

BEST BUYS [££] Vietti Moscato Naturale, [££]–[£££] Barolo and Barbaresco Abbazia dell' Annunziata and Cavallotto, [£££] Brunello di Montalcino Caparzo, [££]–[£££] Rainoldi Valtellinas

David Baillie Vintners

The Sign of the Lucky Horseshoe TEL (0392) 31351
Longbrook Street, Exeter, Devon (answering machine outside office hours)

OPEN Mon–Sat 9 am–6 pm CLOSED Sun, public holidays CREDIT CARDS All accepted; personal and business accounts DISCOUNTS 5% to students on presentation of union card, £1.24 per case cash & carry, 2% cash with order, 5% for 6+ cases DELIVERY Free in Great Britain, min 1 case GLASS HIRE Free TASTINGS AND TALKS Up to 6 organised tastings a year, free (including buffet) CELLARAGE Free if wine bought from them, otherwise £1.20 per case per year

David Baillie's list has always been good, but the autumn 1984 edition has been strengthened with considerably more fine Burgundies and clarets. Clarets, from Nathaniel Johnston, are very reliable, and the list of château-bottled ones goes back, at various quality levels, through 1976/1973/1971 to a range (in limited supply) of classed growths from the 1950s. Prices were very fair for their opening offers of 1983 clarets, Burgundies and Sauternes/Barsac. The extended list still contains many of the old reliable names, plus a few more, both growers and merchants – Tollot-Beaut, Bruno Clair, Jacques Germain – the most expensive of the range being Bâtard-Montrachet, Bienvenues 1982, Henri Clerc, at £15.17 a bottle. The list begins with cheaper wines from £2 to £3 a bottle, but a flip back to the end of the French section will show some reasonable French country wines at the same prices. Alsace wines in the lower price ranges are good value from the Beblenheim co-operative [£]–[££], and Rhônes are well chosen. Basic Germans are sound, and there's a long list of good estate wines. Give the Italians a try, as well – it is an interesting selection. From Spain, you will find the ubiquitous Torres, CVNE Riojas and the less common Olarra Riojas, also good, all quite well priced. There's a sound selection of South African basic and estate wines [£]–[££], a number of Californias, a few Australians [££]–[£££], and one Chilean Cabernet [££]. From nearby Somerset, Colin Gillespie's Wootton Vineyard wines (all three of his grape varieties are here) are at the pinnacle of English wine-making, and good value at a little over £3. And David Baillie have one of the best ranges of almacenista sherries (single cask bottlings) at just over £4. There are lots of good-looking crusting and vintage character ports, Taylor's Chip Dry White and some vintages at prices that are not especially appealing but not expensive either. For an interesting aperitif, try Chambéry Dolin (top quality French vermouth) at £3.62 or Chambéryzette, the same thing flavoured with alpine strawberries for just 20p more. Prices are not particularly cheap, but begin to look very reasonable when you consider that carriage is free to anywhere in Britain for a case or over, and that this may be mixed – so if you live in an out-of-the-way spot, send for a list. Well done, David Sommerfelt and Kenneth (Baillie) Christie, for giving us full details of *every* wine, including the German and Italians, and for helpfully including the VAT in prices this year.

BEST BUYS Most things on the list

Bakewell Vintners

Now at: Upper Town Farm, Birchover near Matlock, Derbyshire

TEL (062 988) 240 (answering machine when office unmanned)

In July 1984, Bob Huddie sold this business to Yorkshire Fine Wines *(see below)*, who now supply Bakewell's Vintners' previous hotel/restaurant customers and list many of the company's best-selling wines. The retail shop in Diamond Court has been closed, but Bob and Liz Huddie are still active in the wine trade – Mr Huddie is a director of Yorkshire Fine Wines – and are acting as agents for them from Birchover, five miles from Bakewell. They hold some stocks of the most popular wines there and can supply any of the company's 1,000+ wines and spirits.

Prices are correct to the best of our knowledge in summer 1984.

Balls Bros of London

313 Cambridge Heath Road, London, E2 TEL 01-739 6466
Associated with Wickham & Co, Bideford, Devon TEL (023 72) 3292

OPEN Mon–Sat 10 am–6 pm CLOSED Sun, public holidays CREDIT CARDS Access/Euro, Visa; credit by arrangement DISCOUNTS 65p per case on 5–10 cases, 90p on 11+ cases, £2.40 per case cash and carry DELIVERY Free in England and Wales, min 2 cases; £1.60 per case for less than two cases; £1 per case in Scotland, £1.60 for less than two cases GLASS HIRE Free
TASTINGS AND TALKS For regular customers by invitation at the 'Wine Centre' headquarters in E2 and an annual City tasting; bi-annual 'City Fellowship' tastings £5 (inc supper), annual tutored tastings (on request) at wine cost
CELLARAGE £1.04 per case per year

Prices are really rather high on the take-home side of wine bar magnates Balls Bros, but delivery on their mail order is cheap, and there's a good discount on cash-and-carry sales from their Wine Centre warehouse in East London. Their 'City Fellowship of Wine' club offers occasional newsletters, and attractive case offers, such as The Christmas Day Case, or The Cabernet Case – a mix of Parducci from California, Concha y Toro from Chile, Craigmore from Australia and Grave del Friuli from Collavini. Over half the list is French, and the best wines are concentrated in the Rhône and South of France, thanks significantly to purchases through the Merchant Vintners, of which they, along with such companies as Adnams, Lay & Wheeler, Tanners and Jones of Banbury, are members. Germans and Italians on the Balls list are boring, Spanish mixed (CVNE, La Rioja Alta and Torres wines are reliable choices, again a bit expensive). The list unhelpfully does not always reveal producers' names, and though some wines that are not yet ready sport a 'laying down' symbol, this is not consistently used. Vintage notes are not very full – or, sometimes, absolutely accurate: both 1977 and 1972 clarets, for example, are described simply as 'light', while 1970 is just 'a very good, consistent vintage'.

BEST BUYS Special mixed cases, personally collected

Augustus Barnett

See CHAINS AND SUPERMARKETS

Barrett's Liquormart

See CHAINS AND SUPERMARKETS

Barretts Liquorstores Ltd

40 Haven Green, London, W5 TEL 01-998 0903

OPEN Mon–Sat 10 am–9 pm Sun 12 noon–2 pm Public holidays 10 am–4 pm CLOSED Never CREDIT CARDS Not accepted DISCOUNTS £1 per case DELIVERY, GLASS HIRE Not available TASTINGS AND TALKS In-store, about 3 times a year CELLARAGE Not available

Barretts Liquorstores (no connection in business terms with Freddy Barrett, though Freddy is this Barrett's father) is a place to hunt for occasional bargains, and to shop for other things on difficult days like Sundays and public holidays, when other sources of the more expensive bulk of the stock are closed. You are likely to find the country's cheapest Champagne here – cheaper than in any of the supermarkets. Prices bottomed out in 1984 at £4.99 for Raymond de Belbal, young but pleasant, and a Champagne called Le Bernard was on sale for £5.59 as we went to press. Other Champagne prices tend not to be particularly cheap. Beware of the more expensive wines, which tend to gather dust – upright – in large banks on the top shelf. Wines are rather jumbled, but you will find some less usual Spaniards – like the reliable Chivite wines from Navarra [£] and some lesser-known Riojas. Vintage ports tend to be on the expensive side, but you may find some late-bottled bargains. We snapped up some Taylors Chip Dry White on our summer visit for just over £5. Barretts do not issue a list, except at Christmas, so next time you're at Ealing Broadway, go ferreting for bargains.

BEST BUYS [££]–[£££] Cheapest Champagnes

Bart's Cellars

56A Great Cumberland Place, London, W1 TEL 01-723 4395

OPEN Mon–Fri 8.15 am–6.30 pm Sat 10 am–12 noon CLOSED Sun, public holidays CREDIT CARDS Personal accounts only DISCOUNTS 2.5% for cash DELIVERY Free in Greater London, min 3 cases (depending on area); elsewhere at cost GLASS HIRE Not available TASTINGS AND TALKS One major tasting a year CELLARAGE On request, at cost

Bart's Cellars sell only by the case, at prices that are quite good, especially in view of their position near Marble Arch. Their main list concentrates on cheaper wines [£]–[££] and spans the better-known regions of France. They ship directly from the Loire and the Rhône. Look out especially for the excellent and good-value Rhônes from La Vieille Ferme [£], Cru du Coudoulet [££] and Ch de Beaucastel [££]–[£££]. The list even includes useful, reliable tasting notes. More extravagant wine buyers should also take a look at Bart's fine wine list, which changes monthly since they buy in small quantities – sometimes as small as a couple of bottles. One recent list stretched back to 1928 Ch Lafite Rothschild, still in bond with duty to pay, at £400 a bottle. Check prices carefully since some are expensive, but there are likely to be some bargains, too. On this list, for Domaine de La Romanée-Conti fans, there was a big range back to 1969 Romanée-St-Vivant. A small range of vintage port went back to 1924, with some good prices worth seeking out.

BEST BUYS [£]–[£££] Rhônes, [£££] Old and rare wines, including vintage port

Barwell & Jones

See CHAINS AND SUPERMARKETS

Thomas Baty & Sons Ltd

37/41 North John Street, Liverpool TEL 051-236 1601

OPEN Mon–Sat 9.15 am–5 pm Chr, Easter extended hours CLOSED Sun, public holidays CREDIT CARDS Not accepted; personal accounts DISCOUNTS Baty's Dozen – 13 in a case; for large quantities, by negotiation DELIVERY Free in Merseyside area, min £20 order; elsewhere £5 per case (inc insurance) GLASS HIRE Free TASTINGS AND TALKS On request; tastings to be organised at Baty's cellars in 1985 CELLARAGE £3 per case per year (inc insurance and advice)

The municipal splendours have not been the only improvements in Liverpool during the past year. Just beside the Cavern Walks development, in Beatles country, Thomas Baty & Sons have renovated their cellar, adding a museum of Edwardian wine antiquities, and they hoped as we went to press soon to be holding tastings and special events there for their customers. The rather special, personal, caring service offered by this independent family firm is reflected in the charming and eager tone of their wide-ranging wine list. But we'd really prefer advice on when to drink the wines, rather than how they are made, and be given some indication of how they taste. We would also like to see growers/producers listed *every* time – they're nearly all present, we admit – and prices which include VAT. Such small grouses apart, this is an excellent selection, and reasonably priced (though do beware of the VAT when you study the list) – particularly in view of the service offered and Merseyside's difficult trading climate. Baty's stock a very good range of petits-châteaux clarets [£]–[££], along with a small selection of more aristocratic growths, going back to the early 1970s, but with rather more choice in more recent vintages. Have a dabble, too, in the short but tempting lists from the Rhône and Burgundy. Baty's are North-West agents for the Domaine de la Romanée-Conti, so their prices for these wines are as fair as you'll find, though you'll find far better value elsewhere on the list. There are some fine German estate wines, mostly QbA and Kabinett, a good few Halbtrocken, and Mondavi California wines at prices only a little above the national average. Ch Musar 1972 from the Lebanon is older than you will see on most lists, and good value at £4.30. The older vintages of Taylor's Quinta de Vargellas are good, too. You could do worse than rely on the

Baty's own-labels, and their special tasting cases are a good way to explore this lovely list. They will also make up and deliver special gift parcels, complete with message.

BEST BUYS £–££ Petits-châteaux, £££ De Venoge Champagne, Rhônes, Burgundies, Germans

Bejam

See CHAINS AND SUPERMARKETS

Bentalls of Kingston

Kingston-upon-Thames, Surrey TEL 01-546 1001

OPEN Mon 9.30 am–5.30 pm Tue–Fri 9 am–5.30 pm Sat 9 am–6 pm CLOSED Sun, public holidays CREDIT CARDS Access/Euro, Amex, Visa; personal accounts DISCOUNTS £2–£4 per case on case sales, depending on price DELIVERY Free, any quantity over a large area of Surrey, and from any of the other 5 branches (which hold no licence but can deliver) GLASS HIRE Free TASTINGS AND TALKS Wines open in wine department Fri & Sat 20–30 weeks in year CELLARAGE Not available

Bentalls' list has been bought with care – but please can we have more details of shippers and producers, and better spelling, next year? There's a spread of traditional French and Germans and a few above-average Italians. Some claret snips were to be found on their last issued list as we went to press, such as Léoville-Las-Cases 1976 at £10.80 and Talbot 1976 for under £9. Good-value sparklers to watch out for are Deinhard Lila, Deinhard's Sparkling Moselle. The Brown Bros range from Australia is a good recent addition ££–£££. Don't expect many bargains at Bentalls, but you may find them good value if you live within their delivery areas.

BEST BUYS ££–£££ Sparkling wines from Deinhard, £££ *some* good clarets

Bergerac Wine Cellar

37 Hill Street, St Helier, Jersey, Channel Islands TEL (0534) 70756

OPEN Mon–Fri 10 am–3 pm, 4 pm–6 pm Sat 10 am–1 pm, 2 pm–6 pm CLOSED Sun, public holidays CREDIT CARDS All accepted DISCOUNTS 10% on case sales DELIVERY Not available GLASS HIRE Free TASTINGS AND TALKS Occasional informal tastings in the shop CELLARAGE Not available

No, this is not a South-West France specialist – the list boasts only an anonymous red and white Bergerac, and a red and white Côtes-de-Duras. It's a long, well-chosen list (with producers generally named) bolstered by a few brands. Prices are fair but not cheap, considering that there's no VAT and lower duty here. The Cellar has been in business for only two years, but the range of clarets is quite extensive, mostly vintages of the last decade, a few 1961s; Burgundies are unexciting. Especially worth trying are the good but expensive Domaine Ott wines from Provence ££–£££, Langlois-Château Loires £–£££, and CVNE Riojas £–££; Ch Carras red, creeping up towards £5, is an excellent wine from Greece, and Courtakis Retsina, one of the best at under £3. The Italian wines are not particularly exciting, but reliable choices include Rocca della Macie Chianti, and Fabbiano Valpolicella and Soave (particularly the Amarone) at under £3; Fontanafredda wines are other possibilities £–££ and the Masi Amaroni are excellent ££–£££.

BEST BUYS £–£££ Italian and Spanish wines

Berkmann Wine Cellars Cellar Shop/Le Nez Rouge Wine Club

12 Brewery Road, London, N7 TEL 01-609 4711

OPEN (Cellar Shop) Mon–Fri 9 am–5.30 pm Sat 10 am–1.30 pm CLOSED Sun, public holidays CREDIT CARDS Access/Euro, Visa DISCOUNTS £1.50 per case cash & carry DELIVERY Free in London postal districts, min 1 case; elsewhere on UK mainland £2.50 on single case deliveries, £2 per case on 2 cases, £1.50 on 3–4 cases, free thereafter GLASS HIRE Free TASTINGS AND TALKS *See entry* CELLARAGE Expensive: £5.20 per case per year

Le Nez Rouge Wine Club was formed in October 1983 as a new retail mail order arm of Berkmann Wine Cellars, longstanding suppliers of many of the top restaurants of London. Burgundy is the main strength of the list, a good half of the extensive range consisting of lighter recent vintages, ready for drinking. Sauzet, Tollot-Beaut and Lafarge are amongst the Burgundian names to look out for £££. Beaujolais are the well-made, easy, fruity wines of Duboeuf, a full range at very good prices ££. The Bordeaux list is interesting, but more modest, with no wines offered *en primeur*. Again, half or more are ready for drinking, many of them petits-châteaux £–£££. The Loire and Rhône lists are short and sound. Sauvion Muscadets are good. The Ch de Quinçay from Oisly et Thésée in the Loire, and the Vacqueyras, Côtes-de-Rhône from the Producteurs Associés, are good and both reasonably priced. There are very short, good-quality Italian and German (up to Spätlese) selections. Little on the list comes for under £3, but the white house wine, Blanc de Blancs Les Caves Geneviève £, is fine value. There are some interesting bin-end and mixed tasting cases. The club membership is to be limited to 500. Life membership costs £35, but this includes a case of Le Nez Rouge House Wine, a free invitation to the next club tasting, and a very smart, expensively produced quarterly magazine (unfortunately a rather dull read). The club is arranging regular tastings, dinners in spring and autumn, and an annual tasting visit to a wine region (the first was to Beaujolais in the summer of 1984).

BEST BUYS [£] Blanc de Blancs, Les Caves Geneviève, [££] Duboeuf wines, [£££] Burgundies – Tollot-Beaut, Sauzet, Lafarge etc

Berry Bros & Rudd Ltd

3 St James's Street, London, SW1 TEL 01-930 1888
The Wine Shop, Houndmills, Basingstoke, Berkshire TEL (0256) 23566

OPEN (London) Mon–Fri 9.30 am–5 pm (Basingstoke) Mon–Fri 9 am–5 pm Sat 9 am–1 pm CLOSED (London) Sat (Both) Sun, public holidays
CREDIT CARDS Access/Euro, Amex, Visa; personal and business accounts
DISCOUNTS 3% on 1–4 cases, 5% on 5–10 cases, 7½% thereafter
DELIVERY Free on UK mainland for 12 bottles or more, may be mixed; Northern Ireland £1 per case; everywhere: one bottle £2.45, 2 bottles £2.95, 3 bottles £3.40, 4–11 bottles £4 GLASS HIRE £1.15 per dozen (includes delivery, collection and washing; hire glasses are often their own excellent glasses *(see our cover illustration)* TASTINGS AND TALKS With tuition, charges by arrangement
CELLARAGE £2.07 per case per year, temperature-controlled, at Basingstoke

Prices are not as expensive at 3 St James's as one might expect in view of the setting and the perfect old-world service. Nothing in the delightful old shop seems to have changed for centuries. With constant traffic roaring past outside, Berry Bros do not encourage collection; they build delivery costs into the prices, so this list is particularly worth studying if you live in some country extremity. Delivery is efficient, particularly rapid in the Home Counties, from their computerised modern bottling, cellarage and distribution centre in Basingstoke, where they also have a small, smart shop, a couple of minutes' drive from the town centre. Bordeaux is the major speciality – they have their own manager permanently stationed in Bordeaux. Some claret prices are very good, some expensive – it's worth spending a bit of time comparing lists. Apart from a separate *en primeur* list, there's a fair range of clarets back to 1975, lots of the *not* recommendable 1972s, a few odd wines back to 1964, plus a few mature magnums. Burgundies are either *négociants'* wines or Berry Bros' own generic selection, bottled in Basingstoke: some mature wines, and a few magnums again. Alsace wines are from Hugel. Muscadet-sur-lie Jacques Guindon has lovely fruit and a bit more weight than most. A fairly extensive German list includes some mature sweet wines. Berry Bros have recently introduced a range of cheaper French wines: four pages under £4, many under £3, generally well chosen and good value. Perhaps best value are the Berry Bros' own-label wines: their 'Good Ordinary Claret' is firm but fruity, lightly tannic, with good Cabernet character, at under £4. Own-label sherries and ports are, extraordinarily nowadays, shipped in cask to Basingstoke for bottling. Mixed sample cases at a special discount are good value, as are the occasional bin-end sales. The neat little pocket list usefully indicates whether the wines are ready to drink, are ready but will keep, or are for laying down.

BEST BUYS [££] Berry Bros Good Ordinary Claret, [££] Muscadet-sur-lie Jacques Guindon, [£]–[£££] some clarets, and sampling cases

Bibendum Ⓥ

113 Regents Park Road, London, NW1 TEL 01-586 9761

OPEN Mon–Sat 10 am–8 pm Sun 11 am–6 pm CLOSED Public holidays (exc Good Friday) CREDIT CARDS Access/Euro, Visa DISCOUNTS 5% per case unmixed cases, £1 per case cash & carry DELIVERY Free ('immediate') in Greater London, min 1 cse; elsewhere in mainland UK £1 per case, min charge £6 for 1–11 cases; 50p per case thereafter GLASS HIRE Free TASTINGS AND TALKS 'Festivals' organised CELLARAGE £2.76 per case per year

Christopher Collins transferred his financial expertise and his fortune from perfume to wine when, seven years ago, he sold his majority share in Goya to ICI. Bibendum, aptly billed 'wine emporium' in Primrose Hill, North London, is the two-year-old retail division (case sales only) of his wine investment company Collins Wines. But wine at Bibendum is certainly not reduced to commodity status: there is a fine selection from all over France (Rhône: Chave, Paul Jaboulet Aîné, and many more [£££], many domaine Burgundies [£££]), a fairly long and well chosen Italian list (Capezzana, Masi, Lungarotti [£]–[£££]), a good choice of recent vintages from the USA, and an interesting scattering from the rest of the world – at reasonable prices, too. Many of the wines offered are 'parcel buys', particularly the fine and mature clarets, and vintage ports back to 1945. Stocks turn over quickly, so a fine wine supplement to the list is periodically sent out to regular customers. It is a shame the main list gives, unlike the supplement, no indication of when the wines will be ready to drink. If you're after big bottles, Bibendum will spoil you for choice: a couple of dozen double magnums, jeroboams (four-bottle size) and imperials (eight-bottle jumbos) of top châteaux back to 1966 end the fine wine list with a flourish. But Bibendum hold more jumbo stock, so it's worth asking if you're looking for something specific. Bibendum/Collins sell to the trade (restaurants and caterers), to offices and to the public. They offer special business catering and private party services, including help with organising caterers and wine sale or return. There are occasional 'festivals' (tasting, dinners and talks) on specific areas.

BEST BUYS Jumbo bottles of fine claret, most things on the list

Birdham Stores

Main Road, Birdham, Chichester, West Sussex TEL (0243) 512888

OPEN Mon–Sat 8 am–5.30 pm Sun 12 noon–1 pm Public holidays 9 am–1 pm CLOSED Chr Day, Boxing Day, 1 Jan CREDIT CARDS Not accepted DISCOUNTS Mixed case 5%, unmixed 8% DELIVERY Free within 20 miles, min 1 case; elsewhere by arrangement GLASS HIRE Free TASTINGS AND TALKS Chr tasting; in-store tastings some weekends CELLARAGE Not provided

Unimposing on the outside, Birdham Stores is stuffed with goodies both liquid and solid. Tear yourself away from the 60 cheeses, home-cooked hams and terrines and the Jersey cream, and you will find a surprising array of wines and spirits. Prices are good and you will even find some bargains, but beware nevertheless of some elderly vintages – in the Italian whites, for example, and on the German and English shelves; there are also a couple of fairly basic 1975 red Australians at under £4, which are likely to be past it by now. France takes up most room with a range of clarets, some of them mature classed growths, Cattin Alsace wines £–££ and a range from Trimbach, Dopf (sic) and anon, lots of André Simon wines, dependable but unexciting, a good-value table wine at under £2, Champagne at fair prices and Langlois-Château Saumur. Best buys for a celebration are the Deinhard sparklers, Moselle and Lila (£4.40 and £5.65), both delicious, the Moselle being medium dry. There is a range from KWV in South Africa, always reliable, two good-value wines from Bulgaria at under £2, and some California wines from Christian Brothers. Birdham Stores stock 30 malt whiskies, too. They operate a catering service, which can cope with up to 150 people.

BEST BUYS £–££ Alsace wines, ££ Deinhard sparkling wines

Bishops

See under Budgen in CHAINS AND SUPERMARKETS

Bond End Wines

Schwallers Restaurant, 6/8 Bond End, Knaresborough, North Yorkshire — TEL (0423) 863899

OPEN Mon–Sun (except Tue) 10 am–11 pm CLOSED Tue (but telephone is manned) CREDIT CARDS Not accepted DISCOUNTS Negotiable on 10+ cases DELIVERY 'If we are passing'. No mail order GLASS HIRE Not available TASTINGS AND TALKS Regular tastings of about 16 wines, with very good cheese selection, £6.50 per head; gourmet wine evenings in restaurant CELLARAGE Not available

The wine side of Schwallers Restaurant (see RESTAURANTS AND WINE section) came into being only in May 1984. Run from the restaurant and selling principally to satisfied diners, Bond End wines is the local agent for the whole list of Stapylton Fletcher *(see below)*, with just a few Italian and German additions of their own. Quality is good and the range very interesting, especially the dominating French 'regional' wines, and the Spanish, Germans, Bulgarians and Chileans. Bond End sell only by the case, which may be mixed.

BEST BUYS £ French regional wines, £ Spanish wines

> Most wine merchants will supply wine for parties sale or return.

Bordeaux Direct

New Aquitaine House, Paddock Road, Reading, Berkshire TEL (0734) 481718

OPEN Mon–Fri 12 noon–7 pm Sat 9 am–6 pm CLOSED Sun, public holidays
RETAIL SHOPS 87 Caversham Road, Reading, Berkshire TEL (0734) 589990
Shop 2, Dorna House, West End, Woking, Surrey TEL (093 15) 6133
4 Alston Road, Barnet, Hertfordshire TEL 01-441 1255
Arch 36, Goswell Road, Windsor, Berkshire TEL (075 35) 66192
3 Holtspur Parade, Beaconsfield, Buckinghamshire TEL (049 46) 77564
24 Market Place, Henley-on-Thames, Oxfordshire TEL (0922) 77355
19 Denmark Street, Wokingham, Berkshire TEL (0734) 785113

SHOPS OPEN mon–Fri 12 noon–7 pm Sat 9 am–6 pm CREDIT CARDS All accepted; Cellarcard, a Lloyds Bank retail credit scheme, is offered to customers – small regular monthly payments pay interest (0.5% per month) when in credit, and interest is charged at 2% per month on credit up to 18 monthly payments DISCOUNTS None, except on special offers DELIVERY Free on orders over £50, min 1 case; otherwise £2 per case GLASS HIRE Free
TASTINGS AND TALKS Shops organise lots of tastings, talks, wine lessons and dinners (casual); occasional group trips abroad CELLARAGE £1 + VAT if bought from BD, £2 + VAT if bought elsewhere MAIL ORDER SPECIALISTS

Bordeaux Direct has managed to assemble all the elements that make buying by mail order worthwhile: an unusual and varied range, not long but largely exclusive, reliable to excellent quality, and perhaps above all personality and enthusiasm in the well-rounded shape of Tony Laithwaite. Prices are not cheap, but then a lot of loving care (and the enormous expense of monthly mailings) goes into informing you, the customer, of how the wine tastes and why. The monthly *Laithwaite's Great Wine Trek*, sent out with the monthly list, sounds so uncommercial, disjointedly full of childish humour and silly pranks, all rather endearing, that one begins to believe that prices, well, aren't *that* bad. . . . Tony Laithwaite has come of age in his delightful, still amusing and useful little *Wine Buyer's Notebook* in which devotees of the Laithwaite list can 'meet' a selection of the regular grower-suppliers. Take this, part of the entry on their Minervois supplier, Jean Cabrol: 'Jean has just four small concrete vats in a tiny cellar under his house and the only way into them is through trap doors let into his living room, kitchen and bedroom floors. Because they make their wine by the "whole-grape" method, they have to tip the uncrushed grapes into the tops of the vats and Mr and Mrs Cabrol actually have to prop up their bed on to a slant during harvest so they can get those grapes into the vats! Dedication! Take a glass on his terrace from where you can see a river gushing out of an underground cavern 200 ft below you, and one of Jean's vineyards just 200 ft away which takes three quarters of an hour to reach on foot because its on the other side of an impassable chasm – you really will never forget Minerve.' Tony Laithwaite's policy is 'to buy the best wine in a cheap region rather than a simpler wine from an expensive region. I don't care about the name on the label. I can always explain.' And Bordeaux

Direct's strengths are indeed in the £–££ ranges from the more out-of-the-way spots, particularly France, with practically everything in drinkable order now. The list changes constantly (one good reason for those expensive monthly mailings). The French 'country wines' £–££ are worth scrutiny, and the Bulgarian wines are good, especially the Cabernet Sauvignon £. Burton Anderson, author, wine consultant and Italian specialist, has had a hand in choosing the above-average eight-wine Italian selection (including, best of all, the Sankt Magdaleners ££ from Weingut Heinrich Rottensteiner in the South Tyrol or Alto Adige). Basic to middle-priced Burgundies are generally good; the excellent Burgundian Domaine Machard de Gramont ££ makes regular appearances under various appellations. Try also the excellent sherries of Tomas Abad and Maria Loreto Molleda ££ – though other single-cask sherries may replace these particular ones during the course of the year. Leacock's Madeiras are good. There are some unusual spirits on the list, too – domaine-produced Armagnac, Calvados and Cognac and single-barrel whisky. Bordeaux Direct is Britain's second biggest mail order wine company – deservedly so, because apart from the wines themselves, their direct marketing techniques are efficient and sophisticated. Their introductory offers (advertised in national papers) are good value, and clever: 'three bottles free', but it's only after you've paid for and received the initial three that you receive a voucher for the three free bottles in your next full case . . . good value nevertheless. Reports on delivery service range from 'appalling, four to five weeks, despite my phoning' to 'very quick'. The company opened last year as many as seven unusual 'Taste Shops' in the South-East: relaxed, rustic, places in the mould of the French *cave de dégustation*, where you taste at the counter from bottles kept fresh under nitrogen, and buy by the case. There's sherry and table wine on tap. They own a Bordeaux château (in production next year) and have an office in France to organise group shipments. Barbara and Tony Laithwaite also run the Wine Club of the *Sunday Times (see below)* from the same base in Reading.

BEST BUYS £–££ French country wines

Borg Castel Ⓥ

Samlesbury Mill, Goosefoot Lane, Samlesbury, Preston, Lancashire — TEL (025 485) 2128

OPEN Mon–Fri 10 am–5 pm Thur eve 7 pm–9.30 pm 1st Sun in month 12 noon–4 pm CLOSED Sat, Sun (exc 1st in month), public holidays
CREDIT CARDS Not accepted DISCOUNTS Not available DELIVERY Free within 30 miles, min 1 case GLASS HIRE Free TASTINGS AND TALKS Club tastings every two months CELLARAGE By negotiation

Borg Castel supply some lovely wines from a variety of sources – and at some fair prices, although there is plenty of choice in the lower price ranges £. France takes up the larger part of the list. Amongst some beautiful Loires are Gitton's Sancerre, Chaume Domaine de la Soucherie Moelleux, and old vintages of Gaston Huet's excellent

Vouvrays (the 1967 Moelleux for £4.56 and the 1966 for £5.63). There's a good spread of Alsace wines from several houses – Heim, Hugel, Kuenz-Bas and Dopff au Moulin, including the latter's Crémant d'Alsace [££]. Other names to look out for are the expensive Châteauneuf Chante-Cigale in the Rhônes, and Tollot-Beaut Burgundies. Clarets are mostly petits-châteaux with a few top growths. Good value is to be found in the South Tyrol section of the Italian list, and the producer-less Germans reach up to expensive Trockenbeerenauslesen. There's a bargain German Riesling sparkler, Reichsgraf von Plettenberg Gutsriesling at under £5 for both NV and vintage; the Champagne range is small, but Pol Roger is only £9.53. The small range of fortified wines covers port vintages back to 1955: Graham 1955 for £24.13 and Quinta do Noval 1963 for £16 – excellent value. Borg Castel do not encourage mail order, but will post a minimum of six bottles.

BEST BUYS [£££] Old vintage ports, Champagne

Bottoms Up

See CHAINS AND SUPERMARKETS

Bow Wine Vaults

10 Bow Churchyard, London, EC4 TEL 01-248 1121

OPEN Mon–Fri 9 am–6 pm CLOSED Sat, Sun, public holidays CREDIT CARDS Not accepted DISCOUNTS 5% on unmixed cases; 2 free bottles per case on orders of 6+ cases DELIVERY Free on UK mainland, min 2 unmixed cases; single cases £3.45 GLASS HIRE Free TASTINGS AND TALKS Free annual tasting for customers. Two evening tutored tastings and dinners a year for 30 people. 'Tailor made tastings' for City boardrooms CELLARAGE £2.50 per case per year

That half the wine trade haunts the Bow Wine Vaults' wine bar is the best possible advertisement for this company's wine. Quality is high, but so are prices, though still within reasonable bounds. The list is mostly French, apart from a small but good range of California wines, a couple of Australians, some very good German estate wines and the well-made and not too expensive English wines from Wootton in Somerset [££], some mature Riojas, and Ch Musar from the Lebanon. Particularly worth buying (for laying down for some time because it's still very tough) is the Mas de Daumas Gassac Rouge 1982, a lovely deep rich wine from, amazingly, the Hérault, not cheap at around £6 but still good value. The rosé is also good with lesser outlay. The Loire list is interesting, including probably the best Quarts de Chaume, the crystal-sharp but immensely complex wine from Jean Beaumard – though his 1980 is very expensive at £8.30 a bottle. There's a nice range of Marc Brédif Vouvrays [££] – [£££], and Rhônes are fine: P Jaboulet Aîné, Guigal, Vieux Télégraphe [£££]. Lirac Domaine de la Tour is good value at just over £3. Burgundies are rather heavy on Prosper Maufoux, not our favourites. Faiveley wines are sound, as are the Beaujolais of Domaine Joubert and the Bourgogne Blanc Les Clous 1982 of Albert de Vilaine. Tasting notes beneath the wines in the list are useful. Better still would be a consistent indication of when the finer wines are likely to be ready.

BEST BUYS [£££] German wines, [£££] Mas de Daumas Gassac Rouge [£££] Bow Wine Vaults Champagne

The Bowlish House Wine Shop

Bowlish House, Wells Road, Shepton Mallet, Somerset TEL (0749) 2022

OPEN Mon–Fri (inc public holidays) 9 am–12 pm Sat 9 am–6 pm Sun By arrangement CLOSED Sun (exc by arrangement); 4 days Chr CREDIT CARDS Not accepted DISCOUNTS Not available DELIVERY Not normally provided, 'but if we are passing or customers can wait 7–10 days, we will normally deliver free up to Bath/Bristol or into London' GLASS HIRE 'Not usually, but we could' TASTINGS AND TALKS Frequently held at the restaurant for clubs, societies etc CELLARAGE Free for 'investment wines'

Brian Jordan has made an interesting selection from his 400-strong restaurant list to offer for retail sale by the bottle as well as by the case. Prices are not cheap (perhaps 20p+ up on the average for most wines) but quality throughout the list is consistently good. It's worth enquiring after wines on the restaurant list, too; Bowlish House also offer to find you any other wine you are after 'at a competitive price'. Brian Jordan obviously has a sweet tooth – 16 dessert wines are offered by the glass in the restaurant – so turn first to the back of the list for calorie-packed temptation. There are some unusual and delicious Italian dessert wines: Torcolato Maculan is £10.75 and the raisiny Tanit, Moscato Passito di Pantelleria from the co-operative on this island way south of the Sicilian coast – and it's below market price at under £5. There are sweet Austrians, too, from A Unger, and more. The longest section of the list is French. Quinson table wines are good value at just over £2. There are some well-made Burgundies – don't scorn the Buxy co-operative – and a small range of clarets from £3 to £8. Rhônes from Meffre are good, as are Gisselbrecht Alsace wines, and there's the interesting Fitou from Mme Claude Parmentier, also under £3. Italy is a fair test of a buyer's faculties, and the list here is excellent. Try the Brunello di Montalcino Poggio alle Mura; or the Masi wines [££]–[£££], and Frascati Colli di Catone for just over £3. Spain is interesting, too, with the good Penedès wines of Masía Vallformosa as well as the more commonly met Cáceres, Torres, La Rioja Alta and Murrieta. On this list, you can really scarcely go wrong.

BEST BUYS Most things on the list

British Home Stores

See CHAINS AND SUPERMARKERS

Broadwell Vintners

Church Lane, Broadwell, TEL (0451) 30671
Moreton-in-Marsh, Gloucestershire

OPEN Mon–Fri 9 am–5.30 pm Sat 9 am–1 pm CLOSED Sun
CREDIT CARDS All accepted DISCOUNTS £1.50 per case cash & carry, 4% on six cases DELIVERY Free in Cotswolds and surrounding areas, min 1 case; elsewhere on UK mainland free for 6 cases+ GLASS HIRE Free
TASTINGS AND TALKS Tastings twice a year CELLARAGE £2.50 per case per year

Broadwell Vintners have at last come to rest, after much uncertainty, under the sturdy wing of traditional Cotswold wine merchants Edward Sheldon *(see below)*. But their list remains much as before. It is mainly French, from the traditional areas. The German bottles are soundly chosen, with some estate wines, and Spanish wines come, a little expensively (like much of the list), from the reliable cellars of Torres and La Rioja Alta. Hill Smith wines from Australia are very good, too. Their Cabernet Sauvignon 1976, fat and minty, is a good match for many of the (mostly young) clarets of the same price on the preceding pages. For Cotswold whisky-drinkers, there are a dozen malts culminating in 22-year-old Highland Park.

BEST BUYS [££]–[£££] Spanish wines, [££]–[£££] Hill Smith Australians

G E Bromley & Sons Ltd

SHOP AND WAREHOUSE London Street, Leicester TEL (0533) 768471
SHOP 271 Leicester Road, Wigston Fields, Leicester TEL (0533) 882057

OPEN (London Street) Mon–Fri (inc public holidays) 10 am–1.30 pm, 5.30 pm–10 pm Sat 10 am–1.30 pm, 6 pm–10 pm Sun 12 noon–2 pm, 7 pm–10 pm; (Wigston Fields) Mon–Fri (inc public holidays) 10 am–1 pm, 5.30 pm–10 pm Sat 10 am–2 pm, 5.30 pm–10 pm Sun 12 noon–1.30 pm, 7 pm–10 pm CREDIT CARD Visa DISCOUNTS Occasional special offers; 7–10% at warehouse on case sales DELIVERY Free for mixed doz in Leicester city for 3+ cases; up to 2 cases £1 per case in Leicester; in Leicestershire £2 per case, free for 5+ cases; elsewhere at cost GLASS HIRE 25p per doz TASTINGS AND TALKS Not provided CELLARAGE £2.76 per case per year

You can snap up some very good bargains at the moment on the slightly expanded claret list of this family company, particularly if you buy at the case rate from the warehouse behind the old London Street shop – though claret prices on the shelf by the bottle are competitive too. There are lots of good low-priced petits-châteaux [£]–[££] and prices for some classed clarets are very keen (Léoville-Las-Cases 1976 is just over £12, Chasse-Spleen 1979 not much over £6, Cissac of the same vintage not quite £5 if you buy by the case). The light and fruity Pierre Coste clarets are well priced [££]. Retail mark-up varies from seven to ten per cent. Bromleys are members of the sharp-nosed Merchant Vintners buying group (along with Tanners, Lay & Wheeler and others) which enables them to negotiate good bulk-buy prices. But not all the scoops on the list are from this excellent source. Bromleys have made sure they offer plenty of choice in all areas of their range at £4 and way below. French country wines are well chosen, and it's well worth dabbling in the southern French wines under £2.50 (Côtes de Gascogne, Ch de Gougazaud etc). Sauvignon Trois Mouline and particularly Ch Thieuley Sauvignon star amongst the white Bordeaux. There's a sensible, short Burgundy list, concentrating on the lower end of the price range. Rhônes are good (Merchant Vintners again). Italians are mostly unexciting, but there are some good Germans, plain and estate, again fairly priced. CVNE Riojas and the Torres wines are the pick of the Spanish list, but prices of the Don Cortez brand make these wines good value now that their style – except for the very disappointing red – has been freshened up (early in 1984). Beware of vintage port prices, however, which are a bit high.

BEST BUYS [£]–[£££] Clarets, [£] cheaper French wines, [££] Ch Thieuley Sauvignon

Buckinghams

157 Great Portland Street, London, W1 TEL 01-580 1622
1 Sutton Court Road, London, W4 TEL 01-995 1682
71 Abingdon Road, London, W8 TEL 01-937 3996
98 Holland Park Avenue London, W11 TEL 01-727 5148
6 Fulham Road, London, SW3 TEL 01-584 1450

OPEN Varies from shop to shop CREDIT CARDS Access/Euro, Visa; personal and business accounts DISCOUNTS 5% on cases collected DELIVERY Free in London for case orders, or bottle orders within half a mile of each shop; elsewhere at cost GLASS HIRE Free TASTINGS AND TALKS Regular tastings at shops CELLARAGE Limited, on request

The prices are all a little over the odds at Buckinghams' bright, well-run shops in West London. But service is friendly, staff are well informed, the choice is good and the wines sound, with a few especially interesting wines off the French beaten tracks that provide the sources of most of Buckinghams' wines: Israeli wines [££], Linderos Cabernet Sauvignon from Chile (£3.99), the very drinkable Sidi Brahim (£2.50) from Morocco, and some less commonly encountered Australian wines from Bleesdale and Tollano [££]–[£££], and even a Tasmanian Cabernet Sauvignon, St Moorilla Estate 1981, if your pocket can stretch to £13.70. There are good, cheap Bulgarian staples [£] and a few New Zealand wines [££]. From Spain, there's the good-value Valdepeñas Viña Albalí (£2.35) as well as fine names such as CVNE and Torres. Claret is the high spot in terms of range, with a spread of prices, but again ones you could easily beat by shopping around. Special offers and wines of the month, often open for tasting in the shops, can be good value. Chilled wines are for sale, too, for last-minute buys. Buckinghams print a helpful, light-hearted monthly newsletter called *Spittoon*, with background and tasting notes on their wines on offer.

BEST BUYS Spanish wines

Budgen

See CHAINS AND SUPERMARKETS

Bulls Head

See Wines of Interest

K F Butler & Co Ltd/Hiscocks & Co

19B The Birches Industrial Estate, Imberhorne Lane, East Grinstead, West Sussex TEL (0342) 313955

OPEN Mon–Fri 8.30 am–5 pm CLOSED Sat, Sun, public holidays CREDIT CARDS Not accepted; personal and business accounts DISCOUNTS 50p per case cash & carry DELIVERY London & locally up to 20 miles; £1 on single case orders, thereafter free; 20–49 miles £3 per single case, £2 per case on 2–5 cases, £1 per case on 6–19 cases, thereafter free; charges for more distant places on request GLASS HIRE Free TASTINGS AND TALKS Three organised tastings a year; to groups on request CELLARAGE £1 per case per year

Hiscocks & Co closed down their Croydon shop in February 1984 and moved in with wine importers and their buyers-out K F Butler to a by-the-case-only warehouse in East Grinstead. (Cases may be mixed, but then carry a 75p surcharge.) The company offers quite a good range of French wines at fair prices, some of them good. (It would be fairer still to quote VAT-inclusive prices.) Particularly worth a try are the Beaujolais from Pierre Ferraud, the reliable Rhônes of Vidal-Fleurie and Willm wines from Alsace. Ch de Fonscolombe Coteaux d'Aix-en-Provence red, white and rosé are especially good value at the cheaper end [£], and there's a scattering of interesting wines from other parts of the world – Rosemount, for example, from Australia and Ch Musar from the Lebanon. The Austrian Brüder Grill wines are poor in our view. The company runs a wine club, making special selections every three months, which customers pay for in instalments by standing order.

BEST BUYS [£] Ch de Fonscolombe

The Butlers Wine Cellar (V)

247 Queens Park Road, Brighton, East Sussex TEL (0273) 698724

OPEN Mon–Fri (exc Wed) 9 am–5.30 pm Sat 9 am–1 pm CLOSED Sun, Wed, public holidays CREDIT CARDS Visa; business accounts DISCOUNTS Not available DELIVERY Free within 15 miles of Brighton, min 12 bottles; elsewhere, free for 3+ cases on mainland UK; charges on application for smaller quantities GLASS HIRE Free TASTINGS AND TALKS 2 free tastings a year at local wine bar CELLARAGE Not provided

The mind-boggling, mouth-watering lists put out by the Butlers almost every month are amongst the best in the country for finding mature wines at good prices. Specialising in old vintages, this husband-and-wife team buys in small lots, so that turn-over is rapid and no list looks like its predecessor. Don't turn the page if you're interested only in cheaper wines: Syrah de l'Ardèche at £2.35, young, already drinkable clarets at under £3, Muscadet or Alsace basics. But if your palate is fine and your wallet fat – turn over, drool, and spend away. An astonishingly large range of claret on their June 1984 list stretched back to 1924, the 21 sweet Bordeaux back to 1921. Hardly less astonishing was the range of Burgundies, whites back to 1955, reds to 1952. The fine range of nine Alsace wines, nearly all Vendange Tardive or Sélection Particulière or the like included two 1976s, and there were three vintages of the Coulée de Serrant in the Loire from Mme Joly – 1977, 1966 and 1964 (£10.75, £18.40 and £18.40 again). There are 1971 and 1975 Germans, mostly Auslesen, with some sweeter; and old Champagnes, old Madeiras, ports back to 1947. Oddities in June included a Swiss wine – 1971 Romane Dôle Cuvée Spéciale Rouge (Orsat), an unusual experiment for just £4.95, though no doubt over the mountain top by now (and perhaps sold out, since there were only 12 bottles); probably still available, however, will be some of the 72 bottles of 1949 Vinho Tinto Garrafeira Particular (Ferreira) bottled 1966 with wax capsules (listed under Spain, though we are mean to point out a rare mistake) – it no doubt *is* particular, too, but not too expensive a potential disappointment at £8.95.

BEST BUYS [£]–[£££] Most things on the list

Anthony Byrne Fine Wines

(Sales office) Kingscote House, TEL (0487) 814555
Biggin Lane, Ramsey, Cambridgeshire
(Warehouse and collections from) Warboys No 1 Bond, The Old Airfield, Warboys, Huntingdon, Cambridgeshire

OPEN (Warboys warehouse, for collection) Mon–Fri 9am–4 pm CLOSED Sat, Sun (collections may be made from Kingscote House 'at any time')
CREDIT CARDS Not accepted; personal and business accounts
DISCOUNTS 5% for cash & carry DELIVERY Free in the UK, min 2 cases; 1 case £5 GLASS HIRE Free TASTINGS AND TALKS About 1 a month, free
CELLARAGE £1.50 per case per year

There are some good bargains to be had from Anthony Byrne, who does most of his trade with restaurants, but sells also to the public (by the case only, which may be mixed). You can buy anything from his main list, but the bargains are to be found on his periodic 'special offer' lists – mostly clarets and Burgundies. He holds the regional agency for Duboeuf – so stocks the full range – Charles Viénot Burgundies, the good Sauvion Muscadets, and the dependable Vacqueyras Co-operative. The house wines from Duboeuf, Sauvion and Viénot are good. You will also find on the main list and sometimes in the specials list Louis

Michel Chablis, 'clean pure and flinty', as Anthony Byrne says, Jean Durup Chablis, another of the best Chablis producers, Paul Jaboulet Aîné Rhônes, Burgundies from Tollot-Beaut, Sauzet and others, Foreau's excellent Vouvray, some good Spanish and Italian wines and estate Germans (the company holds the national agency for three estates including Paul Anheuser and the fine wines of Reichsgraf von Kesselstatt). If you live in the Cambridge area or buy in quantity (two cases or more are delivered free anywhere in the UK), it is worth putting yourself on the Byrne mailing list.

BEST BUYS Special offers

D Byrne & Co (V)

12 King Street, Clitheroe, Lancashire TEL (0200) 23152

OPEN Mon–Wed & Sat 9 am–6 pm Thur–Fri 9 am–8 pm CLOSED Sun, public holidays CREDIT CARDS Not accepted; personal and business accounts DISCOUNTS £1 on mixed case, £1.20 on unmixed cases; 5% on orders over £250 DELIVERY Free case delivery within 20 miles, min 1 bottle in the town, 12 bottles beyond; elsewhere on UK mainland £3.75 per case GLASS HIRE Free TASTINGS AND TALKS For groups at £2 per head CELLARAGE Not available

Clitheroe wine drinkers are some of the most fortunate in the country. Prices at D Byrne & Co are very good, and the range – covering Europe and the New World – is excellent. Particularly outstanding is the long list of estate-bottled German wines, which concentrates on Kabinetts to Auslesen, mostly of recent vintages, though with some 1976s, and mostly in the £4 to £10 bracket. Bordeaux is well represented with some good-value petits-châteaux £–££ and a good selection of younger clarets for laying down, unhelpfully with no indication of when they might be ready for drinking. There are a few older clarets as far back as 1969. Burgundies, mostly late 1970s and early 1980s vintages, are from a wide range of merchants, Chanson, Jadot and Clair Daü featuring heavily. Beaujolais emphasis is on Duboeuf, there's a good selection from merchants in the Rhône, and a strong Loire list, largely from growers (the best include Vacheron in Sancerre £££, Mme Joly in Anjou £££, and Foreau in Vouvray ££). Mr Byrne obviously likes his Muscadet – seven are on the list. There's a spread of Alsace styles with Hugel, Trimbach and Gisselbrecht. The Spanish range includes fine Riojas and most of the excellent Torres range. Italians are good, too (try Masi, Pio Cesare, Nera and the Chiantis). Two pages of California wines at low prices and a handful of Australians are worth looking at, and three excellent Almacenista (single cask) ££–£££ sherries complete the long list of sherry brands. Also offered are a good range of half-bottles, malt whiskies . . . and wine boxes. In addition to his awards for value and service, David Byrne probably qualifies for our worst-spelt wine list award! And, marathon job as it would be, tasting notes, an index and a sensible order would help the no doubt bemused populace of Clitheroe to find their way around this wonderful list.

BEST BUYS Most of the list, ££–£££ German estate wines

Cachet Wines

12 First Avenue, York, North Yorkshire TEL (0904) 425853

OPEN No retail outlet but one may be opened in York late 1984; orders by telephone or post only CREDIT CARDS Not accepted DISCOUNTS Not available DELIVERY Free within 25 miles approx, min 1 mixed case; remainder of Yorkshire £3 per delivery; elsewhere on UK mainland £5 per delivery GLASS HIRE Free TASTINGS AND TALKS On request CELLARAGE £1.50 per case per year MAIL ORDER SPECIALISTS

This careful list, dispensed from home, provides excellent value, especially in the lower price ranges [£], where there is a wonderful choice. Tasting notes on all the wines are extremely helpful – and reliable. Six wines worth trying, all around £2–£2.50, are the Vin de Pays de Gascogne 1983 Colombard, Union des Producteurs (the 1984 as soon as it becomes available in the spring of 1985); two wines from the Côtes-de-Duras; the Sauvignon du Haut Poitou, Faugères, SCEP St-Félix-de-Lodez; the delicious Syrah Vin de Pays de l'Ardèche from the Cave Co-opérative St-Désirat; and the Vin de Pays de la Dordogne, a blend of Cabernet Franc and Merlot from the Producteurs Réunis. The more traditional and more expensive French list looks interesting, too, and there were some good opening prices in the summer of 1984 for the small range of 1983 clarets and Sauternes. Most of the list is French, but the Italians are also well selected. Names worth noting are Masi (Valpolicella, Campo Fiorín, and Soave), and the best of Frascatis, Colli di Catone, all at under £3. Watch out for bargain bin-end prices. Cachet Wines have only a wholesale licence, so sell only by the case, but this may be mixed any way you choose. They offer especially good value in the free delivery area, but if you live beyond, you can arrange to collect from them. They plan to open a 'retail wine centre' in York at the end of 1984.

BEST BUYS Most things on the list

Cairns & Hickey

17 Blenheim Terrace, Leeds, W Yorks TEL (0532) 459501

OPEN Mon–Fri 9 am–6 pm Sat 9 am–1 pm CLOSED Sun, public holidays CREDIT CARDS Not accepted; personal and business accounts DISCOUNTS 5% on case orders DELIVERY Free within 25 mile radius, min 1 case; elsewhere, single bottles by post at cost, one case or more at carrier's cost GLASS HIRE 35p per doz TASTINGS AND TALKS Informal tastings held on premises CELLARAGE £1.25 per case per year

Cairns & Hickey stock a big, mostly European range, including many branded wines: plenty of sound wines to choose from, but little to warrant a detour, except, perhaps, if you're after sweet wines. There's a good range of mature German, Beerenauslesen and Trockenbeerenauslesen, though rather fewer sweet Bordeaux than previously. They stock a fair range of Burgundies from decent houses, and a modest selection of clarets culminating in 1961 La Lagune. Some of the mature claret prices are quite keen. The Italian range is boring. But the range of malt whiskies (25 at present) gets better and better.

BEST BUYS ££ Alsace Hugel, £££ sweet Germans

Camden Wine & Cheese Ⓥ

214 Camden High Street, London, NW1 TEL 01-482 2553

OPEN Tue–Fri 10 am–6.30 pm Sat 9.30 am–6 pm Sun 12 noon–2 pm
CLOSED Mon, public holidays DISCOUNTS 10% on case orders DELIVERY Free locally for case orders; no delivery elsewhere GLASS HIRE Free
TASTINGS AND TALKS, CELLARAGE Not available

The Champagne prices down in the cellar of Camden Wine & Cheese are hard to beat – and all the more interesting in the local free delivery area. Even the Champagne House *(see below)* can't match many of these prices. There are 52 Champagnes to choose from, including nine rosés, nine vintage 1976s, 12 de luxes, a couple *'sans sucre'* and the delicious Mumm Crémant de Cramant. You can buy some in halves, magnums, jeroboams, rehoboams, methuselahs and salmanazars, too! The rest of the list is very sound, and well priced, if (mostly) less dramatically so. A few good choices are Marqués de Cáceres red and white ££, the Torres wines ££, Valdespino Innocente Fino Sherry (£2.99), the Côtes de Buzet wines, especially Cuvée Napoléon 1980 (£3.99), Cousiño Macul Cabernet Sauvignon 1976 (£4.75) and the light, delicious Muscat de Beaumes-de-Venise Vidal-Fleurie (£6.39). Bin-ends in the lower price ranges are often good value.

BEST BUYS Champagnes

Cape Province Wines Ⓥ

11 Clarence Street, Staines, Middlesex TEL (0784) 51860
1 Broadway, Kingston Road, Staines, Middlesex TEL (0784) 52812

OPEN Mon–Thur 10 am–6 pm Fri 10 am–7.30 pm Sat 9 am–6 pm
CLOSED Sun and public holidays CREDIT CARDS Access/Euro, Visa
DISCOUNTS 5% (approx) on case orders DELIVERY Free within 10 miles for 6+ bottles; elsewhere on UK mainland £4.50 for 6–12 bottles, £3.50 per case for 2–5 cases, 6+ cases free GLASS HIRE Free TASTINGS AND TALKS Twice-yearly tastings with substantial buffet for customers + guest, £3 each
CELLARAGE £2.40 per case per year

Cape Province Wines' two shops in Staines stock one of the best ranges in the country of South African wines. Being independent of the big white chiefs in South Africa, their range is more interesting than those of the other two specialists in London, Collisons (a subsidiary of Stellenbosch/Bergkelder) and The Cape Wine Centre retail outlet, due to close this year, of the South African wine co-operative, the KWV). Cape Province Wines' branded wines include the whole reliable KWV range (with the exception of the wine boxes) [£]–[££], Fleur du Cap from the Bergkelder at prices that beat Henry Collisons' own, the Nederburg brands, and a few more – all at prices to match, or nearly, the rock-bottom rates at Cullens, who stock a small South African range. Prices for the estate wines, of which there are around 40 on the list, are also fairly competitive. Excellent value at just under £3 are the two wines from the Twee Jongegezellen estate in the north of the Cape wine growing area, TJ39 and Schanderl, and the Meerlust reds are very good [£££]. The list also includes sparkling, dessert, and sherry-type wines, brandies and liqueurs, and, interestingly, some old vintages of wines from the Nederburg auctions (back to 1967) at prices up to nearly £23). The free delivery service is worth using if you live within a ten-mile radius of Staines. The company operates a gift service in this country, delivering South African wines from friends and relations in South Africa – and indeed a similar service for Brown Bros Australian wines. They work the scheme in reverse, too, arranging for wines gifts to be delivered to addresses in South Africa, Australia, New Zealand.

BEST BUYS Most things on the list

Carley and Webb Wine Cellars

25 Fore Street, Framlingham, Nr Woodbridge, Suffolk — TEL (0728) 724106

OPEN Mon–Sat 8.30 am–5.30 pm CLOSED Wed pm, Sun, public holidays
CREDIT CARDS Access/Euro, Visa; personal and business accounts
DISCOUNTS 5% on case orders DELIVERY Free within 12 miles for orders £25+; deliveries up to 50 miles on application GLASS HIRE Free
TASTINGS AND TALKS Free tastings for their wine club, at least 8 times a year
CELLARAGE 50p per case per year

In addition to a fairly large spread of clarets back to 1950, and a mixed bag of Burgundies back to 1970, Carley and Webb stock some good sweet German wines, a larger than usual selection of our home-grown wines – Bruisyard St Peter, Brandeston Priory, Magdalen, Heywood etc [££], the good Concha y Toro Chilean reds [£]–[££], a Bulgarian selection very reasonably priced at under £2, and some good Garvey sherries; the Italian and Spanish sections are both unexciting.

BEST BUYS [£££] Clarets [££] Garvey sherries [£] Bulgarian wines

Carrefour

See CHAINS AND SUPERMARKETS

[£] means that a wine costs, from most producers and in most British shops, under £3 a bottle, [££] that it costs between £3 and £5, and [£££] that it costs over £5.

Caves de la Madeleine

301 Fulham Road, London, SW10 TEL 01-351 5863
Associated with Copyhold Farm shop, TEL (073 57) 4220
Goring Heath, Oxfordshire

OPEN (London) Mon–Sat 9.30 am–8.30 pm Sun 12 noon–2 pm CLOSED Public holidays CREDIT CARDS All accepted; personal accounts DISCOUNTS 5% on case sales DELIVERY Free in London, min one case; elsewhere £2 for 1 case, £3 for 2 cases, £4 for 3 cases GLASS HIRE Free TASTINGS AND TALKS Bi-annual tasting of 12 wines for customers. Tastings for clubs by arrangement CELLARAGE Cheap at £1.80 per case per year

Prices are high at Caves de la Madeleine, but within the wide range, best value is to be found amongst the wines of more obscure (mostly French) origin, particularly the South-West of France, and also of the Loire – wines which are not to be found elsewhere. But at least you can rest assured that the quality will be the best available wherever your hand may stray on these neat, well-labelled shelves. The 20 Italian wines are excellent from beginning to end: the Barolo of Cavallotto, good Chiantis [££], particularly the Castello di San Pollo in Rosso, Cabernet Sauvignon Sassicaia – and more. The few Spanish wines are good, with a remarkably good price as we went to press for Marqués de Cáceres: hurry before the Caves discover their mistake! California wines are well represented, but again expensive. On French home ground, prices are still high, despite the fact that owner Stephen Spurrier (author of the useful pocket *French Country Wines* and founder of the Académie du Vin school in Paris) buys also for his Paris shops, wine bars and restaurant. Our choice amongst the Bordeaux are the two cheaper Graves, one from Pierre Coste, and Clos de l'Hôpital [££]. Look out in the Loire for the Sancerres of Vacheron [£££], the excellent Muscadet Domaine des Dorices (£3.75) and Beaujolais from Pierre Ferraud – his Côtes de Brouilly 1983 is delicious, firm but ready to drink this year (£4.65). Rhônes, particularly Guigal and Ch de Beaucastel [££] – [£££], are excellent – and terribly overpriced!

BEST BUYS [£] – [££] Wines of South-West France

Cellarmaster Ltd

Broadhembury House, Jarvis Brook, TEL (089 26) 64400
Crowborough, East Sussex

OPEN (telephone only) Mon–Fri 9 am–5.30 pm CLOSED Sat, Sun, public holidays CREDIT CARDS All accepted DISCOUNTS Not available DELIVERY Free on mainland UK, min 2 cases, £1.50 for 1 case GLASS HIRE Not available TASTINGS AND TALKS Not available CELLARAGE £2.50 per case per year MAIL ORDER SPECIALISTS

Cellarmasters started up in the mail order business half a dozen years ago, offering wine selections to American Express cardholders, but that sole plastic link has been broken now for a couple of years. The wines are well bought from reputable sources such as Hallgarten, Trimbach, and French Wine Farmers, a competent wholesale company dealing in wines from French companies, estates and co-operatives, cultivating special links with Ch Cissac, which features regularly on lists issued by post every two months. The Rhônes of Caves St-Pierre are good. Prices tend to be a little high, and an opening offer of 1983 clarets was very highly priced indeed.

The Champagne House

15 Dawson Place, London, W2 TEL 01-221 5538

OFFICE OPEN (no retail shop) Mon–Thur 9 am–6 pm CLOSED Fri, Sat, Sun, public holidays CREDIT CARDS Not accepted DISCOUNTS For quantity, by negotiation DELIVERY Free in the City of London, Westminster, Kensington and Chelsea, min 12 bottles; elsewhere at carrier's cost GLASS HIRE Champagne flûtes or Perrier-Jouët 'Fin de Siècle' flower-enamelled glasses, both free TASTINGS AND TALKS Given from time to time for selected private customers by invitation only CELLARAGE Not available MAIL ORDER ONLY

If Richard Freeman were headmaster in Champagne, there would certainly be no nonsense at the back of the cellar. Some sharp raps over the knuckles were delivered in the 1984 list from these unique Champagne specialists to those who have been caught with their wines too young or too cheap, declaring vintages out of purely commercial motives; and to wine writers who, it seems, almost always fail the Champagne test. Standards and expectations are high here. But prices are *low*. At £1 to £3 *a bottle* less for the same wines than most other retailers in the country, the Champagne House's wines are a great bargain to anyone wanting to buy Champagne by the case. (They have only a wholesale license, 12 bottles minimum, but they will mix in four threes.) The Freeman discipline is applied also to financial matters (he is a stockbroker, after all). Cash is strictly pre-delivery – which goes some way to explaining their low prices. But customers, nevertheless, 'are generally accepted as a result of personal introductions or recommendations'. Thirty-nine wines are listed, plus a ratafia (a sweet, traditional Champenois aperitif of grape juice mixed with marc de Champagne) at just under £8, and a marc (£10.90), curiously referred to throughout the list as a 'liqueur', though this one certainly isn't sweet. They have the exclusive distribution in this country of the wines of small producer Albert Lebrun of Avize, whose non-vintage (£7.50) and Blanc de Blancs (£8.96) are delicious and very good value. These are their best sellers. Other NVs include Pol Roger White Foil and Roederer; vintages, mostly 1975 and 1976, include Bollinger RD, Deutz, Pol Roger again, and Krug back to 1973, at prices also well below other merchants' lists. Blanc de Blancs rise to the costly heights of the excellent Salon de Mesnil 1973 and 1976, each £20 a bottle; to taste a Blanc de Noirs, the premium shoots up to £48 a bottle for Bollinger Vieilles Vignes Françaises (grown on ancient, ungrafted vines in a small phylloxera-free, walled vineyard). Rosé Charbaut is very good Champagne at £7.98, and there are four vintage rosés. Mumm Crémant de Cramant is not much cheaper than elsewhere. The list winds up with five still Côteaux Champenois. Larger sizes of some wines – up to a 12-bottle equivalent salmanazar, are available on request. The Freemans now label all their non-vintage wines with the landing date – a means others might usefully copy of informing the consumer how long the bottle has been lying around in the UK. Day-to-day business is done by Jenny Freeman, who 'likes to get to know' her customers and will spend 'half an hour on the phone discussing orders'. They offer delivery in London within 24 hours.

BEST BUYS [£££] Everything on the list, particularly Lebrun wines

Champagne de Villages

Wellesley House, Elton Park, Ipswich, Suffolk TEL (0473) 56922

OPEN 'All hours!' CREDIT CARDS Not accepted; personal and business accounts DISCOUNTS Not given DELIVERY Free locally for case orders; elsewhere £3 per case up to 5 cases, thereafter free GLASS HIRE Free TASTINGS AND TALKS On request CELLARAGE Not available

No, not purely a Champagne specialist, though this is how the business began four years ago, and the Westbrooks' glossy list does sport 27 Champagnes from eight small growers at prices from £6.60 to £10, plus a number of halves and larger bottles. They stock purely French wines, though, largely from smallish growers, but from some *négociants* too. But first Champagne: two producers of Coteaux Champenois Rouge, one grower of Blanc, and a Rosé from the village of Riceys, plus a ratafia – freshly pressed grape juice with marc at £8.95 – and a marc de Champagne (£12.30). There's a full range from the excellent Barsac property, Ch Caillou: the 1976, 1978 and 1981 vintages are listed, but older vintages back to 1909, where available, will be obtained on request. A new arrival, Ch Caillou Sec, is a delicious, fragrant, dry wine from the same property, half-Sémillon, half-Sauvignon, wonderful value at just over £3. There follow three Graves properties (Larivet Haut-Brion, Carbonnieux and Domaine de Chevalier); Burgundies from merchant Delaunay and good owner-producer Roger Chapelle at Domaine des Hautes Cornières, Beaune, then small ranges from growers and merchants in the Beaujolais, Loire, Rhône and Alsace, all rounded off with rather special Calvados and Armagnac at rather special prices: £21 and £12.95 per bottle respectively. It is good to see background information on all the growers. Tasting notes and advice on when to drink would be the final touch. Champagne de Villages have a wholesale licence, so sell only by the case, which may be mixed. Tony Westbrook's main occupation is his building and shopfitting business in Ipswich, but his wife Claire runs the wine business during the day – hence the very accommodating hours.

BEST BUYS [£££] Champagnes, [££] Ch Caillou Sec

Chaplin & Son

35 Rowlands Road, Worthing, West Sussex TEL (0903) 35888
OPEN Mon–Sat 9 am–1 pm, 2.15 pm–5.30 pm CLOSED Sun, public holidays
CREDIT CARDS Access/Euro, Visa DISCOUNTS 5% off mixed cases
DELIVERY Free for case orders within 7 miles of Worthing GLASS HIRE Free
TASTINGS AND TALKS For local groups at wine cost CELLARAGE Not available

This is a good, interesting range chosen by Master of Wine Tony Chaplin, some of the wines bought through a small consortium of five Sussex wine merchants, which eases prices, most of which are fair, some good. There are some fine non-vintage ports (the excellent Fonseca Bin 27 is only £5.47), and prices of the small range of vintage ports (back to 1955) are cheap. Try the wonderful Almacenista sherries ££, some of them only just over £3. Clarets are unhelpfully listed in price order, with no indication of when they might be ready to drink, but are in general good value. Nathaniel Johnston wines, red and white, including the house claret, are also good value £–££. Loron Beaujolais are reliable, Rhônes are mostly the middle-weights of Pascal at middle-weight prices ££. In the Loire, Vacheron Sancerres are some of the very best. The 1977/78 vintage reds are more mature than most Vacheron reds on shelves elsewhere, and very reasonable ££. The rest of France is skimpily covered. Look out, though, for the Listel wines – excellent, fresh, fruity vins de pays from the southern French coast, including the fresh, clean sparkler Brut de Listel at just over £3. English wines from Carr Taylor are enjoyable but expensive ££. There are a few fine Germans, including estate wines, and Tony Chaplin offers to scout around for any other German estate wines customers might want – that goes for other areas too. The rich, alcoholic Pasmados 1974 (£3.63) is one of the better red Portuguese wines. Italy is well represented (Masi, Nera) £–£££. Spanish wines are almost exclusively from Torres, not particularly cheap, but some older red vintages than are usually found elsewhere. Brown Bros Australians are good. And there's a scattering from other wine-growing areas. The list of malts is particularly outstanding.

BEST BUYS £ Listel wines, ££ Almacenista sherries, £–£££ clarets, ££–£££ ports

The Château (Belfast)

See CHAINS AND SUPERMARKETS

> We should very much appreciate further comments and suggestions of establishments of particular interest to the wine lover. There are report forms at the back of this book.

Chesterford Vintners

The Old Greyhound, Great Chesterford, Saffron Walden, Essex TEL (0799) 30088

OPEN Mon–Wed 9.30 am–5.30 pm Thur, Fri 7.30 am–7.30 pm Sat 9 am–5 pm CLOSED Sun, public holidays CREDIT CARDS Access/Euro, Visa; personal and business accounts DISCOUNTS 2.5% on 3–6 cases, 4% on 7–10 cases, 6% thereafter DELIVERY Free within 25 miles of Great Chesterford, and in Central London, min 2 cases; elsewhere £3.90 for single cases, £2.40 per case on 2–4 cases, 72p per case on 5–10 cases, thereafter free GLASS HIRE Free TASTINGS AND TALKS Regular tastings at Great Chesterford. Tutored group tastings on request CELLARAGE Charges on request

Chesterford stock a fair range of European wines, mostly French, a very few from the New World, at fairly steep prices. Most of the list is in the ££ range, but the choice at the lower end is perhaps best value: try the Vin de Pays de l'Ardèche, Cépage Syrah from the Producteurs de St-Désirat-Champagne (and Louis Latour's Chardonnay de l'Ardèche, a bit more expensive at £3.98). There are only a few clarets. Burgundies are fair, many in the ££ range. The German range is better and includes such suppliers as the Friedrich-Willhelm Gymnasium, SA Prüm and Dr Weil. There are some good Italians: the delicious but expensive Sassicaia 1980 (£9.44), Chianti Classico Riserva Villa Antinori 1979 (£4.52), the good and cheaper Chianti Classico Rocca delle Maccie 1981 (£2.89), and the reliable wines of Fontanafredda and Fabiano. The Hill Smith range from Australia is excellent £–£££. The old sherries from Gonzalez Byass are good £££, and the Palo Cortado from Cuvillo (£4.89). Rare and interesting spirits abound on Chesterford's list: malts, marcs, eaux-de-vie, Cognacs and vintage Armagnacs.

BEST BUYS £–£££ Hill Smith Australians, ££ Cuvillo Palo Cortado, ££ middle-range Burgundies

Christopher & Co

4 Ormond Yard, London, SW1 TEL 01-930 5557

OPEN Mon–Fri 9 am–5.30 pm CLOSED Sat, Sun, public holidays CREDIT CARDS Not accepted; personal and business accounts DISCOUNTS 6% on case orders DELIVERY Free on UK mainland for 6 bottles or more GLASS HIRE Free TASTINGS AND TALKS On request CELLARAGE Temporarily unavailable as we go to press

If you tread with care through the list of Britain's (reputedly) oldest wine merchant, there are some bargains to be had – and also some occasional high prices, so shop around to check. There are some good and interesting wines on the list, but also many that are rather dull. Surprisingly for a firm with a rather old-fashioned image, good value is to be found at the bottom end of the list. The vins de pays from the Côtes de Gascogne are excellent at just over £2. The Côtes du Lubéron wines are a find at the same price, but make sure the white is the latest possible vintage. There's a fine array of claret, the prices comparing favourably with other reasonably priced lists. Burgundy is less interesting, with lots of Ropiteau; Germans and Italians are boring. Christopher's have the agency for Cousiño Macul Chilean wines [££], and their prices for this good value Cabernet and Chardonnay pair are very competitive, as are also prices of the three Blanquette de Limoux sparklers [££], one of the best outside Champagne, for which they are also agents. Some port prices are good, but beware of the expensive Dow 1970 – surprising considering that Christopher's now belong to Scottish & Newcastle Breweries, who hold the Dow agency. It would be nice to see specific information on the producers and the wines on the list rather than the very general comments on wine areas.

BEST BUYS [£] Vins de Pays, clarets, [££] Blanquette de Limoux, [££] Chilean wines

City Cellars Ltd

3 Upper Paul Street, Exeter, Devon TEL (0392) 214565

OPEN Mon–Thur 10 am–7 pm Fri, Sat 10 am–10 pm Public holidays 10 am–1 pm, 2 pm–4 pm CLOSED 1 day a year CREDIT CARDS Access/Euro, Visa; business accounts DISCOUNTS Ask for separate wholesale list DELIVERY Free in Exeter and London, no min order; elsewhere at cost GLASS HIRE Free TASTINGS AND TALKS Monthly tasting for both trade and private customers, often tutored by one of the winemakers represented CELLARAGE Not provided

This small off-licence in Exeter was recently taken over and transformed by Alasdair Crosby, who had formerly acted as wholesale agent for eight German estates after five years' 'apprenticeship' in the German vineyards. His list, predictably, is hot on Germans, particularly estate wines (Weingut Rappenhof, Dr Muth, Rheinhessen; Fürstlich Castell'shes Domänenamt, Castell, Franconia; Prinz zu Salm-Dalberg, Schloss Wallhausen, Nahe, etc). These rise in sweetness only as high as Auslese, with plenty of Trockens and Halbtrockens, and most vintages are fairly recent, apart from a few 1976s; they span the price ranges, with plenty of interesting choice at the lower levels and rising to a rosé Zell-Weierbacher Abtsberg Spätburgunder Weissherbst Auslese 1976, from Freiherr von und zu Franckenstein, Offenburg, Baden for £9.63; and a Casteller Schlossberg Rieslaner Auslese 1979 from the Fürstlich Castell'sches Domänenamt for £11.69. This is a good place to look if you are after the rarer German grape varieties: you will find oddities such as Schwarzriesling, Lemberger, Trollinger and even the Albalonga (a complicated crossing between the Rieslaner, itself a Riesling/Silvaner cross, and the Silvaner). Italian wines, as we go to press, make up the end of the list, and there, too, Mr Crosby has assembled an interesting array. The Piedmont wines are particularly good. There are top quality Barolos back to 1969 (£12.07) from Giacomo Conterno; his Dolcetto and Freisa are also worth a try [££]: the excellent Carema 1979 of Luigi Ferrando (£4.97), the good Gattinara

1976 (£4.72) from Luigi Dessiliani, and a good Asti Spumante from Tenuta Bertulot (£4.10). The selection ranges over other parts of Northern and Central Italy, and includes probably the best Lambrusco going, Cavicchioli (£2.26), and a very good Frascati Superiore, Villaporziana (Colli di Catone under a pseudonym). A note at the back of the summer 1984 list invited enquiries about their small range of vintage clarets, Burgundies and ports. Alasdair Crosby hopes to extend his French list shortly, and has recently taken on the South-West agency for Listel – so watch out for these good value, fresh Southern French wines. It is worth noting that this company will deliver free (any quantity) in London or Exeter.

BEST BUYS [£]–[££] Listel wines, [££]–[£££] Wines from Giacomo Conterno, [££] Luigi Ferrando

The Clapham Cellars (V)

Arch 19, Grant Road, London, SW11 TEL 01-223 6057 or 6724

OPEN Mon–Fri 10 am–7 pm Sat 10 am–5.30 pm CLOSED Sun, public holidays
CREDIT CARDS Access/Euro, Visa DISCOUNTS Not available DELIVERY £2 per case in Central London, £3 rest of UK GLASS HIRE Free
TASTINGS AND TALKS Wines always open for tasting; major wine tastings every 2 months CELLARAGE £2 per case per year

This new wine cash and carry opened early in July 1984, a sister company to mail order business Goedhuis & Co *(see below)*, who continue as before, with free delivery in Central London, credit accounts etc. There are fewer frills in Clapham, but prices are very good indeed, and the selection of wines (not yet complete as we went to press) is excellent, starting with the table wine at just over £2 a bottle. There are some delightful Rhônes and Burgundies (Côtes du Ventoux La Vieille Ferme, £28.90, Puligny-Montrachet 1982, Sauzet, £94) and a few good Loires, clarets, Beaujolais. Marqués de Cáceres 1976 is well priced at £29. There are Champagnes and a few German wines, too. Opening offers of 1983 clarets through Goedhuis & Co, were very competitive: Ch Chasse-Spleen £45.75, and amongst the three sweet Bordeaux, Ch Rieussec 1983 at £74. (*All prices quoted are per case.*)

Cliffe Cellars

See ELLIS SON & VIDLER LTD

The Clifton Cellars

22 The Mall, Clifton, Bristol, Avon TEL (0272) 730287

OPEN Mon–Sat 9 am–6 pm CLOSED Sun, public holidays (exc Good Fri)
CREDIT CARDS Visa; personal and business accounts DISCOUNTS 4% on case orders DELIVERY Free in city of Bristol, min 1 bottle; elsewhere, £1.75 per bottle,

£2 per case GLASS HIRE Free TASTINGS AND TALKS For major customers on request CELLARAGE £1.50 per case per year

This small, friendly shop was once owned by Morans of Bristol and, though independent now for five years, it still stocks wines supplied by Morans, so benefiting from the Merchant Vintners' buying group terms (other members include Adnams and Lay & Wheeler), as well as a growing range of the Clifton Cellars' own purchases. This is an extremely well-chosen, well-balanced list, if not exactly cheap. Particularly mouth-watering is the Rhône list: Ch du Grand Moulas 1981 (£3.56), Châteauneuf du Vieux Télégraphe 1981 (£6.17), Domaine de Beaucastel 1979 (£6.68), and wines from Guigal and Paul Jaboulet. There's a big range of clarets, beginning with the excellent generics of Nathaniel Johnston at around £3, a lot of first growths of the 1976 and 1970 vintages, a few 1966s, 1955s, and oddments back to 1921 Ch Gruaud-Larose at £83.17. There are some bargains, but if you've a lot to spend, collect a few lists and compare, or check the going rates at auction. The few Beaujolais crus are well chosen (Loron, Sarrau, Duboeuf) and the Burgundy range (lots of Chanson) has been extended to include more growers' wines. Basic Alsace wines are mostly from the excellent house of Kuenz Bas but there are also special wines (Réserve Exceptionnelle, Vendange Tardive) and some older vintages from Domaine Dopff, Hugel, Trimbach and a few mystery houses. A few good French wines of lesser regions are listed, too: Ch de Gourgazaud Minervois (£2.94) and Ch de Fonscolombe Aix-en-Provence (£2.79). Good simple Germans from Müller and Huesgen are supplemented by a range of estate-bottled wines including some from von Bühl, the Diefenhard'sches Weingut, Deinhard estates; and Schloss Vollrads for the drier-toothed. It is unusual to see some of the better Lenz Moser Austrians ££–£££, well worth a try. Italians are also very good: Masi, Tedeschi, Poggio alle Mura; there's Torres and a couple of good Riojas from Spain, the delightful Hill Smith Australians, and a 1967 Ch Musar for £8.91! The Clifton Cellar was hoping to open a second shop and wine bar in Wells, Somerset, in the summer of 1984, just too late for this year's *Guide*.

BEST BUYS £–£££ Rhônes, £ French country wines

College Cellar Ltd

56 Walton Street, London, SW3 TEL 01-584 9855

OPEN Mon–Fri 9.30 am–5.30 pm CLOSED Sat, Sun, public holidays CREDIT CARDS Not accepted DISCOUNTS Not available DELIVERY Free for 5+ cases in London postal districts, £3 per delivery for smaller quantities (min 1 case) GLASS HIRE, TASTINGS AND TALKS, CELLARAGE Not available MAIL ORDER ONLY

If you are looking for very old vintages of claret and port, or even Burgundy, we'd advise you to study the latest list of the College Cellar, compare it with the equally good old vintage list of La Vigneronne *(see below)* and with auction prices. In many cases the College Cellar may well be the cheapest. Lists are issued every month or so because stock turns over quickly, being bought keenly, in lots sometimes as small as one half-bottle. Some wines obviously come from auction, some from the trade, but a number are also marked on the list as being sold for private buyers, who pay a commission to the College Cellar – the great advantage for you is that you pay no VAT. (Don't forget that VAT needs to be added to the other prices and sometimes duty, too.) The bulk of the list is always claret, with vintages perhaps from 1929. Ports go back to 1947, and there's lots of lovely sweet Bordeaux as far back as 1924 on the most recent list we have as we go to press. If you are prepared to take the risk, there are six vintages of Champagne back to 1919, and a collection of 'fiftieth birthday presents': 1934 vintages, of course, including a risky bunch of Burgundies.

BEST BUYS Old and rare wines

Peter Collins Wines & Spirits

12 Shakespeare Street, Newcastle-upon-Tyne, Tyne & Wear   TEL (0632) 325795

OPEN Mon–Sat 9.45 am–4.45 pm CLOSED Sun (except for wholesale), public holidays CREDIT CARDS Access/Euro, Visa; personal and business accounts; Wine Guild Card DISCOUNTS 10% on case sales, and to Wine Guild members on smaller quantities DELIVERY Free within 10 miles of Newcastle, min 1 mixed case; thereafter terms on request GLASS HIRE 5p per glass (includes washing) TASTINGS AND TALKS 10 tastings per year for Wine Guild; tutored tastings on request, £3 per person, min 15 people CELLARAGE £5 per case per year

'My wine business is like a mistress. It costs me dearly but gives enormous pleasure,' writes Peter Collins, who is obviously a poorer selector of mistresses than of wine. 'I am still not convinced that the people of the North-East really want a fine wine merchant. If it were not for my restaurant, I would have gone bust years ago. That is why I have decided to help the public to make wine fun.' The fun in question is to be found at Peter Collins' Wine Guild, a club started in 1984 offering, for £12 a year membership fee, monthly tastings and wine workshops, an enthusiastic newsletter, and ten per cent off wines in the well-stocked shop opposite his restaurant. The choice of wines is admirable in this country of beer drinkers. The list begins with 12 Australian wines, including some unusual names: Michelton, Vignacourt and others [££]–[£££]. From Spain, there are seven of the excellent Torres wines [££]–[£££], and seven Riojas from CVNE [£]–[£££]. The good Italians include the refreshing Santa Margharita varietal wines from the Italian South Tyrol, and a wide selection from Pio Cesare in Piedmont – Dolcetto, Grignolino, Barbera, Nebbiolo, as well as the more commonly encountered Barolo and Barbaresco, plus the interesting white Gavi 1983 (£3.83) from the same cellar, recently imported to this country for the first time. We hope the next list will present the German wines more informatively than 'Riesling Halbtrocken 1982' or 'Morio-Muscat 1983'; even when we get to the better wines, there's not a producer's or bottler's name in sight. The same could be said for many of the lesser-known French wines, but this anonymous section certainly looks worth investigating. There's Fitou of different vintages, Corbières, Clairette de Languedoc, and some interesting-looking varietal vins de pays (Colombard, Merlot, Cabernet Sauvignon, Chenin Blanc – from where, please?). Peter Collins doesn't neglect the 'classic' areas, either, and there are some expensive Burgundies (up to Echézeaux 1976, Alain Constant at £17.50) and a good collection of Bordeaux, mostly from Cordier, including the very good second wines of Meyney, Talbot and Gruaud-Larose [££]. We hope that Peter Collins' affair will long continue.

BEST BUYS [£]–[£££] Italian wines, [£]–[££] lesser-known French wines, [£]–[£££] Spanish wines

Henry C Collison & Sons Ltd

7 Bury Street, St James's, London, SW1 TEL 01-839 6407

OPEN Mon–Fri 9 am–6 pm CLOSED Sat, Sun, public holidays CREDIT CARD Access/Euro DISCOUNTS 5% approx on unmixed case orders DELIVERY Min 1 bottle (£2.15), 1 case £3.20, thereafter 42p per case GLASS HIRE Free TASTINGS AND TALKS To groups on request CELLARAGE Not available

With the exception of Camuset Champagne (also stocked by Yorkshire Fine Wines), this traditional-looking elegantly panelled shop in St James's (the British subsidiary of the large South African Stellenbosch group), now concentrates entirely upon South African wines. Basic wines come under the brand name Fleur du Cap from Stellenbosch fine wine division, the Bergkelder, and are fair value [££]. Best value are the estate wines for which Stellenbosch have the marketing rights. Good choices from this list are the Cabernet and particularly the lovely oaked Bordeaux-style blend from Meerlust at just under £6. Uitkyk (pronounced 'ate-cake') Estate make good reds and whites at a rather lower price [££].

BEST BUYS [£££] Meerlust wines

Connolly's (Wine Merchants) Ltd

166 Edmund Street, Birmingham 3 TEL 021-236 3837

OPEN Mon–Fri 9 am–5.30 pm Sat 9.30 am–11.30 am CLOSED Sun, public holidays CREDIT CARDS Not accepted; personal accounts only DISCOUNTS 5% on 3+ cases DELIVERY Free in Greater Birmingham, min 1 case; elsewhere negotiable GLASS HIRE Free TASTINGS AND TALKS Two week-long in-store tastings a year CELLARAGE Negotiable

Prices are not cheap at this small family business, set up three years ago. Much of the list is courtesy of Sichel: reliable clarets, German wines, Wente Bros Californias, but curiously no Torres (another Sichel agency). Reports, please!

Continental Wine House

25 Edgware Road, London, W2 TEL 01-262 2126

OPEN Mon–Sat 10 am–10.30 pm Sun 12 noon–2 pm, 7 pm–10 pm
CREDIT CARDS All accepted DISCOUNTS 5% on case orders DELIVERY £1 on min £30 order within 3 miles of Marble Arch GLASS HIRE Free, max 120
TASTINGS AND TALKS, CELLARAGE Not available

A vast selection of wines and spirits at all prices is jammed into this bustling family-run shop conveniently placed about 100 yards up the Edgware Road from Marble Arch. It *looks* as if it might be treasure trove like Del Monico *(see below)*: 900 different bottles, they claim – no wonder they print no list. You will find some very good bottles here at all price levels, but beware of prices, which tend to the high side even in the lower ranges, though you will find an occasional bargain. Beware especially of the finer wines, which bear an extremely high mark-up (£51 is asked for a bottle of Mouton 1971, £56 for Romanée-Conti 1975) and port and Champagne prices are high. You will find some good and reasonably (though still not cheaply) priced Italian and Spanish wines, however (Lungarotti, Pio Cesare, Santa Margharita, Venegazzù, Rapitalà; Viña Tondonia, Viña Ardanza, Marqués de Cáceres), and some good cheap French reds, like Rhônes from the Caves St-Pierre, and Chantovent Prestige Cabernet, both under £3. Beware of ageing white wines on the shelves here: turn-over of some has obviously been very slow.

BEST BUYS [£]–[££] Cheaper wines

Co-op

See CHAINS AND SUPERMARKETS

Arthur Cooper

See CHAINS AND SUPERMARKETS

Copyhold Farm Shop

Goring Heath, Oxfordshire TEL (073 57) 4720

OPEN Wed 2 pm–5 pm Thur–Sat 9.30 am–5 pm CLOSED Sun–Tue
CREDIT CARDS Not accepted DISCOUNTS Not available DELIVERY On request

Alongside their smoked salmon, pies and farm produce, Copyhold Farm sell a very small selection of the wines of Caves de la Madeleine in London *(see above)* – dependable house wines, sherry, Champagne and some German wines. Nick Goldsmith, who runs the farm, used to work at the Caves.

Corney & Barrow

12 Helmet Row, London, EC1 TEL 01-251 4051
118 Moorgate, London, EC2 TEL 01-628 2898

OPEN Mon–Fri 8.30 am–6 pm CLOSED Sat, Sun, public holidays
CREDIT CARDS Not accepted, but credit accounts can be arranged DISCOUNTS By arrangement, for quantity DELIVERY Free in Central London for 2+ cases; £5.75 for 1–23 bottles; mainland UK £5.17 for one bottle, £6.32 for 2 bottles, £7.47 for 3–35 bottles, thereafter free GLASS HIRE Free
TASTINGS AND TALKS Not provided CELLARAGE £2.80 + VAT per case per year, in and out of bond

If impeccable service and fine clarets are what you seek from your wine merchant, then you, like various members of the royal household, will be well provided for at Corney & Barrow . . . at a price, of course, though not *quite* as lofty as one might imagine. (But if you're a private buyer, remember that list prices *don't* include VAT.) Pomerol lovers will find particular pleasure in the slim and handsome list. Between the vintage-by-vintage pages of other clarets are interspersed informative sections on the châteaux of the Moueix family, some of whose wines Corney & Barrow represent in this country: Pétrus, La Fleur Pétrus, Trotanoy and one of the premier grands crus of St-Emilion, Ch Magdelaine. Of these, a good range of vintages (six to eight) is listed, mostly just back to 1970, omitting bad years, though magnums of the 1942 vintage are available for La Fleur-Pétrus. (Pétrus vintages 1980, 1979, 1978, 1976 and 1970 are there.) The long introductions to these châteaux, like the long accounts of the vintages, are a good read (more precise information on when specific wines might be ready would be useful, though). There's a mouth-watering pageful of mature vintages of top châteaux, ranging from 1967 down to 1942, with plenty of 1966s and 1961s (prices on application). The Burgundy section is slightly less ample. There are a few wines around £4, but the great concentration is again in the upper price reaches, though in this case not amongst the venerable vintages. Most are recent, only a few reaching back to 1976. Domaine Trapet and Domaine Dujac are worth seeking out in the reds, Pierre Matrot, Domaine Bachelet-Ramonet and particularly Leflaive in the whites. Fifteen vintages of Leflaive wines are listed, from 1979 to 1981, at prices from £9 to £18 or so. The Loire, Alsace and the Rhône are reliably but relatively sparsely covered, with a very few French wines below £3. Germans are quite good at all price levels; five CVNE wines dominate one lone Jumilla in the Spanish section; and an unexciting Soave must be doing little to convert Corney & Barrow customers, who, the list regrets, have not expressed a demand for Italians of any description. The superb Manzanilla de Sanlucar of Barbadillo heads the short sherry list, and there's a small collection (five to eight per vintage) of vintage ports from 1980 to 1963, with reasonably good prices for the more mature vintages. The late bottles and crusting range is well chosen.

BEST BUYS Most things on the list

Côte d'Or Wines

88 Pitshanger Lane, London, W5 TEL 01-998 0144

OPEN Mon–Sat 9.30 am–6 pm CLOSED Wed pm, Sun, public holidays
CREDIT CARDS Not accepted DISCOUNTS 10% approx on case orders
DELIVERY Free in Ealing, Harrow, Gerrards Cross etc, West End and City, min 1 case; elsewhere on request GLASS HIRE Free TASTINGS AND TALKS Annual tasting free to customers CELLARAGE £2.50 per case per year

This small, friendly little shop in Pitshanger Lane is useful for anyone living in North Ealing. Prices are slightly over the odds, but the wines are reliable and service attentive and knowledgeable. Despite the name, and Mr Rogers' evident love of Burgundy and Beaujolais, the Burgundian range is not enormous – around thirty wines from a variety of sources, with plenty of interesting choice at the cheaper end [££]. The emphasis has switched rather to Bordeaux, where Côte d'Or made opening offers of the last two vintages, and stock a small range, mostly of simpler wines [££]. Rhônes are reliable – Vidal-Fleurie and Picard Père et Fils; there's a small range of single-vineyard Alsace wines from Dopff & Irion, good Riojas from CVNE, some sound Bulgarians [£], and three Kosher wines [££] for the curious or the faithful. Two aperitifs worth a try are Chambéry Dolin, up-market French Vermouth at just over £4, and Veuve Clicquot Ratafia – juice from Champagne grapes with marc de Champagne, rather expensive at nearly £10 but a curiosity. Mr Rogers will send out gift packs for you at Christmas. An unusual one is the 'Children's Pack' – a big choice of French *sirops* such as pomegranate, peppermint, cherry or raspberry, which might tempt a few sweet-toothed adults, too.

BEST BUYS Most things on the list

Crawfords

10–11 Crawford Street, London, W1 TEL 01-486 0506

OPEN Mon–Sat 10 am–8 pm CLOSED Sun, public holidays
CREDIT CARDS Access/Euro, Amex, Diners; personal and business accounts
DISCOUNTS 5% on mixed cases, 7.5% on 5+ cases, 10% on 10+ cases
DELIVERY Free in Central London, min order £50 GLASS HIRE Free
TASTINGS AND TALKS 2 or 3 free tastings a year; frequent in-store tastings
CELLARAGE £2 per case per year

Much to the delight of local residents, Crawfords Wine Shop, which had been closed for nearly three years, opened again in the early summer of 1984 under the same ownership as the revamped wine bar beside and below it. The pale, spacious shop contains some delicious wines, many of them supplied direct to the owners, who for some years have been running a wine agency business, selling especially wines of the South of France to the British trade. The wines are of a consistently high standard, priced just a little above the average. Try particularly the delicious Châteauneuf-du-Pape Ch de Beaucastel 1980 (£5.65), and the estate's second wine, also very good, Cru du Coudoulet (£3.75 for the 1982 vintage), and the Ventoux and Lubéron wines from La Vielle Ferme [£] – excellent value. There's a short but good selection of Burgundies and clarets, Champagnes, and two good Italian whites – Frascati Superiore Villa Catone 1982 and Chardonnay di Appiano 1983 [££]. There will probably be a much bigger range by 1985. Crawfords can also supply large quantities of ice. You will find all the wines on sale in the shop in the wine bar below, many of them served by the glass – so you could pop down for a reassuring glassful before you buy.

BEST BUYS Most things in the shop

Croque-en-Bouche (V)

221 Wells Road, Malvern Wells, Hereford & Worcester TEL (068 45) 65612

OPEN By arrangement CREDIT CARDS Access/Euro, Visa DISCOUNTS, DELIVERY, GLASS HIRE, TASTINGS AND TALKS Not available CELLARAGE Free

Restaurant Croque-en-Bouche, as you will read in our RESTAURANTS AND WINE section, has cellars bulging with 600 different wines, of which 400 currently appear on the restaurant list. Though any of these can be bought at £2.20 less per bottle than the restaurant price, it is worth asking for the retail list, too, where 55 of the restaurant wines appear at a better discount. Many of the wines are not unique – some of them the restaurant basics such as Muscadet – but very fair value: Marqués de Cáceres 1978 red is under £3, as is the excellent Côtes-du-Rhône, Ch du Grand Moulas 1982; Vacheron's delicious Sancerre and the excellent Chinon from Charles Joguet are both under £5, there's the good, oaked Côtes de Buzet 1978 from the Cave Co-opérative at just over £3, and the Duboeuf Beaujolais-Villages, Fleurie and Moulin-à-Vent at the standard prices. But perhaps most worth seeking out are the oddities. If the steep climb up the winding lanes to the Co-op of St-Jean-du-Minervois makes you car-sick, this is one of the few other places you will find their Muscat (just under £5), and there's excellent Ratafia, Pineau des Charentes and Chambéry, too. You will also be hard put to find walnut oil for as little as £2.60 a half-litre. Mr Jones plans to start a mail order business in the autumn of 1984, selling from an extended retail list of around 200 wines.

BEST BUYS Most wines on the list

Cullens, W H Cullen Wine Case, Cullens Wine Club, Cullens Wine Merchants

See CHAINS AND SUPERMARKETS

The Cumbrian Cellar

1 St Andrews Square, Penrith, Cumbria TEL (0768) 63664

OPEN Mon–Sat 9 am–5.30 pm Public holidays (exc Chr Day, Boxing Day, Good Fri) 12 noon–2 pm CLOSED Sun CREDIT CARDS Access/Euro, Visa; personal accounts DISCOUNTS 5% on case orders DELIVERY Free for case orders in Cumbria; elsewhere 1 bottle £2.27, 2 bottles £2.90, 6 bottles £4.75, 1 case £5 and each further case £1.50 GLASS HIRE Free TASTINGS AND TALKS On request, free to small groups, £1.50 per head for groups of over 30 CELLARAGE £2 per case per year

The Penrith area was in desperate need of a wine merchant before Kenneth Goar and his wife came along. Turnover has been rising rapidly, and more staff and a computer were due to be installed as we went to press. Right in the centre of Penrith, where parking is virtually impossible, the shop has its own car park. Over 500 wines are stocked – a sound selection, though really special wines are few. There's a big range of Beaujolais (Piat, Paul Sapin) and some Burgundies, including older vintages (Chanson, Ponnelle); lots of the not terribly exciting Schröder & Schÿler Bordeaux generics, but a few good petits-châteaux: Ch de Castéra, Médoc 1979 is just over £5. There's a fair range from the rest of France, plenty of better-than-average Italians, a lot of basic German QbAs and a good selection of Riojas: try the CVNE wines, Viña Ardanza, Viña Alberdi and Viña Arana all from the La Rioja Alta bodega; the Marqués de Cáceres and Rivarey reds are good, too. Christian Brothers and Almaden California wines and William Jacob and Orlando Australians are not the most prestigious those countries produce, but fair quality, worth a try, as is certainly the Lebanese Ch Musar (four vintages [££]) and the cheap Bulgarian Cabernet Sauvignon. Non-vintage ports are a mouth-watering array, particularly the tawnies [££]. Prices are really rather high, but then, you are in a mountain outpost.

The Curzon Wine Co Ltd

11 Curzon Street, London, W1 TEL 01-499 3327

OPEN Mon–Sat 10 am–7 pm CLOSED Sun, public holidays CREDIT CARDS Most cards accepted; accounts by arrangement DISCOUNTS 5% on case sales, except credit sales DELIVERY Free, in Central London, min 1 case; elsewhere, a fixed charge of £5, unless order is over £100 GLASS HIRE Free TASTINGS AND TALKS Facilities for small groups CELLARAGE Not available

Prices are extraordinarily high at this shop, completely and smartly refurbished under new management in the New Year of 1984. The selection is good throughout: a long list of superior Champagnes, excellent Burgundies, clarets frighteningly above market rates, fine Italians, the wonderful Hill Smith Australians, Lebanese Ch Musar. It's all there. But it's elsewhere, too. Much cheaper.

Dakin & Co

333 Central Markets, Farringdon Street, London, EC1 TEL 01-236 1111
OPEN Mon–Fri 8 am–6 pm Sat 10 am–2 pm CLOSED Sun, public holidays
CREDIT CARD Visa DISCOUNTS 5% case orders cash and carry DELIVERY Free in Greater London GLASS HIRE Free with order TASTINGS AND TALKS On request CELLARAGE On request

Prices are quite keen at Dakin & Co's small shop in the City, but quality fluctuates rather throughout the wide European range. Good buys include Ch Chasse-Spleen 1979 (£6.89 – a particularly good price), Marqués de Cáceres wines [£]–[££], the fruity, easy-drinking petits-châteaux wines from Maison Danielle Querre [£]–[££], and a good range from the South of France; the wines of Ets Menjucq are good, and a tough, red Béarn wine, Poule au Pot from Menjucq (£2.45), is worth a try. Last year they started an occasional series of visits for customers to Burgundy/Bordeaux at cheap rates, filling the empty leg of charter flights.

BEST BUYS [£]–[£££] Clarets

Davisons

See CHAINS AND SUPERMARKETS

Davys of London Ⓥ

151 Borough High Street, London, SE1 TEL 01-407 1484
OPEN Mon–Fri 10 am–6 pm CLOSED Sat, Sun, public holidays CREDIT CARDS Access/Euro, Visa; Davys of London Card DISCOUNTS 5% on case orders, special prices for cash and carry and very large orders DELIVERY Free in City of London, min 1 case; elsewhere in London free, min 2 cases; elsewhere on UK mainland, charges on application GLASS HIRE Free TASTINGS AND TALKS Wine for tasting every Tue between 11.45 am and 2.30 pm; to groups on request CELLARAGE Not available

Prices on Davys traditional list are very good. Come here to check for bargains in vintage ports – and rare old vintages back to an 1837 'Unknown Shipper, ex Gladstone Cellar Hand Blown Bottle' (£245) – and in clarets: the fairly short range on the list is well chosen, and well priced, going back to 1938, with a large range of Ch Latour stretching back still further to 1881 (£350 a bottle)! Beaujolais from Loron are good; most of the Burgundies are Louis Latour, but you will find some occasional stars like Faiveley, too. Champagnes (Pol Roger, Bollinger ranges and a few more) are fairly priced, though not the cheapest around. The sherries, of the old dry variety, are expensive but delicious. If your budget is less grand, turn to the beginning of the list – the Davys of London Selection – where you will find very reliable German wines,

Sauvignon and claret for under £3, and Davys Rioja and Muscadet for not much more; the Davys St-Julien is specially bottled for John Davy by the proprietors of Ch Léoville-Barton and Langoa-Barton, and is lovely claret at £5.50. Or turn to the back of the list, where amongst the 'Party Lines' the Bulgarian wines at a little over £2 are good value. The 'Connoisseur's Choice' alongside is a useful mini-selection of fine wines from this very good range.

BEST BUYS Vintage port, clarets

Del Monico Ⓥ

64 Old Compton Street, London, W1 TEL 01-437 2738

OPEN Mon–Fri 9 am–6.30 pm Sat 9 am–4 pm Sun 12 pm–2 pm CLOSED Public holidays CREDIT CARDS Not accepted DISCOUNTS Not available DELIVERY Free in Soho GLASS HIRE Not available TASTINGS AND TALKS Occasional in-store tastings CELLARAGE Not available

You would find it hard to beat the prices in Del Monico's tiny Soho shop – except, perhaps, those of Champagne, though these, too, are cheaper than most. Del Monico do not print a list, even at Christmas, and the range changes constantly. Our summer browse in the window and around the tight-packed shelves revealed mostly French and Italian wines, with a few Spanish and a smattering from elsewhere, all at prices between 20p and £2 lower than in other specialist shops, and beating many of the supermarkets for value. All the right names are there: Corvo, Sassicaia, Pio Cesare, Hugel, Concha y Toro, Torres, Marqués de Cáceres, Listel, with a few Blue Nuns and Bull's Bloods, too. Amongst the more expensive wines were Ch Rieussec 1975, Tokay Aszu Eszencia for £29, Cockburn's 1960 for £20. Look for less usual finds, too, like Ruinart Coteaux Champenois Chardonnay, Listel Sauvignon, Lenz Moser Ruster Beerenauslese Weissburgunder 1982 or Vin Jaune d'Arbois from Henri Maire.

BEST BUYS Everything!

Del Monico's Famous Wine Emporium Ⓥ

23 South Street, St Austell, Cornwall TEL (0726) 3593

OPEN Mon–Sat 9 am–6 pm CLOSED Sun, public holidays CREDIT CARDS Not accepted DISCOUNTS 'We can always do a deal' DELIVERY Free within 25 miles; free elsewhere by arrangement for 6+ cases GLASS HIRE Free TASTINGS AND TALKS 4 times a year to groups CELLARAGE Free

David Del Monico used to run the Del Monico's in Soho *(see above)* but sensibly abandoned the red lights of London in 1971 for a quieter life in Cornwall. Here, he now runs a rather similar operation, with a shorter range, but still buying in special batches and offering them, and the regular wines on his list, at remarkable prices. You will find many brands here, too (Bull's Blood in summer 1984 for £1.80), and heaps of sherries and liqueurs, but it won't be long before you start drooling over the prices of some of the more original wines: Frascati Villa di Catone for £2.40, Olarra 1980 or Lan 1979 for £2.50 or Bollinger NV at £9.79. You are likely these days to find a larger selection of better quality wines, too – demand in the £4 to £8 bracket has grown considerably in the past 18 months, according to Mr Del Monico.

BEST BUYS Most wines in the shop

Rodney Densem Wines

4 Church Lane, Nantwich, Cheshire TEL (0270) 623665

OPEN Mon–Tue 10 am–6 pm Thur–Sat 9 am–6 pm CREDIT CARDS Access/Euro, Visa; personal and business accounts DISCOUNTS Up to 5% for quantity DELIVERY Free in Lancashire, Cheshire and North Wales; elsewhere, approx £3 per case GLASS HIRE Variable charge, depending on wine purchase TASTINGS AND TALKS On request CELLARAGE Not available

Rodney Densem Wines are largely wholesalers, but in this shop they sell a fairly good range at reasonable prices. The company does not produce a list, so you will have to browse on the spot. There's a modest selection from Bordeaux and Burgundy, with Cruse much in evidence, lower-priced Alsace wines from the Cave de Türkheim, and a full range of Hugel wines further around the Alsace spectrum. There are some good German wines, Torres and Berberana from Spain, and a fair range of Champagnes is undercut by some good sparklers: Deinhard Lila, Bouvet-Ladubay and Brut de Listel [££] would never disgrace a celebration.

BEST BUYS Most wines in the shop

F L Dickins Ltd

89–91 High Street, Rickmansworth, Hertfordshire TEL (0923) 773636

OPEN Mon–Fri (exc Wed) 8.30 am–6 pm Sat 8.30 am–5.30 pm CLOSED Wed, Sun, public holidays CREDIT CARD Visa DISCOUNTS About 6% on case orders DELIVERY Under revision: enquire GLASS HIRE Not available TASTINGS AND TALKS In-store tastings CELLARAGE Not available

'Fantastic low prices!!!' the Dickins wine list repetitively exclaims, and Mr Dickins wrote to remind us so, too. Don't be fooled, wine drinkers of Rickmansworth, by the shower of hyperbole. These prices are not particularly low at all, and some – like the vintage port prices – are remarkably high. The list concentrates on France, Germany and Italy. Mr Dickins would do well to omit the 'Shipped DIRECT for DICKINS' beneath almost every wine on his list, and give us more information as to his sources.

Direct Wine Shipments/Duncairn Wines Ltd

RETAIL WAREHOUSE (Direct Wine Shipments) TEL (0232) 238700
5–7 Corporation Square, Belfast
SHOPS (Duncairn Wines Ltd) Downtown TEL (0396) 3392
Shopping Centre, Downpatrick
555 Antrim Road, Belfast TEL (0232) 771694

OPEN (Warehouse) Mon–Wed & Fri 9.30 am–5.30 pm Thur 9.30 am–8 pm Sat 9.30 am–1 pm (Shops) Mon–Sat 10 am–9 pm CLOSED Sun
CREDIT CARDS Not accepted DISCOUNTS 10% on case orders from shops
DELIVERY Free in Northern Ireland, min 2 cases; £2 on single cases
GLASS HIRE Not available TASTINGS AND TALKS For groups of 30+ on request
CELLARAGE No charge for limited duration (12–18 months)

There are plenty of good wines to choose from at this friendly and helpful company, where staff, according to reports, are well informed. Some bottles are rather expensive, but there are definite bargains amongst some of the wines for which they hold the Northern Ireland agency, especially if you buy by the case at the Corporation Square warehouse. Prices for Hungarian wines are good, from Bull's Blood [£] to Tokay 5 Puttonyos [££]. The good Prinz von Metternich German sparklers are cheap here [££], likewise the excellent Masi range from the Veneto [£]–[££]. Spanish wines are good but expensive, from Torres and Marqués de Cáceres; investigate also the Lustau sherries. There are a handful of good, basic, reasonably priced Bordeaux [£]–[££], but in the upper price ranges it's Burgundy that accounts for most bottles (Latour, Remoissenet, Mommesin). Faiveley Burgundies are attractive [£££], and Loron Beaujolais [££]. Loires are largely unexciting wines from Rémy Pannier. It's an adventurous selection, stretching out to the New World: Australians from Brown Brothers, California wines from Mondavi, and, if your politics permit, some good wines from South Africa.

BEST BUYS [£] Bull's Blood, [££] Tokay, [££] Prinz von Metternich sparkling wines, [£]–[££] Masi Italians

Dolamore Ltd

Addington Street, London, SE1 TEL 01-928 4851
15 Craven Road, London, W2 TEL 01-723 8894
Wellington Street, Cambridge TEL (0223) 530929
3 St Mary's Passage, Cambridge TEL (0223) 61687
106 Walton Street, Oxford TEL (0865) 57734

OPEN Hours vary from shop to shop CLOSED Sun CREDIT CARDS Access/Euro, Visa; personal and business accounts DISCOUNTS Variable, on application
DELIVERY Free within own delivery area, min 1 case, elsewhere in England, min 2 cases; free in Home Counties, elsewhere £3 per case on 2 cases or less
GLASS HIRE Free TASTINGS AND TALKS Given at a charge of about £5 per head
CELLARAGE Not available

As we went to press, Dolamore were planning to open a new wine warehouse on Dorking High Street in the autumn of 1984, backing conveniently on to the large car park. They intend to extend their range accordingly, adding more wines in the middle and lower price ranges. Dolamore's current 1984 list is not enormous, but a good selection, at fair (but not cheap) prices (VAT-inclusive prices would help everyone). They offer sound claret selections *en primeur* and a handful of predominantly petit-château wines of the 1981, 1980, 1978, 1976 and 1973 vintages. The College claret, from Nathaniel Johnston, is good, soft wine at just £2.59. The rest of the College range is good value, with the College Madeiras and ports worth trying. Wines in the [£] range are generally reasonably priced. There's a nice selection of Burgundies (try Tollot-Beaut, Domaine Clerget, Dubreuil-Fontaine, Albert Morey [£££] and the good-value generic Burgundies of Clair-Daü [££]. Alsace wines come from the excellent firm of Kuenz-Bas (try the Réserves Personnelles [££]–[£££] and Vendange Tardive at £9). The Mosel wines of Max Ferdinand Richter dominate the German list. Australia and California, never well represented at Dolamore, have temporarily disappeared, the couple of Austrians have moved down-market, and the Bulgarian range has been extended to seven: try the varietals [£]. Ch Guiraud is good value for Sauternes [£££], dry white and the cheaper red [££] – much improved in recent years. Two new Dolamore shops opened last year – a second one in Cambridge, and a second in London, near Waterloo station.

BEST BUYS [£] Clarets *en primeur*, [£] Vins de Pays de L'Ardèche, [£] Bulgarian wines, [£] College claret, [£]–[£££] Kuenz-Bas Alsace wines, [££]–[£££] Ch Guiraud Sauternes, red and white

Domaine Direct (V)

29 Wilmington Square, London, WC1 TEL 01-837 3521

OPEN Mon–Fri 9 am–6 pm Sat 9 am–1 pm CLOSED Sun, public holidays CREDIT CARDS Not accepted DISCOUNTS Not available DELIVERY Free in London, min 1 case; free on UK mainland, min 3 cases; smaller quantities at cost GLASS HIRE Free TASTINGS AND TALKS Not available CELLARAGE By arrangement

Domaine Direct have one of the very best Burgundy selections in the country. 'We buy only domaine-bottled wines from growers we know personally. We buy the wines that we enjoy drinking ourselves, selecting those which best reflect the qualities of their appellation,' they explain in the introduction to their summer 1984 list. Certainly some of Burgundy's most outstanding growers are listed here, some well-known, others less so, though all well introduced in the notes: Tollot-Beaut, Lafon, Jean Durup, René Dauvissat, Sauzet, Melou, Juillot, Vincent. 'We visit the vineyards every month of the year,' one of the directors told the *Guide*, 'and are able to monitor every wine we purchase from vine to barrel to bottle.' The company are main or sole importers for more than half the wines on their list. They set up shop in 1981 to sell fine growers' Burgundies to restaurants, but now have a considerable number of private customers, who buy by the case because of the wholesale licence. The list does not include Beaujolais, but you will find Irancy and Chablis. Prices (note that VAT is not included) are very reasonable, no doubt pinned down more successfully by strict cash-on-delivery regulations; Burgundy lovers should derive much enjoyment from this good-value list.

BEST BUYS [££] Bourgogne Aligoté 1982, P Bernollin; Bourgogne Irancy 1982, Melou; [£££] Chablis Grand Cru, Preuses 1981, Dauvissat; Mercurey Rouge, Clos des Barraults 1980, Michel Juillot; and many more

Peter Dominic

See CHAINS AND SUPERMARKETS

Philip Drake Vintners Ltd (V)

Spinney Cottage, Headley Road, Leatherhead, Surrey TEL (0372) 372181
OPEN Mon–Fri 9 am–5 pm Sat 9 am–1 pm CLOSED Sun CREDIT CARDS Not accepted; personal and business accounts DISCOUNTS 20p per case on 5+ cases, 50p per case on 5+ cases cash and carry DELIVERY Free in Surrey and Central London; elsewhere £2–£4 per case GLASS HIRE Free TASTINGS AND TALKS 3 or 4 tastings a year and 2 tastings/dinners in local restaurant; to groups on request CELLARAGE Not available

'Wine by the case at shipper's prices', it says under the arch of the clever design on the cover of Philip Drake's list: a design which members of the wine trade will recognise as the logo of the London Wine Trade Fair, discreetly borrowed by Mr Drake. It means what it says – the prices are indeed very close to shippers' prices. Compare Marqués de Cáceres white at £2.40, or red at £2.50 with most merchants' prices of over £3, the lovely Sauvignon Trois Mouline at £2.40 with Adnams' £2.82, Fleurie Georges Duboeuf 1982 at £3.40 with most prices starting 30p higher, and Quinta do Noval LBV Port at £4.59 with Victoria Wine's £5.69. There are very good prices, too, for a small collection of Riojas and Torres wines. You will also find some good French bottles, concentrated in the lower price brackets, and small lots on the bin-end list of better clarets of recent vintages. Delivery, amazingly, is free in Central London and Surrey. Philip Drake Vintners have been in operation for only just over a year, but Mr Drake was involved in the wine trade for six years before that, and the business, by all accounts, is very reliable. He keeps his overheads down, he says, by working from home with only one member of staff, 'buying right' and concentrating on local trade.

BEST BUYS Everything!

Duncairn Wines Ltd

See Direct Wine Shipments

George Dutton & Son

Godstall Lane, St Werburgh Street, Chester, Cheshire TEL (0244) 21488
OPEN Mon–Sat 8.30 am–5.30 pm CLOSED Sun, public holidays CREDIT CARDS Access/Euro, Visa; personal accounts DISCOUNTS By arrangement DELIVERY Free in Chester and surrounds for case orders, elsewhere at cost GLASS HIRE Free TASTINGS AND TALKS Tutored tastings on request CELLARAGE £1.04 per case per year

Country wine merchants George Dutton & Son were taken over by Willoughbys of Manchester *(see below)* in June 1983, and now share their extraordinarily good list.

Eaton Elliot Winebrokers

15 London Road, Alderley Edge, Cheshire TEL (0625) 582354
OPEN Mon–Fri 10 am–7 pm Sat 10 am–5.30 pm CLOSED Sun, public holidays CREDIT CARDS All accepted DISCOUNTS 5% on case orders DELIVERY Free within 25 miles, min 1 mixed case; elsewhere £1.15 per case, min 4 cases GLASS HIRE Free TASTINGS AND TALKS Tastings fortnightly CELLARAGE £2.50 per case per year

The Elliots have featured in the *Guide* before for their No 15 Wine Bar *(see this year's WINE BARS section)*, and now richly merit an entry for the interesting wine shop they have built up alongside. They offer a very good range, set out in a helpful list with tasting notes on most of the wines, but why break a fine habit in the Italian section where we are surely in even greater need of notes? There are a handful of interesting Southern French wines [£]; Loires including Vacheron's Sancerres in all three colours [££]; Dépagneux Beaujolais and some good Burgundies including Tollot-Beaut, Sauzet, Caves de Buxy and Chablis from the very good co-operative La Chablisienne. Petit-château clarets rise in price only as far as £5.10. Rhônes are good, mostly Paul Jaboulet Aîné, with the excellent Cru de Coudoulet Côtes-du-Rhône, and Vidal-Fleurie's delicate Muscat de Beaumes-de-Venise. The Italian wines are well chosen, too: Valpolicella, Soave and Bianco di Custoza from Santa Sofia [£] are well above average quality, and Chianti Castelli di Volpaia 1979 is also good (£4.15). Other reassuring names include Rosemount Australians [££], Mondavi, Ch Musar, Cáceres, CVNE, and Alfred Gratien Champagnes – try the Rosé Brut at just over £10 next time you have something to celebrate. There's a short but delicious choice of LBV ports; Fonseca's Escudo Aperitif Extra Dry White Port would be an interesting change (£6.85). All this, and good prices, too! The Elliots also provide an unusual service set out in a booklet bearing a tiny luggage tag – 'Happiness is a Hamper'. The 'social hamper', for example, contains a bottle of Bollinger NV (optional extra), cocktail smoked salmon sandwiches, egg and watercress mousse, whole poached Scotch salmon with hollandaise sauce, rice salad, tomato and chive vinaigrette, mixed green salad, strawberry Pavlova, Brie and Bath Olivers, home-made truffles, coffee and sparkling mineral water, all for £9.50 a head; then come the racing hamper, sportsman's hamper and family hampers, progressively simpler and cheaper down to £6.50 a head. They offer a dinner party service, too, and everything 'from tons of ice to professional barmen for functions'. Fortnightly tastings, held in the shop on Thursday evenings, might be 'Rhône' or 'Spain and Italy'.

BEST BUYS Most things on the list

Ebury Wine Co Ltd

178 Ebury Street, London, SW1 TEL 01-730 8206

OPEN Mon–Fri 9.30 am–5.30 pm CLOSED Sat, Sun, public holidays CREDIT CARDS All accepted; business accounts DISCOUNTS 2.5% on orders over £200 or for cash and carry case sales DELIVERY Free in SW1 and SW3, min 1 case; free within greater London, min 3 cases; elsewhere at carrier's cost GLASS HIRE Free TASTINGS AND TALKS Free tastings held regularly, by invitation only CELLARAGE Not available

Check out the Champagne prices in Ebury Street – you are likely to find some bargains, not least their house Champagne, Comte de Robart Brut NV, which was selling for £5.95 as we went to press; it comes from the sound, traditional Epernay house of Boizel (who also makes Louis Krémer, but tend simply to bottle the same wines under different labels for different clients). Some of the major brands are well priced, too: £8.85 for Perrier-Jouët and £18.98 from Krug Grande Cuvée Brut NV. Otherwise, best value is probably to be found in the vins de pays and cheaper clarets. Look amongst the small but well-chosen claret range for André Lurton's wines, and for Ch La Mouline at just over £3 – and its white cellarmate Sauvignon Trois Mouline (£2.44). The Burgundy range is mostly unexciting (mainly Mommessin), but the Italians are fair to good. The Ebury's Muscat de Beaumes-de-Venise, Domaine des Coyeux at £5.55 is one of the very best. Their tasting notes are useful. They hope this year to extend their private sales, setting aside a part of the warehouse in Ebury Street for private customers.

BEST BUYS [£]–[££] cheaper clarets, [£££] Champagne

Ehrmann's Ⓥ

24–25 Scala Street, London, W1 TEL 01-637 0387

OPEN Mon–Fri 9.30 am–6.30 pm Sat 10 am–1 pm CLOSED Sun; public holidays CREDIT CARDS All accepted; personal and business accounts

DISCOUNTS 5% on case orders or for personal collection DELIVERY Free in London, min 1 case; elsewhere on request (expensive) GLASS HIRE Free TASTINGS AND TALKS Annual tastings at Oxford and Cambridge Universities – German wines CELLARAGE £1.50 per case per year

Ehrmann's small shop just off Tottenham Court Road backs on to and sits over the cellars of its sister company, Viniberia, Iberian specialists, as you might guess. They have been highly successful in selling Mateus look-alikes but also large quantities of good quality basic and fine Spanish and Portuguese wines to Britain's supermarkets. So Ehrmann's Spanish shelves are naturally well stocked, and at good prices. In addition to a fine trio from Rioja Bodega Marqués de Cáceres, there are the pale and interesting Muga Riojas (though avoid the not-so-pale white). Viña Albalí is an exceptional wine for Valdepeñas, and even the 1976 vintage is still under £3. Monte Ory 1983 red from north of Rioja is one of the new fruity Navarra wines (£2.28). And Sanches Romate sherries, especially the up-market range (still only just over £3) are excellent – try the pungent nut-and-spice Fino Marismeno. Italian wines are also very reliable at Ehrmann's. The big Tieffenbrunner range from the South Tyrol is good value at around £3, the Cavit basics are sound, and the Lungariotti wines, Pio Cesare, and Chianti Villa di Vetrici, are worth looking out for. With a German national at the helm, Ehrmann's German list has a head start – look especially at the delicious range of 1983 Riesling estate wines, but also at the cheaper wines. France is here, too. As the front page of the spring 1984 list points out, splendid value and a good cheap example of the Syrah grape is to be found in the 'Pure Syrah' Vin de Pays des Collines Rhodaniennes – hills more generally recognised as Crozes-Hermitage: this wine, rich and perfumed, comes from vines too young for the appellation (£2.89). There are more Rhônes, mostly also at the cheaper end, a few select Burgundies and Beaujolais, some basic clarets and some crus, mostly drinkable now. Amongst the Champagnes, try some of the large range from Bruno Paillard, a new quality house. The NV is good value at nearly £8, and so is the mature 1973 vintage (which should still be in stock when the *Guide* is published) at £10.75. If you can't visit these original shops send for a list. Ehrmann's own both branches of Old Chelsea Wine Stores *(see below)*.

BEST BUYS [£] 'Pure Syrah', [£]–[££] Tieffenbrunner Italians, [£]–[££] Spanish wines, [££]–[£££] German estate wines

Eldridge Pope

See CHAINS AND SUPERMARKETS

> Most wine merchants will hire out glasses free of charge, provided they are collected and returned clean, and that you are buying enough wine to fill them! In most cases, it's first come, first served, so get your order in early to ensure supply.

Ellis Son & Vidler Ltd ☞

57 Cambridge Street, London, SW1 TEL 01-834 4101

Cliffe Cellars

12/13 Cliffe Estate, South Street, Lewes, E Sussex TEL (079 16) 77544

OPEN Mon–Fri 9.30 am–5.30 pm CLOSED Sat, Sun, public holidays CREDIT CARDS Access/Euro, Visa DISCOUNTS 5% on case orders, £1.50 cash and carry DELIVERY Free within London and parts of Sussex, Oxford and Cambridge, min 1 case; elsewhere £3.45 per order up to 4 cases; thereafter free GLASS HIRE Free TASTINGS AND TALKS 2 or 3 a year CELLARAGE £2.53 per case per year

After over 200 years in Hastings, this traditional firm of wine merchants moved in 1984 to new, modern premises in Lewes with temperature-controlled wine storage, which, they say, will enable them to give customers a quicker and more efficient service. They also plan to open a cash and carry division there for cut-price case sales. No changes, meanwhile, in the old-fashioned London offices. Madeira is in the family at Ellis Son & Vidler – you will find a good range from Cossart Gordon, including some old vintages, such as an 1895 Bual (£57.50) or a 1916 Malmsey (£42.09), with quotations for vintages not listed available on request. Look out for some characterful Almacenista sherries [££]. Opening offers of clarets are fairly priced, including the very top growths, and the main list bears a good collection of clarets, too, weighted towards more recent vintages. The rest of France is sparsely covered. Best value at the bottom end is to be found in the Vins de Pays des Sables du Golfe de Lyon, the predominantly Cabernet Domaine de Bosquet and the fresh rosé Gris de Gris, Domaine de Jarras, both at around £3, whilst amongst sparkling wines the Brut de Listel (£3.89) and Blanquette de Limoux (£4.83) are good buys. Capezzana wines from Italy [££] and Torres and CVNE from Spain are good, and the Germans from Müller and others are sound wines of recent vintages.

BEST BUYS [£]–[££] Listel wines, [££] Almacenista sherries, [£]–[£££] opening claret offers, and other wines mentioned above

English Wine Centre

See Valley Wine Cellars

Farr Vintners Ltd Ⓥ

Wheelwrights, 12 Upper Green, Tewin, Hertfordshire TEL 01-892 6716 and (043 879) 307

OPEN Mon–Fri 9 am–6 pm (telephone service only – an answering machine will take calls outside hours) CREDIT CARDS Not accepted; approved accounts only DISCOUNTS Not available DELIVERY Free throughout UK mainland for 6+

cases; London: £2 for 1 case, £1 per case for 2–5 cases; elsewhere £4 for 1 case, £2.50 for 2–5 cases GLASS HIRE Not available TASTINGS AND TALKS, CELLARAGE Not available

Farr specialise in the 'old, rare, fine and odd' – the 'odd' generally also laying claim to the other three qualities. They sell mostly to the trade, but will also sell to the public by telephone, in full cases, though mixed cases are possible from their supplementary single-bottle list. So out with your calculator (because prices here, for the trade, are by the case ex-VAT), and compare Farr's prices with those of other specialists in elderly wines for a pleasant surprise. Farr issue four price lists a year, and there is usually little continuity of stock from list to list, since they buy in small lots of between one and a hundred cases. They are specialising more and more in fine Burgundies, with more young wines now appearing on their lists, though still plenty of good, mature bottles. Names to drool over might be Rion, Clair Daü, Leflaive or, if you're a fan, Domaine de La Romanée-Conti. You will find good current and interesting old vintages of Rhônes, Champagnes, ports, top quality clarets and perhaps ancient Barolo, Ch Musar, or old Jura wines.

BEST BUYS [£££] Burgundies, old and rare wines

Farthinghoe Fine Wine & Food Co (V)

The Old Rectory, Farthinghoe, Brackley, Northamptonshire — TEL (0295) 710018

OPEN Mon–Fri 8.30 am–5 pm Sat, Sun By appointment CLOSED Chr Day CREDIT CARDS Not accepted; personal and business accounts DISCOUNTS 50p per case on 2 cases, 75p a case on 3–5 cases DELIVERY Free on UK mainland, min 1 case GLASS HIRE £2 per 48 doz TASTINGS AND TALKS Tutored and untutored tastings held regularly for customers by invitation CELLARAGE By arrangement MAIL ORDER SPECIALISTS

Farthinghoe's is a tempting list, and you are unlikely to go far wrong if you succumb. Bear in mind that prices include delivery anywhere in the UK, and they are not unreasonable. Apart from the interesting small selection of clarets for laying down, this well-written list includes a fine selection of Alsace wines from Gisselbrecht, Hugel and Trimbach, culminating in some rather special 1976s; a few good Rhônes and Loires; and some good quality co-operative wines on the short Burgundy list in the lower price slots, with some good estate-bottled Burgundies to follow. French regional wines are Louis Latour's Chardonnay Vin de Pays des Coteaux de l'Ardèche (£49.95) and Sauvignon du Haut Poitou VDQS, Hatch Mansfield 1983 (£42.15). There's some single vineyard Beaujolais, good estate-bottled Germans and a tiny but sound selection from Spain and Italy. Farthinghoe are open 'if we are in, and we usually are' but are a small family company, mostly mail order, and not really equipped for hordes of customers on the doorstep; indeed, they offer no discount for personal collection, to encourage mail order sales. The 'food' part of the title is run by Simon

Cox's wife, Nicola, author and cookery demonstrator, who runs cookery courses and a kitchen shop from their Old Rectory house near Banbury, at the above address.

BEST BUYS ££–£££ Alsace wines; most things on the list

Ferrers le Mesurier Ⓥ

'Turnsloe', North Street, Titchmarsh, Nr Kettering, Northamptonshire — TEL (080 12) 2660

OPEN 7 days a week, evenings included, but telephone first CREDIT CARDS Personal and business accounts DISCOUNTS Negotiable for quantity, £1.50 per case cash and carry DELIVERY Free in Central London, Cambridge and within 35 miles of Titchmarsh, min 1 case GLASS HIRE Not available CELLARAGE Free if wine purchased from the company

This rather exclusive one-man firm has a short French list with remarkably good prices – many of which have dropped over the past year by rather more than the Chancellor's 18p. Burgundy is best represented, almost entirely with growers' wines, at the lower end of the Burgundian price range. The list gives details of some good Loires, including Gaston Huet Vouvrays, four good ready-to-drink clarets at £4 and under, and three slightly more expensive well-chosen 1982 clarets for laying down. There are useful tasting notes, and a bit of information on each grower.

BEST BUYS ££ Muscadet de Sèvre-et-Maine sur Lie J Drouard, ££ Bourgogne Chardonnay, Guy Roulot & Fils, ££–£££ Burgundies, ££–£££ Gaston Huet Vouvrays

Alexander Findlater & Co Ltd

Heveningham High House, near Halesworth, Suffolk — TEL (098 683) 274 (mail order)

77 Abbey Road, London, NW8 — TEL 01-624 7311

OPEN (Abbey Road) Mon–Sat 10 am–9 pm CLOSED Sun, public holidays CREDIT CARDS Not accepted DISCOUNTS Variable for quantity; £1 per case cash and carry DELIVERY Free in NW8 and Heveningham, min 1 case; elsewhere, £4.20 per delivery GLASS HIRE Free with wine order, otherwise 10p per glass TASTINGS AND TALKS On request; regular tastings in Heveningham and Abbey Road shop CELLARAGE £3 per case per year

Alexander Findlater, descendant of the Alex Findlater who spawned 20 firms and partnerships in the 1920s (many of them still in existence and incorporating this famous wine trade name) set up this latest independent Findlater wine business in 1983 in conjunction with Michael Schuster, a Bordeaux-trained taster. The shop and cellars in Abbey Road stock an excellent selection, both 'classic' and less usual, at prices a little above the average, but the in-shop service here is a little above the average, too. Shop staff are extremely knowledgeable, ready to advise on setting up a cellar, or on wine investment as well as on the contents of the bottles on their shelves. They run a 'club' (no membership fee) with tastings held in the Abbey Road shop or at Heveningham in Suffolk that are often free if the wines are inexpensive, or £5 or so in the case of 'sherry and port', perhaps, or 'La Chapelle' (write for details). The list is exemplary, with every necessary piece of information included, plus concise and frank tasting notes on every wine. Grand-Puy-Lacoste 1978, for example (£9.35) is the 'first wine made under the new management of Xavier Borie, whose father owns Ducru-Beaucaillou. Deeply coloured; intense blackcurrant Cabernet nose rich and concentrated with characteristic Pauillac spice. A grand wine for the 1990s. Highly recommended.' It's a small range of clarets, but very well selected, as are the Burgundies: 'we have tried to ensure they are all definitely Pinot Noir in character' – try the rich, firm Rion wines [£££]. Beaujolais and Rhône are quite good, and there is a fine collection of vins de pays at under £3 a bottle. Italy includes Antinori wines and the young and fruity (unusually so!) Valpolicella of Fabiano. From Spain, a lot more Riojas have appeared on the latest list, also well chosen: CVNE, La Rioja Alta, Bodegas Beronia, plus Torres and an interesting and fresh if not very exciting dry white made with grapes that might otherwise have become sherry: Castillo de San Diego 1980, Barbadillo [£]. Barbadillo brings us on to the sherry section, which is outstanding. Two Almacenista sherries (*see* THE WINE REGIONS section above) are definitely worth trying – an old oloroso and dry amontillado from the Viuda de Antonio Borrego [£££]. The other sherries are well chosen, too: Barbadillo's Manzanilla, Manzanilla Passada and Fino de Balbaina [££] are some of the best wines to come out of Jerez, and you can choose, too, from a selection of two Palo Cortados, seven dry amontillados and two dry olorosos as well as six sweet sherries for sweet-toothed British traditionalists. There is also a reasonable range of California and Australian wines.

BEST BUYS Most wines in the shop

Findlater, Mackie, Todd & Co Ltd

Findlater House, 92 Wigmore Street, London, W1 TEL 01-935 9264

OPEN Mon–Fri 9 am–6 pm CLOSED Sat, Sun, public holidays CREDIT CARDS Access/Euro, Amex, Visa; personal and business accounts DISCOUNTS 10% on case orders DELIVERY Free on UK mainland, min 1 case; Northern Ireland £2 per case GLASS HIRE 35p per doz TASTINGS AND TALKS By arrangement CELLARAGE £2.93 per case per year

Prices at this fine wine shop (which now belongs to the Beechams drug company) may include VAT, carriage and insurance; they remain expensive nonetheless. Clarets, Burgundies, especially good Rhônes and German estate wines are generally of sound quality. Perhaps best value is to be found in the Italian section – not all of it – but watch out for Corvo, Pio Cesare and the very good Italian Tyrol wines of Santa

Margharita, value-for-money in the £–££ range – though again, you would easily find them cheaper elsewhere.

BEST BUYS £–££ Santa Margharita Italians

Findlater (Wine Merchants) Ltd

149 Upper Rathmines Road, Dublin 6 TEL Dublin 976130

OPEN Mon–Sat 10.30 am–2.30 pm, 3.30 pm–6.30 pm CLOSED Sun, public holidays CREDIT CARDS Access/Euro; personal and business accounts DISCOUNTS By arrangement on 10+ cases DELIVERY Free in Dublin, Wicklow, Kildare and parts of Meath; £5.50 flat charge on 1–4 cases; thereafter free GLASS HIRE £3.50 per 4 doz, inc washing TASTINGS AND TALKS On request CELLARAGE Not available

Like their London counterparts in Wigmore Street, friendly and helpful Findlater of Dublin charge high prices; poor Dubliners, who already have to contend with high taxes *and* 23 per cent VAT. As for content, Findlater's list contains some good wines, but also many which fail to inspire us with great enthusiasm. But Hugel Alsace wines, Jaboulet Rhônes, Pio Cesare Piedmontese Italians and the sound German range (including many at the top end of the sweetness scale) are good bottles, and there is a substantial list of classed-growth clarets. Findlaters operate a world-wide gift service, working with Findlaters of London on a reciprocal scheme. If you are fortunate enough to qualify for diplomatic privileges, ask for their separate Diplomatic List.

Fine Fare

See CHAINS AND SUPERMARKETS

Fortnum & Mason

181 Piccadilly, London, W1 TEL 01-734 8040

OPEN Mon–Fri 9 am–5.30 pm Sat 9 am–5 pm CLOSED Sun, public holidays CREDIT CARDS All accepted DISCOUNTS 5% on 1–4 cases, 7½% on 5–9 cases, 10% on 10+ cases DELIVERY Free within greater London and most of surrounding area, no min order; elsewhere, prices on application GLASS HIRE Not available TASTINGS AND TALKS In-store tasting throughout the year; 'Champagne Season' in May CELLARAGE £3 per case per year

Unless you are after rare, mature Champagnes, a ten-minute taxi ride from Piccadilly to any number of other merchants quoted in this *Guide* will have paid for itself by the time you have selected your first bottle. You naturally pay for such attentive and personal service, smart uniforms and the privilege of shopping in this élite haven on one of London's most expensive sites – but then, having done so, you might rather wonder at the refinements of service that are missing.

Extraordinarily, there are no glasses for hire, delivery is free only in London and surroundings, and theirs is not a particularly informative list. But you can have, at a price, a 'personal export and gift service to most countries, local laws permitting'. In addition to the inevitable traditional range you will find an impressive array of fine and rare Champagnes: Krug Collection 1969 and 1964 if you don't mind blowing £120 on a single bottle; and Alfred Gratien and Pol Roger are also available in vintages back to the '60s.

BEST BUYS Rare Champagnes

Fullers

See CHAINS AND SUPERMARKETS

Galleon Wines

See CHAINS AND SUPERMARKETS

G H Gane & Co ☞

Uplands, Itchen Abbas, Winchester, Hampshire TEL (096 278) 352

OPEN Almost any time, by appointment CREDIT CARDS Not accepted; business accounts only DISCOUNTS Special prices quoted for unmixed cases DELIVERY Free within 15 miles of Winchester, min 1 case; elsewhere £4.50 for single cases, £3 per case for 2–5 cases, thereafter by arrangement GLASS HIRE Free, max 200 TASTINGS AND TALKS Three per year CELLARAGE Possible but not encouraged

Service is helpful and personal from Janet Gane's small business in Winchester. Prices are reasonable, sometimes a little on the expensive side, but good value within the free delivery area, because the selection is excellent. The short Burgundy list includes the fine unoaked Chablis of Louis Michel [£££]. Choosier customers can also select from the extensive O W Loeb list *(see below)*. The marvellous Rhônes from Paul Jaboulet Aîné [££]–[£££], and the very good Vouvrays of Foreau [££]–[£££] come from Loeb too. There are just over 20 clarets, mostly in the [££] price range. Amongst the slightly extended but still small choice of Italians, Villa di Capezzana Riserva 1980 (£4.90) and Capezzana Bianco (£2.70) are the best, and worth trying; the prices are competitive. There are some excellent German estate wines, including a few delicious sweet 1975s and 1976s, also from the Loeb list.

BEST BUYS [££] Villa di Capezzana Riserva, [£££] Louis Michel Chablis, [££]–[£££] Paul Jaboulet Aîné Rhônes, German wines, especially Kiedricher Sandgrube Riesling Auslese 1976 [£££]

The Garland Wine Cellar

20 Craddocks Parade, Ashtead, Surrey TEL (037 22) 75247

OPEN Mon–Fri (inc public holidays) 10.30 am–8 pm CLOSED Wed between 2 pm and 6 pm, Sun CREDIT CARDS Access/Euro, Amex, Visa; personal and business accounts DISCOUNTS Up to 10% on case orders DELIVERY Free locally, min 1 case; elsewhere at postal cost GLASS HIRE Free TASTINGS AND TALKS Informal tasting at shop each Sat; private tastings and talks on request CELLARAGE On request

Still a relatively new company, this shop stocks a widespread range. Most interesting are the Rosemount [££] and Berri Estates wines [££] from Australia, Mondavi's Fumé Blanc 1979 (£6.95), Ch Musar 1977 (£4.75), the Torres Spanish wines and the Bulgarian range [£]–[££]. There is a fair French choice, unexciting Italians and a dozen German wines, half of them good quality Kabinett wines and above, from the Schlosskellerei in Alzei. Prices are fair, only a little over average. Beer drinkers might be tempted by the unusual selection of beers from Austria, Holland, Belgium, the USA, Canada and even Japan.

BEST BUYS [£]–[££] Torres wines, Bulgarian wines, [££] Australian wines

Gateway

See CHAINS AND SUPERMARKETS

German Food Centre

44–46 Knightsbridge, London, SW1 TEL 01-235 5760

OPEN Mon–Fri 9 am–5.30 pm Sat 9 am–5 pm CLOSED Sun, public holidays CREDIT CARDS All accepted; personal and business accounts DISCOUNTS 10% on case orders DELIVERY, GLASS HIRE Not available TASTINGS AND TALKS Bottles open daily in the shop CELLARAGE Not available

Tear yourself away from the Würst and the Lebkuchen and proceed to the cellar basement of the smart German Food Centre. If you are keen to try the more unusual German grapes like Siegerrebe, Bacchus, Huxelrebe or Optima, or German minority interest wines like Weissherbst or Schillerwein, this is the place to come, though prices are hardly cheap. But shame on the German government! Where are the producers' or shippers' names on their lengthy list? Turn to the connoisseur wines at the back for the sweeter wines: Beerenauslesen, Trockenbeerenauslesen and Eiswein – just a few half-bottles, but lots of tempting 1976s and 1971s. Sparkling wines include Deinhard Lila Imperial, delicious but expensive here at £6.10, way above the average retail price, and Fürst von Metternich, also very good at £6.40, again £1 or so more than it is likely to cost elsewhere. The Centre also stocks the entire range of German beers imported to Britain, and a good selection of Schnapps and German liqueurs.

BEST BUYS Unusual wines unobtainable elsewhere

German Wine Club

7 Linkside Avenue, Oxford, Oxfordshire TEL (0865) 58755

OPEN Mon–Fri 9 am–6 pm Sat 9 am–1 pm CLOSED Sun, public holidays CREDIT CARDS Not accepted DISCOUNTS 5% on unmixed cases DELIVERY Free on mainland UK, min 1 mixed case, min 3 bottles of each wine; anywhere else in the world at cost GLASS HIRE Not available TASTINGS AND TALKS Regular tastings of 'pre-shipment' wines *(see below)* in Oxford, group tastings on request CELLARAGE At cost MAIL ORDER ONLY

Anyone interested in exploring the wines of the lesser-known villages or the minor grape varieties of Germany will enjoy him/herself enormously dabbling in the list of The German Wine Club. Prices seem expensive, but they do include delivery, and you may feel they are worth it to secure good, unusual wines, particularly if you live in an area without a good German stockist. The wines listed are mainly from co-operatives (which, in Germany, will generally mean sparkling modern equipment and good standard wine-making), but a number of estate wines also appear, from good producers such as von Buhl, Dr Weil, Deinhard, and Schloss Rheinhartshausen. Of the 200-strong list from a score of producers, in all 11 German areas, less than half are actually stocked in the UK, and the proportion of estate wines on the instantly orderable list is fairly high. Orders for other wines are made on a monthly basis and almost always available within four weeks from a group shipment from Germany. Half the club's business is done in this way. Prices range from £3 to £19 a bottle, with a good range of sweet wines, vintages mostly in the 1980s, some sweet 1975s and 1976s, plus, unusually, 17 red wines and 13 rosés. Particularly interesting and good value are the special mixed cases offered with the quarterly newsletter at worthwhile savings. They follow a theme – a good way to teach yourself German wines: there's the Kabinett case, the Staatsweingut case, the dry case, and regional cases, illustrating the wines of the different growing areas. The club is beginning to extend in a limited way to other German-speaking wine-producing countries. The excellent South Tyrol wines of Tieffenbrunner are already on their list, and they say they will be listing a case from an Alsace and an Austrian producer by Christmas 1984. Club membership is £4 a year, refundable on the first order. The club now has just over 800 members, efficiently served by Matthew Walton and his German wife Barbara.

BEST BUYS [££]–[£££] Special mixed cases [££]–[£££] wines of unusual origins or grape variety [££] Enkircher Stefansberg Riesling Kabinett 1981, Enkircher Winzergenossenschaft; Kapellener Kloster Liebfrauenberg Huxelrebe Spätlese 1981, Winzergenossenschaft Deutsches Weintor; (red) Dernauer Hardtberg Spätburgunder 1982, United Growers of the Ahr

The Gilbey Wine & Food Company

The Eton Wine Bar, 82/83 High Street, Eton, Berkshire TEL (075 35) 54921 or 55182

OPEN Mon–Sat 10 am–10 pm public holidays 10 am–10 pm (at the Wine Bar – ring doorbell if bar is closed) CLOSED Sun; 10 days Chr CREDIT CARDS Access/Euro, Visa; personal and business accounts DISCOUNTS 5% on 5+ cases cash and carry DELIVERY Free on UK mainland for 5+ cases; 1 case £3.50, 2 cases £2.50, 3 cases £1.50, 4 cases £1 GLASS HIRE Free TASTINGS AND TALKS Rarely CELLARAGE Not available

Readers within striking distance of Eton are doubly fortunate. Not only can they sample the wares of one of the country's best wine bars *(see* WINE BARS *below)*, but they can also take advantage of the retail division – the Gilbey Wine & Food Company at The Eton Wine Bar – to buy anything that has taken their fancy, by bottle or case. The Gilbeys run a trade division, too, quite separate, so ship the wines on this short retail list in greater quantities than you might expect from the size of their thriving business. Most of the list is shipped from growers, most of it from France, and it concentrates on the low and middle price ranges, the top price being £6.95 for Meursault 1982, Michel Lamanthe. Quality here is good. Try especially the fine Barbadillo sherries for around £3, and the lovely single-vineyard Beaujolais of the 1983 vintage from Chanut Frères. You buy the take-away wines in the wine bar – but ring the bell if you call out of licensing hours.

BEST BUYS [£]–[££] Barbadillo sherries, [££] 1983 Beaujolais Crus, Chanut Frères

Goedhuis & Co

21 Grant Road, London, SW11 TEL 01-223 6057

See The Clapham Cellars

Gordon & MacPhail

58–60 South Street, Elgin, Morayshire TEL (0343) 45111

OPEN Mon–Fri 9 am–5.15 pm Sat 9 am–5 pm CLOSED Wed pm (Jan–Mar, Sept, Oct) CREDIT CARD Access/Euro DISCOUNTS 10% on case orders DELIVERY Free within 20 miles, no min order; elsewhere by post GLASS HIRE Free TASTINGS AND TALKS, CELLARAGE Not available

Besides its vast range of malts and blended and vatted whiskies and other spirits and liqueurs, Gordon & MacPhail's retail department stocks a big selection of wines. There are some good wines here, some not that interesting, but prices tend to be rather high. Best buys on a budget are probably Ch de Fonscolombe red and white, Coteaux d'Aix-en-Provence at £2.50 and Ch de Gourgazaud from the Minervois at £2.66, or the Torres Tres Torres red and Viña Sol white at around £3. You will find a small range of recent classed growth vintages, and some lesser clarets ready for drinking, an unexciting selection of Italian wines, and rather expensive ports, including rare bottles like Fonseca 1948 (£70.59).

BEST BUYS [£] Fonscolombe, Gourgazaud, [££] Torres

Andrew Gordon Wines (V)

The Old Post Office, Newdigate Road, Beare Green, Dorking, Surrey TEL (0306) 711949

OPEN Mon–Fri 9 am–5.30 pm Sat 10 am–1.30 pm CLOSED Sun, public holidays CREDIT CARDS Not accepted DISCOUNTS £1.50 per case cash and carry DELIVERY Free in Surrey and Central London; elsewhere on UK mainland £4 for 1 case, thereafter £2 per case GLASS HIRE Free TASTINGS AND TALKS Occasional tastings and lectures locally; wines opened for tasting at The Old Post Office; 1 major tasting each year for customers CELLARAGE £1.50 per case per year

Andrew and Edwina Gordon issue four interesting wine lists a year from their attractive old Surrey post office; the wines are mostly French, but with a few from elsewhere. South-West France is literally the Gordons' second home, and their interest in the Bordeaux area is clearly to be seen in the selection of clarets, many of them lesser wines, drinkable now, some classed growths including mature wines and younger wines to lay down. There is a small selection of Burgundy, some interesting château and domaine-bottled Beaujolais and a selection of extremely well-priced ports. But it is worth leaving these beaten wine tracks and trying a few of the oddities. There's 'Ancestral Banyuls Grand Cru 1973' (a dry, port-like wine from the South of France) at £4.50, Ch Carras from Greece, made with Bordeaux grape varieties and well priced at £3.92, Roussette de Savoie for £3.50, Cabernet Sauvignon Domaine de St-Hilaire, Côtes de Varois for £2.50, the refreshing rosé Listel Gris de Gris for £2.50, and from Spain a good Ochoa Tinto from Navarra north of Rioja (£2.08) and CVNE 1980 red for £2.96. They sell only by the case, but you might be reassured by the offer at the front of the list that they will exchange any wine you find disappointing.

BEST BUYS Port, most things on the list

Gough Bros

See CHAINS AND SUPERMARKETS

Why not club together with friends to enjoy volume discounts and free delivery?

Richard Granger (Personal Wine Merchant) Ltd

West Jesmond Station, Newcastle-upon-Tyne, Tyne & Wear TEL (0632) 815000

OPEN Mon–Fri 8.30 am–6.30 pm Sat 8.30 am–3 pm CLOSED Sun, public holidays CREDIT CARDS Not accepted DISCOUNTS Not available DELIVERY Free locally, min 1 case; elsewhere negotiable GLASS HIRE Only for weddings (sterilising of glasses costs 60p per doz) TASTINGS AND TALKS On request CELLARAGE Negotiable

There is little to get really excited about in Richard Granger's shop beside the West Jesmond Metro Station. And if you take his list home to peruse, beware. Prices may look exceptionally good, but they do not include VAT. Nor does the list give many details – 'Sparkling Saumur' or 'Orvieto Secco (Dry)' or 'Fino Bottled in Spain' hardly brings us closer to a decision. Practically everything on the list is ready to drink – a small spread from France, Germany and Italy, a number of Champagnes and a tempting selection of LBV, crusting and tawny ports. Service, we hear from customers, is not always as friendly as one might expect of one's 'personal wine merchant'.

BEST BUYS [£]–[£££] Hugel Alsace wines, [££]–[£££] German wines including Deinhard Lila Sekt, [££]–[£££] Ports

Grape Ideas (Wine Warehouse)

Botley Works, North Hinksey Lane, Oxford, Oxfordshire TEL (086 59) 722137

OPEN Tue–Fri 11 am–6 pm Sat 10 am–4 pm CLOSED Sun, Mon, public holidays CREDIT CARDS Access/Euro, Visa DISCOUNTS Not available DELIVERY Free within Oxford city limits, min 1 case; £1.74 per case to most parts of England and Wales GLASS HIRE Free TASTINGS AND TALKS 3 times a year; outside tastings by request; 6 wines open daily in warehouse CELLARAGE Not provided

Ideas are in short supply in Oxford. So as a change from Dolamore, take a trip out towards the ring road roundabout to discover this new wine warehouse, in operation now for a little more than a year. Many prices are keen. The list scans the world sparsely but interestingly, getting down to rather more serious concentration in Burgundy and Bordeaux. Clarets begin at just over £2, rise to £3.95 for Ch Mazeris, Fronsac 1979 and then shoot off into higher realms with 1973 Ch Grand-Puy-Lacoste (£13), and then a run of seven classed growth 1978s culminating in Ch Cheval Blanc at £36 – prices here are not always competitive: shop around. Rhônes include the delicious Crozes-Hermitage, Domaine Thalabert 1980 and Cornas, 1982 Paul Jaboulet Aîné, and Loires the lovely red and white Sancerres of Vacheron, all at a little under £5. There is a small range of basic Germans from Seidenhaus, and just a few French country wines, including the lovely flowery-fresh Vin de Pays de Gascogne Cépage Colombard 1983 at just over £2; the new vintage will be fruitier as soon as it appears in the spring – these are not wines for keeping. Marqués de Cáceres prices are keen, Italians are cheap and cheerful. And there are a few less traditional wines, such as a 1980 Chardonnay and 1975 Cabernet Sauvignon from Argentina, bargains at under £3, which have both had plenty of time to mature as a result of our recent bout of patriotism – why not swallow all three? Also remarkably cheap are Stanley and Leasingham wines from Australia [£]–[££] and Chilean Cabernet Sauvignon, Viña Linderos 1979 at just over £3; Ch Musar 1977 is well priced, too. Last of the oddities is a New Zealand Müller-Thurgau from Montana at nearly £4, interesting, if not best value on the list. Ports are listed, too, but here, as with the other 'classic' areas, you might well find better bargains elsewhere. Best value here is at the lower end and where owner/buyer/Master of Wine David Stephens has allowed his thoughts to wander further afield.

BEST BUYS [£] Marqués de Cáceres, [£] Argentine wines, [££] Chilean Cabernet, [££] Ch Musar

Great American Food & Wine Co

Haslemere, 8 Silver Lane, Purley, Surrey TEL 01-660 6304
OPEN Mon–Fri 9 am–6 pm CLOSED Sat, Sun, public holidays CREDIT CARDS Personal and business accounts DISCOUNTS Not available DELIVERY Free in London; elsewhere at cost GLASS HIRE Not available TASTINGS AND TALKS Tastings on request; major tasting in spring CELLARAGE Not available

The Brook family – parents, son and daughter, New Yorkers living in Surrey for the past 18 years – set up their Great American Food & Wine Company two years ago. They specialise naturally in California, but are the exclusive importers, too, of the only New York State wines so far available in Britain. The Gold Seal New York State Chardonnay 1981 is particularly worth a try, lighter than most California Chardonnays but still with an intense buttery Chardonnay character (£45.88); the bottle-fermented sparkling Gold Seal is also good at £56.23 (prices given are for a case, the only way the wines are sold). Amongst the rest of their range, the Fetzer California wines are particularly good, especially the more expensive ones: the oaky Fetzer Barrel Select Chardonnay 1982 (£57.27) and the rich, oaky Fetzer Estate Bottled Cabernet Sauvignon (£65.09) both have extraordinarily long-lasting flavour.

BEST BUYS [£££] Gold Seal Chardonnay, [£££] Fetzer wines above

> The range of wines available and the prices asked are likely to change in the course of the year. The information given is correct in summer 1984, and we hope it serves as an indication of each restaurant's approach to wine. If you want to drink a particular bottle, it is best to ring beforehand, not only to ensure that it is served correctly, but also to check that it is still in stock.

Peter Green & Co

37A/B Warrender Park Road, Edinburgh TEL 031-229 5925

OPEN Mon–Fri (inc public holidays) 9.30 am–1 pm, 2 pm–6.30 pm Sat 9.30 am–7 pm CLOSED Sun, some local holidays CREDIT CARDS Not accepted; personal and business accounts DISCOUNTS 5% on unmixed case orders DELIVERY 50p per delivery anywhere within the Edinburgh boundary; elsewhere £3.20 for 1 case, £2.10 for subsequent cases GLASS HIRE Free TASTINGS AND TALKS To groups on request, at wine cost less 10% CELLARAGE Currently not available

Some of the very best value in the country is to be found at Peter Green & Co, whose fascinating range could keep most minds happily boggling and match most cooks' repertoires, certainly for the lifespan of this *Guide*, without returning twice to the same bottle. Infinite time and patience have obviously been spent in putting together such an assortment from so many different sources, and care has gone, too, into arranging the list in the way people are likely to go about their wine-hunting: the unusually large Alsace range under grape variety, the Germans arranged under sweetness categories within their regions – though a little verbal encouragement and tasting notes on at least some of the wines would help the less knowledgeable. Prices are very competitive. The clarets are a mouth-watering selection of classed growths, a few more mature wines back to 1961, with lots of younger mature *'petits'* as well. Ch Chasse-Spleen 1979 at £5.95 should be snapped up. There are a dozen Chablis from a good producer, Rémon, plus some other carefully chosen Burgundies from other sources, mostly *négociants*. The Beaujolais include many wines from the fine cellars of Loron. It would be hard to go wrong amongst Peter Green's Rhônes (Guigal, Paul Jaboulet Aîné, Meffre, Vidal-Fleurie, Perrin) especially amongst the Châteauneufs. Loires are good, the sweet ones in particular. Fine Champagnes are to be found in profusion, too, at good if not bargain prices, and a series of larger sizes culminates in a Methuselah (eight bottles' worth in one) of Pol Roger for £80. There's some very fair value to be found in the £ price range of 'other French' wines. Beyond the French borders, a long list of German wines spans the regions and the quality levels very thoroughly, and there are many delicious-looking sweet 1975s and 1976s, and some highly respected estate names like von Schorlemer, Bergweiler Prüm, von Kesselstadt and many more. Portuguese wine lovers will find a big selection here of some of the better wines. Unusually, there are three of Jose Maria da Fonseca's Moscatel de Setúbal wines: the (to us most delicious of the three, and the cheapest) young wine at £4.50, the 25-year-old at £7.99 and the 50-year-old at £25 a bottle. There is a fine choice from Spain, especially from Rioja, many of the wines from Berberana: old vintages back to the 1952 at £9.49 might be interesting for a special occasion (though bear in mind that Spaniards of old made fairly free with vintage dates, so you may not *really* be drinking the wine of your birth-year . . .). Look out amongst the Riojas for the wines of La Rioja Alta, very well priced here (Viña Arana, 1978, for example, for £3.39, or Viña Ardanza 1976 for £3.59) and for the wines of Marqués de Cáceres at well under £3. Torres and León are the stars in the Penedès section £–£££, and the wines of Valladolid if expensive are rich and unusual, peaking in the Vega Sicilia 1969 at £18.25. Look out amongst the Italians for the wines of Frescobaldi ££ and Carmignano Villa di Capezzana Riserva 1978 (£4.55). It is unusual in Britain to find any effort being put into the selection of wines from Austria – these come from several good sources £–££. Further afield, try the Australians from Brown Bros, Rosemount, Tahbilk; California wines are less interesting, mostly from Masson and Almaden, but a good introduction to these wines, nevertheless, at just over £3. From Chile come some fresh wines made by the Torres firm of Spain, Cooks and Marlborough wines from New Zealand, and cheaply priced Lebanese wines from Ch Musar (£3.89 for the 1977, £6.99 for the 1966). Plenty of half-bottles and, as befits an Edinburgh merchant, a fine malt whisky collection, round off this fine list.

BEST BUYS Most things on the list, especially clarets, Rhônes, and Spanish wines

Greens Ltd

34 Royal Exchange, London, EC3 TEL 01-626 8801
36 Duke Street, London, SW1 TEL 01-930 1383

OPEN Mon–Fri 9 am–5 pm CLOSED Sat, Sun, public holidays
CREDIT CARDS Not accepted DISCOUNTS 2.5% on 1–4 cases, 5% on 5+ cases
DELIVERY Free in Central London, min 1 case; elsewhere 1 case £6.32, 2–10 cases £4.02 per case GLASS HIRE £1.32 per doz TASTINGS AND TALKS For groups on request; annual 2-day tasting for customers CELLARAGE £3.39 per doz per year

Greens is another of those old established City merchants who offer an old-fashioned, gentlemanly service, a well-balanced and more than reliable list – and high prices (note that VAT is to be added to the prices – but even before you get out your calculator, they are not cheap). Best value here apart from the reliable house wines are the vins de pays – try the Colombard and the Syrah £, the small Rhône range, Spanish and Australian wines, some good domaine-bottled Burgundies, the excellent Chablis from Domaine la Jouchère and an interesting selection of the 'second wines' of some famous Bordeaux châteaux, as well as a reasonable selection of petits-châteaux and classed growths of recent vintages, with a few back to 1964. You can sample their wares before you buy at their two wine bars, The Greenhouse at the Royal Exchange and Green's Champagne and Oyster Bar in Duke Street, both of which are worth a visit *(see* WINE BARS*)*.

BEST BUYS Own-label wines, sherries and ports

£ indicates wines under £3, ££ wines £3–£5 and £££ wines over £5.

AOL Grilli Wines

Little Knoxbridge, Cranbrook Road, Staplehurst, Kent TEL (0580) 891472

OPEN 'All hours' CREDIT CARDS Not accepted; business accounts only DISCOUNTS 80p per case cash and carry, £2.50 per case on 3–8 cases DELIVERY Free anywhere on UK mainland, min 1 mixed case GLASS HIRE Free TASTINGS AND TALKS For groups on request, at wine cost CELLARAGE Not available

AOL Grilli Wines ('run from home so we are always open') are of special interest for their Portuguese wines, of which prices, already good when compared with other Portuguese wine stockists, are extraordinarily low when you consider that delivery is included for a mixed case anywhere in the UK. Portuguese wines can be terribly tough (as in the rest of the list, there's a tasting note for every wine, which in Colares, for example, is an honest 'rough and tough' or 'stony character will go on for years'), but you will find here some of the very best reds: Garrafeira Particular Caves Dom Theodosio Reserva 1968 (£4.15) is a well-made heavyweight, and the Pasmados 1971 (£3.71) and 1974 (£3.26), both rich, ripe, alcoholic wines, are worth a try. Moscatel de Setúbal, both the 1978 and the 25-year-old, are well priced (£4.42 and £7.68) – lovely dessert wines. Try as an alternative the Muscat de Beaumes-de-Venise (presumably the Co-operative's at this price of £5.07). Selling so much by mail, Mr Grilli would do well to provide more details of producers throughout the rest of his list, which offers a smattering of modest wines from France, Germany and Italy, sherry, Madeira, the delicious Chambéry vermouth (£4.14) and olive oil – descriptions, admirable as they are, are not enough! But turn to his fine wine supplement for a regularly changing selection of clarets, German estate wines and good Burgundies.

BEST BUYS [££] Portuguese reds, particularly Dom Theodosio and Pasmados, [££]–[£££] Moscatel de Setúbal

Hadleigh Wine Cellars

The Maltings, Duke Street, Hadleigh, Suffolk TEL (0473) 827670

OPEN Mon–Fri 9 am–5.30 pm Sat 9 am–2.30 pm CLOSED Sun, public holidays CREDIT CARDS Not accepted; personal accounts DISCOUNTS 8% on case orders, which may be mixed, cash and carry DELIVERY Free locally, min order negotiable GLASS HIRE Free TASTINGS AND TALKS On request CELLARAGE £2 per case per year

This company was set up a year ago by Patrick Brady of the Brady wine bar group, who was joined by Jonathan Hare of Lay & Wheeler. It is largely a wholesale business, but they do have retail premises here at the Hadleigh Maltings. Their range is fairly small, but widespread, taking in briefly Australia, the Lebanon, California, Spain and Italy as well as the major areas of France and Germany. Good value is to be found in the French regional section, and there are lots of good Jaboulet Rhônes, Loron Beaujolais, a few Burgundies, and a small, select range of clarets spanning the price ranges in good vintages back to 1961. Their short list of 1983 clarets *en primeur* was rather expensive at the time, and some other prices are quite high, though the rest of the pricing is average, or even very good. Vintage ports particularly are well priced.

BEST BUYS [£] French regional wines, [£££] vintage ports

The Halesworth Vintner

26 Quay Street, Halesworth, Suffolk TEL (098 67) 3829

OPEN Mon–Sat 9 am–6.30 pm CLOSED Sun, public holidays CREDIT CARDS All accepted DISCOUNTS 5% per case; large orders by negotiation DELIVERY Free locally; elsewhere at cost GLASS HIRE Free TASTINGS AND TALKS Occasionally on request CELLARAGE £2 per case per year

The young 'everyday' wines in this Suffolk shop are really very expensive, but Andrew Low and John Price (trading under the names John Andrew or The Halesworth Vintner) really specialise in elderly wines – old Madeira, sherry, very old claret, Burgundy, all listed (monthly now) in an extraordinarily higgledy-piggledy fashion: sherry–port–claret–port and then perhaps an oddity like Luis Martini's 1960 Private Reserve California Mountain Barbera (£50) which is followed by – yes, there is some logic in it after all, the wines are in vintage order – a 1960 Harvey's Bristol Milk, bottled 1960 (£11). Unusually amongst fine and rare wine companies, The Halesworth Vintner prints a tasting note (where possible), and details of ullage (any loss of wine from the bottle during ageing), and the condition of the label and so on, plus any tasting notes they have come across by the likes of Edmund Penning-Rowsell or Hugh Johnson; they even point to the page on which a 'discouraging tasting note' may be found in Michael Broadbent's *Vintage Wine Book*. They are well placed to give such literary guidance, because their other speciality is wine books, new and old, and books on cookery and wine-growing.

BEST BUYS Mature wines

If your favourite wine merchant is not in this section, write and tell us about him or her. There are report forms at the back of the book.

Special awards

(V) means bargain prices (good *value* may be obtained from merchants without this symbol, of course, if you are prepared to pay for service)

[bottle] means that the merchant stocks an above-average range

[hand] means that extra-special service is offered: helpful advice, informative lists and newsletters, tastings etc.

Hampstead Wine Warehouse

111 West Heath Road, London, NW3 TEL 01-458 4388
(at the corner with Finchley Road)

OPEN Mon–Fri 11 am–8 pm Sat, public holidays 10 am–7 pm Sun 11 am–5 pm CLOSED Chr Day, New Year's Day CREDIT CARDS All accepted; personal and business accounts; own charge card DISCOUNTS 3% for case orders, cash and carry DELIVERY Free in London GLC area, min 1 case, which may be mixed; elsewhere on mainland UK £5 for 1 case, thereafter £3 each. GLASS HIRE Free TASTINGS AND TALKS Bottles open daily in warehouse; wine club tastings CELLARAGE £2 per case per year

The former North West Vintners retail warehouse was taken over in September 1983, changed its name to the Hampstead Wine Warehouse, and greatly extended its range. In this charming old building, formerly the Hampstead stables of Unigate Dairies, French wines account for about half the range of 500 or so different wines, and are a sound if not particularly inspired selection, mostly in the [££] range. Best value in the lower echelons are probably the Listel wines [£], including the sparkling Brut de Listel at just over £3. The Loires are consistently good: try the lovely Savennières 1981 of Jean Beaumard at just over £4 and Sauvion & Fils Muscadets at just over £2. Most interest is to be discovered, however, in the rest of the world: some good Austrian wines, sweet and dry, Bulgarians, Spanish wines from Torres and Marqués de Cáceres at good prices, California wines including Geoffrey Roberts Reserve at under £3. The Alto Adige wines are the best buys amongst the Italians. Some of the prices are quite good, though many are not particularly keen. About four wines are always open for tasting in the warehouse during the week, more at weekends, and Hampstead have started to run special wine tastings for their wine club, some tutored, some 'free'. They also sell a selection of wine food such as mustards, oils, vinegars and cheeses. As we went to press, they were hoping to open another small retail outlet in the Kensington area.

BEST BUYS [£] Listel wines, [£]–[££] Loires, [££] Spanish wines

Gerard Harris Ⓥ ☞

2 Green End Street, Aston Clinton, TEL (0296) 631041
Aylesbury, Buckinghamshire

OPEN Mon–Sat 9.30 am–8 pm Public holidays 11 am–2 pm CLOSED Sun CREDIT CARDS Access/Euro, Visa; personal and business accounts DISCOUNTS 10% on case orders, and on cash and carry DELIVERY Free within 20 miles of Aston Clinton, min 1 case (but £3 for immediate despatch outside van's schedule; elsewhere in England (excluding Devon, Cornwall and some parts of Wales) £3 per consignment, Scotland approx £5–£6 per case; elsewhere at cost GLASS HIRE Free TASTINGS AND TALKS 3 tastings a year, free to regular customers CELLARAGE Limited, £3.50 per case per year

The retail wine shop of the Bell Inn in Aston Clinton near Aylesbury *(see* RESTAURANTS *section)* stocks a very good range of wines, predominantly French but with a good representative selection from elsewhere at prices which are always competitive, sometimes better. The fine range of clarets reaches back to 1961; there are Burgundies, more recent, from a series of good *négociants*; a big selection of northern Rhônes from Paul Jaboulet Aîné (including some magnums), a few from Meffre and others, some very good Loires and Alsace wines and an interesting small selection from the South of France. German wines include some very good estate wines of the 1975 and 1976 vintages. The small range from the rest of the world includes well-chosen California wines from Phelps, Trefethen, Heitz, Shaefer and others, Australians from Brown Bros and Tahbilk and even a couple of Swiss wines, which might suit those with well-lined bank safes in the country of origin.

BEST BUYS ££–£££ Rhônes

Roger Harris Wines

Loke Farm, Weston Longville, Norfolk TEL (0603) 880171

OPEN Mon–Fri 9 am–5 pm CLOSED Sat, Sun, public holidays CREDIT CARDS Access/Euro, Visa; personal and business accounts DISCOUNTS 50p per case for 3+ cases, £1 per case for 5+ cases, £1.20 per case for 10+ cases DELIVERY Free on UK mainland, min 1 case; elsewhere at cost GLASS HIRE Not available TASTINGS AND TALKS On request CELLARAGE Not available

Roger Harris specialises in wines from the Beaujolais, selling by the case only, which may be mixed. The wines are largely from small-scale growers, but some are from co-operatives. Beginning with Beaujolais and Beaujolais-Villages, the list deals with each of the nine crus in turn, a dozen or so wines from each of either the latest or recent vintages, with useful tasting notes on each, and information on the growers. Turn to the back to find some unusual brandies: Marc Extra Egrappé, Pur Bourgogne and Fine Bourgogne (distilled from the grape skins and fermentation residue, and from finished wine, respectively) both from Vincent Jacoulot (£11.65 and £12.30). Special offers, sent out to customers once a month, and soft-sells almost to point of half-heartedness, are worth a look.

BEST BUYS The 1983 vintage crus, certainly until the 1984 vintage appears in spring and summer of 1985; ££ Beaujolais Jean Garlon, £££ Ch du Moulin-à-Vent 1883, Bloud, £££ Morgon Cuvée Jean-Claude Aucoeur 1983

The Wine Standards Board is the trade's disciplinary department and wine watchdog. Their inspectors are responsible for rooting out any malpractices – but they are concerned largely with labelling irregularities. If you have genuine reason to suspect that the wine in a bottle is not what the label claims it is, contact the Board at:
68½ Upper Thames Street, London EC4V 3BJ; TEL 01–236 9512.

Harrods

Knightsbridge, London, SW1 TEL 01-730 1234

OPEN Mon, Tue, Thur, Fri 9 am–5 pm Wed 9.30–7 pm Sat 9 am–6 pm
CLOSED Sun, public holidays CREDIT CARDS All accepted; Harrods account
DISCOUNTS 12 bottles for the price of 11; 15% off list price (single bottles) during Jan/July sales DELIVERY Free within 20 miles of Harrods, any quantity; elsewhere on UK mainland, £3.75 for 1–4 bottles, £5.25 for 5–6 bottles, £5.50 for 7–12 bottles and £2.50 for each additional case GLASS HIRE Not available
TASTINGS AND TALKS In-store tastings every day, 11 am–3 pm
CELLARAGE Not available

Perhaps the best value from Harrods' wine department is to be had by those who live within their van delivery area, a 20-mile or so radius of Knightsbridge: Harrods will deliver any quantity (even one bottle) free – a useful service, especially at Christmas. This apart, no one, presumably, shops at Harrods for bargains. And at prices sometimes eccentrically £10 above the going rate elsewhere, sometimes only a little over, the very good range includes such oddities as a half-dozen Moroccan wines, the odd Swiss, Lebanese, Chinese, Chilean or New York State surprise, but perhaps not so much exotica as one might expect. France takes up most of the elegant shelf space, with a good selection of clarets, fewer but nonetheless desirable Burgundies, and some good single-vineyard Beaujolais. Rhônes, a small assortment, include Châteauneuf Mont Redon and a few Jaboulet wines; there are very good Loires; Domaines Ott [£££] and Fonscolombe wines [£] from Provence and good-value vin de table from Listel in the bottom price ranges [£]. Ports go back to 1955, some well over-priced. Dessert wine drinkers will find some fine sweet German wines too. The Italian wines are exceptionally well chosen, though Spanish wines are undeservedly few and far between. Harrods' list, produced by *Decanter* magazine, enterprisingly includes articles on wines and spirits – and advertisements. Tasting notes and more relevant advice on what to drink and when would be a useful addition – or substitute.

BEST BUYS [£] Listel wines, Ch de Fonscolombe; wines you cannot find elsewhere

G C Harvey

77–81 Ber Street, Norwich, Norfolk TEL (0603) 23531

OPEN Mon–Sat 9 am–6 pm CLOSED Sun, public holidays CREDIT CARDS Not accepted; personal and business accounts DISCOUNTS 5% on case orders
DELIVERY Free in Norwich and within 30 miles, min 5 cases; otherwise at cost
GLASS HIRE Free TASTINGS AND TALKS Free in-store tastings every week; 13-week wine appreciation courses Oct–Jan (£60); for groups on request
CELLARAGE £1.50 per case per year

A lot of care has obviously gone into the compilation of G C Harvey's wine range; their list is rather bald, however: no comment, no tasting notes, though the vital details of producers and vintages are generally there in full. Harveys have sold ten of their retail outlets over the past year, but have revamped their Norwich shop, where their business is now concentrated. Prices are rather high, but quality on the whole is very good. French country wines are a short but interesting collection. You will find some excellent Burgundies, both recent and venerable, some mature single vineyard crus Beaujolais, and good Rhônes. The list of estate-bottled German wines is impressive, and there is a good list of Champagnes. The long Italian range is anonymous. Perhaps most extraordinary is the lengthy selection of Madeiras, including old solera and vintage wines back to the last century from a variety of houses (at rather high prices). There are some very interesting elderly sherries, too.

BEST BUYS Burgundies, Rhônes

John Harvey & Sons Ltd

27 Pall Mall, London, SW1 TEL 01-839 4695
12 Denmark Street, Bristol TEL (0272) 23759
16 The Hard, Portsmouth (area order office) TEL (0705) 825567

OPEN Mon–Fri 9 am–5.30 pm CLOSED Sat, Sun, public holidays
CREDIT CARDS All accepted DISCOUNTS On 3 or more cases (on some wines only) DELIVERY Free on UK mainland for case orders; 1 bottle £2.64, 2 bottles £2.93, 3 £3.33 and 4–11 £3.85 GLASS HIRE Free TASTINGS AND TALKS Twice a year for customers in London, Bristol and Portsmouth; also by arrangement CELLARAGE £2.01 per case per year

Harveys may have added 78 new wines to their 1984 list, but it still remains rather less inspiring than in years gone by. Our large tasting of their lower and middle-priced wines yielded little of great interest, though all were sound, pleasant drinking. And there are really few if any bargains are to be found – after you have read the tiny print and discovered that VAT is not included in the list prices. Anyway, the latest list begins well, with some useful – if sometimes a little over-complimentary – tasting notes on Harvey's own sherries. Try the delicious Harvey's Palo Cortado (£51.66 + VAT) and the old bottled sherries (Bristol Cream bottled 1973, £64.58, Bristol Milk bottled 1973, £61.13, and Very Old Oloroso bottled 1964, £75.38 – all per case plus VAT) which bear no resemblance to the modern brands, and in which time has dried out a lot of the sugar. But after that, tasting notes dry up too – and the list is so short that it really would be quite possible to annotate every wine. Port stretches back very skimpily to 1963, and clarets, too, are skimpier than they used to be, mostly of the recent few vintages. Harveys own nearly a quarter-share of Ch Latour, and list every vintage since 1971, plus 1967, and also five vintages of Latour's second wine, Les Forts de Latour (no discounts on these Latour wines, the footnote stresses). Moillard and Jadot pop up a lot in the Burgundy list; Régnard's Chablis are worth a try (though the 1982s are rather soft, flabby and untypical). German wine lovers should be fairly happy with the estate-bottled German range. John Harvey's 'Personal Selection' was sent out a few times to chosen customers last year – bin-ends and small parcels of wine too small to be put on the main list; anyone interested can ask to be put on the mailing list.

BEST BUYS [££]–[£££] Old bottled sherries

Richard Harvey Wines (V)

The Auction House, East Street, Wimborne Minster, Dorset TEL (0202) 881111

OPEN Mon–Fri 9.30 am–5.30 pm (Wed till 1 pm) Sat 9.30 am–1 pm CLOSED Sun, Wed pm, public holidays CREDIT CARD Visa DISCOUNTS 2.5% on 1–5 unmixed cases, 5% on 6+ unmixed cases DELIVERY Free in Dorset, Hampshire and Central London for 3+ cases; free elsewhere on UK mainland for 6+ cases; Dorset, Hampshire and Central London £2.30 per case for 1–2 cases; elsewhere on UK mainland £4.60 per case for 1–2 cases, £2.30 per case for 3–5 cases GLASS HIRE Free TASTINGS AND TALKS Main tasting once a year, regional tastings 3 or 4 times a year with food, £5 per head; to groups on request, at wine cost. CELLARAGE £1.50 per case per year

Though MW Richard Harvey's list is not long, there is plenty of choice – we at least are tempted by practically everything there! You must buy by the case from this Dorset merchant, since he has only a wholesale licence; prices are quite keen, especially if you live within the mixed-case free delivery area, with plenty of choice in the lower price bracket [£]. Most parts of France are represented: there is a very interesting selection of good French regional wines, a few well-chosen clarets; try the white Ch Thieuley (especially the 1982 if there's any left, and the 1983), delicious fresh Sauvignons at just under £3. Burgundies, particularly the whites, are good, the list is littered with names like Leflaive, Thévenin, and the reliable co-operatives of La Chablisienne and Cave de Buxy. There are good Rhônes and Loires, Alsace wines selected from a number of different producers, fine estate Germans, mostly of recent vintages, sound to good Italians, and a few excellent Spanish wines. The only non-European contender is Brown Bros from Australia, who supply four well-made wines. Amongst the sparkling wines try the Saumurs of Gratien & Meyer [££], mixed, perhaps with a spot of Gabriel Boudier's Cassis, Framboise or Myrtille (bilberry) liqueurs (£6.50). They also supply oils – walnut and olive. Look out for good prices in Richard Harvey's bin-end sales.

BEST BUYS Most things on the list

Special awards

(V) is for bargain prices

(bottle) is for a very good range of wines

(hand) is for exceptional service.

Hatch, Mansfield & Co Ltd

64/65 Cowcross Street, London, EC1 TEL 01-253 8172

OPEN Mon–Fri 9 am–5 pm CLOSED Sat, Sun, public holidays CREDIT CARD Visa DISCOUNTS For quantity, on application DELIVERY Free in GLC area, min 4 cases GLASS HIRE Not available TASTINGS AND TALKS By invitation CELLARAGE Not available

The prime business of this fine wine subsidiary of Allied Breweries is with restaurants and clubs, but they also sell to private customers who have agreed a special account with them. Offers mailed to private customers are generally bin-ends or wines otherwise surplus to requirements, and bargains are sometimes to be found amongst their agencies. These include the Alsace wines of Preiss-Zimmer, Louis Jadot Burgundies, Spanish Marqués de Riscal and the good-value wines of Raimat: dry white Casal and red Abadía, which contains Cabernet Sauvignon and is well worth trying. Victoria Wine belong to the same group, so sell many of the same wines, which you will occasionally find on the VW shelf cheaper than by the case from Hatch Mansfield, so check before you buy.

BEST BUYS Agency wines mentioned above

The Hay Wine Co Ltd

The Market Place, Corby Glen, Lincolnshire TEL (047 684) 420 or 476
Lillie House, Conduit Street, Leicester, Leicestershire TEL (0533) 545389

OPEN (Corby Glen) Tue–Fri 10 am–6 pm Sat 10 am–3 pm Sun 12 noon–1 pm (Leicester) Mon–Fri 10 am–5.30 pm Sat 10 am–3 pm CLOSED Mon, Sun pm, public holidays CREDIT CARDS Not accepted; personal accounts DISCOUNTS 2.5% on 5+ cases, 5% on 10+ cases DELIVERY Free in Central London for 2+ cases; £2.50 for 1 case; elsewhere free for 3+ cases, £2.50 for 1–2 cases GLASS HIRE Free TASTINGS AND TALKS Monthly tastings and regular 'customer days'. Lectures free of charge; talks and tastings at 25p per sample per head CELLARAGE £1.15 + insurance per case per year

This business has a split personality in more ways than one. Their basic wine list – a sparse span of the world with a decidedly French accent – is generally not very exciting, some of it very mediocre, and all of it expensive, especially when you take into account that the listed prices are case prices, on which many companies already charging less would give a discount. But then turn to their fine wine list, expanded this year, and you might find some very keen prices for vintage ports back to 1960 and clarets, mostly top growths, back to 1966, but largely good vintages of the '70s on the latest list we were sent before going to press. Before you get *too* excited – VAT has to be added to this fine wine list, and on wines marked 'IB' you will be charged duty, though wines marked 'PS' are being sold through the company by private individuals, and so are not liable for VAT. From the retail shop in Corby Glen, you can buy by the single bottle (but then at prices about five per cent higher still), wheras the Leicester outlet, having only a wholesale licence, sells only by the case.

BEST BUYS £££ Clarets and ports from the fine wine list

Haynes Hanson & Clark

Head office and wholesale warehouse
17 Lettice Street, London SW6 TEL 01-736 7878
Shop 36 Kensington Church Street, London, W8 TEL 01-937 4650

OPEN (Warehouse) Mon–Fri 9.15 am–7 pm Sat 9.15 am–1 pm (Shop) Mon–Sat 9.30 am–7 pm BOTH CLOSED Sun, public holidays CREDIT CARDS Not accepted; personal and business accounts DISCOUNTS 10% off retail prices on unmixed cases DELIVERY Free in Central London, min 1 case; elsewhere £2.80 per single case, £2 per case for 2 cases, thereafter free GLASS HIRE Free TASTINGS AND TALKS Regular tastings for customers at Lettice Street by invitation. Bottles open for tasting in warehouse CELLARAGE Can be arranged in public warehouses

Haynes Hanson & Clark are serious wine merchants. Their long French list in particular is strewn with good finds, some of them available only from this source, and at prices which, though never a give-away, are mostly fair. At the wholesale price, ten per cent down, prices are good, and now that their warehouse is operational in the back streets of Fulham, collection is easier than from the cramped little shop in busy Kensington Church Street. And bottles are always open for tasting in Fulham, too. Wines span all price ranges. Clarets are a speciality, and *en primeur* offers are very competitive. There's a good selection of petits-châteaux ready for drinking ££. At just above £5 (at case rate), Ch la Tour du Mirail (Haut Médoc) 1979 is delicious, still a fat, fruity, tannic wine which will be lovely towards the end of 1985. On each wine in the long range of clarets for laying down – as indeed for every wine on the list – there's a detailed, honest tasting note, and a good indication of when to start trying it. You would expect one so critical of most things Burgundian as infamous author Anthony Hanson to winkle out a few exceptions to his rule. Stars amongst his selection are certainly the deep, dark, sturdy but fruity reds of Domaine Mussy, a small estate with very old vines. At under £8.50 (case price) per bottle, his Beaune Epenottes and Pommard 1981 are excellent value, but will need three or four years' keeping, at least. St-Romain from Gras-Boisson £££ and the Côtes de Nuits wines of Rossignol £££ are very good. Look out also for the Chablis of the two Raveneau and Durup ££ – £££, and the very reasonable St-Véran 1982 from the Cave de Prissé (£4.26). (The vintage will no doubt change in the spring of 1985.) Rhônes are good from Guigal, Paul Jaboulet Aîné and Domaine du Vieux Télégraphe, but so also is the much cheaper Coteaux du Tricastin Domaine de Grangeneuve (£2.99). Pierre Vaudon Champagne from the co-operative at Avize at under £7.50 a bottle (case price) is good value. Haynes Hanson & Clark run the John Arlott Wine Club in conjunction with *Guardian* Publications *(see above)*.

BEST BUYS Clarets *en primeur*, [£££] Mussy Burgundies

Hedges & Butler

153 Regent Street, London, W1 TEL 01-734 4444

OPEN Mon–Fri 9.30 am–5.30 pm CLOSED Sat, Sun, public holidays CREDIT CARDS All accepted DISCOUNTS 5% cash and carry, 5% wines, 2½% spirits on 2–4 cases delivered; 7½% wines, 5% spirits on 5–7 cases delivered; 10% wines, 5% spirits on 8+ cases delivered DELIVERY Free within Central London; elsewhere £4 per case GLASS HIRE, TASTINGS AND TALKS, CELLARAGE Not available

This retail showcase for Bass's wine and spirit division sells mainly the group's own brands and agencies, which include a number of fine wines. Most interesting are the Bordeaux and the Italian wines. Hedges & Butler hold the agency for Mouton, which includes the not-so-interesting Mouton Cadet, Ch Mouton-Baronne-Philippe and the great Mouton itself, as well as a number of petits-châteaux and bourgeois wines from the firm, not the man, Alexis Lichine. Ch Castéra is particularly good (£4.40 for the 1980). Of the Italian wines (all of which Hedges & Butler distribute to restaurants and retailers throughout Britain), try the good Corvo wines from Sicily, the Chianti Riserva Ducale 1979 from Ruffino (£3.50) and the Gold Label Riserva Ducale (£5.20). Madeiras are of special note: there is an interesting range of old solera wines and vintages starting at £20 a bottle and rising to £63 for Blandy's Vintage 1880 Malmsey. There are ports, too, but why should Hedges & Butler, who can manage to charge some fair if not cheap prices for some of their agency wines, ask £11.20 for Warre 1975 and £14.20 for the 1977 when they are so well connected with the ports of Warre?

BEST BUYS [£] Corvo Sicilian wines, [££]–[£££] Ruffino Chiantis

Hicks & Don

4 The Market Place, Westbury, Wiltshire TEL (0373) 864723
Park House, Elmham, Dereham, Norfolk TEL (036 281) 571

OPEN (Wiltshire) Mon–Fri 9 am–5.30 pm Sun By appointment CLOSED Sun, public holidays (Norfolk) Open usually during office hours, otherwise answering machine will take calls CREDIT CARDS Access/Euro, Visa; personal and business accounts DISCOUNTS On selected wines for quantity; £1 per case cash and carry DELIVERY Free to private or business addresses anywhere in mainland UK, min 3 cases, which for fortified wines may be mixed; £1 per case for 1–2 cases GLASS HIRE Free TASTINGS AND TALKS To groups on request, charges negotiable CELLARAGE £1.32 per case per year

'We try to take the risk out of wine buying,' write Mr Hicks and Mr Don at the beginning of their 1984/85 wine list. This they are well qualified to do, both holding the ultimate wine trade title of Master of Wine. They have sniffed out an unusual range of fine wines, not only from throughout France, but from Spain, Italy and the New World (including a wine from Oregon) plus some interesting oddities like the Greek Ch Carras 1978, Greece's best red, made from the Bordeaux grape varieties and rich and fruity (£4.37) and, for retsina lovers, one of the best, Kourtakis (£3.22), and a good-value Yugoslav Gewürztraminer (£2.73). Spain is one of the strongest points of this strong list. Rarities here include the fresh Castillo de San Diego 1983 (£2.18), a dry table wine made by the firm of Antonio Barbadillo from grapes that might otherwise have become sherry. Another unusual white worth trying is the Gran Fuedo from the firm of Chivite in Navarra (£3.42). Better, however, are the more familiar Viña Ardanza Rioja 1976 (£4.19), the Cabernet Sauvignon 1979 from Jean Léon (£6.05) and the Torres wines [£]–[££]. And best of all, in our view, are the wonderful sherries of Antonio Barbadillo in Sanlucar – a specialist in Manzanilla. Try some of the Manzanilla range, which includes a rich, concentrated, old dry Manzanilla Amontillada (£4.35); but, equally, don't miss the Fino de Balbaina, a light, fresh fino, one of the very best and excellent value at £3.26. The Italian range is also very good: look out for wines from Lungarotti, Antinori, Terre del Barolo and Cá del Bosco. The reliable wines of Rudolf Müller feature frequently in the German list, along with some excellent German estate wines. No less originality has gone into the selection of the French wines. Burgundies concentrate on some carefully selected wines of lesser Burgundian appellations at around the £5 mark, and clarets are bourgeois and petit-château wines. Amongst the white Bordeaux, Ch Thieuley 1983 (£3.12) is delicious. There's good value, too, from the Rhône and Loire, and a number of wines worth trying from other French regions [£]. The finer wines from all countries tend to be offered at 'opening' prices when they first appear on the market, so it is a good idea to put yourself on the mailing list for offers of claret, Burgundy, Rhônes, German wines and port for laying down. Prices are not the cheapest at Hicks & Don (and note that delivery is now free only if you order three cases or more) but nevertheless, a pin stuck at random into the list, or reliance on the lengthy tasting notes and admirable advice on when to drink, should not fail to bring you a satisfying glass.

BEST BUYS Most things on the list, but especially [££] the Barbadillo sherries

High Breck Vintners (V) ☞

Spats Lane, Headley, Bordon, Hampshire TEL (0428) 713689

AGENTS

Nalders Wine Agency, North Berkshire TEL (0734) 332312
The Berkshire Wine Agency, East Berkshire TEL (0734) 343264

Beeston Hall Cellars, East Anglia TEL (0692) 630771
Worthing and South Coast TEL (0903) 32629
North West Sussex TEL (0403 72) 2357
Thames Valley TEL (07357) 2624

OPEN Mon–Fri 9.30 am–6 pm Sat 9.15 am–1 pm Sun and public holidays by appointment only CLOSED Chr Day CREDIT CARDS Not accepted; personal and business accounts DISCOUNTS 2.5% on single drops 11+ cases, 3.75% on 21+ cases; for annual purchases of over £600, terms on application DELIVERY Free within 25 miles, min one case; elsewhere £3 for 1 case, £1.50 per case thereafter GLASS HIRE Free TASTINGS AND TALKS About 30 at Headley per year, no charge. Tutored talks and tastings by arrangement CELLARAGE Limited, £2 per case per year

Retired advertising man and gastronome Tom Johnson chooses his wines with flair and prices them with great modesty. He and his team of local ladies welcome customers to the High Breck hide-away in the woods of the Hampshire–Surrey border with a quiet charm well matched to the setting. (Customers living in the areas of the six agents – *see above* – can deal through them.) France is his main area, and here he has many small-grower agencies which are consequently good value. There are some wonderful and well-priced Alsace wines from the Riquewihr grower Wiederhirn [££]; amongst the many Loires, Jean-Pierre Tijou's sweet Quarts de Chaumes are very good, fresh, clean wines, less sulphured than many Coteaux-du-Layons and excellent value in the older vintages, particularly 1973 and 1974 [££]. Tijou's Domaine de Bellevue Chenin-and-a-bit-of-Chardonnay blend Anjou blanc is good, too, at just over £3 (but his red is less interesting). High Breck have the agency for the Ch la Jaubertie Bergeracs of British former stationery shop magnate Nick Ryman, so prices are low for these very good bursting-with-fruit wines made for early drinking, whites (£3.06 and £3.16), red (also just over £3), and a good sparkler (£4.73). There are many more clarets on the list now for laying down. An unusual find in this country is the sweet Muscat from St-Jean-du-Minervois; and Chambéry vermouth is very good. There's a fine selection of Beaujolais from the Eventail des Vignerons (a promotional grouping of good-quality individual producers); good Germans from Deinhard; and the fine sherries of Lustau have replaced La Riva. Bauget Jouette Champagnes are also good value, starting at £7.52. The useful notes on all the wines in the list include occasional suggestions for food partners, and the odd quirky but nice cooking tip. Chip dry white port [£££], for example, 'should be drunk iced as an aperitif and is most elegant and refreshing. After a few hot peppers have been steeped in it for six weeks or so it makes a marvellous additive to meaty soups. NB This works with dry sherry too.' Tom Johnson's culinary tastes have been put to good use in his selection of oils, mustards and a delicious alternative to smoked salmon, smoked sea trout (which is also available by post).

BEST BUYS [££] Ch la Jaubertie Bergeracs, [£]–[££] Beaujolais, [££]–[£££] sherries

J E Hogg

61 Cumberland Street, Edinburgh TEL 031-556 4025

OPEN Mon, Tue, Thur, Fri 9 am–1 pm, 2.30 pm–6 pm Wed, Sat 9 am–1 pm CLOSED Wed pm, Sat pm, Sun, local holidays CREDIT CARDS Not accepted DISCOUNTS Not available DELIVERY No free delivery; 60p per case in Edinburgh, £3 per case outside Edinburgh + 1% insurance premium on certain items GLASS HIRE Free, limited stock TASTINGS AND TALKS On request, at wine cost CELLARAGE Not available

This good-value family business has put a lot of effort into amassing a wide selection of wines from very many different suppliers in the world's major wine-growing countries, and sells them at prices which must warm the cockles of Edinburgh wine-drinkers' hearts. Beginning with France, some good Loires include three delicious sweet wines, all between £6 and £7 a bottle: 1969 Coteaux du Layon, Clos Ste-Catherine, Baumard, the same grower's Quarts de Chaume 1975, and Foreau's sweet 1971 Vouvray, Clos Naudin. The unusually large range of Alsace wines comes from a number of producers, as do the Burgundies, where you will find the produce of Bouchard Père, Tollot-Beaut, Michel Rémon, plenty of Moreau and others. Beaujolais are also from a number of reliable sources, mostly single vineyard wines. Good Rhônes include many from Paul Jaboulet Aîné. A modest range of classed growth clarets includes plenty of 1970s and 1971s, plus one or two older wines. The Italian range is of mixed quality, but try the Ruffino Chiantis, including the light Aziano for around £2.70, Valtellina wines from Negri and the Barolos of Pio Cesare and Ratti £££. From Spain, Riojas have been well bought, especially the wines of La Rioja Alta, Viña Ardanza and Viña Alberdi £ – ££ – and there is some good value to be found from Catalonia, from the firms of Torres and León. The cheaper, more basic German wines from Deinhard are very reliable, backed up by estate wines up to Trockenbeerenauslese level, including an unusually good selection of mature 1975s and 1976s. You might also dabble here in California and Australia, amongst wines priced from below £3 up to nearly £11. Whisky-lovers will find a good spread of malts.

BEST BUYS Most things in the shop

Hopton Wines

Hopton Court, Cleobury Mortimer, Hereford & Worcester TEL (0299) 270482

OPEN Mon–Fri 9 am–5.30 pm Sat 9 am–1 pm CLOSED Sun, public holidays CREDIT CARDS Not accepted; 30 day payment DISCOUNTS 50p per case cash and carry; 2% for 'prompt payment' DELIVERY Free within 50 miles of Cleobury Mortimer and Chester, min 1 case; elsewhere £4 for 1 case, £7 for 2 cases, thereafter free GLASS HIRE Free TASTINGS AND TALKS At least 3 tastings a year at Hopton Court for customers; for groups on request CELLARAGE Usually free

This little company, set up just over four years ago, offers by the case (mixed or unmixed) a small, reliable selection of mostly French wines which represent good value since they are delivered free within the 50 mile delivery radius, though prices in general are not especially keen. However, Pol Roger Champagne was excellent value on their summer 1984 list at £9.21 for the NV and £10.94 for the 1976 vintage.

BEST BUYS [£££] Champagne, [££]–[£££] Loires

House of Austria

73 Northwood Street, Birmingham TEL 021-233 1112

OPEN Mon–Fri 10 am–5 pm CLOSED Sat, Sun, public holidays CREDIT CARDS Not accepted DISCOUNTS Negotiable DELIVERY Free in Midlands, min 2 cases; elsewhere on application GLASS HIRE Free TASTINGS AND TALKS To groups on request, £1.50 per head CELLARAGE £1.20 per case per year

The House of Austria offers a very small range of German, French and Austrian wines, the choice of the latter being disappointingly small, considering the company's name. However, this is where the best value is to be found on the list, especially the wines from the Krems co-operative [£]–[££].

BEST BUYS [£]–[££] Krems co-operative wines

Ian G Howe

35 Appleton Gate, Newark, Nottinghamshire TEL (0636) 704366

OPEN Mon–Sat 9.30 am–7 pm Good Fri 12 noon–2 pm, 7 pm–8.30 pm CLOSED Sun, Chr Day, public holidays (exc Good Fri) CREDIT CARDS Access/Euro, Visa DISCOUNTS 2.5% on 1–2 cases, 3.5% on 3+ cases, which may be mixed DELIVERY By arrangement GLASS HIRE Free TASTINGS AND TALKS On request; organised tastings periodically CELLARAGE Free, but limited space

This is a friendly small business run by a husband-and-wife team, offering a good selection of well-chosen wines at prices which range from good to sometimes a bit over the average. Areas of greatest interest are the Loire and Rhône, especially the latter. Someone here likes Muscat de Beaumes-de-Venise: four are listed including the delicious Domaine Coyeux (£3.65 for a half-bottle) and Domaine Durban (£5.65). Hugel Alsace wines are good, as is the Chablis of Bacheroy-Josselin amongst the Burgundies [£]–[£££]. There are some good estate wines from Germany, too, up to Auslese level and back to 1975. The Marc de Chablis and Ratafia de Chablis are worth a try amongst the unusually varied short range of eaux-de-vie.

BEST BUYS [£]–[£££] Rhône wines

Howells of Bristol

17 Small Street, Bristol TEL (0272) 211223

OPEN Mon–Fri 9 am–5.30 pm CLOSED Sat, Sun, public holidays
CREDIT CARDS Personal and business accounts DISCOUNTS 5% on case orders
DELIVERY Free in Bristol, min 1 case; elsewhere £4.02 for 1 case, £3.62 for 2–4 cases; thereafter at cost GLASS HIRE Free TASTINGS AND TALKS Occasionally for invited customers CELLARAGE £1.56 per case per year

Howells, the oldest of the many Bristol wine merchants, are now under the ownership of the Namara group; their marvellous vaulted stone cellars have been used by wine merchants since the 15th century. Their list is fairly traditional, with some good clarets and white Bordeaux, and some fine Germans up to Auslese level and back to 1976: look out particularly for Nahe wines from Anheuser and Palatinates from Bürklin-Wolf, as well as the Mosel-Saar-Ruwer wines of the Bischhöflichen Weingüter in Trier. There is also a smattering of good wines from outside France and Germany. As well as the traditional business, Howells have been branching into new areas: their Bin Club Scheme for laying down wine for future consumption funded by regular monthly bankers' orders, with special credit account arrangements, appears to be popular. Offers of at least ten different wines a year within the scheme might include good petits-châteaux or classed growths, Rhônes, California wines, port, or even 55-year-old Cognac. A scheme for wine investment is under consideration.

BEST BUYS [£]–[£££] Petits-châteaux, [££]–[£££] German wines, [£££] Coteaux du Layon, Domaines Baumard

The Hungerford Wine Company

128 High Street, Hungerford, Berkshire TEL (0488) 83238

OPEN Mon–Fri 9 am–1 pm, 2 pm–5.30 pm Sat 9.30 am–5 pm CLOSED Sun, public holidays CREDIT CARDS All accepted; personal and business accounts DISCOUNTS 5% on case orders, 10% on orders £500+ DELIVERY Free on UK mainland, min 3 cases (may be mixed); 1–2 cases within 10 miles of Hungerford, £2 per case; within 60 miles (inc Central London) £3.50 per case; elsewhere £4 per case GLASS HIRE Free TASTINGS AND TALKS Occasionally; more regular tastings, wine evenings and wine weekends planned for 1985 CELLARAGE £2.87 per case per year MAIL ORDER SPECIALISTS

It is presumably Nick Davies's good-value opening claret offers that have spread Hungerford's mail order net well beyond the home patch. It is worth writing for details of Hungerford's opening offers 'commitment scheme'. Since you commit yourself to buying the wines from specific chateaux (below your own ceiling price), and since you pay early, Hungerford can buy in Bordeaux knowing that they will not have to finance the wines themselves, so pass on much of the saving to you. They print their main list once a year, usually in the late autumn, and will generally hold prices till the following year, which means that fine wines are often better value as the year progresses. The regular special offers are often good value, too, accompanied by useful tasting notes and briefings on the progress of the latest batch of clarets in the Bordeaux cellars. Hungerford's is a well-written list, with plenty of helpful advice. And the wines are well selected from table wines (both French and Spanish) upwards. The main emphasis is on Bordeaux, but Beaujolais from Loron are good, Rhônes are sound from Paul Jaboulet Aîné and Guigal, Loires are a tempting selection. The Frescobaldi range from Italy is very good (try the fresh white Pomino, £3.85) and so, too, are the Rioja collection from CVNE and Marqués de Cáceres. Brown Bros Australians and a mix of good California wines round off the list. The Champagnes have recently been supplemented by Hungerford's own-label Champagne from Duval-Leroy at under £6 a bottle.

BEST BUYS *En primeur* clarets, most things on the list

Hurlingham Vintners

96 Ramsden Road, London, SW12 TEL 01-673 4439

OPEN Mon–Sun 10 am–7 pm CLOSED Never CREDIT CARDS, DISCOUNTS Not accepted DELIVERY At postal or carrier's cost GLASS HIRE Not available TASTINGS AND TALKS On request; affiliated to Wine & Dine Society CELLARAGE Nominal charge, by arrangement

Jeffrey Benson's fine and rare wine company, dealing in small quantities, issues a list each month – on which the prices tend to be rather high, sometimes alarmingly so, compared with some of his competitors in this élite field. Earlier in 1984, you might have bought here, for example, Ch Coutet 1934, Barsac premier cru for £85, only to be more than peeved to find it on the shelves of La Vigneronne for £48.50, or at auction for £27.50! But this is one of the most extreme cases, and amongst the fine list of venerable clarets, Burgundies, Sauternes particularly (Mr Benson has written a book on Sauternes) and Germans, you might find specific rare wines you are after at nearer market prices – but do shop around. Expect to see old Rhônes and Champagnes, old vintage ports, oddities like 1911 Pouilly-Fumé (£20), ancient Madeira, half-bottles of Grand Marnier 1920 (£18), hors d'age Calvados (£16.75), old Cognacs and Armagnacs and the like.

BEST BUYS Oddities you cannot find more cheaply elsewhere

Hurlingham Wines

5A Station Approach, Ranelagh Gardens, London SW6 TEL 01-731 2571

OPEN Mon–Sat 10.30 am–2.30 pm, 4 pm–8 pm Sun and public holidays 12 noon–2 pm CLOSED Chr Day, Easter Mon CREDIT CARDS Personal and business accounts DISCOUNTS 5%–10% DELIVERY Free delivery in the Fulham and Putney area, min 1 bottle; within 15 miles £1 per 1–5 cases, 30 miles £1.50,

50 miles £2. 5+ cases free GLASS HIRE Free TASTINGS AND TALKS Free to selected customers CELLARAGE Not available

This little shop in the backwaters by the Putney Bridge tube contains a tempting selection of wines at very reasonable prices. Hurlingham is closely tied with the importers of Marqués de Cáceres, so prices of these excellent Riojas, red and white, and the second-label Rivarey, are keen. The range of table wines from Picard Père et Fils at between £1.75 and £2.80 is very sound. Australians from Taltarni are good [££]–[£££], as is the big range of California wines from Jekel, Zaca Mesa, Burgess and, especially, Fetzer [£]–[£££]. A small well-selected group of clarets includes the good-value wines of Larose-Trintaudon (1976, £4.90 and 1975, £5.25); Burgundies, a bigger range including a few maturer wines, are mainly from Chanson, Picard Père and Mazilly Père et Fils, and co-owner of the company and co-author of *Burgundy*, Christopher Fielden, has obviously had a hand in the selection here. For sweet wines, a sound choice is the Bonnezeaux, la Croix de Mission 1982 at £3.65, though this wine really needs time to show at its best. Better for drinking now is perhaps the Gewürztraminer Beerenauslese 1979 from Lenz Moser (£5.70). Kir lovers should look out for the excellent Cassis of Gabriel Boudier, and try the Liqueur de Framboises or Myrtilles as a refreshing alternative to the Cassis; Gabriel Boudier's Marc de Bourgogne and fruit eaux-de-vie are also good. Look out here for special bin-end buys, since Hurlingham now and then buy in special parcels from the trade or from private individuals, and make an offer of 8 to 16 wines, some from the regular list, once a month in a newsletter mailed to customers.

BEST BUYS [£] Marqués de Cáceres Riojas, red and white

Hynard Hughes & Co Ltd

HEAD OFFICE, SHOP, WAREHOUSE TEL (0533) 769496
4–6 Overton Road, Leicester

BRANCHES 99A Hinckley Road, Leicester TEL (0533) 541771
6 Church Square, Market Harborough, Leicestershire TEL (0858) 66168
OPEN Mon–Thur 9 am–6 pm Fri 9 am–6.30 pm Sat 9 am–4 pm CLOSED Sun, some public holidays CREDIT CARDS Access/Euro, Visa; business accounts DISCOUNTS Special offers, mainly coupled with tastings DELIVERY Free in Leicestershire and immediate surroundings for orders of £50+, otherwise £1.50 per case; elsewhere up to 10 cases, £1.15 per case (min £4) GLASS HIRE 45p per doz TASTINGS AND TALKS Free monthly tastings CELLARAGE £1 per case per year

This family company has condensed its retail operation in the past year, closing down five of the shops in the Leicester area and concentrating business at the head office in Overton Road, though the Hinckley Road, Leicester and the Market Harborough shops still operate. Prices are rather expensive, with only a very small reduction for mixed cases. Their interest in good sherries is clear, and there are some good buys here: Lustau's VO Amontillado, Valdespino Innocente Fino and a small range of interesting Almacenista sherries *(see Sherry in* THE WINE REGIONS *above)*. There is a big range of Burgundy and Bordeaux; try the Chablis from Domaine la Jouchère. Spanish wines are reliable from Torres (Viña Sol and Gran Coronas) and CVNE Riojas, and there's a small sprinkling from elsewhere.

BEST BUYS [££]–[£££] Sherries, particularly the Almacenista ones

Ilkley Wine Cellars

52 The Grove, Ilkley, West Yorkshire TEL (0943) 607313

OPEN Mon–Fri (inc public holidays) 10 am–10 pm Sat 9 am–10 pm Sun 12 noon–2 pm CLOSED Sun pm CREDIT CARDS All accepted DISCOUNTS 5% on 1 case, 7.5% on 3+ cases DELIVERY Free within 25 mile radius of Ilkley, min 1 bottle; elsewhere on UK mainland £2.50 per case for 1–2 cases, £1.30 per case for 3–4 cases, thereafter free GLASS HIRE Free TASTINGS AND TALKS Monthly tastings, £2, refundable on order; wines open every day for tasting CELLARAGE Free

The Ilkley Wine Cellars choose their wines with care, and pass them on to fortunate Ilkley folk at ungreedy prices. The Loire is obviously a particular love of the proprietors – this is an unusual variety of very well-chosen wines: Chaume, Domaine de la Soucherie (1979, £4.57 or, far better value, 1971 for £6.72), a selection of different Vouvrays including some very old wines at very reasonable prices, and the fine wines of Gaston Huet; Sauvion Muscadets and Gitton Sancerres are amongst the best, too. Bordeaux has produced a spread of classed growths, mostly of the '70s. Burgundies are a rather mixed bag, but you shouldn't be disappointed by Michel Rémon, or the many wines from Tollot-Beaut and Sauzet. Kuenz-Bas and Heim Alsace wines are here in profusion – some fine examples, too. Apart from a few Nederburg South Africans, the selection is restricted to Europe, but the expertise doesn't stop at France. Amongst the Italians, you should find some pleasure in the Tedeschi range, and the Ferrari sparkling wines (made largely of *real* Chardonnay) are good even if approaching fine Champagne prices. But try especially the range of Riojas from La Rioja Alta [£]–[££]. A fine selection of malts rounds off the list, along with a number of real ales available in cask.

BEST BUYS [£]–[£££] Loire and Alsace wines, wines from La Rioja Alta

Imbibers Wines

Lairg House, Brill Road, Oakley, Nr Aylesbury, Buckinghamshire TEL (0844) 237233 (answering machine); (0844) 237861

OPEN Mon–Fri 9 am–6 pm Sat, Sun, public holidays By appointment CREDIT CARDS Access/Euro; personal and business accounts DISCOUNTS 2.5% on 6–20 cases DELIVERY Free within 5 miles of Oakley or Oxford, min 1 case;

Bucks, Berks & Oxon £1.80 per case; elsewhere in England & Wales £2.50 per case; Scotland £3.50 per case GLASS HIRE 5–10p per glass
TASTINGS AND TALKS On request to local groups; regular tastings organised by the company CELLARAGE Not available

This still fairly new company sells principally to the trade but will also sell by the case to the public. It's worth sending for a list, because this is an interesting and original selection, put together with care, and prices are moderate to good, especially if you live in the Oakley/Oxford area, where delivery is free. Imbibers are to be praised for including a tasting note under every wine, and although these are sometimes a little general, they are reliable. Fine wine sleuth Christopher Tatham MW helped Imbibers put their French list together. It briefly but competently spans all the major French areas. The Burgundy list only just pops over £5, but you will find some good wines in the lower price brackets, too: Lamblin's 1983 Chablis, for example, is very reasonable at £3.76, or the good co-operative wines of La Chablisienne and the Vignerons de Buxy [££]–[£££]. There is a small list of lesser-known, inexpensive clarets. Some good Loires include the sweet Chaume 1981 Domaine de la Soucherie, Tijou at £4, Vacheron's excellent Sancerres, red, white and rosé [££]–[£££] and the nearby Blanc-Fumé Les Griottes (1982 on the latest list as we went to press for £4.13 – the 1983 will be better). Rhônes include Guigal wines and the light, sweet Muscat de Beaumes-de-Venise of Vidal-Fleurie. In the Italian section, try some of the many Santa Sofia wines [£]–[££], and Castello di Volpaia Chianti Riserva 1979 (£4.58). The New World wines on this list are also impressive. Amongst the American wines, the Gold Seal Chardonnay from New York State is extremely good, and unusual, for under £5, and there are some powerful Zinfandels. From Australia, there's a full list of the tasty Penfolds wines, including the famous Grange Hermitage 1975 for just over £20. Montana wines from New Zealand are also worth a look [££]. The company always has a very small stock of top growth clarets and a few good Burgundies, some mature, at fair, sometimes very good prices, and will circulate interested customers with this in addition to their main list and bi-monthly newsletters and offers.

BEST BUYS [££]–[£££] Burgundies, [£]–[£££] Loires and Rhônes; fine wines

International

See CHAINS AND SUPERMARKETS

J H James (Knightsbridge) Ltd

130 Brompton Road, London, SW3 TEL 01-584 7777

OPEN Mon–Fri 9.30 am–7.30 pm 9.30 am–7 pm CLOSED Sun, public holidays
CREDIT CARDS Not accepted; personal and business accounts for local addresses with references DISCOUNTS 10% on case orders; larger quantities by

arrangement DELIVERY Free in SW1, SW3, SW7, min 1 case; elsewhere at cost GLASS HIRE Free TASTINGS AND TALKS Occasional tastings for regular customers CELLARAGE Not available

J James, the Jimmie of Jimmies Wine Bar down the road in the Kensington Barracks wall on Church Street *(see WINE BARS section)*, is a handy source of peace offerings for repentant erring Romeos. If they can fight their way through the flowers that share this tiny shop with the wine, champagne (house) is here probably the cheapest they will find in this over-priced area (£8.80). The deeply repentant might try Salon Le Mesnil 1976 at £21.95. But prices, as you might expect here in Harrods' shadow, are generally not so keen, so think before you buy, though watch out for occasional bargains such as Gould Campbell 1962 vintage port at £17.50. Mr James buys small lots of wine as well as his standard staples to supply both wine bar and shop, so the shop's frequently changing range is always worth perusing.

BEST BUYS Champagne

Robert James Son & Co Ltd

79 Aslett Street, London, SW18 TEL 01-870 2222
CASH AND CARRY: World Wines, at the above address TEL 01-874 1201
OPEN Mon–Fri 8.30 am–1.30 pm, 2.30 pm–5.30 pm Sat 8.30 am–1.30 pm
CLOSED Sun, public holidays CREDIT CARDS Access/Euro, Diners, Visa
DISCOUNTS Cash and carry 50p per bottle on wines not on special offer; £2 per case on 2–4 cases; £2.50 per case on 5–9 cases DELIVERY Free on UK mainland, 1 case (may be mixed) GLASS HIRE Free TASTINGS AND TALKS On request CELLARAGE Not available MAIL ORDER SPECIALISTS

Robert James is a mail order company, but largely the same wines are available from their World Wines warehouse off Garratt Lane in SW18. You will find some interesting, rarely encountered wines here, mostly from the major areas of France and Germany (including some good, sweet, mature wines). Beware, however, of prices. Who wants to pay £8.05 for Muscat de Beaumes-de-Venise, Vidal-Fleurie? Or £4.49 for Machanudo Fino Sherry (nearly £2 less at Liquorsave . . .)? and these are the cash and carry warehouse prices.

BEST BUYS French wines from growers whose wines are otherwise unobtainable in Britain

Johnson Marr

See TD Vintners

Cellarage is generally provided at the rates quoted only when the wines have been bought from the merchant concerned.

S H Jones & Co Ltd

27 The High Street, Banbury, Oxfordshire TEL (0295) 51177

OPEN Mon–Fri 8.30 am–5.30 pm Sat 9 am–1 pm CLOSED Sun, public holidays CREDIT CARDS Personal and business accounts DISCOUNTS 5% on case orders, and on cash and carry DELIVERY Free in the Banbury area and along main delivery routes within 50 miles, min 2 cases; smaller orders £2; elsewhere in England £2.50 per case for 1–4 cases, thereafter free; Scotland and Wales at cost GLASS HIRE 30p per doz TASTINGS AND TALKS Annual free tasting in November; to groups on request, at wine cost CELLARAGE £2.50 per case per year

France is the mainstay of this high street family business, whose range has expanded over the past year. Look out for some good French country wines in the £2 to £2.50 bracket, and some very good Burgundies at all price levels, including a handful of Chablis from the reliable Rémon. Clarets from petits-châteaux, through classed growths of the last decade including some top 1970s, are well chosen. In the Rhône, the Merchant Vintners buying group's stars, amongst others, shine out in the Rhônes: these include Ch du Grand Moulas 1983 (£2.99) and a big selection of vintages of Chateauneufs from the Domaine du Vieux Télégraphe and Château de Beaucastel [££]–[£££], as well as a fine Northern Rhône selection from Guigal, Ozier and Paul Jaboulet Aîné and Caves St-Pierre. There are some good Spanish wines from Torres, CVNE, Olarra and Marqués de Murrieta [£]–[£££], and look out for – in our experience – Britain's tastiest wine boxes: Australian Berri Estates' Cabernet Shiraz (£8.79), and Riesling and the aptly-named Fruity Gordo at £8.63.

BEST BUYS [£] French country wines, [£]–[£££] clarets, [££]–[£££] Châteauneuf-du-Pape

Justerini & Brooks ☞

61 St James's Street, London, SW1 TEL 01-493 8721

OPEN Mon–Fri 9 am–5.30 pm CLOSED Sat, Sun, public holidays CREDIT CARDS Amex, Diners, Visa; personal account DISCOUNTS 7.5% on 2–5 cases, 10% on 5–8 cases, 12.5% on 9+ cases DELIVERY Free on UK mainland, min 5 cases; otherwise in London £2.88 for less than 1 case, 58p for 1 case, £1.15 for 2 cases, £1.75 for 3 cases; elsewhere £2.88 for 1 case, thereafter roughly double London rate GLASS HIRE Free TASTINGS AND TALKS To groups on request; special wine dinners; annual tastings by invitation CELLARAGE £3 per case per year + insurance

The service – and the wine quality – inside the imposing portals of Justerini & Brooks in St James's Street perfectly live up to the promise of the smart bow-fronted shop front; and so do the prices, but then, this is no ordinary man's merchant. Grand Met's finest wine arm has much to offer on its surprisingly balanced list. The clarets are to be expected: a good choice of mature wines in the 'older wines' section of the list back to 1952, with magnums back to 1959, then a big selection of recent vintages. Old Burgundies go back to 1947; amongst the more recent years you will find very good names such as Clair-Daü and Domaine Machard de Gramont, and lots of sound Chablis from Bacheroy-Josselin. Rhônes are good and obviously popular since the list has been greatly extended, and you will come across some very fine Germans, too. Less expected, perhaps, are the good Italian wines, including Villa di Capezzana 1979 (£3.95), and small ranges of California, New Zealand and Australian wines. The 'everyday wines' are an interesting selection, too: they include, for example, Veltliner, Schloss Grafenegg from Austria for £3.50, and the fresh white Ch de Fonscolombe from Aix-en-Provence for £2.90. Look for big reductions in the January sales, and for special case offers. In addition to general advice to callers from well-qualified staff, J & B have more organised ways of helping you develop your wine cellar. For those willing to put themselves at the tender mercies of their merchant, the 'Unit Wine Investment Scheme' allows you to choose on a regular basis (paid for by banker's order) 'units' of three or four cases at total prices ranging from around £180 to £744, the latter the inclusive price of a recent offer of one case each of Ch Lafite 1975, Bâtard-Montrachet 1979, Louis Latour, and Ch Cheval-Blanc 1978. Each wine is annotated with a tasting note and an indication of when it should be drunk. For those who might find this restricting, J & B have introduced a 'Personal Cellar Plan' offering advice and wines *en primeur*.

BEST BUYS Older wines

Kabinett Wine Co

8 Meadow View Road, Boughton Monchelsea, Maidstone, Kent — TEL (0622) 44709

OPEN 'We never close!' CREDIT CARDS By arrangement DISCOUNTS 5% on 7+ cases (2.5% QbA); cash and carry £1.50 per case DELIVERY Free in Kent area, min 1 case (may be mixed); elsewhere £3.45 for 1 case, thereafter free, but mixed cases £3.45 per case GLASS HIRE Free TASTINGS AND TALKS On request CELLARAGE Not available MAIL ORDER ONLY

This small mail order business specialising in German wines is run from home by Ron and Jenny Glaiser. It began, Mr Glaiser explains, when two years ago, after the death of his German grandfather, he 'suddenly realised that it was impossible to obtain fine Mosels at sensible prices in the UK'. All the Glaisers' wines are imported directly from Germany 'selected on basis of quality before price' and wines made from anything other than the Riesling grape are strictly 'not entertained'. The Glaisers have stuck to their original predilections, and import and sell only wines from the Mosel–Saar–Ruwer. To the small growers of their earliest lists, some more familiar names have now been added, however: the exemplary Sankt Niklaus Hospital estate in Bernkastel and the Staatsdomänen in Trier. They have also kept to their original intention of providing good wines at reasonable prices: there is plenty up to Kabinett level below £3, though you could pay £23.33 a bottle for a 1976 Maringer Sonnenuhr Riesling Trockenbeerenauslese from Dietz-Fritzen, or £12.85 for a 1975 Maringer Honigberg Riesling Eiswein Auslese from the same grower. A 'taste' column on the list usefully assesses with between one and six stars the sweetness of the wine, which ranges from the most luscious down to several trocken wines and one even officially labelled 'Diabetiker' – Graacher Himmelreich Riesling Kabinett – yet again from the enterprising Herr Dietz-Fritzen. Overall, this list seems to be excellent value, especially for Kent customers who can take advantage of the free delivery.

BEST BUYS [£]–[£££] Most things on the list

Myles Kehoe & Son (Enniscorthy) Ltd

7 Castle Hill, Enniscorthy, Co Wexford, Ireland TEL Wexford 33588

OPEN Mon, Tue, Wed, Fri 10.30 am–6 pm Sat 10.30 am–8 pm CLOSED Thur, Sun, public holidays CREDIT CARDS Not accepted DISCOUNTS Not available DELIVERY Free in Enniscorthy and environs GLASS HIRE Free TASTINGS AND TALKS Occasional in-store tastings CELLARAGE Free

Myles Kehoe stock a very reasonable collection of wines from all the major European countries, with an emphasis on claret: classed growths of particularly the 1976, 1978 and 1979 vintages, a few earlier. Best buys here are the Torres and Marqués de Cáceres wines from Spain, Paul Jaboulet Rhônes, Chianti Classico Ducale, Ruffino (£5.20) and Chianti Classico Riserva 1978, Antinori (£4.95), but look also for less regular wines, not included in the list.

BEST BUYS [£££] Torres, Marqués de Cáceres, [££]–[£££] Chiantis from Antinori and Ruffino, [£££] Jaboulet Rhônes

Kendals

PO Box 60, Deansgate, Manchester TEL 061-832 3414

OPEN Mon–Fri 9 am–5.30 pm Sat 9 am–6 pm CLOSED Sun, public holidays CREDIT CARDS All accepted, plus House of Fraser DISCOUNTS 5% on case orders DELIVERY Free within Greater Manchester and Cheshire, min £10; elsewhere at postal cost GLASS HIRE Not available TASTINGS AND TALKS Weekly in-store tastings on Fri, Sat; annual tasting in Oct CELLARAGE Free NO MAIL ORDER

Wine is obviously taken very seriously at Kendal Milne's. The range has been extended since last year and a selection of Kendal's own-label wines was planned as we went to press. And we have received favourable reports of helpful service from knowledgeable staff. Best value here is still to be found in the traditional areas of Bordeaux, particularly (Ch Chasse-Spleen 1979 at £6.09 should be snapped up and there are some well-priced mature clarets, too). Burgundy offers some goodies, though these are a mixed bag, and Champagne presents a tempting choice at prices that are lower than Kendals' shoppers might expect; there are plenty of magnums, halves and quarters, too. German wines tend to be mostly brands and basics from Hallgarten and Deinhard, with a few up the sweetness and quality scale. There are old and recent vintage ports to be found here, but prices are rather higher than you might find elsewhere. The range of over 60 malt whiskies is exceptional. At Christmas, it is worth noting that Kendals sell a big range of special gift packs, which you can have engraved with a name of your choice, supplied ready for posting!

BEST BUYS £££ Clarets, Champagne

Kershaw's Wine Warehouse Ⓥ

74 Totteridge Lane, London, N20 — TEL 01-446 2128 or 445 7785

OPEN Mon–Thur 10 am–8 pm Fri 10 am–9 pm Sat 10 am–10 pm Sun and public holidays 12 noon–2 pm CLOSED Sun pm, public holidays pm
CREDIT CARDS Access/Euro, Visa DISCOUNTS 5% on case orders
DELIVERY Free within 5 miles, min 1 case wine/spirits; other London postal areas £5 for 1–5 cases, 75p per case for 6–14 cases; outside London £5, min 1 case GLASS HIRE Free TASTINGS AND TALKS Occasional free tastings
CELLARAGE £1 per case per year

There's a delightfully balanced range of well-chosen wines to suit most tastes and pockets in this new North London wine warehouse set up just over a year ago by former managing director of Seagram (UK), Stuart Kershaw. Mr Kershaw and his wife, and now an assistant, have rolled up their working sleeves over the past year, not only manning the counter for the long hours the shop is open, but also putting together a very interesting list. The Seagram connection lives on in a number of Seagram brands around the shop – not least the spirits, of which there is a large range here, as well as beer, cider, nuts, mixers, ice etc. The sound new range of Sandeman sherries, Sandeman ports, Paul Masson Carafes and Redwood Hill California wine in cans are all products in which Mr Kershaw must have once had a marketing hand. But the company are already shipping 80–90 per cent of their French wines direct. You will find a small but good spread of clarets from the young-and-ready to a few classed growths still with time to go; Loron, Chanson and Louis Latour Burgundies, Loron and Duboeuf Beaujolais; Léon Vatan Sancerre amongst the Loires (£4.95 for the 1983 vintage) is very good. Prices for Torres and Marqués de Cáceres wines in the Spanish quarter are keen; and try the Gavi from Pio Cesare (£3.95 for the 1983) for an interesting new white. You will find Champagne at cheap prices here: the house Champagne is very reasonable at £5.99 for the NV, £7.99 for the pink or the 1976 vintage. Kershaw's Wine Warehouse is a definite boon for wine-drinking locals, and worth a quick search in the *A to Z* and a small detour, perhaps.

BEST BUYS Most things on the list

Key Markets

See Gateway in CHAINS AND SUPERMARKETS

Richard Kihl

WINE ACCESSORIES SHOP AND OFFICE: TEL 01-586 3838 or 0873
164 Regents Park Road, London, NW1

OPEN Tue–Fri 9.30 am–5 pm Sat 11 am–5 pm CLOSED Mon, Sun, public holidays CREDIT CARDS Not accepted DISCOUNTS 5% on 5+ cases DELIVERY Free in London postal districts, min 5 cases; UK mainland (not Scotland) £2.50 per case, min charge £10 per delivery GLASS HIRE Free TASTINGS AND TALKS On request CELLARAGE £2.50 per case per year MAIL ORDER ONLY

Richard Kihl's business is three-fold: everyday wines, fine wines and, most interesting, a shopful of wine accessories both ancient and modern – corkscrews, decanters, fine glasses, pictures, maps, books and more. (An illustrated brochure is available from the above address.) As for the wines, Richard Kihl sell only by the case, only by mail order, and the £5 delivery charge in London, minimum £10 outside for less than five cases make this a rather expensive way to buy your wine, particularly on the 'wines for everyday drinking' list. This latter homes in mostly on the South-West of France, many of the wines from producers uncommonly encountered in the UK, but prices are rather high. The computer-printed fine wine list is published regularly, since the small lots of wine naturally turn over rapidly. Expect to find a vast selection of classed growth clarets from the venerable to the still-in-cask (arranged by the helpful computer in alphabetical order, so much easier to find for those with a fine palate but less than encyclopaedic memory of which château is in which commune or on which rung of the Bordeaux social ladder); there will be old Burgundies, too, including some very desirable names and some old vintages, and old Sauternes. But do shop around and compare prices carefully with other companies' dealing in this market – you may find yourself paying just £3 or so above the odds elsewhere, but it would be sad to overstep the market price by £10 or more . . .

BEST BUYS Rare wines you cannot find more cheaply elsewhere; wine accessories

Luc Lacerre et Fils Ltd

78/80 City Road, Cardiff TEL (0222) 482302

OPEN Mon–Sat 9 am–5.30 pm CLOSED Sun, public holidays CREDIT CARDS Not accepted DISCOUNTS Not available DELIVERY Free (min 1 case) in South, Mid and West Wales, West of England, Birmingham, and anywhere within 30 miles of M4 between Cardiff and London, and the whole London area; elsewhere

£3 per single case, £2 per case for 2–5 cases; thereafter free GLASS HIRE 50p per doz TASTINGS AND TALKS To groups on request; annual tasting of about 90 wines in Cardiff for up to 2,000 people CELLARAGE £2 per case per annum in bond or duty paid

France provides the bulk of Luc Lacerre's fine list – and bulky it is, too, the enormous stocks supported by the company's extensive wholesale trade, which was bolstered over the past year by a new wine warehouse operation in Wales and the West, offering rather lower-priced wines than the main Luc Lacerre business. Prices at Luc Lacerre are fair, not cheap, but then the range is exceptional, the quality exemplary, and it's worth noting the company's large free delivery area – a great boon to those who live off the beaten track in Wales. Claret and Burgundy are the biggest sections. The huge range of clarets omits the poorer vintages. There are plenty of 1970s and 1966s, and bits and expensive pieces back to 1952. Amongst the many Burgundies, white and red, it will probably be most rewarding to leave aside the better-known names, the none-too-exciting Mommessin and Henri de Villamont, and dabble in the obscurer wines, some from growers. Ask for advice. Vintages are mostly of the 1970s, but there are a few older wines, back to 1937 in the reds. The range of white Burgundy is also unusually large. The rest of France is well covered, too. Alsace wines are good value from Gisselbrecht and Faller. Try Faller's Vendange Tardive Gewürztraminer 1976 for just over £6. The Loire list is good, including Moulin Touchais back to 1949 (£12.07), the luscious Bonnezeaux of Jacques Boivin in vintages back to 1978, still too young to drink, for between £8 and £9, and the reds from Mme Joly's Ch de la Roche, interestingly back to the 1975 vintage [££], as well as the Savennières property she formerly cultivated, in the Coulée de Serrant. There's a big selection of lovely Rhônes, too, including some older vintages and an outstanding collection of whites. Beaujolais come from a variety of producers and include some single property wines and some older crus back to 1978. For those with tighter purse-strings, there are some very interesting wines from properties in the South of France. Outside France, the Italians are not very exciting, but basic Germans are sound, and a larger range of estate-bottled Germans was promised as we went to press. There is vintage port back to 1945, at some very keen prices. The Spanish wines are few but interesting and include the 1969 vintage of Vega Sicilia (£162 a case) and the estate's second wine, Valbuena, at £66 a case for the third year and £108 for the fifth. The list of 35 California wines contains some unusually old vintages (1974/5); there's Cooks New Zealand, Brown Bros Australian and even Inniskillin wines from Canada [££] . . . and the local Welsh Croffta [££]. The evil-looking Calvados is worth a try, too.

BEST BUYS Loires and Rhônes, wines of Southern France

[£] means that a wine costs, from most producers and in most British shops, under £3 a bottle, [££] that it costs between £3 and £5, and [£££] that it costs over £5.

Lakeland Vintners

Ash Street, Bowness-on-Windermere, Cumbria — TEL (096 62) 6321 or 4228

OPEN Mon–Sat 9 am–5 pm CLOSED Sun, public holidays CREDIT CARDS Not accepted; credit accounts DISCOUNTS 50p per case on 1–9 unmixed cases; thereafter £1 per case DELIVERY Free South Lakes, min 1 case; elsewhere min delivery 5–10 cases, free GLASS HIRE Free TASTINGS AND TALKS Not available CELLARAGE Free

Lakeland Vintners stock the usual spirits, mixers and brands plus a not terribly exciting range of wines largely from the predictable areas of France. If you are buying at a distance, beware: prices in the list do not include VAT. Bordeaux comes mostly from Eschenauer, Burgundy from Chanson and Latour, Loire from Rémy Pannier. The Italian range is unimpressive. Perhaps best value are the Spanish wines from Marqués de Cáceres and CVNE, that promiscuous pair again, and German wines from Deinhard. An unusual find at the end of the list is a couple of Swiss wines, one white, one red, from Alphonse Orsat, a fairly expensive experiment at over £6 apiece.

BEST BUYS ££ Spanish wines

Laymont and Shaw Ltd

Ⓥ

The Old Chapel, Millpool, Truro, Cornwall — TEL (0872) 70545

OPEN Mon–Fri 9 am–5 pm CLOSED Sat, Sun, public holidays CREDIT CARDS Not accepted DISCOUNTS £1 per case on 1–2 cases, £1.50 per case on 3–4 cases, £1.75 on 5–9 cases and £2 on 10+ cases DELIVERY Free on UK mainland GLASS HIRE Free TASTINGS AND TALKS By invitation CELLARAGE On request MAIL ORDER SPECIALISTS

Britain's best Spanish merchant, shipping and selling exclusively Spanish wines, celebrated their tenth anniversary this year by inviting the first 200 of their customers to apply for places on a three-hour May celebration cruise down the Thames from Westminster to Greenwich and back, at which they were liberally fed and 'watered'. This friendly, helpful company runs an efficient mail order business: note that delivery to any address on the UK mainland is included in their prices, which makes them very competitive. For personal collection, there is a £1 per case allowance. You will find good-quality representatives here of all the major and some of the minor wine areas of Spain, but best value is nonetheless to be found in Rioja, especially from La Rioja Alta, for whom Laymont & Shaw are UK agents – the Viña Ardanza 1976 is delicious wine now but of great potential, still young (£3.65); the rest of the Rioja roll-call is top flight, too: Muga, CVNE, Marqués de Cáceres, López de Heredia, Murrieta, Alavesas, Riojanas, Beronia and El Coto. Penedès wines are a fine selection, too, beginning with the extraordinary wines of Jean León – the rich, oaky Chardonnay 1981

(£6.56) and the fragrant, tannic, powerful Cabernet Sauvignon 1979 (£5.31); then the contrasting light Masía Vallformosas at a contrasting price of around £3, and of course the full range of Torres wines [££]. From Navarra, the Chivite wines are best value [£]; and though expensive, the Ribero del Duero wines are often good, sometimes remarkably variable [£££]. Of the fortified wines, the Barbadillo sherries are exceptional in all the styles [££] and the Gonzalez Byass Apostoles is very good; the lovely aromatic, long-flavoured Solera 1885 Scholz Málaga at £3.98 makes an interesting, different dessert wine. For those unfamiliar with Spanish wines, Laymont and Shaw's tasting notes are reliable and very helpful, the selection of half-bottles is useful, and so are the mixed 'tasting dozens' which qualify for case discounts.

BEST BUYS [£]–[£££] Wines of Rioja and Catalonia

Lay & Wheeler (V)

HEAD OFFICE AND WINE SHOP — TEL (0206) 67261 or 571386
6 Culver Street, Colchester, Essex (24-hour answering service)

WINE CELLARS AND PAY & CARRY SHOP — TEL (as head office)
Gosbecks Road, Colchester, Essex

CLIPPER CASH & CARRY — TEL (0708) 578267
Peddars Close, Colchester, Essex

LAY & WHEELER AT KEDDIES — TEL (0708) 64123
Market Place, Romford, Essex

LAY & WHEELER AT KEDDIES — TEL (0702) 616880
High Street, Southend-on-Sea, Essex

LAY & WHEELER AT KEDDIES — TEL (0206) 563722
Queen Street, Colchester, Essex

OPEN (Culver Street) Mon–Fri 8.30 am–5.30 pm Sat 8.30 am–5 pm CLOSED Sun, public holidays (opening hours of branches varies) CREDIT CARDS Access/Euro, Visa DISCOUNTS 2.5% on 4+ cases; 5% on 12+ cases; special small discounts in list for cheque with order or cash and carry DELIVERY Free within 30 miles of Colchester, min 1 case; free in England, Scotland and Wales, min 4 cases; for smaller orders £3.97 for 1–3 cases GLASS HIRE Free TASTINGS AND TALKS Regular wine workshops tutored by leading producers and authors; tutored tastings to groups on request, charge about £2.50 per head CELLARAGE £2.76 per case per year (inc insurance)

In all respects, Lay & Wheeler's wine list is one of the finest in the country – high praise which extends to the prices, too, which are average or below average, with delivery costs very reasonable. Beginning at the bottom, there is an excellent choice of table wines – for a good-value red, try Pierre Coste's Costevin, firm, fruity and fresh for just £2.17. A good selection of French country wines includes a full and fruity Côtes du Ventoux, Domaine des Anges (£2.38) and other tempting bargain-basement wines such as Ch la Jaubertie Bergeracs [£], the Aix-en-Provence wines of Ch de Fonscolombe [£] and an unusual range of four single-variety wines from the co-operative of Neuville-du-Poitou – Gamay, Cabernet, Sauvignon and Chardonnay –

all under £3. Though the list nets some fine examples from most of the world's wine-producing regions, its greatest strengths are Bordeaux and Burgundy. The splendid list of clarets includes plenty of half-bottles, a vast collection of magnums and a few larger still, a wide choice of recent vintages at all price levels (short on poor vintages, but usually with one representative), and plenty of 1970s and 1966s and a few earlier. In dry white Bordeaux, Ch Thieuley and Sauvignon Trois Mouline (£2.98 and £2.40) are both extremely good value, particularly the former. Burgundy lovers will be happy at Lay & Wheeler, too, amongst the fine choice of mostly young but also a few older vintages – including some mature whites – many domaine-bottled wines and wines from highly respectable merchants. The Beaujolais selected by top French chef Paul Bocuse from the Duboeuf cellars are very good – try some of the particularly fine 1983s (especially the Juliénas, £3.93). The Rhône list is very sound, again including some older, mature wines and so are the Loires, where especially good value is to be found in the sweet Coteaux du Layon of Ch du Breuil, four mature vintages back to 1959, with the 1959 costing only £10.25. (Lay & Wheeler were promising to improve their Loire section as we went to press.) Cheaper Alsace wines come from Blanck, but there is also a fair selection of the fine, more austere Schlumberger wines and a wider choice of producers in older vintages, which include a number of the fat 1976s. Germans are well selected, too, with a good choice of mature sweet wines; but Morandell is a disappointing choice from Austria. Bigger than usual ranges from CVNE, Marqués de Cáceres and Torres in Spain are well priced and need no commentary; Italians are good, too, on an admirably varied and long list. And California, North West USA, Australia, New Zealand, the Lebanon and Bulgaria are more briefly but also well represented. Spirit drinkers might turn to the back of the list to find some single-vineyard Cognacs and a range of eaux-de-vie from Alsace producer Blanck. All this in a beautifully designed list complete with when-to drink symbols, tasting notes on many of the wines, and brief commentary on the producers. Look out for bin-end sales and specially selected case offers (Lay & Wheeler will make up gift packs, too). Their prices for *en primeur* clarets, Burgundies and Rhônes tend to be on the high side, but then they generally include some less than usual finds, such as fine dry white Bordeaux. Lay & Wheeler also run a 'personal wine investment plan' in conjunction with Lloyds, offering special credit for wine buying as well as life insurance with tax relief and a cash-payment at term.

BEST BUYS [£] Costevin Rouge; Côtes du Ventoux, Domaine des Anges; Ch Thieuley Sauvignon Blanc 1983; Les Sables, Syrah, Vin de Pays des Collines Rhodaniennes; Ch Reynon Blanc Sec 1983, [££] Sancerre, 1983 André Dézat; Paul Bocuse Beaujolais, and too many more to mention

Laytons

HEAD OFFICE 20 Midland Road, London, NW1 TEL 01-388 5081
SHOP 28 Midland Road, London, NW1 TEL 01-388 5996

OPEN Mon–Fri 9 am–5.30 pm CLOSED Sat, Sun, public holidays
CREDIT CARDS Not accepted; personal accounts DISCOUNTS Not available
DELIVERY Free UK mainland, min 3 cases; under 3 cases £2.50 per case
GLASS HIRE 5p per doz + VAT TASTINGS AND TALKS Junior Tasting Group and Ladies' Tasting Circle meet 3 times each per year; to other groups on request
CELLARAGE £4.50 per case per year

Laytons' bright, attractive shop under the arches behind St Pancras Station is well stocked with the traditional good things of France, and is well manned by efficient, polite, informed staff. Burgundies and clarets are the main inhabitants of the neat stacks, many of the Burgundies from Prosper Maufoux under the secondary name of Marcel Amance – wines which have been less than exciting in recent times. The rest of the fairly large Burgundy selection, mostly recent vintages with a few older wines, comes from a range of merchants – Sauzet, Chanson, Drouhin, Louis Latour, with some good single property Burgundies, too. The Chablis from Lamblin are excellent. Clarets are a mix in recent vintages of classed growths and more modest wines, with a few in the early '70s, '60s and '50s, and some quite good prices amongst them – particularly in the periodic bin-end offers and sales, which are worth looking out for. Laytons' 1983 opening prices were a bit expensive, however. Anyone in search of good, dry white Graves might be satisfied here. Laytons have the agency for Deutz Champagne, so you will find it here at good prices, and their prices for other Champagnes are fair, too. They operate an unusual scheme for laying down vintages of Deutz in France to be disgorged and shipped in a few years' time, having had longer on-the-deposit maturation than the standard vintage wines. There is good value to be found outside the classic areas, too – some lovely wines in the French Regional section, good Rhônes, and Loires include the delicious, pure Quarts de Chaume 1975 of Baumard for £5.66. Estate-bottled Germans go back to 1971, a fine selection of sherries, and a range of not particularly well priced vintage ports. The most unusual feature of Laytons' list is the extraordinary catalogue of eaux-de-vie and old and rare brandies, which are sometimes seen on special 'bin-end' offers too: oddities like 1945 Vieux Marc du Ch Rayas, Châteauneuf-du-Pape (£21 earlier in 1984), and modern eaux-de-vie from Théo Cattin in Alsace, an enormous selection that includes less common varieties like 'Sorbier de Montagne' (rowanberry).

BEST BUYS Deutz Champagne, clarets, Rhônes

Lennons

See CHAINS AND SUPERMARKETS

Littlewoods

See CHAINS AND SUPERMARKETS

O W Loeb

15 Jermyn Street, London, SW1 TEL 01-734 5878

OPEN Mon–Fri 9 am–5.30 pm CLOSED Sat, Sun, public holidays
CREDIT CARDS Personal and business accounts DISCOUNTS 5% on case orders, 5% on cash orders over £40 DELIVERY Free in Central London, min 1 case, outer London and country, min 2 cases; otherwise Central London £2, outer London and country £4 GLASS HIRE, TASTINGS AND TALKS Not available
CELLARAGE In-bond only, £2.76 per case per year

From the old-fashioned Jermyn Street offices of O W Loeb are distributed some of the finest wines on sale today in Britain: some to the restaurant trade, some deeper into retail channels, some direct to a discerning public. Most stunning on this impressive list (which now thoughtfully includes VAT) are the German wines, a mind-boggling array of fine estate wines, with a wealth of sweet wines of the 1976 vintage. Or are the Burgundies perhaps more impressive after all? A long list of the lovely unwooded Chablis of Louis Michel ranges from £5 to £8.50, and amongst the many estate- or grower-bottled wines are the excellent wines of Tollot-Beaut and Sauzet. Loeb's hold the agency for Paul Jaboulet Aîné and so naturally can boast the country's most impressive Jaboulet list, including some old vintages: 1961 Hermitage La Chapelle could be yours for just £51.63 a bottle. Look out amongst the Loires for the best Chinon we have tasted from Charles Joguet, a selection of vineyards at just over £5, and the Vouvrays of Foreau. Loebs have also ventured out as far as the Jura, listing old and new vintages from Jean Bourdy: 1964 Vin Jaune de Garde is £16.12.

BEST BUYS Most things on the list

London Wine Brokers (V)

Chelsea Wharf, 15 Lots Road, London, SW10 TEL 01-352 5843

OPEN Mon–Fri 9.30 am–8 pm Sat 10 am–6 pm Sun 11 am–5 pm
CLOSED Public holidays CREDIT CARDS Access/Euro, Amex, Visa
DISCOUNTS Not available DELIVERY No free delivery; Chelsea, Fulham, Putney, Barnes and Central London £1 per case, min £4 GLASS HIRE Free
TASTINGS AND TALKS Free tasting for mailing-list customers 3 times a year
CELLARAGE Not available

So many 'wine warehouses' cash in on the public's supposition that warehouse wines must be cheap that London Wine Brokers are a refreshing discovery down by the Chelsea Embankment. No delivery, discounts or other such nonsense: plain by-the-bottle prices, cash-and-carry, these are some of the very best you will find, and for good quality wines. How many other companies have the confidence to publish that they offer 'sale or return for any quantity, and will gladly exchange or refund any wine for any reason'? It is unusual, too, to see that staff are given 'weekly blind tastings'. Lucky staff. And fortunate, too, are those who live within reach of the Chelsea Wharf, whatever their wine aspirations may be. At the bottom end, good value is to be found from Italy in the Càvit range from this well-run co-operative in North-East Italy – sound 'varietal' wines [£]. You will find Marqués de Cáceres wines here at prices hard to beat elsewhere (£2.50 for the red 1978, £2.45 for the white 1982 as we went to press). Or there's Siglo Saco Rioja (not as good) but 'rich and oaky – despite its hideous overcoat!' also for £2.50. Francophiles will find Sauvignon Trois Mouline (a lovely fresh Bordeaux Sauvignon) for £2.45, or Pascal's Muscat de Beaumes-de-Venise for £4.60, while the more affluent (with a good nose for a bargain, nevertheless) might wander down to the river bank to pick up some of the country's best-value ports (Graham 1977 at £8.60 or Fonseca 1975 at just £6.65 – no, we haven't forgotten to add in the VAT); or mature classed growth clarets; or Bollinger NV at £9.95. Bottles are always open for tasting, too, so don't just believe your eyes. . . .

BEST BUYS Everything

Lorne House Vintners Ltd

Unit 5, Hewitts Industrial Estate, Elmbridge Road, Cranleigh, Surrey — TEL (0483) 271445

OPEN Mon–Fri 10 am–6 pm Sat 10 am–1 pm CLOSED Sun, public holidays CREDIT CARDS Not accepted DISCOUNTS £1 per unmixed case cash and carry DELIVERY Free in Central London and within 25 miles of Cranleigh, min 2 cases; otherwise £3.50 for 1 case, £2 per case for 2–5 cases, £1.25 per case for 6–11 cases, 11+ cases free GLASS HIRE Free TASTINGS AND TALKS Regular tastings at the warehouse CELLARAGE Not available

'A pleasant set-up to buy from within their list limitations,' one reader writes – the limitation being that the wines here tend to be in the under-£5 bracket, and ready for drinking now, rather than laying down: and there's nothing wrong with that! Readers report a friendly and helpful reception at this Surrey warehouse; the regular newsletter is equally warmly informative. The shortish list, of slightly uneven quality (but generally good), covers the main French areas, with a number of reliable German wines from Zimmerman-Graeff, CVNE Riojas and the good sherries of Real Tesoro. Champagne is keenly priced, beginning with a house brand at just £6.15, and culminating in the lovely 1973 vintage and rosé of Bruno Paillard for just £8 and £7.70. Lorne House Vintners offer an unusual service which other merchants might profitably copy: their Shipping Club offers 10 per cent off wines ordered by a given date, pre-paid for subsequent shipping within four or five weeks to members who pay a £5 annual membership fee. We have received good reports, too, of the company's 'relaxed, informal' open house tastings, held regularly at the warehouse.

BEST BUYS [£££] Bruno Paillard Champagnes

Mackie & Co

4 Apothecary Street, London, EC4 TEL 01-236 7080

OPEN Mon–Fri 10.30 am–6.30 pm Sat 10.30 am–2 pm CLOSED Sun, public holidays CREDIT CARDS Access, Visa; personal and business accounts DISCOUNTS 5% on case orders; club members an additional 5% DELIVERY Free in London, min 2 cases; elsewhere on UK mainland free, min 3 cases; charges for smaller quantities on request GLASS HIRE Free TASTINGS AND TALKS 4 tastings a year for wine club, membership £5.50 CELLARAGE £2.16 per case per year

Mackie & Co's well-balanced range provides not only young and mature wines of the classic areas, but plenty of interesting oddities, too, like the very drinkable Sidi Brahim from Morocco (£1.98), and the delicious Mas de Daumas Gassac rosé and red (£3.75 and £5.15 for the still-too-young red 1981) – Vins de Pays de l'Hérault of a very superior kind, as the prices suggest; or Corsican Coteaux Porto Vecchio, Domaine Terraccia (£2.69), one of the few really good wines made on that island. Loire wines are a speciality here, and you will find some of the very best wines of Anjou: the two Anjou Cabernets of Domaine Richou – rich, fruity, full wines (£3.37 and £3.75 for the 1982 vintage of the 'ordinary' and the 'vieille vignes') – and the Richou white 'Chauvigné', which contains some Chardonnay (£3.25). There are some fine sweet Loires, too. Mackie are connected with Hurlingham Vintners and Jeffrey Benson Wines *(see above)* and share their strengths in sweet Bordeaux. They hold the agency for the lovely wines of Ch Rieussec, and sell exclusively in Britain the château's 'second' Sauternes Clos Labère (made with the property's young vines), as well as its good dry whites [£]–[£££]. As always, be circumspect before snapping up any of the fine old wines in the Burgundy and claret list: you may find some rare and interesting old bottles, but some of these prices seem very high. Schlumberger Alsace wines and a couple of sweet Lenz Moser Austrians round out the choice. And this is a good source of interesting old Cognacs, Armagnacs and Calvados.

BEST BUYS [£]–[££] Loire wines, especially Richou red and white, and the range from the Coteaux du Layon, [£££] old Cognac, Armagnac and Calvados

Majestic Wine Company

See CHAINS AND SUPERMARKETS

Malmaison Wine Club

28 Midland Road, London, NW1 TEL 01-388 5996

OPEN Mon–Fri 9 am–6 pm Sat 9 am–4 pm CLOSED Sun, public holidays
CREDIT CARDS All accepted DISCOUNTS 5% to members, cash or cheque
DELIVERY Free on UK mainland, min 1 case GLASS HIRE 50p per 12 glasses
TASTINGS AND TALKS Regular club tastings and dinners CELLARAGE £5 per case per year

Malmaison's shifting range of wines has passed fleetingly across the palates of a succession of wine buyers over the past few years. And if recent tastings (spring 1984) of their own label and cheaper wines have disappointed, maybe things will change now that Stephen Spurrier, formerly associated with the London Caves de la Madeleine *(see above)* is settling into the buying rôle as joint MD with Graham Chidgey. There are many good quality wines to be found at Malmaison: this is a good place to buy clarets, which are very well priced and well selected, and Sauternes is good value, too. Elsewhere on the list, bearing in mind that charges include transport to your door, prices are fair, sometimes perhaps a little high. Burgundies are rather less exciting than the clarets, with a lot of Remoissenet wines; amongst some good Loires, try the powerful gooseberry-redolent Sancerre Domaine de la Mercy Dieu 1982, Bailly Reverdy (£5). Rhônes are very good and reliable, from the beginning at just over £3 to the end at just over £14; the Muscat de Beaumes-de-Venise Domaine des Coyeux, deep and intensely flavoured, is one of the very best (£6.50). There are high-quality German wines, good Spanish, and a small spread from Bulgaria, the Lebanon, Chile, California, Australia and New Zealand: this is one of the few firms that stock the Cooks' 1982 Chardonnay (£6.50).

BEST BUYS Clarets and Sauternes

The Market

See CHAINS AND SUPERMARKETS

Market Vintners

11–12 West Smithfield, London, EC1 TEL 01-248 8382

OPEN Mon–Fri 8.30 am–6 pm CLOSED Sat, Sun, public holidays
CREDIT CARDS Access/Euro, Visa; personal and business accounts
DISCOUNTS 5% on 3+ cases, £1 per case cash and carry DELIVERY Free in Central London, min 1 case; elsewhere at cost GLASS HIRE Free
TASTINGS AND TALKS On request CELLARAGE £2.50 per case per year

Robert Rolls' shop, offices and cellars in West Smithfield offer wines selected to a very high standard at reasonable prices. The stock is principally French: young Alsace wines from a number of producers, some good Burgundies including wines from Albert Pic in Chablis and Etienne Sauzet. Loires include the lovely Sancerres of Vacheron [££], and the Rhône list is particularly strong, from Guigal, Chapoutier and Paul Jaboulet Aîné in the North, with more Jaboulet from the South, and the concentrated Châteauneufs from the Domaine de Beaucastel [£££]; look here, too, for some older Southern Rhône vintages from the early 1970s. From Bordeaux, the only white is the delicious Ch Thieuley at just over £3. The interesting list of young clarets on the main list – petits-châteaux to bourgeois and second wines of major châteaux – is supplemented by a regular fine wine list, clarets of the better growths here going back in some cases to 1953, along with a few older Burgundies, Champagnes, ports and the occasional foreign body such as a 1968 Brunello di Montalcino, Il Greppo, Biondi-Santi (£18). The Italians on the main list are few but worth trying, including the light, white Tieffenbrunner wines from the South Tyrol at just over £3, and the top of Antinori's range [£££]. Spanish wines, also few, are hand-picked from La Rioja Alta and Jean León. Bruno Paillard Champagnes are good value, as are the unusual Almacenista sherries [££]–[£££].

BEST BUYS Most things on the list, especially wines mentioned above

Marks & Spencer

See CHAINS AND SUPERMARKETS

Martinez & Co

36 The Grove, Ilkley, West Yorkshire TEL (0943) 607705
The Ginnel, Parliament Square, Harrogate,
North Yorkshire TEL (0423) 501783

OPEN (Ilkley) Mon 12 noon–7 pm Tue, Wed, Thur 10 am–7 pm Fri 10 am–8 pm Sat 9 am–6 pm (Harrogate) Mon–Thur and Sat 9 am–6.30 pm Fri 9 am–8 pm CLOSED Sun, public holidays CREDIT CARDS All accepted at Ilkley; Access/Euro, Visa at Harrogate DISCOUNTS (Not if paid by Amex or Diners card) 5% on case orders, and on cash and carry DELIVERY Free within van area, min 1 case; elsewhere £4.50 per case for 1–3 cases, £2.50 per case for 5–10 cases GLASS HIRE 50p per doz TASTINGS AND TALKS For groups on request; 2 or 3 organised tastings a year CELLARAGE £2.50 per case per year

Juan Martinez (John after 30 years in Britain) and his wife Christine Evans left their careers as export marketer and embassy interpreter only three years ago to turn their hobby into a small wine business in Ilkley. It has obviously grown rapidly, because in 1984 they opened a second shop three times the size of the Ilkley one in a large Harrogate cellar. Spain has always been the mainstay of the list: a fine selection of Riojas includes CVNE, Marqués de Murrieta, La Rioja Alta, López de Heredia, Marqués de Cáceres, Campo Viejo and more, and has been greatly extended on the September 1983 list; in addition to the old

Berberanas back to 1952 (£16.50) from previous lists, there are now many more old and rare Riojas, such as Murrieta 1960 at around £12, Faustino 1964 at just below £10, and Tondonia 1970 at £7.50. From the Penedès, the Torres wines are better than the sound but unexciting Conde de Caralt assortment, for which Martinez hold the agency. Try also the Marqués de Riscal white from Rueda (£3.50) and perhaps for a very special occasion one of the Vega Sicilia wines: the 1966 is £24.75! Amongst the excellent range of sherries, the De Soto Fino is rather special, lower in alcohol than other sherries imported here, fresh and delicate, and the old Gonzalez Byass sherries are very good, too. The scope of this little business has been widening, however, in countries covered as well as number of wines. A lot of effort has obviously gone into putting together a tempting array of clarets, some classed growths of the 1976, 1978 and 1979 vintages now as well as the petits-châteaux, bourgeois and generics that appeared last year. Amongst the Burgundies are some very good-value wines from the Groupement des Producteurs de Prissé, the St-Véran 1982 (£4.30) in particular being a delicious wine; Chablis from Domaine la Jouchère [££] and Moreau [£££] are good. There are some enjoyable Hugel wines from Alsace. The adventurous might like to try some of the Languedoc-Roussillon wines, such as a Clairette du Languedoc 1983 from the Vignerons du Ceressou or a Fitou from the same source. Best value amongst the sparkling wines is the Blanquette de Limoux (£4.85) but the big range of Champagnes is fairly if not cheaply priced. Martinez have recently taken on 20 German estate wines from Deinhard of the 1976, 1979 and 1983 vintages, plus a number of mature Trockenbeerenauslesen to Auslesen from elsewhere. A different wine is opened daily in both the shops, which should make an exploratory visit even more enjoyable.

BEST BUYS [£]–[£££] Riojas, [££] De Soto Fino, [££] Burgundies from the Producteurs de Prissé, [£]–[££] clarets

Mayor Sworder & Co Ltd

21 Duke Street Hill, London, SE1 TEL 01-407 5111

OPEN Mon–Fri 9 am–5 pm CLOSED Sat, Sun, public holidays CREDIT CARDS Personal and business accounts DISCOUNTS By arrangement DELIVERY Free in London postal districts, min 1 case; elsewhere negotiable GLASS HIRE Free TASTINGS AND TALKS Annual tastings for customers CELLARAGE £2 per case per year

Mayor Sworder's old cellars stretching out beneath London Bridge Station are stacked with an individual assortment of cases, because most wines on this soberly and traditionally presented list, from Burgundy to the Mosel, are from small growers imported direct by the company and in many instances unavailable elsewhere. Quality is good. We do not recommend the table wines, but amongst the other cheaper wines, try the Domaine de Bosc Long, Gaillac Blanc 1983 (£2.65), a light, fresh white, and the red Domaine de Belles Eaux 1980, Vin de Pays de Caux (£2.70), an intense, tannic but fruity red.

Burgundies, growers' wines from recent vintages, include Bernard Michel's deliciously intense and complex Montagny premier cru 1982. There are a few interesting-looking Rhônes, red and white, a small collection of clarets from 1976 upwards, mostly modestly and competitively priced (though the own-label claret is unexciting). The Loire is an individual selection, again of small growers; the red Sancerre Clos du Grand Chemirin 1982 (£4.98) is a firm, meaty wine. The Alsace wines from the small firm of Becker are good and the selection of Champagnes is quite well priced. After France, Germany is a speciality – some lesser-known small growers again, bought to a high standard, judging from our tasting. The Masi Soave and Valpolicella are very fair amongst the Italians [£]. Note that VAT is not included in the prices in the list – Mayor Sworder have little to hide, however; their prices are very fair, certainly compared to some of the other old-established city firms. Anyone put off by the unfamiliar names can taste many of the wines at Cuddeford's Wine bar, next door *(see* LONDON WINE BARS*)*, which is owned by the company.

BEST BUYS [£] Domaine de Bosc Long, Domaine de Belles Eaux, [££]–[£££] Burgundies and German wines

Andrew Mead Wines Ⓥ ☞

Shovelstrode, Presteigne, Radnorshire TEL (054 76) 268

OPEN Variable CREDIT CARDS Not accepted DISCOUNTS 5% on case orders DELIVERY Free within 15 miles, min 1 case; elsewhere free, min 3 cases *(but see below)* GLASS HIRE Free TASTINGS AND TALKS Occasional tastings and wine weekends CELLARAGE Not available (except by special arrangement)

'Do you run a wine club for your customers?' we asked Mr Mead. 'All my customers,' came the reply, 'are regular buyers who receive all our literature and I make a point of getting to know every one of them – you could say they are a club.' Andrew Mead accomplishes this feat by making his deliveries himself on regular nationwide trips, three cases delivered free, one case locally, though the more exigent must pay Roadline rates, and a £4 delivery charge may be levied on smaller deliveries. This still puts him at an advantage to most mail order companies, however, because prices are keen, and the wines an original, personal selection. One could be happy on most 'everyday' days with the 'under £3' selection. German wines are sensitively bought (the *Guide*'s editor must declare an interest: she was first reluctantly introduced to wine in the Neumagen cellars of Carl Schloeder at the age of thirteen-and-a-half, later to be convinced of their quality!); there are other German growers' wines, plus some from

Prices and price categories were correct to the best of our knowledge as we went to press. They, and ranges of wines stocked, are likely to change during the course of 1985, and are intended as a rough indication of an establishment's range and prices.

the reliable firm of Guntrum. Look out for some super Rhônes, Burgundies from small, little-known growers, a small selection of extraordinarily well selected clarets (including in 1984 a number of clarets at competitive opening prices; vintage port at (beatable?) prices; and some very reasonable wines in the small selections from Italy and Spain. Mr Mead was for many years a school teacher. We give him nine-and-a-half out of ten, though we would hate to mark his exam papers – he could perhaps do a little home-work on his hand-writing.

BEST BUYS Most things on the list

J H Measures & Sons Ltd

Ⓥ

The Crescent, Spalding, Lincolnshire TEL (0775) 2676

OPEN Mon–Sat 9 am–6 pm CLOSED Sun, public holidays CREDIT CARDS Not accepted DISCOUNTS 5–10% on case orders DELIVERY Free in Boston and Peterborough; elsewhere arranged through parent company G E Bromley & Sons, Leicester GLASS HIRE 25p per doz TASTINGS AND TALKS Occasionally on request CELLARAGE Not available

J H Measures & Sons are a wholly-owned subsidiary of G E Bromley & Sons of Leicester *(see above)* and stock the same range at the same very competitive prices.

Michael Menzel Wines

297/299 Ecclesall Road, Sheffield, South Yorkshire TEL (0742) 683557

OPEN Mon–Sat 10 am–9 pm Sun, public holidays 12 noon–2 pm, 7 pm–9 pm CLOSED Chr Day CREDIT CARDS All accepted (retail price only) DISCOUNTS 1% on 10–15 cases DELIVERY Free locally, min 3 cases; elsewhere free, min 5 cases GLASS HIRE Free TASTINGS AND TALKS Occasionally, by invitation only CELLARAGE Not available

Case lots, which can be mixed, are the best way to buy wines here since single bottles attract a 10–15 per cent surcharge; the list quotes prices exclusive of VAT (converted by us below), so you may need to play with your abacus to come up with the final figure and find out whether or not you've got a bargain. France is Michael Menzel's longest suit and Bordeaux seems to be trumps, with youngish clarets from 1978 onwards and £4.50 upwards, including Ch Lynch-Bages 1978/79 at £11.50 and an ace Ch Mouton-Rothschild at just over £46 for either the 1971 or 1978 vintage. Some five- or six-year-old red Burgundies, and 1982/83 whites that need keeping, are mostly either from Louis Latour, whose red Ch Corton-Grancey 1979 is £16.67, or from Joseph Drouhin, who also supplies the 1983 Beaujolais-Village. Rhônes are less exalted, although Chapoutier's 1979 Côte-Rôtie (£8.33) would take some beating, and the Ch du Nozet Pouilly-Fumé Baron de L (the 1981 is £10.35) stands out amongst the Loires, but if you feel that's a lot to pay, the Ladoucette 1982 is about £4 cheaper and not a bad second. There is a good range of QbA and QmP wines from a spread of vintages from both the Rhine and Mosel, including a 1976 Spätlese at £9.77 from the prestigious state-owned Steinberg vineyard in the Rheingau. Italy features some of Pio Cesare's Piemonte wines like the good-quality white Gavi (1983 is £3.68) and the very drinkable red Barbera d'Alba (1980/81 for £3.45). Three vintages of Ch Musar bring up the rear.

BEST BUYS 1978/79 clarets and other wines mentioned above

Mi Casa Wines

77 West Road, Buxton, Derbyshire TEL (0298) 3952

OPEN Mon–Fri 5 pm–10 pm Sat and public holidays 11 am–10 pm Sun 12 noon–2 pm, 7 pm–10 pm Chr Day 12 noon–1 pm CREDIT CARDS Not accepted DISCOUNTS 5% on case sales DELIVERY Free in the Buxton area on case orders GLASS HIRE Free TASTINGS AND TALKS On request CELLARAGE Not available

For Buxton folk tired of the ranges of Victoria Wine and Peter Dominic, or for Spanish lovers within striking distance of the town, there's a wealth of exciting wines to discover at Mi Casa. The Casa in question is in fact two cottages. Four customers easily fill the shop. But never fear – there are more wines than meet the eye, more even than the printed list reveals: tucked away behind the shop are 24 red Riojas (three labelled 1964, from £8.50 to £14.75) in addition to the six on the list, and other wines besides. The wines come from many different Spanish importers, and prices, considering the scale of the business, are very reasonable. There's something from most parts of Spain: try the Protos 7th year (£6.95) and Ribera Duero 2nd year (£3.35) from Valladolid, the powerful Jean León wines from Catalonia and the interesting Castillo de San Diego, a fresh, dry white made in deep-South Andalucia from sherry grapes. The whole Torres range is stocked, too. A few Germans and Austrians (Beerenauslesen and Eiswein) add a sweet foreign touch. Since there's no passing trade, Mi Casa opens in the evenings only, all day on Saturday, and on Sunday during licensing hours; but don't be afraid to take Tony and Annette Moore up on their suggestion: 'When closed, please ring the bell.' They live next door in the other tiny cottage. They also run a catering business – and the Buxton Transport Museum.

BEST BUYS Most wines in the shop

Millevini

3 Middlewood Road, High Lane, Stockport, Cheshire TEL (06632) 4366

OPEN 24-hour answering service CREDIT CARDS Not accepted DISCOUNTS 2% on unmixed half-case, 4% on 1–4 unmixed cases, 5% on 5–9; a further 3% for cash and carry DELIVERY Free within 20 miles ie Greater Manchester area, min

1 mixed case; elsewhere £5 per delivery for 1–5 cases, thereafter free GLASS HIRE Free TASTINGS AND TALKS To groups on request, samples at 5% discount CELLARAGE Not available MAIL ORDER SPECIALISTS

'Our aim is to supply and satisfy an increasing consumer need for the better quality wines to be found in the more southerly regions of Italy, where, we believe, many fine wines have still to be exploited.' You will indeed find many good wines here from the Italian South: Mastroberardino wines from Campania [££]–[£££], Corvo from Sicily [££], the raisiny, sweet Moscato di Pantellerìa, Tanit, Agricoltori Associati from an island way south of the Italian coast (£5.49); and some good wines [£] from the Abruzzi, on the eastern side of Italy, on a level with Rome, if you still count this as 'South'. But there are many good wines from more northerly parts, too. Moving up-country, there's the (only?) excellent Frascati, Colli di Catone (£3.66), the very good wines of Capezzana in Tuscany, including their Chianti [££]–[£££], Pieropan Soave (£4.26), a selection of the very tasty Masi wines from the Veneto [££], Venegazzù (£3.97), a couple of the fresh white Tieffenbrunner wines from the South Tyrol [£]+ and Nera's rich, alcoholic Sfurzat (£4.97) from the Valtellina mountains in Lombardy – all these particular recommendations amongst an extraordinarily wide and sound range. This is a well-written list, incorporating useful tasting notes for every wine, and (perhaps in desperation at the died-in-the-Gallic-wool Mancunians?) it ends with a 'comparability study', drawing comparisons between body and style of French and Italian wines. Millevini used to stock French and German wines, too, but have now decided to concentrate entirely on Italy, though they do offer to get hold of any specific French, German or Spanish, or indeed other Italian wines, that their customers are unable to find themselves. They sell only by the case, which may be mixed, largely by mail order, but it is possible to collect, thereby gaining a small discount, from their Marple warehouse.

BEST BUYS [£]+ Tieffenbrunner whites, [££] Masi wines, [££]–[£££] Capezzana wines

Milroy's

3 Greek Street, London, W1 TEL 01-437 0893

OPEN Mon 9 am–6 pm Tue–Fri 9 am–7 pm Sat 9.30 am–5 pm Sun 12 noon–2 pm CLOSED Sun (Jan–Nov), public holidays CREDIT CARDS All accepted DISCOUNTS 5% on 4–14 cases, 10% on 15+ cases DELIVERY Free within London area and surrounding counties, min 2 cases; £2 for smaller quantities; elsewhere on UK mainland £4 for 1–4 cases GLASS HIRE 50p per doz TASTINGS AND TALKS Regular in-store tastings CELLARAGE Not available

'Fine malt whiskies,' proclaims the fine old sign over the back of the Milroy's poky little shop in Soho (otherwise known as the Soho Wine Market). On their list, two double-columned tightly-typed sheets run from Ardbeg 1965 (£13) to American Wild Turkey (£12.65): this is one of the finest whisk(e)y lists in Britain, and that includes Scotland, too!

But they have nevertheless managed to squeeze plenty of wine on to the shelves, and a little bit more around the floor in higgledy-piggledy heaps of cartons: mostly French and mostly traditional Englishmen's fare. Burgundies are good, many from individual growers, Beaujolais are from Duboeuf and there are clarets – *'petits'* and recent classed growths, plus a rapidly changing selection of older bottles at good prices. Champagne, a fair range, is quite well priced. Rhônes include the tasty Domaine Chante-Cigale 1979 at £5.36 and Germans from Guntrum are good, sound wines.

BEST BUYS [££]–[£££] Burgundies, clarets, [£££] Champagne, malt whisky

Mitchell & Son

21 Kildare Street, Dublin 2 TEL Dublin 760766

OPEN Mon–Fri 9 am–5.30 pm Sat 10.30 am–1 pm CLOSED Sun, and Fri–Mon when there is a public holiday CREDIT CARDS Access/Euro, Amex, Visa; personal accounts DISCOUNTS 10% on wine, 5% on port, sherry, Champagne for 5+ cases DELIVERY Free in Dublin City and County, min 2 cases; £1.95 for less; elsewhere £3.10 for 1 case, £3.60 for 2 cases, £4.60 for 3 cases, £6.15 for 4 cases, thereafter free GLASS HIRE 95p per doz TASTINGS AND TALKS In-store tastings; bi-annual tastings of Deinhard wines for customers; for groups on request CELLARAGE Not available

This family wine business is the place to come to buy German wines from the fine Deinhard list – Mitchells are the agents in Ireland for Deinhard. Deinhard Lila amongst the sparkling wines is delicious and good value. There is a reasonable collection of clarets, including some classed growths, back to 1976, but we find it difficult to raise much enthusiasm for the Rhônes, Burgundies and Beaujolais, very largely from Mommessin.

BEST BUYS Deinhard German wines

Morans of Bristol

See TD Vintners

Moreno Wines

11 Marylands Road, London, W9 TEL 01-286 0678
2 Norfolk Place, London, W2 TEL 01-262 4714

OPEN Mon–Sat 9 am–10.30 pm Sun 12 noon–2 pm, 7 pm–9.30 pm Public holidays (Marylands Road only) 9 am–9.30 pm CLOSED Public holidays at Norfolk Place; Chr Day and Boxing Day at Marylands Road CREDIT CARDS Access/Euro, Visa DISCOUNTS 5% on case orders cash and carry DELIVERY Free locally, min 1 case; elsewhere in the UK £5 for 1–2 cases, thereafter free GLASS HIRE Free TASTINGS AND TALKS Spanish tastings and talks to groups on request, with optional tapas CELLARAGE Not available

Formerly only wholesalers of Spanish wines, the Moreno family, or rather the younger generation, have branched out into two West London retail shops that now account for about a quarter of their business. Spanish wine lovers have good reason to give them their custom: their shelves display the wines of 25 Rioja bodegas, four Penedès bodegas, seven cava houses, nine sherry houses and eight brandy distilleries, as well as a few liqueurs, and behind the scenes is a stock of older wines. In their latest list, notes on the bodegas – their styles, and pointers to their best wines – have been added honestly and usefully. Most enjoyment is probably to be found in the lists from Rioja, Penedès, Rueda, Ribera del Duero, Alella and Valdepeñas, but this is the place to come to discover what other areas of Spain have to offer. Our top vote in the sherries goes to the Barbadillo wines, not to be confused with the Bobadilla selection that follows. You are unlikely to find elsewhere a comprehensive Rioja vintage chart (vintages *do* matter in Rioja), and there are vintage recommendations in tabular form for red and white Penedès wines, too. Prices at Moreno's are mostly keen(ish) to keen, though there are occasional inexplicable price leaps.

BEST BUYS Wines from the areas mentioned above

Philip Morgan Ltd Ⓥ

126 Wyndham Crescent, Cardiff TEL (0222) 31570
13 Windsor Road, Penarth, South Glamorgan TEL (0222) 704164

OPEN (Wyndham Crescent) Mon–Sat 10 am–10 pm Sun 12 noon–2 pm, 7 pm–10 pm (Windsor Road) Mon–Wed 9 am– 6 pm Thur–Sat 9 am–7 pm
CLOSED Sun (Windsor Road), public holidays CREDIT CARDS Not accepted
DISCOUNTS 10% on mixed cases DELIVERY Free within Cardiff area; elsewhere free for 5+ cases; smaller orders £5 GLASS HIRE Free TASTINGS AND TALKS Every sun L (Wyndham Crescent) CELLARAGE Only in bond

These small shops stock a wide range of wines from around the world, usually at competitive prices. Their more adventurous customers will appreciate the fact that the assortment changes regularly, being bought in from around the trade as good deals arise. So clarets, red and white Burgundy, Rhônes, Alsace, Champagne, and wines from more far-flung places, too, tend to come from different sources, and do not appear on the list. But wine drinkers of habit will be pleased to find constantly on show at Philip Morgan a small selection of wines, mostly from the Loire (a co-operative and a reliable large company, the CVL) and the South-West of France, reliable wines at around £2 a bottle; and, well priced here, the excellent Riojas of Marqués de Cáceres (the delicious white 1983 is £2.68, the red £2.89 and Reserva 1973 £4.12).

BEST BUYS Variable, but always [£]–[££] Marqués de Cáceres Riojas

Send us **your** views on the report forms at the back of the book.

Morris & Verdin Ⓥ

28 Churton Street, London, SW1 TEL 01-834 5282

OPEN Mon–Fri 9 am–5.30 pm CLOSED Sat, Sun, public holidays
CREDIT CARDS Not accepted; personal and business accounts
DISCOUNTS £1.20 per case on 5+ cases, which may be mixed, £2.40 per case on 10+ cases DELIVERY Free in London and Oxford, min 1 case; on UK mainland £2.30 per case for 1–4 cases; thereafter free GLASS HIRE Free
TASTINGS AND TALKS Not available CELLARAGE £1.15 per case

Some finely tuned palates have put together the French-only list of Morris & Verdin. It is difficult to know where to start, since every section has something rather special to offer. However, in these days of lily-livered Burgundies, Morris & Verdin's fine Burgundian list is perhaps an obvious starting point. Most outstanding are the wines of Daniel Rion, mostly reds from Vosne-Romanée and Nuits-St-Georges – rich, clear, fragrant concentrated wines at prices that are high but very competitive and excellent value. In the whites, the wines of the Domaine des Comtes Lafon are exceptional, but so are the fresh, unwooded Chablis of Louis Michel and the Puligny Montrachet, Les Combettes 1982, Domaine Etienne Sauzet (£13.50). Rhônes are well priced and mouth-watering from start (£2.60 for Côtes du Ventoux, La Vieille Ferme 1981), to finish (£8.25 for Hermitage, La Chapelle 1982, Paul Jaboulet Aîné), with other excellent wines from the Perrin brothers and Jaboulet in between. Dessert wines include the fine, sweet-sharp Bonnezeaux of Jacques Boivin (£5.35 and £4.75 for the 1979 and 1980 vintages). The rest of the Loires are good value, too. Champagnes and the couple of vintage ports are fairly priced, and the table wines that begin the list under the heading 'House Wines' are also above average, especially the Blanc de Blancs (£1.90) table wine from Chablis producer Lamblin and the Mas de Lavabre Coteaux du Languedoc (£2.20). The company moved in the summer of 1984 from cramped premises in Chelsea to Churton Street, where they now have a showroom as well as offices and greater storage space.

BEST BUYS [£] House wines, [£]–[£££] Rhônes, [£££] Rion Burgundies

Morrisons

See CHAINS AND SUPERMARKETS

Mowat Wines Limited

15 Acorn Walk, Milton Keynes TEL (0908) 604455

OPEN Mon–Wed 9.30 am–6 pm Thurs, Fri 8.30 am–8 pm Sat 8.30 am–6 pm Public holidays variable CLOSED Sun CREDIT CARDS Access/Euro, Amex, Visa; personal and business accounts DISCOUNTS 5% on case orders DELIVERY Free in Milton Keynes, Buckingham, Northampton and environs, min

1 case; elsewhere £4 per case for 1 case, £3 per case for 2 cases, £2 per case for 3 cases, £1 per case for 4 cases, thereafter free GLASS HIRE Free TASTINGS AND TALKS On request CELLARAGE Not available

Mowat's is a carefully chosen range from around the traditional areas of Europe, nowhere with a great choice in terms of volume, but there's something to satisfy most customers, including many wines from lesser-known French growers – though it would be nice (and a sales pitch, too?) to know quite *who* produces the Côtes du Roussillon-Villages, matured in oak casks by 'probably the best wine makers of this region'. Many growers' and producers' names are revealed, to be fair, and this looks an interesting selection to explore. Table wines are good, and there is an unusual collection from Beaujolais, Burgundy and the Loire. German wines are from Hallgarten, a wide-ranging choice within the small range, and Italian wines from Santa Sofia are very good. Some of the best value on the list comes from Spain – Viña Alberdi, Ardanza and Leonora [£]–[££] from La Rioja Alta, delicious wines, and it is nice to see that already on their March 1984 list, Mowats were offering our own fresh 1983 Breaky Bottom Seyval Blanc. Lustau's Pilarita sherries are good value, as are the wood and late-bottled ports from Smith Woodhouse and Warre. By the bottle, prices are not the cheapest, but become very reasonable if you live within the free delivery area and are prepared to buy by the mixed case. (For the indecisive, Mowat offer some tempting pre-mixed cases, too.) Certain wines on special promotion come in 'bakers' dozens'. They have added a delicatessen to their town-centre shop during the past year, and offer a food service ('cooked at home by Charlotte Mowat and a number of qualified cooks') for parties as well as 'a wide range of services to help your party or promotion go with a swing'.

BEST BUYS [£]–[££] Riojas, [£££] Wood ports

The Noble Grape Ⓥ

26 The Highway, London, E1 TEL 01-488 4788

OPEN Mon–Wed 10.30 am–7 pm Thur, Fri 10.30 am–8 pm Sat, Sun and public holidays 10 am–6 pm CLOSED Chr Day, Boxing Day CREDIT CARDS Access/Euro, Visa DISCOUNTS 2% on orders £150+ paid by cash or cheque DELIVERY Free within 15 miles, min 1 case; elsewhere, rates on request GLASS HIRE Free TASTINGS AND TALKS May start soon; bottles always open in warehouse CELLARAGE £4 inc insurance per case per year

Prices are *cheap* at the Noble Grape, and if you live within 15 miles of this bustling Wapping warehouse, there is some extraordinary value to be had, delivered free. It is worth coming here for Champagne – a few are listed, but you will find more on display: Moët was £8.85, Lanson Black Label £7.95 last summer. The Noble Grape import 90 per cent of their wines themselves, and you may not recognise many of the names on the bottles, but never fear: there are always many wines open for tasting. 'We have decided,' the Grape's MD wrote to us, 'to give up the research for the world's perfect wine from Outer Mongolia, Outer

Hebrides, Zimbabwe and Utopia, as we find they are rarely good value even if they are drinkable.' So the bulk of the list is now French, covering the major regions, with rather more classed growth claret than in the past, of recent vintages. Burgundies and Beaujolais are predominantly Mommessin, but Duboeuf, at good prices, are the Beaujolais to go for. A small, not so exciting selection from the rest of Europe completes the list, but there tends to be a rapidly changing stock of fine wines in addition, bought in small lots, so ask. Beer drinkers should easily be persuaded to make the trip to Wapping by the vast range of beers from sources as far afield as Singapore, Mexico, China, Australia, New Zealand, Czechoslovakia and Luxembourg. The warehouse is open seven days a week, selling by wholesale licence only by the case; no yellow lines on the road outside, either.

BEST BUYS £–££ Duboeuf Beaujolais, £££ Champagne

Northgate Wines

HEAD OFFICE Northgate, Warwick, Warwickshire TEL (0926) 492468
OPEN 'All hours' with help of answering machine CREDIT CARDS Not accepted DISCOUNTS Not available DELIVERY Free in Midlands, Yorkshire, London and Home Counties, min 1 case GLASS HIRE Free TASTINGS AND TALKS On request CELLARAGE Not available

The Phillips' list is short and specialised, and they sell by the case only. Loire and Alsace are the only French wines available, with those reliable Gisselbrechts, Louis and Willy, supplying the latter at around £3 to £4. Loire suppliers include René Renou whose sweet white Bonnezeaux is good – the 1982, which will keep and improve, is around £3.50; the wealth of red, white and rosé wines is well represented between £2.50 and £4.50 or so, and other good producers include the Confrérie des Vignerons de Oisly-et-Thésée and Langlois-Château. Regions of Northern and Central Italy account for the remainder of the list and there are excellent producers such as Lungarotti whose white Torre di Giano is here (the 1982 is under £4) as well as the top class red Rubesco Riserva 1974 from the Monticcio vineyard (over £8) which should be at its peak about now. Amongst good producers like Badia a Coltibuono and Antinori are the latter's light, crisp white Galestro (under £3.50), Tignanello and the cousin's Sassicaia 1978 at about £9. From the North-East, the wines are less expensive but offer novelties for the adventurous drinker rather than merely bargains, like Bianco di Custoza 1982, Tomassi (£2.71) or Teroldego Rotaliano 1980, Zeni (£4.50), as well as some varietals from classic French grapes. Mixed tasting cases are available.

BEST BUYS £–£££ Italian wines

Oddbins

See CHAINS AND SUPERMARKETS

Old Chelsea Wine Store

56 Lambs Conduit Street, London, WC1 TEL 01-405 3106
358 Kilburn High Road, London, NW6 TEL 01-624 8922

Owned by Ehrmann's Ltd, the Old Chelsea Wine Store's two branches stock the same excellent range and trade on the same terms *(see under Ehrmann's above)*.

Old Compton Wines

64 Old Compton Street, London, W1 TEL 01-437 2738

See Del Monico above

The Old Maltings Wine Co Ltd

The Old Maltings Wine Shop, Long Melford, Sudbury, Suffolk TEL (0787) 79638

OPEN Mon–Sat 9 am–1 pm, (exc Wed) 2 pm–5 pm CLOSED Sun, Wed pm, public holidays CREDIT CARDS Personal and business accounts DISCOUNTS 5% on case orders DELIVERY Free throughout England, min 3 cases; for less, £3 per case anywhere in the UK GLASS HIRE Free TASTINGS AND TALKS On request CELLARAGE In bond, charges on request

To the Old Maltings' predominantly French list have been added during 1984 a few well-chosen wines from other countries: a red and white Rioja from Olarra at around £3, Hill Smith Shiraz and Riesling from Australia, both under £4, Chilean Antiguas Reservas Cabernet Sauvignon 1977 from Cousiño Macul, good value at £4.16, and a few more, including a few basic Germans. There is a short list of clarets, 'as we prefer to make lying down (sic) offers at opening prices' and the long list of Burgundies is dominated by many wines from Mommessin, not the most exciting. Look rather to the northern Rhônes from Guigal and Noyer, and the good Willm wines from Alsace. This is a helpful company with well-informed staff.

BEST BUYS [£]–[£££] Rhônes, [££] Hill Smith Australians, [££] Cousiño Macul Cabernet

Pallant Wines

Main Road, Birdham, Chichester, West Sussex TEL (0243) 512888

OPEN Mon–Sat 10 am–5 pm Sun 10 am–1 pm
CREDIT CARDS Access/Euro, Visa

This wine-by-the-case and wholesale business was just starting up in the building adjoining Birdham Stores *(see above)* as we went to press, offering principally Théo Cattin Alsace wines, Louis Latour Burgundies and KWV South Africans, plus a few clarets, Riojas, German and Italian wines. They intend to hold monthly in-store tastings 'with attractive monthly offers'. *(See Birdham Wines for further details.)* More reports, please!

The Pantiles Vintry

7 The Pantiles, Tunbridge Wells, Kent TEL (0892) 27335

OPEN Mon–Fri 9 am–5.30 pm Sat 9 am–1 pm CLOSED Sat pm, Sun, public holidays CREDIT CARDS Personal and business accounts DISCOUNTS 5% on case orders DELIVERY Possibly free on the route from London to Tunbridge Wells, depending on quantity, value and urgency of order; elsewhere in UK £3.50 per case GLASS HIRE Free TASTINGS AND TALKS On request CELLARAGE £1.56 per case per year plus insurance

Whilst the modest spread of young wines from the major French areas, Italy, Germany, Spain and Portugal are mostly on the expensive side at Pantiles Vintry, there are some bargains to be found amongst the fine, mature wines, both on the regularly issued fine wine lists and on the main list: elderly clarets, sweet Bordeaux such as d'Yquem 1973 at £35 a bottle, old vintage port, and younger, immature port, too, at generally reasonable to very good prices.

BEST BUYS Mature wines

Jeffery Phillips (Wine Merchant) Ltd

22 Station Street, Lymington, Hampshire TEL (0590) 74548

OPEN Mon–Fri 9 am–1 pm, 2.15 pm–5.30 pm Sat 9 am–1 pm CLOSED Sun, public holidays CREDIT CARDS Not accepted DISCOUNTS Not available DELIVERY Free locally (mail order prices include delivery) GLASS HIRE Free TASTINGS AND TALKS, CELLARAGE Not available

This small company specialises in South African wines, stocking the Fleur du Cap range from Stellenbosch and the reliable wines of the KWV [£]–[££] in addition to a number of estate wines, of which the Meerlust Cabernet Sauvignon, cryptically labelled 'vintage', looks probably the most interesting at £5.68. Prices here are fair.

Presto

See Argyll Stores in CHAINS AND SUPERMARKETS

Ptarmigan Wines

Leaston House, Humbie, East Lothian TEL (087 533) 219

OPEN Mon–Sat all day CLOSED Sun, public holidays CREDIT CARDS Not accepted DISCOUNTS 2% on 6–12 cases, 4% on 13+ cases DELIVERY Free in Lothian, Borders and Fife, min 1 case; free for 6+ cases on mainland UK; smaller quantities negotiable GLASS HIRE Free TASTINGS AND TALKS 1 large annual free tasting for 300 customers in November; for groups on request CELLARAGE Free at present

The quality across the range is excellent at Ptarmigan, and prices are reasonable, very good in the case of vintage ports. There's some good value to be found in Bulgarian and French wines at under £3; some very fine Riojas and the interesting fresh Castillo de San Diego made from sherry grapes (£2.50). A wide Italian range includes wines from Frescobaldi, Corvo and Terre del Barolo. A consistently good Rhône list is followed by Beaujolais from Loron, and small but reasonable selection of clarets back to 1971. The Burgundies include the fine Chablis of Louis Michel, and Loires are also worth trying. This is probably one of the best American selections north of the border, including wines from Washington and Oregon states. Look out at the end of the list particularly for the sherries of Barbadillo at between £3 and £4. Ptarmigan sell by the case only.

BEST BUYS £££ Vintage ports

Pugsons Food & Wine

82 Wandsworth Bridge Road, London, SW6 TEL 01-736 6145

OPEN Mon–Fri 10 am–7 pm Sat 10 am–6 pm CLOSED Sun, public holidays CREDIT CARDS Access/Euro, Visa; personal accounts DISCOUNTS Not available DELIVERY Free in Central London, Fulham, Wandsworth, Clapham, min 1 case; elsewhere £5.25 for 1 case, £2 for 2–5 cases, £1.85 for 6–9 cases, thereafter free GLASS HIRE Free TASTINGS AND TALKS Bi-annual tastings from whole range; Sat am in-store tastings CELLARAGE £1 per case per *month*

'Although I have only bought at the cheaper end of Mr Pugson's wine list, the quality and value seems to me to be outstanding. His shop has been open for about a year now, and is great fun, offering a wide range of food and wines from France . . .,' writes one *Guide* reader. Peter Pugson used to work at the famous Moulin des Mougins restaurant under chef Roger Vergé, and now, in Wandsworth Bridge Road (and through his hotel and restaurant supply business) sells the range of preserved foods selected by Roger Vergé – unusual mustards, vinegars, herbs, oils, soups and sauces, as well as cheeses, English hams, cookery books – and wine. Quality here is good, the wines from well-selected growers in Burgundy, the Loire and Rhône, plus a few very respectable *négoçiant* wines such as Claret Réserve Nathaniel Johnston (£2.51). Saturday morning in-store tastings or the Pugson sampling case at £38 could be a good way of getting to know a few unfamiliar names. The company also makes opening offers of clarets.

BEST BUYS [££] Sancerre 1983, Henri Natter, Mâcon-Clessé 1982, Gilbert Mornand; Morgon 1981, Domaine de Pillets

Arthur Purchase & Son

31 North Street, Chichester, West Sussex TEL (0243) 783144

OPEN Mon–Sat 8.45 am–5.30 pm CLOSED Sun, public holidays
CREDIT CARDS Access/Euro, Visa; personal and business accounts
DISCOUNTS 5% on case orders DELIVERY 75p per consignment within Chichester, £1 outside locally GLASS HIRE Free TASTINGS AND TALKS To groups on request CELLARAGE £1 per case per year

This 18th-century shop in the town centre ('The Wine Merchant of Chichester since 1780', the list cover proclaims) stocks a number of brands and a big range of beers and spirits as well as a fair list of other wines at prices which seem a little expensive in a national comparison, but not excessively so. Some Champagne prices, however, are quite keen. There is a small and unexciting claret range, but Loron Beaujolais are very good, as are the couple of Trimbach Alsace wines, and Vacheron Sancerre in the Loire section. Outside France, the Bulgarian wines offer good value at just over £2.20, as do the Riojas from CVNE at just over £3. The Lustau wines are good amongst the sherries, and Chambéry vermouth from Dolin (£3.17) is way up the vermouth market for flavour. For those who prefer to take their list away to study at leisure, it would be a kindness on the part of Messrs Purchase to include *all* the vintages, and rather more than the few scattered producers' names that appear on their latest list. Would it be too much to ask for some tasting notes, too, from a family of such venerable experience in the wine trade?

BEST BUYS [£] Bulgarian wines, [££] CVNE Riojas, Loron Beaujolais, Trimbach Alsace wines, [£££] Champagne

Quellyn Roberts

15 Watergate Street, Chester TEL (0244) 20515

OPEN Mon–Sat 8.45 am–5.30 pm CLOSED Sun, public holidays CREDIT CARDS All accepted; personal and business accounts DISCOUNTS 13 bottles for the price of 12 DELIVERY Free within approx 25 miles of Chester, min 3 cases; elsewhere at cost GLASS HIRE Free TASTINGS AND TALKS In-store tastings up to 3 times a week in season CELLARAGE £2.76 per case per year

You are unlikely to find bargains at Quellyn Roberts but, large range of brands apart, the choice is wide: 1,500 items, they boast. Clarets are a speciality – plenty of young classed growths, bourgeois and petits-châteaux; the Alsace section is good, from Hugel and Trimbach, as are Loron Beaujolais. The Spanish wines are worth trying: Torres, Marqués de Murrieta and a few more Riojas, a touch over-priced again.

Little catches our eye from elsewhere. Their Spring 1984 list was particularly uninformative, giving away few producers and trying to sell Champagne under the heading 'Vintage' without bothering to tell us which! Quellyn Roberts put on series of wine lectures in their attractive 12th-century crypt, and they will also give special tastings and talks there for private groups, charging £4.75 inclusive of six or seven wines, bread and cheese for a minimum 30-head charge.

BEST BUYS [££] Alsace and Spanish wines

Arthur Rackhams

See CHAINS AND SUPERMARKETS

Reid Wines

The Mill, Marsh Lane, Hallatrow, Bristol, Avon TEL (0761) 52645

OPEN Mon–Fri 9.30 am–5 pm, other times by appointment CREDIT CARDS Not accepted DISCOUNTS Not available DELIVERY Free in Bristol area, elsewhere by arrangement, anywhere for 9+ cases; otherwise £1.75 for 1 bottle, £3 for 2–3 bottles, £3.50 for 4–6 bottles, £4.50 for 7–11 bottles, £4.50 per case for 1–2 cases, £3.50 per case for 3–5 cases, £3 per case for 5–9 cases GLASS HIRE Not available TASTINGS AND TALKS, CELLARAGE Not available

This has always been a list for the unashamedly self-indulgent, or for restaurants and hotels with such customers: it is for those with both money *and* sense. A gentle breeze of change is blowing, however, and Bill Baker promises that without altering the character of his operation, he is about to extend the range into less esoteric wines and will also offer a few Bordeaux wines *en primeur*: a new list incorporating these will soon be available. In the meantime, the list continues to charm and tantalise. Should you spend your £100 (plus VAT since the prices do not include it) on two bottles of 1920 Ch Branaire-Ducru, a case of Ch Smith-Haut-Lafitte 1978, or put it as a down-payment towards a bottle of Ch d'Yquem 1945? Or perhaps you should eschew Bordeaux altogether and take your pick of the most prestigious Burgundy producers from the Domaine de la Romanée-Conti downwards, spanning over 50 years? That their customers know a good thing when they see one is testified by the much diminished Rhône section, and Reids offer crocodile tears for an apology: 'as soon as we get hold of anything half decent, you snap it up'; it serves them right for stocking the likes of wonderful Paul Jaboulet Aîné wines such as the 1982 Hermitage La Chapelle at £7.25 (even when there's VAT to be added). There are rich Alsace wines from Hugel, a range of vintage and NV Champagnes, vintage ports from 1900 onwards including a few 1963s at around £20, and some 19th-century solera Madeiras. California wines go all the way back to a 1974 Mondavi Reserve Cabernet Sauvignon, nearly £70 (+ VAT) for a magnum, and Reids are agents for Clos du Val wines. Don't be afraid to ask for advice, which is generous, competent and given with a smile. We hope you will have reason to smile back, because prices here are often very good.

BEST BUYS Mature wines

La Réserve

56 Walton Street, London, SW3 TEL 01-589 2020
47 Kendal Street, London, W2 TEL 01-402 6920

OPEN Mon–Fri 10 am–7 pm Sat 9.30 am–5.30 pm CLOSED Sun, public holidays CREDIT CARDS Access/Euro, Visa; personal and business accounts DISCOUNTS 5% on case orders, 10% on case orders of house wines DELIVERY Free in London postal districts, min 1 case GLASS HIRE Free TASTINGS AND TALKS Wines open in shops on Sat; tastings in shops for regular customers once or twice a year CELLARAGE Not available

The bottles that line La Réserve's well-designed shelves have become increasingly cosmopolitan over the past year. You will still find a vast range of good claret, and old vintages, too, of claret, champagne, port etc routed via La Réserve's fine wine wholesaling company, College Cellar Ltd, but you can now also choose from a superb range of a dozen Italian wines (Pieropan, Biondi-Santi, Oddero [£]–[£££]), a handful of good California whites (Firestone, Edna Valley, Martha's Vineyard, Stag's Leap [££]–[£££]), Rosemount Australian wines, Lebanese Ch Musar, and a more general range of French wines. Quality is always good here, but prices tend to be on the high side, so best value is probably to be found in the lower price brackets – such as the three wines from La Vieille Ferme, a Côtes du Lubéron Chardonnay (£2.85), Côtes du Ventoux at (£2.85) and a Côtes du Rhône (£3.50), or try La Réserve's claret (£2.65) or their fresh Blanc de Blancs Fruits de Mer, Louis Barrault (£1.79). Up the price range, the 'Rhônes and Southern French' section is consistently good, beginning with the delicious Domaine de Trévaillon, Coteaux des Baux-en-Provence 1980 (£4.99) and peaking at Ch Rayas Châteauneuf-du-Pape (£16.99). Alsace wines at the moment are four soft 1982s from Gisselbrecht. Moving back to the clarets upon which La Réserve built its reputation, there are plenty of classed growth 1980s 'for drinking now and for the next few years', then a few hand-picked wines back to 1960, though more are always available than the shop shelves or the (now much more readable and informative) list would imply, and 'we can find any 1983, 1982 and 1981 Bordeaux which you may be looking for, though by the case only', they boldly offer. La Réserve is one of the few sources here of sparkling Clairette de Die; the Brut 1981 at just over £4 is one of the tastier Champagne alternatives, and sweeter tooths might try the even less common Clairette de Die Tradition 1982 at the same price.

BEST BUYS [£] House wines, La Vieille Ferme, [££] Clairette de Die

[£] indicates wines under £3, [££] wines £3–£5 and [£££] wines over £5.

Russell & McIver ☞

The Rectory, St Mary-at-Hill, London, EC3 TEL 01-283 3575

OPEN Mon–Fri 9 am–5.30 pm CLOSED Sat, Sun, public holidays
CREDIT CARDS Not accepted DISCOUNTS Not available DELIVERY Free in London, min 1 case, and in Home Counties, min 4 cases; elsewhere on UK mainland £3 for 1 case, £1 for 2–3 cases GLASS HIRE Free
TASTINGS AND TALKS Several times a year in London and country for customers CELLARAGE £2.40 per case per year

Seriously intent upon passing on every tiniest detail of their wine experience to their customers, Russell & McIver produced last summer yet another fine pale blue and cream tome, weighed down by adjectives, a lengthy tasting note on every wine, a helpful vintage chart, advice on when to drink, hints on serving, combinations with food, background on the growers and stories of how R & M discovered this refreshing and most satisfying glass of claret one fine morning when. . . . This traditional City firm sells mostly to City Institutions, Livery Companies, banks and finance houses, restaurants and clubs, but a second column in the list throughtfully caters for VAT-paying individuals, too. It is a well-bought listful of wines, and though particularly strong on Burgundy, it is well balanced, in the lower price ranges, by a carefully chosen list of French country wines: try the two varietal Vins de Pays d'Oc from the Caves des Salins du Midi, a Sauvignon 1982 and a Cabernet, both deliciously fresh and fruity at £2.65; or the Vin de Pays des Côtes de Gascogne, Cépage Colombard 1983, fragrant and fresh, for £2.42. There are good Rhônes and Alsace wines, too, and some fine Beaujolais from Duboeuf and Loron, while clarets range temptingly from the *petit* to the fairly *grand*, from 1983 (opening offers were rather expensive) sparsely back to a couple of examples from the 1950s and 1960s. But the Burgundy list is the main strength of their French collection, a shortish but fine list of growers' wines beginning at £3.68 for a Domaine St-Prix 1982, Bourgogne Passetoutgrain des Coteaux de St-Bris, Louis Bersan, to £14.95 for the 1979 vintage of Clos Vougeot Grand Cru Ch de la Tour, Domaine Morin. German wines, likewise, have been bought from many sources, firms and estates. From Spain, the Torres and Riojanas wines are good, as are the Rosemount Australians, though prices here are a bit expensive – value from this list is to be found on the exclusive and less common wines. Two unusual finds are the Cognac aperitif Pineau des Charentes Ch de Beaulon, of which the white is unusually made of solely Sauvignon-based wine and the red from Cabernet Sauvignon (both are £5.98); and, an interesting after-dinner alternative to Cognac, Vieux Marc de Bourgogne, Domaine Dubreuil Fontaine (£12.08).

BEST BUYS [£] French country wines, [£]–[£££] own-label wine, [££]–[£££] Burgundies

Prices are correct to the best of our knowledge in summer 1984.

Safeways

See CHAINS AND SUPERMARKETS

J Sainsbury & Co

See CHAINS AND SUPERMARKETS

David Scatchard

4 Temple Court, Liverpool TEL 051-236 6468

OPEN Mon–Fri 9.30 am–6 pm Sat 9.30 am–2 pm CLOSED Sun, public holidays CREDIT CARDS Not accepted; personal and business accounts DISCOUNTS Case orders qualify for trade prices; £1 for cash and carry DELIVERY Free in UK, min 5 cases; £4.50 for up to 4 cases, IOW £1.50 and IOM £1 surcharge GLASS HIRE Free TASTINGS AND TALKS On request, charges between £1 and £3 per head CELLARAGE Not available

David Scatchard has been wheeling and dealing in the wine business for many years, and Spanish wines have been his first love ever since he moved out of the Spanish fruit trade 20 years ago. He moved again last year, with the new financial backing of brewers Greenall Whitley, from his old cellars under the former Liverpool fruit exchange into larger premises in Victoria Street. David Scatchard doesn't issue a list – specialising in bin-ends and special offers, he finds stock turnover too unpredictable. The De Soto range of sherries is uniformly excellent, from a wonderful, subtle, very dry, delicate fino, lighter in alcohol than most finos in this country, through a glorious dry and nutty Oloroso, to one of the few readily available Pedro Ximenez wines found in the UK [£]–[££]. For fans of this producer, the Medium Dry Montilla from his Iberia range is another example of its concentrated, raisiny fruit overlaid with the dark, slightly burnt flavour typical of Montilla. Mr Scatchard is the importer of Campo Viejo Riojas, wines which never cease to amaze in their consistency, coming as they do from a winery of factory-like proportions. The range starts with a light, easy 1978 Crianza (£2.19) and proceeds through very good, plummy, 1976 Reserva (£2.95) and 1973 Gran Reserva (£3.95) to the top wine, the 1970 Marqués de Villamagna (£5.52), a sweet, concentrated, oaky giant of a wine. You will also find, at rather high prices, the excellent Riojas of La Rioja Alta, CVNE and Cáceres and the full Torres range. Mr Scatchard does his own bottlings of single malt whiskies bought in bond and matured, and finds he can make an adequate return selling 12-year-olds at about the same price one would pay for an ordinary blended Scotch. At our last scouting, he had a Highland Park and a Glen Rothes, both at £7.95, and a 15-year-old Macallan at £9.95. Early last summer, he was blending his own port, too, variously dubbed 'Father's Blend', 'Scatchard's Special' or 'Old Man's Mix', from young Taylor ruby and some older tawny port that had thrown a sediment – and was selling it on tap. For a novel party drink, try his punch, blended at the end of the week from whatever is at hand, and as likely to contain whisky as wine.

BEST BUYS [£] Fino Soto, [££] Campo Viejo Tinto Crianza 1978, [£££] 10/15-year-old malt whiskies from the barrel

Seckford Wines

41 Martlesham Heath, Ipswich, Suffolk TEL (0473) 626681

OPEN Tue–Sat 10 am–6 pm Sun 10 am–1 pm CLOSED Mon CREDIT CARDS Not accepted DISCOUNTS Not available DELIVERY Free in London and Suffolk for 5+ cases; elsewhere £1.50 per case for 1–5 cases, £1.25 per case for 6–10 cases GLASS HIRE Free TASTINGS AND TALKS In-store tastings CELLARAGE On request

'Taste before you buy,' declares the slash across the front of this three-year-old company's slim-line folded list. If you do, there are some interesting wines shipped from the property amongst their French selection, including the rich and complex Châteauneuf-du-Pape Ch de Beaucastel 1980 (£5.65) and its second wine, Côtes-du-Rhône Cru de Coudoulet 1982 (£3.50), and the star of the Hérault, Mas de Daumas Gassac 1981 (£4.95). The list hops in utter confusion from country to country, area to area, wines being listed in several random batches of white and red and then white wines again, only price dictating the order within each batch. Seckford's greatest strength is their list of over 70 clarets, back as far as 1947; there are one or two old Burgundies, too, and ports going back like the clarets to 1947, with some particularly good prices for the younger ports. Prices in general are not low, however, on the list of this Suffolk merchant.

BEST BUYS [£££] Vintage ports

Sélection Gault Millau

HEAD OFFICE Whiclar Wines, Mill Lane, Bridge, Canterbury, Kent TEL (0227) 830439
Ford Farm Wines, Ford Farm, Aldbourne, Marlborough, Wiltshire TEL (0672) 40206
Gallery Wines, Station Road, Halstead, Sevenoaks, Kent TEL (095 93) 2439
Just in Case Wines, 17 Thornvale, Abram, Wigan, Lancashire TEL (0942) 861856
Christopher Laws Wines, 86B Bancroft, Hitchin, Hertfordshire TEL (0462) 36881
Markham House Wines, Markham House, Martcombe Road, Easton in Gordano, Bristol, Avon TEL (027 581) 2276
Old Wine Shop, 127 Lambourne Road, Chigwell Row, Essex TEL 01-501 3414

Perfect Partners, The Green, Saltwood, Hythe, Kent TEL (0303) 65330
Platform Wines, Station Approach, East Horsley, Surrey TEL (048 65) 4968
St Lawrence Wine Cellar, 5 High Street, St Lawrence, Ramsgate, Kent TEL (0843) 593947
Sandell Wines, 7 Cinnaminta Road, Headington, Oxfordshire TEL (0865) 61446
Studio 54, 54 St Leonards Road, Windsor, Berkshire TEL (075 35) 66961
Sutton Courtenay Provisions, 5 High Street, Sutton Courtenay, Oxfordshire TEL (0235) 848320
Tettenhall Wine Merchants, Rock House Cellars, Old Hill, Tettenhall, West Midlands TEL (0902) 741801
Vinopoly, 17B Lower Road, Chalfont St Peter, Buckinghamshire TEL (0753) 888781
Warrior Wines, 15 London Road, St Leonards-on-Sea, East Sussex TEL (0424) 432393
Wine Rack, 38C Cambridge Street, Wellingborough, Northamptonshire TEL (080 12) 3154

CREDIT CARDS Access/Euro, Amex, Visa DISCOUNTS 2.5% on orders over £200
DELIVERY £3 per case anywhere in UK GLASS HIRE Not available
TASTINGS AND TALKS On request CELLARAGE Not available
MAIL ORDER ONLY

This efficient, large-scale mail order business was sold in the summer of 1984 to Kent wine wholesalers Whiclar Wines, who intend to continue to buy the range selected by famous French gastronomes Gault and Millau and the UK company's former proprietor Chris Dolley, though there may be a few changes to the range later in 1985. The Gault Millau selection in Britain is an interesting mix of good wines from the better and the lesser-known wine regions of France. Many of them are wines that have appeared in the *Gault Millau* magazine, others are Dolley 'finds' that have been submitted to Gault and Millau for tasting. Nearly but not every wine on the list is labelled with its grower's name, but this list is extraordinarily helpful, despite these few small oversights, in giving a tasting note for each wine, a when-to-drink symbol, a fruitiness factor for red wines (tannic wines being on the low end of the scale, fruit or no, but we know what they mean) and a sweetness factor for whites. Look for good-value, low-priced wines amongst the 'country wines for everyday drinking', especially the Cabernet Sauvignon Vin de Pays des Coteaux de l'Ardèche (£2.30) and the Colombard, Vin de Pays des Côtes de Gascogne (£2.30), and others from the South of France. Most of the wines are in the lower price ranges £–££, with just a few squeezing over £9, and prices by the single case delivered are fairly competitive. Every case will cost you £3 delivery, however, so it may be best to shop around if you are buying in any quantity. The 12 shops listed above also stock almost exclusively the same range, selling only by the case, and are your best source of these wines if you live near enough to collect.

BEST BUYS Vins de Pays

Selfridges

400 Oxford Street, London, W1 TEL 01-629 1234

OPEN Mon–Wed 9 am–5.30 pm Thur 9 am–7 pm Fri–Sat 9 am–5.30 pm
CLOSED Sun, August Bank Holiday, Easter, Chr Day, Boxing Day
CREDIT CARDS All accepted DISCOUNTS Not available DELIVERY Free in Central London for orders over £10; 50p for smaller quantities GLASS HIRE Not available TASTINGS AND TALKS Regular in-store tastings CELLARAGE Not available

Selfridges' wine pavilion, next to their food department, stocks, at prices surprisingly less over the top than one might expect, a fair range of classics – plus a few surprising exotics. This is one of the best places to come to discover Israeli wines (from a variety of producers) and even an Israeli brandy. There is a real Chinese wine (as opposed to the Bordeaux Sauvignon that often masquerades under a Chinese label), the German-style, medium white Dynasty (£4); Japanese Sake; four different Cornish Meads; plus a tempting selection of unusual syrups such as cerise, grenadine, orgeat and gomme as well as a scattering of wine brands and an array of spirits, liqueurs and pre-mixed or mix-your-own cocktails. Head for the 'Connoisseurs' Collection' under glass wraps at the back of the department if your wallet is fat and you need something special: classed growth clarets are mostly of immature vintages, but there are a few more mature bottles back to 1962; and some interesting Burgundies for £9 a bottle and over share a cabinet with Hugel's Gewürztraminer 1976 Vendange Tardive at £18.95. Ports last summer went back to Cockburn's 1955 at £42. Back on the common shelves, the Loire collection is good: try the sweet Clos Ste-Catherine Coteaux du Layon 1981 (£4.75), the Ladoucette wines [£££] and the excellent Sancerres of Vacheron at just over £5. Italy is the best represented country outside France (and Israel!) though much of the range is unexciting. Try the Chardonnay Atesino, Santa Margharita 1981 (£3.40), Chianti from Vicchiomaggio [££] and Barolos from Pio Cesare [£££]; and for a special occasion, the 1980 Sassicaia (£9.75). Spain is rather sparsely covered. Champagnes, a medium-sized range, are not too expensively priced, and there are some good sparklers: Deinhard Lila Imperial at £5.45 and Langlois-Château and Gratien & Meyer Sparkling Saumurs at around £5. The German range includes a number of mature, sweet 1976s. Below the 'Under £2.70 a bottle' sign, the Selfridges' own-label table wines from Loron are reasonable value at just over £2. Especially with the wines arranged in such a haphazard fashion, Selfridges would do well to provide some information on the shelves about how the wine tastes, and to produce a regular list: no doubt they would sell more, too!

BEST BUYS Unusual bottles such as Sake or Israeli wines

Which? Wine Guide does not accept payment for inclusion, and there is no sponsorship or advertising.

Seymour Ramsay

Southmede, Widmore, Wooburn Green, High Wycombe, Buckinghamshire TEL (062 85) 27210

OPEN Mon–Fri 8.30 am–6 pm Sat 8.30 am–12 midnight CLOSED Sun, public holidays CREDIT CARDS Not accepted; personal and business accounts DISCOUNTS 5% on 5 cases, £1 cash and carry DELIVERY Free within 15 miles for 1 case, free on UK mainland for 5+ cases; otherwise £5 for 1 case, £3 for 2–3 cases, £2 for 4 cases GLASS HIRE Free TASTINGS AND TALKS 5 times a year CELLARAGE Free for first year (except insurance), thereafter by negotiation

The best bargains on the comprehensive list of Master of Wine Jan Critchley-Salmonson are the vintage ports: good 1977s start at under £8 including VAT and 1975s at under £7 – good value particularly within the local single-case free delivery area, but at these prices you will easily beat most other merchants' fetch-and-carry prices if you need two cases or more delivered to your door. But you can extend your California repertoire here with the good value wines of Louis Martini and Felton Empire [£]–[£££]; and the few Australians and Cooks New Zealand wines are worth a try. The short Spanish list comes from a reliable trio of bodegas (La Rioja Alta, CVNE and Marqués de Cáceres), and amongst the Italian wines look out for 1979 Tignanello from Antinori at under £4, and the delicious 1979 Sassicaia at around £9. A modest spread from the major regions of France includes a comprehensive collection of good Alsace wines from Heim, and some very good Burgundies. Prices here are fairly average, and there is plenty of reliable choice amongst the 'everyday drinking wines' that start the list.

BEST BUYS [£££] Vintage ports

Edward Sheldon Ltd

New Street, Shipston-on-Stour, Warwickshire TEL (0608) 61409 or 61639

OPEN Mon–Fri 8.30 am–1 pm, 2 pm–5.30 pm Sat 8.30 am–1 pm CLOSED Sun, Sat pm, public holidays CREDIT CARDS Not accepted; credit against banker's reference DISCOUNTS 5% on case orders, 10% on 6+ cases DELIVERY Free to neighbouring counties, min 1 case; elsewhere in UK mainland and Northern Ireland £2.50 for 2–4 cases, £2 for 5–9 cases, thereafter negotiable GLASS HIRE 40p per doz TASTINGS AND TALKS Spring and autumn tastings CELLARAGE £2.50 per case per year

This traditional family business, which bought out Broadwell Vintners *(see above)* early in 1984, charges fairly high prices for a range which is a little spotty in its quality, but which contains plenty of excellent bottles. This is a good place to come for jumbos. The modest range of Champagnes is rounded off by some immodestly sized bottles, culminating in a salmanazar of Charles Heidsieck NV for £161.69; and a good hoard of magnums, including some older vintages, completes a good range of tempting clarets mostly of the 1970s, but with a fair choice of older vintages back to 1934. Amongst the Beaujolais and Burgundies, look out for Loron, Faiveley and Noëllat. A long list of German estate wines includes some lesser-known as well as some of the top stars, and Deinhard's sparkling Mosel (£4.90) is the best-value sparkler, though Edward Sheldon have not priced it particularly keenly. Spanish wines are uniformly good – a handful each from the La Rioja Alta bodega and Miguel Torres, plus the rich Scholz Hermanos Solera 1885 Málaga (£5.20) and the 10th year Vega Sicilia if your pocket can stretch to £22.84 a bottle to meet your curiosity.

BEST BUYS [££]–[£££] Red Burgundies from Faiveley and Noëllat, Spanish wines

Sherston Wine Company

HEAD OFFICE Sherston, Malmesbury, Wiltshire TEL (0666) 840644
10 shops in the South

OPEN (variable) Mon–Sat 10 am–1 pm, 2 pm–6 pm (Sat 7.30 pm) Sun 12 noon–2 pm CLOSED Public holidays CREDIT CARDS Access/Euro, Visa; personal accounts DISCOUNTS 5% on 5 cases, 5% on cash and carry of case orders, 5% for wine club members DELIVERY Ask locally; normally £1.50 per case, min £3, UK mainland GLASS HIRE Free TASTINGS AND TALKS On request CELLARAGE Not available

Sherston's emphasis is still on Spanish wines, particularly from Rioja, but they now offer a larger selection from France together with Italian, German and a few others from around the world. They run a version of the franchise system, whereby the shops are independently owned by the people running them and no money is creamed off for the privilege of using the name: a sensible and workable framework for bringing their wines to a wider public at generally reasonable prices. The annotated list helpfully indicates the range of Rioja styles from fresh youthful wines that have never seen the inside of a cask such as the white Marqués de Cáceres at around £3, to Gran Reservas like the attractive Cerro Anon 1975 at a little over £5; there's also a good range of light and moderately oaked wines around £3 to £4 such as the flavoursome Viña Ardanza 1976 from the producer La Rioja Alta, or the balanced white Monopole. Penedès offers a selection of Champagne method cava wines including the Codorníu and Freixenet ranges, as well as Torres reds and whites, although the Black Label 1976 is a shade expensive at over £11. From France there are petits-châteaux clarets from 1975 onwards, a few Burgundies from Jadot and Viénot amongst others, and a quick canter round the other regions. Odd nuggets like the dry Tuscan red Villa di Capezzana (over £5) enliven the Italians, and there is the sweet Moscatel de Setúbal from Portugal. From California come Paul Masson's Carafes and varietal wines including the Chardonnay at a not unreasonable £3.50.

BEST BUYS [£]–[£££] Wines from Rioja and the Penedès

André Simon

14 Davies Street, London, W1 TEL 01-499 9144
21 Motcomb Street, London, SW1 TEL 01-235 3723
OPEN Mon–Fri 9.30 am–7 pm Sat 9.30 am–1 pm CLOSED Sun
50–52 Elizabeth Street, London, SW1 TEL 01-730 8108
OPEN Mon–Fri 9.30 am–8.30 pm Sat 9.30 am–7.30 pm Sun 12 noon–2 pm

Annabel's Wine Cellars, 66 Fulham Road, London, SW3 TEL 01-589 1238
OPEN Mon–Fri 9.30 am–7 pm Sat 9.30 am–6 pm CLOSED Sun
CREDIT CARDS Access/Euro, Amex, Visa; personal accounts DISCOUNTS 5% on case orders, more on large orders DELIVERY Free in Central London, min 1 case GLASS HIRE Free TASTINGS AND TALKS For groups on request CELLARAGE Not available

Claret, Burgundy, Champagne and port dominate Ray Gough's central London shops. In Bordeaux the petits-châteaux are well represented and provide reasonable and inexpensive wines for drinking now or in the near future. The classics are here as well, mostly from 1970 onwards, although there are limited stocks of even earlier vintages. Beware of some Mayfair prices like a hefty £19 for Ch Cantemerle 1971. Sauternes and Barsac come in both bottles and halves. Red Burgundies mostly back to 1971 and whites to 1978 are generally well chosen: there are some impressive bottles from producers like Bonneau de Martray and Leflaive, with whites showing particularly well, eg Louis Latour's Puligny-Montrachet Les Folatières 1979 (over £12); but there are reasonable buys at the other end of the scale from amongst their two agency labels, like Sapin's fruity Beaujolais-Villages, Les Champs, Bouthier 1983 (£3.35) and decent straight Chablis 1983 from Rémon (£4.25). You can have a beano in Champagne with over a dozen each of NV and vintage (Salon Le Mesnil 1976 is around £21) and nearly as many pink ones. Elsewhere in France, the list is less distinguished. Italy, although short, has some lovely reds like Sassicaia 1980 (about £10) and Tignanello 1979 (over £8) down to Lungarotti's excellent Rubesco Torgiano 1978 (£3.90). Germany, Spain California and Australia are all short but shouldn't be overlooked. Ports are very good, spanning 50 years from the great 1927 to the great 1977 but are not for penny-pinchers (Taylor 1955 is £60 and the younger vintages are expensive, too). The André Simon label is independently owned by Courtenay wines and the shops stock some, but not all of this sound but mostly unexciting range. Not all prices are at Mayfair level, but don't come here, nevertheless, for bargains.

BEST BUYS £–£££ Italian and Spanish wines

> We should very much appreciate further comments and suggestions of establishments of particular interest to the wine lover. There are report forms at the back of this book.

Soho Wine Market

See Milroy's

Stapylton Fletcher Wines ⓥ

North View, Oast Forge Lane, East Farleigh, Maidstone, Kent TEL (0622) 20200

OPEN Mon–Fri 8 am–6 pm Sat 8.30 am–12.30 pm CLOSED Sun, public holidays CREDIT CARDS Not accepted; personal and business accounts DISCOUNTS £1 per case on 6–10 cases; special cash and carry prices DELIVERY Free in Kent, East Sussex, London, min 1 case; elsewhere on UK mainland and Isle of Wight £1 for up to 2 cases, thereafter free GLASS HIRE Free TASTINGS AND TALKS To groups on request; 1 major local tasting each year, free CELLARAGE By negotiation MAIL ORDER SPECIALISTS

This small business is an efficient mail order operation with a very interesting and good-value list, especially in the French 'regional' spread, which is its speciality. You can also buy cash and carry at better prices at the above (new) address. There are good ranges of single grape variety wines from co-operatives in Haut Poitou and the Ardèche [£], Ch la Jaubertie wines, very good value from Bergerac at just over £3, a good selection of 1983 Beaujolais crus from individual producers, some low-priced Alsace wines [£]–[££] from the co-operative at Ribeauvillé, and in 1984 there was an offer of 1983 clarets of lesser stature than those normally offered elsewhere *en primeur* at low prices. Note how fresh the vintages are, switching early after the harvest, a big plus point as far as white wines are concerned. Outside France, the sherries are good but expensive, and there are some nice estate Germans, mostly of recent vintages, good value Spanish wines (but less interesting Italians), and the Bulgarians and Chileans are worth trying, too. An unusual find is the delicious fortified Stanton & Killeen Muscat à Petit Grain from Australia. The company are now mailing customers every month with bin-ends and other special offers.

BEST BUYS [£] French wines

Louis Stefan Wines

OFFICE, NOT SHOP: The Stable House, California Lane, Bushey Heath, Hertfordshire TEL 01-950 9515

OFFICE OPEN (for telephone calls) 9 am–6 pm, including weekends CREDIT CARDS Not accepted; personal and business accounts DISCOUNTS 5% on 5 cases DELIVERY Free within 15 miles, min 1 case; elsewhere at cost GLASS HIRE £6 per 100 TASTINGS AND TALKS Free quarterly tastings by invitation CELLARAGE £2 per case per year MAIL ORDER ONLY

Louis Stefan Wines are mail-order-only wholesalers – selling mixed or unmixed full cases to the surrounding population of Hertfordshire, who can take advantage of the free local delivery. They specialise particularly in Bordeaux, their short list of mature classed growths backed up by a longer list of lesser-known bourgeois growths and petits-châteaux. The company is rather prone to superlatives: that Louis Roederer is 'one of the finest growers in the world' we are willing to concede, but we have our doubts that 'Lebreton' is 'the finest grower in the Loire'. (He seems to 'grow' from Muscadet right along the Loire to Sancerre, and anyway, we know a number of Lebretons.) Pricing seems to vary, but is generally quite fair, with some bargains – such as Roederer Crystal 1977/8 for £22.13 (inc VAT – note that prices in the list are ex VAT). Interested locals might enquire about the occasional free tastings of wines from the list.

BEST BUYS Champagne

Stonehaven Wines

Grayshot Road, Headley Down, Bordon, Hampshire — TEL (0428) 712700

OPEN Tue–Fri 9 am–1 pm, 2 pm–5 pm Sat 9 am–12.30 pm CLOSED Sun, Mon, public holidays CREDIT CARDS Not accepted DISCOUNTS 5% on unbroken cases, 2.5% on 2+ mixed cases, £1 per case cash and carry DELIVERY Free on UK mainland, min 6 cases; £4.95 for 1 case, £5 for 2 cases, £1.90 per case for 3–5 cases GLASS HIRE Free TASTINGS AND TALKS Approx once a month at Stonehaven CELLARAGE Not available

This family business is celebrating its tenth anniversary as a fine Italian wine merchant as we go to press, its anniversary list and friendly newsletters showing just how good the best Italian wines can be. Stonehaven stock a wide range, importing some wines themselves, buying in others from this country, covering thus all but five southern Italian wine-producing provinces. A particular area of strength for Stonehaven – though a serious area of weakness for Italy in general – is the Veneto, source of many a mouth-puckering Valpolicella and Soave. Stonehaven's Le Ragose (£3.83) is possibly the best of the ordinary Valpolicellas, and the Masi wines are excellent, too [£]–[££], as is the Soave Classico from Pieropan (£4.11) – all things being relative, because Soave cannot be an exciting wine. Try also the Venegazzù, especially the new 1980 vintage when it appears. Tuscany is another area to explore – not only the familiar Antinori wines but also the fruity, well-made Badia a Coltibuono (several vintages are available, but only the mature 1968 Riserva [£6.50] appears in their current list); also the numerous wines from Capezzana (Chianti and Carmignano) and the interesting Montecarlo Bianco 1979, Mazzini (£4.17), one of the best of these Tuscan whites. Look out as well for Italy's most expensive sweet wine and experiment if you dare – we have excellent reports, but have never tasted Picolit 1981 from Butussi (£14.95).

BEST BUYS [£]–[£££] Wines from the Veneto and Tuscany

Stones of Belgravia

6 Pont Street, London, SW1 TEL 01-235 1612
4 Symons Street, London, SW3 TEL 01-730 3346
20 Connaught Street, London, W2 TEL 01-724 1986

OPEN Mon–Sat 10 am–9 pm CLOSED Sun, public holidays CREDIT CARDS Access/Euro, Amex, Visa; monthly personal accounts DISCOUNTS 5% on case orders, 10% on large orders DELIVERY Free in Central London, any quantity; elsewhere in the UK £4.92 for 1 case, £2.61 per case for 2–5 cases GLASS HIRE Free TASTINGS AND TALKS Regular in-store tastings CELLARAGE £2 per case per year

It is perhaps to be expected that mark-ups will be high in such smart shops in such smart parts of town. There are some occasional surprises amongst the more modest of the impressive array of Champagnes – Lanson Black Label, for instance, at £8.99, or Pol Roger at £9.49. But who wants to pay £17.50 for Taylors 1970 Vintage Port? (Maybe someone who appreciates same day free delivery of a single bottle order over the phone . . .?) Other services include bags of ice, and a variety of glass-types, lent free with wine orders. A few recent additions, highish up the price range, add interest to a not terribly imaginative selection: from Washington State, there's Quails Run Johannisberg Riesling 1982 (£6.67) and from Oregon, Knudsen Erath Pinot Noir 1980 (£9.44), one of America's very best Pinots, as it should be at this price; also new are some expensive Rothbury and Petaluma Australian wines [£££]. Best value is to be found amongst the Spanish wines: Marqués de Cáceres, CVNE and Bodegas Beronia, though you would not have to stray far to find these cheaper. Italians from Antinori, Pio Cesare and Frescobaldi are good, too. More shelves are lined by clarets and Burgundies, however, the Burgundies are unexciting, the clarets rather overpriced once more.

BEST BUYS [££] Riojas, [£££] some Champagnes

Tanners Wine Ltd (V)

HEAD OFFICE 26 Wyle Cop, Shrewsbury, Shropshire TEL (0743) 53421

BRANCHES

Shropshire Tanners Cellars Shop, 26 Wyle Cop, Shrewsbury (0743) 61370; Tanners, 72 Mardol, Shrewsbury (0743) 66389; Tanners, 39 Mytton Oak Road, Shrewsbury (0743) 66387; Tanners, 36 High Street, Bridgnorth (074 62) 3148; The Wine Centre, 15 Market Square, Wellington (0952) 55297; Tanners, Southwater Arcade, Telford Town Centre (0952) 504494; **Hereford & Worcester** Pulling & Co Ltd, 4 St Peter Square, Hereford (0432) 272044; Tanners, 5 Bargates, Leominster (0568) 4486; **Wales** Tanners, The Old Brewery, Welshpool, Powys (0938) 2542; Tanners, 10 High Street, Newtown, Powys (0686) 27290; Tanners, 3 Imperial Buildings, King Street, Wrexham, Clwyd (0978) 358334

OPEN Mon–Sat 9 am–5.30 pm CLOSED Sun, public holidays; Newtown and Wellington shops closed all day on towns' early closing day; Wrexham open morning only early closing day CREDIT CARDS Not in shops; Access/Euro, Visa for mail order DISCOUNTS £1 per case cash and carry, £1.20 per unmixed case on 6+ cases, £1.80 per unmixed case on 12+ cases DELIVERY Free in an area from Manchester to Gloucester to the mid-Wales coast to Lichfield (see map in price list) – min 1 case, which may be mixed; elsewhere, 1 case £3.97, 2 cases £3.34 per case, thereafter free GLASS HIRE Free, but 58p per doz for delivery and/or washing TASTINGS AND TALKS £2 per head to groups CELLARAGE Not available

Tanners' fine, extensive autumn 1983 list leaves us on the last page with the quotation from John Ruskin: 'It is unwise to pay too much, but it's worse to pay too little. When you pay too much, you lose a little money – that's all. When you pay too little, you sometimes lose everything, because the thing you bought is incapable of doing the thing it was bought to do.' You are unlikely to pay too little at Tanners – not, we hasten to add, that they overcharge. On the contrary, prices at the lower end [£]–[££] are very competitive, especially with the mixed case wholesale discount, though it's worth shopping around a few other lists before you plunge into any quantity of the finer, mature clarets and vintage ports, as some of these prices are a little over the top. Interesting special mixed cases at regular intervals (The Claret Drinker's Case, Spain and Italy, Everyday French Red, Christmas Dozen) carry an extra case discount on the wholesale price for either four or a dozen different wines. You could reasonably, perhaps, expect to pay more for the sort of service Tanners give: ready, reliable advice to callers or by phone from well-trained staff ('ten of our sales staff have a combined service of 250 years'). Their mail order business was extended over the past year (they now say they mail 12,000 households). Their informative annual autumn list, updated in abbreviated form in April, tells you much more about the wines than vintage, producer, shipper and other basics which others are prone to omit. They offer a special service for weddings and parties, including special discounts on Champagne prices which are already good, and 'all services connected with serving the wine' and will also suggest '. . . the names of some excellent caterers and marquee hire firms'. Quality is good from the bottom up – the clean, fresh Loron table wines at just over £2, and the fresh Chanterelle wines from Chantovent at under £2. Southern French wines are good value here: Ch de Fonscolombe, Coteaux d'Aix-en-Provence red, white and rosé are excellent value at just over £3, and the Minervois wines from the Ch de Gourgazaud [£], and Côtes de Buzet from the excellent co-operative [£]–[££] are good buys, too. Loires are tempting, as are Alsace wines from an unusually wide selection of producers (Kuehn, Hugel, Blanck, Boeckel, Trimbach), while the Rhônes follow the fine trail of the Merchant Vintners, the bargains here too numerous to mention. Burgundies are tempting, too, from Loron, Sauzet, Henri

> [£] means that a wine costs, from most producers and in most British shops, under £3 a bottle, [££] that it costs between £3 and £5, and [£££] that it costs over £5.

Germain, Lafon, Leflaive, with some older Chanson vintages back to 1972. The fine list of clarets is well selected, and, omitting poor vintages, reaches back through half a dozen or more wines of each vintage to 1961. But clarets begin at under £3 with Tanners' own house claret, a lovely, fruity, herby wine with good Cabernet Franc character. The Italian section is still rather disappointing (but try the Antinori and Vicchiomaggio Chianti [££] and Corvo wines [££]). Spanish wines are good, with some snappy prices for Torres, Marqués de Cáceres and CVNE Riojas. There's a small but worthy Californian collection, peaking at the 1976 vintages of Martha's Vineyard and Bella Oaks from Heitz, both at £29.66 a bottle; a few Australians, some South Africans, including one or two good estates like Meerlust; and Ch Musar and Concha y Toro [££] from the Lebanon and Chile. The selection of Madeiras comes unusually from a number of producers (Rutherford & Miles, Cossart Gordon, Leacocks, Blandys). Vintage ports go back to 1955 (but Tanners are certainly not the cheapest source), and the new selection of Tanners' own-label sherries is worth trying. Malt lovers might find an unusual dram or two rounding off the list: there's Sheep Dip eight-year-old from Islay, and Highland malts Mortlach 12, Glen Mhor 8, Old Pulteney 10 and Balbair 10. Tanners richly deserves its triple award.

BEST BUYS Most wines on the list

TD Vintners (Morans and Johnson Marr)

HEAD OFFICE AND WAREHOUSE

4 High Street, Nailsea, Bristol, Avon	TEL (0272) 855166
Morans, 42 Welshback, Bristol, Avon	TEL (0272) 25033
Morans, 6 Trimwood Parade, Stoke Bishop, Bristol, Avon	TEL (0272) 684385
Morans, 41 Forest Hill, Yeovil, Somerset	TEL (0935) 27611
Johnson Marr, 7 Bridge Street, Kingsbridge, Devon	TEL (0548) 3025
TD Vintners, 42 Mill Street, Bideford, Devon	TEL (023 72) 77641
TD Vintners, c/o Perriams Stores, 6 Fore Street, Budleigh Salterton, Devon	TEL (039 54) 3531

OPEN Variable CREDIT CARDS Access/Euro, Visa; personal and business accounts DISCOUNTS Enquire locally DELIVERY Free within a small radius of the shops, min 1 case; elsewhere at cost GLASS HIRE Free TASTINGS AND TALKS On request CELLARAGE Not available

Although mainly wholesalers dealing with the hotel and restaurant trade, TD Vintners have six retail shops and a warehouse – two of the shops and the warehouse in Bristol, the four others scattered through Somerset and Devon. Their shop on Welshback, the cobbled quayside where cargoes destined for Wales used to be loaded, carries most of the range, and a range of cheaper bin-ends. Run by John Moran post-TDV takeover, Morans have a good and varied selection. Chantovent wines from the South-West of France complement some good clarets, with the excellent Nathaniel Johnston Bordeaux generics mid-way.

Germany is heavy with Huesgen Liebfraumilch, but Italians are very well chosen, the short range including 1974 Brunello di Montalcino, Poggio alle Mura (£84.92), 1961 Brunello di Montalcino, Biondi-Santi 1961 (£678.50), the fresh Frascati Colli de Catone (£34.84) and wines from Masi, including his deliciously rich 1977 Amarone Recioto della Valpolicella (£67.50) – all prices are per case and are given here to include VAT. There are good Alsace wines from Kuenz-Bas, fine Riojas from Marqués de Cáceres and Bodegas Gurpeguí, and the odd fine Australian from Hill Smith.

BEST BUYS [£] Ch de Gougazaud, Minervois, red and white, [£]–[££] Nathaniel Johnston Bordeaux generics

Tesco

See CHAINS AND SUPERMARKETS

Threshers

See CHAINS AND SUPERMARKETS

Henry Townsend & Co

Chalk Pit House, Coleshill, Amersham, Buckinghamshire TEL (024 03) 3823
44 Hurlingham Road, London, SW6 TEL 01-736 8729

OPEN (by appointment or telephone) Mon–Fri 8.30 am–10 pm Sat, Sun 9 am–10 pm CLOSED Public holidays CREDIT CARDS Not accepted; personal and business accounts DISCOUNTS 5% on unmixed cases DELIVERY Free in South Buckinghamshire, Ascot and Windsor and Berkhamsted areas, Central London, City of London, Hampstead, Highgate, Fulham and Chelsea, min 1 mixed case; elsewhere £4.50 for 1 case, £3.15 for 2–5 cases, £2.55 for 6–10 cases, £2.15 for 11+ cases GLASS HIRE Free TASTINGS AND TALKS Locally and in London for customers CELLARAGE £2.90 per case in first year, thereafter £2.50 MAIL ORDER Available

Wine drinkers have obviously become more and more appreciative of the excellent value offered by Henry Townsend, because as we went to press, details were being finalised for their move into larger premises, manned by more staff, in Beaconsfield. (New customers should contact Philip Henry Townsend Eyres at his Amersham home address above, or his new partner John Casson at his London home address for details of the company's whereabouts in 1985.) Henry Townsend sell only by the case, and if mixed cases are very well priced, prices for unmixed cases are very competitive indeed, especially to anyone living within their free delivery area – a large slice of London and within 20 miles or so of their Buckinghamshire base. The list is long and well balanced, with an emphasis on France and Germany but with plenty of wines of excellent quality to keep the adventurous happy, too. Supplementary lists offer wines for laying down – Rhônes and Germans as well as the more usual *en primeur* Burgundies and clarets of varying stature. The 'possible maturing date' on these young-wine lists is useful. Champagne prices are good here, beginning with an assortment of the lovely wines of Bruno Paillard at £7.80 for the Brut, through a number of well-priced better-established names like Roederer, Krug and Alfred Gratien to an unusual collection of vintage Champagnes back to 1970. Young white Burgundies include the fine Chablis of Louis Michel as well as wines from Jadot and Latour; reds 'for drinking' in the main list are from more varied sources back to 1976, including quite a few domaine-bottled wines. From Bordeaux, there's a good choice of dry whites: don't miss the delicious wines of Ch Thieuley, Entre-Deux-Mers Sec at just over £3; but look for more expensive dry Graves, too. Clarets go back to 1966. The Rhône section of the Townsend list has been extended this year to include Chapoutier and Guigal as well as Paul Jaboulet Aîné, and both reds and whites are a tempting if small array. Loires include the fine Foreau Vouvrays [£££], and there is a mixture of interesting Alsace wines, largely from Trimbach. The German list is as impressive as the French – a pure, unadulterated Riesling list concentrating mostly on Kabinett, Spätlese and Auslese with a large proportion of mature 1976s and famous names in abundance: Maximin Grünhaus, von Schubert, Friedrich-Wilhelm Gymnasium. . . . From the rest of Europe, there's a very full range of Torres wines including some of the older and finer reds; the only other Spanish contenders are two wines from La Rioja Alta – the 1976 Viña Ardanza is excellent value at £3.60. South Tyrol whites from Tieffenbrunner and Kettmeir are very refreshing, mostly around £3, and the two dry white Austrians from Lenz Moser and Bründelmeyer, new to the list, are worth trying at around £4. From further afield, try the Concha y Toro wines of Chile [£]–[££], something from the small but well-chosen bunch of California wines, or Brown Brothers Australians. Port here is fairly well priced, whether for laying down or, from vintages from 1960 to 1968, for drinking now.

BEST BUYS Most things on the list

T & W Wines

51 King Street, Thetford, Norfolk TEL (0842) 63855

OPEN Mon–Sat 9.30 am–5.50 pm Sun, public holidays by arrangement CLOSED Sun, public holidays CREDIT CARDS All accepted DISCOUNTS Not available DELIVERY Free within 15 miles of Thetford, min 1 case; elsewhere £4 for 1–2 cases, thereafter free GLASS HIRE Free TASTINGS AND TALKS Organised wine trips to France CELLARAGE £2.75 per case per year

The initials may sound impersonal, but this is a courteous, friendly and helpful little business, which specialises in old vintages of claret, Burgundy, port and other wines, but which also sells fine wines for laying down, and a selection of younger medium to high-priced wines like Sancerre and Chablis for drinking now. Prices are not as keen as they used to be at T & W (note that VAT is to be added to prices in the bi-monthly list). It takes dedication and substantial capital, however, to put together such an immense list of mature wines, which begins as it means to go on with a bottle of 1863 Latour for £1,200 + VAT. Nine large pages later, we round up with Mouton 1982 for £35 + VAT, followed by a page of white Bordeaux, sweet back to 1900, dry back to 1971. Burgundies young and old, a shorter but still substantial list, come principally from the Domaine de la Romaneé-Conti, with a consort of Doudet Naudin and younger vintages from Louis Latour, plus a wider selection of whites, including again a few elderly Doudet Naudins. Doudet Naudin pops up again in the Rhône with more old vintages; his Châteauneuf is £14 + VAT; and you will find some old Germans (probably more pleasant now to look at than to drink) amongst the recent vintages, and old Madeiras and ports at prices a little over the average.

BEST BUYS Mature wines

Unwins

See CHAINS AND SUPERMARKETS

Valley Wine Cellars

Drusilla's Corner, Alfriston, East Sussex TEL (0323) 870532

OPEN Mon–Fri 9 am–5 pm Sat, Sun By appointment Public holidays By appointment CLOSED Sat, Sun, public holidays (exc by appointment) CREDIT CARDS Not accepted; personal and business accounts DISCOUNTS 5% on case orders DELIVERY Free within Central London and 15 mile radius of Alfriston, min 5 cases; elsewhere on request (but expensive) GLASS HIRE Free TASTINGS AND TALKS On request CELLARAGE By arrangement

The main interest of the Valley Wine Centre is the English wine list, the most extensive in the country, and a good selection from some of the best winemakers. This is a good place to come for the freshest vintages (so many shops seem to stock tired and aged English wines as turnover is slow) – only 1982s and 1983s were quoted on the Centre's summer 1984 list, and there were to be more 1983s on the next list, and lower prices, too, since the sun shone so extraordinarily kindly on the English vines in 1983. Don't miss the foot-note in the list – prices exclude VAT – do only companies, the extra profitably self-employed and mathematicians have a taste for English wines? VAT-less prices range from £29.75 a case for Sussex County 1983, the first 'generic' English wine, to £44.42 for Westbury Rosé 1982. The Valley Wine Centre has only a wholesale licence, so you can buy only by the case, but 'samples will be invoiced at list price and credited should an order result from the tasting'. There is a vineyard here, too, well equipped to deal with tourists, even down to a small wine museum. The English

Wine Festival is held here early every September. You will also find quite a fair selection of foreign wines at Drusilla's Corner, a bit expensive, but useful if you live locally. Mead is an interesting oddity at £2.44 (+37p VAT).

BEST BUYS English wines

Helen Verdcourt Wines (V) ☞

Spring Cottage, Kimbers Lane, Maidenhead, Berkshire — TEL (0628) 25577

OPEN All the time (24-hour answering machine) CREDIT CARDS Not accepted DISCOUNTS 5% on 12+ cases DELIVERY Free in Central London, Berkshire, Buckinghamshire, Hampshire and Surrey, min 1 case; free occasionally to other areas – enquire GLASS HIRE Free TASTINGS AND TALKS Regular tutored tastings CELLARAGE Not available

Helen Verdcourt's business is based entirely on tutored tastings to her regular monthly clubs in Maidenhead and Egham, plus other occasional tastings elsewhere. Quality is generally good, prices generally low, and readers report 'personal, prompt service and attention (she remembered a passing telephonic query and got an individual quote for me on a specific wine I had been unable to find)'. A wine tour organised for 20 people last summer by this obviously very hard-working one-woman band went to some respected growers (her suppliers) in Chablis, Burgundy, the Rhône and Sancerre. Not all the wines in stock are listed. They include, at the bottom end, a good red and white from the Ch de Gourgazaud in the Minervois (both £2.35) and good Gamay and Syrah de l'Ardèche from the St-Désirat co-operative (£2.65). From the Loire there is Sauvion's excellent 1983 Muscadet (£2.60), and from Burgundy, the lovely wines of Tollot-Beaut and Beaujolais from Georges Duboeuf. Jaboulet dominates the Rhônes, and the pleasant dessert wine Muscat de Rivesaltes from Aphrodis is quite well priced at £4.60. There's a fair selection of good, younger clarets (though *some* of the prices here are rather higher that one might expect in view of the very reasonable prices on the rest of the list). Alsace wines come from Gisselbrecht, and the exceptional 1983s were on sale by the summer of 1984. Spanish suppliers include Torres and León, both good value, and there's some well-priced Marqués de Cáceres – especially the red 1983 at £2.80. The Italian range is equally impressive: Tieffenbrunner South Tyrol wines at around £3, Capezzana wines from Tuscany £–££ and Lungarotti's Rubesco Torgiano from Umbria (£4.05) are all worth trying. An Australian contingent is largely from Brown Bros, bolstered by a few others ££–£££.

BEST BUYS £ Marqués de Cáceres and Rivarey wines, £££ Tollot-Beaut Burgundies

Victor Hugo Wines

19 Halkett Street, St Helier, Jersey TEL (0534) 78173
15 Bath Street, St Helier, Jersey TEL (0534) 20237

OPEN Mon–Sat 9 am–5.30 pm CLOSED Sun, public holidays CREDIT CARDS Not accepted; personal and business accounts DISCOUNTS 5% on 5+ cases DELIVERY Free, min 1 case all over the Island GLASS HIRE Free TASTINGS AND TALKS 4 tastings a year for private customers; for groups on request CELLARAGE £1 per case per year

These helpful shops are the retail outlets of Ann Street Brewery's wine division. The tax-haven prices look most alluring to mainland eyes, as do some of the Victor Hugo agencies, which include the elegant, austere Schlumberger Alsace wines, Laurent-Perrier Champagne, and the good sparklers of Gratien, Meyer & Seydoux from Saumur, clarets from Sichel, Burgundies from Louis Latour, sound German wines from Guntrum and the always reliable Márques de Cáceres Riojas, along with their second wines, Rivarey. Alongside a number of good wines from Sichel are more well-chosen clarets – such as Larose-Trintaudon, Camensac and Castéra, with an especially large choice of 1979s. The Italian and Portuguese ranges are unexciting. Go for the Fetzers in the California section. You will find some interesting spirits and liqueurs here, too.

BEST BUYS [£]–[£££] Schlumberger Alsace wines, [£] Marqués de Cáceres and Rivarey, [£]–[£££] clarets

The Victoria Wine Company

See CHAINS AND SUPERMARKETS

La Vigneronne

105 Old Brompton Road, London, SW7 TEL 01-589 6113

OPEN Mon–Sat 9.30 am–11 pm Sun and public holidays 12 noon–2 pm, 7–10 pm CLOSED Christmas Day and Boxing Day CREDIT CARDS All accepted DISCOUNTS 5% on cash and carry case orders, 10% on selected lines DELIVERY Free in Kensington, Chelsea, Battersea, Notting Hill, Victoria, Bayswater, Shepherds Bush, Hammersmith, Westminster, City, West End – min half-bottle; other London postal districts £2 per case on 1–23 bottles, £1.50 per case on 24–59 bottles, free for larger orders; on UK mainland £4 per case on 1–23 bottles, £2.50 a case for 24–59 bottles, larger orders free GLASS HIRE Free TASTINGS AND TALKS *See below* CELLARAGE Not available

It is unlikely that you will ever be disappointed with wines you buy from La Vigneronne. Younger wines tend to be on the light side, fruity, well chosen. But if you're after old vintages, La Vigneronne comes into its own. There's a fascinating selection in this little treasure trove in the Old Brompton Road, where you could browse for hours amongst well-selected wines from all over the world, shelves filled with vintages back to the 19th century, but nevertheless a good selection of some of the best wines hot off more modern presses. About a third of the stock in the shop is bought at auction or from private cellars. With careful buying, Liz Berry MW and her ex-merchant-banker husband Mike Berry manage to put wines on their shelves at prices little higher than those at auction. The selection changes constantly. Older vintages are a speciality in most of the regions they stock. There's a huge range of clarets back to 1904, red Burgundies back to 1920, whites back to 1949, Amarone back to 1958, and an 1866 Sercial amidst the long Madeira list. Bordeaux and Italy are particularly well covered, as is the Loire, with a mouth-watering selection of sweet whites. The Rhône section is good. La Vigneronne concentrates on older vintages in Germany and, unusually, in California, where the Berrys bought heavily when they set up shop four years ago. The California list goes back to 1975. There's a whole page of Australians, too, also concentrating on the older vintages. Not a branded wine in sight, though one recent list did offer Mouton Cadet: at £33.90 a bottle for the first ever vintage, 1934! The list is now annotated with advice on when each wine will be ready to drink. Long as the list is, the Berrys say they will extend their range again this year. They are already importing a lot more wines direct, rather than buying from wholesalers, which makes for a more interesting and exclusive choice. They also offer their services as wine sleuths to seek out for you any wine you cannot find. Good-value, by-the-case offers are made every two months to customers by mail. And La Vigneronne wine tastings are held almost weekly at prices between £5 and £20 in a hotel near the shop, tutored by 'famous names' in the wine world.

BEST BUYS [£] Syrah de L'Ardèche, house claret, [££] Sauvignon de St-Bris, [££] Gigondas L'Oustaù Fauquet, [£££] Ch Chasse-Spleen 1979, Muscat de Beaumes-de-Venise, Domaine de Coyeaux

El Vino Co Ltd

47 Fleet Street, London, EC4 — TEL 01-353 6786
6 Martin Lane, Cannon Street, London, EC4 — TEL 01-626 6876
30 New Bridge Street, London, EC4 — TEL 01-236 4534

OPEN Mon–Fri 11.30–3 pm, 5 pm–8 pm Sat (Fleet Street only) 11 am–3 pm CLOSED Sun, public holidays CREDIT CARDS Access/Euro; personal and business accounts DISCOUNTS Negotiable for quantity; for cash and carry £1 per case up to £50, thereafter £2 DELIVERY Free in the City; elsewhere £2.65 for 1–3 bottles, £4.60 for 4–23 bottles, thereafter free GLASS HIRE Free TASTINGS AND TALKS 2 or 3 times a year at all branches CELLARAGE £1.50 per case per year

Regular drinkers in El Vino's three EC4 wine bars *(see* WINE BARS *section)* will no doubt have tasted the wines of their choice before slipping into the tiny cubicle-shops to place their take-away orders.

Nevertheless, a company with such long experience in the wine trade might at least take the trouble to annotate its list properly with producers' names for the benefit of armchair buyers and men of little memory. It simply isn't enough to tell us that the wines are 'with appellation' or 'without appellation' as the list sections are ridiculously headed. El Vinos have taken a bold step outside the traditional areas of France, Germany, Oporto and Jerez with a solitary Rioja Viña Reál 1980 (£3.70). But quality, from our bar-side tastings, is good, prices, though a bit eccentric, sometimes low, sometimes very high, are often fair, and free delivery within the City is a boon for thirsty business folk.

BEST BUYS Own-label wines

The Vintage House

42 Old Compton Street, London, W1 TEL 01-437 2592
328c Kilburn High Road, London, NW6 TEL 01-624 2064
48 Chapel View, South Croydon, Surrey TEL 01-651 2557
44 East Hill, Dartford, Kent TEL (0322) 76782

OPEN Variable CLOSED Chr Day only CREDIT CARDS Not accepted; personal and business accounts DISCOUNTS For large orders paid cash with order DELIVERY Free within London postal districts for orders over £30 GLASS HIRE Free TASTINGS AND TALKS Approx 1 a month CELLARAGE Not available

Most interesting in this small chain of shops is the range of Australian wines from Brown Bros, Stanley, Penfolds, Leasingham and Great Western. There are plenty of clarets, too, including some mature vintages and a number of magnums. Much of the Burgundy comes from Geisweiler, sound but unexciting. There is an assortment of 15 sweet, mature German wines. The Italian range is rather dull, however. The company is due to launch a new fine wine section in the autumn of 1984.

BEST BUYS ££–£££ Australian wines

Vintage Wines of Nottingham

116 Derby Road, Nottingham, Nottinghamshire TEL (0602) 476565

OPEN Mon–Fri 9 am–5.30 pm Sat 9 am–1 pm CLOSED Sat pm, Sun, public holidays CREDIT CARDS Access/Euro, Visa; personal and business accounts DISCOUNTS 5%+ on mixed case orders cash and carry, 13 bottles for the price of 12 for unmixed cases DELIVERY Free within 30 miles of Nottingham, no min GLASS HIRE Free TASTINGS AND TALKS Occasionally, by invitation; to groups on request CELLARAGE £1 per case per year

It is sad that a company once so keen on Spanish wines has been driven, presumably by local apathy, to reduce their Spanish list to so few bottles, good as the wines of Marqués de Cáceres and CVNE are. No one section of the Vintage Wines list is now particularly long, but it competently covers Europe, with a few oddments to round things off from the rest of the world, including some brands. Prices are rather high in this dark, oak-fitted shop, but bear in mind, if you can't face the haul part way up the Derby Road towards the University, that delivery of any quantity within a 30-mile radius is free, though we have every sympathy when they tell us that they 'get a bit sniffy if it's one bottle'. Impoverished students would do well to head for the tasty Listel range at around £2.70, all reliable, and might celebrate with the good-value Pierre Vaudon Champagne at £8.95 (note that this 'established shipper of advancing reputation' is in fact a highly respectable co-operative, who also supply Marks & Spencer, amongst others). Other Champagnes include lots of lovely Pol Roger – though Champagne prices here are a little higher than you might expect. So are prices of vintage port. There are a small number of clarets, a mix of respectable *négociants'* Burgundies, a big range of Hugel wines from Alsace, including some expensive but delicious 1976 *vendage tardive* wines. There are some good German wines at the higher price levels, and some fair Italians. Vintage Wines offer a very helpful service, which includes gift packaging, advice on wines and catering.

BEST BUYS [£] Listel wines, [££]–[£££] Spanish wines

The Vintners Wain

14 Buckingham Palace Road, London, SW1 TEL 01-828 3967

OPEN Mon–Fri 9.30 am–6.30 pm CLOSED Sat, Sun, public holidays
CREDIT CARDS Access/Euro, Visa; personal and business accounts
DISCOUNTS 5–10% on case orders DELIVERY At cost GLASS HIRE Free
TASTINGS AND TALKS In-store tastings; for groups on request CELLARAGE Not available

Our interest in this little shop in Buckingham Palace Road lies in its big selection of English wines: 42 at the last count, from 27 different vineyards. When this *Guide* appears, most listings should be changing to the 1983 vintage, and this is the one to go for. There are some good wines in the rest of the range – Lustau sherries, vintage ports, Deinhard Germans, Trimbach Alsace and the wine boxes of Berri Estates in Australia – and some uninteresting bottles, too – but they all seem rather more expensive than even the proximity of Buckingham Palace can justify.

BEST BUYS English wines

Waitrose

See CHAINS AND SUPERMARKETS

Most wine merchants will supply wine for parties sale or return.

Waters of Coventry

29 High Street, Coventry, West Midlands TEL (0203) 26657
3 Southborough Terrace, Leamington Spa TEL (0926) 21270

OPEN Mon–Sat 10 am–10 pm Sun and public holidays (Leamington only) 10 am–2 pm, 6 pm–10 pm CLOSED (Coventry) Sun, public holidays CREDIT CARDS Not accepted; personal and business accounts DISCOUNTS Approx 10% on case orders DELIVERY £1 locally for delivery of cut-price goods, otherwise free; elsewhere on UK mainland £4 for 1–4 cases, £1 per case for 5–10 cases GLASS HIRE 20p per doz TASTINGS AND TALKS Organised occasionally CELLARAGE 50p per case per year

Waters of Coventry are expensive, though you may find some bargains on their occasional lists of special offers. But quality is good if money is no object: Lustau sherries, clarets, Bacheroy-Josselin Chablis [££]–[£££], excellent Rhônes [£]–[£££], a short list of good Germans, fair Italians, Mondavi and Brown Bros from California and Australia respectively; and amongst the Spanish wines, go for the Riojas, if you are prepared to pay the highest prices we have come across in the country for the excellent wines of Marqués de Cáceres.

Weavers of Nottingham

1 Castle Gate, Nottingham, Nottinghamshire TEL (0602) 580922

OPEN Mon–Sat 9 am–5.45 pm CLOSED Sun, public holidays CREDIT CARDS All accepted; personal and business accounts DISCOUNTS For case orders, on request DELIVERY Free within 25 miles of Nottingham, min 6 bottles; elsewhere approx £2.95 per case, min 1 case GLASS HIRE 10p per doz TASTINGS AND TALKS On request CELLARAGE Not available

This friendly and helpful company, whose shop and cellars burrow into the Nottingham Castle rock, stock a reasonable range from the major countries of Europe at bottle prices which range from the very keen to the very expensive, but which all or nearly all become keen once the variable but generous case discounts have been applied. Some of the own-label wines are well worth a try: their Germans come from Müller [£] and Meffre makes their Côtes-du-Rhône (£2.89). There is plenty of claret and Burgundy to choose from in the middle to upper price categories, though the Burgundies are not particularly exciting. There is a big range of Hugel wines, including many reserves. You will find some other good Germans, one or two good Italian wines; the Riojas are all worth trying, particularly the big CVNE range, as are the Torres wines from the Penedès. Outside Europe, the more expensive California wines are worth a try, and the Hill Smith Australians are good value. Not all the wines are listed or even displayed, so ask for something special if it doesn't appear to be there. It would be helpful if Weavers included full information of all the producers (including the poor, forgotten Germans and Italians) on the list.

BEST BUYS [£]–[£££] Riojas; wines by the case

Whitesides of Clitheroe

Shawbridge, Clitheroe, Lancashire TEL (0200) 22281

OPEN Mon, Tue, Thur, Fri 9 am–5.30 pm Wed, Sat 9 am–5 pm CLOSED Sun CREDIT CARDS Access/Euro, Visa; personal and business accounts DISCOUNTS 3–5% on unmixed case orders DELIVERY Free in NE Lancashire; elsewhere at cost GLASS HIRE Free TASTINGS AND TALKS For groups on request; biennial comprehensive tasting for customers, entrance fee refundable against order CELLARAGE £1.50 per case per year

Whitesides of Clitheroe stock a good, large assortment of wines from the traditional wine regions, with emphasis on the major French production areas and Germany, at reasonable prices. The wide range of classed growth claret stretches back to 1960. Burgundies, back to 1970, are dominated by the sound wines of Emile Chandesais; Alsace is from Sipp. Loires comprise a fair selection – try especially Jean Beaumard's delicious Savennières 1979 (£4.60) and Quarts de Chaume 1974 (£5.60). Amongst a number of wines from the South-West of France, the Côtes de Buzet co-operative wines are very good £–££. The German list is particularly impressive, with plenty of mature vintages of better quality levels from highly respected names such as Bürklin-Wolf and the Diefenhard'sches Weingut, and there is an unusual selection of Tokay, too, going back to a 1964 Tokay Aszu Eszencia. The big Italian range is unexciting, however. Perhaps the standard of foreign language teaching in Clitheroe is to blame – but if we give our 'worst spelling award' to nearby David Byrne, our 'worst use of accents award' must, we fear, be bestowed upon Whitesides.

BEST BUYS ££–£££ German wines, £–£££ clarets

Whittals Wines

See CHAINS AND SUPERMARKETS

Willoughby's Ltd

53 Cross Street, Manchester TEL 061-834 0641
100 Broadway, Chadderton, Oldham, Lancashire TEL 061-620 1374

OPEN Mon–Fri 9 am–6 pm Sat 9 am–5 pm (Chadderton branch Wed and Sat till 1 pm) CLOSED Sun, public holidays CREDIT CARDS Access/Euro, Visa; personal and business accounts DISCOUNTS For quantity, sometimes, by arrangement DELIVERY Free for full cases within Greater Manchester, elsewhere at cost GLASS HIRE Free TASTINGS AND TALKS 10 a year for Willoughby's Wine Society, lunchtime tastings for businessmen, regular in-store tastings; tastings to groups on request CELLARAGE £1.04 per case per year

You could spend pleasurable hours scouting around the shelves of this fine Manchester merchant, subsidiary since 1968 of Lees the brewers. Behind the counter you will find sound product knowledge, swift, courteous service and advice. Prices are fair, not cheap, apart from some remarkable bargains amongst the well-selected sherry brands and the sparkling wines: no fewer than 45 sparklers at very good prices. There's an extraordinary sparkling range: Saumur; Blanquette de Limoux; others from Italy, Spain, California, South Africa and even two from the Crimea £££ (which we don't recommend!). Deinhard Lila is definitely worth a try amongst the sparkling Germans ££ – perhaps the best of all the sparkling range – though German prices are not such bargains. That's not to mention Champagnes, of which there are 82 different brands, sizes and vintages back to 1973 – again fair prices here, not exactly cheap, but what a choice! Clarets are the other major speciality, wide-ranging in price, with a fine range back to 1973 and thereafter a scattering back to 1964. (What a pity the wines are all mixed up within the vintage lists; some advice on what is ready, and how long to keep them would be welcome.) On the long but less outstanding Burgundy list (Chandesais, Chanson and Drouhin prevail) are to be found quite a lot of older vintages (back to 1969) at very reasonable prices. There's a fine choice of 11 Hugels ££ – £££ from Alsace, including two delicious 1976 Vendange Tardive wines, Riesling and Gewürztraminer at well over £10. There are plenty of good German wines (lots from Deinhard, again, and Sichel). The Torres range ££ – £££ is the pick of the Spanish section (why no vintages on the list?); try their wines from Chile, too ££. We find the Morandell Austrians rather 'toffeeish' and not to our taste. Nine English wines are a rarity so far north of the growing regions, and one it seems that Mancunians are slow to appreciate: beware old vintages if they have not moved on by the time the *Guide* is published from the tired old 1979s, 1980s and even a 1977 Huxelrebe! South Africa, your politics permitting, is represented by some good estates. Try the lovely sweet Moscatel de Setúbal from Portugal, particularly the fruitier five-year-old (£4.20); or Tokays up to the 1975 Five Puttonyos ££. Red Ch Carras in the Greek section is very good (Bordeaux grapes) and worth a try, but not a repeat, perhaps, at over £4. There are also Kosher wines, Bulgarian wines, sensibly still Argentine wines and a selection from Ch Musar. Willoughby's are one of very few companies in the country who sell Swiss wines – we wonder who buys them at between £4 and £7. You may enjoy a not too expensive browse on the California shelf, and try the New Zealand whites from Cooks, Montana and Marlborough. You would search far and wide for a better selection of malts and vatted whiskies, vintage Armagnacs and liqueurs, too.

BEST BUYS £ – ££ Sparkling wines, ££ sherries, most things on the list

Windrush Wines Ⓥ

The Barracks, Cecily Hill, Cirencester, Gloucestershire TEL (0285) 67121

OPEN Mon–Fri 9 am–5.30 pm Sat By appointment CLOSED Sun, public holidays CREDIT CARDS Not accepted: personal and business accounts DISCOUNTS 75p per case cash and carry; 5% on 5+ cases DELIVERY Free locally;

free elsewhere for 5+ cases, £3 per case for 1–2 cases, £2 per case for 3–4 cases GLASS HIRE Free TASTINGS AND TALKS On request, wines at list price; free tastings for club members CELLARAGE £1.50 per case per year

It might have been difficult to pick out an area in which to start our praise of Mark Savage MW's list of fairly priced wines of exemplary quality had he not specialised some years ago in the wines of the North-West USA: the states of Washington, Oregon and Idaho north of California. These wines are generally lighter than those from California, more elegant owing to a cooler climate. Try the Riesling 1982 (£4.98) from Tulatin; Associated Vintners' tough Bordeaux look-alike 1981 Cabernet Sauvignon, Red Willow Vineyard 1981 (£8.59); Knudsen Erath Pinot Noir 1980 (£6.99), far superior to any Pinot Noir we have yet tasted from California and tasting rather more of Pinot Noir than many a Burgundy. Windrush also stock a number of California wines; they are agents for Conn Creek, Matanzas Creek and St Clement and also sell Far Niente, Round Hill and Cuvaison. But back across the Atlantic, look also on this well-written, personal and informative list for a fine selection from the major areas and also for a few out-of-the-way wines such as the Cahors, Clos la Coutale – much more drinkable than most – for just over £3. Amongst the cheaper wines, good value is to be found in the Oisly-et-Thésée Cabernet and Sauvignon from the Loire at under £3, and in the Loron table wines which start the list at around £2. Mr Savage might helpfully make clear which clarets are/will be ready for drinking when – the list is heavily on the younger vintages, from 1982 to 1971, and is a tempting selection with special emphasis on Chx Cissac and Ausone; there are selected vintages of the latter from 1967 to 1983, as well as vintages of Chx Belair and Roc Blanquant, which both belong to the owner of Ch Ausone. Beaujolais are all domaine or single vineyard wines from a variety of growers, including a number from the reliable Loron. Amongst an interesting list of high quality growers' Burgundies, look out especially for the Aligoté 1982 from Rion (£3.74) and his Nuits-St-Georges, Premier Cru, Les Haut Pruliers 1980 (£12.70) for another example of what Pinot Noir *really* tastes like. The Mâcon-Clessé 1982 from Thévenet is good value at £4.22. The few Rhônes are well worth trying, and so is the lovely Bandol, Domaine Tempier 1980 (£4.74). Gitton Sancerres are amongst the best ££. It is difficult to find the lovely clean, elegant Rieslings of Balthazar Ress of Hattenheim elsewhere in this country; look out for wines with unusual labels, like the delicious, mature Hattenheimer Wisselbrunnen Riesling Auslese 1976 with its decorated piece of sandpaper for a label (£11.26). There are some other fine German estate wines, too. From Spain come the fine Riojas of La Rioja Alta £–££ and powerful Chardonnay 1981 and Cabernet 1979 from Jean León in the Penedès (£7.25 and £5.73). For a refreshing dessert wine, try amongst the Italian range Vietti's Moscato Naturale del Piemonte (£3.46) a high quality almost still version of Asti Spumante; the Tieffenbrunner wines of the SouthTyrol are good value at just over £3, as are the lovely but tough and rather expensive Barbarescos of Gaja ££–£££. Sherries from Barbadillo are delicious, the fino excellent value at under £3, and the rich, nutty dry Amontillado Principe (£4.29) makes a very good, unusual aperitif. There are some old wines, too, from the fine bodega of La Riva. Domaine Cognac and Calvados, and white spirits from Alsace such as eau-de-vie de Gewürztraminer or Framboise Sauvage, in half-bottles, might tempt you at the end of the list.

BEST BUYS Most things on the list, especially wines mentioned above

The Wine Case Place

56 Bedford Street, Leamington Spa, Warwickshire TEL (0926) 881421

OPEN Tue–Wed 10 am–6 pm Thur–Sat 10 am–7 pm CLOSED Mon, Sun, public holidays CREDIT CARDS Access/Euro, Visa DISCOUNTS 5% on mixed cases, 10% on unmixed cases DELIVERY Free within 25 miles, min 5 cases; elsewhere for smaller quantities £4 for 1–4 cases, £1 for each subsequent case GLASS HIRE Free TASTINGS AND TALKS Free tasting each month, by invitation CELLARAGE Not available

This new wine warehouse opened its doors in December 1983, stocking largely the same range as Waters of Coventry *(see above)*, and aiming to attract 'both the experienced wine lover and the novice who is perhaps deterred by the "stuffy" image of the traditional wine merchant'.

The Wine Club (of the Sunday Times)

New Aquitaine House, Paddock Road, Reading, Berkshire TEL (0734) 481713

OTHER DETAILS *See Bordeaux Direct, above* MAIL ORDER ONLY

The Wine Club is owned by the same company as Bordeaux Direct *(see above)*, run under contract for *The Sunday Times*, but only a score or so of wines span both lists, and this one sports more merchants' wines than its sister company's. Hugh Johnson is club president, and advises on wine buying. If you're searching for something specific, the list is hard to follow because wines are arranged, red, white and rosé separately, in ascending order of price, with the countries all mixed up. Each wine has a useful tasting note, and a symbol to indicate when to drink – including such lengthy sophistications as: 'Wine enjoyable now, although young, but which will be more interesting when it gets a bit of the flavour of age. Will develop over six months/two years. Early decanting is a major benefit to these wines'; or: 'A mature wine which won't come to harm if kept up to two years.' The 'Young wine intended for laying down' symbol appeared only three times on the list that came out as we went to press – the Wine Club serves mostly the instant drinker. The Italian range is now shorter but excellent, selected by Italian specialist Burton Anderson. On the summer 1984 list, the excellent Rocche dei Manzoni Bricco Manzoni (£5.75) from the

Piedmont; that rare beast, a good Valpolicella – the Classico Superiore (£3.39) from Allegrini, and Pieropan Soave (£4.21) were worth a try (though we're not sure we would annotate this last wine, good as it is, with 'World's most delicate white wine. Appleskin ultra-clean and freshly bottled'). French wines abound, with plenty in the [£] price range. The bottled-for-the-club Torres wines [£]–[££] are quite good value, as is the Rioja (listed as Don Sebastian Tinto, but actually from Marqués de Cáceres at quite a good price). Domaine Machard de Gramont Burgundies are good [£££], as are Abad sherries, and the Almacenista (single cask) amontillado [££]. Prices are not cheap, but not extortionate, and the selection is good. The club puts on tastings nationwide, organises a 'Vintage Festival' annually in London, which many growers attend, and runs regular tutored wine tours to wine-growing areas.

BEST BUYS [£]–[£££] Italian wines

Wine Growers' Association

230 Great Portland Street, London, W1 TEL 01-387 6839
1 The Aldwych, London, WC2 TEL 01-836 5581
135 Western Road, Brighton, East Sussex TEL (0273) 28408
5 Castle Meadow, Norwich, Norfolk TEL (0603) 27112
MAIL ORDER Freepost, London, NW10 1YA TEL 01-451 0981

OPEN Mon–Fri 9 am–6 pm CLOSED Sat, Sun, public holidays
CREDIT CARDS (Shops) Access/Euro, Visa; (Mail order) Access/Euro, Amex, Visa
DISCOUNTS £1 per unmixed case; £2 on wine of month DELIVERY Free locally from shops, min 2 cases; elsewhere on UK mainland and Isle of Wight £3 for 1 case, £5 for 2 cases, £2 per case 3–5 cases, 6+ cases free GLASS HIRE Free
TASTINGS AND TALKS Not available CELLARAGE £2.40 per case per year
MAIL ORDER SPECIALISTS

Never mind the rest of the world – turn straight to the fine Italian range at the back of the Wine Growers' Association's list. Since the arrival a couple of years ago of the group of companies that includes the Association of Italian specialist Richard Hobson MW with his Italian Wine Agencies, this is one of the best retail lists of Italian wines in the country – note the many references to the firm in the Italian section of THE WINE REGIONS above. Particularly good value are the wines from the Italian South Tyrol, especially the Chardonnay di Appiano and Gewürztraminer Tenuta Trattmannhof, both 1983 as we went to press and both just over £3. Look out also for Tedeschi and Cesari wines, and Frascati Villa di Catone, the best on the market at £2.95. Sparkling Ferrari is a good, mature Champagne method wine made from the Chardonnay grape (£6.10 for the NV and £7.65 for the 1979), and for an interesting change at the end of a meal, try the sweet, intensely raisiny Moscato Passito di Pantelleria (£4.85) made on a little island way south of the Sicilian coast. France outweighs Italy in list length, but there's little to get excited about here. Their 1983 opening offer of clarets was not very competitively priced – indeed, all prices are rather high on the

Wine Growers' Association's list. Whatever you do, don't buy your port here – these are some of the highest port prices we have ever seen. And the own-label wines have never given us much pleasure.

BEST BUYS [£]–[£££] Italian wines, especially from the South Tyrol

The Wine Shop

7 Sinclair Street, Thurso, Caithness, Highland TEL (0847) 65657

OPEN Tue–Sat 9.30 am–12.45 pm, 2.30 pm–5.30 pm CLOSED Mon, Sun
CREDIT CARDS Access/Euro DISCOUNTS Approx 15% on half a case
DELIVERY Free within 10 miles, £1 for rest of Caithness, minimum half a case
GLASS HIRE Minimum 1 dozen with wine order, 35p per breakage
TASTINGS AND TALKS 4 tastings per annum, in-store tastings by arrangement
CELLARAGE Not available

This competently bought range spans France and the rest of Europe and hops briefly over to Brown Bros in Australia – and must be a godsend to the people of Caithness. Despite a prolonged illness at the beginning of 1984, Mr Collett, who runs Britain's most northerly wine merchants business single-handed, has managed to extend his German, Rhône and Burgundy ranges. Look out for Beaujolais from Sarrau and Sapin, Alsace wines from Heim, the good-value semi-sweet dessert wine Bonnezeaux 1981 from René Renou (£4.40) amongst the Loires, and those Brown Bros Australians [££], as well as a good selection of clarets (with tasting notes thoughtfully provided for the lesser-known petits-châteaux and bourgeois growths) and Burgundies. Amongst the many Eastern European wines, the Bulgarian Cabernet is best value at £2.69.

BEST BUYS [£] Bulgarian Cabernet, [££]–[£££] Burgundies and clarets

The Wine Society

Gunnels Wood Road, Stevenage, Hertfordshire TEL (0438) 314161 (24 hours)
53 Bolsover Street, London, W1 TEL 01-387 4681

OPEN Mon–Fri 9 am–5 pm Sat (pre-Chr only) 9 am–1 pm CLOSED Sat (exc pre-Chr), Sun, public holidays CREDIT CARDS Access/Euro, Visa DISCOUNTS £1.20 per case on unbroken cases, or for cash-and-carry at Stevenage or London offices DELIVERY Free in UK and Northern Ireland for full cases, may be mixed; smaller orders, £2, but some small orders eg Chr gifts, are priced to include delivery GLASS HIRE Free TASTINGS AND TALKS A London-based ws dining society and tastings at Stevenage and London, £4–£10 CELLARAGE £3 per case per year in excellent temperature-controlled conditions MAIL ORDER ONLY

Prices are now much more competitive than they used to be at The Wine Society. The list is good and extensive (500 wines), though there are not as many exclusive agencies as one would hope for from a business which exists entirely to do mail order: one can, after all, buy Hugel Alsace wines all over the country. But The Wine Society is a *society* (you must be recommended by a member, and buy a £10 share for life membership) so presumably the members are happy with their very reasonable lot. The Wine Society is particularly good value for those in distant places, because delivery is free in the UK and, unusually, in Northern Ireland. All readers' reports on delivery from the recently fully computerised depot in Stevenage are glowing: wines arrive in a matter of days, and service in the Home Counties with the Society's own fleet of delivery vans is especially swift. At the lower end of the list, the Society's own-label wines are generally sound, sometimes unexciting. Their Burgundy and Rhône 'own-labels' are usually particularly good. 'Sampling cases' carry a small discount. A large chunk of the profit seems to have been sunk in years past into wines for laying down at Stevenage, because there's a fair range of older wines on offer, though fewer now than a couple of years ago. However, clarets go back only to 1970, with a few older bottles available on request. There's a good range of ready-to-drink petits-châteaux. The Burgundy list, after a big offering of the difficult 1983 vintage *(see the Burgundy section of* THE WINE REGIONS*)* now beats the clarets for length. Remoissenet dominates the list, but look out for the lovely wines of Roumier, Dujac, Sauzet, and Domaine de la Pousse d'Or – a good selection. Rhônes are fine, dominated by the excellent wines of Paul Jaboulet Aîné [£££]; try also Chave's Hermitage and the traditional Châteauneuf-du-Pape, Domaine de Mont Redon [£££]. Vacheron Sancerres are excellent in the Loire [££] and good value. The Italian list is extraordinarily sound: the South Tyrol wines of Hofstatter [££], Antinori wines [££] – [£££], Franco-Fiorino Barbaresco and Barolo [£££], Torgiano Rosso 1978 from Lungarotti (£3.85), Vino Nobile di Montepulciano 1977 from Fassati (£4.50) – and more. The Spanish list is fair, inexpensive, but very short. Worth a try at just over £5 are the relatively delicate (for Australia) Koombahla Vineyard Cabernet Sauvignons from Brown Bros. The Wine Society's list and literature are some of the best designed in the wine trade. But there are occasional lapses: now and then no producer's name, or no indication of when to drink the wine. But information, including a tasting note for each wine, is generally excellent.

BEST BUYS [££] – [£££] Italian wines, [£££] the Society's Champagne, other wines mentioned above

The Wine Studio

9 Eccleston Street, London, SW1 — TEL 01-730 7596

OPEN Mon–Fri 10 am–7 pm Sat 10 am–2.30 pm CLOSED Sun, public holidays CREDIT CARDS Access/Euro, Visa DISCOUNTS 5% on case sales DELIVERY Free for case orders in London; on UK mainland, £3 per case for 1–4 cases; thereafter £2.50 per case or part-case GLASS HIRE Free TASTINGS AND TALKS Regularly organised, open to all on advance application CELLARAGE Not available

Cool, smart, modern, the Wine Studio's shelves are lined with Britain's best range of California wines and, since 1984, the best range of

Australian wines, too, over 30, many from small wineries previously scarcely heard of here, plus a small range of French and Spanish wines for those of us still inextricably stuck in the mud of the Old World. Dare we risk another superlative? The Wine Studio's list is one of the most helpful in Britain in explaining how the wines taste – and even which foods they might best accompany! A key runs through the list: A is for 'Soft wines, low acid and tannin. Straightforward drinking or bland food'; D is for 'rich wines with medium to high acidity. Shellfish and rich sauces'; H means 'Blockbuster, strap in chair, do not drive! Barbecued spare ribs, curry . . .' The 17 'Studio Selection' wines, in addition, have full tasting notes, some of the best we've seen – whoops, there we go again – as do the good value De Lahaye Champagnes. From California, over 170 wines are listed, arranged by grape variety and then by vintage with a short explanation above each section of how the varieties perform differently there from their European counterparts. There are also wines from the North-West USA (Washington, Oregon and Idaho), and some very respectable Gold Seal wines have appeared recently from New York State. You can dabble quite painlessly in the Goeffrey Roberts house wines, still below £3 as we went to press, and there are other cheaper California wines [££] too, but prices soon leap to £8 plus, reflecting the dollar's continuing strength. Some prices have come down, however, since last year, a marketing ploy by some Americans, alarmed as their UK market seemed likely to fold under pressure of prices. Sweet California wines are sensibly available in halves, and worth a try, though often very expensive (£16.75 for a half?). Don't miss some good-value bin-ends. Australian prices range from £4 to £14. Some little-known examples include Balgownie, Saltram, Stanley Leasingham, Gawler River and Hungerford Hill. And back in Europe, Marqués de Cáceres is cheap at under £3, and the extraordinary, rich Mas de Daumas Gassac, Vin de Pays de l'Hérault is an expensive but exciting wine at up to £6.50, depending on vintage. The Wine Studio puts on very good tastings, generally at around £10 a head, sometimes with dinner as an optional extra. These could be 'Exotic Chardonnays', '1978 Cabernet Sauvignons', or selections for individual wineries, more often than not tutored by their visiting owners or winemakers, otherwise by such celebrities as Jancis Robinson, Christopher Fielden or Geoffrey Roberts. At Christmas, look out for the Wine Studio's tasting cases, presentation boxes, and good present ideas like a portable picnic Champagne cooler stuffed with one bottle of NV and one of pink Champagne.

BEST BUYS [£] Geoffrey Roberts house wines, [£] Marqués de Cáceres, [££]–[£££] Australian wines, [£££] California wines

> The Wine Standards Board is the trade's disciplinary department and wine watchdog. Their inspectors are responsible for rooting out any malpractices – but they are concerned largely with labelling irregularities. If you have genuine reason to suspect that the wine in a bottle is not what the label claims it is, contact the Board at:
> 68½ Upper Thames Street, London EC4V 3BJ; TEL 01–236 9512.

The Winery

4 Clifton Road, London, W9 TEL 01-286 6475
2 Charleville Road, London, W14 TEL 01-385 3528

OPEN Mon–Sat 9 am–8 pm (Clifton Road), 11 am–9 pm (Charleville Road) CLOSED Sun, public holidays CREDIT CARDS Access/Euro, Visa; business accounts DISCOUNTS With case orders – variable DELIVERY Free within Central London; elsewhere on UK mainland £3.95 for 1 case, £1.95 for subsequent cases GLASS HIRE £1 per dozen TASTINGS AND TALKS Free tastings every 4 months CELLARAGE £3 per case per year

Most prices are a bit on the high side in these two smart shops, but the wines are reliably selected. This business was set up by an Australian several years ago, and the Australian influence still remains in a choice of a dozen Aussie wines from various sources. Most of the list is French, however, with a short list of clarets including a few mature classed growths, reliable Burgundies from Duboeuf, Louis Latour and others, supplemented by a 'fine and rare' section of old Burgundies, clarets and Ch d'Yquem. There are reliable wines from the major French regions, well-chosen Champagnes, including Bruno Paillard at the lower end of the price bracket, good Rhônes, Hugel Alsace wines. Look out for some fine German estate wines, the ubiquitous trio of good-quality Spanish wines, Torres, CVNE and Marqués de Cáceres; and amongst a not terribly exciting Italian range, the best of two generally boring denominazioni: Soave Classico from Pieropan (£3.95) and Frascati Colli di Catone (£3.45) – they should have moved on to the fresher 1983 vintage of both of these wines by the time this *Guide* is published. The Winery operates the mail order wine business for Habitat.

BEST BUYS Wines mentioned above

Wines of Interest Ⓥ

46 Burlington Road, Ipswich, Suffolk TEL (0473) 215752

OPEN Wed–Fri 9 am–5.30 pm Sat 9 am–1 pm CLOSED Sun, Mon, Tue, public holidays CREDIT CARDS Not accepted DISCOUNTS Not available DELIVERY Not normally free, but can be arranged locally or for large orders; otherwise £1.72 per case in most of England, Wales and Southern Scotland
GLASS HIRE Free TASTINGS AND TALKS Monthly organised tastings in London, Ipswich and Norwich; private tastings on request CELLARAGE Not available

Tim Voelcker's flimsy folded sheet, tightly typed with a hundred or so wines, changes quarterly and is worth perusing – you never know what you might find. One thing you *will* find is good prices, especially if you buy by the mixed case (add 20p a bottle otherwise to case rates, and you still often have a bargain). You might find Torres, Ch Musar, Hill Smith Australians, the well-made Wootton Schönburger from Somerset, sparkling Blanquette de Limoux, Bulgarian Cabernet Sauvignon, Merlot, Riesling and Pinot Chardonnay (all the Bulgarians are under £2), Moulin Touchais 1959 at just over £6, some mature lower-priced clarets, mostly [££], good Beaujolais from Sarrau and Rhône from Guigal, German estate wines, and vintage ports, often at good prices, too. Wines of Interest hold regular tastings, two or three times a month in London at the Bulls Head, 80 Leadenhall Street, EC3 (01-283 2830), twice a month in Norwich and once a month in Ipswich, on themes like 'Pudding Wines' (£7.50 a head including food), eight different vintages of Ch Gruaud-Larose: 1976 to 1959 (£7.50) or Portuguese reds (£3.25). All comers are welcome, so write to them for details. The Ipswich side of the business moved into bigger premises last year on the main A12 route into the town centre, where there's plenty of parking space – one reason Wines of Interest can keep its prices down is their policy of (almost only) cash and carry sales.

BEST BUYS Most wines on the list

Wines of Spain

4 Temple Court, Liverpool TEL 051-236 6468

See David Scatchard above

Wines of Westhorpe (V)

54 Boyn Hill Road, Maidenhead, Berkshire TEL (0628) 21385

OPEN (office, no shop) Mon–Fri (inc public holidays) 9 am–6 pm Sat (almost always) 9 am–6 pm CLOSED Sun CREDIT CARDS Not accepted DISCOUNTS For 10+ cases cash and carry, 11+ cases delivered, on application DELIVERY Free on UK mainland, min 5 cases; £5 per order on 1–4 cases GLASS HIRE Not available TASTINGS AND TALKS, CELLARAGE Not available

Alan Ponting is, we presume, accurately counting on the probability that his low margins will ensure a profitably ample flow of wines through the small business he runs in the time left over from his maths coaching. Or is it the other way round? Mr Ponting specialises in Hungarian and Bulgarian wines, selling only by the case, at very low prices. His Hungarian wines are more interesting than the general run-of-the-state-farm bottles we usually see on the British shelves, but the Bulgarians represent much better value, from the basic Mehana red and white at £17.40 to the star of the varietals, Sakar Mountain Cabernet 1976 (£29.90). Special mixed cases are also available. Delivery of small quantities is rather expensive, so Berkshire locals can pick up the best bargains.

BEST BUYS [£]–[££] Bulgarian wines

> Why not club together with friends to enjoy volume discounts and free delivery?

Witton Vintners

610 Blackburn Road, Astley Bridge, Greater Manchester TEL (0204) 58618

OPEN Mon–Fri 11 am–6.30 pm Sat 10.30 am–6.30 pm CLOSED Sun, public holidays CREDIT CARDS All accepted DISCOUNTS 5% on case orders, cash and carry DELIVERY Free locally, min 1 mixed case; elsewhere £3.50 per case GLASS HIRE Not available TASTINGS AND TALKS Occasional tastings by invitation; to groups on request CELLARAGE Not available

Witton Vintners stock a most impressive range for a two-year-old company – a range, indeed, of which many old-established wine merchants might be justifiably proud. And prices are average to good here, too. The shop is primarily of interest to locals, since Witton do not yet produce a list, though they hope to do so by 1985. They stock a growing collection of California wines – bravely, with the North in its current unhappy financial state – which includes a selection of grape varieties but principally Chardonnays and Cabernets from a large number of wineries of varying stature; there's the excellent Pinot Noir 1980 from Knudsen Erath in Oregon (£8.50). From Australia, there are the fine Hill Smith wines – the minty Cabernet Sauvignon 1976 is well worth £6.95 – and Taltarni and a couple of other wineries are also represented. The Italian range is expanding, too: amongst an interesting selection, try the range from Lungarotti in Umbria, Nera in Valtellina and Pio Cesare in the Piedmont. Germany is covered by many Deinhard wines and wines from a number of other estates, including plenty of sweet, mature 1976s. There are good Riojas and a big range of Torres wines, vintage port at good prices and an assortment of sherries that might well have popped straight out of the top ten of this *Guide*'s tasting for its newsletter, *Which? Wine Monthly*, plus the delicious old sherries of Gonzalez Byass. But France still takes up most shelf space: come here for top classed growths, many of the 1970 and 1975 and 1978 vintages, a good range of sweet Bordeaux that includes some 1976s and 1975s, a fine selection of Burgundies and Chablis from Remon; Rhônes from Jaboulet, a short but very good Loire section including the clean sweet Layon of Tijou, Vouvrays from the reliable Huet and Foreau, the lovely Gitton Sancerres, both red and white, and Alsace from Hugel, including plenty of ripe, mature 1976s. Champagne is well chosen, though prices here are not as keen as elsewhere on the list: there are ranges from Alfred Gratien, Pol Roger, Roederer, Bollinger and Krug.

BEST BUYS Most things on the list

We have tried to make the *1985 Which? Wine Guide* as comprehensive as possible, but we should love to hear from you about any other establishments you feel deserve an entry, or your comments on existing entries. Write to us either by letter or using the report forms supplied at the back of the book.

Hedley Wright

The Old Maltings, Sawbridgeworth, Hertfordshire BM2 9JX — TEL Bishop Stortford (0279) 723344

OPEN Mon–Fri 9 am–5.30 pm Sat 9.30 am–1.30 pm CLOSED Sun, public holidays CREDIT CARDS Not accepted; personal and business accounts DISCOUNTS 5% on 5+ cases, £1.50 per case cash and carry DELIVERY Free within 25 miles of Sawbridgeworth and Central London, min 1 case; elsewhere in UK £2.50 per case GLASS HIRE Free TASTINGS AND TALKS 2 free tastings and wine talks for customers a year CELLARAGE £2.50 per case per year

A limited but interesting and original range of wines is to be found in this Hertfordshire warehouse, where wines are always (reassuringly) open for tasting – or take away the helpful if strong-sell list, which includes labels, tasting notes and information on wines that Hedley Wright particularly recommend. If you arrive on the wrong day to taste something, you can rely on the generic clarets and petits-châteaux clarets from Nathaniel Johnston, and there are some more exalted clarets of light, recent years. Other French regions are covered mostly by growers' rather than merchants' wines. There are a few basic Germans from recent vintages, the tasty Torres range from the Penedès area of Spain and a selection of Georges Goulet Champagnes, rounded off by a few wines from elsewhere.

BEST BUYS Clarets

Peter Wylie Fine Wines

Valelands, West Chiltington Lane, Billingshurst, West Sussex — TEL (040 381) 3533

OPEN All hours except 'usual sleeping hours' CLOSED Very rarely CREDIT CARDS Not accepted DISCOUNTS Not available DELIVERY Free in London and within 15 miles of Billingshurst, min 2 cases; elsewhere and for smaller quantities £3.45 per case GLASS HIRE, TASTINGS AND TALKS Not available CELLARAGE £3 per case + insurance

Considering the immense stock of fine old wines held by this small company, it is surprising that prices are so reasonable – indeed that there are bargains to be found in the lengthy lists issued every couple of months or so. Lafite, Latour and their peers are much in evidence on the – as Peter Wylie puts it none too modestly – 'perhaps unequalled' July 1984 list; clarets reach back to 1878 and up and on for another 102 years through stacks of 1945s, 1953s, 1959s to pagefuls per vintage from 1961 onwards, tailing off in the poorer and the immature vintages. Two large pages of sweet Bordeaux stretch back to 1890, Burgundies, a shorter list, back to reds of the 1955 vintage and whites of 1959; vintage Champagne goes back to 1928, vintage port to 1908. Clarets come in bigger sizes, too, both old and new vintages: eight-bottle imperials, six-bottle jeroboams and plenty of double magnums. Those who live outside the free delivery areas and object to a £3 per case delivery charge can arrange to collect their wines from the London Bridge warehouse (ask when you order). Peter Wylie and his wife Sheila run the business from home. They are also willing to advise on wine investment and were hoping to start a fine wine tasting group as we went to press.

BEST BUYS Mature wines

Yapp Brothers

The Old Brewery, Mere, Wiltshire TEL (0747) 860423

OPEN Mon–Fri 9 am–1 pm, 2 pm–5 pm Sat 9 am–1 pm CLOSED Sun, public holidays CREDIT CARDS Not accepted DISCOUNTS £1.20–£2.40 per case cash and carry DELIVERY Free on mainland Britain, min 1 unmixed case; £2.50 per case for mixed cases GLASS HIRE Free TASTINGS AND TALKS Tastings and wine dinners around Britain CELLARAGE £2.50 per case per year
MAIL ORDER SPECIALISTS

Customers who make a pilgrimage to the Yapps' attractive Old Brewery in the depths of the Wiltshire countryside might leave with something of a feeling of having dropped in to buy *'vente directe'* down some little country lane in France. Those (as most do) who buy by post will find the Yapps' catalogue an evocative substitute. The snaps of the growers at work or tables have been replaced temporarily in the latest list by Greek etchings and snippets composed in the fifth and sixth centuries BC by selected Greek poets on the subject of the wines of the Brothers Yapp. But the lengthy tales of the winemakers, their cellars and their surroundings still have a thick French accent. Thicker still this year, because doctor and dentist Judith and Robin Yapp have greatly extended the small Provence section. The tempting selection includes lesser-known appellations such as Bellet, Palette and Coteaux de Pierrevert, as well as fine examples of more familiar wines (in name at least) such as Bandol and Cassis, and the firm, rich, fruity Coteaux des Baux, Domaine de Trévallon (between £4 and £4.25 for vintages 1980–1982). The Rhône and the Loire remain, of course, the Yapp mainstays, backed up now also with the very good Champagnes of Jacquesson and Alsace wines from Charles Schléret. Quality here is always more than reliable and service fast and personal.

BEST BUYS Most things on the list

The Wine & Spirit Education Trust is the body in charge of educating those in and on the fringes of the wine trade. They offer a series of courses right up to Master of Wine level, the more basic of which are open to non-trade members who can convince the Trust of their intention to enter the wine trade. Contact them at:
Five Kings House, Kennet Wharf Lane, Upper Thames Street, London EC4V 3AJ; TEL 01–236 3551.

Yorkshire Fine Wines

Nun Monkton, York, North Yorkshire TEL (0901) 30131

OPEN Mon–Fri 8.30 am–5.30 pm Public holidays 8.30 am–3 pm
CREDIT CARDS All accepted DISCOUNTS 4% cash on delivery; case rates variable, on request DELIVERY Free between Scottish Borders (South) and Nottinghamshire (South), min 1 case, may be mixed; elsewhere £4 for 1 case, £3.50 for 2 cases, £3 for 3 cases, thereafter free GLASS HIRE Free
TASTINGS AND TALKS On request, and arranged periodically CELLARAGE £1.25 per case per year

The wines really are fine at Yorkshire Fine Wines, and if prices are a bit high, they begin to look very fair if you live within the large free delivery area and take advantage of their weekly delivery service. Greatest emphasis is on French wines. There's a big selection of good Burgundies, lots of the excellent, firm Beaujolais of Sarrau, many first growth clarets back to 1961, with plenty available in magnums, good Rhônes including the Beaucastel and Coudoulet wines, and Loires including the very good Sancerres and Pouilly-Fumés of Vatan and Ch du Nozet, and a varied selection of Alsace wines. German wines are concentrated largely in the lower levels of sweetness, mostly Rieslings, and good quality wines. There is a small but interesting clutch of Spanish wines: León, Torres and Vallformosa from Catalonia ££ – £££ and a few good Riojas. From outside Europe, Hill Smith Australians ££ – £££ are very good, as are the Mondavi wines ££ – £££ from California.

BEST BUYS Mixed tasting cases, French, Spanish and Australian wines

Chains and supermarkets

Many people, for convenience, buy wine *only* in supermarkets and the specialist chains. The supermarkets alone now account for over half the unfortified wines sold in this country, with Sainsbury's dealing with a hefty 15 per cent chunk. So we have included in this year's *Guide* a comprehensive survey of what they all have to offer, reviewing even those we cannot recommend. Standards of wine-buying in both supermarkets and chains vary enormously, from those, like Oddbins, Victoria Wine, Sainsbury's and Waitrose which rival some of the better specialist, individual wine merchants, to the few who simply buy down to a price, with apparently no regard whatsoever for their customers' pleasure.

Argyll Stores

HEAD OFFICE Millington Road, Hayes, Middlesex TEL 01-848 8744
1,100 licensed branches nationwide, including Lipton, Presto, Locost, Mojo, Templeton, and Galbraith
CREDIT CARDS Not accepted DISCOUNTS Not available

A stodgy diet of brands and generic wines is currently being enlivened with a few own-labels. Only the five-strong German range, all £2 or under, was on the shelves as the *Guide* went to press, and we found them acceptable drinking if rather monotonously indistinguishable from each other; the clean, fresh, 1983 Niersteiner Gutes Domtal had marginally more body and better balance than the rest. About 15–20 French (including Champagne) and Italian wines are due to be added to the range soon.

ASDA

HEAD OFFICE Asda House, Britannia Road TEL (0532) 539141
Morley, Leeds
100 licensed branches mostly in the North but expanding South
CREDIT CARDS Access/Euro, Visa DISCOUNTS Not available

ASDA's range consists mostly of familiar names, and in most stores there is little to tempt even the slightly adventurous drinker; if this is your main source of supply, you will have to settle for a diet of Ch Malijay 1981 (£2.49) from Côtes du Rhône, Chablis Premier Cru Mont de Milieu 1982 (£4.35) from Chanson, and one or two others, as your brightest hope. Some, like Duboeuf Fleurie 1982 (£4.45) or good value Chianti Classico Lamole 1981 (£2.69) are restricted to a small number of branches. But developments are just around the corner. Antonia Hadfield has taken over from Bill Gunn as wine buyer, and is supervising the introduction of a new range of own-label wines, mostly from Germany, which should be in the stores before Christmas 1984 but which came on stream too late for us to evaluate. A Vintage Choice range of six white and six red domaine wines, exclusive to ASDA and all under £4, is also on its way to all stores: keep your eyes peeled for a 1983 Sancerre and a surprise from Spain. A restricted number of stores will again get jam on it, too, in the form of a further dozen vintage goodies.

BEST BUYS [£]–[££] Wines mentioned above

Ashe & Nephew

HEAD OFFICE Ellis Ashton Street TEL 051-480 5678
Huyton Industrial Estate, Liverpool
320 branches in the North West, Yorkshire, Midlands, London, North Wales

OPEN Mon–Sat 10 am–10 pm Sun 12 noon–2 pm, 7 pm–9.30 pm CLOSED Chr Day CREDIT CARDS Access/Euro, Visa; accounts DISCOUNTS 5–10% according to quantity DELIVERY Ask locally GLASS HIRE Ask locally

Peter Carr MW is wine buyer for this new Whitbread acquisition and his carefully selected range of wines steers a firm and successful course between popular saleable names and fashionable esoteric finds at reasonable prices; he seems to be leading his customers gently in the right direction. For example, no High Street chain can survive without Liebfraumilch, of which there are eight to choose from here, but this is balanced by the quality of a Kaseler Nies'chen Riesling Auslese 1976 from Bischöfliches Priesterseminar at £6.80; or from Italy there are the simple but all too rare delights of a Barbera d'Alba from Pio Cesare, at just over £3 or Venegazzù at just under £4. From Spain there are Monopole, Torres and Marqués de Cáceres wines as well as Marqués de Riscal and the good Viña Albalí (but we have not enjoyed the own-label Ashe's range); from California, Inglenook as well as Paul Masson; from Australia, Brown Bros. Similarly in France, the largest section, it is a delight to be able to pick up a bottle of Paul Jaboulet Aîné wine like the Crozes-Hermitage 1979 (£4.10) from the corner shop. Claret ranges from a drinkable generic version from Jean-Paul Bartier at £2.31 through a very good value Ch Dillon 1979 (soon to be 1981) at £3.10 to a 1978 Shatto Smith Ho Lafeet Graves Croo Klassay, as their staff notes put it, at around £8. They are agents for Pierre Olivier wines, and you can enjoy the warm, ripe fruit of his Bourgogne Rouge 1981 for £3.60 (but avoid his Chablis), or be tempted by Duboeuf Beaujolais-Villages

1982 (£3.50), Durup Chablis (the premier cru Fourchaume 1982 is £4.80), or Jadot, Latour, Moillard and Tollot-Beaut Côte d'Or wines at ungreedy prices. They are in the process of introducing a wine selector coding which will follow the standard practice of grading whites from one to nine in increasing order of sweetness, and are experimenting with a 'bodyweight' scale for reds. Do note that as usual in chains, not all wines are available off-the-peg in all branches.

BEST BUYS Wines other than the Ashe & Nephew own-label range

Augustus Barnett

See Bass Off-Licences

Barretts Liquormart

HEAD OFFICE 76 Goldhawk Road, London, W12
6 licensed outlets in London and one in Bucks

OPEN (Variable) Mon–Sat 9.30 am–7.30 pm (Sat till 8.30 pm) Sun 12 noon–2 pm, 7 pm–9 pm CLOSED (Some branches) Mon CREDIT CARDS Not accepted DISCOUNTS Not available TASTINGS AND TALKS Regular free in-store tastings

A small publicity-shunning chain in which Freddie Barrett cuts the price of wine by the bottle rather than by the case so that everybody can benefit. A wide range of countries is represented, as are many branded wines, and some Grande Marque Champagne is competitively priced. This is a good place to come for cheap, more basic Champagne, too. Their house Champagne was £5.49 a bottle as we went to press.

BEST BUYS [£££] Champagne

Barwell & Jones

HEAD OFFICE 24 Fore Street, Ipswich TEL (0473) 56751
18 shops in Norfolk, Suffolk, Cambridgeshire and Essex

OPEN Varies, ask locally CREDIT CARDS Visa; personal and business accounts DISCOUNTS Variable for 1 case or more DELIVERY Free to Norwich, Cambridge, Ipswich, Bury St Edmunds; elsewhere not available GLASS HIRE Free TASTINGS AND TALKS Occasionally in-store CELLARAGE Free

There is some very good value to be found in the 18-strong chain of Barwell & Jones shops (the retail arm of Tolly Cobbold Brewers) if you look beyond the more 'obvious' names from France. Perhaps best value are the Southern French wines, like the lovely rich, fruity and tarry Ch d'Alvariche from the Côtes du Roussillon at around £2.50, or Ch Belingard, Bergerac and for just a few pence more, Ch Montauriol, Côtes du Frontonnais or Commanderie de la Bargemone, Coteaux d'Aix-en-Provence, or Domaine de la Rouillère, Côtes de Provence, at nearer £3. Pierre Sparr Alsace wines are excellent, too, and not expensive [££]–[£££]. The small range of Italian wines is consistently well above average, and they also hold the agency for the Montecillo Rioja.

BEST BUYS [£] Southern French wines, [££]–[£££] Pierre Sparr Alsace wines

Bass Off-Licences

HEAD OFFICE North Woolwich Road Silvertown, London, E16 TEL 01-476 1477
875 branches nationwide, including Augustus Barnett, Galleon Wine, Wine Sellers and Underwoods

OPEN (Variable) all week 10 am–2 pm, 5 pm–10 pm
CREDIT CARDS Access/Euro, Visa in some shops DISCOUNTS 5% on non-promotional prices of table and sparkling wines CELLARAGE Enquire locally TASTINGS AND TALKS Regular in-store tastings

The ranges in this group have been standardised since brewers Bass took over the large Augustus Barnett chain early in 1984. A substantial proportion of the 200 or 300 items per shop is accounted for by brand names, including a lot of Hedges & Butlers', with Italian and French wines predominating. But from Bordeaux, there are one or two rays of sunshine like three vintages of Ch Lascombes (the 1976 is under £10), or Ch de Pez 1979 knocking on for £9. Grande Marque Champagnes like Moët, Bollinger and Lanson at around £9 to £12 are not the cheapest available, but there are a couple of vintages of Chablis from Laroche [££]–[£££]. In addition to the Sicilian Corvo wines at around £3, Italy offers Ruffino's fresh white Galestro at about £2.50, and there are Portuguese Grão Vasco wines including a 1975 Garrafeira for well under £3. This chain has followed Victoria Wine's lead in marking all white and rosé wines on a one to nine sweetness scale, and providing descriptive shelf cards for the majority of the wines.

BEST BUYS [££]–[£££] Clarets, wines mentioned above

Bejam

HEAD OFFICE 1 Garland Road, Honeypot Lane Stanmore, Middlesex TEL 01-952 8311
170 licensed branches

CREDIT CARDS Access/Euro, Amex, Visa DISCOUNTS Not available

The small range of about two dozen very basic, inexpensive wines is split roughly half and half between Colman's brands and Bejam's own-labels. There are more whites than reds on offer, and we recommend that you stick to Bejam's own Germans [£], like the rather sweet Liebfraumilch from Rheinhessen, or the particularly good value Niersteiner Gutes Domtal 1983, made from Müller-Thurgau and Silvaner, which is clean, fresh and well balanced.

BEST BUYS [£] Own-label Germans

Blayney Wines

HEAD OFFICE Riverside Road, Sunderland TEL (0783) 484488
65 Branches, including Liquormart, in North East

OPEN (Variable) Mon–Sat 10 am–10 pm Sun 12 noon–2 pm, 7 pm–9 pm
CREDIT CARDS Access/Euro, Visa DISCOUNTS Not available GLASS HIRE Free
TASTINGS AND TALKS On request

Blayney's is the retail wing of Vaux Brewery and its shops stock a range of European wines, mostly under £3.50, with an emphasis on France and Germany. White Bordeaux is from Yvon Mau, and the petit-château clarets are extended in some shops, or to order, by a small selection of classed growths. Rather more expensive Burgundies come from a variety of producers including Les Caves de Champclos and the dependable Faiveley. Loires are from Rémy Pannier and Alsace from Muré. Gustav Adolf Schmitt has the virtual monopoly of their German wines which are predominantly from recent vintages, rarely cost more than £3, and include one or two odd items like a trocken rosé. Italy is standard, Spain poor, but there are some inexpensive Portuguese Dãos and a small selection of Poças Ports.

BEST BUYS [£]–[£££] French wines

Bottoms Up

HEAD OFFICE 40 Victoria Way, Charlton TEL 01-858 2000
London, SE7
18 branches London and South

OPEN Mon–Fri 10 am–10 pm Sat 9 am–10 pm Sun 12 noon–2 pm, 7 pm–10 pm CREDIT CARDS All accepted DISCOUNTS For quantity on request
DELIVERY Within reasonable distance of shops for reasonable-sized order
GLASS HIRE Free

This is a list and a half. There is no mail order, so if you don't live near a branch, consider moving house, although Edward Butler Vintners, who own Bottoms Up, intend to open a few more 'wine superstores' as they justifiably call them, soon. Regrettably, prices are not always displayed on the shelves of the pleasantly cluttered shops so you may have to ask for assistance, or a copy of their 1,000-strong single sheet list, and a microscope. By way of compensation, the sophisticated till receipt tells you everything, including the time of day. There are some expensive wines and plenty of choice for people who drink Champagne only by the Nebuchadnezzar, as well as some for those with only a bit of loose change in their pocket, but the strength lies not so much in knock-down cheapies as in range and choice at realistic prices. For instance, the acceptable Ochert Carte Jaune NV Champagne (under £6) is only about £1 dearer than Champagne method wines from the Loire or Spain, but you can escalate through a good NV range (Lanson, Pol Roger, Mumm) at under £10 to vintage Taittinger Comtes de

Champagne at under £20 and so on through the roof. From otherwise humble Italians, it is well worth seeking out Pio Cesare's Piemonte wines like his 1974 Barbaresco at under £6, Walsch's Gewürztraminer from the Italian South Tyrol (£3.49) and the Chardonnay Santa Margherita (£3.65). Spain offers reliable red and white Torres wines and Riojas including Campo Viejo and CVNE at very good prices, and from Portugal, there are a couple of the better 10-year-old Garrafeira reds for less than the price of Mateus. There are a couple of dozen Germans under £3, mostly QbA like a pretty, light Bereich Bernkastel 1983 from Schmitt, but some Spätlesen too, and another three dozen spanning the range from Kabinett via Eiswein to Trockenbeerenauslese, mostly from either Schmitt or Stolz. From France, there are Kuentz-Bas Alsaces, and pedigree Chablis like Moreau's premier cru Vaillons 1982 [£££]; in fact Moreau is a bit like sand at a picnic – he gets everywhere. There is village Beaujolais; Rhônes from Domaine des Chanssaud and Durieu (and Moreau) – Durieu's 1982 Côtes-du-Rhône (£2.85) is big and tasty; and amongst the Côte d'Or reds, look out for the producer Dujac as well as the more familiar Latour. From Bordeaux (apart from Moreau) there is a good spread of petit-hâteau clarets up to £4 or £5, like the earthy Ch Caronne St-Gemme 1978; a clutch of 1980s featuring a couple of second-growths at about £6.50 and a good range of 1978s. Listel wines represent good value amongst the 'French Regional Wines'. You will find plenty of opportunity at Bottoms Up to experiment in the lower price ranges of California wines – Wente and Paul Masson [££], and even greater choice from Australia; try particularly the Brown Bros Wines and Berri Estates Wines, including the two bag-in-box wines, especially the red at £7.99 for three litres. Amongst the sparkling wines, Brut de Listel is best buy at £3.29. Ports are rather expensive here, but two interesting dessert alternatives are Muscat de Rivesaltes, Aphrodis (£4.55) and Muscat de Beaumes-de-Venise, Domaine Durban (£5.89). Since the list doesn't offer any information about vintage styles or when to drink what, you are left to your own devices. Single malt whisky drinkers are also well catered for.

BEST BUYS [£] Listel wines, [££] Sparkling Listel, [£]–[£££] Spanish wines, [££]–[£££] Australian wines, [£££] Champagne prices are fairly good

British Home Stores

HEAD OFFICE Marylebone House TEL 01-262 3288
129–137 Marylebone Road, London, NW1
38 licensed branches nationwide

CREDIT CARDS Not accepted DISCOUNTS Not available

A small range of about 15 very basic own-label wines, which they call a 'Classic Collection', is the best you can hope for at BHS apart from literally one or two others, and own-label sherries. Shelf or label information is sparse or non-existent, prices are mostly between £2 and £3 per bottle, and the wines in the Classic Collection, whilst nothing to write home about, do offer an average Beaujolais 1983, a Germanic style Bordeaux Blanc and a grapy Liebfraumilch 1983 from Rheinpfalz.

Budgen

HEAD OFFICE PO Box 9, Stonefield Way South Ruislip, Middlesex TEL 01-422 3422
136 licensed branches London, Home Counties and East Anglia
CREDIT CARDS Not accepted DISCOUNTS Not available

Budgen have recently swallowed up Bishops' stores and are in the process of merging the two under the Budgen facia. Their range includes a dozen own-labels, quite a few brands and generic wines, leaving Europe only for Paul Masson's carafes; there are also a couple of more interesting bottles like Marcilly Bourgogne NV at well under £4, and Chablis 1982/1983 from the reliable co-operative La Chablisienne at a little over £4. There are one or two from southern France including Listel [£], Villa Cerna's Chianti Classico [£], and Lamberhurst from the Isle of Wight. Of the own-label wines, we found the white Vin de Table dull and fruitless, but the youthful, robust, if rather hard red at under £2 was more drinkable; amongst the undistinguished Germans, the Niersteiner Gutes Domtal and Piesporter Michelsberg, both 1983 and both around £2, were clean but neutral in our summer 1984 tasting and lacking character. Perhaps the shake-up will include a review of these.

BEST BUYS [£] Listel wines

Carrefour

HEAD OFFICE St Georges House St Georges Street, Winchester, Hampshire TEL (0962) 68351
8 licensed branches in the South East, South West, Midlands and Yorkshire
OPEN Mon–Sat 9 am (Mon 12 noon)–8 pm (Fri 9 pm) CREDIT CARDS Not accepted DISCOUNTS Not available TASTINGS AND TALKS Weekly tastings of new and promoted wines

Subject to the usual caveats about availability of particular wines in particular stores, Carrefour, part of the Dee Corporation, generally stock a wide range of brands but also have a few more interesting wines at quite competitive prices. Germany offers QbA wines from Schmitt and Hallgarten mostly under £3, but there are some of Hallgarten's QmP wines from Kabinetts at around £3 through to a couple of 1976 Beerenauslesen at about £8. The Italian range is basic and includes Enotria's Ambra wines; Spain is represented almost exclusively by Paternina, but there are some halves of their Banda Azul and Banda Dorada Riojas at an inexpensive £1 a throw. From France there is a handful of classed-growth clarets and upmarket Burgundies from Henri de Villamont, as well as a range of generic wines shipped and bottled exclusively for Carrefour, and the attractive Listel Domaine du Bosquet rouge 1980 at just over £2. There is a little from Eastern Europe, but possibly more interest from Paul Masson's varietals (as well as carafes) like his Pinot Chardonnay for just under £3, and Australians from Orlando and Berri Estates.

BEST BUYS [£] Listel and Bulgarian wines, [££]–[£££] better German wines, [££] Berri Estate Australian wines, especially the red

The Château

HEAD OFFICE 439 Lisburn Road, Belfast BT9 7EY TEL (0232) 662874
12 licensed branches in Newtownards, Lurgan, Portadown, Newry
OPEN Mon–Sat 11.30 am–11 pm CLOSED Sun, Chr Day CREDIT CARDS Not accepted DISCOUNTS 20% on 6 bottles, 5% on case orders
GLASS HIRE Free TASTINGS AND TALKS On request

The Château provides a helpful catalogue, asking, and briefly answering, such basic questions as 'What is wine?', dealing with alcoholic strengths, outlining the AC system, etc, and suggesting guidelines for matching wines with food. The full list has a short but good range of clarets, particularly strong on 1978s, such as Ch d'Angludet (under £8), Ch Lynch-Bages (under £15) or Ch Margaux (under £25), but there are also petit-château and generic red and white wines shipped by Borie-Manoux and Calvet for well under £5. Straight and village Beaujolais wines are from Pasquier-Desvignes, who also supply red and white Burgundies, Rhônes and VDQS, vin de pays and vin de table wines. Loires from Muscadet to Sancerre and Pouilly are mostly from the reliable Sauvion, and are generally under a fiver. Of the two dozen modestly priced German QmP wines the best are probably Sichel's Spätlesen and Auslesen, and from Italy, there are Veneto wines, Soave, Bardolino and Valpolicella, from Villa Girardi. A few wines from Spain, Portugal and California are also listed.

BEST BUYS [£]–[£££] Loires, clarets

Co-op

HEAD OFFICE CWS, New Century House TEL 061-834 1212
Corporation Street, Manchester
2,400 licensed branches nationwide
CREDIT CARDS Sometimes accepted DISCOUNTS Sometimes

The regional co-operative societies throughout the UK are semi-independent entities, hence the range of wines stocked, and prices, may vary from one region to another. Most of the wines are own-label and are arranged by country of origin under brand headings, like Lohengrin (Germany), Carissa (Italy), Karlova (Yugoslavia) and so on. At our summer 1984 tasting of a small representative range, we found no merit in the wines whatsoever. If you must buy wine at the Co-op, we would advise you to find a store that stocks the very few 'Special Reserve' wines like Ch Laborde 1979 (£3.59) from Lalande de Pomerol, or Ch Cissac 1975 (£5.29) or 1977 (£4.05).

Arthur Cooper and Roberts Off-Licences

HEAD OFFICE Imperial Retail Shops Ltd TEL 01-965 8844
17 Cumberland Avenue, London, NW10
420 branches mostly in the South

OPEN (Variable) Mon–Sat 10 am–7 pm, but check locally CLOSED Most on Sun
CREDIT CARDS Access/Euro, Visa DISCOUNTS 5% on promoted table wines
GLASS HIRE Free

Both retail chains are part of Imperial Retail Shops, which in turn is part of the Courage/Saccone & Speed group; Arthur Cooper carries about 90 per cent of the range of Roberts of Worthing. The wines are generally inexpensive and rather standard, with France predominating. From Bordeaux, 1978/79 petit-château and generic Louis Eschenauer wines provide most of the drinking [£]–[££], and the brightest stars are the lesser and more forward vintages of one or two classed growths like Ch Rausan-Ségla 1974 for under £8. The two Alsace wines are from Hugel, and there are a few French regional wines including a light and fruity although still tannic 1982 Corsican, Vin de Pays de l'Île de Beauté (£2.29). Brands abound, especially from Germany. Half a dozen Champagnes include Piper-Heidsieck NV at around £9 and the 1976 at £13. There is a helpful nine-point sweetness indicator for white wines.

BEST BUYS [£]–[££] Riojas, [£] Bulgarian wines, [££] well-priced standard brands of sherry

Cullens Ⓥ

HEAD OFFICE Parsonage House, Station Road TEL (0306) 880099
Dorking, Surrey
48 licensed branches in London and the South

OPEN Mon–Fri 9 am–6 pm, 8.30 am–4.30 pm Sat 8.30 am–4.30 pm
CLOSED Sun, public holidays OTHER DETAILS *See Cullens Wine Merchants*

The licensed grocers in the Cullens group carry a small range from the excellent value Cullens Wine Merchants list *(see below)*. You can arrange to collect wines on the longer list from any of these outlets. Amongst the best buys on the shelf here are the Bulgarian Cabernet and the Mehana red and white, also from Bulgaria, and all three very cheap [£].

BEST BUYS [£] Bulgarian wines

W H Cullen Wine Case

HEAD OFFICE 142 Battersea Park Road, London, SW11 TEL 01-622 4467
SHOPS 103 Queens Road, Weybridge, Surrey TEL (0992) 47926
The Droveway, Hove, East Sussex TEL (0273) 500267

OPEN Mon–Fri 10 am–8 pm Sat, Sun 10 am–5.30 pm Public holidays CLOSED 2 days in year CREDIT CARDS Access/Euro, Visa DISCOUNTS 7% off retail price for case orders, 10% for Club members *(see below)* DELIVERY Free in local area; elsewhere £4.25 for one case, £3.25 for 2–5 cases, £1.75 thereafter GLASS HIRE Free TASTINGS AND TALKS At least 10 wines open every day, regular tutored tastings, tastings also organised on request for outside groups

After their one-year trial at Weybridge, Cullens decided last year to extend their wine warehouse operation: the first multiple chain to venture into this growing business. Wines from the extensive and good-value Cullens list are always open for tasting – around ten different wines each day. Staff are helpful and generally well informed, educated on in-house wine training courses. *See Cullens Wine Merchants for details of wines.*

Cullens Wine Club

142 Battersea Park Road TEL 01-622 4467 or 01-834 9090 (24 hours)
London, SW11

CREDIT CARDS Access/Euro, Visa DISCOUNTS 10% off retail price, 12.5% off for 10 cases DELIVERY Free to any of the Cullens branches: licensed/unlicensed grocer, Wine Case, Wine Merchants; elsewhere £4.25 for one case, £3.25 for 2–5 cases, £1.75 thereafter GLASS HIRE Free TASTINGS AND TALKS Four London tastings per year, three tutored tasting-dinners per year

Cullens' prices are hard to beat anyway, but all the more so if you are buying by the case from their Wine Club – provided, that is, that you collect your wine from one of their large chain of wine shops or grocer/delicatessens throughout London and the South. Wines will be delivered to the shop of your choice within eight days of ordering. Otherwise, delivery is expensive. Since last summer Club members (£2 membership fee per year) have also been able to select mixed cases at any of the branches at a ten per cent discount on production of their membership card. 'Mixed parcels' offered monthly enjoy an additional small discount. There are five mailings a year of the list, along with a no-nonsense newsletter. It's distressing to find that such a clued-up company doesn't annotate its list consistently with producers'/suppliers' names. And an indication of when the wines might be ready to drink would be useful in some areas of the list. *See Cullens Wine Merchants for details of the wines.*

> Cellarage is generally provided at the rates quoted only when the wines have been bought from the merchant concerned.

Cullens Wine Merchants

HEAD OFFICE 142 Battersea Park Road TEL 01-622 4467
London, SW11
40 shops in London and the South

OPEN Mon–Fri 10 am–9 pm Sat 9 am–9 pm Sun 12 noon–2 pm, 7 pm–9 pm Public holidays at managers' discretion CLOSED Varies
CREDIT CARDS Access/Euro, Visa DISCOUNTS 5% on case orders
DELIVERY Not available *(but see Cullens Wine Club)* GLASS HIRE Free
TASTINGS AND TALKS Four times a year in each shop on Sat

Cullens' specialist wine shops have all had a lick of paint over the past year, and changed their name to Cullens Wine Merchants from the cheap-and-nasty-sounding W H Cullen Winemarts. Not that there was ever anything nasty about Cullens. The wines – concentrated at the least expensive end of the market with a good range of more expensive wines too – are excellent value, and cheap indeed, compared with most lists in the country. Best value in the lower price ranges are Bulgarians [£], Chileans [£]–[££], lesser French wines. Ch Musar from the Lebanon is priced low [££]. Try the lovely fresh 'nouveau' Riesling from Hill Smith in Australia, which as we go to press just squeezes into the [£] range. Higher up the price range, still excellent value, Cullens is one of the best places to go in search of Australian wines, with a fairly full range from Rosemount, Brown Bros and Hill Smith (try particularly Hill Smith's rich, minty Cabernet Sauvignon [£££]). The few up-market Austrians (Kabinett+) are good value [£]–[£££] and Cullens stock one of the best ranges of Cooks' New Zealand wines [£]–[££]. There's a well-chosen scattering from elsewhere in Europe and the rest of the world, too.

BEST BUYS [£] Bulgarian Cabernet, [£] Syrah de l'Ardèche, [£]–[££] petit-château wines from Bordeaux, Bergerac and surrounds, [££] Vacheron Sancerre, [£££] Mondavi California wines

Davisons

HEAD OFFICE 7 Aberdeen Road, Croydon, Surrey TEL 01-681 3222
85 branches London and the Home Counties

OPEN (Variable) Mon–Sat 10 am–2 pm, 5 pm–10 pm Sun 12 noon–2 pm, 7 pm–9 pm, but check locally CREDIT CARDS Access/Euro, Visa; personal accounts DISCOUNTS 8½% on case orders, which may be mixed DELIVERY Free near most branches for a case or more GLASS HIRE Free
TASTINGS AND TALKS Ask locally

Part of the same Leonard Tong buying group as Unwins, Cullens etc, Davisons' strongest suit is France, particularly petit-château claret and Burgundy, with prices ranging from a little over £2 to about £10, generally a bit over the average. The nice thing about this bunch of cheaper clarets is that you don't have to hide them in a cellar until your grandchildren come of age: they can be drunk, the clarets that is, straight from the shop, though many will come to no harm if you want to keep them a while, since they are mostly from the better vintages of the late 1970s, like a mature, fruity Ch Picard 1979 from St-Estèphe for around £6; or you can dig a little deeper into your pocket or purse for an attractive Ch La Lagune 1976 (around £10). Red Burgundies offer the contrasting styles of traditional Dufouleur and ultra-modern Boisset, as well as a nugget or two from Louis Latour; Georges Duboeuf Brouilly and Fleurie are around £4. The Vin de Pays de Vaucluse red and especially the white were poor in summer 1984. Outside France, interest begins to wane a little; Germany and Italy are unexciting, and the rest of the world has token representation in Eastern Europe, the Iberian peninsula and the New World. The ten Champagnes are mostly NV, and the three vintage ports are good value: try ready-for-drinking Cockburn 1967 at just over £11. White and rosé wines are helpfully graded and coded for sweetness, and reds for fullness.

BEST BUYS [£]–[£££] Clarets, [£££] vintage ports

Peter Dominic

HEAD OFFICE Vintner House, River Way TEL (0279) 26801
Harlow, Essex
460 shops nationwide

OPEN (Variable) Mon–Sat 8.30 am–5.30 pm CLOSED Sun, public holidays
CREDIT CARDS All accepted, plus Grand Met and Peter Dominic accounts
DISCOUNTS 5% on case orders DELIVERY Free locally for orders over £20; 50p locally for orders under £20 GLASS HIRE Free TASTINGS AND TALKS 3–4 Wine Festivals a year; in-store tastings; *See also Peter Dominic Wine Mine Club below* CELLARAGE £3.35 per case per year

Peter Dominic stock a wide range of sound wines at fair, if rarely cheap, prices with a strong emphasis on France. Not every shop stocks every wine on their admirably clear, enthusiastic and informative list, but you can order any wine from the warehouse if you are prepared to allow up to three weeks for it to reach your local branch. Those who live or work in London may find their best Peter Dominic source is the Orange Street branch, tucked away behind the National Gallery, just off Haymarket; here you will find a much bigger range of wines, including a few rarities such as the deliciously concentrated, sweet Muscat à Petit Grain from Australian producers Stanton & Killeen. Away from the exotica and back into the ordinary branches, look out amongst the table wines for the good-value Les Chais Rouge and Blanc (£2.59). Many of the wines are Peter Dominic's own-label, or wines shipped exclusively by them, alongside a generous selection of brands, and some other wines. Alsace wines are from Hugel, most of the Beaujolais and Burgundies from the reliable Piat and the very reliable Bouchard Père, the agencies for which are held by sister companies of Peter Dominic within the Grand Met group. Look out, too, for the Chablis from Bacheroy-Josselin. Amongst the Rhônes, the Domaine de

Bel Air, tarry and full, is good value at £2.59. Peter Dominic are perhaps strongest on clarets, stocking some good petits-châteaux as well as classed growths, including a few older vintages. Dry white Bordeaux are worth a look, too, coming from yet more sister companies: try particularly the white wine from their Ch Loudenne (£4.25 for the 1983 vintage). Peter Dominic seem to have rounded up most of the major Liebfraumilch brands, but stock some better Germans, too, up to some mature Beerenauslesen. Stars amongst the Italians are Carmignano, Tenuta di Capezzana 1981 (£3.29), Ruffino Riserva Ducale 1977 (£4.10) and, on the assumption that it will approach the quality of last year's, try the Vino Novello from Lamberti when it beats Beaujolais Nouveau to the British shelves in the autumn [£]. There is a smattering of wines from elsewhere in the world. For those who want to learn more about wine, Peter Dominic run a tasting club, and produce regular newsletters *(see below)*.

BEST BUYS [£] Les Chais red and white, [£]–[££] petit-château clarets, [£]–[££] Italian wines mentioned above, [££]–[£££] Bouchard Père Burgundies

Peter Dominic Wine Mine Club

Vintner House, River Way, Harlow, Essex TEL (0279) 26801
DISCOUNTS AND DELIVERY *See Peter Dominic above*
TASTINGS AND TALKS Regularly in London, Wilmslow and Edinburgh

Operating from the Peter Dominic shops, the Wine Mine Club provides a basic information service for its members, as well as organising some interesting tastings. It also makes special offers from time to time of wines from the general Peter Dominic list, which may include brands such as Mateus as well as more interesting offerings and *'en primeur'* clarets. The quarterly newsletter contains features on wine areas and storing, serving and tasting wine, etc, aimed at the beginner or near-beginner, and occasional book reviews.

Eldridge Pope

HEAD OFFICE Weymouth Avenue TEL (0305) 64801
Dorchester, Dorset
13 branches in southern England

OPEN Mon–Fri 8.30 am–5.30 pm Sat 9 am–1 pm CLOSED Sun, public holidays CREDIT CARDS Not accepted DISCOUNTS On application DELIVERY Free in trading area GLASS HIRE Free TASTINGS AND TALKS Four tutored tastings per year for their own Dorset Wine Society CELLARAGE £1.20, min 20 cases

Eldridge Pope have told us to tell you to expect a dramatic change in their operation in the near future: they are completely revamping the whole range but were unable to supply details in time for this year's

Guide. If their two MWs Joe Naughalty and Jack de Carteret intend cutting the Independent Wine Buyers' Consortium apron-strings, then their customers could be even better served than in the past, although Eldridge Pope have always maintained a wide and interesting selection of other wines too, including particularly fine claret, good Burgundy, sherry and whisky, and have encouraged the appreciation of the finer things in life through their Dorset Wine Society.

Fine Fare

HEAD OFFICE Gate House, Fretherne Road TEL (07073) 28140
Welwyn Garden City, Hertfordshire
285 licensed branches particularly in the North East and Scotland
CREDIT CARDS Not accepted DISCOUNTS Not available

The task of changing all their wines 'from top to bottom' was still in progress as the *Guide* went to press, and Fine Fare were not able to provide us with information about their new look.

Fullers

HEAD OFFICE Griffin Brewery TEL 01-994 3691
Chiswick Lane, London, W4
About 60 branches in West London and the Home Counties
OPEN (Variable) Mon–Sat 10 am–2 pm, 4 pm–9 pm
CREDIT CARDS Access/Euro, Visa DISCOUNTS 5% on case orders
DELIVERY From some shops within reasonable distance GLASS HIRE Free
TASTINGS AND TALKS On request

A few clarets constitute the jam on Fullers' bread and butter list, and they are not particularly cheap. Ch Meyney 1979 at £7.50 heads the petit-château and generic wines, and the classed growths are mostly from lesser vintages like 1977 and 1980, with another Cordier wine, Ch Talbot 1977, at around £8. Burgundies are from Servant and Loron, Loires from the sparkling firm of Ackerman-Laurance, Rhônes from the big *négociant* David & Foillard, Alsace from Hugel, and there are a few French country wines. Germans are from Rudolf Müller and include a short range of QmP wines, mostly 1981 and 1982, with Auslesen around £4.50. Italians are basic and the rest of the world receives scant attention.

BEST BUYS ££ Alsace wines

Galbraith

See Argyll Stores

Galleon Wine

See Bass Off-Licences

Gateway

HEAD OFFICE PO Box 197, Cater Road, Bishopsworth, Bristol, Avon TEL (0272) 785555
About 300 licensed outlets

Gateway recently took over Key Markets and are in the process of rationalising the two wine ranges.

Gough Brothers

HEAD OFFICE Durham House 12 Upper Green West, Mitcham, Surrey TEL 01-640 5131
155 licensed branches in Greater London and the Home Counties
OPEN (Variable) Mon–Sat 9 am–9 pm Sun 12 noon–2 pm (some open in evening) Public holidays 11 am–2 pm CREDIT CARDS Access/Euro, Visa; personal accounts DISCOUNTS 5% on 1 case, 7½% on 2 cases, 10% on 3 cases DELIVERY 30p per mile, min 1 case GLASS HIRE Free
TASTINGS AND TALKS Ask locally

Sold by Scottish & Newcastle during 1984 to Seagram, Gough's, in common with many other chains, have different grades of shop, combined with a system of obligatory and optional items based on what they believe they can sell through each outlet; see if you think they've got it right when you pop into your local branch. Prices are a bit over the average, but Champagnes are well priced. Their forte is inexpensive wines, with French predominating, and the range includes quite a few brands as well as some which are shipped with Gough's name but which are not strictly own-label. The few 'Gough' wines we tasted suggested there was little to get excited about, but you may derive marginally more enjoyment from the reds than the whites; amongst these, Les Faisans red (under £2) is a light vin de table with some backbone, and Ch Haut-St-Romain 1981 (£2.75), an English bottling, is okay if you like fairly tough, hard claret; their Piesporter Michelsberg 1983 (£2.49), with a clean Germanic grapiness, is verging on pleasant. Italy is dull and Spain mostly the Corrida brand, but Hungary and Bulgaria get a look-in, as does the New World with Paul Masson California carafes and a couple of New Zealand wines from Cooks. White wines are marked with a nine-point sweetness indicator.

BEST BUYS [£££] Berri Estates three-litre bags-in-boxes, [£££] Champagne

Prices are correct to the best of our knowledge in summer 1984.

International

HEAD OFFICE Ocean House, Bracknell, Berkshire TEL (0344) 483111
330 licensed branches in southern England and Wales
CREDIT CARDS Not accepted DISCOUNTS Not available

There is unfortunately nothing for the serious wine buff amongst the small range of brands, the best of which might be Paul Masson California Carafes, Domecq Domain Rioja or Harvey's No 1 Claret £–££, nor amongst the uninspiring own-label wines from France, Germany, Italy and Spain, although one of the latest additions to the range, a Hock Tafelwein (£1.69) shows a slight and welcome improvement in quality. In addition they stock spirits, fortified wines, beer, lager and cider. Prices are quite keen.

BEST BUYS £–££ Standard brands

Key Markets

See under Gateway in this section

Lennons Ⓥ

HEAD OFFICE Corporation Street TEL (0744) 23216
St Helens, Merseyside
115 licensed branches in Merseyside and Greater Manchester
OPEN (Five-sixths) Mon–Sat 9 am–6 pm (and closed Sun) (One-sixth) Mon–Sat 9 am–9.30 pm Sun 12 noon–2 pm, 7 pm–9.30 pm CREDIT CARDS All accepted DISCOUNTS 5% on unmixed cases DELIVERY £2 per case on mainland UK GLASS HIRE Free CELLARAGE On request

Lennons is neither strictly a supermarket nor strictly a chain. The wine and spirit division is a subsidiary of Lennons PLC; 98 of its outlets are independent of the supermarkets, and about one-sixth operate more typical off-licence hours. This special status is reflected in the range of wines available, particularly from France, at mostly very fair prices: there is choice of Grande Marque Champagnes at under £10, clarets from Calvet and Cordier, including the latter's Sarget de Gruaud-Larose and Connétable de Talbot, and good, if not always cheap, offerings like Ch de Pez 1978 (£8.50). Burgundies are from the larger and less exciting *négociants* like Chanson and Patriarche, and the André Simon range is available, but they have some impeccable Alsace from Hugel. Italians are mostly generic, from Italvini, whilst Spain and Germany are relatively less well represented. Although Lennons is a bit more of an Aladdin's cave than many supermarket competitors, all that glisters isn't gold: there are a lot of brands, and a rather dull sheen on their own-label wines, with the possible exception of a gutsy house claret, AC Bordeaux rouge, and a clean, crisp Sauvignon

AC Bordeaux blanc (both around the £2 mark). Most shops stock most wines, but in any case, they all helpfully carry a stock-list so that you can order your vintage claret or Champagne if it isn't on the shelf.

BEST BUYS [£] House claret, Bordeaux Sauvignon, [£££] Champagne

Lipton

See Argyll Stores

Littlewoods

HEAD OFFICE JM Centre, Old Hall Street, Liverpool TEL 051-235 3109
105 licensed branches nationwide

CREDIT CARDS Not accepted DISCOUNTS 5% on unmixed cases

Little would induce one to rave about this short but inexpensive range; among the brand names, Harvey's No 1 Claret at £3.35 is the most expensive, and one of the best. The company hopes that '1985 will show the public that behind the knickers and socks in Littlewoods lurk some excellent wine buys'. Of their own-label wines, which are much in evidence, there is frankly little to get in a twist about, and no frills: Liebfraumilch from Rheinpfalz (£1.99 a bottle, £2.65 a litre) is about the best of the generally disappointing whites; but if you're in piggy-bank vein, you could do worse than try one of the slightly better reds like Full French Vin de Table (good value at £1.69), Vin de Pays d'Oc (£1.79) or Claret (£2.19).

BEST BUYS [£] The more expensive of the reds

Majestic Wine Warehouse (V)

Colina Mews, Park Road, London, N15 TEL 01-889 9380
OPEN Every day 10 am–8 pm

Albion Wharf, Hester Road, London, SW11 TEL 01-223 2983
OPEN Every day 10 am–10 pm

West Ealing Station, Hastings Road, London, W13 TEL 01-567 9251
OPEN Mon–Sat 10 am–8 pm Sun 10 am–5 pm

Arch 84, Goding Street, London, SE11 TEL 01-587 1830
OPEN Mon–Sat 10 am–8 pm Sun 10 am–4 pm

79 Sumner Road, Croydon, Surrey TEL 01-681 8130
OPEN Mon–Fri 11 am–9 pm Sat 10 am–8 pm Sun 10 am–7 pm

381 Cowley Road, Oxford, Oxon TEL (0865) 716959
OPEN Mon–Sat 10 am–8 pm Sun 10 am–5 pm

7–9 Coldhams Lane, Cambridge TEL (0223) 313133
OPEN Mon–Fri 10 am–8 pm Sat 9 am–7 pm Sun 10 am–4 pm

CREDIT CARDS Access/Euro, Visa DISCOUNTS Negotiable on orders over 30 cases DELIVERY Greater London and Cambridge £2.50–£5 per case for up to 9 cases; thereafter free GLASS HIRE Free TASTINGS AND TALKS Free in-store tastings

Majestic's breezy approach blows away a few cobwebs. You could throw caution to the winds, step into their fine wine section and walk out with, for example, any of the good range of classed-growth clarets from 15 vintages (how about a magnum of Ch Pape-Clément 1970 at £52?). But that is not what they are really about: if you can stand up to the gale force hype, you will find that their considerable strength lies in inexpensive wines for everyday drinking rather than prestigious names to grace your cellar. Petit-château clarets [£], including some 1982s, are very much for quaffing, and there are some light 1979s and lesser 1977s and 1974s like their Pauillac 1974 scoop – austere, tannic, but big and stylish – and the third wine, would you believe, of Ch Latour (£6.99). It is perhaps even more difficult to find sound, inexpensive wines from Burgundy, but in this shorter section there are some interesting whites from Clair-Daü as well as Chablis from Lamblin and Pic [££]–[£££]. Rhônes include a drinkable if unrefined Côtes-du-Rhône 1979 [£] from the Co-op at Rasteau. There are light reds and whites from all over the South of France costing 'no more than a couple of pints of bitter'; in the case of Vin de Pays de l'Hérault blanc, however, take the bitter. They are agents for Brems German wines, most of it QbA under £2, and there are middle-of-the-road Mergler & Engel wines, mostly from the 1981 vintage [£] for garden swigging. Sparklers are a mixed bunch, Champagnes are nearly all NV, but their House Champagne, Telmont Brut, although a bit coarse, is recognisably Champagne and under £6. Spain offers some well-priced Riojas, mostly from CVNE, and the good, cheap Valdepeñas wines of Viña Albalí (£1.89 and £2.59). They reckon that the jewels in the Majestic crown are the Bulgarians; see if you agree by trying the 1976 Sakar Mountain Cabernet (£2.69). Sherries are particularly good value, such as the lovely, aromatic Fino Marismeno, well priced at £3.29, and, for a special treat, the Almacenista sherries [£]–[£££]. California and South Africa get a look in, as does Australia with Brown Bros and Rothbury wines, but if you're not sure what you like from this catholic collection, go along to one of their free tastings. What you save on wine bargains you can spend on coffee, oils and tinned Roux brothers' pâté.

BEST BUYS [£]–[£££] clarets, [£]–[££] Spanish wines, [££]–[£££] sherries

The Market/Le Provençal

Ⓥ

The Market, 213–215 Upper Street, London, N1	TEL 01-359 5386
The Market, 700–702 Fulham Road, London, SW6	TEL 01-736 4348
The Market, 32–34 Highgate High Street, London, N6	TEL 01-348 2422
The Market, 12 Craven Road, London, W2	TEL 01-723 6965
The Market, 165 Haverstock Hill, London, NW3	TEL 01-722 6521
Le Provençal, 167 Haverstock Hill, London, NW3	TEL 01-586 7987

OPEN Mon–Sun 9 am–9 pm public holidays 9 am–9 pm CLOSED Chr Day, Boxing Day CREDIT CARDS Not accepted DISCOUNTS 10% on unmixed cases and cases made up in multiples of 3 bottles, unless already promotionally discounted DELIVERY Free in Central London, min 6 cases; no deliveries outside central London; £3 for smaller orders GLASS HIRE Free
TASTINGS AND TALKS In-store tastings 6 times a year

Don't be fooled by the supermarket-look exterior – you'll get supermarket service all right (unless you *ask*, and then you might find the staff have been taught a thing or two); but you will also find a consistently good-value range of wines from all over Europe, with particular emphasis on the superior wines of Italy. Wine buyer Nicholas Belfrage MW's book on Italian wines should appear by the end of 1985, and his literary research has obviously been put to good use. On The Market's list (prices here are at the mixed case rate, ten per cent down on shelf prices), Italian wines take up a whole large page, half as much as France! Look out especially for the Tieffenbrunner wines from the South Tyrol at around £3, Valpolicellas from Masi and Soave from Pieropan, and the Chiantis: Villa di Vetrice, Castellare, Villa di Capezzana [£]–[££]; Lungarotti's Torgiano is a good, full, fruity wine (£2.39 a bottle at case price), as are the Pio Cesare wines of North-West Italy [£]–[£££]. Iberian wines are good here too. At the case price, Marqués de Cáceres is to be had here cheaper than from most other British retailers (£2.28 for the white and £2.43 for the red 1978); there's the lovely Viña Ardanza 1976, not *so* cheap but still only £3.70, and a good basic Rioja at just £1.89. Viña Albalí (£1.75) is one of the best Valdepeñas we have tasted (a bit of friendly expertise swapping here with Spanish experts Ehrmanns – *see SPECIALISTS above*). And there are very few Portuguese wines we would wholeheartedly recommend apart from the attractive Dão Conde de Santar 1978 (£2.31) and the rich, remarkably young-tasting Garrafeira Caves Velhas 1968 (£2.56). At the cheaper end, the Bulgarian wines present some of the best value [£]. Back to those two pages of French wines, there's also good value to be had here, mostly in the lower price brackets [£]–[££]. Look out especially for Gitton Sancerre and Pouilly Fumé (£3.98 and £4.10), the artfully labelled Ch Toutigeac 1981 (£2.31), some good-value clarets, many well bought from poor vintages, excellent Rhônes and good 'French regional wines'. Champagnes are well priced. Last summer you could have found Roederer NV for £9.16, Alfred Gratien for £9.09, or for the more frugal, the very acceptable Blanc de Blancs, Michel Gonet, for just £5.58, or, more frugal still, the sparkling Saumurs of Gratien & Meyer (£4.31 and £4.73). The Market's list, with its full details of producers (but where are the names of the Germans who produced these 'wines of excellent breeding'?) and concise, helpful tasting notes, is (nearly) exemplary. The company closed three unprofitable shops during the past year, in Streatham, Kings Mall and Hammersmith – and the wine drinkers in those areas are so much the poorer.

BEST BUYS Most things on the list, especially by the case; [£]–[££] Italian wines, [£££] Champagne

Marks & Spencer

HEAD OFFICE Michael House TEL 01-935 4422
47–67 Baker Street, London, W1
260 licensed branches throughout UK

CREDIT CARDS Not accepted DISCOUNTS Not available

Provided you don't want a wide choice and are prepared to take what is available, M & S are almost bound to have something you'll like in their range of about 35 European wines and half a dozen sherries. Their Full French Red (£2.99 a litre) has received much favourable publicity, and rightly so: it is a solid, fresh, flavoursome blend of Carignan and Grenache (actually an AC Côtes du Roussillon-Villages) and rather outshines the French Dry White from Anjou at the same price. Amongst the whites, the Chablis at £3.99, one of a short Vintage Selection range, is well worth the price, as is the attractive, plummy red Pomeral Rioja at £3.19. Not all stores carry the Vintage Selection wines, however, and you may have to content yourself with the standard offerings, in which case you will enjoy fairly reliable if unexciting drinking, at prices that can easily be beaten elsewhere.

BEST BUYS [£] Full French Red, [££] Chablis, Rioja

James Mellor and Mellor & Pattison (V)

HEAD OFFICE 127 Duke Street, Liverpool TEL 051-236 8651
Mellor & Pattison 2/4 Tithebarn Street, Liverpool TEL 051-236 7001
20 licensed branches on Merseyside

OPEN (Variable) Mon–Sat 10.30 am–1 pm, 5 pm–10 pm Sun (some closed) 12 noon–2 pm, 7 pm–10 pm CREDIT CARDS Not accepted; personal accounts DISCOUNTS 10% on case orders DELIVERY 1 case or more free within 20 miles of Liverpool; elsewhere on UK mainland £5 per delivery, min 1 case
GLASS HIRE Free TASTINGS AND TALKS Four a year for trade and private customers

Followers of Izaak Walton, and auction prices will understand the significance of a bottle of Ch Cheval-Blanc 1975 at a mere £26, or a Dow 1955 port at £12. These are, or were, part of the small and constantly changing stock of the two Mellor & Pattison shops where MD David Winepress (sic) sportingly uses them to tempt customers to browse through his other goodies; there is no mail order, and there may only be the odd bottle available, but wherever you are in the country, you stand a good chance of paying for your train fare with the savings on a couple of well-chosen purchases, and you could also take home Burgundies from the Domaine de la Romanée-Conti, Geisweiler, Jaffelin, Drouhin or Loron, as well as Chanson, Patriarche and d'Esgrigny. Not all the James Mellor shops on Merseyside carry the exalted items of stock, but they will obtain them for you. More usual fare might include generic Bordeaux from Schröder & Schÿler and one or two petit-château clarets, Alsace wines from Hugel, Paul Masson carafes and varietals from California (the Chardonnay, for example, is around £4), a choice of half a dozen Liebfraumilchs, a standard range of Italians, and a list of brands as long as your arm. But for wine buffs the Tithebarn Street shop looks the sort of place you could easily get hooked on.

BEST BUYS Most of the range is well priced

Mojo

See Argyll Stores

Morrisons Ⓥ

HEAD OFFICE Young Street, Thornton Road TEL (0274) 497421
Bradford, West Yorkshire
34 branches in Lancashire and Yorkshire, all licensed
CREDIT CARDS Not accepted DISCOUNTS Not available

Morrisons have a good range of predominantly European wines (but no own-labels) and they are nothing if not eclectic: you might come across anything from a humble but drinkable Minervois or a Corbières from the co-opérative at St-André for well under £2, to a 1979 Ch Margaux or Ch Lafite, both at just over £20, with quite a lot in between. Best value from the Italian assortment is to be had by passing over the ordinary Chianti or Frascati, with a choice of two or three of each up to about £2.50, and the umpteen assorted, mostly European, brands, and paying just a little bit extra for, say, the Montepulciano d'Abruzzo (£2.59) from the Adriatic coast, a Gattinara (£2.99) from Piemonte, or Venegazzù (£3.45). Wines from the south of France, like Roussillon, Lubéron and the Listel range (the attractive Domaine du Bosquet is £2.31) nestle cheek by jowl with Burgundies from Chanson and village Beaujolais from Duboeuf and the odd bottle of something more exciting. A good range of standard sherries includes Harvey, Gonzalez Byass, Sandeman, Williams & Humbert and others. Prices of most wines are very competitive.

BEST BUYS Most things on the list are keenly priced; £–£££ French wines, £–££ the less 'standard' Italians

Morris's

HEAD OFFICE Stirling Road TEL 021-704 3415
Cranmore Industrial Estate, Shirley, Solihull, West Midlands
25 licensed branches in the Midlands including Astral Wines
OPEN (Variable) Mon–Sat 10 am–2 pm, 6 pm–10 pm Sun 12 noon–2 pm, 7 pm–10 pm CREDIT CARDS Amex in all branches, Access/Euro, Visa in some shops DISCOUNTS By negotiation DELIVERY Free within 30 miles of

Birmingham, then £3 for 1 case, £4 for 2 cases, £1.50 per case for 3–10 cases, thereafter £1 per case GLASS HIRE 20p per dozen, £6 deposit required TASTINGS AND TALKS Occasionally CELLARAGE Free

France is by far the strongest section in this range of mostly European wines, with a token handful from Eastern Europe, California and South Africa, and whilst there is no shortage of brand names, they are balanced by well-chosen and more interesting bottles from the Merchant Vintners' range, of which Morris's are members. Clarets, for example, include the deliciously fruity red Graves Cuvée Pierre Coste 1979 (£3.49) and his 1978 Domaine de Gaillat(£5.49), as well as a good mix of classed and lesser growths from most of the good vintages of the 1970s; there are a few vintages of Ch Ducru-Beaucaillou and Cordier's Ch Gruaud-Larose, with the latter's 1976 at around £10. From Burgundy, Morris's stock Côte d'Or reds of good pedigree from Roumier, Dujac, Latour and Drouhin, with a preponderance of 1978s and 1979s, but quality doesn't come cheap and there is very little under £10; whites from recent vintages include a choice of Meursaults, Puligny-Montrachets and others, from a variety of producers. Rhônes are few but combine inexpensive Côtes-du-Rhône, Lubéron and Ventoux from the south with quality Hermitage and Crozes-Hermitage from Paul Jaboulet, Guigal and Chapoutier in the north. Italy consists of standard Ambra and Bolla wines, Spain is brand-heavy, but Germany offers a more balanced selection with QmP wines from Deinhard and Peter Mertes. There is a short but comprehensive range of vintage ports from 1955 to 1977, although the prices here are not really for bargain-hunters.

BEST BUYS [£]–[££] Cheaper clarets, [£]–[£££] Rhônes

Oddbins

HEAD OFFICE 80 Wapping High Street, London, E1 TEL 01-488 0109
57 branches nationally

OPEN Variable, but generally 10 am–8 pm CLOSED Sun, public holidays CREDIT CARDS Access/Euro, Visa DISCOUNTS Not available in shops; mail order £1 per case for 2 cases, £1.75 per case for 3–4 cases, £2 per case for 5+ cases DELIVERY No delivery from shops; free on UK mainland from mail order list GLASS HIRE Free TASTINGS AND TALKS Monthly in-store tastings in London and environs; elsewhere occasionally CELLARAGE Not available

Canadian booze giant Seagram's taking a three-quarters share in Oddbins seems to have brought little change, in these early stages at least, to their policy of stocking a wide and interesting range in *all* their 57 branches, at very keen prices. In addition to the shops, Oddbins by Post, celebrating its second birthday in 1985, offers a selection of this 400 to 500-wine range from an admirably informative list incorporating good tasting notes on almost every wine; orders are taken by mail or by phone to these new premises into which the company moved early in 1984. We can confidently say that Oddbins are the only wine merchants to employ a full-time art department – of five artists, each with an individual style, who dream up and keep up the distinctive Oddbins shops, and provide all the posters and signs for in-store promotion and information. Oddbins is a good place to go for something out of the ordinary, but you will find at least a few fine pickings from most of the better-known wine regions of the world, too. Amongst an interesting list of French country wines, the light, prickly white Apremont from Savoie is worth a try (£3.83, shelf price). Loires are good, some of the best value coming from the co-opérative of Oisly-et-Thésée, a light, well-made, fresh Sauvignon de Touraine 1983 (£2.70) and a lovely, light, juicy-fruit Cabernet de Touraine (£2.65). Look for the good cheaper clarets, a reliable Rhône and Burgundy range. Champagnes are good value: for those on a tight budget, the appley-fresh Comte de Blanzac Champagne is perfectly adequate at £5.99, and the Philiponnat range begins at £8.82. German wines include a number of grower and estate wines back to 1976 and up the sweetness scale to Auslesen, and include the excellent wines of Bert Simon, von Bühl and others. Rioja is an Oddbins speciality: don't ignore the cheapest: Vega 1980 is a good oaky-gamy wine at £2.43, and the white Rioja Gran Vendema 1983 (£2.35) is really Marqués de Cáceres in disguise. Some interesting Italians include wines from Masi, Nera and Ceretto [£]–[£££]. Portuguese wines have obviously taken Oddbins' fancy, too: best value are the Garrafeira 1974, Caves Velhas, almost over-rich and still young-tasting (£2.85), the ripe, intense Pasmados 1971 (£4.69) and Garrafeira 1974, Cavalho Ribeiro & Ferreira (£3.95). Watch out for the sherries of Barbadillo and Lustau [£]–[££], some well-priced ports, and bits and pieces from Chile, Morocco, Bulgaria, California, Australia, and Lenz Moser sweet Austrians. Oddbins staff tend to be well-trained, too, so ask for advice.

BEST BUYS Most wines, especially those mentioned above

Presto

See Argyll Stores

Le Provençal

See The Market

Arthur Rackham's Ⓥ

HEAD OFFICE Winefare House, Byfleet, Surrey TEL (093 23) 51585
15 shops in London and Surrey

OPEN (Variable) Mon–Sat 9 am–6 pm or 10 am–2 pm, 5 pm–10 pm Sun 12 noon–2 pm, 7 pm–9 pm Public holidays 11 am–3 pm CLOSED Wed pm CREDIT CARDS Discount Club cards and credit cards through the Vintners Wine Club DISCOUNTS 13 bottles for the price of 12; 10% on 10+ cases

DELIVERY Free in London and Surrey, min 5 cases; for smaller quantities and elsewhere on UK mainland £3 per case, 10+ cases free GLASS HIRE Free TASTINGS AND TALKS Frequent in-store tastings; annual tasting August Bank Holiday at Foxhills Golf and Country Club; specialist organised tastings; for groups on request

The shelves of Arthur Rackham's Wine Shops have never been the most exciting to peruse because of Rackham's policy of buying almost exclusively from one supplier within a specific area, though of course this has obvious price advantages. But things have been changing over the past year, and whilst the old Rackham favourites still hog a large amount of the shelf space, over 70 new wines have been added, so these multi-coloured shops now offer much more interesting browsing. For one thing, Rackhams have become champions of the English wine cause, and have taken on a remarkably large collection of English wines which they hope to promote heavily over the coming year: several Ditchling, Staple St James, Spots Farm and Tenterden wines of the 1982 and 1983 vintages, all under £4. A number of 1976 classed growth clarets have been added to the predominantly Cordier collection (which includes the 1981 vintages of the three 'second wines' of Cordier, good value at £4.59. A few more interesting Burgundies (Marchand de Gramont and others) have broken Louis Latour's exclusivity, whilst more German wines – from Guntrum and Schloss Rheinhartshausen – have come in alongside old favourite Müller (concentrating still on sweetness grades reaching only as high as Spätlese). CVNE wines now make an appearance alongside the well-priced Marqués de Cáceres on the Rioja shelf, and yet more of the cheap and reliable Chantovent wines are to be found amongst the French regionals. Even places down under are getting a look-in: Rosemount wines, Berri estates, including the tasty bag-in-box Cabernet/Shiraz at £7.69, are well worth a try, as is the lovely Matawhero Gewürztraminer 1982 from New Zealand (£3.99), and Ch Musar 1977 at £4.29 from the Lebanon. Hardest sell of all is reserved perhaps for the fine Champagnes of Alfred Gratien, for which Rackhams hold the agency. Look for old vintages back to 1961 (£47.50) as well as big bottles: you could blow £124 on a NV Salmanazar. Rackhams were about to launch a new mail order venture as we went to press, characteristically linked in with a small number of suppliers which include Cordier and Dom Ruinart.

BEST BUYS Prices generally are keen; [£]–[££] Riojas, [££] Australian and New Zealand wines, [££] 'second wines' of Cordier

Roberts of Worthing

See Arthur Cooper

Prices were current in summer 1984 to the best of our knowledge but can only be a rough indication of prices throughout 1985.

Safeway

HEAD OFFICE Beddow Way, Aylesford TEL (0622) 77822
Maidstone, Kent
OPEN Mon–Fri 8 pm (some later) Sat 8 am–6 pm
CREDIT CARDS Not accepted DISCOUNTS, DELIVERY Not available

Safeway stock a large range, including some brands at often rather high prices, but mostly own-label wines or wines bottled specially for them, which are much better value. Last summer, the Safeway litres of Vin de Table Rouge from René Rousseau, light with liquoricy fruit, was very good value at £2.35, though hardly, as they say on the label, 'a full-bodied red wine'. German wines from Zimmermann-Graeff are clean and fresh; there are other German wines from a variety of suppliers. The Loire wines from the Celliers de la Loire are dull, as are the Hungarians. But the light Côtes-du-Rhône (£1.99) and the fruity and firm Rioja (£2.25) were good at these prices. Try Safeway's young, blackcurranty claret (£2.29) if you like reds with plenty of tough tannin. Best value is to be found in this middle price range of their own labels rather than under the 'Fine wines at low prices' sign. The latter come mostly from Reine Pédauque in Burgundy and Roger Joanne in Bordeaux, plus a few rather highly priced bourgeois and classed growths, often of lesser vintages.

BEST BUYS £ Own-label claret, Vin de Table Rouge, Rioja

J Sainsbury & Co

HEAD OFFICE Stamford House TEL 01-921 6000
Stamford Street, London, SE1
About 250 licensed branches mostly London and the South
CREDIT CARDS Not accepted DISCOUNTS Not available

Along with only two or three other supermarkets, Sainsbury's are at the heart of the current revolution in the British public's wine-buying habits. The better supermarkets all stock their shelves with a combination of own-label wines for everyday drinking and a selection of top quality, more expensive wines such as we normally associate with the traditional wine merchant; this policy has certainly paid off for Sainsbury's, who are the biggest UK retailer of light wines, accounting for about 15 per cent of the market. The own-label wines have no pretensions above being sound, drinkable, value-for-money bottles, and that is more or less how we found them; the range is impressive, getting on for 100 in the better-stocked stores, with a good variety from France particularly, followed by Germany. Their big-selling Liebfraumilch is a non-vintage blend of Silvaner and Müller-Thurgau from the Rheinpfalz at under £2, and is clean, scented and palatable. You can have fun navigating the backwaters of France, but leave room in your trolley for some mainstream Claret, a fruity

Bordeaux Supérieur at under £2. Spanish reds include a reasonable, own-label Rioja, La Rioja Alta's Viña Alberdi (£2.25), the less familiar Valdepeñas (the excellent Viña Albalí, £2.25) and excellent Jumilla (£1.95), but Italy is less well represented. From Portugal, however, there's the delicious claret-style Quinta da Bacchalôa. A good selection of sparklers includes their own-label Champagne at around £6. Some stores are blessed with a rack of well-chosen Vintage Selection wines; with rare exceptions, these range in price from £3 to about £7 or £8; are understandably mainly from vintages within the last five years; and may include petit-château clarets (with a classed growth if you're lucky), good producers like Louis Latour, Hugel and Chanson, and 1976 German Auslesen. Constant updating of the range keeps regular customers on their toes. Consult the nine-point sweetness indicator, applicable to all white, rosé and sparkling wines, if in any doubt; and pick up any leaflets that are going to keep yourself amused whilst waiting at the checkout.

BEST BUYS Own-labels, most things on the list

W S Sanderson

HEAD OFFICE Hope & Anchor Brewery TEL (0670) 57521
Morpeth, Northumberland
21 branches in Northumberland, Tyne & Wear, North Durham

OPEN Mon–Sat 10 am–10 pm Sun 12 noon–2 pm, 7 pm–9 pm
CREDIT CARDS Access/Euro, Visa; personal accounts DISCOUNTS 2½% on mixed cases, 2½% cash on delivery, 50p per case cash & carry DELIVERY Free in Northumberland, Durham, Carlisle and Borders, min 1 mixed case, elsewhere £3.95 per case GLASS HIRE £2 per 10 dozen thereafter 15p per dozen
TASTINGS AND TALKS One free tasting per year, smaller ones at £1.25 per head
CELLARAGE £1.56 per case per annum

Sanderson, a Merchant Vintners' company, has an interesting and eclectic range of wines set out in a helpfully annotated catalogue. Clarets are mostly from the decade of the 1970s, but there are one or two from earlier years as well as 1981s, 1982s and 1983s; their selection from the 1970 vintage ranges from a Ch Meyney at under £9 to a Ch Beychevelle at over £26, the 1978 vintage from Ch Cissac at over £7 to Ch Ducru-Beaucaillou at over £14. Red Burgundy includes Beaujolais from Pasquier-Desvignes and Sarrau, and wines from Antonin Rodet such as Bourgogne Rouge, Gevrey-Chambertin, and their domain Mercurey, Ch de Chamirey, all from the large but attractive 1979 vintage, and from £3.50 to £7.50; white Burgundies are mostly from 1980 onwards. There are few Rhônes, but they include the Merchant Vintners' Ch du Grand Moulas (the 1982 is under £3), and there is a handful of Loire, Alsace and French regional wines. Deinhard and Guntrum supply many of the German wines which range from plentiful 1982 QbAs at around £2 to £3 back to some very rich 1976s. Amongst the Italians, Tuscany comes up trumps with white Vernaccia di San Gimignano, and reds Vino Nobile di Montepulciano and Brunello di Montalcino as well as a choice of good Chiantis. Spain is not neglected, offering Marqués de Murrieta and CVNE Riojas [£]–[££]; and as well as a few Eastern European, California and South African wines, there are half a dozen Cooks' New Zealand wines, Tollana wines from Australia and Cousiño Macul 1976 (under £4.50) from Chile. Vintage and NV grande marque Champagne (NV mostly £10 or under) and vintage ports for both laying down and drinking, bring up the rear.

BEST BUYS [£] 'Lesser French Regional Wines', [£]–[££] Rhônes

Templeton

See Argyll Stores

Tesco

HEAD OFFICE Tesco House, Delamare Road TEL (0992) 32222
Cheshunt, Hertfordshire
358 licensed branches nationwide

CREDIT CARDS Not accepted DISCOUNTS Not available

There has been a big upward swoop in quality at Tesco over the past year and a bit, thanks to the arrival of senior wine buyer Adrian Lane, a fledgling of the fine Sainsbury's nest. In addition to a large selection of branded wines, Tesco have launched 50 own-label wines, with more to come. Prices are keen and there's good value to be had in the lower price ranges, well below £2, where the quality is still sound. Tesco's labels are amongst the best-designed and prettiest in the whole wine world. Those who lose their appetite at the sight of a supermarket label on their dining table will be pleased to note that the Tesco's crest is so discreet as to be hardly noticeable. More and more Tesco's wine departments are moving over to self-service. But the little Tesco Good Wine Guide booklet is, in our view, almost useless.

BEST BUYS [£] Table wines and lower-priced wines, Loire, Rhône.

Threshers

HEAD OFFICE Sefton House, 42 Church Road TEL (070 73) 28244
Welwyn Garden City, Hertfordshire
400 branches, mainly in the North West, South and South East

OPEN (Variable) Mon–Sat 9 am or 10 am–9 pm or 10 pm Sun and public holidays 12 noon–2 pm, 7 pm–9 pm CREDIT CARDS Access/Euro, Visa DISCOUNTS 5% for 1–4 cases, 10% for 5 cases and over DELIVERY Ask locally GLASS HIRE Free

Whether you get wheat or chaff at your local branch of Threshers may depend to some extent on your manager, since not all shops stock the full range. You may strike lucky and come across the likes of Ch Lynch-Bages 1979 at £8.69, but much more likely is a good range of less ambitious but acceptable wines like the own-label full-bodied young Côtes du Roussillon-Villages (£2.49) or straight commercial claret (£2.59). Most of the numerous Burgundies and Bordeaux are pitched at under a fiver, like a Côte de Beaune-Villages Réserve de la Grosse Tour 1979 at £4.79 or the bourgeois Ch de By 1981 at £3.49, and there should be just enough of interest, such as the very good Corsican Domaine Torraccia at £2.59, to steer you away from the brands. But even there, as well as the superbores, you will find the better Domecq Domain Rioja (£2.79), for example.

BEST BUYS Wines mentioned above

House of Townend

HEAD OFFICE Red Duster House, York Street, Hull TEL (0482) 26891
30 branches in Humberside

OPEN (Variable) Mon–Sat 10 am–10 pm Sun 12 noon–2 pm, 7 pm–9.30 pm
CREDIT CARDS Access/Euro, Visa; accounts DISCOUNTS 10% on non-promotional mixed cases DELIVERY Free within 3 miles of any branch, min 1 case, thereafter by arrangement GLASS HIRE 25p per dozen
TASTINGS AND TALKS Bi-annual tasting by invitation; frequent local tastings: ask branch manager CELLARAGE £2.30 + insurance and VAT

If you can make it to the head office cash-and-carry and buy by the case, the range of wines will be greater and the prices may be lower than in the shops, where, as always, they are geared to very local demand. Townends are part of the Merchant Vintners buying group, and their full range reflects the strengths and weaknesses of the group. Good Bordeaux include the dry white Ch Reynon 1982 (£2.99) and classed growth clarets from 1970 onwards, with less expensive petits-châteaux of the 1978, 1979 and 1981 vintages, which may be drunk now or kept for a short while, including Ch Cissac 1978 (£5.99) and 1979 (£5.49) as well as the light, fruity Pierre Coste wines. A small selection of good white Burgundy from Loron, Latour and Rémon, and reds from Chanson, Boisset et al, span a wide price range. Rhônes include a few vintages of Brunier's very drinkable Châteauneuf-du-Pape Domaine du Vieux Télégraphe, at around £5.60 for the 1977, 1979 and 1980 vintages, and French country wines are few but well chosen, such as Minervois Ch de Gourgazaud (£2.92) and Côtes de Buzet 1980 (£2.99). The short German range shows an eye for quality amongst the QmP wines in both shippers and vintages, but may set you back a bob or two, like the Schloss Vollrads Kabinett 1982 at £7.35 from the Rheingau, or some of von Schubert's Ruwer wines such as a 1976 Maximin Grünhauser Abstberg Spätlese (£9.59). Italy is more basic, there are some 1970 and 1975 ports, and beyond Bulgaria you fall off the edge of the world.

BEST BUYS [£] Ch Reynon white Bordeaux, [£] French country wines, [£]–[£££] clarets

Underwoods

See Bass Off-Licences

Unwins

HEAD OFFICE Birchwood House TEL (0322) 72711
Victoria Road, Dartford, Kent
285 branches in London and Home Counties

OPEN (Variable) Mon–Sat 10 am–2 pm, 4 pm–9 pm (or 10 pm) Sun 12 noon–2 pm, 7 pm–9 pm CLOSED Usually one day per week (Tue or Wed, check locally) CREDIT CARDS All accepted DISCOUNTS 1 case 5%, more for larger orders DELIVERY Free in North and Central London, some outlying areas, and within 70 miles radius for bulk orders; otherwise at cost, plus packing and insurance GLASS HIRE Free with order TASTINGS AND TALKS On request CELLARAGE On application

A broad spectrum of wines is on offer from this serious High Street chain, from bread and butter stuff at around £2 a bottle up to first-growth claret (Chx Haut-Brion, Latour and Mouton-Rothschild are £35 each for the 1978 vintage). Prices tend to be rather high, compared even to many of the independent specialist merchants. France is by far the strongest section, and Bordeaux figures prominently: a straight Bordeaux Rouge 1982 (£2.29) bottled for them by Albert Bichot, for whom they are UK agents, is a lively, fruity, everyday wine. The three dozen fine clarets are mostly between five and ten years old and many will need to be kept for a while before drinking, although if you have an eye for the lesser and more forward vintages you will find Ch Léoville-Las-Cases 1974 or Ch Malescot St-Exupéry 1977, at under £10 a bottle, worth a try. Bichot Burgundies such as the Santenay 1981 (£6.72) do not seem to justify the high prices, but there are plenty of others to choose from. Germany, likewise, offers a selection from bland brands through to some fine QmP wines like Hallgarten's Wehlener Sonnenuhr Spätlese 1982 (£5) or Deinhard's Winkeler Hasensprung Riesling Auslese 1976 (£12.50). Spain is unadventurous with Marqúes de Murrieta topping the bill (£4.79), whilst in Italy Rosso Piceno 1982 (£3.60) peeps through a chink in the solid wall of standard names. Eastern Europe, South Africa, Australia, New Zealand, and a Ch Musar 1977 (£5) from the Lebanon bring up the rear. If your local branch has only a modest stock, they will obtain any of the other wines for you, and also offer to seek out any wine you care to name; if it is imported into Britain they will get hold of it for you.

BEST BUYS French wines, but prices are high

The Victoria Wine Company

HEAD OFFICE Brook House, Chertsey Road TEL (048 62) 5066
Woking, Surrey
800 branches nationwide

OPEN Variable CREDIT CARDS All accepted DISCOUNTS 5% on case orders of wine, sparkling wine and vintage port, 3% on 6 bottles DELIVERY Free locally (every shop) for purchases over £25; £1 for smaller quantities GLASS HIRE Free

Many of the Victoria Wine shops have been rejuvenated over the past few months, and the whole 800-strong chain will have taken on the same cool, white-and-green super-modern look a couple of years from now. Along with the 'Habitat' look, conceived by Victoria Wine's new MD Lister Fielding (former MD of Mothercare Europe) has come a completely original approach to wine retailing. Victoria Wine now arrange white wine on the shelves by sweetness and reds and sherries by weight and firmness, according to the 'wine selector' scales they introduced a year or so ago. To the wine beginner – most of the British nation – this can be an enormous help. But it might take those who *know* the wine they're after a while longer than usual to establish its whereabouts. A doctor amongst our readers wrote to complain that his local branch had become 'a total shambles, wines being classified according to their *sweetness* – French, Spanish, Italians, etc all jumbled together'. But our friends in the wine trade dealing with obscurer regions report that the system is leading people to experiment with the more unusual wines, which are prominently displayed, a tasting note on the shelf below them, instead of being tucked away on the bottom shelf – and that can't be a bad thing. Victoria Wine's list looks most impressive (now also arranged in the same organised 'jumble' as their shops) but of course not all the wines are available at every branch. Most, in fact, stock around half the listed range, of which many wines are own-label, and the rest, starred on the list, can be ordered and obtained within a week or so. Victoria Wine employ a very competent buying team, and quality here can be relied upon to be extremely good. For bargains, look out for their own-label wines – the Côtes-du-Rhône (£2.19) is excellent, the claret (£2.19) good – but elsewhere, check prices carefully if you have another possible wine source, because some of them are rather high – clarets, for instance, brands in general, Champagnes and vintage ports. At the bottom of the price range, their fragrant Vin de Pays Catalan is excellent value at £1.79, and their Corbières (£2.19) is unusually soft. The Muscadet de Sèvre-et-Maine Ch de la Cassemichère 1983 (£3.19) is a lovely fresh, rich wine and the Gatão Vinho Verde (£2.49) has recently improved, drier now. German wines, the cheaper ones from the very reliable Sankt Ursula Weinkellerei, with a good (orderable) selection of estate-bottled wines from Kabinett to Trockenbeerenauslese level, are good, and Spain offers some safe bets, including the newly improved Don Cortez wines, especially the rosé. There are some good (orderable) Italian wines, too, and wines (some orderable, some ubiquitous) from Australia and New Zealand. All Victoria Wine shops' cash registers should be plugged into a stock control computer by the time the *Guide* is published, the largest system of its kind in Europe, the company claims. As Christmas approaches, it's worth noting, especially in view of the far-flung locations of the branches, that they offer a gift token scheme.

BEST BUYS Own-label wines, especially Côtes-du-Rhône

Waitrose

HEAD OFFICE Doncastle Road TEL (0344) 24680
Southern Industrial Area, Bracknell, Berkshire
76 branches in South East England, North as far as Leicester, West as far as Bristol

OPEN Mon 12 noon–6 pm Tue, Wed 9 am–6 pm Thur, Fri 9 am–8 pm Sat 8.30 am–4 pm CLOSED Sun, public holidays DISCOUNTS 5% on orders of £500 + GLASS HIRE Free

Waitrose's wide assortment of wines is bought to a very high standard, whether own-label or under producers' labels, and some very interesting wines are to be found here, especially amongst the reds, at very keen prices. Though France dominates the shelves, there is plenty to choose from elsewhere, and prices range from the very cheap to claret and Burgundy at nearly £7. Good buys on the Waitrose shelves in the summer of 1984 included own-label Alsace Gewürztraminer (£2.55), a fragrant white Vin de Pays des Côtes de Gascogne 1983 (£1.79), the fruity Cuvée Valclair Rouge (£1.75), 1.5 litre bottles of Dolianova Vino da Tavola from Sardinia, fruity with a nice, slightly bitter finish (£3.49), a light red Côtes de Duras (£1.95), and the excellent Ch de Rivard AC Bordeaux 1982 (£2.35). The soft Pinot-and-Cabernet Cooks' New Zealand Dry Red is delicious at £2.55. Higher up the price range, try the Venegazzù at £3.45, the full, rich, easy Haughton Supreme from Australia (£3.65) or, for a special occasion, the Clos du Château, Ch de Meursault 1979 white (£6.55).

BEST BUYS Wines mentioned above

Whittalls

HEAD OFFICE Château Pleck, Darlaston Road TEL (0992) 36161
Walsall, West Midlands
75 Branches, mainly in the Midlands

OPEN Mon–Sat 10 am–10 pm (some branches close pm) Sun 12 noon–2 pm, 7 pm–10 pm CREDIT CARDS Not accepted DISCOUNTS Case prices by negotiation DELIVERY Large quantities only GLASS HIRE 50p per dozen CELLARAGE By arrangement

This selection is designed to provide standard drinking from a limited range of producers, with few shocks to the system; so provided you like these particular producers' wines and don't wish to explore further, you should be all right. Most of them come through the Independent Wine

Buyers' Consortium (IWBC), of which Whittalls are members along with companies like Eldridge Pope, Thomas Baty and Willoughbys. Louis Sipp provides the four Alsace wines of which the 1979 Gewürztraminer (£3.59) is attractively scented with spicy honey; modestly priced Loires are mostly from Robert Noël, house Champagne is de Venoge, and so on. The trouble with relying almost exclusively on IWBC is that there is some pretty dull stuff, like the house Bordeaux wines, Delamère Claret and Ch Tanesse white; but by way of compensation there is a small but sensible selection of classed-growth clarets from most of the vintages of the 1970s, with a special crop of 1978s including a Ch Gruaud-Larose at around £9. Would that there were similar relief from Roger d'Esgrigny's white Burgundies and Emile Chandesais' reds (although the ubiquitous Moreau provides the Chablis) and from the undistinguished Michael Schneider Germans. Their range from Italy isn't particularly exciting but at least it knocks spots off Spain. The rest of the world gets short shrift although the meagre offerings from Australia (Tollana), New Zealand (Cooks') and California (Wente) are better than nothing. There are good ports from 1963, 1970, 1975, 1977 and 1980, and slightly higher than average prices.

BEST BUYS ££ Alsace and New Zealand wines

Wine Sellers

See Bass Off-Licences

Yates Brothers

HEAD OFFICE 54 Carnarvon Street, Manchester TEL 061-834 4691
20 branches mostly in the North West and Yorkshire

OPEN (Variable) Mon–Sat 10.30 am–5.30 pm CLOSED Sun CREDIT CARDS All accepted DISCOUNTS Not available DELIVERY Not available GLASS HIRE Not available TASTINGS AND TALKS Not available CELLARAGE Not available

These bastions of the North West, offering their traditional road to oblivion paved with own-label sweet Australian fortified wines, were perhaps the originators of the Wine Bar, and their off-sales are still inextricably linked with the Wine Lodges. Own bottlings of Ports, especially Crusted, have been justly popular and they bottle their own sherries too. Clarets are few and of lesser vintages but there is good Chablis from Albert Pic including a Premier Cru (£4.50) and a Grand Cru (£7), both 1981. Marqués de Cáceres red and white 1979 Rioja is £3.25 (expensive for the white particularly), and for a little extra, there is an Australian 1978/79 McLaren Vale Shiraz.

BEST BUYS £ – £££ Albert Pic Chablis, £££ Own-label Crusted Port

Wine at auction

Why buy at auction? At the expensive end, many of the mature wines such as 1959 or 1966 clarets or rare old vintaged Madeira or Cognac may not be available from wine merchants, so this may be your only source. Prices may be high from a specialist merchant, even if he does have such wines. At the cheap end, however, you can sometimes pick up at really bargain prices young wines sold off by merchants as surplus to their requirements, or, sadly abundant these days, wines being sold off by the Receiver. It's worth clubbing together with friends to bid. Fine, old wines may be sold in single bottle lots, but younger wines will be in lots of on average three cases.

The small print at the front of the catalogues may seem complicated. Your first bid in a crowded auction room may be daunting. Go along to an auction or two before you think of buying and settle into the system. It's really quite simple. It can be fun. And it may well save you some money.

Auction procedures differ between auction houses. The following is a novice's guide to the goings-on at the two London auction houses Christie's and Sotheby's. You may find conditions of sale are different at country auction houses, which are discussed separately at the end of this section.

Good value at auction in 1985

The auction market in general as we go to press is fairly firm. But there are one or two areas where snips are to be found. For investment, young classed growth Bordeaux are always undervalued at auction and invariably cheaper to buy than anywhere else – largely because the big-spending Americans are interested only in wines that are drinkable now. Since October 1984, the 1981 clarets have been coming on to the market, good wines at relatively low prices that reflect interest in the excellent 1982s and 1983s that followed. 1970 vintage ports are also excellent value at around £10 a bottle, but are likely to fetch much higher prices in the next few years. And they are very good, too. The excellent 1977 ports are fairly well priced at auction, but it's early days for anyone buying them as an investment to sell later on – vintage port prices only begin to fetch high prices at least ten or more years after their vintage year.

For drinking now, good quality German estate wines are almost always to be found at bargain prices.

Pre-sale information

Sale dates Consumers' Association's newsletter *Which? Wine Monthly* gives dates and times of forthcoming sales, as does *Decanter* magazine, and both Sotheby's and Christie's advertise their sales in the national press. The safest way is to put yourself on an auction house's mailing list, which, for a small fee, will provide you not only with pre-sale catalogues but may also bring other subscribers' perks, like previews of the pre-sale tastings. *See below for further details of both London and Country auctioneers.*

Getting a cagalogue Catalogues are generally available three weeks or so before the sale. If you are not a subscriber, you can buy catalogues individually, by post, or call in to collect one.

Bidding by post Postal bidding forms will arrive with your catalogue, and the auction house provides a free postal bidding service. Simply mark the maximum price you are prepared to pay beside the lot. The auctioneer will secure the lot for you at a lower price if possible. You may find it difficult to pitch the bid. Remember that the estimates in the catalogue are based on prices fetched most recently for the same or a similar wine at this auction house or elsewhere, and the vendor may well have fixed a reserve minimum price, probably somewhere near the bottom of the estimate bracket. So you are unlikely to get your wine if you bid below the estimate. If you are determined to buy it, or if you really want a bargain, it's better to attend the sale. Auctioneers will generally accept either/or bids – so you can give an alternative in case you are unlucky with your first choice. The maximum amount to be spent can also be specified. You should indicate on your form if you would like to take up options (*see below*) and whether you would like your wine delivered.

Pre-sale tastings These are mostly held the day before, except for Christie's South Kensington sales, where they are held immediately before. You are unlikely to find tasting samples of very expensive wines, very small lots, wines sold in bond (*see below*) or wines that will sell easily on their reputation alone. But vendors are surprisingly generous, and you may well be able to taste younger vintages of second growth clarets, and decent Burgundies, and certainly less expensive wines. Christie's generally put out a tasting sample for parcels of five cases and over. (The first lot will usually be less than five cases, however.) If you specifically want to taste a wine before taking the plunge, telephone the auctioneer to make sure it's going to be available for tasting (if it isn't, he will probably be able to offer you his advice), and do arrive early, before the gannets have got to work. (But remember that catalogue subscribers are allowed in first.)

Which? Wine Guide does not accept payment for inclusion, and there is no sponsorship or advertising.

Understanding the catalogue

Read the list carefully. Be cautious – don't take the price at face value. We list below some of possible extra charges and explain a few other possibly confusing details:

VAT The list prices do not include VAT. If the vendor is a merchant registered for VAT, you will have to pay the 15 per cent in addition to the list price, and this will be indicated on the list (with a little dagger symbol in Sotheby's and Christie's lists). No VAT is charged on wines sold by private individuals who are not registered for VAT – fortunately, mature wines generally fall into this category.

Duty paid Wines marked 'duty paid' have simply been cleared by Customs, and the price already includes excise duty. Foreign buyers will not be too eager to pay these prices, so you will be bidding only against British buyers.

In bond The excise duty has not yet been paid, and the wines are still under the Customs Officer's eagle eye. Foreign buyers may be bidding (and prices are particularly cheap to the Americans at the moment, with the exchange rate to their advantage). For a small fee, the auctioneer will normally take care of the Customs procedures on your behalf.

Duty paid available in bond Bidding will be at duty paid prices, and for the British buyer there is no extra duty cost. Overseas or trade buyers may choose to take the wine 'in bond', and the duty will be subtracted from their bill.

FOB Freight on Board is a term used for wine that is sold when it is still overseas. The vendor pays all packaging and delivery costs to the nearest railhead or container depot, and the buyer is responsible for subsequent freight, duty, VAT and customs clearance charges. The auction house will generally arrange shipment on your behalf, and will specify charges in the catalogue.

Estimates Based on most recent prices fetched by this or a similar wine at auction.

Ex cellar Sometimes, wine is offered 'ex cellar' ie lying in the cellars of the château or estate. This can be the cheapest way of buying good recent vintages – but not if the quantities are small.

Bidding at the sale

What *precisely* are you bidding for? If the lot consists of just a few bottles, bidding is per lot. If it's one or more cases, you bid 'per dozen' and it will be multiplied up.

Bid steps A table in the catalogue will set out the 'bid steps', the amounts by which each bid raises the price within each price segment. At Christie's, for example, bids go up in single pounds up to £30, or sometimes even to £50, then jump £2 a time up to £100, £5 a time up to £200 and so on. By the £2,000 level, you'll be leaping up as much as £100 a time.

Reserves may have been set by the vendor, usually towards the lower end of the estimate bracket in the catalogue.

Options The option may be offered to the buyer of one lot in a series of lots of the same wine to buy all the remaining lots at the same price. This is really for the benefit of trade buyers, who will generally need to secure larger quantities of any particular wine. So if you really want the wine, you must bid for the first lot. If options are taken up, this can make the sale go at a rattling pace, so make sure you don't miss the later lot you were waiting to bid for. Not all sales offer options. If they are going to, it will be printed in the catalogue and announced at the start of the sale, though the auctioneer may choose to offer an option anyway, mid-sale. Christie's offer options only to purchasers of the first lot of a series (parcel) of the same bottle size. Sotheby's also offer options mid-parcel.

Mistakes If you have a twitch, don't worry that you might accidentally find yourself burdened with a £2,000 bottle of Ch Lafite. If the auctioneer is in any doubt whether you are bidding, he will ask you. If you find you have bid on the wrong lot, tell an auction room employee *at once* so that the lot can be re-auctioned. Legally, it's yours once the hammer has dropped. But the auctioneer will generally agree to re-auction it if he is informed before the end of the sale.

How to bid Simply, clearly, raise your hand, or wave your catalogue, or, in rare desperation, call out. Once the auctioneer has seen you bidding, he'll continue to keep an eye on you until the bidding stops for that lot.

Your address Once the hammer is successfully down on your bid, an auction-room assistant will ask you for your name and address. Only the lot number, not a verbal description, will appear on the form. So double-check that you have bought the right lot!

Payment and delivery

Buyer's premium On some categories of goods sold at auction, the buyer has to pay a ten per cent premium plus VAT to the auction house. Sotheby's introduced a ten per cent buyers' premium for the first time in 1984. No such premium is levied on wine at Christie's, and they have no intention of introducing one, so for the small-scale private buyer, it is certainly advantageous now to buy at Christie's. (The vendor of course pays commission in all auction houses, usually 15 per cent, on the 'hammer price'.)

Delivery or collection The catalogue will say where the wine is being stored. Smaller lots in particular, often stored at the salesroom, will generally have to be collected. Delivery of other wines can mostly be arranged, and delivery charges will be found in the catalogue.

Payment Invoices are posted after the sale, and the wine may be collected or delivered only after payment. Pay straight away and get the wine; any problems can then be sorted out before the auction house pays the vendor.

Faulty wine Inform the auction house straight away. The auctioneer cannot be expected to examine every bottle, and is not personally responsible, being only an intermediary between you and the vendor. But he will generally be willing to help in negotiations with the vendor.

The London auctioneers

London auctionners Christie's and Sotheby's are the only wine auctioneers of any significant size in the UK (*but see also* COUNTRY AUCTIONEERS *below*), and Christie's wine turnover is far greater than Sotheby's. Since Sotheby's added their ten per cent buyers' premium in the summer of 1984, the best bargains for the private buyer are more likely to be found at Christie's, though of course there may be special bargains at any auction depending upon who else is bidding, and a low hammer price at Sotheby's may well outweigh the ten per cent surcharge.

Christie's

8 King St, St James's, London TEL 01-839 9060
Held 11 fine wine sales in the 1983/84 season, 11 claret sales, 13 for inexpensive wines and trade remnants, and six more abroad. They expect to hold as many in this current season. They handle all types of wine from every conceivable source – private, trade, UK, overseas, grower, collector, liquidator, for trustees/estates etc, with the main emphasis on vintage wines. Christie's is the main world dealer in old, rare, fine, mature wines. They have a large, specialised wine staff. Their King Street sales (fine wines) are held on Thursdays at 11 am, plus some afternoon sessions at 2.30 pm, with the pre-sale tasting the previous day at 12 noon–1 pm. The 'inexpensive' sales at South Kensington (63 Old Brompton Road, SW7; tel 01-581 2231) are held on Mondays at 6 pm, with the pre-sale tasting immediately before, from 4.30 to 5.45 pm. You will see their sales advertised weekly in *The Times* and *The Daily Telegraph*, and each month in *Decanter* magazine. Catalogue subscriptions to UK addresses are £20 for the fine wine auctions, £18 for claret, £10 for 'inexpensive' sales, all including the mailing of after-sale price lists. Addition perks of subscribing to Christie's catalogue are the preview tastings at 11 am on auction days, special events such as tastings, a pre-publication discount on all new Christie's wine books, and special offers on others. If you are selling wine, Christie's will also advise you on the best time to sell ('We often say "wait"'), and on the present market value and market prospects.

Christie's run wine courses and tastings in conjunction with Stephen Spurrier (write to the above address for details). UK vendors pay 15 per cent to Christie's on the hammer price for small quantities of wine, 12.5 per cent for larger amounts.

Sotheby's

34–35 New Bond Street, London, W1 TEL 01-493 8080
Held 17 sales in London in the 1983/4 season, and just their Christmas sale out of London in Pulborough, West Sussex, plus a few overseas in Switzerland and South Africa. They expect to hold about the same number in the 1984/5 season. Sotheby's sales invariably take place on Wednesday mornings at 10.30 am, with a pre-sale tasting the day before from 11.30 am to 1 pm, often with more bottles open for tasting than at Christie's, since Sotheby's sales, all fine wines, are wider ranging. Catalogue subscribers are not generally allowed in early. The wines Sotheby's handle come from all the same types of source as Christie's, but Sotheby's do not deal in the cheaper end (as Christie's do at South Kensington), and tend to attract a few more rarities. Their sales are advertised in *The Times* and the *Daily Telegraph* on the Monday before the sale and also occasionally in *Decanter* magazine. Annual subscription to the catalogue is £20, which includes price lists after the sale. There are no special subscribers' perks – except for a big saving in the cost of the catalogue. Sotheby's wine department, manned by a large number of wine experts, will offer free advice on pricing, balancing your cellar, where to find specific wines, what to buy. They hold rather up-market tutored tastings (write to the above address for details) and organise one visit a year to a wine-growing area for members of the public. With the arrival of the buyers' premium of ten per cent in June 1984, the commission charged to vendors also changed. If you are selling small quantities, you will still be charged 15 per cent on the hammer price; but at prices over £500, this will be lowered to ten per cent, and you may be offered even lower trade rates for even bigger parcels. Sotheby's will deliver anywhere in the UK at a flat rate of £3 per case; but there is a minimum charge of £9 per drop including insurance, and of £6 a drop without.

P W Silverstone

210–212 Brick Lane, London, E1 TEL 01-739 3764
Held no sales last season, but expect to hold six or seven in 1984/5. They specialise in liquidation and receivership stock, and stocks seized by Customs & Excise, and advertise only in trade papers, but you can subscribe to their catalogues for an annual £7.50. They can organise delivery if required, and charge 15 per cent to vendors. They have wine specialists on their staff.

The country auctioneers

All the country auctioneers deal principally in other goods, but a few hold one or two wine auctions a year. If you intend to buy at a country auction, study market values carefully beforehand. (Christie's publish an annual price guide, available by post from their address above for

£6 – 1984 edition – inc postage and packing). You *can* snap up wines amazingly cheaply in these out-of-the-way sales. You can also pay outrageously high prices.

Colliers, Bigwood & Bewlay
The Old School, Tiddington, Stratford-upon-Avon TEL (0789) 69415
Held four sales during the 1983/4 season, and intend to hold six in 1984/5. Sales take place on Thursday evenings, quarterly, with an occasional one interspersed, with a pre-sale tasting from 4 pm onwards. The company accepts wines of all categories from most sources. You many see their sales advertised in *Decanter*, the *Birmingham Post*, the *Daily Telegraph, Daily Mail* and local press, or you can subscribe to their mailing list for an annual £6. There is no buyers' premium, and the vendors' commission varies from 8 to 15 per cent depending on quantities entered in the sale. Wines must generally be collected from the saleroom, but delivery can sometimes be arranged. Colliers employ two specialised wine consultants.

Charles Hawkins & Son
Lynn Road, Downham Market, Norfolk TEL (0366) 382112
Hold three or four auctions per season, advertised in local papers, always on Friday evenings, occasionally with pre-sale tastings. Wines come from trade and private sources. Charles Hawkins will deliver nationwide. Annual subscription to their mailing list is free, and vendors pay a ten per cent commission. There is a wine specialist on the staff.

Lacy Scott
1 Cornhill, Bury St Edmunds, Suffolk, IP33 1BA TEL (0284) 67121
Hold one sale a year, always on Friday evenings at 7.15 pm, the first after we publish on 30 November 1984. Wines come from all sources, and sales are advertised from six to two weeks before the sale in *Decanter, East Anglian Daily Times,* other local papers and the *Financial Times*. Subscription to the catalogue is free, no delivery can be arranged, and there is no wine specialist on the staff. Vendors pay 12.5 per cent commission.

Lithgow, Sons & Partners
The Auction House, Station Road, Stokesley, Middlesbrough, Cleveland TEL (0642) 710158
Hold three sales each season on the last Wednesday in September, the first Wednesday in December and the first Wednesday in July, all fine wines from trade and private sources. Sales are advertised locally, and you can be put on their mailing list for an annual £3, which includes tastings. Lithgows do not deliver – wines must be collected from Stokesley, but may be stored there. Vendors pay between 7.5 per cent and 15 per cent commission, depending on quantity. There is a wine specialist on the staff.

Osmond, Tricks & Son

Regent Street Auction Rooms, Clifton, Bristol TEL (0272) 737201
Hold on average one or two wine auctions a year 'whenever we are fortunate enough to be asked to sell a parcel which we consider to be appropriate', and forthcoming sales are advertised in *Decanter* and the local press. The mailing list is operated free of charge. There is a pre-sale tasting whenever possible, and delivery can be arranged to any part of the country. Normal commission for vendors is ten per cent, and there is no buyer's premium. The company uses a Master of Wine as consultant for its wine sales.

Phillips, Son & Neil

39 Park End Street, Oxford OX1 1JD TEL (0865) 723524
Phillips used to hold very regular wine auctions, then stopped for some years before starting up again with two sales in 1983. They intend to hold four in the 1984/5 season, perhaps more. Wines tend to be a mixture of everyday and fine wines, from both trade and private sources. Sales are held on either Tuesdays or Thursdays, with a pre-sale tasting open to any catalogue holder on the day of the tasting. They are advertised in *The Times* and *Telegraph, Decanter* magazine and *Country Life*, or you can subscribe to the mailing list for £4.80. There is no buyers' premium, and the 15 per cent vendors' commission is to be reviewed at the end of 1984. Phillips run an investment advisory service; they employ a wine consultant. Wines must be collected from the saleroom.

Part III

Drinking out

Wine bars

Dear Wine Bar Manager

Do your customers know something you and your staff don't know? We believe so, in the majority of cases, after visiting wine bars the length and breadth of Britain and trying (often in vain) to discover from ill-informed bar staff and utterly uninformative lists just what you offer that we might enjoy and recommend. 'Valpolicella £5' or 'Mâcon Blanc £6' tells us even less than 'Real Ale 90p a pint'. Wine drinkers, like beer drinkers who care what they get, want to know more. There are so many filthy, thin, acetic Valpolicellas around that few experienced wine drinkers would take the risk of buying an anonymous one. There are a few super ones, too – but even they are sometimes listed simply as Valpolicella, full stop.

The British are drinking more wine each year (in fact there are now more wine than beer drinkers in Britain); they are choosing better wines; and they are rapidly learning more about them. Your staff should be ahead of them, helping. So often, however, the blind are leading the partially sighted, as well as those with a first rate eye for a good wine – if they're shown it. OK, your counter staff come and go. But it wouldn't take long, or cost much, to train them in a few basics. It's not only that they don't know what the wines taste like, what to offer as an alternative, that a particular Pinot Blanc comes from Alsace and not from Portugal; counter staff can rarely provide the knowledgeable wine drinker with the vital statistics he needs to make his choice – vintage and producer or shipper – without wasting everyone's valuable time on a trip to the wine rack. Worse, many managers we quizzed for basic details were stumped, even when they stocked only a simple list of a couple of dozen wines; and few, even some of the very best bars, had taken the trouble to write such information into their list.

Surely, this is the solution – to provide a detailed wine list to which the staff, as well as the customers, can refer. We apologise in advance to the country's best bars for this blanket criticism: perhaps one in ten of Britain's wine bars (no more) consistently provides the information we need. The very best add a note of advice on what to choose, and how the wines will taste. Many of the other 90 per cent of you do know your stuff, we're sure: so tell us, write it into your list! And if you can't cope, ask your wine merchant to do it – properly.

We don't mean to say that we, the public, know it all. One good way of extending your customers' repertoire of wines is to offer a different 'wine of the week' by the glass in addition to the house wines – if it's good and properly promoted, it can't fail to sell well, so you're unlikely to be left with half-empty bottles turning slowly to vinegar. House wines offered by the glass are anyway so often dull and mediocre. Most of us would jump at the chance to experiment.

And please, make it clear how much we're getting when we buy 'a glass'. We don't like being given a minute glass for 95p – and probably sha'n't come back for more. At least if you tell us, we will have plumped deliberately for a couple of expensive gulps. Wine lovers are unhappy, too, with tiny glasses brimming over, leaving no room for the smallest of noses. So after your next smashing session, why not replace little glasses with good eight-ounce Paris goblets, and fill them two-thirds full?

Prices are a sore point, too. How many wine bars passed on the spring 1984 duty reductions to their customers? Scarcely any that we know of. (Wine merchants were much more magnanimous here, most dropping prices even of wines already in stock, upon which they had already paid duty.) In a wine bar with a mark-up of 100 per cent or more, the saving to the customer should *have been 36p per bottle. Any wine bar should now be able to put a good house wine on its list for under £4.*

At least wine bar food is better, on the whole, than food in pubs. But food standards, we find, have deteriorated. Many of the bars recommended in the Guide *are serving delicious fresh food, both hot and cold, some of the best value in the country – all praise to the caring and the adventurous. But by far the greater proportion – including many of our recommended bars – have resorted to frozen quiche and bought-in tubs of salad, and serve the same cold cut meats and cheeses session after session, drier by the hour. How much better to have wine bar food that's utterly simple – but also incredibly good: fine beef, ham and cheese, simple, well-dressed salads, and excellent bread and butter, and nothing more. Good coffee is always welcome, too, but an unusual find in a wine bar. Again, we would quibble over prices in a lot of bars – most are counter-service, after all.*

But wine is surely your main priority. The public are beginning to know and care more about the wine they drink. Are you?

Dear Wine Bar Customer

Our main criterion for including the bars recommended in the pages that follow was the quality of the wines they serve: we looked for a selection (not necessarily large) of bottles a wine lover would be likely to enjoy. Some bars in poorly served city areas or small country towns would not have won their place in the Guide *had they been in the West End, say, or Chelsea or Central Manchester, where a five or ten minute walk would take you to a far better bar (though some of the bars we have judged best* are *in small country towns – including one of the nation's few three-star bars, in Inverness!). We looked also, of course, for a cheerful atmosphere, friendly, efficient and well-informed service and, with disappointingly little success, for very good food.*

All the recommended bars are licensed to serve wine alone, without food. (Some 'bars' have been excluded because they have only a restaurant licence, including the few 'wine bars' in Northern Ireland, where licensing laws do not permit the sale of wines alone; though none of the Northern Ireland bars would anyway have reached the Guide*'s standards.) Even if a bar does serve wine without food, it is often difficult to determine if it really is a wine bar, and not a hamburger joint, bistro, pub, disco or cocktail bar – so many bars, especially outside London, are being invaded by the cocktail. Not that we have any objection to any of these, so long as their presence in no way detracts from the quality of the wine service and the standard and range of wines offered.*

This year, 150 new bars made the grade for the Guide*. Every bar (plus many more rejected ones) has been inspected at least once by the* Which? Wine Guide*'s inspectors during the summer of 1984, many of them on several occasions.*

London bars are listed alphabetically by name; bars in the rest of the country will be found under town name. Prices are correct to the best of our knowledge as we go to press, but some are sure to change during the Guide*'s life, as, indeed, are specific wines and vintages offered; but our comments will give you a good indication of the standard and range to expect. Bars we judge to be above average in the range, value and service they offer sport the* Which? Wine Guide *special awards.*

We are always eager to hear your views, reports on the bars selected here, or others you feel deserve an entry. Meanwhile, happy hunting amongst this year's choice.

London

Albertine

1 Wood Lane, W12 TEL 01-743 9593
OPEN Mon–Fri 11 am–3 pm, 5.30 pm–11 pm Sat 6 pm–11 pm CLOSED Sat L, Sun, public holidays CREDIT CARDS Access/Euro, Amex, Diners
UNDERGROUND Shepherds Bush, White City WHEELCHAIR ACCESS Yes
VEGETARIAN DISHES At least one special main dish daily

At lunchtime you may find yourself in the thick of celebrating BBC types, in the evening as part of the local clan that gathers most evenings for the live pop/rock music. Whenever, the friendly informality is the same; so, unfortunately, is the smoky stuffiness. The wine list is sensibly put together: a good, substantial selection with no frills, just dependable value. The wide range of basic house wines, served in both small and large glasses as well as by the bottle, includes the Geoffrey Roberts California Reserve (red and white) at a very reasonable £4.45 (or 90p and £1.30 a glass). For a white wine by the bottle, you can rely on Duboeuf Burgundies and the Deinhard Moselles and hocks, but for a more adventurous choice, try the Vouvray 1981 La Peu de la Moriette Demi-Sec (£7.10), the Venegazzù Pinot Grigio 1982 from Conte Loredan (£5.40) or the excellent Sauvignon Fumé Blanc 1981 from Robert Mondavi (£8.45). The reds include an attractive quartet of competitively priced Beaujolais Crus – catch the Duboeuf 1982 Fleurie Domaine des Quatre Vents for £6.85, or try the Ch Rahoul 1979, Graves, which is ready and very good now (£7.20). From Italy, you might choose the Barbera d'Alba 1980 by Pio Cesare (£5.30), but if you are looking for a smoother wine, perhaps a Rioja Berberana 1979 (£4.50) will fill the bill. And don't forget to check the list of half-bottles; the Ch La Grolet from the 1975 vintage is definitely worth a go at £3.40. Food seems to vary somewhat in quality, but is always reasonably priced and imaginative. Vegetarians are well looked after, and might be tempted by a broccoli mousse (95p) or leek and potato soup (70p); there's always a special vegetarian main dish. Carnivores might choose kidneys in mustard sauce (£1.95) or pork and apple pie (£1.10). Sweets are all inexpensive (85p) but it's the banana cream pie that gets the popular vote. A new room was to be opened upstairs as we went to press. This should help to relieve some of the congestion and allow pre-booking of tables.

Special awards

(V) is for bargain prices

is for a very good range of wines

is for exceptional service.

Alexander's

37–39 Horseferry Road, SW1 TEL 01-834 2907

OPEN Mon–Thur 11 am–3 pm, 5.30 pm–11 pm Fri–Sat 11 am–3 pm, 5.30 pm–12 pm CLOSED Sun CREDIT CARDS Access/Euro, Amex, Visa UNDERGROUND Victoria, Westminster WHEELCHAIR ACCESS Yes VEGETARIAN DISHES Salads

One of the more recent arrivals on the wine bar circuit, Alexander's is a brother establishment to Cosy Griffs in EC2 and has a similar selection, including some quality wines at good prices. The Montagny Louis Latour 1979 (£8), and the Chablis Ier Cru Prosper Maufoux 1981 (£9.75) are both sharp buys. And the excellent Alsace Riesling 1981 from Trimbach is worth every bit of the reasonable £6.45. The red Bordeaux section contains just six wines, ranging from an inexpensive £5.35 for a Ch de Fayolle 1979 to a showy Ch Grand-Puy-Lacoste 1961 for £45! In between, the Ch La Gurgue, Margaux 1979 is an attractive wine at an attractive £9. Amongst the red Burgundies, an unidentified Auxey-Duresses 1979 stands out and arouses curiosity for its price of just £9.75, while the Gigondas 1980 from Ogier is a good, honest wine at £6.35. None of the wines is available by the glass but a few half-bottles and a decent range of sherries, Madeiras, Armagnacs and ports are listed. Buffet food is the usual wine bar fare – pâté and bread (£1.75), ham salad (£2.95), lasagne (£2.75) – but it is well presented and helpings are generous. Alexander's is an ideal party place, and, every Saturday night, that's exactly what it becomes. There is lots of space, live music and a helpful staff: to judge by the crowds, a successful combination.

Almeida Theatre Wine Bar

(V)

1 Almeida Street (off Upper Street), N1 TEL 01-226 0931

OPEN Mon–Sat 11 am–3 pm, 5.30 pm–11 pm CLOSED Sun, public holidays (unless the theatre is open), all August CREDIT CARDS Not accepted UNDERGROUND Angel, Highbury & Islington (& BR) WHEELCHAIR ACCESS Yes VEGETARIAN DISHES Very good

This very Islington wine bar is attached to the theatre next door, a proximity which seems to create a refreshingly informal atmosphere. The stripped pine decor is relieved by a collection of pretty green plants and an upright piano in the corner, used for occasional live music sessions. The fairly standard wine list, chalked on the blackboard, includes the house wine (£3.95/75p), a Valpolicella (£4.15), a Petit Chablis (£6.95), a Beaujolais-Villages (£5.95) and a Vouvray (£5.45). However, it is worth a visit for a relaxed glass or two and the cheap, wholesome food – you feel healthy just looking at it: carrot soup or stuffed spud (80p), spinach crunch (£2.45) or a large mixed salad (£1.75). Carrots are obviously the 'in' thing here as they appear again in the puddings with a carrot cake (95p); wine lovers might be a bit dubious about the chocolate and red wine pud (90p)!

Bar des Amis

11/14 Hanover Place, WC2 TEL 01-379 3444

OPEN Mon–Sat 11.30 am–3 pm, 5.30 pm–11.30 pm CLOSED Sun
CREDIT CARDS All accepted UNDERGROUND Covent Garden
WHEELCHAIR ACCESS Impossible VEGETARIAN DISHES Some

Apart from the uninspired decor, the Bar des Amis is *très français*. Most of the wines are supplied by Les Amis du Vin *(see the* MERCHANTS *section)* who own the bar as well as the brasserie and restaurant of the same name upstairs. The emphasis is on good value wines, so you will not find many illustrious names or châteaux on the list but instead a commendable selection of decent quality. Try the dependable Vin de Pays de l'Hérault (£4.95) or the Gamay de l'Ardèche 1983 (£4.95). Many of the wines are Les Amis 'special selections': their hock is pleasant at £1.05 a (14cl) glass or £4.95 a bottle, and the Claret Les Amis is very drinkable (£5.25/£1.10). The Touraine Sauvignon 1982 (£5.35) is attractively fresh, and the Chinon 1982 (£5.75) and the Sancerre Rosé (£8) are slightly more unusual. From Spain comes the crisp, 'new-style' white Rioja of Marqués de Cáceres 1982 (£5.50) and an admirable Viña Albina 1976 Rioja Reserva (£5.75). Both the Geoffrey Roberts red and white California Reserves are good drinking for a very reasonable £4.95. The food at Les Amis is above-average wine bar fare. The menu includes typically French home-made soups (soupe de pêcheur £1.10), salads, saucissons and pâtés. The hot *plats du jour* might feature pork chops normande (£3.95) or filet de saumon à la laitue (£4.55). And, for a snack or to end a meal, £1.95 will present you with a sample of five *fromages*. Lunch-times here are busy with Covent Garden shoppers and evenings can be positively crowded, since the bar is popular with opera- and theatre-goers as well as the regular *amis des Amis*.

Angela & Peter's

300 Battersea Park Road, SW11 TEL 01-228 6133

OPEN Mon–Sat 12 noon–3 pm, 7 pm–11 pm CLOSED Sun, public holidays
CREDIT CARDS Not accepted BR STATION Clapham Junction
WHEELCHAIR ACCESS Not easy VEGETARIAN DISHES Some

This looks more like a restaurant than a wine bar, and you do feel rather guilty occupying a table with just a glass of wine, although no one attempts to hurry you. Between the stripped pine walls, the Battersea locals obviously feel at home as they flock here for their evening meal. The wine list is short and simple, with a conspicuous lack of information, even vintages. But the prices are very reasonable, with house wine £3.95/85p, and a Côtes-du-Rhône and Côtes-du-Roussillon Villages £4.75. Sparkling Veuve Chaudray (£5) looks particularly good value and the Campo Viejo Rioja (£4.95) would make a good supper wine. Starters include deep-fried clams (£1.95), cream of sweetcorn soup (£1), aubergine salad (£1.65) and garlic mushrooms (£1.95). Spinach quiche (£1.75), spaghetti al tonno (£2.75) or lemon sole in watercress and cream sauce (£3.25) give a clue as to why the locals find it such a convenient spot.

The Archduke

Concert Hall Approach, South Bank, SE1 TEL 01-928 9370

OPEN Mon–Fri 11 am–3 pm, 5.30 pm–11 pm Sat 5.30 pm–11 pm
CLOSED Sat L, Sun CREDIT CARDS Access, Amex, Diners, Visa
UNDERGROUND/BR STATION Waterloo WHEELCHAIR ACCESS Yes
VEGETARIAN DISHES Some

One of London's more spectacular wine bars – architecturally at least. Instead of featuring in food guides when it opened, its high-tech railway arch infill made headlines in the architectural press. It has mellowed and settled in since then, and now could do with a bit of repolishing here and there, especially in the cramped downstairs bar. It is extremely noisy, what with the trains trundling overhead, the very loud pianist or duo in the evenings, plus the hard acoustics. More a place for silent communion with one's partner than for a spirited conversation! The house selection is as good as ever – and the Champagne is fine value at £10.55 (rosé at £12.15). There's an interesting selection of Loire wines – Sancerre at £7.90; from St-Véran a 1982 produced by Corsin at £8. From Spain, Utrero Divisa Gran Reserva Rioja 1978 is £5.40, the same price as last year. Aperitifs include Ratafia de Champagne at £1.70 a glass. Food on the ground floor comes from a salad bar with quiches and pies as standards. On the top floor, the restaurant has hot food, which can be disappointing, including the house speciality of a variety of sausages, variously described by readers as 'an acquired taste', 'rather spicy and dry' and even 'unspeakable'. The soufflé omelette and the chicken and avocado salad are recommended. But then, there is little else on this side of the river near the South Bank complex.

L'Artiste Musclé

1 Shepherd Market, W1 TEL 01-493 6150

OPEN Mon–Sat 12 noon–3 pm, 5.30 pm–12 pm Sun 7 pm–11 pm CLOSED Sun
CLOSED Sun L, Chr Day, Boxing Day, Good Friday CREDIT CARDS All accepted
UNDERGROUND Green Park WHEELCHAIR ACCESS Yes
VEGETARIAN DISHES Salads

A cramped but popular upstairs and downstairs wine bar in the picturesque backwater of Shepherd Market. There is a lively lunch-time trade, but regulars also seek out L'Artiste for an evening with friends. The wine list is brief and not particularly distinguished but suits the unpretentious nature of both decor and menu. The Muscadet de Sèvre-et-Maine 1982 is well priced at £4.90 and the

Pouilly Fuissé 1982 Comte de Montfort is also a good buy for £8. Red wines are a more varied selection. The 1982 Brouilly, Domaine des Nazins (£6.50), or the Ch La Pervenche, Lalande de Pomerol 1979 (£6.30) are both good value. Look out for the 'specials' chalked up on the blackboard: you might find a Vosne-Romanée, Bouchard, 1972 for just £12.50 or a not-so-familiar Touraine Gamay 1982 for £4.50. Food is all home-made and simple. Choices may include a smoked chicken salad (£3) or boeuf bourguignonne (£3.50) as well as a variety of cheeses, pâtés and ragoûts.

Ashbee's

22 Hogarth Place, SW5 TEL 01-373 6180

OPEN Mon–Fri 12 noon–3 pm, 5.30 pm–11 pm Sun 7 pm–10.30 pm
CLOSED Sat, Sun L, probably two weeks Aug CREDIT CARDS Not accepted
UNDERGROUND Earls Court WHEELCHAIR ACCESS Impossible
VEGETARIAN DISHES Interesting cheeses and quiches

Just a hop, skip and jump from Earls Court Station and at the edge of that Kensington Village called Kenway Road lies this attractively muralled cellar bar run by two brothers, Conrad and Kim Marshall-Purves. Kim isn't always there in the evenings because he still follows his first career, the stage. There are about 60 wines listed, mostly from France, though all major wine-producing countries are represented. It is worth casting your eye over the shelves because they are always adding fresh and unusual wines: on our visit, for example, a red Bergerac from Ginestet with at least seven years' bottle age (£5.50) and a Nederberg Cabernet Sauvignon from South Africa (£5.95). There is good house red from Pasquier Desvignes (£4.25/95p) and house claret (£5.25/£1.25). Among the whites is a house Muscadet (£4.50/£1), an excellent Mâcon Villages 1983 from the Cave Co-opérative at Viré and a tank method sparkler, Duc de Dreux, at £5.75. For an extra 20p, they will throw in a carafe of orange juice to make a version of Buck's Fizz. There is no printed menu. The blackboard changes daily, offering food like smoked prawns and smoked quails' legs, both at £1.95, Stilton and celery quiche and salad (£2.25) or the more down-to-earth chilli con carne (£3.25). There is a very good, changing selection of French and English cheeses at £1.50. Altogether one of the more cheery watering places in this part of London.

We should very much appreciate further comments and suggestions of establishments of particular interest to the wine lover. There are report forms at the back of this book.

Do **you** know of any more bars that deserve inclusion in next year's *Guide!* If so, write and tell us on the report forms at the back of the book.

Bacchus's Bin

Ⓥ

5–9 Leytonstone Road, E15 TEL 01-534 2066

OPEN Mon–Thur 11 am–3 pm, 5.30 pm–10.30 pm Fri Sat 5.30 pm–11 pm with 1 hour's extension for restaurant suppers CLOSED Sun, public holidays CREDIT CARDS Access, Amex, Visa BR STATION Maryland; UNDERGROUND Stratford WHEELCHAIR ACCESS Yes VEGETARIAN DISHES Good range

The Valente family run the Broker and Five Lamps wine bars in the City, and this new opening in 1984 brings a similar quality and range of choice to a previously ill-served area. Though it lies on a busy main road, the bar is nonetheless well insulated from the noise and bustle outside. The main floor has the bar area on one side and dark wood nooks on the other. Downstairs, similar booths offer a quieter restaurant atmosphere for full meals, and the licence there runs for an hour longer in the evening. The wine list is extensive, with some fine opportunities to explore. Château-bottled wines start at 1980 and £4.60, up to 1974 Third Growth Cantenac-Brown at £23. Ch La Noë Muscadet is £5.25, and there is 1977 Vosne-Romanée at £11.90. Several half-bottles are very interesting – 1976 Châteauneuf-du-Pape (£2.50), 1977 Côtes-de-Beaune-Villages (£2.50) and Chablis (£3.75). The 1970 Barolo Gagliardo is remarkable value at £7.40, considering that bottles of that wonderful vintage are now very hard to find. Alsace Sylvaner is very reasonable at £3.95 as is 1978 Marqués de Cáceres Rioja (£4.80). There are six house wines, including a rounded Burgundy-style red with a nice bite, and a soft, gentle Burgundy-style white (£3.50/90p). The house claret lacks Cabernet character and, although pleasant, finishes short, but there is a tangy, aromatic Italian white with much better length (£3.50/90p). The menu gives a splendid choice of snacks and classic dishes. Four different salamis, mortadella and ox tongue (£2.50), four spicy smoked sausages (all £1.55) and an unusual range of a dozen cheeses, including Pecorino Romano and Provolone (£1.10) show the spread of colour and flavour. Taramosalata (£1.10) is a typical bar dish of the day and you may eat your cold lobster (£8.75) where you please – at the bar or in the restaurant proper.

Prices are only a rough indication, and were current in summer 1984.

We have tried to make the *1985 Which? Wine Guide* as comprehensive as possible, but we should love to hear from you about any other establishments you feel deserve an entry, or your comments on existing entries. Write to us either by letter or using the report forms supplied at the back of the book.

Every wine bar in this *Guide* has been anonymously inspected.

Balls Brothers

Ⓥ,

3–6 Budge Row, Cannon Street, EC4 TEL 01-248 7557
UNDERGROUND Mansion House WHEELCHAIR ACCESS Impossible

5–6 Carey Lane, off Gutter Lane, EC2 TEL 01-606 4787
UNDERGROUND St Paul's WHEELCHAIR ACCESS Yes

6–8 Cheapside, EC2 TEL 01-248 2708
UNDERGROUND St Paul's WHEELCHAIR ACCESS Yes

Laurence Poutney Hill, EC4 TEL 01-283 2947
UNDERGROUND Mansion House WHEELCHAIR ACCESS Impossible

In the Great Eastern Hotel, Liverpool Street, EC2 TEL 01-626 7919
UNDERGROUND Liverpool Street WHEELCHAIR ACCESS Yes

Moor House, London Wall, EC2 TEL 01-628 3944
UNDERGROUND Moorgate WHEELCHAIR ACCESS Yes

2–3 Old Change Court, St Paul's Churchyard, EC4 TEL 01-248 8697
UNDERGROUND St Paul's WHEELCHAIR ACCESS Yes

St Mary at Hill, EC3 TEL 01-626 0321
UNDERGROUND Monument WHEELCHAIR ACCESS Impossible

142 The Strand, WC2 TEL 01-836 0156
UNDERGROUND Temple WHEELCHAIR ACCESS Impossible

42 Threadneedle Street, EC2 TEL 01-283 6701
UNDERGROUND Bank WHEELCHAIR ACCESS Impossible

OPEN Mon–Fri 11.30 am–3 pm, 5 pm–7.30 pm CLOSED Sat, Sun, public holidays CREDIT CARDS Access/Euro, Amex, Visa
VEGETARIAN DISHES Sandwiches

Balls Bros are, after Davy's, the biggest chain of wine bars in London and evidently they have found a successful formula. This is not to say that they are all the same but, generally speaking, they reject the old oak and sawdust. Many are in the process of being refurbished, with air-conditioning now installed. Some command stunning views like that in Old Change Court which looks on to St Paul's Churchyard and where tables and chairs are put out on fine days. The branch in the Strand has a Law Courts atmosphere; and the branch in Cheapside has tables and chairs in the adjacent gardens. A new Edwardian style branch (with a listed ceiling), quite unlike all the others, was opened mid-1984 in the Old Abercorn Bar of the Great Eastern Hotel, at the corner of Liverpool Street and Bishopsgate.

Balls Bros are also wine merchants, so it is natural that the list is extensive in all their establishments. The emphasis is on France and particularly on Bordeaux: from Ch La Tour Michèle (£4.65 a bottle/95p a glass) stretching up to Ch Ducru-Beaucaillou 1966 at £14.50 a bottle.

It would be hard to buy it at Sotheby's at that price! This is the key, perhaps, to their success: thundering good value. Take, for example, the Ch de Fonscolombe Coteaux d'Aix-en-Provence for £4.60, or the Clos Madeleine Sauvignon Sec from Bordeaux at £4.65. Sherries and ports feature strongly: Gran Manzeda Manzanilla (60p a glass), and Quinta Gold Cap, Tawny (£1 a glass). Food is simple, principally pâtés at about £1.25 or sandwiches at about £1, but in some establishments, like Carey Lane, Budge Row and Moor House, there are grills, rump steak (£4.50, vegetables 45p) and cold buffet, roast beef at £2.30 and salads (60p). The new Liverpool Street bar serves only sandwiches, but of an imaginative and substantial kind. It is possible to use the Balls Bros bars for parties till 10 or 11 pm by private arrangement.

The Bar

33 Old Bailey, EC4 TEL 01-236 2101

OPEN Mon–Fri 11.30 am–3 pm, 5 pm–8 pm CLOSED Sat, Sun, public holidays CREDIT CARDS All accepted UNDERGROUND Blackfriars, Aldgate, St Paul's WHEELCHAIR ACCESS Yes VEGETARIAN DISHES Some salads

None of the hidden nooks and crannies here so typical of most City wine bars. 'The Bar' is one large and spacious room, plainly decorated with pleasant hanging greenery. It has an almost colonial air, helped by interesting silk screen prints, which are for sale. It is good to see that all six English wines, supplied by Palace wines and including a Pinot Noir Rosé from Northesk (£5.25), are reasonably priced: the 1982 Felstar Seyval Blanc and Chardonnay are the most expensive at £5.30. German wines, though few, are *slightly* more interesting than in most bars: the 1982 Dexheimer Doktor Silvaner Kabinett, Dry, QmP (£5.50) is worth trying if you are partial to the German dry wines. The list is generally well balanced but with no surprises. House wine, Le Bourdon, red and white, is £3.95 with a choice of either large (£1.30) or small (£1) glass. You might be tempted to try one of the wine cocktails, 'Kickback' – a combination of Champagne and blackberry brandy (£2). Fresh fruit juices are available (90p/60p), again in a choice of glass. As for food, daily specials are chalked up on the blackboard, such as devilled kidneys and rice (£2.80); tuna fish pie (£1.60); a wide choice of salads including cheese (from £1.50) or smoked mackerel (£1.95); chocolate fudgy cheesecake (£1.20). During happy hour, 5 pm–7 pm, there's a £1 bottle discount (except for Champagne).

Bar du Musée

17 Nelson Road, Greenwich, SE10 TEL 01-858 4710

OPEN Mon–Sat 12 noon–3 pm, 6.30–11 pm Sun, public holidays 12 noon–2 pm, 7 pm–10.30 pm CLOSED Chr Day CREDIT CARDS All accepted WHEELCHAIR ACCESS Yes VEGETARIAN DISHES Cheese, salad, quiche

The Bar du Musée has a comfortable, lived-in atmosphere and decor with assorted, sometimes antique, artefacts on the dark walls. There's a pretty back garden, and spiral wrought-iron stairs lead down to the Cellar Bar which, with several candlelit tables, is better for hand-holding (despite the proximity of the serving area). Music is unobtrusive but loud enough to enjoy if you're interested. The wine list verges on the expensive, given the ten per cent service charge on all bills and not much attention to the Chancellor's March (1984) reduction. The house red has a good, plummy flavour and nice finish, but the white is a bit too yeasty and short on acidity (both £3.95/80p). The house Champagne is very reasonably priced at £10.60. Claret (£5/94p) is authentic and has a bit of bite, and comes in half-bottles, too (£2.65). Rioja at £6.20 seems a bit pricy, but worth investigating is a brace of South African wines including the sweet 1981 Nederberg at £5.50. The menu's special-feature dishes are changed daily, while others remain fairly constant. Again, food is a little expensive: steak au poivre (£6.95); cheeseburger, chips, salad (£3), chicken in cream and wine sauce (£3.50) and succulent horseradish and mackerel pâté (£1.30). The 'mousse poisson and toast' (£1.50) is delicious. Service is a little slow, but gracious and friendly.

Barnes Wine Bar

7 White Hart Lane, Barnes, SW13 TEL 01-876 5336

OPEN Mon–Fri 12 noon–3 pm, 5.30 pm–11 pm Sat 12 noon–3 pm, 7 pm–11 pm Sun 7 pm–10.30 pm CLOSED L Sun & public holidays
CREDIT CARDS Not accepted BR STATION Barnes Bridge
WHEELCHAIR ACCESS Yes VEGETARIAN DISHES Soup and occasional dishes

This wine bar, in the middle of Young & Co country, is six boat-lengths from the river and a short sprint from the finish of the Oxford and Cambridge race. Although it is on ground level, it feels like a cellar, with steps leading down to the back bar and a ceiling decorated with raffia. The wine selection is restricted, with house wines £3.70 a bottle/70p a glass; there is usually a special monthly wine offer. Limited food, but a handsome welcome from the proprietors.

Le Beaujolais Wine Bar

25 Litchfield Street, WC2 TEL 01-836 2277

OPEN Mon–Fri 12 noon–3 pm, 5.30 pm–11 pm CLOSED Sat, Sun, public holidays CREDIT CARDS Access UNDERGROUND Covent Garden, Leicester Square WHEELCHAIR ACCESS Yes VEGETARIAN DISHES Rarely

This small bar, surprisingly unpopulated considering its location in theatreland, tries hard to create a Gallic atmosphere. Naturally, the wine list features Beaujolais – a reasonable collection imported by the Burgundian owner Joël Defaut from small *négociant* Juillard, which ranges from the basic to Brouilly (£6.85) through the nine different crus to Moulin-à-Vent (£8.75). Perhaps someone might tell them that the simpler Beaujolais are best chilled – especially in summer. The list is not so chauvinistic as to exclude wine from other areas: there are the usual basic German wines, but from the Loire you might try the Vouvray Maison Verdi (£5.45) or if Bordeaux (heaven forbid!) is more your style, Le Beaujolais broadmindedly offers a choice of four – Ch Ligaue 1979 will cost you £6.50. Food is satisfying and freshly prepared – apart from the vegetables, which are likely to be frozen, even in high summer. The menu changes every month or so and might include merguez (£2.45), cold salmon salad (£2.85) or a respectable chicken in red wine sauce (£2.95). Cheeses are sometimes very good, sometimes rather tired. You can immortalise your visit by donating your tie (or suspenders?) to the continuously expanding collection above the bar.

Bert's Wine Cellar

44A Floral Street, WC2 TEL 01-836 1868

OPEN Mon–Fri 12 noon–3 pm, 6 pm–11.30 pm Sat 6 pm–11.30 pm
CLOSED Sat L, Sun, public holidays, August CREDIT CARDS All accepted
UNDERGROUND Covent Garden WHEELCHAIR ACCESS Difficult
VEGETARIAN DISHES One or two, quite interesting

Bert's candlelit cellar, just underneath Bertorelli's Restaurant, is particularly Italian in flavour. Not surprisingly, Italian wines are the thing, but there are a few token French wines on offer too. No half-bottles, but the glass size is larger than average, so you might settle happily for a round of Rosso Piceno Salvalai at £1 or the Frascati Cantina San Matteo at £1.15. The house wines (95p a glass) at the time of our visit had little to recommend them. Geographically, the wine list is somewhat erratic, no vintages are given and producers barely acknowledged. Still, do not be deterred: try the Chianti Antinori Classico (£6.25) or the Trebbiano Salvalai at a reasonable £4.25. Alternatively, you could experiment with one of the Sicilian Corvos at £5.80. The food is comfortably predictable, with good tagliatelle and cannelloni al forno, and excellent crespoline di ricotta. The main dishes are usually better value than the slightly skimpy appetisers but all is worthwhile for the pleasant, intimate atmosphere. An ideal pre- or post-theatre staging-post (sample the range of Italian liqueurs) or a place to linger with the gentle entertainment provided by their guitarist-singer.

Bill Bentley's

239 Baker Street, NW1 TEL 01-935 3130

OPEN Mon–Sat 11.30 am–3 pm, 5.30 pm–11 pm CLOSED Sun, public holidays
CREDIT CARDS All accepted UNDERGROUND Baker Street
WHEELCHAIR ACCESS Yes VEGETARIAN DISHES Some

Whatever you may say of Mr Bentley's establishments, you cannot accuse them of being standardised. All three have their own unique atmosphere. In Baker Street, a few cricket pitch lengths from Lords, you might think yourself in a Thames Valley pub. The dark, carved oak panelling and bars and the discreet, efficient service of Italian waiters in scarlet bum-freezers come straight from a high class hostelry in Cookham or Marlow. The wine bar food is similar to that in the other establishments: excellent smoked salmon, Arbroath smokies, cold beef and a good array of cheeses. There are about a dozen table wines by the glass: Sauvignon Blanc, Bordeaux (£1.15), Crustacé Alsace (£1.35), a Ch Ségonzac from Bordeaux (£1.30) and sparkling Blanc de Blancs at £1.40. Fino San Patricio is £1 a glass and Fonseca 1968 vintage the most expensive fortified wine at £2.50. If you have a mind to drink a bottle, try Ch Loudenne 1976 from the Médoc (£6.95), Chénas 1982 (£6.85) or Hugel Gewürztraminer 1981 from Alsace (£8.50). For a special occasion, there is Savigny-lès-Beaune 1979 by Louis Latour at £15.

Bill Bentley's

31 Beauchamp Place, SW3 TEL 01-589 5080

OPEN Mon–Sat 11.30 am–3 pm, 5.30 pm–11 pm CLOSED Sun, public holidays
CREDIT CARDS All accepted UNDERGROUND Knightsbridge
WHEELCHAIR ACCESS Impossible
VEGETARIAN DISHES Not provided

Bill Bentley, a Free Vintner and a member of the family which was noted for its oysters and fish, opened this complex of restaurant, oyster bar and wine bar among the smart boutiques of Beauchamp Place some fifteen years ago. It is a very clubby place with books on shelves behind the bar and a delightful small garden at the back. The clientèle are urbane, regular and faithful. A stranger might think he had gatecrashed a private party, until, of course, he received his bill, though it will be quite moderate by SW3 standards. The emphasis is on French wines, with a sprinkling of hocks, Moselles, and Champagne but, of course, as this bar is run under Vintners' privilege, no spirits. There are nearly 30 wines served by the glass, including Rémy Pannier's Muscadet (£1.20), a Côtes du Ventoux (£1.15) and a sparkling Blanc de Blancs (£1.40) as well as Fino San Patricio and old landed Tawny Port, both at 95p. By the bottle, there is Mâcon-Lugny 1982 (£6.80), a Sancerre Chavignol 1982 (£8.30), and a Fleurie 1982 from Georges Duboeuf (£7.70). Excellent cold food includes cream of oyster soup (£2), country pâté (£1.25), roast beef and baked potato (£3.95). There are no hot main dishes, but then you have only to climb the stairs to find a very good restaurant.

Special awards

Ⓥ is for bargain prices

is for a very good range of wines

is for exceptional service.

Bill Bentley's

18 Old Broad Street, EC2 TEL 01-588 2655

OPEN Mon–Fri 11.30 am–3 pm, 5 pm–8.30 pm CLOSED Sat, Sun, public holidays CREDIT CARDS All accepted UNDERGROUND Bank, Liverpool Street (and BR station) WHEELCHAIR ACCESS Impossible VEGETARIAN DISHES Some

Old Broad Street houses a very impressive collection of wine bars: Capataz and Pontac's through Coates down to the Greenhouse (which, though strictly not in Old Broad Street, dominates it from the Mansion House end). Tucked in rather modestly next to the impressive portals of the City of London Club is the City face of Bill Bentley. The restricted wine bar area has something of a nautical flavour with its brass clocks and dark wood bars and deck. We visited very shortly after its opening, so all was ship-shape and Bristol fashion. You will find a reasonable range of house wines from Rémy Pannier, red, white and rosé (£4.15 a bottle/£1.05 a glass), and about ten other wines from France and Germany at slightly higher prices, culminating in Champagne Chaumel NV (£10.80 a bottle/£2.15 a glass). As you would expect from Bill Bentley, a very good list of ports and sherries is on offer, with Taylors Vargellas 1972 at £2.50 in the starring role. You can eat smoked salmon (£5.50), Arbroath smokies (£2.50) or ham cut from the bone, and ox tongue and beef (£4.50–£5.75). Sandwiches cost about £1. But, beware, the bar has a beautiful view over a terrace attached to the downstairs oyster bar, so you may well be tempted to spend much more on food and drink there. This is an elegant and stylish addition to City lunching places.

Blakes Wine Bar

34 Wellington Street, Covent Garden, WC2 TEL 01-836 5298

OPEN Mon–Sat 11.30 am–11 pm Sun 12 noon–10.30 pm CLOSED Christmas & Boxing Days FOOD SERVED 11 am–10.30 pm WINE SERVED Mon–Sat 11.30–3, 5.30–11 Sun 12–2, 7–10.30 CREDIT CARDS Access, Amex, Barclay UNDERGROUND Covent Garden WHEELCHAIR ACCESS Difficult but possible VEGETARIAN DISHES Good selection

Just around the corner from Covent Garden market, the small street front gives no hint of the size of the establishment: two large, simply but attractively furnished rooms upstairs, and a more dimly lit piano-bar downstairs, where there is live music every evening (except Sunday). Blakes is a popular watering-hole for young professionals at lunch and a good excuse for delaying the homeward journey later. At weekends, the crowd is more mixed, but still lively and friendly. A simple, wholesome buffet has a good range of game pies, quiches, pâtés and smoked mackerel as well as attractive fresh salads. These and the puddings are produced locally, but the hot dishes such as chicken curry and shepherd's pie are made on the premises. Helpings are generous and reasonably priced. The wine list is unadventurous but adequate:

there are several ever-dependable Georges Duboeuf wines. No half-bottles, but of the wines by the glass, try the California House White, Geoffrey Roberts' selection (£1.25) or the red Côtes-du-Rhône, Paul Deloux at £1.05. The premises can be booked for private parties.

Bleeding Heart Wine Bar and Restaurant

Bleeding Heart Yard (off Greville Street), EC1 TEL 01-242 8238

OPEN Mon–Fri 11 am–3 pm, 5.30 pm–11 pm CLOSED Sat, Sun and public holidays; Chr–New Year CREDIT CARDS All accepted
UNDERGROUND Farringdon, Chancery Lane WHEELCHAIR ACCESS Only to outside tables VEGETARIAN DISHES Some

Question: 'Why is it called Bleeding Heart Yard?' Answer: 'Because it is bleeding hard to find.' Don't even bother to consult your *A–Z* for this one – it's not there! However, perseverance is rewarded when you arrive at this newly opened first-class cellar bar (through a narrow opening halfway down Greville Street on the left, with your back to the North). Probably because most of the customers arrive exhausted by their attempts to find it, there is very efficient waitress service and plenty of tables and bar stools. An outside cobbled yard has seating for fine weather eating and drinking, but you'll be lucky to get a free table, such is the place's popularity. (A 'drawing room' may be booked for private parties.) The extensive wine list, with a good selection of half-bottles, starts with Cuvée Jacques Mathiot as house wine (£3.95/80p). Vin de Pays is well represented in both red and white: try the Domaine de la Grange Cabernet Sauvignon (£4.50) or the Domaine de la Gardie, Grenache Blanc (£4.50). The Brouilly, Jacques la Chevalière (£6.65) looks good value or, for a change, the 1982 Beaujolais Blanc, Domaine du Creuse Noir (£6.50). The two Australian wines, a Shiraz and a Riesling (£7.25) from the reputable Hill Smith, are certainly worth looking at. Perhaps it is the vicinity of Hatton Garden and all those engagement rings that makes Champagne so popular here: eight brands are on offer, headed by a very reasonable Jacques Martin NV at £9.95. The food is rather more original than in most wine bars – even the humble baked potato is dressed up with salmon and cream cheese (£1.50), or Danish caviar and sour cream (£1.35), and a healthy serving it is, too! Salads include prawn and mussel (£1.95), or spinach with bacon and croûtons (£1.45). There are various 'special' sausages, and dishes of the day, a firm favourite being the seafood crêpes (£2.75). Charles Dickens' novel *Little Dorrit* features Bleeding Heart Yard, and on display on the walls of the attractive arched cellar are more than 100 old editions of Dickens' books, and more than 20 first edition prints.

Blenheims

12 Blenheim Terrace, NW8 TEL 01-624 5313

OPEN Mon–Sun in summer 12 noon–3 pm, 7 pm–11 pm CLOSED Sat L in winter CREDIT CARDS Access, Visa UNDERGROUND St John's Wood, Maida Vale WHEELCHAIR ACCESS Yes VEGETARIAN DISHES Good choice

Yet another wine bar that has changed management in the last 18 months, Blenheims is a friendly, relaxed 'neighbourhood' bar – but everyone is made welcome. The wine list is very simple – house wines are Vins de Pays de L'Ardèche for £4.50 a bottle/90p a glass, and house Champagne is Louis Henry for £11.80. Other wines are relatively expensive, particularly by the glass: Niersteiner Gutes Domtal (£1.40), a Muscadet 1982 (£1.30). But if you're having a bottle, try the Mâcon-Villages 1982 (£7.50) or the Côtes-du-Rhône Benoît 1982 for £5.50. Gazpacho (£1.60) is a perfect summer appetiser, or guacamole (£2); Blenheims specialities include Swiss raclette (£3.50) – a welcome novelty on a wine bar list – and stuffed potato skins with a variety of fillings (£3). For extra good value try the *prix fixe* (£6) traditional three-course Sunday lunch. Constant taped jazz except on Friday nights, when there is live music in the downstairs section. Blenheims can be booked for a private party.

Boaters Wine Bar

56/60 Park Road, NW1 TEL 01-402 8979

OPEN Mon–Fri 11 am–3 pm, 5.30 pm–11 pm CLOSED Sat, Sun, public holidays CREDIT CARDS All accepted UNDERGROUND Baker Street WHEELCHAIR ACCESS Yes VEGETARIAN DISHES Salads

There have been some changes at Boaters in the last year. A recent redecoration has given it an appearance rather reminiscent of a high-class hotel bar (could it be the vibrant carpeting or perhaps the recorded pop music?). The wine list has also undergone some reconstruction and – remarkably – the prices have gone *down*! Morgan Furze supply the majority of the list, including Piat de Beaujolais (£5.30) and the Chablis Bouchard Père et Fils (£6.75). A Hugel Sylvaner is reasonably priced at £5.40, and a Ch La Croix de Gay adds some class from Pomerol. Only house wines are available by the (7 fl oz) glass (£1) and half-bottles are no more plentiful, but, for people without expense accounts, it is worth noting that on Tuesdays and Thursdays between 6 and 7 pm all bottles over £4 are reduced by £2. Food is simple, mostly charcoal grills and a cold buffet. The giant country herb sausages with straw potatoes (£1.50) are a popular choice, or there is grilled sirloin steak for £2.75. Prices are kept low and the sweet of the day might be almond mousse for just 40p. Boaters is available for private functions on Saturdays and Sundays.

Boltons

198 Fulham Road, SW10 TEL 01-352 0251

OPEN Mon–Sat 11 am–3 pm, 5.30 pm–11 pm Sun 12 noon–2 pm, 7 pm–10.30 pm public holidays 11 am–3 pm, 5.30 pm–11 pm CLOSED 4 days Chr, 2 days Easter CREDIT CARDS All accepted UNDERGROUND Gloucester Road, Earls Court (10 minutes) WHEELCHAIR ACCESS Impossible VEGETARIAN DISHES Salads and occasional specials

There has been a wine bar on this site since the early '70s, but this is now the newest and the smallest addition to the Ebury group (*see also the Ebury Wine Bar and Draycotts*). Light stripped pine gives the place a Scandinavian air and a small terrace at the rear affords a little more air on hot days. Late breakfasters can linger over cappuccino and croissants till midday, and brunch with the papers is the thing on Sundays. On the short wine list, at least a dozen are offered by the glass. These include a good Rioja Utrero, Bodegas José Palacios (£4.95 a bottle/£1.15 a glass), and a crisp Muscadet, Cuvée de Cardinal 1983 (£4.50/£1.10). From Bordeaux, Ch Hestrille 1981 is £5.50 a bottle. Scrambled eggs with ham or smoked salmon are £1.80, smoked haddock kedgeree is £2.50 and croissant with melted cheese and ham £1.80. Otherwise, the food, prepared in a miniscule kitchen, is less ambitious than at the Ebury: a *plat du jour* with salad (£3.50) or rare roast beef (£3.95). As in the other bars in the group, the service is bright, young and enthusiastic.

Boos

1 Glentworth Street, NW1 TEL 01-935 3827

OPEN Mon–Fri 11.30 am–3 pm, 5.30 pm–8 pm Sat L in summer CLOSED Sat, Sun, public holidays, 3 weeks Sept, 2 weeks from 25 Dec CREDIT CARDS Amex, Diners UNDERGROUND Baker Street WHEELCHAIR ACCESS Yes VEGETARIAN DISHES Soup

Boos is tiny and quickly becomes congested, especially at lunchtime. But for such a diminutive establishment, it has a remarkable wine list, both in length and quality. Wines are almost exclusively French, the list simply divided into white, red and sparkling. Of the whites, the 1981 Mâcon-Lugny, Les Genièvres (a Louis Latour selection) is a delicate Mâcon, fairly priced at £7.15. The 1981 Chablis Grand Cru, Les Clos from René Dauvissat is also a good buy at £10.50. In the reds is the rare chance to sample a truly aged Châteauneuf-du-Pape – the 1969, Comte de Lauze – which is intriguingly only £11.10. There are more remarkable bargains. The 1979 Louis Latour Chassagne-Montrachet is only £9.50 – it sells for more in the shops! – if your penchant is for an intense, full, alcoholic wine. Amongst the clarets, there are yet more goodies – some fine châteaux and excellent vintages at great prices. Try the 1975 Ch du Cauze, St-Emilion for only £7.95, or the 1975 Ch Monbousquet, Grand Cru St-Emilion for £10.50; but then again, for the same price, you could taste a 1970 La Rose, Pauillac which should be at its peak right now. For more moderate lunchtime drinking, there is a range of good quality half-bottles, and for celebrations, an unusually reasonable selection of Champagnes: Bollinger Special Cuvée NV (£13.20) or Louis Roederer Extra Dry NV (£12.65). Although food plays second fiddle, simple pâtés, cheeses and brown bread sandwiches can all be had for under £2, soups (in winter) are excellent, and cheesecake buffs have sniffed out a good one here.

The Boot & Flogger

10–20 Redcross Way, SE1 TEL 01-407 1184

OPEN Mon–Fri 11.30 am–3 pm, 5.30 pm–8.30 pm CLOSED Sat, Sun, public holidays CREDIT CARDS All accepted UNDERGROUND/BR STATION London Bridge WHEELCHAIR ACCESS Impossible VEGETARIAN DISHES Not provided

Despite the name, this is not the re-creation of a medieval torture chamber: the boot was used for mulling wine and the flogger for coaxing bungs from barrels. Originally opened in Borough High Street in 1965, the wine bar is now tucked away in a back street, but that evidently does not deter customers particularly at lunchtime and also in the weeks leading up to Christmas. It is run personally by John Davy under the privilege accorded to members of the Vintners Company to do so without a licence. There are a limited number of house wines by the glass: Sauvignon (£1.10), Muscadet (£1.40) and house claret (£1.10), but an amazing collection of rare wines available to be decanted at the bar. One client remembers drinking the legendary Quinta do Noval 1931 at £7 a bottle, more than a decade ago. It still features, even though the price has increased seven-fold. This is only one of 80 vintage ports stretching back to 1860. There are 70 clarets extending back to the 19th century, 17 wines from the Domaine de la Romanée-Conti, 24 vintages of Latour, all available for purchase provided that they are decanted and drunk at the bar. The food (all cold) takes second place here: beef, ham and salads of excellent quality, and very good cold salmon in season. A proper 19th-century atmosphere pervades.

Booty's Riverside Bar

92A Narrow Street, Limehouse, E14 TEL 01-987 8343

OPEN Mon–Fri 11 am–3 pm, 5 pm–11 pm Sat 7 pm–11 pm public holidays CLOSED Sun, Chr CREDIT CARDS Amex, Diners, Visa BR STATION Mile End WHEELCHAIR ACCESS Impossible VEGETARIAN DISHES Some

Booty's long, narrow dark-wood room with a view on to the Thames's bobbing jetsam gives you the impression of being between decks on HMS Victory. It is serendipity, given the area, and tranquil, with blessedly distant music. By-the-glass wines are limited to seven, three of them German, and the Muscadet had run out when we were there.

Glasses are priced between 80p and £1.10, and French house wine bottle prices encouraging at £3.75. The white is pleasant, and the red has a slightly baked taste but is soft and acceptable – both much better than the more expensive (£5.25/£1.05) house claret from the Ebury Wine Company which neither smells nor tastes like claret. At £7.95, 1976 Ch Gruaud-Larose (Bordeaux) and Mâcon-Lugny (Burgundy) seem good value and there is a domaine-bottled Pouilly Blanc Fumé at £8.80. Champagne (choice of four) starts at £14.25. Best wine value, however, is 1971 Ch Coutet, the Barsac Premier Cru dessert wine at £7.25. Food is limited and a little desultory. Chilli con carne (£2.25), ham and leek pie with jacket potato (£2.90) and rare roast beef (£3) may be the best bets, or the cheeseboard trio – Dolcelatte, Brie and Stilton.

Le Bouzy Rouge

221 Kings Road, Chelsea, SW3 TEL 01-351 1607

OPEN Mon–Sat 11 am–3 pm, 5.30 pm–11 pm CLOSED Sun CREDIT CARDS All accepted WHEELCHAIR ACCESS Impossible UNDERGROUND South Kensington VEGETARIAN DISHES Limited

Le Bouzy Rouge, a basement bar on the Kings Road, believes it was London's first wine bar (1954) – an assertion that some may wish to dispute – but its management is one of the latest. Throughout, there is a curious combination of the mundane and the eccentric. The decor is uninspired and the music is of the airport lounge variety, but the menu is in French Creole style and there are one or two Ethiopian specialities thrown in for good measure. 'Salade jamaïque' (prawns, asparagus and citrus fruit) is listed as a starter for £2.40, and zigni (a chicken and beef combination) can be sampled for £3.70. Paella, starting at £8 for two, to eat in or to take away, can be ordered with 24 hours' notice. The specialities are even written in Amharic at the back of the menu. The wine list is severely limited, but it does feature (surprise, surprise) a 1980 Bouzy Rouge (£10.50), the rare wine made from 100 per cent Pinot Noir in Champagne, and there is also a not-so-common Sancerre Rouge 1982 (Domaine de la Caillerie) for £7.60. Beware of wines by the glass, which come in tiny portions. There is evidently someone around with 'different' ideas, and more planning and co-ordination would go a long way to realising the wine bar's potential.

Bow Wine Vaults

10 Bow Churchyard, EC4 TEL 01-248 1121

OPEN Mon–Fri 11.30 am–3 pm, 5 pm–7 pm CLOSED Sat, Sun, public holidays CREDIT CARDS Not accepted UNDERGROUND Mansion House, Bank WHEELCHAIR ACCESS Easy VEGETARIAN DISHES Not provided

This busy City wine bar is a wine merchants' bar. It even earns ungrudging respect from other proprietors. It searches out and imports lesser-known French wines; 95 per cent of the extensive list is shipped directly and the house wines are brought over in bulk and bottled by them. About 100 wines are listed and about 20 are available by the glass. There is an attractive Sauvignon de St-Bris at £5.30, and at the other end, a great rarity, Vouvray Moelleux 1947 of Marc Brédif, at £34 a bottle. Amongst the reds is an unusual Rully 1979 at £8. Every two months, a special region is featured, and dinners are arranged from time to time to show special wines. Go early at lunchtime, since the Vaults fill up rapidly with the City-suited, and you must be adept at balancing plate, fork and knife, for there is little space to sit down. Typical dishes are mackerel and lime pâté (£1.80), spicy beef with mushrooms and cumin (£2.95), and don't miss the hazelnut meringue gâteau (£1.50), made by the proprietor's wife in her own kitchen. There is a busy restaurant and a wine shop under the same roof (*see above in the* WINE MERCHANTS *section*), as well as private dining rooms for hire.

Bradys

Hillgate House, Seacoal Lane, EC4 TEL 01-248 3741
OPEN Mon–Fri 11.30 am–3 pm, 5 pm–8 pm CLOSED Sat, Sun, public holidays
CREDIT CARDS All accepted UNDERGROUND/BR STATION Blackfriars
WHEELCHAIR ACCESS Yes VEGETARIAN DISHES Not provided

In the summer, Bradys has a distinct advantage over most wine bars: the large doors that form the front of the bar fold back to create a pavement café and a light, airy interior. The marble flooring and bar, set off by the pretty duck-egg blue paintwork and the stunning floor-to-ceiling mirror make this bar calm and elegant. The wine list is short and fairly simple, the house white (£4.30/90p) is very drinkable and does not really have a serious bargain-price contender except for the house claret (£4.65). A step up in price, the 1982 Syrah, Vin de Pays de L'Ardèche (£5.25) is worth trying, as is the Bordeaux Sauvignon Trois Mouline (£5.35). Ch Calon-Ségur 1970, Cru Classé St-Estèphe looks rather out of its depth at £25 compared with the rest of the list, though there are three white Burgundies at £7+, including a 1976 Meursault from Louis Latour (£15.90). House Champagne, Chaudron NV is a reasonable £9.50, especially when the only other Champagne, Veuve Cliquot NV is £16.20; Bouvet Ladubay Brut from Saumur, good as it is, costs £7.95. The menu is as short as the wine list: only 'Frishbees' – a whopping wholemeal roll filled with salad and a choice cheese (£1.10), ham (£1.25) or roast beef (£1.35), are available in the wine bar, although there is a restaurant upstairs offering beef and Guinness pie and various grills. The second Bradys, downstairs in the Barbican Tavern, Lee House, Monkwell Square, EC2, was being re-vamped as we went to press. The same wines are on sale there.

Every wine bar in this *Guide* has been anonymously inspected.

Brasserie Mode

15 Great Castle Street, W1 TEL 01-580 2125

OPEN Mon–Fri 11 am–3 pm, 5.30 pm–11 pm CLOSED Sat, Sun, public holidays
CREDIT CARDS All accepted UNDERGROUND Oxford Circus
WHEELCHAIR ACCESS Yes VEGETARIAN DISHES Salads

With a change of ownership, this site has undergone a metamorphosis, emerging as a very stylish cocktail/wine bar/restaurant on two storeys, convenient for Oxford Circus. The upstairs is for expense account lunches, downstairs for lounging elegantly at the Art-Deco (-ish) bar or sampling some of the well-prepared buffet food in the back room – smoked salmon quiche and salad (£4), ham, apple and chutney pie (£3.20). The wine list is predominantly French, with many good-value La Chevalière Burgundies. The Bourgogne Aligoté 1982 (£5.95) is a reliable, full-flavoured white wine and the Pouilly-Fuissé 1982 reasonably priced at £9.90. The Brouilly 1982 (£6.75) is another to look out for. A surprisingly reasonable £7.95 is asked for the attractive Chablis 1er Cru, Montée de Tonnerre 1982, while the Binger St Rochuskapelle Spätlese 1982 can be had for £6.50. There are no half-bottles but a fair number of wines can be bought by the glass: house wines are from Jacques Mathiot at £4.95 a bottle/85p a glass; the house Champagne is Jacques Martin NV for £13. If you only have time to 'perch' at Brasserie Mode before your next appointment, you can still keep up your strength with the sandwiches or a few of the complimentary nibbles.

The Brentham Vineyard

124 Pitshanger Lane, W5 TEL 01-998 6810

OPEN Mon–Thur 11 am–3 pm, 5.30 pm–10.30 pm Fri & Sat 11 am–3 pm, 5.30 pm–11 pm Sun 12 noon–2 pm, 7 pm–10.30 pm (Restaurant Tue–Sat from 7.30 pm) CREDIT CARDS Access, Visa UNDERGROUND Hanger Lane (5 minutes), Ealing Broadway (15 minutes) WHEELCHAIR ACCESS Yes
VEGETARIAN DISHES Always one special

Not much competition nearby, and as much beer, spirits and cocktails seem to be dispensed here as wine. Rooms lead into more rooms, becoming rather ramshackle towards the restaurant and wooden-benched yard at the back. The wine list is largely Italian and French, and contains enough small stars to keep the wine lover moderately happy – particularly since most bottles are under £5, and many of the Italian wines under £4. You will have to ask to see the labels because no details of the wines are given. The food is nothing special, even if you pay the premium and eat in the cavernous, darkened, crudely painted and cat-bestrewn Cats Restaurant: mushroom salad (£1.95), whitebait (£1.95), grilled grapefruit (£1.55), fisherman's pie (£3.95), grilled rainbow trout (£4.25). Barbecues on hot summer evenings are a slightly safer bet.

The Broker Wine Bar

16 Byward Street, EC3 TEL 01-488 0131

OPEN Mon–Fri 11.30 am–3 pm, 5 pm–8.30 pm CLOSED Sat, Sun, public holidays CREDIT CARDS All accepted UNDERGROUND Tower Hill WHEELCHAIR ACCESS Yes VEGETARIAN DISHES Not provided

Run by the same management as Bacchus's Bin and Five Lamps just a few minutes' walk away, the Broker offers the same food and wine list in an oak-panelled and marble bar. Not as large as the Five Lamps (what could be?), it is a good intimate lunchtime retreat with efficient and pleasant staff.

Bubbles

41 North Audley Street, W1 TEL 01-499 0600

OPEN Mon–Fri 11 am–3 pm, 5.30 pm–11 pm Sat 11 am–3 pm CLOSED Sat D, Sun, public holidays CREDIT CARDS All accepted UNDERGROUND Marble Arch, Bond Street WHEELCHAIR ACCESS Yes VEGETARIAN DISHES Always a selection

Just round the corner from the American Embassy in Grosvenor Square, this is quite the smartest address amongst the Hewitson team of wine bars (Cork & Bottle, Shampers and Methuselah's, *see below*) – no longer run by the don himself but by David and Susan Nicholl. But Don Hewitson's influence is everywhere evident in the wine on offer and the way it is promoted. Like the other bars in the group, Bubbles follows the seasons and the fashions, but is lighter and more elegant, with a spacious layout of tables downstairs as well as on the ground and upper floors. The range of hot dishes will be familiar to fans of the other establishments and it is likewise very busy in the early evening (and, like Shampers, a refuge at sale time). If you feel like 'bubbles' you can drink a half-bottle of Veuve Clicquot for £6 or a bottle of Perrier-Jouët Belle Epoque Rosé 1978 for £25. If, on the other hand, pay-day's a little way off, perhaps Trovador Rosé Pétillant from Portugal (£4.95) might do the trick.

The Bull's Head

80 Leadenhall Street, EC3 TEL 01-283 2830

OPEN Mon–Fri 11.30 am–3 pm, 6 pm–9 pm CLOSED Sat, Sun, public holidays CREDIT CARDS All accepted UNDERGROUND Aldgate, Tower Hill WHEELCHAIR ACCESS Impossible VEGETARIAN DISHES Not provided

How, you wonder, can a pub, wine bar and restaurant be squeezed into this narrow-fronted Dickensian City pub? You soon find out as you follow the stairs up and up. The wine bar is on the first floor, although the same list is available in the 'pubby' bar downstairs; the restaurant is at the top. A coat of paint would not go amiss, but wine is the serious business here, not interior decoration. What a selection and where to start! A 1979 Bulgarian Merlot was the wine of the week (£3.60/66p) and a fondness for the very good value wines from this Eastern European country is continued with a Riesling (£3.50) and a Pinot Chardonnay (£3.60). There are far too many good buys to list individually. However, special mention must be made of the Bouchard Père 1972 Santenay (£5.25) and the Lebanese 1977 Ch Musar (£6.35). 1976 Cru La Lagune (£5.60) – don't get it mixed up with Ch La Lagune – makes an appearance in the Claret section, along with 1970 Ch d'Yquem, Côtes de Bourg (£5.85), a mature wine but still full of life. 1981 Hill Smith Estate (£4.60) and 1977 Firestone Pinot Noir (£6.60) are the Australian and Californian contenders, both well-made wines and good examples of their kind. The food equals the wines only in cheapness – soup of the day (50p) and ham or beef salad £2. Enquire about their special wine tastings.

Butlers Wine Bar

Shakespeare Tower, Barbican, EC2 TEL 01-920 9610

OPEN Mon–Sat 11.30 am–3 pm, 5 pm–11 pm Sun; public holidays 12 noon–2 pm, 7 pm–10.30 pm CLOSED Chr, Boxing Day CREDIT CARDS All accepted UNDERGROUND Barbican, Moorgate (and BR station) WHEELCHAIR ACCESS Impossible VEGETARIAN DISHES Cheese

One of London's most intractable problems is how to sustain yourself with food and drink on visits to the Royal Shakespeare Company or a concert in the Barbican. Some people solve it by taking a picnic, but one possible solution, with a little skill in orienteering, is to find the compact Butlers wine bar at the corner of the Shakespeare Tower, overlooking a large piazza. It is a friendly place where you are served generous helpings of unambitious food: game pie, cold roast beef, lasagne, shepherd's pie, all for about £2.50. You also have the choice of 100 or so wines, ranging from decent red and white carafe wine (£3.90 a bottle/£1.10 a glass), through Ch de By 1981 Médoc (£7.25), Santenay 1979 from Joseph Drouhin (£12) to Latour 1973 at £33.

Café St Pierre

29 Clerkenwell Green, EC1 TEL 01-251 6606

OPEN Mon–Fri 7.30 am–12 pm Sat 10.30 am–12 pm Sun 11 am–4 pm CLOSED Public holidays, 24 Dec–1 Jan CREDIT CARDS All accepted UNDERGROUND Farringdon WHEELCHAIR ACCESS Yes VEGETARIAN DISHES Salads or special order

As the name and the opening hours suggest, this is first and foremost a café/brasserie. To start the day, the full English breakfast (£2) is worth a detour to Clerkenwell Green. But, within licensed hours, this bustling café welcomes wine drinkers with an exceptional list of 150 wines, all carefully chosen by proprietors Will and Caroline Thompson, manager David Gleave and consultant, Master of Wine Nicholas Belfrage. Wonderful notes describe every wine, with further information available from the tasting panel. There is a choice of good French or Italian house wines, all at £4.50 a bottle, but it would be a shame not to venture beyond. Bank balance permitting, the Bordeaux section will dazzle you: 1966 Ch La Lagune (£43.95) or, more reasonably, 1978 Ch Fourcas-Hosten, Listrac (£10.25) or 1974 Ch Léoville-Barton (£12.90) show what good buying and careful tasting can produce. Burgundy fans can have an equally splendid time starting with a 1978 Hautes-Côtes de Nuits (£8.95) and rising to a 1964 Romanée-St-Vivant (£43.25) with a 1980 Savigny-lès-Beaune (£11.25) or the more unusual red 1980 Chassagne-Montrachet (£13.95) in between. This must be London's best wine bar listing of Italian wines, Nicholas Belfrage's speciality. Of particular excellence are the Tieffenbrunner wines of South Tyrol (£6–£7), Pio Cesare Barolos (£8.75 and £13.65 for the 1979 and 1978 vintages), 1978 Torgiano (Lungariotti) for £5.95, and many more. Even the Valpolicella, in most wine bars fit only for the vinegar pot, is excellent here: try the Serègo Alighieri 1980 Valpolicella (£9.95), or the 1978 Capitel San Rocco of Tedeschi at £8.55. Auslesen, Trockenbeerenauslesen and Eiswein leap out from the German selection. California is also something of a speciality with some classy wines like 1980 Chardonnay, Chalone (Monterey County) (£21.95) and Phelps 1979 Johannisberg Riesling, Late Harvest at £17.65 for a half-bottle (it's a shame that there are not more half-bottles). Parducci's 1979 Pinot Noir (£8.35) is worth trying, but then you would have to return to compare it with the Trefethen 1978 Pinot Noir (£12.95). The only way to appreciate the wine list at Café St Pierre is to see it for yourself. And while you are there, try the three-course menu at £7.50, or the gammon and strawberry salad (£5.25), followed by a home-made ice-cream or sorbet (£2). Food can be excellent, sometimes disappoints, but is certainly above wine bar average. The menu changes twice a day: make sure you look at the blackboards for the specials and the cheeses of the day. There is a separate restaurant too.

Capataz

89 Old Broad Street, EC2 TEL 01-588 1140

OPEN Mon–Fri 11.30 am–3 pm CLOSED Sat, Sun, public holidays
CREDIT CARDS Not accepted
UNDERGROUND/BR STATION Liverpool Street
WHEELCHAIR ACCESS Yes NO FOOD

An old city wine bar enclosed in a time capsule. You negotiate a steep staircase to find a plainly furnished bar where riper citizens drink excellent sherry or Madeira at 70p a glass, or sparkling French wine at £4.50 a bottle/£1 a glass. Some clients have been doing so for 40 years or more: certainly the inhabitants of J B Priestley's *Angel Pavement* would recognise it. In the tradition of such places, no food is served, and it disdains to open for the after-office drinker. The wine list is short, with some remarkable bargains. We daren't hope that Pontet-Canet 1970 at £9.50 a bottle or Nuits-St-Georges 1972 at £10 over the bar can survive the publication of the *Guide* but perhaps they will be replaced by other treasures.

Captain Wooduck's

285 Northfield Avenue, W5 TEL 01-840 2740
OPEN Mon–Fri 11.30 am–2.30 pm, 5.30 pm–11 pm Sat 5.30 pm–11 pm Sun 12 noon–2 pm, 7 pm–10.30 pm CLOSED Sat L, Chr Day evening
CREDIT CARDS All accepted UNDERGROUND Northfields
WHEELCHAIR ACCESS Yes VEGETARIAN DISHES Quiche and salads

'*Evening Standard* Wine Bar of the Year', the barmaids' backs proclaim. We can't imagine why. Captain Wooduck's has a fair but unexciting and badly annotated list, loud music (live or piped) and mediocre food (undressed green salad, salad of tinned bean shoots, rather ordinary chilli con carne). We can think of scores that are better. But service here is exceptionally friendly, the atmosphere, even mid-week, buzzes and sparkles, and the charcoal grill, where you watch over your own duck, chicken or tender steak, is novel and fun. Captain Wooduck's draws crowds of obviously contented Ealing and Northfields youth. Amongst the sparse names on the wine list are Duboeuf and Torres, and the Sauvignon Blanc Chevalier de Védrines is quite good value at £4.95. House wines by the 80p glass are not very good, and don't be misled by the boxes highlighting certain wines on the list – it's simply that those wines are supplied by the merchant who arranged the printing. And don't be caught out by the darkened exterior – the bar may be open after all: the multi-coloured lighting is too weak to shed as far as the pavement.

Carriages Wine Bar

43 Buckingham Palace Road, SW1 TEL 01-834 8871
OPEN Mon–Fri 11 am–3 pm, 5.30 pm–11 pm Most Sats (Apr–Nov) 11 am–3 pm, 5.30 pm–11 pm CLOSED Sat (Dec–Mar), Sun, 4 days Chr
CREDIT CARDS All accepted UNDERGROUND/BR STATION Victoria
WHEELCHAIR ACCESS Yes VEGETARIAN DISHES Only occasionally

With the brick walls and metal railings that partition the ground-floor room into separate dining areas, Carriages has attempted to provide an 'outdoors' feeling inside. The result puts you in mind of concrete city gardens, yet it is not unpleasant. There is more conventional and elegant decor in the smoky basement. The wine list is varied and reasonably priced, with a good selection of middle-range wines. The five Alsace ones are all made by Gisselbrecht and his Riesling Grande Réserve 1982 is a particularly attractive offer at £5.75. Also available is his most unusual Alsace Pinot Noir 1982 (£5.60) – a light red wine, best served chilled. From the Graves comes the Ch Coutet Sec 1983 (£6.50), a light but full wine with a dry finish. The Sauvignon de Touraine 1982 (£4.75), on the other hand, although made from the same grape variety, is a fresh, clean, almost aggressive wine that might be a perfect accompaniment to Carriages' fish pie (£2.95). Another crisp wine, but of a much softer nature, is the Tocai Friuliano 1982 (£4.60), while from closer to home comes the Staple St James Huxelrube 1982 – a Kentish wine for £5.95. Amongst the seven red Bordeaux are some pleasant petits-châteaux: highly recommended is Ch les Rambauds 1978 (£6.75) and Ch du Bousquet 1982 at a pound less, although this last is still a little young. The Beaune, Clos des Fèves 1973 (Chanson) £11.50 is good now, or choose one of the many Rhône wines – perhaps the Hermitage Rouge 1976 (L Mousset) for just £9.50. The house Champagne changes periodically (but was Eugène Clicquot at the time of our visit) and costs only £10 – excellent value! Watch out for Carriages' special features – a selection of wines from a particular area offered throughout the month. The Brasserie menu has daily-changing specials as well as club sandwiches, croque-madame and other snacks. Live music (7 pm to 10 pm, Tuesday to Friday) varies, but may include blues, jazz and contemporary.

CJ's

8 City Road, EC1 TEL 01-606 0064

OPEN Mon–Fri 12–3 pm, 5.30 pm–11 pm CLOSED Sat, Sun, public holidays, 25 Dec–1 Jan CREDIT CARDS All accepted UNDERGROUND/BR STATION Old Street WHEELCHAIR ACCESS Impossible VEGETARIAN DISHES Salads

CJ's is one of those places unable to decide whether it is a hamburger restaurant or a wine bar. The multitude of tables covered with (plastic) green checked tablecloths and a large Pepsi Cola sign may be off-putting but it is worth staying around to examine the wine list and special selections. Eight house wines are offered by both bottle and glass, starting with Cuvée Rouge/Blanc at £3.90/80p, and rising to a Minervois at £4.50/90p. CJ's keeps its options open with the house Champagne (£9.95), so if you are fussy about your Champagne, ask which the current brand is. The wine list does try to be adventurous, but the offerings from Australia, California, South Africa, England and Hungary are rather plain examples and the 1979 Wraxall will certainly be getting rather tired by now. The fine wine selection at the back of the list is a little disappointing, too, although the 1972 Ch Meyney (£10.95) and the Delacroix 1978/9 Châteauneuf-du-Pape (£8.75) are exceptions. The place to look is the blackboard: 1967 Ch Gruaud-Larose (£18) and 1968 Ch Latour (£22.50) were on offer during the *Guide*'s visits. As far as food is concerned, CJ's knows it is really a hamburger bar after all. There are charcoal-grilled beefburgers with chips and salad for £2.95 or a whopping 12 oz rib steak for £4.50. Attractive quiches (£1), pâtés and salads (70p or 40p a half-portion) are also available for a quick snack and the sweet-toothed would be satisfied by chocolate walnut log or apple and apricot crumble (both £1).

Cork & Bottle

44–46 Cranbourn Street, London WC2 TEL 01-734 7807

OPEN Mon–Sat 11 am–3 pm, 5.30 pm–11 pm CLOSED Sun, Chr Day, Boxing Day, New Year's Day, Good Friday CREDIT CARDS All accepted UNDERGROUND Leicester Square WHEELCHAIR ACCESS Impossible VEGETARIAN DISHES Excellent salads

Almost in Leicester Square, tucked in among steak houses, amusement arcades and cinemas, the two entrances to the best, most lively wine bar outside the City are very easy to miss. At lunchtime, publishers and art directors negotiate the precipitous spiral staircase into the cramped cellars; in the evening, the place is invaded by theatre-goers and a younger set, so arrive early after work to get a seat (though the crush eases as theatre curtains go up). This was wine bar supremo Don Hewitson's first venture, later joined by Shampers, Bubbles and Methuselah's (*see above and below*). The wine list is stuffed with information, and is mind-boggling in its variety, from Australian Ch Tahbilk Marsanne 1980 (£5.50) to Anjou Rouge 1981 (£7.50), a fresh flowery Cabernet from Jean Baumard, and too many other interesting wines to mention. In any case, the wine list is ever changing. Beaujolais is celebrated twice a year, first when the new wine arrives in November and then in spring when the Beaujolais crus are ready. At other times, the range of wine on special offer will be Italian, perhaps, or even New Zealand. You may broach a bottle of Ch Margaux 1970 at £36 which includes in the price two glasses of Champagne 'while the wine breathes'. A fine variety of salads is on offer, and vegetarians can take on a large selection for £3.95, or an American gourmet salad of avocado, prawns and other delicious things in a red Stilton dressing (£4.25). For others, there is grilled Scotch sirloin served with Calvados, mustard and Roquefort butter at £5.95, although many dishes are much cheaper. There are sweets and coffee, too. Though the service may seem pressed, it is always cheerful and efficient.

Corney & Barrow

118 Moorgate, EC2 TEL 01-628 2898

OPEN Mon–Fri 11.30 am–3 pm, 5 pm–8.30 pm CLOSED Sat, Sun, public holidays CREDIT CARDS All accepted UNDERGROUND Moorgate WHEELCHAIR ACCESS Difficult NO FOOD

The bar is in the elegant complex set up by leading City wine merchants Corney & Barrow. The wine shop, restaurant, and Champagne bar have pressed the wine bar into rather a small but dramatically lit space. House wines are the ones to go for, as you would expect: Corney & Barrow red Bordeaux is £4.65 a bottle/£1 a glass and their white Burgundy is the same price. Since this is the City, the house port at £8.40 a bottle/£1.40 a glass is worthy of mention. Lunchers or diners are expected to eat in the restaurant.

Corts

84–86 Chancery Lane, WC2 TEL 01-405 3349

OPEN Mon–Fri 12 noon–3.30 pm, 5.30 pm–9 pm CLOSED Sat, Sun, public holidays CREDIT CARDS All accepted UNDERGROUND Holborn, Chancery Lane WHEELCHAIR ACCESS To restaurant only VEGETARIAN DISHES Salads

The legal eagles collect in this large basement wine bar where even the decoration reminds you that you are now deep in law land. The splendid three-dimensional mural looks realistic enough to frighten you off your solicitor for good. The house wine, bottled in Burgundy, is a fair £4.10/95p and there are one or two other good buys at the cheaper end, such as 1982 Côtes du Ventoux, Bellière (£4.80), Aveleda Vinho Verde (£4.90) and even a Côtes de Bourg, 1979 Ch Plaisance (£5.30), but the smarter wines do seem to be a bit on the pricy side – a simple 1982 Beaujolais-Villages is £7.35. Kir (£1) and Kir Royale (£1.20) are relatively good value and might make a pleasant change if you just wanted a glass of something. The food is a fairly standard wine bar cold buffet: cheese and pâté, smoked mackerel from £1.30, mixed salads (£1.50) or pies and cold meats. But there's plenty of room in the upstairs restaurant for those who have worked up an appetite during a morning in court.

Corts

34 Brook Street, W1 TEL 01-629 2471

OPEN Mon–Fri 7.30 am–10 am (for breakfast), 11.30 am–3 pm, 5.30 pm–11 pm Sat 11.30 am–3 pm CLOSED Sat eve, Sun, public holidays CREDIT CARDS All accepted UNDERGROUND Bond Street WHEELCHAIR ACCESS Impossible VEGETARIAN DISHES Salads

This West End off-shoot of the Chancery Lane Corts draws in a smart crowd from nearby Bond Street. The very roomy premises offer plenty of seating to rest weary legs, and a chance to admire the imaginatively framed and expensive-looking carrier bags from the local boutiques in South Molton Street (reasons for an even bigger spree!). The wine list is the same as the City branch *(see above)* although the food does look more adventurous, offering poached salmon salad (£4.50), beef Wellington salad (£4.50), or dressed crab and salad (£3) as well as ham from the bone, cold roast turkey, pâtés and cheeses. The separate restaurant has a set menu for £9.95, which looks as smart as its surroundings.

Ⓥ means a bar has wine at bargain prices

shows a bar has an above-average range of wines

☞ indicates especially good service, which includes friendliness, good wine knowledge, an informative list, and good food.

Cozy Griffs

11 Sun Street, EC2 TEL 01-247 9445

OPEN Mon–Fri 11.30 am–3 pm, 5.30 pm–8 pm CLOSED Sat, Sun, public holidays CREDIT CARDS Access/Euro, Amex, Visa UNDERGROUND/BR Moorgate, Liverpool Street WHEELCHAIR ACCESS Two low steps VEGETARIAN DISHES Salads and cheese

An unusual wine bar to find so close to Finsbury Square. While most City bars have bare floors and cask ends, this has soft lights, comfortable chairs and looks for all the world like an afternoon club. It is a place for the serious wine drinker: as we went to press, it was planning to introduce wine by the glass containing a full quarter bottle. The present measure, a little less, costs £1 for Belair Sauvignon Sec (£4.50 for the bottle). Sandeman's House Claret 1978 is £5.50 a bottle/£1.25 a glass, Kir £1.25. Further up the list, we were delighted by a Gigondas Ogier 1980 at £6.35, and promised ourselves a return visit one affluent day for Domaine de Chevalier 1975 Graves at £19. There is an excellent range of Trimbach Alsace wines, including the Riesling 1981 at £6.45. Fairly conventional food is served in generous quantity: smoked salmon (£4.25), fried scampi (£4.50), steak sandwich (£2.75), to which you must add a little under £1 for vegetables or salad. Service is friendly, welcoming and efficient.

Crawford's

10–11 Crawford Street, W1 TEL 01-486 0506

OPEN Mon–Fri 11 am–3 pm, 5.30 pm–11 pm Sat 12 noon–3 pm, 5.30 pm–11 pm CLOSED Sun (but may do Sun brunch in 1985) CREDIT CARDS All accepted UNDERGROUND Baker Street WHEELCHAIR ACCESS Impossible VEGETARIAN DISHES Fair selection

Under new management (the same as Crawford's wine shop upstairs – *see* MERCHANTS SECTION), this former dark green dungeon has been transformed into a cool, basement bar, and the wine list has been drastically upgraded. The regional French wine selection is the strength of the list. The Ch de Fonscolombe from Coteaux d'Aix-en-Provence (both red and a very attractive Sauvignon-like white) is a bargain at £4.50 a bottle but rather expensive by the glass (£1.20 small/£1.65 large). The sound house wines are exceptionally low-priced at £3.60/95p. Also available by the glass is the delicious La Vieille Ferme Côtes du Ventoux at £1.25 or £1.75. Cru du Coudoulet 1982 Côtes-du-Rhône and Ch de Beaucastel 1980 Châteauneuf-du-Pape are both delicious if still really too young (£6.75 and £9). A Chablis Grand Cru 1982 Domaine le Jouchère is well priced at £8.50 and the St Emilion Grand Cru Ch Destieux 1979 is also reasonable at £9.75. Red Marqués de Cáceres 1978 is good value at £5.50, or try the Geoffrey Roberts Red California Reserve (£5.25). The attractively presented cold buffet offers a good but fairly routine selection of salads, pâtés and terrines, including a vegetable one. Everything is freshly prepared on the premises – even the mayonnaise – and is reasonably priced, especially considering the W1 location. There is also a table d'hôte menu (£6.50 for two courses, £7.50 for three), waiter-served in the large back area; the good choice might include crudités with tarragon marinade, grilled chicken supreme with lime butter, and cheese, fruit salad or 'sweet of the day' to finish. And even at the busiest times, you'll never be an unwilling party to the conversation at the next-door table: Crawford's is refreshingly spacious. Now that there is a wine shop above the bar, customers will be able to take home more of anything that has taken their fancy at a ten per cent discount per case.

Crispins Ⓥ

14 The Green, High Street, W5 TEL 01-579 6912

OPEN Mon–Sat 11 am–3 pm, 5.30 pm–11 pm Sun 12 noon–2 pm, 7 pm–10.30 pm (365 days a year) CLOSED Never CREDIT CARDS All accepted UNDERGROUND South Ealing, Ealing Broadway
WHEELCHAIR ACCESS Underground VEGETARIAN DISHES Quiche, salads, omelettes

Since Crispins changed hands in 1983, the list of this dark, narrow, bow-fronted bar beside Ealing Green is the best in the area despite the continuing omission of shippers' names and vintages. But if you ask the knowledgeable staff behind the bar, you'll be in for some pleasant surprises, at penny-pinching prices. The list is not long, but the wines are consistently good. The house wines are very respectable (Cuvée Jean-Paul at 75p a glass, £3.95 a bottle, the red made in the Rhône from vines too young for the Côtes-du-Rhône appellation). The Sancerre 1983 is from Marcel Gitton, one of the best growers (£7.95), or a cheaper alternative might be a Sauvignon Vin de Pays du Jardin de la France 1982 from Pierre Frain for £4.25. There's a good range of Alsace wines from Heim, a few petits-châteaux, respectable Burgundies and a Chablis, all between £4.95 and £7. The Italian wines, unusually, are very good, too. Bardolino, Valpolicella and Soave are all from Lenotti and all under £5, the Chianti from Frescobaldi is £4.95, and Frascati Colli di Catone is, we think, the best that comes out of the area (£4.95). The Rioja is delicious CVNE at £4.50, and there are the good Freixenet sparklers for between £5.35 and £6.75, if the house Champagne at £13.75 is beyond your pocket. Watch out, too, for off-list specials chalked up on the board: on our visit, for instance, there was CVNE Imperial 1973 for £6.95. The cheap, food is home-cooked, basic and often disappointing, however. Ham and mushroom or chicken and mushroom crêpes (£1.95), sirloin steak in pepper sauce (£4.50), moussaka (£2.50), all include salad in the price. Pâtés and cheeses with French bread or crackers are £1. Crispins had just obtained planning permission as we went to press to extend their garden into the one next door to make an outdoor bar, and were about to do up the dingy but pleasant interior, too. (Don't, by the way, confuse this little Crispins with the noisy pub-like bar on the Mall.)

Crocodile Tears

660 Fulham Road, SW6 TEL 01-731 1537

OPEN Mon–Sat 12.30 am–3.30 pm, 5.30 pm–11 pm Sun 12 noon–2 pm, 5.30pm–10.30 pm CREDIT CARDS Access/Euro, Barclay
UNDERGROUND Parsons Green WHEELCHAIR ACCESS Not to lavatories
VEGETARIAN DISHES Some

An attractive, informal wine bar with a neighbourhood feeling, Crocodile Tears has a good following of regulars (and a memorable spiral staircase). The list has a fair sprinkling of wines from several countries in addition to France. Spain in particular is well represented, with five red wines including the dependable Marqués de Cáceres 1978 (£5.75) and the very attractive Viña Réal 1980 (£5.50). There is a good range of reasonably priced German wines, all under £5, and a few New World offerings from California, as well as South Africa, and an Australian Coonawarra Cabernet Sauvignon 1978 (£7) from Wynns. One or two petits-châteaux worth investigating include a Ch Latour-Prignac 1981 (£6.95) and a Ch Cazet-Beauchêne 1978 (£7), while the Mâcon Blanc-Villages 1982 (£6.95) was very drinkable on our visit. For a crisper, finer wine, try the Sancerre Clos de la Perrière 1983 (£8.25). Keep an eye open for the wine 'specials' chalked up on the blackboard – you might find a Meursault 1980 at £9.95, or a Bardolino 1978 at £4.50. Food is all home-made and offers more than the usual pâtés and quiches. Try potato skins and sour cream (£1.35); the house special, 'crocburger' (£2.95) is always dependable, or you might prefer grilled salmon trout (£4.50 with vegetables), with walnut cheesecake (£1.45) to finish.

Cuddefords

20 Duke Street Hill, SE1 TEL 01-403 1681

OPEN Mon–Fri 11.30 am–3 pm CLOSED Every evening, Sat, Sun, public holidays CREDIT CARDS All accepted UNDERGROUND Monument, London Bridge (and BR station) WHEELCHAIR ACCESS Yes VEGETARIAN DISHES Soups and a large range of cheeses

The City wine merchants Mayor Sworder own and run this cool, dark retreat next door to their offices in this wine-redolent area of Tooley Street and London Bridge, where most of London's wine used to be imported and where a great deal is still stored 'underneath the arches'. Cellars below the bar are often used for special tastings and it is not unusual for unfinished bottles to find their way to Cuddefords bar, to be sold for about £1 per glass. There are about a dozen red and white wines always open by the glass. In particular, Sauvignon Cru la Fontaine 1982 (£1.15) and the red Côtes du Ventoux were good on our visit. Amongst the 60 or so wines by the bottle, there is much of interest from dry white Lirac 1981 (£6.20) up to the magnificent Lynch-Bages 1966 (£18). The bar is also strong on sherries and ports.

You would expect the food to be plain and so it is: cold beef or ham, £3.60; but the servings are a bit meagre, which you might not expect. The hot menu changes every day.

Daly's

210 Strand, WC2 TEL 01-583 4476

OPEN Mon–Fri 11 am–3 pm, 5.30 pm–9.30 pm CLOSED Sat, Sun, public holidays CREDIT CARDS All accepted UNDERGROUND Aldwych WHEELCHAIR ACCESS Yes VEGETARIAN DISHES Quiches and salads

Daly's cheerful, airy interior – cane chairs, wooden tables, white paint, hanging plants – is a welcome alternative to the sawdust-strewn, murky 'snugs' around the Strand area. The wine list is simple and reasonably priced. Many wines are from Georges Duboeuf, including Cuvée Duboeuf Blanc (fair value at £5.50) and his good Beaujolais-Villages 1982 for £7.05 (the 1983 will be better). House wines are Les Caves Geneviève and are dependable choices for £4.30 (or 90p for a small glass), especially the white, while the Chablis 1982, Gloire de Chablis, is generous at £7.75. Bordeaux gets only a brief look-in with three petits-châteaux, and Germany, Spain and Italy have just two wines each – the Bardolino Boscaini would be an enjoyable bottle at £4.65. Daly's menu has some interesting and affordable starters – chef's pâté with brandy (£1.50) is popular, and the 'scallop surprise', with grapes in a creamy Champagne sauce (£2.85) is worth making a trip for. Main courses are more substantially priced: poached halibut steak with mousseline sauce (£4.75) and noisette of lamb with cream and peppercorns (£4.90) are two to be recommended, while the prime fillet steak in a pastry case with Madeira sauce, not inexpensive at £6.75, is in a class of its own. Many of the inmates of the nearby law courts make a regular lunchtime trip here and it is equally popular with office workers on the homeward journey. After 9.30 pm and at weekends, Daly's is available for private functions.

Special awards

Ⓥ is for bargain prices

is for a very good range of wines

is for exceptional service.

Do **you** know of any more bars that deserve inclusion in next year's *Guide?* If so, write and tell us on the report forms at the back of the book.

Every wine bar in this *Guide* has been anonymously inspected.

Davy's of London ⓥ

All branches are closed Sat, Sun and public holidays except where stated to the contrary. All branches accept all credit cards and Davycard.

Arch '9'
Seacoal Lane, EC4 TEL 01-248 0110

OPEN Mon–Fri 11.30 am–3 pm, 5.30 pm–8.30 pm UNDERGROUND Blackfriars, Farringdon, St Paul's WHEELCHAIR ACCESS Yes VEGETARIAN DISHES Salads

Bishop of Norwich
91 Moorgate, EC2 TEL 01-920 0857

OPEN Mon–Fri 11.30 am–3 pm, 5 pm–8 pm
UNDERGROUND/BR STATION Moorgate WHEELCHAIR ACCESS Impossible
VEGETARIAN DISHES Salads

The Bishop's Parlour
91 Moorgate, EC2 TEL 01-588 2581

OPEN Mon–Fri 11.30 am–3 pm CLOSED Evenings
UNDERGROUND/BR STATION Moorgate WHEELCHAIR ACCESS Impossible
VEGETARIAN DISHES Salads

Bottlescrue
Bath House, Holborn Viaduct, EC1 TEL 01-248 2157

OPEN Mon–Fri 11.30 am–3 pm, 5.30 pm–8.30 pm UNDERGROUND Chancery Lane WHEELCHAIR ACCESS Yes VEGETARIAN DISHES Salads

Bunghole
57 High Holborn, WC1 TEL 01-242 4318

OPEN Mon–Fri 11.30 am–3 pm, 5.30 pm–8.30 pm UNDERGROUND Chancery Lane WHEELCHAIR ACCESS Yes VEGETARIAN DISHES Salads

Burgundy Bens
102 Clerkenwell Road, EC1 TEL 01-251 3783

OPEN Mon–Fri 11.30 am–3 pm, 5.30 pm–7.30 pm UNDERGROUND Farringdon
WHEELCHAIR ACCESS Impossible VEGETARIAN DISHES Salads

Champagne Charlies
325 Essex Road, N1 TEL 01-226 4078

OPEN Mon–Fri 11 am–3 pm, 5.30 pm–10.30 pm Sat 11 am–3 pm, 5.30 pm–11 pm BR STATION Essex Road WHEELCHAIR ACCESS Yes
VEGETARIAN DISHES Salads

Chopper Lump
10c Hanover Square, W1 TEL 01-499 7569

OPEN Mon–Fri 11.30 am– pm, 5.30 pm–9 pm UNDERGROUND Oxford Circus
WHEELCHAIR ACCESS Impossible VEGETARIAN DISHES Salads

City Boot
7 Moorfields High Walk, EC2 TEL 01-588 4766
OPEN Mon–Fri 11.30 am–3 pm, 5 pm–8 pm
UNDERGROUND/BR STATION Moorgate WHEELCHAIR ACCESS Yes
VEGETARIAN DISHES Salads

City Flogger
120 Fenchurch Street, EC3 TEL 01-623 3251
OPEN Mon–Fri 11.30 am–3 pm, 5 pm–7 pm UNDERGROUND Bank
WHEELCHAIR ACCESS Impossible VEGETARIAN DISHES Salads

City FOB
Lower Thames Street, EC4 TEL 01-621 0619
OPEN Mon–Fri 11.30 am–3 pm, 5 pm–7.30 pm UNDERGROUND Monument, (and BR station) London Bridge WHEELCHAIR ACCESS Impossible
VEGETARIAN DISHES By arrangement

City Pipe
Foster Lane, EC1 TEL 01-606 2110
OPEN Mon–Fri 11.30 am–3 pm, 5 pm–7.30 pm UNDERGROUND St Paul's
WHEELCHAIR ACCESS Impossible VEGETARIAN DISHES Salads

City Vaults
2 St Martins Le Grand, EC1 TEL 01-606 8721
OPEN Mon–Fri 11.30 am–3 pm, 5 pm–7.30 pm UNDERGROUND St Paul's
WHEELCHAIR ACCESS Impossible VEGETARIAN DISHES Salads

Crusting Pipe
27 The Market, Covent Garden, WC2 TEL 01-836 1415
OPEN Mon–Sat 11.30 am–3 pm, 5.30 pm–11 pm UNDERGROUND Covent Garden WHEELCHAIR ACCESS Impossible VEGETARIAN DISHES Salads

Davy's Wine Vaults
165 Greenwich High Road, SE10 TEL 01-858 7204
OPEN Mon–Thur 11.30 am–3 pm, 5.30 pm–10.30 pm Fri 11.30 am–3 pm, 5.30 pm–11 pm Sat 12 noon–3 pm, 7 pm–11 pm BR STATION Greenwich
WHEELCHAIR ACCESS Difficult VEGETARIAN DISHES Salads

Grapeshotts
2–3 Artillery Passage, SE1 TEL 01-247 8215
OPEN Mon–Fri 11.30 am–2.30 pm, 5 pm–7 pm
UNDERGROUND/BR STATION Liverpool street WHEELCHAIR ACCESS Ground floor only VEGETARIAN DISHES Salads

Gyngleboy
27 Spring Street, W2 TEL 01-723 3351
OPEN Mon–Fri 11.30 am–3 pm, 5.30 pm–8.30 pm
UNDERGROUND/BR STATION Paddington WHEELCHAIR ACCESS Yes
VEGETARIAN DISHES Salads

Mother Bunch's Wine House
Old Seacoal Lane, EC4 TEL 01-236 5317
OPEN Mon–Fri 11.30 am–3 pm, 5.30 pm–8.30 pm UNDERGROUND St Paul's, Chancery Lane WHEELCHAIR ACCESS Impossible VEGETARIAN DISHES Salads

Skinkers
40 Tooley Street, SE1 TEL 01-407 9189

OPEN Mon–Fri 11.30 am–3 pm, 5.30 pm–8.30 pm
UNDERGROUND/BR STATION London Bridge WHEELCHAIR ACCESS Impossible
VEGETARIAN DISHES Salads

The Tappit Hen
5 William IV Street, WC2 TEL 01-836 9839

OPEN Mon–Fri 11.30 am–2.30 pm, 5 pm–7 pm
UNDERGROUND/BR STATION Charing Cross WHEELCHAIR ACCESS Ground floor only VEGETARIAN DISHES Salads

The Tapster
3 Brewers Court, Buckingham Gate, SW1 TEL 01-222 0561

OPEN Mon–Fri 11.30 am–3 pm, 5.30 pm–8.30 pm UNDERGROUND St James's Park WHEELCHAIR ACCESS Impossible VEGETARIAN DISHES By arrangement

The Udder Place
Russia Court, Milk Street, EC2 TEL 01-606 7252

OPEN Mon–Fri 11.30 am–3 pm, 5.30 pm–8 pm UNDERGROUND St Paul's, Bank
WHEELCHAIR ACCESS Impossible VEGETARIAN DISHES Salads

The Udder Place Wine Rooms
Russia Court, Milk Street, EC2 TEL 01-600 2165

OPEN Mon–Fri 11.30 am–3 pm, 5.30 pm–8 pm UNDERGROUND St Paul's, Bank
WHEELCHAIR ACCESS Yes VEGETARIAN DISHES Salads

From that ambitious acorn the Boot and Flogger *(see above)*, which John Davy still runs under his Vintner's privilege and which boasts the most prestigious wine list of any bar in London, has sprung this magnificent oak, the largest chain of wine bars in London. There were 23 Davy's wine bars at the time of going to press; there will doubtless be more by the time you read this. Unlikely spots have been converted, like Mother Bunch's, running under arches off Farringdon Street, and Skinkers, similarly and cunningly placed under London Bridge station. Possibly the most exciting is the Crusting Pipe (nothing to do with tobacco) on several levels of the refurbished Covent Garden. It is topped by Mullins coffee house, which opens only in fine weather, and also operates as a wine bar. These enterprising interiors are mostly furnished in the same fashion with oak tables and chairs, dark wood bars, low lights, small windows, if any, and sawdust on the floor. The food is simple: smoked salmon, roast beef and other cold cuts with salads, good cheeses. There is a good range of sherry – fino, manzanilla, oloroso – all at about 80p a glass, and vintage character port at £1.25, Davy's Sauvignon from Bordeaux (£4.70/£1.20), or Davy's claret (£4.75/£1.25). The Muscadet-sur-Lie 1981 Domaine de l'Augerie at £5.60/£1.40 is a find. Further up the list, there is Trimbach's Riesling d'Alsace 1982 at £6.75 a bottle, or St-Amour, Domaine des Billards 1982 from the Beaujolais at £6.45. Mr Davy has also persuaded the owners of Châteaux Léoville and Langoa-Barton to bottle a St-Julien for him at £7.95. With 24 hours' notice, you can order in wines from the Boot and Flogger list. Don't bother to look for anything outside the classic areas – they won't be there.

Déjà Vu

89 Haverstock Hill, NW3 TEL 01-722 1819

OPEN Mon–Sat 11 am–3 pm, 5.30 pm–12 pm Sun 12 noon–2 pm, 7 pm–11 pm CLOSED Some public holidays CREDIT CARDS All accepted UNDERGROUND Belsize Park, Chalk Farm WHEELCHAIR ACCESS Yes VEGETARIAN DISHES Special salads

This well co-ordinated wine bar – everything, including the wine list matches – seems to be where lonely Hampstead batchelors come for supper, attracted more, one hopes, by the atmosphere in this small bar than by the provocative pictures on the wall. The wine list has a sharp, modern appearance and misses out on such useful information as vintages and makers' names; and it does seem bizarre to list Rosé d'Anjou (£4.50) under a 'Various' heading alongside sherry and port. The short selection includes a red and white California wine (£4.80), and a white Rioja (£4.95) with the usual standbys of Muscadet (£5.10), Côtes-du-Rhône (£4.75) and Beaujolais (£5.50), but one might feel slightly apprehensive about buying the St-Emilion (£6.10) or the Chablis (£6.45) without knowing a bit more about them. Food is well presented and offers a vegetarian special salad (£2.30), jacket potato with cheese or chilli (£1.50), or a plate of charcuterie, including honey-roast ham, pâté, salami and garlic sausage for £2.95. For afters, there is a chocolate fudge cake (£1.20). The supper licence enables Déjà Vu to stay open until midnight.

Dover Street Wine Bar

8–9 Dover Street, W1 TEL 01-629 9813

OPEN Mon–Fri 12 noon–3 pm, 5.30 pm–1 am Sat 5.30 pm–1 am CLOSED Sat L, Sun, public holidays CREDIT CARDS All accepted UNDERGROUND Green Park WHEELCHAIR ACCESS With assistance VEGETARIAN DISHES Interesting

As you descend the stairs, instead of finding a small, pseudo-arty room, you come across an unusually large, rather frayed, basement made to appear even more spacious by some cunning positioning of mirrors. The appallingly mis-spelt wine list, some 60 wines, hides a well thought-out selection that would appeal to all types of patron – and all types certainly make their way down here. The choice ranges from the house Pontanet Burgundies (£4.10) and the basic Liebfraumilch (£4.50) to an erudite Ch Latour 1er Grand Cru Classé Pauillac 1977 for £22.50. In between, there are some pleasant surprises, such as the 1982 Sauvignon de St-Bris from Simonet-Fèbre (£8.75) or a Bouzy Rouge from the Coteaux Champenois – the 1979 is offered at £11.95. The rest of the list is by no means run-of-the-mill, but the prices are noticeably high: the Bourgogne Rouge, for example, is £6.95, and Ch La Vigeraie 1980, Bordeaux Supérieur £7.90. Food is also costly for wine bar fare, but is all home-made and comes in generous helpings. After the curried vegetable pie (£2.75) or the excellent marinated char-grilled pollo alla diavola (£3.95), you could try the 'dietician's delight' for a chocolate overdose, or perhaps a more moderate bowl of wickedness – the Dover's own honey and brandy ice-cream (95p). Perhaps the main reason Dover Street is usually crowded in the evenings is that every night except Monday there is some form of live music ranging from New Orleans style boogie to bop and blues (sets start at 9 pm and 10.45 pm). Suddenly prices no longer seem so high.

Down's

5/6 Down Street, W1 TEL 01-491 3810

OPEN Mon–Sat 12 noon–3 pm, 5.30 pm–12 pm Sun 12 noon–3 pm, 7 pm–11.30 pm CREDIT CARDS All accepted UNDERGROUND Hyde Park Corner WHEELCHAIR ACCESS Yes VEGETARIAN DISHES On request

Suavely impersonal yet attractive, Down's is a convenient base for the inhabitants of Mayfair and the more temporary 'locals' staying at plush hotels nearby. Considering the neighbourhood, one should not be surprised at the prices. The wine list, featuring only French and German wines, is well set out in an attractive booklet, with relevant maps and comments. There is a very good Loire selection (try the Sauvignon de Touraine, £4.95) and an appealing range of 14 Bordeaux at not-so-appealing prices. At the lower end of the range is a Ch du Bousquet 1979 for £6.95; in the middle bracket a Ch Léoville-Poyferré 1976 (£17.60); and a 1971 Ch Haut Brion would indeed 'make for perfect drinking now' – as the list comments – but at a cool £37! The Burgundies are more 'middle range': Chablis Premier Cru, Vaillon 1978 (£10.05), Meursault 1979 (£12.35), Vosne-Romanée 1972 (£16.50). From the Rhône, a 1979 Châteauneuf-du-Pape (£9.15) would be a good partner, perhaps, to a sirloin steak au poivre (£5.95), and one of the country wines from the South of France (Fitou 1976, £6.15) would go nicely with one of Down's home-made beefburgers (£3.35 with baked potato). German wines are from Dr Wilkomm and represent the best value. The Klusserather St Michael Kabinett 1980 comes at £4.90, while a Bernkastel-Kueser Weissenstein Auslese (estate-bottled by St Niklaus Hospital) can be had for £7.50. House wines are also reasonably priced (£3.95/90p), especially the red, an attractively plump Vin de Pays de l'Hérault. In addition to the steaks and burgers, there is always a fish dish and a *plat du jour*, which might be médaillon de veau (£4.95) or tagliatelle verde (£2.95). The cold buffet offers smoked salmon (£4.95) and marmalade ham (£3.75). For a lively end to the evening, you may like to take to the dance floor downstairs where there is a disco from 8.30 pm to midnight.

Downs of Mayfair

40 Wimbledon Hill Road, SW19 TEL 01-946 3246

OPEN Mon–Fri 12 noon–3 pm, 5 pm–2 am Sat 12 noon–3 pm, 7 pm–2 am
CLOSED Sun CREDIT CARDS All accepted
UNDERGROUND/BR STATION Wimbledon WHEELCHAIR ACCESS Yes
VEGETARIAN DISHES Not specially provided

Despite the name, there's no longer any connection between this wine bar and the one that actually is in Mayfair! This is at the bottom of Wimbledon Hill, near the railway station and in the shopping centre – the heart of suburbia rather than the heart of the metropolis. There's a ground-floor bar and restaurant, a garden and a basement restaurant with late-night disco. Downs is noisy, busy and popular with the young trendies of Wimbledon; not a place for a quiet drink, although the wine list is long and homes in disproportionately on Bordeaux and Burgundy: Léoville-Poyferré 1976 (£18.40), Brane-Cantenac 1970 (£20.50); Latour 1973 (£31), Vosne-Romanée 1972 (£22). Apart from these two areas, the list offers reasonable choice in France – three Alsace, six Beaujolais (no merchants or producers and multiple choice vintages). Outside France, it all comes to a very ordinary halt. The menu is vast, especially the sweets, which are bought in. Good if rather badly presented are pork Oliver (fillets of pork fried in butter, mushrooms, onions and sliced olives with lemon and white wine) at £4.55; and kidneys à la crème (full marks for having offal at all) at £3.55.

Draycotts

114 Draycott Avenue, SW3 TEL 01-584 5359

OPEN Mon–Fri 11.30 am–3 pm, 5.30 pm–11 pm Sat 11.30 am–3 pm, 6 pm–11 pm Sun 11 am–3 pm, 7 pm–10.30 pm Public holidays 12 noon–2 pm, 7 pm–10.30 pm CLOSED 4 days Chr, 2 days Easter CREDIT CARDS All accepted
UNDERGROUND South Kensington WHEELCHAIR ACCESS Impossible
VEGETARIAN DISHES Not provided

Probably the most colourful of the group of wine bars which started with the Ebury in the early '70s, this one is very much part of the Sloane Ranger circuit. It is always crowded, the decor has a faded turn of the century elegance, and the consumption of Champagne is high. The Champagne bar upstairs boasts the latest dispensing machine, which draws off wine a glass at a time, filling the space left with nitrogen, thereby excluding oxygen, so that rare and expensive wine is available by the glass and doesn't spoil. On a more modest level, a Listel Vin de Pays red (£4.50 a bottle/£1 a glass), and a Muscadet de Sèvre-et-Maine (£1.30 a glass) are excellent. Food is good and interesting: brochette of monkfish and bacon with garlic butter (£4.25), and really rare roast beef with potato salad (£4.50). Sunday brunch has become a local institution.

Ebury Wine Bar

139 Ebury Street, SW1 TEL 01-730 5447

OPEN Mon–Fri 11.30 am–3 pm, 5.30 pm–11 pm Sat 11.30 am–3 pm, 6 pm–11 pm Sun 12 noon–3 pm, 7 pm–10.30 pm Public holidays 12 noon–2 pm, 7 pm–10.30 pm CLOSED 4 days Chr, 2 days Easter CREDIT CARDS All accepted UNDERGROUND/BR STATION Victoria WHEELCHAIR ACCESS Poor VEGETARIAN DISHES Not specially provided

Although in existence for 24 years, the Ebury really took off in its present form when acquired by the two Nigels, Messrs Windridge and Pullen, both already well grounded in the wine trade. Two other associated wine bars have since sprouted, Draycotts and Boltons *(see above)*. In many ways, this is the most successful and the food, all home cooked, is of a higher order than in the other two establishments. (To be certain of a table at lunchtime, come early or late.) The decoration is plusher and the clientèle a touch older and better heeled. This is, after all, the heart of Belgravia. The wines are mainly French, some 20 or so sold by the glass; very good house red or white at £4.20 a bottle/£1 a glass. Ch Bonnet 1981 from Bordeaux (the beautiful château where the owner of Brane-Cantenac and Clos Fourtet actually lives) is £6.95 a bottle/£1.45 a glass. Or go for excellent Gigondas 1981 from the Rhône at £6.90 a bottle and a lovely Gewürztraminer 1979 at £6.95. Finer wines are also featured temporarily: on our visit, there was Ch Léoville-Barton 1979 at £13.50 and Clos Vougeot 1980 at £15.75. It is worth eating the *plats du jour*, always garnished with vegetables. Veal escalope with Madeira sauce, new potatoes or French beans is £4.95; a selection of grills sets you back between £4 and £7, vegetables extra. There's a good range of starters: fish soup, Stilton and walnut tart, and chicken terrine chinoise are all under £2.

El Vino

47 Fleet Street, EC4 TEL 01-353 6786

OPEN Mon–Fri 11.30 am–3 pm, 5 pm–8 pm Sat 10 am–3 pm CLOSED Sat evening, Sun, public holidays UNDERGROUND/BR STATION Blackfriars

New El Vino
30 New Bridge Street, EC4 TEL 01-236 4534

OPEN Mon–Fri 11.30 am–3 pm, 5.30 pm–8 pm CLOSED Sat, Sun, public holidays UNDERGROUND/BR STATION Blackfriars

Old Wine Shades
6 Martin Lane, Cannon Street, EC4 TEL 01-626 6876

OPEN Mon–Fri 11.30 am–3 pm, 5 pm–8 pm CLOSED Sat, Sun, public holidays CREDIT CARDS Access/Euro UNDERGROUND Monument WHEELCHAIR ACCESS Impossible in all three bars VEGETARIAN DISHES Cheese and sandwiches

El Vino, the world-famous haunt of journalists that became the target of women's lib because it refused to serve women at the bar, has now consigned this unhappy practice to oblivion. Nevertheless, some rules remain: at both old and New El Vinos, gentlemen must wear jacket and tie and ladies must not wear jeans or cords. Both bars are very clubby, Fleet Street always crowded and the recently opened New Bridge Street establishment catching up. Being traditional bars, they are strong on sherry: no fewer than eight own brands are offered. The list of French wines is strong and Germany is represented but no other country. A very different atmosphere reigns at the Old Wine Shades, housed in a 1730 building near London Bridge. As you sip your glass of Madeira, you can imagine Mr Pickwick or Samuel Weller sidling up behind you. Wooden wine cases serve as bottle racks, and there are small bottle-glass windows and a red turkey carpet. Food in all three establishments is confined to well-filled sandwiches, though there is also a restaurant in the New Bridge Street branch.

Fenchurch Colony Wine Bar

14 New London Street, EC3 TEL 01-481 0848
OPEN Mon–Fri 11.30 am–3 pm, 5 pm–8 pm CLOSED Sat, Sun, public holidays
CREDIT CARDS All accepted BR STATION Fenchurch Street
UNDERGROUND Tower Hill WHEELCHAIR ACCESS Impossible
VEGETARIAN DISHES Salads

If you feel nostalgic for the *Jewel in the Crown* colonial atmosphere, a visit to the Fenchurch Colony will revive you. Wicker tables and chairs, with prettily covered sofas, and a staggering number of plants that thrive in the light from the large windows easily make this the most attractive wine bar in the City. Judging from the busy lunchtime trade, the EC3 crowd think so as well.

Not content with creating a perfect setting, proprietors Hugh Bethell and David Cleave have provided an exciting and well-annotated wine list, too. Eleven house selections include not only the usual red and white quaffing wine (£4.30/£1.10) but also 1980/81 CVNE Rioja (£5.20/£1.40), Mâcon Rouge (£5.50/£1.50), 1976 Ch La Grolet, Côtes de Bourg (£5.70/£1.60) and Gatão Vinho Verde (£4.90/£1.30). If you are celebrating, try the house Champagne, Duc de Lavigny NV, at £10.90, or, for real extravagance, 1975 Pol Roger Rosé (£16). The more dedicated claret drinker would also be happy here with 1974 Ch Laroque Grand Cru St-Emilion (£6.50), and 1974 Ch Mouton-Baronne-Philippe (£7.90) – both need to be drunk before too long, hence the reasonable prices. If Burgundy is more your style, the Moreau-Fontaine 1978 Mercurey (£7.50) and the Jadot 1978 Côte de Beaune-Villages (£8.50) are well priced, as is the 1982 Meursault (£9.50). Two Paul Masson varietals, 1981 Cabernet Sauvignon and 1982 Pinot Chardonnay, both at £6.20, are California's contribution and make a pleasant change from Bordeaux or white Burgundy. Various vintage ports are decanted to order from such impressive years as 1955, 1960, 1963 and 1966. Fonseca Bin 27 is available by the glass (£1.50) as is the ten-year-old tawny (£1.80), but for a great dessert wine, try the 1959 Anjou Moulin Touchais (£10.50/£1.60).

Sandwiches filled to bursting start at £1.15 for egg and bacon, with beef and horseradish at £1.70. Tuna mousse is £1.70, with freshly made salads or baked potatoes both 60p. Hot dishes like chilli con carne (£2.50) change daily.

Five Lamps

3 St Katherines Row, off Fenchurch Street, EC3 TEL 01-488 1587

OPEN Mon–Fri 11.30 am–3 pm, 5 pm–8.30 pm CLOSED Sat, Sun, public holidays CREDIT CARDS All accepted BR STATION Fenchurch Street UNDERGROUND Tower Hill WHEELCHAIR ACCESS Impossible VEGETARIAN DISHES Not provided

Once you have vaulted the major hurdle and found the Five Lamps, tucked away on St Katherines Row, you are in for a big surprise. This vast cellar (at least half of it must sprawl out under Fenchurch Street Station) is a busy lunchtime meeting spot. The wine list is short. Vintages make a fleeting appearance, but they are the only information forthcoming. House red and white are an average £4.20 a bottle, £1.10 a glass, but the house claret is very drinkable at a price that won't break the bank (£4.50/£1.20). A few more words about the St-Emilion (£5.60) would have been useful. However, the 1976 Ch St-Paul (£5.90) and the 1978 Ch La Tour St-Vincent (£7.80) should be drinking well. Burgundy and Rhône are the mainstays of the list, our main quibble here being a 'Marcel Amance' (£4.85) – presumably a table wine – sandwiched between such well-known but anonymous names as 1980 Beaune, Les Theurons (£11.50) and 1981/2 Fleurie (£7.15). It is, in fact, a subsidiary brand of Prosper Maufoux, a well-known Burgundian wine merchant. Four Germans, two Riojas and two Italians are as far as this list strays out of France – so don't go looking for anything too exotic. The blackboard tells of special Champagne offers; at the time of our visit, Piper Heidsieck and Charles Heidsieck were £11, a saving of £2 on the list price. There is a good selection of bar food. Sandwiches start at 80p, baked potatoes (60p), or a plate of 'shell-on' prawns (£1.40). The smoked chicken (£2.40), with salad (60p) looked appetising.

Fox's ☞

176 Stoke Newington Church Street, N16 TEL 01-254 2709

OPEN Mon–Sat 12 noon–3 pm, 5.30 pm–11 pm Sun 12–2 pm, 7 pm–10.30 pm Public holidays 12 noon–3 pm, 5.30 pm–11 pm CREDIT CARDS Access/Euro, Visa BR STATION Stoke Newington WHEELCHAIR ACCESS Yes VEGETARIAN DISHES Some

Plenty going on at this local meeting place: if a notice board with exhibitions and accommodation or 'baby sitter wanted' adverts is not enough to occupy you, a heap of magazines and newspapers ranges from the *Beano* to *The Listener*. A small garden is another useful addition to this friendly bar, where you really are made to feel welcome and not just a customer passing through. Look at the back of the list for the wine of the month, usually a slightly more up-market wine from the rest; you will also find a pageful of first-class information about it. We award Fox's bonus points for stating on the list whether bottles contain 70 or 75 cl; it would be good to see more wine bars adopting this practice. Surprisingly, on such an informative list, vintages make only a fleeting appearance, but at least the owner, Robbie Richards, makes no pretence when a wine is Tafelwein. There is quite a batch of André Simon wines including Mâcon Supérieur (£6.20), Beaujolais (£5) and claret (£4.50). As well as the usual collection of Italians and Germans there are two Bulgarians, a Riesling (£4.25) and Cabernet Sauvignon (£4.25). House wine is served by the glass (75p), half-litre (£2.90), or the litre (£5.75). Food is home-made in the busy kitchen, with a menu that changes daily, and is cheap, with salads at 65p, hot harvest pie (95p) or, for the very hungry, steak and kidney pie with green beans and new potatoes (£2.50). Puddings include a delicious-sounding treacle and nut pie with cream (95p).

Frannies Ⓥ

75 East Dulwich Grove, SE22 TEL 01-693 3549

OPEN Mon–Sat 12 noon–2.30 pm, 7 pm–12 pm Sun 12 noon–2 pm, 7 pm–10.30 pm CREDIT CARDS Not accepted BR STATION East Dulwich WHEELCHAIR ACCESS Yes VEGETARIAN DISHES Omelettes, pizzas

A small, friendly wine bar with a list to match that deserves a special mention for passing on the 1984 duty decreases to their customers, making the Cuvée Jacques Mathiot house wine one of the cheapest around at £3.50/80p. The short list does not try to be anything fancy, but does have a spark of individuality with a Bulgarian Cabernet Sauvignon (£3.80), a Rumanian Merlot (£4.50), and a Syrah from the Côte de l'Ardèche (£4.40). For white wine drinkers, there is the lovely 1982 Viña Esmeralda from Torres. The menu offers both an English and Continental ploughman's lunch, the latter consisting of garlic sausage and smoked cheese (£1.50), or there are home-made pizzas (£1.25) and various omelettes and salads from £1.20.

French's

55 East Hill, SW18 TEL 01-874 2808

OPEN Mon–Sat 11.30 am–3 pm, 5.30 pm–11.45 pm Sun 7 pm–11 pm CLOSED Sun L CREDIT CARDS Access/Euro, Visa UNDERGROUND East Putney WHEELCHAIR ACCESS Yes VEGETARIAN DISHES Some

It's spot-the-ancestor time along a wall full of photographs from the turn of the century, an interesting and fascinating collection that makes the space invader and fruit machines look very out of place. A lengthy but simple wine list offers pleasant house wine (£3.95/75p)

with Bergerac and Provence coming in at £4.50. 1983 Vouvray (£4.95) is reasonable, or if you prefer red, the 1979 Chianti Classico Riserva (£4.95). The famous black crock Black Tower Liebfraumilch is one to forget at £5.75, especially when compared with the ordinary Liebfraumilch (£4.20). Bar food is good and plentiful and includes clam fries (£1.60), fisherman's platter (£1.85), jumbo king prawns in hot garlic butter (£2.80) or bacon, lettuce and tomato and club sandwiches (£1.20, £1.75).

French Wine Bar

Trocadero, Shaftesbury Avenue, W1 TEL 01-439 8476

OPEN Mon–Sat 12 noon–3 pm, 5.30 pm–11 pm Sun 12 noon–2 pm, 7 pm–11 pm CREDIT CARDS All accepted UNDERGROUND Piccadilly Circus WHEELCHAIR ACCESS Impossible VEGETARIAN DISHES Quiches, soups, cheese

Wine buffs, shoppers and sightseers in the new Trocadero Centre just off Leicester Square might well bypass the not terribly exciting range of wines in the Italian Wine Bar in the Italian Village and make for the attractive French Wine Bar above the French Restaurant, predictably in the French Quarter. French accordion music floats up from the restaurant and spindly chairs and little square tables complete a fairly authentic scene that might have popped out of a modern French text book. The wine list has been supplied by Duboeuf importers Berkmann Wine Cellars and, though brief, is consistently excellent. Almost everything comes in half-bottles as well as bottles. There are two very good house wines by the glass: Blanc de Blancs Les Caves Geneviève, a light, clean, fresh table wine from Muscadet producers Sauvion (£3.90/£1.95 a half/70p a glass), and Rouge de Champlos, Co-opérative Val d'Orbieu, Roussillon, a firm, fairly fruity, medium-bodied red with a pleasantly bitter finish, for the same prices. Not surprisingly, there's a predominance of Duboeuf Beaujolais and Burgundies, up to a single domaine Beaujolais, Domaine de Coubillaty 1982 for £7.10. You might also choose Chablis, Ch de Maligny, Jean Durup (£8.45/£4.40 a half) or a Rosé de Provence 1983 from Les Maîtres Vignerons de St-Tropez (£6/£3 a half/£1 a glass). Best value for a sparkling celebration – though this is, after all, a shopping centre and perhaps not the place to celebrate (try the Cork & Bottle across the Square) – is the Georges Duboeuf Crémant de Bourgogne NV (£9.50/£1.70). Mumm Cordon Rouge is very expensive at £17.80. The food, sadly, is less interesting. It would be so easy in this area to produce an excellent cheeseboard but though this one contains, as the menu says, Pont l'Evêque, Roquefort etc, it was all rather tired and dull on our visit (£1.75 for a selection). There are a number of pâtés: pâté de lapereau en croûte (£1.95) or mouse de mackerau (sic) at £1.95. Quiches (spinach and Alsace onion) were all eaten up when we called. Jambon de Bayonne (£2.50) was good, served in copious quantities with a tiny salad of chicory and radicchio. The dressing comes in separate oil and vinegar pots. A good, atmospheric spot for a glass or a bottle of good wine while out shopping.

Frogs Legs

264 Battersea Park Road, SW11 TEL 01-228 3794
OPEN Mon–Sat 12 noon–3 pm, 5.30 pm–11 pm CLOSED Sun, public holidays L
CREDIT CARD Visa BR STATION Clapham Junction (10 minutes)
WHEELCHAIR ACCESS Yes VEGETARIAN DISHES Pizzas

If you remember the solid old wicker chairs that used to appear as garden or nursery furniture, you would feel nostalgically at home here. Michoub Benotmane (if you think that is a mouthful, call him Slim), is the proprietor of this cosy wine bar, worth a visit for the beautifully decorated froggy blackboard and friendly service. Daily papers are there for the reading and, should you so wish, a board on which to leave your visiting card. The wine list is well presented and informative. The main supplier is Berkmann Wine Cellars, which means lots of Duboeuf Beaujolais and the very good Les Caves Geneviève house wine (£4.30/95p). Try the 1983 Côtes de Duras (£5.20) or the 1981 Côtes du Frontonnais (£5.20) as a change from the house wine or, a little more up-market, the 1983 Saint-Amour, Cru Beaujolais (£6.85) and the 1983 Sancerre (£6.80). Liebfraumilch lovers may be disappointed not to see their favourite here, but they can always try the 1982/3 Oppenheimer Krötenbrunnen (£4.95), which they should enjoy as much if not more. As for food, what else would you expect to be offered but frogs' legs in garlic butter (£2.80)? If you don't fancy that (and with the adorable frog looking down on you from the blackboard you might feel a little guilty), try the red mullet al cartucho (£4.50) or the chicken Kiev (£3.95). There is also a large selection of pizzas and, for pudding, hot chocolate tart and cream (£1.15).

The Gallery Ⓥ

122/123 Newgate Street, EC1 TEL 01-606 3570
OPEN Mon–Fri 11.30 am–2.30 pm, 5 pm–11 pm CLOSED Sat, Sun, public holidays CREDIT CARDS All accepted WHEELCHAIR ACCESS Impossible
VEGETARIAN DISHES Not provided

The aptly named Gallery (that is precisely what it is) is really an appendage to the restaurant next door. Bar stools form the main seating arrangement and seem to please the mainly businessman clientèle. The wine list, perhaps because of the close proximity of the restaurant, is extensive, with a commendable selection of half-bottles. A large glass of very acceptable house wine is £1.20 (£4.40 a bottle). With a Beaujolais at £5.50 and Pierre Sparr's Gewürztraminer £7.40, even the better class wines look reasonable. The real goodies are in the Bordeaux section. Someone has obviously done some careful buying: the 1966 Ch Bel Orme (£18.50) looks very inviting, with 1978 Ch Lynch Moussas coming in at £12.50. It is good to see that 1974 Ch Nairac, second growth Barsac, is available not only by the bottle (£5.95) but also by the glass (£1.50), a very well priced wine for the pudding.

Food, prepared in the open-plan kitchen at the end of the bar, seems a little expensive – until you see the hefty helpings. Fillet steak sandwich and chips (£3.65) or home-made lasagne (£2.75) are good lunchtime fillers. If you prefer more of a snack, sandwiches start at 90p, pâté and toast (£1.65) or a plate of prawns at £1.75. The Gallery offers an off-sale service (cases only) on most of the wines available at the bar.

Garrick Wine Bar

10–12 Garrick Street, London WC2 TEL 01-240 7649

OPEN Mon–Fri 12 noon–3 pm, 5.30 pm–12 pm Sat 6 pm–12 pm CLOSED Sat L, Sun CREDIT CARDS All accepted UNDERGROUND Covent Garden WHEELCHAIR ACCESS Possible but difficult, to upstairs bar only VEGETARIAN DISHES Always one special

A friendly, homely bar with red-checked tablecloths and half-window lace curtains upstairs, a few tables on the pavement, and a tiny-roomed cavernous cellar down the winding stair, dimly lit with coloured bulbs, and buzzing with life. The wine list is short on information on half the wines, but there is quite a good selection from a number of different merchants, and plenty of choice under £5, though some of the prices are not cheap. There are a few good Italians, three English wines, four Beaujolais from Pierre Ferraud (£6.55 to £8.85), some pleasant Rhônes and a short list of clarets, plus a few of the wine bar staples such as anonymous Piesporter Michelsberg (£4.85), and a smattering of wines from other countries. House Champagne is good value at £9.80/£2.20; and watch the board for special offers and that week's wine by the glass, which may be Rémy Pannier table wine (85p), Italian Tocai del Veneto from Cesari (90p), and a Cabernet Sauvignon from the Aude, 1982 from Foncalieu (90p). Food, apart from a few of the sweets, is freshly made on the premises and is good value. Starters may include creamy garlic mushrooms, hot croissant with bacon and Camembert, or taramosalata with crudités and pitta bread, all at £1.50, while main courses may be chilli con carne with jacket potato or pasta or garlic bread at £2.50, 'poet's fare', soup, Cheddar cheese, salad and French bread (£1.90) or rump steak, salad and baked potato for £4.50.

Gate Street Wine Bar

10 Gate Street, WC2 TEL 01-404 0358

OPEN Mon–Fri 12 noon–3 pm, 5 pm–12 pm CLOSED Sat, Sun, public holidays CREDIT CARDS All accepted UNDERGROUND Holborn WHEELCHAIR ACCESS Yes VEGETARIAN DISHES Vegetarian burgers, quiches

Gate Street is an attractive wine bar (with full restaurant upstairs) tucked away from the turmoil of Holborn. It offers an informally elegant atmosphere with al fresco dining in summer. The wine list tends to the pricy but the wines are good quality and sensibly selected.

There is a pleasing assortment of petits-châteaux, of which the Ch Ferrande 1979, Graves (£8.85) or the Ch La Marche-Canon 1974 are possibly the best value, while the Ch du Cauze 1979, St-Emilion Grand Cru, is simply an attractive wine even if it is priced at £12.90. The Beaujolais Cru prices are also too high, but try the Beaujolais Ste-Odile 1982 for £5.95. The red list is topped by the Corton Renardes 1974 (£17.80) – not the best vintage. The white wines include a reasonably priced Puligny-Montrachet 1979 (£13.90), and an unexciting Pouilly Fumé 1982 from Rémy Pannier for £8.20, but a fair deal is the Chablis Chauvot-Labaume 1982 Premier Cru at £9.85. Wines by the glass are inexpensive and offer a decent choice. The French house wines are straightforward and good value at £3.95/75p. Food at Gate Street is a strong point. Everything is prepared on the premises. An enterprising full menu is on offer in the first-floor restaurant, while snacks are available in the wine bar. These might include whitebait (£1.75), champignons panés (£1.85) or potted shrimp (£2.10), with kiwi sorbet (£1.10) or lemon syllabub (£1.45) for afters. In the two years since it opened, Gate Street has gathered a faithful following. It is popular for business lunches and in the evenings attracts office workers and straying theatre-goers. It also specialises in Christmas parties and observes Pancake Day and St Valentine's Day in its own imaginative way.

The Gazebo

10 Argyll Street, W1 TEL 01-734 2929

OPEN Mon–Sat 11 am–3 pm, 5.30 pm–11 pm CLOSED Sun
CREDIT CARDS Access/Euro, Amex, Visa UNDERGROUND Oxford Circus
WHEELCHAIR ACCESS Yes VEGETARIAN DISHES Some

This is one of the more successful examples of the new breed of wine bars to spring up in London over the past two years. Painted in pastel greens and pinks, the Gazebo's garden atmosphere is accentuated by potted plants, skylights and an attractive mural. Part of this street-level room is reserved for a tea and coffee bar (open all day from 8 am) though the majority of space is given over to the wine bar. French wines of moderate price predominate – a Ch Giscours 1979 is the most costly at £12, while a La Cour Pavillon goes for £5.75 and a highly recommended Ch Loudenne, Médoc 1981 is a reasonable £7.95. The Burgundy selection is lean, but the reliable Bouchard Père et Fils provide a Pouilly-Fuissé and the Chablis 1982 (both £6.70). A crisp Sancerre from Henri Brochard is £7.40, while the Cru la Galissonnière is an attractive example of Muscadet. From both Germany and Italy come several predictable wines but their main attraction is their modest price – Valpolicella 1982 for £4.75, Soave Classico DOC 1982 for £4.75. The food is prepared on the premises and could not be called expensive. Quiche is 95p, pickle and mushroom pie with two veg costs £2.20, while salad platters range in price up to £2 for chicken with salad. Friendly and helpful staff.

Gordon's Wine Bar

47 Villiers Street, WC2 TEL 01-930 1408

OPEN Mon–Fri 11.30 am–3 pm, 5 pm–9 pm CLOSED Sat, Sun
CREDIT CARDS Not accepted UNDERGROUND Embankment, Charing Cross (and BR station) WHEELCHAIR ACCESS Impossible VEGETARIAN DISHES Some

Contrary to some other claims, Gordon's has to be London's oldest wine bar. It was first granted a Royal Charter in 1364 and was exempt from regular licensing law until nine years ago, when it was bought by the present owner (another Gordon). For an authentic taste of Dickensian tavern-life, this is definitely the place to go. In an old cellar, it is delightfully dilapidated with crumbling brick and peeling paint and a bevy of suitably dusty bottles – not to mention the eccentric collection of taps and the gramophone speaker hanging from the ceiling! Gordon's was originally a sherry bar and today it still has a range of its own specially blended sherries served from the cask for 85p and £1.50, depending on the size of the glass, as well as Madeiras, Pineau des Charentes, and Hallgarten's Strawberry Cup for delaying the return to work. The main wine list is simple and unexciting and includes Gordon's house wine for £4, Aveleda Vinho Verde at £4.65 and a Spanish Siglo Sacco Rioja for £5.20. There are also seasonal selections, which offer more variety – perhaps a Sardinian Torbato (£4.50) or a Domaine du Bosc 1979 (£4.35). Food is hugely imaginative, wholesome, and attractively presented. Avocado mousse, fresh salmon (with salad £3.30) and game pie (£3.25) are all dishes to agonise over, on which you pile your choice of salads. You can eat inside, or sit at tables outside in Watergate Walk in summer.

The Greedy Grape

3 Victoria Street, New Barnet, Herts TEL 01-441 2869

OPEN Mon–Sat 12 noon–2.30 pm, 7 pm–10.30 pm Sun 7 pm–11 pm
CLOSED Public holidays CREDIT CARD Barclay
WHEELCHAIR ACCESS Impossible VEGETARIAN DISHES Some

Obviously popular with the locals, the Greedy Grape has retained a lot of its Victorian charm (it was once a bakery), helped by Laura Ashley wallpaper and pretty lights. The cosy ground floor is anyway worth a visit to view the lovely watercolours for sale, painted by a local artist. The wine list is a 'top of the pops' collection with such all-time favourites as Mateus Rosé (£6), Mouton Cadet (£7.85) and Cordon Negro sparkling Spanish (£9). The house wine, Cuvée de Grangeon (£3.95/70p) is acceptable and an extra 25p buys a pleasant Soave (£4.20) or Valpolicella. The red and white Marqués de Cáceres Riojas (£5.50) are very good. It's the simple home-cooked food that squeezes the Greedy Grape into the *Guide*. Hot dishes change daily. Soup (75p) was good and nourishing, and the open sandwiches (starting at 85p) are served with a generous helping of salad. Considerable will power is needed to resist the chocolate fudge cake and lemon soufflé cake (85p). The larger cellar bar serves the 'greedy hamburger' at lunchtime – for 90p you get a combination of beef, onion, herbs and wine in a fresh, seeded bun.

Green's Champagne Bar

36 Duke Street, St James's, SW1 TEL 01-930 1383
OPEN Mon–Fri 11.30 am–3 pm, 5.30 pm–7.30 pm CLOSED Sat, Sun, public holidays CREDIT CARDS All accepted UNDERGROUND Piccadilly Circus/ Green Park WHEELCHAIR ACCESS Impossible VEGETARIAN DISHES Salads

A sister establishment to the Greenhouse at the Royal Exchange, but quite different. It is several times larger, and food is more important here: oysters, lobster, salmon, gulls' eggs and crab sandwiches in season, cold roast beef – none of them cheap but all of impeccable quality. The bar is under the personal supervision of its director, Simon Parker-Bowles. Its similarities to the City establishment are its mahogany panelling and, of course, a wine list supplied by Green's, on which the house Champagne, Floquet, is good value. Many visitors to London treat this bar as the club it really is (though there is no subscription).

The Greenhouse

16–17 Royal Exchange, EC3 TEL 01-626 8801
OPEN Mon–Fri 11.30 pm–3 pm, 5 pm–8 pm CLOSED Sat, Sun, public holidays CREDIT CARDS Not accepted UNDERGROUND Bank VEGETARIAN DISHES None

We would tip this luxurious mahogany-lined bar to win a competition for the smallest and most crowded bar in London. A Boston stockbroker was amazed on Christmas Eve to see stockbrokers' clerks ten deep on surrounding pavements spending their bonuses on bottles of Champagne. This is the key to this establishment: though the short wine list is backed up by its owners, Green's, one of the leading City wine merchants, Champagne consumption (house Champagne at £10.50 a bottle/£2 a glass) is the game played here. Food takes second place – smoked salmon sandwiches (£1.95), Mediterranean prawns (£3.35) are designed merely to give you the strength to order the next bottle. This is likely to be white, an excellent Chablis perhaps, at £7 a bottle/£1.30 a glass, since very little red wine is consumed here. As well as inhabitants of Lloyds and the Stock Exchange, you are certain on weekday lunchtimes to meet members of the London wine trade.

Every wine bar in this *Guide* has been anonymously inspected.

Les Halles

57 Theobalds Road, EC1 TEL 01-242 6761

OPEN Mon–Fri 10 am–11 pm (normal licensing hours apply) Sat 5.30 pm–11 pm CLOSED Sun, public holidays CREDIT CARDS All accepted UNDERGROUND Holborn WHEELCHAIR ACCESS Difficult VEGETARIAN DISHES Quiches and salads

Manager Pascal Niqueux exudes Parisian charm, and immediately one feels at ease in this small, prettily French bar. The French influence extends to the wine list – indeed, wines from any other country would look positively foreign here. The excellent house red (£4.70/95p) is light, fresh and fruity and puts many other house wines to shame. The short list encourages wine by the glass, with a choice of nine available. Duboeuf's Beaujolais are a dominant feature: Côte de Brouilly is £7.95. There's 1983 Côtes de Duras (£6.85/£1.35) or Corbières (£5.95/£1.20), perhaps a little on the pricy side, but at least you don't have to buy your ticket to Paris. A daily visit to Billingsgate market means that fish usually features as a hot dish, perhaps lemon sole with vegetables alongside navarin d'agneau (both £4), or there is home-made soup (90p), salade niçoise (£1.60) or a plate of charcuterie (salami, garlic sausage and pâté) for £2.30. The restaurant through the connecting archway looks well worth a visit.

Hamptons

15 Whitcomb Street, WC2 TEL 01-839 2823

OPEN Mon–Sat 11.30 am–3 pm, 5.30 pm–11 pm CLOSED Sun, public holidays CREDIT CARDS All accepted UNDERGROUND Leicester Square WHEELCHAIR ACCESS Yes VEGETARIAN DISHES Some

A handy place to recuperate after queuing at the Leicester Square theatre ticket booth: Hamptons provides lots of tables and chairs so there is no need for a precarious balancing act with a glass of wine and a plate of pâté. The light, airy feel to this large room is created by lots of windows which open in the warm weather to give the illusion of a secluded patio. The wine list opens with French-bottled house wine at £4.35/95p, although the 'German style' white at the same bottle price leaves you wondering exactly what is being offered. Although the rest of the list is not desperately exciting, there is plenty of choice, reds being rather better represented than the whites. The 1974 Siglo Gran Reserva looks good value at £7, especially when compared with a 1979/80 Mouton Cadet (£7.95), but if it is claret you want, try the 1978 Ch Ferrasses (£5.90). There are also three much smarter wines, looking a little out of place on this list, starting with 1974 Ch Pichon-Longueville-Lalande (£15.75). Cheese and pâtés start at a reasonable £1.15, but the rest of the menu is a little on the expensive side. Helpings are generous, though, and the hot croissant Cordon Bleu with salad garnish (£1.65) would be an adequate lunchtime snack. Hot dishes change frequently; chicken curry, with rice and cucumber salad (£2.95) is a typical example.

Hiccups

3 Crown Buildings TEL 01-524 7282
The Green, E4

OPEN Mon 6.30 pm–10.30 pm Tue–Thur 12 noon–3 pm, 6.30 pm–10.30 pm Fri 12 noon–3 pm, 6.30 pm–11 pm Sat 6.30 pm–11 pm Sun 12 noon–2 pm, 7 pm–10.30 pm CLOSED Mon L, Sat L, Chr D CREDIT CARDS Access/Euro, Visa UNDERGROUND Walthamstow Central WHEELCHAIR ACCESS Yes VEGETARIAN DISHES Ploughman's, salads

There's not much seating here, with standing room only on ultra-busy weekend evenings, when the bar gets hot and noisy. The range of wines is slightly above average, with no real surprises, apart from Chablis (£8.50), perhaps a little unexpected in a wine bar with such a 'pubby' atmosphere. Vouvray (£4.95) and Muscadet (£4.40) are better bets than the house wines (£3.50/70p): the white (French) had an artificial baked vanilla flavour and no fruit, while the red tasted of stewed fruit and was oxidised. Perhaps the bottle had been open too long. A fruity Frascati (£4.30/85p) with above-average finish showed them both up. Food is mainly snacky (scampi and chips £2.95, chicken curry, £1.95) but steak, chips and peas at £5.95 is always available. The chilli and rice is tasty (£1.95). This bar was formerly called Jacey's.

Hilltop

58 High Street, Pinner, Middlesex TEL 01-866 3181

OPEN 7 pm–10.30 pm, (Fri, Sat till 11 pm) CLOSED Chr Day, Boxing Day CREDIT CARDS Not accepted UNDERGROUND Pinner WHEELCHAIR ACCESS Yes VEGETARIAN DISHES Food may be available from autumn 1984

This wine bar has a pleasant westerly aspect looking out on to the small green at the top of Pinner High Street. Pavement tables give it a continental air. Inside, it is on three levels, the bar area occupying the first room with other rooms going into the back of the building – rather gloomy but intimate once the candles are lit. The decor is dark beams and white plaster, and a brick bar with some interesting old prints of Pinner. Proprietor for six years, Tony Dabiran does a range of 23 (anonymous) wines and three cocktails, one bottled beer and some spirits and aperitifs. There's a range of Italian staples for around £5: Chianti from San Lorenzo (£5.25/95p); Chablis from Thorin (£7.50), Muscadet from Edouard Angenault (£5.15) and more at similar prices. Staff were friendly and courteous on our visit and the atmosphere was relaxed, with piped music. This is a pleasant place for the first drink of the evening but, without any food to soak up the alcohol, you would want to move on. However, Mr Dabiran hopes to open a restaurant next door before the end of 1984, and says he will provide 'French cuisine', with bar snacks as well.

Hobson's

20 Upper St Martin's Lane, WC2 TEL 01-836 5849

OPEN Mon–Fri 11 am–3 pm, 5.30 pm–11 pm Sat 5.30 pm–11 pm Sun 7 pm–10.30 pm CLOSED Sun L CREDIT CARDS All accepted UNDERGROUND Leicester Square, Covent Garden WHEELCHAIR ACCESS Impossible VEGETARIAN DISHES Some

A 'Dickensian' wine bar with magnificent wooden beams and sawdust on the floor (beware! it can be extremely slippery). No doubt the location (between theatre district and Covent Garden) is responsible for the somewhat elevated prices: Bordeaux Rouge for £5.60, Beaujolais-Villages 1982 (£7.40) and Sancerre Clos du Paradis 1981 for a frightening £10.35. But there is a small range of basic house wines at around £4.50, and by the (6 oz) glass for more penny-pinching prices: house wine is £1.02, Bardolino £1.12, Liebfraumilch £1.22 . . . what happened to those good old round numbers? Bargains are not to be found on the wine list; instead, keep an eye on blackboards and the occasional oak beam to find chalked-up offers such as three-star Cognac for just 90p. Food is a stronger point. There is a very attractive display of imaginative dishes which change daily but might include turkey, ham and tarragon pie (£2.95) or cauliflower pie (£2.60) and a good selection of cheeses.

Hollands Bar

6 Portland Road, W11 TEL 01-229 3130

OPEN Daily 11 am–3 pm, 5.30 pm–11 pm CREDIT CARDS Access/Euro, Visa UNDERGROUND Holland Park WHEELCHAIR ACCESS Yes VEGETARIAN DISHES Some

A highly popular bar, both for friendly business lunches and for evening rendezvous and dinners. Indeed, Hollands is such a hive of activity that it is wise to reserve a table, although sipping wine in the pleasant downstairs section whilst waiting is scarcely a hardship. The upstairs is cleverly and attractively designed, and has recently benefited from the addition of a delightful glass-walled conservatory, which is particularly appealing for a sunny Sunday brunch. This features a roast and 'extras' (£4.85), kedgeree (£2.95), or a variety of croissants (95p–£1.15). The wine list is a sensible, basic selection, adequate but not adventurous. The house wine is on the expensive side (£4.35 or 95p for a small glass) but the white, Blanc de Blancs Maison Caurette, is attractive. A Gisselbrecht Pinot d'Alsace 1981 is well priced at £5.35, and Ch Larose-Trintaudon 1976 is tempting at £9.75. Food is good, traditional English fare but distinctly costly. Soups are home-made and imaginative (cold walnut soup, for instance) but you get only a small bowl for £1.25. On our visit, the chicken liver pâté (£1.35) came in a more satisfying portion and with a basket of fresh mixed bread. Main courses feature grilled sirloin steak (£5.45), home-made steak and kidney pie (£4.35) and, although the menu changes weekly, there is also a selection of cold meat salads for about £3.10. In spite of these prices, Hollands is relaxing but invigorating – a good place to spend an evening with friends.

Jacksons

291 Sandycombe Road, Richmond, Surrey TEL 01-940 3590

OPEN Mon–Sat 12–3 pm, 6.30 pm–11 pm CLOSED Sun, public holidays
CREDIT CARDS None accepted WHEELCHAIR ACCESS Impossible
VEGETARIAN DISHES Good, changed daily

A very enthusiastic lady named Jackie owns this homely wine bar where fresh flowers on the tables help to give the impression that you are drinking in someone's front room. The homely feeling extends to the wine list, which is as basic as they come. However, house wine is cheap enough at £3.65/75p. Sadly, vintages and shippers remain a mystery and even the identity of the Lussac St-Emilion (£6.95) is not revealed. According to Jacksons, Beaujolais has moved from Burgundy to Bordeaux, although Brouilly Ch du Chapitre (£7.65) does find its rightful place in the Burgundy section along with a simply named Mâcon (£5.15) – whether it is red or white we are left guessing. The food is good and home cooked, the hot dish changing daily. Caribbean lamb, beef and mushroom pie or chicken and mushroom pancakes are the sort of thing to expect. With cheese from £1 and chicken liver pâté with port £1.20 it could be worth a lunchtime stop if you are in the area.

JB's City Brasserie

Plantation House, Mincing Lane, EC3 TEL 01-623 8234

OPEN Mon–Fri 11.30 am–3 pm, 5 pm–8 pm CREDIT CARDS All accepted
WHEELCHAIR ACCESS Impossible VEGETARIAN DISHES Not provided

Deep in the basement of Plantation House lies JB's City Brasserie. It is predominantly a restaurant, but an area is set aside for the wine and cocktail bar. Be warned – wine is at the more expensive restaurant prices and the air of exclusivity makes you feel that you have to be on your best behaviour. Duboeuf is the supplier for the house wines, and Burgundy, the Cuvée Blanc/Rouge is £5.10 a bottle. Even a plain Bergerac Rouge is £5.95 here. If your pocket can't take the strain, there is a good selection of half-bottles: 1982/3 Beaujolais-Villages (£3.95), 1982 Fleurie (£4.60) and even a 1982 Mâcon-Lugny. Burgundy is much better represented than Bordeaux, the latter offering 1982 Ch Pérenne,

Premières Côtes de Blaye at £7.50 or, at the top end of the scale, 1976 Ch Talbot (£18.80). Food is also on the costly side: eggs Benedict, barbecued spare ribs, chilli con carne and salad niçoise are all £2.95. Beefburgers with chips or salad are also available.

James Wine Bar

46–48 James Street, W1 TEL 01-487 4847

OPEN Mon–Sat 11.30 am–3 pm, 5.30 pm–11 pm CLOSED Sun, public holidays CREDIT CARDS All accepted UNDERGROUND Bond Street WHEELCHAIR ACCESS Yes VEGETARIAN DISHES Quiche, salads, sometimes hot dishes

Handy for concert-goers, just round the corner from the Wigmore Hall, this cool, crisply decorated wine bar opened early in 1984. In summer you can sit outside under the large apricot-coloured awning. The wine list is of the uncommunicative type, but ask the staff, some of whom know their stuff, and you will find some reasonable if not top-flight bottles. House wines from Bouchard Père et Fils are very fair at £3.95 a bottle/85p a glass. Bouchard Père supply a couple of the Burgundies, too: Hautes-Côtes-de-Beaune 1978 (£8.50) and Hautes-Côtes-de-Nuits for the same price. There are a couple more Burgundies and a couple of Rhônes from the reliable JP Brotte, or you might try Brouilly Ch de la Pilonnière 1981 from David & Foillard. Alsace wines come from Muré, and the Loires look interesting, including the good Muscadet Domaine des Dorices 1982 (£6.50). You might finish with Fonseca Bin 27 or Taylors LBV at £1.25 a glass, or a choice of Madeira styles at £1. The food is variable, so it is probably best to stick to the cold table: ham off the bone (£2.65), fresh smoked mackerel (£2.40), smoked chicken (£2.80), all served with a mixed salad. And beware – on our evening visit, salads and some other dishes had run out by 9.30 pm and it took some persuasion before we were given cold meats (excellent) and bread.

Jimmies

Kensington Palace Barracks,
Kensington Church St, W8 TEL 01-937 9988

OPEN Mon–Sat 12 noon–3 pm, 5.30 pm–11 pm Sun 12 noon–2 pm, 7 pm–10 pm CLOSED Chr, Boxing Day CREDIT CARDS Not accepted UNDERGROUND High Street Kensington WHEELCHAIR ACCESS Yes VEGETARIAN DISHES Some

Owned by an ex-army captain, Jimmies is literally part of the wall of Kensington Palace Barracks. It seems to be busy at all hours: at lunchtime, it is full of local business people, and in the evenings, it becomes a popular spot for singles attracted by the live music from 8–11 pm. It is an unpretentious place – as is the very basic wine list. But for more interesting wines, it is always worth keeping an eye on the blackboard, because Jimmies can produce some off-year bargains:

Ch Gruaud-Larose 1972 for £7.50, Ch Lagrange 1972 at £8.50; or Ch Léoville-Barton 1974 at £9.50 are just three on recent offer. There are even some half-bottles of fine wines (a regrettably infrequent occurrence in the majority of wine bars). Last summer, for example, there was a 1973 Nuits-St Georges or 1973 Vosne-Romanée, both for a mere £5. Be a little wary of old vintages and lesser years of fine wines, however – they may not be such a bargain. Food, prepared on the premises, is simple and inexpensive; the meat cuts (T-bone £3.90, lamb chops £2, home-made sausage 95p), grilled to your exact specifications over a charcoal fire, are a particularly good option on the daily-changing menu, and the salads are all attractively presented.

Julie's Bar ☞

137 Portland Road, London W11 TEL 01-727 7985

OPEN Mon–Sat 11 am–11 pm Sun 12 noon–10.30 pm CLOSED Chr, Easter
CREDIT CARDS Not accepted UNDERGROUND Holland Park
WHEELCHAIR ACCESS Yes VEGETARIAN DISHES Always cheeses and salads, sometimes more

Julie's Bar, just next to the restaurant of the same name, has been a popular gathering place for young and not-so-young 'successfuls' over the past 13 years. It is the sort of place where you can linger over a traditional Sunday lunch (newspapers provided); meet for a quiet afternoon tea in the conservatory overlooking the secluded garden; or join the evening hum with a group of friends. The wine list has been sensibly chosen, a good mixture of unremarkable 'dependables', and one or two more unusual offerings. In this last category, the Ch Rahoul, Graves 1979 (£7.75) is worthy of note, as is Le Chouan Chardonnay 1981 from the Loire (£4.65). There are token representatives from several other countries, including California and Chile but, surprisingly, only two Champagnes, and these are highly priced. Food is wholesome and mainly traditional, although with several imaginative touches. The menu changes daily, and you might find a pea and ham soup (£1.10) or blue Brie in puff pastry (£1.75) amongst the starters. As a main course, Julie's excellent steak and kidney pie with spiced red cabbage and new potatoes (£3.70) is always a popular choice. Finish with one of the tempting desserts and some good fresh coffee, served with jugs of real cream by a friendly and efficient staff. The wine list on its own is not sufficient reason for a visit to Julie's but, combined with the menu suggestions and the delightfully eclectic decor, this bar is certainly worth a small detour.

Special awards

Ⓥ is for bargain prices

is for a very good range of wines

☞ is for exceptional service.

Just Williams

6 Battersea Rise, SW11 TEL 01-228 9880

OPEN Mon–Fri 12 noon–3 pm, 5.30 pm–11 pm Sat 12 noon–3 pm, 6.30 pm–11 pm Sun 7 pm–10.30 pm Public holidays 12 noon–2.30 pm, 7 pm–11 pm CLOSED Sun L, 4 days Chr, Easter Sun CREDIT CARDS All accepted WHEELCHAIR ACCESS Yes VEGETARIAN DISHES Some

Almost next door to the well-known Pollyanna's restaurant and run by the same partnership, Just Williams has won considerable popularity with the Battersea crowd and it is easy to see why. The light, airy interior with Spanish style arches and white walls opens out on to a pretty patio, a great attraction on a warm summer's evening. Wines are bought from a variety of suppliers: house wines (£3.95/75p) are French, with a house claret at £4.75, sensibly also available in halves (£2.65). Two French country wines, Vin de Pays des Pyrénées (£4.10) and Ch de Millegrand, Minervois (£4.25) look particularly good value, as does the Sichel's Bordeaux Sauvignon (£4.25). For the curious, there is a 1982 Beaujolais Blanc, Marcel Amance (£8.95), once a popular wine but rarely seen these days. Bordeaux offers one or two treats, with 1978 Ch Lyonnat (£9) and 1976 Ch Rausan-Ségla (£14.95); and even the 1971 Ch La Lagune (£16) does not seem too expensive for the quality. The delightful Torres Viña Esmeralda, a blend of Gewürztraminer and Muscat grapes (£5.25), would be lovely to drink as the sun goes down over the patio, or you might prefer the California 1981 River Oaks Vineyard (£6.95). Most of the food is made on the premises and is served at lunchtimes and from 7.30 pm in the evening. The barbecue grill offers hamburger and salad (£2.50), steak with salad and jacket potatoes (£4.25) or kebabs with salad and rice (£3.85). Slimmers can start with blue cheese dip and raw vegetables (£1.50) and make up the calories with carbonnade of beef with vegetables and dumplings (£2.95). Cheese and pâté are both £1.20 and home-made quiches and salad £1.95.

Korky's

319–321 King St, W6 TEL 01-741 2458

OPEN Mon–Fri 12 noon–3 pm, 5.30 pm–11 pm Sat 7 pm–11 pm Sun 7 pm–10.30 pm CLOSED Sat and Sun L CREDIT CARDS Access/Euro, Visa UNDERGROUND Ravenscourt Park, Stamford Brook WHEELCHAIR ACCESS Yes VEGETARIAN DISHES Some

Korky's is a friendly neighbourhood wine bar attractively furnished with plain pine. Its trade-mark is the wide variety of excellent home-made beefburgers, but don't let that blind you to the diversity of the wine list. The French section is fairly lean but the Chablis 1982 from Lamblin for £7.80 is worthy of note and a Ch de Cordaillon 1977 from Graves (£7.25) is an attractive petit-château. Do a bit of armchair travelling and try a Cooks Chardonnay from New Zealand (£5.40) or an

Australian Dry Muscat 1982 from Brown Bros (£5.40). South Africa, Spain, Portugal, Germany and Italy all provide at least two or three representatives at reasonable prices, while from England there's Lamberhurst Priory 1981 for £6.20. Half-bottles are not plentiful but there is a good range of wines by the glass. The Italian house white is just 75p and a good dry wine with which to start an evening, or try the house speciality – Korky's Fizz: sparkling wine, orange juice and grenadine (£1.30). To finish, a glass of Muscat de Beaumes-de-Venise at 90p shouldn't drain the kitty.

Lautrec

52 Cannon Street, EC4 TEL 01-248 1019

OPEN Mon–Fri 11.30 am–3 pm, 5 pm–10 pm CLOSED Sat, Sun, public holidays
UNDERGROUND/BR STATION Cannon Street

31 Eastcheap, EC3 TEL 01-623 1477

OPEN Mon–Fri 11 am–3 pm, 5 pm–11 pm CLOSED Sat, Sun, public holidays
UNDERGROUND Monument

Lautrec Bis 163 Moorgate, EC2 TEL 01-628 6521

OPEN Mon–Fri 11 am–3 pm, 5 pm–11 pm CLOSED Sat, Sun, public holidays
UNDERGROUND/BR STATION Moorgate CREDIT CARDS All accepted
WHEELCHAIR ACCESS Impossible VEGETARIAN DISHES Not provided

The wallpaper and posters at the third and most recent in the Lautrec series of wine bars in Cannon Street (formerly Cousins) leave you in no doubt as to the wine bar's name. Tables and chairs are on raised platforms, which leaves adequate room for those who prefer to stand at the bar. Popular with the many office folk in the vicinity (maybe it's those intimate tables for two), the Vin de Patron house wine is £3.85/£1. A few pence extra buys the Blanc de Blancs (£4.10) or the house claret (£4.45). The wine buyer for Lautrec is obviously keener on Burgundy than Bordeaux. The Jules Bernard 1979 Meursault (£11) and 1980/81 Puligny-Montrachet (£11.50) are expensive treats but worth sampling. If you are looking for red wines, Benoît Latreille 1982 Beaujolais (£4.95) and Fleurie (£7.50) are reasonably priced, and a Moreau 1979 Côte de Beaune-Villages (£10) is not unduly expensive. The Italian section shows a few faceless favourites, with Soave at £4 and Chianti £4.30. America makes a token appearance with a French Colombard and Zinfandel at £5.65. A usual selection of cold food, pâtés (£1), quiche and salad (£2.20) is supplemented by a daily change of hot dishes and baked potatoes (£1) or by cheese (£1.30).

Do **you** know of any more bars that deserve inclusion in next year's *Guide*? If so, write and tell us on the report forms at the back of the book.

Leadenhall Wine Bar

27 Leadenhall Market, EC3 TEL 01-623 1818
OPEN Mon–Fri 11.30 am–3 pm, 5 pm–8 pm CLOSED Sat, Sun, public holidays
CREDIT CARDS Amex WHEELCHAIR ACCESS Impossible
VEGETARIAN DISHES Not provided

The floor-to-ceiling casement windows of this large, elegant room give a bird's-eye view of the comings and goings in Leadenhall market. Looking inwards, the coral pink walls and old-fashioned prints hint at the exclusivity of a gentlemen's club. An extensive, mostly French, wine list offers some interesting clarets, and although considered an 'off' vintage, the 1977 Ch La Tour de By (£8.80) seems very reasonable. 1976 Ch Montrose (£16.35) should be drinking well now and for a real treat, try the 1977 Ch Latour (£22.15). It is good to see Pouilly Fumé feature on a wine bar list: there's 1982 Pouilly Fumé, Les Moulins-à-Vent (£9.15), as well as 1982 Sancerre, Clos Paradis (£8.15). Further down to earth, house white and red are £4.50/£1.05 with a house claret and hock being offered at £5.75 and £4.65 respectively. There is a pleasant Blanquette de Limoux at £7.65 and Champagne starts with Duc de Lavigny NV at £10.65/£2.40. The lunchtime cold buffet is a substantial open table at £4.50 per head; or for the less hungry, there is home-made pâté (£1.75) or a selection from the cheeseboard (£2.50). No food is served in the short after-work session.

Marlows

Lloyds Avenue, EC3 TEL 01-481 1168
OPEN Mon–Fri 11.30 am–3 pm, 5 pm–7 pm CLOSED Sat, Sun, public holidays
CREDIT CARDS All accepted WHEELCHAIR ACCESS Impossible
VEGETARIAN DISHES Some

There is seating a-plenty in this large, modern basement, which is brightened by the attractive David Hockney posters and friendly service. Certainly worth a stop for a leisurely glass of wine. The list is uncomplicated. The Marlows red and white from Loron at £4.20 a bottle/95p a glass is very drinkable, but for a little more excitement, try the 1975 Imperial Reserve Rioja (£7.35) or the 1981 Louis Latour Montagny (£8.10). There are some nicely priced wines from the Rhône: 1982 Côtes-du-Rhône, Domaine des Aires Vieilles (£4.85) or the white Crozes-Hermitage £6.15. Party-goers can order a litre of Bucks Fizz at £6.65, a nice idea as a starter.

The counter service is open only at lunchtime and has a good selection of cold specials plus two hot dishes daily, such as veal and vegetable pie (£2.85) or pasta bolognese (£2.95). The duck, endive and avocado salad with lemon dressing (£2.35) sounds very inviting. Puddings are a speciality, and the gâteau russe would go very well with a glass of Muscat de Beaumes-de-Venise (£1.50).

Maxim Chinese Wine Bar

7 Boston Parade, Boston Road, W7 TEL 01-567 9708

OPEN Mon–Sat 12 noon–3 pm, 5.30 pm–11 pm Sun 12 noon–2 pm, 7 pm–10.30 pm (including public holidays) CLOSED 25–28 Dec
CREDIT CARDS All accepted UNDERGROUND Boston Manor
WHEELCHAIR ACCESS Easy, but very crowded at night
VEGETARIAN DISHES Noodles, salads

Tucked into a row of dingy shops opposite the Boston Manor tube, the green, plant-bestrewn Maxim Chinese wine bar is smart enough to have gained an entry in the *Guide* even if we'd found it in the middle of Covent Garden, where the competition is tough. Here, just off the Great West Road and a short trip by car down from Ealing and Acton, Maxim is a godsend in an area where gastronomes could previously resort only to the other (related) Maxims, the Chinese restaurant down the road. 'Maxim was created,' we were told by manager Dave Chin, 'to maximise the customers' pleasure by giving the best of both worlds – western wines and Chinese cuisine.' The marble-green wine list was selected for them by the Ebury Wine Company, and offers a very good choice, each wine (nearly) identified in all its details, with even a tasting note of the most useful kind beneath each. Watch vintages, however, which may be switched without telling you. The house wines are some of the best value at £3.95/85p, the red, a Vin de Pays de l'Hérault, being particularly good. There's the Ebury's House Claret 1982 – oddly scented and quite unlike anything bordelais we've ever tasted, but pleasant nevertheless at £4.80/£1. The short but sound collections from Bordeaux and Burgundy range from £4.50 to £10.30, and other French regions are each represented by a couple of fair to good bottles, as are other European countries and Australia and China, the latter by the light, sweetish German-style Dynasty. This is made by winemakers from Rémy Martin in co-operation with the Chinese Government – a drinkable experiment, but at £8.90 amongst the worst value on the list. 'We always have at least one fine vintage port,' the list assures. On our visit, however, all that could be offered was late-bottled vintage. The food at Maxim is excellent, and beautifully presented. Begin, perhaps, with delicious crisp sesame prawn fingers (£3), bang bang chicken salad with sesame dressing (£1.80) or soup of the day (80p), and continue with Canton roast duck (£2.80), griddle-sizzled lamb (£3.20), griddle-sizzled prawns (£3.50) or the regional casserole of the day (£2.60). Perhaps best vâlue, and equally delicious, are the 'snacks' from the sandwich bar: sliced duck (£1.80) or char siu pork loin (£1.80) come in wholewheat bread. There's a good cheeseboard 'for Western Devils'. 'So,' the menu concludes, 'Chin Chin (which has always sounded suspiciously Chinese to us) and Gan Bei (bottoms up) to you.' There's loud live music (free) four nights a week, and loud (deceased pop) at lunchtimes.

Every wine bar in this *Guide* has been anonymously inspected.

Maynard's

22–23 Woodstock Street, W1 TEL 01-499 0216

OPEN Mon–Fri 11 am–3 pm, 5.30 pm–11 pm Sat 11 am–3 pm CLOSED Sat eve, Sun, Chr Day, Boxing Day, Good Friday CREDIT CARDS All accepted UNDERGROUND Oxford Circus, Bond Street WHEELCHAIR ACCESS Yes VEGETARIAN DISHES Salads

After the noise and traffic of Oxford Street, it is a relief to walk into the airy and attractive surroundings of Maynards. Wooden furniture and green plants create a pleasant setting for a bite in either the self-service or waitress-service areas. But, beware, the food is expensive: pork and garlic pâté (£3.75), roast beef with salad (£4). The wine list, on the other hand, although quite brief, does give value for money – house wines are good quality, the white a Philippe Bouchard and the red a Michel Trielle, both for £3.95. Chevalier de Védrines 1979 is a dependable red Bordeaux for £5.45, while the Beaujolais Supérieur from Ch du Grand Talence is very reasonably priced at £6.45. The full-flavoured Chablis Ancien Domaine Auffray 1983 is also good value (£7.95), as is the Meursault, lès Poruzots, 1977 at £9.95. Staff morale seemed low at the time of our visit but perhaps this was merely a temporary affliction – especially since several of the other customers were evidently regulars.

Methuselah's

29 Victoria Street, SW1 TEL 01-222 0424

OPEN Mon–Fri 9 am–11 pm Sat, Sun 9 am–6 pm CLOSED Chr Day, New Year's Day, Boxing Day, Good Friday CREDIT CARDS All accepted UNDERGROUND St James's Park, Victoria (and BR STATION) WHEELCHAIR ACCESS Difficult VEGETARIAN DISHES Some

A recent addition to Don Hewitson's stable, and attractively refurbished, Methuselah's has a Division Bell to call back truants to the nearby Houses of Parliament. The main wine bar is small and at basement level. On the ground floor is another bar and a sea of white-clothed tables (some 200 or more covers). Half wine bar, half bistro, it is now beginning to blossom under the influence of the new enthusiasm, after a rather hesitant start. Every two months, there is a new range of one region's wines. An interesting feature is the selection of second wines from famous Bordeaux châteaux, Gombeaude 1979 (£8.50) from Ch Lascombes, and Ch Lalande-Borie 1977 from Ch Ducru-Beaucaillou (£8.95). From Burgundy, there is Joseph Drouhin's Chorey-lès-Beaune 1979 and a good white Chardonnay de Bourgogne 1981 at £5.95. Good named house selections feature at £4.95 per bottle. There's a large variety of food with a regularly changing menu, but in this, Methuselah's has not so far come up to the high standards of the other bars in the same group *(see below)*; Methuselah's seafood Mornay (£4.25) and noisettes of lamb with sweet rosemary sauce (£5.95) were nevertheless praised by one inspector. In deference to Don

Hewitson's Antipodean past, there is always Pavlova. Consult the entries for other bars in the group, Cork & Bottle, Bubbles, and Shampers, for other wines you are likely to find.

Le Métro

28 Basil Street, SW3 TEL 01-589 6286

OPEN Mon–Sat 11 am–3 pm Mon–Fri 5.30 pm–11 pm public holidays 12 noon–2 pm, 7 pm–10.30 pm CLOSED Sat eve, Sun CREDIT CARDS Amex UNDERGROUND Knightsbridge WHEELCHAIR ACCESS Via rear entrance VEGETARIAN DISHES On request

Le Métro is a stylish newcomer to the wine bar scene. One look at the excellent wine list and a quick assessment of the simply chic (chicly simple?) decor will convince you that this is a carefully thought out operation. The list is entirely French, with wines from all the regions. It has been knowledgeably selected, combining 'essential' wine bar wines from good quality merchants, with more obscure, interesting items. The Pouilly Fuissé 1982 is a Georges Duboeuf (£9.95); from Alsace comes Hugel's 1981 Riesling (£7.95), and Louis Jadot has his name on the Côte de Beaune-Villages 1979 (£9.50). Of the more unusual wines, the five red Loires are the most immediately obvious: Bourgueil Caslot-Galbrun 1978 (£7.70) or Chinon Ch de la Grille 1980 (£11.50) are unexpected finds. But do not overlook the still Coteaux Champenois Chardonnay, Blanc de Blancs NV (Ruinart Père et Fils) at £13.25 or the Connétable Talbot 1980, the dry, full-bodied, elegant second wine of Talbot. It is priced a little high at £8.50, as indeed are many of the other clarets – especially since they come from less than exciting years (1977 and 1980). More curiosities are dispensed – by the glass – from Le Métro's *cruover* machine. This expensive collection is in fact the only source of wines by the glass, a drawback further compounded by the total absence of any half-bottles on the list. Nevertheless, the wines are fine and the selection changes frequently. Last year, for example, there were five red 1979 Burgundies (£5 per glass) and five Louis Latour white 1981 Burgundies. Food is French provincial with specialities such as salade tiède de foies de volailles (£1.50), terrine de lotte aux poivrons (£1.75) and filet d'agneau dijonnaise (£5). All are well prepared on the premises. Yes, the prices at Le Métro are high but, considering the attractive decor, the good service and the location (just round the corner from Harrods) they are at least justifiable.

We have tried to make the *1985 Which? Wine Guide* as comprehensive as possible, but we should love to hear from you about any other establishments you feel deserve an entry, or your comments on existing entries. Write to us either by letter or using the report forms supplied at the back of the book.

Mildred's

135 Kensington Church Street, W8 TEL 01-727 5452

OPEN Mon–Fri 12 noon–3 pm, 5.30 pm–11 pm Sat 7 pm–11 pm CLOSED Sat L, Sun, two weeks end Aug to early Sept CREDIT CARDS Not accepted UNDERGROUND Notting Hill Gate WHEELCHAIR ACCESS Yes VEGETARIAN DISHES Some

Mildred's is a wine bar/restaurant whose menu (mostly grills and red meat dishes) seems to have influenced the wine list. Whilst there are some potentially good whites (only 'potentially' because they are unspecified), the reds include a small but attractive range of detailed clarets and some reasonable (although, again, mostly unspecified) Burgundies. The Ch Laroque 1981 Grand Cru St-Emilion is good value at £9.95 (also available in half-bottles) and, for a more mature wine, the Ch Patache d'Aux 1976 is not overpriced at £9.50. For special occasions you could try a bottle of Ch Talbot 1966 (£29) but a less expensive alternative might be the Volnay, Clos des Chênes 1980 (£16.50) or the Gevrey-Chambertin 1981 (£15). For everyday drinking, the Rioja Faustino V (£5) is to be recommended, as is the house College Red from Dolamore (£4.50/£1 per glass). These would make fine accompaniments to one of Mildred's 'Specials': perhaps roast pork with spicy green peppercorn sauce (£4.95), diced lamb in sour cream and orange sauce (£4.75), or sirloin-Stilton (£7.25). Salads and cold dishes are also available or, for just £4.50, you could enjoy a three-course lunch. For those with smaller appetites, an omelette (£2.50), marinated mushrooms with herbs (£1.50), or prawn, celery and walnut cocktail (£1.95) would make a light snack with one of the several half-bottles on offer. Mildred's has a friendly, informal atmosphere; an added attraction is the changing display of paintings by contemporary artists.

Mithras

35 Bucklersbury, EC4 TEL 01-248 6030

OPEN Mon–Fri 11.30 am–3 pm, 5 pm–8 pm CLOSED Sat, Sun, public holidays CREDIT CARDS Amex, Diners UNDERGROUND Bank WHEELCHAIR ACCESS Impossible VEGETARIAN DISHES Salads

You could be forgiven for thinking that Mithras is tiny as you step in off the street, but the crowded corridor opens out to a more spacious area and a trip down the stairs takes you into a rabbit warren of rooms with plenty of stools and elbow room. The wine list is long, and is sometimes off-beam, describing Chenin Blanc AC Touraine as 'the classic wine of Alsace'. The wines are generally reasonably priced, starting with the house red and white at £4.20/£1.10. The Bordeaux section runs from 1981 Ch Bel Air (£5.50) to 1972 Ch Chasse-Spleen and 1979 Ch Brane-Cantenac (both £14). Shippers' names are noticeably lacking from the Burgundy section, but the 1982 Beaujolais look good value at £5, as does the 1982 Mâcon-Villages (£5.90). Rhône wines include Crozes-Hermitage red and white at £7.50. The German selection is short and rather sad, offering Liebfraumilch, Bereich Bernkastel, Niersteiner Gutes Domtal and Piesporter Michelsberg (about £4.50). Mithras is a popular place to eat. A wide range of cold meats and salads starts at £3 and hot food, including steaks, veal escalopes or the more basic lasagne and quiches, looks quite appetising. Freshly prepared sandwiches start at £1.10.

Motcombs

25 Motcomb Street, SW1 TEL 01-235 9170
OPEN Mon–Fri 11 am–3 pm, 5.30 pm–11 pm CLOSED Sat, Sun
CREDIT CARDS All accepted UNDERGROUND Knightsbridge, Sloane Square
WHEELCHAIR ACCESS Yes VEGETARIAN DISHES Salads

This wine bar is for graduates of the Sloane School. Popular at lunchtime and packed to overflowing in the evening, Motcombs has been happily established for 11 years now and does not have to prove a thing. The wine list is lean but 'well-toned': a good house Champagne for a very reasonable £11; Pinot Blanc, Hugel 1982 (£5.75); Fleurie 1982, Paul Sapin for £7.75, and a somewhat more unusual Ch La Gurgue 1979 (£9). Apart from one sparkler, you can buy only house wine by the glass (90p), and as there are only three half-bottles on the list, people tend to linger over a bottle at lunchtime, sampling a smoked chicken and almond salad (£3.25) or pasta in one of its many forms (£2.50), perhaps even some oysters in season. No coffee (too much caffeine) and no puddings (bad for the figure), but in the evenings you can make up for such virtue by munching on the complimentary potato chunks and sour cream dip. There's no danger of going totally overboard – dinner is not served!

Mother Goose

65 Lordship Lane, SE22 TEL 01-299 1921
OPEN Mon–Fri 12 noon–3 pm, 6 pm–11 pm Sat eve 7 pm–11 pm
Sun 12 noon–2.30 pm, 7 pm–10.30 pm CLOSED Sat L, most public holiday evenings CREDIT CARDS All accepted BR STATION East Dulwich
WHEELCHAIR ACCESS Yes VEGETARIAN DISHES Some

Mother Goose was once a David Greig grocery and the attractive thistle tiling and marble shelves remain intact to give some interest to this high street wine bar. The original shop has a connecting doorway to what once must have been the store room, so there is plenty of space. The wine list, although not exciting, does include such firm favourites at reasonable prices as Claude Sarment 1982 Beaujolais Villages (£5.25) and a 1983 Sauvignon Blanc de Touraine (£4.25). Four Italian wines, including Soave and Bardolino, are all £4.25, as is the Décas Père et Fils 1982 Bordeaux Rouge. The brand of Champagne remains a mystery at £11.95, but the unpleasant Moc Baril sparkling

Saumur is worth avoiding at £6.95. With French-bottled house wine at £3.75/75p, Mother Goose certainly will not break the bank. Sunday lunch is a speciality: roast beef and Yorkshire pudding or roast lamb with potatoes and vegetables are a snip at £2.95, and anyone really missing mother's home cooking can follow that with jam roly-poly and ice-cream (95p). If you can't make Sunday lunch, the daily menu includes courgettes au gratin (£1.25), lamb and apricot pie (£2.50), Burgundy pie (£2.25) or macaroni cheese (£1.75).

Mr Garraways

46 Gresham Street, EC2 TEL 01-606 8209

OPEN Mon–Fri 11.30 am–3 pm, 5 pm–8.30 pm CLOSED Sat, Sun, public holidays CREDIT CARDS All accepted UNDERGROUND Bank WHEELCHAIR ACCESS Yes VEGETARIAN DISHES Salads

Swift spoke of the original Mr Garraway's tea house as 'the place where dealers and brokers met to prey upon the public'. Happily, this is not apparently true of the present-day wine bar with its relaxed atmosphere and spacious rooms thoughtfully filled with enough tables and chairs to accommodate the busiest lunchtime crowd. A huge bottle of Champagne reclines in one of the wall alcoves, telling of the emphasis on bubbly here. A mixture of seventeen *marques* and sizes are available, starting with Pommery & Gréno NV at £10.75 and rising to 1976 Krug (£33). This handsome, mainly French, list, has some interesting wines in its Bordeaux section. Garraways Cellars Claret (£4.65) is also offered by the glass (90p) and double large glass (£1.70). There are four petits châteaux at under £7 a bottle and a 1977 Ch Vignelaure from Provence (£8.99), which is certainly worth a try as it is made by Georges Brunet, who used to own Ch La Lagune. It seems that 1976 is a favourite year here, with Ch La Lagune (£15.67), the delicious Ch La Dominique (£13.66) and Ch Lynch-Bages (£16.98) all available. It is good to see a wine bar paying attention to the cru Beaujolais, with six on offer from 1983 Beaujolais-Villages (£5.55) to 1981 Moulin-à-Vent (£6.96). Best buy amongst the white Burgundies is François Paquet's 1982 Mâcon Blanc Lugny, St-Denis (£6.36); Burgundies are otherwise rather unexciting – far better to go for the 1982 Chardonnay Latour from the Ardèche (£6.52). There is a good selection of Blandy's Madeiras and Taylors ports, all except the Crusted available by either bottle or glass. A fine array of seven salads (70p a portion, 40p a half-portion) would go well with the fidget or Cumberland pie (£1.60) or the traditionalist's preference, quiche (£1.35). A hot dish (from £1.90) changes daily. This bar is under the same management as Mr Pontac's *(see opposite)*.

Ⓥ means a bar has wine at bargain prices

shows a bar has an above-average range of wines

☞ indicates especially good service, which includes friendliness, good wine knowledge, an informative list, and good food.

Mr Pontac's

45 Old Broad Street, EC2 TEL 01-628 7929

OPEN Mon–Fri 11.30 am–3 pm, 5.30 pm–8 pm CLOSED Sat, Sun, public holidays CREDIT CARDS All accepted UNDERGROUND/BR STATION Liverpool Street WHEELCHAIR ACCESS Impossible VEGETARIAN DISHES Not provided

This is a modern building set low among the City skyscrapers, for all the world like a berthed luxury liner complete with angled gang plank. It is a marvel that this newly built complex (expensive retaurant above, modestly priced one below, no food in the wine bar itself) can afford the rents and rates in the heart of the financial district. The shipboard feeling persists inside the wine bar with views through the large windows, and the bustle suggesting the moments before the announcement 'all visitors ashore'. There is a short list of wines by the glass: excellent Garraways Cellars Claret, a Bordeaux Sauvignon, Beaujolais and Muscadet, all at 90p per glass (£1.70 per large glass). But there are some real bargains further up the list: Ch Grand Verdus 1979, Bordeaux Supérieur (£6.95), Ch Vignelaure 1977 (£8.99) from Provence, and a Juliénas 1981 (£6.76) by Paquet from the Beaujolais. Particularly enterprising is the listing of Chardonnay Latour 1982 (£6.52), a wine made in the Ardèche by the famous Burgundy house of Louis Latour. Mr Pontac was a famous proprietor of Ch Haut-Brion and has at least one Bordeaux château named after him (Ch Pontac-Lynch).

Mulford's Wine Bar

127 Shepherd's Bush Road, W6 TEL 01-603 2229

OPEN Mon–Fri 12 noon–3 pm, 6 pm–11 pm Sat 6 pm–11 pm Sun & public holidays 7 pm–10.30 pm CLOSED Lunchtimes on Sat, Sun, & public holidays, 24 Dec–3 Jan CREDIT CARDS All accepted UNDERGROUND Hammersmith WHEELCHAIR ACCESS Impossible VEGETARIAN DISHES Not provided

After a decade in the wine trade, Peter Mulford decided to open this wine bar at the corner of Brook Green. Since he represented the Burgundy house of Geisweiler, wine from that duchy is the backbone of his list, from the Blanc de Blancs of Armand Lafont at £3.95 a bottle/85p a glass to a Savigny-lès-Beaune 1979, Domaine du Château de Meursault (red) at £10.20. Patriarche's Bonne Auberge Rouge at £4.70/£1 slips down very well. There are a few wines from California, Bordeaux and even Wootton Vineyard 1982 (£6.95) from England but it is better to follow the *patron*'s enthusiasm. Venetia Mulford is responsible, one imagines, for the simple lime green decoration with its photographs of old Hammersmith. But she is certainly accountable for the imaginative food, Green Dragon Balls and rice, meat loaf with blue cheese filling, both £2.85, and pork and bacon cassoulet with garlic bread (£3.10). This is not an over-populated part of London for wine bars, so BBC people from White City gratefully pile in; a number of them seem to congregate at lunchtime. There are fewer people in the evening, but it's early days yet.

No 77

77 Mill Lane, NW6 TEL 01-435 7787

OPEN Mon–Wed 12 noon–3 pm, 6 pm–11 pm Thur–Sat 12 noon–3 pm, 6 pm–12 pm Sun 7 pm–10.30 pm CLOSED Sun L, public holidays
CREDIT CARDS All accepted UNDERGROUND West Hampstead
WHEELCHAIR ACCESS Difficult VEGETARIAN DISHES Good choice

Recently extended, No 77 is a collection of light, airy rooms filled with an assortment of tables and chairs. In good weather, the large doors roll back and a few tables appear on the outside pavement. Blanc de Blancs and Rouge de France house wine heads the list at £4.05/85p, the elderflower country wine, red and white (£4.25), or the sparkling gooseberry wine (£9.50) are certainly different! There are also two New Zealand wines, 1982 Chasselas (£7.45) and 1982 Müller-Thurgau (£7.45); otherwise, it is back to the usual collection of anonymous Côtes-du-Rhône, Frascati and Liebfraumilch, with La Cour Pavillon a bit expensive at £7.35. A few more vintages and makers' names would be welcome, although the year does frequently appear on more expensive wines such as the 1978 Côtes de Nuits-Villages (£8.15). Look at the blackboard for the daily menu: pissaladière (£1.45), lasagne (£2.55), or the speciality, No 77 hamburger (£3.25). Puddings might be sorbet (90p) or chocolate and ginger roulade (£1.35).

Odettes

130 Regents Park Road, NW1 TEL 01-586 5486

OPEN Mon–Sat 12 noon–3 pm, 5.30 pm–11 pm CLOSED Sun, public holidays, 10 days Chr CREDIT CARDS All accepted UNDERGROUND Chalk Farm
WHEELCHAIR ACCESS Impossible VEGETARIAN DISHES Yes

Down in the basement below the restaurant of the same name, Odettes wine bar has a capacity of little more than a couple of dozen places. It is attractively decorated – old paintings and photographs line the walls and the tables are set with fresh flowers and candles. Only house wines (£1) and Champagne cocktails are sold by the glass but there are some excellent half-bottles, and the general selection is such that you will probably want more than one glass anyway. Admittedly, prices are on the high side, yet all the wines are good quality and well chosen. The Mâcon Blanc-Villages 1982 is rather expensive at £8.75, as is the Chablis Domaine le Verger 1983 at £10.95, and the Montagny 1981 Louis Latour at £12.25. For a good, crisp wine, try the Sancerre 1982 Ch de Thauveney (£9.95) or go for more flavour in the Gewürztraminer 1982 Léon Beyer (£8.50). The red wine section has several alluring suggestions: the Fleurie 1982 Collin et Bourisset (£9.25) is a beautiful example of a Beaujolais Cru, while the Ch Belcier 1979 is an attractive, inexpensive Bordeaux Supérieur at £5.75. Several other Bordeaux wines stand out, such as the Ch Le Tour Figeac Grand Cru St-Emilion 1976 (£12.95). A Ch Brane-Cantenac 1970 is just at its peak right now, but at

£26 you will probably need a very special occasion to try it out. From Burgundy comes an Auxey-Duresses Clos du Moulin aux Moines 1979, Domaine Roland Thévenin (£13.95); but perhaps some of the best buys are from the Rhône: the Châteauneuf-du-Pape, Ch de Beaucastel 1979 (£13.20) is a robust wine and fleshy enough for drinking this year, and the second wine of Beaucastel – the Cru du Coudelet – is a very good buy for £7.50, although the 1981 is still a bit young. The wine bar menu is simple but imaginative. Non-meat-eaters have several choices: perhaps a bowl of hot carrot soup (£1.25) or some onion and cream tart (£1.60). Salads include smoked cheese and cucumber (£2.50) and honey-roasted ham and coleslaw (£2.95), while 'specials' feature dishes such as chicken hot-pot (£3) and a vegetarian moussaka (£2.50). Save room for some brown bread ice-cream (£1.30) or 'wet chocolate cake' (£1.65). Worthy of note is that between 5.30 pm and 7.30 pm house Champagne is offered at just £9 a bottle.

Old Compton's

21 Old Compton Street, W1 TEL 01-437 3292

OPEN Mon–Sat 11.30 am–3 pm, 5.30 pm–11 pm CLOSED Sun
CREDIT CARDS All accepted UNDERGROUND Leicester Square
WHEELCHAIR ACCESS Yes VEGETARIAN DISHES Salads

Old Compton's is a mixture of incongruities. It has an olde worlde tavern flavour, and yet the recorded music is piped pop. The service is basic and yet the wine list is of a high general quality, sensibly selected (by the Wheelers' restaurant group) and thoughtfully put together, even with annotated maps. Old Compton's main list is not very exciting but includes a sound range of Bouchard Père and Louis Latour Burgundies. There are also a few New World wines, such as Brown Bros 1977 Cabernet Sauvignon from Australia (£6.60) and the Riveroaks Premium White (£6.05) from California. Fino sherry is an attractive alternative unusually offered in half-bottles and served chilled in authentic Jerez style (£2.25). Annexed to the main list is a smaller selection 'for the connoisseur'. Check the ice bucket, too, and behind the bar for the unwritten extras. There may be Niersteiner Klostergarten Kabinett 1978 (£4.80) or Corton-Charlemagne B Martray 1979 (£19.80), with several interesting Burgundies in between, including Wheelers' own 1981 Chablis, François Laday (£6.50/90p). Perhaps most interestingly, customers are encouraged to bring their own wine (£2.10 corkage) and may have it chilled or decanted if delivered in advance. Since Old Compton's is owned by Wheelers' restaurant next-door, it is scarcely a surprise to discover that fish is the house speciality. But the cold buffet tends to be more appetising than the hot dishes. A generous wedge of the excellent chicken and ham pie comes for £1.80, or you might sample some of the home-made pâtés. Only the salads seem unenterprising and expensive at 80p a portion.

192

192 Kensington Park Road, W11 TEL 01-229 0482
OPEN Mon–Sat 12.30 pm–3 pm, 5.30 pm–11.30 pm CLOSED Sun
CREDIT CARDS Access/Euro, Amex, Visa UNDERGROUND Ladbroke Grove
WHEELCHAIR ACCESS Yes VEGETARIAN DISHES Some

The futuristic decor, *nouvelle*-ish *cuisine* and pleasant background of classical music or jazz are a little incongruous in a neighbourhood that has seen much redevelopment but has still a long way to go. The wine list is not extensive but quality is good. French wines predominate, with just one Mosel – a Bereich Bernkastel Riesling 1982, Müller (£5.50). The Bordeaux section offers some attractive clarets: for example, a juicy Domaine de Gaillat, Graves 1978 (£8); a Ch la Clotte, St-Emilion Grand Cru 1980 (£9.50), is also a good, light 'lunchtime' wine. Burgundy is sparsely represented, but the flag-bearer is a Gevrey-Chambertin 1980 (Domaine Louis Trapet) for £14. A 1982 Georges Duboeuf Brouilly Ch de Nevers is a versatile Beaujolais Cru (£7.50), while his Mâcon-Prissé 1982 is worthwhile at £7.25. One drawback to the list is the absence of any half-bottles, but several wines are available by large as well as standard glass. Amongst these are the good, buxom vins de table of Madame Lamour at Domaine St-Louis-la-Perdrix 1982 (90p standard/£1.80 large). The daily-changing menu is enterprising and pricy. It might include marinated squid salad (£3), steamed salmon with ginger and spring onion (£6), or cold poached rump of veal with tuna sauce, anchovies and capers (£4.45). Finish your meal, perhaps, with some strawberry tart (£2) and a (rather expensive) glass of the Muscat de Beaumes-de-Venise (£2.20).

Ormes

67–69 Abbeville Road, London SW4 TEL 01-673 2568
OPEN Mon–Sat 12 noon–3.30 pm, 6.30 pm–12.30 am Sun 12 noon–3.30 pm, 7 pm–12 pm Public holidays 12 noon–3.30 pm, 6.30 pm–12.30 am
CREDIT CARDS All accepted UNDERGROUND Clapham South
WHEELCHAIR ACCESS Only to bar VEGETARIAN DISHES Always a special dish

Ormes has two entrances – one for its restaurant and the other for the wine bar; the two meet somewhere at the back. The bar is unobtrusively decked out on a green and red theme with tiled floor and bare boards, and the restaurant, which occupies most of the space, is split level with an interesting back section of curtained alcoves for secluded, romantic evenings. If you are after just a quick glass of wine, there is a bigger than average range of house wines – four whites and reds, ranging from £3.99/80p for the 1983 Pinot Blanc Vin de Pays de Loire to £4.50/90p for a 1982 German Silvaner Riesling Trocken, or a 1980 Utrero Rioja; try the good, full-flavoured Cabernet Sauvignon Vin de Pays de l'Aude at £3.95/80p. The list is vast (around 125 wines) and includes everything from English elderflower to fine, mature clarets.

These begin at Ch Bel Air 1981 Bordeaux AC at £4.95, followed by a few petits châteaux, and rise to the heights of Ch Larcis-Ducasse 1971 for £13.95 or the tough Ch Phélan-Ségur 1975, St-Estèphe for £12.95. Remarkably, the list actually tells you it's tough: there's a useful tasting note on almost every wine. Try the 1978 Ch Larose-Trintaudon, still young but delicious (£9.95), or 1980 St-Julien, Anthony Barton (£8.95). There are single vineyard crus Beaujolais, mature Burgundies, good Rhônes; some of the Italians are good too: Torgiano Rosso from Lungarotti is £5.65, or try the fresh white Tenuta di Pomino from Frescobaldi. What a shame, as so often, that producers are suddenly missing from the Italian list. Torres wines are well priced, and there's the lovely Marqués de Murrieta 1979 for £6.95. Hill Smith Australians are very good indeed, especially the minty 1976 Cabernet Sauvignon, worth every penny of £9.95. And there's a scattering from elsewhere. For those who have paced their drinking, there is a selection of ports (tawny, old tawny and crusted) and even real (not late-bottled vintage) vintage port, ready decanted – Dow 1970 for £2.25 a glass; or a couple of Madeiras at 95p a glass for the less extravagant. The menu, which changes every two weeks, offers a good range of starters including deep-fried mushrooms with garlic mayonnaise (£1.45) and a varied selection of main courses, such as smoked haddock and prawn lasagne (£3.95) or beef stirfry (£4.35). There are all the trimmings like garlic bread (65p), new potatoes (65p), and slim-line mixed salads at 75p. The selection of sweets (around £1.40) is good, with lots of fresh fruit and, specially recommended, ice-cream made on the premises. There are no cocktails or happy hour. Ormes is for the serious eater and drinker, and it is worth booking in advance for Friday and Saturday evening.

Partners

25 Newman Street, W1 TEL 01-631 3174

OPEN Mon–Fri 11 am–3 pm, 5.30 pm–11 pm CLOSED Sat, Sun
CREDIT CARDS All accepted UNDERGROUND Tottenham Court Road, Oxford Circus WHEELCHAIR ACCESS Yes VEGETARIAN DISHES Some

This is your hard-core, smoky, noisy – and popular – wine bar! The wine list does not concern itself with names of producers or many vintages, so a fair amount of pot-luck is involved, unless you can corner one of the busy staff for long enough to get some details. Prices are remarkably reasonable – especially given the W1 address – and all wines, bar the Champagnes, are under £7. There are no half-bottles but several wines are available by the glass. House wines are French and quite drinkable (£4.35 a bottle/90p a glass), and house Champagne – Cordillon Pontillart Brut – is a very reasonable £10.50 or £1.60 a glass. The unidentified Chablis is the most expensive item on the list at £6.95, followed by an equally enigmatic Sancerre (£6.85). Both are probably worth the gamble, likewise the Fleurie 1980 (£5.95). Italy has several representatives, of which the Frascati Superiore (£4.70) or the Barolo 1979 for £6.10 would be a safe bet. And from Spain comes the very acceptable Siglo Saco Tinto 1979 (£5.90). With the food, on the other hand, there is no doubt where it was made (on the premises) or when (it is all fresh). Smoked salmon or mackerel pâté with toast (£1.60) or guacamole (£1.40) make delicious starters, while the steak and kidney pie (£2.95) and the cannelloni (£2.60 with salad) are good main courses. Salads and cold meats are all attractively presented and very tempting. There are fresh strawberries and cream (£1.40) when in season, or chocolate fudge cake (£1.20) to finish.

Penny's Place

6 King Street, WC2 TEL 01-836 4553

OPEN Mon–Fri 11 am–3 pm, 5.30 pm–11 pm Sat 5.30 pm–11 pm
CLOSED Sat L, Sun, public holidays CREDIT CARDS Access/Euro, Visa
UNDERGROUND Covent Garden WHEELCHAIR ACCESS Yes
VEGETARIAN DISHES With notice

Penny's is a three-in-one package. There is an arty French-style bistro upstairs, and a new, racy VIP cocktail/wine bar downstairs, with an elegantly subdued dining room in an adjoining cellar. The wine and food selections are fairly similar throughout, although there is a slight variation in price from one bar to the next. The wines are principally French but almost all details of producers and vintages have been omitted – entirely, in the case of the very basic bistro list. The VIP list makes for more illuminating reading and from this the Ch Sablons 1977 (£6.60) or the Ch des Landes, Lussac St-Emilion 1979 (£8) are good offers. There is also a range of Beaujolais Crus but at very high prices – the Fleurie Clos des Moriers 1981/82 is £10.25, while the Moulin-à-Vent Domaine des Petites Caves 1982 is a cool £10.75. It seems that the more imaginative touches have been reserved for the food, all prepared by their chef from Alsace. Pâté de crabe (£2) and scampi et bacon brochette (£3.65) are starters you might find on the monthly changing menu. Poulet fumé (£3.95) and chilli con carne (£4.50) are house specials. In typical French style, the cheese selection is excellent; there are also attractive seasonal offers such as strawberries and Chantilly cream served with a glass of Champagne (£3). Penny's has built up quite a following in the eight years of its existence. And, in spite of the high prices, many of the regulars use it like a club for its convenient location near Strand offices and the theatres.

Pissarro's

1–5 Kew Green, Richmond, Surrey TEL 01-940 3897

OPEN Mon–Sat 11.30 am–3 pm, 5.30 pm–11 pm Sun 12 noon–2 pm, 7 pm–11 pm CLOSED Chr Eve, Chr Day, Boxing Day, Easter Sun
CREDIT CARDS Access/Euro, Visa WHEELCHAIR ACCESS Lavatory facilities difficult VEGETARIAN DISHES Some salads

There are some wine bars you go to for want of something better, some you like, and some you love. Pissarro's is definitely in the last category.

The two large and one smaller adjoining rooms are furnished with solid wooden tables of all shapes and sizes and an assortment of good old-fashioned chairs. The Pissarro reproductions and the soft classical music lend an air of gentility. The beautifully scripted wine list starts with house wine at £4.20/80p and includes Muscadet, Beaujolais and claret at £5. All the wines are reasonably priced, with the Duboeuf 1981/2 Fleurie excellent value at £6.75. Moreau's 1979/81 Chablis (£6.95) and a 1982 Côtes-du-Rhône-Villages £5.60 are worth investigating, but the blackboard is the place to find real goodies from the 'directors' bin'. The 1977 Ch Lynch-Bages (£10) is a bargain, and the magnums of 1976 Gevrey-Chambertin (£30) are not expensive. Food is served at lunchtimes and in the evenings from 6.45 pm. The advantages of sharing an owner with Jasper's Bun in the Oven next door is soon obvious in the extensive menu and carefully prepared food. The cold buffet looks appetising and hot food includes such favourites as sausage and mash (£2), steak and kidney pie (£3.50) or lamb casserole (£2.50). Fish lovers would be happy with seafood casserole (£3) and fish pie (£2). Some readers have formed the service slow.

Plums

129 Brackenbury Road, W6 TEL 01-748 0107

OPEN Mon–Fri 12 noon–2.30 pm, 5.30 pm–10.30 pm Sat 5.30 pm–10.30 pm Sun 12 noon–2.30 pm CLOSED Sat L, Sun eve CREDIT CARDS Not accepted UNDERGROUND Hammersmith (20 mins) WHEELCHAIR ACCESS Yes VEGETARIAN DISHES Some

One of the more obscure wine bars tucked away off King Street, Hammersmith, in a quiet, residential street where children play football. It is a simply and attractively furnished offshoot of Plummers Restaurant and has a lot to offer. The food is of a very high standard, freshly prepared on the premises and attractively presented. The choice is often imaginative and reasonably priced: home-made soups at 95p, smoked cod's roe (80p) or perhaps some smoked chicken and home-pickled spiced peach (£1.95). Fresh fruit salad and cream (£1.20) makes a pleasant finish to a good meal. The wine list is no less enterprising. A great deal of thought goes into the constantly changing selection, but we suspect it is not fully appreciated by many of the local clientèle. It is a pity that there are not more wines by the glass, but the bottle list (actually a blackboard) has many interesting features. Worthy of note is the uncommon Sauvignon de St-Bris 1982 and an Irancy Blanc Bourgogne. The Bernard Michel 1982 Montagny at £6.45 is a good bargain, not to mention the Bouzereau 1979 Chassagne-Montrachet for a reasonable £9. There is also a fair range of non-French wines. A very unusual and surprisingly good New York State Gold Seal Chardonnay (£6.05) and a Bel Arbres Zinfandel (£5.80) from California are two New World examples worth investigating. England gets a look-in with a Müller-Thurgau 1982 from Spots Farm for £5.60. The back room with an open fire is particularly charming and can be hired for private parties.

Punters

Ⓥ

5 Abchurch Yard, Abchurch Lane, EC4 TEL 01-623 2355

OPEN Mon–Fri 11.30 am–3 pm, 5 pm–8 pm CLOSED Sat, Sun, public holidays
CREDIT CARDS All accepted WHEELCHAIR ACCESS Impossible
VEGETARIAN DISHES Some salads

With the house Champagne at £10.25, it is not surprising that the City regulars at Punters make good use of the extensive Champagne list. The bar is larger than it first appears with plenty of space in the back arches, although at lunch-time you do need to get there early if you want a seat. Kir Royale and Bucks Fizz can be made with either Champagne or sparkling wine. Bravely, proprietor Caroline Mack refuses to list Liebfraumilch and will guide alarmed Liebfrau drinkers to Niersteiner Gutes Domtal (£4.85) or Bereich Bernkastel (£5.10). A large glass of wine means 18.75 cl (a quarter of a bottle), which makes the house wine at £1.15 very good value, although it is still cheaper to buy a bottle (£4.45) if you intend to down four glasses. Happy hour-and-a-half, 5 pm to 6.30 pm, means £1 off any bottle of wine. The 1979 Coonawarra Cabernet Sauvignon (£6.80) is certainly worth a try, but if you prefer your Cabernet Sauvignon to come from Bordeaux, look for the 1977 Ch Grand-Puy-Ducasse (£12.80). The 1966 Ch Fourcas-Hosten, Cru Bourgeois Supérieur Listrac, mentioned in last year's *Guide*, is still available, but at the more expensive price of £19.90. The lunchtime buffet offers an excellent selection of home-cooked food, cold rare roast rump of beef being the star at £3.25. The unusual pies are good fillers: pork, apple and chutney is £2.95. Pâté maison starts at £1.50 for a very generous helping, and smoked mackerel pâté is £1.65. The hot dishes change daily, as do the gooey puds, which can be washed down with a (large) glass of Paul Jaboulet Muscat de Beaumes-de-Venise (£2.35), or an Australian liqueur Muscat (£2.25). For those who prefer port to go with the cheese, there is a good selection with a decanted vintage port always available. The small restaurant offers excellent value for a three-course set meal at £8.85 – a real bargain for the quality and quantity of food served.

Ruby's Wine Bar

28 Sussex Place, W2 TEL 01-262 4654

OPEN Mon–Fri 12 noon–3.30 pm, 5.30 pm–12.30 am Sat 12 noon–3.30 pm, 7 pm–12.30 am Sun 12 noon–3.30 pm, 7 pm–12 pm CREDIT CARD Amex
UNDERGROUND Lancaster Gate, Marble Arch WHEELCHAIR ACCESS Yes
VEGETARIAN DISHES Salads, cheeses and one hot dish daily

Ruby's is the sort of place everyone likes to think is their own secret, but while it may be known by 'The Select' it is certainly not restricted to 'The Few'. This small, attractive wine bar is lively at all times, Wednesday evenings being particularly popular for the free live music. The wine list is unpretentious and predominantly French. From the generous selection of wines by the (6 oz) glass, the house wines (£1) by Sichel and the Bordeaux Blanc (£1.25) are good options. By the bottle, the Gevrey-Chambertin 1979, available at a reasonable £9.50, is an attractive offer, and the house Champagne is a decent wine for a decent £10.95. All the food is prepared on the premises and changes daily. Again, it is unpretentious, but the general standard is dependable. Good home-made soups (£1.10), attractive salads (£2.95), but more beans than mince in the chilli con carne (£2.95). Vegetarians are well catered for with the wide selection of salads and cheeses, and usually a hot dish, such as macaroni cheese, on offer. Watch out for Ruby's seasonal parties (Hallowe'en, for instance) or book it for your own private party. Staying open late (till 12.30 am during the week and midnight on Sundays), Ruby's is a useful last call.

Russell's

44 High Street, E11 TEL 01-530 2302

OPEN Mon–Sat 12 noon–3 pm Mon–Thur 6 pm–10.30 pm Fri 6 pm–11 pm Sat 7 pm–11 pm Sun 7 pm–10.30 pm CLOSED Sun L CREDIT CARDS Not accepted UNDERGROUND Wanstead, Snaresbrook WHEELCHAIR ACCESS Impossible VEGETARIAN DISHES Good selection

Two wine bars within a few doors of each other need to be complementary if both are to survive, and Russell's certainly has its own original touches (*see also Woodbine Wine Rooms*). A glossy black window (flecked at night with what look like yellow flower petals which turn out to be the light from the candles inside) creates a cosy penumbra in the spacious interior. Tables of varying lengths, church-pew seating, wine barrels to hold the spare cruets and wall-prints which include 'The Boyhood of Raleigh' give a comfortable, relaxed atmosphere. The wine list shows quite a bit of thought and points out that brand-names are avoided since the wines are selected for their quality and not in compliance with media advertising. A splendid 16 wines are available by the glass, and if you buy a bottle and do not finish it, the staff will cork it for you to take home. Sweet Coteaux du Layon (£4/£1) shows how well they know the unsung quality areas worth offering, and there are two KWV Afrikaaners, Chenin Blanc (£4.65/£1) – 'very popular' – and Roodeberg (£4.95/£1.10). Mercier Champagne is £13. Soave and Lambrusco, at £4.50, are the cheapest wines, and the house wines are £4.95/85p and £2.50 for a half-litre. The white is lightly aromatic and well balanced while the house claret (£5.25/£1.10), with a soft, toasted character, is pleasant but not really clarety. The menu is limited and more interesting for vegetarians than meat-eaters – vegetable curry, lasagne and quiche are among the dishes changed each week.

Prices are only a rough indication, and were current in summer 1984.

Scamps Wine Bar

32 Vanston Place, Fulham Broadway, SW6 TEL 01-381 3782

OPEN Mon–Sat 11.30 am–3 pm, 5.30 pm–12 pm Sun 7 pm–11 pm
CLOSED Sat L, Sun CREDIT CARDS Access/Euro, Visa
UNDERGROUND Fulham, Broadway WHEELCHAIR ACCESS Yes
VEGETARIAN DISHES Salads

Scamps is an attractively furnished wine bar and brasserie: mirrors and bentwood chairs combine with hanging plants and large skylights to give a comfortable yet stylish impression. Beer connoisseurs will be glad to discover that Scamps specialises in that particular brew, with cocktails as a second string. The wine is basic but drinkable: Beaujolais (Paul Beaudet) is £4.75 and Frascati (Cecchi) (£4.45). Chianti (Cecchi) costs £4.20, while the Rioja (Bodegas Velazquez) runs at £6.50. The house Champagne changes frequently but the price remains a steady £9.90. Food is served in the brasserie at the rear – a variety of steaks, hamburgers and kebabs, all charcoal-grilled. Chilli con carne costs £2.25 and there is a familiar selection of appetisers around the £1.50 mark. Every last Thursday of the month is Fancy Dress Night, when anyone participating in appropriate garb receives a free cocktail. Between 6 and 8 pm each evening is 'Happy Hour' whilst on Friday and Saturday nights, a DJ keeps the joint jumping.

Scandies

4 Kynance Place, SW7 TEL 01-589 3659

OPEN Mon–Fri 12 noon–3 pm, 6 pm–11 pm Sat 12.30 pm–3 pm, 7 pm–11 pm Sun 12.30 pm–2 pm, 7 pm–10.30 pm CLOSED Chr Day, Boxing Day, public holidays L CREDIT CARDS Not accepted UNDERGROUND Gloucester Road WHEELCHAIR ACCESS Impossible VEGETARIAN DISHES Very limited

It is easy to miss this unobtrusive turning off Gloucester Road. But Scandies is a happy oasis in this area not over-endowed with wine bars. It has a South of France air about it, which extends to the food: garlic bread and pâté, stuffed tomatoes, pasta romaine (all about £2.50 a serving). They are serious about the wine, too, for in addition to house wine (£4.05 a bottle/85p a glass), there is a fine range of claret and Burgundy in the £5–£10 bracket; Ch Fombrauge 1979 is £6.95 and Gevrey-Chambertin 1979, £8.65, but there is also a 'connoisseurs' list' of older vintages. Spain, South Africa and Italy are represented (try the Chianti Classico Riserva Rocca delle Macie at £5.45), and even California contributes a Jordan's Chardonnay 1980, very overpriced, however, at £14.50.

Do **you** know of any more bars that deserve inclusion in next year's *Guide?*
If so, write and tell us on the report forms at the back of the book.

Shampers

4 Kingly Street, W1 TEL 01-437 1692

OPEN Mon–Fri 11 am–3 pm, 5.30 pm–11 pm Sat 11 am–3 pm CLOSED Sat evenings, Sun, public holidays CREDIT CARDS All accepted UNDERGROUND Oxford Circus, Piccadilly WHEELCHAIR ACCESS But very cramped at lunchtime VEGETARIAN DISHES Always a selection

This big ground-floor room and basement just a few yards from Carnaby Street is miles away from it in atmosphere, a haunt for publishers and art directors rather than punks and tourists. The same exciting range of wines as at the Cork & Bottle *(see above)* and similar tasty dishes of the day are presided over here by Tom and Sue Glynn. A rather bigger menu is served downstairs, by waiters. Upstairs, the service (largely self) is friendly and efficient, too. Shampers is a handy refuge during the sales, where you can sip at a bottle of Pinot Blanc d'Alsace 1982 (£5.25) while your partner lays siege to the bargain basements. *As well as the Cork & Bottle, see also the other two bars in the group, Bubbles and Methuselah's.*

Smithy's

28 Brittania Street, WC1 TEL 01-278 5949

OPEN Mon–Fri 11.30 am–3 pm CLOSED Sat & Sun CREDIT CARDS All accepted UNDERGROUND King's Cross WHEELCHAIR ACCESS Yes VEGETARIAN DISHES Some

Smithy's is a weekday lunchtime-only spot, always popular with local office workers who fill the two large, airy rooms. The wine list is not the place's strength, but the unidentified generic wines are all reasonably priced: Muscadet (£4.60), Valpolicella (£4.30), Beaujolais (£5.50) and the most expensive wine – a Chablis – at just £7.80. There are no half-bottles but most wines are available by the glass, and the dependable house wine is £1.10. Food is the main attraction. It is all prepared on the premises, is inexpensive and comes in very generous helpings. Quiches and pies are wholesome, the ploughman's lunch is £1, while beef salad costs £2.40. There is a buffet which has a tempting display of help-yourself salads (£1.40) but for a more filling meal there are steaks (£4) charcoal-grilled to your specifications. Cheesecake and chocolate cake (both 80p) are institutions here and worthy of a detour on the slightest excuse. Also worth noting is that Smithy's can be booked for private parties in the evenings – they provide free nibbles.

Readers' reports submitted to *The Good Food Guide* as well as *Which? Wine Guide* have been used to supplement official inspectors' reports in compiling this section.

Solange's Wine Bar

11 St Martin's Court, WC2 TEL 01-240 0245

OPEN Mon–Sat 11 am–3 pm, 5.30 pm–11 pm CLOSED Sun CREDIT CARDS All accepted UNDERGROUND Leicester Square WHEELCHAIR ACCESS Yes VEGETARIAN DISHES Some

An authentically decorated French-style bistro/wine bar with an atmosphere to match, Solange's just happens to be in the heart of London's theatre district and is extremely convenient for a meal before or a 'light bite' after a performance. Hot dishes might include gigot d'agneau (£2.65) or ravioli niçoise (£1.85) whilst cold dishes tend towards the more typical wine bar fare, but all are well prepared and presented. The wine list comes with comments so cheeky and amusing that they could sell the wine regardless of the actual quality. The Chablis 1982 is 'important, strong, almost immortal' (and costs £8.90); the Frascati Superiore DOC 1982 is 'a promiscuously cultivated favourite' for £5.15, while the Beaune Clos de l'Écu 1976 Jaboulet Vercherre (£15.50) is simply 'unrepeatable'. There are also some less frivolous inclusions, such as the intense Gewürztraminer 1978 Réserve, Hugel for £9.75, or the Mâcon-Lugny 1981 Les Genièvres from Louis Latour, good value at £8.60. There is also a less-than-common selection of clarets, of which the Ch du Cauze 1979 Grand Cru St-Emilion stands out at £9.50. The several wines by the glass include a Valpolicella 1980 for 95p and a very decent Grand Véraux Cuvée Anniversaire which is the (slightly pricy) house Burgundy for £1.10.

Sopers

13 Well Court, Queen Street, EC4 TEL 01-248 8388

OPEN Mon–Fri 11.30 am–3 pm, 5 pm–7 pm CLOSED Sat, Sun, public holidays CREDIT CARDS All accepted UNDERGROUND Mansion House WHEELCHAIR ACCESS To upstairs bar VEGETARIAN DISHES Some

If you are looking for somewhere in the City to sit down, Sopers is certainly the place. The small upstairs bar, which serves only wine, gives no clue to the enormous restaurant/bar area in the basement. Down here, tables and chairs are abundant and are sensibly spaced to allow private talk. The wine list, although unexciting, concentrates steadily on France, Germany and Italy, with a California wine, Almaden Cabernet Sauvignon, creeping in at £5.75. There are some regularly changing 'specials' on the blackboard, drawn from all over the wine-producing world. The house wine starts at £4.15, with a generous glassful available at £1.10. The 1982 Chablis looks a good buy (£6.40) as does the 1981 Crozes-Hermitage Champs la Dame (£5.95). The Saumur sparkler, Ackerman 1911 Méthode Champenoise Brut is tempting (£6.70) but with the house Champagne at £8.95, it is really worth spending the extra or certainly indulging in a glass (£1.75). There is a pleasant range of pâtés and fish mousses (smoked salmon £2.50 or crab

£1.80) and good salads starting at 60p for a generous serving. For more exotic tastes, try smoked chicken and beanshoots (£2.20) or tandoori chicken (£2.20). Daily changing hot dishes are also available. The restaurant area offers a '50 minute lunch' (£6.50) or a more formal set menu (£9.85 two courses, £11.35 three courses). Sopers can be booked for parties and holds 100+ for buffets or more formal meals.

The Source

106 Blackheath Road, SE10 TEL 01-691 1010

OPEN Mon–Sat 12 noon–3 pm, 7 pm–11 pm Sun 12 noon–2 pm, 7 pm–10.30 pm
CREDIT CARDS Not accepted UNDERGROUND New Cross
WHEELCHAIR ACCESS Impossible VEGETARIAN DISHES Not provided

This brave little wine bar in a beer-and-skittles patch is due to undergo a reincarnation – Bus Stop – with the decor based on the Marilyn Monroe movie. There are plans, too, for the patio terrace at the back downstairs. Holders of a Gilbey Vintners Winelist of the Year award in 1982, The Source had to close for six months after a fire but reopened early in 1984. The list covers most of the predictable areas. Some prominence is given to Italian – a choice of nine – and there is a Fleurie (£7.35), a Saumur Brut (£3.75) and a 1980/81 Sancerre (£7.25). The house red is from the Loire and soft enough to tempt the most entrenched white wine drinker, while the white, from Rémy Pannier, was oxidised and lacked acidity when we called. The Zimmerman-Graeff German selection, particularly the grapy Piesporter (£4/75p) is good, with more assertive flavour than many. A practical idea is their mini-bin-end selection of take-away bottles at a uniform £2. The food is limited in scope and geared to the majority of the potential passing clientèle. Chicken curry and spaghetti bolognese are popular, Lancashire hot-pot too. (All hot main courses are £3.) Excellent trifle (£1).

Southeys Wine Bar

144 Chiswick High Road, W4 TEL 01-747 1946

OPEN Mon–Thur 12 noon–3 pm, 6 pm–11.30 pm Fri, Sat 12 noon–3 pm, 6 pm–12 pm Sun 12 noon–3 pm, 7 pm–11.30 pm Public holidays 12 noon–3 pm, 7 pm–11 pm CLOSED Chr Day CREDIT CARDS All accepted
UNDERGROUND Turnham Green, Chiswick Park WHEELCHAIR ACCESS Yes
VEGETARIAN DISHES Some

Carry on west from Hammersmith Broadway and you find yourself in the middle of a parade of high street shops amongst which is Southeys, where stuffed owls survey the country tables and chairs. John and Sally Southey enlist knowledgeable and welcoming girls to serve; enthusiasm is evident on the wine list, too: over 125 different wines, and more selections appear on blackboards. A few wines are sold by the glass, including the house La Cordaine red and white and dry Rosé de

Loire, all at £1.20. The mark-up on bottles is reasonable, so one is tempted by Ch Beausoleil 1978 at £5 from Bordeaux, Lirac Domaine des Causses 1978 at £5.70, St Véran 1982 at £7.50 and Gros Plant from the mouth of the Loire (£5.25). This bar concentrates on French wines, but there are also wines worth trying from Germany, Italy and Spain like the Viña Pomal 1977 at £6.10, Marqués de Cáceres red at £5.70, the good white Marqués de Riscal (£5.30) and from Italy Tignanello from Antinori, well worth the extra at £9. The *plats du jour* are cooked in small quantities throughout the very generous opening hours (till midnight on Friday and Saturday) and one can pick modestly at tzatziki and pitta bread (£1.50) or indulge in a porterhouse steak with salad or baked potatoes for £5.

Spats Wine Bar

237 Earls Court Road, SW5 TEL 01-370 6899

OPEN Mon–Sat 12 noon–3 pm, 6.30 pm–12.30 am Sun 7 pm–10.30 pm Public holidays 12 noon–3 pm, 6.30 pm–12.30 am CREDIT CARDS Not accepted UNDERGROUND Earl's Court WHEELCHAIR ACCESS Yes VEGETARIAN DISHES Few

An elegantly furnished wine bar at the southern end of the Earl's Court Road at its boundary with the Old Brompton Road. Its great charm is the patio – an oasis on hot days and, for the late-night drinker, a licence which extends to 1.30 am. A bouncer bars the way to over-indulged refugees from the Earls Court pubs. The wine list is not exhilarating, and does not reveal producers' names, but prices are modest: house wines 85p per (14 cl) glass, £4.50 a bottle, nothing special. The Australian Hardy's dry white at £5.20 presumably finds a market. There is a selection of cold food and salads as well as hot dishes: chicken winglets (£3.50) and steak (£4.75). At lunchtime, they offer a glass of house wine with the dish of the day for under £3.

Tappit Hen

97 Maple Road, Surbiton, Surrey TEL 01-390 4742

OPEN Mon–Fri 11.30 am–2.30 pm, 5.30 pm–10.30 pm Sat 11.30 am–2.30 pm, 5.30 pm–11 pm Sun 7 pm–10.30 pm CLOSED Sun L CREDIT CARD Visa WHEELCHAIR ACCESS Tricky (two steps and awkward corner to negotiate) VEGETARIAN DISHES Quiche, salads, ratatouille

This is a light, narrow bar on the ground floor done out in unfussy Victoriana: bare floorboards, bentwood chairs and framed sepia photographs of school and stern great-grandparents. Brown oilcloths bedeck the tables, each with a candle and a spray of pinks. Downstairs is a larger but more intimate room with bare brick walls, deliciously cool in summer. Service is cheerful and helpful: they genuinely wanted to know what some regular customers thought of the cheesecake from a new supplier. Disceet background music adds rather than detracts from the pleasant, relaxed atmosphere. The wine list is a slightly wider than usual collection of basics, including a Sauvignon de Touraine (£5.30), a Chinon (£5.95), a Vouvray (£5.20), Freixenet sparklers and Maison Caurette's Club Claret. No vintages! No producers or shippers! Even the proprietors don't know the answers without a long hard stare at the bottle and claim that no one can tell the difference anyway between one Liebfraumilch and the next. The menu includes taramosalata (£1.05), garlic mushrooms (£1.40) and various pâtés, then jacket potatoes (with ratatouille £1.25, Cheddar, Stilton or sour cream and chives, all £1.05). As a main course, ratatouille topped with cheese is £1.85, moussaka and salad, £2.40. Smoked loin of pork salad is £2.50 or there is the usual quiche, ham or prawns. Daily blackboard specials might be kidneys Turbigo (£2.95) or goulash (£3.10). Passion, chocolate or cheese cakes are all 95p, citrus sorbets or cheeses £1.05 each. Apart from the cakes and ices, it is all freshly home-made, and recommendable in the area.

Tiles

36 Buckingham Palace Road, SW1 TEL 01-834 7761

OPEN Mon–Fri 12 noon–3 pm, 5.30 pm–11 pm CLOSED Sat, Sun, public holidays CREDIT CARDS All accepted UNDERGROUND/BR STATION Victoria WHEELCHAIR ACCESS Yes VEGETARIAN DISHES Yes

For a wine bar so close to Victoria Station, Tiles is remarkably free of luggage-towing travellers. Rather, it is a popular lunchtime spot for local office workers, and in the evenings, it attracts faithful followers who come for the informal atmosphere, good food and wine. The wine list is well structured with quality wines at very good value prices, so you can 'drink thy wine with a merry heart' (*Ecclesiastes* 7) as one of the many drunken quotations on the wine list suggests. Fizz is always a good way to start. You could choose one of the Spanish sparklers: from Freixenet there's Carta Nevada (£6.25), Brut Rosé 1975 (£6.35) or Paul Masson's good quality California Brut (£6.25). The house Champagne is excellent value for £10.95 and the Canard Duchêne 1975 is equally well priced at £15. White wines include a Sauvignon de Touraine (£5.45) and one of the increasingly popular white Rhônes, a 1981 from Vidal-Fleury (£6.35). Don't miss the excellent Chablis 1981 from Joseph Drouhin (£8.95) or the Alsace wines from the top class house of Hugel: Pinot Blanc 1981 (£5.85) and Gewürztraminer 1981 (£7.98). Amongst the reds, the Côtes du Roussillon-Villages is a full-bodied wine at a good price (£4.55), and the Ch Plaisance 1979 is a bargain at £4.95. Torres Gran Coronas 1979 (£5.75) is well priced. In addition to the regular list, there are also wine specials each month. These might feature an unusual but delightful Beaujolais Blanc 1982 (£6.95), a Morey-St-Denis 1973 (£8.45) or a Ch Lartigue 1976 (£6.25). There are no half-bottles on the list but there is a very good selection of wines by the glass – the light French house wines, Le Terral, cost 80p. Food is all home-made, reasonably priced and imaginative. The menu changes daily but might include tuna, egg and lemon mousse and bread (£1.75), chicken, celery and almond pie with mashed potato topping and tarragon cabbage (£3.45); and oranges in sherry or fresh pear cheesecake £1.50) to finish. Special events at Tiles have included an Italian day, a Corsican week, and a Californian month.

Tracks

170 Soho Square, W1 TEL 01-439 2318
OPEN Mon–Fri 10 am–11 pm Sat 5.30 pm–11 pm CLOSED Sun
CREDIT CARDS All accepted UNDERGROUND Tottenham Court Road, Leicester Square WHEELCHAIR ACCESS Yes VEGETARIAN DISHES Salads and quiches

The location of this café/wine bar in a corner of Soho Square probably accounts for much of its popularity. The wine list is basic and refuses to concern itself with such minutiae as vintages, vineyards or producers. But it does have some great throw-away lines in the guise of wine descriptions: their (unspecified) Rioja has no qualms about declaring itself 'the best in Spain'. Food, however, prepared on the premises, is attractive and wholesome. Salads and substantial quiches look appetising and there is always at least one hot dish of the day. Prices for both wine and food are high, but Tracks is a good retreat from Oxford Street shopping or en route to cinemas or theatres.

Tropics

37 Kensington Park Road, W11 TEL 01-343 0666
OPEN Mon–Sat 11 am–3 pm, 5.30 pm–12 pm Sun 7 pm–11 pm CLOSED Sun L
CREDIT CARDS All accepted UNDERGROUND Ladbroke Grove
WHEELCHAIR ACCESS Yes VEGETARIAN DISHES Occasional specials

The '1940s Singapore Raffles' decor is possibly the greatest attraction of this unusual bar – it certainly isn't the wine list. In fact, since February 1983, when a full licence was granted, the emphasis has been less on wine than on cocktails. Tropics is now better known for its 'Homicide Rouge' than it is for its house red. Nevertheless, this drinkable red Bordeaux (90p a glass) is a better choice than the unexciting St-Emilion La Garette for £1.20. The 1981 Chablis costs £6.80 and their Fleurie goes for £7.90. The basic menu is of the simple quiche and pizza (£1.50) variety, but 'home-made specials' change daily and might include ocean pie (£2.95), chicken and asparagus pie (£2.95) or chilli con carne (£2.95) – with Black Forest gâteau or bananas and cream (£1) afterwards. Tropics is an ideal party venue and can easily accommodate up to 120 people in its downstairs (basement) room.

Prices are only a rough indication, and were current in summer 1984.

Tuttons Brasserie

11–12 Russell Street, WC2 TEL 01-836 1167

OPEN Mon–Sat 9 am–11.30 pm Sun 12 noon–11.30 pm CLOSED Chr Day
CREDIT CARDS All accepted UNDERGROUND Covent Garden
WHEELCHAIR ACCESS Yes VEGETARIAN DISHES Vegetable coulibiac, good salads

Tuttons copes remarkably well over the fourteen and a half hours that it's open, catering for the morning shopper, the exhausted tourist, the newly released office worker, the theatre-goer. Tuttons is really a large brasserie-restaurant with a relatively small bar area, but the same wine is served throughout. The list is short and basic, with no mention of producers at all. Bordeaux is represented exclusively by three 1979 petits-châteaux (eg Ch Beau Vallon, St-Emilion, £8.70) whilst the two 'Burgundies' are in fact a Beaujolais 1982 (£6.90) and a Beaujolais Cru – Brouilly 1982 (£9.50). An expensive Chablis 1980 (£12) and a St-Véran for £9.70 are the sole representatives of Burgundian white. Germany and the Loire provide the majority of wines; the Vouvray 1981 is an attractive offer for £6.80, but the German wines are all over-priced. Still, Tuttons does offer some good half-bottles, including the house Champagne (Beaumet NV) for £8, and their house wines are decent but again pricy for their type – Celliers du Prieuré from the Loire (£4.50/95p for a 14 cl glass). The bar offers only basic snacks: pâté (£1.30) and quiches. For a more varied or filling choice, the brasserie and restaurant serve a complete menu.

The Village Wine Bar

14 Queens Parade, Queens Drive, W5 TEL 01-997 0206

OPEN Mon–Sat 11 am–3 pm, 5.30 pm–11 pm Sun 12 noon–2 pm, 7 pm–10.30 pm CREDIT CARDS Amex, Diners UNDERGROUND North Ealing
WHEELCHAIR ACCESS Yes VEGETARIAN DISHES Always one special

There's little choice in this part of West London, and The Village, small, pale and unimaginative, is certainly better than the pub and pizzeria lookalike wine bars that line the approaches to Ealing. 'Bergerac Bordeaux Rouge' chalked up on the board was the first indication on our visit that the staff could lay no claims to wine knowledge. And after much searching and a few attempts to obtain out-of-stock listed wines, we plumped, intrigued, for a Portuguese Pinot Blanc, 'a fruity wine': at £5 an excellent Pinot from Alsace. Take the trouble to ask to see the bottles, and you'll find some good wines: Sauvignon Trois Mouline (£5), Dolamore's College Claret (£5) and some fair Rhônes and Loires. Food is edible, if sloppily served, and the barmaids pleasant. The Village is certainly not worth a detour, but worth a try if you're parched and confined to the northern reaches of Ealing.

West 11 Wine Bar

120 Kensington Park Road, W11 TEL 01-727 4093

OPEN Mon–Fri 11.30 am–3 pm, 5.30 pm–11 pm Sat 9 am–3 pm, 6 pm–11 pm
CLOSED Sun, public holidays CREDIT CARDS Access/Euro, Amex, Visa
UNDERGROUND Notting Hill Gate WHEELCHAIR ACCESS Yes
VEGETARIAN DISHES Salads and vegetarian quiche

The West 11 Wine Bar, just one block from Portobello antiques market, has been in its renovated state for a year now. The Finch's corner retail store was converted to create an upstairs section – more reminiscent of a coffee-pâtisserie shop than a wine bar – while the original cellar has been attractively renovated. With its numerous intimate candlelit alcoves, it is an ideal place for a tête-à-tête. There is live jazz music at no charge on Wednesday and Friday evenings, and old (sometimes scratched) records the rest of the time. The house red is much better than the watery house white. Both are French and 90p a glass. France is broadly represented, and we would recommend the Chablis (A Pic) 1982 at £7.50. The Georges Duboeuf Morgon 1982 (£6.65) and Fleurie 1982 (£7.80) are good, dependable wines and the Rioja Royal 1973 is reasonably priced at £5.95. Apart from two South African Nederburg wines, the list does not show much originality, but there is something to suit most tastes, helped by an unusually large selection of half-bottles. There are sparkling wines (eg President Brut NV at £6.65) and Champagne (eg Bollinger NV for a rather expensive £16.50). Sherry and port are available by the glass, ranging from 90p for an Amontillado or a Finch's Tawny Port to £3.50 for Quinta de Vargellas 1972. Food is cooked locally and changes daily. Again, originality is not the strong point but the dishes are attractively presented, even if the main courses are a trifle dear: game pie and fresh salads (£3.50), king prawns in garlic butter with salad (£4.50). Service can be a little off-hand, but when the place livens up later on in the evening, the atmosphere invites one to linger.

Whipps Wine Bar

883 Lea Bridge Road, E17 TEL 01-521 5023

OPEN Mon–Sun 12 noon–3 pm Sun–Thur 7 pm–11.30 pm Fri, Sat 7 pm–12 pm (After normal licensing hours it is necessary to order food with wine)
CLOSED Some public holidays CREDIT CARDS All accepted BR STATION Wood Street WHEELCHAIR ACCESS Yes VEGETARIAN DISHES Omelettes and quiches

Pampas grass and potted plants fill the bow-fronted windows of Whipps wine bar, the attractive bare brickwork inside giving an almost rustic appearance. There are plans to extend this already quite roomy bar into the premises next door, which will make it very spacious indeed. Since Whipps is owned by the adjacent wine merchants, Swainsons, it came as a surprise to see that the Burgundies and Rhônes had got mixed up with the clarets in the list. Remove the Eastern interlopers, and the

Bordeaux section is rather depleted. You might choose 1973 Ch Smith Haut-Lafitte (£13.50) and 1970 Ch Canon La Gaffelière (£16.50), both of which require rapid drinking before they are past their best. House wines include Vin du Patron, Blanc Océan and Vin de Pays de Vaucluse, all at £4.40 with a choice of large (£1.20) or medium (90p) glass. The 1971 Châteauneuf-du-Pape, Comte de Lauze (£11) could be a very interesting wine – it is not often one comes across a mature example like this on a wine bar list. The 1972 Savigny-lès-Beaune (£10.75) is one of the better buys too, although don't forget that you'll find it under claret. The small kitchen produces a fine array of food, from snacks to main meals: jacket potato with chilli (£1), spaghetti bolognaise (£1.85) or for those with a good appetite, chicken in white wine and cream sauce (£3.25) and Dover sole (£6).

Whispers

823 Romford Road, E12 TEL 01-478 2663

OPEN Mon–Sat 6.30 pm–12 pm CLOSED Sun CREDIT CARDS Not accepted
BR STATION Ilford, Manor Park WHEELCHAIR ACCESS Yes NO FOOD

A splendid awning in the style of those gracious New York apartment buildings ushers you into Whispers, inaptly named, perhaps, considering the thumping music coming off the walls. Part of a complex which includes a separate restaurant and drama/dance studios, the wine bar is a long, high-ceilinged room with tables on one side and a long bar on the other. Wall-mounted bottle-racks and reddish-orange lighting give a clubby, late-night atmosphere, even when it is daylight outside. In addition to the usual fare, the wine list features high-class claret and Burgundy so prices are high. The tough 1972 vintage of fifth-growth Bordeaux Ch Camensac is £11.10, and Pernand-Vergelesses from the same year is £13.90. There is a first-growth 1978 Chablis at £10.50 and although not too many will want to pay £15.15 for a bottle of 1979 Nuits-St-Georges, it is nice at least to be offered such an opportunity. The 1978 Châteauneuf-du-Pape is £8.65. Bottle prices start at £4.40 for the Bereich Bernkastel, but only two wines are available by the glass – red and white French from the respectable house of Boisset (both £1). Their Perrier (unclear from the list whether Laurent- or -Jouët) Champagne is a reasonable £11.10. The cocktail selection is large. No food is available in the wine bar itself.

Prices are only a rough indication, and were current in summer 1984.

Special awards

Ⓥ is for bargain prices

is for a very good range of wines

is for exceptional service.

Whittingtons

21 College Hill, Cannon Street, EC4 TEL 01-248 5855

OPEN Mon–Fri 11.30 am–3 pm, 5 pm–7.30 pm CLOSED Sat, Sun and public holidays CREDIT CARDS All accepted UNDERGROUND Mansion House WHEELCHAIR ACCESS Impossible VEGETARIAN DISHES Not provided

Turn again Whittington, off Cannon Street and down College Hill, negotiate a flight of stairs and a long passage and you'll arrive at these authentic cellars, no doubt in need of refreshment after such a trek. Sir Richard certainly lived in College Hill, though his house was burnt in the Great Fire, and this is probably where this legendary and hospitable man kept his wine. It first opened as a wine bar in the late '60s and now, having passed through different hands, is firmly established as a London drinking den. 'Good wine needs no bush' and though the bar is tricky to find, it's well attended at lunch-time, less so in the evenings; but then, Cannon Street and its surroundings afford plenty of competition. There are about 50 wines on the list, ten or so offered by the glass; house red and white at £4.20/80p and the blackboard announces a daily selection: on our visit Aveleda Vinho Verde (£5.35/95p) and California Ch Saint Jean 1982 (£1.80). South Africa featured with Koopmanskloof (try that when you've had a bottle) at £7.50/£1.25. We enjoyed Fleurie 1982 from Georges Duboeuf at £8.50. The menu changes weekly and you can eat well here: saddle of lamb (£4.75), quenelles of sole and salmon in cream sauce (£4.50), vegetables extra, cheerfully served, both wine and food, by largely Antipodean staff.

Wine Butt ☞

91–95 Clerkenwell Road, EC1 TEL 01-242 3246

OPEN Mon–Fri 11.30 am–3 pm CLOSED evenings, Sat, Sun and public holidays CREDIT CARDS Not accepted WHEELCHAIR ACCESS Impossible VEGETARIAN DISHES Not provided

It is worth fighting your way through the crowded and boisterous Leather Lane street market to reach the Wine Butt, which has one unique feature – service. No jostling at a crowded bar here, the friendly cellar bar is all table service (which means you can reserve in advance). You are guided to table, and a dish of nuts and crisps appears for you to nibble while you make your choice of wine or food. The Wine Butt is owned by the Italian importers Cantina Augusto, so it is no surprise to see Italian wine dominating the list, and good value it is, too, with house wine at £3.40 a bottle/85p a glass. There is also a special weekly selection and the 1982 Mâcon-Villages (£4.60) looked stunning value. High spots from a short list are the 1982 Pinot Bianco (£5.10) and the 1978 Barolo (£6.20). The list itself could do with some attention as far as presentation is concerned. Wines are loosely grouped under red and white in a confusing jumble of countries and districts. Food is the weak point at the Wine Butt. Sandwiches start at 90p with a more substantial veal and ham pie and salad at £2. Ham cornets stuffed with rice salad or beef cornets with Russian salad are the remaining choice.

The Wine Gallery

49 Hollywood Road, SW10 TEL 01-352 7572

OPEN Mon–Sat 11.30 am–3 pm, 5.30 pm–11 pm Sun 12 noon–2 pm, 7 pm–10.30 pm CLOSED Public holidays CREDIT CARDS Not accepted UNDERGROUND Earls Court WHEELCHAIR ACCESS Yes VEGETARIAN DISHES Few

A new wine bar in this street known for restaurants; its owners run successful Brinkley's next door. The emphasis is on the food, which is good and inexpensive – just as well since they don't like you to drink without eating. On our visit, smoked fish and gravad lax at £3 were the dearest, while an excellent soupe de poissons cost £1.50, moussaka £2.50 and cassoulet £2.70. On the short wine list (to be extended during the year), the most expensive, as is often the case, is the best value: Ch Lascombes 1977 at £10. House wines are £3.90 a bottle/£1 a (12.5 cl) glass. Most wines are available by the glass. The room is airy; pale wood abounds and the clients are young and cheery, more fun than Sloane Ranger. It's unusually brightly lit for a wine bar, but this suits its character. As the name implies, a rotation of paintings decorates the walls.

The Wine Press Ⓥ

161 Fleet Street, EC4 TEL 01-353 9550

OPEN Mon–Fri 11.30 am–3 pm, 5 pm–10.30 pm CLOSED Sat, Sun, public holidays CREDIT CARDS All accepted UNDERGROUND Blackfriars WHEELCHAIR ACCESS Impossible VEGETARIAN DISHES Good choice

The Wine Press has become a favourite Fleet Street watering hole and deservedly so. No slouching here. A good-looking wine list offers a choice of 71 wines often, irritatingly, with no indication of producer or shipper. France forms the backbone of the list, but Italy, Iberia, Germany and Austria are well represented – the two Australian wines, 1980 Hunter Valley Cabernet Sauvignon (£6.95) and the 1982 Chardonnay Show Reserve from Rosemount Estate (£8) are excellent examples of Australia's high quality. Alsace kicks off with five wines from Gisselbrecht, including a Pinot Blanc (£4.95) and a Pinot Noir (£5.60), and the Rhône section offers a 1981 Crozes-Hermitage for only £5.50 or Mousset's 1976 Hermitage Rouge at £9.50. More temptation comes from Bordeaux with a fair petit château from Côtes de Bourg, Ch du Bosquet (£5.75), or 1979 Ch Moncets, Lalande de Pomerol (£7.85). 1976 Viña Ardanza, Rioja Alta, (£6.95) is certainly worth visiting the Wine Press for, as is the Austrian 1982 Gewürztraminer Spatlese,

Bürgenland (£6.50). As might be expected in such a professionally run establishment, the food is of an equally high standard: carrot and orange soup (£1.30), courgette mousse (£1.40) or port and Stilton pâté (£1.35) together with well-filled baps (from £1.05). The good selection of cheeses is a more than adequate lunchtime filler. There is an informal restaurant with an imaginative menu, changed weekly. Booking is advisable.

The Wine Press

Basement of White House Hotel, Osnaburgh Terrace, NW1 TEL 01-387 1200

OPEN Mon–Fri 11 am–3 pm, 5.30 pm–11.30 pm CLOSED Sat, Sun, public holidays CREDIT CARDS All accepted UNDERGROUND Great Portland Street WHEELCHAIR ACCESS Yes VEGETARIAN DISHES Fair choice

The basement of the White House Hotel is not the first place you might think of looking for a wine bar. Do not be deterred – the Wine Press is not a half-hearted hotel lobby, but an unpretentious tavern with something of a teutonic flavour. The wine list is short (26 wines) and basic but it is also remarkably inexpensive – one suspects there must be some hefty subsidy here. Only house wines come by the glass so, unless you settle for Mouton Cadet halves (red £3.10, white £2.40), you have to opt for full bottles. Try the Barolo 1975 (£5.25), the Utrero Rioja 1980 (£4.60) or Vinho Verde for just £3.90. There are two house reds: a Cuvée le Bosq at a very reasonable £3.40 and the most acceptable Cuvée le Grange for £3.80. House whites are similarly priced: branded Renaissance and the clean Vin de L'Ecaillère. Food is also inexpensive. Home-made leek and potato soup is just 50p; salads and quiches are all freshly made, and the hot dish of the day, usually around £2.50, may be a spaghetti bolognese. The Wine Press is definitely not just a bolt-hole for hotel inmates but has attracted a regular following of lunchtime office refugees, too.

Wives of Bath

5 Pilgrim Street, EC4 TEL 01-248 2255

OPEN Mon–Fri 11.30 am–3 pm, 5 pm–8 pm CLOSED Sat, Sun, public holidays CREDIT CARDS All accepted UNDERGROUND St Pauls, Blackfriars WHEELCHAIR ACCESS Impossible VEGETARIAN DISHES Quiches and salads

A skilful use of mirrors makes this small bar look larger than it actually is. There is also a room downstairs, open only at lunchtime, part of which forms an intimate restaurant. Obviously popular with the local clientèle, the Wives of Bath has a relaxed and friendly, rather cosy atmosphere. Dishes of nuts and olives are liberally offered – a welcoming touch. The house wine, Les Templiers, is £4.35 a bottle/£1.30 a glass, with a house claret at £4.95. A bit more information on the list about the wines would be appreciated – the Beaujolais and the Gewürztraminer missed both vintage and shipper. France is certainly the predominant source. The 1982 Mâcon-Lugny (£6.95) looked a real snip and the 1979 Ch Canteloup (£6.25) was reasonable enough. Spain is rather weak with a lonely Rioja, 1978 Campillo available at £5.85. The short Italian wine section offers 1981 Frascati Secco Superiore (£5.95) or 1981 Aziano Chianti Classico (£5.95). English wine gets a look in with 1982 Crazies Hill (£7.95), unfortunately not available by the glass. The sweet Loire 1959 Anjou Moulin Touchais is relatively cheap, as ever (£10.95/£1.65), and the Taylors Chip Dry Fine Old Aperitif is interesting (£10.95/£2.10). Full marks for offering Bucks Fizz and Kir Royale with either Champagne or sparkling wine and the suggestion of Framboises or Fraises des Bois as a change from Cassis. Food, served downstairs, looks crisp and appetising. The hot dish, changed daily, is served with potatoes or rice and three salads (£3.95). The rare roast beef which really was rare, is also served with the three salads (£3.95). For something lighter, try the smoked fish pâté (£1.95).

Wolsey's Wine Bar

52 Wells Street, W1 TEL 01-636 5121

OPEN Mon–Fri 11 am–3 pm, 5.30 pm–11 pm CLOSED Sat, Sun, public holidays, 25 Dec–1 Jan CREDIT CARDS Access/Euro, Amex, Diners
UNDERGROUND Oxford Circus, Tottenham Court Road
WHEELCHAIR ACCESS Yes, but not to lavatories VEGETARIAN DISHES On request NO-SMOKING ROOM

Wolsey's popular wine bar is situated above the associated French bistro called 'The Cardinal'. Together, they watch over a considerable flock. Most of the extensive wine list is French, although there is a short list of Germans, which includes Sittman's Forster Mariengarten Riesling Spätlese 1976, remarkably good value at £5.50. There is a wide range of *grande marque* Champagnes: the house Montaudon is £11, while Roederer is well priced at £14. The choice of clarets is equally pleasing, from the house claret, Ch des Graves 1977 at £5, all the way up to a Ch Ausone 1971 at £22. Look out, too, for the wide selection of Beaujolais Crus from Benoît Lafont at reasonable prices and some big Côtes-du-Rhones. The largest selection is of Burgundies, including Louis Trapet's Gevrey-Chambertin (his Chambertin 1970 is £17.50), and Moine-Hudelot's Musignys (Chambolle-Musigny, Les Amoureuses 1974 is £11.50). There is an Aloxe-Corton 1971 (£12.75) and a Beaune, Clos de la Mouche 1979 (£11.30). Then, when you are about to despair of ever making a decision, you realise that there are many high quality half-bottles (top marks for Wolsey's) so maybe you might try a Nuits-St-Georges 1976 (£6.24) *and* a Volnay, Les Angles 1er Cru 1979 (£5.95). Cold buffet foods include home-made raised pie, smoked fish, quiches, and a great variety of cheeses. Imaginative hot food might be a pasta dish, boeuf bourguignonne or lamb chops.

The Woodbine Wine Rooms

36 High Street, E11 TEL 01-989 0552
OPEN Mon–Sat 11 am–3 pm, 5.30 pm–10.30 pm (11 pm Fri, Sat) Sun 12 noon–2 pm CLOSED Sun eve CREDIT CARDS Access/Euro, Barclay
UNDERGROUND Wanstead WHEELCHAIR ACCESS Yes
VEGETARIAN DISHES Salads

Owned by the Webster family, famous for their pubs around this area, the Woodbine bears more than a passing resemblance to the Davy chain of City wine bars. A first-class wine list and good food are the main attractions that draw customers into these wine rooms. Except for a few German wines, like the 1982 Eitelsbacher Marienholz (£7) and 1982 Zeltinger Himmelreich Auslese (£9), the list is definitely French, but look out for the blackboards that proclaim the monthly offers and bin-ends, a round-the-world mixture. House wines, of which there are nine, start with a French dry red or white (£4/80p) and include a Blanc de Blancs (£4.25/85p) and a 1981/2 Beaujolais-Villages (£5/£1). For the real goodies it's back to the list. Bordeaux and Burgundy are both well represented, although some of the red Burgundies are a little young. However, you can always drink claret, starting with a modest Cru Bourgeois, 1976 Ch Potensac (£7.50), and then decide between 1976 Ch Pavie, 1er Grand Cru St-Emilion or 1976 Ch Montrose 2ème Cru St-Estèphe, both at £14.75. If you really want to splash out, try the 1967 Ch Latour (£28.75) or even the magnum of 1976 Ch Brane-Cantenac (£26.00). The white Burgundies are attractively priced, making the choice difficult between Louis Latour 1981 Montagny (£8.50) and Long Depaquit's 1982 Chablis 1er Cru Les Vaillons (£9.75). Maybe the latter might just win. 1963 port is obviously popular here: four different shippers' 1963s include Delaforce (£21) and Taylors (£28), or there is the 1966 Taylors (£23.50) or a 1968 Grahams Malvedos (£16). Food is served either in the small restaurant or from the cold buffet. A short but wholesome selection includes avocado 'Dr Butlers Head' with prawns and smoked salmon, half a lobster (£4.80), roast sirloin of beef (£2.90) or freshly carved ham (£2.70). On Sunday lunchtimes, come here for a traditional roast – it's well worth a trip to Wanstead!

Country

ALDERLEY EDGE Cheshire

No 15 Wine Bar

15 London Road TEL (0625) 585957
OPEN Mon–Sat 12 noon–2 pm, 7.30 pm–10.30 pm CLOSED Sun
CREDIT CARDS Access/Euro, Visa WHEELCHAIR ACCESS Easy to the drawing room VEGETARIAN DISHES Not always available

You could be forgiven for thinking as you enter the hall of No 15 that you had strayed into someone's home. From the pretty, walled garden, with wrought-iron tables and chairs around the lawn, through the long, low dining area downstairs to the drawing room above, the tasteful fittings create an intimate and relaxed 'period' atmosphere. Care has also been taken in compiling the wine list. There are adequate house wines, with Chantejoie at 80p a glass (which may have changed by now to blended red and white Beaune). But on closer inspection, Maurice Bailly's excellent Blanc Fumé, Les Griottes 1982 (£6.05) or Caronne Ste-Gemme 1978 (£6.65) also seem well within reach. The 1978 Mercurey Clos Fortoul from Remoissenet looks interesting at £7.35. However, vintages are not listed and it would be wise to check on the year currently available. Food-wise, there are two blackboard menus, a 'specials' board that changes daily and offers a selection of hot and cold dishes like chicken coronation salad at £3.25 or beef bourguignonne at £3.75, and a board of such standards as moussaka (£2.95) or fish pie (£3.10). Sweets such as chocolate meringue or treacle tart also change daily and are fairly priced at £1. Helpings are generous and well presented. No 15 is a pleasant place, though a rather more adventurous wine list and menu might raise it to greater heights.

ALDRIDGE West Midlands

Hop 'n' Grape

Anchor Parade TEL (0922) 58051
OPEN Mon–Thur 11.30 am–2.30 pm, 6 pm–10.30 pm Fri–Sat 11.30 am–2.30 pm, 6 pm–11 pm Sun 12 noon–2 pm, 7 pm–10.30 pm CLOSED Chr Day eve CREDIT CARDS Not accepted WHEELCHAIR ACCESS Yes
VEGETARIAN DISHES Salads and quiche

Part of the West Midlands Taverns chain *(see Horts, Edgbaston)*. On the ground floor, you can drink real ales to the sound of hit songs whilst you watch the film-of-the-song on one of the umpteen videos; indeed, you have little choice. The wine bar is upstairs, open in the evenings only, and offers cocktails as well as the standard WMT grub.

ALTRINCHAM Cheshire

Gander's

2 Goose Green TEL 061-941 3954

OPEN Mon–Sat 12 noon–3 pm, 7 pm–10.30 pm (Sat till 11 pm) Sun 7pm–10.30 pm CLOSED Sun L CREDIT CARDS Access/Euro, Visa WHEELCHAIR ACCESS Impossible VEGETARIAN DISHES Good selection

Interesting barn-like premises on the first floor, with high ceilings, exposed beams, unobtrusive floral wallpaper and simple wooden furnishings. But any dreams of rustic tranquillity are shattered by the energetic young staff and continuous pop music. A fairly short wine list does contain the occasional surprise, like Pouilly-Vinzelles (£5.95) in amongst old standards like Niersteiner Gutes Domtal (£4.35) et al. House wines are Cuvée Jean-Paul at £4.95 a litre, 70p a glass. There is a good 1981 Côtes-du-Rhône from Rasteau (£5) and a reasonable Barolo Dogliani 1977 for £5.60 (though the list reveals few vintages or suppliers). The occasional special could be Portuguese (Vinho Verde, etc) or Buck's Fizz at 75p a glass. Food is pleasant bistro-style: starters might be avocado and crab (£1.80) or pastrami with green figs (£1.85); main courses beef goulash (£2.35), chilli (£2.35) or the house speciality, fondue bourguignonne (£11.50 for two, £4.75 each for four or more). Sweets include sherry trifle and profiteroles (both 80p). *(See also Gander's Go South, Manchester.)*

AMBLESIDE Cumbria

De Quincey's

Regent Hotel, Waterhead TEL (0966) 32254

OPEN Mon–Sat 12 noon–2.30 pm, 7 pm–10 pm Sun 12 noon–2 pm, 7 pm–10 pm Public holidays 12 noon–2.30 pm, 7 pm–10 pm CLOSED Thur eve, all month Jan CREDIT CARDS Access/Euro, Amex, Visa WHEELCHAIR ACCESS Yes VEGETARIAN DISHES Some

When we visited, De Quincey's bar was still serving wine only with food, but they have been granted a full licence from 1985. Done out in Mediterranean style, with a red-tiled floor, wooden tables and chairs and a separate area for pre-dinner drinks, the bar may have been redecorated by the end of 1984 as part of the hotel's refurbishment plans (a swimming pool and cocktail bar are planned alongside the wine bar). Sadly, the once excellent list has been trimmed over the past year down to the more common wine bar wines, anonymous Valpolicella and Liebfraumilch, with a few brands, but a couple of clarets and some Rhônes and Italians at reasonable prices might keep the wine lover happy. Food is good and copious: spinach and mushroom noodles (£2.50), paprika beef (£4.50) or moussaka (£3.95). Service is efficient and friendly. Not a great bar, but worth a visit in this land of water and little wine.

BAKEWELL Derbyshire

Aitch's Wine Bar & Bistro

4 Buxton Road TEL (062 981) 3895

OPEN Mon–Sat 11.30 am–2.30 pm, 7 pm–11 pm Sun (summer only) 7 pm–11 pm Public holidays 11 am–3 pm, 7 pm–11 pm CLOSED Sun L, all day Sun in winter CREDIT CARDS Not accepted WHEELCHAIR ACCESS Easy VEGETARIAN DISHES Always some

Though the wine list is short and far from exciting, Aitch's wine bar is an oasis in this mid-Derbyshire desert – complete, indeed, with a real palm tree. An 18th-century oak-beamed Derbyshire gritstone clothing factory was converted 18 months ago to the bar downstairs and a simple, attractive function room (for up to 70) above. The bar is pleasantly decorated in yellow and green (palm-tree wallpaper and yellow brick walls with wooden benches), and the atmosphere is young and lively. Few clues in the wine list to the source of the wines. Many are from the André Simon range, or sister brand Courtenay wines: Côtes du Roussillon (£4.25), very basic Italians (£4+); and two Beaujolais and a Côtes-du-Rhône from Quinson (£5.75, £4.95, £4.45). Best buys are the Listel rosé Gris de Gris and red Domaine de Bosquet (both £4.45), and Bulgarian Cabernet Sauvignon (£4.45). Sauvignon Blanc de Touraine is good at £4.45. You can have only house wines by the glass (65p) – acceptable, just. The kitchens have been rebuilt in the past year, and the cooking has become a little more adventurous, especially in the evening. Second in command in the kitchen is a vegetarian, so her ilk are well catered for (vegetarian crumble £1.85, cauliflower cheese £1.45). Lunches are simple: copious helping of lasagne (£1.95), steak and kidney pie (£2.25), half-tandoori chicken (£3.65); but there's more in the evening: stuffed local trout (£2.75), duckling (£4.75), lemon sole in prawn and dill butter (£3.80), rack of lamb (£4.85). Puddings are good (home-made cheesecake 75p, home-made fruit pies 85p).

BEACONSFIELD Buckinghamshire

Bucks Fizz

3 Warwick Road TEL (049 46) 71582

OPEN Mon–Sat 11 am–2.30 pm, 7 pm–12 pm (10.30 pm last order) CLOSED Sun CREDIT CARDS All accepted WHEELCHAIR ACCESS Yes VEGETARIAN DISHES Some

With its change of ownership, Bucks Fizz has lost its pretentiousness. The atmosphere is pleasantly homely and pubby and, unusually, one can escape into a small Weingarten at the rear. The wine list has considerably improved, now less obviously devoted to the great god 'profit-margin', and the inclusion of wines from Australia is to be commended. The rest of the selection is standard, but that must be seen as no criticism as each wine seems well selected. House wines are from 80p a glass, with white Rioja or Vinho Verde 90p; house Champagne is £1.50 a glass. Food is advertised on a blackboard – a standard menu with daily specials. The fare is predictable wine-bar food – prepared beforehand and reheated, and served in reasonable helpings that are tasty but hardly overwhelming bargains. The service is discreet, almost to the point of being self-effacing and, though friendly, Bucks Fizz does give the impression of a certain forced conviviality – perhaps more revealing of Beaconsfield society than of the particular regime.

BERWICK-UPON-TWEED Northumberland

Foxton's

1 Sydey Court TEL (0289) 302621

OPEN Mon–Fri 10 am–3 pm, 6 pm–10.30 pm (Sat till 11 pm) CLOSED Sun, early Oct CREDIT CARDS Not accepted WHEELCHAIR ACCESS Yes VEGETARIAN DISHES Good

To be the best wine bar in Borders country is not a difficult task – but David Foxton would qualify for the top notch given quite stiff competition. His friendly, relaxed wine bar, hidden away in a courtyard off the main street by the Stonegate and open only for two years, already seems to be one of the town's main attractions. 'The whole place is immaculate,' writes one customer, 'even at 10 pm on a Saturday night when most of Berwick seems to congregate there, often whole families, including Granny.' The wine list is extensive, drawn from a number of excellent sources. Best amongst the house wines, unusually, is the rosé from Listel, 75p for a 5 fl oz glass, £1.30 for 9 fl oz, or in lovely locally made decorated jugs at £2.75 for a half-litre, £5.35 for a litre. Other wines by the glass change weekly. There are generally ten, which might be Torres Viña Sol (90p), Pinot Grigio, Collavini (85p), Muscat d'Alsace, Gisselbrecht (£1.20), Cabernet Sauvignon Concha y Toro (75p) and Torres Gran Sangredetoro (95p). The list ranges in price from the fruity Viña Carossa from the Penedès at £3.80 a bottle to Ch Mouton Rothschild 1970 at £60. David Foxton knows his wines well, and is always at hand to help and advise. There is a wide variety of food, too – simple, delicious and beautifully presented. There might be spiced carrot soup (75p), cauliflower and Stilton soup (75p), mushroom and Mozzarella quiche (95p), aubergines baked in yoghourt (£2.40, with green salad) and a choice of original salads, such as cauliflower, apple and peanut in lemon yoghourt, carrot and wholewheat, and many more. Vegetarians will appreciate not only the meatless dishes: there's always a special vegetarian hot dish such as cassèrole of courgette, or leek and mushroom lasagne (£2.10, with green salad). This exemplary wine bar takes our inspectors happily on a long detour from their habitual tracks, so if Foxton's is your local, do help us by sending in *your* views.

BILLERICAY Essex

Webbers

2 Western Road TEL (027 74) 56581

OPEN Mon–Thur 11.30 am–2.30 pm Mon 7 pm–10.30 pm Tue–Thur 6 pm–10.30 pm Fri & Sat 11.30 am–2.30 pm, 6 pm–11 pm Public holidays 7 pm–10.30 pm CLOSED Sun, public holidays L CREDIT CARDS Access/Euro, Diners, Visa WHEELCHAIR ACCESS One step to front door VEGETARIAN DISHES Excellent choice

No one could accuse the proprietor of this attractive wine bar of skimping on his wine list. No fewer than 133 are listed, from all areas of Europe and from as far afield as Australia and California. Full marks for nine interesting French country wines, including a white Bergerac, Domaine de Grand Champ 1982 (£6.25) and Ch Cap de Fouste Roussillon rouge (£6.75). Amongst a fine range of red Bordeaux, the excellent, firm, fruity 1970 Ch Chasse-Spleen is £13.25. Yapp's provide a number of delicious Rhônes and Loires: Savennières Domaine du Closel at £6.85 is splendid value. Roger Harris Wines are responsible for most of the Beaujolais: Meziat's 1982 Chiroubles at £7.65 is the pick of a fine bunch. There are sixteen Italian wines: Masi's 1974 Campo Fiorin at £6.25 is most reasonable for this well-made wine. A better than average selection of German wines is offered, but only two Alsace wines. This is a minor lapse, however, on a thoughtful, varied and well-laid-out list. Twenty-one wines are available by the glass – 87p for Loron's reliable vins de table, 90p for Liebfraumilch, 96p for Muscadet. House wines by the bottle are £4.60. The range of food is equally enterprising. A printed menu of cold dishes is always available and includes cold chicken and ham pie (£2.15), quiche Lorraine (£1.25) and wheatmeal pizza (£2.25). The frequently changing blackboard of hot and cold specialities is always interesting: rabbit with bitter orange sauce, veal with leeks and raisins, and squid provençale. Vegetarians are catered for with vegetable terrine with tarragon cream, and baked potatoes with various fillings. Sweets are £1.10 to £1.25: home-made ice-cream is particularly recommended. You can even complete your meal with Earl Grey tea at 40p a pot. Well done, Webbers – keep up the good work.

BIRMINGHAM West Midlands

Hawkins Café-Bar

King Edward Building, 205–219 Corporation Street TEL 021-236 2001

OPEN Mon–Fri 11 am–11 pm Sat 10 am–11 pm Sun 5 pm–10.30 pm Public holidays 7 pm–10.30 pm CLOSED Chr Day, Boxing Day, New Year's Day CREDIT CARDS All accepted WHEELCHAIR ACCESS Yes VEGETARIAN DISHES Few

This bright and characterful café-bar with its cosmopolitan clientèle and easy-going style is open for something or other most of the day.

Apart from house wines (£4.10/75p) and about eight Champagnes (£10–£25), there are nearly fifty varied wines on offer, mostly between £4 and £8. There are few departures from the beaten track apart from the more expensive wines like Ch Rocher Calon 1964, or Hattenheimer Heiligenberg, 1976 Auslese, both £10. Germany is well represented but, as we went to press, Californians were about to be dropped and French wines extended. You can get your teeth around 4 oz of home-made hamburger with a choice of wine, blue cheese or onion sauce, plus the trimmings, and still have 25p change from £3. The pizzas are 'hand-built, including the dough' on the premises and come with six toppings in two sizes (£2.30 and £2.75). Hawkins also offer steaks, baked potatoes, salads and a lot of cakes – they obviously intend that no one should go away hungry. Some Tuesday and Wednesday evenings may produce live jazz concerts. They are terribly proud of the up-to-the-minute laser lighting display and powerful digital sound system, so if that's your style, try a weekend visit.

La Galleria

Paradise Circus TEL 021-236 1006

OPEN Mon–Thur 12 noon–2.30 pm, 5.30–10.30 pm Fri & Fat 12 noon–2.30 pm, 5.30–11 pm CLOSED Sun, public holidays CREDIT CARDS All accepted WHEELCHAIR ACCESS Yes VEGETARIAN DISHES Various

The 60-seater restaurant and the three or four areas of the capacious wine bar are separated, in mock Italian fashion, by wrought-iron dividers draped with plastic vegetation and raffia-covered bottles. The same kitchen serves all eaters, and wine bar customers get a particularly good deal: a choice of several fish including fresh grilled sardines (£2.35) or calamari marinara (£4.40), fresh asparagus in season (£2.50), a dozen good salads edging towards the £3 mark, half a dozen pizzas and pasta dishes, and special Italian treats like osso buco at £4.50. The pizza toppings would look good in the back streets of Naples, although the base on our visit was disappointingly flat and much nearer to home. No wonder, though, that it is difficult to get one of the many seats, nor that the extremely pleasant service may take a little while at peak times. Italian wines get undeservedly short shrift on so many wine bar lists that it is refreshing to see one that is Italian-inspired. Details are as usual very sparse, but the designations NV (non-vintage) or Vin (vintage) go some way towards being helpful. Italian prices range from £4 all the way up to £4.95, with the exception of a Barolo, Vin, £5.40, and include the very drinkable Sicilian Corvo, red and white, at £4.95, and a sweet white Orvieto Abboccato, Vin, in both full and half-bottle (£4.20/£2.15). Although not on the list, a delightful Valpolicella Amarone was changing hands rapidly for £6. House wines are available in glass (70p), goblet (£1), half-litre (£1.95) or litre (£3.65). Oh, and there are some French and German wines, too.

Willie's

Fleet Street TEL 021-236 2977

OPEN Mon–Thur 12 noon–3 pm, 5.30 pm–10.30 pm Fri & Sat 12 noon–3 pm, 5.30 pm–11 pm CLOSED Sun, public holidays, Chr Day CREDIT CARDS Not accepted WHEELCHAIR ACCESS Impossible VEGETARIAN DISHES Some

Positively buzzing with life (you didn't really want to sit down, did you?), Willie's is dark greenish inside with about four or five different kinds of wallpaper, pasted many years ago. But as there are so many people you can't really see much of it and in any case, what matters is the animation and the mix: professional and city gents, arty types, students, office girls, all setting the world to rights – very cheaply. Apart from Champagne, Chablis at £7.65 and a couple of Bordeaux, you needn't go over a fiver for any of the 30 or so wines on offer (try Martini Asti Spumante at an utterly reasonable £4.65), and if you're saving hard for your next Lamborghini, you should go during the happy hour, 5.30–6.30 weekday evenings, when they knock a further £1 off all bottle prices, and 10p off a glass, normally around 75p, of claret, Liebfraumilch, Beaujolais, Tafelwein and house wine. The management is obviously too busy to put details of vintage or shipper on the list, but in any case, there are no pretentions beyond standard and branded wines. As to the food, you take pot luck: it may be a mix of Greek dips with pitta bread for £1.10, or steak and kidney pie for £2, or then again it may not ('We can't keep everything on all the time, dear'). Service by girls kitted out in fetching black is calm and helpful.

BRADFORD ON AVON Wiltshire

The Georgian Wine Lodge

25 Bridge Street TEL (022 16) 2268

OPEN Mon–Sat 12 noon–2.30 pm, 7 pm–11 pm CLOSED Sun, public holidays, two weeks after Chr CREDIT CARDS Access/Euro, Diners, Visa
WHEELCHAIR ACCESS Through side entrance
VEGETARIAN DISHES By arrangement

More than ten years ago, Philip Ridge turned his back on a career in the West End wine trade and with his wife Carole set out on a remarkable venture in the elegant Georgian house at one end of the town's medieval bridge, complete with pilgrims' chapel. His early days in the wine trade are reflected in the careful choice of wines. Although many of the real treasures have gone *'derrière les fagots'*, the genial *patron* can be persuaded to reach beyond his list by those who show a sympathetic interest in the finer points of eating and drinking. However, his present list is still quite exceptional for a wine bar – 24 clarets with a good balance between communes and vintages – the château-bottled wines range from Ch du Marquisat 1979, Côtes de Bourg (£7), just ready, to the rich, velvety, fully developed Ch la Croix-du-Casse 1964, Pomerol, an affordable treat at £20. There are also seven Sauternes, five sensibly in half-bottles, led by Ch Coutet 1966 (bottles only) at £25 for the unashamed sybarite. Red and white Burgundy are also well represented – whites starting with a young, fresh Moillard Aligoté (£6.20/£1.05) and rising to Bouchard Père's Corton Charlemagne 1979 (£22) and just under 30 reds from throughout the region. Other French regions are there, with a rare spread of four single vineyard 1976 Châteauneuf-du-Papes – Fine Roches (£13) and Fortia, Mont Olivet and la Solitude (all £14), which present the problem of how to justify a comparative tasting. The rest of Europe and new wine countries are not neglected, although, as might be expected, the list's strength lies in the more traditional areas. The Ridges have now opened three well-appointed double bedrooms overlooking a courtyard, each with private bathroom, so those eager to 'dine where they sleep' can indulge themselves in the Wine Lodge's remarkable port list – vintages from 1950 through to 1970, seventeen in all. The prices are somewhat daunting but, alas, represent the market value. There is also a list of old solera Madeiras – very much in the luxury price bracket. Back to earth, there is a good and varied range of wines by the glass. The French house wine is a reasonable 70p, the house Champagne, shipped from Epernay, £2, and a California sweet Muscat, Christian Brothers' Ch la Salle (£1.05). French AC wines hover around the £1 mark. There is also a good range of half-bottles conveniently listed separately. Philip Ridge has the assistance of a chef in the kitchen, but the ample menu is very much his own inspiration, and the influence of a Salcombe weekend cottage is easily discernible. The main menu is augmented by a blackboard of daily specials dependent on availability in the local markets. Fresh grilled sardines (£1.80) are a safe starter, and cottage pie (£2.60) is a satisfying continuation. A successful choice was a fresh cod steak with anchovy sauce (£3.80). The cheeseboard (£1.60) is more inspired than most, and the imaginative puddings are augmented by daily specials – a good moment to remember those half-bottles of Sauternes. You can choose whether to eat downstairs in the lively atmosphere of the bar or more quietly at upstairs tables. Salads and sandwiches are also available at the bar. A very attractive private dining room with a bow window overlooking the courtyard can accommodate up to 12 people for private functions.

BRAINTREE Essex

Thirty Four

34 New Street TEL (0376) 45615

OPEN Tue–Fri 10 am–3 pm, 7 pm–11 pm Sat 7 pm–12 pm CLOSED Sun, Mon, public holidays CREDIT CARDS All accepted WHEELCHAIR ACCESS Impossible VEGETARIAN DISHES Some

Customers are drawn from some distance to Steven Garnsey's attractive wine bar, tucked away from the bustle of this market town. Is it by coincidence or design that thirty-four still wines are offered?

There is also an impressive selection of ten Champagnes, ranging from 'house' Montaudon (£11.95) to Dom Pérignon (£33.95). House wines (£4/75p) are French red and white, hock, Mosel and Rosé d'Anjou. No other wines are sold by the glass, but seven are available by the half-bottle. Popular wines listed include Liebfraumilch, Niersteiner, Piesporter, Muscadet and Beaujolais – all under £5. There is also a well-chosen list of fine wines but it is a pity the selection ('mainly from Lay & Wheeler, Colchester') of Burgundy, Rhône and Loire fails to show growers, as there are some first-class producers represented. The menus are changed monthly; starters on the lunch menu have recently included curried mushroom parcel (£1.75) and fresh grilled scallops (£2), to be followed by lasagne (£2.25) or smoked salmon crêpes (£1.95). In the evening, you can choose from the sensibly sized and varied menu: char-grilled Mediterranean prawns are £3.95, home-made onion soup is 85p with main course char-grilled saddle of lamb cutlets with rosemary (£4.95) or breast of chicken in tarragon cream (£5.25). Desserts are £1. There are also good coffee and freshly squeezed orange juice. It is essential to reserve tables for Saturday evenings.

BRIDGNORTH Shropshire

Baileys

78 High Street TEL (074 62) 3445

OPEN Mon–Sat 11 am–2.30 pm, 6 pm–11 pm Sun 12 noon–2 pm, 7 pm–10.30 pm CLOSED Chr Day and Boxing Day CREDIT CARDS Not accepted WHEELCHAIR ACCESS Impossible VEGETARIAN DISHES Good salads and quiches

The building dates from the middle of the 17th century and has recently been completely gutted, exposing a network of oak beams. A large oak staircase connects the split-level ground floor to two heavily beamed rooms upstairs. Candle-lit tables set the atmosphere. The wine list is uninspiring and really caters only for popular choice, although it is good to see that Baileys have taken the trouble in most cases to list shippers and vintages. House wines are reasonably priced (£3.25/60p) – just passable on our visit. There is a big if unexciting range of wines by the glass: Piesporter Michelsberg (80p), Liebfraumilch (75p), Beaujolais and house claret (80p), Laski Riesling (75p) and Bucks Fizz, whose 60p price tag warns you that it is made with sparkling wine and not Champagne. Baileys specialise in German wines, and even list two red wines from Germany. Best value in the German whites must be Binger St Rochuskapelle Kabinett 1982 (£4.95). For a drier white, try the Ch Tanesse 1981 by Cordier; their house claret (£4.35) is also worth a try. The food, served on the ground floor, is displayed with the dishes of the day on a hot-plate; the cold meats and salads are in a glass display cabinet. There are usually three hot dishes at lunchtime, such as quiche and salad (95p), and leeks wrapped in ham (£1.25), with different ones in the evening: chicken 'champignon' (£2.95), boeuf en daube (£2.95). Salads and cold dishes are also shown on a large board at the back of the bar. Turkey, ham, beef and pork cost £1.50 for an extremely generous 'small' helping, £2.25 for a large. There is a wide selection of well-presented salads at 40p each.

BRIGHTON East Sussex

Crusts

24 Prince Albert Street (off Market Square) TEL (0273) 23807

OPEN Mon–Sat 12 noon–2.30 pm, 6 pm–11 pm Sun 12 noon–2 pm, 7 pm–10.30 pm CLOSED Never CREDIT CARDS Not accepted
WHEELCHAIR ACCESS Impossible VEGETARIAN DISHES Not provided (no food)

Now that the Market Wine Bar, Brighton's original '60s wine bar, has become a restaurant, Crusts is the only place where you can drop in just for a drink – there's no food, because that is provided, with a very limited selection of wines, at Crusts Restaurant opposite (which is open till midnight). Upstairs in the wine bar, the walls are covered with 'antique' articles, pots and various bits and pieces which the gentleman behind the bar described to our inspector as 'naff'. Yet they do add up to 'fun' surroundings. The music tends to be a little loud but is appropriate to this trendy spot. The cocktail bar is sensibly separate, however, downstairs, for the use of the real trendies. Crusts' wine list is of the anonymous, generic type, with one or two more interesting wines than the usual wine bar run: Corbières (£4.50), Pouilly-Fuissé (£9.25), Fleurie (£7.55) – and prices tend to be rather high. Thirteen wines, including Rioja, claret and Côtes-du-Rhône, are sold by the glass. Hardly an interesting list, but the best you will find in Brighton.

BRISTOL Avon

Pinafore

9 Park Street TEL (0272) 25148

OPEN Mon–Sat 12 noon–2.30 pm, 5.30 pm–10.30 pm (Fri & Sat till 11 pm) Sun 12 noon–2 pm CLOSED Sun eve, public holidays CREDIT CARDS Not accepted
WHEELCHAIR ACCESS Yes VEGETARIAN DISHES Always one

Now in their fifth year, Stephen and Jane Samuel began with two advantages – the decoration of the wine bar and its adjacent rooms, put together in the thirties with pillars and panelling saved from the 1907 version of the transatlantic liner SS Mauretania, and secondly the depths of Messrs Averys cellars, both owing much to the late, great and distinctly eccentric Ronald Avery, whose successors *(see the MERCHANTS section)* run their old-established wine merchants in the same building. The wine list is well set out and reasonably comprehensive, with some unexpected wines from the new wine countries (via Averys upstairs) – two McWilliams wines from New South Wales and another from New Zealand, Cooks Cabernet Sauvignon 1979 (£6.60, on the light side but with plenty of style and flavour), and an offering from Canada. There are some treats from nearer home, too – a 1980 Savennières (£6.55), Brouilly 1979 (£6.55), and a distinct bargain, Crozes-Hermitage, Salavert, 1980 (£5.45). Spain, Italy and Germany are well enough represented and there is a good sprinkling of halves. Rather fewer wines are available by the glass – this seems to depend on the whim of the bar-person – but a bottle on most of the tables is the order of the day. The menu is fairly basic, although the choice is good by wine bar standards, and is complemented by weekday lunchtime specials displayed on the blackboard. In the evenings, the scene is more lively, the resident pianist adjusting his music according to the look of the customers. Helpings are generous, even bread and cheese (choice of several) describing itself as a 'hungry' ploughman's lunch – Cheddar or Stilton (£1.65). The milkmaid's lunch is crispbread and cottage cheese at the same price. Main dishes include grills, curries and pasta, all around the £3 mark, served with a choice of vegetables or salad, and there is always one vegetarian dish on the blackboard.

The Vintner Ⓥ

Crusader House, St Stephen's Street TEL (0272) 291222

OPEN Mon–Fri 7.30 am–10.30 am (breakfast), 10.30 am–2.30 pm, 5.30 pm–8.30 pm CLOSED Sat, Sun, public holidays CREDIT CARDS Access/Euro, Visa WHEELCHAIR ACCESS Impossible VEGETARIAN DISHES Plenty of choice NO-SMOKING AREA

Vintner must be the most overworked word in the *Wine Guide*, embracing all manner of establishments, but here its use is well merited. Jim Hood is a liveryman of the Worshipful Company of Vintners but he has chosen not to exercise his right as a Free Vintner and the bar's licence is granted by the local bench. He is also a director of Bristol's oldest wine merchants, Howells *(see* MERCHANTS *section)*, which ensures a well-balanced and more than adequate choice of wines. Most of the building that was above ground has suffered the combined disasters of wartime bombing and post-war planning but the patchwork masonry of brick and stone below incorporates part of the old city walls and, far from being draughty and austere, the narrow, vaulted cellars are cosy with nooks and niches and a handsome display of wine artefacts. When the weather is benign, there is welcome overflow into a courtyard adjoining St Stephen's church. The wine list contains about fifty wines, all under £6 and mostly drawn from the middle ranks of French vineyards. Sound bets are the VDQS's such as Sauvignon de St-Bris 1982 (£5.75) and the red and white Costières du Gard 1981, Domaine St Louis la Perdrix (£5.10/90p). There is a separate list of sixteen wines by the glass, goblet or jumbo – the latter being about a quarter of a bottle, and a very satisfying quantity to drink of the Ch Beauregard, AC Bordeaux, the most expensive at £2.25. The house wines are good, too, and reasonably priced (70p/95p/£1.60/£3.80). Finally, there is a supplementary 'fine wine' list of about a dozen wines of more than passing interest. An excellent 1978 Alsace Muscat (£5.75) is star of the whites, and the reds include Marqués de Cáceres 1973 Rioja Riserva (£6.80), Ch Musar 1977 (£6.05) and a Chilean Cabernet Sauvignon, Viña Linderos 1979 (£6.25). The Ch Broustet, Barsac 1971 (£7) provides a splendid accompaniment to the enterprising list of puddings. The moving spirit of the food side is Jim Hood's wife Janet, who, rather unexpectedly, presides over a battery of microwave ovens. But take heart – all the food is prepared the same day by a cohort of the Hoods' friends in their own kitchens. The homeworkers certainly come up with the goods: the reheated results are hard to fault. Favourites include stuffed mushrooms (£1.80) and a delicious, if prosaically named, 'Portuguese fish dish' (£3.30). Fish is very much a speciality, and locally caught Severn salmon is good in season. The blackboard menu changes frequently and features casseroles, moussaka and other satisfying dishes around the £3 mark, and a good selection of vegetables and salads. Those who bemoan the relatively early evening closing (the Vintner is very much in the business centre of the town) can always make an early start the next day and tuck into a hearty British breakfast.

BROADWAY Hereford and Worcester

Goblets

The Lygon Arms TEL (0386) 852255
OPEN Mon–Sat 11.30 am–2.30 pm, 6 pm–10.30 pm (Fri & Sat till 11 pm) Sun 12 noon–2 pm, 7 pm–10.30 pm Public holidays 11.30 am–2.30 pm, 6 pm–10.30 pm CLOSED 6 days at Chr CREDIT CARDS All accepted
WHEELCHAIR ACCESS Yes VEGETARIAN DISHES Prepared on request

Next door to, and owned by, The Lygon Arms, this small wine bar with attractive stone exterior and big inglenook fireplace, black-painted wooden beams and pillars, appeals perhaps not surprisingly to more than a few transatlantic visitors who flock to Broadway. They are met by an atmosphere of relaxed decorum and a list of just over 20 wines. Considering the stock of the parent establishment, the list is disappointingly short, but the wines are well chosen and the management thoughtfully displays vintages and other details. Apart from Lanson Black Label at £15.75 (a relatively low mark-up for them), bottle prices range from £4.75 for a Trockener Sekt Schloss Böchingen from the Rheinpfalz through a 1979 Bordeaux Supérieur, Ch Le Grand Verdus at £6.60, to a 1982 Pouilly Fumé at £8.45 from Monmousseau. A blackboard menu, which may offer curried egg mayonnaise at £1.25 or mushroom omelette with potatoes for £2.50 (made with free-range eggs), extends the printed menu's choice of dishes, such as barbecued spare ribs (£1.95) or sweet-and-sour chicken with rice (£3.50). Preparation is done at the Lygon, and heating and cooking to order at the wine bar.

Send us **your** views on the report forms at the back of the book.

BUNTINGFORD Hertfordshire

Bacchus

30 High Street TEL (0763) 72886

OPEN Tue–Sat 10.30 am–2.30 pm, 7.30 pm–10.30 pm (Fri & Sat till 11 pm) Sun 12 noon–2.30 pm, 7.30 pm–10.30 pm Public holidays 12 noon–2.30 pm
CLOSED Mon, public holiday evenings CREDIT CARDS Not accepted
WHEELCHAIR ACCESS One small step VEGETARIAN DISHES Variety of salads and pizzas

The warmth of the reception at this comfortable, oak-beamed wine bar in rural Hertfordshire makes it a favourite with locals and visitors alike. Care has been taken in selecting nearly fifty reasonably priced wines from around the world, and the list gives an informative note on most. Vintages are hand-written, as are late additions and prices. Regrettably, however, there is no indication of the shipper. Worth trying is the white Ch Loudenne 1979 (£6.30), the Chablis 1982 from Louis Bonard (£6.80) and the fifth-growth Ch du Tertre 1974 (£7.20). On a more modest scale, there is a Côtes-du-Rhône 1982 (£4.10) and Verdicchio dei Castelli di Jesi Classico (£4.20). Half-bottles of Piesporter (£2.50), Chablis (£3.50) and Médoc (£2.50) are also available for the abstemious. The food is wholesome and excellent value: sustaining home-made chicken and mushroom pie (£2.50) or moussaka (£1.90) and various salads, plus a mouth-watering selection of desserts, including an exotic raspberry Pavlova (90p) and very popular hot brandied peaches with cream (£1.50).

BURY ST EDMUNDS Suffolk

The Decanter

74–75 Whiting Street TEL (0284) 64488

OPEN Mon–Sat 12 noon–2 pm, 6 pm–11 pm Sun 12 noon–2 pm, 7 pm–10.30 pm Public holidays 12 noon–2 pm, 7 pm–11 pm CLOSED Chr Day
CREDIT CARDS Not accepted WHEELCHAIR ACCESS Impossible
VEGETARIAN DISHES Some

This is a splendid, cosy little wine bar, where a friendly welcome is given to all, service is attentive and the home-prepared food is of good quality and well presented. The wine list, which at the time of our visit was soon to be revised, offered 35 wines at most reasonable prices. House wines were 75p per glass, and favourite wine bar bottles from Germany and the Loire were under £5 a bottle. The new wine list will show a range of recently purchased Riojas at attractive prices, we are assured. The blackboard menu varies daily. At our visit, there was avocado and prawns (£1.50) as a starter, half a dozen snails in garlic (£1.50), chicken liver pâté with toast (95p) or canteloupe melon with port (£1.50). Main courses included chicken and ham Tetrazzini (£2.25), lamb kidneys in sherry served with vegetables and rice (£2.25) and mushroom quiche with jacket potato and salad (£1.95). Among the sweets at 75p you may find treacle tart and ice-cream, pear Bakewell and rum baba.

CAISTOR Lincolnshire

Caistor Wine Bar

9 South Street TEL (0472) 851206

OPEN Mon–Sat 11.30 am–2.30 pm, 7 pm–11 pm Sun 12 noon–2 pm, 7 pm–10.30 pm CLOSED Chr Day, Boxing Day CREDIT CARD Visa WHEELCHAIR ACCESS Yes VEGETARIAN DISHES By arrangement

You could if you wished come here once a week for three years and try a different wine each time. At that rate, it would take you four months just to get through the house wines, of which about a dozen are available by the glass from 55p; further delays may be caused by the proprietor's habit of having other interesting bottles open for you to try. You would find enough Champagne and sparkling wines to celebrate all Christmases and birthdays during that period twice over, including, for example, a Spanish Cordon Negro at £6.30. Spain otherwise offers mainly Torres wines from the Penedès; Italy is poorly represented, but you can while away your time in France with good clarets like Ch Meyney 1966 (£16.80), Ch Lagrange 1966 (£17.55), or 1976 (£16). The wine bar is by no means expensive, though, with plenty to suit all tastes and pockets. Likewise the food: they will do you anything from a double-decker cheese or ham sandwich (80p), through a Coggyburger (named after the local butcher, Cogham, who makes them) with chips and peas for £1.55, to a range of steaks from 8 oz to a staggering 24 oz (ring for an estimate). 'His 'n' Hers' gammon steaks provide unequal opportunities to gorge yourselves; availability of other dishes seems to depend on which chef is on duty. There are a couple of brollied tables outside – there are bound to be a few fine days in three years. Then you can start all over again.

CAMBERLEY Surrey

Rackhams

23 High Street TEL (0276) 29291

OPEN Mon–Thur 11.30 am–3 pm, 5.30 pm–10.30 pm Fri & Sat 11.30 am–3 pm, 5.30 pm–11 pm CLOSED Sun, public holidays CREDIT CARDS All accepted WHEELCHAIR ACCESS Yes VEGETARIAN DISHES Good range

The dark green brick façade of Rackhams is sandwiched in a parade of shops in the main shopping street of Camberley. Inside, the one spacious bar is simply furnished with bare boards and furniture built from wood taken from a redundant church; French café-style curtains blot out the street and hanging plants and fresh flowers on the table give a bit of colour. The wine list is basic and gives no details of vintage or supplier, but offers a fair range of French, Spanish, Italian and German generic wines for under £5 a bottle. House red, white and Tafelwein are £3.95/80p, and other wines available by the glass include Valpolicella and Chianti, both 85p. Though the list is uninspired, this is certainly the best of Camberley's wine bars. All the food is freshly prepared on the premises and the menu, which changes daily, could feature stuffed aubergines (£1.50), fisherman's lunch (£2.45) and pork Normandy (£2.45).

CAMBRIDGE Cambridgeshire

Brookes

25–26 Bridge Street TEL (0223) 321052

OPEN Mon–Sat 11 am–12.30 pm, 6 pm–11 pm Sun 12 noon–2 pm, 7 pm–10.30 pm CREDIT CARD Access/Euro WHEELCHAIR ACCESS Impossible VEGETARIAN DISHES Not provided (but fish and seafood)

Barry Dubas has been in the Cambridge wine-bar trade for six years but opened Brookes only last May. He seems to have got his sums right. The decor is very modern and pleasant with just the right amount of light and colour balance. Prints of country scenes hang unobtrusively on the walls. The wine bar is downstairs but there is also a small, enclosed courtyard. The wines are principally from Dolamore, and the house wine is an own-label French red and medium-dry white from Henri Gaillard (£3.60/65p). There is a Rosé de France vin de table from Vivienne Mackenzie, and plans for an own-label Champagne from Bernard Roland may by now have materialised. Fifteen wines are available by the glass, ranging from a Côte du Ventoux from Bellière at 80p to a sparkling French at £1.10, and a strawberry wine at 80p a glass. Bourgogne Blanc and Rouge from Clair Daü are just over the £8 mark and a cru bourgeois Margaux – Ch La Tour de Mons 1979 – just creeps in at under £10. The food is strong on seafood and shellfish, with prawns and Cromer crab well in evidence. They also offer their own home-made pâté and hot dishes such as lasagne and the chef's special dish of the day. The upper floor has been converted into a small, oak-beamed restaurant, seating about 70 people, and the menu offers the same basic selection as the wine bar, with the addition of some steak dishes. There are plans for private functions and parties as well as special 'gourmet evenings'. More reports, please!

Crusts

21 Northampton Street TEL (0223) 353110

OPEN Mon–Sat 12 noon–2.30 pm, 6 pm–11 pm Sun 12 noon–2 pm, 7 pm–10.30 pm CLOSED Chr Day CREDIT CARDS Access/Euro, Visa WHEELCHAIR ACCESS Yes VEGETARIAN DISHES Plenty

Plants, Victorian kettles, various bric-à-brac hanging from the ceiling, and the wines chalked up in psychedelic colours on blackboards in various nooks and crannies as well as upon the low wooden beams (mind your head), set the scene. Crusts is part of a group of six wine bars scattered over the country, with this Cambridge site the latest venture. There are plans for a gentlemen's club upstairs, complete with leather seats and draped curtains. The restaurant offers a wide selection of steaks, pies, burgers, chilli con carne, etc. The menu has a good choice, with extra daily specials chalked up on the bar. Sadly, though, the wine list is still lacking in character and originality. The Crust group buys exclusively from Grierson Blumenthal and the nondescript Arc de Triomphe house wine is well in evidence again, as on so many wine bar lists (£3.95 a bottle, red, white and rosé or 85p a glass). There is a basic range of 32 wines, eight available by the glass. The Olarra Rioja at £1 a glass looks interesting and there is a Côte de Beaune 1979 at just under £10 a bottle. There were plans in the outrageous cocktail bar to produce the ultimate cocktail, costing £100, to be served in an enormous Victorian pot. One wonders, however, whether, despite all these new gimmicks, their time would not be better spent in getting back to their wine-bar roots and producing a more noteworthy list.

Flambards

4–6 Rose Crescent TEL (0223) 358108

OPEN Mon–Sat 10.30 am–2.30 pm, 6 pm–11 pm Sun 12 noon–1 pm, 7 pm–10.30 pm CREDIT CARDS Not accepted
WHEELCHAIR ACCESS Impossible VEGETARIAN DISHES Plenty

You can sit outside in the precinct and watch the tourists and trendies go by, or descend the narrow steps into the cellar bar for its typical bistro-style atmosphere. Of two things you can be assured: friendly, courteous service and a good selection of wine and food. There is a choice of sixty wines, all supplied by Turner Fanshaw of Essex. The house wine is the Caves des Tonneaux, red/white/rosé at £3.95/80p. There are half a dozen other house wines by bottle and glass, but no half-bottles. A small bin-end list is worth studying. On our visit, it yielded a Volnay, Champons 1979 (£15.60) and a good value Mercurey 1978 from Domaine Maurice Protheaux (£9.60). Italy and Germany are also well represented. A small salad bar offers 20 different salads as well as a typical cold buffet. There is also a set lunch for £2.50. The menu changes daily and vegetarians are well catered for by a special vegetarian pie, ratatouille, and curried bananas. Live music every lunchtime, usually by a local pianist, but occasionally other artists, and there is also a Monday night disco. Watch out also for special events such as Bastille Day and Chinese New Year, well celebrated here in authentic style and costume.

> Readers' reports submitted to *The Good Food Guide* as well as *Which? Wine Guide* have been used to supplement official inspectors' reports in compiling this section.

The Last Resort

59 Hills Road TEL (0223) 312022

OPEN Mon–Fri 12 noon–2.30 pm, 7.30 pm–12 pm Sat 12.30 pm–2.30 pm, 7.30 pm–12 pm Sun 7.30 pm–10.30 pm CLOSED Sun L, public holidays CREDIT CARD Amex WHEELCHAIR ACCESS Yes VEGETARIAN DISHES On request

We are told that on some evenings an English voice is nowhere to be heard at this wine bar in the heart of the language school community. The upstairs area is used as a coffee bar during the day, with a small cocktail bar in the back that opens in the evening, and a disco downstairs. The wine bar on the ground floor has a selection of sixty inexpensive wines ranging from the house Italian Merlot at 70p a glass to a Portuguese Barrocão Garrafeira 1960 at £8 a bottle (which, we are told, needs 24 hours' notice). Portugal and Italy are well represented, but beware: no vintages specified. Any wine under £5 is also available by the glass and there are some half-bottles, too. Daniel Merecki has a particular fondness for Swiss wines and is constantly off to Switzerland, importing his own, to be served in a small Swiss-style bistro that is to be opened soon. At lunchtime, there is a good selection of cold meats and salads as well as simple hot dishes such as lasagne and moussaka. In the evening, the food is more French bistro style, with dishes such as fillet steak cooked in Armagnac, and frogs' legs, etc.

Shades

1 King's Parade TEL (0223) 359506

OPEN Mon–Sat 11.30 am–2.30 pm, 6 pm–11 pm Sun 12 noon–2 pm, 7 pm–10.30 pm CLOSED 4 days Chr CREDIT CARDS All accepted WHEELCHAIR ACCESS Impossible VEGETARIAN DISHES Some available, with notice

David Carter has been running Shades Restaurant opposite King's College Chapel for the last 12 years and has achieved his success through consistency in his selection of wines and the quality of his food – you wouldn't make a detour for the wine. The wine bar is downstairs; a white-walled cellar with intimate atmosphere for students, visitors and businessmen alike. Mr Carter offers a diverse choice of wines by the glass, ranging from his vin de table from the Loire valley (65p) to Bourgogne La Vignée (£1). Germany and France are best represented on his list in a selection of approximately 50 wines, but no half-bottles are available. At lunchtime, a selection of cold meats, pies and about ten different types of salads are offered, wholesome and nicely presented. Seasonal foods are always on offer, often smoked mackerel when it's at its best in the winter, and the pâtés are all made locally. Vegetarian food can be prepared, if prior notice is given. Unobtrusive classical music against a term-time buzz of students.

CANTERBURY Kent

Alberry's

38 St Margaret Street TEL (0227) 52378

OPEN Mon–Sat 12 noon–2.30 pm, 6.30–12 pm CLOSED Sun, public holidays
CREDIT CARDS Access/Euro, Visa WHEELCHAIR ACCESS Yes
VEGETARIAN DISHES Always available

A Roman wall has been exposed in Alberry's cosy cellar bar. It is cool in summer, warm in winter, and a welcoming retreat for locals or visitors to the cathedral just a few hundred yards away. The wine list is comprehensive, starting with French table wine at 70p a glass and house wines at 90p (a selection of five including a red and white Burgundy AC from Colcombet Frères at £5.40), and rising modestly to Ch La Tour de By at £8.15, with Champagnes from G Pannier NV at £14 to Dom Pérignon 1975 (£35). Apart from the Champagnes, all the wines on the list are reasonably priced. Wines are anonymously listed, but you might end with Loires and Rhônes from Moreau, Beaujolais and Burgundies from Dépagneux, Alsace wines from the Cave Co-opérative d'Ingersheim, or CVNE Riojas, and some better Germans than usual, too. The late happy hour between 6.30 and 9 pm (Monday to Saturday) is worth aiming for. Alberry's is always full of people tucking into moules provençale, chilli or lasagne, garlic spare ribs or 'chicken mole' (spices and chocolate and a few other secret ingredients!). The dishes change daily, and most hungers can be satisfied for £1 to £3.75. Classical music or jazz at lunch-time, pop in the evening (live on Mondays, Tuesdays and Thursdays). Helpful proprietors are always on hand.

CARDIFF South Glamorgan

La Brasserie Ⓥ ☞

60 St Mary Street TEL (0222) 372164

OPEN Mon–Sat 12 noon–3 pm, 7 pm–12.30 am CLOSED Sun CREDIT CARDS All accepted WHEELCHAIR ACCESS Yes VEGETARIAN DISHES Not provided

If Champers Wine Bar (next door to La Brasserie – *see below*) is the outstanding wine bar specialising in Spanish wines, then the cosmopolitan Brasserie would be the French equivalent in the principality. Simplicity and value for money is the successful formula here. The wine list is comprehensive, though sometimes not quoting shippers' names, and the overall standard of wines is excellent. Prices are also more than fair. Star buys include Louis Gisselbrecht Riesling (£6.50), André Dézat Sancerre (£7.50) and an outstanding Muscadet (Serge de Berthenais) at £5. The reds include a fine range of Beaujolais from Maison Faye, all fairly priced, but rises to the expensive heights of Ch Ducru-Beaucaillou 1975 at £18, and Ch Haut-Brion 1966 at £46. La Brasserie had a house Burgundy when we called, Savigny-lès-Beaune Le

Village 1980 from Henri de Villamont (£7.95). The house Champagne, Laurent-Perrier, is £9.95. The food is simple, but great value for money: it includes spit-roasted suckling pig, honeyed crispy duck, fresh sea bass (most days), all at £5.95. Starters are interesting, but limited. There are no sweets, but a small selection of French cheeses, which could be increased and improved. All the main courses are served with a jacket potato and a selection of salads. A walk-in cellar has recently been opened where customers are invited to select their claret from a list of thirty or so leading wines of the Médoc, ten Graves and twenty St-Emilions and Pomerols. The vintages include all the classics since 1970 and customers are encouraged to order 24 hours in advance so that the wine can be brought to the correct temperature. It seems that every effort has been made to improve the quality of wines on offer. This is one of the few establishments which actually take a pride in their 'ordinary' German wines. It is a shame that the house red and white cannot be recommended (£3.85).

Champers Ⓥ

61 St Mary Street TEL (0222) 373363
OPEN 12 noon–3 pm, 7 pm–12.30 am Sun 7 pm–12.30 am CLOSED Sun L
CREDIT CARDS All accepted WHEELCHAIR ACCESS Yes
VEGETARIAN DISHES Not provided

The happy atmosphere and the bonhomie of the staff is equalled only by its twin next door *(La Brasserie)*. The food is along traditional UK lines, simple but outstanding value for money, though lacking in the Spanish flavour you might expect from a wine bar owned by a Spaniard and specialising in the finest Spanish wines. Starters include shrimps served in pint pots (£1.95) or hot with garlic sauce (£2.35), dressed crab (£2.25), sardines (£2.35). For the main course, you might choose the wonderful pork kebabs at £2.35, unusual but very tasty fish kebabs (£3.20), huge spare ribs (£2.35), home-made hamburgers (£3.25) or top quality steaks and pork chops. All dishes are barbecued and served with jacket potato. The wine list is built around an outstanding selection of Rioja, which includes Vega Sicilia Gran Reserva 1962 at £150 per bottle – any takers? – but the list of attractive and low-priced Rioja is too large to mention individual wines. Suffice it to say that it is unequalled in the UK. Unfortunately, house red and white are very ordinary (£3.85), though the German list has shown an improvement in quality over the past year. The house Champagne, Laurent-Perrier, is very reasonable at £9.95. Well worth a detour.

Special awards

Ⓥ is for bargain prices

[bottle symbol] is for a very good range of wines

[hand symbol] is for exceptional service.

Trillium

40 City Road TEL (0222) 463665

OPEN Mon–Sat 11.30 am–3 pm, 5 pm–11 pm CLOSED Sun
CREDIT CARDS Access/Euro, Amex, Visa WHEELCHAIR ACCESS Yes
VEGETARIAN DISHES Limited choice

This interesting wine bar opened in the late spring of 1984. The main room is decorated in the old-fashioned style of a London gentlemen's club reading room and library. A further room, contrasting dramatically with this, is like a conservatory, each table surrounded by trellises and plants. The wine list is outstanding by any standards, running to wines from fifteen different countries. House wines include a range of excellent vins de table (£3.75), where quality has obviously been uppermost in the proprietor's mind. An interesting selection of French country wines and German wines is available by the glass at reasonable prices (70p to £1.10). In addition to the high quality Muscadet, Vouvray and Sancerre in the Loire section, there is Coulée de Serrant 1964. Amongst the white Bordeaux, Ch d'Yquem 1976 is listed at £57 a bottle, but probably the best value for money here is the Sauvignon Trois Mouline, extremely refreshing at £5 a bottle. On the white Burgundy list, Chablis Grand Cru Bouguerots from Domaine Jouchère seems very reasonable at £10.35. There is an interesting list of Southern French reds, plus a good house claret at £5.60. The section of ten classified growths dates from as far back as 1952: Ch Léoville-Las-Cases (£50) and Ch La Lagune 1966 (£30.50). The Beaujolais come from both Mommessin and Maison Faye, the Rhône from good sources, including Côte-Rotie, Chapoutier, 1959 at £27. The Burgundy section, starting with Mâcon Rouge from Henri de Villamont at £5.70 and finishing with Gevrey-Chambertin from Docteur Barolet, 1937 at £69.75, also has some mouth-watering wines; between these extremes, you can find Bonnes-Mares, Domaine Drouhin Laroze, 1976, Morey-Saint-Denis from Chauvenet, 1969, and Clos de Bèze, Domaine Drouhin Laroze, 1961. The choice of food is limited to four or five dishes per day, but each is individually cooked on demand. The Welsh proprietor's years spent on the other side of the Atlantic are reflected in the menu, so you might be offered French Canadian onion soup (£1.50), New England clam chowder (at £2 the best clam chowder to reach the principality), Kentucky burgoo (£3.25), a most unusual lasagne verde ragoût (£3), and an interesting selection of vol-au-vents, which are a meal in themselves. The service is as impeccable as the wine and food.

If you disagree with us, please tell us why. You will find report forms at the back of the book.

CHELTENHAM Gloucestershire

Forrest

1 Imperial Lane TEL (0242) 38001

OPEN Mon–Sat 10.30 am–2.30 pm, 6.30 pm–11.30 pm CLOSED Sun, Chr and Easter bank holidays CREDIT CARDS Not accepted WHEELCHAIR ACCESS Yes VEGETARIAN DISHES Good

A typed menu, which changes daily, is the welcoming sign displayed outside this long-established wine bar. An adventurous variety of three hot dishes at different price levels is offered. One dish is always vegetarian, such as gnocchi, layered gratin, stuffed cabbage rolls (£2.50), and other choices might be marinated lamb kebabs with spiced rice (£3.50) or grilled rump steak (£5.50). There is also a good range of cold dishes. This gastronomic boost may be needed, as the wine bar is windowless. Inside, the dark brown paintwork is rather oppressive, making for gloom rather than intimacy. Combined with the wipe-clean furnishings, the effect is more coffee bar than wine bar. But the moment you open the informative wine list you are left in no doubt as to the true nature of the establishment. The bias is towards the costlier wines from the traditional areas: of the nine clarets on the list, only one is under £8 and on the list as a whole, nearly half the wines are in double figures. There's Mouton 1970 at £96.80, Ducru-Beaucaillou 1970 at £46.65, Montrose at £33 – all more than 100 per cent up on top prices at auction, and in some cases nearer to 300 per cent. You can drink Tollot-Beaut Burgundies, Ch de Beaucastel Châteauneuf-du-Pape, Guigal and Paul Jaboulet Aîné Rhônes. You could have bought a whole case of Moulin Touchais 1959 at auction a couple of years ago for the price of just over three bottles here (£17.25 each). But anyway, the bar simply doesn't provide the environment in which to enjoy such wines and would do better to provide more choice at lower prices. Currently, the best of these are in the Spanish section – Viña Ardanza 1976 (£6.13) and a good range of Torres wines; or try the Vacqueyras 1981 from the Producteurs Associés (£6.30). The excellent Hill Smith Shiraz and Riesling are perhaps best value on the list at around £6.

CHEPSTOW Gwent

The Grape Escape

24 St Mary Street TEL (029 120) 70959

OPEN Mon–Sat 10 am–3 pm, 5.30 pm–11 pm Sun 12 noon–2 pm, 7 pm–10.30 pm CREDIT CARDS Not accepted WHEELCHAIR ACCESS Yes VEGETARIAN DISHES Usually some

Philip Major's delightful wine bar set in the pretty town of Chepstow continues to be well recommended. The standard of food, at one time above criticism, has lately elicited criticisms of careless serving, not to mention re-heated main dishes. There is a special daily dish, which can be spicy chilli, plentiful steak and kidney pie or goulash, though there have been grumbles about the rabbit in white wine, and spare ribs fit for dieters only. The wine list is still comprehensive, though the cheaper range of both French and German now come from poorer quality sources. The main body of the list includes interesting petits-châteaux and a few wines from the satellites of Bordeaux, plus all the first growths from leading vintages of the 1960s and 1970s. One questions the popularity amongst the local farmers of Ch Pétrus 1971 at £99.35 a bottle, or the most expensive wine, Ch d'Yquem 1947, at £195.50. The Beaujolais section is unfortunately built around the 1979 and 1981 vintages, which seems both unnecessary and rather strange as most leading merchants are offering the 1982 and superior 1983 vintages. It is also strange that a list supposedly concentrating on top quality wines should offer only 1980 and 1981 vintages of white Burgundy, and not a single 1978 or 1979. When we visited, Muscadet de Sèvre-et-Maine was available at £6.30, but the only other quality Loire white was the Anjou Blanc 1964 from Moulin Touchais. Of all the white wines available, probably the pick of the bunch is the Muscat d'Alsace 1981 from Louis Gisselbrecht at £6.60. The list also includes wines from Portugal, Hungary, South Africa, California and lesser-known wine-growing districts, such as John Bevan's 1982 Croffta, probably the only commercial wine made in Wales. This establishment is still worth a visit, but it is sad to see the overall standard of the wines declining unnecessarily, especially as the prices have not been reduced with the introduction of some inferior products.

CHESTER Cheshire

Clavertons

37 Lower Bridge Street TEL (0244) 319760

OPEN Mon–Sat 11 am–3 pm, 5.30 pm–10.30 pm Sun 12 noon–2.30 pm, 7 pm–10.30 pm CLOSED Chr Day CREDIT CARDS Not accepted WHEELCHAIR ACCESS Very difficult VEGETARIAN DISHES One dish daily, changed 2 or 3 times a week

This wine bar is owned by the Grosvenor Hotel, Chester. The bar down one side of the large room serves beers, lagers and spirits as well as wine. Perhaps more than the other Chester wine bars, Clavertons has two distinct types of customer: at lunch-times, it serves shoppers, office workers and businessmen. At night, it is more of a young people's pub with mostly beer and lager sold. The house wines are good and drinkable Litre Vin (£2.50 per half-litre/65p), supplied by Duttons of Chester. The Côtes-du-Rhône is also worth drinking and is served by the glass (85p); it is more interesting than the other wines sold by the glass: Anjou Rosé, Valpolicella, and Lambrusco (70p), Muscadet, claret, Beaujolais (85p), and Liebfraumilch (75p). Some wines are featured as special offers: at the time of our visit these were Bordeaux Blanc and Corbières VDQS (£3.65), and Jules Mignon Champagne (£9.60). The hot dishes change daily, but are available only at lunchtime: chicken à la king and rice (£1.95), baked potatoes and mushroom sauce (95p), Cumberland sausage with salad (£1.95). The evening cold food service of turkey, pâté, beef, quiche, game pie, chicken, cheese and mackerel fillet (£1.95) is more than adequate but stops at 8 pm, sometimes earlier. Ask about the salads even if they're not on display.

Dukes

18 Mercia Square TEL (0244) 23469

OPEN Mon–Sat 11.30 am–3.15 pm, 5.30 pm–10.30 pm CLOSED Sun
CREDIT CARDS Not accepted WHEELCHAIR ACCESS Impossible
VEGETARIAN DISHES Salads or quiche

Up in this elevated square over the shopping precinct, Dukes, one of the Deering Restaurant chain, overlooks Chester Cathedral. To one side is a restaurant, to the other a real ale bar. The decor is modern, and dim lights reveal one or two recesses along one wall, and old pub tables. The wine list is unimaginative and although the list states 'vintage years may vary', no vintages are listed. But the wines are reasonably priced. You might be happy with Côtes du Roussillon-Villages (£3.85), Sauvignon de Touraine (£4), sparkling Saumur Brut or Demi-Sec (£6.25) or house claret (£4.10). The house red and dry white are both French, 'Les Chevaliers': the white is commercial, clean and fresh, the red rather dull (and not very nice). Also by the glass are Muscadet (70p), Côtes-du-Rhône (80p), Valpolicella (67p) and Yugoslav Riesling (65p), and larger glasses are on hand for 93p. At lunch-time, you can help yourself to a choice of twelve salads displayed on a tile-covered counter, and appetising ham, cheese, prawn, quiche or mackerel to go with the salads (£2.30 to £2.50). Different dishes are also available: kidneys, tomato and mushrooms in a wine sauce served on a bed of rice (£2), scampi and chips (£2.30), rump steak, salad and chips (£3.75). These hot dishes are also available in the evenings, as are salads, but made to order (£1.20). Beware! Dukes stop serving food at 7 pm.

Pierre Griffe

4–6 Mercia Square TEL (0244) 312635

OPEN Mon–Fri 11.30 am–3 pm, 5.30 pm–10.30 pm (Fri till 11 pm) Sat 11 am–3 pm, 5.30 pm–11 pm Sun 12 noon–2 pm (May–Sept), 7 pm–10.30 pm
CLOSED Chr Day, Boxing Day, New Year's Day, Good Fri, Easter Mon L
CREDIT CARDS Not accepted WHEELCHAIR ACCESS By ramp to Mercia Square upper level VEGETARIAN DISHES One special dish changes daily

Pierre Griffe is a busy wine bar, with plenty of seating outside on the patio overlooking Chester city walls and the Cathedral. Inside, scrubbed wooden tables, and blackboards everywhere proclaim dishes of the day, wine offers and even £1 off every bottle (or 20p off a glass) at 'happy hour' – 5.30 to 7.30 pm. The standard list offers a reasonably priced selection of popular wines with a sprinkling of the more unusual, like a 1979 red Dão (£4.50) and a 1978 Zinfandel (£4.70). (Can we have shippers'/producers' names on the list, please?) There is also a specials list of five red and five white wines, offering such rarities as unusually mature vintages (1972/3) of Ch Musar red (£6.50), Ch Dutruch Grand Poujeaux 1977 (£5.45) or the refreshing 1983 Hill Smith Estate Australian Riesling (£5.40). Cold food consists of a choice of cheese, pâtés and pies with mixed salad and will cost you around £2, while inexpensive daily hot dishes such as spicy Italian meatballs (£2.20), coq au vin (£2.25) or beef in Guinness and orange sauce (with rice and side salad) are £2.35. It's best to eat at lunch-time or before 8.30 pm (serving stops at 9 pm). Any later, and you get to play sardines with the Chester under-30s set.

CIRENCESTER Gloucestershire

Shepherd's

Fleece Hotel, Market Place TEL (0285) 68507

OPEN Mon–Sat 10.30 am–3 pm, 7 pm–11 pm Sun 10.30 am–3 pm, 7–10.30 pm CLOSED Chr Day CREDIT CARDS All accepted WHEELCHAIR ACCESS Yes VEGETARIAN DISHES Various

Centrally situated in the Market Square, Shepherd's Wine Bar, part of the Fleece Hotel, recreates a rustic past with lots of wood and panelling, and sawdust on the floor. It is cool in summer, warm in winter, and central alcoves make nice snugs in which to settle with a bottle. The range of wines is good, including such essential lunchtime wines as a Bourgeuil 1982 (£5.95) and some good Cru Beaujolais. Some of the wines go back surprisingly far, such as a Bourgogne Rouge (Caves Buxy) 1976 (£6.95) and some very reasonably priced stunners such as a Côte-Rôtie (Domaine de Vallouit) 1979 (£10.20). Some excellent California wines are also represented (Clos du Val Zinfandel 1978, £10.75), Australian (McWilliams Cabernet-Shiraz 1978, £6.35) and New Zealand (Cooks' rich, buttery Chardonnay 1980, £9.20). There is a printed menu with dishes of the day both cold (including a variety of smoked fish) and hot (several good pies) which can include some filling casseroles. Service, however, can sometimes be less than friendly.

COLCHESTER Essex

Troupers

21 Head Street TEL (0206) 47474

OPEN Mon–Sat 11 am–2.30 pm, 6 pm–11 pm CLOSED Sun, public holidays CREDIT CARDS All accepted WHEELCHAIR ACCESS Impossible VEGETARIAN DISHES Salads

Troupers received an enthusiastic report in the *1984 Guide* but this year's visit proved to be a little disappointing. The flair and style that were evident last year seemed to be missing on the day of our inspection. Forty-four wines are offered on a list which is much the same as, if not identical to, last year's. Most wines carry descriptions, but house rosé, for example, bears the illuminating comment, 'You don't have to be in Juin les Pins to enjoy it.' House wines are reasonably priced – between £4.05 and £5.75 a bottle/82p and £1.17 a glass, and are well chosen to suit most tastes. Popular German wines range from £4.35 to £4.85, Muscadet is £5.05, Bourgogne Aligoté £6.75 and Loron's Ch de Fleurie £7.05, from a list drawn mainly from Lay & Wheeler and Turner Fanshawe. The menu is interesting. You can kick off with winter chowder (medium £1.50, large £3) or mussels, amongst a variety of starters. Of the more enterprising main dishes, cheese fondue (minimum two people) is £2.25 per person or try the barbecued spare ribs (medium £1.50, large £3). There are also traditional dishes like beefsteak, potato and onion pie with chips and peas – good value at £1.95. Sweets or cheese are 95p and coffee 35p.

CONGLETON Cheshire

Odd Fellows

20 Rood Hill TEL (026 02) 70243

OPEN Mon–Sat 12 noon–2 pm, 6.30 pm–10.30 pm (Sat till 11 pm) CLOSED Sun, Chr Day, Boxing Day, New Year's Day, public holidays CREDIT CARD Amex WHEELCHAIR ACCESS Ramp at rear VEGETARIAN DISHES Good selection

What this former pub may lack in polish it more than makes up for in enthusiasm. The attempts to please the customer extend even to offering to exchange a bottle if you simply don't like the wine you've ordered. The list gets off to a good start with ten Alsace wines, usually a sign that the host takes more than a passing interest in his wares; these include Gewürztraminers from Gisselbrecht, 1981 (£6.95) and Hugel, 1979 Réserve Personnelle (£11.95). Burgundies are few, but Bordeaux offers a 1979 red Graves, Ch de l'Etoile for £6.35, and the Rhônes are mouth-watering: Châteauneuf-du-Pape, Domaine du Vieux Télégraphe 1980, £9.65; Cornas, Paul Jaboulet Aîné 1980, £9.80. From Germany there is a balanced selection of mostly young Rhine and Mosel wines, with a couple of dry Franken wines for interest, eg Stettener Stein Kabinett 1979, £9.45. Italy and Spain are comparatively dull, although there is a Torres Gran Coronas 1979 for £7.85. South Africa is unusually featured with half a dozen KWV wines: a Steen/Chenin Blanc 1981/82 at £5.35, and Cabernet Sauvignon 1979, Roodeberg 1980 and Pinotage 1978, all at £5.75. Champagne and sparklers, and a couple of Australians, bring up the rear of a generally well-assembled 100-strong list, which gives welcome details of vintages and shippers. Most wines are reasonably priced at under £8 but a few special bottles pop up, like Ch Talbot 1978 (£16.95). In addition, the bar offers a vinous surprise of the week, available by the glass, to keep one step ahead of the regulars. When we visited, it was a rather unexciting Rioja Cruzado 1979 (£4.60/75p) but other weeks' may be better. The food is not the cheapest you'll come across, but it is made on the premises, varies frequently, and helpings are generous; you might enjoy the likes of aubergine and potato casserole (£2.85), tandoori chicken salad (£3.95) or 'drunken bullock' with rice (£4.85). Toffee and apple crumble, hot chocolate fudge cake and lemon dreams are all £1.05.

COVENTRY West Midlands

Clarets

Warwick Row, Greyfriars Green TEL (0203) 22623

OPEN Mon–Thur 11.30 am–2.30 pm, 6 pm–10.30 pm Fri–Sat 11.30 am–2.30 pm, 6 pm–11 pm Sun 11.30 am–2.30 pm, 7 pm–10.30 pm CLOSED Chr Day L, Boxing Day L, public holidays L CREDIT CARDS Not accepted WHEELCHAIR ACCESS Difficult, and lavatories downstairs VEGETARIAN DISHES Salads and quiche

Part of the West Midlands Taverns chain *(see Horts, Edgbaston)*. From leafy Warwick Row, you enter what appears to be a sedate country-house living room with big fireplace and bookshelves; but if you are hoping to find a gentle atmosphere at Clarets, you must choose your time of the week with care. On a weekend evening, Bulls' Blood rather than claret would be more appropriate to describe the feel of it, as young lads pile in as if through a turnstile at a Cup Final; to survive the thumping disco sounds, you need to be young and trendy – or possibly old and deaf. *(See Horts for details of the wines.)* The menu is mostly routine, but if you can stand the culture clash, you could treat yourself to a black pudding pizza for £1.10.

Corks

4/5 Whitefriars Street TEL (0203) 23628

OPEN Mon–Sat 11 am–2.30 pm, 6 pm–11 pm Sun 7 pm–10.30 pm Public holidays 7 pm–11 pm CLOSED Sun L and public holidays L CREDIT CARDS All accepted WHEELCHAIR ACCESS Yes VEGETARIAN DISHES Some

What Corks' fabric may lack in sparkle, with its dark wood and brick, softened by a little greenery and green paint, is likely to be made up for by its decorative clientèle. There are plenty of tables, and enough space, to accommodate quiet twosomes as well as lively hen parties. Service is friendly. Highlights in an otherwise straightforward list of 30 wines mostly in the £4 to £7 price range include a Cahors at £5.50, a Champagne (Henri Goutorbe) for a very reasonable £9.15 and a Ch Montrose at £10.15. Faustino Rioja (£5) and a 1982 Chablis (£6.90) from Thorin appear good value; white Burgundy includes a Pouilly Fuissé and a Meursault. Sadly, no details of vintages or shippers are given on the list. Apart from a Bereich Bernkastel (68p/£4.15), the only wines available by the glass are the dependable house wines which come in glass (65p), goblet (90p), half-litre (£2.55) and litre (£4.90). Value for money extends to the food, where even garlic bread is a snip at 16p. Pizzas (£1.10) are good: the base is first-class and rather more authentic than the topping. If you don't fancy lasagne (£1.30), chilli con carne (£1.30), salads (£1.30–£1.95) or whatever the daily special happens to be (£3), you can trade up into the restaurant for one of a variety of steaks at under £6.

COWBRIDGE Glamorgan

Farthings Old Wine House

54 High Street TEL (044 63) 2990

OPEN Mon–Sat 11.30 am–3 pm, 5.30 pm–12 pm CLOSED Sun
CREDIT CARDS Not accepted WHEELCHAIR ACCESS Yes
VEGETARIAN DISHES Always something interesting

This tastefully modernised wine bar is the central meeting place of the local community. Morning coffee and afternoon teas are served in addition to the normal wine bar business. Wines from twelve countries include outstanding house red and white (80p a glass). A comprehensive list of Loire and Beaujolais star in the French section, all from the leading producers in each area: these include Sancerre from André Dézat at £9.95, Vouvray at £6.50 and Fleurie from Mommessin and Ch des Tour, Brouilly, both at £8.50. Most of the German wines come from impeccable sources (unusually). This pretty wine bar, so full of atmosphere, and run in such a friendly manner, is let down by indifferent food, but should go from strength to strength when/if improvements to the menu are introduced.

CREDITON Devon

Grapevine

1 St Lawrence Green TEL (036 32) 4107

OPEN Mon, Tue 7 pm–12 pm Wed–Fri 12.30 pm–2 pm, 7 pm–12 pm
Sat 7 pm–12 pm CLOSED Mon & Tue L, Sun, public holidays, 3 weeks early spring CREDIT CARDS Not accepted WHEELCHAIR ACCESS Yes
VEGETARIAN DISHES Several starters, always one main dish

This handsome building was once a Victorian dairy. The yard at the back, where the cows were milked, is set with tables for summer use. The wine bar, now in its fourth year, has been in the *Guide* before but has recently changed hands. Reportedly, the new regime has had its teething problems, the result as much of over-enthusiasm as anything else, but now seems to have settled down – although describing Rougemont Castle Red and White, not recommended even at £3, as English wine is unlikely to endear the Keens to West Country vineyard owners. Otherwise, the wine list is straightforward and reasonably priced although a bit of a City Vintagers look-alike. The house wines, all French – two white, a rosé and a red – cost 70p for a fairly generous glass and are the only half-bottles (£2) on the list. In the well-equipped kitchens, Mrs Keen, working with local ingredients, puts her previous experience in outside catering to good effect. There is a short and sensible menu, changed weekly, and reduced to three main course dishes at lunchtime. The home-made pâté (95p) was appetising and beef in red wine (£3.90), with an attractive salad, warm and satisfying. More reports, please.

DATCHET Berkshire

Chez Petit Laurent

Country Life House,
Slough Road TEL (075 35) 49314

OPEN Mon–Sat 11 am–2.30 pm, 6 pm–10.30 pm (Fri & Sat till 11 pm)
CLOSED Sun and public holidays CREDIT CARD Visa
WHEELCHAIR ACCESS Yes VEGETARIAN DISHES Some

Wooden case ends and a profusion of bottles in their racks in the bar area *chez* Petit Laurent contrast with the bare brick decor and spartan seating, like pews from a modern church. Though hardly extensive, the wine list offers a token presence from the various major wine-producing areas of the world. All wines are reasonably priced, and both vintages and descriptions are clearly shown. Most commendably, each section boasts a non-standard brand or name, thus encouraging a little experimentation. House red is Domaine de Petit Chaumont, house white a Blanc de Blancs (both £3.90/75p). The place appears to be a haunt of the lively local beautiful set, but they probably avoid the food; and the myopic amongst them will find choosing difficult from the blackboards. The choice seems limited to highly spiced dishes; the food itself betrays its microwave history: bland, tasteless and pathetically limp on the plate. Portions are depressingly minute. Moral – come here for a drink, but eat elsewhere.

DARLINGTON Co Durham

Newbus Arms Hotel

Neasham TEL (0325) 721071

OPEN Mon–Sat 12 noon–3 pm, 6.30 pm–10.30 pm Sun 12 noon–2 pm, 7 pm–10.30 pm CLOSED Chr Day, Boxing Day CREDIT CARDS All accepted
WHEELCHAIR ACCESS Yes VEGETARIAN DISHES Some

In the entrance hall of this imposing hotel, John and Amanda Willmott have successfully created a wine bar and bistro for those not wishing to step beyond to the restaurant. The tables are small and cluttered, but for the atmosphere of this little room with log fire and panelled walls, you can put up with a certain amount of discomfort. The blackboard menu is changed regularly: there are always two 'chef's specials' of the day, perhaps excellent home-made soup (65p), snails (£2 per half-dozen), steak and mushroom pie (£2.95), deep-fried frogs' legs (£2). Speciality of the house is fondue (£5.95), and sweets are home-made (£1). Wines of the week, with useful tasting notes, range from French house wine (£4), through Australian Barossa Valley red and white (£6.50) and excellent Fine Traditional Claret (£5.90), to Côtes du Lubéron red and white from Provence at 75p a glass. The full wine list has 97 very well chosen wines, 71 from France, the rest from Germany, Italy, Portugal, Australia, California and Spain. Prices tend to be on the high side: mark-up here is obviously a percentage. Chablis 1983 from Robert Sarrau is £8.40 per bottle and Ch Cissac 1973 £13. Jean Vatan's good red Sancerre is £9.95. For smaller budgets, try Côtes du Ventoux, La Vieille Ferme 1982 for £5.95, or, surprisingly low-priced, the delicious Hill Smith Riesling (£6.50) or Hill Smith Estate Red from Australia (also £6.50).

DENHAM Buckinghamshire

Tapas (V)

Station Parade TEL (0895) 833048

OPEN Mon–Fri 12 noon–2.30 pm Mon–Sat 6 pm–10.30 pm CLOSED Sat L, Sun CREDIT CARDS Access, Amex, Diners, Visa WHEELCHAIR ACCESS Yes VEGETARIAN DISHES Some

Tapas has been tacked on to the side of La Capelle restaurant as a more informal off-shoot, and as a means for the Spanish owners to promote a little more actively the food and wine of the Peninsula. You could be forgiven for failing to realise that a wine bar actually exists here, swallowed up in the façade of La Capelle as it is. And even those who go inside might wonder if they have come to the right place. If you are after the buzz of trendy bars, or the romance of candlelit corners, you will not be thrilled by Tapas. This bar is unashamedly devoted to food and wine. You provide your own entertainment. The wine list offers an enterprising range of Spanish wines, both red and white, not only from Rioja, but also from Navarra and Valdepeñas. No single wine merits specific recommendation – all are worth trying and well priced in the £5 to £6 bracket. There is a token French and German list, but surely no one comes here specially for them. Food reveals the same Spanish orientation – squid, mussels and fabulous sardinas a la plancha for under £3. All the ingredients come fresh from the market. Helpings are not generous, but satisfying anyway. Praise goes also to the service, which is obliging and delightfully friendly. For those who seek the taste of Spain without the castanets, this is the place to go.

Do **you** know of any more bars that deserve inclusion in next year's *Guide*? If so, write and tell us on the report forms at the back of the book.

DEVIZES Wiltshire

The Grapevine

13 High Street TEL (0380) 6681

OPEN Tue–Sat 10.30 am–2.30 pm, 7 pm–11 pm Sun 12 noon–2 pm
CLOSED Sun eve, all day Mon, Chr Day and New Year's Day
CREDIT CARDS Access/Euro, Visa WHEELCHAIR ACCESS Yes
VEGETARIAN DISHES At least one daily

The High Street is about the smallest and hardest to find in this very conservative market town. A system of one-way streets renders navigation redundant as drivers seem to be inexorably funnelled into a vast central car park. The Grapevine is an oasis in a far corner of it. The building is old and attractive, almost qualifying as quaint, with a warm atmosphere and a loyal set of customers. An ingenious double-sided fireplace both divides and brings together the bar and eating areas. An enthusiastic calligrapher has produced a wine list with more flourish than accuracy but there are unexpected treasures within: Ch Calon-Ségur 1971 (£18.50) is a tempting pearl, but there is a sad lack of vintages and information elsewhere. The house wines, red and dry, medium and sweet white (75p/£2.90/£5.80 – the last a half-litre and litre respectively) are sound and good value. France, Germany and Italy are there, followed by a 'Wines of the World' section – as cosmopolitan as you like. From the blackboard menu you can choose anything from a simple snack to the equivalent of a four-course meal, with satisfying dishes such as steak and kidney pie, cooked in the local Wadworth's 6X brew, lasagne and moussaka (all £1.95) somewhere in the middle. Things get a bit more exotic in the evening. Strangers may take second place to regulars when the service is pressed, but the overall impression is one of cheerful friendliness.

DOVER Kent

McCartneys

8/9 1st Floor, Church Street TEL (0304) 215484

OPEN Mon–Sat 10.30 am–2.30 pm, 6.30 pm–11 pm Sun 7 pm–10.30 pm
CLOSED Sun L; 25–30 Dec CREDIT CARDS Amex, Visa
WHEELCHAIR ACCESS Impossible VEGETARIAN DISHES Salads

Limited space is used economically, with comfortable and functional seating, in this clean and tidy wine bar, where modern fittings intermingle with local memorabilia. The wine list contains around 28 mainly generic wines. The house wine is acceptable, but for a few pence more you can enjoy something much better. For non-wine drinkers, there's the house Bière de Garde and a Luxembourg lager. The food is very basic, ranging from home-made soup to various salads; steak and kidney pie is good and filling. The quantities served are very reasonable and you can eat your fill for around £3 per head.

DUBLIN

Gallery 22

22 St Stephen's Green TEL Dublin 686 169

OPEN Mon–Fri 10.30 am–4.30 pm Sat 11 am–4 pm Thur–Sat 6.30 pm–11 pm CLOSED Sun, public holidays CREDIT CARDS All accepted WHEELCHAIR ACCESS Impossible VEGETARIAN DISHES Special salad on request

This light and airy wine bistro/art gallery facing St Stephen's Green is apparently favoured by senior officials from the nearby departments of Foreign Affairs and Justice. It belies its basement location with attractive black and white tiled floors, pink tablecloths and lots of greenery. Husband and wife owners Gerry and James Cobbe still have a fairly small bill of fare, but are keen to add to the soup of the day, perhaps fresh cream of watercress (£1.10), quiche, a salad plate and one hot speciality (the escalope of ham Cordon Bleu (£3.95) was especially good and came with a crunchy, freshly made salad alongside). The small wine list of six reds and six whites, taken entirely from Gilbey's lesser range, Piat d'Or et al, presents no challenge. The house wine is currently the pretty ordinary Pedrotti red or white at £1.10 for a generous 14 cl glass. The best wine on the list is probably the Jaboulet Crozes-Hermitage (£8.95) but you might feel slightly infanticidal drinking the 1982. The proprietors say they will be expanding the wine list as customers reveal their tastes, and hope to be importing their own house wines before the end of the year. More reports, please.

Mitchell's Cellars

21 Kildare Street TEL Dublin 680 367

OPEN Mon–Fri 12.15 pm–2.30 pm Sat 12.15 pm–2.30 pm (winter only) CLOSED evenings, public holidays, Sun; Sat in summer CREDIT CARDS Access/Euro, Amex, Visa WHEELCHAIR ACCESS Yes VEGETARIAN DISHES On menu from time to time; salads or pizza on request.

A popular cellar bar beneath one of Dublin's oldest family-run wine firms, with dark beams and subdued lighting contributing to the vault-like atmosphere. No bookings, so if you arrive at the lunch-hour peak time, you may have to wait rather a long time in the cask-enclosed furthest recesses which house the bar. However, the staff are very good about keeping you in the picture and service is eventually fast and cheerful. The Mommessin carafe is £6/£1.25, with a crisp Anjou rosé and a pleasant Soave also available by the glass at £1.30. Interesting bottles include a Portuguese 1979 Dão white at £6.90 and a rich Chilean Cabernet Viejo Roble 1976 at £8.25. About ten wines on the list of 38 are available in halves. Lunch might be a soup, a homely beef casserole or bacon and mushroom pie with tossed salad (£4.50) with a particularly good range of sweets (£1.40): profiteroles, melting-moist chocolate cake and fresh fruit-laden Pavlova. Latecomers often have to make do with the comprehensive cheeseboard, which is usually in good condition, but portions at £1.60 can vary wildly, so try to get the board left at your table for self-service.

Shrimp's

1 Anne's Lane TEL Dublin 713 143

OPEN Mon–Sat 12 noon–11 pm CLOSED Sun, public holidays
CREDIT CARDS All accepted WHEELCHAIR ACCESS Yes
VEGETARIAN DISHES Salads and pizzas on request

The trendy Shrimp's continues to hum with *jeunesse dorée* and the not-so-young affluent set, and even in the off-peak afternoon hours it gives shelter to a few perennial Bertie Woosters, as well as a sprinkling of late-lunching businessmen and Brown-Thomas rangers, refreshing themselves with excellent sparkling Blanquette de Limoux (£2.10 per glass). House wines change fairly frequently – an acceptable Vieux Papes red from Gilbey's when we called, or a blandish dry white Yvecourt at £6.50/£1.25. A fair selection of half-bottles gives further scope to abstemious patrons, from a Beau Rivage vin de table at £3.50 to Veuve Clicquot NV at £12.50. The menu is simply divided between hot and cold dishes. Hot dishes vary daily and might include croque-monsieur (or madame) at £3.15 (£3.40), or chicken and marrow provençale at £5.75. Excellent smoked salmon pâté is £3.10 and a seafood salad bowl is £6.25. The cheeseboard runs to four or five well-selected cheeses, including a reliable Stilton, but there's no way of knowing whether you're going to be charged £1.85 or £2.35 or anywhere in between – perhaps it depends on how greedy the waitress thinks you've been.

EASTBOURNE East Sussex

Bilbo Baggins

53 South Street TEL (0323) 21713

OPEN Daily 10.30 am–2.30 pm, 6 pm–11 pm (normal licensing hours)
CLOSED Chr Day, Boxing Day L CREDIT CARD Amex
WHEELCHAIR ACCESS Yes VEGETARIAN DISHES Salads, some special dishes

The white lights here are slightly harsh but the place is more than appealing with its terrariums and fish tanks, and cushioned church pews. The service is extremely friendly, and the only disadvantage for the dedicated imbiber might be the juke-box, though no one seemed to object on the night we called. The menu and wine list of 20 wines are written up on a board. Rather than the house wine (£3.70), it is well worth plumping for the Listel wines – excellent, refreshing wines from the South of France – at £4 a bottle/80p a glass. There are various good clarets, and Champagne is reasonable at £11.50. Four bitters, two lagers, and draught cider add something of a pubby air. The menu includes cheeses, sausages and omelettes at about 80p, with chips at 80p a portion – very popular with Bilbo Baggins' clientèle. Quiche, salad and chips on our visit were good value at £1.10, and the taramosalata and pâté were decent versions.

The Bodega

6 Church Street TEL (0323) 25503
OPEN Mon–Sat 10 am–2.30 pm, 6 pm–11 pm (till 10.30 pm Mon–Thur in winter) Sun 12 noon–2 pm, 7 pm–10.30 pm CLOSED Chr Day
CREDIT CARDS Not accepted WHEELCHAIR ACCESS Yes
VEGETARIAN DISHES Always on menu, and prepared to order

This friendly, atmospheric bar undergoing sensitive renovation in the old town of Eastbourne serves also as a pub, stocking numerous beers and spirits. Barry Baulcomb's wine suppliers have provided a very adequate list: Gewürztraminer – 'unique and very fruity' – is £4.50, there's Coteaux du Layon at the same price, Chablis at £8.70, Minervois at £3.50, some more French and German wines, and some Australians and Californians – all anonymous and without vintage, but many looking worth investigating. Maureen Baulcomb produces good and reasonably priced fresh food, and the menu changes regularly. You might find locally caught rainbow trout almondine (£4.25), whole fresh mushrooms in garlic and herb butter (£1.20), or lasagne topped with prawns in garlic (£1.95).

Mike's Wine Bar ☞

8 Bolton Road TEL (0323) 23023
OPEN Mon–Fri 10 am–2.30 pm, 6 pm–11 pm (winter till 10.30 pm, Fri till 11 pm, also in winter) Sat 10 am–2.30 pm, 6 pm–11 pm Sun 12 noon–2 pm, 7 pm–10.30 pm Public holidays 10 am–2.30 pm, 6 pm–11 pm CLOSED Chr Day
CREDIT CARDS Amex, Diners, Visa WHEELCHAIR ACCESS Impossible
VEGETARIAN DISHES Good choice

This busy wine bar in a semi-basement near the centre of Eastbourne is a real find. Opened two and a half years ago, it has developed a loyal following under the knowledgeable and friendly owner/manager Mike Mullens. Clean, fresh and modern with red hessian walls, wicker seats, wood-topped tables, panelled bar front and tiled floor, the bar is relatively small, but in summer, good use is made of the garden behind. There is lively music and a very helpful, well-trained and cheerful staff. The food is straightforward but well served and invitingly presented: 15 snack dishes range from £1.50 to £5.25 for such dishes as lamb steak in a green peppercorn sauce, pork fillet with mushroom and white wine sauce, taramosalata, jacket potatoes with four different toppings, and often interesting fresh fish dishes. There is a daily vegetarian dish such as ratatouille, rice salad with three sauces or courgette bake. If your wine budget is limited, your only choice will be two Corsican Sélection des Garrigues, red and white, at £3.95/70p, or a Loire Vin de Pays Sauvignon at the same price. Otherwise, there's Ch Meaume 1982

Bordeaux Rouge Supérieur (£5.20/95p), Ch Bonnet 1982 white (£5.25/95p), Beaujolais – no vintage, no shipper – at £5.75/£1.05, Utrero Rioja 1980 or Chilean Concha y Toro Cabernet/Merlot, both at £5.55, plus some fair Germans from Zimmermann-Graeff for under £4.50 and some uninspiring Italians. And if your pocket will stretch that far, you might try Ch la Dominique, St-Emilion 1976 (£14.50) or one of a trio of 1971 clarets: Beychevelle, Léoville-Barton or Talbot for £26.50/£24.50/£23; or Champagnes from £11.95 up to £26.50 for Perrier-Jouët Belle Epoque 1975.

EDGBASTON West Midlands

Horts Five Ways

Harborne Road TEL 021-454 4672

OPEN Mon–Fri 12 noon–2.30 pm, 5.30 pm–10.30 pm Sat 12 noon–2.30 pm, 7 pm–1.30 pm Sun 12 noon–2 pm, 7 pm–10.30 pm CLOSED Chr Day, Boxing Day L, public holidays L CREDIT CARDS Not accepted WHEELCHAIR ACCESS Yes VEGETARIAN DISHES Salads and quiche

Horts seems to be the flagship of this successful chain of wine bars, owned by West Midlands Taverns Ltd, with wines mainly supplied by Seligman & Co. Other bars listed here are Flints (Sutton Coldfield), Clarets (Coventry), Bar Roussel (Warwick), Hop 'n' Grape (Aldridge), The Bank (Leeds), Heaths (Hanley), and Horts (Manchester). Their formula is straightforward and effective. The decor is always stylish, combining materials like rustic brick, good carpets, a bit of glass, modern prints and fittings, and often some book-lined shelves to give an air of mock seriousness. The wine list, about 40 strong outside house wines and sparklers, most of them around £4 to £5, is the same in all the bars: straightforward, sound but unremarkable stuff for the most part (four out of the six Rhine wines are Liebfraumilch), typically devoid of information about shippers, vintages, producers etc, with the exception of six wines which form a Connoisseurs' Selection and which just about bring the whole thing to life. These include a Sancerre, Cuvée Clos du Roc 1981 (£6.20), an attractive-sounding Merler Stephansberg Auslese 1975/76 from near Zell in the Lower Mosel (£7.80), and Cordier's cru bourgeois from St-Estèphe, Ch Meyney 1974 (£9.30). Apart from house wines (£3.60/65p), four others are available by the glass: Muscadet from Bougrier (£4.30/75p), Beaujolais from Chandesais (£4.60/80p), Liebfraumilch Falkenburg (£4.10/75p) and Piesporter Michelsberg (£4.30/75p). Moët & Chandon Première Cuvée NV is a not unreasonable £11.90 (£23.50 the magnum). There are other clarets (anonymous on the list) from the reliable Cordier, equally reliable Burgundies from Chandesais, and a good Chablis from Moreau (£7.50), Rhônes from Malbec and Masson Californians. As an added attraction, food is invariably fresh and well made, not expensive: at Horts, York or marmalade-baked hams with a selection of salads can be yours for under £2.50, fish might include mussels or pickled herring, and a hefty chunk of pizza at 90p is very tasty with a generous topping of ham and cheese. And the final common touch: all bars have recorded pop, which ranges from loud to deafening. Unlike the other bars, Horts has a small Champagne and Port Bar, where you can buy Champagne by the bottle, from Charles Heidsieck NV at a very generous £9.95, through to Dom Pérignon 1976 at £27.50, and some, if they can find an ice bucket big enough, in Jeroboam, Methuselah and Salmanazar; or ports by the glass, such as late-bottled Quinta do Noval, 70p, and by the bottle, like Cockburn 1967 (£16.75) or Taylor's late-bottled vintage (£7.95/80p).

EDINBURGH

L'Alliance

7 Merchant Street (off Candlemaker Row) TEL 031-225 2002

OPEN Mon–Sat 11 am–2.30 pm, 6.30 pm–10.30 pm CLOSED Sun, public holidays CREDIT CARDS Not accepted WHEELCHAIR ACCESS Yes VEGETARIAN DISHES On request

Le Caveau

13b Dundas Street TEL 031-556 5707

OPEN Mon–Sat 11 am–2.30 pm, 6 pm–10 pm CLOSED Sun, public holidays, 1st two weeks July CREDIT CARDS Not accepted WHEELCHAIR ACCESS Impossible VEGETARIAN DISHES On request

Le Monde

16a Queen Street TEL 031-226 3396

OPEN Mon–Sat 10 am–7 pm CLOSED Sun, public holidays CREDIT CARDS Not accepted WHEELCHAIR ACCESS Impossible VEGETARIAN DISHES On request

The 'doyen' of the Scottish Wine Bar trade, François Aliane is as French as his name implies, and his three establishments offer much that is enjoyable in relaxed French eating and drinking. Both Le Caveau and Le Monde are easy to find, just North of Princes St, but L'Alliance is more tricky – Candlemaker Row runs from the Grassmarket to Greyfriars Bobby in George IV Bridge, and the cul-de-sac Merchant Street leads off there. It is 14 years since M Aliane opened Le Caveau, presumably his busiest of the three since the ground-floor restaurant opens in the evening to provide substantial meals. A 'prix fixe' meal at £7.75 including starter and sweet or cheese offers a good range with main courses like salmon in a pastry case (the menu reads *'dans son kilt'*), escalope Le Caveau, lamb cutlets. Lunchtime is catered for in an attractive bar just below pavement level. Le Monde is less ambitious in its meals, with a good range of open sandwiches at £1.75, and cold meat and seafood platters at £2.95. Note its early closing hour at 7 pm. L'Alliance is perhaps the most attractive of the three, being built in the foundation archway of the George IV Bridge. Here, there is space, light and room to enjoy the modestly priced lunchtime menu of soups, pâtés, salads, ragoûts, and so on. In the evenings, an augmented menu of daube de boeuf or sole au vin blanc (both £3) continue to offer good value for money. At all three places, the wine lists show similar wines and acceptable prices, all French and nearly all fifty or so supplied by Quien et Cie, Bordeaux, for whom M Aliane is agent. Pouilly Fumé 1979 (£6.40), Gëwurztraminer 1980 (£5.80), Ch Maillard 1981 (£4.70) are good examples. A Chambolle-Musigny 1977 at £11.30 is the most expensive. An adequate number of the wines is available in half-bottles. The house red is easy to drink, the white less so, but still good value at £4.50 for a litre (60p a glass). Monsieur Aliane knows his Edinburgh, and runs his wine bars with skill; he also sells his wines to take away by the case.

Doric Tavern

15 Market Street TEL 031-225 1084

OPEN Mon–Fri 7 am–1 am Sat 7 am–11.45 pm Sun 12.30 pm–2.30 pm, 6.30 pm–11 pm CLOSED Chr Day, New Year's Day
CREDIT CARDS Access/Euro, Amex, Visa WHEELCHAIR ACCESS Impossible
VEGETARIAN DISHES Salads only

Long since a haunt of the newspaper fraternity (one of Scotland's dailies is produced a few doors away), the Doric was taken over in the spring of 1984 by the go-ahead proprietors of the Edinburgh Wine Bar *(see below)*. So at the time we went to press, it was early days to judge, but the food seemed less assured than the wine – our lunchtime soup was of indeterminate taste, and the chicken, bacon and mushroom pie's over-fired pastry obscured the taste of the other ingredients. The wine list shows around 130 items, and while some cross-pollination with the Edinburgh Wine Bar has taken place, this list needs time to settle. It would be worth looking beyond the £4.30/£1.25 (large glass)/75p (small glass) house wine. For the sweet palate, there are three 'goodies': Ch Bastor-Lamontagne 1976 Sauternes at £8.80 per bottle, Ch Rayne-Vigneau 1975 Sauternes at £5.50 per half-bottle, and Binger Osterberger Scheurebe Beerenauslese 1975 at £9.50 per half-bottle. Other Germans on the list are fairly modest (but so are the prices) while Italy, Australia, California, Spain and Portugal are given token coverage. France, on the other hand, is well represented, with some fairly infrequent wine bar bottles offering the chance for inexpensive exploration: Tavel Rosé 1982, Mommessin (£5.50), Gigondas 1978, Meffre (£6.80), Bourgueil 1982, Guillot (£5.70). The claret page is well graded in price and quality, with likely bargains in Ch Cissac 1975 at £8.60 a bottle, Ch Léoville-Barton 1974 at £9.20 and indeed the dearest, Ch Giscours 1975 at £14.20 per bottle, although this will still be improving next year and thereafter. Reports, please!

Which? Wine Guide does not accept payment for inclusion, and there is no sponsorship or advertising.

Edinburgh Wine Bar

110 Hanover Street TEL 031-226 3009

OPEN Mon–Thur 11 am–12 pm Fri 11 am–2 pm Sat 11 am–12 pm Sun 6.30 pm–11 pm CLOSED Chr Day, New Year's Day CREDIT CARDS All accepted WHEELCHAIR ACCESS Difficult VEGETARIAN DISHES Salads and cheeses

The comfortable, dark-red Edinburgh Wine Bar has got its relaxed feel about right, and it suffers no identity crisis over whether it's a wine bar, cocktail lounge or pub – a frequent confusion. Food is solid rather than inspired but good value for the youthful appetites of its customers: abundant Grosvenor pie, potato salad, and mushroom, tomato and cucumber salad all for £2.70. House Blanc de Blancs by Calvet is £1.14 for a 20 cl glass, house red a Côtes-du-Rhône at the same price (or you can have smaller glasses for 68p) but it might be better to look further. Worthwhile 'specials' on our visit were Saumur Champigny at £5.50 per bottle, and a Cordier half-bottle of St-Emilion at £2.40. Watch the blackboard above the bar for other interesting extras. This Wine Bar is sister to the Doric Tavern *(see above)*, but at the Edinburgh, the list is more inclined to the adventurous. For example, a Champagne method sparkler from André Simon might not be for the bubbly perfectionist, but at £6.90 seems worthwhile. Mildara Cabernet Sauvignon 1979 from the Australian 'Médoc', Coonawarra, has to be interesting at £6.90 per bottle. Italy's Rubesco de Torgiano, 1978, Lungarotti at £5.30 would pleasantly ease away an hour or so. Burgundy and the Rhône get fairly short recognition, and even the claret section could do with a boost. Ch La Rose Puyblanquet, 1976, St-Emilion (£6.40) might be a good buy, and Ch Bourgneuf-Varon, 1976, Pomerol, at £8.50 is not expensive for this normally high-priced commune. Try also the white Bordeaux, or, for a good, dry white, the Muscadet, Ch de la Galissonnière, 1982 in bottles and halves (£5.30/£2.90).

Nimmo's Ⓥ

101 Shandwick Place TEL 031-229 6119

OPEN Mon–Sat 11 am–2.30 pm, 5 pm–11 pm (Sat till 11.45 pm) CLOSED Sun, Chr Day, Boxing Day, New Year's Day, some local holidays CREDIT CARDS All accepted WHEELCHAIR ACCESS Easy to wine bar area VEGETARIAN DISHES Various

Nimmo's comprises a lounge bar and wine bar at pavement level, and the Bistro Restaurant downstairs. The wine bar is a popular venue for the nearby business community, where service is quick and cheerful. The wine list is elegantly printed by wine bar standards, although the descriptions are spasmodic and brief. Nevertheless, there are one or two items of interest besides the unremarkable Fleurie-style Vin du Patron by the litre/half-litre/20 cl glass at £4.70/£2.50/£1. Roger Joanne's Sauvignon Blanc 1981 (£3.90) would provide good lunchtime drinking, while the red Rioja lover might enjoy Marqués de Riscal 1978 (£4). The big Italian red, Amarone Recioto della Valpolicella 1976 (£5.60) has to be a good buy, though perhaps not if you have to go back to the office in the afternoon. For the claret traditionalist, there is nothing of note, and even less for the Burgundy fiend, with only Beaujolais in red. Quinson, however, provides two of the Beaujolais, a straight AC at £4, and his Beaujolais-Villages, 1982 Rougelons at £4.30. At the top is Moulin-à-Vent, 1978 by Groffier-Léger, for £5.55. The occasional 'special' augments the list, so watch the blackboard; tourists might have been drawn to the 'special' current on our visit, Scottish Country Wines from Moniack Castle: silver birch, elderflower and so on for £4.25 a bottle. On the board was also Kir – at £1.10 per glass, the ideal aperitif. Bob Nimmo's forthcoming list promises new additions in his constant effort to tempt the public beyond the familiar stand-bys from Germany and Italy. He talks of the Penedès, Bulgaria, the Cape and Australia. Food is flavoursome and attractively presented, though mixed salads have more than their fair share of mayonnaise. Downstairs in the Bistro Restaurant, wine prices are only marginally higher than in the wine bar, and lured by promising Bistro menus both at lunch and dinner, you might be more comfortably rewarded by taking the downward steps.

Waterfront (V)

1c Dock Place (off Commercial Street), Leith TEL 031-554 7427

OPEN Winter: Mon–Wed 11 am–11 pm Thur & Sat 11 am–12 pm Fri 11 am–1 am Summer: Mon–Sat 11 am–12 pm+ Sun 6.30 pm–11 pm CLOSED Sun in winter, Chr Day, Boxing Day, 1 & 2 Jan, some public holidays
CREDIT CARDS Not accepted VEGETARIAN DISHES Various

Tucked almost out of sight, this small former dock building has been transformed into one of Edinburgh's most exciting wine bars (find where the Water of Leith reaches Leith Docks, then ask). Some problems arise at lunchtime peak periods since wine is served only from the bar, while food orders are taken only at the tables (hot food is served 12 noon till 2.30 pm, 6 pm till 10 pm; cold food 12 noon till 10 pm). Given the three separate rooms, the young but willing staff can't always pick out the hungry from those already eating. The bar area is crowded, too, since customers for refills and coffees keep coming back. The menus are attractive and inexpensive, the modest wine list equally so. Two people sharing a £10 note could go for smoked salmon (£2 each) and a bottle of Chablis (£6). The pâté au Cognac, served in ramekins, was delightfully piquant, the poached prawn mayonnaise plentiful and tasty. Salads were fresh and interesting. Our initial glass, McKinlay McPherson's Vin de Pays du Tarn was disappointing, lacking fruit, flavour and bite. It comes in bottles (£3.90) and two glass sizes (£1.15/70p). A much better buy is the Marqués de Cáceres white (the best in the new white Rioja style) at £4.80/£1.35/80p, while its red partner, at the same price, was a very good version. Other attractive possibilities are Pinot Grigio (£4.50), Pouilly Fumé (£6.80), and indeed,

Blanquette de Limoux NV, a more than adequate lunchtime sparkler (£6.80). On the red side of the board is an easy-to-drink St-Saturnin NV (from the South of France via Howgate Wines), well priced at £4.20; Torres Coronas 1979 (£5), and Chianti Classico 1980, Brolio (£4.50) should be good medium-range drinking, the most expensive red being Fleurie at £7 per bottle. If you are looking for solid clarets, Burgundies, and Rhônes, you will not find them here. But the Waterfront more than compensates with less 'classic' bottles, and with its atmosphere, liveliness and ability to please, three basics other establishments might do well to copy.

EPWORTH South Yorkshire

The Epworth Tap

9–11 Market Place TEL (0427) 873333

OPEN Mon–Sat 7.30 pm–11.30 pm CLOSED Lunchtime, Sun, Chr Day, New Year's Eve, 1st week Aug CREDIT CARDS Access/Euro, Amex, Diners
WHEELCHAIR ACCESS Except to lavatories VEGETARIAN DISHES Starters always, main dishes on request

The Epworth Tap is a wine bar with the emphasis on *wine*. Over 100 are generally listed, though the list changes from week to week, ranging, perhaps, from house wine at around £4 a bottle up to Ch Citran 1961 at £18 and Beaune Marconnets 1976 (£12). Wines are gleaned from a large number of merchants plus frequent forays down to Sotheby's auctions. Rhônes looked particularly delicious on our visit: Gigondas 1980 L'Ousveau Fauquet, Roger Gerbe (£6.99), Ch du Grand Moulas 1982 (£5.50), Crozes-Hermitage 1980, Thalabert, Jaboulet (£7.75), and more. Italians were good, there was Lebanese Ch Musar 1969 for £7.99 or 1975 for £7.80, some good estate Germans, as well as fine and affordable Burgundies and clarets. Proprietor John Wynne is by day a schoolmaster, but his interest in wine becomes quite apparent when he mans the 'Tap' of an evening. He also arranges wine tastings and gourmet meals every two months and wines are available to take away by the case, mixed if you like. Cooking is by Helen Wynne, who prepares nearly everything on the premises, offering a sensibly short but still varied and sometimes quite exotic choice. There might be courgettes niçoise (£1.15), baked spare ribs (£1.15), watercress or fennel soup (80p), keema curry (£2.50), breast of chicken in cider with mushrooms and fresh ginger (£3.50), or pork olives stuffed with Parmesan and garlic and cooked in red wine (£4.25). The cheeseboard is extensive and five vintage ports are available, some by the glass. The 'Tap' is fairly small and intimate, well patronised despite being rather out in the sticks. If you're coming any distance and want to eat, do book (for Saturdays a fortnight in advance!) – the tiny dining room, complete with old kitchen range, seats only 18. Expect to dine to the sounds of Ben Webster, Red Allen and the like: John Wynne is a jazz expert, too.

ETON Berkshire

Eton Wine Bar

82/83 High Street TEL (07535) 54921 or 55182

OPEN Mon–Thur 11.30 am–2.30 pm, 6 pm–10.30 pm Fri–Sat 11.30 am–2.30 pm, 6 pm–11.30 pm Sun & public holidays 12 noon–2 pm, 7 pm–10.30 pm CLOSED Easter Sunday and 1 week Chr CREDIT CARDS Access/Euro, Visa WHEELCHAIR ACCESS Yes VEGETARIAN DISHES Salads, quiches, soups, sometimes main courses

The *Guide* thought it had made a blunder arriving here on 31 May which, as everyone (who's anyone) knows, is actually 4 June in Eton parlance. But no, the clientèle was mostly quiet and non-College. This has been one of the *great*, impeccably run wine bars of England for about ten years. Food is imaginative and *really* home-produced: quiches of asparagus (£2.45), cheese and onion (£1.75) and tuna (£2.45), pork and aubergine cocotte. But Stilton-flavoured Brie is either an exciting new cheese or the result of lack of space in the larder. Puddings are excellent and often gooey. The wine list is wide-ranging, imaginative and excellent value. Côtes-du-Rhône 1983 is only £5.20 and Mercurey (Paul-Jean Granger) a mere £9.50. Chanut house wines are fair, but why are only they (and omnipresent Liebfraumilch) available by the glass? Surely a changing 'wine of the day' would draw customers to experiment further on this exciting list. The Gilbey Brothers, the Hon Michael and the Hon William, and their wives serve tirelessly and without fuss. The *Guide* observed an Australian gentleman returning a bottle of claret with loud protestations. 'Yes sir, certainly does taste sharp, sir.' It was whipped away and replaced, the charm absolutely brimming over. That the returned wine was perfectly sound and subsequently consumed with relish by our inspector, who asked to try it, earns the Gilbeys yet another star for fortitude in the face of extreme provocation.

EVESHAM Hereford & Worcester

The Vine

16 Vine Street TEL (0386) 6799

OPEN Mon–Sat 11.30 am–2.30 pm, 7 pm–11 pm Sun 12 noon–2 pm, 7 pm–10.30 pm CLOSED Sun (Nov–Easter), Chr Day, Boxing Day, New Year's Day CREDIT CARDS Not accepted WHEELCHAIR ACCESS Relatively easy VEGETARIAN DISHES Some, particularly salads

Compilers of many a wine bar list, when looking for inexpensive bottles, seem to be magnetically attracted by the mass-produced stereotypes. Although there are some of these here, the light, airy, congenial and not too noisy Vine also provides an interesting 30-strong list at reasonable prices, albeit without vintages. One of the most expensive still wines is a Beaujolais Ch de Néty at £5.95, and a South

African KWV Pinotage weighs in at £5.50; a Westbury White, £4.25, from Berkshire, keeps the flag flying. Furthermore, about 20 wines are available by the glass at something between 65p and 90p; since not all these appear on the list, you may need to ask what is on offer. The rarest and tastiest piece of cold roast beef that has come our way in a long time was served up with a selection of salads for about £3; there are a dozen variants on this theme, including game pie, and vegetarians can make free with as many salads as can be heaped on a plate for £1.50. For the same price, you could dip your pitta bread into taramosalata and Feta cheese, or try one of the half-dozen pizzas. The cheese board is a welcome solution at the end of the meal – puddings on show were obviously not made on the premises. Otherwise, all food is generous, well presented and very good value. It's a pity that the service is not more attentive.

EXETER Devon

Bottlescreu Bill's

White Hart Hotel, South Street TEL (0392) 37511
OPEN Mon–Sat 12 noon–2.30 pm, 7 pm–11 pm CLOSED Sun, public holidays
CREDIT CARDS All accepted WHEELCHAIR ACCESS Yes
VEGETARIAN DISHES By prior arrangement

The application of the Davy's well-tried formula *(see the LONDON BARS section)* to Devon's county town has been sympathetically achieved. A summertime open-air charcoal grill might be out of place in the capital, but not here in the courtyard of the White Hart, a 14th-century coaching inn. The wine list is not long, but a high proportion of the wines are available by the glass and attractively priced bin-ends – even the occasional old vintage of first-growth claret – feature on a blackboard. Ch Maquin St-George, St-Emilion, 1976, on the main list was also a distinct bargain at £5.95. The list starts with Davy's French White and Red 'Ordnary' offering sound basic quality (£4.10/£1.10) and there is a fair choice of middle-range wines between £5 and £6. The glasses are generous, approaching a quarter of a bottle, which tempers criticism of the lack of halves. The menu doesn't try to upstage the main hotel dining room, in whose kitchens most of the food is prepared, but high spots are delicious toasted fingers – anchovy, sardine or Stilton at 25p each, with a bargain offer of six (two of each) for £1.20 – and their excellent steak and oyster pie (£3.30). The decoration of the bar, the helpful service, Champagne and Buck's Fizz in tankards and generous pourings of port and sherry follow the Davy's pattern and price.

Have we included your favourite spot for eating *and* drinking? If not, or if you disagree with our assessment, tell us about it either by letter or on the forms at the back of the *Guide*.

FOLKESTONE Kent

Harvey's Wine Bar

Langhorne Garden Hotel TEL (0303) 57233
10–12 Langhorne Gardens

OPEN Mon–Sat 11 am–2.30 pm, 7 pm–10.30 pm (Sat till 11 pm) Sun 12 noon–2 pm CREDIT CARDS All accepted WHEELCHAIR ACCESS Very difficult VEGETARIAN DISHES Some

A friendly crowd of regular customers seems to inhabit this bar from opening to closing time. Beyond the clean and tidy wine bar is a cocktail bar (waitress service only), which may also be hired for private parties and business functions. The wine list is long but apart from the unspecified house wine only Liebfraumilch or Lambrusco are sold by the glass (70p). A blackboard of better options fills the wall beside the bar: Ch Bel Air, Roger Joanne 1979 is good value at £5. A late happy hour between 7 and 8 pm is worth noting. The food is all prepared and cooked on the premises by the brother-owners and ranges from the usual wine bar lasagne and spaghetti to their speciality, locally caught trout. Good value, too, are the roasts and a summer cold buffet.

GERRARDS CROSS Buckinghamshire

La Même Chose

25–27 Station Road TEL (0753) 889000

OPEN Daily 10 am–5 pm, 7 pm–12 pm (normal licensing hours)
CREDIT CARDS All accepted WHEELCHAIR ACCESS Yes
VEGETARIAN DISHES Some

Not the same thing by any means, La Même Chose, half wine bar, half bistro, and opened as recently as May 1984, seems already set on the path to success. Its bare-brick walls and a profusion of pot plants, enhanced by the uniformity of its ample modern (and comfortable) chairs and tables, exemplify the attractive side of contemporary design. The wine list is enterprising and clearly laid out, each wine carrying a short description but, as is too often the case, vintages are not marked. In each of the national sections there is a wide choice of wines and, most encouragingly, apart from the predictable German offerings, this extends beyond the standard names. You might choose, for example, a good Rioja Reserva, a better than average range of Bordeaux châteaux, or a Burgundy such as an Hautes-Côtes de Beaune or a Savigny-lès-Beaune for under £7. A range of cocktails is also offered. The limited blackboard menu changes daily. An interesting selection of starters is as well presented as the generous main courses, which might be ham and parsley sauce with new potatoes. Temptation does not end there, for the list of sweets can easily prove irresistible: perhaps a glass of port with your slice of passion cake? Friendly but not overpowering service.

GLOUCESTER Gloucestershire

Corkers

43 Barton Street TEL (0452) 413328

OPEN Mon–Sat 10.30 am–3 pm; 6 pm–11 pm Sun 12 noon–2.30 pm; 7 pm–10.30 pm CLOSED Chr Day CREDIT CARDS Not accepted
WHEELCHAIR ACCESS Yes VEGETARIAN DISHES Some

Corkers looks like a little old tea shop from the outside but when you go in it goes on and on, past several bars, until you reach a great barnlike interior at the back. But its hugeness is well broken up and doesn't become overwhelming. The wine list is a relatively uninteresting compilation of generic titles from the usual places, redeemed by the occasional glint of something more individual such as Ch d'Olivéry, Corbières (£4.10) and Aveleda Vinho Verde (£4.10). Cocktails are on offer, too. Hot food is served at a queue-with-a-tray canteen type counter, but you can see what you're getting and it's all enjoyable, filling stuff, if not haute cuisine: turkey curry, pork in mustard, seafood Mornay, coq au vin or moussaka will cost you between £2.50 and £3.50. A special tip to *Which? Wine Guide* readers: the door to the loos is a massive garage-like affair. Don't, flushed with success at opening it, then fall down the step inside.

Taster's

22 London Road TEL (0452) 417556

OPEN Mon–Fri 12 noon–2.30 pm; 7 pm–10.30 pm (Fri till 11 pm) Sat 12 noon–2 pm; 7 pm–11 pm CLOSED Sun; public holiday L, Chr Day, Boxing Day CREDIT CARDS All accepted WHEELCHAIR ACCESS Impossible
VEGETARIAN DISHES Good selection

Climbing up the steps from the street into this small bistro-like wine bar, with its jumbled appearance of pine, cork and posters, is a bit like entering student digs, but the place is unatmospheric for all that. Don't be put off, because within strictly European confines, the wine list's range is broad, the prices reasonable and the quality excellent, even if producer details are in short supply. Amongst 11 wines available by the (5 oz) glass, best value by far is Tanners House Claret at 95p. A daily changing menu provides an interesting choice of carefully prepared hot and cold dishes, such as Boston aubergines (95p), osso buco and rice (£2.45), and spiced lamb and rice (£2.45). The house wines are French, (£4.50/84p), and a light fruity red, soft dry white and medium dry rosé are available as well as a good range of other wines by the glass, including Jean Perico sparkling white at £1.30. Otherwise the very short list offers a sound, basic range of French, German and Italian wines all very reasonably priced: Sancerre, for example, is £7 a bottle. Recent house specials have included a good range of petit-château Bordeaux wines from the 1975 and 1976 vintages at under £6 a bottle.

GUILDFORD Surrey

Rowley's Wine Bar

124 Tunsgate TEL (0483) 63277

OPEN Mon 12 noon–3 pm Tue–Fri 12 noon–3 pm, 6.30 pm–11 pm Sat 12 noon–3 pm, 6.30 pm–11 pm CLOSED Sun, Mon eve, public holidays CREDIT CARDS Diners, Visa WHEELCHAIR ACCESS Impossible VEGETARIAN DISHES Salads

This popular businessman's haunt is housed in a Grade Two listed building overlooking the cobbled High Street and the town clock. After finding the door in the Tunsgate arch you have to negotiate a small flight of stairs to reach a series of interconnecting first-floor rooms with uneven wooden floors. Balustrades, irregular white-painted walls and beamed ceilings all add historic charm. Ham, beef, game pie, Pastrami, quiche and turkey breast served with a selection of salads from a buffet are always on offer at prices between £2.75 and £3.95, plus seasonal specials like dressed crab salad. Hot dishes such as moussaka, lasagne, chicken curry, chilli and fisherman's pie are available for around £3, mainly during the winter months, and home-made sweets like treacle or butterscotch tart (£1.10) or a very good selection of cheeses (95p to £1.70).

HANLEY Staffordshire

Heaths

Albion Street TEL (0782) 272472

OPEN Mon–Thur 11.30 am–3 pm, 7 pm–10.30 pm Fri–Sat 11.30 am–3 pm, 7 pm–11 pm Sun 7 pm–10.30 pm CLOSED Sun L, Chr Day, Boxing Day, public holidays CREDIT CARDS Not accepted WHEELCHAIR ACCESS Yes VEGETARIAN DISHES Salads and quiche

Part of the West Midlands Taverns chain *(see Horts, Edgbaston)*, Heaths sports attractive dark bamboo furniture and an intimate little 'library' as well as a short blackboard menu that might offer pork and pineapple curry with rice (£1.90), a range of salads including prawn, £1.95 (the prawns were tasteless on our visit but the salads are okay), and for pudding you might try a hot chocolate brownie. If you're a cocktail person, you can choose from a separate list of about 20.

> We have tried to make the *1985 Which? Wine Guide* as comprehensive as possible, but we should love to hear from you about any other establishments you feel deserve an entry, or your comments on existing entries. Write to us either by letter or using the report forms supplied at the back of the book.

HARROGATE North Yorkshire

The Drum and Monkey

5 Montpellier Gardens TEL (0423) 502650

OPEN Mon–Sat 12 noon–1.30 pm, 7 pm–10.15 pm CLOSED Sun
CREDIT CARDS Access/Euro, Visa WHEELCHAIR ACCESS Impossible
VEGETARIAN DISHES Various

The Drum has the atmosphere of a city seafood restaurant, and is run very much on the lines of Bill Bentleys in London. It is almost always busy, both in the ground floor wine bar and the small restaurant above, but they always seem able to squeeze a few more in. William Fuller, the proprietor, does all the cooking himself and then presides over the bar. The wine list is fairly short but excellently chosen and unusually well compiled, with shippers and producers revealed in *nearly* every case. Prices are perhaps a little elevated, but then quality is reliably good, and standards in all things are high in this bar. The list begins with Champagnes, full and half-bottles of Lanson Black Label (£12.95/£6.95), Lanson 'Pink' NV (£15.05), Bollinger NV (£16.25) and Taittinger Blanc de Blancs 1975 (£28.25) for anyone who really has something to celebrate. White Burgundies are from Duboeuf, Boisset and Abel Garnier and Chablis from the fine cellars of Louis Michel (prices range from £6.95 to £15.55); the couple of Alsace wines come from Gisselbrecht, there's a Crozes-Hermitage 1982 from Paul Jaboulet Aîné, an anonymous Sauvignon de Touraine, Listel's good value Blanc de Blancs at £5.55, a few Loires and some anonymous Germans for the unadventurous. Reds number just two in such a fishy place – Duboeuf's Beaujolais (£6.05) and a Côtes-du-Rhône (£5.15). House wines are fair value – Duboeuf white (£4.65/80p) and Gaston Laselle red for the same price. The food does full justice to the wines. Lobster and Dover sole are the specialities, done in several delicious ways. Or you might choose king prawns marinated in spices, grilled and served with rice (£5.15), scallops wrapped in bacon with garlic butter, pineapple and rice (£5.65), cold seafood platter, including half a lobster (£9.75) or seatrout with asparagus hollandaise, in season (£4.75). Oysters are a speciality, too (£3.45 for half a dozen Pacific in summer, £5.25 for a half a dozen Number One in winter), or you might start with salmon and watercress délice, a casing of watercress mousse filled with salmon, egg and lettuce in mayonnaise (£1.45), tarragon fish soup (£1.05) or smoked mackerel and spinach mousse (£1.55). You will often see other restaurateurs tucking in at the Drum – perhaps the best compliment that can be paid.

Have we missed your favourite bar? We hope not, but if so, or if a new bar opens in your area, tell us about it on the report forms at the back of the book.

HASTINGS East Sussex

Briefs

High Street TEL (0424) 427000

OPEN Mon–Sat 11 am–2.30 pm, 7 pm–11 pm CLOSED Sun CREDIT CARDS All accepted VEGETARIAN DISHES Better than average

Briefs is well placed in the back streets of Hastings old town, and with its original oak beams and (gas-fired) log fire is likely to become a favourite meeting place for those with a taste for the grape. There is no printed menu or wine list, and virtually no information on the boards apart from the generic name of the wine. Briefs plan to develop the list beyond the present dozen, which include house wines (£3.90), basics such as Niersteiner (£4.40) and a few more interesting offerings like Brouilly by Bouchard Père et Fils (£6.95). Food includes home-made pasta (spaghetti with seafood or bolognese, or lasagne at £2.95). Smoked mackerel and salad is £1.95, and locally smoked salmon and granary bread £2.95. For the sweeter toothed, the hot chocolate fudge cake and cream at 95p is worth trying.

HENLEY-ON-THAMES Oxfordshire

Barnaby's Ⓥ

2 New Street TEL (0491) 572421

OPEN Mon–Sat 12 noon–3 pm, 7 pm–10.30 pm Sun 7 pm–10.30 pm
CLOSED Sun L; Chr Day CREDIT CARDS Access/Euro, Visa
VEGETARIAN DISHES One or two every day

'Wine, vittals and pizzas' is what John Whitton serves at his brothel-red, half-timbered dive just down the street from Henley Brewery. It's about the best place to meet in the town. Mr Whitton is usually at the charcoal grill or the computer, and buys his wines mostly from the Gilbey Wine and Food Company in Eton,– they seem to cost less here than they do there. Try the St Nicolas de Bourgueil 1982 (£6.20), Bergerac Sauvignon (£5.20), and a lovely Chablis, Montée de Tonnerre 1982 for only £8.95. Belgian dry cider at 65p a glass is a speciality here. Basic red, Chanut, is 80p a glass but for 95p you get a very pleasant château-bottled 1980 claret – Ch Haut-Castenet. There is a 'wine of the week' – Gewürztraminer for £5.85 on our visit. Food is good and varied. Starters include fresh oysters (£3.95 for six) and good moules marinière (£2.20). Main courses of truite verte (watercress sauce) (£3.75), chicken kopita (£3.95), porc polonaise, filet bordelaise and poulet basquaise are all very international and all good value. We liked the merguez at £3 but couldn't taste the wine afterwards!

Send us **your** views on the report forms at the back of the book.

HEREFORD Hereford & Worcester

Saxtys Ⓥ ☞

33 Widemarsh Street TEL (0432) 57872
OPEN Mon–Sat 12 noon–2.30 pm, 7 pm–10.30 pm Sun 12 noon–2.30 pm
CLOSED Sun eve, public holidays CREDIT CARDS Access/Euro, Visa
VEGETARIAN DISHES Always a few

Saxtys is obviously one of the 'in' places to be in Hereford. An extremely busy wine bar within easy reach of the city centre and popular with people of all ages, it caters in its large and varied wine list and ever-changing menus for all kinds of tastes. A large bar stretches down the side of one wall, and here the wine imbibers congregate. There is an area at the end of the room for diners and a further recently opened drinking area at the back of the building. Called 'The Library', it has one wall covered with about two thousand books; it has its own bar, and is ideal for functions and parties. There is a large selection of wines from most wine-producing countries, particularly strong in Spanish (Torres Coronas is £5.65), and French country wines, such as the delicious Ch de Fonscolombe, Rosé (£4.95). Also listed are wines from California (Zinfandel is £7.45), the excellent Cabernet Sauvignon Viña Linderos (£6.35) from Chile and a fair Australian red, William Jacob (£5.35). The house wines are all sold under the Saxtys label. 'As far as our house wines go, we feel that every establishment should stand or fall on their good value.' They are indeed all exceptional value (£3.60/65p). Saxtys may by now have added a range of half-bottles to their list, joining a small selection of magnums, Ch Vincent, Côte de Fronsac, 1978 (£11.95), for one. At lunch-time there are always two hot dishes, perhaps cider sausages, lasagne or courgette and spinach bake (£1.95 to £2.30) and a range of ten different salads, cold meats, pâté and quiche (£1.50 to £2.50). In the evening, the restaurant menu is available, and very good it is, too: garlic potted prawns (£1.95), walnut and Stilton soufflé (£1.60), or Saxtys' soup of the evening (85p), salmon tarragon (£6.75), lamb pancakes (£5.90), roast guinea fowl (£5.95) or the ever popular Saxtys' charcoal rump steak (£6.25), which is cooked *exactly* how you order it.

HIGHWORTH Wiltshire

The Wine Cellar at Highworth Ⓥ ☞

10 High Street TEL (0793) 763828
OPEN Mon–Sat 12 noon–2.30 pm, 7 pm–11 pm Sun 12 noon–2 pm, 7 pm–10.30 pm CLOSED Never CREDIT CARDS Not accepted
WHEELCHAIR ACCESS Impossible VEGETARIAN DISHES By arrangement only

Since the last *Guide*, the management of the former Highworth Wine Bar has been taken over by the freeholder, a local architect, and his partner Christine Howell, who have accepted the challenges with enthusiasm. The attractive building facing on to the town's market square is of very uncertain date; the owner invites discussion on this point, but the long narrow cellar has proven medieval origins and there is even a blocked-up subterranean passage with an engraved stone saying 'to the church' (which is a good 100 yards away). The house wines (£3/50p) – French Red and White, Liebfraumilch and an enterprising North Italian Merlot – must be among the best value in the country. There is a certain irreverence in the wine list – 'Wines to Guzzle', and 'Wines to Quaff' can be had by bottle or glass, 'Wines to Savour' by bottle only. The list, in all its parts, is short but well balanced and the lack of vintages and information on shippers and origins is to some extent compensated for by the helpful and informed staff. The price reductions under the new regime have certainly brought the customers back and, in the words of one of them, the 350-year-old cellars have lots of character – and that includes the staff and other customers. The food is prepared behind the bar from fresh, top quality ingredients. There is a menu, but the emphasis is on the £2 dishes of the day supported by more mundane grills. An excellent dish of cannelloni (£2) followed by an original home-made grapefruit and cider sorbet justified a detour off the M4. A good selection of sandwiches and bar snacks is also available. Regular wine tastings are held on the first Tuesday of each month.

HIGH WYCOMBE Buckinghamshire

Fagin's Wine Bar & Restaurant

25 Easton Street TEL (0494) 444095

OPEN Mon–Sat 11 am–2.30 pm, 6.30 pm–11 pm CLOSED Sun
CREDIT CARDS Not accepted WHEELCHAIR ACCESS Difficult
VEGETARIAN DISHES Some

Fagin's has an almost pubby atmosphere, perhaps because the bar is quite separate from the dining section, and it gets most of the basics right, which include being the only wine bar in a town as large as High Wycombe. The wine list is impressive for its range – 57 wines are listed and there is a particularly extensive selection of reasonably priced sparkling wines along with some attractive-looking Italians, a more adventurous than usual choice of Bordeaux and Burgundy, and the trusty favourites from the KWV range. Prices are reasonable – £5 to £6 in the main – and there is in addition a section devoted to budget wines. Most commendably, each wine bears a helpful description, which should encourage experimentation, but no vintages are shown, which will discourage splashing out on the higher-priced wines. The food selection matches the wine in its variety. There are snacks, jacket potatoes with fillings for around the £2 mark, regularly varied specials and full-priced meals – steaks, etc. In general, the food dishes give a 're-heated' impression, but no one can argue with the generous nature of the helpings and the straightforward value for money that each represents. Service is friendly and attentive.

HORSFORTH West Yorkshire

Stuart's

166 Town Street TEL (0532) 582661
OPEN Mon–Sat 12 noon–3 pm, 6.30 pm–10.30 pm CLOSED Sun, public holidays CREDIT CARDS Not accepted WHEELCHAIR ACCESS Yes VEGETARIAN DISHES Salads

Stuart's is considered by many to be the best wine bar in the Leeds area. Owner/manager Stuart Haigh has been in the wine trade for longer than he may care to remember, and is always on hand. He also owns the retail shop next door, the Horsforth Wine Centre *(see the* MERCHANTS *section)*, and extra wines regularly makes their way from it into the wine bar to supplement an already very respectable list. You may sometimes find 'specials' in the bar, bought in small batches, which never find their way into the shop. House wines, Hallgarten's red and Deinhock from Deinhard, are £5 a litre/60p for a 4 oz glass. Beaujolais from Georges Duboeuf are good, easy drinking, from Beaujolais 1983 (£5.25) through most of the crus to Chiroubles at £7.25 – and the excellent 1983 vintage was already on sale by early summer. Germans come from Hallgarten and Deinhard, a fair selection of Rhônes from Salavert; there's a range of Nederburg, South Africans under £6, Mondavi's Zinfandel at £5.75, a short list of Burgundies rising to an anonymous 'La Romanée' 1970 at £30, and a number of clarets, including some classed growths, often of 'off vintages', so consult the bar staff before you take the plunge. The choice of sparkling wines is good, with Deinhard's Lila Imperial exceptionally good value at £6.50. Food is particularly good, too, centring on joints of cold beef, ham and pork, carved before your eyes in generous helpings (with salad, £3.25). The salad selection is exemplary, and hot dishes are more adventurous than most wine bar fare: prawns in garlic butter (£1.40), frogs' legs (£2.95), half roast duck with orange salad (£5.95), salmon and prawn pancake in cheese sauce (£4.25).

ILFORD Essex

Harts

545 Cranbrook Road, Gants Hill TEL 01-554 5000
OPEN Mon–Fri 11.30 am–3 pm, 7 pm–11 pm Sat & Sun 7 pm–11 pm
CLOSED Sat L, Sun L, Chr Day, Boxing Day L, public holidays L
CREDIT CARDS All accepted WHEELCHAIR ACCESS Impossible
VEGETARIAN DISHES By arrangement

Harts has an odd mix of military prints and only just bearably loud disco music in its dimly lit, stone-tiled room. Local business people fill the place at lunchtime, local youth at night, and the short wine list is geared to local tastes: no great bottles, and only basic descriptions ('Chablis, £7.10, dry, soft and mellow'). But if you ask, they'll show you what they have. There are four Champagnes, Sancerre (£8.50), Pouilly-Fuissé (£9.25); four of the five Germans are available at 90p/95p per glass; anonymous house wines, too, come by the glass. Cocktails are rather more in Harts' line: 24 are listed, but they'll mix to order anything you can dream up; spirits and beer are also on offer. The local youth probably go for the home-made chilli con carne (£2.85), and leave the 8 oz fillet steak with vegetables or salad (£6.75) and Dover sole (from £7.95) to the expense account lunchers.

INVERNESS Highland

Brookes

75 Castle Street TEL (0463) 225662

OPEN Mon–Wed 10.30 am–11 pm Thur–Sat 10.30 am–1 am Sun 12.30 pm–2.30 pm, 6.30 pm–11 pm CLOSED Chr Day, Boxing Day, New Year's Day, 1st Mon of month (Nov–Mar) CREDIT CARDS Not accepted
WHEELCHAIR ACCESS Easy, but not to lavatories
VEGETARIAN DISHES Various

The decor may be too fancy for some at this gently lit, comfortable wine bar with barely audible music, but the food is a major draw, changing twice daily, with all ingredients fresh and home-cooked: perhaps good vegetable quiche (£1.90) with a beautiful salad of apple, orange, mushroom and tomato, or Italian ham (£2). Afternoon callers will be offered more traditional Scottish fare: fruitcake and shortbread, tea and coffee, with the added bonus of being able to eat it in a non-smoking area – all too rare a possibility. (The bar is air-conditioned, too.) As for the wines, Justerini & Brooks' dry house white is modest drinking, but clean, crisp, and well priced at £3.75 a bottle. The wine list, 80 wines long and wisely hand-written rather than permanently printed, is informative, interesting and certainly not over-priced. Most bottles are from France, but Italy, Germany, Australia and California are all represented. The German section includes Wehlener Sonnenuhr Riesling Kabinett 1981 (£7.45) and Kaseler Nieschen Riesling Spätlese 1981 (£8.40), two Mosels well worth trying. Alsace is supplied by Hugel, and his Cuvée des Evêques, Gewürztraminer 1981 is a good buy at £7.25. A reasonable-sized glass of Muscat de Beaumes de Venise 1982 is only £1.50. On the red side, Guigal's Côte-Rôtie 1978 at £13.25 must surely still be developing, but Brookes offer 15 per cent discount for off-sales. Three generic Burgundies – Mercurey, Beaune (Bouchard Père et Fils) and Volnay – are all from the lowly 1977 vintage but modestly priced at £7.75, £9.25 and £10. Perhaps the best claret should be the Ch Boyd-Cantenac 1976 at £14, but a Ch Montalivet 1978 (£7.25), and Ch L'Abbaye 1979 (£6.60) provide cheaper but good-drinking red Bordeaux. There are 28 wines by the glass (lead crystal tulips, no less!). For the brave at heart, cocktails by the jug are offered (six to eight glasses' worth), from Buck's Fizz at £5.75 to the provocative Bosom Caresser at £7.25; the non-alcoholic Cinderella is £3.25.

IPSWICH Suffolk

Butts

33–37 St Nicholas Street TEL (0473) 215721
OPEN Mon–Fri 11.30 am–2.30 pm, 5 pm–11 pm Sat–Sun 5 pm–11 pm
CLOSED Sat & Sun L, public holidays CREDIT CARDS Access/Euro, Amex
WHEELCHAIR ACCESS One step down from pavement
VEGETARIAN DISHES Small range

A popular lunchtime haunt for nearby office workers and at night a bustling meeting place for Ipswich wine-lovers, who seemed to be the under-thirties on our evening visit – attracted, perhaps, more by the rather loud music than by the food and wine. The interior of Butts has certainly been smartened up by the new owners: the ground-floor bar has recently been augmented by a smaller side area with four or five tables; there is also an upstairs room which gets rather congested at weekends. House wines (French red and dry white plus EEC Tafelwein) at £3.95/75p are reasonably priced and of palatable if unexciting quality. Sparkling wine is 90p a glass. There is anonymous Muscadet (£4.95), Beaujolais (£5.90) and Gewürztraminer (£5.95); Liebfraumilch, Bereich Nierstein, Bereich Bernkastel and Piesporter are all under £5 a bottle. The menu is limited but adequate and there should be something to please all. Home-made soup is 75p, and to follow there's prawns with salad and French bread (£1.75), lasagne (£1.85), beef or ham salad (£2.50), various burgers around 95p and – for vegetarians, salads which range in price between 65p and £1.35. Sweets are 75p to £1.

KENILWORTH Warwickshire

Inky's

101–103 Warwick Road TEL (0926) 56275
OPEN Mon–Sat 12 noon–2.30 pm, 6 pm–11 pm Sun 7 pm–10.30 pm
CLOSED Sun L, Chr Day, Boxing Day, New Year's Day
CREDIT CARDS Access/Euro, Amex, Diners WHEELCHAIR ACCESS Yes
VEGETARIAN DISHES Various

For 85p, Inky's will still mix chilled Mosel with soda water, ice and a twist of lemon in their Moseltzer version of Queen Victoria's favourite thirst-quencher. Mosel-lovers in fact do rather well here with a Kabinett (£5.20) and Spätlese (£6.65) from the Apotheke vineyard at Trittenheim. If you prefer your sparkle to be made the hard way, you may be tempted by the not unreasonable £17.95 for a 1976 Veuve Clicquot Champagne, more so, perhaps, than by the same vintage of Dom Pérignon at £29. Vintages throughout the list of about 50 wines are otherwise conspicuous by their virtual absence. For around 65p, you can tuck into a glass of any of the eight house wines such as Soave (£3.55 a bottle) or Jean Cordillac Vin de Table (£4.80 a litre). Apart from the connoisseurs' short list, which is subject to availability, and the bubbly, you would be hard put to fork out more than £8 a bottle. Why Inky's is inky we can't imagine, but the name may perhaps refer to the policy of fitting ten-watt light-bulbs; such illumination as there is can be found concentrated behind the bar, where it enables you at least to study the blackboard menu. Asterisks help to distinguish the home-made items, and for £2.50 you can tuck into a plateful of the likes of chilli con carne, chicken casserole, beef curry, moussaka or lasagne with salad; an asparagus quiche and salad (£2.25 or £1.35 for just the quiche) had soggier wholemeal pastry than was probably intended, but was determinedly asparagussy in flavour. A small area is set aside 'strictly for diners only'.

KINSALE Co Cork

Max's

Main Street TEL 010-353 21 72443

OPEN Mon, Wed–Sat 12.30 pm–2.30 pm, 7.30 pm–11 pm Sun 12.30 pm–2.30 pm, 7.30 pm–10.30 pm CLOSED Tue, mid-Jan to end Feb; Oct to mid-Dec
CREDIT CARDS Not accepted WHEELCHAIR ACCESS Yes
VEGETARIAN DISHES A few

Two hundred years ago, Kinsale was a successful and prosperous trading post. It is now enjoying a revival as a trendy fishing and yachting resort teeming with little restaurants, bars and knick-knack shops. On one of the side streets, called, naturally enough, Main Street, a good meeting place is Max's, run by Wendy Tisdell and named after her dog. It is tiny (just eight tables), spotlessly clean, friendly and efficient. The short, intelligent wine list includes Antinori Chianti and Orvieto by the glass or jug (£1.15/£6.50), some interesting and inexpensive wines from Chile, and a Morey-St-Denis 1976 (no shipper named) at £14. Max's is one of the most pleasant drinking places in the area, and certainly one of the best places to eat at. Children are tolerated if they are well behaved, but not encouraged. The menu is simple, the food good and nicely presented, ranging from home-made soup (£1), crab claw salad (£3.50) or spare ribs (£4.50) to a fillet steak at £7.50.

KNAPHILL Surrey

Froggies Food and Wine Bar (V)

42–44 High Street TEL (048 67) 80835

OPEN Mon 12 noon–2.30 pm Tue–Thur 12 noon–2.30 pm, 7 pm–10.30 pm Fri–Sat 12 noon–2.30 pm, 7 pm–11 pm CLOSED Sun
CREDIT CARDS Access/Euro, Visa WHEELCHAIR ACCESS Yes
VEGETARIAN DISHES Soups, quiches, special dishes with prior notice

Frogs positively abound in this friendly, busy wine bar run by Robin and Debbie de Winton. A large china frog squats on the bar, a debonair silk model hangs on the wall and in all there are some 150 of the ilk round the bar area. The de Wintons knocked together a butcher's and a greengrocer's to create three adjoining rooms, including a panelled dining room which also caters for private functions. The low-ceilinged bar area is simply furnished with pale-green walls, and outside, a small courtyard has been turned into a garden area with tables, chairs and a barbecue. The fairly short wine list changes frequently but is above average in interest and quality and includes German, Italian and Spanish wines, although the main emphasis is on France. House wines, a fruity Minervois (£4.15/75p) and a crisp Blanc de Blancs, are always supplemented by a good range of blackboard wines by the glass such as English Adgestone (95p). Details of growers and vintages are added to the list by hand as Robin de Winton likes to alternate suppliers to give a choice of interesting wines at good prices, but selections when we visited included Ch Les Moulins 1976, Puisseguin St-Emilion at £7.20 and Crozes-Hermitage at £5.95. The wine bar has built up a good local reputation for food, even at lunch-time when the fare is simpler: home-made soups, pâtés, stuffed potatoes and salads. Debbie de Winton's dinner menus are based on a few favourites like Roman roast shoulder of lamb (£4), daily supplemented with seasonal specialities. These could include poached Scotch salmon with hollandaise for £5 or a whole sea bass for two (£10.50). All main-course prices include potatoes and salad. Starters might be baked cheese and cream soufflés (£1.30) or gravad lax with dill and mustard sauce (£2), and the trolley of sweets, all home-made, offers a good selection for £1.

LEAMINGTON SPA Warwickshire

Wildes

7 The Parade TEL (0926) 36732

OPEN Mon–Fri 12 noon–2.30 pm, 7 pm–11.30 pm Sat 7 pm–12 pm Sun 1 pm–2.30 pm CLOSED Chr Day, Boxing Day, Sat L, Sun eve
CREDIT CARDS Access/Euro, Visa WHEELCHAIR ACCESS Impossible
VEGETARIAN DISHES Few

We are pleased to note that James Walker's enthusiasm for wines continues unabated. He offers a choice of around 60 wines ranging from the humble but good Jaboulet-Vercherre house wines (£5/80p) through a good value Premières Côtes de Bordeaux, Ch Péconnet 1979 (£6.95) and a 'superlative, hefty' Chassagne-Montrachet 1979 (£12.95), to the show pieces of the (rich) 'Connoisseurs' List': a 'long-lived' (it had better be) 1947 Gevrey-Chambertin from Doudet Naudin (£35), Geisweiler's 1961 Chambolle-Musigny (£25), or 1970 clarets like Ch Beychevelle, £40, or Ducru-Beaucaillou, £45. But you needn't pay so much to enjoy yourself: 95 per cent of the wines on the main list are priced between £5 and £8. Whether you are taking lunch inside or on the rustic benches out at the back, you will find a continental meat platter good value, with a bit each of Parma and Black Forest hams, pastrami, sapocka, Italian salami and Parisian sausage, all for £1.95; or try a vegetable lasagne (£1.65) or gloriously rare roast beef salad (£3.50). In the evening, a range of about eight rather more substantial dishes is added. These might include chicken livers sautéed with limes and fresh ginger (£2.95), fillet steak au poivre (£7.25) or lamb kebabs with rice (£3.95). All the food is made on the premises and occasionally kitchen and cellar combine in a celebration of one of the regions of France (bookings only), when you are likely to find a well-researched six- or seven-course meal for a reasonable £12 per head, with a good selection of matching wines.

LEEDS West Yorkshire

The Bank Wine Bar & Bistro

Sovereign House, Park Row TEL (0532) 434539

OPEN Mon–Thur 11.30 am–3 pm, 5.30 pm–10.30 pm (Fri & Sat till 11 pm) Sun and public holidays 7 pm–10.30 pm CLOSED Sun & public holidays L, Chr Day
CREDIT CARDS Not accepted WHEELCHAIR ACCESS Impossible
VEGETARIAN DISHES Salads and vegetable quiche

This large basement bar, still very popular at lunch-time with office staff and businessmen, is not a bar to seek out specially, but it is useful in its area. In the evenings, it is completely transformed, with different clientèle, music and a light show, including lasers, masterminded by the resident disc jockey. As well as wines, The Bank offers cocktails, sales of which are copious, and a range of 20 different bottled lagers. The wine list is a collection of mostly tedious-looking anonymous wine bar staples, often with misleading notes: Sancerre Clos du Roc, for example, is 'similar in style to some white Burgundies, but much less expensive'. You will nevertheless find some drinkable basic wines here, if stuck in the area. The food is similar to that offered by other wine bars in the West Midlands Taverns Chain (*see Horts, Edgbaston*).

> Have we included your favourite spot for eating *and* drinking? If not, or if you disagree with our assessment, tell us about it either by letter or on the forms at the back of the *Guide*.

Parkers Wine Bar

12 Park Place TEL (0532) 456087

OPEN Mon–Sat 11.30 am–3 pm, 5.30 pm–10.30 pm CLOSED Sun
CREDIT CARDS Not accepted WHEELCHAIR ACCESS Impossible
VEGETARIAN DISHES Salads

Steep steps lead down to this den of draught beers, lagers and spirits, fruit machines and video games. There's little choice in the area, however, and Parkers' limited range of wines is extremely well priced – 16 are available at below £4 a bottle. An anonymous, unvintaged Médoc is £4.25, a St-Emilion £4.95, a Côtes-du-Rhône £3.95, the sound Moreau Blanc £3.70. House wine (the Partager brand) is 75p a glass. There is reasonable hot and cold food, with a good choice of salads. Because Parkers is in the heart of the city, it tends to fill up at lunch-time from nearby offices. As an encouragement to evening stragglers, spirits are served between 5.30 and 8 pm at 70p a double . . . could wine drinkers please have a happy hour, too?

LEOMINSTER Hereford & Worcester

Roots

Royal Oak Hotel, South Street TEL (0568) 2610

OPEN Mon–Sat 10.30 am–2.30 pm Fri–Sat (only) 7 pm–11 pm CLOSED Sun, Mon–Thur evenings, Chr Day CREDIT CARDS Access/Euro, Visa
WHEELCHAIR ACCESS Impossible VEGETARIAN DISHES On request

Rescued from disuse and disrepair and carefully and sympathetically restored by John and Sue Pallant, Roots, with its arched brick alcoves in the basement of the Royal Oak Hotel, is a comfortable and elegant location for a meal and a glass or two of wine. The wine list is comprehensive, well laid out, with something for everyone. House wines are the good value French Chantarel red, dry white and sweet white from Tanners of Shrewsbury and are sold in five-ounce glasses (£3.70/70p). Of special interest are the superb Châteauneuf-du-Pape, Domaine du Vieux Télégraphe 1981 from Brunier et fils (£6.75); Côte de Buzet, Cuvée Napoléon 1978 (£5); Ch Durfort-Vivens 1970 (£18), and from the local Herefordshire vineyard, Bodenham Reichensteiner 1983 (£8). The food is less interesting but still sound; try the delicious rare beef sandwiches (£1.35), Stilton ploughman's (£2), home-made quiche Lorraine (£3.20), prawn omelette (£3.65), seafood platter (£3.25) or fillet steak (£6.50). The daily special on our visit was gammon with new potatoes, salad and apple chutney (£1.60).

Readers' reports submitted to *The Good Food Guide* as well as *Which? Wine Guide* have been used to supplement official inspectors' reports in compiling this section.

LEWES East Sussex

Carmichaels

197 High Street TEL (079 16) 77879

OPEN Mon–Sat 9 am–11 pm (Fri & Sat till 12 pm) CLOSED Sun, some public holidays CREDIT CARDS All accepted WHEELCHAIR ACCESS Yes VEGETARIAN DISHES Interesting choice

Carmichaels, from being a 'promising new venture' in the last *Guide*, is becoming very much an institution where food is as important as the wine; yet a great effort is obviously made to ensure that the restaurant does not overpower or indeed detract from the Edwardian atmosphere of the wine bar. There are regular special theme weeks, such as a British Week featuring traditional English food and six English wines, including Sussex County (£4.95), Cuckmere (£5.50) and Breaky Bottom (£6.95). As we went to press, the very reasonable list was drawn totally from the Ebury Wine Company, and included the fresh Ch Bonnet Blanc 1982 (£4.85), Gewürztraminer Réserve Spéciale 1979 from Gisselbrecht (£6.95), Ch Bonnet 1979 red at £6.75, and a score of other reasonable wines. But proprietor Michael Carmichael tells us that his new list will come from other suppliers, too. Food is well prepared by a Lyonnais chef: lunchtime specialities might be salade niçoise (£1.80), seafood pie (£3.30), and various casseroles. In the evening, prawns with aïoli (£2.70), seafood à la bretonne (£3.30), casserole of lamb with flageolet beans (£3.50), with a selection of vegetables, salads, and garlic bread, might be the options. The menu changes constantly, and all the food is cooked on the premises. There are tables outside in summer.

LINCOLN Lincolnshire

Straits

8/9 The Strait TEL (052 29) 20814

OPEN Mon–Sat 12 noon–2.30 pm, 7 pm–11 pm CLOSED Sun, Chr Day, Boxing Day, New Year's Day CREDIT CARDS All accepted WHEELCHAIR ACCESS Reasonable VEGETARIAN DISHES Some

A relaxed and friendly wine bar in one of Lincoln's narrow old streets leading up the steep hill towards the Cathedral: you won't need crampons until you get nearer the top. The two-roomed ground-floor bar is stocked with about three dozen fairly young wines, still without any answer on the list to the question: 'Little wines, who made thee?', apart from a worthy 1978 Grand Bourgeois Exceptionnel from the central Médoc, the relatively slow-to-come-round Ch Dutruch Grand Poujeaux, at £10.25. The list at the time of writing is very similar to last year's, as are the prices with, for example, a 1980 Montlouis at £5.25/£1.15, a 1981 Trittenheimer Altärchen Auslese at £7.95, and a Pierre Ponnelle Crozes-Hermitage 1981 at £7.90; there are encouragingly about a dozen wines available by the glass, and a dry tank method sparkler at £5.45/£1.10 is a very pleasant way to start an evening; house red is from Quinson (£3.50/75p), and house claret from Nathaniel Johnston (£5.20/£1.15). But a planned new wine list may be in operation by the time you read this – they are to change the German section and highlight some of the good value lesser-known wines of France. Food is served upstairs. The more substantial dishes appear in the evening, and you will find a good range of salads including tongue or sugar-baked ham at £2.70, and hot garlic prawns with toast or garlic bread at £1.80 (unfortunately the bread goes into the microwave too, and to consume the result is like trying to chew through a sponge). What the lamb bhajees with curry sauce and rice (£2.80) may lack in authenticity they make up for in taste; vegetable lasagne is £2.20, and beef Dijon may be on the board at £2.85, or oriental pork at £2.70. Hot chocolate fudge cake is a snip at 95p.

LLANGOLLEN Clwyd

Gales

11 Bridge Street TEL (0978) 860089

OPEN 1 June–15 Sept: Mon–Sat 12 noon–1.45 pm, 6 pm–10.15 pm Sun 7 pm–10.15 pm; 16 Sept–31 May: Tue–Sat 12 noon–1.45 pm, 6 pm–10.15 pm CLOSED First 2 weeks Nov, (6 Sept–31 May) Sun & Mon
CREDIT CARDS Not accepted WHEELCHAIR ACCESS One step up
VEGETARIAN DISHES Plenty

This small, panelled wine bar, bustling with activity, has a tremendous atmosphere and a noble pricing policy for the excellent wine list – all wines carry a flat ten per cent mark-up. The house wines are a soft red Côtes du Ventoux 1981 and a fresh, dry vin de table white both at £3.60/65p. Yugoslav Riesling and Liebfraumilch are also available by the glass (65p). At the next step up, you might consider the Crozes-Hermitage Blanc 1981 (£4.75), Muscadet 1982 (£3.95) or Torres Coronas 1979 (£4.95). Some wines come in half-bottles (Médoc 1981, £2.70, Bereich Bernkastel Riesling 1981, £2.60), and there's a large and unusual selection of liqueurs. The fine wine list featuring clarets from the 1957/1961/1966/1970 vintages, vintage ports and a good range of Burgundies, also carries a mere ten per cent mark-up on auction room prices, so the more you spend the better value you get. Gales' wholesale licence enables them to sell any of the wines listed, in unbroken or mixed cases, at good discounts. Take-away wines from the fine wine list cost ten per cent more than the wine bar price. The interesting menu is on the wall at the back of the bar and a *plat du jour* is always featured (boeuf provençal with rice, £2.45). Other choices offering excellent value might be red pepper and onion quiche (95p), smoked salmon and apple mousse (£1.20), chicken liver and herb pâté served with granary bread (£1.10). There is a range of home-made ice-cream (70p) with lemon and mocha the favourites. It's all well presented, and the service is friendly and efficient, even when the place is at its most hectic.

LONG MELFORD Suffolk

Canes Ⓥ

Hall Street TEL (0787) 78213

OPEN Mon–Sat 7.30 pm–11 pm CLOSED L, Sun CREDIT CARDS Access/Euro, Visa WHEELCHAIR ACCESS Yes VEGETARIAN DISHES Salads and cheeses; other dishes if notified in advance

This charming and busy wine bar/bistro, decorated with old photographs, lies on the main street of this pretty Suffolk village. Neville Cox, the proprietor, offers 72 wines diverted from the list of his own wine business. House wines at £3.95/70p are better than are generally found at this level and the entire list has been well chosen and clearly presented. The 1983 Muscadet de-Sèvre-et-Maine Sur Lie, Clos d'Orfeuilles is fresh and crisp, with Sancerre (£5.60) and Alsace Riesling (£4.95) also good buys, but probably the best value amongst the whites is the 1983 St-Véran from Sylvan Fessy, excellent at £5.95. The wide range of reds includes Nick Ryman's splendid Bergerac, Ch la Jaubertie 1981 (£4.95) and the Brouilly 1983, Sylvan Fessy at £5.40; Côtes Roannaises (£4.75) is soft and grapy and particularly recommended. The menu, which changes weekly, normally shows a choice of six starters, main courses and sweets. Food is well prepared and not over-priced. On the day of our visit, avocado vinaigrette, mushrooms with garlic butter and smoked mackerel mousse were all £1. Main courses included spaghetti bolognaise (£2.25), chicken with plum sauce (£3.25) and cod Mornay (also £3.25). Amongst the selection of sweets at £1 were rhubarb and ginger crumble, cheesecake and chocolate and brandy mousse. Cheese was £1.20.

MACCLESFIELD Cheshire

Harlequins Ⓥ

68a Chestergate TEL (0625) 32657

OPEN Mon–Sat 10.30 am–3.30 pm, 6.30 pm–12 pm (Fri, Sat till 12.30 am) CLOSED Sun, Chr Day, Boxing Day CREDIT CARDS Access/Euro, Visa WHEELCHAIR ACCESS Yes VEGETARIAN DISHES A few

An ambitious set-up in an old stable in the centre of town, this is something of an oasis in the Macclesfield area. It's a pleasantly fronted building with a well-maintained courtyard garden. Harlequin motifs are rampant. The place is worth a visit for its choice of wines by the glass alone: sound house wines (Cuvée Jean-Paul), especially a peppery Rhône-style red at 65p, a 1978 Campo Viejo Rioja at £4.50/75p, plus a frequent weekly special – on our visit, a 1982 Nussdorfer Bischhofskreuz Kabinett, again 75p. The full list, constantly up-dated to include the proprietors' new discoveries, lives up to this promise, with around 150 wines from most major wine-producing countries. There are such temptations as a 1979 Grand Cru St-Emilion Ch d'Artus

(£6.40), a Wachenheimer Königswert Auslese 1976 (£6.50), a 1979 Barolo from Cantina Terre del Barolo (£5.70), and even a Vendange Tardive Gewürztraminer 1979 (A Heim) (£10.30). The proprietors list up to ten Riojas (three of them Gran Reserva) and are thinking of specialising in this area. All the food is cooked on the premises (even some of the bread!) and at lunch-time, the blackboard menu, changed daily, offers cold cuts and salads and various hot dishes: ham risotto (£1.50), chicken cacciatore (£1.75), and a few vegetarian dishes, such as leeks in cheese sauce at £1.50. There are set price evening meals (between £6 and £9.50 for starter, main course and sweet), changing every three weeks and offering generous bistro-style food. The delicious-looking home-made gâteaux cry out for the glass of Muscat de Beaumes de Venise available for £1. Members of Harlequins' wine club are entitled to discount prices on take-away bottles and the use of a comfortable lounge, as well as special tasting evenings. The atmosphere is relaxed and informal, the service friendly.

MANCHESTER

Bligh's

5 Old Bank Street, Royal Exchange TEL 061-832 6146

OPEN Mon–Sat 11.30 am–3 pm, 5.30 pm–10.30 pm (Fri, Sat till 11 pm)
CREDIT CARDS Not accepted VEGETARIAN DISHES Few

Is this cellar, off fashionable St Anne's Square, dimly lit just to hide the gaudy wallpaper? A scaffold structure of wooden beams proudly bears some fascinating bottles, sadly empty, of past weekly specials. These include some classed growth clarets and other finery and vary according to recent bargains. The main list is no more than adequate, but it does include the odd welcome surprise, like a 1979 Graves de Vayres, Ch Bussac at £5.20 and the Chianti, a 1978 Putto Riserva from the fine house of Pasolini (£4.95). Some of the house wines are good, the Cabernet d'Anjou Rosé Moulin Touchais (£3.60/67p) and the crisply fruity dry white Le Compagnon (£4.65 per litre/65p) are both from the Touchais family. Unusually, too, you can buy decent port by the glass – Taylor's crusting or Taylor's ten-year-old at 80p. Food is staple stuff and revolves around pâtés, quiche and cheeses at up to £1.30 and a small selection of hot dishes, like home-made steak and kidney pie with chips and peas at £1.85. Bligh's is under the same ownership as Duke's in Chester, where the wine list is sadly much more limited.

> Prices were current in summer 1984 to the best of our knowledge but can only be a rough indication of prices throughout 1985.

> If you disagree with us, please tell us why. You will find report forms at the back of the book.

Cellar Vie I Ⓥ

20 Lloyd Street TEL 061-834 9696
OPEN Mon–Fri 12.30 pm–3 pm, 8 pm–midnight Sat 8 pm–2 am

Cellar Vie II Ⓥ

20 Charlotte Street TEL 061-236 6006
OPEN Mon–Fri 12.30 pm–3 pm, 9 pm–2 am, Sat 9 pm–2 am

CLOSED (Both wine bars) Sat L, Sun, public holidays CREDIT CARDS Not accepted WHEELCHAIR ACCESS Yes VEGETARIAN DISHES Some

Cellar Vie I was Manchester's first wine bar and, 11 years on, is still going strong. Others may have overtaken it in terms of the range offered, but value given is still reasonable. The wine list is limited to the sort of generic wine most enthusiasts cut their teeth on (Côtes-du-Rhône at £4.25, Muscadet at £4.70, or Liebfraumilch at £4.20) with neither vintages nor suppliers listed. However, if you persist, it will be revealed that the anonymous Riojas at £6 a bottle are Marqués de Riscal 1979 and Marqués de Murrieta 1979. Bollinger (*that* name at least was worthy of inclusion) is one of the three Champagnes offered at a reasonable £14.50. At Cellar Vie II, the influence of the Spanish manager is apparent in two wines from Torres, Viña Sol and Sangretetoro, both £4.50, and red and white Riojas: 1976 Domecq Domain Reserva at £4.75 and Marqués de Murrieta Blanco 1980 at £5.50.

The menu is more varied at Cellar Vie I. In addition to a fine array of cold cuts and salads at lunch-time (costing between £2.35 and £3 for poached salmon, inclusive of bread and salad), there is a blackboard menu of hot foods under £3: fettuccine, duck in orange sauce and satay beef. Sweets are simple and good value at 75p for fresh fruit salad or cheesecake. There are even free cold buffets on Wednesday and Thursday evenings, and the occasional gourmet evening. Cellar Vie II offers a simpler menu of cold dishes: gala pie and salad (£2.20) or tuna and salad (£2.75); and limited hot dishes like barbecued ribs or Cumberland sausage at £1.95. Evenings at both bars are generally given over to pop music and a younger clientèle, and the food is more restricted.

Which? Wine Guide does not accept payment for inclusion, and there is no sponsorship or advertising.

The Wine Standards Board is the trade's disciplinary department and wine watchdog. Their inspectors are responsible for rooting out any malpractices – but they are concerned largely with labelling irregularities. If you have genuine reason to suspect that the wine in a bottle is not what the label claims it is, contact the Board at:
68½ Upper Thames Street, London EC4V 3BJ; TEL 01–236 9512.

Gander's Go South

1/3 Barton Arcade, Barton Square TEL 061-832 8360

OPEN Bistro: Mon–Sat 10 am–8 pm (licensed between 11.30 am–3 pm, 5.30 pm onwards) Bar and Restaurant: Mon–Sat 12 noon–3 pm, 5.30 pm–11.30 pm Sun 7 pm–11.30 pm CLOSED Bistro: Sun Bar and restaurant: Sun L Both: Chr Day, Boxing Day, public holidays CREDIT CARDS Access/Euro, Amex, Visa WHEELCHAIR ACCESS To Bistro only VEGETARIAN DISHES Salads

One to watch, under the same ownership as Gander's in Altrincham *(see above)* and Bramhall, this new venture (open since March 1984) is dominated by a Southern States theme both in food and decor. Downstairs in the bar/restaurant, it's all New Orleans French Quarter with wood balustrading, bare brick columns, fans and jazz prints. When we called, the temporary wine list (to be developed as trading patterns become clear) offered, in addition to fair house wines (the ubiquitous Cuvée Jean-Paul at £4.35/75p), a reasonable selection from the Loire (Sauvignon Vin de Pays at £5.75), a Premier Cru Chablis Mont de Milieu 1982 at £8.75, a Moulin-à-Vent Domaine de la Tour de Bief 1980 at £6.35 and a growing selection of château-bottled clarets: Ramage la Batisse 1980 and Clos de la Cure 1979 Grand Cru St-Emilion (£7.55 and £8.95 respectively). Also worth trying is the 1981 Côtes-du-Rhône from the Vignerons de Rasteau (£5.85). Food downstairs is taken seriously, even to the extent of butchering and hanging their own beef for specialities like 16 oz char-broiled rib-eye steaks (£5.95). Starters include clam chowder (£1.20) and deep-fried chicken wings (£1.80). Main courses continue the Creole theme with jambalaya (£5.75), lemon sole Orleans (£4.35) and lamb with minted peppers (£4.85). Sweets are the likes of blueberry pie (95p) and fudge cake (£1.10). There is also a three-course lunchtime special for £4.50. Upstairs, the food is less unusual: baked potatoes with various fillings, salads, even a children's menu and a daily choice of hot dishes (kromesky in barbecue sauce at £2.35 – well, less southern, at least.) And yes, goose will be served in season. We hope this imaginative place, set in the recently restored, civic-design-winning Barton Arcade, lives up to such early promise.

Hort's Continental Wine Bar and Bistro

18 St Ann's Square TEL 061-832 4241

OPEN Mon–Sat 11.30 am–3 pm, 5.30 pm–10.30 pm (Sat till 11 pm) Sun, public holidays 7 pm–10.30 pm CLOSED Sun L CREDIT CARDS Not accepted WHEELCHAIR ACCESS Impossible VEGETARIAN DISHES Quiche

This popular Art Deco wine bar at basement level is the lunchtime and early evening haunt of businessmen. After 8 pm, the lights go down and the music goes up to suit a younger clientèle. The wine list is a fair mix of popular standards, without vintages or suppliers. French house wines are cheap (£3.60/65p) and come from Yvon Mau. A few other wines are available by the glass – on our visit, there was a fair 1982

Muscadet and a 1982 Piesporter (both 75p). The red Burgundies are from Chandesais and include a 1978 Côte de Beaune-Villages at £6.50; the whites are from Moreau: 1979 Chablis, for example, at £7.50. There is a limited and largely branded choice of wines from other countries such as Vinho Verde (Aveleda) at £4.10. What lifts the list from the ordinary is the 'Connoisseur's Selection' of six wines, including a Sancerre Clos du Roc 1981 at £6.20, a Merler Stephansberg Auslese 1976 at £7.80 and a 1978 Gevrey-Chambertin by d'Esrigny for £13.40. Food (on sale between midday and 2.30 pm) is plentiful and cheap. Four daily hot dishes might be chicken in orange and tarragon sauce (£1.95, including rice) or cannelloni (£2.30). There is a cold buffet with cold cuts, game pie, smoked mackerel etc, all £2.30, inclusive of salad and French bread. The choice of sweets is limited to staples such as chocolate fudge cake or cheesecake, all 95p and served with cream. You could round off your meal with a glass of Taylor's ten-year-old for 95p.

MANNINGTREE Essex

Bucks

Cattawade TEL (020 639) 2571

OPEN Mon–Sat 11.30 am–2.30 pm, 5.30 pm–11.30 pm Sun 12 noon–2 pm, 7 pm, 10.30 pm CLOSED Chr Day (possibly) CREDIT CARDS All accepted WHEELCHAIR ACCESS Impossible VEGETARIAN DISHES Salads and some starters

The Bucks Horne public house at Cattawade has become Bucks Restaurant and Wine Bar. Opened in March 1984 by Paul Lewis (late of Robert Carrier's Hintlesham Hall), it has rapidly become a favourite haunt for those seeking high quality food and interesting, reasonably priced wines. Service is friendly and prompt and the smallish bar is crowded most lunch-times and evenings. The wine list shows sixty wines (double that in the adjoining 30-seater restaurant). House wines (£3.95/70p) are the well-made and fruity Pinot Chardonnay and full-bodied soft Cabernet Sauvignon from Bulgaria, and Huesgen's Tafelwein. The 'personal selections' (four white, seven red, a rosé and a Champagne) include a delicious Alsace Pinot Blanc (£6.70) and a fruity, fresh Gold Medal-winning Gamay de l'Ardèche (£5.90). There is a good range of Bordeaux and Burgundy, with Pierre Coste's Domaine de Gaillat 1981 at £8.45 and Louis Tête's 1982 Fleurie looking particularly good value. Alsace, Rhône and Loire are represented and popular German wines are in evidence. The menu, which changes regularly, is painted on the mirror above the log fire. Starters might include watercress soup (60p), garlic stuffed mushrooms (50p) or smoked salmon mousse (90p). Seafood pancake (£1.50) is a popular main dish served with a crisp, well-dressed salad and chips. Ham in Madeira (£3.10) looked appetising, and steak and mushroom pie with new potatoes and peas at £2.20 was good value. The future looks bright. More reports, please!

MARKET BOSWORTH Leicestershire

Softleys

Market Place TEL (0455) 290464

OPEN Mon–Sun 12 noon–2 pm Tue–Sat 7.30 pm–10.30 pm CLOSED Sun eve
CREDIT CARDS Not accepted WHEELCHAIR ACCESS Difficult
VEGETARIAN DISHES Some

Softleys, in a corner of the village square, is a clean, well-run, two-roomed little place, with a smack of individuality about the decor. It seems to act as the unofficial village pub. If you've a mind for cocktails, are prepared to part with £2.50 and don't blush easily, you could ask for a Long Sloe Comfortable Screw Against The Wall. On the very standard list of 24 wines, clearly presented with vintages indicated (but without shippers or producers), Bordeaux fares as well as anywhere, reds including Ch Baron 1979 (£5.75) and Ch Guimbertau 1978 (£7.95). House wines from way down south in Roussillon are £3.50/60p and a welcome glass of Fonseca Bin 27 is 80p. Lunchtime food might include Lancashire hot-pot (£2), convincingly home-made with tasty lamb chops. In the evening, the fare becomes more ambitious with perhaps turkey breast in a hazelnut and cream sauce (£3.80). Service is friendly and efficient.

MIDDLETON Greater Manchester

Jacques Wine Bar and Bistro

7/11 Market Place TEL 061-653 2993

OPEN Mon–Fri 11.30 am–3 pm, 5.30 pm–10.30 pm Sat 5.30 pm–11.30 pm
Sun 7 pm–10.30 pm Public holidays 11.30 am–3 pm, 5.30 pm–10.30 pm
CLOSED Sat & Sun L, Chr Day CREDIT CARDS Access/Euro, Visa
WHEELCHAIR ACCESS Yes VEGETARIAN DISHES Available on request

Jacques is an old police station, no less, imaginatively revamped to offer a variety of settings – a bar, a homely restaurant and an indoor Vineyard Café (complete with umbrellas and garden furniture). The wine list, however, is not nearly as imaginative as the setting deserves, and is unevenly priced, but for a lunchtime glass (or bottle), you search long and hard for alternatives in North Manchester. House wine is cheap at £5 a litre/65p a glass, and comes in five styles. A non-vintage Médoc costs £7 while a 1979 Ch Ramonet is £4. Soundly priced wines include a 1982 Côtes-du-Rhône from Malbec at £3.95, a Chenin Vin de Pays from the Loire at £3.70, a 1979 Condal Rioja at £4.10 and Moreau's Petit Chablis 1982 at £6.90 (but, once again, neither vintages nor suppliers are listed). Food in the Vineyard Café is reasonably priced: starters include tuna and onion salad for 95p or spare ribs at £1.50. Home-made pizzas cost up to £2.20 for the Vineyard Special, there are charcoal-grilled steaks (£4.75 for rump, £6 for T-bone) and the other hot food is standard bistro fare: moussaka (£1.75), beef Stroganoff (£4.50).

MIDDLEWICH Cheshire

Tempter's

11 Wheelock Street TEL (060 684) 5175

OPEN Tue–Sat 7 pm–10.30 pm (Fri, Sat till 11 pm) CLOSED L, Sun, Mon, 1 week mid-Mar, 2 weeks mid-Oct CREDIT CARDS Access/Euro, Visa WHEELCHAIR ACCESS Impossible VEGETARIAN DISHES Very good selection

The soft, low-key colours of the decor, the pleasing wooden furniture and the friendly, unobtrusive service provide the setting for food and wines chosen with equal deliberation. Tempter's wine list is not over-long and tries to avoid the obvious. (More details of wine producers would be appreciated.) There are a couple of Reserva Riojas from Bodegas Artacho (Ramona 1976 at £5.45 and Vinador 1975 at £5.30), a 1978 Gigondas for £8.10 and some interesting French regional wines from Tanners of Shrewsbury – Côtes de Buzet at £5.65 or a VDQS Corbières Montrabech 1980 for £3.85. The whites have a Germanic flavour (Deinhard is well represented) but do include the occasional rarity like a Domaine St-Martin 1980 Montlouis at £5.80 and Côtes-du-Rhône, Les Héliades at £6.50. The French house wines are reasonably priced at £3.10/60p. Other wines are available by the glass, too: Deinhock at 70p or Saumur 1980 at 65p. The cooking shows an admirably individual touch. Starters include baked egg in Stilton sauce or spiced chicken livers (both £1.20). Main courses may be boeuf provençale for £2.50 or émincés de boeuf for £3.50 – but watch for the separate specials board, which might offer an excellently presented Leicestershire chicken or honeyed lamb, both £4.50; the price includes two (more like eight!) vegetables cooked *al dente* to perfection. Sweets include orange Boodle or raspberry meringue Chantilly, £1.05 each. Tempter's maintains a high standard throughout, with careful service. It's well worth a detour.

MORETON-IN-MARSH Gloucestershire

The Greedy Grape

3 Oxford Street TEL (0608) 50039

OPEN Mon–Sat 10 am–3 pm, 6 pm–12 pm Sun 12 noon–3 pm, 7 pm–12 pm Public holidays 12 noon–3 pm, 7 pm–11 pm CREDIT CARDS Access/Euro, Amex WHEELCHAIR ACCESS Yes VEGETARIAN DISHES Some

We want good wine bars to continue trading, and must spare a thought for their particular economic circumstances. So, despite the name, the fact that this Cotswold village wine bar marks up all its 60-odd wines by 100 per cent and, paradoxically, the more expensive wines by more than that, does not necessarily mean it is greedy. But it does mean that you won't find any bargains here; nor will you find many surprises. However, the range of choice at least means that a couple of Paul Masson California wines get a look in – Pinot Chardonnay is £7 and

Cabernet Sauvignon £6.78; and an Alsace Gewürztraminer 1981 (£7.31) from Jules Muller has got to be better value than a bottle of Blue Nun at £7.38! Own-label Les Frères house wines are available in two virtually indistinguishable glass sizes, 4 oz (70p) and 5 oz (80p), served brimful, as well as half-litre (£2.70) and litre (£5.10) carafes. The list is clearly presented, with detailed and helpful comments about the source and style of each wine. Food isn't cheap here either, but helpings are generous; salads and fish dishes are plentiful, grilled steaks are good. Prices (£4.75 to £7.55) are inclusive of coffee, and specialities like gravad lax, £3.50, are enterprising.

NEWCASTLE UNDER LYME Staffordshire

Candles

Paradise Street TEL (0782) 617585
OPEN Mon–Sat 10 am–3 pm, 7.30 pm–11 pm Sun 7.30 pm–11 pm
CLOSED Sun L, Spring Bank Holiday, Chr Day, Boxing Day CREDIT CARDS Not accepted WHEELCHAIR ACCESS Yes VEGETARIAN DISHES Quiche and salads

A bustling, no-nonsense shoppers' rendezvous on market days, rather than the intimate, seductive setting that its name might evoke, Candles offers no frills. The most you can pay for one of the 20 items on the blackboard menu is £1.75, which would get you a plateful of steak and kidney pie with baked potato, perhaps, or a smoked mackerel, ham or beef salad; crabmeat on toast is £1.30. The 40-odd wines on the less than fully detailed list are similarly modestly priced, with little over £6 a bottle; both half-bottles and wines by the glass are plentiful, if rather unadventurous. Still, there is a Côtes de Bourg, Ch La Tour Camillac 1979 at £5.30, a Marcel Sautejeau Muscadet-sur-Lie, Domaine de l'Hyvernière 1982 (£4.75), dependable Domecq Domain Rioja (£4.65 the white, £5.05 the red), and a couple of good value Paul Masson California wines – Pinot Chardonnay 1981 (£5) and Zinfandel 1979 (£4.80).

NEWCASTLE-UPON-TYNE Tyne & Wear

Bewicks Wine & Cheese Bar

24 The Cloth Market TEL (0632) 619872
OPEN Mon–Sat 11.30 am–2.30 pm, 5.30 pm–10.30 pm Sun 7 pm–10.30 pm
CLOSED Never CREDIT CARDS Not accepted WHEELCHAIR ACCESS Yes
VEGETARIAN DISHES Large selection of good cheeses

The 'cheese' suffix is not for nothing – this bar specialises rather more in cheese than in wine: the cheese list has tasting notes! There's 'Walton – a strong, rich cheese made from Cheddar and Blue Stilton coated with walnuts' (goes with Worthington, the list suggests) or 'Caerphilly – creamed and mild with a delicate flavour. Matures in only two weeks. Its mildness makes it easily digestible and leaves a clean, fresh taste on the palate. A gentle cheese'. It seems rather a shame to drink the recommended Liebfraumilch. . . . The 30 listed cheeses are mostly English but with a few interesting foreigners (£1.50 for a substantial selection with dill cucumber and butter). Home-made pâtés are the alternative (£1.50 again), all served with good wholemeal bread from an excellent local baker. The wine list is fair, supplied by Hedges & Butler, the wine division of Bass, who own this bar – the only traditional wine bar they do own in the North, in fact. House red (£3.80/70p a glass or 95p for a large glass) is Bâton Rouge, and the white for the same prices is 'Minette' – a nice, crisp Sauvignon. A glass of Lanson Black Label is £2.10 and Warre's Nimrod Port is just 75p. If you are having a bottle, there is Côtes du Lubéron VDQS (£4.35), Alsace Gewürztraminer (£7.65), Aveleda Vinho Verde (£4.90), 'Vouvray AC Vintage' – more we are not told – for £5.50, Minervois (£4.20) or Côtes-du-Rhône (£4.85). The tasting notes on the wines are accurate, too, but Hedges & Butler might like to annotate their next list properly, with origins and vintages. Bewicks is an enjoyable bar, converted from the old Imperial Hotel pub, with a long, mahogany bar and brass fittings. The lighting is low, and on the walls are copies of prints by Thomas Bewick – the 18th-century artist and engraver whose former workshop is 50 yards from the wine bar. Bewicks can be booked for wine and cheese parties.

Dennhöfer's Wine Bar

44 Leazes Lane TEL (0632) 614060
OPEN Mon–Sat 12 pm–3 pm Tue–Sat 7 pm–12 pm (food till 10.30 pm)
CLOSED Sun CREDIT CARDS Access/Euro, Amex, Visa
WHEELCHAIR ACCESS Difficult but possible VEGETARIAN DISHES Quiche, cheeses

Number 44 Leazes Lane is an old converted synagogue, and Heinz Dennhöfer has fitted it out remarkably well. He moved here from his original wine bar in the Handyside Arcade, and is an old pro in the wine trade; his wines have always been of a reasonable standard. More wine bar managers and proprietors might do well to copy his excellent idea of sticking actual wine labels on to the list – the simplest way of providing all the necessary information – attractive and tempting, too. German wines are from a variety of sources, and include a 1981 Hochheimer Stein Riesling Trocken from the Verwaltung der Staatsweingüter, Eltville (£6.45) and a 1981 Wehlener Sonnenuhr Riesling Kabinett from M J Clüsserath in Mehring am Mosel (£5.50); there's even a German red and rosé, plus a few French wines and a couple of uninteresting Italians, a sparkling German and a Champagne. The menu is decidedly Teutonic, too: pork Schnitzel for just over £4, Bratwurst mit Sauerkraut (£3.75), German salads and a tempting selection of Kuchen, Torten and special ice-creams.

Send us **your** views on the report forms at the back of the book.

Fitzgerald's

Ⓥ

60 Grey Street TEL (0632) 615038

OPEN Mon–Sat 11.30 am–2.30 pm, 5.30 pm–10.30 pm Sun 7 pm–10.30 pm Public holidays 7 pm–10.30 pm CLOSED Sun & public holidays L
CREDIT CARDS Access/Euro, Visa WHEELCHAIR ACCESS Yes
VEGETARIAN DISHES Some

Fitzgerald's is tastefully done out in traditional Victorian/Edwardian oaky design, with a rather earthy atmosphere, and loud music. If you can think of something to celebrate, Champagnes are really very well priced here: Baron de Beaupré (house Champagne) is £8.60, Moët £10.60 and Bollinger NV Cuvée Spéciale just £11.70 – cheaper than you would find it on a lot of wine merchants' lists. Some of the best value on the wine list is hidden at the end, in the Iberian section: Domecq Domain Rioja is £4.90, and white Marqués de Riscal is £5.05. Aveleda Vinho Verde is a pleasant, off-dry white at £4.60, and the William Jacob wines from Australia are very drinkable, too, at £4.15, along with the Masson California Cabernet and Chardonnay at just over £5. The usual French wine bar staples – Mâcon-Villages, Côtes-du-Rhône, Rosé d'Anjou – fill out the list. Food on our visit included vegetarian lasagne with green salad (£1.80), a selection of salads for £1.80 and substantial sandwiches. Sweets are a speciality: home-made blackberry mille-feuille, chocolate and orange choux ring, or home-made coffee ice-cream (80p), cooked by the resident Cordon Bleu cook.

Lazers

1 Grey Street TEL (0632) 616106

OPEN Mon–Sat 11.30 am–2.30 pm, 7 pm–10.30 pm Sun 5.30 pm–10.30 pm public holidays 5.30 pm–10.30 pm CLOSED Sun & public holidays L
CREDIT CARDS Access/Euro, Visa WHEELCHAIR ACCESS Up three steps
VEGETARIAN DISHES Good choice

If loud music and jabbing laser beams are your style, Lazers is the place for you – though you will find the wines more reasonably priced just up the street *(see above)*. Bollinger NV here is £17.40 and Moët nearly £15. The list is heavy on Champagnes, in fact, but most of the other French wines are better priced at under £5 for the usual wine bar names, plus Chiroubles 1978, anon, at £7.65. Perhaps most interesting on the list, politics permitting, is the South African Pinotage (£5.25). The two retsinas include an unusual red one called Kokkineli. The sudden appearance here of a producer's name is no doubt explained by the owner's nationality – reflected also in the simple grilled-and-fried Greek food. Vegetarians should be happy here with vegetarian stuffed vine leaves and peppers, hummus, Feta cheese, omelettes; and there are shish kebabs (£2), moussaka (£1.85) or chicken supreme (£2.20) for meat-eaters.

NEWPORT Shropshire

Rogues

St Marys Street TEL (0952) 814085

OPEN Tue–Sat 12 noon–2.30 pm Mon–Sat 7.30 pm–11 pm CLOSED Sun, Mon L CREDIT CARDS Visa WHEELCHAIR ACCESS Very easy to wine bar; large steps up to restaurant could prove difficult VEGETARIAN DISHES Unexciting

Rogues, a 17th-century building in St Marys Street just off Newport High Street, is a cross between a pub and a wine bar and, by the time the *Guide* is published, will have taken a step further – the wine bar was undergoing alterations at the time of our visit to turn the first floor into a small cocktail bar for diners. The place seems to cater mostly for the young and for local farmers. A large bar takes up the whole of one wall, and as well as wine, beer and spirits are much in evidence. The house red wine by Chantovent is excellent (£3/60p) and the French white at the same price is also good, but they are the only wines available by the glass. The rest of the wine list is unimaginative, and vintages served may not be the ones listed. The only half-bottles are Mateus Rosé (£2.50) and Graves (£2.45). The food is served in a small back room decorated with unframed wine maps. Like the wine, it is rather plain, such as cold roast beef or lasagne (£2.25, including three help-yourself salads). This is the only wine bar in Newport and for many miles around – useful in the area, but not worth a detour.

NEWPORT PAGNELL Buckinghamshire

Glovers Ⓥ

18–20 St John's Street TEL (0908) 616398

OPEN Tue–Sat 11.30 am–2.30 pm, 6.30 pm–11 pm CLOSED Sun, Mon CREDIT CARDS Access/Euro, Visa WHEELCHAIR ACCESS Very difficult VEGETARIAN DISHES Some

Adrian and Eve Glover's tiny wine bar (there's more room upstairs) is an attractive brick, wood and tile construction just behind their restaurant, displaying some colourful batik which is for sale. The wine list is perched above the bar, and chalk and duster allow it to be kept up to date. In addition to Lamberhurst Priory (£6) and a standard European range, California varietals are pleasingly in evidence with a Cabernet Sauvignon (£5.40), Greystone Zinfandel (£4.90/£1) and a well-balanced Paul Masson Chardonnay (£5.40/£1.10). It's good to find that well over half of the two dozen wines, moderately priced between £3.50 and £5.50, are available by the glass at about a fifth of the bottle price: Rioja (£4.85/£1), a tank method sparkler, Comte de Lauvère (£4.70/95p) and a Liebfraumilch (£3.20/65p). Although there is some overlap, you can extend your choice a little by consulting the restaurant wine list. The kitchen that serves the restaurant also supplies the wine bar with a good range of salads, small pizzas, vegetable quiche with wholemeal pastry, extremely good value at 75p, shepherd's pie at £2.25, and the unlikely sounding Gloverburger.

NORTHALLERTON North Yorkshire

Tontine Inn

Staddlebridge TEL (060 982) 207

OPEN Mon–Sat 12 noon–3 pm, 7 pm–11 pm Sun 12 noon–2 pm, 7 pm–10.30 pm CLOSED public holidays CREDIT CARDS All accepted WHEELCHAIR ACCESS Impossible VEGETARIAN DISHES Some

Teesside trendies patronise the cellar bar and bistro at the Tontine Inn, where the candlelit pine tables, low ceilings and 1930s music create a lively but easy atmosphere, like a German Weinkeller. It is advisable to book. The blackboard menu is changed daily, offering an array of superbly cooked food served by young, somewhat casual but very efficient staff. You might choose home-made soup (£1.10), excellent rough pâté (£1.95), pastrami (£2.30), crispy spare ribs or lasagne (£3.25), tandoori chicken (£5.95), or a selection of steaks from £6.45 – all are served with salad and new potatoes. Various home-made sweets are £1.50. Three own-label house wines are on sale in litres (£6.55) or by the large glass (90p): a full French red, a crisp clean French white, and a German Tafelwein. Special wines of the month are advertised on blackboards; these might be Touraine Sauvignon 1982 Clos Roche Blanche from Catherine Roussel (£5.25), or Beaujolais 1983, Georges Duboeuf (£5.85). Wines on the main list, though not cheap, are well chosen, particularly the 1970 clarets and white Burgundies.

NORWICH Norfolk

Skippers (The Wine Cellar)

18 Bedford Street TEL (0603) 22836

OPEN Mon–Sat 12 noon–2.30 pm, 6 pm–11 pm CLOSED Sun, public holidays CREDIT CARDS All accepted WHEELCHAIR ACCESS Impossible VEGETARIAN DISHES With prior notice; always quiches and salads

Skippers' long association with the wine trade is immediately evident as you enter this pleasant wine cellar/restaurant. Some 36 different light wines, 14 fortified wines, and four Champagnes and sparkling wines are available by the glass at prices ranging from 68p to £1.35. You might immediately begin to worry about oxidation with such a varied choice, but Mr Skipper assures us that all wines opened within a day are sent to the kitchen, and we're inclined to believe him, judging by the frequent use of alcohol in the 'daily specials'. The main menu is changed every three months but each day there is a choice of three special dishes. These might be mushrooms sautéed with onion and garlic and finished with cream and brandy (£2.35), cucumber and cream cheese mousse (£2.05), kidneys in sherry sauce (£3.50), or boeuf bourguignonne (£4.50). It sounds enterprising, but the results can be disappointing. Skippers also has a regular 'mid-week treat' on Wednesdays, such as Far Eastern food, 'A taste of Old England' or an Italian evening (£15 for two). The wine list is attractively presented and the wines thoughtfully chosen, though prices are sometimes a little high. Besides the mandatory inclusions, there is a 1976 Pinotage from South Africa (£6.50) and a Chardonnay from Bulgaria (£4.25). House wines are £3.25 a half-litre carafe or 68p a glass and the choice is either an Italian-bottled Merlot Castelbello DOC, a dry white Soave del Colle DOC, or a medium or sweet French-bottled wine, and one rosé. A much wider selection of wines is available for retail sale in the new wine shop immediately above the wine cellar.

The Wine Press

Woburn Court, 8 Guildhall Hill TEL (0603) 612874
OPEN Mon–Sat 9 am–3 pm CLOSED Evenings, Sun, public holidays
CREDIT CARDS Not accepted WHEELCHAIR ACCESS Impossible
VEGETARIAN DISHES Salads, quiche

The Wine Press is conveniently situated just off Norwich's Market Square and serves coffee from nine in the morning, then lunch, but not supper. The atmosphere is bustling and the range of wines limited, but very good as one would expect – the Haynes family of Haynes Hanson & Clark *(see MERCHANTS section)* own the bar. The list comprises just 13 wines, all reliable, five of which are available by the glass. The most unusual is an Abbey Knight Müller-Thurgau from Suffolk (£5.50/90p). The house wines are £3.90/65p – there's a house red, Blanc de Blancs, Rosé d'Anjou and a Liebfraumilch, R Müller 1983. Apart from these, there are two fruity young clarets – Les Thuilleries at £5.90 and Ch Gaussens at £3.35 (half-bottles only), a 1983 Beaujolais-Villages (£6.35), one Mâcon, one Rhône and one Loire. House sparkling white at £6.95 is sound, and Champagne Pierre Vaudon Brut at £13.70 is good. But shame on Haynes Hanson & Clark – where are the producers' names for half of these wines? All the food is freshly cooked. Dishes of the day might be chicken and mushrooms in sauce with rice, curries, and an assortment of quiches, salads, pâtés and puddings.

OSWESTRY Shropshire

The Good Companion

10 Beatrice Street TEL (0691) 655768
OPEN Tue–Sat 11 am–3 pm, 7.30 pm–11 pm CLOSED Sun & Mon
CREDIT CARDS Not accepted WHEELCHAIR ACCESS Yes
VEGETARIAN DISHES Excellent

Food is a speciality at this small gas-lit wine bar housed in a 17th-century building, and the proprietor takes justifiable pride in the fact that it is all home-made. It is also excellent value. On our visit there were spare ribs in barbecue sauce (£2.65), chilli con carne and rice (£3) and moussaka and salad (£3.95) – the last two came with pitta bread. Vegetarians are very well catered for here: hummus dip and pitta bread (£1.15), cauliflower and courgette savoury with garlic bread (£2.45), prawn pancakes, salad and French bread (£3.20), seafood lasagne, salad and garlic bread (£3) or mixed nut salad (£2.50). Fudgy banana pie, crêpes with maple syrup or praline filling, and blackcurrant and raspberry Pavlova, all at 85p, are further attractions. The wine list is good, too, and covers a wide range: Côtes-du-Rhône (£4.05), Crozes-Hermitage, Domaine de Thalabert from Paul Jaboulet (£8.46), Pouilly Fumé, J Moreau 1980 (£6.32), Côtes de Buzet de Gueyze 1979 (£4.98), Wiltinger Scharzberg Kabinett 1982 (£5.45). The house wine is a very good French vin de table, Chantal (£2.50 a half-litre, 75p a glass). They also have a house claret from Nathaniel Johnston (£4.46/95p) well worth trying. There are four different whites and three reds available by the glass, and half-bottles of St-Emilion 1981 (£2.65) and Liebfraumilch (£1.95). Service is both friendly and efficient. The proprietors also have a larger room at the back of the wine bar, where they can cater for parties and functions.

Wine in the Willows

45 Willow Street — TEL (0691) 659140

OPEN Tue–Sat 12 noon–2.30 pm Mon–Sat 7 pm–12 pm CLOSED Sun, Mon L CREDIT CARDS Access/Euro, Visa WHEELCHAIR ACCESS Easy VEGETARIAN DISHES Several well-chosen dishes

Like its counterpart above, Wine in the Willows nestles in a 17th-century listed building in one of Oswestry's quieter streets. The bar is divided into three small panelled rooms with a wealth of oak beams and a small compact bar. The wines of Spain are something of a speciality here. The house wines are either French Red and White Litre Vin, or, much better value, the Viña Bonita red and white (£3.60/60p) from La Mancha. There is also an excellent red Rioja Campo Viejo 1981 (£4/70p) and a Marqués de Monistrol Gran Reserva 1977 (£6.40) from Penedès. On a comprehensive list of about 100 wines, most are under £5 a bottle and are available by the glass too, although this is not always stated. The good selection of low-priced home-cooked dishes ranges from tuna fish flan (£1.50) to smoked trout salad (£2.50), all served with jacket potatoes (30p extra), fresh French bread, and generous, well-prepared salads. But there are also steak and seafood dishes ranging from prawn provençale (£3.50) to steak au poivre (£5.90). Service and attention are good.

Do **you** know of any more bars that deserve inclusion in next year's *Guide?* If so, write and tell us on the report forms at the back of the book.

OTLEY West Yorkshire

Korks Wine Bar & Bistro

40 Bondgate TEL (0943) 462020

OPEN Mon–Thur 12 noon–2 pm, 7 pm–10.30 pm Fri–Sat 12 noon–2 pm, 7 pm–11 pm Sun 12 noon–2 pm, 7 pm–10 pm CREDIT CARDS Access/Euro, Visa WHEELCHAIR ACCESS Yes VEGETARIAN DISHES Some

Korks is a roomy establishment with plenty of bar area (a bit like a saloon in a Wild West movie) and a restaurant area capable of seating 72 people. Philip and Marjorie Sedgwick are constantly on hand to look after their customers. Their wine list gives details of around 75 bottles, plus ten house wines. 'Bag in box' Italian wines are sold on draught by the glass (65p), half-carafe (£2.50) or carafe (£4.80), whilst French and German house wines can be sampled by bottle or glass (£3.95/70p). Otherwise, there are Georges Duboeuf wines (Beaujolais-Villages £6.50), Robert Sarrau Chablis (£6.95) and Lucien Lannay's delicious Touraine Sauvignon (£6.50). The New World is represented by Mission Creek in California and the excellent Hill Smith Estate in Australia (Shiraz £7.25). Various blackboards offer bin-ends, some of which may be rather by-passed by the bargain-minded Otley folk – Ch Talbot 1973 (£12.50), Arnheimer Adelberg Trockenbeerenauslese 1976 (£11.75). The Sedgwicks were revising the list at the time of our visit, dropping some of the everyday wines (Beaujolais, Muscadet, Côtes-du-Rhône) in favour of quality wines from better-known shippers/growers, which will certainly boost the existing list. All the food is home-prepared and cooked and is wholesome, well presented and cheap. There are lunch and evening menus, the more exotic courses changing regularly.

OXFORD Oxfordshire

Emperors

22 Broad Street TEL (0865) 723642

OPEN Mon–Fri 12 noon–2.30 pm, 6 pm–10.30 pm Sat 12 noon–2.30 pm, 6 pm–11 pm Sun, public holidays 12 noon–2 pm, 7 pm–10.30 pm CLOSED Chr Day & Boxing Day CREDIT CARD Access/Euro WHEELCHAIR ACCESS Difficult VEGETARIAN DISHES Various pies

Arguably Oxford's prime wine bar site, smack opposite Trinity, one of the University's Sloaniest colleges. After some misadventures, the re-opened Emperors is now in the safe hands of wine merchants Morris & Verdin although the young manager, William Walter, has a licence to buy outside as well. Adventurously, his house wines (all £4.50/£1) include Geoffrey Roberts' brace of own-label California wines, and a balanced but not distinguished Sauvignon from Annabels. He knows his market: Pimms at £1.80 a pint draws crowds of Henries and their Lucies to the tiny but welcoming garden. They would do well to go for the house claret, 1980 Ch Fayau (£4.50/£1), a Bordeaux Supérieur which is a model light luncheon claret, and the Rioja Ederra of the same year at the same price. More serious drinkers can start with an excellent Madeira, then contemplate the fine Domaine Daniel Rion Burgundies imported by the owners, or Ch Ducru-Beaucaillou 1970 at £22.50, and end with a vintage Cognac or a 1965 Macallan. Food, like the wines, is imaginative but not always perfect: a cheering bouillabaisse with saffron and coriander (£1.95), but not enough aubergine in the moussaka (£2.65). But it is all home cooked.

George's

11 Wheatsheaf Yard, Blue Boar Street TEL (0865) 250440

OPEN Mon–Sun 12 noon–2.30 pm Sun–Thur 6 pm–10.30 pm Fri & Sat 6 pm–11 pm (supper licence till 12 pm) CLOSED Chr Day, Boxing Day
CREDIT CARDS Access/Euro, Visa WHEELCHAIR ACCESS Two shallow steps into bar, lavatories upstairs VEGETARIAN DISHES Cheese and salads

Down an alley off the High at the back door of Christchurch, George's is a remarkably unpretentious place, a sympathetic mixture of wine bar and pub serving almost as much beer (Morrell's Varsity) as wine; its most unusual, and most sold, drink is Grolsch's Dutch ale at £1.20 for one of those old-fashioned bottles holding three quarters of a pint. Many of the wines (mostly from André Trépel and Hedges & Butler) are routine: a fresh, fruity house white at £3.85/70p, Vinho Verde at £4.20/75p, a couple of ordinary hocks. But there are one or two goodies. The 1981 Chablis (£8.50) comes from Joseph Drouhin, and so does the Beaujolais Nouveau. The Ginestet Médoc (which once upon a time contained a spoonful or two from Ch Margaux) is good value at £6.50, the 1978 Marqués de Cáceres is recommendable at £5.75. The food, like the drink, has its routine items (the chilli con carne at around £2, the ploughman's lunch, the salads, the commercially bright pink taramosalata, at around £1.20). But the fish salad at £1.95 was fresh and delicious, and the spaghetti carbonara at the same price would not have disgraced a classy Italian restaurant.

PLYMOUTH Devon

Barbican Wine Lodge

5 The Quay, Barbican TEL (0752) 660875

OPEN Mon–Sat 11 am–2.30 pm, 6 pm–11 pm Sun 12 noon–2 pm, 7 pm–10.30 pm CLOSED Never CREDIT CARDS All accepted
WHEELCHAIR ACCESS Difficult VEGETARIAN DISHES On request

On the quayside of Plymouth's Elizabethan Barbican quarter, this extraordinary three-storeyed building has played many parts in its 400 years. Originally a powder store, subsequently a coppersmith's shop and a sail loft, it is now a lively wine bar. The upper levels (only one is in use as part of the wine bar) have original flooring and the tables have ingenious adjustable legs so that bottles and glasses keep on an even keel. Peter Standyk, the extrovert, newish owner – he claims to have been the previous incumbency's best customer, and his timber trade origins are betrayed by copious quantities of sawdust on the floors – would not deny a little eccentricity, but any amateurism is compensated for by the infectious enthusiasm shared by his young and cheerful staff. The place is always bustling and noisy, near anarchy prevailing at the time of the start of the transatlantic and other yacht races. The wine list is in two parts, the first available at the bar by the bottle and, in most cases, by the glass (17 in all), and the second on offer to those taking a more serious meal. Like the lists of other Devon establishments, both of these have a City Vintagers identikit look about them. The basic house wines (72p for a 14 cl glass) are safe and good value, but with the wonderful range of fresh fish available – the catches are landed across the quay from the bar – it would be nice to see rather more enterprising dry whites. Perhaps they will come in time. There is a large evening à la carte menu, changing about once a month, with a page each for starters, main meat courses and those fish dishes. Some are unusual and it's good to see monkfish, John Dory, red mullet and squid there. At lunch-time, things are more simple, but there is always an adequate daily blackboard selection: on our visit, an enjoyable crab salad (£2.95).

REIGATE Surrey

Scutts Caves

6 London Road TEL (073 72) 22177

This extraordinary bar changed hands at the end of the summer, so we hope that the previously tedious and expensive wine list may improve during the life of this *Guide*. Improvements or no, Scutts Caves are worth a visit for the sheer novelty of the place alone. Descend several flights of steps from the upstairs bar and you'll find yourself in an extensive labyrinth of 17th-century silver sand mines, where, in two additional bars, Scutts can seat 100 people. Reports, please!

ROSSETT Clywd

Churtons Wine & Food Bar Ⓥ

Machine House, Chester Road TEL (0244) 570163

OPEN Tue–Fri 12 noon–3 pm, 7 pm–11.30 pm (if eating) Sat 12 noon–3 pm, 7 pm–12 pm (if eating) CLOSED Sun, Mon, from Chr Eve to 1st Tue after New Year CREDIT CARDS All accepted WHEELCHAIR ACCESS Yes, two steps VEGETARIAN DISHES Salads

A meal and a bottle of wine will cost you a few pounds more than at most wine bars. But then, this is no ordinary wine bar. Midway between Wrexham and Chester on the main road (A483), it was opened two years ago by Nicholas and James Churton, who converted an old barn into this remarkable place. The atmosphere envelops you as you walk in. The panelled downstairs room is heavily beamed and decorated with many old artefacts of the wine trade: copper measuring jugs hang round the well-designed bar and in one corner stands a spittoon, unused, because the wine here is too good to spit out! There are eight assorted tables downstairs and the same again upstairs, arranged round a gallery overlooking the bar. Hunting prints and the stuffed heads of Cape buffalo, stag, bear and giant eland adorn the walls. At the bottom of the stairs and opposite the bar is the large blackboard with the day's menu. All the food is home-cooked, such as smoked trout and horseradish pâté (£1.65), chicken liver and peppercorn pâté (£1.65), Churton-style caviare (£1.40) or Morecambe potted shrimps (£1.45) for starters. The main courses are equally delicious: fresh local Dee salmon with seafood and wine sauce (£5.25), beef Stroganoff (£5.95), wine-sauced kidneys, bacon, celery, mushrooms, topped with cheese (£4.25). All are served with attractive salads or vegetables and all are unconditionally excellent. The wine list is as good as the menu. And it is nice to drink from decent, tall-stemmed thin-glass glasses instead of the usual commercial ones. The house wines are particularly good value. The red Côtes du Ventoux are from Salavert (£3.95/75p), and from the Loire a dry Blanc de Blancs from Martin Jarry. There are also a further five wines available by the glass, including a spicy Edelzwicker from Alsace (85p). The list is particularly strong in Rhône wines, all from the house of Salavert, 1981 Côtes-du-Rhône, Goutte Vermeille (£4.85) being particularly good value. Burgundy is well represented, and there is a good choice of fine clarets: Ch Chasse-Spleen 1975 (£12), Ch Pontet-Canet 1970 (£14.80). The house Champagne, Jacquart Brut Tradition, is also very good value for £9.50. Churtons gets extremely busy and you may have to wait for a table if you want to eat. But waiting here is no hardship.

RYE East Sussex

The Peacock

Lion Street TEL (0797) 223161

OPEN Mon–Fri 11.45 am–2.30 pm, 6.45 pm–10.30 pm Sat 11.45 am–2.30 pm, 6.45 pm–11 pm Sun (June–Oct) 12 noon–2 pm, 7 pm–10.30 pm Public holidays 11.45 am–2.30 pm, 6.45 pm–11 pm CLOSED (Dec–Easter) Sun–Thur eve (open L); 3 days Chr, 1 week Feb & June CREDIT CARDS Access/Euro, Diners, Visa WHEELCHAIR ACCESS Yes VEGETARIAN DISHES Good selection

Not far from the famous Mermaid Inn, the Peacock, with its oak beams, polished tables and gleaming brass, feels perhaps more like a pub. There is table service for all drinks and food. We sampled crab pâté and coarse meat pâté, both with hot toast and salad (£2) – thumbs up for the first, thumbs down for the second. Traditional English dishes dominate the menu: soup (90p), Cotswold cottage pie and steak and kidney pie (both £2.10), fisherman's pie (£2.20), and puddings (95p). Unlimited coffee is 55p. Vegetarians are well catered for here, with three vegetarian dishes from £1.35 to £2.20. The Peacock lists 38 anonymous wines, with unhelpful comments such as 'popular fruity white wine', covering nine French regions as well as oddments from seven other countries. English wine is represented by a Lamberhurst Vineyards Seyval Blanc (£5.10). Claret is £4.30, Rioja £4.70, California Cabernet £5.75, Corbières £4.25, Alsace Sylvaner £5.75 and Gewürztraminer £6.15 – good prices. Ask to see the bottles to discover who made them. House wines are reasonably priced at £3.85 – and there are six wines served by the glass. Children are welcomed in the restaurant half of the bar.

ST HELIER Jersey

La Bastille Taverne

4 Wharf Street TEL (0534) 74059

OPEN Mon–Fri 10 am–8 pm Sat 10 am–5 pm CLOSED Sun, public holidays CREDIT CARDS Not accepted WHEELCHAIR ACCESS Possible through back, lavatory down two steps VEGETARIAN DISHES Salads, quiches

The seafood is very good at the Bastille, even attracting locals. The wine list is lengthy and includes a 'connoisseurs' list', with a good choice of white wines to accompany the seafood – many dry whites from the Loire, and Gewürztraminer and Pinot Blanc (Hugel) from Alsace. House wines are Ch Grand Seuil Coteaux d'Aix-en-Provence red, white and rosé at £3.30 and Côtes-du-Rhône Pierrodin Larbalestier at £4. Champagne ranges from Charles Heidsieck Brut at £9 to Dom Pérignon at £23. The Bordeaux are from Echenauer, Burgundies from Labourie-Roi and Germans from Julius Kayser. The list includes three Riojas. House wine is available by the glass (50p), sparkling wine and Muscadet (60p). A bottle of Fonseca 1970 costs £16/£1.20. The service is attentive and wine well looked after and correctly served. If you shun the spider crab salad (£4.50) or dressed crab salad (£5) there is always a daily speciality like steak and kidney pie (£2.50), or you could plump for assorted saucissons (£1.80) or entrecôte steak (£4).

La Bourse

Charing Cross TEL (0534) 77966

OPEN Mon–Sat 11 am–11 pm CLOSED Sun CREDIT CARDS All accepted WHEELCHAIR ACCESS Difficult VEGETARIAN DISHES By arrangement

We might have been 'better off in the restaurant upstairs' as the bar staff suggested, but this small wine bar, with eight seats at the bar and a shelf around the walls so that you can eat standing up, is a jolly place. It serves more beer and spirits than wine, but on request, the wine list, then the wine, will be sent down in the dumb waiter, as was our Sauvignon Blanc Alexis Lichine (£4). Two other guests' aperitifs, meanwhile – two glasses of Muscadet Sèvre-et-Maine 1983 at 60p each were served with unsolicited lumps of ice – better, no doubt, than drinking it warm. The list offers three white and four red Burgundies, the best being Côte de Beaune Mommessin at £9.80. The claret section does not list vintages: the wines ranged on our visit from Ch La Mote (£4) to Ch Rausan-Ségla (£12.65). Italy is well covered on this list, the whites beginning with Orvieto Bigi (£4.30) and rising to an anonymous Verdicchio Castelli di Jesi (£5.45); reds range from Chianti Ambra (£4.30) to Amarone Bolla (£9.80). House red, white and rosé Le Caveau is only £2.50, and Muscadet by the bottle, with or without ice, is £3.60. Champagnes are rather expensive: Charles Heidsieck (£12.70) and Lanson Black Label (£13). Food is fair: king prawns in garlic with side salad (£3.70), steak sandwich £1.80, quiche and ham salad (£2.90).

Lido's

Clarendon Hotel, 6 Market Street TEL (0534) 22358

OPEN Mon–Sat 10.30 am–10 pm CLOSED Sun, some public holidays, Chr
CREDIT CARDS Not accepted WHEELCHAIR ACCESS Yes
VEGETARIAN DISHES Some

Lido's Bar was opened in its current form in October 1983. Before that, it was a market traders' pub, and it has been owned by the same family since the 1930s. The bar is decorated in subdued colours with original watercolours and lithographs on the walls and little pots of flowers on the tables. Background music is often French jazz. The wine list and menu are thoughtfully compiled, the wine list extending to 58 wines, from the house white, Ch Bauquière, a reliable Côtes-de-Provence (£3.20/70p), to more expensive finds such as Ch Lagrange, St Julien 1976 (£9.75) or the exotic but typically low-priced Coteaux du Layon J Touchais 1959 (£10.05). Champagnes are a speciality. Though the list is mostly French, there are a few good German wines from Louis Guntrum, white Marqués de Cáceres (£3.70), and half a dozen good Italians (Chianti Classico Castelli Vicchiomaggio 1979, £4.40). Producers' identities are (in most cases) revealed. This is a very inviting wine bar in which to linger over a morning coffee and croissant, and to return to in the evening for gratins and pies from £1.50 or many cold dishes. There is an emphasis on fish and shellfish in the summer. The menu changes weekly and some dishes daily: starters might include pâté d'Alsace en croûte (£1.35) and moules poulette (£1.85), with main courses such as lasagne de fruits de mer (£1.85), 'crabe farcie au calvados flambée' (£3.75) and poulet aux crevettes (£2.55).

Ⓥ means a bar has wine at bargain prices

▭ shows a bar has an above-average range of wines

☞ indicates especially good service, which includes friendliness, good wine knowledge, an informative list, and good food.

SAWBRIDGEWORTH Hertfordshire

Beatons

Bell's Walk, 47–49 London Road TEL (0279) 722460

OPEN Mon–Sat 12 noon–3 pm, 6 pm–10.30 pm (Sat till 11 pm) Sun 7 pm–10.30 pm CLOSED Sun L; Chr Day WHEELCHAIR ACCESS Impossible VEGETARIAN DISHES Excellent selection

This first-floor bar-cum-restaurant in a shopping precinct deservedly appeals to more than just local shoppers and business customers from Harlow, five minutes down the road. Most people are here for a meal, eating at one of the dozen or so tables that are separated by high-backed wooden-stalls. The City Vintagers wines are unexciting but sound. The house red, the Les Frères range, in two-glass sizes – 80p/£1.05 (£3.95 a bottle) – is better than the dry white. There are five German wines also available by the glass: try Nussdorfer Herrenberg 1983 £1/£1.25 (£5 a bottle). Of the short, standard list of names, the claret Ch de Chartres 1981 (£5.35) or Vinho Verde dry white (£3) are safe. The blackboard menu, which changes constantly, is more enterprising and the food is attractively and freshly prepared. You can begin with home-made pâté (£1.25), or grilled sardines (£1.25), and the baked-potato skins with sour cream (£1) are tasty, too. Salads (garlicked chicken, £2.95, 'Waldorfish', £3.25) are inventive and recommended; but a variety of more elaborate dishes, like veal calvados (£4.25) and chicken Wellington (£4.75), is available. Beatons in Epping and Stamford are under the same ownership.

SHEFFIELD South Yorkshire

The Victoria

395/397 Ecclesall Road TEL (0742) 660690

OPEN Mon–Fri 12 noon–3 pm, 6.30 pm–10.30 pm Sat 12 noon–3 pm, 6.30 pm–11 pm CLOSED Sun CREDIT CARDS All accepted WHEELCHAIR ACCESS Except to lavatory VEGETARIAN DISHES Regularly provided

A warm atmosphere is to be found in this smart, Victorian-style wine bar, attached to a bistro, not far from the City Centre. Manager Pompeo Corso has built up its reputation, particularly for his selection of Italian wines. The Sicilian house wine (one of only three wines available by the glass at £3.95/60p) is good, but move on to the Spanna Gattinara 1978 (£5.50) or the Villa Antinori Chianti Classico 1978 (£6.40) if you are staying to sample the bistro's entrecôtes, part of a wide and attractive menu with additional specialities available each day. For those with an evening to spare, the intense and well-matured Barolo Juta special reserve 1975 (£9.25) is ideal with food. Amongst the white wines, the German hocks look very good value and the Victoria won a prize last year from German vintners for the selection and display of their products. The assortment of French wines in the medium-price bracket has recently improved, and these are good complements to the excellent variety of beautifully presented fresh seafood, veal and game, and various other bar snacks.

SHREWSBURY Shropshire

The Cornhouse

59A Wyle Cop TEL (0743) 241991

OPEN Mon–Sat 12 noon–2.30 pm, 6.30 pm–11 pm Sun 7 pm–10.30 pm CLOSED Sun L CREDIT CARD Access/Euro WHEELCHAIR ACCESS Difficult, but possible VEGETARIAN DISHES Plenty

The entrance to the wine bar is in St Julians Friars (a side street) where it is difficult to stop, let alone park. It is a four-storeyed 1850s red brick building at the bottom of Wyle Cop, and the ground and first floors were used to store grain until the early part of this century. The wine bar is on the ground floor, and a hand-built, twisting iron staircase leads to the restaurant on the second floor. The specialities of the day are listed on a blackboard – perhaps celery, tomato and pepper quiche (£1.80), pork n'Marsala sauce (£3.10), calamares (£1.20) or souvlakia kebabs (£3.10). All main courses are well prepared and served with jacket potatoes or rice, and mixed, diced salads. Prices in the separate restaurant are only slightly higher: pork saltimbocca or boeuf bourguignonne (both £4.15). Vegetarians are well catered for. The sixty or seventy wines on the list range from Greek Demestica (£4.15) to Ch Cantemerle 1976 (£12.46). The house wines are all French. The dry white changes frequently but the red is Arc de Triomphe (£3.95/80p) – hard, thin and to be avoided. Extra large glasses (about 10 oz) are available at £1.50. The only other wines available by the glass are generic German.

The Raven Real Ale & Wine Bar

62–63 Mardol TEL (0743) 57061

OPEN All day for food and soft drinks outside licensed hours Mon–Wed 11 am–3 pm, 6 pm–12 pm Thur–Sat 11 am–3 pm, 6 pm–1 pm Sun 12 noon–3 pm, 7 pm–11 pm CLOSED Chr Day, May Day, from mid-June to mid-Sept, Dec, Jan 1–14, school half-term holidays CREDIT CARDS Access/Euro, Visa VEGETARIAN DISHES Quiches and salads, more interesting dishes with advance notice

The builders had only just moved out of The Raven (formerly Just Williams) real ale and wine bar at the time of our visit. Owners Peter and Cecile Williams, and their daughter, Nicola (who used to run Just Williams), have completely transformed the building, exposing all the old beams in one of Shrewsbury's most ancient buildings, which dates from the early 15th century. The wine and real ale bar is on the ground floor – a light and pleasant room with a tiled floor, wooden chairs and marble-topped tables. The basement is being turned into a disco, which will have its own bar and entrance, so should not interfere with the wine bar or restaurant. Just post-transformation, the wine selection was very poor, but Mr Williams assures us that once the building has been completed there will be a full range of wines, a score of them available by the glass – reports, please. By the early summer (1984), the bar was specialising in Riojas – fifteen including Reservas and Gran Reservas (£4.50 to £6.50). There was also a good list of clarets, from house claret (£3.95) to Ch Cissac 1978 (£8.50) to the heights of Ch Margaux 1962 for a modest £22.75. Cold food and salads are on display: quiche (75p), continental salad with ham, turkey or beef (£2.95 to £3.50). Hot food is also available: rainbow trout (£2.95), mini steak (£2.95), spring lamb loin chops (£2.85), all served with chips or jacket potatoes and mixed salads. On Tuesday to Saturdays, you can dine instead in the upper restaurant, a pretty little room with low, curved ceilings and old settles. Everything on this separate menu is reasonably priced, for example, noisette of lamb (£3.95), fillet steak (£5.25).

SOUTHEND-ON-SEA Essex

The Pipe of Port

84 High Street TEL (0702) 614606

OPEN Mon–Fri 11 am–2.30 pm, 6 pm–11 pm Sat 11 am–2.30 pm, 7 pm–11 pm
CLOSED Sun, public holidays CREDIT CARDS All accepted
WHEELCHAIR ACCESS Impossible VEGETARIAN DISHES Special salads

The Pipe of Port is a family-run wine bar with that all-important ingredient – atmosphere. Half wine casks line the walls and furnish the bar down in this subtly lit cellar; several small rooms, seating 12–15 people, allow for private gatherings and parties, without losing the atmosphere of the whole. The Jones's list boasts no fewer than 72 wines, which include a good range of fortified wines: fino sherry is served chilled and vintage port is available by the glass or bottle. Unusually, three Madeiras are offered; there are five Champagnes, and still wines range from Loron's very drinkable Vins de Table (£3.90/£1.15) to 1976 Ch Latour at £30.90. Emphasis is placed on French wines, and these have been well chosen. Steve Jones presumably enjoys claret: five classified Médocs are offered. Germany is adequately represented – house hock and Moselle at £4.40/£1.15 – and there are interesting wines from Italy, Spain, Austria, California, Australia, New Zealand and Chile; and how pleasing to see producers' names listed. Dopff Au Moulin's Perle d'Alsace (£5.40), Jaboulet Aîne's 1980 Crozes-Hermitage (£6.95) and delicious dry Beaujolais Rosé (£6.80) all look good value. All wines are also offered on an off-sales list at reduced prices and can be delivered in the Southend area at a nominal charge. A wide range of snacks and sandwiches is available; for a more substantial meal you may wish to start with excellent toasted Stilton fingers (six for £1.25) or home-made soup (65p). Pies (hot and substantial) are a speciality, perhaps steak, kidney and mushroom

(£3.15), or chicken and chestnut (£2.80), served with jacket potatoes. The cold table has meat, seafood and salads in plenty, including a vegetarian salad at £3.25. There is live music occasionally, and wine tastings are held monthly in this well-run and popular establishment.

SUTTON COLDFIELD West Midlands

Flints

Belwell Lane, Mere Green TEL 021-308 5148

OPEN Mon–Thur 12 noon–2.30 pm, 6 pm–10.30 pm Fri–Sat 12 noon–2.30 pm, 6 pm–11 pm Sun 12 noon–2 pm, 7 pm–10.30 pm CLOSED Chr Day
CREDIT CARDS Not accepted WHEELCHAIR ACCESS Yes
VEGETARIAN DISHES Salads and quiche

Part of the West Midlands Taverns chain *(see Horts, Edgbaston)*. By way of a change from the smart interior decor, you might sit outside at one of the wooden bench-tables and watch the world watching you watch the world go by. There is the usual inexpensive range of food to choose from: maybe a slice of quiche (95p), or pizza (80p), or you might try a simple hot pasta dish (£1.20), or a steak sandwich (85p).

SWANSEA West Glamorgan

Corks Wine Bar

39 Uplands Crescent, Uplands TEL (0792) 470235

OPEN Mon–Thur 12 noon–3 pm, 5.30 pm–10.30 pm Fri & Sat 12 noon–3 pm, 5.30 pm–11 pm CLOSED Sun CREDIT CARDS Not accepted
WHEELCHAIR ACCESS Yes VEGETARIAN DISHES Always available

This pleasant wine bar came under new ownership recently and both the food and wine have noticeably improved. The wine list includes all the normal favourites, and though rather dull, they at least all come from the best vintages and leading shippers. The Beaujolais is from Mommessin 1982/83, at £6.50, and the Burgundies come from Henri de Villamont (Hautes Côtes de Nuits 1978, £8.50). Much more interesting are some top quality country wines, including a Côtes de Buzet Napoléon 1979 (from the excellent co-operative) at £6.50, Ch de Haute Serre Cahors 1978 at £7 and, perhaps best value of all, the red Domaine d'Ormesson, Vin De Pays de L'Hérault 1981 at £4.95. Amongst the whites, the Muscadet comes from Martin Jarry at £5.50. Try the outstanding Sauvignon Trois Mouline (Bordeaux) at £5.75, and a 1982 Chablis from Domaine Jouchère, reasonably priced at £7 a bottle. There are also various Italian, California and German wines. As you might expect in this part of the world, there is a Croffta 1983 (made in Groes-Faen Vineyard, just outside Cardiff), at £6. The food is limited to home made soups (£1.50), pâté (£1.75) and salads, the main attraction at £2, but the new management is increasing this range, and standards are already very high within the limited choice.

1266 Wine Bar ⓥ

1–2 St Marys Street TEL (0792) 51603
OPEN Tue–Sat 11.30 am–3.30 pm, 6.30 pm–10.30 pm (Fri & Sat till 11 pm)
CLOSED Sun, Mon CREDIT CARDS All accepted
WHEELCHAIR ACCESS Impossible VEGETARIAN DISHES A selection always available

Colin Pressdee, the proprietor of this simple but tastefully decorated wine bar, has always taken his food and wine seriously, and this new venture is no exception. Unlike many wine bar owners and restaurateurs in the area, Mr Pressdee is not afraid to charge high prices for his wines, many of which he imports himself, but the quality of most ensures that they still represent value for money. Unlike his restaurant list (for the Drangway), this list specialises in wines from the Loire, but a few exciting bottles are available from other regions, including classic vintages from Bordeaux such as 1961 Ch Batailley (£21), Ch Lynch-Bages (£25), and the better wines from off-vintages including 1977 and 1980. Burgundies come from Latour and Jadot and the Beaujolais from Duboeuf. In season, Pembroke oysters are offered (£2.10 for six), laver bread, a traditional Welsh dish, is usually included in the menu somewhere, and other fresh fish from Pembrokeshire is normally available. Mr Pressdee ships both Muscadet and Gamay Primeur every autumn and numerous lunchtime parties follow, when his regulars have a comparative tasting of these wines and Beaujolais Nouveau.

TAVISTOCK Devon

Betsy Grimbal's

4 Barley Market Street TEL (0822) 2268
OPEN Mon–Sat 11.30 am–2.30 pm, 7 pm–10.30 pm (Fri & Sat, and weekdays in summer till 11 pm) CLOSED Sun, unspecified annual closure
CREDIT CARDS Not accepted WHEELCHAIR ACCESS Yes
VEGETARIAN DISHES Sometimes

Betsy Grimbal was a 16th-century lady of the town who came to a sticky end in the medieval tower which bears her name, which also lives on in this small, cheerful and well-decorated wine bar run by the Chapmans, who opened here some five years ago. The building has a lot of old-world charm; there's an upstairs section for private functions. The wine list is recognisably like others in this part of the world, by courtesy of City Vintagers, but the range is rather larger and it is well set out, although the headings 'Beginners', 'Middlers' and 'Enders' are a bit twee. Rather more white than red wines are available by the glass and there are two sizes, 5 oz and 6⅔ oz for 75p and 90p respectively, for the basic house wines. It would be easier to choose the wines if a clearer distinction were made between red and white. The blackboard menu offers plenty of choice; lunchtime dishes are simpler than the more substantial ones served in the evenings. Everything is home-cooked and shows imagination. Tavistock is somewhat isolated on the edge of Dartmoor, but the West Country traveller will be sure of a warm welcome here with good food and wine.

TUNBRIDGE WELLS Kent

La Galoche ⓥ

The Common TEL (0892) 26823

OPEN Mon–Sat 11.30 am–2.30 pm, 6 pm–11 pm Sun 12 noon–2 pm CLOSED Sun eve CREDIT CARDS Not accepted WHEELCHAIR ACCESS Yes VEGETARIAN DISHES Always available

Once you have found the private road to the Mount Edgcumbe Hotel, you drive a short distance to the large car park, also part of the parent hotel. There are seats and tables outside for those who can't bear to leave the scenery, which is really quite superb considering that this is the heart of Tunbridge Wells. But you really shouldn't miss the unusual construction of the wine bar, hewn from the famous sandstone rocks which have the advantage of keeping the bar cool in summer and warm in winter. House wines are well chosen and good value at £3.50. The rest of the list also shows care. The range is vast, from the usual generics for between £4 and £6, to 1966 Ch Beychevelle at £40 a bottle. The food is good, too: always a wide choice of fish, and David Barnard's fruits de mer a bargain at £4. The cheeseboard on our visit held 36 different cheeses and at £1.50 the helping was very good value. The menu changes regularly and you can eat from as little as £1 up to £10 per head. The Galoche occasionally holds well-advertised regional tasting evenings, where the food of the area is also served and a guest speaker is on hand to answer questions.

The Grape Vine ⓥ

8 Chapel Place TEL (0892) 34219

OPEN Mon–Sat 11 am–2.30 pm, 6 pm–11 pm Sun 12 noon–2 pm, 7 pm–10.30 pm CLOSED Boxing Day, New Year's Day CREDIT CARDS All accepted WHEELCHAIR ACCESS Yes VEGETARIAN DISHES Always on menu

At the bottom of the High Street is a cobbled pedestrian walk and about ten yards down on the right-hand side is this large, informal wine bar. John Cullen's careful menu changes regularly and may include such unusual dishes as quails' eggs, locally caught trout, and prawn and cucumber pâté, the latter made by his mother; or you might choose crab pâté, coronation chicken and Atholl Brose (whisky, cream and honey) all for about £4.75 and all washed down by wine rather better than the average wine bar bottle. Mark-up here is not on a percentage basis, so the more expensive the wine, the better value you get. There's

1er Cru Chablis at £8.40 and Meursault at £10.30. The house wines are very drinkable, and there are about 50 different wines, a good range from France and a few from elsewhere – Italy, Germany and the very reasonable Beronia 1978 Rioja from Spain (£4.85). Some but not all of the French producers are listed: Beaujolais is mostly from Loron (Brouilly 1982, £7.40), Burgundies from Moillard, Moreau and Duboeuf – the latter being the best buy (Mâcon-Prissé 1982, £7.08). The Côtes-du-Rhône 1982 from Caves St-Pierre is good value at £4.50, as is the Côtes du Ventoux at £3.90. Blanquette de Limoux is good but expensive at £8.70, as are the Champagnes – house Champagne (£12) or Charles Heidsieck (£14). Best value is to be found in the cheaper still wines. Downstairs, there is an intimate, relaxed and well-furnished restaurant. On Wednesdays, live jazz is played at no charge.

UCKFIELD East Sussex

Percy's

119 High Street TEL (0825) 61366

OPEN Mon–Fri 12 noon–3 pm, 7 pm–11.30 pm Sat 12 noon–3 pm, 7 pm–12 pm Sun 12 noon–2.30 pm public holidays 12 noon–3 pm CLOSED Sun eve, public holiday eve CREDIT CARDS Access/Euro, Visa WHEELCHAIR ACCESS Yes VEGETARIAN DISHES Salads and cannelloni

Percy's has a delightful indoor-outdoor atmosphere. It is Victorian in style, one large room with a gallery dining area on high reached by a heavy staircase, which at the same time divides the downstairs into two areas. The floor is tiled, the tables covered with pastel green cloths, each bearing a candle. There are 65 wines on the list including ten wines in half-bottle and six by the glass. Among these are Domaine des Cadenières Vin de Pays des Maures (£4.25/75p), Listel's good red Domaine du Petit Chaumont (£4.25/75p), and a Cabernet Sauvignon Vin de Pays de l'Aude (£4.75/80p). Full marks to Percy's for including very nearly every piece of information about their wines a wine-lover might look for. Much of the list comes from Morgan Furze – good, reliable wines. Clarets begin with Morgan Furze NV (£4.90) and rise to Ch Giscours 1979 at £13.30. Beaujolais and Burgundies look interesting: Brouilly, Ch de la Chaize 1982 (£7.60) up to Nuits-St-Georges, Les Vaucrains from Bouchard Père at £18. We are even told that the basic Germans come from M Kleeback Weinkellerei in Trier, and the good 1983 vintage was on sale early summer 1984, when most bars were still using up old, tired stock. There are Alsace wines from Hugel and Laugel, Viña Ardanza from Spain, the lovely Schloss Grafenegg Grüner Veltliner from Austria (£5.80), a few Californias, the very good Twee Jongegezellen '39' white from South Africa (£4.85) and Lamberhurst Priory from nearer home (£7.10 – can this really be the 1978/79 vintage? Avoid it if it is!). Although the food is all home-made with pasta the speciality, two dishes we tried were undistinguished. The bar food menu offers onion soup (80p), baked potatoes with chicken and mushroom (£1.50), lasagne (£2.20), ploughman's (£1.50), cauliflower cheese (95p). From the restaurant menu, you might choose potted shrimps (£1.95) or crêpes de fruits de mer (£4.55) with ratatouille (95p), or rump steak (£4.80). Presentation is good and service friendly. On Fridays and Saturdays, when there is live piano music, you will be charged £1 extra.

WALLINGFORD Oxfordshire

Lamb Wine Vaults

Lamb Arcade, Castle Street TEL (0491) 39606

OPEN Mon–Sat 10.30 am–2.30 pm, 6.30 pm–10.30 pm CLOSED Sun
CREDIT CARDS Access/Euro, Visa WHEELCHAIR ACCESS Impossible
VEGETARIAN DISHES Plenty

A warm welcome is guaranteed at this low-ceilinged hideaway – indeed, Nick and Carole Treadaway *insist* that new customers make themselves known. Decor is somehow very 1950s, in this subterranean world of wine and good living. There are always six or more interesting wines available by the glass and a 'wine for the day' chosen to match the *plat du jour*: Cocumont's excellent Marmandais Sauvignon *does* go very well with smoked trout vol-au-vent. The food choice is not exciting and could become repetitive for regulars, but the helpings are generous and freshly prepared. There's a big list (76 wines) and all may be purchased at roughly £2 less per bottle to take away – ask for the wholesale price list. They give good support to local enterprise, listing both Henley's Crazies Müller-Thurgau Bacchus 1983 (£5.96) and Pangbourne's Westbury Müller-Thurgau Seyval 1982 (£6.15). Wines appear to come from a variety of sources, with a wealth of classed-growth clarets, domaine Burgundies and Rhônes, and the apparent strength in Loire and Dordogne wines perhaps indicates the Treadaways' choice of holiday locale. Service is first-rate.

WARWICK Warwickshire

Bar Roussel

Market Square TEL (0926) 491983

OPEN Mon–Thur, Sun 12 noon–2.30 pm, 7 pm–10.30 pm Fri–Sat 12 noon–2.30 pm, 7 pm–11 pm CLOSED Chr Day CREDIT CARDS Not accepted
WHEELCHAIR ACCESS Yes VEGETARIAN DISHES Salads

Part of the West Midlands Taverns chain *(see Horts, Edgbaston)*, and probably the one with the lightest touch. There are a couple of comfortable sofas amongst the varied small tables where a man can take a contemplative pull at his pipe and read the newspaper; there is a bright but gentle feel to the place, and it is tasteful, relaxed and civilised, as befits Warwick. There is the usual pedestrian menu with, for example, soup (60p), pâté (85p), prawn cocktail (£1.20), half a dozen salads for under £2, and one hot dish of the day.

WEST DRAYTON Middlesex

SJ's

Canal Cottages
Packet Boat Lane, Cowley TEL (0895) 441596

OPEN Mon–Fri 12 noon–3 pm, 7 pm–12 pm Sat 7 pm–12 pm Sun 12 noon–3 pm, 7 pm–12 pm CLOSED Sat L, Chr Day, Boxing Day, public holidays L CREDIT CARDS Access/Euro, Diners, Visa WHEELCHAIR ACCESS Yes but lavatories difficult VEGETARIAN DISHES Some on menu and others cooked to order

Beside the Grand Union Canal next to a hump-backed bridge, this five-year-old wine bar was originally two derelict cottages. A well-laid-out garden next to the canal offers tables and chairs, good car parking and a pleasant grassy area where children can play. Inside, the atmosphere is cosy: tiled floor, beams, plenty of plants, plain wooden tables and church pews. SJs is popular with local business people at lunch time and the younger set at night, particularly on Friday and Saturday disco evenings. The staff are very helpful and efficient in the two bars (one for wine, the other for cocktails). French house wines, at under £1 a glass, are of reasonable quality. Also by the glass, there's Beaujolais-Villages 1983, Thorin (£1.05). Champagnes are expensive: Charles Heidsieck NV (£13.95) or Veuve Clicquot NV (£16). The rest of the wines, covering the main French, German, Italian, Portuguese and Spanish areas, hold no outstanding gems. Food is wholesome: home-made celery and pea soup (£1.25), spaghetti bolognese (£3.75), chunky-topped pizza (£2.45), honey-roast ham salad (£3.50), a four-course roast lunch every Sunday, and frequent summer barbecues. All food eaten outside carries a ten per cent service charge.

WETHERBY West Yorkshire

The Old Wine Bar

Castle Gate TEL (0937) 65220

OPEN Tue–Fri 12 noon–2.30 pm, 7 pm–10.30 pm Sat 12 noon–3 pm, 7 pm–10 pm Sun 7 pm–10 pm CLOSED Sun L, Mon evening CREDIT CARDS Not accepted WHEELCHAIR ACCESS Impossible VEGETARIAN DISHES Some

On the evening the *Guide* visited this wine bar, a lively jazz session was in progress, making for a relaxed and friendly atmosphere without drowning the conversation. Jazz is on the menu on Wednesday nights and Saturday lunchtimes, and local folk groups make an appearance on Sunday evenings. Most of the wines on the list of 98 are under £5 and nine countries are represented, including two bottles from Greece. However, no serious attempt to define the wines is made: more vintages should be given and the list would be enhanced by a few better wines, particularly from Burgundy and Bordeaux, where the choice is narrow. A large wall-mounted board serves to display the menu, a basic range of dishes at reasonable prices: ploughman's lunch (£2.70), fisherman's fayre (£3.70). The clientèle is a cross-section of customers of all ages and types.

WEYBRIDGE Surrey

Berkleys Wine Bar and Restaurant

20 Baker Street TEL (0932) 51333
OPEN Mon–Fri 12 noon–2.30 pm, 7 pm–10.30 pm Sat 12 noon–2.30 pm, 7 pm–11 pm CLOSED Sun, public holidays L, Dec 25–31
CREDIT CARDS Access/Euro, Amex, Diners WHEELCHAIR ACCESS Yes
VEGETARIAN DISHES Soup, quiche; special dishes on request

Berkleys Wine Bar is near the centre of Weybridge and the range of wines and the sophisticated approach reflects the affluence of this stockbroker belt location. The spacious ground-floor wine bar, newly decorated with a refurbished kitchen area at the back, is like a cellar, with mellow brickwork and attractive archways. It's a place in which to eat as well as drink: three chefs provide a varied menu, which changes every six to eight weeks. Starters are likely to be devil's choice (£1.90) – marinated whitebait seasoned with cayenne pepper – or Camembert special (£1.80) – wedges of the cheese wrapped in bacon and deep-fried, served with gooseberry preserve. Main dishes include a range of crisp salads: Arabian Nights (£4.90) is chargrilled marinated lamb kebab served with rice. Sweets – described on the menu as 'Sweet Sins' – might include meringue mirage at £1.90. Blackboard specials feature seasonal specialities, particularly fresh fish and game, and during the lunchtime period cheaper dishes are available. But whilst the food is good and attractively presented, it is the list of over 120 wines that makes Berkleys worth a visit. The list is clearly printed with full details of vintages, growers and domaines where applicable – except, as nearly always, in the German section. Whilst Berkleys specialise in Bordeaux and Burgundy, the list also offers Rhône, Loire and Alsace wines with German, California and one Spanish wine. The house wines are a dry, fresh and very crisp white Vin de Pays de l'Aude and complementary fruity red for £4.90/90p, and a house claret, currently a 1978 Côtes de Castillon, at £5.50. Over the years, owner John Laverack has amassed an enviable cellar of classic Bordeaux and Burgundy wines, which he offers to his customers at very reasonable prices. His list of classed-growth Bordeaux ranges from Ch Latour 1959 at £98 a bottle to Ch Beychevelle 1970 (£25), Ch d'Angludet 1971 (£12.50) to Ch Meyney 1976 at £9.90. Most wines are from good vintages, but there are also several selected wines from off-vintages and special offer wines carefully chosen through Mr Laverack's expertise and good wine trade contacts. The Burgundy list is equally tempting to the palate – and the affluent pocket. Berkleys' cellar includes good stocks of 1955, 1960 and 1963 ports with one always available by the glass. On our visit, Feuerheerd 1963 was on offer at a very reasonable £1.90.

WINDSOR Berkshire

Tracks

Ⓥ ☞

4 Goswell Hill TEL (075 35) 58090

OPEN Mon–Sat 12 noon–2.30 pm, 6 pm–11 pm (food served 7 pm–10.30 pm)
CLOSED Sun, public holidays CREDIT CARDS Access/Euro, Amex, Visa
WHEELCHAIR ACCESS Impossible VEGETARIAN DISHES Always some; special dishes by prior arrangement

Underneath Brunel's great viaduct, this is a highly successful wine dive. Not perhaps the place for the chap looking for nice old crus classés, but it has terrific atmosphere, the service is impeccable and the prices are keen. House Champagne – 'how ya like it, pink or white?' – is a tenner. Choosing wine is hard, partly because the list is nailed up in the brick vault. Clos de la Baronne 1980 Meursault at £12.50 is the most expensive; Côtes-du-Rhône 1982 at £5.50 seemed good value, as did Chianti Classico, but a certain 'B Cock' (they economise on words) Blanc de Blancs Rosé is new to us. The food is international, ranging as far afield as guacamole and natchos (£2.10); fresh grilled sardines go down well with the £10 Champers and '60s Motown music. A warm, cosy place for all its size.

WOODSTOCK Oxfordshire

Brotherton's

1 High Street TEL (0993) 811114

OPEN Mon–Thur, Sun & public holidays 12.30 pm–2.30 pm, 7 pm–10.30 pm Fri & Sat 12.30 pm–2.30 pm, 7 pm–10.45 pm Morning coffee is served 10.30 am–12.30 pm, teas 2.30 pm–6 pm CLOSED Chr week CREDIT CARDS All accepted WHEELCHAIR ACCESS Two shallow steps
VEGETARIAN DISHES Change daily

An agreeable, informal, pine-tabled brasserie is reached through an equally pleasant wine bar in the middle of touristy Woodstock. The place is certainly ideal for relaxing over half a bottle of Bollinger (£7.50) after the slog round Blenheim, but it's also worth a visit for the food alone: the sensibly short menu, changed quarterly, offers not just steaks but rabbit pie (£4.25) and sweet-and-sour spare ribs (£3.95). A short list of daily specials includes a vegetarian dish like non-meaty moussaka, leek and celery pie or deep-fried broccoli in beer batter at £3.75. Carnivores can savour lamb steaks with herbs and fresh vegetables not, for once, over-cooked. Appetising sweets include 'really solid' bitter chocolate mousse and fresh cherry cream at around £1. The wines are, sadly, less remarkable than the food. Stick to the house wines, which include a nourishing French-bottled Cabernet Rosé d'Anjou from Henri Chouteau, properly light but with more fruit than the usual rosé, a decently grapy Hainselder Ordensgut Kabinett 1981 and a very correct, if austere, house claret, all at £1 a glass, £5.25 a bottle. The main wine list is selected from respectable suppliers like Dolamore and Edward Sheldon, but it is short and unimaginative. The Sauvignon de Touraine at £5.95 is probably the best value.

YORK North Yorkshire

Oscars

Little Stonegate TEL (0904) 52002

OPEN Mon–Sat 11 am–11 pm (wine served in normal licensing hours) Sun 12 noon–2 pm, 7 pm–11 pm CLOSED Chr Day CREDIT CARDS Access/Euro, Amex, Visa WHEELCHAIR ACCESS Yes VEGETARIAN DISHES Special dish each day

The entrance to Oscars is through an attractive walled garden with tables and seats in summer and a barbecue on warm days. A jazz trio plays every Monday, and there is occasionally other live music. Although at first sight the place does not seem large, it is on two floors and can seat up to 150 people. Prices of the wide selection of wines are very reasonable. No list, but a selection is written on the blackboard. House wine is 65p or 95p for a large glass. There are brands in abundance, but plenty of good staples, too, many of them from Gilbey Vintners (which belongs to the same group as Peter Dominic and supplies many of the same wines). Burgundies from Bouchard Père et Fils are excellent, there are some from Piat along with Piat Beaujolais, Hugel Alsace wines, and a scattering from around France and elsewhere. Bulgarian Cabernet and Chardonnay were good value on our visit at £4 a bottle. Ten hot dishes and ten pick-your-own salads are always available, all served with jacket potato and a good selection of fillings at around £2 a serving. Oscars is open from 3 pm, once licensing hours are over, for cakes, other snacks, tea and coffee.

Wine in restaurants

Dear Restaurateur,

You know what we're going to say; but we'll say it again: mark-ups of 100 per cent and more push wine prices way out of proportion to the cost of the food. The better the wine, the more distorted the relationship; restaurant prices of expensive wines become quite ridiculous when the cost price is multiplied by two or three, especially when 15 per cent VAT *(why don't you* all *include it?) and 10 per cent service are calculated on top. But before you start to fume (B . . . . . journalists again, without the first idea of the hidden costs of running a restaurant: the depreciation, the rent, rates, insurance, energy, maintenance, capital tied up in expensive stocks and repayments to the bank manager, as well as the waiters, the kitchen staff, the cleaners and dishwashers, administrators and managers; not to mention the time spent travelling to and from wine tastings, and slurping and spitting for your benefit) – what of those articles in catering papers quoting restaurateurs who, having put, say, a standard £5 or 50 per cent mark-up on their more expensive wines, report that their wine* and *food turnovers improved enormously when they made the switch? And what about the success of places like Kenwards in Lewes, Sussex* (see below) *with its standard £2 mark-up, and the Tate with its 40 per cent? If such margins seem altogether too tight for your business, you could perhaps start by offering a better-than-house white and red each week or each month at a lower mark-up; it could be that the larger number of bottles drunk bring greater overall profit. Or, if large stocks supplying a very extensive list prove an impossible burden of interest or tie up too much capital to allow such generous pricing, why not reduce an enormous list to sensible proportions – and pass on the savings to the customer?*

Our other major grouse – one that is echoed in our WINE BARS *section – is the lack of information on so many restaurant lists. Any customer who knows a little about wine wants to be told not just the wine's name, but also the vintage, and the name of the grower or shipper. Restaurant lists, even some of the best included in the* Guide, *are especially poor at revealing growers or shippers of their Italian and German wines. It might* once *have been the case that most Italian wines were so poor that it simply wasn't worth knowing who had made them, but no longer. It may take up an extra line to add 'Weingut Heinrich Becker' to the already space-greedy Dinkelsheimer Pinkelberg Gewürztraminer Trockenbeerenauslese 1976, but it* does *make all the difference to the buying decision of anyone who knows his Germans well – because, as we all know, the Dinkelsheimer Pinkelberg is owned by as many as 45 growers, some of them crooks, some of them idle, some of them producers of excellent wines. Name your house wines, too. If your list is quite short, one solution is to include the labels under plastic covers; if you have your list printed, consider reproducing labels at reduced size.*

But to the many customers who know less, and who panic at the sight of your list, there is much more help you can give. What the customer wants is a wine that will go with his food and that he will enjoy at the price he is prepared to pay. Ideally, of course, the staff should be able to advise. Some can, but many simply do not know how the wines they are serving taste (a good reason to involve them as much as possible in the wine buying, and to encourage them to attend tastings and tasting courses). It will help only the knowledgeable customers if you list your wines under the traditional geographical headings – Bordeaux, Burgundy, Italy – with no indication of how sweet, dry or full-bodied they might be. How much better to list them under taste categories – 'light, dry whites', or 'full, fruity reds', perhaps like the taste categories in the WINE WITH FOOD *section – always, however, making it clear where the individual wines are from. Better still, or in addition, an individual tasting note beneath each wine is enormously useful if it is competently and honestly written. The length of your list may make this impractical (though take heart from the Croque-en-Bouche in Malvern Wells, which manages to provide notes for each of its wines – all 400 of them!); in which case it is helpful to pull out a dozen or so wines, listing them at the front with useful comments so that people can choose with confidence. Consult your wine merchant if you can't cope; failing that, restaurants with any pretension to a serious wine list might reasonably be expected to pay for the list to be annotated by an expert consultant. It will sell your wines for you, too – especially the lesser known ones. Best of all are the restaurants (like Café St Pierre in London EC1 and Rothay Manor in Ambleside) which suggest one or more specific wines under each dish or group of dishes on the menu. Tasting notes might also encourage you to remove from the list any wines that are not yet ready for drinking. What are 1978 and 1975 classed growth clarets doing on the wine list in 1984 and 1985? So, you're rich? But we don't really need to know for a few years yet that these are in your cellar. All we want to see are the wines that are drinkable* now.

Another way to help your customers, and particularly regulars, is to offer each week one better wine by the glass – if the choice is limited, there will be little lost in part-finished bottles. More wines by the half-bottle would also lead to experimentation, and solve the predicament of diners whose partners have chosen unmatched dishes.

Lastly, the service. Glasses need to be large enough to hold a decent amount when filled just half or two-thirds full. Rinse and polish them, and don't store them upside down full of stale air and vapours from the starch or the furniture polish. Decanting cradles and baskets are pretentious; they are pointless for younger wines and a positive nuisance when used to present mature wines at table, serving only to stir up the sediment as the wine sloshes back into the bottle after pouring. Wine with a sediment needs to be properly decanted, away from the table. But how many restaurants ask *the customer* when *he would like his wine decanted? So many simply open the bottle as the customer begins his aperitif, and many fine old wines have passed their best by the time the main course arrives (*see 'Decanting' in WINE WITH FOOD*). Some people like wine as an aperitif: be aware of the need to take the order and bring the wine speedily. Be alert also to customers who want both white and red wine served at the beginning of the meal with two glasses for each person. What generally happens is that the wine is all poured out before the starters are over, and the poor person hoping for white wine with his main course finds that there is little left. Bring the wine list and menu simultaneously: some may care more about their wine than their food, and may wish to choose the food to match the selected wine. And when you have brought the wine, don't top up the glasses over-fast.*

And please – be sensitive; work out who is paying. It might well be the woman, and these days she might well know more about wine than her guest.

Dear Restaurant Customer,

Choosing the wine while the waiter hovers can be embarrassing and bewildering, especially if, as we complain above, the list gives you little help. But it really is unnecessary to be embarrassed by diminutive wine knowledge. If you are unfamiliar with the Indian or Italian dishes on a menu, you probably have no qualms about asking for explanations. It's no more shameful to ask about the wine, and any waiter or fellow guest who thinks less of you for it is the one who should be ashamed. In any case, you can safely assume in most restaurants, even in some of the poshest, that the waiter knows as much as or less than you do about how the wines will taste. If he does seem to know what he's talking about, ask for advice; tell him what you have chosen to eat, what sort of wine you like, and, if you have eaten there before, what you drank, and whether you liked it. He will then be in a much better position to advise, and should suggest a choice at different price levels. Don't let him price you up beyond your means. But if the waiter is as little use as the wine list, don't panic. For a start, why choose the wine in silent secrecy? Your guest(s) might enjoy sharing the task; they might know more than you do and help you out, or they might defuse the embarrassment by admitting their *vinous shortcomings. Don't disregard the house wine – it might be good, especially if it's not too cheap. In most restaurants, avoid the upper price ranges anyway. It's best to drink better wines when you're at home: £8 wines marked up 100 per cent to £16 are ridiculously poor value compared to a good, basic £2 wine marked up to £4.*

Once you have made your choice, particularly if the wine waiter doesn't *know his stuff, make sure the vintage and producer are the ones you ordered. Vintages must, of course, change some day, and a* younger *basic wine may well be fruitier and better than its predecessor. The purpose of the tasting ritual is to enable you to detect faults in the wine – like mustiness or vinegar – not to decide if you like it; you might not like a wine which is perfectly sound. Once you have plenty of experience, you'll be able to tell on the smell alone if the wine is sound. If you are in any doubt, taste it, too. And don't be afraid to complain if, tasting in peace after accepting the wine under the waiter's eagle eye, you realised you made a mistake and there's something wrong with it after all – though the wine waiter is unlikely to be sympathetic if you have downed half the bottle before making up your mind!*

A word to smokers: spare a thought as you puff a cigarette with your aperitif or a cigar with the port for the poor people trying to enjoy their food elsewhere in the room; and wait till later. Non-smokers do *mind, even if they're too polite to say so.*

We have considerably increased the number of restaurants in this year's Guide, *but our selection of Britain's best restaurants for wine is still stringent. On the assumption that people go to a restaurant principally to eat, we have included only those restaurants with a very good wine list where we would also strongly recommend the food – and we have added a short assessment of the sort of food you can expect. Our special awards go to restaurants within this élite which offer above-average wine ranges, above-average value or particularly good wine service. Following the main entries is a list of restaurants with notably good wine lists, whose food falls short of our high standards. The restaurant section ends with a new feature, a list of restaurants around the country with no wine licence, where you can take your own wine. Again, restaurants have been excluded if we feel the food is below acceptable standard, though our expectations are much lower for this style of establishment. If we have missed your favourite bring-your-own-bottle haunt, do let us know.*

London

Boulestin

1a Henrietta Street, WC2 TEL 01-836 7061 or 3819

OPEN 12 noon–2.30 pm, 7 pm–11.15 pm CLOSED Sun, Sat L, 1 week Chr, last 3 weeks Aug CREDIT CARDS All accepted UNDERGROUND Covent Garden, Charing Cross VEGETARIAN DISHES Yes TDH L £14 ALC FOR TWO £45

Grand Met's elegant flagship is a luxurious and clubby basement in Covent Garden, with fat-stock prize-winners on the walls looking down on the fat cats below enjoying discreet business lunches or more frivolous dinners. Prices are fierce but at least the move to all-inclusive meals will mean fewer unpleasant shocks when the bill is presented. The menu is French, with *nouvelle cuisine* overtones; there are occasional lapses which should not occur at this level, but people have liked the delicate scallop mousse with Champagne sauce, oysters in a buttery leek purée, various plainly cooked fishes, and magret de canard normandie. Service is mostly unobtrusive and considerate, and wines are treated with respect. The six house wines include Haut Poitou Sauvignon and Gamay, both 1982, at £9 and £10 respectively. There is a fair choice at £12 or under (Louis Latour Morgon 1978 at £11, for example) but the temptation is to explore the higher reaches of the mainly French list: Alfred Gratien Champagne, NV (£17), a relative bargain; Meursault Charmes, Cuvée Grivault, 1979, Thévenin (£30); Ch Léoville-Las-Cases 1966 (£53); Ch Coutet 1975 (£18). There are half-bottles and magnums, and a handy list of bin-ends tucked in the menu. Leave a copper or two for the fine vintage ports, mainly 1963 (Croft, £32), with Fonseca 1955 at £40. And if vintage Armagnac is your poison, Casterède 1881 is £16 'a large measure'.

Capital Hotel Restaurant

22–24 Basil Street, SW3 TEL 01-589 5171

OPEN 12.30 pm–2.30 pm, 6.30 pm–10.30 pm CREDIT CARDS All accepted UNDERGROUND Knightsbridge WHEELCHAIR ACCESS Yes VEGETARIAN DISHES Yes PIPES Not allowed in restaurant TDH L £14.50 ALC FOR TWO £40

A discreetly smart Knightsbridge hotel with a newly refurbished French dining-room, all swags, engraved mirrors and handsome Limoges china. Service tends to be correct if impersonal, and it is worth asking advice about unfamiliar dishes to avoid duplicating ingredients or sauces. The *Michelin* star was earned by such fancies as terrine de ris de veau sauce aux cervelles (£4.50); moussette de volaille au basilic (£4); cailles farcies au foie gras frais (£12); and carré d'agneau persillé aux herbes de Provence (£25 for two). Sweets are imaginative, cheeses competent, and 'the chocolates with coffee the best ever'. The menu lists six appropriate wines, including Chablis Montmains 1981, Raoul Gautherin (£12.50), and Ch Lestage 1961, CB (£15), and there is a separate list of splendid dessert wines, several of which are available by the glass each day (Johannisberg Riesling Selected Harvest 1978, Firestone's Ambassadors Vineyard, £20). The main list of close to 200 bottles repays leisurely study. The Bordeaux section reads like the 1855 classification (Latour 1967 seems a relative bargain at £47); Volnay Caillerets 1972, Bouchard Père et Fils, is £40 a magnum; and other celebrations could be launched on all styles of Champagne, including Laurent-Perrier Rosé (£25.50), and Veuve-Clicquot-Ponsardin Rich (£22.50).

The Connaught

Carlos Place, W1 TEL 01-499 7070

OPEN 12.30 pm–2.30 pm (restaurant), 6.30 pm–10.15 pm CLOSED Sat (grill room), Sun, public holidays CREDIT CARD Access/Euro UNDERGROUND Bond Street WHEELCHAIR ACCESS Yes TDH (Restaurant) From about £17.50 ALC FOR TWO (Grill) £50

London's finest old-fashioned hotel, in many people's view, with a pair of dining-rooms offering not dissimilar menus: in the handsome, mahogany-panelled restaurant, you pay according to your choice of main course; in the grill room, the choice is straight *à la carte*. The Connaught is the place for fine English dishes, from roast beef to game, but because the chef, Michel Bourdin, is French, you may also enjoy croustade d'oeufs de caille Maintenon (still the best version in town of this much copied pastry boat with duxelles, soft-cooked quails' eggs and hollandaise), rendezvous de pêcheur sauce légère nantaise, truite saumonée ou saumon sauvage 'au choix', fricassée d'agneau du Kent à l'estragon, fraises et framboises Romanoff, and even a savoury (Scotch woodcock, champignons sur toast). There are clubby regular standbys for weekday lunches (Friday is oxtail) and a few specialities which must be ordered in advance (mousse de homard Neptune). Fifteen wines cost under £10 among the 150 or so on the list: three of them are Liebfraumilch, one sparkling hock and another Mateus Rosé, so if you are economising, perhaps it would be best to stick with the house French carafes at £6.75 a pint. Otherwise, consider the four Alsace wines: Gewürztraminer 1982, Beyer (£12) and Riesling, Cuvée des Ecaillers, 1979 (£13). The Italian page is unexpectedly trendy, with Venegazzù 1976, Villa Gasperini Loredan (£11) and Gavi 1982, Conti della Cremosina (£16). Other possibilities include Gigondas 1978, Delas (£13.30); Chablis Vaudésir 1981, Fèvre (£17); Mazis-Chambertin 1976, Faiveley (£33.50); Bouchard's Fleurie and Juliénas 1982 (£13); Ch La Tour-de-By 1978 (£15); Vieux Ch Certan 1966 (£46.50); Ch Pavie 1961 (£91); Ch Haut-Brion 1961 (£160). There are various half-bottles and magnums, sometimes of a different vintage to the full bottle (not always a disadvantage: for example, a 1978 Meursault is likely to be showing better than the 1981). Champagne starts at £20.50 for

Laurent-Perrier Brut, NV, and rises to £46.50 for Roederer Cristal 1977. At the other end of the meal, there are 20 ports, from three 1955s (Fonseca, Cockburn and Tuke Holdsworth) at £41 to Kopke 1919 at £71. For lesser mortals, Taylor's Crusted is £1.60 a small glass. The Connaught serves an outstanding breakfast, but even its many American guests have not persuaded the management to produce it before the normal working day begins.

D'Artagnan

19 Blandford Street, W1 TEL 01-935 1023

OPEN 12.30 pm–2 pm, 7 pm–10 pm CLOSED Sat L, Sun, Aug CREDIT CARDS All accepted UNDERGROUND Baker Street WHEELCHAIR ACCESS Yes TDH £12.50 ALC FOR TWO £33

A small, recently refurbished restaurant, with tables rather too close together, offering *cuisine bourgeoise*, either *à la carte* or in a set meal devoted to one region. Service can be chilly or warm, and the cooking similarly uneven, but when it *is* on form people like the croustade d'oeufs de caille, terrine de lapereau aux noisettes, saumon à l'oseille, magret de canard aux noix et citron, noisettes d'agneau en croûte sauce paloise, and passion-fruit sorbet. The wine list offers few bargains, but there are a sensible number of VDQS or vins de pays, including Marcilly Spécial, NV, Marcilly Frères (£6.90); Coteaux de l'Ardèche, NV (£6); Cheverny 1982, Jean Guéritte (£7.50); and Côtes du Tarn, NV, Labastide de Lévis (£6.30). Further up the scale, there are still interesting regional wines: Cahors, Ch de Cayrou, 1981 (£8.90, though it would be infanticide to drink it: the 1934 is still on splendid form!); Cassis, Clos Ste-Magdalaine, 1981 (£10.80). With the unevenness of the cooking, and the often dominant sauces, you might think twice about spending much on fine red wine, but no claret is younger than 1976, no red Burgundy younger than 1978, so there are interesting opportunities. The Bas Armagnacs draw the eye too, from Ch de Ravignan 1972 (£2.50 a glass), to Croix de Salles, Domaine de Pyrelongue, 1924 (£7.50 a glass). You are cautioned that many of these are 100° proof, and the measure large.

Dorchester Hotel

Park Lane, W1 TEL 01-629 8888

OPEN (Grill) 12.30 pm–3.30 pm, 6.30 pm–11.30 pm (Terrace) 6 pm–1 am CLOSED Sun L CREDIT CARDS All accepted UNDERGROUND Hyde Park Corner WHEELCHAIR ACCESS Yes VEGETARIAN DISHES (on request) Grill TDH £14.50 ALC FOR TWO £42 Terrace TDH £21 ALC FOR TWO £46

The Dorchester is a many-splendoured thing, from its marble-floored 'Promenade' for afternoon tea, to its 'Provencal pâtisserie' bar for good sandwiches and other snacks, the Grill Room for more-or-less English cooking, and the rococo Terrace for *nouvelle cuisine* and beyond, either *à la carte* or as a *'menu surprise'* (six light courses, £54 for two). Throw in a pianist till 10 pm and a trio for foxtrotting thereafter, and you ought to be set for a memorable evening. It might be wise to avoid the *menu surprise* on Saturday, when the masterly Mosimann hand is sometimes absent, and remember that the Grill feels more alive at lunch. Unsurprisingly, the English triumphs include smoked salmon, rib of beef and bread-and-butter pudding, the weaknesses overcooked vegetables and disappointing cheeses. The Terrace pleases with sweetbreads and crayfish in puff pastry, mignons de veau au Stilton, turbot braisé aux legumes, and its passion-fruit soufflé. Service is, for the most part, friendly and professional, though the pacing of wines needs more thought. The Grill Room includes a half-litre of house French in the set lunch; it would cost you £6.50 at dinner. Otherwise, the list is the same in both restaurants, with no half-bottles except of Champagne in over two hundred mainly French wines; magnums are available. Prices are not greedy (and service is included): consider Alsace Riesling 1980, Léon Beyer (£12); Beaune Clos des Mouches 1978, Joseph Drouhin (£30); Ch Fombrauge 1978 (£12); and Ch Coutet 1975 (£24). Good digestifs, again mainly restricted to bottles (Cockburn 1955, £70), but Warre's 1974, late-bottled, is £1.80 a glass.

Dulcinea

29 Ebury Street, SW1 TEL 01-730 4094

OPEN 12 noon–3 pm, 6.30 pm–11.30 pm CLOSED Sat L, Sun, public holidays, 1st 2 weeks Aug CREDIT CARDS All accepted UNDERGROUND Victoria WHEELCHAIR ACCESS Yes VEGETARIAN DISHES On request NO-SMOKING ROOM TDH L £6.75 D £7.50 ALC FOR TWO £32

This Spanish restaurant feels like coolly elegant Belgravia, but it is only two convenient steps from Victoria station. It is surprisingly empty in the evening, and it may be lack of custom that has discouraged the *chef/patron* and led to a certain unevenness in the cooking. But when he is on form, Longinos Benavides turns out a fine garlic or fish soup, a dazzlingly fresh and generous paella (£15 for two), and some good duck and veal dishes. But the wines are the thing: the 20-page list is three-quarters Spanish, and it seems pointless to stray further, since such an opportunity arises so seldom in the UK. The respectable house Rioja is £4.75, but with so many others under £10, it is tempting to opt for something more interesting: Muga (Rioja Alta) 1978 (£7); 904 Reserva 1970 (£9.50); Marqués de Murrieta 1975 (a fine, old-style fat, oaky white Rioja, £8.75); Legitimo Marfil Tinto 1976 (from Alella, £5.50); Peñafiel Fifth Year (from Valladolid, where the proprietor was born, £8.50); Codorníu Non Plus Ultra Brut (£9.25); Jean León Cabernet Sauvignon 1978 (£8.75). The great names are there in double figures: Torres Gran Coronas Reserva Black Label 1975 (£22.75); Vega Sicilia Unico 1966 (£26.50). Although there are no half-bottles, you will probably be encouraged to drink what you wish from a full one.

L'Escargot

48 Greek Street, W1 TEL 01-437 2679

OPEN (Brasserie) 12.30 pm–3 pm, 5.30 pm–11.15 pm (Restaurant) 12.30 pm–2.30 pm, 6.30 pm–11.15 pm BOTH CLOSED Sat L, Sun CREDIT CARDS All accepted UNDERGROUND Tottenham Court Road VEGETARIAN DISHES On request ALC FOR TWO (Brasserie) £20, (Restaurant) £30

Nick Lander's smart restaurant/brasserie on several floors of this genuine 'old Soho' establishment (it was l'Escargot Bienvenu for the previous half-century) is cool, smart and popular, whether you drop in for a light meal in the ground-floor brasserie or a more formal one in the restaurant. The menus in both are appealing: terrines, quiches, Cumberland sausages, fishy dishes in the brasserie; upstairs, perhaps, spring salad; seafood bisque; feuilleté of snails with a garlic beurre rouge; seafood sausages of Dover sole, pike and brill with a cider sauce; roast quail stuffed with oranges and almonds; ragout of sweetbreads, morels and cream; mocha gâteau. There are some misses among the hits, however, and occasional off-days. Service is also variable: don't expect to get out swiftly, even from the brasserie. The wine list, on the other hand, is a paragon of every kind of virtue: clear, well organised, succinct in its tasting notes, offering an interesting range of wines at reasonable prices. Nick Lander's wife, Jancis Robinson, founder of this *Guide*, displays the same pithy commonsense in her own writings and TV programmes, and L'Escargot's list serves as a refreshing reminder that it is possible to be informative about wine without being a candidate for Pseud's Corner. There are over fifty wines, clearly set out under headings, starting with a pair of respectable house wines: Loron white and Dulong Frères red (£4.95/£1). Then follow four sparklers, the Paul Masson Sparkling Brut 1981, roughly half the price of the house Champagne (£12.95). There are half-bottles and magnums (Louis Michel's Chablis Premier Cru 1982, £5.50; Gigondas 1967, Paul Jaboulet, £9.50 – both in halves; Beaune, Cuvée Maurice Drouhin, Hospices de Beaune, 1973, Drouhin, £30 a magnum). White wines are divided into 'light fruity', 'dry flinty' and 'Chardonnay'; reds into 'light fruity', 'rich fuller', 'classic wines' and 'aristocratic Cabernet Sauvignons', all with those punchy tasting notes: Galestro Antinori 1982, 'lemon-fresh dry white from the Tuscan hills' (£5.75); Alsace Pinot Blanc 1982, Trimbach, 'pungent racy stuff from a punctilious winemaker' (£6.50); Syrah, Domaine de Vallouit, 1982, 'this juicy red, that would be called something much grander if the vines were a year or two older, is a real find' (£5.75); Meursault Charmes 1980, Garnier, 'good, rich white Burgundy, true Meursault character' (£14); Ch La Cardonne 1978, 'very well-made example of this vintage from the Rothschilds of Ch Lafite' (£9.50). Dessert wines include Mondavi's Moscato d'Oro 1982 (£12/£2 a glass).

Please comment on the *service* of wine as well as taste, cost, etc.

La Giralda

66 Pinner Green, Pinner TEL 01-868 3429

OPEN 12 noon–2.30 pm, 6.30 pm–10.30 pm CLOSED Sun D, Mon, Aug
CREDIT CARDS Access/Euro, Amex, Diners UNDERGROUND Pinner
WHEELCHAIR ACCESS Yes VEGETARIAN DISHES Yes TDH L £5.50 SUN L £8 (Children £4) D £8

Avoid Saturday nights at David Brown's suburban Spanish place if you like a leisurely meal, otherwise you may feel rushed and fussed. The atmosphere is unpretentious, service often scatty, and the food heavy on garlic, with other vinous hazards such as fruity starters and chocolate puddings. Praise for hot seafood cocktail, salmon, sole, fried chicken, and crème brûlée. The dessert menu lists sweet wines by the glass (Montilla Pedro Ximenes, £1.15). Over a hundred Spanish wines, from Sherston Wine Company and Arriba Kettle, are stored in an air-raid shelter, presumably immune to vibration and sudden temperature change. House Santyago red and white are £4.60 a bottle, and then you progress through carefully classified white wines, including a strong list of cavas, to two pages of reds, all from Rioja, and listed by age in cask, from the *marcas* at less than a year (Rivarey 1980, Marqúes de Cáceres, £6.35) to the *gran reservas* with more than three years in cask: Reserva 904 1970 (£8.85); La Calzada 1968 (£9.35), according to the list 'refined and smooth, beautifully developed, cedary'. Beware – some bottles are still lovely, some now going over the top. Only seven wines in half-bottle. Tastings and dinners are arranged through the Cofradia Riojana, 'a society for the appreciation of the wines of Rioja', and wine is available wholesale by the case.

Hilaire

68 Old Brompton Road, SW7 TEL 01-584 8993

OPEN 12 noon–2.30 pm, 7 pm–11.30 pm CLOSED Sat, Sun, Aug
CREDIT CARDS All accepted UNDERGROUND South Kensington
WHEELCHAIR ACCESS Yes VEGETARIAN DISHES Yes TDH L £9.50 D £17.50

Kennedy Brookes, having backed Simon Hopkinson's new venture, have left him and partner John Solway to get on with it. Hopkinson has been chef, restaurateur and restaurant critic – all before his thirtieth birthday – and people are enjoying this relaxed *restaurant du quartier* with its cool walls, good linen, potted palms and classical music on tape. Lunch is a simple meal with limited choice of, perhaps, crab pancake with ginger sauce, linguine con pesto, tête de veau aux lentilles, saucisson chaud aux pommes lyonnaise, poulet au vinaigre, lemon bavarois or bread-and-butter pudding. The dinner menu, changed weekly, moves further into *haute cuisine* (and a fair number of supplements), with sauté of duck liver with fresh fig, bresolles de lapin au foie gras et à la ciboulette, bream with basil sauce, passion-fruit bavarois. Salads include posh French leaves. Service is good on the whole, though you may have to serve your own white wine from an ice bucket which can become messy. There are about seventy rather steeply priced wines – always a problem for a new restaurant – but at least they are interesting, whether New World like Petaluma Chardonnay 1981 (£22.50), and Firestone Cabernet Sauvignon 1978 (£13.25); or Old World: Maxim's Champagne, NV (£17); Côte de Duras Sauvignon 1982 (£9.25); Gewürztraminer 1982, Preiss-Henny (£10.50); Les Forts de Latour 1976 (the second wine of Ch Latour, £28.75); Ch Coutet 1971 (£31.50). The house wine, from Georges Duboeuf, costs £6.25/£1.75. The impressive list of *digestifs* includes Marc de Gewürztraminer (£3 a glass).

Lampwicks

24 Queenstown Road, SW8 TEL 01-622 7800

OPEN 12.30 pm–2.30 pm, 7.30 pm–10.30 pm CLOSED Sat L, Sun, public holidays, Aug 18–Sept 9 CREDIT CARDS All accepted BR STATION Queenstown Road WHEELCHAIR ACCESS Yes VEGETARIAN DISHES With notice TDH £16

Queenstown Road is becoming the Chelsea of the South Bank in gastronomic terms, and this newest recruit is a worthy addition. Alan and Ann Bennett have created a prettily flowered interior, spacious and comfortable, in which to enjoy Alan's talented French set menu (note that you may eat only two courses at lunch if you wish, for £10.50). Dishes praised include sorrel soup, croustade d'oeufs de caille aux asperges, timbale aux riz de veau, foie et rognons de veau au basilic, canette aux quetches, fine cheeses from Philippe Olivier in Boulogne, and the sorbets and tarts. The French wine list is workmanlike, with no great bargains, but several wines which go well with the food: Alsace Pinot Blanc 1982, Kuentz-Bas (£6); Sauvignon de Touraine 1982 (£7.75); Blanquette de Limoux, Cuvée Aldéric, NV (£10.50); Ch Fourcas-Hosten 1976 (£16.90); Muscat de Beaumes de Venise, Domaine de Durban (£12/£2 a glass). A complimentary Kir appears with the savoury nibbles when you sit down: would it be churlish to ask them to improve it?

Lichfield's

Lichfield Terrace
Sheen Road, Richmond TEL 01-940 5236

OPEN 12.15 pm–2 pm, 7 pm–10.45 pm CLOSED Sun, Mon, 1 week Chr, 1 week Whitsun, 2 weeks Sept CREDIT CARDS Access/Euro, Amex UNDERGROUND/BR STATION Richmond WHEELCHAIR ACCESS Not to lavatories VEGETARIAN DISHES On request TDH L From £13 ALC FOR TWO £42

A surprisingly sophisticated restaurant to find in a suburban row of shops: quietly elegant and uncluttered, with an English proprietor, Stephen Bull, cooking French food in what he describes as 'the modern, free-ranging style'. The short menu is particularly strong on fish: ceviche of monkfish with coriander; mille-feuille of salmon and leeks in white wine; panaché of red mullet and brill with lobster sauce. Game and offal are tempting also: sweetbread and salsify tart; hot venison and pigeon pie with apples and game sauce; fillets of saddle of hare with beetroot, orange and sour cream. Vegetables are imaginative 'though stingily served at the price', and hot lemon tart a favourite pudding. The wine list is mainly French, with a good selection of whites for the fish: Quincy 1982, Pierre Mardon (£7.50); Gewürztraminer 1978, Hugel (£9.50); Chablis Fourchaume 1981, Dupas (£14.50); Puligny-Montrachet, Clos de la Mouchère, 1979, Boillot (£18). For the game and exotic sauces, you might fancy Bourgueil La Hurolaie, 1982, Caslot-Lebrun (£7.75), or the Spanish house wine, from Penedès, at £6.50 a bottle. However, there are classy clarets for the asking: Ch Pontet-Canet 1966 (£28) at one end of the list, and Ch Montalivet 1978 (£7) at the other. Red Burgundies include Santenay, Les Gravières, 1976, Berry Bros (£14). Four dessert wines by the glass: Ch de Septy 1977 (Monbazillac) is £1.20.

Mabileau

61 The Cut, SE1 TEL 01-928 8645

OPEN 12 noon–2 pm, 6 pm–11.15 pm CLOSED Sun, Sat L, Chr & Boxing Day
CREDIT CARD Amex UNDERGROUND/BR STATION Waterloo
WHEELCHAIR ACCESS Yes VEGETARIAN DISHES Prefer notice
ALC FOR TWO £26 PRE-THEATRE MEAL £8.75

An offshoot of RS J, handy for the Old Vic and the South Bank complex, this is a 30s-style restaurant with a range of menus (lunch, pre- and post-theatre, as well as the standard *carte*) offering *cuisine moderne*: lovely for summer, and if it's lunch or pre-theatre, you should stay awake after your meal. Praise for spinach and crêpe, calf's liver with lemon and rosemary or with a sorrel sauce, supreme of guinea-fowl cassis, cold lemon soufflé, pot au chocolat. Vegetables can be rather tasteless. The service is young, well scrubbed and helpful. There are over 60 wines, with more whites than reds. A special Loire section offers the delicious Anjou Rouge 1982, Richou (£6.26) – the best red from the area; Bourgueil, Domaine des Raguenières, 1978, Paul Maître (£11.95); Savennières, Coulée de Serrant, 1971, Mme Joly (£18.75); and Coteaux du Layon, Faye d'Anjou, Ch Montbenault, 1976, Leduc (£11.75). From the rest, consider, perhaps, Blanc de Blancs, Les Caves Geneviève (£4.95); Dão Branco 1980, Dom Ferraz (£5.65); Ch Côtes de Plaisance 1978 (£7.05); Gigondas 1980, Les Producteurs à Vacqueyras (£8.85); Ch Brane-Cantenac 1976 (£14.95); and Ch Doisy-Védrines 1979 (£8.25 a half-bottle). Glasses are large, thin and tulip-shaped.

Some restaurants may be willing to send you a list by post, so that you can choose at leisure if you want to drink special wines from a lengthy list.

Martin's

88 Ifield Road, SW10 TEL 01-352 5641

OPEN 12.30 pm–2 pm, 7 pm–11.30 pm CLOSED Sun, Sat L, last 2 weeks Aug, public holidays CREDIT CARDS Access, Master, Visa UNDERGROUND West Brompton, Earls Court VEGETARIAN DISHES With notice TDH L £8.50 D (two courses) £14.50

A smart little restaurant comfortably furnished in warm pink, with a *nouvelle cuisine* set menu, priced for two courses, with pudding or cheese extra. Presentation is attractive, vegetables undercooked, combinations sometimes unusual: mousseline de volaille au crabe, lotte au moules, magret de canard au fumet de cèpes, coquilles St Jacques au safran, marquise au chocolat. Service is friendly and capable, though it can become very slow at times. Most of the sixty wines are French, none at give-away prices. The house Bordeaux and Côtes de Duras are £7.50/£1.50 and thereafter you may choose from Sancerre 1982, Jean Vacheron (£12; £6 a half); Mâcon Villages 1982, Collin et Bourisset (£8.50); Ch Nénin 1976 (£18); and Châteauneuf-du-Pape, Clos de L'Oratoire, 1980, Amouroux (£12.50). Muscat de Beaumes de Venise and Ch Fayau 1981 are available by the glass, and there are several sweet half-bottles: Ch Filhot 1976 (£10).

Pollyanna's

2 Battersea Rise, SW11 TEL 01-228 0316

OPEN 1 pm–3 pm (Sun only), 7 pm–12 pm CLOSED L (except Sun), Dec 24–27, Jan 1 CREDIT CARDS All accepted BR STATION Clapham Junction VEGETARIAN DISHES Yes TDH SUN L £6.95 ALC FOR TWO £28

A pretty place on various levels where the informality leads many people to expect bistro cooking and house plonk. Instead, they are fed *nouvelle cuisine* and faced with a serious wine list. Popular dishes include terrine of scallops and sea bass with an orange sauce, fricassée of seafood in port and cream, best end of lamb on a pink peppercorn sauce with hollandaise, and dark and white chocolate mousse with a coffee-bean sauce. There are over 100 wines, now entirely French, starting with an impressive collection of ten vintages of Ch Gruaud-Larose, from 1976 (£14.75) to 1961 (£64). Champagnes include the delicious Deutz Blanc de Blancs 1979 (£18), and a rosé version from the same year (£19). For the fish, consider St Véran, Domaine de Vignemont, 1982, Paul Sapin (£8.20); Chablis Blanchots 1978, Laroche (£14.95); Touraine Sauvignon 1983 (£6.50); Pouilly Blanc Fumé, Domaine Thibault, 1983, Andre Dezat (£9.95). And for the lamb, Ch Patache d'Aux 1979 (£7.95); Ch Rauzan Gassies 1970 (£21.50); Pernand-Vergelesses, Les Vergelesses, 1976, Verry Père et Fils (£12.50); Clos Vougeot 1961, Noëllat (£29.50); Cornas 1979, Delas Frères (£9.50); with the pudding, perhaps a half-bottle of Ch Rieussec or Ch La Tour Blanche, both 1978 and £6.95; if there are lots of you, Moulin Touchais

1961 is £12.50 a bottle. French house wine is £4.95 a bottle. During special regional food and wine weeks, Norman Price has the enlightened policy of offering a dozen appropriate wines by the glass: for a Bordeaux week he produced, among others, Ch Grand Puy Lacoste 1976 (£2.15; £13.25 a bottle); Ch Rauzan-Gassies 1966 (£4.25); Ch Calon (a Montagne St Emilion) 1961 (£3.25); Ch La Louvière 1981 (£1.90); and Ch d'Yquem 1976 (£5).

The Ritz

Piccadilly, W1 TEL 01-493 8181
OPEN 12.30 pm–2.30 pm, 7 pm–11 pm CREDIT CARDS All accepted
UNDERGROUND Green Park VEGETARIAN DISHES Yes TDH L £16 D £21.50
ALC FOR TWO £45

Famed in song, story and various gastronomic guides, the Ritz has a lot to live up to. The stunningly beautiful rococo dining-room never fails to impress; the service does occasionally; but the cooking seems to be getting on more of an even keel under Michael Quinn. The style is both English and French, reflected in the menu's offering a 'bill of fare' with smoked salmon, dressed crab, Dover sole, salmon hollandaise, mixed grill, liver and bacon, steak béarnaise, as well as 'suggestions for your own composition' with more *nouvelle* dishes: marinated salmon with dill sauce; sweetbread terrine with crayfish sauce; mousse of lobster with lobster and saffron sauce; breast of chicken with vegetable mousseline and beetroot sauce; fillet of duck, chicken and veal with a Brouilly sabayon; fresh lime mousse with mango sauce; hot glazed fresh strawberries. You are urged to gamble by choosing the set dinner sight unseen (as at the Dorchester, but there the odds are different). The wine list – chosen by Harry Waugh, another legend – is distinguished, lengthy, and informative. Each section is preceded by notes on the characteristics of the wines, with vintage evaluations and maps. The page of Champagnes begins with the Ritz Cuvée Privée (seen on several lists around the country) NV (£19), 1976 (£23) and Rosé (£21). Traditionalists may opt for a double magnum of Perrier-Jouët Belle Epoque 1976 at £145.50. There are almost 60 clarets, with sensible petits-châteaux at the lower end (Ch Haut Sociondo 1979, £10), several very appealing bottles under £20 (Ch La Tour-Pibran 1978, £17.25; Ch Gazin 1976, £19.50), and a roll-call of great names and vintages thereafter: Ch Canon 1966 (£26.50); Ch Pavie 1971 (£29.75); Ch Trotanoy 1971 (£55.25); Ch Latour 1959 (£71.50); Ch Latour 1961 (£190 – a relative bargain); Ch Pétrus 1967 (£115.50). Red Burgundies begin with Beaujolais-Villages, Ch de Corcelles, 1983 (£11.75), and progress through Chorey-lès-Beaune 1980, Tollot-Beaut (£17) to Gevrey-Chambertin 1978, Lefort (£30) and Chambertin, Clos de Bèze, 1971, Averys (£48.25), culminating in Lâ Tache, Domaine de la Romanée-Conti, 1971 (£115.50). Whites start with Rully 1981, de Suremain (£11.25), pass through some curiously youthful Chablis to Meursault Perrières 1979, Comte Lafon (£23.50) and Le Montrachet

Baron Thénard 1972, Averys (£73.25). A lightning tour round the remainder of the list produces reliable Germans, stronger in Moselles; two outstanding Alsace wines (Hugel's Gewürztraminer Vendage Tardive 1976, £25.75); decent Rhônes; a couple of Prince Poniatowski Vouvrays in the Loire section; two fine Cabernet Sauvignons from California, both 1978 (Mondavi at £14.75 and Stag's Leap at £21.75); and token representatives from Spain, Italy, South Africa and England. Culminate, perhaps, with the superb Ch Guiraud 1976 at £17.75 a half-bottle, or save yourself for the page of ports, going back from 1966 (Warre or Sandeman, £35.50) to 1924 (Taylor, £69.75). Three 1960s are available by the glass at £4.25, as well as tawnies and a ruby at rather less. There are fine Cognacs and Armagnacs.

South of the Border

8–10 Joan Street, SE1 TEL 01-928 6374

OPEN 12 noon–2.30 pm, 6 pm–11.30 pm CLOSED Sun, Sat L CREDIT CARDS All accepted UNDERGROUND/BR STATION Waterloo WHEELCHAIR ACCESS To restaurant only VEGETARIAN DISHES Yes ALC FOR TWO £19

This converted warehouse near the Old and Young Vics is a cheerfully relaxed place, where an Australian chef produces 'Australasian and Pacific Basin' food. The menu, changed monthly, might offer satay and empanadas as well as more familiar pâté as starters, with South Seas sausages, vegetarian coulibiac, rabbit and pigeon pie and baked sea bream to follow. French house wines start at £4.50 a bottle, and thereafter the sixty or so wines, on a modest and rather sparsely annotated list, include sparkling Saumur (£8.50/£1.70 a glass); Hardy's Nottage Hill Shiraz 1979 (£9.40); Ch Fourcas-Dupré 1975 (£15.50).

Tate Gallery Restaurant Ⓥ

Millbank, SW1 TEL 01-834 6754

OPEN 12 noon–3 pm CLOSED Dec 24, 25 & 26; Jan 1; Apr 5; May 6
CREDIT CARDS Not accepted UNDERGROUND Pimlico
WHEELCHAIR ACCESS Yes VEGETARIAN DISHES With notice
NO-SMOKING AREA Yes ALC FOR TWO £30

The Tate is *the* wine merchants' watering-hole, since the wines are not only imaginatively chosen but also modestly priced and carefully served. Join them at the linen-clad tables under the Rex Whistler murals for a lunch of mainly English dishes, of which the simplest are generally the best cooked: roasts of beef or lamb, potted crab, poached salmon or salmon trout, skate with black butter. Steaks and pies are other favourites, vegetables and cheeses are served *à point*, and the puddings include a good fruit tart. Luckily there are many half-bottles on the list, so that you can try several without breaking the bank: Pouilly Fumé, Comte Lafond, 1982 (£3.90); Ch Ducru-Beaucaillou 1976

(£9.50); Santenay Les Gravières 1978, Remoissenet (£3.50). But to explore the list in greater depth, take additional friends and funds and try, perhaps, Corton-Charlemagne 1978, Chanson Père et Fils (£12); Wehlener Sonnenuhr Spätlese 1975, J J Prüm (£9.50); Ch Latour 1973 (£24.50); Merlot 1977, Stag's Leap (£16). It will take several visits to appreciate the latest additions to the list: 18 wines from three Bordeaux châteaux, just bought by the Tate straight from the cellars: Ch Baret, Villenave d'Ornon 1906 (£39.50); Ch Gruaud-Larose 1950 (£49.95 a magnum); Ch Talbot 1952 (£37.98). Champagne is another bargain: Charles Heidsieck, NV (£9.50), for example. There are four distinguished white Bordeaux in half-bottle (Ch Coutet 1973, £6.50), and vintage port as well (Cockburn 1955, £25). Warre's Warrior is 60p a glass, and there are Alsace eaux-de-vie too, even Vieille Prune matured in oak (£1.20). The house wines are not to be despised either: Papagni Zinfandel 1974 (£4.80) and Muscadet-sur-Lie, Domaine de la Maretière, 1983 (£4.80). If only they were open for dinner . . .

Tourment d'Amour

19 New Row, WC2 TEL 01-240 5348

OPEN 12.30 pm–2 pm, 6.30 pm–11.30 pm CLOSED One week from 24 Dec
CREDIT CARDS All accepted UNDERGROUND Leicester Square, Charing Cross
WHEELCHAIR ACCESS Yes VEGETARIAN DISHES Yes TDH (2 courses) £12.50, (3 courses) £16

A spruce little restaurant on the fringes of Covent Garden, offering careful and original French cooking with a reasonable choice of dishes on the two- or three-course menus: soupe glacée de pommes au curry, kiwi d'oeufs brouillés, tartare de thon frais, escalope de barbue au moutarde et à la tomate, foie de veau aux trois poivrons, carré d'agneau au jus d'olives, glace de yaourt au café, mousse à la mangue. There are about 90 wines, mainly French of course, and not all fully enough annotated. However, there are plenty to choose from: Sauvignon de St-Bris 1982, Brocard (£8.50 – let's hope they have now moved on to the better 1983); Chassagne-Montrachet 1981, Louis Latour (£17); Ch La Clotte 1980 (£13); Ch Fourcas-Hosten 1976 (£14); Corton Clos de la Vigne au Saint, 1978, Marcel Amance (£23); Rioja Siglo 1979 (£8.50); Muscat de Beaumes de Venise (£1.75 a glass).

Country

ALFRISTON East Sussex

Moonrakers

High Street TEL (0323) 870472

OPEN D only, 7 pm–9.15 pm CLOSED L, Sun, Mon, Jan 15 to Feb 13
CREDIT CARDS Not accepted WHEELCHAIR ACCESS Impossible
VEGETARIAN DISHES On request TDH D £11.40

Candle-light, flowers and wood fires brighten this ingle-nooked cottage, and you can relax in the garden in summer. Elaine Wilkinson cooks the set dinners, which offer a considerable choice: blue Brie parcels (in puff pastry), watercress soup, hot Sussex smokie, Burgundy pie, lamb cassoulet, raspberry trifle, crème de menthe and grapefruit sorbet. The wine list starts with Corney & Barrow French house wines (£4.80/90p). Guy de Chassey Champagne is £14.50, C&B's Champagne method Sparkling Blanc de Blancs, £7.20. Other wines include the dry version of Ch Doisy-Daëne 1981 (£6.90); Sancerre, Clos du Roi, 1983, Millerioux (£7.80); Gewürztraminer, Bollenberg, 1981, Cattin (£8.10); Chardonnay 1978, Simi (California, £10.60); the English Carr-Taylor Gutenborner 1982 (£6.50); Ch Maquin-St-Georges 1978 (£7.80); Côtes du Ventoux 1980, Chival (£6.40); Chianti Classico Riserva, Villa Antinori, 1978 (£6.40). There are some tempting bin-ends, few half-bottles.

AMBLESIDE Cumbria

Rothay Manor

¼ m SW of Ambleside, on A593 TEL (0966) 33605

OPEN 12.30 pm–2 pm, 8 pm–9 pm CLOSED 3 weeks Jan, 1 week Feb
CREDIT CARDS All accepted WHEELCHAIR ACCESS Yes
VEGETARIAN DISHES On request NO SMOKING IN THE DINING-ROOM
TDH D £15 SUN L £8 BUFFET L From £1.50

A charming Regency house is the setting for the Nixon family's self-confident operation. Rooms are comfortable, service is friendly and very efficient, the cooking is successful and the wines treated with care. The menu offers a limited choice of English and French dishes, many based on local game: Stilton beignets with hot Cumberland sauce, poached Windermere char with herbed hollandaise, cream of lettuce soup, local roast leg of lamb with apple-mint jelly, braised mallard with rowan jelly tartlets, jugged hare, guinea-fowl normande, chocolate fudge cake, nutty pineapple. The menu lists an inexpensive but appropriate wine beside the main courses: Bulgarian Cabernet Sauvignon 1979 (£4.70) with the jugged hare, for example, and Madiran 1976 (£6.30) with the braised brisket and dumplings.

French house wines, by litre, half-litre, quarter-litre and 6-oz glass, cost from £6 to £1. Otherwise, you may drink half a full bottle at three-fifths the bottle price – or pay the full price and take the 'bottom half' home. There are about 150 wines, covering most wine-growing areas: Australia is represented by, among others, Brown Bros Muscat Blanc 1980 (£8.80) and Penfolds Grange Hermitage 1975 (£18.30). Clarets yield Ch Castéra 1975, Lichine (£9.40); Ch Léoville-Las-Cases 1970 (£23.70). Other tempting bottles include Chambolle-Musigny, Les Charmes, 1978, Remoissenet (£14.20); Gratien & Meyer's Crémant de la Loire, NV (£8.60); Ch de Pech-Redon 1981, Delombe (£5.90); Hermitage 1979, Chave (£13.20); Oppenheimer Krötenbrunnen Auslese 1976, Kurprinz (£8.70); Ch Bastor-Lamontagne 1976, Sauternes (£4.90 a half-bottle). The winter programme of special-interest dinners and weekends always includes several wine events, either wines from one area or château, or tutored varietal tastings.

ANDOVER Hampshire

Keys Ⓥ

Swan Court, East Street TEL (0264) 52830

OPEN 12 noon–2.30 pm, 7 pm–10.30 pm CLOSED Mon CREDIT CARDS All accepted WHEELCHAIR ACCESS Yes VEGETARIAN DISHES Yes
ALC FOR TWO £20–£28

A relaxed and welcoming spot where prices are reasonable, service efficient and the menu interesting (young boar Vosges style, £6.50). Over a hundred wines on a frequently updated and carefully annotated list, with particular strengths in Bordeaux and the Palatinate. Too few halves, especially in dessert wines. Try the 1976 clarets (Ch Fonplégade, £7.50; Ch Potensac, £6.90) or some of the newly imported von Bühl Germans (Forster Ungeheuer Riesling Spätlese 1982, £7.90; Deidesheimer Herrgottsacker Riesling Beerenauslese Eiswein 1978, £22). The heavies, like Ch Cheval Blanc 1970 (£38), need 24 hours' notice. House wines, imported direct from France and unappealingly named Red and White Satin, are £5 a litre, £2.75 a half. The Bernard family hold wine tastings several times a year, sell by bottle or case, and act as consultants too.

Have we included your favourite spot for eating *and* drinking? If not, or if you disagree with our assessment, tell us about it either by letter or on the forms at the back of the *Guide*.

The range of wines available and the prices asked are likely to change in the course of the year. The information given is correct in summer 1984, and we hope it serves as an indication of each restaurant's approach to wine. If you want to drink a particular bottle, it is best to ring beforehand, not only to ensure that it is served correctly, but also to check that it is still in stock.

ASHFORD Kent

Eastwell Manor

Eastwell Park TEL (0233) 35751
OPEN 12.30 pm–2 pm, 7.30 pm–9.30 pm CREDIT CARDS All accepted
WHEELCHAIR ACCESS Yes VEGETARIAN DISHES Yes NO PIPES OR CIGARS IN DINING-ROOM TDH L £9 D £20 ALC FOR TWO £45

You don't come to this handsome manor house in its 3,000 acres of grounds if you need to count the pennies. It is luxurious, even pretentious, and its prices are high. That said, for a glorious wallow with service that seems impeccable except at breakfast, and a chef who handles a weighty menu with finesse, it may be worth it. The cooking is 'modern', a mixture of *nouvelle* and classical dishes: smoked salmon comes with celery and walnut foam; seafood hot-pot with saffron; grilled salmon with crayfish and truffle sauce; pheasant with foie gras, oysters and port; poached pear with puff pastry, kirsch sabayon and blackcurrant sauce. The so-called *'menu dégustation'* is no more than a choiceless five-course dinner, beginning, sometimes, with Parma ham and melon, as cliché'd a dish as ever came out of the Home Counties. The wines, from Grants of St James's and others, start with house French wine at £7.95 and £8.50 the bottle, and from them on you would be hard put to it to stay in single figures: Muscadet-sur-Lie, Ch de la Cassemichère, 1982 (£9.50); Ch de la Jaubertie Rouge 1981 (from Bergerac, £9.75); and Cook's Chenin Blanc 1981 (£9.75). Of the three English wines on offer, the Lamberhurst Priory 1982 Müller-Thurgau (£9.75) is weighty enough – and delicious enough – to match the food. If the sky is the limit, consider Louis Roederer Cristal 1978 (£41.50); Pouilly Fumé, Baron de L, 1981, Ladoucette (£27); Musigny Cuvée Vieilles Vignes 1978, de Vogüé (£59.50); Ch Pétrus 1970 (£130); and Ch d'Yquem 1976 (£98). Since this is a relatively new establishment, its fine wines are often unfortunately young.

ASTON CLINTON Buckinghamshire

The Bell

On A41 TEL (0296) 630252
OPEN 12.30 pm–1.45 pm, 7.30 pm–9.45 pm CLOSED Mon (exc residents)
CREDIT CARDS Access/Euro, Visa WHEELCHAIR ACCESS Yes
VEGETARIAN DISHES By arrangement ALC FOR TWO £35

Michael Harris's roadside inn is very grand these days, a worthy member of the *Relais et Châteaux*. New dishes are added to the menu, but regulars return to enjoy Bell Inn smokies, lobster terrine, pantoufle périgourdine, three fillets Médicis, saddle of venison, roast duck and roast beef. Vegetables and sweets win approval too. Service is rather stately. The adjacent wine shop, Gerard Harris Ltd (*see* MERCHANTS), reminds us that it was Michael's father who first made the Bell a place of pilgrimage for wine-lovers. Those with slim purses can settle for the sound Red and White Bell (£4.20): note that none of the prices on the list includes VAT. Even so, it is easy to reach double figures on such fine wines as Erbacher Siegelsberg Auslese 1976, Schloss Reinhartshausen (£13.95); Chablis Vaudésir 1981, Louis Michel (£13.80); Coulée de Serrant, Ch de la Roche aux Moines, 1979, Mme Joly (£12.51); Ch Chalon 1969, Jean Bourdy (£27.75) – the rare Jura vin jaune; Johannisberg Riesling, Ambassadors Vineyard (Selected Harvest), 1978, Firestone (£13.32); Corton 1976, Viénot (£18.76), and the same wine in the 1967 vintage (£21); Chambertin, Clos de Bèze 1966, Drouhin Laroze (£75 a magnum) for a very special party; Hermitage La Chapelle 1961, Jaboulet (£38.20 – £39.26 for a magnum of 1971 if you want to make comparisons). Clarets require a section to themselves, since there are four pages of them, almost all highly covetable. At the modest end of the price range, Ch des Moines 1976 is £8.85, and Ch Guineau 1978, £6.55. But it is tempting to climb through familiar names such as Ch Langoa-Barton 1976 (£15.50); Ch Haut-Brion 1973 (£32); Ch Malescot-St-Exupéry 1971 (£19.50); Ch Pichon-Longueville 1970, CB (£25); Ch Gruaud-Larose 1967, CB (£18.50); Ch Brane-Cantenac 1966, CB (£32); Ch Calon-Ségur 1961, CB (£55); and even back to Ch Pape-Clément 1926, CB (£70): keep us posted if you try it. Dessert wines include more great names: Ch Coutet 1971 (£16). It would be unfair to the Bell and its customers not to pick out some of the more modest wines on the list: various cru Beaujolais under £10; Rhônes at about the same price (Gigondas, Domaine des Bosquets, 1979, Meffre, £7.99); Sauvignon Blanc, Côtes de Duras, 1982 (£5.35); Côtes de Buzet, Ch de Padère, 1981 (£6.75); Viña Reál Reserva 1973, CVNE (£8.82); Lamberhurst Priory 1981 (£8.55); Allesverloren Swartland 1977, a powerful red from South Africa, £6.55; and Muscat Blanc 1982, Brown Bros (in Australia) at £7.58. As you might expect, there are several weighty ports listed (Cockburn 1963, £39), with, for example, Warre's Nimrod tawny at £1 a glass. Wine tastings are organised in conjunction with the wine shop.

BARNSLEY South Yorkshire

Brooklands (V)

Barnsley Road, Dodworth TEL (0226) 299571
500 yd W of M1, junction 37

OPEN 12 noon–2 pm, 6.30 pm–9.30 pm CLOSED Dec 25 & 26
CREDIT CARDS All accepted WHEELCHAIR ACCESS Special entrance with ramp
VEGETARIAN DISHES Few TDH L £4.80 ALC FOR TWO £24

This former transport café with a motel attached is cheerfully unassuming, and unashamedly successful, with a loyal local following as well as those from further afield who count the journey worthwhile. Helpings are enormous and the friendly waitresses urge you to further excesses. If you fancy the Barnsley chop – 'saddle of lamb cut in three;

one served per portion, £7.30' – you should forego the rather routine starters (minestrone, prawn cocktail, spaghetti bolognese) and don't expect to be able to face the peach Melba or sherry trifle, either. Other popular main courses include steaks, game and veal. Vegetables may disappoint. Two surprises in such a down-to-earth place are the dazzling display of exotic fruits which runs the length of one room; and the wine list, which could paper a wall. Spelling may be eccentric, several wines are from off-years, and too many are stored in the dining-room, but prices are benevolent and some of the older wines irresistible: ask about them when you arrive, since they are not all listed. But actually on the list are: Ch Gloria 1976 (£9.98); Deutz Champagne 1970 (£32.70 a magnum); Sancerre Rosé, Clos du Roi, 1982 (£5.80); Brauneberger Kurfurstlay Auslese 1976, von Schorlemer Lieser (£5.50). And if you fancy something from Cyprus, Hungary, Turkey or Chile, you'll find it. Italian house wine is £3.10 a bottle, 50p a glass.

BARWICK Somerset

Little Barwick House

E of A37, 2 m S of Yeovil TEL (0935) 23902

OPEN 7 pm–9.30 pm CLOSED L; Sun; Chr CREDIT CARDS All accepted
WHEELCHAIR ACCESS Yes VEGETARIAN DISHES Yes TDH £11

This elegant Georgian dower house is a relaxing place to stay, with a peaceful garden outside and friendly staff within. The set menu changes with the seasons, and is supplemented by the day's shopping – or catch. Roast game is a recurring favourite, and venison appears with Francatelli's sauce (Cumberland plus cinnamon, by the sound of it). Otherwise, choose from soup, avocado, cream smokies, steaks in various ways, roast poussin, assorted pies, gratin de langoustines, and creamy or fruity puddings. There are forty or so wines, on a rather chaotic-looking list which includes punchy tasting notes where appropriate. The house wines are from Georges Duboeuf and Lamblin (£5 a bottle); Georges Goulet's Champagne, NV, is £12.50; David Baillie's Claret, NV (£5.50); Ch Verdignan 1975 (£9); Gewürztraminer 1981, Baron de Hoen (£7.50); Ch Liot 1970, a delicious Barsac, is a bargain £9.50. Most Burgundies and Rhônes lack sources on the list. Five German wines, with lengthy typewritten descriptions, include Piesporter Goldtröpfchen Riesling Trocken 1981, Reichsgraf von Kesselstatt (£8). They hope to start wine dinners during the winter.

Prices and wines listed may change as the year progresses. Our examples are intended only as an indication of each restaurant's approach to wine.

TDH Table d'Hôte (set meal for one) ALC FOR TWO A la carte Estimate of the probable cost of an à la carte meal for two *excluding* wine L Lunch D Dinner.

BATH Avon

Hole in the Wall

16 George Street TEL (0225) 25242
OPEN 12 noon–2 pm, 7 pm–10 pm CLOSED Sun (exc residents), 2 weeks Chr
CREDIT CARDS All accepted WHEELCHAIR ACCESS Yes
VEGETARIAN DISHES With notice NO-SMOKING ROOM Yes TDH £13.50 (2 courses), £16 (3 courses)

The Hole is literally in the wall, making some of the alcove tables actually sub-pavement. A by-word in the 1950s under George Perry-Smith, this carefully tended 'restaurant-with-rooms' generally pleases people under two of his former trainees, Tim and Sue Cumming, previously at Crane's in Salisbury. The cooking is French provincial, with a daily changed set menu, offering two or three courses. It is supplemented by a handsome cold table and extra dishes, according to shopping and the chef's last-minute inspiration. People have enjoyed the paglia e fieno alla ghiotta; the boudins blancs aux épinards; soupe de poissons; calf's liver with honey, ginger and grapefruit; sirloin with cream and peppercorns; and the Armagnac and prune soufflé. The waitresses are pleasant and helpful, though the wine service is not always entirely formal: check temperatures of white wine. The wines, mainly from Yapp and Reid Wines, are mostly French, with a good covering of the major areas at all price levels. The house Ardèche and Loire wines are £6/£1.20, and Jacquesson Champagne is also available by the glass at £2.40. If you like old Champagne, there's Veuve Clicquot 1947 at £55. Meursault 1978, Remoissenet, is £20 (£10.50 a half), and Lamblin's Petit Chablis 1982, £4.25 a half. The Loires range from St Pourçain-sur-Sioule 1980 from the Caves Co-opératives (£6) to Bonnezeaux, Ch des Gauliers, 1947, Mme Fourlinnie, at £40, with a Sancerre Rosé 1981, Jean Vatan, at £8.80 in between. Alsace provides Riesling, Les Murailles, 1979, Dopff & Irion (£8). Red Bordeaux has sadly few halves at the lower end of the price range (Ch Latour St Bonnet 1975, £12.50 a bottle, £6.50 a half), but a (last?) chance to try Ch La Mission-Haut-Brion 1964 at £24 a half. Ch Gruaud-Larose 1973 (£36 a magnum) should be worth celebrating with. Red Burgundies are well represented, with Chorey-lès-Beaune 1979, Tollot-Beaut at £10, and Latricières Chambertin 1961 (Averys French-bottled) at £40. The page of Rhônes is worth contemplating too, from Bandol Rosé, Mas de la Rouvière, 1980, Bunan (£7.65), to Châteauneuf-du-Pape, Chante Cigale, 1980, Christian Favier (£10). Finish with one of the impressive list of sweet Bordeaux, perhaps Ch Coutet 1971 (£20). Occasional dinners are organised in co-operation with their wine-shippers.

Readers' reports submitted to *The Good Food Guide* as well as *Which? Wine Guide* have been used to supplement official inspectors' reports in compiling this section.

Priory Hotel

Weston Road TEL (0225) 331922

OPEN 12.30 pm–2 pm, 7.30 pm–9.15 pm CLOSED First two weeks Jan
CREDIT CARDS Access/Euro, Amex, Visa WHEELCHAIR ACCESS Yes
VEGETARIAN DISHES To order NO CIGARS AND PIPES IN DINING-ROOM
TDH SUN L £15.50 BUFFET L From £16.50 TDH D From £16.50

An elegant hotel in formal gardens on the outskirts of Bath. Owner John Donnithorne is always present, supervising his efficient staff, and the whole operation ticks over smoothly. The menu is sophisticated French: beignets de fromage sauce andalouse, crème de celériac gratinée, mousseline de coquilles St-Jacques, suprême de canard au cassis, foie de veau Düsseldorf (with bacon, apples and onions), darne de saumon grillé sauce mousseline, soufflé glacé praliné, parfait au chocolat sauce café. This is one of few places to offer a savoury: croûte épicure (Stilton with egg and brandy on toast). There are over 130 wines, from first-class sources. Unfortunately, prices are quoted without VAT, so add 15 per cent to those given here. Ten Champagnes start with René Lancier's Cuvée Spéciale, NV (£12; £7.75 a half-bottle sounds punitive) and goes up to Dom Pérignon 1975 (£34.10). Most of the white Burgundies are young, but there are two 1978s, both from Remoissenet: Puligny Montrachet, Les Folatières (£20.25), and Corton Charlemagne (£30.50). Reds climb equally steeply: try, perhaps, Mercurey, Les Sazenay, 1979, Genot (£10.75). The two dozen clarets are much more approachable: Ch Pitray 1975 (£8); Ch Cissac 1973 (£13.10); Ch Le Tour de Mons 1971 (£22.50); with Ch Lynch-Bages 1961, CB, for those with £47.60 (plus VAT) in their pockets. The Rhônes include some distinguished bottles: Châteauneuf-du-Pape, Ch Rayas, 1957 (£23.75); Gigondas 1967, Jaboulet (£9.60 a half-bottle). Outside France, the Italian section yields most of interest: Venegazzù 1977 (Conte Loredan), at £7.40, and Sassicaia 1979, Marchese della Rochetta, at £15.30. There are also French house wines from £6/£1.35. Occasional wine tastings are held.

BEARWOOD West Midlands

Franzl's

151 Milcote Road TEL 021-429 7920

OPEN D only, 7 pm–10.30 pm CLOSED L; Sun, Mon, Aug
CREDIT CARDS Access/Euro, Visa WHEELCHAIR ACCESS Yes
VEGETARIAN DISHES Yes ALC FOR TWO £20

A small, friendly Austrian restaurant where Adolf Geiregger pleases customers with gebackener Käse (deep-fried Swiss cheese served with tartare sauce), Eier mit Rahm (eggs baked with cheese and sour cream), gefüllter Schweins Lungenbraten (pork fillet stuffed with pâté and deep fried), Kalbsleber Tiroler Art (liver with onions, mushrooms, white wine and sour cream), as well as Wienerschnitzel (of course), venison casserole, and plain fillet or sirloin steak for the timid. Sweets are rich and creamy; an alcohol-soaked chocolate sponge is a particular favourite. There are two dozen moderately priced Austrian wines (listed mostly without producers): house Grüner Veltliner, Riesling, St Laurent and Zweigelt, at £5.80 a litre, 75p a glass (and put in a gravity dispenser unless you object); Johan Kattus sparklers (Hochriegl Trocken, £7.75); Muskat Ottonel 1981 (£5.85); Nussberger Hoehenweg Traminer Kabinett 1979, Kattus (£6.20); Ruster Blaufränkisch Spätlese 1979 (£7.10).

BIRMINGHAM West Midlands

Jonathans'

16–20 Wolverhampton Road, Oldbury, Warley TEL 021-429 3757

OPEN 12 noon–2 pm, 7 pm–10 pm CLOSED Sat L, Dec 26 CREDIT CARDS All accepted WHEELCHAIR ACCESS Yes VEGETARIAN DISHES Yes TDH SUN L £8.50 ALC FOR TWO £30 SNACK LUNCH From £2.50

Self-consciously Victorian, even to giving prices in shillings and pence (for which read pounds and multiples of 10p), Jonathans' remains popular for the interesting – if rather coarse – English cooking it provides, as well as a great deal of fun and fact in its chatty menu and wine notes. You can eat in the garden, or even on the roof if you belong to their luncheon club: salmon pie, Benton eggs (with mustard, horseradish and cream), smothered rabbit, calf's liver with ginger, strawberry and rhubarb ice-cream, Spotted Dick with Cumberland rum butter. Jonathans' lists about a hundred wines, mainly French, starting with Cuvée Georges Duboeuf as house wine (£5.10/£1). Spelling and annotation are hit-and-miss, but there are some fine wines: Ch Montrose 1970 (£25.60); Chassagne-Montrachet 1981, Labaume Aîné (£10.60); Côte-Rôtie, Les Jumelles, 1979, Paul Jaboulet (£11.80). The house Champagne is £12.50: you feel you've earned it after translating the typing errors and the shillings and pence . . . .

BIRTLE Greater Manchester

La Normandie

Elbut Lane TEL 061-764 3869
Off B6222, 2½ m NE of Bury

OPEN 12 noon–2.30 pm, 7 pm–9.30 pm CLOSED Sat L, Sun D, Dec 26–Dec 30 CREDIT CARDS All accepted WHEELCHAIR ACCESS Yes VEGETARIAN DISHES On request TDH L £7.50 D £13.50 ALC FOR TWO £30

The old blackstone beer house at the end of a long cul-de-sac overlooking Manchester and the Pennines is now lost amid the glass structure that surrounds it. Inside, all is Laura Ashley and friendly service. Other transformations have also taken place: while the familiar *carte* offers the familiar smoked salmon, avocado vinaigrette, salmon, Dover sole, duck, steaks and creamy puddings, there is a *nouvelle cuisine* set dinner on Fridays, introducing sceptics to Parma ham with paw-paw, lamb with rhubarb, saddle of hare in a semi-sweet sauce, and poire Tatin. Occasional *haute cuisine* dinners are planned. The wine list has been revamped by their consultant, David Wolfe, whose helpful tasting notes may reconcile you to the prices: Champagne, NV, Jules Mignon (£13.50); Crémant d'Alsace, NV, Dopff Cuvée Julien (£10.70); Chablis Fourchaumes 1981, Pic (£13.60); Sancerre, Clos du Paradis, 1982, Vacheron (£10.50); Viña Esmeralda 1983, Torres (£7); Rosemount Chardonnay 1983 (£10.40); Ch Montalivet 1978 (£8.90); Ch Giscours 1970 (£25); Santenay, Clos Rousseau, 1979, Chevrot (£13.70); Juliénas, Les Envaux, 1981, Pelletier (£9.10); Castel San Michele 1979, Instituto Agrario Provinciale (the classic blend of Bordeaux grapes – £11); Cousiño-Macul Cabernet Sauvignon Antiguas Reservas 1976 from Chile (£9.20). There are two interesting non-vintage Rhône wines from Chapoutier, better described, says David Wolfe, as reserve wines, since they are blends of mature vintages, marketed only when ready to drink: Crozes-Hermitage, Les Meysonniers (£18 a magnum), and Châteauneuf-du-Pape, La Bernadine (£27 a magnum). Dessert wines include the splendid Bailey's Liqueur Muscat Special Reserve (from Australia), at £11.80/90p, and Warre's 1963 Port at £29.50/£2. There are several useful half-bottles, and house wines include Le Chouan Chardonnay 1982 (£6.20/£1). A recently formed dining club, Patrons de la Normandie, holds special dinners every two months.

BOTALLACK Cornwall

Count House Ⓥ

Off B3306, 1 m N of St Just TEL (0736) 788588

OPEN 12.30 pm–1.45 pm (Sun only), 7.30 pm–10 pm CLOSED Sun D, Mon, Tue, 2–3 weeks winter CREDIT CARDS All accepted
WHEELCHAIR ACCESS Restaurant only VEGETARIAN DISHES With notice
TDH Sun L £5.95 ALC FOR TWO £25

Ian and Ann Long now have their daughter Suzanne working with them in this peaceful stone house 'on the edge of the coast', with views of the engine-houses, the cliffs and the sea. Inside all is flag-stones, whitewash, heavy beams and polished furniture, with various pictures and posters for sale. Sunday lunch is a bargain, offering a choice in each course: the main one might be home-spiced topside in red wine or roast leg of lamb with prune and pork stuffing. Dinners offer a wider choice, with many adventurous – and successful – combinations: swede and gooseberry soup, triple-layered mousses (cheesy, fishy or a combination of these with vegetables), pork and woodcock terrine, rolled lemon sole with grapefruit cooked in white wine, ballotine of duck in red wine, pigeon breast topped with a chicken mousse and baked in puff pastry, best end of lamb with apricot purée. There is always a steak or something else plain for the conventional – or wine-lover. An impressive display of elaborate sweets tempts most people to a taste of more than one. There are about forty wines on the workmanlike list, carefully annotated and with helpful tasting notes. French house wines (François Paquet) are £4.20 a litre, 65p a glass. There is also a house claret, Ch Haut-Puynormand 1979, Pierre Jean (£5.95); three others are picked out for special mention at the start of the list: St-Pourçain-sur-Sioule 1982 (£6.10); Côtes de Provence, Blanc de Blancs (£4.20); and half-bottles of Ch Bastor-Lamontagne 1976 (£6.45), popular with those showy puddings. Other appealing wines include Ch Peyraud 1976 (£7.70); Beaujolais St-Amour 1978, Sarrau (£7.15); Pouilly-Fuissé 1982, Paquet (£7.90); the English Reichensteiner 1982, Rock Lodge (£6.75); Vinho Verde, Aveleda (£4.95); Banda Azul 1978, Paternina (£4.10). Occasional wine dinners are held.

BOWNESS-ON-WINDERMERE Cumbria

The Porthole Eating House

3 Ash Street TEL (096 62) 2793

OPEN D only, 6.45 pm–11 pm CLOSED L, Tue, mid-Dec to mid-Feb
CREDIT CARDS All accepted WHEELCHAIR ACCESS Impossible
VEGETARIAN DISHES With notice ALC FOR TWO £27

The Berton family's warm and friendly beamed cottage in the middle of the village is always packed with regulars appreciative of the pleasant staff and competent cooking. The basic menu is Italian but many of the dishes on the weekly one are French borrowings, especially strong on fish: fettuccine with julienne of smoked salmon (£3); escalope of salmon Troisgros. A dozen wines are listed on the back of the menu, but it is worth asking for the serious list and browsing before ordering: over thirty Italians, with a dozen Brunello di Montalcino (Il Greppo Dr Biondi Santi Riserva 1968, £18.50); Bordeaux from Ch Plagnac 1975 (£8), to Ch Margaux 1961 (£165), with a useful sprinkling of half-bottles; several of the rare Hugel 1976s (Gewürztraminer Vendange Tardive, £19.50); a page of Germans, mostly from distinguished houses (some inadequately annotated); not to mention the fine Burgundies and, Signor Berton's newest interest, Rhône wines (Gigondas, Domaine St Gayan 1980, Roger Meffre, £9). There are some venerable wines marked 'prices on request', and jereboams of Ch La Lagune 1973 (£84). The house Merlot and Trebbiano are £6 a litre.

Special awards

Ⓥ is for bargain prices

is for a very good range of wines

is for exceptional service.

BRISTOL Avon

Bistro Twenty-One

21 Cotham Road South, Kingsdown TEL (0272) 421744

OPEN D only, 7 pm 'till late' CLOSED L, Sun, Mon, 1 week Chr, 1 week Easter, 3 weeks Aug CREDIT CARDS Not accepted WHEELCHAIR ACCESS Restaurant only VEGETARIAN DISHES With notice ALC FOR TWO £22

An unassuming little bistro where one of George Perry-Smith's long-ago protegées turns out dishes reminiscent of the master and Elizabeth David, as well as others revealing his own imaginative flair. Stephen Markwick changes his menu every day so that what you eat are fresh ingredients, simply cooked: Provençal fish soup with aïoli and rouille, aubergine fritters with tomato sauce, salmon in pastry with currants and ginger, ragout of monkfish and scallops, noisettes of pork with prunes, scallops of venison with gherkins and sour cream, sweetbreads with bacon and Madeira, civet of hare, St-Emilion au chocolat, walnut and treacle tart. The wine list lacks many details you might expect in other than a bistro, but for a small, informal restaurant it is admirably succinct, and helpfully arranged in 'white' and 'red' with geographical sub-divisions. House French is £4.80 or £5 a litre, 75p a glass. Thereafter, choose from Azay-le-Rideau 1981 (£5.40); Reuilly 1981, Cordier (£6.50); Hugel Gewürztraminer 1978 (£10; £5 a half); Marqués de Cáceres 1982 white (£4.75); Ch de la Rivière, Fronsac, 1975 (£8.50); Fleurie 1982, Moreau (£6.50), Châteauneuf-du-Pape, Chante Cigale, 1980 (£8); Rioja, Reserva 904, 1970 (£7.50). There is a 'special oddments' page of fine wines in smaller quantities. The menu suggests Muscat de Beaumes-de-Venise (£1.20) or Muscat de Rivesaltes (90p) with your sweet, and there is also vintage port from £2 a glass.

BURGHFIELD Berkshire

Knights Farm Ⓥ ☞

(see below) TEL (0734) 52366

OPEN 12.30 pm–1.45 pm, 7.30 pm–9 pm CLOSED Sat L; Sun; Mon; 1 week Chr; 3 weeks Aug CREDIT CARDS All accepted WHEELCHAIR ACCESS Yes VEGETARIAN DISHES Yes TDH L £10.95 D £13.95

Though this elegant Georgian house is hard to find (ask when you book), it is soothing and restful once you get there, with unobtrusive service of both food and wine and a knowledgeable proprietor, Charles Trevor-Roper. The set-price menus, changed every two months, tend to the 'eclectic modern': hot chicken liver and grape salad; mosaic of sole and salmon; duck with two mousses; fruit and pastry box. Praise for carefully cooked vegetables, fish and vegetarian dishes (aubergine charlotte, for example). The frequently changed wine list, with a bias towards France, has a maximum mark-up of £5 on expensive wines, thus making many of them very good value. The eighty or so wines are classified according to sweetness for whites and weight for reds. House Le Chouan Chardonnay and Gamay de l'Ardèche are £5.50/£1.20. Try the Australian Rosemount Chardonnay 1983 (£7.95); Les Forts de Latour 1976 (£17.65); and one of the pudding wines offered by glass or half-bottle (Ch Doisy-Védrines 1979, £6.50 a half). Interesting aperitifs and digestifs. Off-sales licence, restaurant customers only.

BURNHAM MARKET Norfolk

Fishes'

Market Place TEL (0328) 738588

OPEN 12 noon–2 pm, 7 pm–9.30 pm CLOSED Mon, Sun D (winter), 24 to 28 Dec
CREDIT CARDS All accepted WHEELCHAIR ACCESS Yes
VEGETARIAN DISHES With notice TDH L £5.95 (Sun £6.95) ALC FOR TWO £22

A simple – but not unsophisticated – fish restaurant within easy reach of mussels, crabs, lobsters and sea-trout. 'We grow our own oysters.' The atmosphere and the service are relaxed and friendly but cooking standards are rather uneven. However, people like the oysters, salmon fishcakes, seafood au gratin, smoked trout and orange salad, and lemon cake. The wine list is sensibly short, weighted towards white, and mainly French, with fairly helpful tasting notes. The three house wines are Martin Jarry's Blanc de Blancs, a Loire Chenin Blanc 1983, and a Loire Gamay, all £4.25/85p. Other possibilities include Rüdesheimer Rosengarten 1982, Erben (£4.25); the local Elmham Park 1983 (£5.90); Rully Blanc, Domaine du Prieuré, 1982, Monassier (£9.50); Joseph Perrier's Champagne, NV (£15.50); and Ch de Padère, Côtes de Buzet, 1982 (£6.50). It is wise to book in summer and at weekends.

CALLANDER Perthshire

Roman Camp Hotel

East end of Main Street TEL (0877) 30003

OPEN 12.30 pm–1.55 pm, 7 pm–8.55 pm CLOSED Early Dec to early Feb
CREDIT CARDS Not accepted WHEELCHAIR ACCESS One shallow step to dining-room VEGETARIAN DISHES By arrangement NO SMOKING IN DINING-ROOM TDH £14 SUN L £9.50 WEEKDAY LUNCH From £3

The Denzlers left their successful Edinburgh restaurant for this charming 17th-century hunting-lodge which looks, with its various tiled towers, like a tiny Loire château transported to the River Teith (you may fish if you wish). The hotel has been gently refurbished in appropriate period and national style, although the dining-room, with its pale maple tables and panelling, looks 'rather Swiss'. The set meals also reflect Sami Denzler's Swiss heritage, with other European influences – even Scottish ones: écrevisses hollandaise, cock-a-leekie, gazpacho, escalope de veau valaisienne (with mushrooms, cream, cheese and asparagus), saumon zougoise (with cream and herbs), poulet poché Stanley (in a lightly curried sauce with banana and almonds), Apfelstrudel, Black Forest cake, and Callander Mist (enlightenment welcome). Mr Denzler imports a few Swiss wines seldom seen outside Switzerland: Yvorne, Haut Combe, 'a medium-dry white wine from a favoured site in the Swiss Rhône valley near Geneva', at £12.50, and Dézaley, L'Arbalète, from the same area, at £13.50. His four Austrian wines come from the Klosterneuberg monastery: Klosterjuwel Predigstuhl Muskat-Ottonel 1981 (£5.90), and Kahlenberger Weisser Burgunder Auslese 1977 (£8.25). There are over a hundred others, all with careful notes: Italian Lugana 1981, DOC (£5.15); Reserva 904, Rioja Alta, 1970 (£8.20); Hallgartener Schönhell Spätlese 1976 (£8.05); Gewürztraminer 1980, Quien (£7.55); Cornas 1978, Jaboulet (£11.55); Ch Lalande 1979 (£8.35); Ch Grand-Puy-Lacoste 1970 (£15.50); Chambolle-Musigny 1969, Faiveley (£5.95). There are some attractive dessert wines, with the winner perhaps Quarts de Chaume 1973, Baumard (£8.80).

CARTMEL Cumbria

Aynsome Manor

Off A590 at High Newton TEL (044 854) 276

OPEN 1 pm (Sun only), 7 pm–8.30 pm CLOSED L (exc Sun), first 3 weeks in Jan CREDIT CARDS Access/Euro, Amex, Visa WHEELCHAIR ACCESS Dining-room only VEGETARIAN DISHES With notice TDH D £10.50 SUN L £6.50

The Varleys work hard in their small manor house set in lovely countryside. Everything sparkles, service is attentive, and the reasonably priced set meals are very popular locally. You may be offered seafood vol-au-vents or pancakes, good home-made mushroom soup, roast duckling or lamb, salmon with prawn and parsley sauce. Sweets are heavily creamy, cheeses adequate. The wines are also reasonably priced, and the list of 80 or so, though lacking some essential details, is clearly set out and covers several countries, all European except for South Africa. House wines – Italian, German and Spanish as we went to press – are £5.30 a litre, 75p a glass. Others include eight 'table wines', recommended as value for money: Vin de Pays des Pyrenées Orientales (red and white), is £3.75; Austrian Falkensteiner, £4.10. Climbing up the list, we find: Gatão Vinho Verde (£4.50); Steiner Bergher Rheinriesling 1982 (£5.50); Montagny 1981, Louis Latour (£9); Muscadet, Marquis de Goulaine, 1982 (£5.95); Marc Brédif's Sparkling Vouvray (£9.10); Côtes-du-Rhône 1978, Viénot (£5); Ch Smith-Haut-Lafitte 1978 (£16.85); Rioja Alta Reserva, Marqués de Cáceres, 1973 (£7.60). Lots of half-bottles, very dull dessert wines.

If you know of a good restaurant where it is possible both to eat *and* to drink well, please let us know if we have not listed it. There are report forms at the back of the book.

CHAGFORD Devon

Gidleigh Park

2 m W of Chagford TEL (064 73) 2367

OPEN 12.30 pm–1.30 pm, 7 pm–9 pm CREDIT CARDS Not accepted
WHEELCHAIR ACCESS Impossible VEGETARIAN DISHES With notice
TDH D £23 ALC L FOR TWO £36

Gidleigh Park, on the edge of Dartmoor, offers a fine menu and – more important – an outstanding wine-list. Summed up by its American proprietor Paul Henderson as 'designed for and run by affluent connoisseurs', it has become a place of pilgrimage, even for the not-so-affluent who appreciate the value for money and save up to savour Kay Henderson's and John Webber's innovative cooking and a wine or two from the 24-page list. (It's worth sending £3 for a copy so that you can plan ahead.) Lunch is à la carte, dinner a set meal, but at either you will have a choice of about six dishes in each course: Billi-Bi (mussel and cream soup), perhaps; or 'ragout' of monkfish, turbot and lobster, cooked in white wine and cream; or sautéed veal kidneys with mustard; or lamb with leeks and rosemary sauce; or sweetbreads in lettuce parcels with ham and tomato sauce; finish with 'splendid' cheeses or sorbets and exotic fruits if the sweets trolley seems too much of a challenge. Service is obliging, occasionally obtrusive.

The wine list is truly *embarras de richesse*: where to start? (Note that all prices are ex-VAT.) Paul Henderson is especially proud of his Alsace wines: from Muscat Réserve 1982, Trimbach, at a modest £7, through Riesling Clos Ste Hune 1979, also Trimbach (£12), nine of the dazzling 1976s, with Hugel's three 'Sélection des Grains Nobles', and the 1971 version of Clos St Hune (£25); and Schlumberger's delicious dessert wine, Gewürztraminer 'Cuvée Christine' (£21). The two pages of Champagnes and sparkling wines include Joseph Perrier's Cuvée Royale at £12.50 (£2.50 a glass); Mumm's Crémant de Cramant Blanc de Blancs at £16; a clutch of older Champagnes from 1969 back to 1949 at £35 to £60; and Schramsberg's Blanc de Noirs 1978 at £17. California wines are a particular strength, with many listed which are no longer around in the US, and at ungrasping prices. Consider a comparative tasting of Chalone Chardonnay, for example: 1981, 1980 and 1979, between £18 and £20. More modest purses could settle for the Edna Valley 1981 at £11. The Cabernet Sauvignons are equally distinguished: Firestone 1978 (£12); Ch Montelena 1974 (£30); and a trio of Mayacamas, 1975, 1974, and 1973. Other varietals include Clos du Val Merlot 1979, £15. The solitary Oregon wine, Chardonnay 1979 from Eyrie Vineyards, is lighter than the Californians and worth a try (£16). Paul Henderson thinks his Burgundies better value than his clarets, and who would disagree with Louis Michel Chablis 1982 at £8.50, his Vaudésir 1981 at £10, and Montmain 1978 at £17? Many fine shippers' names appear in both the white and red lists: Corton Les Bressandes 1978, Tollot-Beaut (£25); Nuits-St-Georges, Ch Gris, 1959, Lupé-Cholet (£29), and many more. German wines, many from Loeb, also merit study: Wachenheimer Mandelgarten Scheurebe Auslese 1976, Bürklin-Wolf (£13); Ayler Herrenberger Auslese 1971, Bischöfliches Konvikt (£13). Australia boasts the Rothbury Estate 'Individual Paddock' Semillon 1976 at £9.50. The Rhône section has Ch Rayas 1971 for £16 among the whites, and many fine Paul Jaboulet elders among the reds: Châteauneuf-du-Pape Les Cèdres 1957 is £32. One should not ignore the fine Bordeaux, with a drinkable Ch Potensac 1978 (£10) at one end of the list, and Ch Haut-Brion 1934 (£100) at the other. Dessert wines, ports and digestifs are worthy codas. Go and find out for yourself – or at least send for the list and dream a little. Special wine weekends, with authoritative speakers, are held from time to time.

CHEDINGTON Dorset

Chedington Court

Ⓥ

Off A356 at Winyard's Gap, 4½ m SE of Crewkerne — TEL (093 589) 265

OPEN D only, 7 pm–9 pm CLOSED L; annual holiday CREDIT CARDS Amex WHEELCHAIR ACCESS Yes VEGETARIAN DISHES Yes TDH D £15

A handsome stone house set in ten acres of grounds from which you can see three counties. Mrs Chapman's carefully balanced five-course dinners are popular for such dishes as tarte provençale, watercress soup, mushrooms in garlic butter, turbot in white wine sauce, salmon hollandaise, beef in various ways, rack of lamb with mushrooms and cream, tongue with Madeira, and a dazzling display of creamy sweets. Vegetables are good. Service is agreeable and unobtrusive, though some find the waits between courses too long. But wine drinkers can pass the time agreeably, since Mr Chapman's lengthy hand-written list has some interesting finds at reasonable prices: Ayala Champagne, NV (£15, £8.20 a half); Gigondas Rosé 1980, Roger Meffre (£7.60); Wraxhall 1981 (from Somerset) (£7); Rothbury Estate Semillon, 1976 (£9.60); Hermitage Blanc 1980, Chave (£13.70); St-Véran, Les Grandes Bruyères, 1982, Roger Luguet (£9.10); Gewürztraminer, Baron de Huen, 1981 (£8.80). The three German pages deserve special study, since they offer many of the delicious 1971s and 1976s: Niersteiner Hipping Auslese 1976, Schmitt (£12.50); Mettenheimer Schlossberg Beerenauslese 1971, Wissman (£16.50); and Wiltinger Schwarzberg Auslese 1976, Hallgarten (£10.20). Red wines are equally eclectic, many of them seldom found on restaurant lists: Loire Coteaux d'Ancenis (Gamay) 1981, Jacques Guindon (£6.20); Colares Reserva 1976, Real Vinicola (£6.30). There are many cru Beaujolais, and an ancient Averys-bottled Richebourg 1928 at £35 a half-bottle, as well as a healthy showing of mature (but younger!) Burgundies: Beaune Grèves 1970, Remoissenet (£28.50). Clarets considerately include almost as many half-bottles as full ones: Ch Lyonnat 1966, CB (£14.50); Ch Giscours 1970 (£9.20); Ch Batailley 1978 (£8) – all halves. French house wines are £4.60 a bottle, £1.20 a glass.

CHITTLEHAMHOLT Devon

Highbullen

Off B3226, 5 m SW of South Molton TEL (076 94) 248
OPEN D only, 7.30 pm–9 pm CREDIT CARDS Not accepted
WHEELCHAIR ACCESS Impossible VEGETARIAN DISHES With notice
NO SMOKING IN DINING-ROOM TDH D £10.50

An informally relaxed hotel with fine views and splendid sports facilities: a nine-hole golf course, indoor and outdoor swimming-pools, tennis, squash, croquet, billiards, saunas and spa baths. Luckily, you can enjoy the peace and quiet doing nothing at all if you wish, and many do. Mrs Neil's dinner menu offers a generous choice in each course, many of them old favourites: cream of lettuce soup, marinated kipper fillets, guacamole, chicken with tarragon and almonds, leg of lamb with spinach and béarnaise, feuilletés aux ris de veau, escalope of veal tapénade, raspberry soufflé, apricot and hazelnut meringue cake. The list of 150 wines starts with 30 of Christopher Piper's, recommended as value for money: the house wine, Mouflon d'Or, NV (£5.80 a litre, 85p a glass); St-Pourçain 1982 (£5.20); Brouilly, Ch des Tours, 1982 (£6.25); Chenin Blanc 1980, Parducci (£7.90); Côtes-du-Rhône, Domaine des Moulins, 1982, Georges Duboeuf (£5.25); Zinfandel 1976, Inverness (£5.95). From the remainder of the list, consider St-Amour 1982, Georges Duboeuf (£8.50); Eltviller Sonnenberg Auslese 1976, Fischer (£9.75); Cabernet Sauvignon, Wynns Coonawarra Estate, 1978 (£8.80); Sarget de Gruaud-Larose 1979 (the château's second wine) at £11; Fixin, Clos du Chapître, 1976, Guyot, at £13.50. The impressive claret section runs from 1978 (Ch Chasse-Spleen, £11.60) back to 1952 (Ch Rouet, London-bottled, £9.50), with many distinguished stops in between: Ch Pape-Clément 1970 (£17.50); Ch Lynch-Bages 1961, London-bottled (£39.50).

CHRISTCHURCH Dorset

Splinters Ⓥ

12 Church Street TEL (0202) 483454
OPEN D only, 6.30 pm–10.30 pm CLOSED L; Sun CREDIT CARDS Amex, Visa
WHEELCHAIR ACCESS Yes VEGETARIAN DISHES Yes NO SMOKING IN DINING-ROOM ALC FOR TWO £26

Splinters, for the last 20 years a tiny restaurant in a cul-de-sac by the priory, has now happily expanded into the place next door, thus increasing the comfort all round without diminishing the charm of the flowery pinè surroundings. Juanita Franke cooks a huge menu of French dishes with more innovative *plats du jour*: deep-fried Dover sole roes with tartare sauce, palm hearts with pastis and cheese sauce, écrevisses chinoise (with a ginger and sherry sauce), poussin aux abricots, trout cooked with prawns, capers and brown butter. The local fish is particularly good, and there are careful steaks for meat-eaters; sweets are mostly creamy and fruity. John Carter has built up his stock of 23,000 bottles over many years, and is so far resisting his accountant's advice to send the lot to Sotheby's. The emphasis is on French wines, with a few Germans 'to fill a gap in the French spectrum'. Mark-ups are low, quality is high: even the house wines are of interest, with Anjou Rouge 1979 (Cabernet) and Blanc 1982 (Chenin) at £4.75 a bottle, £1.25 a glass. (They have off-sales facilities – but hate parting with the oldest wines: the house wines are £29.95 a case.) The list begins with detailed notes each month on two of the less usual wines, for example, Jasnières, Caves aux Truffières, 1976, Pinon (£8.75), and Preiss-Zimmer's Pinot Noir d'Alsace 1978 (£7.60). After that it's into the bubbly, with a dozen Champagnes, from Bollinger, NV (£15), to a magnum of Dom Pérignon 1969 (£56); there are four useful half-bottles. White wines include Corton-Charlemagne 1979, Louis Latour (£18.50); St Nicolas de Bourgueil, Clos de la Contrie, 1982 (£6.50); Riesling, Cuvée Tradition, 1982, Kuentz-Bas (£7.25); Klusserather Bruderschaft Auslese 1976 (no shipper given) (£13); Deidesheimer Herrgottsacker 1979 (£7.75). The two pages of clarets are beguiling: from Ch Rouet 1973 (Fronsac) at £6.75 to Ch Rauzan-Gassies 1961 at £30, there is surely something for every taste: Ch Haut-Marbuzet 1978 (£8.75); Ch Gruaud-Larose 1966 (£22); Ch Latour 1948 (£20 a half-bottle). Red Burgundies are also appealing: Beaune Grèves 1964, Chanson (£16); Santenay, Domaine St-Michel, 1978, Maufoux (£9.50; £5 a half); Corton Reynards 1966, Pasquier-Desvignes, 1966 (£19.50); and a pair of 1962 wines from the Hospices de Beaune, each £25 – Pommard, Cuvée Billardet, and Volnay, Cuvée Général Muteau. Rhônes are nicely varied in style and price, including Grand Hermitage 1962, Chapoutier (£17.50), Côtes-du-Rhône 1979, Loron (£7.50), and a medium-dry sparkler, Clairette de Die, NV, Archard-Vincent (£8.75). Dessert wines encompass several Sauternes (Grand Mayne 1973, £7.75; Ch Filhot 1975, £6.50 a half-bottle); Quarts de Chaume, Ch de Suronde, 1959, £19; Muscat de Beaumes-de-Venise, Domaine de Durban (£8.90; £4.75 a half); and Dirmsteiner Mandelpfad Trockenbeerenauslese 1976, Faber (£9.75 a half-bottle). There are several vintage ports by bottle or half-bottle, Taylor's LBV 1978 and Old Tawny (£1.25 a glass). Occasional French regional evenings are held, with an appropriate dinner preceded by a serious tasting. Mr Carter should consider including tasting-notes for more wines on his list.

COATHAM MUNDEVILLE Co Durham

Hall Garth

Ⓥ

TEL (0325) 313333

OPEN 12.30 pm–1.30 pm, 7.30 pm–9.15 pm CLOSED Sun, Dec 23–Jan 2
CREDIT CARDS All accepted WHEELCHAIR ACCESS Yes
VEGETARIAN DISHES Yes NO SMOKING IN DINING-ROOM TDH L From £6.50 D From £10.95

This mainly Georgian hall, set in a deer park, is relaxed and unpretentious, serving good, fresh, hearty food in ample Northern helpings, thus appealing to locals and hungry tourists alike. Soups are popular, as are leek and ham gratinée, beef and red wine pie, roast rump of beef with mushroom and sherry sauce, lamb chops with apricot sauce, and game in season. Vegetables are well cooked and sweets imaginative. Service is cheerful and efficient, and the lack of taped music 'lets you talk to your companions'. There are over a hundred wines, mainly French, with a few others worth looking at: Marqués de Murrieta 1975 (white) at £7.20; Freixenet sparkling Cordon Negro at £6.75; Robert Mondavi's Pinot Noir 1977 at £11. Halves are thin on the ground, but at least bottle prices are not grasping: Sancerre 1982, Jean Vatan (£8.20); Saumur Champigny, Domaine de Pillintreau, DB, 1980 (£6.50); Hermitage Blanc 1979, Chave (£12.45; his red of the same year is £11.50); Clairette de Die, NV, Frachet (£7.25); Ch Castera 1976 (£7); Ch Giscours 1970 (£15). Burgundies and German wines should be more fully annotated.

COGGESHALL Essex

The White Hart

Market End TEL (0376) 61654

OPEN 12.30 pm–2.30 pm, 7.30 pm–9.30 pm CLOSED Mon, Aug
CREDIT CARDS All accepted WHEELCHAIR ACCESS Yes
VEGETARIAN DISHES Yes ALC FOR TWO £36

A comfortable, family-run timbered inn with a worryingly long menu but some very respectable food: home-smoked salmon, Mersea oysters, local game, steak-and-kidney pudding, pork fillet in white wine and cream. Garnishes sometimes go over the top: black cherries with roast duckling in orange, lemon and port sauce; avocado and orange with calf's liver in Madeira sauce. The charcoal-grilled meats are popular. There are several hundred wines on the French-biased list, which sensibly offers 40 half-bottles at the front: Ch d'Angludet 1978 (£6.25); Chablis 1982, Albert Pic (£5.95). And there are magnums at the back for those who think big: Vosne-Romanée, Les Suchots 1971, Joseph Drouhin (£57.95). In between come sonorous clarets (Ch Gruaud-Larose 1973, £18.95, and 1966, £39.95) as well as other fine wines: Meursault-Charmes 1979, Louis Jadot (£19.75); Trefethen Chardonnay

1979 (£17.95); Hermitage 1976, Ozier (£15.95); Ch Rieussec 1971 (£18.75). The Lay & Wheeler French house wine is £5.75 a bottle, £1 a glass.

CORK Co Cork

Arbutus Lodge

Ⓥ ☞

St Luke's Cross, Montenotte TEL Cork 501237

OPEN 1 pm–2 pm, 7 pm–9.30 pm CLOSED Sun, 24 to 30 Dec CREDIT CARDS All accepted VEGETARIAN DISHES Yes/NO PIPES OR CIGARS IN DINING-ROOM TDH L IR£13.75 D IR£16.95 ALC FOR TWO IR£48

This suburban Georgian hotel overlooking a well-groomed garden and the River Lee provides some delightful surprises in both food and wine. The Ryans are creative enthusiasts, always learning, always changing their ideas. The cooking is mainly *nouvelle cuisine*, and there is even a special tasting menu for two or more people (seven dainty courses, IR£19.95). The plates are picture-book pretty: vegetable terrines, hot oysters with various garnishes, fillet of sole with sea-urchin sauce, breast of chicken with cream lime sauce, with every last tiny vegetable perfectly cooked and placed. For heartier appetites, the local shellfish includes lobster from the vivarium (buttered or grilled, IR£12.55 a pound), as well as the local crubeens vinaigrette (pigs' trotters) and pavé de boeuf aux echalottes. Service is unassuming and friendly. Patsy Ryan guides you through the wine list knowledgeably. The dozen house wines include Ayala Champagne, NV (IR£15.90, IR£8.15 a half); Chilean Santa Digna 1982 (IR£8.25); Merlot Grave del Friuli, 1977 (IR£8.15); and Robert Mondavi Red 1981 (IR£9.99). The New World has impressive representation with, among others, Mayacamas Chardonnay 1976 (IR£29.70), and Chalone Pinot Noir 1975 (IR£26.80 – one of the few successful California wines made from this grape); and Rothbury Estate Individual Paddock Hermitage 1975 (IR£10.95). The Italian section includes Traminer Aromatico Alto Adige 1982, Vaja (IR£8.75), and Venegazzù 1975, Conte Loredan (IR£15.20), which will fizz when first opened. Germans, many from Deinhard, include Schloss Johannisberg 1978, Furst von Metternich (IR£11.70), Schloss Böckelheimer Felsenberg 1980, Hans Crusius (IR£9.85), and Wehlener Sonnenuhr 1979, Deinhard (IR£10.25). Clarets and Burgundies are not neglected either: Ch Dutruch Grand Poujeaux runs from 1973 to 1981 (IR£21.70 to IR£10.70); Ch Margaux 1904, for gamblers (IR£64); Ch d'Angludet 1976 (IR£17.70); several vintages of the 'Irish' clarets, Ch Léoville-Barton and Ch Langoa-Barton; six fine Chablis from Albert Pic (Valmur 1979, IR£18.70); ancient and modern Burgundies (Corton Grancey 1953, Louis Latour, IR£35.50; Gevrey Chambertin, Clos St Jacques 1978, Clair-Däu, IR£29.50). Rhône and Loire are covered more than adequately also, and there are several classy dessert wines to finish with: Ch Rayne-Vigneau 1975 (IR£14.75); Ch Filhot 1978 (IR£9.25 a half); Quarts de Chaume, Château de L'Echarderie 1961 (IR£22.90); and Oestricher Doosberg Beerenauslese Eiswein 1971, Deinhard (IR£30.50).

CORSE LAWN Gloucestershire

Corse Lawn House Hotel

On B4211, 5 m SW of Tewkesbury TEL (045 278) 479

OPEN 12 noon–2 pm, 7 pm–10 pm CLOSED Sun D, Mon, Chr Day, Boxing Day
CREDIT CARDS All accepted WHEELCHAIR ACCESS Yes
VEGETARIAN DISHES Yes TDH L £8.50 D £11.75 ALC FOR TWO £35

The Hines' (of Cognac fame) Queen Anne house in a quiet village is set between a duck pond and the vegetable garden. There are just four bedrooms, but the restaurant is busy, and there are good bar snacks as well (soups, pies, shellfish, terrines, salads). Baba Hine and Andrew Foley cook in the French style, a mixture of provincial and modern dishes, for example: terrine of crab beurre blanc, hot shrimps en croustade, tournedos of veal with Noilly Prat and mushroom mousseline, roast duckling with apricot sauce, calf's liver with pleurottes (oyster mushrooms) and chives, home-made sorbets and ice-creams and several other desserts based on exotic fruits. The list of over 200 wines begins with 11 'budget wines', including the French house wine at £5 (white) and £5.50 (red). The clarets include a useful number of half-bottles and an enticing magnum, Ch d'Angludet 1978, at £30.70. Other possibilities on the rather confusing list include Pouilly-Vinzelles 1981, Loron (£11); Chénas 1981, Louis Latour (£13.40); Sancerre, Clos les Perrières, 1982 (£10.60); Rioja Reserva 904 (£19.70/£11.50); Rothbury Estate Shiraz 1980 (£11.45). As you might expect, the digestifs are distinguished, with five early-landed Hine Cognacs by the glass: Grande Champagne 1951, landed 1952, bottled 1969 for Wolverhampton & Dudley Breweries, Ltd (£3.20). Straight vintages include Grande Champagne 1918, at £4 a glass. If you stay, don't miss breakfast, which offers home-made croissants and jams, as well as free-range eggs, home-made sausages, and kidneys in cream.

DARTMOUTH Devon

The Carved Angel

2 South Embankment TEL (080 43) 2465

OPEN 12.30 pm–1.45 pm, 7.30 pm–10 pm CLOSED Sun D, Mon, Jan
CREDIT CARDS Access/Euro, Visa VEGETARIAN DISHES By arrangement
TDH D £18 SUN L £15 ALC Also (weekday lunch)

From the dining-room of the elegant Angel, overlooking the Dart estuary, diners enjoy a reassuring view of Joyce Molyneux and her assistants in the kitchen. Her former partner Tom Jaine writes about their constant search for prime raw materials, new recipes, and their wine philosophy and discoveries in *Twelve Times a Year*, compulsive reading for followers of Roy Shillabeer, the butcher and Rear-Admiral Haynes, supplier of tomatoes. The menu, changed daily, features local fish of course (John Dory with sorrel mousseline, turbot with prawn sauce), but there is praise too, for example, for the home-made pasta with various delicate sauces, kid cooked with Marsala, oxtail with prunes, and rare roast beef (for two). Puddings are no less tempting: rhubarb baked in honey and saffron custard, brandy-snaps with kumquat cream. The changes in management were still under way as we went to press. There is no reason to believe that there will be radical alterations in the previous wine policy of intelligent selection, reasonable mark-ups and careful service, but we must wait and see. Reports on this old favourite will be particularly welcome.

DEDHAM Essex

Le Talbooth

Off A12, 7 m NE of Colchester TEL (0206) 323150

OPEN 12.30 pm–2 pm, 7.30 pm–9.30 pm CREDIT CARDS All accepted WHEELCHAIR ACCESS Through kitchen VEGETARIAN DISHES Yes TDH L £9.25 ALC FOR TWO £35

Gerald Milsom is a complete professional, who has nicely calculated the blend of rustic charm and over-the-top luxury in his timbered restaurant by the Stour, and in its sleeping accommodation, Maison Talbooth, half a mile away. Similarly, the menu offers a wide choice of dishes, some as traditional as smoked salmon, crab with tomato and cheese topping, and steak and kidney pie; others as *nouvelle* as vegetable terrine with tomato sauce, chicken breast stuffed with sweetbreads in a tarragon cream sauce, Dover sole poached in Mosel with leeks, and hot passion-fruit brûlée. Service of both food and wine is friendly and well trained. The Lay & Wheeler list of 140 mostly French wines starts with a page of Milsom's recommendations, with tasting notes: the Cuvée Duboeuf, red and white, are £5.55; Marqués de Cáceres Blanco 1982 is £6.65, and Tinto 1978, £7.45. Other attractions include Puligny-Montrachet, Les Referts, Louis Jadot, 1980, at £16.10; Graves Rouge, Cuvée Pierre Coste, 1981, at £8.05 and Santenay, Remoissenet, 1978, at £13.50. A flamboyant touch is the house Champagne, as served by the Ritz and the QEII, at £14.50. French house wine is £5.20 a bottle, £1.20 a glass.

Prices were current in summer 1984 to the best of our knowledge but can only be a rough indication of prices throughout 1985.

TDH Table d'Hôte ALC A la carte D Dinner L Lunch.

Some restaurants may be willing to send you a list by post, so that you can choose at leisure if you want to drink special wines from a lengthy list.

DINGLE Co Kerry

Doyle's Seafood Bar ⓥ

John Street TEL (066) 51174

OPEN 12.30 pm–2.15 pm, 6 pm–9 pm CLOSED Sun, Nov to Mar
CREDIT CARDS All accepted WHEELCHAIR ACCESS Yes
VEGETARIAN DISHES No ALC FOR TWO IR£25

There is a sophisticated simplicity about John and Stella Doyle's fish restaurant: they gave up taking bookings when they found themselves turning away potential customers one Bank holiday, while reserved tables stayed empty; they offer only fish as a main course. But what fish: absolutely fresh, naturally, and presented in simple ways which enhance the flavour rather than masking it: oysters, smoked salmon, crab cocktail, grilled black sole; grilled or boiled lobster, crab claws beurre blanc, poached salmon with sorrel sauce, brown trout with mushroom sauce. Home-baked bread and a salad come with the fish, and potatoes at dinner. Sweets include home-made ice-cream, rhubarb tart, lemon and wine custard. John Doyle takes his wine seriously, having visited vineyards in the New World as well as the Old: he even worked in Napa Valley for three months. He bemoans the Irish system which puts almost £2 duty on a bottle of wine, plus 23 per cent VAT, and does well in that situation to offer the wines he does, mainly white, of course, but with a healthy showing of Spanish reds: Marqués de Riscal 1974 (IR£10.25); Penedés Sangre de Toro 1978, Torres (IR£8.80). There are French, German, Australian and Spanish whites to choose from: Chablis Montmains 1978, Piat (IR£13.70); Clos de l'Arlot Blanc 1979, Jules Belin (IR£24); Saint-Joseph 1980, Grippat (IR£12); Carta de Plata 1975 (IR£6.50); Gewürztraminer 1978, Geyser Peak from California (IR£8.50); Seppelt 'Reserve Bin' Rutherglen Chardonnay 1982 (IR£10.50); Ch Liot 1972 (IR£9.50). French house wine is IR£10 a litre, IR£2.50 a glass. Small tastings of new wines are arranged for regular customers.

DODWORTH see Barnsley

DRYBRIDGE Banffshire

The Old Monastery ⓥ

2½ m south of Buckie, junction of A98 & A942 TEL (0542) 32660

OPEN 12 noon–2 pm, 7 pm–9 pm CLOSED Sun, Mon, 2 weeks Jan, 2 weeks Oct
CREDIT CARDS Not accepted WHEELCHAIR ACCESS Yes
VEGETARIAN DISHES By arrangement ALC FOR TWO £21

The Craigs' converted chapel with its splendid views over the Moray Firth should have its full licence by now, so that you can buy to take home any wine you particularly fancy. In four years, these southern emigrants have established themselves with neighbours and customers alike, and there is a relaxed informality about their dining-room, with its pine tables echoing the original pitch pine roof. Their menus lean heavily on the fine local produce, cooked in French and Scottish ways: ham'n'haddie (ham and smoked haddock in cheese sauce), pheasant pâté, skewered scallops in bacon with mushrooms, Aberdeen Angus sirloin with a Dijon mustard sauce, poached sole with salmon mousse in cream and wine, braised haunch of venison, Speyside salmon, summer pudding, blackcurrant mousse. Anthea Craig has put together a list of over 100 wines, with 80 per cent costing under £10 a bottle, an example for others to follow: her mark-ups are between £2.50 and £5 a bottle. There are seven house wines, available by bottle and glass: Costières du Gard (£4.60/92p); Bourgogne Aligoté 1982 (£5.60/£1.15). Start, perhaps, with Gratien & Meyer's Sparkling Saumur (£7.05), or Christian Brothers' Chardonnay (£6.45), or Riesling, Cuvée des Evêques, 1981, Hugel (£6.75). The German page offers Eitelsbacher Marienholz 1982 at £6.40, and Kaseler Herrenberg Spätlese 1976 at £8.75 (no makers' or shippers' names are given). Burgundies are also erratically annotated, but include St-Véran 1981, Caves de Prissé (£7.60), and Vosne-Romanée 1976, Bouchard Père et Fils (£11.55). Clarets include Ch Figeac 1976 (£13.60), and Ch des Templiers 1978 (£6.60). Outside France, there are other bargain reds: Castillo Los Molinos 1978, Jumilla (£4.50); Alexander Valley Zinfandel 1978, Simi (£7.95); Coonawarra Cabernet Sauvignon Show Reserve, Hungerford Hill, 1979 (£8.65). A couple of pages of half-bottles yield Binger Osterberg Scheurebe Beerenauslese 1976 (£8.30); Ch La Tour-du-Pin-Figeac 1962 (£8.05), which the list suggests is still robust. Three ports are available by the glass.

DUBLIN Co Dublin

Le Coq Hardi

35 Pembroke Road, Ballsbridge TEL Dublin 689070

OPEN 12.30 pm–3 pm, 7 pm–11 pm CLOSED Sun, Sat L, 2 weeks Chr, 2 weeks Aug CREDIT CARDS All accepted WHEELCHAIR ACCESS Yes VEGETARIAN DISHES On request TDH L IR£11.75 ALC FOR TWO IR£65

An elegant restaurant, spacious, comfortable – and expensive. However, many people think the cooking amongst the best in Ireland, and the wines are even more outstanding, so worth saving up for a special occasion if your expense-account lunches don't extend to this league. The cooking is French – classical, *bourgeoise* and *nouvelle* – and the menu a lengthy printed affair with hand-written daily additions. John Howard's *menu dégustation* (IR£20.50) is considered good value, since the seven small courses allow you to explore many different tastes. Otherwise make your own choices from a plethora of dishes including smoked salmon, pâtés and soups, before, for example, sweetbreads and kidneys with chestnuts, calf's liver with fresh apricots, sea-trout en papillote, steaks in various fancy ways, and fruity puddings. Guinness sorbet has appeared as a palate-cleanser: reports welcome. Mr Howard is a wealthy and dedicated wine-buyer (1978, 1981 and 1982 clarets were the latest purchases as we went to press), and his 33-page list deserves study, if you are a wealthy and dedicated wine-lover. If you are merely dedicated, consider his eight house wines, among them Sauvignon du Haut Poitou 1981, and Olarra Tinto 1978, each IR£9. Other relatively cheap bottles include Brolio Reserva Chianti Classico 1977 (IR£10.50); Marqués de Cáceres 1978 red (IR£11) and 1982 white (IR£10.50); Ch Musar 1977 (IR£11.50); Oppenheimer Schloss Silvaner Trocken 1980, Guntrum (IR£11.50). But let's pretend we've scooped the pools and can consider the 13 pages of superb clarets, and hang the expense: ignore Ch Ségur 1981 (IR£11.75), and push on to Ch de Pez 1978 (IR£19.75); Ch Talbot 1976 (IR£26.75); Ch Mouton-Rothschild 1973 (IR£48); Ch Ausone 1971 (IR£57); Ch Cheval-Blanc 1970 (IR£85); Ch Pétrus 1967 (IR£95); Ch Figeac 1966 (IR£55). There are 20 1961s, from Pavie to Pétrus (IR£66 to IR£307), a page of various 1950s vintages, nine 1945s, and then a few showings back to 1878 Ch Mouton-Rothschild (recorked) at IR£1,875 a magnum, and the 1870 for IR£1,000 a bottle. Unless you have won the Derby as well as the pools, best not think about the double magnums . . . It is almost a relief to read that the complete collection of Ch Mouton-Rothschild is not all for sale, but on view to anyone who wishes to admire the artist-designed labels. As you would expect, there are several classy white Bordeaux, with eight vintages of Ch d'Yquem (1976 to 1878). The Burgundies are also impressive, with many wines from the Domaine de la Romanée-Conti (Grands Echézeaux 1978, IR£80). The Loire and the Rhône are naturally overshadowed, but Anjou Rablay 1928 from the Prunier sale is IR£48, and there are two vintages of Châteauneuf-du-Pape, Ch Rayas, 1976 and 1978, each IR£31 for the white, IR£35 and IR£36.50 for the red. John Howard has opened a fine wine shop along the road at 1 Pembroke Street, selling to retail and wholesale customers, and organising tastings on a regular basis: definitely worth investigating.

Locks Restaurant

1 Windsor Terrace, Portobello TEL (01) 752025

OPEN 12.30 pm–2 pm, 7.15 pm–11 pm CLOSED Sun, Sat L, 1 week Chr
CREDIT CARDS Amex, Diners, Visa WHEELCHAIR ACCESS Yes
VEGETARIAN DISHES With notice ALC FOR TWO IR£36

The Douglases' canalside restaurant feels pleasantly French, with *cuisine moderne* to match: salmon and monkfish terrine with a Pernod sauce; beignets of Camembert with a cherry sauce; smoked salmon; sweetbreads and prawns in an orange butter sauce; grilled lamb cutlets vert-pré; ribbons of roast duck with a sweet-and-sour sauce; salmon en papillote with Noilly Prat and lettuce sauce; game in season; home-made ices; Irish cheeses. Richard Douglas restricts his wine list to about three dozen bins because he likes to know them himself and he also wants to store and serve them correctly. The present scarcity of mature claret in Ireland has forced him to start laying some down: he currently lists five, including Ch Branaire-Ducru 1976 (IR£17.95), and Ch Gruaud-Larose 1970 (IR£34.50). More modest reds include two Paternina wines: Banda Azul 1980, IR£7.85, and Gran Reserva 1973, IR£11.75. Robert Mondavi's Table Wine 1981, rarely seen on this side of the Atlantic, is IR£11.25, and Antinori's Tignanello 1980 is IR£15.25. Whites include Muscadet-sur-Lie, Domaine des Morines, 1982, Martin Jarry (IR£8.95); Mâcon-Lugny, Les Genièvres, 1982, Louis Latour (IR£12.35); and Oestricher Doosberg Spätlese 1976 (IR£10.95). House wines are from Maison Calvet, at IR£6.75 a bottle, IR£1.30 a glass, and there are three half-bottles on the list. Perhaps Mr Douglas should consider incorporating tasting notes in his list, since he is obviously well qualified to produce them.

DUNBLANE Perthshire

Cromlix House

Off B8033, 4 m N of Dunblane, ½ m N of Kinbuck

TEL (0786) 822125

OPEN 12.30 pm–1.45 pm, 7 pm–9.30 pm CLOSED Few days Chr/New Year
CREDIT CARDS All accepted WHEELCHAIR ACCESS Yes
VEGETARIAN DISHES With notice TDH £23

This handsome Scottish-Baronial pile of granite in its own 5,000-acre estate entertained Edward VII when feathered game was on his mind. It will satisfy you, too, if you wish to be treated right royally for an evening – or a day or two. The rooms are large, and appropriately furnished, but such is the warmth and friendliness of the staff that you feel comfortable rather than overwhelmed. The choiceless four-course meals combine country house style with more modern ideas, using the fine local produce: asparagus tips with strawberry vinaigrette; cream of venison soup; crayfish tails with curry cream; fresh noodles with smoked bacon and wild mushrooms; lamb with aubergine charlotte; breast of duck with fried pears and raspberry vinegar sauce; hot Amaretto soufflé with a fresh nectarine sauce; gratinée of oranges and pink grapefruit. The cheeses include the good Dumfriesshire ewe's milk Barac. The wine list is staggering, in both riches and price: perhaps you should prepare yourself with a suitably Edwardian bottle of Ritz Champagne Rosé, NV, at £17, while browsing through the 80 clarets and 50 Burgundies. The youngest clarets, and there are only three, are 1976 (Clos du Clocher, Pomerol, £12); the oldest is 1945 (Ch Léoville-Las-Cases, £98). In between, you can find many famous names: Ch Lafon-Rochet 1970 (£24); Ch Palmer 1962 (£50); Ch Lascombes 1961 (£39 a half-bottle); Ch Citran 1966 (£20). The red Burgundies are hardly less impressive, with many 1971s and 1976s, and even a couple of 1961s: Christopher's Gevrey-Chambertin at £12.75 a half-bottle (worth a gamble?). The 1971s include Chambolle-Musigny, Chanson (£19); Vosne-Romanée, Doudet-Naudin (£18.50); and Beaune-Marconnets, Averys (£22; £11 a half). Other bottles at less daunting prices include an ageing Moulin-à-Vent 1978, Louis Latour

(£12); Sancerre Rouge 1978, Vacheron (£13.50); Gewürztraminer, Cuvée St Hubert, 1981, Kuehn (£10); Côtes-du-Rhône, Goutte Vermeille, 1978, Salavert (£9); Wachenheimer Bischofsgarten Auslese 1976, Bürklin-Wolf (£15.50); Gran Viña Sol Reserva, Green Label, 1979, Torres (£11); Zinfandel 1978, Joseph Phelps (£12.50); and the English Müller-Thurgau 1982, Breaky Bottom (£9.25). The house wines include the sound Côtes-du-Rhône, Ch du Grand Moulas 1980 at £7 (£1.25 a glass).

EAST GRINSTEAD West Sussex

Gravetye Manor

Vowels Lane, Sharpthorne (A264/B2028) TEL (0342) 810567

OPEN 12.30 pm–2 pm, 7.30 pm–9 pm CREDIT CARDS Not accepted
WHEELCHAIR ACCESS Impossible VEGETARIAN DISHES No ALC FOR TWO £48

'The platonic ideal of an English country house', this Elizabethan manor in its William Robinson garden on Forestry Commission land has handsome wood panelling, log fires, spacious rooms, fine antiques and considerate service. Such luxury does not come cheap, and a few guests complain that prices do not include VAT (though they *do* include a 15 per cent service charge), that vegetables are charged extra when they are meagre enough to rate as no more than a garnish, and that breakfast is charged by individual items. Most, however, just lie back and enjoy being cosseted. Although the menu sounds rich and elaborate, helpings are not overfacing, and the exemplary quality of the raw materials might tempt you to take advantage of the offer on the menu that they are prepared to cook more plainly if you prefer. This is particularly true if you fancy one of the best wines and are faced, for example, with a choice of roulade of salmon ('salmon and spring cabbage layered with a salmon mousse, rolled and served with vermouth sauce') and breast of chicken with crabmeat, a sweetcorn pancake and shellfish sauce. Hazelnut and carrot cake is praised, and there are savouries as well as the best of English and French cheeses. Peter Herbert finds updating his wine list a never-ending task, 'like painting the Forth Bridge', and it repays careful study, since there are strengths in most sections, and, happily, enough half-bottles to make comparative tasting possible. Consider some of these wines, among many: Chablis, Les Clos 1978, Louis Michel at £16.40 (plus VAT); Puligny-Montrachet, Les Folatières 1979, Louis Latour (£20.20); Forster Kirchenstück Riesling Auslese 1976, Bürklin-Wolf (£21.70); Ch Cissac 1971 (£39 a magnum); Ch Rauzan-Gassies 1976 (£16.50); La Tâche, Domaine de la Romanée-Conti, 1971 (£75); Ch Rayas 1976 (£20.50). There are many more expensive wines listed, and also cheaper ones well worth drinking: two from the Cave Co-opérative at Buxy, for example, and any of the Alsace wines. Digestifs are in keeping with the high standards. Tastings and dinners are held during the winter.

EDDLESTON Peebles-shire

Cringletie House Hotel

2½ m N of Peebles, off A703 TEL (072 13) 233

OPEN 1 pm–1.45 pm, 7.30 pm–8.30 pm CLOSED Jan, Feb CREDIT CARDS Not accepted WHEELCHAIR ACCESS Impossible VEGETARIAN DISHES On request SMOKING Discouraged in dining-room
TDH SUN L £8.50 D £13 ALC WEEKDAY L FOR TWO £15

This Scottish-Baronial mansion, set in 28 acres of grounds, provides comfort and relaxation. The Maguires and their staff are friendly and efficient, and if you stay, you can enjoy huge breakfasts and home-baked teas as well as the light lunches and four-course dinners. Local produce is used whenever possible, and a typical meal might include leek and Gruyère savoury, spiced tomato soup, sole with white wine and mushroom sauce, and fresh lime mousse (there is a limited choice in each course except the soup). Medallion of beef with tomato and basil sauce, and loin of pork with prunes and fresh sage are other popular main courses. There are 100 wines, starting with an impressive page of clarets: Ch Gazin 1970 (£16); Ch Malartic-Lagravière 1975 (£13.50); Ch Pavie 1976 (£16.50); Ch Citran 1978 (£9.50). Rhônes offer better value than Burgundies: Domaine des Bosquets 1976 (£8.50). Things tail off rather after that: it would be helpful to have a few good Sauternes in half-bottle to enjoy with Mrs Maguire's excellent puddings, and the German section should be more carefully annotated. German and French house wine is £6 a litre, 80p a glass.

ELY Cambridgeshire

Old Fire Engine House (V)

25 St Mary's Street TEL (0353) 2582

OPEN 12.30 pm–2 pm, 7.30 pm–9 pm CLOSED Public holidays, 2 weeks from 24 Dec CREDIT CARDS Not accepted WHEELCHAIR ACCESS Impossible VEGETARIAN DISHES On request ALC FOR TWO L £16 D £19

East Anglia knows what it likes, and it likes this pretty brick house (which still functioned as a fire station at the turn of the century) for its unpretentious atmosphere, friendly service, and large helpings of good, plain English cooking at reasonable prices. There are occasional hiccoughs – muddled orders when they are particularly busy, a stuffy dining-room at the end of the evening, a bony rabbit casserole – but for the most part, people are delighted by such dishes as terrine of pork, smoked salmon pâté, lamb cutlets in pastry cases, local pike with cream and white wine, venison pie, and various fruit pies and meringues, dealt with a generous hand. The list of about 60 wines, with an impressive addition of bin-ends, encourages customers to try unfamiliar, moderately priced wines rather than the mediocre: Bulgarian Cabernet Sauvignon 1979 (£3.85); Chante-Cigale Blanc de

Blancs 1982 (£4); Chilean Cabernet Sauvignon 1979, Concha y Toro (£5.20). Tasting notes, generally helpful and always enthusiastic, guide you through: Sancerre Le Grand Chémarin 1982, Balland (£7.90); Clos du Marquis 1976 (the second wine of Ch Léoville-Las-Cases) at £11; Chablis, Montée de Tonnerre, 1981, Croix-Bequet (£7.90); Aloxe-Corton 1979, Jadot (£12.50); Ch Coutet 1973 (£6.80 a half-bottle). French house wine is £4.80 a litre, 80p a glass. They are particularly proud – and justifiably so – of their single-vineyard cognac, Fine Petite Champagne, Réserve du Templier, Lhéraud at £1.30 a glass.

EVERSHOT Dorset

Summer Lodge

Summer Lane TEL (093 583) 424

OPEN D only, 8 pm CLOSED L; 1 Dec to 1 Jan CREDIT CARDS Access/Euro
WHEELCHAIR ACCESS Impossible VEGETARIAN DISHES On request TDH £12

The Corbetts live in the Earl of Ilchester's former dower house and run it so much like a private house rather than a hotel that you might find it difficult to get your bill. The well-equipped bedrooms and well-cooked Cordon-Bleu-style dinners are popular, despite the lack of choice: local asparagus, smoked mackerel pâté, spinach roulade, onion and cheese quiche, roast leg of lamb with rosemary, gammon in cider with Cumberland sauce, beef Wellington béarnaise, steak and kidney pie, meringue Dacquoise, chocolate roulade, sherry trifle. Cheese is served before or after pudding, as you wish, and generally includes Blue Vinney and a local goat. French house wines range from £4.25 to £4.85 a bottle, and thereafter you have about 80 to choose from: George Goulet's Champagne, NV (£11.80); Sauvignon, Côtes de Duras, 1981 (£5.55); Ch Fombrauge 1978 (£9.45); Ch Beau-Site 1971 (£12.75); Echézeaux 1976, Alain Constant (£15.50); Pouilly Fumé 1982, Charles Deloire (£7.85); Forster Bischofsgarten Huxelrebe Auslese 1976, Forst (£6.35); Ch Liot 1976 (£7.35).

FADMOOR North Yorkshire

Plough Inn Ⓥ ☞

Off A170, 2½ m N of Kirkbymoorside TEL (0751) 31515

OPEN 12 noon–1.30 pm (bar Sat & Sun only), 7.30 pm–8.30 pm CLOSED Sun, Mon, Chr, 1 week May, Oct & Feb CREDIT CARDS Not accepted
WHEELCHAIR ACCESS Impossible VEGETARIAN DISHES By arrangement
TDH D £8–£10 BAR L About £3

The Browns' whitewashed inn on the edge of the moors is the village pub as well as a restaurant offering well-cooked food and modestly priced wines. You have your aperitif among the darts players and then go through to the oak-and-tapestry dining room for an Anglo-French meal priced according to the main course (with too many irritating supplementary charges). Dishes praised include mushrooms en cocotte, mousseline of smoked salmon with sorrel sauce, duckling with lemon compote, king prawns armoricaine, and the various home-made ice-creams and sorbets. Mr Brown discusses and serves his wines carefully. The list of over a hundred (from Yorkshire Fine Wines) is mainly French, eccentrically spelled and annotated, but worth deciphering for such bargains as Bulgarian Merlot 1979 for £4; Meursault 1979 (Louis Latour) for £12.80; Ch Fourcas-Hosten 1966 (CB) for £13.20. Note the many half-bottles and also the clutch of wines from South-West France, including Côtes du Lubéron, Madiran and Côtes de Buzet. House French and Italian are £4.20 and £4 respectively, 65p a glass.

FLITWICK Bedfordshire

Flitwick Manor

Church Road TEL (0525) 712242

OPEN 12 noon–2 pm, 7 pm–9.30 pm CLOSED Sun D CREDIT CARDS All accepted WHEELCHAIR ACCESS Yes VEGETARIAN DISHES Yes
ALC FOR TWO £28

Somerset Moore has moved from the nearby White Hart in Flitton to this handsome listed building which is to have six letting bedrooms before the end of the year. As before, his menu is mainly fishy, from salmon caviare with a glass of Highland malt (£3.75), home-cured dill salmon, and Helford oysters to tandoori fillet of turbot with pilaf, poppadum and pickles (£6.50), scallops fried with bacon and Noilly, and 'our superior plate of fresh shellfish' with half a lobster, crab and various smaller shellfish (£12.50). Meat-eaters can settle for smoked chicken terrine, cassoulet of duck, pork and white beans, calf's liver with calvados and cream; vegetarians have a special menu (£6.90) with tagliatelle al pesto as its main course. A gourmand (sic) menu lurches through Sevruga caviare, oysters, lobster with truffles and brandy, and wild strawberry ice-cream, with vodka, Champagne and Cognac at appropriate moments (£45). Alternatively, you may settle for a 'light meal' – one of the starters – with a glass of wine. All the 70 wines are French, half of them white: house Saumur 1982 from the cave co-opérative (£5.50); Muscadet-sur-Lie 1983, Chéreau (£8.40; £4.50 a half); Condrieu 1983, Georges Vernay (£18.50); Alsace Riesling Les Murailles 1981 (£10.50); Corton-Charlemagne 1977, Bonneau de Martray (£24). The reds include ten clarets (Ch Beauséjour 1976, £9.30; Ch Calon-Ségur 1961, £65); Tricastin, Domaine de Grangeneuve, 1982, Bour (£8.20); Bourgogne Irancy 1982, Melou (£9.90); Sancerre, Sentier de St-Romble, 1981, Jean Vatan (£11.80). As so often in new restaurants, the mark-ups are pretty fierce: the Tricastin is £3.15 a bottle on Yapp's list. Note also that if you pay by credit card, '12½ per cent will be added (for service) unless otherwise requested'.

FORT WILLIAM Inverness-shire

Inverlochy Castle

4 m N of Fort William, on A82 TEL (0397) 2177
OPEN 12.30 pm–1.45 pm, 8 pm CLOSED Mid-Nov to mid-Mar
CREDIT CARDS Access/Euro, Visa WHEELCHAIR ACCESS Impossible
VEGETARIAN DISHES Yes NO SMOKING IN DINING-ROOM TDH D £20

This noble Victorian pile in the lee of Ben Nevis pleased the (contemporary) monarch: she wrote in her diary, 'I never saw a lovelier or more romantic spot.' The Castle exterior has, in fact, faint overtones of the Tower of London but, inside, all is antique elegance and dazzlingly professional service. Some find the luxury oppressive, but the set menus, at least, show elegant simplicity: four choiceless and well-balanced courses are suggested, with a few alternatives written underneath for the picky. The cooking is a highly accomplished blend of *nouvelle* and classical *cuisine* with a Scottish accent where appropriate: quenelle of turbot Nantua, turban Neptune with chive sauce, consommé Mikado, poached sea-trout or wild salmon sauce mousseline, roast Aberdeen Angus beef, medallions of veal with sage sauce, stuffed saddle of lamb with port sauce, chocolate marquise with orange sabayon, rhubarb crumble. The wine list is part Bible, part historical document: so many fine old clarets and Burgundies, many far beyond the purse of the average drinker. However, they are there, and it is worth recording the fact: there are few places in Britain where one could count on appropriate surroundings, service and cooking for their appreciation. Enjoy, then, in theory if not in practice: Dom Pérignon 1970, 1973, 1976, each £45 (plus VAT, an iniquitous habit); Ch Ducru-Beaucaillou 1966 (£85); Ch Cantenac-Brown 1949 (£55); Ch Lafite 1961 (£100); Ch Léoville-Barton 1955 (£36); Le Montrachet 1971, Averys, French-bottled (£63); La Tâche, Domaine de la Romanée-Conti 1970 (£75); Beaune, Vignes Franches, 1961, Louis Latour (£36); Bonnes-Mares 1966, Pierre Ponnelle (£30). Turning now to the rest of us, consider Crémant de Bourgogne Blanc, NV at £9.80; Ch Macquin 1975 at £6.75 (the 1978 vintage is £7.80, a prohibitive £5.20 in half-bottle); the dry wine from Ch Doisy-Daëne 1981 (£7.30); Schloss Böckelheimer Königsfels Auslese 1976 (£12); Muscadet, Ch de la Galissonnière, 1982 (£6); Beaujolais, Moulin-à-Vent, 1982 (£10.50); Châteauneuf-du-Pape, Domaine de Mont Redon, 1980 (£10.50); Gewürztraminer, Vendange Tardive, 1976, Schmidt (£13.50); Ch Bastor-Lamontagne 1976 (£6 a half-bottle). (The list is generous with its half-bottles.) Port comes in halves: Averys 1960 (£12.40); Croft 1963 (£21). Taylor's Crusting (bottled 1973) is £1.30 a glass. The house wine is Averys French at £1.55 a glass. Mark-up here is very high.

Have we included your favourite spot for eating *and* drinking? If not, or if you disagree with our assessment, tell us about it either by letter or on the forms at the back of the *Guide*.

FRANT East Sussex

Bassetts

35 High Street TEL (089 275) 635

OPEN D only, 7 pm–8.45 pm CLOSED L; Sun, Mon, Tue, 3 weeks June
CREDIT CARDS Access/Euro, Amex, Visa WHEELCHAIR ACCESS Yes
VEGETARIAN DISHES With notice NO PIPES OR CIGARS IN RESTAURANT
TDH D £9.75 (two courses, Wed & Thur), £10.95 (three courses)

The Bassetts' comfortable and cosy restaurant is peaceful on the whole, though strains on the service are sometimes visible. The set menu sensibly allows the choice of two courses or three, with original dishes as well as traditional ones, many difficult to match to wine: aïoli; curried parsnip soup; pied de porc grillé, sauce vinaigrette; chicken with honey and oranges; pork fillet with plum and ginger sauce. There are over 80 bottles, mainly French, rather patchily annotated, with twenty or so halves. In the latter, Sauvignon du Haut Poitou is a bargain £2.95, and Ch Malescot-Margaux-St Exupéry 1977 (£5.95). In bottles, try perhaps Sauvignon de St-Bris 1981, Vannier (£6.85); Fleurie La Madonne 1982, Georges Duboeuf (£8.20); Ch Latour 1973 (£28.50). Duboeuf house wine is £3.95 a bottle, £1 a glass.

FRENCHBEER Devon

Teignworthy

3 m SW of Chagford TEL (064 73) 3355
(follow signs to Fernworthy & Kestor)

OPEN 12.30 pm–2 pm, 7.30 pm–9 pm CREDIT CARDS Not accepted
WHEELCHAIR ACCESS Yes VEGETARIAN DISHES Yes SMOKING Discouraged in dining-room TDH D £17.50 SNACK LUNCHES From £5

Lutyens' Castle Drogo nearby inspired the style of this handsome stone house on the moors, with superb views and its own pretty gardens. The Newells have created a relaxed atmosphere, with friendly, unobtrusive service, which has people coming back for more – and that includes the delicious breakfast kedgeree. Gillian Newell's set dinners offer a reasonable choice: lettuce, watercress and parsley soup; fresh langoustines baked with olive oil and basil butter; quails braised with coriander; noisettes of lamb with mushroom sauce; red mullet en papillote; honey and walnut flan; home-made ice-creams. The wine list is workmanlike rather than pretentious, about 90 wines, clearly annotated, and starting with eight house wines, all with tasting notes, all available by the glass: Champlos Rouge and Blanc at £5.20 a litre (£1 a glass); Georges Duboeuf's Cuvée de L'Amitié Rouge and Blanc (£4.50/£1.10); Crémant de Bourgogne Brut, from the Mâcon-Lugny co-opérative (£1.40 a glass). Thereafter, there is something for the high-flyer as well as the more canny: Ch Martouret 1982, Dominique Lurton (£5.50); Ch Camensac 1978 (£11.30); Ch La Lagune 1971

(£19.50); Chorey-lès-Beaune 1979, Tollot-Beaut (£11.60); Puligny Montrachet 1981, Henri Clerc (£13); Juliénas, Domaine de la Seigneurie, 1983, Duboeuf (£7.95); St Pourçain 1982, Cave des Producteurs (£5.30); Riesling 1982, Gisselbrecht (£5.95); Forster Pechstein 1979, Shultz & Wagner (£6.10); Venagazzù 1974, Conte Loredan (£8.50); Rothbury Estate's Individual Paddock Semillon 1976 (£7.90).

FRESSINGFIELD Suffolk

Fox & Goose

On B1116 TEL (037 986) 247

OPEN 12 noon–1.30 pm, 7 pm–9 pm CLOSED Tue, 21–28 Dec
CREDIT CARDS All accepted WHEELCHAIR ACCESS Impossible
VEGETARIAN DISHES With notice TDH From £11 ALC FOR TWO £35

An ancient half-timbered inn where the Clark family offer food for gargantuan appetites: since they encourage you to order ahead by phone, this can pose problems. However, they have recently introduced a short *carte* and a seasonal set meal as well, so that at least you can back down if overfaced early on. There has been praise for fish and, especially, game, whether pheasant, partridge, wild duck or venison, all treated simply. More elaborate dishes include sweetbreads in pastry, cailles en Madère, boeuf en croûte, veau portugaise, hot raspberry soufflé with raspberry sauce. The mammoth wine list has many venerable bottles at fairly stiff prices: arrive early enough to browse by the fire in the bar. The list begins in style with several single-vineyard Champagnes: Jean-Paul Arvois Brut 1975/76 (£18). There are such curiosities as Fressingfield Dry White 1981, from Wood Farm, at £7.06, and Red Velvet Sparkling Burgundy from Jaboulet-Vercherre, at £10.60, but the heart of the list is the fine claret collection: five pages, with nothing older than 1945 (Ch Margaux, CB, £250) and nothing younger than 1976 (Ch Les Carmes Haut-Brion, £25 a magnum). In between, you find ten 1961s (the *premiers crus* at £100 a half-bottle, Ch Lyonnat, £30), eight 1962s, ten 1966s (Ch Brane-Cantenac, £42), 18 1970s (Ch Giscours £34, Ch Haut-Brion, £90). Burgundies also reach for the heights, but come down to earth with, for example, Rully Blanc 1975, Jaboulet-Vercherre (£6.50), and Beaune 1973, Bouchard Père et Fils (£14). If you can afford them, there's Richebourg 1955, Domaine de la Romanée-Conti (£100), and Romanée-St-Vivant 1971, Arnoux (£54). Everything else seems an anticlimax, but there are French and Italian house wines (£5.40/£1.10). A trio of Moulin Touchais, the delicious Anjou dessert wine, includes the 1929 vintage (£40). Otherwise, finish with Ch Caillou 1967 (£12.50 a half-bottle) or port going back to Burmester 1948 (£30).

Estimated prices in the information panel *exclude* wine.

GITTISHAM Devon

Combe House Hotel

2½ m SW of Honiton TEL (0404) 2756

OPEN 12 noon–2 pm, 7.30 pm–9.30 pm CREDIT CARDS All accepted WHEELCHAIR ACCESS Yes VEGETARIAN DISHES With notice TDH D From £14 SUN L £8

An Elizabethan manor in 3,000 acres, where the Boswells provide rich French food at moderate prices, though the set dinner has many supplements. However, with no extras you could try avocado ceviche or toast aux crevettes Rothschild, brochettes de St Jacques or entrecôte béarnaise. Smoked salmon, Dover sole and roast duck would add £4.70 to the set price. Bar lunches are served during the week, a set roast lunch on Sunday. The fifty or so wines, many from Corney & Barrow, start with French house wine at £5.30 a bottle, £1.45 a glass, and include Ch St Gérome 1978 (£8.10); Ch Fombrauge 1976 (£14.50); red Burgundies mostly from lesser years, but a good youthful Chablis in Vaillons 1982, Michel Robin (£12.60); Gewürztraminer 1981, Bernard Heydt (£9.10) and Cabernet Sauvignon 1976, Simi (in Napa Valley) at £12.50. Corney & Barrow's sherry, Champagne and Cognac could nicely round out an evening.

GLASGOW Strathclyde

Ubiquitous Chip

Ashton Lane TEL 041-334 5007

OPEN 12 noon–2.30 pm, 5.30 pm–11 pm CLOSED Sun, 25 to 31 Dec, 1 & 2 Jan CREDIT CARDS All accepted WHEELCHAIR ACCESS Yes VEGETARIAN DISHES Yes ALC FOR TWO L £20 D £30

Consistently good food and attentive service have been far from ubiquitous at the Chip during the past year, but the staff suffered various bouts of illness which might explain some of the problems. Let's hope that all is now well with them, and that we can again expect to enjoy relaxed and delicious meals in these airy, outdoorsy converted stables in a winding mews. The menu is 'Scots/international' with the emphasis on fish and game: ham and lentil soup, haggis and neeps, pike in white wine with orange mayonnaise, wholewheat cheese and onion flan, Guinness carbonnade, roast mallard with port and orange, roast quail with liver canapés, noisettes of lamb with prawns and béarnaise, chocolate and brandy pot, apple and Calvados crumble with egg custard. Avoid the 'blue' red cabbage. Service is amiable, though often mistimed. The wine list is one of the best and cheapest in Scotland, and the glasses are large, thin, and the correct shape. French house wines are £3.95 a bottle, 80p a glass. There are over 200 other wines listed, with a couple of pages of clarets worth the detour from almost anywhere: ten (too young) 1978s in half-bottle (Ch Malescot-

St-Exupéry, £5.65); in bottle there are a dozen 1976s, from Ch Livran (£6.85), via Ch Lafon-Rochet (£9.85), to Les Forts de Latour (£16.25); in 1975 there's Ch Carbonnieux (£9.50); in 1971, Ch Mouton Rothschild (£36); and in 1970, Ch Gloria (£18.85). Earlier vintages are sparser but can still raise Ch Montrose 1966, CB (£26) and Ch Baret 1953, CB (£24.65). Red Burgundies include Aloxe-Corton 1978, Louis Latour (£14.15), and Beaune Marconnets 1976, Remoissenet (£17.25). There are five Loron Beaujolais (Moulin-à-Vent, Yvonne Couibes, 1978, £6.25); and appealing Rhônes, many of them from Paul Jaboulet: Châteauneuf-du-Pape, Les Cèdres, 1966 (£15.95). The California section includes Firestone Cabernet Sauvignon 1979 (£7.80), and Zaca Mesa Chardonnay 1979 (£8.35). Other appealing whites include Ch Nairac 1976 (Barsac) at a bargain £10.35; Mâcon-Lugny 1982, Louis Latour (£2.95 a half-bottle); Savennières, Coulée de Serrant, 1979, Mme Joly (£10.85); Châteauneuf-du-Pape, Cuvée des Félibres, 1982, Domaine de Mont Redon (£6.65); Riesling, Clos Ste-Hune, 1979, Trimbach (£9.35); a Champagne method Austrian sparkler, Hochriegl Alte Reserve, NV, Johann Kattus (£6.45); Grüner Veltliner 1980, Klosterdawn (£4.50); Schloss Vollrads Weissgold Auslese 1976, Graf Matuschka-Greiffenclau (£16.80); Brauneberger Juffer Sonnenuhr Beerenauslese 1976, Von Schorlemer (£25.85). If you are still thirsty, there's a wealth of single malts to quench you, as well as ports, armagnacs and Polish fruit – and herb – flavoured vodka. The adjacent pub does a nice line in venison sausage, game pâté, and various other cold dishes, with eight wines by the glass, from 80p, and Belhaven ales. Occasional tutored wine dinners are held during the year.

GRASMERE Cumbria

Michaels Nook

East of A591, behind the Swan — TEL (096 65) 496

OPEN 12.30 pm for 1 pm, 7.30 pm for 8 pm (7 pm & 9 pm Sat in season) CREDIT CARD Amex WHEELCHAIR ACCESS Yes VEGETARIAN DISHES By arrangement TDH L £14.50 D £19

Reg Gifford's fine Victorian stone house overlooking Grasmere valley is all country-house elegance and atmosphere, an impression enhanced by his fine antiques, aristocratic Great Dane and chatty parrot. You will find more residents than 'casuals' for meals, all looked after firmly by Mr Gifford and his team. The set meals are 'modern French/English with light sauces': smoked trout soufflé, home-cured salmon, sweetbreads in white wine and cream, local loin of lamb en croûte in a distinguished Madeira sauce, with crisp vegetables, and various cream and fruit desserts to finish. There are about 100 wines, mainly from Youdell of Kendal, with prices which seem gentle: they are unchanged since last year. Thus you can feel ritzy with the Ritz Champagne, NV, at £15, and make a smaller splash with Muscadet, Marquis de Goulaine 1982 (£5.80); Gewürztraminer 1979, Hugel (£7.80); Kreuznacher Brückes Riesling Auslese 1976 (no shipper listed) at £8.70, or Caillou

Blanc du Ch Talbot 1978 at £6.50. Red Burgundies are dominated by Louis Latour: Chénas 1981 is £8.25 (compare it, perhaps, with a half-bottle of the 1978, £4.40); Santenay 1976 (£11.90); Chambertin, Cuvée Héritiers Latour, 1971 (£33). Sixteen clarets provide a wide range of style and quality: Haut-Médoc 1979, Lalande (£5.80); Ch Plagnac 1975 (£8.10); Ch La Mission-Haut-Brion 1970 (£37); and Ch Latour 1966 (£55). Two tawny ports are available by the glass, and Gonzalez Byass 1960 Vintage is £14 a bottle.

White Moss House

Rydal Water, off A591 TEL (096 65) 295

OPEN 7.30 pm for 8 pm CLOSED L, early Nov to mid-Mar CREDIT CARDS Not accepted WHEELCHAIR ACCESS Yes VEGETARIAN DISHES With notice NO SMOKING IN DINING-ROOM TDH D £13.50

This small country house is cosy and comfortable, with every sign of care in furnishing, cooking and wine-buying. The set dinners, with a choice only at the pudding stage, are English-based, with local Crummock Water char appearing in May, as well as duck and Marsala soup, loin of veal with wild rice and lovage stuffing, fillet of beef with green peppercorn béarnaise sauce, Sussex Pond pudding, brown bread ice-cream, and a wide range of English – and Scottish – cheeses, including Barac, Cotherstone, and Somerset Brie. Mr Butterworth and his daughter serve with efficiency and charm. Many of the mostly French wines on the not terribly exciting main list come from Youdell of Kendal *(see under* MERCHANTS*)*; his Bordeaux, Burgundy and Rhine house wines are £6.50 a litre, 75p–80p a glass. The main list is dominated by Latour Burgundies, of which the recent vintages to be found here have been rather disappointing. The majority of the clarets are still rather tough (1978s and 1975s). However, amongst the others, Marqués de Cáceres Reserva 1973 is good value at £7.95. But there's greater pleasure to be found on the special list: a fair selection of clarets back to 1948, Burgundies back (possibly too far) to 1964. Ch L'Angélus 1961 is £11.25 a half; Pernand Vergelesses 1973, Chanson is £5.50 a half; amongst the Rhônes, there's the excellent Domaine Chante Cigale 1979 for just £8.75 and amongst the many reliably good Jaboulet wines, Châteauneuf-du-Pape, Les Cèdres 1969 (£7.30 a half); in the Loire Gitton's excellent Sancerre Les Belles Dames 1982 (£8.50) and Vouvray Clos du Bourg 1970, Gaston Huet (demi-sec) (£9.85). Muscat de Beaumes de Venise is sensibly offered on the menu at 95p a glass.

> The range of wines available and the prices asked are likely to change in the course of the year. The information given is correct in summer 1984, and we hope it serves as an indication of each restaurant's approach to wine. If you want to drink a particular bottle, it is best to ring beforehand, not only to ensure that it is served correctly, but also to check that it is still in stock.

GREAT DUNMOW Essex

The Starr

Market Place TEL (0371) 4321

OPEN 12 noon–1.30 pm (Sun only), 7 pm–9.30 pm CLOSED L (exc Sun), Sun D, Mon, Dec 24–Jan 7, 3 weeks Aug CREDIT CARDS All accepted WHEELCHAIR ACCESS Yes VEGETARIAN DISHES Yes TDH SUN L £12.50 ALC 3 COURSES FOR TWO £32

An open fire, pale green linen, fresh flowers and an impressive display of fish straight from Billingsgate make this an appetising restaurant. The blackboard menu changes daily, but might include fish soup, venison terrine, sea bass steamed with elderflowers, noisettes of veal with cream and herbs, duck or game in various ways, and good home-made ices and chocolate truffles. Service is almost too attentive with frequent enquiries to check that you are satisfied. There are about 150 wines on an informative list, which includes an assessment of vintages in Bordeaux and Burgundy, an explanation of the German labelling system, and short notes on various shippers. Five wines are offered as 'house' wines, including Côtes du Rhône, Caves des Vignerons de Vacqueyras, NV (£6.35, £1.30 a glass). Clarets include Ch Lynch-Bages 1976 (£21.40), and the 1961 vintage at £65. Most of the crus Beaujolais are represented, in either 1981 or 1982 (Juliénas 1981, Ernest Aujas, £10.95); red Burgundies include Volnay Chevret 1976, Boillot (£18), and Chablis Valmur 1978, Fèvre (£16). Hugel's Gewürztraminer Réserve Personnelle 1976 is a reasonable £16. Most of the wines are French, but Viña Arana Rioja 1973 is £7.20. There are several useful halves, including Ch Climens 1976 (£12). Informal tastings are held for regular customers.

GRIMSTON Norfolk

Congham Hall

Off A148, follow signs to Grimston TEL (0485) 600250

OPEN 12.30 pm–2 pm, 7.30 pm–9 pm CLOSED Sat L, Sun D, Chr and New Year CREDIT CARDS All accepted WHEELCHAIR ACCESS Yes VEGETARIAN DISHES With notice TDH L £9.50 D From £18

This Georgian manor house in 44 acres of grounds, complete with fine flower and vegetables gardens – and a swimming-pool – is very white outside and has an exceptionally pink dining-room: everyone comments on it before describing their meal. The dinner menu, priced by choice of main course, changes seasonally and runs to eight small courses. They involve what sound like bizarre combinations, many of them apparently successful: paw-paw and brown shrimp cocktail; lamb fillet with raisins and cassis in an almond pancake and puff pastry served with a mustard sauce; beef fillet with scampi and fennel in a lobster sauce. Venison liver with mustard and juniper sauce, or saffron scallops, sound a safer bet for the conventional. Sweets tend to be fruit or ice-cream-based. The 60-item wine-list is much more conventional, mainly from Barwell & Jones, and offering, for example: Muscadet, Domaine des Dorices, 1982, Boullault (£6.50); Dexheimer Doktor Kabinett Trocken 1982, Sittmann (£5.15); Gewürztraminer 1981, Sparr (£7.35); Ch Ormes-de-Pez 1978 (£14.35); Côte-Rôtie Brune et Blonde 1979, Jaboulet-Vercherre (£14.15). A short connoisseurs' list includes two bargain dessert wines: Anjou Moulin Touchais 1959 (£10.85), and Ch Rayne-Vigneau 1976 (£12.50). There are plenty of halves, and French house wine at £5 (85p a glass).

GUIST Norfolk

Tollbridge

On B110, 10 m SW of Holt TEL (036 284) 359

OPEN 12 noon–1.45 pm, 7 pm–9.30 pm CLOSED Sun, Mon, Jan
CREDIT CARD Visa WHEELCHAIR ACCESS Yes VEGETARIAN DISHES By arrangement TDH L £6.50 ALC FOR TWO £22

The Starks' pretty restaurant on the Wensum was a toll-house till 1938, and their dining-room enjoys placid views of river and meadow, 'very Constable-like'. The Wensum provides pike, eel and crayfish to enrich the menu, which also sports local lobster, either as a first course gâteau à la nage or whole with garlic butter or salad. Non-fishy treats include smoked pork fillet, spinach soup with toasted almonds, steak of duck with fresh figs, fillet of lamb with lime and chive sauce, charcoal-grilled entrecôte béarnaise, home-made Champagne sorbet and gratin of kiwi-fruit. There are about 60 wines, starting with Hicks & Don's French at £4.60 a bottle, 80p a glass. After that, Mr Stark helpfully lists first white wines and then red, rather than grouping geographical areas; his tasting notes are useful, the range is good, and his prices are reasonable: Sauvignon de St-Bris 1983 (£7); Muscadet, Clos des Barillères, 1982, Bouchereau Frères (£6); Falkensteiner Hofberg Auslese 1976, Friedrich-Wilhelm Gymnasium (£9.75); Sparkling Saumur, Henri Chouteau (£7.50); Brouilly, Ch des Tours, 1982, CB (£8); Cabernet Sauvignon 1978, Louis Martini (£8.50); Viña Alberdi 1980 (£5.75); Ch Les Trois Croix 1978, Guillou Keredan (£9); Vacqueyras, Domaine des Lambertins, 1978 (£6.70); Ch Rieussec 1976 (£7.50 a half-bottle). Two dessert wines and two ports are offered by the glass.

Special awards

(V) is for bargain prices

is for a very good range of wines

is for exceptional service.

GULLANE East Lothian

Greywalls

Off A198, at west end of village TEL (0620) 842144

OPEN 12.30 pm–2.30 pm, 7.30 pm–9.30 pm CLOSED Nov to Feb
CREDIT CARDS All accepted WHEELCHAIR ACCESS Yes
VEGETARIAN DISHES On request TDH D £17.50 ALC FOR TWO £42

This small hotel is a superb Lutyens house in local Rattlebags stone overlooking Muirfield golf-course and the Firth of Forth. The cleverly decorated interior feels cosily small, but it can be cool in early spring, so take your plaids. Service is notably efficient and pleasant. The menu is mainly *nouvelle cuisine* with the usual flour-free sauces, sweet-savoury combinations and kiwi-fruit or tomato-rose garnish. People have praised the fish, the duck and the vegetables, but the test meal, sadly, produced some dull and carelessly seasoned dishes, with particularly poor vegetables. Perhaps best to stick to the good, plain salmon, steak or lamb, and enjoy the splendid wines the more. The long and distinguished list is French-oriented, with 90 clarets classified by commune as its opening salvo: a run of seven Ch Cissac (1971 to 1979), and something for everyone between Ch Peyrouze 1979 (£5.50), and Ch Léoville-Poyferré 1929 (£120). The white Bordeaux section less helpfully lumps Graves and Sauternes together. Other treasures include Ch Rayas 1957, the fine Châteauneuf-du-Pape from Reynaud (£37); Heitz Cabernet Sauvignon, Martha's Vineyard 1977 (£35.95 – you can't find that in *California* any more); and five Bollingers, including Vieilles Vignes Françaises 1975 (£48.30) made from ungrafted French vines. The house wines are Justerini & Brooks' Bordeaux and white Burgundy at £7.50, and a good bet to match the complex *nouvelle* tastes is Muscat de Riquewihr Réserve 1981, Dopff au Moulin (£9.45). Wine weekends are held several times a year.

La Potinière Ⓥ ☞

TEL (0620) 843214

OPEN 1 pm, 8 pm (Sat only) CLOSED Dinner (exc Sat), Wed, Sat L, 1 week June, Oct CREDIT CARDS Not accepted WHEELCHAIR ACCESS Yes
VEGETARIAN DISHES No NO SMOKING TDH L £9.50 D £13.50

A paragon among restaurants, this pretty little place in the village main street. It is, above all, honest and unpretentious in every respect, and David and Hilary Brown are realistic about what they can do well. Note that they serve only one dinner and five lunches each week, starting from scratch each day to compose and shop for the choiceless menu which Hilary cooks and David serves. Most meals start with soup, intriguingly spiced cauliflower or tomato, perhaps, and then comes a delicate mousseline of fish or white meat, or a tiny soufflé, cheese or courgette, or whatever seems appropriate that day. Main-course favourites include tarragon chicken and steak in a cream sauce. Gratin dauphinoise potatoes aren't always appropriate to a creamy main course, but the imaginative and varied salads are popular. At lunch, you choose either a perfectly ripe Brie or a pudding; at dinner, you are offered both. It seems ironic that this is one of the few restaurants in the *Guide* which reporters praise for its wine service when it is David Brown who squeezes in the wine waiting between serving the food, answering the 'phone, welcoming people and seeing them out. The list is obviously composed by a lover of wine rather than a lover of profit. It is almost invidious to pick out specific examples. However, a few highlights from the thirty pages includes four vintages of Perrier-Jouët Belle Epoque Champagne (1976, £21; 1966, £30); 11 Alsace Rieslings (Réserve Personnelle, 1976, Hugel, £10.50); 21 different Chablis, reading like a roll of honour (Fourchaume 1981, Pic, £9.25). White Burgundy yields 20 from Louis Latour as an introduction to the others, divided by commune, with, for example, seven Aloxe-Cortons (Corton-Charlemagne, 1978, Tollot-Beaut, £21); 11 Meursaults (Clos Richemont 1979, Darnat, £11.50); 11 Chassagne-Montrachets (Le Montrachet 1973, Lafon, £27). Reds are equally thorough and distinguished. White Rhônes include seven Hermitages (Chave 1981, £10.75) and five Châteauneuf-du-Papes (Domaine de Mont Redon 1978, £9.50). The forty red Rhônes include six Hermitage la Chapelle, Jaboulet, from 1959 to 1972, and five Domaine de Mont Redon, from 1964 to 1972. There are seven cru Beaujolais, seven pages of mouth-watering red burgundies offering a chance to taste Chambertin, Clos de Bèze, Clair-Däu (£24); Chambolle-Musigny 1969, Faiveley (£18.75); Corton, Les Maréchaudes 1966, Doudet-Naudin (£17.50); and Volnay, Champans 1966, Marquis d'Angerville (£25). Red Bordeaux are listed by commune, with most of the grands crus making one or more appearances, from 1977 back to 1961. Where else, if you had the cash, could you compare the following 1961s: Ch Montrose, Ch Lynch-Bages, Ch Grand-Puy-Lacoste, Ch Gruaud-Larose, Ch Léoville-Barton, Ch Lascombes, Ch Brane-Cantenac, Ch Haut-Brion, Ch Gazin (from £25 to £70, with most under £30). There are, of course, other lesser wines at more modest prices . . . The 13 dessert wines, six in half-bottle, include Ch Rayne-Vigneau 1975 at £5.50 the half. This is above all a restaurant where you can ask for advice and know that you will get the most appropriate recommendation. Drink, and enjoy.

HADLEIGH Suffolk

Tavitons

103 High Street TEL (0473) 822820

OPEN 12 noon–2 pm, 7.30 pm–9.30 pm CLOSED Mon, Sat L, Sun D, Dec 25–28, Oct 20–31 CREDIT CARDS Access/Euro, Amex, Visa
WHEELCHAIR ACCESS Impossible VEGETARIAN DISHES By arrangement
TDH L £8.75 D £11

The Wilsons are settling nicely into this beamed cottage in the High Street, and are continuing their predecessors' pattern of serving a frequently changed five-course dinner, with limited choice and at moderate cost. You might encounter to start with mussels in garlic butter with mushrooms and ham, or crab mousse, followed by soup ('lovely cream of fennel'), and then chicken supreme in lemon sauce, or lamb cutlet in puff pastry, or baked salmon steak in cream and herbs. Salad and cheese are served together, and the puddings are appealing enough to keep space for: plum compote with almond cake, rhubarb cream, chocolate velour. The eighty clearly tabulated wines, mostly from Lay & Wheeler, start with house Burgundy at £5.25 (90p a glass) and go on to include Pouilly-Fuissé 1982, Loron (£8); Crozes-Hermitage Mule Blanche 1981, Jaboulet (£8.60); Muscat 1981, Hugel (£8.55); Cuvaison Chardonnay 1979 from Napa Valley (£11.25); Sancerre Rosé 1982, Jean Vatan (£8.85); Ch Franc Borie 1979 (£8.60), perhaps the easiest to drink of the rather young clarets; St Joseph 1979, Ogier (£9.90); Cabernet Sauvignon 1976, Cuvaison (again), at £10.45, a vintage you probably could no longer find in California; Ch Terfort 1976 at £6 a half-bottle for those puddings. An occasional wine tasting and buffet is laid on in co-operation with Hadleigh Wine Cellars.

HAMBLETON Leicestershire

Hambleton Hall

3 m SE of Oakham, off A606 TEL (0572) 56991
OPEN 12.30 pm–2 pm, 7.30 pm–9.30 pm CREDIT CARDS All accepted
WHEELCHAIR ACCESS Two steps VEGETARIAN DISHES Yes TDH L £18 D £25

A stylish but welcoming Victorian mansion on the shores of Rutland Water, Tim and Stefa Hart's hotel reflects their own enthusiasm for quality in both food and wine. Ingredients are first-class and always fresh – the menus are done from scratch each day – and only very occasionally is too heavy a hand noted in the cooking. The set meals (four courses at lunch, five at dinner) offer a sensible choice, and you might enjoy some of the following: warm salad of asparagus, puff pastry pillow of scallops, terrine of veal and sweetbreads with Cumberland sauce, calf's liver with blood oranges, whole grey mullet baked with fresh dill, steamed chicken breast with chive sauce, well-kept cheeses, iced rhubarb soufflé with raspberry sauce, and 'two hearts of cream'. Service tends to the formal. Tim Hart's wine philosophy is to offer good wines which are delicious *now*. Thus he held back his 1978 white Burgundies until last year, since he felt they showed less well than his 1979s, and is introducing them only gradually: Bâtard Montrachet, Leflaive, is £50 a magnum, Chablis Les Grenouilles, Louis Michel, is £21. The well-organised list is strongest on French wines, and begins with a useful dozen chosen for those who don't want to thumb through the full 21 pages. These include Ch Tauzinat l'Hermitage 1975 (a St-Emilion), at £8, and Pouilly-Vinzelles 1979, Georges Duboeuf, at £9. A leisurely read might lead you to Joseph Perrier Champagne 1976 (£10.50 a half-bottle); Ch La Garde 1970 (£12); Ch Cheval-Blanc, also 1970 (£70); Ch La Clotte 1978 (£28 a magnum);

Chambolle-Musigny 1971, Chanson Père et Fils (£23); Ch Rayas 1957 (white), Reynaud (£25); Graacher Domprobst Auslese 1976, Friedrich-Wilhelm Gymnasium (£14.50); Riesling Clos Ste Hune 1971, Trimbach (£28); Cabernet Sauvignon 1977, Robert Mondavi (£14). Ch d'Arche 1970, an attractive Sauternes (£9.50 a half-bottle). French house wines are £7.50/£1.50, and house Champagne is £15.50/£3.50. Three serious wine dinners are held in the winter months.

HARLECH Gwynedd

The Cemlyn

High Street TEL (0766) 780425

OPEN 7 pm–10 pm (lunch by arrangement only) CLOSED Oct to Feb (except Sat D, Oct 1 to Jan 1) CREDIT CARDS Amex, Diners WHEELCHAIR ACCESS Yes VEGETARIAN DISHES With notice CIGARS AND PIPES DISCOURAGED ALC FOR TWO £22

Ken Goody's restaurant, with views of Harlech Castle and the sea, is a 'treasure-trove of pottery and paintings' inside. The atmosphere is friendly and informal, the cooking interesting but erratic, using good local materials cooked with a French accent: scallops in cream and gin, lasagne with home-made pasta, turnip and dill soup, chicken with tarragon cream sauce, honey-basted Welsh lamb with cider and mint sauce, grilled brill béarnaise, strawberry Pavlova, chocolate marquise. There are over 100 wines, with French house wine at £5 a bottle. Prices are reasonable, minor areas of France are covered as well as major, and there are some scattered bottles from most wine-producing countries: Chilean Cabernet Sauvignon, Viña Linderos, 1979 (£7.25) to compare with the Bulgarian 1979 version at £6 and the Lebanese Ch Musar 1977 at £7.75. From France, try Pouilly Fumé, Ch de Tracy 1982 (£8); Corsican Domaine de Torraccia 1978, Imbart (£6); Ch Gloria 1971 (£11.50); Alsace Riesling Réserve 1979, Louis Sipp (£6.75); Gigondas 1977, Malbec (£7.75). On Saturdays during the winter, food and wine evenings are held, devoted to a single country.

HARRIS Western Isles

Scarista House

On A859, 15 m SW of Tarbert TEL (085 985) 238

OPEN D only, 8 pm CLOSED L, Sun, Nov to Mar CREDIT CARDS Not accepted WHEELCHAIR ACCESS Impossible VEGETARIAN DISHES By prior arrangement NO SMOKING IN DINING-ROOM TDH £12.50

Everyone's idea of an enchanted island hotel, this former manse overlooking miles of Atlantic beach is a handsome setting for the quietly sophisticated endeavours of Alison and Andrew Johnson. Bedrooms, whether in the main house or the extension, are well furnished and comfortable, and the dining-room gleams with candlelight, polished wood and silver. The choiceless set dinner menus are carefully balanced and make use of the local fish, shellfish, mutton and game. A spring menu yielded cream of cucumber soup; aubergine charlotte; scallops in oatmeal with gratin dauphinoise, stir-fried carrots and courgettes; strawberries and cream with brandy-snaps; cheeses; dessert. Breakfasts offer a further wonderful display of local produce, including black, white and fruit puddings. The hotel was granted its licence only during 1983 and has already produced a praiseworthy list of about sixty wines with brisk tasting notes. Prices are ungrasping: Alsace Riesling 1980, Schleret (£6.80); Marqués de Murrieta 1979 white, (£7); Chenin Blanc, Cooks Te Kauwhata 1981 (from New Zealand £6.50); Ch Cissac 1979 (£7.10); Aloxe-Corton 1978, Tollot-Beaut (£19.50); Rioja Viña Arana (no vintage given, £5.70). Older wines are not ignored: Ch Boyd-Cantenac 1970 (£22); Chambolle-Musigny 1971, Chanson Père et Fils (£16.50). Of the nine dessert wines, six come in half-bottle, one also by the glass, and as well as the predictable, but delicious, sweet Bordeaux (Ch Coutet 1973, £5.80 a half), there are three Loires (Anjou Rablay 1928, Caves de la Maison Prunier, £12 a half). Leave head-space for a fine sherry – San Patricio, or Palo Cortado or Dry Oloroso from Barbadillo (85p a glass) – and a digestif, whether malt whisky, port or Madeira.

HARROGATE North Yorkshire

Russell Hotel, Hodgson's Restaurant

29/35 Valley Drive TEL (0423) 509866

OPEN D only, 7.30 pm–10.30 pm CLOSED L, Sun, Mon CREDIT CARDS All accepted WHEELCHAIR ACCESS Yes VEGETARIAN DISHES On request TDH From £12.75

The Hodgson family successfully aim their Victorian terrace hotel and elaborately panelled and gilded dining-room at Harrogate's many visiting businessmen as well as locals. The formal tone is partially softened by the friendly service. The frequently changed menu, which 'interprets *nouvelle cuisine* for the English palate' (they say), may yield terrine of venison and veal, smoked halibut with salad in hazelnut oil, pork fillet in a Calvados cream sauce, stuffed roast guinea-fowl, roast loin of lamb with rosemary and redcurrant stuffing, caramelised pear pastries, and lemon and lime mousse. The lengthy wine list, hand-written on parchment, starts with a dozen Champagnes (Louis Krémer Brut, NV, £13), and the cheaper options of Henkel Trocken, NV (£8.75), and Champagne method Touraine, Domaine des Echardières, NV (£8.95). Clarets and red Burgundies each stretch to a page, the former including Ch Troplong-Mondot 1979 (£11.50), and Ch Talbot 1947 (£57); the latter, Vougeot, Clos de la Perrière, 1976, Bertagna (£16.75). (The many alternative vintages on the list are particularly irritating in the red Burgundy section.) Turning to whites, one could do well in Alsace (Gewürztraminer 1982, Gisselbrecht, £8.30), the Loire (Sancerre, Clos du Chêne Marchand, 1982, £9.75), Germany

(Wachenheimer Gerümpel Auslese 1976, Bürklin-Wolf, £10.95), Austria (St Margarethener Beerenauslese 1981, £8.95) or California (Riesling 1980, Stag's Leap, £9.50). Dessert wines include a half-bottle of Ch St-Amand 1979 at £7.50, Tokay Aszu, 5 puttonos at £8.20 (half-litre bottle), and Christian Brothers' Ch La Salle, NV (£6.50): on a list of this length, it would be helpful to find them grouped together. French house wines are £5.90 a litre, 85p a glass. They hope to run 'fine wine breaks' for residents during the winter.

HARWICH Essex

The Pier at Harwich

The Quay TEL (0255) 503363

OPEN 12.30 pm–2 pm, 6.30 pm–10 pm CLOSED Dec 25 & 26 CREDIT CARDS All accepted WHEELCHAIR ACCESS Yes VEGETARIAN DISHES Yes
TDH L (2 courses) £5.75, (3 courses) £6.75 SUN L £8.25 ALC FOR TWO £18–£26

You have glimpses of the harbour in this pleasantly informal fish restaurant (related to *Le Talbooth* in *Dedham*). Service is courteous and friendly, the fish is fresh and carefully cooked, and even the brown bread and salads win praise. Three steaks for carnivores, otherwise a diet of, for example, gravlax, prawn Alabama, local lobster and crab, fish pie (£6.25), skewered salmon hollandaise, and fairly routine desserts. Weekday buffet lunch, set lunch on Sunday. The eighty wines on the Lay & Wheeler list are, naturally, more white than red, and most are French, with a considerate number in half-bottle. The cheapest house wines are Georges Duboeuf red and white at £5.55 (£1 a glass), and thereafter you could choose from Hugel Pinot Blanc 1982 (£8.80); Gamay and Sauvignon du Haut Poitou, both 1982, at £7.15 and £7.50 respectively; Fumé Blanc 1981, Robert Mondavi (£14.85); or Corton-Charlemagne 1979, Louis Jadot (£23.30). Avoid the tables nearest the piano if you want to hear your table-mates' conversation.

HELFORD Cornwall

Riverside Ⓥ ☞

Off B3293 TEL (032 623) 443

OPEN 7.30 pm–9.30 pm CLOSED End-Oct to mid-Mar CREDIT CARDS Not accepted WHEELCHAIR ACCESS Possible, not easy VEGETARIAN DISHES Yes
TDH D £19.50

George Perry-Smith and Heather Crosbie succeed in their stated aim: to provide in their simple white house by the pretty Helford creek 'an unobtrusive background of comfort, very good food and an interesting wine list, with enough personal attention to make you feel at home but unfussed'. Perry-Smith, who acknowledged his debt to Elizabeth David when he opened the Hole in the Wall in Bath over thirty years ago, is in turn recognised as the inspiration of many of the best chefs in the country. The style at the Riverside is still recognisably Elizabeth David, 'natural but imaginative', and the daily hand-written menu might beguile you with, for example, fennel and cucumber soup, smoked salmon tart, or terrine of salmon, lobster and mushrooms, followed by bourride of monkfish with aîoli and rouille, poulet au riz basquaise, or the famous salmon in pastry with currants and ginger. Cheeses include the fine Chewton Mendip Cheddar, and sweets 'the definitive St Emilion au chocolat', iced lemon soufflé, and a wicked walnut treacle tart. Service 'couldn't be nicer', and you get advice when it's needed. There are over 200 bins on the reasonably priced wine list, many of them French, but with something of interest in most sections: Pilton Manor 1982 (£8.50); Viña Ardanza 1976 (six years in cask, £7); Venegazzù 1979, Conte Loredan (£8.50 – this tasty Cabernet Sauvignon wine has a natural tendency to re-ferment slightly, so don't blame it on the storage); Ménétou Salon 1982, Jean Teiller, £8.50: Wachenheimer Mandelgarten Scheurebe Auslese 1976, Bürklin-Wolf (£15); Châteauneuf-du-Pape Les Cèdres 1969, Paul Jaboulet (£9 a half-bottle); Pernand-Vergelesses 1970 Baron Thénard (£20); Ch de la Rivière 1975, Fronsac (£11.50); Ch Climens 1971 (£18). There are plenty of half-bottles and magnums, and house wines by glass (£1.20) and bottle (£7).

HESWALL Merseyside

Les Bougies ⓥ

106 Telegraph Road TEL 051-342 6673

OPEN D only, 7.15 pm–9.45 pm CLOSED L, Sun, Mon, 'most of Aug', 1st week Jan CREDIT CARDS Access/Euro, Amex, Visa WHEELCHAIR ACCESS Yes VEGETARIAN DISHES On request when booking ALC FOR TWO £24

Judith and Alvar Jones run a convincing French Provincal restaurant in a row of Victorian sandstone cottages. It is unassuming, 'but somehow stylish', and Judith's cooking of the seasonally changed menus is very competent: boudin noir à la normande, terrine de canard aux raisins, crème de choufleur, darne de saumon sauce mousseline, daube avignonnaise, estouffade de pigeon au céléri et genièvre, chevreuil au vin rouge, sorbet au citron, tarte aux cerises noires. The wine list comes in three separate folders: red, white, and half-bottles (rosé sneaks in on the red section). There are about 100 wines from various sources, not greedily priced, starting with house French, Cuvée J-C Boisset (£4.20) and house Spanish, Viña Bonita (£3.95). Others include Muscadet 1982, Ackerman Laurance (£4.95); Chablis, Blanchots, 1978, Laroche (£12.60); Mâcon-Lugny, Les Genièvres, 1982, Louis Latour (£6.95); Winkeler Hasensprung Spätlese 1976, Allendorf (£7.85); Marqués de Murrieta 1979 white (£6.85); Châteauneuf-du-Pape, Ch Fortia, 1980 (£9.70); Ch Plaisance 1979 (£6.60); Ch Léoville-Barton 1967, CB (£12.90); Rioja, Campo Viejo Gran Reserva, 1973 (£6.95); Barolo 1974, Pio Cesare (£8.90). The halves include Sauternes AC 1973, Schröder & Schÿler (£3.15), probably a better bet than Ch Coutet from the sorry 1974 vintage (£5.95).

HINTON CHARTERHOUSE Avon

Homewood Park

5½ m S of Bath, off A36 at sign for Freshford/Sharpstone TEL (022 122) 2643

OPEN 12 noon–1.30 pm, 7 pm–9.30 pm CLOSED Dec 24 to Jan 17
CREDIT CARDS All accepted WHEELCHAIR ACCESS Yes
VEGETARIAN DISHES As required ALC FOR TWO £37

An enchanting 18th-century house with Victorian additions in lovely countryside and its own well-groomed and much beflowered gardens, Homewood Park feels like everyone's ideal country-house hotel, all quietly tasteful elegance and friendly and efficient staff. There is a fishy set dinner on Thursday because that is fish-delivery day; otherwise, the *carte* offers a generous choice of fairly *nouvelle* dishes, some of which are curiously seasoned: wild rabbit sausage with flageolets in garlic and cream had dominant allspice one night, whereas the vegetables lacked salt. Roast saddle of venison, admirably high, pink and tender, was overwhelmed by a heap of blackcurrants when only three or four might have worked wonders. But there is praise for leek and wild chive soup, Roquefort cheese and walnut soufflé, grilled duck breast with coriander peaches, calf's kidneys with purée of French parsley, lemon soufflé tart, and the delicately fruity ices and sorbets. The wine list, from many good sources, starts with a dozen house wines, including Marcilly Vin de Table (£5.75), and Geoffrey Roberts California Reserve, both red and white, at the same price. Other fine bottles include Savennières, La Roche aux Moines, 1982, Soulez (£10.80); Jean Vatan's Sancerre Rosé 1982 (£9.60); Montagny 1979, Amance (£8.95); Marqués de Murrieta 1975 (£7.50); Viña Ardanza 1976 (£6.95); Merlot, Ambassadors Vineyard, 1977, Firestone (£12.50); Beaune Grèves 1966, Remoissenet (£17.50); Ch de la Rivière 1976 (£13.50); Ch Giscours 1971 (£27.50); Ch Filhot 1976 (£12.50). Three dessert wines are sensibly listed on the sweets menu.

HOLT Norfolk

The Flask Ⓥ

7/8 Chapel Yard TEL (026 371) 3968

OPEN 12 noon–2 pm, 7 pm–9.30 pm CLOSED Sun D, Mon
WHEELCHAIR ACCESS Yes VEGETARIAN DISHES On request
ALC FOR TWO L £11 D £20 TDH SUN L £7.25

A bright and cheerful bistro recently taken over by Ian McEwan, a former wine-broker. He offers simple lunches, a Sunday roast (with fishy alternative), and more elaborate dinners, using fresh local produce whenever possible: garlic mushrooms, asparagus hollandaise, sole with Pernod and prawns, spiced lamb with almonds, redcurrant sorbet, chocolate pots, biscuit tortoni. The fifty wines start with a dozen 'for everyday drinking': Muscadet 1983, Vigron (£3.30 a bottle, 65p a glass); Cuvée Doudet-Naudin Vin de Table (£4.95); Blaye, Prince de Guyenne, 1979 (£4.30; £2.30 a half); Rioja, Grand Condal Reserva, 1974 (£3.80). On the main list – almost entirely Bordeaux and Burgundies – mark-ups are equally kind, and the brief tasting notes helpful: Ch du Glana 1975, 'drinking very well' (£8); Ch La Croix 1976 (£10); Ch Cos d'Estournel 1966 (Berry Bros, £25); Ch Fourcas-Hosten 1961 (£22); Corton Bressandes 1971, Masson (£24); Pernand-Vergelesses 1976, Verry (£12); Barolo Reserva 1971, Conterno (£14). Ports include Warre 1945 at £75 and Cockburn 1967 ('declared by only four shippers, but plenty of breeding') at £14. Champagne is also well chosen and modestly priced, with Ayala NV at £9.75 and Pol Roger 1973 Extra Dry (£18).

HORTON Northamptonshire

French Partridge Ⓥ

On B526, 6 m SE of Northampton TEL (0604) 870033

OPEN 7.30 pm–9.30 pm CLOSED L, Sun, Mon, 2 weeks Chr, 2 weeks Easter, 3 weeks summer CREDIT CARDS Not accepted
WHEELCHAIR ACCESS Yes NO-SMOKING ROOM Yes TDH £12.50

This 16th-century coaching inn has made an unpretentious setting for the Partridges for over twenty years. David Partridge's cooking is mainly French Provincial, but the four-course set dinner menus include such dishes as salade tiède de poulet, foie de veau au citron vert and délice de chocolat aux fraises, as well as the more familiar mussel soup, blanquette de veau, and prune and armagnac ice-cream. Vegetables are home or locally grown, and there are good supplies of game in season. Mary Partridge buys the wine, with considerable flair, as witnessed by the modest prices and also, for example, by the five 1970s in a short list of Bordeaux (Ch Pape-Clément, £18.50) and the eight 1976 red Burgundies (Volnay, Chavout Labaume, £16.50). The 21 house wines, chosen to cover a wide spectrum of tastes and grape varieties, include Sauvignon du Haut Poitou 1982, and Lirac Les Garrigues 1980 (both £5.90). There are also two dozen half-bottles: Chablis, Montée de Tonnerre 1981, Durup (£4.90); Ch Chasse-Spleen 1978 (£5.90). Other interesting bins include Rosé de Marsannay, 1979, Clair-Däu (£6.50); Azay-le-Rideau 1982, G Pavy (£5.90); Crémant de Bourgogne 1980, Grégoire (£9.50); Merlot 1977, Veedercrest, from California (£7.90); Ungsteiner Honigsackel Auslese 1971, Seidel (£9.50); Langenloiser Heiligenstein Spätlese, Grüner Veltliner, 1979 (£6.50); and Ch Trillon 1976 (£5.50 a half) for the puddings. Obviously Mrs Partridge buys from many sources and the list changes frequently, although the wide range remains.

Please comment on the *service* of wine as well as taste, cost, etc.

HORTON-CUM-STUDLEY **Oxfordshire**

Studley Priory

TEL (086 735) 203 or 254

OPEN 12.30 pm–1.30 pm, 7.30 pm–9.30 pm CLOSED Mon, 1–20 Jan
CREDIT CARDS All accepted WHEELCHAIR ACCESS Yes
VEGETARIAN DISHES With notice NO PIPES OR CIGARS IN RESTAURANT
TDH D £16 SUN L £12 ALC FOR TWO £50

The 12th-century Benedictine nunnery has come a long way, via a starring role as Sir Thomas More's home in *A Man for All Seasons*, to its present-day status of luxury hotel with an impressive wine list. The cooking is *nouvelle cuisine*, with such dishes as home-cured breast of duck on a spinach and orange salad, mousseline of lobster and scampi with tarragon beurre blanc, roast saddle of rabbit on cabbage with a rosemary-flavoured sauce, stuffed breast of guinea-fowl with lime sauce, hot passion-fruit soufflé with marinated mango. Not much of it makes an easy marriage with the many fine wines, so choose carefully. There are hundreds of wines – send for the list in advance if you want to do it justice. It begins encouragingly with Geoffrey Roberts' California Reserve white and red as house wines, at £5.50 a bottle, followed by a dozen half bottles, several of them distinguished: Ch Pavie 1970 (£18); Châteauneuf-du-Pape, Les Cèdres, 1967, Paul Jaboulet (£12.15). For those who think big, magnums include Ch Latour 1970 (£100). The list has sensible, helpful tasting notes provided by the proprietor: for example, Ch Guimberteau 1976, one of the cheaper Bordeaux at £7.50, is 'noted for its characteristic Pomerol taste. Good accompaniment for lightly sauced dishes'. With 12 1970s to evaluate, most people need some guidance to choose between, say, Ch Potensac at one end of the scale (£15.55) and Ch Ducru-Beaucaillou at the other (£35). The latter can also be sampled in six other vintages (1953, £70). Red Burgundies start with the first-rate Pinot Noir from the co-opérative in Buxy (£7.95); and include Pommard, Clos Micault 1976, Domaine Parent (£25), and Clos Vougeot 1976, Remoissenet (£27.50). The Rhône yields such delights as Ch Grillet 1981, Neyret-Gachet (£28); Ch Rayas Blanc 1976, Louis Reynaud (£20.50); Côte-Rôtie Les Jumelles 1979, Paul Jaboulet (£14.15). The Alsace section includes Gewürztraminer 1981, Willm (£8.75), and two of Hugel's Vendange Tardive Gewürztraminers, the 1976 at £30 and the 1967 at £55. It would be difficult elsewhere to compare two 1967 Sauternes: Ch Coutet and Ch Guiraud (Barsac), each £30. Set foot out of France and you come across some distinguished German wines (Wehlener Sonnenuhr Auslese 1971, J J Prüm, £19.50); California's Champagne-method Blanc de Blancs 1980 from Schramsberg (£20.30), and Firestone Cabernet Sauvignon 1978 (£10.75); Australia's Rothbury Individual Paddock Semillon 1976 (£8.95) and the same estate's Cabernet Sauvignon 1979 (£7.90). There are vintage ports and Madeiras, too. Further good news is that the wine glasses have been improved, and the serious wine-tasting weekends will continue.

HUNTINGDON Cambridgeshire

Old Bridge Hotel

1 High Street TEL (0480) 52681

OPEN 12.15 pm–2.30 pm, 7.15 pm–10.30 pm CREDIT CARDS All accepted
WHEELCHAIR ACCESS Impossible VEGETARIAN DISHES On request
ALC FOR TWO £32 BUFFET LUNCH From £4

Once a bank, this fine ivy-covered hotel by the Ouse is part of a small East Anglian Group, Poste Hotels Ltd *(see also Stamford)*. They combine fine oak panelling with friendly service, and provide a mixture of informal eating from a generous buffet in the lounge and bar and more formal restaurant meals, famed for their trolley traffic: smoked fish, roast joints, and sweets. Other dishes include fresh salmon and dill mousse, monkfish with rosemary in a tomato cream sauce, fresh grilled tuna steak with a Chianti and basil sauce, rack of lamb seasoned with lavender and served with raspberry gravy, chocolate mousse and mille-feuille. The wine list and menu are combined, making it easy for them to suggest a glass of Moulin-Touchais 1959 (£1.50) with the puddings, and a glass of one of four ports (Cockburn 1970, £1.60) with the Red Leicester or Stilton (yes, another trolley, with whole cheeses). The 90 wines cover France, Germany and Italy, with clarets and red Burgundy dominating: Beaune, Les Champs Pimont, Coron (£12.60); Ch Birecourt 1978 (£8.45); Ch Rauzan-Gassies 1976 (£15.35). There are also four good Alsace wines from Sparr, and Touraine sparkling Blanc-Foussy (£8.95).

INVERNESS Inverness-shire

Dunain Park

On A82, 3 m SW of Inverness TEL (0463) 230512

OPEN 12.30 pm–2 pm, 7.30 pm–9 pm CLOSED End Oct to end Mar
CREDIT CARDS Not accepted WHEELCHAIR ACCESS Yes
VEGETARIAN DISHES On request
SMOKING DISCOURAGED IN THE DINING-ROOM TDH D £16
SNACK LUNCHES From £5

Ten years of hotel-keeping have not dampened the enthusiasm of Michael and Judith Bulger: their elegant, mainly 19th-century home, in six acres of well-tended and highly productive gardens, still provides a warm welcome and relaxing environment for tourists, mainly American in summer. Judith Bulger cooks interesting set dinners, with a limited choice, using their own and local produce as far as possible. Many agree with them that their salmon from the Ness, smoked by a neighbour, is 'the best ever'. The menus are eclectic and may offer Stilton and onion flan, ratatouille vinaigrette, artichoke or beetroot soup, roast haunch of venison, lamb chops with anchovy butter, mango sorbet in a brandy snap, walnut pie. There are over 100 wines, offering a reasonable choice of both price and area: Ch de la Rivière 1976 (£12.65); Ch Guimberteau 1978 (£8.65); Santenay Gravières 1978, Remoissenet (£13.25); Pouilly-Fuissé 1982, Loron (£9.75); Côte-Rôtie Brune et Blonde 1979, Guigal (£19.65); Muscadet, Ch de la Galissonnière, 1982, Lusseaud (£6.20); Riesling 1981, Hugel (£9.20); Dom Avelsbacher Auslese 1971, Hohe Domkirche (£14.50); Venegazzù 1979, Conte Loredan (£8.15); Zinfandel 1976, Inverness (£8.65); Ch Rieussec 1978 (£8.15 a half-bottle). Vintage ports include Delaforce 1963 (£25), and there are a dozen malt whiskies to choose from, as well as a fair range of other digestifs. Carafino by the glass is £1.

JERSEY Channel Islands

Longueville Manor Hotel

St Saviour TEL (0534) 25501

OPEN 12.30 pm–2 pm, 7.30 pm–9.30 pm CREDIT CARDS All accepted
WHEELCHAIR ACCESS Yes VEGETARIAN DISHES On request TDH £11.50
ALC FOR TWO £40

This comfortable member of *Relais et Châteaux* is a 13th-century creeper-clad manor house, sensitively updated: note the 16th-century oak panelling in the dining-room. The menu is mainly *nouvelle cuisine*, but in Channel-Islands-sized helpings, so expect *two* barquettes of quails' eggs with duxelles and hollandaise (chef John Dickens worked at the Connaught in London), *four* lamb cutlets with sweetbreads and onion marmalade. The cooking is careful, the pace of service slow, the waiters not always well informed. The list of over 80 wines is particularly strong on claret: Ch Cissac 1976 (£12.75); Ch Lascombes 1970 (£30.50); Ch Léoville-Las-Cases 1955 (£58.50). The ten Champagnes include Perrier-Jouët Belle Epoque 1976 (£28.25). White wines worth considering: Chablis Vaudésir 1978, Marcel Amance (£36.50 a magnum); Pouilly Fumé, Château de Nozet 1981 (£9.25; £4.75 a half) and its superior cellar-mate 'Baron de L' 1981, certainly one of the best Pouilly Fumés, if expensive at £14.25; and the local Clos de la Mare 1982 (£5.75). Red Burgundies include Beaune Grèves 1971 (Protheau), at £29.50, and Savigny-lès-Beaune 1976, Louis Latour, at £28.50 a magnum. French house wine is £3.25 a bottle, and others at the lower end of the scale include Côtes du Rhône, NV, Lichine (£4.75), and Paul Masson's Pinot Chardonnay 1979 (£4.75).

The Wine & Spirit Education Trust is the body in charge of educating those in and on the fringes of the wine trade. They offer a series of courses right up to Master of Wine level, the more basic of which are open to non-trade members who can convince the Trust of their intention to enter the wine trade. Contact them at:
Five Kings House, Kennet Wharf Lane, Upper Thames Street,
London EC4V 3AJ; TEL 01–236 3551.

JEVINGTON East Sussex

The Hungry Monk

Village centre, on B2106 TEL (03 212) 2178

OPEN 12 noon–2 pm (Sun only), 7 pm–10 pm CLOSED L (exc Sun), 24–26 Dec
CREDIT CARDS Not accepted WHEELCHAIR ACCESS Impossible
VEGETARIAN DISHES Yes NO CIGARS IN THE DINING-ROOM
TDH SUN L £9.48 D £10.29

This cosy and cottagy restaurant offers generous set meals (including a glass of port) in an informal setting. You may need a walk on the Downs afterwards if you allow yourself to be tempted by the blackboard menu, enticingly described by the staff before you order: feuilletage of cheese with mustard sauce; roulades, either plain or spinach, with fishy fillings; pancakes, terrines and quiches, again often fishy; pies, stews and roasts; and some novelties, like sirloin steak with buttered squid. Puddings are rich, too, if you can stay the course. The eccentrically spelled and patchily annotated wine list starts sensibly with a list of half-bottles and a selection from the main list for those unwilling to plod right through. House wines are Alexis Lichine's Vins de Table at £5.23 (£1.15 a glass). Others worth considering include Ch Fonplégade 1976 (£11.93); Gigondas, Domaine des Bosquets, 1980, Meffre (£9); Bourgogne Aligoté 1982, Lamblin (£6.52); Ch Rieussec 1979 (£7.20 a half-bottle).

KILCHRENAN Argyllshire

Ardanaiseig

Off B845, 4 m NE of the village TEL (086 63) 333

OPEN 12.30 pm–2.30 pm, 7.30 pm–9 pm CLOSED End Oct to Easter
CREDIT CARDS All accepted WHEELCHAIR ACCESS Impossible
VEGETARIAN DISHES On request TDH D £20 ALC LUNCH FOR TWO £20

Gracious living is at its most remote and elegant in this handsome stone mansion set in one of Scotland's finest gardens (try for the azalea or rhododendron season), with views of Loch Awe and Cruachan. It is fine walking country, with the hotel's boats on hand for fishing or island picnics. The set dinner menu offers a limited choice – one fish main course, one meat – with optional variations, at a price. Start, perhaps, with potted salmon, baked Brie or gazpacho, before going on to quenelles of pike in Noilly Prat or roast Aberdeen Angus, with fruit brûlée or mango parfait, and cheese to finish. There are five house wines, carefully described and reasonably priced, including Cuvée des Gaulois 1982 and Colombard 1982 (Coteaux de Gascogne), both £5.90, £1.50 a glass. The Ritz Champagne Rosé is as ubiquitous as tartan in Scotland's stately homes: here it is £15.45; alternatively, try J&B's Champagne method Blanc de Blancs (£9.50). Clarets include Ch Chasse-Spleen 1976 (£9.70); Ch La Lagune 1970, CB (£27.39); and Ch

Latour 1967 (£42.25). From Burgundy, there are Bâtard-Montrachet 1979 (£30); Fleurie 1983, Georges Duboeuf (£10.90); and Volnay, Les Chevrettes 1976, Boillot (£10.42 a half-bottle). The German section lists Winkeler Hasensprung Auslese 1976, Nagler (£17.90), and Ayler Kupp Auslese 1976, Bischofliches Konvict (£17.50). There are several vintage ports by the bottle, and also a decanter of Croft's LBV 1978 in the drawing-room: pour for yourself, and fill in the chit.

KILLARNEY Co Kerry

Gaby's Seafood Restaurant

17 High Street TEL Killarney 32519 (no reservations)

OPEN 12.30 pm–2.30 pm, 6 pm–10 pm CLOSED Sun, Mon L
CREDIT CARDS All accepted WHEELCHAIR ACCESS Impossible
VEGETARIAN DISHES With notice ALC FOR TWO IR£32

The Maes family's smart and cheerful white-walled restaurant specialises in fish straight from the Kerry boats, with a couple of steaks for non-believers. The simplest dishes are most liked: oysters, smoked salmon, grilled lobster. But those with a weakness for butter and cream also enjoy the chef's special salmon, turbot and lobster, as well as the vegetables. Sweets are mainly combinations of fruit and alcohol. Service is friendly and efficient, especially helpful over the choice of wine. There are over 200 bins on the list, starting with 11 house wines, all available by glass (IR£1.80) as well as bottle (IR£8): Pinot Grigio, Grave del Friuli 1982; Banda Azul 1978, Paternina. The Sauvignon du Haut Poitou 1978 is surely far over the hill by now. The *cru classé* Bordeaux represent good value and include: Ch Léoville-Las-Cases 1976 (IR£19.05); Ch Pichon-Lalande 1966 (IR£26.20). Other areas of France are less fully represented: Riesling d'Alsace 1979, Emile Kugler at IR£12 (halves of the 1981, IR£6.20); Aloxe-Corton 1973, Louis Latour (IR£18.50). Consider also the three vintages of Torres Gran Coronas Black Label (1971, IR£15); Château Musar 1975 (IR£12); and Ch Rieussec 1979 (IR£9.20 a half-bottle).

KINTBURY Berkshire

Dundas Arms

Station Road TEL (0488) 58263

OPEN D only, 7.30 pm–9.30 pm CLOSED L, Sun, Mon, Chr to New Year
CREDIT CARDS All accepted WHEELCHAIR ACCESS Yes
VEGETARIAN DISHES With notice ALC FOR TWO £34

The Dundas Arms is popular for its pub beer and bar-snacks as well as for its Anglo-French cooking and fine wines in the restaurant. Inspectors have praised tomato mousse with quail eggs, escalope of warm duck's liver on a potato pancake, gravad lax with mustard and dill sauce, fillet of lamb with wild mushrooms, saddle of hare with raspberry vinegar sauce, calf's liver with bacon and red pepper conserve, various delicious home-made ices and sorbets, and St-Emilion au chocolat. The lengthy wine list is strong on Bordeaux, listed by commune: Ch Bel Air 1978, Borie (£7); Clos du Moulin 1976 (£8.50); Ch Duhart-Milon-Rothschild 1970 (£19); Ch d'Issan 1976 (£16.50); Ch Cheval Blanc 1966 (£45). Burgundy offers Chorey-lès-Beaune 1979, Tollot-Beaut (£11); Santenay Les Gravières 1978, Remoissenet (£13.50); Chablis, Les Clos, 1979, Louis Michel (£13.50); Beaune, Clos des Mouches, 1982, Drouhin (£19.50). Other possibilities include Muscat, Les Amandiers, 1982, Dopff & Irion (£9); Châteauneuf-du-Pape, Les Cèdres, 1979, Jaboulet (£12.50); Schloss Vollrads 1978, Graf Matuschka-Greiffenclau (£7.20).

KIRKBY FLEETHAM North Yorkshire

Kirkby Fleetham Hall Ⓥ

1 m north of village TEL (0609) 748226

OPEN 12.30 pm–1.30 pm (Sun only), 7 pm–9 pm CLOSED L (exc Sun)
CREDIT CARDS Not accepted WHEELCHAIR ACCESS Impossible
VEGETARIAN DISHES With notice TDH SUN L £6.95 D £12.50

In their peaceful and handsome country house hotel, David and Chris Grant offer five-course set dinners, the only concession to local taste being the serving of cheese after sweet: beef consommé with sherry, or tomato and orange soup; smoked haddock and prawn roulade, hare terrine with gooseberry relish, or brioche with smoked trout; lamb steak with orange, ginger and garlic or pork fillet with apples, Calvados and cream; prune ice-cream or lime soufflé. Arrive early to absorb the 40-page wine list, which begins with a table analysing both the weight and degree of sweetness of over 60 wines. There are also maps, explanations of the 1855 Médoc classification and German labels, and tasting notes. David Grant is a genuine wine enthusiast who tends to leave prices static until a wine has to be replaced. He comments ruefully that the mention of Ch Lafite 1961 in last year's *Guide* brought him phone calls from London dealers eager to buy it by the case and his bank-manager, interested in knowing what he had paid for it. It's all gone now . . . The clarets are dazzling, starting gently with Ch de Bouchet 1978 (£7.95), and progressing upward through Ch Fonbadet 1976 (£13), and Ch du Tertre 1970 (£17), to Ch La Mission-Haut-Brion 1961 (£49). The final claret page tabulates Haut-Brion, Margaux, Lafite, Latour and Mouton-Rothschild, 78 of them in all, with Ch Haut-Brion 1971 the cheapest at £18, and Ch Latour 1945 the most expensive at £140 – and still a bargain. Burgundy is less well represented with many off-years; however, there are Savigny-lès-Beaune, Les Guettes, 1969, Doudet-Naudin (£15.50), and Chablis, Valmur, 1978, Fèvre (£16.25). From other regions, consider Ch Chalon 1973, Bourdy (perhaps as an aperitif for a large party) at £22; Sancerre Rosé 1982, Vatan (£9.95); Châteauneuf-du-Pape, Domaine de Mont-Redon 1976 (£15.50); Gewürztraminer 1979, Humbrecht (£7.95); a dozen Champagnes, including Roederer Cristal 1976 (£24). Nor is Germany neglected, though the precious 1971s mostly lack shippers. Port ranges from Cockburn's 1920 (£35) to Sandeman's 1963 (£19). The list finishes with 2½ pages of half-bottles, including Ch Filhot 1975 (£6.95). There *are* house wines – Bouchard Père French at £5 a bottle, £1 a glass – but it seems a pity to pass up the opportunity to explore the full list.

KNARESBOROUGH North Yorkshire

Schwallers

6–8 Bond End TEL (0423) 863899

OPEN 12.30 pm–2 pm (Sun only), 7 pm–10.30 pm CLOSED L (exc Sun), Tue, 26 Dec to 30 Jan CREDIT CARDS Access/Euro, Visa
WHEELCHAIR ACCESS Impossible VEGETARIAN DISHES Yes
NO SMOKING IN DINING-ROOM TDH £8.75 ALC FOR TWO £27

A relaxed and friendly place radiating the enthusiasm of its young owners, Martin and Caroline Schwaller. There is a comfortable ground-level bar with lots of books and menus for browsing through, and the first-floor restaurant is pretty and uncramped. Both table d'hôte and à la carte menus change daily, according to supplies, and Martin's cooking marries his Swiss heritage to modern ideas: cheese and herb pâté, stuffed mushrooms, fondue neufchâteloise, rendezvous de fruits de mer sauce safran, poulet aux deux moutardes, roast quails Souvaroff (flamed in gin and served in a red wine and juniper sauce), brown apple Betty, raspberry Pavlova. Good fresh vegetables come in generous helpings. The Schwallers' enthusiasm extends to their wine list, loose-leaf so that it can be kept up to date. It starts with a minor triumph: they have persuaded their sherry shippers to produce half-bottles of Bodega Marqués del Reál Tesoro, £3.75, in Fino, Manzanilla and Amontillado, all dry, and a semi-sweet cream sherry. Then follow ten house wines, all carefully annotated, including tasting notes, and available by glass (90p) as well as bottle: Gaillac Perlé, NV, from the Caves Co-opératives (£4.70); Viña Real 1978 (£4.95). Ten sparklers run the gamut from Bollinger 1976 (£19.75) to the Touraine Champagne method Blanc Foussy (£6.90). Clarets include Ch Coufran 1977 (£8.20), as well as the interesting Cuvée de la Commanderie du Bontemps 1978 (leading proprietors' contributions to the commanderie, blended by the manager of Ch Latour) at £8.10. Red Burgundies start with Hautes-Côtes-de-Nuits 1978, Geisweiler (£10.35), whites with Montagny 1981, Louis Latour (£9.75). A 'typically earthy' Côtes-du-Rhône comes from the Caves des Vignerons de Bourg-St-Andéol (£4.90). The Loire offers Gros Plant, Ch de la Galissonnière, 1982 (£6.50) and Ménétou-Salon 1982, Mellot (£7.50). There is a healthy showing of German wines: Burg-Layer Rotenberg Auslese 1976, Schaffer (£8.95); Ockfener Bockstein Spätlese 1979, Rheinhart (£9.90). The list also includes three Gran Reservas from Spain; Moscato d'Oro 1980, Robert Mondavi's sweet dessert Muscat (£8.95); Chilean Cabernet Sauvignon 1979, Concha y Toro (£6.20);

Austrian Ruster Blaufränkisch Spätlese 1977 (£7.15); and a few Australians. As well as the 15 dessert wines available by the bottle, others are offered each day by the glass: if you are lucky it may be the Austrian St Margarethen Beerenauslese 1981 (£1.25), or the Australian Muscat à Petit Grain, Stanton & Killeen (£1.30). The Schwallers organise tastings in tandem with their new wine business, Bond End Wines *(see* MERCHANTS *section)* basically an agency for Stapylton Fletcher, one of their main suppliers.

LACOCK Wiltshire

At the Sign of the Angel Ⓥ

Church Street TEL (024 973) 230

OPEN 1 pm–1.15 pm, 7.30 pm–8 pm CLOSED Sat L, Sun D, 22 Dec to 1 Jan
TDH L £11 D AND SUN L £14.50

In a National Trust village, a 15th-century wool-merchant's house, where all the wood gleams and the flowers are fresh. Have aperitifs in the garden on sunny days before settling down to vast helpings of traditional English food, served by 'lovely ladies'. Start with good home-made soup or various mousses and pâtés, go on to the roast of the day with carefully cooked vegetables, then to delicious home-made ices or treacle lick, before truckles of Cheddar and Stilton. It may have been a happy accident of the common name that the Levis family discovered the Gaillac co-opérative, Labastide de Lévis, but they have had the wines on their list for many years: currently, both red and perlé are £6 a bottle, £1.50 a glass. The other 80 or so wines are sometimes sketchily annotated, but intelligently chosen, moderately priced, and correctly served: house claret (£6.20); Ch Cissac 1975 (£11); Ch Phélan-Ségur 1973 (£14); Georges Duboeuf Beaujolais are well represented (Moulin-à-Vent 1982, £7.50); Mercurey 1978, Bouchard Père et Fils (£7.50); Bourgogne-Matterre 1979, Parrisot (£8); Sancerre Rosé 1981, Jean Vatan (£10); St-Joseph 1980, Grippat (£9); Bandol 1979, Bunan (£9.20); Viña Ardanza 1976 (£7.50). If it's treats time, why not have a bottle of Deutz Champagne, NV (£15) as an aperitif, and a half-bottle of the luscious Dirmsteiner Mandelpfad Optima Trockenbeerenauslese 1976 (£12) with – or before – the pudding.

LAKE ULLSWATER see Ullswater

Send us **your** views on the report forms at the back of the book.

We should very much appreciate further comments and suggestions of establishments of particular interest to the wine lover. There are report forms at the back of this book.

LEDBURY Hereford & Worcester

Hope End

2½ m N of Ledbury, just beyond Wellington Heath TEL (0531) 3613
OPEN 7.30 pm–9 pm CLOSED L, Dec to last weekend Feb CREDIT CARDS All accepted WHEELCHAIR ACCESS Yes VEGETARIAN DISHES By arrangement NO SMOKING IN DINING-ROOM TDH £14

John and Patricia Hegarty like you to feel you are staying with friends in their peaceful hotel in its forty acres of grounds, where one of our consumer reporters 'met only rabbits and pheasants'. Patricia cooks five-course dinners with a choice in only the first and last courses, using as far as possible their own and local produce. Dishes praised include Gloucester Old Spot ham omelette, broad bean and lemon soup, grilled lamb with medlar jelly, civet of venison, grilled and honeyed pears, and Parson Woodforde's Charter custard. A light salad is served between main course and cheese, often the local Single Gloucester or Belvoir Blue. There are over a hundred wines, and John Hegarty is particularly proud of his range of half-bottles – and keen to expand it: Ch Laville-Haut-Brion 1980 (£16); Savigny-lès-Beaune, Les Marconnets 1979, Bize (£6); Chablis, Montée de Tonnerre 1980, Durup (£4); Châteauneuf-du-Pape, Domaine de Mont Redon, 1980 (£5); Rioja Viña Real Gran Reserva 1970 (£5.50); Ch Caillou 1976 (£8). Clarets range from Ch Lague 1978 (Fronsac) at £6 to Ch Léoville-Las-Cases 1970 at £32. The Rhônes include Condrieu 1982, Vernay (£14); Gigondas Rosé 1980, Roger Meffre (£7.50); Châteauneuf-du-Pape, Domaine du Vieux Télégraphe 1980 (£8.50); and the Tain co-opérative's sparkling St-Péray, NV (£6.50). Robert Mondavi represents California with his Cabernet Sauvignon 1977 (£11.50) and the luscious Moscato d'Oro 1981 (£7 a half). The French house wine is £4 a bottle, 70p – £1 a glass; Moscatel de Setúbal is £1.60 a glass.

LEWES East Sussex

Kenwards Ⓥ

151A High Street, Pipe Passage TEL (0273) 472 343
OPEN From 7.30 pm (lunch by arrangement only) CLOSED Sun, Mon, 24 Dec to 1 Jan CREDIT CARDS Amex WHEELCHAIR ACCESS Impossible VEGETARIAN DISHES Yes TDH £7.95 ALC FOR TWO £24

John Kenward is a campaigner, and in his attractive beamed and stripped-pine restaurant you may find yourself persuaded to try strong and unusual flavours from his seasonal menu: celeriac and mace soup, sweetbreads with cabbage, lemon sole with buttered mussels, turnips stuffed with Blue Cheshire and celery, as well as all sorts of game in season. There is a choiceless three-course set meal for £7.95. He feels strongly about wine too, and has even persuaded his local wine-maker at Breaky Bottom to bottle some halves, which are selling well: Seyval

Blanc and Müller-Thurgau, both 1982 (£5.30 a bottle, £2.80 a half). His list is strongest in French wines, and the modest mark-ups encourage experimentation: Savennières, Clos du Papillon 1982, Jean Baumard (£6.75); Alsace Riesling 1979, Trimbach at £3.85 a half (but avoid the Muscats which are too old – 1974 to 1979 – to have retained their character); Ch Branaire-Ducru 1967 (£11.20); Richebourg 1961, Paul Bouchard (£15.90); Viña Ardanza 1976 (£6; £3.20 a half). There is a separate list of dessert wines, strong on Germans, with Graacher Himmelreich Riesling Auslese 1976, J J Prum at £16, and Ch Doisy-Védrines 1970 at £7 a half. Even in Mr Kenward's absence, the wine is discussed intelligently and treated sensibly. Wine by the glass is £1.05. If you are walking home, there are tempting single malts, eaux-de-vie and marcs.

LINCOLN Lincolnshire

Harveys Cathedral Restaurant ⓥ

1 Exchequer Gate, Castle Square TEL (0522) 21886

OPEN 12 noon–1.45 pm, 7 pm–9.30 pm CLOSED Sun; lunch Sat and public holidays; 1 to 4 Jan CREDIT CARDS Access/Euro, Visa
WHEELCHAIR ACCESS Impossible VEGETARIAN DISHES Yes
ALC FOR TWO £27 LUNCH About £6 per person

Bob and Adrianne Harvey's relaxed and friendly place beside the Cathedral offers simple, reasonably priced lunches and more elaborate five-course dinners, priced according to the main course. At midday, choose from soups, salads, ploughman's and various other platters, with a roast and a casserole or two (lamb in white wine, £3.40). At night the breezy style of the menu deters some, but others enjoy smoky pot, Greek fish and shellfish mayonnaise, tropical pineapple (with fruit and nut curry inside), Burgundy beef, Chinese duckling, planked steak, and various exuberant sweets. The 24-page wine list introduces you gently to a few bargain bin-ends, and with the house wines, French and Austrian (£5.50 a bottle), you pay pro rata for what you drink. Eight basic wines then follow, and a useful page of 'Halves for Solos': Chablis Vaillons 1981, Bernard Defaix (£5.50); Hautes Côtes de Beaune 1976, Caves Co-opératives (£5.95). Bob Harvey has put together an interesting cluster of 20 Wines from the Cape: Theuniskraal Gewürztraminer 1982 (£7.50); Uitkyk Carlsheim 1981 (£6.50); Allesverloren Tinta Barocca 1978 (£7.25); Meerlust Cabernet Sauvignon 1976 (£9.75). German wines run from basic Liebfraumilch 1982 (£6.50), to Erdener Treppchen Auslese 1976, Weingut A E Erben (£13.50). White Burgundies include St-Aubin, La Pucelle 1982, Roux (£8.75), and Meursault, Charmes 1979, Julien Coche-Debord (£12.50). French reds make a powerful showing: from the Loire, Cheverny Rouge, Domaine Gaudronnière, 1982 (£5.95), through Gigondas, Domaine de la Chapelle, 1978 (£9.50) and Gevrey-Chambertin 1978, Moillard (£12.25), to the three pages of Bordeaux, which include Ch Rouet 1979 (a Fronsac) at £7.50; nine 1973s (Ch Talbot, £11.50); five

1971s (Ch La Lagune, £16.50); and four 1970s (Ch d'Issan, £15). There are promises of more Burgundies, and a page of Gran Riserva Riojas, to come. Good range of aperitifs and digestifs.

LINLITHGOW West Lothian

Champany

2 m NNE of Linlithgow, junction of A904 and A803 TEL (050 683) 4532

OPEN 12 noon–2 pm, 7.30 pm–10 pm CLOSED Sun D, 2 weeks from Chr Eve
CREDIT CARDS All accepted WHEELCHAIR ACCESS Yes
VEGETARIAN DISHES Yes ALC FOR TWO £32 TDH SUN L £10.50
CHOP-HOUSE About £5

The Davidsons, already acclaimed as purveyors of the best steaks in the country, have changed the bar of their handsome round-house (a converted horse-mill) into a chop and ale-house with a lunchtime cold buffet, hamburgers, sausages and pizza as well as fine chops and steaks (the ale is Belhaven 70/- and 80/-). The main restaurant has polished mahogany tables, fresh fruit and flowers – and a view of the chef at his grill through a glass screen. There is also a 1,000-litre fish tank to ensure the supply of lobsters, oysters, mussels, crayfish and prawns. As well as those and the famed steaks (hung for three weeks), plain or with various sauces, you can enjoy gravad lax alone or with smoked salmon (to end the debate as to which is best?), Cullen skink (smoked haddock soup), spit-roasted duckling, fresh tuna steaks, with good fresh vegetables and a choice from a laden salad table. Fresh fruit seems the wisest option thereafter, but there is a sweets trolley. Such highly-flavoured food requires some meaty wines: luckily South African Clive Davidson has chosen well. The list begins with Georges Duboeuf Beaujolais (majors – bottles, super majors – magnums, and majorettes – 50 cl): all 1983 as we went to press – Morgon (£8.45), Juliénas (£8.75), Chiroubles (£8.75) and Fleurie (£9). Then follow four pages of red Burgundies, from Bourgogne Cuvée Latour 1982 (£9.85), to La Tâche, Domaine de La Romanée-Conti, 1976 (£90.45). Beaujolais Blanc 1979, Louis Jadot, is £10.50; Beaune, Clos des Mouches, 1982, Drouhin, £18.40; Bâtard-Montrachet 1979, Louis Latour, £29.45. The clarets select good years at reasonable prices: Ch Gionne 1979 (£9.15); Ch des Templiers 1978 (£9.75); Ch Liversan 1977 (£9). You can fly much higher if you wish. The most interesting – because least familiar – part of the list is the South African section, with succinct one-liners to indicate the style: red wines are classified by grape variety; for example, under Cabernet Sauvignon you find Groot Constantia 1979 (£9.20) – 'superb; well balanced, with a long after-taste'. You could, if you wish, compare it with the same company's Pinotage 1980, 'soft with fine bouquet; finished in wood' (£9.25). 'Blended wines' include KWV Cap Foret, Coastal Region, 1982 (£7.25) – 'off-dry and refreshing'. The page of Spanish and Portuguese wines includes several which would suit the cooking style admirably, for example, Colares,

Companhia Real Vinicola, Reserva, 1973 (£8.65). The 20 Champagnes offer NV, 1976, 1975, and 1973 from various houses, culminating in Krug Private Cuvée 1973 at £41.50. The only sweet half-bottle on the list is Muscat de Beaumes-de-Venise 1982 (£8.05). South African house wines cost from £7.05 in the restaurant, £5.50 in the chop-house, £1.50/95p a glass. As the *Guide* went to press, the Davidsons opened Champany Inn Town, 2 Bridge Road, Colinton (in Edinburgh) with the same steaks and wines, some of the latter more fiercely priced.

LLANDEWI SKIRRID Gwent

Walnut Tree Inn ⓥ

3 m NE of Abergavenny, on B4521 TEL (0873) 2797

OPEN 12.30 pm–2.30 pm, 7.30 pm–10.30 pm CLOSED Sun CREDIT CARDS Not accepted WHEELCHAIR ACCESS Yes VEGETARIAN DISHES Yes ALC FOR TWO £28

The Taruschios' endearing whitewashed pub at the foot of a bracken-covered hill is a combination of restaurant, bistro and bar. Most people favour the bistro, since it is less formal – and better served – than the restaurant, more comfortable than the bar. The food is the same. Franco Taruschio is a creative perfectionist, and his menu, based on mainly local produce and his own Italian background and varied interests, springs constant surprises: oysters gratiné with laverbread, carpaccio St Angelo with truffles, bavarois of smoked salmon with the salmon roe (smoked separately) inside, grilled lobster with Vin Santo, salmon with rhubarb, quails Rossini, spumoni Amaretto, plums in vodka . . . the invention seems endless. Fish and game are the special strengths, but some local businessmen go back once a week for the lasagne. There are 22 pages of wines, starting with house Italian at £5.95 a litre, and covering most of Europe's wine-growing areas, as well as California. Pride of place must go to the Italian section, where you can choose between Vernaccia di San Gimignano 1980 (£5.50); Rapitalà 1980, from Alcoma in Sicily (£6); Favorita 1979 (from Alba) at £6.25; a dry Picolit di Monte Fano 1979 (£6.50); Rosso Piceno di Monte Fano 1980 (imported by the restaurant) for £5.95; Venegazzù 1977 (£8.20); and Brunello di Montalcino 1973 (£10.50). The six pages of clarets include Ch Castéra 1975 (£10.10); Ch Coufran 1973 (£8.50); Ch La Garde 1970 (£14.25); and Ch Haut-Brion 1967 (£25). Others to consider include Moulin-à-Vent 1978, Loron (£9.25); Vougeot, La Perrière 1976, Bertagna (£18); Chablis, Les Clos 1979, Louis Michel (£16.50); Gewürztraminer 1980, Schleret (£7.50); Ruppertsberger Gaisbohl Spätlese 1976, Dr Bürklin-Wolf (£11); Cabernet Sauvignon 1978, Trefethen (£15.50).

Prices and wines listed may change as the year progresses. Our examples are intended only as an indication of each restaurant's approach to wine.

LLANDUDNO Gwynedd

Bodysgallen Hall ☞

On B5115, towards Conwy TEL (0492) 84466
OPEN 12.30 pm–2 pm, 7.30 pm–9 pm CREDIT CARDS All accepted
WHEELCHAIR ACCESS 2 low steps VEGETARIAN DISHES Yes
TDH L £8.30 D £13.50 ALC FOR TWO £35

A 13th-century watch-tower, stone mullioned windows and Edwardian bathrooms all add to the pleasure of staying in this fine listed building, most of it 17th-century, set in the midst of a walled rose garden, a 17th-century knot garden and a productive vegetable garden. The set menus vary daily, the à la carte one seasonally, both of them offering mainly English cooking based on fresh local produce: Stilton fritters with gooseberry sauce; crab, sorrel and tomato tart with a butter sauce; fried brill with herb butter; sirloin in port and mushroom sauce; duck with apples and lime; syllabub; apple and almond tart. Service is skilled and unobtrusive. The list of about 150 wines is strongest in Bordeaux, with a special list of the dozen best vintages of Ch Gruaud-Larose, from 1957 (£23.50) to 1979 (£16.70). Ch Lafite 1967 seems a relative bargain at £18.50 a half-bottle. Wines from other regions include: Nuits-St-Georges, Les Didiers, 1976, Chandesais (£15.30); Châteauneuf-du-Pape, Chante Cigale, 1980 (£10); Chablis, Les Clos, 1981, Moreau (£13); Muscat 1982, Wiederhirn (£7); Torres Gran Coronas Reserva 1973 (£14.20); Ch Musar 1977 (£10.20). There are too few half-bottles, especially in white and sweet wines. The house wines are Corney & Barrow Vin de Table at £6.30 a bottle, and Nathaniel Johnston's Bordeaux Rouge, NV, at £6.70. A wine-tasting weekend is organised annually.

LLANRWST Gwynedd

Meadowsweet Hotel

Station Road TEL (0492) 640732
OPEN 12.15 pm–1.45 pm, 6.30 pm–9.30 pm CREDIT CARDS Access/Euro, Amex, Visa WHEELCHAIR ACCESS Yes VEGETARIAN DISHES With notice
NO SMOKING TDH L £5.95 D £10.95

John and Joy Evans' well-furnished Victorian villa on the edge of this small market town overlooks the Conwy valley and the mountains beyond. The dinner menus have a French accent (Sunday lunch is firmly British): foie de veau en gelée de poivre, roulades aux fromages, boeuf en daube, rouget provençale, gigot d'agneau aux olives, walnut cheesecake, cherry clafoutis, raspberry parfait. Service is friendly and efficient. The wine-list is being improved each year: let's hope it gets no longer, since its several hundred hand-written items take longer to absorb than one can generally spare before a meal. Nine wines by the glass include Choix du Roy (£1.20), and house Champagne (£2.50).

Then follow two dozen wines under £6: Minervois, Cuvée Jean Alibert, NV (£5.95); Ch de Fonscolombe, NV (£5.95). Six pages of clarets encompass 1978 (Ch de la Gurgue, £11.95) and 1961 (Ch Pavie-Macquin, £29.95) with all the good vintages in between, and many half-bottles. There is an impressive list of Beaujolais, especially 1978: Moulin-à-Vent, Lucien Charvet (£11.30). Red Burgundies make a healthy showing in 1976: Beaune, Vignes Franches, Louis Latour (£19.25). An intriguing contrast of two vintages of Condrieu would be Georges Vernay's 1982 (£16.95) and 1973 (£25.50). The Loire covers all possible colours and styles. In the Spanish section, Marqués de Murrieta appears in both red and white, 1979 and 1978 respectively, each £9.95. If you survive to the last page, you will find an interesting list of cognacs, eaux-de-vie and malt whiskies. Special food and wine weekends are organised from time to time.

LODDISWELL Devon

Lavinia's

On the north side of the village TEL (054 855) 306

OPEN 7.30 pm–9.30 pm (lunch by arrangement only) CLOSED L, Sun, Mon, end Oct to Easter CREDIT CARDS Access/Euro, Visa
WHEELCHAIR ACCESS Impossible VEGETARIAN DISHES On request TDH £17

Lavinia and Jeremy Davies' elegantly converted barn down a leafy lane appeals more to smart holiday-makers and weekend sailors or cottagers than to locals: can it be the taped Bach? Lavinia's cooking is French-influenced, and though much of the produce is local and fresh, the set menu changes little: rolls of smoked salmon filled with avocado mousse, vol-au-vents of sweetbreads in tarragon sauce, salmon and brill 'en tresse' (interwoven, in a ginger cream sauce), lamb en croûte with watercress and hazelnut stuffing, steak au poivre, coffee and hazelnut meringues, chocolate cups with orange liqueur mousse. An interesting hot savoury is offered: profiteroles filled with a creamy Stilton sauce. There are over 60 wines, starting with St-Pourçain red and white from the co-opérative (£6.80/£1.20). Thereafter, most wines are French, pleasant drinking but with few bargains: Ch Bel-Air 1978 (£8.30); Ch Cissac 1971 (£21.30); Morgon 1981, Thévenin (£8); Meursault, Genevrières 1979, Michelot-Buisson (£21.75); Sancerre 1983, Laporte (£9); Crozes-Hermitage 1978, Thierry (£8.85); Riesling, Grande Réserve, 1982, Gisselbrecht (£7.50); Merlot, Ambassadors Vineyard 1979, Firestone (£10.20).

LOUGHGALL Co Armagh

The Bramley Apple ⓥ

Main Street TEL (076 289) 318
OPEN From 7.30 pm CLOSED L, Sun, Mon, 12 and 13 July, 25 and 26 Dec
CREDIT CARDS Access/Euro, Diners, Visa WHEELCHAIR ACCESS Yes
VEGETARIAN DISHES With notice ALC FOR TWO £28

A pleasant surprise to find this smart little restaurant with peat fires and candles in an old schoolhouse set amongst apple orchards. The short menu tends to the elaborate: chicken and mushroom crêpes topped with cheese and bacon, loin of lamb with lemon and herb crumb coating and Marsala sauce, duck with walnut and raisin stuffing and apricot and brandy sauce. The vegetables are fresh and the sweets appetising. The list of 90 wines divides into three parts, the largest French, the rest German (mainly QmP) and Italian, the latter from Cynthia Bacon of Petersfield *(see* MERCHANTS *section)*. Moderate prices and intelligent selections enable you to enjoy, say, Ch Haut Sociando 1979 (£6.25); Ch Filhot 1978 (£6.95 a half-bottle); Châteauneuf-du-Pape, Le Vieux Télégraphe 1981 (£10.30); Mörzheimer Herrlich Ortega Auslese, Gebeits-Winzergenossenschaft 1980 (£8.30); and Vernaccia di San Gimignano Riserva Pietrafitta, 1981 (£7.22). A considerate number of halves, and Georges Duboeuf house wine (£4.50/90p).

LYMINGTON Hampshire

Stanwell House Hotel, Railings Restaurant

15 High Street TEL (0590) 77123
OPEN 12.30 pm–2 pm, 7 pm–9.30 pm (10.30 pm Sat) CLOSED 4 days Chr
CREDIT CARDS All accepted WHEELCHAIR ACCESS Impossible
VEGETARIAN DISHES With notice TDH L £6.25 D £9.25 ALC FOR TWO £32

A comfortable hotel, much used by summer yachtsmen, with its dining-room overlooking a walled garden. They concentrate on fresh food, cooked mostly in simple English ways: mushroom soup, liver and walnut pâté, fried plaice tartare, grilled veal kidneys with sherry sauce, breast of duck vin rouge, apple crumble, various Pavlovas and home-made ice-cream. Service is prompt but unhurried. The rather expensive wine list has two unusual features. It begins with ten wines with helpful notes at £5.95 a bottle: Bulgarian Cabernet Sauvignon 1978; Marqués de Cáceres, also 1978; Ch Moulin de Launay 1982, a crisp Sauvignon from Entre-Deux-Mers; and the rather soft Sauvignon de St-Bris 1982, Moreau (the 1983 will be better). At the other end of the price scale are wines shipped specially from Ch Langoa by Anthony Barton: Ch Langoa-Barton from 1948 to 1974 (1953 is £32.50); Ch Léoville-Barton from 1943 to 1976 (1947 is £38.20). Tasting notes from *Decanter* magazine are provided: perhaps they should be updated? The rest of the list includes a good range of claret (Ch Latour 1961, £155, for a very special party), some sound Burgundies (Clos Vougeot 1966, Charles Noëllat, £38.15); Meursault, Les Casse-Têtes 1978, Thévenin, £24.50; and a few examples from other regions of France, Germany, Italy, England, Spain, South Africa, California, Lebanon and Australia. French house wine is £4.50 a bottle, 90p a glass. There is a Léoville-Barton wine club, which holds an annual dinner (£55 a head).

MALVERN WELLS Hereford & Worcester

Restaurant Croque-en-Bouche Ⓥ

221 Wells Road TEL (06845) 65612
OPEN D only, 7.30 pm–9.15 pm CLOSED L, Sun, Mon, Tue, Chr
CREDIT CARDS Access/Euro, Visa WHEELCHAIR ACCESS Yes
VEGETARIAN DISHES Yes NO PIPES OR CIGARS IN THE DINING-ROOM
TDH £16.60

This neat stone villa on the main road is run *by* perfectionists *for* enthusiasts. On their side, Robin and Marion Jones seldom fall down, but his disappointment is evident if customers seem insufficiently interested in what they are eating and drinking. Marion Jones is a talented and imaginative chef and puts together dinner menus which are nicely balanced: impeccable soups, followed perhaps by ceviche of turbot with avocado and pimento, or asparagus beurre blanc, or salmon sauce paloise; then leg of lamb with ginger, rosemary and soy, or chicken bourride or medallions of venison Francatelli; next come many-leaved salads and French cheeses in perfect condition, before exquisite fruit tarts or sorbets. Robin Jones does all the front-of-house tasks, from welcoming to wine-waiting, and for the most part things go very smoothly. The 52-page wine list is worth studying: you can buy a copy for £1.50 and thus be well prepared for your second visit. . . . Each of the 400 wines has a succinct tasting-note, and several which the Joneses think especially good are marked 'recommended'. On an outstanding list, the particular strength has always been the Loire, and this year Mr Jones nominates Vouvray and red Loires as his special interests: ten dry and medium-dry Vouvrays (Clos Naudin 1973, Foreau, £10; Brédif's 1964, £15.60); a mousseux and a pétillant (Brédif again, £8.80); and five medium or sweet wines, culminating in Brédif's 1921 at £72, 'still perfect'. The red Loires include Chinon, Domaine Olga Raffault, 1978 (£9.50), and Saumur-Champigny, Vieilles Vignes 1982, Domaine Filliatreau (£8.95). Other Loires are also worth considering, and so, too, are the two pages of Alsace wines – apart from a weakness for ageing Muscats, the list offers very fine wines indeed: Riesling Cuvée Spéciale 1981, Gisselbrecht (£7.95); Riesling, Clos Ste-Hune 1971, Trimbach (£25); Gewürztraminer, Cuvée des Seigneurs de Ribeaupierre, 1976, Trimbach (£14.20); and four vendange tardive wines (Riesling 1976, Dopff & Irion, £16.80). The eight Chablis include Valmur 1978, Jean Moreau (£15), and there are also attractive 1978s in white Burgundy: Meursault, Charmes, Pierre Morey (£16.60). A bargain white is the dry version of Ch Doisy-Daëne 1981 (£6.75), and for those who like the lighter style of modern Spanish whites, there is Marqués de Cáceres 1982 (£5.20). The California whites include some wines not well enough known in the UK: Riesling 1979, Jekel (£7.95); Chardonnay 1977, Cuvaison (£11.90). There are three pages of sweet wines, from the Coteaux-du-Layon, Monbazillac, Minervois, Alsace and Hungary, as well as Bordeaux. It would be pointless to evaluate the remaining red wines in so much detail. Sufficient to say that there are good, solid clarets, from Ch les Tourtes 1978 (£7.70), to Ch Mouton-Rothschild 1959 (£130), with plenty in between, including several halves. The Rhône section is strong on Jaboulet (Côtes-du-Rhône, Parallèle 45, 1962, £14); red Burgundies stretch over four pages and 48 years; the dozen California reds, like the whites, come from a variety of distinguished growers (Cabernet Sauvignon 1975, Clos du Val, £14); Italy and Spain both offer interest and bargains. Even choosing your aperitif demands concentration, since over a dozen are listed, including Pineau des Charentes, Lillet, Ratafia de Champagne, and a home-made vin de noyer. And to finish, there are seven pages of fine ports (going back to Martinez 1927, £75), Madeira, Armagnac (Ch de Percenade 1893, £6.50 a glass), Cognacs, brandies, Calvados (the superb Groult, Doyen d'Age, is £4 a glass), Marcs (Marc de Champagne, Veuve Clicquot, £1.20, is recommended), 19 eaux-de-vie, and a page of liqueurs, including a home-made ratafia of cherries, raspberries and redcurrants. Note that prices include service. Mr Jones also has a retail wine list (minimum order 12 bottles) and almost all the wines on the restaurant list may be bought at £2.20 less than the restaurant price. *See also the Croque-en-Bouche entry in the* MERCHANTS *section.*

MANCHESTER

Moss Nook Restaurant

Ringway Road TEL 061-437 4778

OPEN 12 noon–2 pm, 7 pm–10 pm CLOSED Sun, Mon L, Sat L, 2 weeks from Chr CREDIT CARDS All accepted WHEELCHAIR ACCESS Impossible VEGETARIAN DISHES Yes TDH £17.50 ALC FOR TWO £45

You might expect to find a red-plush-and-panelled restaurant two minutes from the airport full of businessmen at lunchtime, but would you expect *nouvelle cuisine* and a fine wine list too? That's what you get from the Harrisons, who are enthusiastic about all aspects of their work. (Pauline was a vegetarian for ten years and this is one place where you will not be offered the usual unimaginative dishes: not one is repeated within six months.) The enthusiasm spills on to the menu with over-long descriptions: five lines for scampi au citron et miel, four for filet aux poivres roses et verts. Some dishes that might need explanation are the soft-shelled crabs from Maryland (you eat the lot), Lancashire black pudding served with a mustard sauce and chutney, tresse de saumon et barbue (interwoven strips of salmon and brill in a mango and tomato sauce), venison steaks on a red wine and raspberry sauce. Vegetables are imaginatively cooked, puddings mainly creamy and fruity. The Harrisons are *compagnons, commandeurs* and whatever of various French wine groups, and visit wine-growing areas each year. Their list reflects this degree of interest, and they are particularly proud of the many individual growers they have discovered. The list is a leather-bound book with label illustrations and helpful tasting notes. It starts with a bang: ten Champagnes (Alfred Gratien 1973, £18.50) and six rosé Champagnes (Alfred Gratien still £18.50 but NV this time). Earning one more descriptive line than the scampi, Gaillac, Domaine de Mazou, 1982, is £6.50. Clarets include Ch Charmail 1979 (£10.50); Ch La Fleur Cravignac 1978 (£14.50); and Ch Ducru-Beaucaillou 1976 (£25). White Burgundies are all youthful: Montagny 1981 from the Cave des Vignerons in Buxy (£8.95); Chablis Vaudésir 1981, Long-Depaquit (£15); Corton-Charlemagne 1982, Bichot (£29). Bichot's Bourgogne Rouge 1980 (£8.50) has the 'tastevinage' label. La Romanée 1975 (£30) is apparently 'a jewel of a wine'. The Rhône section shows the harvest of those trips: various interesting Côtes du Ventoux, Côtes-du-Rhone and Tavel wines from small shippers, all at modest prices. Other jewels include Alsace Riesling, Les Eglantiers, 1979, Heim (£10.50); Briederner Römergarten Trocken 1981, Otto Görgen (£6.90); Kallstadter Kobnert Kerner Auslese 1976, Winzergenossenschaft (£10.50); a red Swiss St-Saphorin Grand Croix 1980 (£10.50); Ch Romer du Hayot 1955, a little-known Sauternes (£30). 'Derek's private cellar' (worth studying) tantalises you with some fine wines of which there may be only one or two bottles left and, at the other extreme, the postscript is a German de-alcoholised white wine at £4.50: the fact that it comes from Schloss Boosenburg in Rudesheim should not make you dismiss it as a joke. House wines are available at £6.50/£6.95 a bottle, £1.50 a large glass.

MATLOCK Derbyshire

Riber Hall

1 m off A615 at Tansley TEL (0629) 2795

OPEN 12 noon–1.30 pm, 7 pm–9.30 pm TDH L £8 ALC FOR TWO £34

This handsome Elizabethan manor house set in its own grounds, with a pretty walled garden and orchard, comes complete with a stable block housing half-timbered, four-postered bedrooms, a fridge-bar and patchwork quilt in each, whirlpool baths in two. There's also a helicopter pad, useful for businessmen in a hurry. The dining-room is furnished in Jacobean style; the cooking is more *nouvelle* than that. There is special praise for the fine meat served and a dazzling light hand with pastry (if you stay, you meet it again in the breakfast croissants). The menu might offer terrine of lobster with cucumber sauce, snails in puff pastry with cream and garlic butter, fisherman's soup (wearing a pastry sou'wester), scallops in cream and ginger sauce, roast duckling with glazed pineapple, guinea-fowl with Ricard and cream, noisettes of lamb with honeycomb and thyme, chocolate and hazelnut crêpes, or a savoury – mind you, shrimps in curry sauce on toast will *not* flatter the port. . . . We have a few complaints to make about the wine list: first, prices include neither VAT nor service, thus requiring one to add 25 per cent or so 'in one's head', if choosing to a budget; second, the list is too long for easy comprehension before a meal and several wines chosen have not been available; third, despite the proprietor's good intentions, several people report having a different wine to the one ordered brought to them with no prior discussion. That said, there are some fine wines to ponder over: what better than the rousing list of 20 Champagnes, running from the house Camuset Brut Réserve, NV, at £13.10 (plus VAT, etc) to Bollinger Vieilles Vignes Françaises Blanc de Noirs 1975 (made from the rare French ungrafted vines) at £48.75. Other sparklers include the Loire de Meyran Brut White Foil (Champagne method), at £7.50. House claret is Henri Rodier's Bordeaux Supérieur (£6.05; £3.10 a half-bottle); thereafter take pot luck with Ch Cissac 1973 (£13.95); Ch Peymouton 1979 (a 'forward' St-Emilion), at £8.95; Ch Rausan-Ségla 1970, CB (£29.80); and Ch Latour 1964 (£64). House Burgundy is Raoul Clerget's Bourgogne Rouge 1982 (£8.35); others include Chiroubles 1982, Sarrau (£8.60); Savigny-lès-Beaune 1979, Louis Latour (£13.85); and Grands Echézeaux 1976, Domaine de la Romanée-Conti (£62.25). A feature is made of several 1976 Burgundies from Robert Clerget, from St-Aubin (£13.65) to Chambolle-Musigny (£20.95). Slimmer purses might consider, for example: Touraine Sauvignon, Clos Roche Blanche, 1982, Rousell (£6.10); Côtes du Ventoux, La Vieille Ferme, 1982, Perrin (£6.05); Hugel's 1982 Riesling (£8.10); any of the Deinhard Rhine wines, from about £6 upwards; the white Rioja, Viña Leonora, 1982 (£6.35); a Rumanian Pinot Noir, Marmarot 1980, Gerhardt (£8.60); the three Provence wines from Domaines Ott (Ch de Selle Rosé 1982, £11.60); or Hill Smith Estate Riesling 1982 (£6.60). There are several half-bottles, dessert wines included, and port 'per decanter' (Croft 1960, £30), as well as a daily vintage port by the glass (£2.50).

MAYFIELD East Sussex

The Old Brewhouse

High Street TEL (0435) 872 342

OPEN 12.30 pm–1.45 pm, 7.30 pm–9.30 pm CLOSED Sun, Mon, Tue L, 'variable' annual closures CREDIT CARDS Amex, Diners, Visa WHEELCHAIR ACCESS Yes VEGETARIAN DISHES With 24 hours' notce TDH L £5.75 D £10.90

A modest family-run restaurant, all beams and ingle-nooks, in a very pretty village. The cooking is mainly French and offers a fair choice in the reasonably priced set meals. Home-made watercress soup or gazpacho might lead on to chicken Mère Michel, kidneys in mustard and cream or seafood florentine, with imaginative vegetables. Sweets are mostly rich and creamy. Bottles or half-litres of French wine are available at lunchtime only (£4.80 and £2.80 respectively). Otherwise, choose, perhaps, Bourgogne Aligoté 1982, Paul Reitz (£7.75); Ch

Chasse-Spleen 1979 (£11.05); Nussdorfer Bischofskreuz 1981 (£7.25). Croft 1963 is available at 24 hours' notice (£25) but as an impulse buy with the pudding, have Muscat de Beaumes de Venise (£1.10 a glass).

MOFFAT Dumfries & Galloway

Beechwood Country House Hotel

Turn left at top of Harthope Place TEL (0683) 20210

OPEN 12.30 pm–1.30 pm, 7.30 pm–9.30 pm CLOSED Jan CREDIT CARDS All accepted WHEELCHAIR ACCESS 2 steps (no access to lavatories) VEGETARIAN DISHES Yes NO SMOKING IN DINING-ROOM TDH L £6.50 D £10

Keith McIlwrick's headmasterly manner does not please all his guests in this former girls' school, set in ten acres of handsome beech trees, and his wife Sheila's cooking is not universally approved either, but when things do go well, people praise the simple well-cooked set dinners, appetisingly presented. The choice is sensibly restricted to three first courses (chicken livers in Madeira sauce, perhaps), soup (tomato is liked), a roast (loin of pork with white wine sauce) and a baked main course, and several puddings (almond tart with Jersey cream). Scottish cheeses feature regularly. (Note that the set lunch is served to booked customers only; others have cold food.) The extensive wine list has a good showing of 1976 and 1978 clarets: Ch d'Angludet 1976 (£9.20); Ch La Tour St Bonnet 1978 (£7.35; £3.92 a half-bottle). Other wines include Chablis, Les Fourchaumes, 1978, Fèvre (£11.70); Gaillac Perlé, NV (£4.88); Rioja Reserva 904 (£19.70/£8.80). Both Burgundy and German sections would be improved by fuller annotation of shippers and so on. Italian house wines are £4.40 a litre. Several special dinners are held throughout the year, and Mr McIlwrick hopes to introduce monthly tastings. Another new venture, due to be launched as we went to press, is the Moffat Wine Shop, 15 Well Street, Moffat; tel: (0683) 20554, with a list similar to the hotel's.

MOULTON North Yorkshire

Black Bull Inn

1 m south of Scotch Corner (A1) TEL (032 577) 289

OPEN 12noon–1.30pm, 7pm–10.15pm CLOSED Sun CREDIT CARDS Not accepted WHEELCHAIR ACCESS Not all 3 restaurants VEGETARIAN DISHES On request ALC FOR TWO £20

An attractive country pub with three small restaurants, one of them a fish bar, another a restored coach from the Brighton Belle. Regulars return for the warm welcome and friendly service as well as the seasonal produce, cooked simply for the most part, as long as you count lashings of cream and butter as 'simple'. Dishes liked include the lobster soup, snails in garlic, sole in half-a-dozen ways, lobster 'especially thermidor', brains in pastry, and game in various styles. The local unpasteurised Swaledale cheese is popular, and so are the brandy-snaps. George Pagendam runs a wine company too (Pagendam Pratt and Partners Ltd of Wetherby) and naturally most of the restaurant wines come from that source. They are strong on Georges Duboeuf Beaujolais and Burgundies and Louis Métaireau Muscadets. The list is erratically annotated, making it hard to distinguish value, but Gisselbrecht's Gewürztraminer 1982 (£7) and Ch Guiraud 1971 (£9.50) are obvious bargains. Georges Duboeuf Cuvée Blanc or Rouge is £5 a bottle. The wine company organises a tasting once a year.

NAIRN Nairnshire

Clifton Hotel

Viewfield Street TEL (0667) 53119

OPEN 12.30 pm–2 pm, 7 pm–10 pm CLOSED Nov to Mar CREDIT CARDS All accepted WHEELCHAIR ACCESS Yes
VEGETARIAN DISHES Yes NO-SMOKING ROOM
ALC FOR TWO £24 BAR SNACKS From £2.50

This well-groomed Victorian house overlooking the sand dunes and the Moray Firth is as rich as Aladdin's cave inside, and a worthy setting for its colourful owner, Gordon Macintyre, who stages plays, concerts and recitals here during the winter. If you fancy a formal fishy lunch with the family silver, you must book; otherwise there are soup and sandwiches in the comfortable bar. Dinner offers a wide choice, much of it based on local fish and shellfish, as well as game in season. There is praise for Roquefort mousse, saumon au beurre blanc, pigeonneau en croûte, and rognons de porc Henri IV. Vegetables, sweets and cheeses are all 'fresh and good'. The long, rather sketchily annotated, wine list is French-oriented, with solid clarets and Loire wines, but sadly no half-bottles. The house Quinson French wine is £5.10 a bottle (£1 a glass). Among the others are: Muscadet Ch de la Galissonnière 1982 (£7.50); Barolo 1977, Fontanafredda (£8); Ch Gloria 1970, CB (£20); Schramsberg, Blanc de Noirs, 1977 (a very good Champagne-method sparkler from California) at £35.20. English wines without vintages – and many others without growers or shippers – make this a frustrating list to read: at least in the restaurant you can ask for further details.

If you know of a good restaurant where it is possible both to eat *and* to drink well, please let us know if we have not listed it. There are report forms at the back of the book.

Hear about the best wine bargains all year round with *Which? Wine Monthly*, Britain's only wine newsletter. See the back of this book for more details and a subscription form.

NAYLAND Suffolk

The Bear

Bear Street TEL (0206) 262204
OPEN 12.30 pm–2 pm (Sun only), 7.30 pm–9 pm CLOSED L (exc Sun), Mon, Sun D, last week Mar, last week Aug CREDIT CARDS Access/Euro, Amex, Visa WHEELCHAIR ACCESS Yes VEGETARIAN DISHES With notice
TDH D From £12 SUN L £5.75

A half-timbered hotel with a wood-panelled dining-room, all pink linen and matching flowers, makes a relaxed and pleasant setting for the Naismiths' mostly English dinners, set meals priced according to the main course: duck rillettes, salmon and haddock pâté, celery and almond soup, roast fillet of beef in Madeira sauce, monkfish in cream and vermouth, pork tenderloin fried in a nut coating, peach brûlée, strawberry mille-feuille. There are almost 100 wines, many from Lay & Wheeler, starting with a dozen recommended house wines, the cheapest being Liebfraumilch, NV (£4.95), the best buy Chablis 1981, Jean Durup (£7.60). Others listed include Sarget de Gruaud-Larose 1979 (the château's second wine) at £10.80; Ch Haut-Batailley 1975 at £18.20; Juliénas 1981, Aujas, at £8.20; Pouilly-Fuissé, Ch Fuissé, 1978, at £13; Sancerre 1982, Raimbault, at £8.60; Ch La Jaubertie 1982 (Bergerac), red or white, at £6.50.

NETHERFIELD East Sussex

Netherfield Place

2 m W of Battle TEL (042 46) 4455
OPEN 12.30 pm–2 pm, 7 pm–9.30 pm CLOSED Sun, last 2 weeks Jan, 1st week Feb CREDIT CARDS All accepted WHEELCHAIR ACCESS Yes
VEGETARIAN DISHES Yes TDH D £13.50

The Katnic family have been followed by loyal customers from London (Oslo Court, NW8) to this fine house in its own 30 acres near Battle. Some even pop over the Channel from France for a taste of the country-house atmosphere, complete with panelled dining-room, fresh flowers and a warm welcome. Rajko Katnic has created a colourfully international menu: crab La Rochelle (in pastry with cream and brandy), boudin blanc (made from chicken breast and truffles in a tarragon sauce), duck Bosnaka (crisply roast, stuffed with its own liver, fruit, pine kernels, rice and lemon, served with a cherry sauce), fried calf's liver and sweetbreads in tarragon sauce with home-made pasta, guinea-fowl Poire Williams. Grand Marnier soufflé is worth waiting for. June Katnic has put together a splendid wine list, no longer cheap, but still offering wines hard to find elsewhere: for example, the clarets include nine 1961s (Ch Haut-Bages, £27.50; Ch Pichon-Longueville-Baron, £79), Ch Haut-Brion 1959 (£102), and Ch Cheval-Blanc 1947 (£228). The magnum of Ch Latour 1961 is now edging £400. Luckily for the average diner, there are also some well-chosen petits-châteaux: Ch La Gurgue 1978 (£16.20). Red Burgundy starts with Louis Jadot Réserve 1977 (£8.50), and climbs rapidly through Beaune-Theurons 1976, Louis Jadot (£17.50), to Richebourg, Domaine de La Romanée-Conti, 1969 (£75). White Burgundy seems relatively good value with Chassagne-Montrachet 1973, Morey (£16.50), and Corton Charlemagne 1973, Louis Latour (£32). Those with slimmer purses should look to Alsace, where Riesling 1979, Preiss-Zimmer, is £8.50, or to the Rhône, where Châteauneuf-du-Pape, Domaine de Valori, 1980, is £11.50. California is well represented, but overpriced. Australia fares better, with Rothbury Estate Cabernet Sauvignon 1979 (£9.50). Spain is worth a try: CVNE Rioja Tinto 1978 (£6.50); Castillo Jumilla 1980 (£7.50). There is an impressive list of half-bottles, especially strong – once again – on clarets, and with some useful sweet wines: Ch Filhot 1975 (£5.50). Vintage port ranges from 1931 (Quinta de Noval, £60) to Taylor's 1963 (£26). To come right down to earth, Jaboulet-Vercherre house Burgundy is £6 a bottle.

NEW MILTON Hampshire

Chewton Glen Hotel

Lymington Road, on A337 TEL (04252) 5341

OPEN 12.30 pm–2 pm, 7.30 pm–9.30 pm CREDIT CARDS All accepted
WHEELCHAIR ACCESS Yes VEGETARIAN DISHES On request
NO PIPES OR CIGARS IN DINING-ROOM TDH L £10.50 D £21.50
ALC FOR TWO £50

An opulent and well-groomed hotel – naturally a member of *Relais et Châteaux* – near the New Forest, where the high prices seem almost justified by the number of well-trained staff who minister to your needs. There must be even more of them in the kitchen, since the set lunch offers a dozen items in each course, the set dinner has four or five, and the *carte* is also lengthy. However, they cook the French classical and *nouvelle* dishes to order, so you should be pleased with your terrine of rabbit with small yellow plums and Mirabelle liqueur, turban of assorted fish with lobster butter sauce, and creme brûlée with pears (on the lunch menu), or, in the evening, salade de coquilles St Jacques au basilic, marbré de ris de veau et de homard au Sauternes, rouelle de saumon sauce oseille, délice de pintade au coulis de framboise, pigeon en fricassée à l'ail, tarte chaude aux myrtilles, or marquise au chocolat. David Burns supplies the wines, which start with Bordeaux and Loire house wines at £5.45/£5.85 (£1.60 a glass). Although the main strength of the lengthy list lies in France, there are interesting representatives from Italy, Germany and California as well, and a few token appearances from Spain, South Africa and Australia: Brunello di Montalcino, Tenuta Poggio alle Mura, 1974 (£13.50); Picolit 1977, Collavini, 1977 (£28.25); Avelsbacher Altenberg Auslese, Hohe Domkirche, 1976 (£14.75); Merlot 1978, Firestone (£11.20);

Chardonnay 1980, Trefethen (£22.65); Viña Esmeralda 1982, Torres (£8.15); Rothbury Estate Individual Paddock Hermitage 1975 (£13.95). The three pages of Bordeaux run the gamut from Nathaniel Johnston's Claret, NV (£5.35), through some middle-of-the-road bottles (Ch Smith-Haut-Lafitte 1976, £17.40) to the heights of Ch Latour 1966 (£108), Ch Branaire-Ducru 1961 (£65), and Ch Lafite-Rothschild 1952 (£125). White Burgundies yield Meursault Les Casse-Têtes, 1978, Thévenin (£28.05), and reds, Volnay-Caillerets 1976, Jean Clerget (£30.40). Cru Beaujolais are reasonably priced (Fleurie 1982, Robert Sarrau, £10.20), and Loire, Rhône and Alsace are also worth studying. In sum, this may be a hotel for the rich, but a cautious wine-lover can drink well without breaking the bank.

NEWTON Warwickshire

Tabuteau's Ⓥ

Newton Grange
On B5414, 3 m NE of Rugby TEL (0788) 860348

OPEN D only, 7.30 pm for 8.15 pm and 8.30 pm for 9.15 pm CLOSED L, Sun, Mon, 1st week Jan CREDIT CARDS Access/Euro, Amex, Visa
WHEELCHAIR ACCESS Yes VEGETARIAN DISHES Yes TDH D £11.95

The Tabuteau-Harrisons run their elegant restaurant like a private house, so be a polite guest and arrive on time: there are two dining-rooms which 'go in' an hour apart. Mrs Tab's cooking is dinner-party in style, with a French flavour: homely vegetable soup, crab au gratin, duck with apricot, lamb with an orange sauce, porc catalane, chocolate hazelnut flan, apple pie. The wine list has painstaking introductions to areas, styles, vintages, and is one of the few hand-written lists to be wholly legible and punctiliously annotated. There are about 140 wines, mainly French. Clarets seem reasonably priced and from most of the good vintages of the past 15 years: Ch Tronquoy-Lalande 1978 (£9.45); Ch Kirwan 1975 (£13.50); Ch Gloria 1971 (£9.84); Ch Chicane 1978, Famille Coste (£6.59); Ch La Cardonne 1970 (£8.96). Red Burgundies include Fixin, Clos Napoléon, 1979, Pierre Gelin (£7.87); Echézeaux 1976, Mongeard-Mugneret (£17.50); Côtes de Beaune-Villages 1978, Parisot (£6.53). Rhônes are represented by several 1979s: Gigondas, Pascal (£5.87); Hermitage, Guigal (£11.70). Three 1975 Riojas, all under £7, include the oaky Marqués de Murrieta and Marqués de Riscal, an interesting comparison, perhaps. White Burgundies seem a good buy: Pernand-Vergelesses 1981, Laleure-Piot (£9.54); Chablis, Valmur, 1978, Fèvre (£11.50). Other whites include Gewürztraminer 1977, Gisselbrecht (£6.05), and the sweet Moulin Touchais 1959 (£8.65). The German section is the weakest on the list, in terms of poor years and lack of shippers' details. Mr Tab should also add some decent half-bottles, especially since the French house wine is available only by the glass (85p).

OXFORD Oxfordshire

Cherwell Boathouse

Bardwell Road TEL (0865) 52746

OPEN 1 pm–2 pm (Sun only), 8 pm–10.30 pm CLOSED L (exc Sun), 1 week Chr
CREDIT CARDS All accepted WHEELCHAIR ACCESS Yes
VEGETARIAN DISHES Best with notice TDH £9.50 SUN L £8.25

Unpretentious place on the river (approach by water or down the lane by the Dragon School playing-fields), currently undergoing much-needed refurbishment. The modestly priced set meal offers two choices in each course: a recent menu was cream of tomato soup or Brie tart; grilled red mullet with herb sauce or Armenian lamb with pilaf; topaz sorbets or mille-feuille; coffee, cheese, fruit. Anthony Verdin, the owner, is half of the Morris and Verdin wine company, and his interest shows in the restaurant list, from the Tarn and Vaucluse house wines at a reasonable £3.50 a bottle to Ch Cheval Blanc 1967 at £45 a magnum. There are over a hundred wines, carefully tabulated, most from good years and shippers. They include: Ch Macquin St-Georges 1978 (£6.50); Muscat, Les Amandiers, 1981, Dopff & Irion (£7.50); Maximin Grünhäuser Abtsberg 1976, von Schubert (£12.50); Hermitage La Chapelle 1976, Jaboulet (£15); and the very good Bourgogne Passe-Tout-Grains 1982, Daniel Rion (£6). Dessert wines are worth considering, too, with Bonnezeaux, Ch des Gauliers, 1964, Mme Fourlinnie (£14), and even the possibility of comparing the same grower's 1947 vintage (and also with brother Jean Boivin's 1947, each £30). The final page of rare wines has temptingly venerable premier cru clarets, a Vosne-Romanée 1937 from the cellars of Dr Barolet (£34), and for those who believe it prolongs life, Tokay Eszencia 1889 at £250.

La Sorbonne

130a High Street TEL (0865) 241320/242883

OPEN 12 noon–2.30 pm; 7 pm–11 pm CLOSED Chr to New Year
CREDIT CARDS All accepted WHEELCHAIR ACCESS Yes
VEGETARIAN DISHES Yes ALC FOR TWO £40

Uneven standards of both food and service are reported in Monsieur Chavagnon's restaurant and snack-bar. But the 17th-century surroundings are appealing, the atmosphere is very French, and on a good day you will enjoy many of the classical dishes: soupe au pistou (£2.80); omelettes au choix (£4.40); entrecôte béarnaise (£8.50); canard à l'orange (£9); soufflé glacé (£3). (Note that vegetables are extra.) The wines, mainly from Morgan Furze, are almost all French, and not as fiercely priced as the food: Chiroubles 1981, Reynier (£10.45); Chablis, Fourchaume 1982, Lamblin (£10.10); Ch Liversan 1978 (£10.95). The French house wine is £3.30 for 50 cl, 85p a glass. Several half-bottles, but none, annoyingly, in sweet Bordeaux. Le Casse-Croûte is the adjacent snack-bar where prices are more modest (tarte à l'oignon, £1.90; civet de lièvre with vegetables, £3.50) and a dozen of the wines are available.

PADSTOW Cornwall

The Seafood Restaurant

Riverside TEL (0841) 532485

OPEN 12 noon–2 pm, 7.30 pm–9.30 pm CLOSED Sun (exc Easter), Sat L, Nov to mid-Mar CREDIT CARDS All accepted WHEELCHAIR ACCESS Yes VEGETARIAN DISHES Yes TDH £8.75 ALC FOR TWO £30

The Steins' informal quayside restaurant is spacious, cool and pretty enough to make you think you are on the French rather than the Cornish Riviera. The bustle is cheerful rather than intense, and staff cope well with large numbers, even taking time to instruct a novice on dismembering the crab on his plateau de fruits de mer. The accent is, naturally, fishy, and Richard Stein likes to keep dishes simple and sauces light so that the fresh tastes can shine out: grilled John Dory with chive and fennel dressing; terrine of brill, salmon and sorrel; grilled Dover sole, Padstow lobster or crawfish; ragout of scallops and turbot with basil. A soup and a main dish are added daily: you may be lucky enough to find bouillabaisse on the blackboard – definitely a main course. There are two meaty dishes for carnivores, and the set meal is rated both delicious and a bargain. The wine list is strong on appropriate whites at reasonable prices, with Richard Stein's comments to help you choose. The two house wines are Vin de Table Blanc, Loron, at £4.95 (95p a glass) and Sauvignon du Haut Poitou 1983, at £5.30 (£1.05). Thereafter, choose from the Loire Gros Plant 1982, Henri Poiron (£5.50), or the same shipper's Muscadet, Domaine du Manoir, 1982 (also £5.50), or experiment with Ménétou Salon 1982, Jean Teiller (£6.95). Others of interest include a white Châteauneuf-du-Pape, Domaine Font de Michelle 1982, Gonnet (£8.75); Meursault 1978, Remoissenet (£14.85); Alsace Riesling 1981, Heydt (£6.90). The reds include a St-Nicolas de Bourgueil, a good, rich Spanish, Viña Ardanza 1976, several clarets and Burgundies, and there are also sparklers, and even Cornish farmhouse cider, 80p a half-litre if you prefer to think yourself in Normandy.

PEAT INN Fife

The Peat Inn (V)

At junction of B940 and B941, 6 m SW of St Andrews TEL (033 484) 206

OPEN 12.30 pm for 1 pm, 7.30 pm–9.30 pm CLOSED Sun, Mon, 1st week in Jan, 1 week Apr, 1 week Oct CREDIT CARDS Amex, Visa WHEELCHAIR ACCESS Yes VEGETARIAN DISHES No NO-SMOKING ROOM TDH L £8.50 ALC FOR TWO £28

Wine-lovers at least should not complain about having to wait some time for their meal in this former post-office in the middle of nowhere, since the list deserves long and careful study. The small restaurant has recently been revamped, the welcome is still warm, the cooking is in the modern French style, using the best and freshest ingredients in highly skilled and original ways, and the prices are modest for what you get: lobster with 'posh' salad leaves, prawn and lobster cake, chartreuse of pigeon and pigeon livers in a cabbage leaf, salmon with butter sauce, superb grouse and wild duck, fine loin of lamb with port sauce, delicious Tayberries, irresistible ices. The choiceless four-course lunch is a real bargain. David Wilson loves his wines and regrets the difficulty of replacing the older clarets and Burgundies, many listed at near auction price and thus popular with knowledgeable customers. The 1970 clarets, for example, are tempting: Ch Cantenac-Brown, CB (£16); Ch Croizet-Bages, CB (£14); Ch La Fleur (£11.50). These are just a few among many: seven vintages of Ch Pichon-Longueville-Lalande, from 1977 (£12) to 1959 (bottled by Gloag of Perth), at £19.50; ten grand and premier cru Chablis, including Montmain 1981, Louis Michel (£10.50) and Valmur 1978, Maurice Fèvre (£15); a mouth-watering page of Côte de Beaune white Burgundies, including Meursault, Charmes 1978, Comte Lafon (£15.50); fine red Burgundies as well – Chambolle-Musigny 1969, Faiveley (£22). Other areas of France are also well represented, and the two pages of German wines, though almost shorn of the 1971s of previous years (a happy exception is Winkeler Hasensprung Spätlese, Deinhard, £9.80), still boast several 1976s: Wiltinger Rosenberg Auslese, Forster (£8.50). Other countries typify David Wilson's policy, 'short selection, top estates', with South Africa represented by, for example, Meerlust Cabernet Sauvignon 1976, Nicolas Myburgh (£9), and California by Stag's Leap, Trefethen and Chalone (the latter's Pinot Noir 1979, £14.80). The last – the 18th – page lists half-bottles for those concerned about their livers or their mortgages: Riesling Les Murailles 1981, Dopff & Irion (£4.25); Châteauneuf-du-Pape, Domaine Nalys, 1976 (£5.90); Ch Rayne-Vigneau 1975 (£6). Note that prices include service as well as VAT. There will probably be wine dinners during 1985: enquire.

PINNER see under London

POOL IN WHARFEDALE West Yorkshire

Pool Court

3 m E of Otley TEL (0532) 842288

OPEN D only, 7 pm–9.45 pm CLOSED L, Sun, Mon, 2 weeks Chr, 2 weeks July/Aug CREDIT CARDS All accepted WHEELCHAIR ACCESS Yes VEGETARIAN DISHES With notice CIGARS AND PIPES Discouraged in restaurant TDH £10 ALC FOR TWO £38

A very smart restaurant-with-rooms – very smart rooms, they are, too. Attention to detail is apparent in every aspect of Michael Gill's enterprise, including the service. There is a choiceless three-course meal (£10); otherwise you pay, according to the cost of the main dish, for four interesting courses, showing signs of *nouvelle cuisine* as well as the chef's native wit: warm pigeon salad, mousse of chicken with Roquefort, cream of leek and watercress soup, carrot and chervil terrine, mignons de boeuf au raifort, calf's liver with avocado and sage, breast of duck with cider and glazed turnips, caramel ice-cream, deep-fried Brie. There are about 250 wines on an interesting list which has been 're-thought' since our last edition, and now offers some good bargains. The house wines are more distinguished than most: Champagne from Boizel, NV (£15.15); white from Hugel in Alsace (£9.75); Bordeaux Supérieur from Alexis Lichine (bottled by Louis Frémont) at £8.70; Rhône from J-P Perrin (owner of Ch de Beaucastel) at £7.95. There is also a list of 14 'everyday wines', all at £5.75: Chenin Blanc Sec 1983, Fleur du Cap; Sélection Clerget Rouge, Raoul Clerget; La Grollière Rosé, Mommessin. Another innovation is the introduction of several vintages of Ch Cissac, which – as Mr Gill rightly says – produces excellent wine even in difficult years: the 1978 is £14.90; 1973 in Imperial (the equivalent of eight bottles) is £155. Conspicuous consumption also shows in the list of Champagnes, but there is subtler attraction in the white Burgundies: Chablis, Bougros, 1979 (£17.20); Bâtard-Montrachet 1979, Raoul Clerget (£32.30). This is the place, too, for Condrieu, Vendange Tardive 1976 Alsace wines, Trockenbeerenauslese Rhines from the superb 1976 vintage, and weighty clarets and red Burgundies. Provence is unexpectedly well represented, with Côtes du Lubéron, Fleur du Printemps, both red and white, from François Peyret, at just over £5, and three wines from Domaines Ott (Ch de Selle Rosé 1982, £14.30).

PORT APPIN Argyll

Airds Hotel

TEL (063 173) 236

OPEN 12.30 pm–2 pm, 7.30 pm–8 pm CLOSED Mid-Nov to end Mar
CREDIT CARDS Not accepted WHEELCHAIR ACCESS Yes
VEGETARIAN DISHES On request NO SMOKING IN RESTAURANT
TDH £15 BAR LUNCHES From £2

The Allens' 'wee holiday hotel', as they modestly describe it, is much more than that to its grateful guests. As well as its beguiling setting overlooking Loch Linnhe, they provide a relaxed and peaceful atmosphere, punctilious and friendly service, and particularly good food and wine. Local produce, scallops, prawns, halibut and netted salmon, is off to a good start, and when it is cooked *à point* with light and interesting sauces and herbs from the garden, you have memorable meals. Scotch beef and lamb, and roast saddles of local hare and venison also make their appearance. The puddings are rich but often down to earth: brown-bread ice-cream, date pudding with butterscotch sauce. Twenty pages of wines built up from scratch in six years is an impressive score, especially when they are both well chosen and clearly annotated. The main strength lies in France, especially the clarets, listed by commune. The house claret is a Bordeaux Rouge, NV (£5.50), and then one can take off into Ch Lyonnat 1979 (£8.60); Ch Gazin 1970 (£19); Ch La Mission-Haut-Brion 1976 (£32); Ch d'Angludet 1978 (£12, and really rather too young). Red Burgundies include Gevrey-Chambertin, Clos St-Jacques, 1976, Clair-Däu (£18.80); Beaune, Clos des Mouches, 1978, Drouhin (£13.20); and in Beaujolais, Juliénas 1981, Aujas (£9.50). Amongst white Burgundies are four attractive Chablis (Fourchaume 1981, Remon, £10), as well as the white Clos des Mouches 1976 (£15). Rhônes offer Condrieu 1979, Guigal (£14); Cornas 1979, Jaboulet Aîné (£9.50); and Châteauneuf-du-Pape, Les Cèdres, 1967, Jaboulet Aîné (£16) – this must be one of the last full bottles in the country, since elsewhere it is listed only in halves. Respectable Loires include Savennières, Clos de la Coulée de Serrant, 1981, Mme Joly (£12.80), Pouilly Fumé, Ch du Nozet, 1981, Ladoucette (£10). Good German bottles stretch back to the fine 1975s (Brauneberger Juffer Kabinett, Bergweiler Erben, £9.50). Other countries are briefly represented: South African Allesverloren Tinta Barocca 1978 at a bargain £6.50; Brunello di Montalcino 1976, Barbi at £10. Champagne starts at £15 (Moët & Chandon, NV) but there's also Sparkling Saumur from Gratien & Meyer (£8.40). The useful four pages of half-bottles includes Ch Rayne-Vigneau 1975 (£6).

PULBOROUGH West Sussex

Stane Street Hollow

Codmore Hill, on A29 TEL (079 82) 2819

OPEN 12.30 pm–1.15 pm, 7.15 pm–9.15 pm CLOSED Sun, Mon, Tue L, Sat L, 3 weeks May, 3 weeks Oct, 24 Dec to 5 Jan WHEELCHAIR ACCESS Yes VEGETARIAN DISHES With notice TDH L (2 courses) £4.25 ALC FOR TWO £26

The Kaisers' charming old cottage is a rural idyll, with a duck-pond, free-range hens, a vast vegetable garden, and an unselfconsciously homely interior 'that is almost cluttered, but not quite'. The menu changes every month to take advantage of seasonal produce. In spring, you might be offered a pancake stuffed with home-smoked haddock, galantine de canard, casseroled rabbit in white wine, lamb with sweetbreads and kidneys in red wine, the famous Quark Kuchen (cheesecake) with their own rhubarb, or various home-made ices. There are over sixty wines, with French house wine at £6 a litre (75p a glass). You will find some bargains: Saivigny-lès-Beaune 1979, Louis Latour (£10.25); Sancerre, Clos de Chêne, 1982, Marchand (£7.95); Ch Fombrauge 1978 (£9.75); Chianti, Villa Antinori 1978 (£6.95). The four Swiss wines – from the Kaisers' native land – include St Saphorin 1980, J B Testuz (£9.45), with the tasting note, 'a red wine of character and charm'.

Estimated prices in the information panel *exclude* wine.

ROSS-ON-WYE Hereford & Worcester

Pengethley Hotel

On A149, 4 m N of Ross-on-Wye TEL (098 987) 211
OPEN 12.30 pm–1.45 pm, 6.30 pm–9.15 pm CREDIT CARDS All accepted
WHEELCHAIR ACCESS Yes VEGETARIAN DISHES Yes
SMOKING DISCOURAGED IN RESTAURANT TDH L £9.50 D £14.50
ALC FOR TWO £48

A starkly white Georgian house in 15 acres of grounds, which produce many of the vegetables and some of the lamb for the table. Friendly service of the basically English cooking with French overtones. There are 24 pages of wines, from which monthly wine-tastings are organised. The tasting notes throughout the list are confusing rather than helpful, but it is certainly possible to find several attractive bottles, not too greedily priced: Viña Esmeralda 1981, Torres (£7.85); Fumé Blanc 1980, Robert Mondavi (£14.45); Beaune, Clos du Roi, 1971, Chanson Père et Fils (£20.50); Châteauneuf-du-Pape, Domaine du Mont-Redon, 1976 (£17.50); Ch St Amand 1979 (£4.85 a half-bottle).

RUGBY Warwickshire

Andalucia

10 Henry Street TEL (0788) 76404
OPEN 12 noon–2.30 pm, 7 pm–10.30 pm CLOSED Sun D, 'some public holidays'
CREDIT CARDS All accepted WHEELCHAIR ACCESS Yes
VEGETARIAN DISHES Yes TDH L £5.10 ALC FOR TWO £27

The original owner has retired to Spain but his chef and other staff have taken over and many regulars are still pleased with the friendly welcome and the Spanish food and wine. Thursday night is Spanish fish night with a three-course meal for £8.75. The full menu is eclectic, to say the least, with ravioli, prawn cocktail, minestrone, mixed grill, and Black Forest gâteau with Royal Chocolate Mint. Stick to the house specialities, all Spanish: Dover sole with white wine and prawns, duckling with cherries and peaches or with oranges and honey, pacopepper (fillet steak with sauce espagnole flavoured with port, cream and peppercorns), zarzuela de mariscos ('an aquarium of shellfish,' says Chef), arroz con pollo, paella, either fishy or vegetarian, and fruit- or ice-cream-based sweets. Most of the wines are Spanish, with more Riojas than anything else. Reds include Paternina Banda Azul 1980 (£6.50); Faustino V 1976 (£8.75); Marqués de Murrieta 1975 (£9.50); Reserva 904 1968 (£14.50). Whites offer Olarra Rioja Blanco 1976 (£6.50); Viña Esmeralda 1978 (£8.25); Marqués de Riscal 1978 (£7.75). Cordon Negro Brut 1971 is £8.50. There are a few half-bottles, and Spanish house wine is £6.50 a bottle, 85p a glass.

RUSHLAKE GREEN East Sussex

The Priory

Off B2096 at Three Cups corner TEL (0435) 830553

OPEN 12.30 pm–2 pm, 7.15 pm–9 pm CLOSED Chr Eve to mid-Jan
CREDIT CARDS Not accepted WHEELCHAIR ACCESS Impossible
VEGETARIAN DISHES Yes TDH L £10.29 D £16.04

This handsomely restored Augustinian priory in vast grounds pleases visitors with its peaceful atmosphere and friendly, if amateurish, staff. Some are less happy about the chilly stone-floored dining-room (no problem elsewhere in the house), the uneven standard of the cooking, and the ignorance about the listed wines. It is country-house cooking with some *nouvelle* touches: crab and watercress mousse, oxtail soup with Guinness, turkey paupiettes with a lemon sauce, grilled duck breast with spiced, fresh fig sauce, lemon and kiwi mousse, cinnamon and apple pancakes. Nick Clarke, MW, is wine adviser, and has composed an interesting list of about 140 wines, grouped by vintage within each region, with helpful notes. All prices are minus VAT, an infuriating practice inappropriate to a restaurant list, but many of the prices will nevertheless delight lovers of fine wine since mark-ups tend to be a standard amount per bottle rather than a percentage. Under 'Priory Reserve' are 'small parcels of wine which we believe will interest the serious drinker': Ch Pape-Clément 1961, CB (£51.60); Ch Gruaud-Larose 1962, CB (£22.50); Ch Lynch-Bages 1967, CB (£15.50); Musigny, Vieilles Vignes, 1969, de Vogüé (£41.65); the same wine from the 1971 vintage (£38.80); an impressive range of Charles Noëllat Burgundies, and many others, ending with two Meerlust Cabernet Sauvignons (1975 and 1976) for under £10. The main list glances at England, California, South Africa and Germany, but its strength lies in France, and especially Bordeaux and Burgundy: Ch Haut-Brion 1973 (£25.50); Ch Larrivaux 1976 (£9.05); Vougeot, Clos de la Perrière, 1976, Bertagna (£20.35); Hautes Côtes de Nuits 1978, Cave Co-opérative (£7.95). Gigondas 1978, Pax (£8.10); Sancerre, Clos Paradis, 1982, Fouassier (£8.30). There is a good selection of half-bottles, and the French house wine is La Borie (£6.25 a bottle, £1.40 a glass).

RYE East Sussex

Monastery

6 High Street TEL (0797) 223272

OPEN 12.30 pm–2 pm (weekends only), 7 pm–9.30 pm CLOSED L (exc weekends), Tue, Mon (Nov to Easter), Chr Day CREDIT CARDS Not accepted
WHEELCHAIR ACCESS Yes VEGETARIAN DISHES Yes SMOKING Discouraged
TDH SUN L (2 courses) £5.50 ALC FOR TWO £25

Steeped in as much atmosphere as Rye itself, Don Moore's restaurant is becoming something of a gothic fantasy in its decor. But the menu lists enough old favourites to reassure the regulars: brandade, mussels in cream sauce, the superb roast loin of Romney lamb (£10.50 for two) and charlotte Malakoff, for example. The more adventurous might wish to try grilled lemon sole with oyster sauce or braised lamb's liver with beetroot and onions. There are about fifty sensibly chosen and priced wines, starting with Cuvée St Pierre, Mommessin, at £4.25 (85p a glass). Several others are also relative bargains: Chablis Vaillon 1983, Servin (£9.20); Côtes-du-Rhône, Les Grangères, 1982, Labaume (£4.95); Rioja, Faustino V, 1978 (£4.95). You'll find a useful number of halves, and Muscat de Beaumes de Venise at 95p a glass for the puddings.

ST AUSTELL Cornwall

Boscundle Manor

2 m E of St Austell, off A390 TEL (072 681) 3557

OPEN 7.30 pm–9.30 pm CLOSED L, Sun, 23 Dec to 8 Feb (approx)
CREDIT CARDS Access/Euro, Amex, Visa WHEELCHAIR ACCESS Reasonable
VEGETARIAN DISHES On request ALC FOR TWO £28

Local business people as well as holiday-makers enjoy the comfort and friendly welcome the Flints provide in their 18th-century manor with its many fine antiques but 20th-century comforts. Mary Flint cooks local produce in straightforward ways, with some rich sauces on occasion. Her soups are good, and the grilled steaks and fish are also popular. Other possibilities are salmon hollandaise, duck with oranges, pork Normandy style, chocolate mousse and French apple flan. There are very few half-bottles on the wine list, and much of it seems more appropriate to the businessman than the holiday-maker (what sort of successful deal might be consummated with the Imperial of Ch Pontet-Latour 1975 at £85?), but the house wine is the very drinkable Listel from Provence (£5 a bottle, £1.25 a glass). Otherwise, splash out, perhaps, on Gewürztraminer, Les Sorcières 1976 (£12.75); Marqués de Riscal 1978 (red) at £7.25; Châteauneuf-du-Pape 1979, Pierre Ponnelle (£11.50); or one of the attractive clarets – Ch La Lagune 1976 (£14.75).

ST SAVIOUR see Jersey

SHANAGARRY Co Cork

Ballymaloe House

2 m E of Cloyne, on the Ballycotton road TEL Cork 652531

OPEN 1 pm–2 pm, from 7 pm CLOSED 24 to 26 Dec CREDIT CARDS All accepted WHEELCHAIR ACCESS Yes VEGETARIAN DISHES On request
TDH L IR£8 D IR£16.50

A relaxed country house – with its own farm, swimming-pool, tennis court and croquet lawn – where Mrs Allen cooks the fresh local ingredients with care and inspiration and Mr Allen buys some exceptional wine. The set menus might include lettuce and mint or artichoke soup; locally smoked eel; monkfish with green pepper sauce; sauté'd calf's liver with whiskey and tarragon; roast lamb, beef or pork; and 'today's catch' of lobster, well worth the IR£2 supplement. Sticky brown bread is delicious, vegetables crisply fresh, and do leave room for the excellent sweets. Service is pleasant, the pace leisurely. The strength of the rather eccentrically spelled wine list lies in its clarets, still impressive in 1970s and 1972s: Ch Latour du Pin Figeac 1970 (IR£17.50); Ch Beauregard 1971 (IR£19.50). There are several halves (Ch Beau Rivage 1979, IR£4.60). Burgundies are less exciting, but there are some interesting Rhônes: Hermitage 1978, Chave, IR£16; Condrieu 1980, Guigal, IR£18. The heavy VAT impost makes prices seem high, especially for non-vintage Champagne (Veuve Clicquot, IR£22). House red and white Burgundy are IR£8 a bottle.

SHEPTON MALLET Somerset

Bowlish House

Wells Road TEL (0749) 2022
OPEN 7.30 pm–10.30 pm CLOSED L, 4 days Chr CREDIT CARDS Not accepted
WHEELCHAIR ACCESS Yes VEGETARIAN DISHES Prefer notice
NO PIPES OR CIGARS IN RESTAURANT TDH £10.50 and £13

A mother being pestered with questions by her child said, 'Why don't you ask your father'; the reply was, 'I don't want to know *that* much about it.' You may have a similar reaction when you visit Brian Jordan's 18th-century wool-merchant's house: he is an enthusiast, with all the advantages and some of the disadvantages that implies. The hotel is comfortable, the new conservatory charming, the staff friendly and efficient, and Mr Jordan is concerned to give you value for money: 'More than you expect for less than you'd think.' The cooking – country-house style in the main – is done by committee, with staff rotating jobs, and the set meals testify to the success of the scheme: vegetable terrine; avocado with whitebait and anchovy cream; noisettes of lamb with three sauces; plaited brill fillets with white wine, cucumber and courgettes; kidneys with German sausage in port and paprika sauce; pot-au-feu; good cheeses, and lavish puddings. The wine list really should be published: it is a book of wine lore as well as a lengthy list of interesting wines, but one needs leisure to study the grape varieties of the world, the comparison chart of relative sweetness and weight, the statistics about wine-consumption and production, the explanations of labels, the analyses and maps for each region . . . . All good stuff, mind you, as are the wines themselves. To help you cope with the tome, Brian Jordan divides his list into sections. The first offers 15 wines at £3.50 each, Penedès Masía Vallformosa 1981, Métaireau's Anjou Rosé, and Chianti Putto, Colli Sensi, 1979 among them. Then come the 'quick lists', the top twenty white and red wines chosen most often during the past three years: Mülhofener Rosenberg 1981, Dyck (£5.50); Brouilly, Cuvée Anne de Millière, 1978, Hospice de

Beaujeu (£8.10); Colares Reserva 1974 (£4.80). Then comes the 'standard list', 145 wines from £4.50 to £9.95, colour-coded on white and pink paper, and with regional notes opposite each section; red dots indicate special value, for example, Fleurie, Les Terres Dessus, 1982, André Colonge (£7.80); Côte de Beaune-Villages 1977, Audiffred (£7.85); Sauvignon de St-Bris 1982, Brocard (£6.20); Eltviller Sonnenberg Spätlese 1976, Hans Lang (£6.70); Rapitalà Rosso 1981, Conte della Gatinais (£4.95); Marqués de Cáceres 1973 (£6.25); Bulgarian Cabernet Sauvignon 1978 (£4.45). It is also good to see litre bottles of the excellent red from the Caves Co-opératives at Fronton, Côtes du Fronton, at £4.50. The 'very special wine list' (from £8 to £25) follows next, with, for example, Châteauneuf-du-Pape, Domaine du Vieux Télégraphe, 1977, Brunier (£12.85); Knudsen Erath Pinot Noir 1978 (£11.45); Vouvray 1970, Marc Brédif (£11.75). Two pages of fine Italian wines include three vintages of Brunello di Montalcino, five of Sassicaia from Marchese Mario Incisa della Rocchetta (1979, £12.30); Gavi, 1981, Tenuta San Pietro (£10.15); Chardonnay di San Michele, Vigneto Zaraosti, 1982, Zeni (£8.20). Fifteen dessert wines are offered by the glass: Italian Vin Santo, Portuguese Moscatel de Setúbal, Italian Tanit, Austrian Bouvier Trockenbeerenauslese, all between £1 and £2. No, son, this isn't the end: there's a separate list of fine clarets, Burgundies, German wines, dessert wines and Champagnes. The clarets run from Ch Branaire-Ducru 1958 (£20.20) to Ch Calon-Ségur 1973 (£12.60), with many fine names and vintages in between; the German list is mostly the excellent 1971s and 1976s; the dessert wines include three vintages of Ch d'Yquem (1950, £78.65), three Tokays and even a 1964 Eszencia, £39.65 (50 cl); the Champagnes run from Georges Goulet NV at £10.95 to Bollinger, Vieilles Vignes Françaises 1970 (pre-phylloxera vines) at £46.80. Those with stamina (next week *War and Peace*?) will now reach the dozen impressive ports, and deserve them: Taylor 1945 (£53.20); Cockburn 1970 (£12.05).

SHINFIELD Berkshire

Milton Sandford

Church Lane TEL (0734) 883783

OPEN 7 pm–9.30 pm CLOSED L, Sun, last week July, 1 week Aug
CREDIT CARDS All accepted WHEELCHAIR ACCESS 4 steps
VEGETARIAN DISHES With notice TDH £16.75

Richard Sandford's former vicarage is coolly elegant in the modern manner, the spacious dining-room and bar softened by fresh flowers – and a fire in winter. His cooking is modern too, a blend of English and French, offering a wide choice on the set dinner menu: Brixham scallop and puff pastry tart, fillet of sole filled with leek soufflé, hot beetroot soup with almonds, French beans with crispy bacon; followed by roast saddle of lamb and garlic, calf's liver avocado, roast poussin on a raspberry butter sauce, or roast suckling pig with glazed turnips. There are good French cheeses before home-made ices or sorbets, or more decadent chocolate concoctions. Wine-lovers in particular are irritated by the habit of serving a 'surprise' sorbet between the first and second courses. Richard Sandford now has well over 200 bins, many of them red Burgundy, since he is keen to persuade his customers that other wines exist besides claret. The special Burgundy list is mainly made up of individual growers who bottle their own wine. He thinks that though many of the wines are young, they are very drinkable now: from Domaine Armand Rousseau, Gevrey-Chambertin 1978 and 1979, at £14.80 and £14.60; from Domaine Marquis d'Angerville, Volnay-Champans 1978 (£17.10); nine wines from Tollot-Beaut, including Chorey-lès-Beaune 1979 (£12.40); eight from Leroy (Volnay, Santenots, 1976, £25.25); from Domaine Dujac, Morey-St-Denis 1978 (£18.25); and from a new estate, Domaine Machard de Gramont, Pommard, Les Vignots, 1976 (£15.50). The main list begins with excellent house wines at rock-bottom prices: Viña Ardanza and Chardonnay du Haut Poitou (£5.50; £2.75 a half-bottle). Others are equally well chosen: Bourgogne Rosé de Marsannay 1979, Clair-Däu (£7.80); Morgon, Domaine des Versauds, 1983, Georges Duboeuf (£7.35); Ch St-Jérome 1978 (£7.30); Ch de Sales 1976 (£13); from 11 1970s, Clos l'Eglise, CB (£22); Chablis, Montée de Tonnerre, 1982, Durup (£12.50); Hermitage 1979, Guigal (£13.90); Graacher Himmelreich 1979, Friedrich Wilhelm (£9.75); California Pinot Noir 1979, Sanford & Benedict (£16.90); Gewürztraminer, Les Sorcières, 1979, Dopff & Irion (£3.95 a half). As well as the special list of dessert wines by the glass, the main list offers Vouvray Moelleux 1971, Foreau (£11.80); Veuve Clicquot 'Rich England', NV (£16.25); and Gewürztraminer, Sélection de Grains Nobles, Vendange Tardive, 1976, Hugel (£23).

SOUTH MOLTON Devon

Stumbles

134 East Street TEL (076 95) 3683

OPEN 12.30 pm–2.30 pm, 7.30 pm–10 pm CLOSED Chr Day
CREDIT CARDS All accepted WHEELCHAIR ACCESS To wine bar only
VEGETARIAN DISHES Yes ALC FOR TWO £22 WINE BAR LUNCH About £5

The lively young Potters run this complex of restaurant, wine-bar and hotel, with a 'sun-trap' courtyard and children's playground thrown in. Lunch in the wine bar – or courtyard – offers grills, salads, toasted sandwiches, and such innovations (for a wine-bar menu) as garlic-grilled mussels, guacamole, and crab Voltaire. There's granary bread, sticky sweets and good coffee, too. Dinner is more ambitious, with aillade, tagliatelle carbonara, ceviche, venison and mushroom pâté, veal escalope with kidney and Stilton, poached brill with Champagne sauce, lamb cutlets béarnaise, and more of those delicious sweets. The wine bar has eight wines by glass or bottle, including the house Mouflon d'Or (red and white) at £5.50 a litre, 80p a glass. The full list is available if you wish. There are over 60 sketchily annotated wines, several in half-bottle, and none greedily priced: Crémant de Bourgogne £8.50; Muscadet-sur-Lie, Domaine de la Cognardière, 1982 (£6.60); Cabernet Sauvignon 1976, Souverain (£11.50).

STAMFORD Lincolnshire

George of Stamford

71 St Martin's TEL (0780) 55171

OPEN 12.30 pm–2.30 pm, 7 pm–10.30 pm CREDIT CARDS All accepted
WHEELCHAIR ACCESS Yes VEGETARIAN DISHES On request
ALC FOR TWO £32 BUFFET LUNCH From £3.75

This ancient inn – part of a small East Anglian group, Poste Hotels Ltd *(see also Huntingdon)* – offers a generous buffet in the Garden Lounge and bars: roast joints, venison sausages on sauerkraut, baked salmon, pies, and salads. The oak-panelled restaurant is more sedate, with a busy traffic in trolleys: one for pâtés, one for smoked fish, and one for the massive sirloin, a speciality. Other dishes include Gruyère fritters, salmon quenelles with watercress sauce, seafood pot, half a roast duck with orange sauce, osso buco, and various creamy puddings. A list of a dozen Italian wines, all DOC, is suggested with the buffet food: Vernaccia di San Gimignano 1983 (£6.95); Chianti Classico 1980, Lilliano (£5.90). The restaurant list has about 70 bottles: Touraine Blanc Foussy Brut (£8.95); Gewürztraminer 1982, Pierre Sparr (£8.25; £4.15 a half); Crozes-Hermitage Rochefine 1981, Jaboulet-Vercherre (£8.10); Ch Rausan-Ségla 1978 (£15.50). Full marks for offering (on the menu) glasses of Moulin Touchais 1959 at £1.50. Warre's 1960 Port is £2.50 a glass.

STONHAM Suffolk

Mr Underhill's

On A140, 300 yds S of junction with A1120 TEL (0449) 711206

OPEN D only, 7.30 pm–8.45 pm CLOSED L, Sun, Mon CREDIT CARD Visa
WHEELCHAIR ACCESS Yes VEGETARIAN DISHES With notice
NO SMOKING IN RESTAURANT TDH £15.95

The Bradleys aim at running a sophisticated 'London-style' restaurant in the heart of the country, and they do better than succeed, since this elegant little place with its good linen and lithographs is much more appealing – and much better value – than many London equivalents. The style is *nouvelle cuisine*, a choiceless set menu, based on the day's shopping and the recipes of the masters – Vergé, Bocuse, Guérard, et al: harlequin omelette Roger Vergé, gravad lax with mustard sauce, boudin noir, carrot tourte; fillet of beef with green peppercorn sauce, suprême of chicken with garden herbs, bitter chocolate granita, rhubarb tart with clove cream. The house wines, all Loire, are imported direct from Domaine des Eschardières, in the Launay family for 150 years: Sauvignon 1983, Vin Gris de Pineau d'Aunis 1982, Gamay 1982, and Cabernet 1981, all £5.75 a bottle. There are also house Champagnes from Bonnaire of Cramant: a Blanc de Blancs, a Crémant, a demi-sec and a 'non-dose' at £12.50, and a 1978 Brut at £13.75. Other highlights include Montlouis, Domaine des Liards, 1980 (£7.45); Chablis Blanchots 1978, Laroche (£13.05); Riesling, Cuvée Speciale, 1981, Gisselbrecht (£7.60); Ch des Moulinettes 1975 (£8.45); Ch Potensac 1970 (£14.60); Blagny, La Piece sous le Bois, 1978, Pernot (£12.45); St-Joseph 1978, Noyer (£8.75); Sassicaia 1977 (£13.95); Christopher's Barsac, NV (£6.80). There are bin-ends, special food and wine evenings, a newsletter, and the offer for sale of the fine mustards and oils used in the kitchen.

STORRINGTON West Sussex

Manleys

Manleys Hill TEL (090 66) 2331

OPEN 12 noon–2 pm, 7 pm–9 pm CLOSED Mon, Sun D, 1st week Jan, last week Aug, 1st two weeks Sept CREDIT CARDS All accepted
WHEELCHAIR ACCESS Yes VEGETARIAN DISHES On request ALC FOR TWO £35
TDH SUN L £11.50

Karl Loederer, the former distinguished chef of plush Gravetye Manor *(East Grinstead)*, opened up his own plush little restaurant in a Queen Anne house. It feels slightly cramped, though comfortable. The menu is still on the grand Gravetye scale, classical French cooking with Austrian overtones. The result is rich: petit flan de homard en habit rouge (the 'habit' is a lobster-flavoured soufflé), gâteau de foies de volaille sauce Nantua, délices de sole aux langoustines et son coulis au vin rouge, venison steak with red cabbage and a red wine sauce, Rahm Geschnetzeltes mit Käse überbacken und Spinat Spätzli (strips of veal in a piquant sauce, baked with cheese and served with green noodles), magret de canard grillé à la savoyarde (with shredded Chinese leaves and smoked ham), gratinée de sabayon au Crème de Menthe, Salzburger Nockerln ('lemon-flavoured soufflé cooked in honey and cream' doesn't begin to describe this superb pudding). The hundred wines are far from cheap, but they have been carefully chosen and annotated. For white, consider Schwarzhofberger 1979, Egon Müller (£11.40); Johannisberger Klaus Spätlese 1975, H H Eser (£10.50); the Austrian Neuburger 1983, Ing H&M Buck (£6.20); Muscadet, Ch de l'Oiselinière, 1982 (£6.20); Corton-Charlemagne 1981, Tollot-Beaut (£24.90). There are some classy reds, difficult to match to such elaborate food: Ch Cantemerle 1967, CB (£22.50); Ch Nénin 1971 (£19.50); Beaune, Clos du Roi, 1981, Tollot-Beaut (£16.50); Pommard, Les Grands Epenots, Domaine de Montille 1979 (£60.50 a magnum). The strong showing of Paul Jaboulet Rhônes might be a good choice: Côtes-du-Rhône-Villages 1970 (£13.40); Côte-Rôtie, Les Jumelles 1978 (£16.90); Châteauneuf-du-Pape, Les Cèdres, 1969 (£25). Finish with a toast to the Austrian chef in the luscious Ruster Trockenbeerenauslese 1979, Sepp-Höld (£21.80).

STRANDHILL Co Sligo

Knockmuldowney

Culleenamore TEL Sligo 68122

OPEN D only, 7.30 pm–10 pm CLOSED L, Sun & Mon (exc public holidays), late Jan to early Mar CREDIT CARDS All accepted WHEELCHAIR ACCESS Through kitchen VEGETARIAN DISHES On request TDH IR£10 ALC FOR TWO IR£27

The Coopers' old house, overlooking the sea, has pigs and hens as well as trees and roses. The atmosphere is pleasantly relaxed and the cooking straightforward: smoked salmon, leeks tartare, chicken broth, poached salmon, sirloin steak with mushroom sauce, blackcurrant fool, raspberry Pavlova. The French house wine is IR£6.60 a bottle, IR£1.50 a glass. Thirty clarets dominate the wine-list: Ch Livran 1978 (IR£9.20); Ch Phélan-Ségur 1975 (IR£18.80), Ch Malartic-Lagravière 1970 (IR£24.60). Other reds worth noting include: Ch de Haut Serre 1978 (Cahors) at IR£10.80; Moulin-à-Vent 1976, Georges Duboeuf (IR£15.50); Monthélie 1978, Lupé-Cholet (IR£19.50); Hermitage 1981, Chave (IR£14.60). Marqués de Riscal 1975 (IR£9.20); Ch Musar 1972 (the earliest vintage extant?) at IR£9.90. White wines include Meursault Blagny 1978, Jadot (IR£16.40); Riesling, Cuvée des Evêques, 1980 (IR£8.90); Binger St Rochuskapelle Spätlese 1979, Guntrum (IR£8.90); Johannisberg Riesling 1978, Ch St Jean (IR£9.20), a delicious bargain from California.

SWANSEA West Glamorgan

Drangway Restaurant

66 Wind Street TEL (0792) 461397

OPEN 12.15 pm–2.15 pm, 7.30 pm–10 pm CLOSED Sun, Mon
CREDIT CARDS All accepted WHEELCHAIR ACCESS Yes
VEGETARIAN DISHES Yes NO-SMOKING ALCOVE
TDH L From £5.45 D From £8.95 ALC FOR TWO £27

Colin Pressdee's bentwood and green restaurant makes a relaxing, garden-like setting in which to enjoy his *nouvelle*-style cooking, whether in the leisurely *menu dégustation* which introduces a series of small courses (£13.95) or from the other menus, a flexible mixture of *à la carte* and *table d'hôte*. Fresh local ingredients are used as far as possible, and it is good to see cockles as well as mussels given the marinière treatment, and Welsh cawl and laverbread flan making an appearance, either here or in the adjacent 1266 Wine Bar *(see the WINE BARS section)*. Other popular dishes include fish market terrine with beurre blanc, salmon with sorrel, fillet of beef 'en chevreuil', crème brûlée, and various ice-creams and sorbets. Standards appear to have been uneven during the past year: is Mr Pressdee devoting too much time to his new ventures? (These include canning laverbread and opening another wine-bar in Mumbles.) Luckily there is nothing uneven about the wine or its service. Much of the 100-bottle list is imported by the proprietor; others are also well chosen. Ch de la Cassemichère is represented by its Muscadet-sur-Lie 1982 (£6.75) and Le Chouan (Chardonnay) 1982 (£5.45). Others include magnums of Santenay Les Gravières 1973, Prosper Maufoux (£25.95); Ch de Selle Rosé 1980, Domaines Ott (£10.95); Wehlener Sonnenuhr Auslese 1982, Bergweiler (£8.95); Saumur Champigny 1981, Fonteyn (£6.25); Savigny-lès-Beaune Les Guettes 1970, Doudet-Naudin (£15.25); Ch Pitray 1975 (£8.95); Ch Batailley 1961 (£21.95). And what a chance to compare 1966 and 1948 Latour, each £39.75! French house wine is £5.45 a litre, 75p a glass.

TAUNTON Somerset

Castle Hotel

Castle Green TEL (0823) 72671
OPEN 12.30 pm–2 pm, 7.30 pm–9 pm CREDIT CARDS All accepted
WHEELCHAIR ACCESS Yes VEGETARIAN DISHES On request
TDH L From £6.90 D £14.90 ALC FOR TWO £50

The Chapman family believe in Highly Visible Management in their Norman fortress hotel, 'divine in wistaria season'. Everything is Highly Visible at the Castle, including the prices, but the comfort and luxury are certainly there, and obviously enjoyed by the many transatlantic visitors. The chef produces a set 'dinner of the week' as well as a short *carte* which changes less frequently: dishes in the *nouvelle* style, with rather verbose description ('warm calf's brain finished with shallots, chives and its own juices, presented on a salad'). Start with a creamy soup, mousse, terrine or fishy salad, before, say, 'fillet of fresh huss, placed on a peppered cream sauce served with crisp spinach', or veal steak in Madeira, or loin of lamb wrapped in a caul with its sweetbreads, laid on a rosemary sauce. Vegetables at inspection were so *al dente* they bounced off the plate when prodded. Some dishes are erratic, and service is also hit-and-miss at times. The wine list is a massive 400 or so bins long, with something for everyone, or at least everyone who can afford to eat here. The carafe wines are Thévenin and Lamblin's red and white vin de table, at £5.40 for 50 cl, 85p a glass. Twenty house wines include Ch Millegrand, NV, a Minervois from Eldridge Pope (£5.05); Averys Clochemerle Rouge and Blanc, NV, at £5.95, and Barton & Guestier's Sauvignon de Bordeaux, NV (£4.65). Eight pages of clarets start gently with, for example, Ch Segonzac 1979 (£7.60) and Ch Le Piat 1978 (£10). But it would be easy to be bewitched by Ch La Lagune 1976 (£22.50) or Ch Cos d'Estournel 1971 (£29), to say nothing of the runs of premiers crus from 1953 – or earlier – to 1976 (Lafite-Rothschild, Mouton-Rothschild, Latour – with the 1934 thrown in at £125; Margaux, Haut Brion – the 1934 is £99.50 for this one, and

Cheval Blanc). There are others in single figures when you come down to earth again. The Beaujolais are mostly 1982s (Moulin-à-Vent, Ferraud, £9), red Burgundies much older: Peter Chapman revises a section of his list at a time, on the painting-the-Forth-Bridge system, and the list we have on file was having its Burgundies revamped. As with clarets, there are impressive names and vintages: Bonnes-Mares 1961, Comte de Vogüé, at £70 a magnum; Vosne-Romanée Les Suchots 1972, Averys at £21.75; and a youthful Givry, Clos du Cellier aux Moins, 1982, Delorme at £10.50. White Burgundies include Puligny-Montrachet 1978, Remoissenet (£17.90). Jaboulet Hermitages and Châteauneufs from Loeb dominate the Rhône section. The reputedly long-lived Ch Rayas (white) from Reynaud is present in its 1962 vintage for testing. The Loire and the German sections also make good reading – and drinking – and it is encouraging to see listed seven Somerset wines: Müller-Thurgau 1982 could be compared from Wootton (£8.50) and Pilton Manor (£8.80). There is a page of fine Champagne, another of New World wines, yet another of port, starting with Cockburn 1927 at £130 and listing several 1960s and 1966s by the glass – only one or two can be opened at the same time, but Cockburns Special Reserve and Taylor's LBV Reserve, 1976, are always available (£1.20 a glass), as are Averys Finest Old Sercial and Bual. To end at the beginning, don't neglect the splendid range of sherries, including Don Zoilo Fino and Oloroso, at £1.10 a glass; Averys Elizabetha (£1.10); La Guita Manzanilla (£1); and Averys Palo Cortado (£1.10). A wine weekend is held in November.

THORNBURY Avon

Thornbury Castle

At the north end of the village, behind the parish church tower — TEL (0454) 412647

OPEN 1 pm–2 pm, 7 pm–9.30 pm CLOSED Chr CREDIT CARDS All accepted WHEELCHAIR ACCESS Yes VEGETARIAN DISHES No TDH L £15.50 ALC FOR TWO £40

Henry VIII, Anne Boleyn, and Mary Tudor slept here (not all three together), and you may, too, now that Kenneth Bell has converted some of the rooms in his handsome castle into luxurious bedrooms. The baronial dining-rooms, the crenellated walls overlooking Mr Bell's vines (his Müller-Thurgau 1983 is on the wine list, £9.50), the Jacob sheep and the wild boar, all switch you into a time warp. Prices are distinctly inflation-modern, but the menu boasts many old English dishes, as well as some more *nouvelle*: iced strawberry soup, Dover sole and crayfish in puff pastry with a saffron sauce, Severn salmon poached with wild asparagus, turbot baked with fresh ginger and lime, mint and blackcurrant sorbet, hot treacle tart. Note that there is a cover charge of £1.50 four evenings a week in the large dining-room to finance the pianist: many guests would prefer silence. Service is polished and considerate. The Thornbury wine list runs into hundreds of items, and Kenneth Bell has considerately extracted fifty bins under £10 for those unwilling to plough through the considerable riches of the main list. These include Viña Ardanza 1976 (£7.50); Ch La Tour Bicheau 1981 (£8.50); Viña Esmeralda 1982, Torres (£6.50); and St Véran 1983, Louis Tête (£8.75). French listings are particularly strong, but few restaurants can better the two pages of California wines, starting with Paul Masson litre carafes at £7.05, and continuing with five Chardonnays (Rutherford Hill 1979, £16.25); six Johannisberger Rieslings, three of them late-harvest wines (Firestone Selected Harvest 1978, £18.25); six Zinfandels (Ch Montelena 1977, £15); and 11 Cabernet Sauvignons (Iron Horse 1978, £19.75). Spain's two dozen include Jean León's distinguished Chardonnay 1981 (£14.50), and Viña Zaco 1969 (£9.75). Sixty Bordeaux are evenly divided between bottles and half-bottles, another consideration seldom shown the drinker who wishes to try more than one wine. These range (in bottle) from Sichel's Bel Air Claret (£6.40), to Ch Calon-Ségur 1961, CB (£70), via Ch Chicane 1979 (£7.40), Ch Coufran 1976 (£16.90), and Ch Ducru-Beaucaillou 1966, Berry Bros (£46); and in halves: Ch Chasse-Spleen 1979 (£6.05); Ch Trottevieille 1953, Averys (£10.50); Ch Latour 1960 (£19.50), and 1948 (£28). Twenty sweet Bordeaux leave you embarrassed for choice: Ch St-Armand 1979 at £4.75 a half-bottle; Ch Rayne-Vigneau 1975 at £14.50; Ch Coutet 1918 at £77.50. Red Burgundies include Bourgogne Pinot Noir 1978, Parisot (£8); Volnay Santenots 1971, Sichel (£19.75); and Nuits-St-Georges, Clos de la Maréchale 1976, Faiveley (£18.50). Amongst red Rhônes are Ch de Ruth 1976 (£8.50), and Châteauneuf-du-Pape, La Bernardine, 1978, Chapoutier (£13.50). Haut Poitou is represented by four wines, a Sauvignon, a Chardonnay, a rosé de Cabernet and a Richaumoine, all between £4.75 and £6.15. Alsace is remarkable for the eight Hugel Vendange Tardive wines (Gewürztraminer 1969, £24). Passing over some decent Sichel and Loeb German wines, we arrive breathlessly at the page of ports. Warre's Nimrod is a reasonable £10.75; once into vintage port, you can choose from, among many others, Taylor's Crusted 1963 (£27), Cockburn 1960 (£30), Guimaraens 1946 (£45), and Warre 1924 (£65). There are two pages of bin-ends, equally beguiling, but they will have changed by the time you read this. . . .

TOTNES Devon

Elbow Room

6 North Street TEL (0803) 863480

OPEN 12 noon–2 pm, 7.30 pm–9.30 pm CLOSED Sun, Mon, Sat L, Tue D, 2 weeks Feb, 2 weeks Nov CREDIT CARDS Amex, Visa
WHEELCHAIR ACCESS Impossible VEGETARIAN DISHES On request
ALC FOR TWO £26

The Sellicks' converted cider-press makes a relaxed and attractive restaurant, and there is a garden for summer lunches or evening aperitifs. The eclectic menu offers crab chowder, pineapple japonaise, rognons d'agneau au Roquefort, turbot Marguéry, roast duck with sage and onion stuffing, roast lamb with lemon and walnut stuffing, and some delicious creamy puddings, the meringues being a special favourite. Simpler lunches include hot roast joints, sandwiches, pies and salads. There are 90 wines, not fully enough annotated, and strongest in claret: Ch Segonzac 1976 (£8.35); Ch Cantemerle 1967 (£24.50). Others worth trying include Côtes du Ventoux, NV, Thévenin (£5.80); Alsace Riesling 1981, Domaine d'Engelgarten (£7.95); Oppenheimer Schloss Beerenauslese 1976, Herman Martin (£30.15). French house wine is £4.65 a bottle, 85p a glass.

ULLSWATER Cumbria

Sharrow Bay Hotel

2 m S of Pooley Bridge, signed Howtown TEL (08536) 301/483

OPEN 1 pm–1.45 pm, 8 pm–8.45 pm CLOSED Dec, Jan, Feb
CREDIT CARDS Not accepted WHEELCHAIR ACCESS Yes
VEGETARIAN DISHES Yes NO-SMOKING AREA
TDH L £16.50 D £22.50

It's a Lakeland institution, this cherished and burnished house overlooking Ullswater, richly antiqued and richly catered. Dinner can seem like an alumni reunion as regulars compare notes on favourite dishes. The set meals offer an unnerving choice of over 20 first courses, with relative restraint in the half-dozen main ones, and a mere eight sweets; the fish course and sorbet are choiceless. The style is English country house with a French flavour, helpings are generous and cream hard to avoid. Roasts are very popular, whether Scotch beef sirloin and fillet, or poulet à l'estragon; local salmon and lamb are well treated, and various creamy concoctions of sweetbreads, guinea-fowl or pork are also praised. This is the place for real puddings: chocolate pye, sticky toffee sponge, bread-and-butter pudding, lemon honeycomb mould. There are over 140 wines, about half of them in half-bottle (a worthy example to other restaurateurs), with the emphasis on France. Pick your way through the alternative vintages (the signature of a list compiled mainly by Youdell of Kendal): if money is no object, there are many mature first-growth wines; if you have to watch the pennies, there are still appealing bottles. Burgundies, drawn mostly from Louis Latour, include Chassagne-Montrachet 1979 (£19.60); Santenay 1976 (£15.65); and Aloxe-Corton 1971 (£50 a magnum). Clarets start with Ch des Tuileries 1978 (£6.90), rise through Ch Plagnac 1975 (£11.30), and Ch L'Angélus 1970 (£40.75) to Chx Margaux, Mouton-Rothschild and Lafite 1961 (£298). The attractive German section offers Zeltinger Sonnenuhr Auslese 1976, Freiherr von Schorlemer (£13.60) and Bretzenheimer Vogelsang Beerenauslese 1971, Graf von Plettenberg (£30). From other areas, choose from Sauvignon de Touraine 1983 (£6.15); Vouvray 1978, Marc Brédif (£10); Alsace Cuvée les Amours, Pinot Blanc de Blancs 1981 (£7.10); Marqués de Cáceres Reserva 1973 (red, £8.75). Champagne starts with Perrier-Jouët Grand Brut, specially bottled for the *Relais et Châteaux* (£19.75). A half-bottle of Ch Lafaurie-Peyraguey 1975 (£9.90) would see off one of the puddings in great style. There are various good digestifs by the glass, and also several vintage ports by the bottle: Cockburn 1955 (£45). Note the final page of bin-ends.

UPHALL West Lothian

Houstoun House

On A899, West of Uphall TEL (0506) 853831

OPEN 12.30 pm–2 pm, 7.30 pm–9.30 pm CLOSED 1 & 2 Jan
CREDIT CARDS Access/Euro, Amex, Diners WHEELCHAIR ACCESS Impossible
VEGETARIAN DISHES With notice TDH L £9.50 D £14

The Knights' hotel, 13 miles from Edinburgh, is an ancient laird's house, sensitively adapted to its modern function. The bar is stone-floored with a vast fire-place, the first-floor dining-rooms quietly elegant. The set meals provide a reasonable choice of mostly French food, with some leaven from Russia, North Africa and the Caribbean: timbale of scallops in an orange cream, 'true' rissole of lambs' sweetbreads and mushrooms (a delicate deep-fried pastry concoction), cromesquis of seafood polonnaise, duck breast with raspberries and green pepper, venison braised in port, roast pheasant with Gewürztraminer and mushrooms, Virgin Island fruit pie with rum, home-made fruit ices. Standards are rather uneven – vegetables seem to pose problems. The service is not always paced to customers' needs, and it is sometimes difficult to get a given wine to table at the same time as the food it is to accompany. This can impede one's enjoyment of one of the best wine cellars in the country. The list runs to 35 pages, impossible to absorb in a few minutes, so it is worth arriving early enough for a leisurely read in the bar and ordering well before the meal. It is possible to drink cheaply here, but the eye is constantly drawn to the rare treasures also on offer. From Bordeaux you could settle for a Fronsac, Ch Roc St-Bernard 1978 (£6), or take the opportunity to try Ch La Fleur Pétrus 1964 (£22), or Ch Ausone 1961 (£60), or Ch Giscours 1961 (£25). That would leave almost 30 1961s for future visits. Red Burgundies begin modestly enough with Bourgogne Rouge 1976, Drouhin (£9), but soon the choice includes Le Chambertin, Domaine Louis Trapet, 1969 (£26.50); Corton, Les Pougets 1949, Louis Latour (£40); Beaune, Clos des Mouches, 1969, Drouhin (£20), and so many more. Jumping over some fine Beaujolais and Rhônes – and pausing at 'Other French reds' only long enough to note a bargain, Corsica's best wine, the fruity, characterful Domaine de Torraccia 1979, at £4.30 – one lands in Italy, where there are Sassicaia 1977, Marchese della Roccheta (£14), and Brunello di Montalcino 1971, Biondi-Santi (£30). California makes a strong showing with, for example, Firestone's Merlot 1978 (£8), and Australia's listing includes Brown Brothers' Milawa Koombahla Cabernet Sauvignon 1979 (£9.50). The white wines are equally distinguished, with several dry white Bordeaux (Ch

Malartic-Lagravière 1979, £11.40); 11 good Chablis; three pages of mouth-watering white Burgundies (Meursault, Les Poruzots 1961, Bouchard Aîné, £21 – and still going strong?); a page of Loires with slightly elderly Muscadet but a bargain in the sweetly delicious Moulin Touchais 1959 (£9); two pages of Alsace wines (Gewürztraminer, Les Sorcières, 1979, Dopff & Irion, £9.20); three of German wines, carefully annotated in a way too rarely seen (Waldracher Sonnenberg Auslese 1976, Scherf, £10.90, and Bernkasteler Doctor Auslese 1971, Bergweiler-Prüm, £26). California and Australia are not neglected – nor is the solitary drinker, since the last four pages list half-bottles, from £3 to £47.50. If you have the stamina, repair to the bar for one of the many fine malt whiskies it stocks.

UPPINGHAM Leicestershire

The Lake Isle ⓥ

16 High Street East TEL (0572) 822951
OPEN 12 noon–2 pm, 7.30 pm–10 pm CLOSED Mon, Sun D
CREDIT CARDS Access/Euro, Visa WHEELCHAIR ACCESS Yes
VEGETARIAN DISHES Yes TDH D £12.50 SUN L £6.50 SNACK LUNCH £4.50

The Whitfields plan major refurbishments and the introduction of two guest bedrooms before 1985. This is a plain high-street restaurant with few pretensions, set meals cooked to an acceptable standard, and a wine list with some fascinating bargains. The French menus offer a limited choice in each course: potato and leek or broccoli soup, perhaps; pigeon salad or sole with basil butter; gigot with spinach, poussin grillé au Roquefort or rendezvous de fruits de mer à la crème de Chambéry; up to a dozen English and French cheeses; and home-made ice-cream, banana and walnut tart, or lime soufflé. The wine list is sketchy on spelling and annotation, but a great deal can be forgiven in the face of such ungrasping prices (the mark-up is a fixed one) and such interesting bottles. Le Dauphin from Reynier is the basic house wine at £5.50 a litre, but another dozen also listed as house wines include Dopff & Irion's Crystal d'Alsace, NV (£4.85), and Castillo de Tiebas 1975 (from Navarre) at £4.60. There are many other wines under £6: Ch de Ruth 1980, Meffre (£5.85), for example, and Clos de Ste-Catherine 1981, a honeyed Coteaux de Layon (£6.50). From number 100 on the list, things become more serious, with several pages of fine Bordeaux and Burgundy: Ch Phélan-Ségur 1959 (£27.50); Ch Coufran 1967 (£9.75); Ch Croizet-Bages 1971 (£13.70); Ch La Tour-Blanche 1970 (£13.75); Beaune, Marconnets 1961, Bouchard Père et Fils (£21.10); Chorey-lès-Beaune 1978, Joseph Drouhin (£11.25); Chablis, Les Clos 1979, Louis Michel (£12.75). There are several worthwhile half-bottles, to say nothing of the ten vintage ports: Warre, Croft and Cockburn's 1960 (from £23 to £25.85) and five 1963s. Five ports are offered by the glass each evening. A bin-ends list may tempt you further, and there are gastronomic dinners during the winter, wine and cheese evenings in the summer.

WATERMILLOCK Cumbria

Leeming on Ullswater Country House Hotel

On A592 TEL (085 36) 444

OPEN 12.30 pm–1.45 pm, 7.30 pm–8.45 pm CLOSED 1 Jan to mid-March
CREDIT CARDS All accepted WHEELCHAIR ACCESS Yes
VEGETARIAN DISHES Yes TDH BUFFET L £5.75 D £16.75

This member of the Prestige Hotel group is a Victorian 'Georgian' manor with velvet lawns rolling down to Ullswater and immaculately maintained rooms. The Fitzpatricks clearly enjoy running the place and the atmosphere is very welcoming. The set dinner offers a generous choice in each course, and the style is country-house with touches of more modern cookery: rabbit and hazelnut terrine with home-made chutney, smoked turkey with tomato vinaigrette, cream of asparagus, roast loin of lamb with apple and redcurrant stuffing, turbot steak with seafood soufflé, pot-roast guinea-fowl with Calvados sauce, Linzertorte, chestnut bavarois. Vegetables are carefully cooked. The wine list – mainly from Youdell of Kendal – has the Youdell weakness of listing too many alternative vintages: a hotel with pretensions ought to be willing to reprint its list as necessary. The house wine, not listed, is a French magnum at £7.16 (£1 a glass). The emphasis in general is French, with several pages of red Bordeaux, listed by commune: Ch Gazin 1975 (£27.60); Ch Beau Site 1970 (£11.80). In Burgundy, Morgon 1981, Louis Latour, is £8.15; Richebourg 1971, Charles Viénot, £31.50; Chablis, Les Clos 1982, Vocoret, £11.53. A page of sparkling wine has, among more conventional offerings, Roederer Champagne Rosé, NV, at £20.98, and Henkell Trocken, NV, at £6.95. Play Russian roulette and order Winkeler Hasensprung Auslese, either 1971 or 1976, Deinhard (£15.57): you can hardly lose. The same cannot be said of Hugel's Riesling Vendange Tardive, either 1976 or 1981, at £27.30 – an acceptable price, perhaps, for the 1976, but not for the 1981, which needs years of maturity. An especially praiseworthy aspect of this list is the large number of halves, showing that it can be done, after all.

WEST RUNTON Norfolk

Mirabelle

Station Road TEL (026 375) 396

OPEN 12.30 pm–2 pm, 7 pm–9.15 pm CLOSED Mon, first half Nov
CREDIT CARDS All accepted WHEELCHAIR ACCESS Yes
VEGETARIAN DISHES With notice TDH L £7 D £10.50 ALC FOR TWO £35

Rather characterless modern building with pleasant staff and a 'continental' menu which mingles fried whitebait, aubergine viennoise, Wienerschnitzel, grilled salmon and cucumber, venison steak with morels, supreme of chicken with Boursin and green pepper, peaches in Champagne sauce, and crêpes Suzette. The wine list lays three main claims to the wine-lover's attention (spelling is not one of them): it is divided roughly in half, with the front nine pages listing only wines under £12 a bottle; it also lists many old vintages now hard to find elsewhere; and, lastly, there is an impressive number of half-bottles. House wines begin with red and white vin de table from Reynier at £4.75 a bottle. From the front section, there is a fair choice in Bordeaux and Burgundy: Ch Malescot-St-Exupéry 1973 (£10.15 a half); Mercurey 1978, Bouchard Père et Fils (£8.50); Caillou-Blanc 1979 (the dry white wine from Ch Talbot) at £10.20. The Alsace section includes three different producers' Gewürztraminer, all under £8; German wines, as so often, lack adequate notation. The ten Austrians include Schloss Grafenegg 1979, Weingut Metternich (£6.55). Moving firmly into double figures allows you to sample clarets back to 1962 (Ch Beychevelle, CB, £27.75); Ch d'Yquem from an off-year (1965, £36.50); red Burgundies back to 1966 (Chambolle-Musigny, Doudet-Naudin, £27.50); white Burgundies back to 1971 (Bâtard Monrachet, Albert Morey, £32.25); and some impressive ports – Graham's 1955 (£35). Occasional wine dinners are held.

WHITWELL-ON-THE-HILL North Yorkshire

Whitwell Hall

On A64 TEL (065 381) 551

OPEN From 7.30 pm CLOSED L (exc by arrangement), 2 weeks Jan
CREDIT CARDS All accepted WHEELCHAIR ACCESS Yes
VEGETARIAN DISHES Yes NO SMOKING IN DINING-ROOM TDH £13

The promise of English cooking in a Gothic mansion in handsome countryside brings the tourists flocking, and they tuck into a four-course dinner (menu changed daily) of, perhaps, kipper pâté, country house soup, local game or fish with fresh vegetables, and gooseberry pie. The forty wines, from Yorkshire Fine Wines, are not greedily priced and offer an adequate choice: Kaseler Kehrnagel Trocken 1982 (£8.75); Rioja Viña Arana 1976 (£6.25); Ch Pontet-Canet 1975 (£17.10). French house wine is £5.40 for 70 cl, £1.05 a glass. They will get in wines for special occasions, if you wish.

WILLITON Somerset

White House

On A39 TEL (0984) 32306

OPEN 7.30 pm–8.30 pm CLOSED L; Nov to May CREDIT CARDS Not accepted
WHEELCHAIR ACCESS Yes VEGETARIAN DISHES No TDH £12

Dick and Kay Smith's hotel is a *very* white house indeed, and the Mediterranean feeling extends to the menu, which, though mainly French provincial, sneaks along the coast to include hummus, aubergine purée, potage à l'andalouse, and even further afield with satay, and safely back to England for the rich and creamy puddings. Favourite dishes include hot crab ramekins; tarte à la moutarde; loin of lamb with a cream and garlic sauce; ragout of prawns, tomatoes and peppers with tagliatelle; and Norfolk treacle tart. Vegetables, perfect specimens to begin with, are perfectly cooked. Dick Smith sensibly leaves a copy of his 18-page wine list in the hotel bedrooms, so that residents at least can give it the detailed attention it deserves (he would send a copy if you asked). The house wines are a red and a white Georges Duboeuf and a Hallgarten Niersteiner Gutes Domtal, all £4.20 a bottle, 75p a glass. Canard-Duchêne Champagne, NV, is £13 a bottle, £2.20 a glass, and the alternative sparkler is the prize-winning Saumur Mousseux from the Cave Co-opérative in St-Cyr-en-Bourg (£7.70 a bottle, £1.30 a glass). Among the high spots, consider Ch Carbonnieux 1980 (£12.50); Hermitage, Chante Alouette, 1975, Chapoutier (£14.50); Penedès Chardonnay 1980, Jean León (£10.50); Waldracher Hubertusberg Auslese 1971, Langenbach (£14); Brouilly , Ch des Tours, 1983, Georges Duboeuf (£7); Ménétou-Salon 1982, Jean Tellier (£6.80); Gigondas 1976, Vidal-Fleury (£8.80); Ch Bahans Haut-Brion, NV, a product of Haut-Brion's young vines, generally blended from two or more vintages, at £10; Tokay 1971, 5 puttonyos, £7.20 for half a litre. We have not yet touched on the four pages of reserve wines, which Mr Smith recommends ordering at least the morning before you plan to drink them, since none is stored at room temperature: clarets back to an Averys-bottled Ch Le Gay 1950 (£32), and also including Ch du Glana 1970, Gabriel Meffre (£16); Corton 'Diamond Jubilee' 1967, Remoissenet (£21); Hermitage La Chapelle 1972, Jaboulet (£20). The Spanish and Italian sections were due for revision as we went to press. Mr Smith's list should be sent to new restaurateurs who wish to learn how to inform the public without patronising them, and how to make their choice as easy as possible. This list is a model of conciseness and clarity, with tasting notes that sound as if they were written by a wine-lover but could be understood by a literate tyro eager to learn.

WINDERMERE Cumbria

Miller Howe

Rayrigg Road (A592) TEL (096 62) 2536
OPEN 8.30 pm (Sat 7 pm and 9.30 pm) CLOSED L; 1 Jan to 9 Mar
CREDIT CARDS Amex, Diners, Visa WHEELCHAIR ACCESS Impossible
VEGETARIAN DISHES With notice NO SMOKING IN RESTAURANT TDH £18.25

People either adore Miller Howe, or they do not: most do. It has its own high style: a handsome house with dramatic views over the lake to the Langdale Pikes beyond; comfortable and thoughtfully furnished bedrooms ('cluttered', say some); and a choiceless (except for dessert) five-course dinner, served at 8.30 pm, apart from Saturdays when the two sittings make for some tension. The food, based on the best and freshest of ingredients, is imaginative, elaborate, and difficult to match to wine, since John Tovey loves novel combinations, especially of sweet and savoury. By the time you reach your American coffee wheatmeal slice with warm walnut apricot sauce, you will have experienced two dozen or more separate flavours: the occasional faint-heart would love to spread dinner over 24 hours and savour each new delight to the full. Remember too that since dinner is so carefully synchronised, you will have little chance to linger over wine. Best in the circumstances to choose something light, fragrant or adaptable: the Hugel Muscat 1981 (£9.10), say, or Pierre Dupond's Fleurie 1982 (£8.95), or Château de Selle Rosé, Domaines Ott, 1981 (£13.50). These are on the main list of seventy wines; there is also a 'private wine list' with about 20 more expensive wines (Beaune-Grèves, 1976, Remoissenet, £20.70) and over 40 South African wines, selected by John Tovey on his winter trips: from KWV's Steen 1981 (£7.25), to Allesverloren Tinta Barocca 1978 (£7.80), with enough porty weight to fight the main course. The staff are well trained and friendly and you may find them offering you a Buck's Fizz before breakfast.

WITHERSLACK Cumbria

Old Vicarage

Off A590, ½ m W of village TEL (044 852) 381

OPEN D only, 7.30 pm for 8 pm CLOSED L, Chr week CREDIT CARDS All accepted NO SMOKING DURING MEAL TDH £13.50 (£14.50 non-res)

A small Georgian hotel in unspoilt Winster Valley, with its own pretty gardens and a relaxed and friendly atmosphere. Local produce is combined into well-balanced five-course dinners: courgette mousse hollandaise, lentil soup, roast loin of pork with orange and ginger sauce, fresh fruit salad and hasty pudding, cheeses. Vegetables are imaginative and carefully cooked. Two sweets are left on each table, and few refuse a taste of each. The wine list, composed with the advice of a Master of Wine and kept up to date by computer, could surely have fewer alternative vintages: many Lakeland restaurants with Youdell of Kendal as one of their suppliers share this weakness. Although there are no house wines as such, you may buy by the glass any wine costing £6.50 or less: for example, Ch des Tuileries 1978 (£5.15); Caillou Blanc du Ch Talbot 1978/81 (try for the latter), at £5.85; Mâcon Rouge 1982/83, Mommessin (£5.60); Muscadet-sur-Lie, Marquis de Goulaine, 1982 (£5.95); Côtes-du-Rhône-Villages, Caves des Papes, 1978 (£4.80); Bernkasteler Kurfürstlay 1982, Carl Reh (£5.90); Castillo Jumilla 1980, Bodegas Bleda (£4.95); Aveleda Vinho Verde 1982 (£4.60). These give a fair idea of the range of the list, though prices obviously go much higher for the finer wines: Ch Grand-Puy-Lacoste 1978 (£23.65); Ch Lafaurie-Peyraguey 1975 (£8.45 a half-bottle); Chassagne-Montrachet 1978, Raoul Clerget (£14.20); Hermitage Blanc, Chante Alouette, 1981, Chapoutier (£18.15); Brunello di Montalcino 1978, Cecchi (£13.95); Rioja, Gran Reserva 904, 1970 (£12.65); Fumé Blanc 1981, Mondavi (£14.20).

'Bring your own Bottle'

While every wine-lover is delighted to learn of restaurants with good food and splendid wine lists, there are many who have excellent cellars themselves and who welcome the opportunity to enjoy a meal out with rather better wine than they could afford at current restaurant prices; or whose budget is limited and who prefer to avoid high restaurant mark-ups on wine. In other words, there is a need to know about unlicensed places which allow you to take your own bottle in the knowledge that it will not be mishandled and that you will not have to pay a massive corkage charge. The following short list is an encouraging beginning. We hope to hear about many others before the next edition is published.

London

Barocco Bar 13 Moor Street, W1 TEL 01-437 2324 No corkage
Cheap, informal Italian place.

La Gaffe 109 Heath Street, NW3 TEL 01-435 4941 No corkage
Mainly French food with an Italian flavour, specialising in fish.

Good Friends 139 Salmon Lane, E14 TEL 01-987 5541 No corkage
East End Cantonese restaurant, often crowded: book.

Harry's 6 Kingly Street, W1 TEL 01-734 8708 No corkage
For hungry night-owls who like English food: open 10.30 pm to 6 am.

Luba's Bistro 6 Yeoman's Row, SW3 TEL 01-589 2950 No corkage
Hearty Russian food, variable standards, crowded surroundings.

Micro-Kalamaras 66 Inverness Mews, W2 TEL 01-727 9122
No corkage
Informal Greek taverna in a mews off Queensway, usually packed.

Oliver's Café 10 Russell Gardens, W14 TEL 01-603 7645 Corkage 50p
Sometimes you queue to share tables in this simple, relaxed place with a bistro menu, careful cooking (especially of vegetables), slapdash service.

Ooblies 78 Chester Road, N19 TEL 01-263 3899 No corkage
A wide range of delicious pancakes.

Paulo's 30 Greyhound Road, W6 TEL 01-385 9264 No corkage
Family-run place offering Brazilian food.

Seashell 35 Lisson Grove, NW1 TEL 01-723 8703 No corkage
329 Kingsland Road, E8 TEL 01-254 6152 No corkage
Superb fish and chips: greater comfort in E8; expect to queue in NW1 (which may be licensed by the spring).

Tsiakkos Kebab House 5 Marylands Road, W9 TEL 01-286 7896
No corkage
Simple little backroom place with short, standard Greek/Cypriot menu in cramped surroundings.

Windmill 486 Fulham Road, SW6 TEL 01-385 1570 Corkage 30p
A self-service café offering generous helpings of vegetarian food.

Country

Ambleside Cumbria
Sheila's Cottage The Slack TEL (0966) 33079 No corkage
Simple Swiss-style lunches in a 200-year-old cottage.

Birmingham West Midlands
Happy Gathering 54 Pershore Street TEL 021-622 3092 No corkage
Modest prices, long Cantonese menu.

Canterbury Kent
Paradise Café 15 St Dunstan Street TEL (0227) 69839 Corkage 10p
Simple decor, imaginative vegetarian menu.

Dedham Essex
The Mallard Riverside Cottage, Mill Lane TEL (0206) 322066
No corkage
Choose and barbecue your own steak to eat with salads and vegetables.

Dingle Co Kerry
An Cafe Liteartha TEL 51380 No corkage
A bookshop with a decent range of records, newspapers to read, and good light meals – 'excellent home-baking' (closes 6 pm winter, 7 pm summer).

Glasgow
Shish Mahal 41 Gibson Street TEL 041-334 7899 No corkage
Elegant decor in this Indian place near the university: vast helpings at reasonable prices (tandoori comes with rice and salad).

Gunthorpe Nottinghamshire
Mr Toad's Riverfront TEL (0602) 663409 No corkage
Basement bistro with interesting menu and some sound cooking.

Manchester
On the Eighth Day 109 Oxford Road TEL 061-273 4878 No corkage
Popular help-yourself vegetarian place near the fly-over, run by a co-operative which often does vegan dishes.

Oxford Oxfordshire
Munchy Munchy 6 Park End Street TEL (0865) 245710 No corkage
Sparkling Indonesian cafe: six dishes, changed daily according to shopping and mood.

Sedbergh Cumbria

Cross Keys Hotel Cautley TEL (0587) 20284 No corkage
Plain English food, 'all fresh, nothing fancy': duckling, salmon, chicken.

Underbarrow Cumbria

Tullythwaite House TEL Crosthwaite (044 88) 397 No corkage
Book well in advance for sound English cooking in the elegant dining-room of this gentleman-farmer's house. 'Some people even take sherry to have as an aperitif in the garden.'

Walberswick Suffolk

Potter's Wheel Village Green TEL Southwold (0502) 723173
Corkage 50p
A fairly new restaurant in a crafts complex, with a short set menu of interesting food (good stir-fried vegetables).

Liquid Diet

Places where the wine comes highly recommended but we do not consider the food to be quite up to standard for a fully entry:

London

Au Jardin des Gourmets, W1

Tiddy Dols, W1

Country

Bath Avon
Royal Crescent Hotel

Bristol Avon
Harveys

Broadway Hereford & Worcester
Lygon Arms

Chilgrove West Sussex
White Horse

Doddiscombsleigh Devon
Nobody Inn

Inverness Inverness-shire
Glen Mhor House

Poole Dorset
Edelweiss

Scone Perthshire
Balcraig House

Speldhurst Kent
George & Dragon

The Good Food Guide The Good Hotel Guide and *The Good Pub Guide*

Places also listed in one or more of Consumers' Association's other three 1985 guides appear on the following pages. An asterisk indicates establishments that feature in more than one of these guides.

The Good Food Guide 1985

Edited by Drew Smith, this year's edition gives details, descriptions and assessments of over 1,000 of the best restaurants in Britain offering meals from £3 to £30 + a head.

Wine bars

LONDON

The Boot & Flogger
The Cork & Bottle
Corney & Barrow
Gordon's
Green's Champagne Bar
Maxim
Methuselah's
192
Ormes

COUNTRY

Bradford on Avon
The Georgian Wine Lodge

Edinburgh
Waterfront

Eton
Eton Wine Bar

Harrogate
The Drum and Monkey

Llangollen
Gales

Rossett
Churtons Wine & Food Bar

Southend-on-Sea
The Pipe of Port

Wallingford
Lamb Wine Vaults

Restaurants

LONDON

Boulestin
Capital Hotel Restaurant
The Connaught*
D'Artagnan
Dorchester Hotel
L'Escargot
Hilaire
Lampwicks
Mabileau
Martin's
Polyanna's
The Ritz
Tate Gallery Restaurant
Tourment d'Amour

COUNTRY

Alfriston
Moonrakers

Ambleside
Rothay Manor*

Andover
Keys

Ashford
Eastwell Manor

Aston Clinton
The Bell*

Barnsley
Brooklands

Barwick
Little Barwick House*

Bath
Hole in the Wall*
Priory Hotel*

Birmingham
Jonathans'

Birtle
La Normandie

Botallack
Count House

Bowness-on-Windermere
The Porthole Eating House

Bristol
Bistro Twenty-One

Burnham Market
Fishes'

Callander
Roman Camp Hotel*

Cartmel
Aynsome Manor*

Chagford
Gidleigh Park*

Chedington
Chedington Court*

Chittlehamholt
Highbullen*

Christchurch
Splinters

Coatham Mundeville
Hall Garth*

Coggeshall
The White Hart

Cork
Arbutus Lodge*

Corse Lawn
Corse Lawn House*

Dartmouth
The Carved Angel

Dedham
Le Talbooth*

Dingle
Doyles

Drybridge
The Old Monastery

Dublin
Le Coq Hardi

Dunblane
Cromlix House*

East Grinstead
Gravetye Manor*

Edinburgh
Waterfront

Ely
Old Fire Engine House

Evershot
Summer Lodge*

Fadmoor
Plough Inn

Flitwick
Flitwick Manor

Fort William
Inverlochy Castle*

Frenchbeer
Teignworthy*

Frant
Bassetts

Fressingfield
Fox & Goose

Glasgow
Ubiquitous Chip

Grasmere
Michaels Nook*
White Moss House*

Great Dunmow
The Starr

Grimston
Congham Hall

Guist
Tollbridge

Gullane
Greywalls*
La Potinière

Hadleigh
Tavitons

Hambleton
Hambleton Hall*

Harlech
The Cemlyn

Harris
Scarista House*

Harrogate
Russell Hotel,
Hodgson's Restaurant

Harwich
The Pier at Harwich

Helford
Riverside*

Heswall
Les Bougies

Hinton Charterhouse
Homewood Park*

Holt
The Flask

Horton
French Partridge

Huntingdon
Old Bridge Hotel

Inverness
Dunain Park

Jersey
Longueville Manor

Jevington
The Hungry Monk

Kilchrenan
Ardanaiseig*

Kintbury
Dundas Arms*

Kirkby Fleetham
Kirkby Fleetham Hall

Knaresborough
Schwallers

Lacock
At the Sign of the
Angel*

Ledbury
Hope End*

Lewes
Kenwards

Lincoln
Harveys Cathedral
Restaurant

Linlithgow
Champany

Llandewi Skirrid
Walnut Tree Inn*

Llandudno
Bodysgallen Hall*

Llanrwst
Meadowsweet Hotel*

Loddiswell
Lavinia's

Lymington
Stanwell House Hotel,
Railings Restaurant*

Malvern Wells
Restaurant
Croque-en-Bouche

Manchester
Moss Nook Restaurant

Matlock
Riber Hall*

Mayfield
The Old Brewhouse

Moffat
Beechwood Country
House Hotel*

Moulton
Black Bull

Nairn
Clifton Hotel*

Nayland
The Bear*

Netherfield
Netherfield Place*

New Milton
Chewton Glen Hotel*

Newton
Tabuteau's

Oxford
Cherwell Boathouse

Padstow
The Seafood Restaurant

Peat Inn
The Peat Inn

Pool in Wharfedale
Pool Court*

Port Appin
Airds Hotel*

Pulborough
Stane Street Hotel

Ross-on-Wye
Pengethley Hotel

Rugby
Andalucia

Rye
Monastery

Shanagarry
Ballymaloe House*

Shepton Mallet
Bowlish House

St Austell
Boscundle Manor*

Shinfield
Milton Sandford

South Molton
Stumbles

Stamford
George of Stamford*

Stonham
Mr Underhill's

Storrington
Manleys

Swansea
Drangway Restaurant

Taunton
Castle Hotel*

Thornbury
Thornbury Castle*

Totnes
Elbow Room

Ullswater
Sharrow Bay Hotel*

Uphall
Houstoun House*

Watermillock
Leeming on Ullswater Country House Hotel

Williton
White House

Windermere
Miller Howe*

Witherslack
Old Vicarage*

The Good Hotel Guide 1985

Edited by Hilary Rubinstein, this year's edition describes nearly 1,000 places to stay in Britain and Europe, ranging from small, friendly guest-houses to sumptuous grand hotels.

LONDON

Connaught*

COUNTRY

Ambleside
Rothay Manor Hotel*

Aston Clinton
Bell Inn*

Barwick
Little Barwick House*

Bath
Hole in the Wall*
Priory Hotel*

Callander
The Roman Camp Hotel*

Cartmel
Aynsome Manor Hotel*

Chagford
Gidleigh Park Hotel*

Chedington
Chedington Court*

Chittlehamholt
Highbullen Hotel*

Cork
Arbutus Lodge Hotel*

Corse Lawn
Corse Lawn House*

Dedham
Maison Talbooth*

Dunblane
Cromlix House*

East Grinstead
Gravetye Manor*

Evershot
Summer Lodge*

Fort William
Inverlochy Castle*

Frenchbeer
Teignworthy*

Gittisham
Combe House

Grasmere
Michael's Nook*
White Moss House*

Gullane
Greywalls Hotel*

Hambleton
Hambleton Hall*

Helford
Riverside*

Hinton Charterhouse
Homewood Park*

Kilchrenan
Ardanaiseig Hotel*

Kintbury
Dundas Arms*

Lacock
At the Sign of the Angel*

Ledbury
Hope End Country House Hotel*

Llandudno
Bodysgallen Hall*

Llanrwst
Meadowsweet Hotel*

Lymington
Stanwell House Hotel*

Matlock
Riber Hall*

Moffat
Beechwood Country House Hotel*

Nairn
Clifton Hotel*

Nayland
Bear*

Netherfield (Battle)
Netherfield Place*

New Milton
Chewton Glen Hotel*

Pool-in-Wharfedale
Pool Court Restaurant with Rooms*

Port Appin
The Airds Hotel*

Rushlake Green
The Priory Country House Hotel

St Austell
Boscundle Manor*

Shanagarry
Ballymaloe House*

Stamford
The George of Stamford*

Taunton
The Castle Hotel*

Ullswater
Sharrow Bay Country House Hotel*

Uphall
Houstoun House*

Windermere
Miller Howe*

Witherslack
The Old Vicarage*

The Good Pub Guide 1985

Edited by Alisdair Aird, this year's edition describes around 1,200 of the most distinctive pubs in Britain and lists another 1,500 more that have been recommended by readers.

Kintbury
Dundas Arms*

Llandewi Skirrid
Walnut Tree*

Nairn
Clifton Hotel*

Port Appin
Airds Hotel*

Stamford
George*

Gazetteer of places outside London

KEY
W Wine bar
R Restaurant
M Merchant

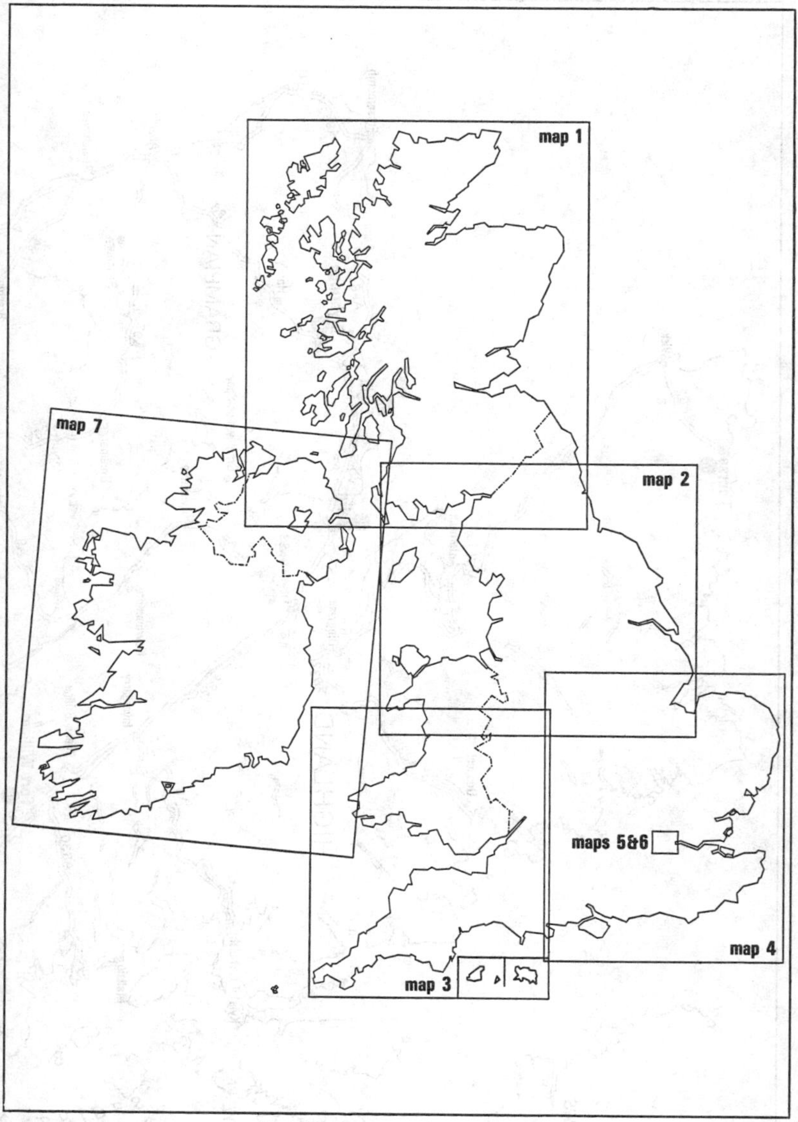
map 1
map 7
map 2
maps 5&6
map 4
map 3

Map 1 Scotland

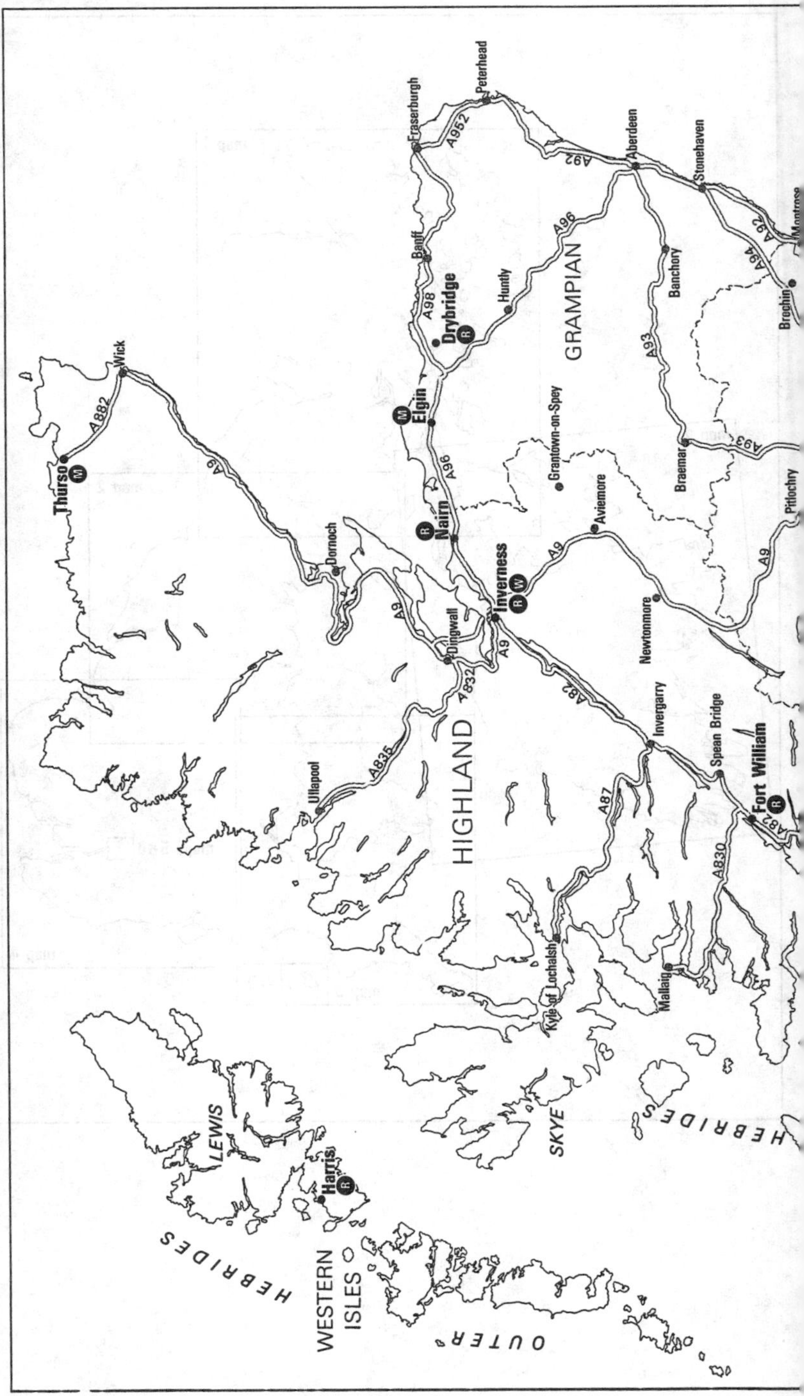

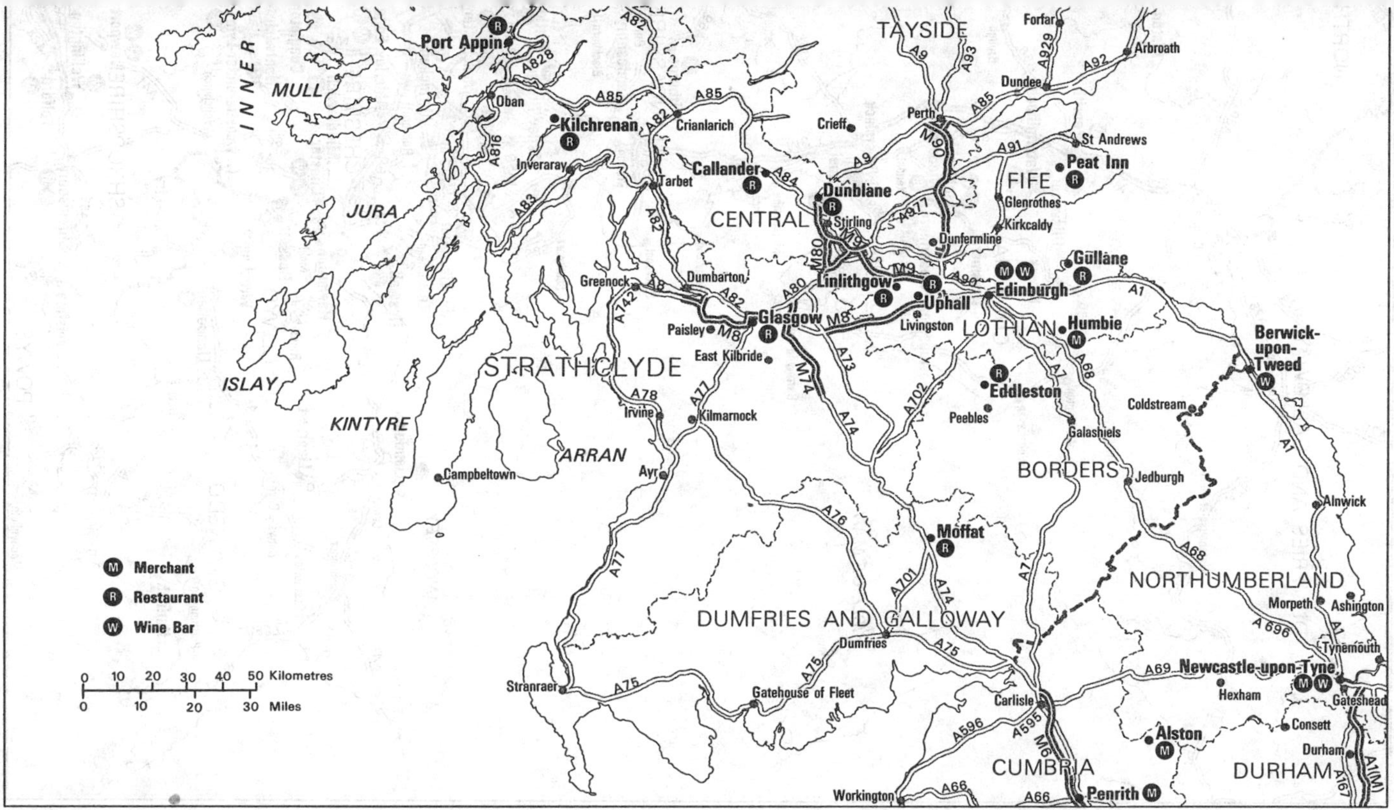
INNER
MULL
JURA
ISLAY
KINTYRE
ARRAN
TAYSIDE
FIFE
CENTRAL
STRATHCLYDE
LOTHIAN
BORDERS
DUMFRIES AND GALLOWAY
NORTHUMBERLAND
CUMBRIA
DURHAM
Port Appin
Oban
Kilchrenan
Inveraray
Crianlarich
Tarbet
Callander
Crieff
Perth
Forfar
Dundee
Arbroath
St Andrews
Peat Inn
Glenrothes
Kirkcaldy
Dunfermline
Dunblane
Stirling
Gullane
Edinburgh
Linlithgow
Uphall
Livingston
Humbie
Greenock
Dumbarton
Glasgow
Paisley
East Kilbride
Irvine
Kilmarnock
Ayr
Campbeltown
Eddleston
Peebles
Galashiels
Coldstream
Berwick-upon-Tweed
Jedburgh
Alnwick
Moffat
Morpeth
Ashington
Tynemouth
Newcastle-upon-Tyne
Gateshead
Hexham
Consett
Durham
Alston
Penrith
Carlisle
Dumfries
Gatehouse of Fleet
Stranraer
Workington
A82
A828
A85
A816
A83
A84
A9
A93
A929
A92
M90
A91
A977
M9
M80
A90
A1
A8
A80
A742
M8
A73
M74
A74
A702
A7
A68
A78
A77
A76
A701
A75
A596
A595
M6
A66
A69
A696
A167
A1(M)
Merchant
Restaurant
Wine Bar
0 10 20 30 40 50 Kilometres
0 10 20 30 Miles

Map 2 North of England

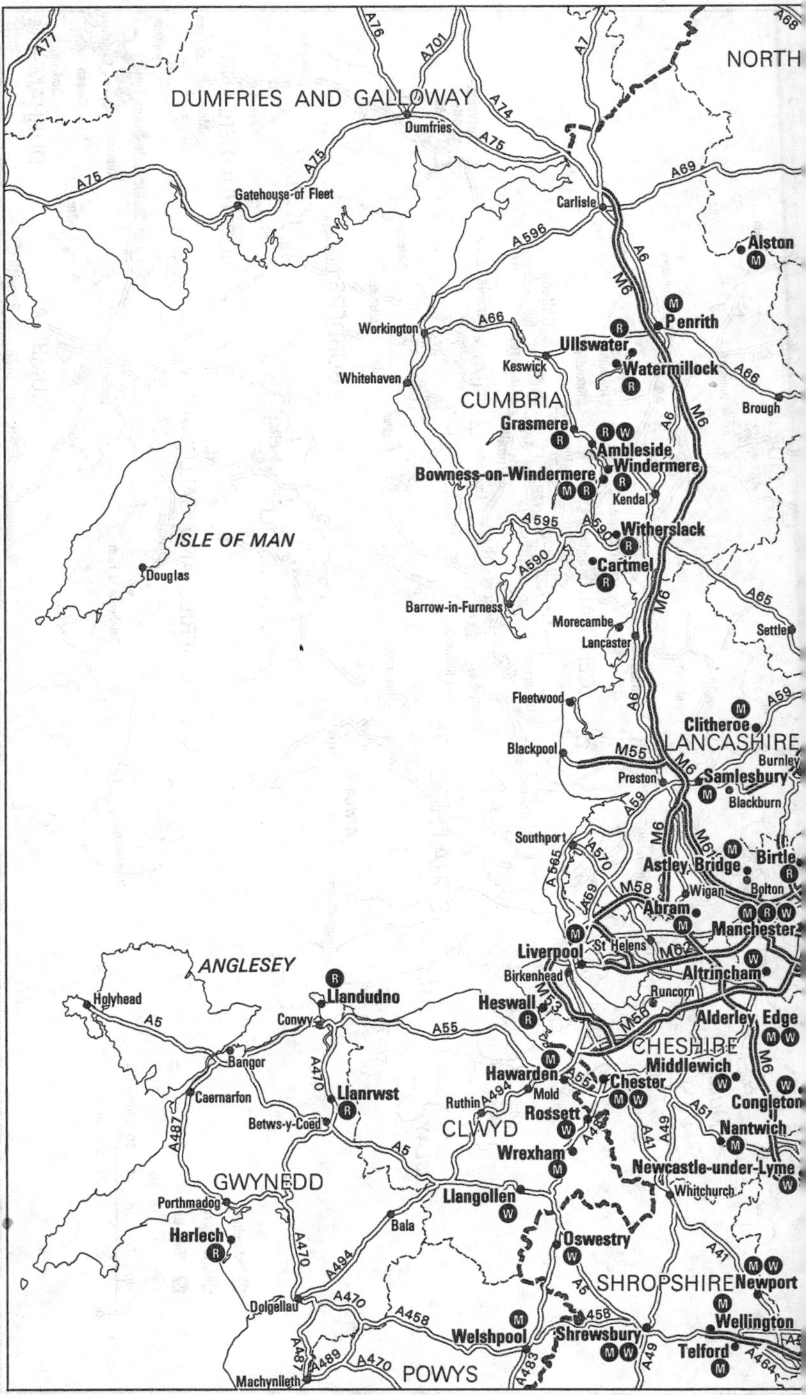

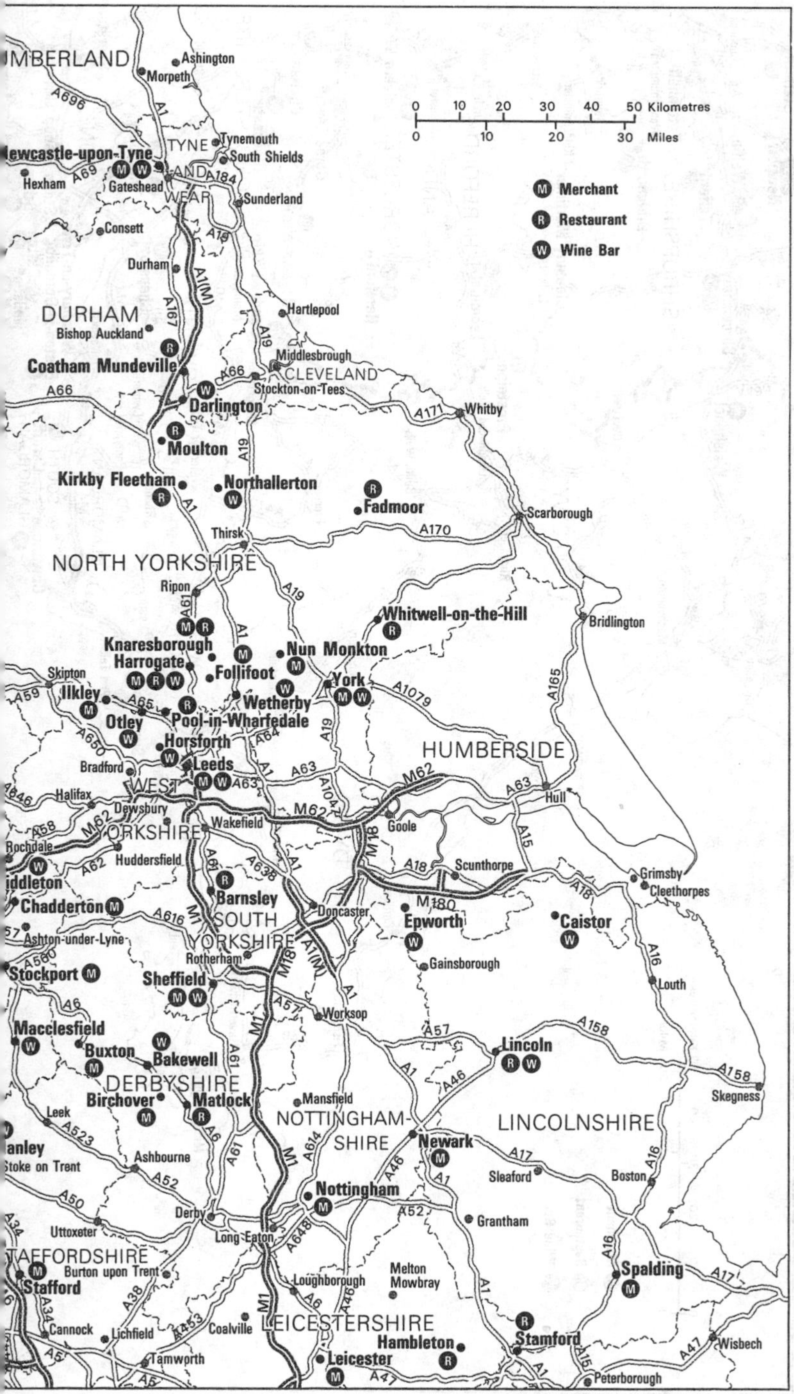

0 10 20 30 40 50 Kilometres
0 10 20 30 Miles
Merchant
Restaurant
Wine Bar
DURHAM
CLEVELAND
NORTH YORKSHIRE
HUMBERSIDE
WEST YORKSHIRE
SOUTH YORKSHIRE
DERBYSHIRE
NOTTINGHAMSHIRE
LINCOLNSHIRE
LEICESTERSHIRE
Ashington
Morpeth
Tynemouth
South Shields
Hexham
Gateshead
Sunderland
Consett
Durham
Hartlepool
Bishop Auckland
Coatham Mundeville
Middlesbrough
Stockton-on-Tees
Darlington
Whitby
Moulton
Kirkby Fleetham
Northallerton
Fadmoor
Scarborough
Thirsk
Ripon
Whitwell-on-the-Hill
Bridlington
Knaresborough
Harrogate
Follifoot
Nun Monkton
York
Skipton
Ilkley
Otley
Pool-in-Wharfedale
Wetherby
Horsforth
Leeds
Bradford
Halifax
Dewsbury
Wakefield
Hull
Goole
Rochdale
Huddersfield
Scunthorpe
Grimsby
Cleethorpes
Chadderton
Barnsley
Doncaster
Epworth
Caistor
Ashton-under-Lyne
Rotherham
Gainsborough
Stockport
Sheffield
Louth
Worksop
Macclesfield
Buxton
Bakewell
Lincoln
Skegness
Birchover
Matlock
Mansfield
Leek
Newark
Ashbourne
Sleaford
Boston
Nottingham
Derby
Grantham
Uttoxeter
Long Eaton
Burton upon Trent
Stafford
Loughborough
Melton Mowbray
Spalding
Cannock
Lichfield
Coalville
Hambleton
Stamford
Wisbech
Tamworth
Leicester
Peterborough

Map 3 South Wales and South West England

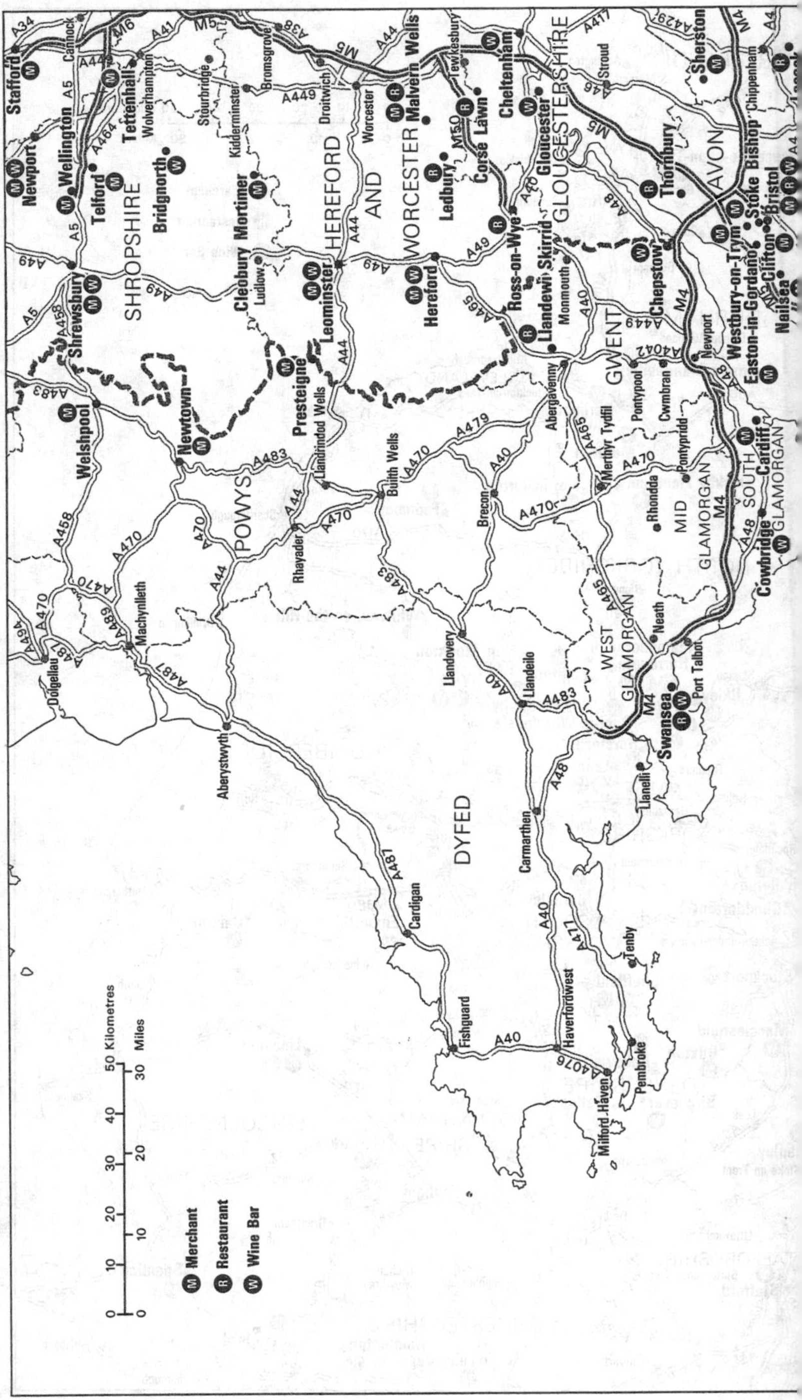

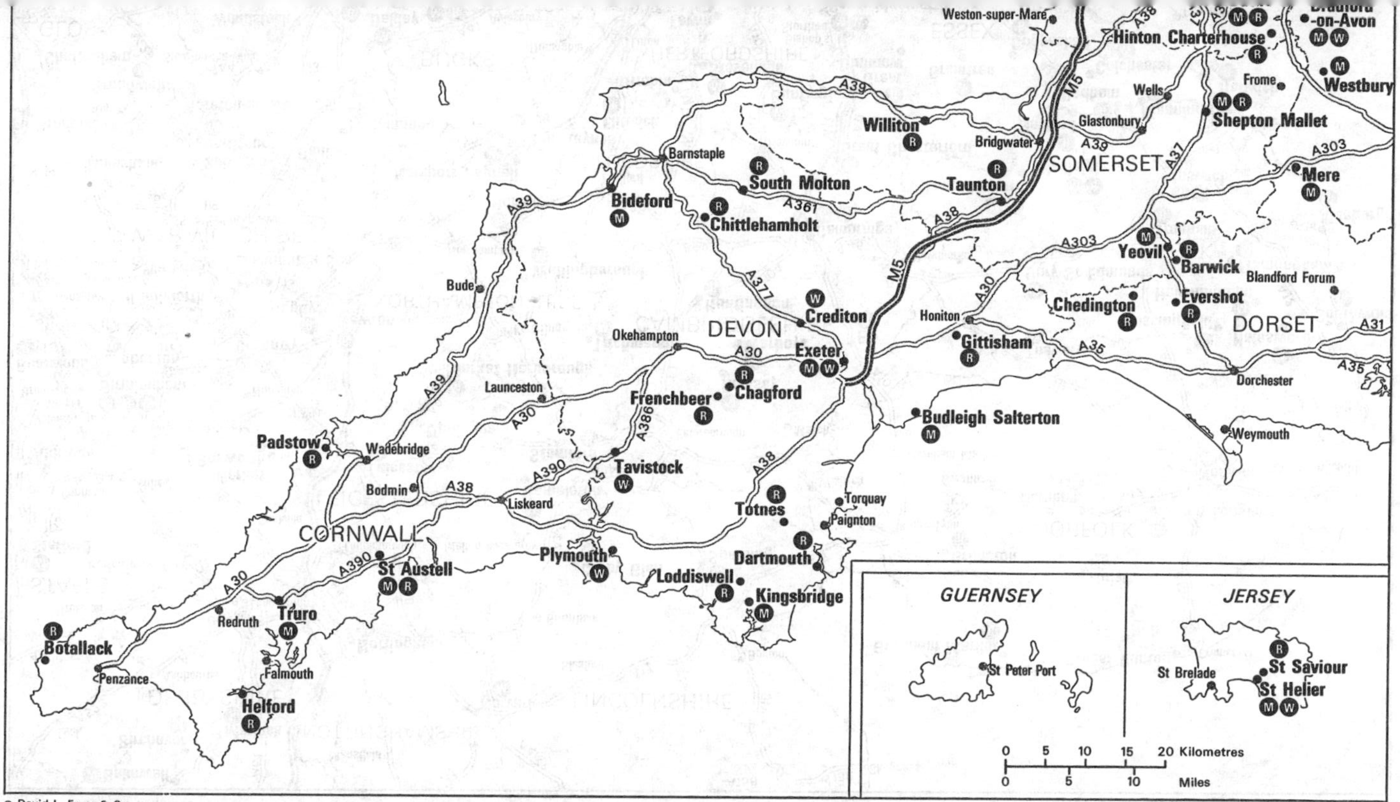
Weston-super-Mare
Hinton Charterhouse
Bradford-on-Avon
Westbury
Frome
Wells
Shepton Mallet
Glastonbury
Williton
Bridgwater
SOMERSET
Barnstaple
South Molton
Taunton
Mere
Bideford
Chittlehamholt
Yeovil
Barwick
Blandford Forum
Bude
Crediton
Chedington
Evershot
DORSET
Honiton
Okehampton
DEVON
Exeter
Gittisham
Dorchester
Launceston
Chagford
Frenchbeer
Budleigh Salterton
Weymouth
Padstow
Wadebridge
Tavistock
Bodmin
Liskeard
Torquay
Totnes
Paignton
CORNWALL
Plymouth
Dartmouth
St Austell
Loddiswell
Kingsbridge
Truro
Redruth
Botallack
Falmouth
Penzance
Helford
GUERNSEY
St Peter Port
JERSEY
St Brelade
St Saviour
St Helier
0 5 10 15 20 Kilometres
0 5 10 Miles
A38
A37
A39
M5
A303
A361
A377
A30
A35
A31
A386
A390

Map 4 Central and Southern England

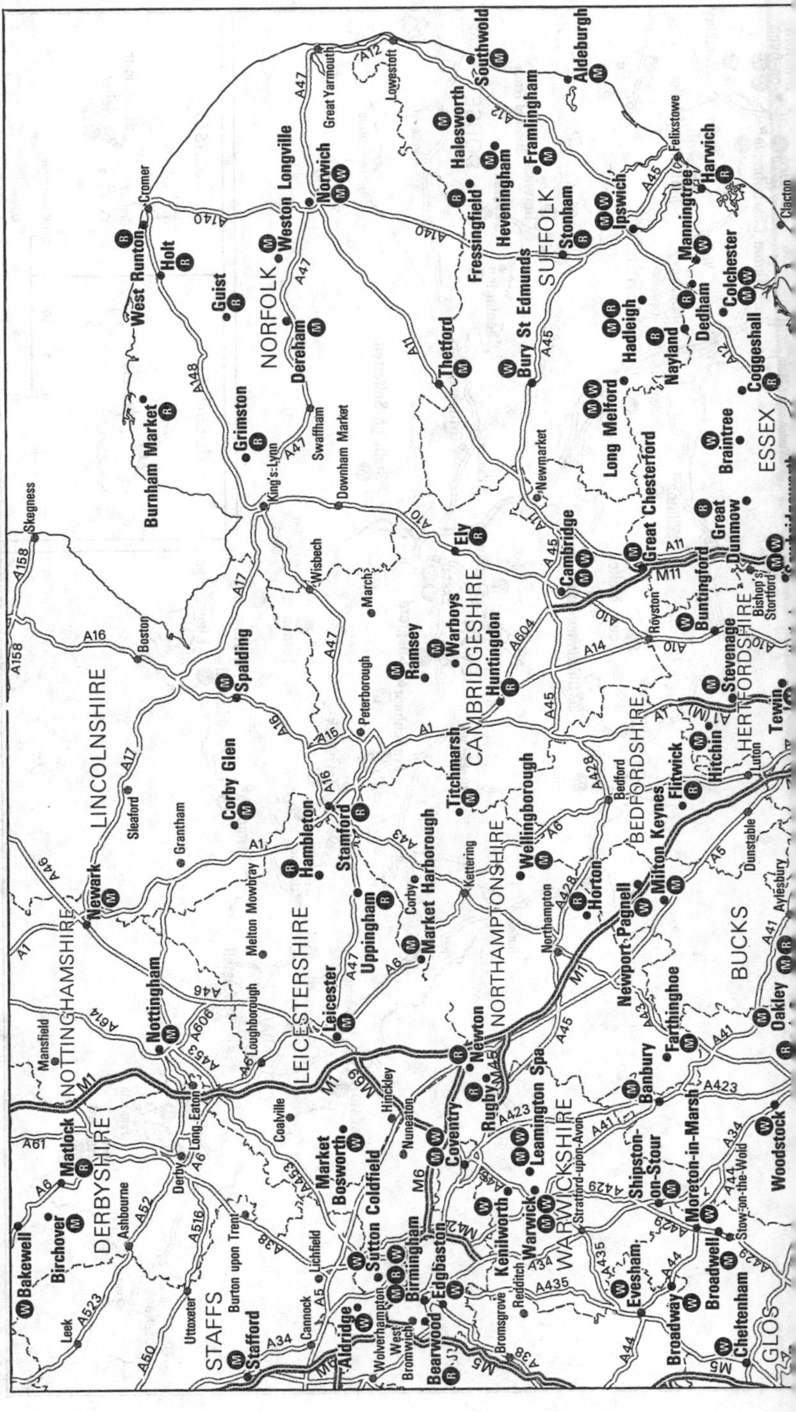

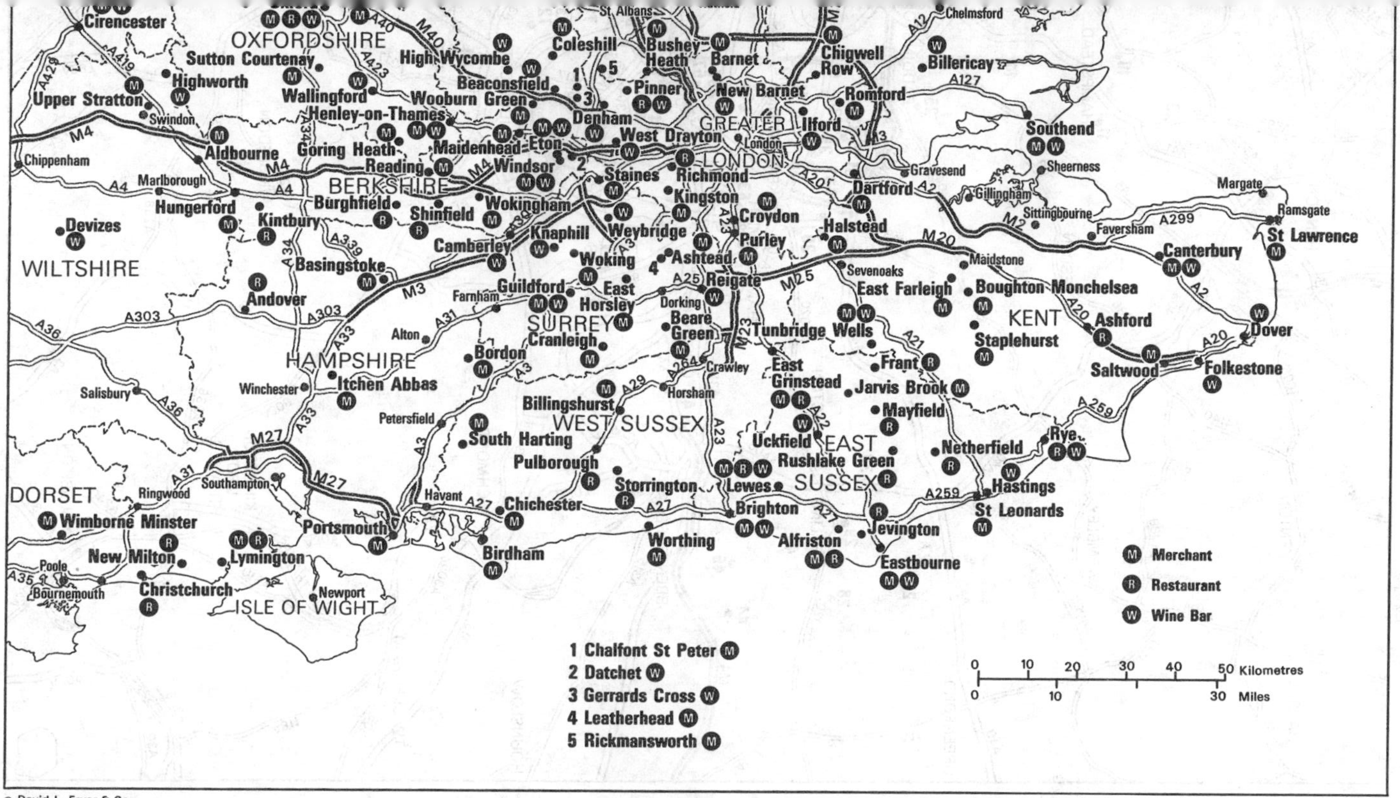
OXFORDSHIRE
BERKSHIRE
WILTSHIRE
HAMPSHIRE
SURREY
GREATER LONDON
KENT
WEST SUSSEX
EAST SUSSEX
DORSET
ISLE OF WIGHT
Cirencester
Upper Stratton
Highworth
Sutton Courtenay
Wallingford
Henley-on-Thames
Goring Heath
Reading
Aldbourne
Hungerford
Kintbury
Devizes
Andover
Basingstoke
Burghfield
Shinfield
High Wycombe
Beaconsfield
Wooburn Green
Maidenhead
Eton
Windsor
Wokingham
Camberley
Knaphill
Woking
Weybridge
Guildford
East Horsley
Coleshill
Denham
West Drayton
Staines
Bushey Heath
Pinner
Barnet
New Barnet
Chigwell Row
Romford
Ilford
Richmond
Kingston
Croydon
Purley
Ashtead
Reigate
Beare Green
Cranleigh
Bordon
Itchen Abbas
South Harting
Billingshurst
Pulborough
Storrington
Chichester
Birdham
Portsmouth
Lymington
Christchurch
New Milton
Wimborne Minster
Worthing
Brighton
Lewes
Uckfield
Rushlake Green
Alfriston
Jevington
Eastbourne
East Grinstead
Tunbridge Wells
Frant
Jarvis Brook
Mayfield
Netherfield
Hastings
St Leonards
Rye
East Farleigh
Boughton Monchelsea
Staplehurst
Halstead
Dartford
Ashford
Saltwood
Folkestone
Dover
Canterbury
St Lawrence
Southend
Billericay
Chippenham
Swindon
Marlborough
Salisbury
Winchester
Southampton
Ringwood
Poole
Bournemouth
Newport
Havant
Petersfield
Alton
Farnham
Dorking
Horsham
Crawley
Sevenoaks
Maidstone
Gravesend
Sheerness
Gillingham
Sittingbourne
Faversham
Margate
Ramsgate
Chelmsford
St Albans
London
M4
M3
M27
M40
M20
M2
M25
M23
A4
A34
A303
A36
A31
A33
A339
A3
A29
A264
A23
A22
A21
A27
A259
A25
A20
A2
A299
A127
A12
A13
A419
A429
A423
A30
1 Chalfont St Peter M
2 Datchet W
3 Gerrards Cross W
4 Leatherhead M
5 Rickmansworth M
M Merchant
R Restaurant
W Wine Bar
0 10 20 30 40 50 Kilometres
0 10 30 Miles

Map 5 Greater London

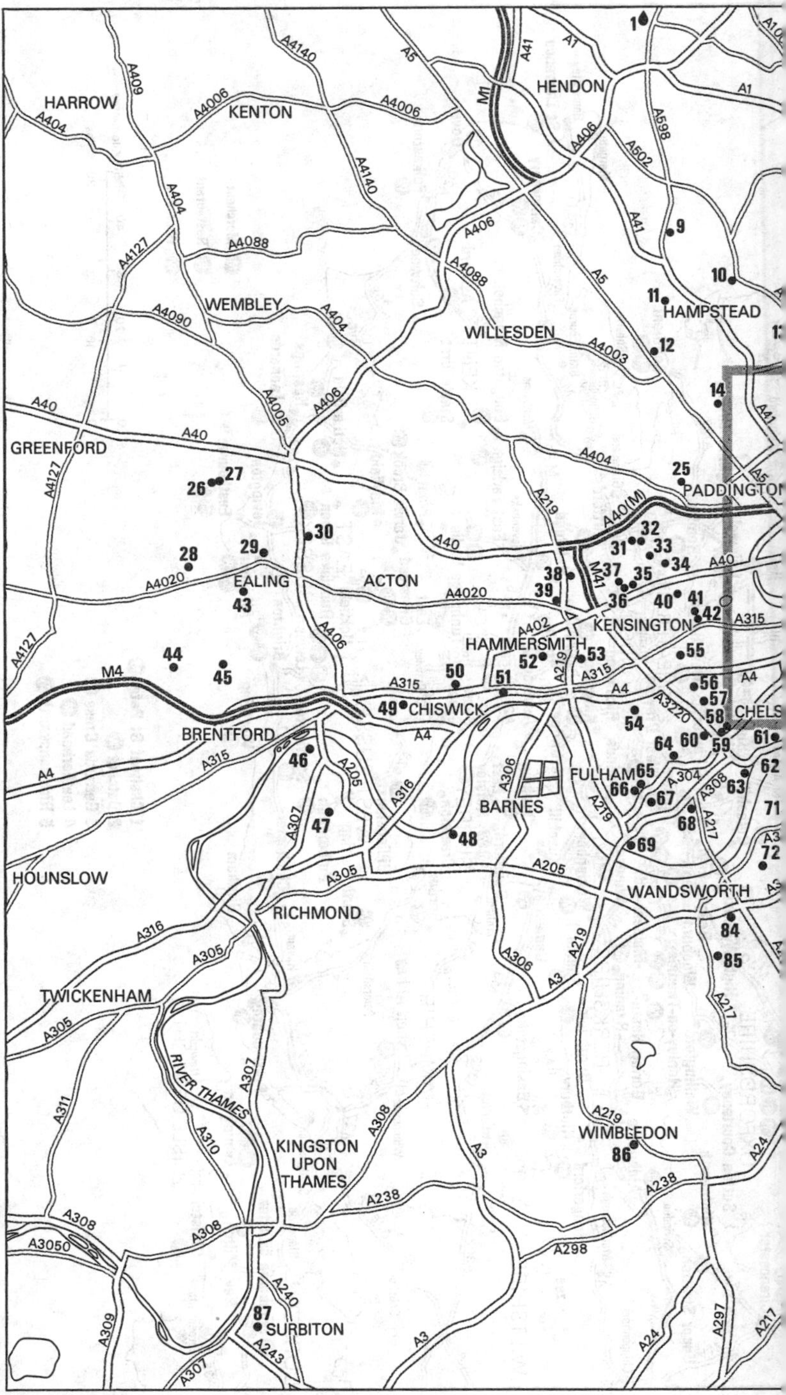

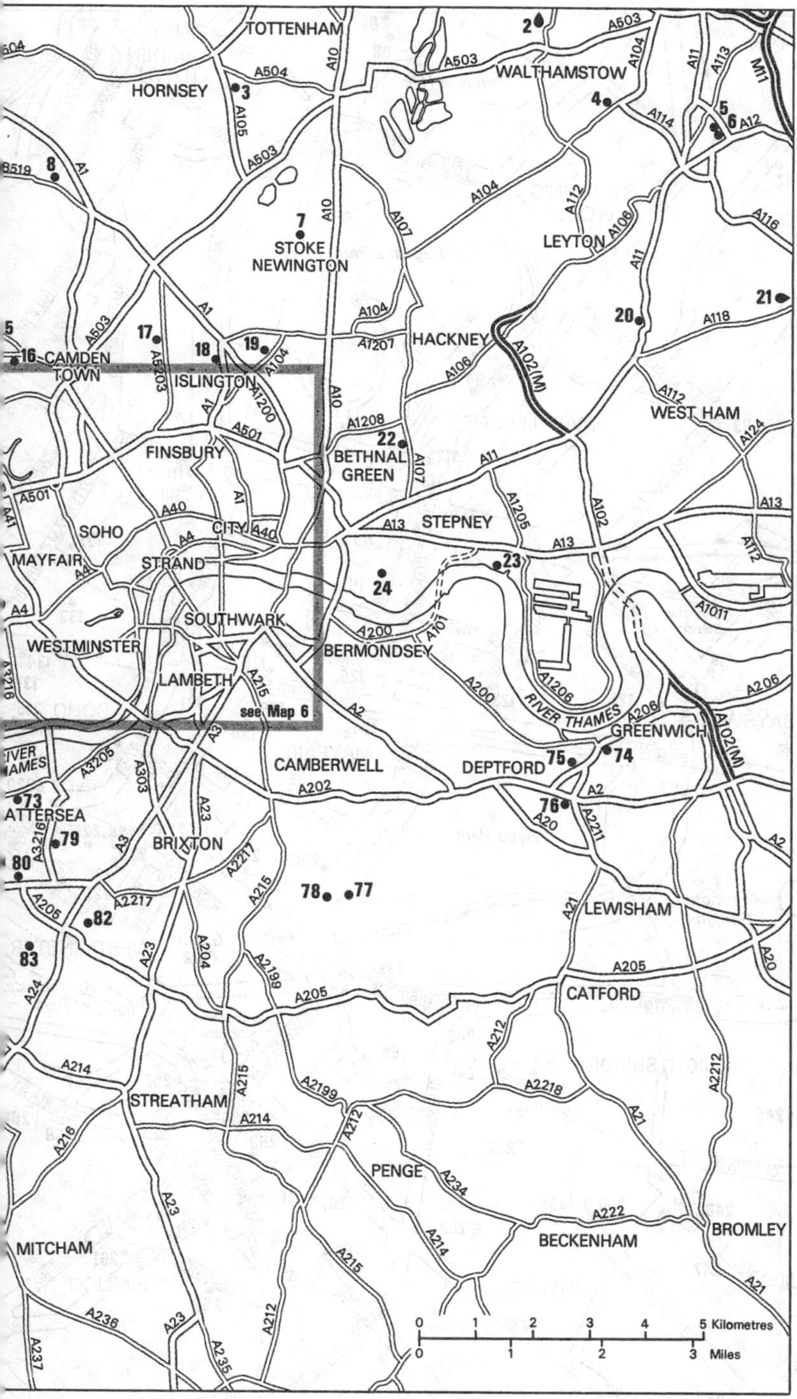
TOTTENHAM
WALTHAMSTOW
HORNSEY
STOKE NEWINGTON
LEYTON
CAMDEN TOWN
ISLINGTON
HACKNEY
WEST HAM
FINSBURY
BETHNAL GREEN
STEPNEY
SOHO
CITY
MAYFAIR
STRAND
SOUTHWARK
WESTMINSTER
BERMONDSEY
LAMBETH
see Map 6
RIVER THAMES
GREENWICH
CAMBERWELL
DEPTFORD
BATTERSEA
BRIXTON
LEWISHAM
CATFORD
STREATHAM
PENGE
BECKENHAM
BROMLEY
MITCHAM
2
3
4
5
6
7
8
16
17
18
19
20
21
22
23
24
73
74
75
76
77
78
79
80
82
83
0 1 2 3 4 5 Kilometres
0 1 2 3 Miles

Map 6 Central London

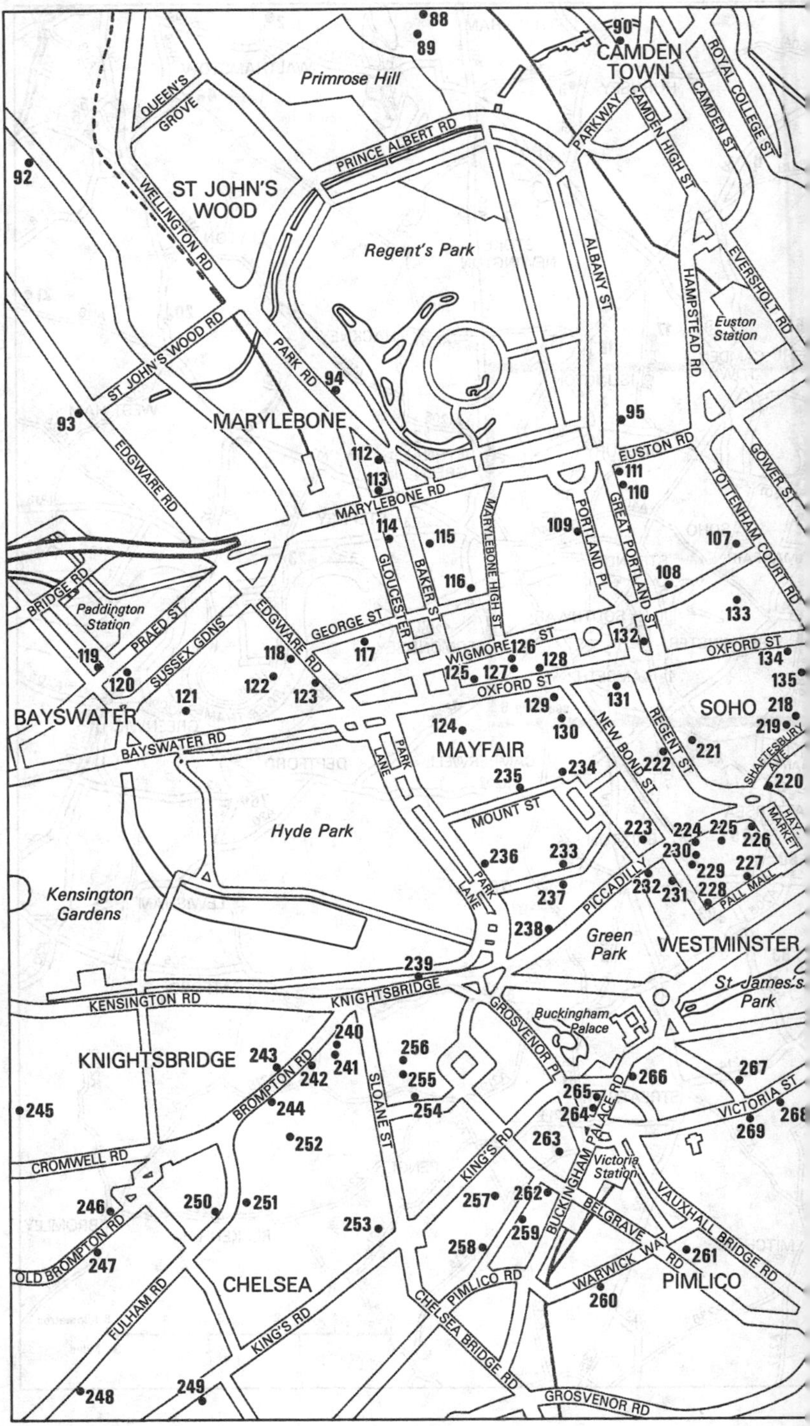

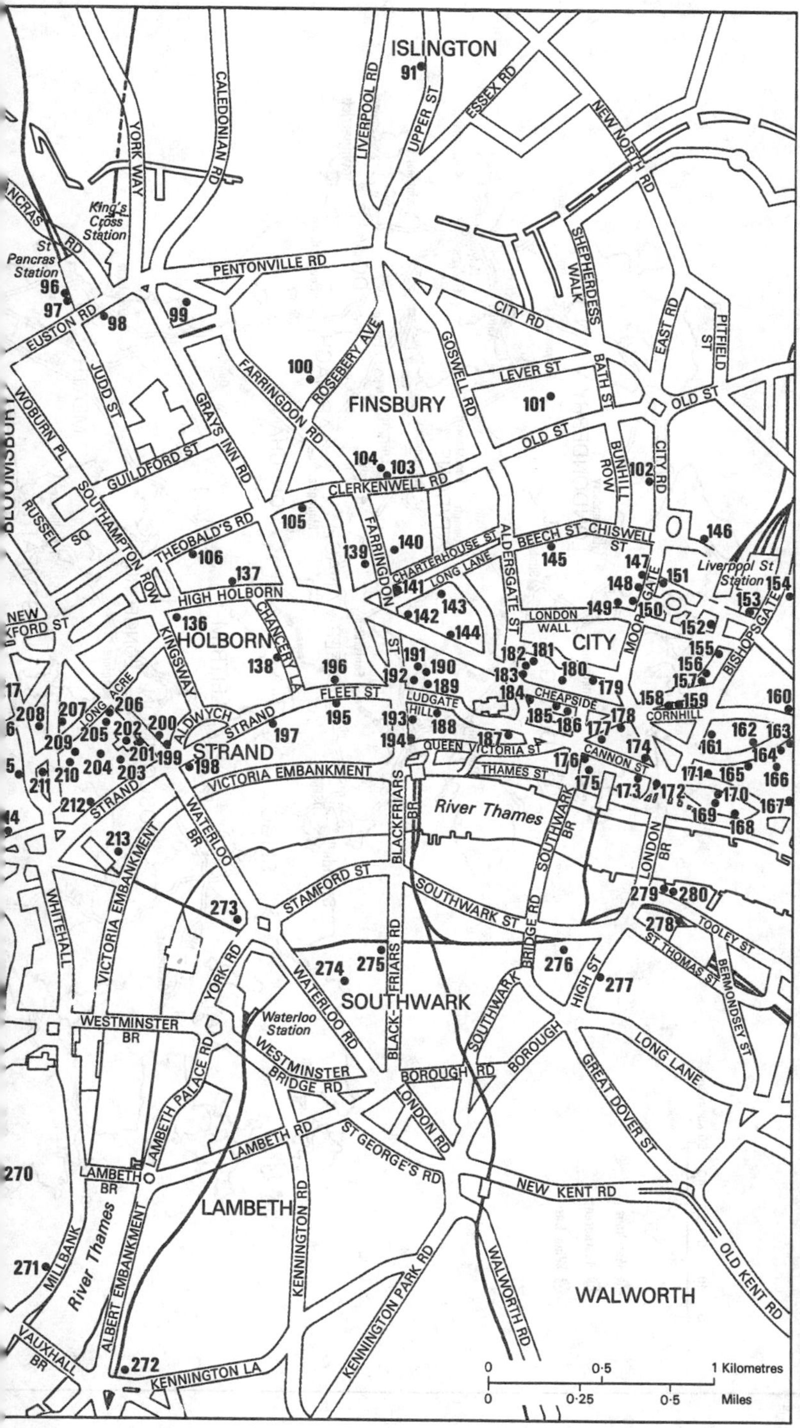

ISLINGTON
FINSBURY
HOLBORN
CITY
STRAND
SOUTHWARK
LAMBETH
WALWORTH
River Thames
King's Cross Station
St Pancras Station
Liverpool St Station
Waterloo Station
CALEDONIAN RD
YORK WAY
LIVERPOOL RD
UPPER ST
ESSEX RD
NEW NORTH RD
PENTONVILLE RD
EUSTON RD
CITY RD
SHEPHERDESS WALK
EAST RD
PITFIELD ST
LEVER ST
OLD ST
BATH ST
BUNHILL ROW
ROSEBERY AVE
FARRINGDON RD
GOSWELL RD
GRAYS INN RD
JUDD ST
WOBURN PL
GUILDFORD ST
SOUTHAMPTON ROW
RUSSELL SQ
THEOBALD'S RD
CLERKENWELL RD
FARRINGDON
CHARTERHOUSE ST
LONG LANE
ALDERSGATE ST
BEECH ST
CHISWELL ST
MOORGATE
BISHOPSGATE
HIGH HOLBORN
CHANCERY LA
KINGSWAY
NEW OXFORD ST
LONG ACRE
ALDWYCH
STRAND
FLEET ST
LUDGATE HILL
LONDON WALL
CHEAPSIDE
CORNHILL
QUEEN VICTORIA ST
CANNON ST
THAMES ST
VICTORIA EMBANKMENT
WATERLOO BR
BLACKFRIARS BR
SOUTHWARK BR
LONDON BR
WHITEHALL
STAMFORD ST
SOUTHWARK ST
TOOLEY ST
ST THOMAS ST
BERMONDSEY ST
YORK RD
WATERLOO RD
BLACKFRIARS RD
SOUTHWARK BRIDGE RD
HIGH ST
BOROUGH HIGH ST
LONG LANE
WESTMINSTER BR
WESTMINSTER BRIDGE RD
BOROUGH RD
LAMBETH PALACE RD
LONDON RD
GREAT DOVER ST
LAMBETH RD
ST GEORGE'S RD
NEW KENT RD
LAMBETH BR
KENNINGTON RD
KENNINGTON PARK RD
WALWORTH RD
OLD KENT RD
MILLBANK
ALBERT EMBANKMENT
VAUXHALL BR
KENNINGTON LA
91
96
97
98
99
100
101
102
103
104
105
106
136
137
138
139
140
141
142
143
144
145
146
147
148
149
150
151
152
153
154
155
156
157
158
159
160
161
162
163
164
165
166
167
168
169
170
171
172
173
174
175
176
177
178
179
180
181
182
183
184
185
186
187
188
189
190
191
192
193
194
195
196
197
198
199
200
201
202
203
204
205
206
207
208
209
210
211
212
213
270
271
272
273
274
275
276
277
278
279
280
0
0·5
1 Kilometres
0
0·25
0·5
Miles

Map 7 Ireland

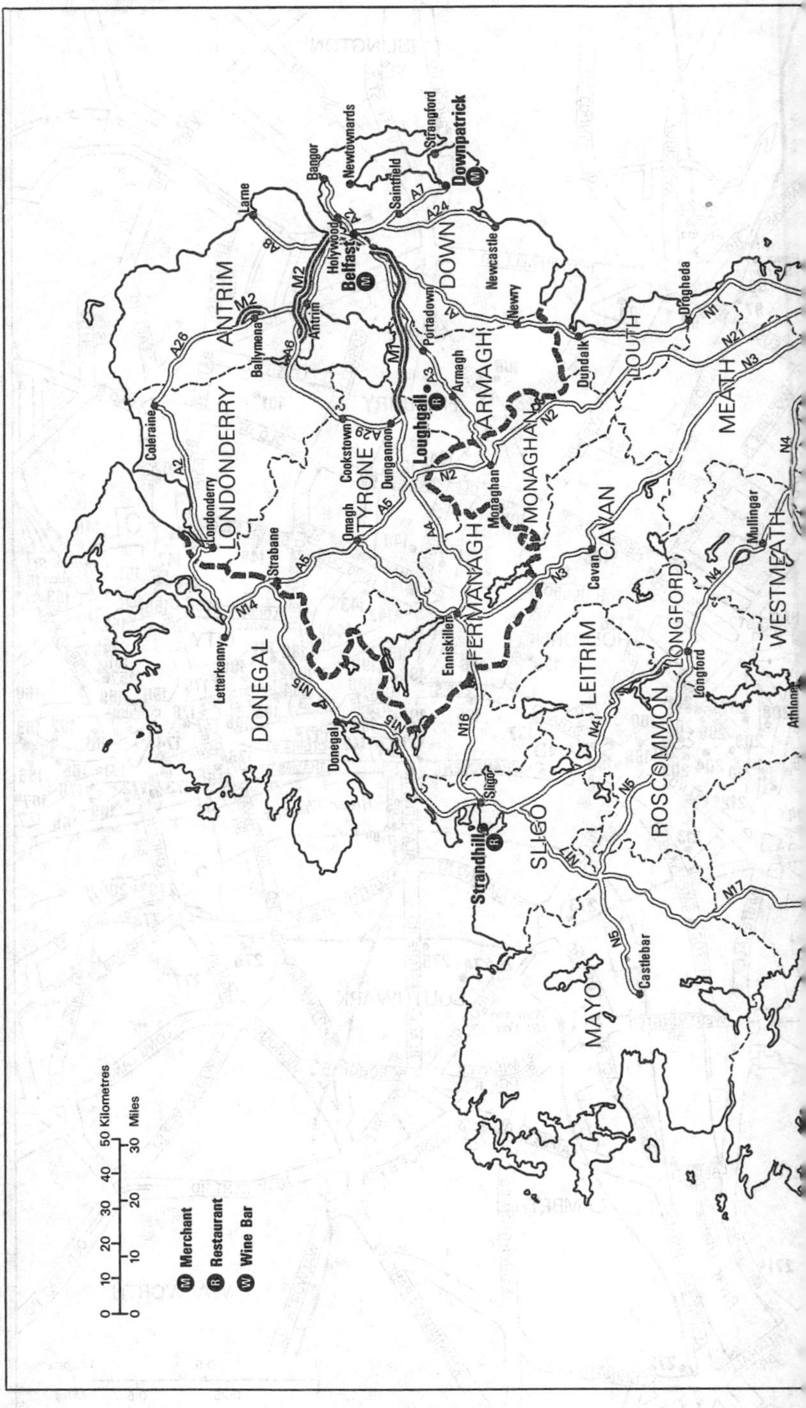

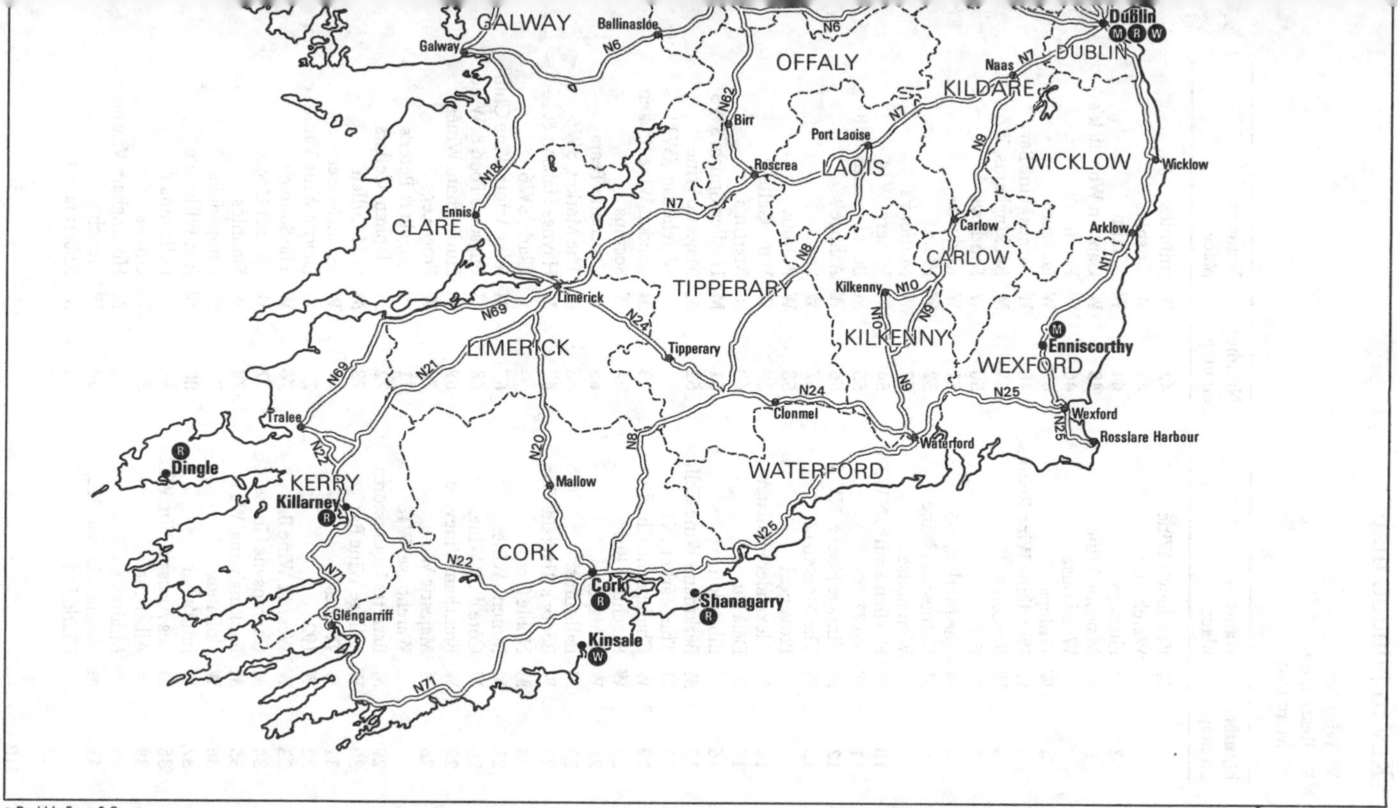
GALWAY
Galway
Ballinasloe
N6
OFFALY
Dublin
DUBLIN
Naas
N7
KILDARE
N62
Birr
Port Laoise
N9
WICKLOW
Wicklow
Roscrea
LAOIS
N18
Ennis
CLARE
Carlow
Arklow
N8
CARLOW
N11
Limerick
TIPPERARY
Kilkenny
N10
N69
N24
KILKENNY
Enniscorthy
LIMERICK
Tipperary
N21
WEXFORD
N25
Clonmel
Wexford
Tralee
Waterford
Rosslare Harbour
Dingle
N22
N20
KERRY
Mallow
WATERFORD
Killarney
CORK
Cork
Shanagarry
N71
Glengarriff
Kinsale

Key to London maps

W Wine bar
R Restaurant
M Merchant

Number on map		Name of place
1	**M**	Kershaw's Wine Warehouse
2	**W**	Hiccups
3	**M**	Majestic Wine Warehouse
4	**W**	Whipps
5	**W**	Woodbine Wine Rooms
6	**W**	Russell's
7	**W**	Fox's
8	**M**	The Market, N6
9	**M**	Hampstead Wine Warehouse
10	**M**	H Allen Smith, NW3
11	**W**	No 77
12	**M**	Vintage House, NW6
13	**M**	The Market/Le Provençal
14	**M**	Alexander Findlater
15	**W**	Déjà Vu
16	**M**	Bibendum
17	**M**	Berkmann Wine Cellars
18	**M**	The Market, N1
19	**W**	Champagne Charlies
20	**W**	Bacchus's Bin
21	**W**	Whispers
22	**M**	Balls Bros
23	**W**	Booty's Riverside Bar
24	**M**	Noble Grape
25	**M**	Moreno Wines
26	**M**	Côte d'Or Wines
27	**W**	Brentham Vineyard
28	**M**	Majestic Wine Warehouse, W13
29	**M**	Barretts Liquorstores
30	**W**	Village Wine Bar
31	**W**	Tropics
32	**W**	192
33	**W**	West 11 Wine Bar
34	**M**	Champagne House
35	**M**	Buckinghams, W11
36	**W**	Hollands
37	**W**	Julie's Bar
38	**M**	Les Amis du Vin, W12
39	**W**	Albertine
40	**W**	Mildred's
41	**M**	Haynes Hanson & Clark, W8
42	**W**	Jimmies
43	**W**	Crispins
44	**W**	Maxim
45	**W**	Captain Wooduck's
46	**W**	Pissarro's
47	**W**	Jacksons
48	**W**	Barnes Wine Bar
49	**M**	Buckinghams, W4
50	**W**	Southeys
51	**W**	Korky's
52	**W**	Plums
53	**W**	Mulford's
54	**M**	Winery, W14
55	**M**	Buckinghams, W8
56	**W**	Ashbee's
57	**W**	Spats
58	**W**	Boltons
59	**W**	Wine Gallery
60	**R**	Martin's
61	**M**	H Allen Smith, SW3
62	**M**	Majestic Wine Warehouse, SW11
63	**M**	London Wine Brokers
64	**W**	Scamps
65	**W**	Crocodile Tears
66	**M**	The Market, SW6
67	**M**	Haynes Hanson & Clark, SW6
67	**M**	John Arlott Wine Club
68	**M**	Pugson's Food & Wine
69	**M**	Hurlingham Wines
70	**W**	Frogs Legs
71	**W**	Angela & Peter's
72	**M**	Clapham Cellars
73	**M**	W H Cullen
74	**W**	Bar du Musée
75	**W**	Davy's Wine Vaults
76	**W**	The Source
77	**W**	Mother Goose
78	**W**	Frannies
79	**R**	Lampwicks
80	**W**	Just William's
81	**R**	Pollyanna's
82	**W**	Ormes
83	**M**	Hurlingham Vintners
84	**W**	French's
85	**M**	Robert James

Number on map		Name of place
86	W	Downs of Mayfair
87	W	Tappit Hen
88	M	Richard Kihl
89	W	Odettes
90	M	Camden Wine & Cheese
91	W	Almeida Theatre
92	W	Blenheims
93	M	Winery
94	W	Boaters
95	W	Wine Press
96	M	Laytons
97	M	Malmaison Wine Club
98	W	Gazebo
99	W	Smithy's
100	M	Domaine Direct
101	M	Corney & Barrow, EC1
102	W	CJ's
103	W	Burgundy Bens
104	W	Café St Pierre
105	W	Wine Butt
106	W	Les Halles
107	M	Ehrmann's
108	W	Wolsey's
109	M	Buckinghams, W1
110	M	Wine Growers' Association
111	M	Wine Society
112	W	Bill Bentley's
113	W	Boos
114	M	Crawfords
114	W	Crawford's
115	M	Les Amis du Vin, W1
116	R	D'Artagnan
117	M	Bart's Cellars
118	M	La Réserve, W2
119	M	The Market, W2
120	W	Gyngleboy
121	W	Ruby's
122	M	Stones of Belgravia, WC2
123	M	Continental Wine House
124	W	Bubbles
125	M	Selfridges
126	W	James Wine Bar
127	M	Les Amis du Vin, WC2
128	M	Findlater, Mackie, Todd
129	W	Maynard's
130	W	Corts, W1
131	W	Chopper Lump
132	W	Brasserie Mode
133	W	Partners
134	W	Tracks
135	M	Milroy's

Number on map		Name of place
136	W	Gate Street Wine Bar
137	W	Bunghole
138	W	Corts, WC2
139	W	Bleeding Heart
140	M	Hatch Mansfield
141	M	Dakin & Co
142	W	Bottlescrue
143	M	Market Vintners
144	W	Gallery
145	W	Butlers
146	W	Cozy Griffs
147	W	Lautrec Bis
148	W	Bishop of Norwich
148	W	Bishop's Parlour
149	W	City Boot
150	W	Balls Bros
151	M	Corney & Barrow
151	W	Corney & Barrow
152	W	Capataz
153	W	Balls Bros
154	W	Grapeshotts
155	W	Mr Pontac's
156	W	Bill Bentley's, EC2
157	W	Balls Bros, EC2
158	W	Greenhouse
159	M	Greens
160	M	Bull's Head
160	W	Bull's Head
161	W	Leadenhall Wine Bar
162	W	City Flogger
163	W	Marlows
164	W	Five Lamps
165	W	JB's City Brasserie
166	W	Fenchurch Colony
167	W	Broker
168	W	City FOB
169	M	Russell & McIver
170	W	Balls Bros, EC3
171	W	Lautrec
172	M	El Vino, EC4
172	W	Old Wine Shades
173	W	Balls Bros, EC4
174	W	Punters
175	W	Whittingtons
176	W	Lautrec
177	W	Balls Bros, EC4
178	W	Mithras
179	W	Mr Garraways
180	W	Udder Place
181	W	Balls Bros, EC2
182	W	City Pipe
183	W	City Vaults
184	W	Balls Bros, EC2
185	M	Bow Wine Vaults

KEY TO LONDON MAPS

Number on map		Name of place
185	W	Bow Wine Vaults
186	W	Sopers
187	W	Balls Bros, EC4
188	W	Wives of Bath
189	W	The Bar
190	W	Bradys
191	W	Mother Bunch's
192	W	Arch 9
193	M	Mackie & Co
194	M	El Vino
194	W	New El Vino
195	M	El Vino
195	W	El Vino
196	W	Wine Press
197	W	Daly's
198	W	Balls Bros, WC2
199	M	Wine Growers' Association, WC2
200	W	Blakes
201	W	Tuttons
202	W	Crusting Pipe
203	R	Boulestin
204	W	Penny's Place
205	W	Bert's
206	W	Bar des Amis
207	W	Hobson's
208	W	Beaujolais
209	W	Garrick Wine Bar
210	R	Tourment d'Amour
211	W	Solange's
212	W	Tappit Hen
213	W	Gordon's
214	W	Hamptons
215	W	Cork & Bottle
216	W	Old Compton's
217	R	L'Escargot
218	M	Vintage House
219	M	Del Monico
219	M	Old Compton Wines
220	W	French Wine Bar
221	W	Lampers
222	M	Hedges & Butler
223	W	Dover Street Wine Bar
224	M	Fortnum & Mason
225	M	Christopher & Co
226	M	OW Loeb
227	M	John Harvey
228	M	Berry Bros & Rudd
229	M	Henry Collison
230	W	Greens, SW1
230	M	Green's Champagne Bar
231	M	Justerini & Brooks
232	R	The Ritz
233	M	Curzon Wine Co
234	M	André Simon
235	R	Connaught
236	R	Dorchester
237	W	L'Artiste Musclé
238	W	Down's
239	M	German Food Centre
240	R	Capital
241	W	Le Métro
242	M	Harrods
243	M	J H James
244	W	Bill Bentley's
245	W	Scandies
246	R	Hilaire
247	M	La Vigneronne
248	M	Caves de la Madeleine
249	W	Le Bouzy Rouge
250	M	Buckinghams, SW3
251	W	Draycotts
252	M	La Réserve
252	M	College Cellar
253	M	Stones of Belgravia, SW3
254	M	Stones of Belgravia, SW1
255	W	Motcombs
256	M	André Simon, W1
257	M	André Simon, SW1
258	M	Ebury Wine
259	W	Ebury Wine Bar
260	M	Ellis, Son & Vidler
261	M	Morris & Verdin
262	M	Wine Studio
263	R	Dulcinea
264	W	Tiles
265	M	Vintners Wain
266	W	Carriage's
267	W	Tapster
268	W	Methuselah's
269	M	Army and Navy
270	W	Alexanders
271	R	Tate Gallery
272	M	Majestic Wine Warehouse, SE11
273	W	Archduke
274	R	Mabileau
275	R	South of the Border
276	W	Boot & Flogger
277	M	Davys
278	W	Skinkers
279	W	Cuddefords
280	M	Mayor Sworder

Reports please

Reports from our readers are one of our most vital sources of information on Britain's wine merchants, wine bars and restaurants. Do let us know if you discover a place you think deserves an entry in the *Guide*, or if you agree or disagree with existing entries. We shall consult every report before writing next year's entry. You can write your report – any length, even just a few lines – on the forms on the following pages, or in a letter if you prefer. It will help us enormously if you use a separate sheet or a separate form for each establishment.

When reporting on restaurants and wine bars, please include details of the food as well as the wine, atmosphere, decor, service, cost and, importantly, whether the staff are knowledgeable about wine. We are particularly interested to hear about the quality of service given by wine merchants, too – such as delivery, advice and tastings.

Unless you indicate otherwise below, we shall pass on any relevant reports to *The Good Food Guide*.

We shall start compiling the 1986 edition of *Which? Wine Guide* in May 1985, so reports received by mid-June are the most useful. But information can often be incorporated right up till August. If you would like more report forms, let us know at the FREEPOST address (no stamp needed if posted in the UK):
Which? Wine Guide, FREEPOST, London WC2N 4BR.

We look forward to hearing from you.

Report to the Editor *Which? Wine Guide*

This is a report on a ☐ wine merchant* ☐ wine bar ☐ restaurant

and is a new recommendation ☐
a comment on existing entry ☐ *please tick as appropriate*

*includes off-licences, supermarkets, licensed grocers, wine clubs, wine warehouses

name of establishment

---

address

---

tel no:

---

please continue overleaf

Are you willing to have your report shared with the *GFG*? yes/no
and to have your name or initials quoted in the *GFG*? yes/no

date of most recent visit

signed

I am not connected directly or indirectly with the management or proprietors

name *in block letters, please*

address

Send to: Which? Wine Guide, Freepost, London WC2N 4BR
(please note: no postage required within UK)

Report to the Editor *Which? Wine Guide*

This is a report on a □ wine merchant* □ wine bar □ restaurant

and is a new recommendation □
a comment on existing entry □ *please tick as appropriate*

*includes off-licences, supermarkets, licensed grocers, wine clubs, wine warehouses

name of establishment

---

address

---

tel no:

---

please continue overleaf

Are you willing to have your report shared with the *GFG*? yes/no
and to have your name or initials quoted in the *GFG*? yes/no

date of most recent visit

signed

I am not connected directly or indirectly with the management or proprietors

name *in block letters, please*

address

Send to: Which? Wine Guide, Freepost, London WC2N 4BR
(please note: no postage required within UK)

Report to the Editor *Which? Wine Guide*

This is a report on a ☐ wine merchant* ☐ wine bar ☐ restaurant

and is a new recommendation ☐
a comment on existing entry ☐
please tick as appropriate

*includes off-licences, supermarkets, licensed grocers, wine clubs, wine warehouses

name of establishment

address

tel no:

please continue overleaf

Are you willing to have your report shared with the *GFG*? yes/no
and to have your name or initials quoted in the *GFG*? yes/no

date of most recent visit

signed

I am not connected directly or indirectly with the management or proprietors

name *in block letters, please*

address

Send to: Which? Wine Guide, Freepost, London WC2N 4BR
(please note: no postage required within UK)